THE

OXFORD
COMPANION TO
AUSTRALIAN
FILM

THE
OXFORD
COMPANION TO
AUSTRALIAN
FILM

Edited by

BRIAN MCFARLANE   GEOFF MAYER   INA BERTRAND

OXFORD
UNIVERSITY PRESS

OXFORD

UNIVERSITY PRESS

253 Normanby Road, South Melbourne, Australia

Oxford University Press is a department of the University of Oxford.
It furthers the University's objective of excellence in research, scholarship,
 and education by publishing worldwide in

Oxford New York

Athens Auckland Bangkok Bogotá Buenos Aires Calcutta
Cape Town Chennai Dar es Salaam Delhi Florence Hong Kong Istanbul
 Karachi Kuala Lumpur Madrid Melbourne Mexico City Mumbai Nairobi
Paris Port Moresby São Paulo Singapore Taipei Tokyo Toronto Warsaw

with associated companies in Berlin Ibadan

OXFORD is a trade mark of Oxford University Press
in the UK and in certain other countries

National Library of Australia
Cataloguing-in-Publication data:

The Oxford companion to Australian film.

Bibliography.
Includes index.
ISBN 0 19 553797 1

1. Motion pictures—Australia. 2. Motion picture industry—Australia.
3. Motion picture actors and actresses—Australia—Biography.
4. Motion picture producers and directors—Australia.
I. McFarlane, Brian, 1934–. II. Mayer, Geoff. III. Bertrand, Ina, 1939–.

791.430994

Edited by Michele Sabto and Edward Caruso
Cover design by Steve Randles
Typeset by Desktop Concepts Pty Ltd, Melbourne
Printed by Kyodo Printing Co. (Singapore) Pte Ltd

PREFACE

The world now thinks of Australia as a film-making country, but it is probably less well known that this country's film-making history is over 100 years old. Rather than providing an encyclopaedic coverage of this history, the aim of the *Companion* is to give a sense of the sweep of cinema in Australia: entries on selected people, films, institutions, and developments throughout the twentieth century convey what Australian cinema is and has been. While a growing body of books focuses on more specialised aspects of Australian cinema, the *Companion* is intended to be comprehensive and to appeal to a wide readership. It will obviously be of special relevance to those with a stake in the film industry and to those actively involved in promoting film culture in Australia. It is, however, above all intended as the book of first reference for anyone interested in the way in which Australian cinema has confronted the realities of Australian life.

Australian cinema got off to a flourishing start at the turn of the twentieth century and this volume seeks to make clear how prolific the early decades of the century were. In the 1930s, Australian cinema came closer to a studio system than at any previous (or subsequent) time, but World War II disrupted local feature production and the industry took more than 20 years to recover. In the interim, the idea of Australian cinema was kept alive by a rich documentary and newsreel tradition. At the same time, Australia became the exotic backdrop for American and British films: the few brave Australian feature film-makers were exceptions who only served to emphasise the comparative drought that swept over a once-thriving feature-production industry. The 'new Australian cinema' that was campaigned for in the 1960s, established in the 1970s and 1980s, and that assumed an international flavour in the 1990s, has been one of the great successes of the world film scene in recent decades and it is a function of this book to convey this success. The *Companion* also acknowledges that this revival has a history and a context and, in drawing attention to processes of distribution and exhibition, it makes it clear that production is only one arm of the film industry.

The revival of the Australian feature film industry in the 1970s coincided with the world-wide surge of interest in film culture and in new ways of considering the production, perception, and reception of film. Consequently, there has been a marked rise in the level of discussion of film in the last third of the twentieth century, and the *Companion* reflects this in the range of critical and historical approaches evident in the longer essays. There are entries on such diverse matters as the representation of Aboriginal life and issues; the role of magazines in the dissemination of film culture; images of rural and urban life; the cinematic treatment of masculinity and femininity; the institutional framework of production, distribution, and exhibition; international participation at various stages of Australian film history; the role of the literary adaptation, melodrama, and genre film-making; and the nature of film comedy. In short, the *Companion* is concerned with whatever contributes to the distinctiveness of Australian cinema, as well as with those matters that ally it with other film-making countries.

Matters such as these—issues relating to film as an art, an industry, a site of pleasure, and a site of critical analysis—are the subject of entries that vary between several hundred and several thousand words. They take up about a quarter of the *Companion*. The rest consists of biographical entries and entries on individual films. Many of the biographical entries are on directors, actors, and producers, but there are also representative selections from a much wider field of film-making activity, including entries on such collaborators as cinematographers,

Preface

scriptwriters, music directors, costume designers, and art directors, as well as certain key figures in the film industry. While the latter may be less well known to the public, it is important in a work of this kind to indicate their significance in the industry.

The criterion for the selection of actors, directors, and others for inclusion as entries was not only that they had a sufficient body of work to warrant a place, but also that the major part of their work has been in Australian cinema. It was not easy to settle on an exact measure in this respect: some who have made only a few films have made more impact than those whose credits contain twice as many titles. It was also important to draw attention to international involvement and to work in other media. Furthermore, some people who seem only to have dabbled in film but have notable careers in other media are included because we believe many readers will want to check on the film record of, say, actors who have given enjoyable performances on stage or television. The length of the entry on individuals is determined less by how prolific they have been than by the nature of their contributions.

The films selected for inclusion have been chosen for a variety of reasons. Most films produced before the coming of sound are lost and therefore is it difficult to determine which films made during this period might warrant our attention today. For this reason we decided to make the survival of a substantial portion of the film the major criterion for entries on films made in Australia between 1896 and 1932. We have deemed only a handful of lost features from this period important enough to merit entries, and in each of these cases the text of the entry indicates that no footage from the film survives. Documentaries and non-fiction from this period are not usually given separate entries: rather, they are discussed in longer, discursive articles, under such headings as Documentary and non-fiction, silent; Silent film, to 1914; and Newsreels. The selection of later feature films was based on many different considerations: some were major commercial successes (even though reviewers may have reviled them); some were influential in their day, either stylistically or because they broke new ground thematically; some represent the work of people who were, or would go on to be, significant figures in Australian, and sometimes in world, cinema; some are included because they won major awards; others because they seem so quintessentially 'Australian'. No two people will draw up the same list, even from the same criteria, but we do believe that the films included all deserve their place for one or more of the reasons suggested.

The three *Companion* editors have written most of the entries, but approximately 80 were commissioned by other film scholars with particular interests. These writers ensure that there is a pluralism of approaches to the vast and complex field of activity that is film and film culture in Australia. At an early stage in the preparation of the volume, a list of entries was drawn up, comprising suggestions for thematic articles as well as lists of people and films. This list was then circulated to several advisers who made recommendations, many of which were followed by the editors. Individual writers were then invited to contribute and we are grateful for the depth and diversity of their insights. In order to give a first-hand sense of those who, in one function or other, made the films discussed, we decided to include a small number of interviews with participants in the industry, as another strategy for arriving at the distinctive flavour of Australian film and its place in the world of cinema.

The *Companion* does not lack predecessors. A number of earlier reference books have different emphases: some are particularly strong on people working in film; others are useful references for actual films; and others provide valuable information on industrial matters. We acknowledge the ground-breaking contributions of these books. In their more specialist ways, these earlier works have been invaluable to us in our enterprise of providing a comprehensive, one-volume companion to film in Australia. We have aimed to make this a lively, readable, and scholarly record of what has been achieved in Australia cinema.

Brian McFarlane
Geoff Mayer
Ina Bertrand
January 1999

ACKNOWLEDGMENTS

A volume of this size owes debts to many people. First, the editors wish to thank all the contributors, particularly the authors of thematic essays, those who wrote multiple shorter entries, and those who agreed to be interviewed. We are grateful for their care and patience. Our thanks are also due to the Monash University Arts Faculty Research Fund; those who provided photographic stills, including Sue Maslin, Natalie Miller, Googie Withers and John McCallum, Arthur Stiles, Cameron's Management, Shanahan Management, Ian Stocks, Diane Naphthali, June Cann Management, Melbourne Artists' Management, Stacey Testro International, Bayside Pictures, Richard Franklin, Jan Epstein, Ken Berryman, Jennifer Mitchell, Ray Edmondson, MTM Management, and the National Film and Sound Archive in Canberra; those who acted as consultants in helping us to determine the headwords and in checking drafts of entries, whether for the list at large or for particular categories; and Monica Maughan, Judy Adamson, John Morris, Jeannette Delamoir, Felicity Cogan, Melinda Hildebrandt, William D. Routt, Graham Shirley, Sophie McFarlane, and Alissa Tanskaya. We also thank the staffs of the Australian Film Institute library, Melbourne, and of the National Film and Sound Archive, Melbourne. In Peter Rose at Oxford University Press we have had an insightful and enthusiastic publisher; we thank him, his assistant Iga Bajer, and her predecessors, Alexa Burnell and Felicity Edge. We also thank the two editors who worked on this book: Michele Sabto and Edward Caruso. Finally, we must thank our partners—Geraldine McFarlane, Lesley Mayer, and Graeme Bertrand—for their forbearance during the very long gestation process attending the production of this volume.

How to Use the Companion

Entries are arranged in alphabetical order, by surname for individuals (**Neill, Sam**) and by first word for film titles (**Head On**), but not under the English definite or indefinite articles (**Sentimental Bloke, The**). Subjects are entered under the key word of the subject (**Adaptation, history of**).

Film entries begin with the following information: title, year of release, director/s, producer/s, scriptwriter/s, director/s of photography, composer/s, length, whether or not the film is black and white (B&W), and selected cast list (actor's name, followed by the character name in brackets).

If information is not available (for example, the length of some early films), that aspect of the entry is omitted. If a film is known to have been made in black and white, that is included: all films not specified as made in black and white can be assumed to have been made in colour. If a film includes both black-and-white and colour footage, this is mentioned in the body of the entry.

Biographical entries appear under the name most commonly used in the film business (Chips Rafferty rather than John Goffage): if a pseudonym is in common use, the original name will usually be provided within the text of the entry, but it is not generally given as a separate headword. When a person is known by both his or her given name and a nickname (Reginald L. ('Snowy') Baker), the given name is provided in the headword and the nickname is referred to in the body of the entry. Second or middle names are provided only when this is how the person is known in the industry (Anna Maria Monticelli), or when the person is also known by his/her initials (A.R. (Alexander Roy) Harwood). Honorifics are not used in headwords, but may be referred to in the body of the entry.

The person's name is followed by birth and death dates in brackets. If neither the birth nor the death date is currently known, the entire date is omitted. If there is a presumption of death but no date is known, or if the date of death is known but not the date of birth, a question mark is used in place of the unknown year (for example, 1942–? or ?–1995). Despite our best efforts, we cannot guarantee the accuracy of these dates: in the entertainment industry such information is notoriously difficult to obtain, and is often unreliable.

Each biographical entry begins with descriptors for that person's major functions. If he or she has made a significant contribution in more than one area, multiple descriptors are used (for example, **Atkins, David** (1955–) ACTOR/DANCER/CHOREOGRAPHER), but if a contribution is minor it may be discussed in the body of the entry rather than listed as an additional descriptor. Where multiple descriptors apply to a single person, abbreviations are used to describe their function in any individual film (see Abbreviations, p. xiii).

An effort has been made to mention in each biographical entry that person's major films, particularly every major Australian film. Sometimes (for example, Arthur and Corinne Cantrill) the body of work is so large that mentioning every film is impractical, in which case this is noted in the entry. For films not mentioned in the body of the entry, a list of additional Australian titles is appended to the entry. The wording 'Other Australian films: …' denotes that we are confident that we have listed all titles. The wording 'Other Australian films include: …' denotes that we are less confident of having listed every possible title. As our concern in this volume is with Australian film, no effort has been made to list all the foreign films made by any person, although their work overseas is often mentioned in the body of the entry. Some films are described as shorts or documentaries. This is not done for every short or documentary film, but only to distinguish the shorts or documentary work of someone whose main output has been in features.

Subject entries are given under broad headings such as **Gay cinema** and **Country towns**. In the case of institutions, entries are listed as the most recent incarnation of that institution (**Australian Film Commission**), with earlier names (for instance, Australian Film Development Corporation) mentioned in the body of the text. In many cases, headword entries for earlier institutional names will refer the reader to the main entry under the most recent name.

Cross-references are indicated by • before a film title or person's surname or institutional name. Some cross-referencing has been provided by additional headwords: for instance, there is a headword entry referring anyone seeking information on Bert Ive to the entry on **Silent film, to 1914**. In the body of the text, bold indicates a film title (including films that may not have had a theatrical release before going to video): italics is used throughout for titles of books, television and radio programs, videos, and plays. Abbreviations are listed on p.xiii. The full name of an institution is spelled out the first time it is used in any entry, and subsequent references in that entry are in an abbreviated form.

Contributors are identified at the end of every entry. For film entries and biographical entries written by one of the three *Companion* editors, initials have been used. For all subject entries, and for all entries written by authors other than the editors, full names have been used. Short biographies of the contributors are provided in the directory of Contributors on p. xvii

ABBREVIATIONS

ABC	Australian Broadcasting Corporation
AC	Companion of the Order of Australia
ACA	Australia Council for the Arts (formerly Australian Council for the Arts)
ACOFS	Australian Council of Film Societies
ACS	Australian Cinematographers Society
ACT	Australian Capital Territory
ACTF	Australian Children's Television Foundation
ACTU	Australian Council of Trade Unions
AFC	Australian Film Commission
AFI	Australian Film Insitute
AFPA	Australian Film Producers Association
AFTRS	Australian Film, Television and Radio School
AGSC	Australian Guild of Screen Composers
ALP	Australian Labor Party
AM	Member of the Order of Australia
AO	Officer of the Order of Australia
APG	Australian Performing Group
ASDA	Australian Screen Directors Association
ASEA	Australian Screen Editors Association
ASEAN	Association of South-East Asian Nations
ASSA	Australian Screen Studies Association
AT&AEA	Australian Theatrical and Amusement Employees Association
ATOM	Australian Teachers of Media
ATSIC	Aboriginal and Torres Strait Islander Commission
AWG	Australian Writers Guild
AWU	Australian Workers Union
BBC	British Broadcasting Commission
BHP	Broken Hill Proprietary Company Limited
CFL	Commonwealth Film Laboratories
DOI	Department of Information
FFC	Australian Film Finance Corporation
FPAA	Film Producers Association of Australia
FQ	Film Queensland

Abbreviations

FTI — Film and Television Institute of Western Australia

MHR — Member of the House of Representatives
MLA — Member of the Legislative Assembly
MLC — Member of the Legislative Council
MPDA — Motion Picture Distributors Association
MPEA — Motion Picture Exhibitors Association
MPTA — Motion Picture Technicians Association

NFB — National Film Board
NFSA — National Film and Sound Archive
NFTA — National Film Theatre of Australia
NIDA — National Institute of Dramatic Art
NSW — New South Wales
NSWFTO — New South Wales Film and Television Office
NT — Northern Territory
NZ — New Zealand

OAM — Medal of the Order of Australia

POW — prisoner of war

QC — Queen's Counsel
Qld — Queensland

RN — Royal Navy
RSL — Returned Servicemen's League

SA — South Australia
SAFC — South Australian Film Corporation
SBS — Special Broadcasting Service
SPAA — Screen Producers Association of Australia

Tas. — Tasmania
TFC — Tasmanian Film Corporation

UN — United Nations
USA — United States of America

VCA — Victorian College of the Arts
Vic. — Victoria

WA — Western Australia
WIFT — Women in Film and Television

Abbreviations used in bracketed references to films

a.	actor
anim.	animation
ass. d.	assistant director
assoc. d.	associate director
assoc. p.	associate producer
c.	cinematographer
co-d.	co-director
co-p.	co-producer
co-w.	co-writer
d.	director
d.o.p.	director of photography
doc.	documentary
ed.	editor
ex. p.	executive producer
nar.	narrator
p.	producer
short	short film
w.	writer

CONTRIBUTORS

Judith Adamson works in documentary film and film history. She wrote a mini-history of Australian film to 1960 under the title of *Australian Film Posters 1906–1960* (1978).

Martha Ansara, a documentary film-maker and former cinematographer, has been researching and writing about Australian film history for a number of years.

Tony Barta is a research fellow in history at La Trobe University, where he founded the History and Film Program. He is the editor of *Screening the Past: Film and the Representation of History* (1998).

Keith Beattie is Director of the Contemporary Studies Program at the University of Queensland. He is editor of the *Australasian Journal of American Studies* and author of *The Scar That Binds: American Culture and the Vietnam War* (1998), a study of the ways in which Hollywood has represented the domestic impact of that war.

John Benson teaches media studies at La Trobe University. He has a keen interest in popular Australian film, which he has expressed in writing study guides for students, researching early film exhibition in Melbourne's western suburbs, and teaching a course on popular film, including Australian features.

Chris Berry teaches in the Department of Cinema Studies at La Trobe University. Together with Annette Hamilton and Laleen Jayamanne, he is the editor of *The Filmmaker and the Prostitute: Dennis O'Rourke's 'The Good Woman of Bangkok'* (1997).

Ken Berryman, a film researcher and historian, works at the National Film and Sound Archive's Melbourne base. He edited *Screening the Past:*

Aspects of Early Australian Film (1995) and is a frequent contributor to *Metro* and *Cinema Papers*.

Ina Bertrand taught film history at LaTrobe University for 25 years. She has written many articles and several books on Australian film, including *Film Censorship in Australia* (1978) and *Cinema in Australia: a Documentary History* (1989). She is co-editor of the online history-and-film journal *Screening the Past*.

Rod Bishop is the Director of the Australian Film Television and Radio School. He produced and co-wrote the feature film **Body Melt** and for five years was film critic for the *Age* 'Green Guide'.

Anne Bittner's PhD thesis focuses on the social and cultural perspectives of the relationship between stage performances and film in Australia from 1920–25. She is an associate editor of the online history and film journal *Screening the Past*.

Ian Britain is an Australian Research Council senior fellow in the Department of History at Monash University. His books include *Once an Australian: Journeys with Barry Humphries, Clive James, Germaine Greer and Robert Hughes* (1997).

Chris Brophy is manager of the Research and Information Centre of the Australian Film Institute and former manager of the State Film Centre of Victoria Film and Video Library (now the Cinemedia Access Collection).

Arthur Cantrill and **Corinne Cantrill** are experimental film-makers whose films have been shown internationally since 1971. They have been editors and publishers of *Cantrills Filmnotes*, a review of experimental film. Arthur Cantrill recently retired from a position as

Contributors

Associate Professor at the Victorian College of the Arts.

Raffaele Caputo is a freelance writer and has lectured in film studies at the Royal Melbourne Institute of Technology and La Trobe University. Between 1989 and 1993 he was assistant editor of *Cinema Papers*. With film-maker Geoff Burton he co-edited *Second Take: Australian Film-makers Talk* (1999).

Felicity Cogan studied at Monash University and at the Chisholm Institute of Technology. She holds an MA in Australian cinema and a Diploma of Film Production (Video) from the Audio Visual College, Richmond, Vic.

Diane Collins is a lecturer at the Sydney Conservatorium of Music at the University of Sydney. She has written *Hollywood Down Under* (1987).

Felicity Collins teaches in the Department of Cinema Studies at La Trobe University and is the author of *The Films of Gillian Armstrong* (1999). She is currently involved in an Australian Research Council-funded research project on Australian film and television comedy.

Ross Cooper is co-author of *Australian Film 1900–1977* (1998). With Nigel Buesst he co-directed the documentary *Jacka, VC*. He has completed a PhD on Australian silent cinema and for many years taught history at La Trobe and Melbourne universities.

Barbara Creed is Associate Professor in the Department of Fine Arts at the University of Melbourne. She has reviewed film for the *Age*, and is the author of *The Monstrous-Feminine: Film, Feminism, Psychoanalysis* (1993).

Stephen Crofts is Director of Postgraduate Studies at the Centre for Film, Television and Media Studies at the University of Auckland. He has published extensively in Australia, the USA, and the United Kingdom, including books on the film **Shame** and on televisual constructions of politics.

Jeannette Delamoir, who has worked in film exhibition in Australia and the USA, is completing her PhD in media studies. Her dissertation is on Australian silent-film actor Louise Lovely. She teaches in the School of Contemporary Communication at Central Queensland University.

Marilyn Dooley organises an academic outreach program with the National Film and Sound Archive, where she has worked since 1984. Formerly a teacher and an opera producer, she specialises in video restorations of Australian silent features.

Anna Dzenis lectures in the Department of Cinema Studies at La Trobe University. She is book-review editor for the online journal *Screening the Past* and is part of the editorial team on the publication *Real Time on Screen*.

Ray Edmondson is Deputy Director of the National Film and Sound Archive of Australia and President of the South East Asia-Pacific Audiovisual Archive Association UNESCO 'Memory of the World' program. He is the author of *A Philosophy of Audiovisual Archiving* (1998) and has taught post-graduate professional courses in audiovisual archiving in Australia and USA.

Jan Epstein has for many years broadcast on the subject of film for the ABC. She also writes for *Cinema Papers* and the *Australian Jewish News*.

Gerard Foley is the film archivist in charge of the Western Australian film collection at the Battye Library, Perth. He is a professional member of the Australian Society of Archivists, and of the international Association of Moving Image Archivists.

Karen Ford is currently completing an MA in cinema at La Trobe University. She lectures with Cinemedia as part of the Screen Education Film as Text unit, and has produced several short films.

Freda Freiberg is a film historian, lecturer, and critic, specialising in Japanese and Australian cinema. She is a contributor to *The Australian Screen* (1989), *World War 2, Film and History* (1996), and the *Oxford Guide to Film Studies* (1998).

Ross Gibson is the creative director of Cinemedia's Screen Gallery at Federation Square in Melbourne. Over the past 20 years he has produced several books, films, and multimedia environments.

Ben Goldsmith is a research fellow at the Australian Key Centre for Cultural and Media Policy at Griffith University. He has published widely on Australian cinema, with a focus on the films and the industrial, institutional, and critical frameworks of the early revival period.

Denise Haslem is a producer and editor with more than 20 years' experience in the film and television industry. She is the president of the Australian Screen Editors, an organisation devoted to protecting, promoting, and improving the role of screen editors.

Wendy Haslem is a PhD student at La Trobe University and is writing a thesis on the American gothic-romance film cycle of the 1940s. She has taught film at Monash and teaches in the Department of Cinema Studies at La Trobe University.

Melinda Hildebrandt is a PhD student at Monash University, researching the tradition of realism in British cinema. She is a research assistant on the forthcoming *Encyclopedia of British Cinema*.

Bruce Hodsdon is senior coordinator of the audiovisual unit at the State Library Of Queensland. For more than 10 years (1968–79) he was involved with the National Film Theatre in various capacities.

Peter Hughes lectures at La Trobe University, in courses dealing with digital media cultures and writing non-fiction forms of television. Documentary film is the focus of his PhD thesis and most of his published articles. He has also worked as an education consultant in film distribution and in secondary education.

Tim Hunter is the film reviewer for the *Melbourne Weekly*, and the *City Weekly* in Melbourne and Sydney respectively. He has worked as editorial assistant for *Cinema Papers*.

Karen Jennings lectured for many years at the University of South Australia, where her special area of interest was Australian cinema. She is the author of *Sites of Difference: Cinematic Representations of Aboriginality and Gender* (Australian Film Institute, 1993) and now works in Adelaide as a freelance writer and researcher.

Paul Kalina is Deputy Editor of *Cinema Papers*. He writes on pay television for the Melbourne *Age*, and was formerly the video columnist at the *Sunday Age*.

Peter Kemp is a writer, broadcaster, and lecturer who has contributed to a range of publications, including *The Bent Lens: A Complete Guide to Gay and Lesbian Film* (1997). He currently lectures in screen studies at the Victorian College of the Arts School of Film and Television.

Barrie King has researched and written about film in Western Australia since the 1960s. He was also part of the film society movement in WA. With John Turner he restarted the Australian Council of Film Societies in 1975 and was involved with its administration until 1999.

Harry Kirchner is a Melbourne-based academic and has been a practising screenwriter, working in film and television since 1980.

Scott J. Knight is Assistant Professor of Film and Television at Bond University, where he has taught film and media studies since 1991. A member of the programming panel of the Brisbane International Film Festival since 1993, he is currently researching a PhD in popular film and television of the 1990s.

Franz Kuna is a professor in the Institut Für Anglistik und Amerikanistik at Klagenfurt University, Austria. Australian cinema is his research area and he co-edited *Studies in Australian Culture: an Introductory Reader* (1994).

Wayne Levy is the author of over 20 books, including *Fred Ott Sneezes For Edison* (1976) and *The Film of the Book and Vice Versa* (1995). He has made medical documentaries in Singapore and Timor.

Chris Long is a film researcher who has written extensively about early Australian film (including a series of seminal articles in *Cinema Papers*). He has made video compilations of these films, and is currently producing and marketing CD-ROMs.

Rose Lucas works at Monash University, where she has taught literature, cinema studies, and gender studies.

Peter Malone is the president of the International Catholic Organisation for Cinema. He has reviewed films for over 30 years and has written books on film, including *Movie Christs and Antichrists* (1988) and *The Values Dimensio;, Australian Directors in their Own Words* (forthcoming).

Sue Maslin is a producer of documentary films (including **Thanks Girls and Goodbye**, 1987;

Contributors

Mr Neal is Entitled to be an Agitator, 1991) and feature films (**Road to Nhill**, 1997). She is also a founder and continuing active member of Women in Film and Television in Victoria.

Geoff Mayer is Chair of the Department of Cinema Studies at La Trobe University. He has published widely on Australian and American film, with a special interest in the development of cinema studies in secondary schools and tertiary institutions.

Mark McAuliffe has taught film and television, and established a cable community television channel for Optus. His doctoral thesis considered the **Mad Max** film trilogy as an expression of Australian masculinity in crisis.

Neil McDonald was a foundation lecturer in film history at the Mitchell Council of Adult Education from 1970–96. He is the author of *War Cameraman: The Story of Damien Parer* (1994) and co-author of *Two Hundred Shots: Damien Parer, George Silk and the Australians at War in New Guinea* (1998).

Joy McEntee is an associate lecturer in the English Department at the University of Adelaide. She studied at Monash University and the University of Western Australia.

Brian McFarlane, Associate Professor in the English Department at Monash University, has published widely on Australian and British film, and on the connections between literature and film. He is compiling *The Encyclopedia of British Film*.

Lisa Milner, a film-maker and academic, is currently completing a PhD in Australian film history at the University of Wollongong.

Bruce Molloy is Professor of Film and Television at Bond University. He was a board member of the Pacific Film and Television Corporation from its inception in 1991 until 1997.

Lorraine Mortimer lectures in sociology and anthropology at La Trobe University, teaching courses on ethnographic film. She has written on Australian film for *Literature/Film Quarterly*.

David Muir has spent 30 years in the film industry and has won awards for cinematography, screenwriting, and direction. He began teaching at the Australian Film, Television and Radio School in 1990. Since then he has lectured at Macquarie University and La Trobe University. He is currently writing a screen-production textbook.

Scott Murray is a co-founder of *Cinema Papers*, a film-maker, and a writer on film. His books include *Australian Film 1978-1994* (1995) and *Australian on the Small Screen 1970-1995* (1996).

Diane Napthali's doctoral thesis traces music in the Australian film industry from 1894 to 1969. She has contributed articles on this subject to encyclopedias in Australia and the USA. She is currently a consultant to the National Film and Sound Archive and is continuing her research into the history of music and the Australian film industry.

Harry Oldmeadow holds degrees in history, comparative religion, and cinema studies, and is a senior lecturer in the Department of Arts at La Trobe University's Bendigo campus. He has published in many journals including *Continuum*, *Quadrant*, and *Asian Philosophy*.

Vincent O'Donnell has worked in film, television, and radio, and is executive producer of the syndicated radio program *Arts Alive*. His PhD research examines the contribution of the state film corporations to the Australian film industry.

Tom O'Regan is Director of the Australia Key Centre for Cultural and Media Policy at Griffith University. His books include *Australian National Cinema* (1996) and *Australian Television Culture* (1992). With Albert Moran he edited *Australian Screen* (1989) and *An Australian Film Reader* (1985).

Barbara Paterson practised law in Melbourne for a number of years. In 1992 she completed an MA in public history. Her thesis was published in book form as *Renegades: Australia's First Film School, from Swinburne to VCA* (1996).

Andrew Pike is co-author of *Australian Film 1900–1977* (1998). He has made several short films and documentaries, including the award-winning *Angels of War* (1982). He now runs the film-distribution company Ronin Films. In 1986 he won the Australian Film Institute's Byron Kennedy Award for services to the film community.

Noel Purdon was educated at the universities of Sydney, Florence, and Cambridge. While at Cambridge, he co-founded and edited the magazine *Cinema*. Besides working in the industry as an actor, writer, and director, he has lectured on cinema at Bristol University and at Flinders University (where he became Head of the Department of Screen Studies).

Neil Rattigan is currently lecturing in film studies and screenwriting in the School of English, Communication and Theatre at the University of New England. He is the author of *Images of Australia: 100 Films of the New Australian Cinema* (1991).

William D. Routt is an honorary associate (research) in the Department of Cinema Studies at La Trobe University and has written extensively on Australian cinema.

Graham Shirley is a documentary film-maker and film historian. He is co-author of the book *Australian Cinema: The First 80 Years* (1983).

Catherine Simpson was co-director of the first Australian Film Festival in Istanbul in 1994. She is currently completing a PhD on gender and location in Australian cinema at Murdoch University.

Alex Stitt, a leading figure in Australian film and television animation, created the 'Life. Be in it.' public-health advertisements on television and co-produced the feature film **Grendel Grendel Grendel** (1981). In 1966, he co-founded the film-production company The Film House.

Ian Stocks was educated at Monash University and the University of Queensland. From the early 1970s he wrote, produced, and photographed documentaries. He has taught in film departments of the Australian Film Television and Radio School, the Victorian College of Arts, and Queensland University of Technology.

Rick Thompson teaches in the Department of Cinema Studies at La Trobe University. He previously taught film in the USA. He has written about animated film, narrative genre, film criticism, American and French cinema, and crime fiction.

John Tulloch is Professor of Media Communication at Cardiff University, Wales. Formerly he was Professor of Cultural Studies at Charles Sturt University. He has published two books on the Australian film industry: *Legends On The Screen: The Narrative Film in Australia 1919–29* (1981) and *Australian Cinema: Industry, Narrative and Myth* (1982).

Graeme Turner is Professor of Cultural Studies at the University of Queensland. He has written widely on Australian film, television, literature, and popular culture; his books include *Making it National* (1994) and (with Stuart Cunningham) *The Media in Australia* (1990, 1997).

John Turner has been involved in the foundation and organisation of film societies since the mid 1950s. He has written articles, film reviews, and film book reviews for various publications.

Quentin Turnour is a freelance writer and curator, and a programmer with Cinemathèque.

Deb Verhoeven lectures in cinema studies at RMIT University and reviews film for the *Melbourne Times*. Her most recent publication is the edited collection *Twin Peeks: Australian and New Zealand Cinema* (1999).

Paul Washington has published several journal articles and book chapters on topics in film studies and literary studies, and he is currently preparing a textbook on film studies. He has taught at the University of Melbourne and at Charles Sturt University.

Deane Williams teaches documentary film theory, television studies, Australian film and television, and Australian film history at Monash University. He is the author of *Mapping the Imaginary: Ross Gibson's 'Camera Natura'* (1996) and is working on the biography of Australian film-maker John Heyer.

A

Abigail (1945–) ACTOR London-born Abigail was, in the late 1960s and the 1970s, a sort of Australian-based version of Diana Dors. She first made her blonde, voluptuous presence felt on television, in the long-running series *Number 96, did several other television series, and appeared on stage in roles that revealed some comedy flair. But it was as a sex symbol that she has her place in new Australian cinema. Her films gave her little chance to show more than her physical charms, and her best work is probably as Esmeralda in Richard *Franklin's sadly comic deflation of male sexual aspiration, **The True Story of Eskimo Nell** (1975). She also filmed in France in the late 1970s.
Other Australian films: *Alvin Purple (1973), Alvin Rides Again (1974), *Eliza Fraser (1976, billed as 'buxom girl'), Summer City (1977), Melvin, Son of Alvin (1984), Breaking Loose (1988), Sher Mountain Killings Mystery (1990). BMcF

Aboriginality and film A historical overview of Australian narrative cinema reveals that there were almost no Aborigines as major characters in its first 70 years. There are, however, a few notable exceptions, such as Charles *Chauvel's *Uncivilised (1936) and *Jedda (1955), and a couple of British co-productions: *The Overlanders (1946) and *Bitter Springs (1950). In early documentaries, Aborigines are often the objects of ethnographic curiosity. Along with Australia's exotic flora and fauna, their ceremonial and hunting life was extensively documented and commodified for White audiences. Early narrative fictions portraying Aborigines also include corroborees, evil witchdoctors, gum-leaf bands, and similar exoticisms. There are also a few recurrent minor-character types. For example, in a number of bushranger films of the silent era, Aborigines appear as sidekicks—loyal, subservient allies of the White heroes.

Examples of such films are the 1907 version of **Robbery Under Arms** and **Dan Morgan** (1911). Often in these films, Aborigines were played by White actors in blackface, a practice that survived until the 1960s, the most remarkable example being a film called *Journey out of Darkness (1967) in which an Aboriginal tracker was played by Ed *Deveraux and an Aboriginal prisoner by Kamahl.

Since the 1970s, representations of Aborigines have been more common, with more than 25 Australian feature films in this period dealing centrally or substantially with Aboriginality. It is difficult to generalise about such a corpus of films, but it is possible to identify recurring patterns and myths. The term 'myth' is used here not to suggest falsehoods, but rather refers to the chain of concepts by which members of a culture understand certain things. Myths typically deflect attention from the historical, social, and political specificity, functioning to make the cultural seem natural—myth naturalises. Myth also has a homogenising quality, constructing categories of diverse and specific phenomena as not only natural, but unitary. As Marcia Langton, an anthropologist and commentator on Aboriginal affairs, has noted (*Well I Heard it on the Radio and I Saw it on the Television*, 1993), on screen Aborigines have often been represented in ways that ignore or deny their historical specificity and disregard the ways in which humans change in response to social interaction and wider culture.

Many Australian films mythologise Aboriginality, presenting rigid categories of racial difference and marking these as natural in various recurring ways. However, many of these films are also ambivalent and contain narrative and representational contradictions and tensions. Others deliberately seek to problematise such differences. They are sites in which racial differences are inscribed in ways that encourage diverse readings. Some of these, discussed later in this entry, are films derived from radical film-making practice and are quite deliberate in their de-mythologising intent.

One recurrent pattern in films about Aborigines is an emphasis on individualised narratives, in which the story of a protagonist is privileged and the character is psychologised. This is in keeping with the imperatives of classical Hollywood cinema. Such characters are de-contextualised—socially, politically, and historically. This pattern is evident in films such as •**Manganinnie** (1980), •**Walkabout** (1971), •**The Fringe Dwellers** (1986) and, to a lesser extent, **Jedda**. John Honey's **Manganinnie** perhaps illustrates the myth most clearly. With its languid, gentle pace and extraordinary lyricism, it celebrates the exotic in its representations of both landscape and people. **Manganinnie** is ostensibly a personal story, a fable of friendship between an Aboriginal woman and a young White girl that transcends race, age, and religious belief. Despite its undoubtedly good intentions, its mythologising gloss prevaricates about Tasmanian history, providing a romanticised tale of rapprochement. While it purports (in its publicity) to document the atrocity of the European massacres of Tasmanian Aborigines, very few scenes actually foreground such violence. **Manganinnie** masks both the historical causes of racial conflict (dispossession of land) and the contemporary political struggle of Tasmanian Aborigines. In this respect it contrasts markedly with Fred •Schepisi's •**The Chant of Jimmie Blacksmith** (1978), which forcefully locates a personal story of oppression within a historical context, and does not shy away from the violence that inevitably ensues.

A second major myth is also evident in **Manganinnie**: the conflation of Aboriginal culture with Nature. **Manganinnie** inscribes racial difference through various contrasting symbols in the film (such as fire sticks and table lamps). The unconstrained world of Nature is continually opposed to the rigidity of civilisation. 'Primitive' Aboriginal culture is conflated with the natural. Similar oppositions are evident in **The Chant of Jimmie Blacksmith** where the 'full-blood' Aborigine, Mort, is repeatedly aligned with Nature and contrasted with the different Aboriginality of his 'half-caste' brother, Jimmie. •**Blackfellas** (1993) also has elements of this dichotomy. In **Manganinnie**, •**Journey Among Women** (1977), •**Eliza Fraser** (1976), •**Storm Boy** (1976), and **Walkabout**, to name a few, an opposition is set up between the bush and White settlements in Australia. Aboriginal culture is repeatedly conflated with Nature and opposed to White culture. To varying degrees the first three of these films operate to subvert populist colonial notions of Aborigines as primitive savages. All are well-intentioned attempts at an anti-racist re-writing of history. In doing so, however, they inadvertently circumscribe Aborigines within the category of 'noble savage'. All these films share a common motif of the

journey or flight of White protagonists from civilisation to the bush, with Aborigines acting as intermediaries or benevolent guides leading the Whites to an accommodation with Nature. Aboriginal characters act as foils to non-Aboriginal characters and, in different ways, all these films privilege perspectives of the latter. Aboriginal culture is invested with meaning only in relation to White/Anglo culture. Aboriginality functions as a signifier of essential difference. The same mythologising and Eurocentric discourse is evident also in •**We of the Never Never** (1982) and •**The Last Wave** (1977). In both these films, as in **Manganinnie**, White go-between characters become 'honorary Aborigines' so that they too can have certain rarefied, 'natural' qualities attributed to them.

A third mythic pattern relates to 'blood'. In films ranging from **Jedda** to **The Last Wave** to **The Chant of Jimmie Blacksmith** to **The Fringe Dwellers**, categorical assertions of differences of 'blood' abound. Marcia Langton has lamented the insidious ideology of the 'full-blood–half-caste dichotomy' and the 'urban-rural-tribal triangle' in anthropological writing. These oppositions are also readily observable in Australian cinema. 'Full-blood' Aborigines are opposed to 'half-castes' (Marbuk and Joe in **Jedda**; Mort and Jimmie in **The Chant of Jimmie Blacksmith**) and urban Aborigines are opposed to tribal Aborigines (most notably in **The Last Wave**). Peter •Weir's **The Last Wave** emphasises spiritual and mystical elements of Aboriginal identity. The task of the lawyer (Richard Chamberlain) is to establish that the urban Aborigines whom he is defending are the real thing—that they have a direct line to the Dreaming and to spiritual dimensions of traditional Aboriginality. Its distinctions aestheticise and mystify Aboriginal spirituality in ways comparable to **Manganinnie**. In **The Last Wave** Aboriginal spirituality is packaged as mysterious 'otherness' to serve the generic requirements of a supernatural thriller. While it works very successfully as a genre film, **The Last Wave**'s thesis is still one of biological determinism centred on a unitary, essentialist notion of Aboriginality, arising from a romantic nostalgia about a 'natural' uncontaminated past.

One film that makes a genuine attempt to depart from this kind of essentialism and that represents Aboriginality as complex and contradictory is Bruce •Beresford's **The Fringe Dwellers**. The community examined in **The Fringe Dwellers** is an Aboriginal fringe camp on the outskirts of a fictional Queensland town. The script is based on Nene Gare's novel of the same name, published in 1961. It tells the story of an Aboriginal family (significantly called the Comeaways), focusing especially on the adolescent daughter, Trilby (Kristina Nehm). Along with **Blackfellas**, **The Fringe Dwellers** is notable for the way in which Aboriginal communal life is central to the film. Similarly, •**Wrong Side of the Road** (1981) makes Aboriginal characters central, but its road-movie form and its focus on members of a band narrows its scope. Unlike the other films discussed so far, there are no significant White roles in **The Fringe Dwellers**. While we see the characters' interactions with White society and White authority figures (police, teachers, employers, and so on), the emphasis is very much on the social microcosm of the fringe camp.

However, in transposing the 1950s narrative of the novel to a 1980s setting, Beresford makes few concessions to changing political circumstances or prevailing ideologies of racial identity. The narrative therefore can be read as anachronistically endorsing a 1950s assimilationist ideology, implicitly rejecting the politicisation of race relations in Australia over the past 30 years. Its concentration on the personal and the particular compounds its dislocation from any geographical or historical specificity. Beresford seems defeated by a contradictory dual desire to construct Aboriginal life as quaint, caring, and picturesque, and to highlight its social problems. Ultimately, the film suggests that assimilation is possible and desirable, but only through individual struggle: that is, the survival of the fittest. Nonetheless, **The Fringe Dwellers** does represent Aboriginality as complex and diverse, and Beresford's willingness to make material that is so often marginalised or ignored central to the action deserves recognition.

Other films that can be seen as working to de-mythologise Aboriginality are films such as •**Backroads** (1977), •**Backlash** (1986), **Wrong Side of the Road**, •**Deadly** (1992) and **Blackfellas**. Phil •Noyce's **Backroads** tells the story of two fringe-dwelling Aborigines, Gary and Joe, in parallel with the story of a White drifter, Jack, who is racist and sexist and, like Gary and Joe, is a social failure and outcast. **Backroads** firmly contextualises these characters in ways that enable it to explore the intersection of class, race, and gender. There is no essentialist representation of Aboriginal no-hopers. **Wrong Side of the Road** demonstrates ways in which non-Aboriginal art forms (music and the films) have been appropriated and converted in the service of resistance politics. The lyrics and dialogue speak of opposition and confrontation. **Wrong Side of the Road** also represents the heterogeneity of Aboriginality. For example, it portrays significant ideological differences between the old and the young, and between women and men.

Like **The Fringe Dwellers**, Bill •Bennett's **Backlash** was released in 1986. Both films focus on rural, non-traditional Aboriginal women. **Backlash** is the story of an Aboriginal woman, Kath (Lydia Miller) who has been arrested in Sydney for murder, and is being escorted back to the scene of the crime in Queensland by two police officers. Wrongful presumptions of guilt set the scene for one of the film's central theses—the fallibility of White, and ultimately also of Black, law and order. **Backlash** works best as a self-deprecating and humorous character study within a plot that combines elements of the picaresque road movie and the thriller. Through the interactions of the three lead characters Bennett acknowledges structural divisions of class and race and the social construction of gender. Kath has bush skills, but these are not romanticised; she is characterised in class and gender terms as much as racial ones. One of **Backlash**'s achievements is that it successfully establishes the complex dynamics between the three main characters. These lead ultimately to harmony but they are frequently traversed by shifting affiliations and divisions of class, race, and gender.

Deadly (written and directed by Esben •Storm) is the story of a flawed White cop sent to investigate a case of a death-in-custody in a country town. The superficial similarities with **Backlash** are immediately obvious. In both films the journey of White police to the country and their contact with Aborigines (specifically with Aboriginal women) is a rite of passage in which they are humanised and enlightened. Both films are very cynical about the White legal system and offer stringent critiques of the racism embedded within Australian institutions and personal relations. Both combine elements of the thriller genre with social commentary. **Backlash** is, however, much lighter in touch than **Deadly**, which administers a hefty dose of didacticism. Storm and co-writers Richard •Moir and Ranald Allan have a very obvious political agenda. Their script is clearly informed by a sympathy with the plight of Aboriginal communities torn apart by the removal of children from their families, by alcohol, racism, repeated imprisonment, police brutality, and deaths in custody. Several characters are given lengthy and eloquent monologues in which they directly address the audience with these issues. **Deadly** contests White histories and White attitudes towards Aboriginality that stereotype Aborigines. Difference within Aboriginal communities is acknowledged and repeatedly asserted. Commonalities between Aboriginal and non-Aboriginal people are highlighted, reminding viewers of the artifice of much racial characterisation. There is an ambitious but ultimately uneasy tension between the heroic conventions of the thriller/cop/action genre and the social-message film.

James Ricketson's **Blackfellas**, based on Archie Weller's novel, *Day of the Dog*, is another contemporary urban story about Aboriginal communal life. Ricketson engaged in extensive consultation with Aboriginal members of the cast and crew, as well as the wider Aboriginal community, and this is evident in the palpable 'insider' feel of **Blackfellas**. **Blackfellas** is aptly named, since the women in the film do little more than occasionally disrupt or guide the men in the narrative. The film successfully highlights many of the complexities of Aboriginal male identities in contemporary Australia, and displays a positive raw energy as it explores the vicious cycles of petty crime and gaol that dominate its

Aboriginality and film

characters' lives. It boldly juxtaposes the untouched outback with the grime of the town, and the legacy of the absent mythologised Aboriginal father with the middle-class concerns of White mothers. However, the boldness of its vision at times teeters on the edge of melodrama, undermining a potentially incisive analysis of race, sexuality, mateship, and power. Nonetheless, **Deadly, Backlash, The Fringe Dwellers**, and **Blackfellas** all acknowledge the social processes of cultural change and racial conflict. They all dramatise the racism institutionalised in the legal system and very explicitly address the larger social system within which contemporary Aborigines live.

More contentious representations of Aborigines are to be found in two comedies firmly located within the popular mainstream, •**Crocodile Dundee** (1986) and **Crocodile Dundee II** (1987). These can be read as de-mythologising some romantic myths about Aboriginality at the same time as they actively work to create new ones. The character of Nev (David •Gulpilil) in **Crocodile Dundee** is constructed as a 'real city boy'. Much of the humour in his interactions with Mick (Paul •Hogan) and Sue (Linda Kozlowski) hinges precisely on his evasion of romantic myths about Aboriginality. Nev's characterisation explicitly subverts myths of Aboriginal affinity with the land, telepathic qualities, and a spiritual affiliation with tribal rituals such as the corroboree. At the same time, however, the film equivocates. The corroboree, for example, is filmed at some length as an ethnographic curiosity, and Mick appropriates the very same Aboriginal mythological qualities that Nev sheds. This transition achieves its fullest expression in **Crocodile Dundee II** where Mick is described as 'more like an Aborigine than a White man'. He's able to use a bull roarer to summon assistance, he comes out of nowhere, moves around the bush like lightning, and his antics are frequently accompanied by didgeridoo music on the soundtrack.

As cultural commentator Meaghan Morris has explained, both Nev and Mick are culturally mobile—they are cultural poachers. This is true also, but to a lesser extent, of Charlie (Ernie •Dingo) in **Crocodile Dundee II**. Often in **Crocodile Dundee**, the depiction of Mick as an honorary Aborigine is undercut, and contributes to the film's playful, self-deprecating humour. It is part of a wider rendition of the Australian comic tradition of the tall story. This is not so clearly the case in **Crocodile Dundee II**, where Mick's characterisation loses that playful edge and is constructed much more tediously as a mythological hero. Not only does Mick appropriate Aboriginal qualities, but he also appropriates the right to speak on behalf of Aboriginal people. Significantly Nev and Charlie never articulate anything much that is autonomous or serious, existing solely as comic foils to Mick. While Mick's delineation of Aboriginal relationship to the land as one of belonging, rather than ownership, may well be true of pre-contact Aboriginality, it denies the validity of cultural change and contemporary Aboriginal experience and aspirations. At the same time as Mick talks on behalf of Aboriginal people, he also rejects Aboriginal land claims, surely one of the central elements of contemporary Aboriginal politics. Ironically, in **Crocodile Dundee II** he emerges himself as owning a large chunk of the Northern Territory—called 'Belonga Mick' and rich in minerals such as gold!

While **Crocodile Dundee** successfully evades and subverts some romantic myths, it also constructs a discourse that itself evades history and politics: that is, it exemplifies the key characteristics of myth. Mick's ostensible apoliticism is, of course, profoundly political. The **Crocodile Dundee** films' constructions of Aboriginality are straw men. In their attempts to naturalise a non-conflictual, apolitical cultural rapprochement, they keep Aborigines firmly in their place. While they have been liberated from the romantic, 'primitive' place of the past, they have not been admitted fully to the present.

Finally, it is appropriate to refer to several short 'independent' films made by, or in collaboration with, Aboriginal film-makers. These have been selected because of their formal experimentation and their explicit agendas to analyse the contemporary politics of Aboriginal identity. Michael Riley's **Poison** (1990) is a visually exciting, experimental exploration of the impact of White culture on Aboriginal lifestyles. In particular, it describes the poisonous influence of drugs and alcohol. Riley's film, produced by the Aboriginal Program Unit of the ABC, uses some of the potentially mythologising contrasts of city and bush discussed earlier. However, the stylised iconography and tableau-like quality of the imagery avoid naturalising, and the film manages to sustain its political, historically informed edge. **Poison** uses a variety of techniques to subvert dominant cinematic conventions. These preclude audience identification with the linear unfolding of the story, and encourage a continual reappraisal of its historical context and moral position.

Tracey •Moffatt's **Nice Coloured Girls** (1987) is an account of three young Aboriginal women cruising Sydney night spots for some diversion at the expense of a boorish and predatory White man. Their progress from pub to restaurant to disco to the taxi is explained in terms of their own world-view and various accounts of the history of sexual exploitation of Aboriginal women that have shaped that outlook. It is a film that seeks to counter dominant stereotypes of Aboriginal women. **Nice Coloured Girls** explicitly denies the victim status of Aboriginal women in White Australia, and celebrates their perceptiveness, ingenuity, skills, and sexual power. It is reductionist to see it simply as a film about three 'coloured girls' who take revenge for 200 years of White oppression by ripping off a symbolic White 'Captain'. Instead, it can be read as a film that establishes a dynamic interplay between a number of binary oppositions : nice girls/nasty girls; White culture/Black culture; the past/the present; predator/prey; exploiter/exploited. **Nice Coloured Girls** deliberately rejects and confronts orthodox histories of colonial race and gender relations, and makes an important contribution to the re-appropriation of that history by Aborigines.

Ros Sultan and Tim Burns's short experimental film **Luke's Party** (1992) is a highly self-reflexive work that foregrounds the film-making process. An Aboriginal woman (Ros Sultan) attempts to give a personal account of her family's history of stolen children and her fear of losing custody of her own child. Her direct address to the camera—a highly familiar and conventional documentary mode—is continually disrupted by exaggerated technical 'difficulties' and absurdist interruptions by a host of representatives of various bureaucracies and institutions of state control. The film oscillates between anarchic comedy and disturbing pathos as the woman's story struggles to break through the barriers of systemic poverty and institutionalised racism.

The problem of who should and can speak for whom raises crucial political issues about representation, representativeness, and exclusivity, and major cultural institutions in Australia are becoming increasingly aware of this. In 1995 the Australian Film Commission established an indigenous production unit and sponsored six short experimental films, all by first-time drama directors. The collection was screened under the title **From Sand to Celluloid**, and was later broadcast on SBS. The six short dramas are stylistically varied, ranging from the naturalistic to the highly stylised, but they share a passion and an impressive boldness of vision. One of the most powerful is Richard Franklin's **No Way to Forget** (1996), a strong impressionistic account of a Koori investigator of Aboriginal deaths in custody, and is based on Franklin's own experiences as a field officer during the Royal Commission into Aboriginal deaths in custody. The film locates stark first-person memories in the surreal and haunting landscape of a literal and symbolic road journey. A more comical journey is the subject of Rima Tamou's **Round Up**, in which two country 'cowboys'—one White, one Aboriginal—go to the city and are forced to confront issues of their own differences and commonalities. Others in this series include Sally Riley's **Fly Peewee Fly** (1995), a whimsical and poignant work that deals with the dilemma of a young boy torn between his White grandmother and his Aboriginal father. Darlene Johnson's **Two Bob Mermaid** (1996) explores similar issues of racial tension and identity for an Aboriginal teenage girl.

Australians are wrestling with complex questions and challenges posed by the Mabo case and the Wik High Court judgment about native title lands and pastoral leases. The 2000 Sydney Olympics are focusing global attention on human rights issues concerning Aborigines. Films that promote the de-mythologising of Aboriginality are more than ever profoundly important. The increasing participation of Aboriginal people in film and video production both indicates and assists such reappraisal. KAREN JENNINGS

Actors Equity,
see **Unions and associations**

Actuality,
see **Documentary and non-fiction, silent**

Adams, Phillip (1939–) PRODUCER Although Phillip Adams is designated as a producer here, his contribution to the growth of new Australian cinema goes well beyond this function. His first film, •**Jack and Jill: A Postscript** (1970), on which he shares (with Brian Robinson) director, producer, script, editing, and cinematography credits, represented the culmination of five years of hard, trouble-ridden work. By the time that this bitter little tale of a mismatched relationship was released, Adams had become a major stirrer of public interest in the prospect of a local industry and, since then, in various newspapers, including the *Australian*, the *Age*, and the *Sydney Morning Herald*, he has acquired a reputation as an often iconoclastic diagnostician of Australian cultural mores, with particular interest in television and the cinema.

In 1968, the Liberal prime minister, John Gorton, appointed him to the Australian Council of the Arts, along with Victorian lecturer and Labor Party member, Barry Jones, to advise on the promotion of an Australian film industry. Gorton sent them and Peter Coleman, Liberal politician and chairman of the Film and Television Committee of the Australian Council of the Arts (see Australian Film Commission), on a fact-finding mission to study how overseas governments assisted their film and television industries. Their recommendations led to the formation of several important organisations, including the Australian Film Development Corporation (which later became the Australian Film Commission), the Experimental Film and Television Fund (see Experimental film), and a national Film and Television School (see Australian Film, Television and Radio School (AFTRS)). Adams was the foundation chairman of the Film, Radio and Television Board of the Australian Council of the Arts, and later of the •Australian Film Institute. There had been other notable voices in the 1960s clamouring for an Australian cinema, but it is arguable that Adams, having the ear of those with real political power, was the most influential in actually bringing about material progress. Throughout this time, he maintained his position as partner in a Melbourne advertising agency.

His name is attached to several key films of the 1970s. He was executive producer on John B. •Murray's •**The Naked Bunyip** (1970), a semi-documentary on sexual

behaviours, which made a profit from the makers' direct exhibition procedures. As producer of Bruce •Beresford's •The Adventures of Barry McKenzie (1972), he also handled distribution personally. The film was a commercial success both here and in the United Kingdom. He produced Beresford's •Don's Party (1976), based on David •Williamson's play, and former Prime Minister Gorton was given a cameo appearance as a gesture towards his support for the arts, and especially film, in Australia. In direct contrast to these varied explorations of 'ockerdom', his next film as producer, again with Beresford as director, was the coming-of-age period piece •The Getting of Wisdom (1977), derived from Henry Handel Richardson's classic of nineteenth-century life in a girls' boarding school. He co-produced the animated feature •Grendel Grendel Grendel (1981) with its scriptwriter-director, Alexander •Stitt, and has acted as executive producer on a number of other films, including •Lonely Hearts (1982), •We of the Never Never (1982), Kitty and the Bagman (1982), and Street Hero (1982). In the 1997 feature •Road to Nhill, he was heard as the voice of God. His own status as participant in, and commentator on, the Australian film industry is perhaps not quite so lofty, but whether or not one agrees with him, there is no gainsaying his importance in the local cultural scene.
Other Australian films: Hearts and Minds (1967, doc.), Impressions of Australia (1970, doc., w.), One Designer, Two Designer (1979, doc.), Alive and Kicking (1980, doc., guest artist), A Toast to Melbourne (1981, short, guest artist), Dallas Doll (1993, actor).

BMcF

Adaptations; critical The raiding of literary texts for films sources is widespread. The large number of critically and commercially acclaimed films thus derived is well documented. The new Australian cinema of the 1970s and 1980s (see Revival, the) highlighted this issue: much of its prestige is due to the fact that many of these films are literary adaptations, and many that were not adapted from novels and plays are nevertheless characterised by 'literary' virtues.

Earlier Australian cinema drew from literary sources but, compared with the new Australian cinema, it took a less respectful attitude to its texts. This was partly a function of the texts chosen, and partly of the period in which the films were made. Although such earlier Australian films as •The Sentimental Bloke (1919, 1932) and •For the Term of His Natural Life (1927) drew on classics of Australian literature, most films were based on texts of more ephemeral and/or popular appeal: for example, •Kid Stakes (1927), based on Syd Nicholls's comic-strip characters; Hills of Hate (1926), based on a novel by E.V. Timms; The Mystery of a Hansom Cab (1925), from Fergus Hume's novel of the same name; and various films based on Steele Rudd's 'Dad and Dave' stories (•Dad and Dave Come to Town, 1938; •Dad and Dave: On Our Selection, 1995; •Dad Rudd, MP, 1940) .

In the new Australian cinema there was a much greater reliance on 'classic' works of Australian literature. Films from this period also display a respect for the original. This may be a by-product of the many television series based on famous novels that were being made at this time. These series had the time to be more 'faithful' to the incidents and characters of the texts on which they were based. It may be that in Australia and elsewhere film-makers of recent decades are less likely than their predecessors to gut novels for plot with little regard for matters of style, atmosphere, and detail. There may also be, in new Australian cinema, a sense of wanting to claim respectability quickly, to maintain distance from 'ocker' images and from the melodramatic framework of many of the earlier adaptations. The result was not always fortunate, and this strain of 1970s film-making has now fallen into some critical disfavour.

Peter •Weir's •Picnic at Hanging Rock (1975) caught the public imagination and helped to establish the idea of a national cinema of a particular kind. It ushered in a series of similar films: based on literary sources, set in carefully recreated pasts, and of a gentle decorous nature that eschewed the genres of the dominant American cinema. At the time, these films seemed to be a reaction against the broad comedies of the early 70s—for example, •Stork (1971) and •Alvin Purple (1973)—and they gestured as much to arthouse as to mainstream cinema. The success of Picnic at Hanging Rock was also interesting in the light of the earlier failure of two fine adaptations to achieve comparable commercial success: •Wake in Fright (1971), directed by a Canadian, Ted Kotcheff, and based on a novel by Kenneth Cook; and •Walkabout (1971), directed by Nicolas Roeg, from the United Kingdom, and based on a novel by James Vance. These two films offer visions of Australia that are at odds with a national mythology that enshrines the bush as the crucible of moral virtues and persistence (predominantly male) in the face of daunting challenges. Wake in Fright represents the landscape as empty and menacing, its inhabitants as brutal and brutalising; Walkabout recognises its awesome beauties but displays them with a poetic sophistication at odds with simple mythologising, and disturbs with its implication that the values of Western civilisation may be inadequate to the challenges of the bush. The adaptations that effectively initiated and sustained the revival of Australian cinema several years later are a different matter. To start with, they are, unlike Wake in Fright and Walkabout, period films. This means that the critiques of Australian society that they offer are safely displaced into the past. Further, with rare exceptions, they belong to a gentler, more decorous school of film-making. Whatever their often considerable virtues, they do not aim to unsettle their audiences.

Picnic at Hanging Rock is important in the history of Australian cinema, not merely because of its popularity at the time, but also because of the influence that, in hindsight, it appears to have exerted on Australian film. It is based on a novel with a strong middle-class appeal; its plotting is essentially episodic, weak in causality, and deficient in closure; and it consciously eschews the melodramatic paradigm that it seems initially to offer and that might have pulled it into tighter narrative shape. It is firmly and decoratively set in the past; it has an informing strain of the rites-of-passage theme so common in Australian fiction; and it shows itself more interested in imagistic effects (visual and aural) and atmosphere than in story. After a provocative opening, the essence of the film lies not in its development of a tightly organised narrative, but in the evocation of an atmosphere, and such coherence as it aspires to lies in the way it explores the conflict implied imagistically in its two key icons: the rock and the college attended by the young women in the film.

Its success locally, and the critical acclaim it elicited overseas, served to legitimate a number of strains in Australian film culture, not all of them in the interests of the growth of a sturdy national cinema. Among the literary adaptations ushered in by **Picnic at Hanging Rock** were films such as •**Storm Boy** (1976), •**The Getting of Wisdom**, •**The Mango Tree** (1977), •**Blue Fin**, •**The Irishman**, •**The Chant of Jimmie Blacksmith** (1978), and •**My Brilliant Career** (1979). Apart from •**Sunday Too Far Away** (1975) and •**Newsfront** (1978), both based on original scripts, it was largely on such adaptations, which foregrounded their sources, that the reputation of the new Australian cinema was founded. These particular adaptations attracted some of the most notable talents of the emerging national cinema: Bruce •Beresford, Fred •Schepisi, and Gillian •Armstrong, as well as Weir. Only Schepisi's **Jimmie Blacksmith** makes uncomfortable viewing; the rest, whatever their virtues, tend to cushion their conflicts in elaborately conceived period *mise en scène* in a deferential attitude to the source text, and in a preference for the pictorial over the dramatic.

It is instructive to consider the kinds of literary texts to which Australian film-makers have been drawn. Unlike American cinema, which has so willingly and successfully ransacked the annals of popular fiction (for example, the genres of detective fiction, romantic melodrama, and the Western), new Australian cinema has been persistently drawn to works of more obviously literary aspirations. Such revered works of Australian literature as Miles Franklin's *My Brilliant Career*, Henry Handel Richardson's *The Getting of Wisdom*, Jeannie Gunn's *We of the Never Never*, Rolf Boldrewood's •*Robbery Under Arms*, Christina Stead's •*For Love Alone*, and D.H. Lawrence's •*Kangaroo* have been translated to the screen with varying success. These, and others that can less securely be called literary classics—for example, Ronald McKie's *The Mango Tree*, Elizabeth O'Connor's *The Irishman*, Beth Roberts's •*Manganinie*, and Sumner Locke Elliott's •*Careful He Might Hear You*—derive from or are firmly set in Australia's past, as is **Picnic at Hanging Rock**. It is worth noting that those few films that addressed themselves to the indocile facts of Australia's present failed at the box office; while there has been a trickle of social realist films through the 1970s and 1980s (for example, •**The FJ Holden**, 1977 and •**Fran**, 1985), they have had difficulty finding audiences, however sympathetic and well observed they are. Furthermore, almost all the literary adaptations exhibit a concern with the rites-of-passage theme (see Rites of passage) that has been endemic in Australian literature (and film), leading one to suppose that Australia as a nation was forever hovering on the brink of puberty. A concern with a 'theme' rather than a firm narrative line is also endemic in these novels, and the films based on them, as if awed by the artistic prestige of the texts, rarely do much to modify their loosely structured narratives. As a result, these films incline towards the arthouse tradition rather than to popular mainstream cinema, a tendency established with **Picnic at Hanging Rock**.

In theoretical terms, Roland Barthes's structural analysis of narratives (*S/Z*, 1974) pinpoints the defects of this dominant school of late 1970s Australian screen adaptation. Barthes identifies five codes at work in all narratives. The adaptations of the new Australian cinema seem to be deficient in the two codes that function in a linear fashion: the 'hermeneutic' code, referring to the enigma, mystery, or puzzle on which our narrative expectations are based, and describing the overall narrative contours of the work; and the 'proairetic' code, referring to the series of actions upon which the narrative is constructed. These two codes are clearly of paramount importance in narrative-driven cinema. They are crucial to the power of melodramatic structuring and to the classical Hollywood cinema. In Australian literary adaptations, it is as though film-makers have wilfully underestimated their power, as if narrative vigour and rigour were somehow vulgar.

Even when post-**Picnic at Hanging Rock** film-makers have been drawn to modern fictions, these have tended to be of the episodic, atmospheric variety, such as Gabrielle Carey and Kathy Lette's •*Puberty Blues*, Helen Garner's •*Monkey Grip*, and Criena Rohan's *The Delinquents* (see Minogue, Kylie). The attraction has been to novels whose strengths lie in the evocation of an ambience rather than in strong plotting, in which character and event work purposively to maintain the narrative drive that is obviously so important to popular cinema. Where popular fictions have been chosen as the basis for films—for example, Barry Oakley's *A Salute for the Great McCarthy* (filmed as **The**

Adaptations

Great MacArthy, 1975), Jon Cleary's *Helga's Web* (filmed as Scobie Malone, 1975), Peter Corris's •*The Empty Beach*, and the two Colleen McCullough romantic melodramas, •*Tim* and •*An Indecent Obsession*—the results have been disappointing. These films are disappointing because they do not have the courage of their convictions: they more or less embrace the melodramatic structures on which they are based, but do not follow them through: they more or less acknowledge genre conventions but, in case these might render them formulaic, they settle for meandering narrative procedures and unsatisfying closure.

The one adaptation that breaks free from the leisurely, literary, episodic rendering of a rites-of-passage story set in the recent past is **Careful He Might Hear You** (1983), derived from Sumner Locke Elliott's novel and directed by Carl •Schultz. It is in several ways an archetypal case of Australian literary adaptation: its source is artistically respectable; it is set in the recent past, beautifully recreated; and it charts a rites-of-passage progress towards a new, explicit sense of identity. However, it organises its material with a confident regard for the conventions of melodrama that saves it from some of the defects of the other adaptations discussed. It follows through the formal structures of melodrama as it charts a young boy's movement towards self-determination, the forces opposing this, and the resolution (in the interests of the boy's growth) of conflicting influences on him.

In the mid 1990s two adaptations of plays had mixed receptions: Michael •Blakemore's •Country Life (1994), which transplants Chekhov's play *Uncle Vanya* to an outback cattle station; and Richard •Franklin's •Hotel Sorrento (1995), derived from a play of the same name by Hannie Rayson. Both have been criticised as offering a return to the stately adaptation ethos of the latter 1970s. Both are concerned with the return to Australia of a successful expatriate, and both raise issues of national identity, daring more in the way of discussion and ideas than is common in Australian, and perhaps any, cinema. There is arguably a literal-mindedness at work in the transplanting of Chekov to an alien setting but **Hotel Sorrento** is exemplary in the discreet acknowledgment of the screen's difference from the stage. But in a contemporary cinema dominated by the successes of, say, •Strictly Ballroom (1992), •The Adventures of Priscilla, Queen of the Desert (1994), and •Muriel's Wedding (1994), adaptation of the kind most often favoured by the new Australian cinema seems likely to have a hard time attracting either customers or even-handed criticism. The recent failure of Gillian Armstrong's •Oscar and Lucinda (1998), based on Peter Carey's novel, offers further evidence of this.

The literary adaptation, looming larger perhaps than its exemplars warranted, was substantially responsible for inducting an almost ostentatiously anti-'ocker' strain, which assumed the status of orthodoxy in new Australian cinema until the big money-making films of the 1980s (•The Man from Snowy River, 1982, •Mad Max 2, 1981, and •Crocodile Dundee, 1986) suggested other directions. In 1975, in view of the success of the ocker comedies, a gently paced, decorative mood piece, in which atmosphere matters more than plot, could hardly have been expected to launch the 'serious' revival of Australian cinema; however, that is essentially what **Picnic at Hanging Rock** achieved.   BRIAN MCFARLANE

Adaptations, history of   Since the earliest days of Australian cinema, film-makers have used a variety of literary sources—such as novels, plays, poems, comic strips, and even newspaper reports—as the basis for their scripts. The Salvation Army's •Soldiers of the Cross (1900) was adapted from a religious text, John Foxe's *The Book of Martyrs*, originally published in 1563; •The Squatter's Daughter (1933), directed by Bert Bailey, was adapted from the play of the same name, which Bailey co-authored; poems and short stories by Henry Lawson were made into films; the *Fatty Finn* comic by Syd Nicholls became the film •The Kid Stakes (1927); Jim Bancks's comic strip *Ginger Meggs* was made into a film; and the film •Mr Reliable (1996) is based on the story of Walter Mellish that has its origins in newspaper reports.

Many fine Australian novels have been used as the basis of the script for feature films. The extremely popular novel •*Robbery Under Arms* by Rolf Boldrewood has been made into five feature films: in 1907, 1911, 1920, 1957, and 1985. The world's first big-selling crime novel, *The Mystery of a Hansom Cab*, written by Fergus Hume, in which the action starts in Collins Street Melbourne, became immensely popular as a book and a film. Charles •Chauvel's novel •*Heritage* won a Commonwealth prize of 10 000 pounds, and he directed a feature film of it in 1935. •*For The Term of His Natural Life*, written by Marcus Clarke, was made into feature films in 1908, 1911, and 1927. The Rev. Richard Cobbold's *The History of Margaret Catchpole* is a classic Raymond •Longford and Lottie •Lyell film of 1911, and Dale Collins's novels *Ordeal* and *The Sentimentalists* became American films in 1929 and 1930.

One feature of adaptation peculiar to Australia is the number of films based on poetry, particularly on long verse-narrative. The classic is, of course, C.J. Dennis's verse-narrative •*The Sentimental Bloke*, a Longford and Lyell feature film of 1919, and also filmed in 1932, 1968, and 1982. Adam Lindsay Gordon's poems *The Sick Stockrider* and *The Wreck*, Thomas E. Spencer's *How McDougall Topped the Score*, John O'Brien's collection, •*Around the Boree Log*, Henry Lawson's *Taking His Chance* and *Trooper Campbell* and the immensely popular •*The Man from Snowy River* by A.B. Paterson have all been made into feature films.

Children's literature has also been popular with film-makers as a source of adaptation. *I Can Jump Puddles* by

Alan Marshall, *Blinky Bill* by Dorothy Wall, •*Dot and the Kangaroo* by Ethel Pedley, •*Seven Little Australians* by Ethel Turner, *Golden Fiddles* by Mary Grant Bruce were all filmed either for the cinema or for television, and *Mary Poppins*, by the Australian novelist Pamela Travers, became a worldwide success, although it is not an Australian film.

Australian authors who have managed to gain an international reputation have had many of their novels filmed. Perhaps the best known was Nevil Shute. His *A Town Like Alice* has been made into a feature film and a television series, and other feature films have been made of his books *Lonely Road*, *No Highway*, *Landfall*, and *The Pied Piper*. But by far the most famous is Stanley Kramer's version of •*On the Beach*. Several of the novels of Morris West have been made into feature films: *The Shoes of the Fishermen*, *The Devil's Advocate*, *Salamander*, *The Naked Country*, and *The Crooked Road*. As is the case with Pamela Travers, it is not generally known that James Clavell is an Australian. His novels *King Rat* and *Tai Pan* have been made into feature films, while *Shogun* became a telemovie. Several novels by Jon Cleary have been filmed: •*You Can't See Round Corners*, •*The Sundowners*, *The High Commissioner*, *The Green Helmet*, *Dust in the Sun*, *Helga's Web*, *Spearfield's Daughter*, and *High Road to China*. Paul Brickhill's extremely well-known books about World War II—*The Dam Busters*, *Reach for the Sky*, and *The Great Escape*—were all made into feature films with international casts and directors. Russell Braddon's novel *The Year of the Angry Rabbit* was made into an American film titled **Night of the Lepus** (1972), and his novel •*End Play* became an Australian film directed by Tim •Burstall.

The contribution made by women authors has been substantial. *The Wilderness Orphan* by Dorothy Cottrell became a film called •**Orphan of the Wilderness** (1936), and her novel *The Silent Reefs* became an American film, **The Secret of the Purple Reef** (1960). Mary Mitchell's *A Warning To Wantons* became a movie, as did Mabel Forrest's *The Wild Moth*, which was renamed •**The Moth of Moonbi** (1926) and was directed by Charles Chauvel. Beatrice Grimshaw's *Conn of the Coral Seas* became a movie entitled •**The Adorable Outcast** (1928) directed by Norman Dawn. Katherine Susannah Prichard's •*The Pioneers*; Henry Handel Richardson's •*The Getting of Wisdom*, *Maurice Guest*, and *The Young Cosima*; Jeannie Gunn's •*We of the Never Never*; and the non-fiction story of Sister Elizabeth Kenny's work with polio victims, *And They Shall Walk*, have all been made into Australian or international films.

Adapted novels range from such classics as Miles Franklin's •*My Brilliant Career*, to more controversial works such as Norman Lindsay's •*The Age of Consent*, which stars British actors James Mason and Helen Mirren. Joan Lindsay's novel •*Picnic at Hanging Rock*, directed by Peter Weir, became

the icon of the rebirth of the Australian film industry in the mid 1970s. The popular novel is represented by Colleen McCullogh's •*Tim*, which stars a young Mel •Gibson, and her love story •*An Indecent Obsession*, which stars Wendy Hughes.

WAYNE LEVY

Addis, Erika (1954–) CINEMATOGRAPHER After studying cinematography at the Australian Film, Television and Radio School in Sydney under Bill Constable and Brian •Probyn, Erika Addis worked with cinematographer Geoffrey •Burton on three feature films. She is now mainly shooting observational documentaries, experimental films, and short films, gaining critical acclaim for such short films as •**Don't Call Me Girlie** (1985). Erika won an Australian Cinematographers Society Golden Tripod Award (Best Cinematography, Short Drama) for **The Nights Belong to the Novelist** (1987) and a St Kilda Film Festival Kodak Award, Best Cinematography, for the short film **My Life Without Steve** (1987). She has photographed one feature film, **Breathing Underwater** (1992). DAVID MUIR

Adele, Jan (1935–) ACTOR The high point in Jan Adele's film career was undoubtedly the role of Bet, Claudia •Karvan's grandmother, in Gillian •Armstrong's •**Hightide** (1987), a bitter-sweet study of three women who come together in a caravan park on the south-east coast of NSW. Adele's skilful performance won her the Australian Film Institute (AFI) award for Best Supporting Actress in 1987. Adele followed this with the lead role in the uneven comedy **Daisy and Simon** (1989). Adele began her career in the entertainment business as a child performer; by the age of 14 she was appearing as a singer and dancer in many of the top nightclubs in Sydney. Adele also spent 12 years as a regular artiste on the *Mike Walsh Show* on television. Her other notable film performance was in the comedy **Wendy Cracked a Walnut** (1990), a performance for which she won the Houston International Film Festival award for Best Supporting Actress.

Other Australian films: •**Caddie** (1976), •**Winter of Our Dreams** (1981), **Fatal Bond** (1992), **Greenkeeping** (1993), •**The Sum of Us** (1994). GM

Adorable Outcast, The
[Black Cargoes of the South Seas]

1928. *Director/Producer/Scriptwriter*: Norman Dawn. From the novel *Conn of the Coral Seas* by Beatrice Grimshaw. *Director of photography*: Arthur Higgins. B&W. *Cast*: Edith Roberts (Luya), John Gavin (Carberry), Arthur Tauchert (Mack).

The **Adorable Outcast** is typical of the island romance genre of its period, with a desirable 'native' woman (often revealed not to be native after all) at the centre of a plot involving

Adventures of Algy

good and evil White men in conflict over the fabulous riches of a tropical paradise. In 1920, Norman •Dawn released a film in the USA through Universal Pictures called **The Adorable Savage**, which apparently has not survived. It starred Edith Roberts. Eight years later he made **The Adorable Outcast**, also starring Edith Roberts, for •Australasian Films. Although the plots of the two films are distinguishable genre variants, the intertitles on the surviving footage from the Australian film show two distinct typefaces, suggesting two different sources. Dawn, who had operated independently for some years in Hollywood, in later life boasted of his ability to make new films from the out-takes that his specially worded contracts assigned to him. Viewed in this light, **The Adorable Outcast** is quite an interesting technical achievement.

WILLIAM D. ROUTT

Adventures of Algy, The

1925. *Director/Producer/Scriptwriter:* Beaumont Smith. *Photographers:* Lacey Percival, Frank Stewart, Syd Taylor, Charles Barton, Edwin Coubray. B&W. *Cast:* Claude Dampier (Algernon Allison), Barthie Stuart (Kiwi McGill).

Preserved today substantially as it was released, Beaumont •Smith's Australian–New Zealand production **The Adventures of Algy** is a spirited romantic comedy/drama, a local folk film, and very much a part of its time and place. The story is perfectly slight. It concerns Algy's meanderings through New Zealand countryside in search of his inheritance and the woman he loves. His prevailing mania, however, is for a seemingly insoluble crossword puzzle. Following a series of misadventures from the streets of Auckland to the oil wells of Taranaki, the film reaches its climax with the opening of an extravagant new show at a Sydney theatre—a marvellously bizarre amalgamation of vaudeville, ballet, fan dance, Maori dance, and even Cossack dancing. In the end, Algy is reunited with Kiwi and solves his puzzle. Claude Dampier made a speciality of 'silly-ass' roles, and local audiences found much to laugh at in the clueless new chum's difficulty in adapting to colonial customs.

KEN BERRYMAN

Adventures of Barry McKenzie, The

1972. *Director:* Bruce Beresford. *Producer:* Phillip Adams. *Scriptwriters:* Bruce Beresford, Barry Humphries. *Director of photography:* Don McAlpine. *Music:* Peter Best. 114 min. *Cast:* Barry Crocker (Barry McKenzie), Barry Humphries (Aunt Edna, Hoot, Meyer de Lamphrey), Peter Cook (Dominic), Spike Milligan (landlord), Dick Bentley (detective), Dennis Price (Mr Gort), Julie Covington (Blanche), Paul Bertram (Curly).

The **Adventures of Barry McKenzie** is based on Barry •Humphries's comic-strip character, which appeared in the British satirical magazine *Private Eye* in the 1960s. The episodic narrative structure of the film resembles the rambling narrative pattern of its source as it contrasts, and exaggerates, the stereotypically crude aspects of the Australian 'ocker' with a similarly caricatured presentation of British characters who are recognisable by their decadence and/or moral corruption. The film suffers from unimaginative direction and a rambling script that reworks the traditional comedy narrative pattern of placing an 'innocent' in an alien setting and then forcing the humour from the juxtaposition of two gross stereotypes, in much the way that •Crocodile Dundee (1986) takes the 'natural' Australian bushman from the Australian outback and places him in New York, although this later film is much less confrontational in its comedic style.

Barry McKenzie, an Australian 'innocent', leaves Sydney for a visit to London where he discovers that corruption and depravity are endemic in English culture, beginning with the taxi driver who takes him from Heathrow airport to his Aussie mates at Earls Court via Stonehenge. Faced with a series of humiliating encounters, ranging from Mr Gort's desire to involve Barry in his public-school flagellation fantasies, to Jesus freaks, corrupt pop promoters, and counter-culture temptations, McKenzie retains his 'virtue' by fleeing from sexually assertive English women and those aspects of English civilisation that offend his simplistic world view. McKenzie's celebration of Australian ('ocker') culture, combined with his rejection of all other cultures, is expressed by his colourful language and, often, a physical response, such as vomiting or urinating. As the audience is encouraged to laugh at both McKenzie's reaction and the presentation of any alternative viewpoints, Humphries's script is consistently nihilistic, or 'democratic', with regard to its targets.

Budgeted at $250 000, **The Adventures of Barry McKenzie** was the first film to be wholly financed by the Australian film Development Corporation (see Australian Film Commission; Cultural policy) and the commercial success of the film, despite initial opposition from the large cinema chains that forced producer Phillip •Adams to distribute the film himself, meant that the production company was able to repay most of the loan within three months of its release. The film's popularity with Australian audiences was duplicated in London and, despite reservations from some quarters in Australia concerned with the film's image of Australia and the effect this might have overseas, **The Adventures of Barry McKenzie** played a crucial part in the resurgence of the Australian film industry in the early 1970s by demonstrating the commercial viability of local production.

GM

Adventures of Dot, The

1927. *Director*: Cyril J.C. Sharpe. *Producer*: Cameo Productions. *Director of photography*: Reginald Young. *Grenfell version*: 15 min. B&W. *Cast*: Sadie Logan (Dot Farley), E.C. Dodd (Bill Cummings), A.E. Anderson (Fire Chief), Roy Roper (Andy Webb). *Temora version*: 15 min. B&W. *Cast*: Myrtle Ruschen (Dot Farley). *Young version*: 25 min. B&W. *Cast*: Molly Armstrong (Dot Farley), William Brown (Bill Cummings), Freddy Cahill (Editor), Bill Briggs (Andy Webb), Constable Eadie (PC 99), G. Spark (Town Clerk).

These short fiction films share the same story, concerning Dot, the new schoolteacher, and her two suitors—Bill and Andy. Amateurs, in a broad, comic style, perform each film, and each has been filmed in a particular town, featuring local streets and local personalities such as the fire chief, newspaper editor, town clerk, and policeman. All the schoolchildren appear, hundreds of them, filmed as they leave primary, secondary, state, and Catholic schools. Of the three versions that survive in the National Film and Sound Archive (NFSA), the version made in the town of Young is the longest and most easily followed, containing intertitles not found in the other two, and longer documentary sections, including local events such as bike races and tennis matches, watched by large crowds, across which the camera slowly pans. At the time, citizens of the towns were eager participants and equally eager spectators when the film was shown at the local cinema: the Young version even opens with footage of the exterior of the Strand Theatre, the film's sponsor. Now, the films provide unique records of the towns at that moment in their history. IB

Adventures of Priscilla, Queen of the Desert, The

1994. *Director*: Stephan Elliott. *Producers*: Al Clark, Michael Hamlyn. *Scriptwriter*: Stephan Elliott. *Director of photography*: Brian J. Breheny. *Music*: Guy Gross. 99 min. *Cast*: Terence Stamp (Bernadette), Hugo Weaving (Tick/Mitzi), Guy Pearce (Adam/Felicia), Bill Hunter (Bob), Sarah Chadwick (Marion), Mark Holmes (Benjamin).

With a brash script, outrageous costumes and a high camp soundtrack, this film was destined to be memorable— exactly what writer-director Stephan Elliott wanted after his début feature, **Frauds** (1993) went largely unnoticed.

Priscilla deserved its success; it is a well-made film. Who would have thought that a film about a bus carrying three drag queens from Sydney to Alice Springs would have had such public appeal? But its well-balanced script, credible actors, stunning visuals (who can forget Guy •Pearce, resplendent in silver lamé atop the travelling bus, silver train billowing behind him, miming opera?), and Oscar-winning costume design managed to make gay drag culture accessible and very entertaining.

However, it does not hold up under too much close scrutiny. Attempts at exploring the whys and wherefores of sexuality are lightweight, and Pearce's mincing performance is a tad too overdone. Terence Stamp as the sardonic trans-sexual Bernadette has some great moments and brings enough gravity to keep the flippant levity in check.

TIM HUNTER

AFC, *see* **Australian Film Commission**

AFI, *see* **Australian Film Institute**

AFI Awards, *see* **Appendix**

After Sundown

1911. *Directors*: W.J. Lincoln, Sam Crews. *Production Company*: Amalgamated Pictures. *Scriptwriter*: W.J. Lincoln. *Director of photography*: Orrie Perry. 60 min.(?) B&W. *Cast*: Leslie Woods (Gilbert Baxter), Godfrey Cass (Western Moore), Frank Cullinane (Davy, the publican), John Ennis (Angas McDougall), Miss Laing-Mason (Betty), Nellie Bramley (Nellie), Ethel Grist (Widow O'Leary).

This was the first of nine features produced in 1911 and 1912 by Amalgamated Pictures. It was a romantic family saga set in a small bush community, with interiors filmed in the company's St Kilda studio and location filming near Healesville. The heroine (Betty) allows her affections to be diverted from her true love (Gilbert Baxter) to a cattle duffer (Western Moore), who is caught in the act, shot, and dies in the arms of the girl he betrayed (Nellie), leaving Betty and Gilbert to wander through the bush arm in arm into a happy future. Surviving fragments show bucolic scenery and some melodramatic action at a dance in the local hall. It was announced for release at the Melbourne Glaciarium, but this does not appear to have taken place. The quality of the film is similar to that of others of the period. IB

Age of Consent

1969. *Director*: Michael Powell. *Producers*: Michael Powell, James Mason. *Scriptwriter*: Peter Yeldham. *Director of photography*: Hannes Staudinger. *Music*: Stanley Myers. 103 min. *Cast*: James Mason (Bradley Morahan), Helen Mirren (Cora), Jack MacGowran (Nat Kelly), Neva Carr-Glyn (Ma Ryan), Lonsdale (Godfrey the dog).

Successful but disillusioned Australian artist Brad Morahan returns from New York seeking solitude and respite from the pressures of the art world. His sojourn on a secluded island on the Great Barrier Reef is transformed when he meets teenager Cora, who lives on the island with her rapacious, alcoholic grandmother, Ma Ryan, and dreams of escaping to Brisbane. Cora's sylph-like innocence captivates

Brad and rekindles his artistic passion. In an argument with Cora over money, Ma falls to her death, which Brad and Cora manage to convince the local policeman was accidental. Brad tells Cora she has 'given me back my eyes', and the film ends as they embrace for the first time. Adapted from a Norman Lindsay novel, Michael Powell's second Australian feature (after •They're a Weird Mob, 1966) was commercially well received, although James Mason's unconvincing performance detracts somewhat from the glorious Dunk Island locations and from an endearing performance by Helen Mirren, already an accomplished stage actor, in her first major film role.   BEN GOLDSMITH

Alexander, Elizabeth (1953–) ACTOR   Elizabeth Alexander is a television, stage, and film actor from South Australia who graduated from the National Institute of Dramatic Art (NIDA) in 1972. After key performances in the late 1970s, including the role of Jenny Abbott, the enigmatic woman who plays a pivotal part in the violent climax to •Summerfield (1977), as well as •The Chant of Jimmie Blacksmith (1978), and The Journalist (1979), Alexander had the best role of her relatively brief screen career in •The Killing of Angel Street (1981). In this film she has the lead role of Jessica Simmonds, the scientist who returns from overseas to her inner-city Sydney roots to find a battle over the fate of the remaining houses in Angel Street. After the murder of her father, Simmonds successfully leads the residents and squatters in the fight against a ruthless property developer, corrupt police, and greedy politicians. Following The Killing of Angel Street Alexander largely withdrew from film acting and became increasingly involved in theatre direction that included a video presentation of the Australian Film Theatre's production of Emmett Stone in 1985. Alexander was also a commissioner in the Australian Film Commission.

Other Australian films include: •Ride a Wild Pony (1975), The Scalp Merchant (1978), Two Brothers Running (1988), Sebastian and the Sparrow (1989).   GM

Alison, Dorothy (1925–92) ACTOR   Most of Dorothy Alison's screen career was in the United Kingdom, where she gave memorable performances in such films as **Mandy** (1952), as a shrewd teacher of deaf children, and **Reach for the Sky** (1956), as Douglas Bader's sympathetic nurse. However, born in NSW, she appeared in •**Eureka Stockade** (1949) and •**Sons of Matthew** (1949) before leaving Australia, as actors wanting film careers were obliged to do then. She returned to make several films in the 1980s, including **Two Brothers Running** (1988), **Rikky and Pete** (1988), •**Evil Angels** (1988, as Lindy Chamberlain's mother), and **Malpractice** (1989). Her last role was in the French production, **Australia** (1989). She had a special skill in imbuing whatever role she plays with naturalness and warmth.   BMcF

Alvin Purple

1973. Director: Tim Burstall. Producer: Tim Burstall. Script: Alan Hopgood. Director of photography: Robin Copping. Music: Brian Cadd. 97 mins. Cast: Graeme Blundell (Alvin Purple), Elli Maclure (Tina Donovan), Penne Hackforth-Jones (Dr Liz Sort), George Whaley (Dr McBurney), Alan Finney (Spike Dooley), Noel Ferrier (Judge).

Alvin Purple was without doubt one of the seminal films of the 1970s. The definitive ocker comedy, it depicts Alvin's attempts to come to terms with his irresistibility to the opposite sex through his school days and time as a waterbed salesman. He is driven to seek the advice of psychiatrist Liz Sort, whose colleague Dr McBurney sees Alvin's remedial potential for his sexually dysfunctional female patients, and sets him up as a sex therapist. When McBurney is exposed as a fraud, Alvin is prosecuted but acquitted. Hounded by the husbands of his clients, Alvin realises his true love for Tina who, disenchanted with the revelations about his activities at the trial, has become a nun. To prove his love for her, Alvin becomes the convent gardener.

With a cast of household and soon-to-be familiar names, **Alvin Purple** survived a critical mauling to become the most commercially successful Australian film of the 1970s. Local audiences responded to the film's blend of innuendo, slapstick, and full-frontal nudity, which pushed the boundaries of recently relaxed censorship regulations. The success of Tim •Burstall's previous feature, •Stork (1971), encouraged the distribution–exhibition conglomerate •Village Roadshow to join forces with the director and his business partners, Robin •Copping and Peter Bilcock, and form •Hexagon Films. **Alvin Purple** was Hexagon's first feature, and represented the first investment in production of the revival by a major distributor or exhibitor. The film spawned two sequels, **Alvin Rides Again** (1974) and **Melvin: Son of Alvin** (1984), and a controversial 1976 ABC television series, and might be credited with creating a space for the period drama to emerge as the genre of choice for the funding bodies (as the antithesis of ocker) from the mid 1970s.   BEN GOLDSMITH

Always Another Dawn

1947. Director: T.O. McCreadie. Producer: T.O. McCreadie. Scriptwriters: Zelma Roberts, T.O. McCreadie. Director of photography: Harry Malcolm. Music: Iris Mason, Hal Saunders. 79 (originally 108) min. B&W. Cast: Charles Tingwell (Terry Regan), Guy Doleman (Warren Melville), Queenie Ashton (Molly Regan), Betty McDowall (Patricia).

This was the first of three features produced by Embassy Pictures, formed by T.O. (Tom) •McCreadie and his elder brother Alec. The film suffers from high-minded dialogue and overly insistent patriotism. Its chief interest is in •Tingwell's first leading role (he had a bit part in •Smithy in 1946), and he acts with the naturalness that become one of his great strengths. He plays Terry Regan, whose naval officer father had been killed in action in 1916. Terry farewells his mother (Ashton can do little with her 'stage-Irish' dialogue) to join the navy at the outset of World War II, does service in the Mediterranean, falls in love with Patricia when he comes home on leave, and is killed in the war with the Japanese. His friend 'Bunny' Warren Melville is left to voice the noble sentiments by which Terry has lived. Action scenes, including training sequences at Flinders Naval Depot, are well staged, but the personal drama lacks conviction. BMcF

Anderson, Robin (1950–) and Connolly, Bob

(1945–) PRODUCERS/DIRECTORS After a career with the Australian Broadcasting Corporation where, during the 1970s, he worked on A Big Country, Bob Connolly contributed to the scripts of David •Bradbury's **From Hiroshima to Hanoi (Public Enemy Number One)** (1981), **Frontline** (1979), **Nicaragua** (1984), **No Pasaran**, and **Chile: Hasta Cuando?** (1985).

The partnership of Robin Anderson and Connolly has since directed and produced a trilogy of films: **First Contact** (1983), **Joe Leahey's Neighbours** (1989), and **Black Harvest** (1992) set in Papua New Guinea. The trilogy is a complex analysis of Papua New Guinea's emergence into modernity. **First Contact** (Academy Award nominee, 1984) traces the initial contacts between New Guinea highlanders and European explorers, Mick Leahey and his brothers, pointing up the complex intercultural negotiations involved. The later two films, through Mick Leahey's son, Joe, examine relations within a cash-crop economy in a post-colonial nation—presenting a society caught between tribal loyalties and the practices of modern commerce in the global coffee trade.

Like these films, **Rats in the Ranks** (1996), an incisive dissection of local politics in Sydney's inner western suburbs, uses an observational style based on a strong central character and a compelling narrative to present its picture of political manoeuvering. Exemplary use of visual storytelling techniques and narrative exposition, creating a rich and emotionally gripping drama, are characteristics of each of these documentaries. PETER HUGHES

Angel Baby

1995. Director and Scriptwriter: Michael Rymer. Producers: Timothy White, Jonathan Shteinman. Director of photography: Ellery Ryan. Music: John Clifford White. 104 min. Cast: John Lynch (Harry), Jacqueline McKenzie (Kate), Colin Friels (Morris), Deborra-Lee Furness (Louise), Robyn Nevin (Dr Norberg).

Harry and Kate meet and fall in love through a day-care therapy group for schizophrenics. Kate receives messages from her guardian angel, 'Astral', through a television quiz show, and both Harry and Kate are troubled by 'voices' and debilitating delusionary spells. Against the odds, they set up house in a grotty Housing Commission flat. Harry finds a job and Kate falls pregnant, but both suffer relapses after abandoning their medications. Birth and death converge in a traumatic hospital-scene climax and its aftermath.

Angel Baby, a stylish and well-received début from Michael Rymer, presents a compassionate and unsentimental dramatisation of the difficulties schizophrenia poses for relationships and for any kind of normal life. However, with a governing interest in character and mood, it transcends the limits of the 'social problem' film through the intensity of the central relationship. John Lynch's performance is striking, and the Melbourne cityscape is well captured by Ellery •Ryan, although the symbolism of the West Gate Bridge is perhaps a little strained. HARRY OLDMEADOW

Animation

In 1907, 22-year-old Pat Sullivan, a modestly talented cartoonist, took off from his native Darlinghurst for London, landed a job as a mule-wrangler on a boat plying the Atlantic, jumped ship in New York, fell into the fledgling animated cartoon trade, and hired a bright young kid called Otto Mesmer who, while Sullivan was spending a year in prison for rape, devised a character called Felix the Cat, for which his boss ever after took credit, fortune, and fame. Animation is a funny business.

The year before Sullivan left home, two other young Sydney artists, Sydney Ure Smith and Harry Julius, opened what was to become a highly successful commercial art studio, Smith and Julius. Ure Smith would eventually become a big name in Australian art publishing, while Harry Julius was attracted to the new medium of the cinema, and became the first artist in Australia to make film cartoons and advertisements, although it was Eric •Porter who established the first local studio dedicated to animation. At 16, Porter was working for Ken •Hall at •Cinesound when a young Frank Packer financed him, along with cartoonist Jim Bancks, to produce a short cartoon film featuring Bancks's popular comic-strip character Ginger Meggs. Soon after, Porter set up his own studio and produced, between commercial assignments, entertainment shorts featuring Willy Wombat and other anthropomorphic Australian animal characters, with little popular success.

The advent of television in the USA provided a whole new market for animation, and Porter's studio began contracting the production of episodes of American cartoon series. This Americanisation of the studio's output is reflected even in the title of its only animated feature, the first made in Australia, **Marco Polo Junior versus the Red Dragon** (1972). Not a wombat in sight. Polish-born Yoram •Gross, on the other hand, who opened a studio in Sydney in 1968, had considerable international success with indigenous characters in •**Dot and the Kangaroo** (1977) and a whole string of sequels. The American market was eagerly cultivated by other local studios, and eventually led to Hollywood's Hanna-Barbera (*The Flintstones*) establishing a studio of their own in Sydney, although 'factory' would be a more appropriate description, since it provided work and experience for Australian animators, but very little joy, since all of what passed for creative input was foreign.

In 1956 everything changed. The advent of television in Australia meant Australian content and, more particularly, Australian commercials. Animation boomed, creativity became a sought-after commodity, and some gifted people entered the business. David Deneen, one of Australia's most stylish animators, had started out as a finishing artist at Smith and Julius. In 1960 he joined the Rowell Greenhalge studio as a trainee animator-designer. As he moved in, Ray Leach, a key figure in this studio, moved out to start his own highly influential studio, Graphik Animation. Deneen also later established his own business, Film Graphics. Also in 1960, Zoran Janjic arrived from Yugoslavia where he had worked at the sophisticated Zagreb studios. He soon joined Wal and Wendy Hucker at Air Programs International (known as API, perhaps as a nod to UPA, the iconoclastic American animation studio of the 1950s).

All of this activity was in Sydney. Melbourne, with no history of animation production to speak of, presented a very different picture. The Owen Brothers (who had once employed a very young Bruce •Petty as an animator) ran a small studio, mostly preparing title cards for newsreels and the like. Apart from one or two individuals, including Alex •Stitt, this was the extent of animation activity in Melbourne. Stitt produced a handful of commercials through 1956 and 1957. When John Wilson, a Los Angeles-based Englishman, persuaded Channel 9 in Melbourne (GTV9) to form a subsidiary company (John Wilson Productions, later named Fanfare Films) to produce animated commercials, Stitt was hired as a designer, and joined a group of highly talented, eminent newspaper cartoonists, illustrators, and the like, all of whom were completely inexperienced in animation. Wilson brought over a team of American practitioners—an animator, a cell painter, a background artist, and a camera operator—to train the staff of Fanfare Films. He also brought with him a number of show reels of American advertisements—work by talents as disparate as John Hubley, Stan Fregberg, and Saul Bass—that had a major impact on the work produced by the team at Fanfare.

One of Fanfare's early clients was Paton Advertising, represented by their television producer Phillip •Adams and his young assistant Fred •Schepisi. Adams had a genuine passion for the medium of animation, and encouraged Fanfare to develop innovative styles and techniques for his clients' work. Stitt's association with Adams, which continued for many years after Stitt had formed a studio of his own, led to the 'Life. Be in it' government fitness campaign (1976 and on) and the animated features •**Grendel Grendel Grendel** (1981) and **Abra Cadabra** (1983).

Many of the Fanfare staff went on to play important roles in the industry. While still at Fanfare, Gus McLaren wrote, directed, and animated Australia's first animated series, *Freddo the Frog*. *Freddo the Frog* ran to 39 five-minute episodes. McLaren later joined API and worked on their homegrown *Arthur and the Square Knights of the Round Table* series. Anne Jolliffe spent many years in London before returning to Sydney to make **The Maitland and Morpeth String Quartet** and, among other things, the title sequence for *Kaboodle*, an ambitious local animation project of the Australian Children's Television Foundation. Frank Hellard acted as animation director on both **Grendel** and **Abra Cadabra**. David Atkinson, a gifted animator, became a fine teacher, joining the staff of the Royal Melbourne Institute of Technology. Maggie Geddes, after a sojourn in London, eventually established The Funny Farm. Bruce Petty produced a string of idiosyncratic films, including the Academy Award-winning **Leisure**, made in association with Deneen. Petty's films, or any of Mesmer's Felix cartoons (which are now almost a century old), clearly reveal that animation—which can be personal, unique, surprising and mysterious—is a medium that ranks with any other art form. Nowadays, however, this idea is almost totally submerged by the wash of commercial animation.

ALEX STITT

Annie's Coming Out

1984. *Director*: Gil Brealey. *Producer*: Don Murray. *Scriptwriters*: John Patterson, Chris Borthwick. Based on the true story of (and a book by) Rosemary Crossley and Anne McDonald. *Director of photography*: Mick Van Bornemann. *Music*: Simon Walker. 96 min. *Cast*: Angela Punch McGregor (Jessica Hathaway), Drew Forsythe (David Lewis), Liddy Clark (Sally Clements), Monica Maughan (Vera Peters), Philippa Baker (Sister Waterman). Tina Arhondis (Annie O'Farrell).

Based on a true story, **Annie's Coming Out** dramatises the plight of Anne McDonald (in the film called Annie O'Farrell), a physically disabled child who is wrongly diagnosed as mentally retarded. A social worker, Jessica Hathaway (in real life Rosemary Crossley, from whose experiences and book the film is derived) takes up her case and determines to rescue the child from the institution to which she has been committed. As in many films of the new Australian cinema (see Revival, the), institutions are unsympathetically depicted, but the film tends to settle for well-tried melodramatic clichés rather than exploring the problem in the sober complex detail it requires.

However, Annie's story is indeed an inspiring one, and Tina Arhondis registers the pain of an acute mind imprisoned in a disabled body. The best of the film is in the relationship between her and her rescuer.   BMcF

Anzacs, *see* War-time film-making; Mateship

Archdale, Alexander (1905–86) ACTOR So long resident in Australia that some reference books describe him as 'Australian actor', Alexander Archdale is, in fact, British-born. His long career has included acting in all the media, teaching at the British Royal Academy of Dramatic Art (RADA) in 1957–60 (during which period he made some British films), and returning to Australia to found the Community Theatre in 1961. His British films included **Lucky Days** (1935) and **The Scapegoat** (1959). He first appeared in films here in Cecil •Holmes's •**Three in One** (1957), in the 'Joe Wilson's Mates' story. Of his later roles, the most prominent was that of the ageing academic who refuses to be intimidated in •**The Killing of Angel Street** (1981). In whichever country, he was almost always cast as a distinguished upper-class man.
Other Australian films: •The Adventures of Barry McKenzie (1972), •Newsfront (1978), •The Night The Prowler (1979).
                    BMcF

Archives In the early twentieth century it was by no means self-evident that films had enduring value and, if they did, that any strategic action was warranted to ensure their preservation. Survival was mostly a matter of chance, albeit assisted by occasional foresight and a growing underworld of private collectors from the 1920s onwards. Occasionally, films were placed in libraries or institutions with the stated intention of preservation, although the task of preservation would have been beyond the technical capability of archivists. None of these films seems to have survived. The 1930s saw the increasing global destruction of silent film inventories rendered commercially valueless by the advent of sound.

A farsighted beginning to government action occurred in 1937 with the establishment of the National Historical Film and Speaking Record Library, under the aegis of the then Commonwealth National Library, but the initiative did not survive the war years. However, the idea re-emerged in the 1950s as a subsidiary activity of the National Library's film division: the division, although primarily a lending library, began a low-key but dogged search for early films, which yielded important discoveries. Also, in Canberra, the Australian War Memorial began actively to include film footage in its assembly of war records.

A moribund production industry—only gradually stimulated by the introduction of television in 1956—and gen-

eral disregard of the cultural, academic, historical, and artistic value of film, made an unpromising climate for archiving. These conditions began to change as the 1970s dawned and a gathering ferment of activism accompanied the renaissance of feature film production and the advent of colour television. In 1972 the National Library of Australia established a separate staff unit to build on the film division's work: collections, skills, and activity rapidly expanded and international norms were adopted. At the same time, other institutions—such as Australian Archives and the State Library of Western Australia—established archival film collections. The Commonwealth Film Unit (now •Film Australia) and ABC television gave serious attention to the care of their own inventories, and commercial production houses and television networks began to follow suit. The accessibility of expanding collections, in turn, stimulated research and the popularity of compilation films and television programs that explored the history of the Australian film industry as well as society in general. In 1981, The Last Film Search, a successful treasure hunt for vanishing film, captured the national imagination and the global attention of film archivists. It had a simple message: 'nitrate won't wait'.

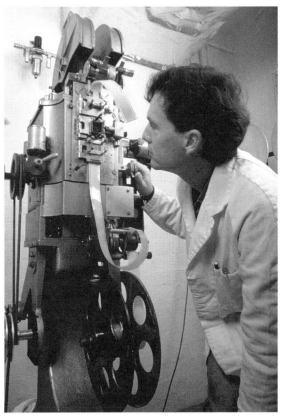

Work in progress at the National Film and Sound Archive

In 1984, after more than a decade of persistent pressure from a broad range of media, as well as from academia, the film and television industry, and other cultural sources, the government hived off the film and sound archive collections and staff of the National Library and re-established them as the National Film and Sound Archive (NFSA), an autonomous institution based in Canberra, with branches in Sydney and Melbourne. Symbolically, this raised and recognised the cultural status of Australia's audiovisual heritage in its own right, and created a central reference point for the further stimulation of the field. It recognised the need for investment in developing the technical facilities, skills, and infrastructure to preserve and provide access to the heritage. The NFSA was renamed ScreenSound Australia (SSA) in 1999.

By the end of the 1990s, the archiving landscape had changed markedly. Collectively, a number of institutions and organisations—both public and private—offered a range of large, high-quality, controlled-storage environments for all audiovisual formats. Computerisation of catalogues and inventories advanced and made access easier. A well-developed policy base set out what institutions should aim to achieve. From the proverbial handful, the number of archival audiovisual collections grew to dozens, operating at the national, state, and local-region levels, and endeavouring to distribute and coordinate the national task in sensible ways.

In recent years, Australia can be said to have moved from a 'country cousin' status in the global archiving networks to one of the more significant players, especially in the area of technical services, training, and professional theory. It plays a pivotal role in the rapidly developing network in South-east Asia and the Pacific. As an example, the SSA laboratories now restore films and tapes for overseas as well as domestic clients and, in 1997, the NFSA and University of New South Wales jointly launched a pioneering internet-delivered course in audiovisual archiving to a global clientele.

There are many challenges for the future. The ever-increasing volume of film and television production signals increased preservation costs. The escalating pace of technical obsolescence requires a constantly expanding skills and equipment base, for archives have to maintain obsolete as well as current equipment. To the traditional problem of nitrate film decomposition, we add the newer, and potentially greater, demands of 'vinegar syndrome'—the degradation of modern acetate film. Digitisation will bring both benefits and new demands. Australia has still not introduced legal deposit arrangements for audiovisual materials, so archives still rely on other acquisition arrangements. The preservation and management task increases annually as collections grow, as does the need to contain costs and work smarter.

As we enter the new century, how may we judge our archival stewardship of our film heritage to date? Sadly, we were too late to capture most of our pre-1930 silent films: only five per cent of the whole (including 10 per cent of the feature films) are known to have survived. We have done better since then: the distributed collection includes most of our feature films, documentaries, newsreels, and short films, and at least a representative coverage of advertising. But there are serious gaps and shortcomings: surviving copies are not always complete, of the best quality, or in exemplary condition. For example, many hundreds of the newsreels lack soundtracks. Current production is being covered reasonably well, although not always promptly. Supporting material—publicity stills and posters, scripts, memorabilia—tends to reflect the same pattern: the older it is, the less there is of it. RAY EDMONDSON

Argall, Ray (1957–) DIRECTOR/CINEMATOGRAPHER In 1990 Ray Argall wrote and directed one of the most attractive Australian films in the low-key realist tradition, •**Return Home**. It centres on a divorced Melbourne businessman who visits his garage-owning brother and family in seaside-suburban Adelaide and finds, in the warmth of familial life, that he has 'returned home' in more ways than one. The freshness of the film's observation, its unobtrusive contrasts between modes of living, and its telling, uncluttered visual style should have marked Argall out as a major new director. In the event, he has to date directed and written only one further feature, the little-seen **Eight Ball** (1992). He came to direction through his work as a cinematographer on such films as **The Plains of Heaven** (1982) and **Tender Hooks** (1989), contributing a great deal to the persuasiveness of these very different milieu studies, the one alpine and the other inner suburban. His versatility extends to writing and editing as well.

Other Australian films: Wrong World (1986, ed., c.), •With Love to the Person Next to Me (1987, ed., c.) The Prisoner of St Petersburg (1990, c.), Stan and George's New Life (1991, c.), Body Melt (1993, c.). BMcF

Argue, David (1959–) ACTOR David Argue's role as Snowy in •**Gallipoli** (1981) established his screen persona as that of a crude larrikin. He repeated this persona as Dicko Baker in •**Razorback** (1984), and later refined it, particularly in •**Backlash** (1986), arguably his finest screen performance.

Argue comes from a show-business family; his parents have long been involved in ice-skating. At the time of his admission, Argue was the youngest person accepted at the National Institute of Dramatic Art (NIDA). He has worked as a comedian, ice-skater, writer, screen, and stage actor. Argue has also performed in many Australian television series, including *Water Rats* and *Corelli*, and he was a regu-

David Argue

lar guest on the *Ray Martin Show*. Argue's first comic novel, *Even the Rats Clapped*, was published in 1995. His screen career has languished since the mid 1980s, when he had key roles in films such as **BMX Bandits** (1983), **Midnight Spares** (1983), **Stanley: Every Home Should Have One** (1984), and **The Coca-Cola Kid** (1985). Although Argue has worked steadily since then, including a pivotal role in •**Blood Oath** (1990), he appears constrained by the screen persona established in his early roles.

Other Australian films: The Return of Captain Invincible (1983), Going Down (1983), Melvin, Son of Alvin (1984), Pandemonium (1988), Crime Time (1992), No Escape (1994), •Angel Baby (1995), •Lilian's Story (1995).   GM

Armstrong, Gillian (1950–) DIRECTOR The longevity of Gillian Armstrong's career as a prominent director can be attributed to a publicly funded production industry that has been prepared to nurture and reward a mix of talent, tenacity, and timing, in the interest of producing quality cinema. In the first of many well-timed moves, Armstrong graduated from Swinburne Technical College in 1971, after switching from theatre costume design to the art school's fledgling Film and Television course. In 1973 she was one of 12 students admitted to the inaugural Interim Program of the newly established Australian Film and Television School in Sydney, winning acclaim for her adaptations of two short stories by Alan Marshall, **One Hundred a Day** (1973) and **The Singer and the Dancer** (1974). The critical and popular success of •**My Brilliant Career** (1979), adapted from Miles Franklin's classic novel of the same name, promoted Arm-

strong to the ranks of internationally citable directors, including Bruce •Beresford, Fred •Schepisi, and Peter •Weir, each of whom contributed to the exemplary body of 1970s Australian period films based on literary sources. As the first Australian feature film directed by a woman in 40 years, **My Brilliant Career** also marked the beginning of Armstrong's collaborative relations with high-profile women producers (Margaret •Fink, Sandra •Levy, and Jan •Chapman) and screenwriters (Eleanor •Witcombe, Laura •Jones, and Helen •Garner). The success of her first feature launched the screen careers of Judy •Davis and Sam •Neill and brought Armstrong to the attention of Hollywood, where she directed **Mrs Soffel** (1984), **Fires Within** (1991), and her most flawless film, the box-office drawcard **Little Women** (1994).

Alternating between Hollywood and Sydney, Armstrong survived the •10BA period and went on to direct •**Oscar and Lucinda** (1998), adapted from Peter Carey's novel and partly funded as the first prestige film from Sydney's Fox Studio. Although Armstrong's oeuvre is dominated by period dramas featuring rebellious women out-of-step with their times, her most compelling films are a documentary series about three working-class women, and the keenly observed family dramas •**Hightide** (1987) and •**The Last Days of Chez Nous** (1992). Armstrong's talent for intimate observation from a self-effacing distance is evident in her documentary series and her fictions. Her eye for milieu and for the way it shapes the everyday life of households gives an expressive dimension to her focus on the generational bonds and conflicts between women. Steering a steady course between the poles of landscape nostalgia and suburban grotesquerie, Armstrong shapes her films around finely tuned performances from promising young actors, notably Davis, Neill, Claudia •Karvan, and Cate •Blanchett. Her unerring ability to transform landscape into milieu, and to integrate milieu and character into a unified performance, defines Armstrong's persistent vision across genres and decades.

Other Australian films: The Roof Needs Mowing (1971, short), Smokes and Lollies (1976, doc.), 14's Good, 18's Better (1981, doc.), •Star Struck (1982), Bob Dylan in Concert (1986, doc.), Bingo, Bridesmaids and Braces (1988, doc.), Not 14 Again (1996, doc.).   FELICITY COLLINS

Armstrong, Kerry (1958–) ACTOR This versatile film–stage–television actor formally trained with Uta Hagen and Anthony Hopkins, and began as a weather girl while still at high school. While filming in Los Angeles her best-known international role as Elena, Countess of Brana in the American television series *Dynasty*, Kerry Armstrong started an experimental group (The Actors Gang), with John Cusack, Tim Robbins, Helen Hunt, and Anthony Edwards. Notable film performances include •**The Getting of Wisdom** (1977), **Amy** (1997), **20,000 Leagues Under the**

Sea (1997), and **Justice** (1997). Other films she has appeared in are: **Key Exchange** (USA, 1985), **Dadah is Death [A Long Way from Home]** (1988), **Hunting** (1991), **Tanker Incident** (USA, 1997), and **Heart of Fire** (USA, 1997). She appeared in the first episodes of *Prisoner* and subsequently many major Australian television series, including the miniseries *Water Under the Bridge* and *Come In Spinner* (1989), as well as starring roles in *Ocean Girl* and *SeaChange*. She has also been active in award-winning short films, such as **The Good Looker** (1996), **Denial** (1997), **Hepzibah Menuhin** (1998), and **Taken** (1998).

Other Australian films include: •Grievous Bodily Harm (1988).

RICK THOMPSON

Around the Boree Log

1925. *Director/Producer/Scriptwriter:* Phil K. Walsh. Based on the book of verse by John O'Brien (a pseudonym; his real name was Father Patrick Hartigan). *Director of photography:* Lacey Percival. B&W.

Around the Boree Log, which survives in more or less complete form, has a deserved reputation for sticky-sweet sentimentality. Yet there is more to the film than that. Like •**The Sentimental Bloke** (1919), **Around the Boree Log** is an almost plotless film based on a book of popular verses and narrated in the first person. In this case, however, it is difficult to locate the 'I' of the verse in the story told by the film, and this circumstance unsettles what one sees ever so slightly. Also, the Australia shown with such fervent nostalgia in the film is one that still lives in small rural communities, is piously Irish Catholic, and implicitly republican. References to the United Kingdom and the Empire are absent, which is not the usual thing in films from this period. Although the verse is overly sentimental and the direction of the anonymous cast of children pedestrian, Lacey •Percival (•**Robbery Under Arms**, 1920, •**Painted Daughters**, 1925) again demonstrates that he was one of the most astute Australian cinematographers of the 1920s with his superbly evocative images.

WILLIAM D. ROUTT

Arrighi, Luciana PRODUCTION DESIGNER   Italian-born Australian Luciana Arrighi has established an internationally distinguished career as a designer of film, television, opera, and theatre. While her experience has been varied, she admits that her passion lies in designing for the cinema. Arrighi is renowned for her extensive research and for her eye for verisimilitude in designing sets that evoke the past.

While training at the BBC from 1963 to 1966 she was commissioned by Ken Russell to design three of his early television specials. Arrighi moved into film with Russell, contributing to the design of his screen adaptation of D.H. Lawrence's **Women in Love** (1969). Returning to Australia, Arrighi designed the visual concept of Gillian •Armstrong's •**My Brilliant Career** (1979). Her intricate and faithful reproduction of rural Australia during the final years of the nineteenth century was recognised with an AFI award for art direction. Arrighi has been most successful in the USA. She won two Academy Awards in successive years for her art direction on the Merchant-Ivory productions **Howard's End** (1993) and **The Remains of the Day** (1994).

Other Australian films: •The Night The Prowler (1979), •Oscar and Lucinda (1998).

WENDY HASLEM

Asia in Australian film   In view of Asia's geographic proximity and popularity as a tourist destination, a surprisingly small number of Australian feature films have been set in South-east Asia. Those that have reveal strong similarities in narrative, characterisation, and use of setting. In nearly all of them, the heroes are Australian investigative, or photographic, journalists. They are crusading heroes—trying to expose injustice and corruption and save oppressed Asians from oppressive Asians. The suspense-thriller format is favoured, often combined with romantic melodrama. Locations are often ill-defined—it could be Hong Kong, Macao, the Philippines, Thailand, Malaysia, or Indonesia. Asian settings provide exotic backgrounds against which Western heroes and heroines play out their heroic or melodramatic destinies; they are beautiful places, full of tantalising mysteries and sensual attractions, but also sinister and/or treacherous. Asian actors, of whatever nationality, are used predominantly in minor roles and in crowd scenes as extras. Asian women tend to be portrayed as sexual and/or political victims of brutal, sinister or oppressive Asian men—necessitating the intervention of White saviours.

In •**Far East** (1982), the expatriate Australian hero (Bryan •Brown) runs a seedy bar, the Koala Club, in what is suggested but not specified to be Manila. Here, other expatriate Australian men congregate to enjoy a chat, a drink, and sexual stimulation—provided by gyrating young Asian female flesh. In a narrative strongly reminiscent of the American Warner Brothers classic **Casablanca** (1942), an old flame from Saigon (Helen •Morse) turns up with her activist journalist husband (John •Bell). Like Humphrey Bogart in **Casablanca**, Brown appears amoral and cynical but deep down his heart is true blue, and he finally sacrifices himself to save his rival, her husband. While the first half of the film intertwines romantic melodrama with exposure of social abuses (the exploitation of Philippine women and children in the streets, factories, and bars), standard elements of the suspense thriller take over towards the end: a gaol escape, a car chase, and a shoot-out. There are two Australian heroes—the intellectual investigative journalist, and the macho action hero. Like the other Asian women in the film, the Asian woman activist, potentially a second heroine, is ultimately reduced to a victim, in this case of rape and brutality.

In *The Year of Living Dangerously (1982), an adaptation of Christopher Koch's novel of the same name, Indonesia's national political crisis is reduced to the setting for a suspense thriller and a testing ground for Australian journalists. Again there are two heroes, a White male political correspondent (Mel *Gibson) and a male Chinese-Australian photojournalist (Linda Hunt), who is infatuated with Indonesian culture and hero-worships Sukarno. The former is embroiled in a romantic melodrama (with British diplomat, Sigourney Weaver) and survives; the latter dies a disillusioned death. Indonesia is portrayed as a land of beauty and terror, of sinister unfathomable politics, populated by hordes of Asian extras. While the decision to cast a White American actress as Billy (the male Chinese-Australian photographer) can be seen as disturbing the categories of gender and race, it can also be seen as a literal enactment of the Western propensity to feminise the Asian male. The feminine maleness of Billy invests the relationship between Hunt, Gibson, and Weaver with complexity, ambiguity, and even perversity; Billy's complex ethnicity (American–Chinese–Australian, immersed in Indonesian culture) helps to mask the confusion of mingled metaphors (political and personal, spiritual, and cultural) evoked by his fascination with *wayang* puppets, the film's major framing device.

In *The Good Woman of Bangkok (1992), the crusading hero is not seen, but he is there behind the camera. He is another version of the Australian investigative journalist, this time in the form of a documentary film-maker—the film's director Dennis *O'Rourke—exposing the dirty business of sex tourism and Thai prostitution through his covert (peeping) camera and overt interviews with patrons and prostitutes. He's also a would-be saviour, but exposes himself as a failed saviour, and his masochistic and exploitative aesthetic mirrors that of Aoi, the Thai prostitute, who stars for him as his melodrama queen.

In **Turtle Beach** (1992, directed by Stephen *Wallace), an adaptation of a novel by Blanche D'Alpuget, an Australian investigative journalist is again the crusading hero. Even if this time (exceptionally) the hero is a woman, her priorities are the same as her male counterparts: getting a good story, exposing oppression and injustice, and saving Asian victims from Asian oppressors. This time the setting is Malaysia and the issue the plight of the Vietnamese boat people. Objections to the film by the Malaysian government are quite understandable, given that in it Malays are unequivocally represented as monstrous murderers of Vietnamese boat people. The crusading heroine (Greta *Scacchi) not only exposes the inhuman behaviour of the Malays towards the boat people but also saves Vietnamese orphans from a watery grave. While their mother, who can't swim, stages a suicidal self-sacrifice, our heroine swims out to the boat and displays her skills as a lifesaver.

On the surface, *Traps (1994) seems to be following the pattern, set by previous Australian films, of using Asian settings and political struggles as a backdrop for the romantic adventures and investigative feats of White Australian heroes and heroines. The film is set in former Indochina, when the Vietnamese struggle for independence against French colonial rule was being spearheaded by the Viet Minh. Yet again the main protagonists are journalists: an Australian husband and political journalist and his English wife, a photojournalist. And yet, while the dramatic action centres on the personal and professional problems of the British–Australian couple, their role is critiqued rather than endorsed. Caught up in the siege mentality generated by the critical political climate, the couple's complicity in racist colonial rule is shown to be connected to economic dependence, sexual desire, emotional hysteria, and fear. In their desperate struggle for personal survival, they cannot function as saviours. No foreign crusader can free the Vietnamese; they must free themselves. This film subjects the imperialist presumption to criticism from the inside.

The Australian crusading hero surfaces again in *Blood Oath (1990), but this time he is a military prosecutor rather than an investigative journalist. **Blood Oath** is a courtroom drama based on war trials conducted soon after the end of World War II on the Indonesian island of Ambon. The Australian prosecuting hero, played by Bryan Brown, exposes the war crimes committed by the Japanese—the brutal treatment of Australian prisoners of war and the unwarranted execution of captured airmen—and attempts to indict the senior officers responsible but succeeds only in punishing a conscientious Christian junior officer. He concludes that power and privilege are the issue, not nationality. Like the emperor of Japan, the man responsible for decision-making on the island, Admiral Takahashi, was exonerated of guilt because he was deemed useful to American policy in occupied Japan.

As steel-cold samurai and hot-tempered oppressor respectively, the admiral and the camp commandant are certainly stereotyped in the manner of Japanese soldiers in World War II Allied propaganda movies, but Tanaka, the Christian junior officer, is romanticised and portrayed as a victim of both American imperialism and the Japanese class system. The revival of the touchy issue of Japanese war crimes in 1990 stirred up anti-Japanese sentiments still harboured by many Australians, but tempered this with a dose of anti-Americanism (also simmering under the surface since the war when Uncle Sam's troops wooed Australian women away from 'Aussie boys') and some social criticism. Cynical observers may see the inclusion of a good, conscientious Japanese, who fortuitously happens to be a Christian as well as a victim, as a sop to both anti-racism and the new economic power of the Japanese.

In a rare departure from the suspense thriller with its investigative hero, **Echoes of Paradise** (1987, directed by Phil •Noyce) is a woman's melodrama. Set in Sydney and Phuket (Thailand), it centres on the personal journey of middle-aged, middle-class housewife and mother, Maria (Wendy •Hughes), towards self-discovery and self-assertion. The heady sights, sounds, and smells of Asia (Phuket) arouse her sensuality, an androgynous Asian gigolo (Chinese-American John Lone as a Balinese dancer) provides her with tenderness and satisfying sex, and her Asian vacation experiences enrich and strengthen her, enabling her to return to Sydney and resume her former life with newfound confidence and respect from her formerly philandering husband. The Asian male is again feminised, this time as a dancer, long-haired, soft, and of ambiguous sexual proclivities, an object of desire for both Western men and women. It's easy to mock this film as a cross between a Thai tourist promotion and a humourless prefiguration of the British film **Shirley Valentine** (1989). But in its use of a fictional space called 'Asia' to explore Australian sexual fantasies, it really is no more laughable than the standard Australian thrillers depicting Asia. It is simply that, in the case of the thrillers, sexual fantasies are accompanied by national–political fantasies. FREDA FREIBERG

Atkins, David (1955–) ACTOR/DANCER/CHOREOGRAPHER In a different kind of film industry (Hollywood, for instance) David Atkins's talents would have been more in demand. However, Australia does not produce many film musicals, so his brilliant dancing and choreography have been more visible on the stage, in productions such as *Grease*, *Guys and Dolls*, *Cats*, and *Hot Shoe Shuffle*; on television in variety performances with Daryl Somers, Don Lane, Mike Walsh, and Bert •Newton; and on videoclips for Elton John. He has choreographed two feature films: •**Star Struck** (1982) and **The Pirate Movie** (1982). He is also an accomplished actor, in both musical comedy and straight roles. His first theatrical performance was as Patrick in *Mame* in 1968–69. He has appeared in many Australian television series, from *Homicide* and *The Sullivans* to *The Young Doctors* and *GP*. His only starring role in film was as the cocky hoodlum Arthur 'Squizzy' Taylor, in Kevin Dobson's **Squizzy Taylor** (1982). This role ideally suited his modest height and his capacity to light up the screen with his energy and self-confidence. He

David Atkins

has won many awards, including the 1995 Oliver Award for choreography and the 1994 Advance Australia Award for his Outstanding Contribution to Musical Theatre. IB

Australasian Films, *see* **Greater Union Organisation; Cinesound**

Australia Calls

1913. *Director*: Raymond Longford. *Production company*: Spencer's Pictures. *Scriptwriters*: C.A. Jeffries, John Barr. *Directors of photography*: Ernest Higgins, Tasman Higgins, Arthur Higgins. 4000 ft. B&W. *Cast*: Lottie Lyell (Beatrice Evans), Frank Phillips (Evans), William E. Hart (Aviator), Andrew Warr (Asian commander); Alfred O'Shea, George Wilkins.

By 1913 Raymond •Longford was an experienced director, ready to tackle an epic theme in a complex production. This story interweaves a romance (the inevitable love triangle) with an Asian invasion of Australia: the airborne attack is defeated by Australian grit—an aviator flying the only plane at that time in Sydney—and the true lovers are united. Lottie •Lyell stars, as in so many of Longford's films, although the other White actors were less well known. The 'Mongolian' invaders were played by members of the Sydney Chinese community. Despite unconvincing special effects (model planes on wires, a model of Sydney destroyed by fire), the film was received enthusiastically by a jingoistic public already gearing up for war, but none of it survives today. IB

Australia Calls

1923. *Director*: Raymond Longford. *Production*: Commonwealth Immigration Office/British Empire Exhibition Commission. *Scriptwriter*: Lottie Lyell. *Director of photography*: Arthur Higgins. 4000 ft. B&W. *Cast*: Ernest Idiens.

Not to be confused with an earlier film of the same name by Raymond •Longford, this was a semi-documentary, structured in a similar way to the Commonwealth Film Unit's later **Capacity Smith** (1951). A farmer (Ernest Idiens) re-enacts his own story of immigration and life in Australia. It was planned as one of four films for display in the Australian pavilion at the British Empire Exhibition. Although at least one other was completed, **Australia Calls** is the only one that we know much about and none of it survives. It may not have been widely distributed in Australia, but drew large crowds at the London exhibition from June to October 1924. IB

Australia Council, *see* Australian Film Commission

Australia's Own

1919. *Director/Producer/Scriptwriter/Director of photography*: J.E. (Jack) Ward. B&W. *Cast*: Nellie Romer, Gary Gordon, the people of Papua New Guinea.

The surviving footage from **Australia's Own** is unedited and may consist of out-takes (that is, footage unused in the released film). Much of it is 'documentary' material, shot in New Guinea, which some Australians considered 'Australia's Own' colony in 1919. A title of the film claims 'This film is an authentic record of Papuan life, made during the eight years of my travels in search of Birds of Paradise in New Guinea'. Some of these 'documentary' scenes have nonetheless evidently been staged for the camera, and one young man in particular is singled out for extensive coverage. In addition, the footage contains dramatic scenes involving a bad man, a good woman, and a good man (all White), added to make the non-fiction material into a feature attraction. Whatever value or interest these fragments of film elicit is most likely to be attached to the Papuan material.

WILLIAM D. ROUTT

Australian Centre for the Moving Image (ACMI), *see* Cinemedia

Australian Council of Film Societies, *see* Film Societies

Australian Film Authority, *see* Australian Film Commission

Australian Film Commission (AFC)

The Australian Film Commission is one of the most powerful film bureaucracies in the country. It originated from lobbying in the 1960s for federal government support for the film industry. In 1970, the three major recommendations of the Interim Report of the Film and Television Committee of the Australian Council for the Arts were put into effect by the federal government: the Experimental Film and Television Fund (see Experimental film), the •Australian Film and Television School, and the Australian Film Development Corporation (AFDC; see Cultural policy). The AFDC provided direct financial assistance to commercial film production: among its early projects were substantial investment in **Stockade** (1971) and the provision of full funding to •**The Adventures of Barry McKenzie** (1972). An inquiry into film and television by the Tariff Board in 1972 considered distribution and exhibition as well as production, and recommended the establishment of a comprehensive Australian Film Authority: when this recommendation was put into effect in 1975 the new body was called the Australian Film Commission. A project branch provided direct financial assistance (in the form of script development funding, production financing by loans and investment, and completion guarantees) on cultural as well as commercial grounds. (In 1979 the Peat, Marwick Mitchell Report initiated a shift towards preference in funding for films judged to have high box-office potential.) A marketing and distribution branch supported the distribution of Australian product overseas, both commercially (primarily at the Cannes Film Festival for instance), and in prestigious festivals and seasons: it also established AFC offices in both the USA and the United Kingdom, starting with Los Angeles in 1978. The Commonwealth Film Unit (later •Film Australia) became another division, in a rather tense relationship that lasted until 1988. The secretary's branch administered the AFC. In 1976, a fifth division was added, the creative development branch. This branch took over the functions of the Film, Radio and Television Board of the Australia Council: support of less commercial areas of film (such as experimental and documentary film), and promotion of film cultural activities such as journals, festivals, and conferences. While division 10BA of the *Tax Act* was the major method of funding feature film (see Finance), the AFC played an important role in judging which films qualified for such tax relief. In 1988, this system of support was replaced by a new funding system, through the Australian Film Finance Corporation (see Finance), which is independent of the AFC. However, the AFC continued to provide cultural funding, and support for groups of film-makers and for particular needs within the film-making community. The research and information branch has gathered data on the industry, and publishes compendiums of these in the irregular series *Get the Picture*. Documentary fellowships were provided for several years in the mid 1980s, and the women's program (which replaced the Women's Film Fund, established by the federal government in 1976) continues to provide training and other material support to women film-makers. From 1993, the indigenous branch supported training programs, and mounted special seasons of films, starting with **From Sand to Celluloid** (see Aboriginality and film). The AFC administered the Commercial Television Production Fund from 1995 to 1998 and, in the 1990s, provided generous assistance to new media projects through the 'new image research' program. Over its long history, there have been criticisms of the AFC: elements of the film community have viewed it as a rigid bureaucracy that encourages cronyism, and some outside the industry have seen it as an inappropriate drain on the public purse, a form of unwarranted subsidy for what should be a commercial activity. But it is undeniable that without this institution, in its various incarnations and with its many offshoots, Australian film production might have continued to languish and Australian film culture might have been far poorer. INA BERTRAND

Australian Film Development Corporation (AFDC), *see* Australian Film Commission; Cultural policy

Australian Film Finance Corporation, *see* Finance

Australian Film Institute (AFI)
Incorporated in 1958, the Australian Film Institute is a non-profit cultural organisation based in Melbourne. It is devoted to the promotion of the moving image as an art form, with a particular focus on the Australian screen industries. Begun as an offshoot of the Melbourne International Film Festival, the AFI was deliberately modelled on the British Film Institute, its primary function being the organisation of annual awards for achievement in the Australian film industry. In the 1960s, the early governors of the AFI successfully lobbied the Australian government to inject funds into the Australian film industry, a move that led to the establishment of the Experimental Film and Television Fund (see the entries on Experimental Film and the Australian Film Commission). In 1969, the AFI began administering this Fund, which ultimately led the Institute to assume the role of film distributor to ensure an outlet for the short films produced with grants from the Fund. The Institute began exhibiting programs in the 1970s, operating cinemas in Melbourne, Hobart, and Sydney. It established its Research and Information Centre in Melbourne in 1978 and, in 1979, took on the operation of the •National Film Theatre of Australia.

The AFI is a membership-based organisation that is governed by a board elected directly by members. Funds for the Institute come from a combination of membership fees,

state and federal government grants, corporate sponsorship, and income-generating activities, including distribution, exhibition, and research. The main activities of the Institute continue to be the organisation of the annual AFI Awards for Australian film and television, the distribution of over 1100 films and videos (predominantly Australian shorts and documentaries), a national exhibition program of first-release and curated seasons, the operation of cinemas in Hobart and Sydney, and the operation of a research library in Melbourne. The AFI also lobbies in concert with other Australian screen culture organisations. CHRIS BROPHY

Australian Film Society, *see* Film societies

Australian Film, Television and Radio School (AFTRS)
Established by an Act of Parliament in 1973, with Jerzy Toeplitz as its inaugural director, the AFTRS has been a fount of talent for the film and broadcast industries. The alumni include directors Jane •Campion, Gillian •Armstrong, Phillip •Noyce, P.J. •Hogan, Jocelyn •Moorhouse, Chris Noonan, Rolf •de Heer, Shirley Barrett, and Alex •Proyas. Nearly all the School's film and television graduates are employed in the industry, and many radio graduates are employed as broadcasters.

The main campus is in North Ryde, Sydney, with regional offices in Melbourne and Brisbane, and representatives in Perth, Adelaide, and Hobart. The school offers postgraduate and graduate diplomas in film and television for approximately 100 full-time students, supplemented by 170 short courses (with 4000 participants), which are offered throughout the country. The school includes training in directing, producing, writing, cinematography, editing, design, sound, screen studies, radio, and digital media.

Student films have won more than 300 awards at over 200 film festivals during the past 25 years. Former AFTRS students produced the winners of the Palme d'Or in 1993 (Jane Campion, •**The Piano**, 1993) and the Camera d'Or in 1996 (Shirley Barrett, •**Love Serenade**, 1996) at the Cannes Film Festival. Eleven feature films directed by graduates and eight shorts by students have been selected for the following sections of the Cannes Festival: Competition, *Un Certain Regard*, and Directors' Fortnight. ROD BISHOP

Australian National Films Board, *see* Film Australia

Australian Screen Editors Association, *see* Editing

Australian Theatrical and Amusement Employees Association, *see* Unions and associations

Students at work at the Australian Film and Television School, 1977

Auzins, Igor (1949–) DIRECTOR Igor Auzins's screen career began as a cinematographer for Crawfords in 1969 and, in the 1970s, he worked there as director and producer on television series such as *Homicide*. His first feature film as director was **High Rolling** (1977), which introduced Judy •Davis to the screen as a feisty hitch-hiker. Later television projects included the telemovies *All at Sea* (1977) and *The Night Nurse* (1978), the acclaimed miniseries *Water Under the Bridge* (1980), and the short-lived soap opera *Taurus Rising* (1982). He made documentaries for the •South Australian Film Corporation and many television commercials, but he is best known for two feature films: •**We of the Never Never** (1982) and •**The Coolangatta Gold** (1984). IB

Avalon, Phillip (1945–) ACTOR/WRITER/PRODUCER Male model Phillip Avalon's first film credit was for a small role in **Inn of the Damned** (1975). He then became a producer, running his own company (Avalon Films/Avalon Film Productions), making first the telemovie *The Double Dealer* (1975, which he also wrote and acted in), then **Summer City** (1977), in which he co-starred with Mel •Gibson as one of four surfers on a wild weekend. A leading surf-ski athlete, and founder of the magazine *Tracks*, Avalon made a series of surfing documentaries and continued with the surfing theme in the feature films **Breaking Loose** (1988) and **Exchange Lifeguards** (1993) which he also wrote. Another common element of his films is the violence of their outsider protagonists: there are horrific murders in **Sher Mountain Killings Mystery** (in which he also played the leading role, 1990), **Fatal Bond** (which he also wrote, 1992), and **Tunnel**

Vision (1994), and vicious thuggery in **Signal One** (1993, unreleased). But what ties his work together more than themes is a certain B-movie style, a rawness, that often confines the films to the video shelves, but occasionally rises above that (as with the leading performances of Jerome Ehlers and Linda Blair in **Fatal Bond**). IB

Avenger, The

1937. *Director:* A.R. Harwood. *Production company:* New Era Film Productions. *Scriptwriter:* Bert Hollis. *Directors of photography:* Arthur Higgins, Tasman Higgins. *Music:* Frank Chapple. 55 min. B&W. *Cast:* Douglas Stuart (Terry Druton), John Fernside (Max Hart), Karen Greyson (Della, the Maid), Marcia Melville (Gwen), Marshall Crosby (Detective Sergeant O'Neill), George Lloyd (Happy), Raymond Longford (Warren).

Reformed burglar Terry Druton marries socialite Gwen, and takes a job with wealthy industrialist Warren, leaving former colleagues Max and Happy to face gaol. On his release, Max seeks revenge, but Terry turns the tables on him. The complications of this plot are not always easy to follow. Performances are uniformly wooden, except for George Lloyd, still sounding and looking uncannily like George •Wallace. What little credit the film warrants should go to the •Higgins brothers, for some convincingly sinister camera work and lighting, in both interiors and street scenes at night. The film was accepted under the NSW quota provisions, but not widely distributed in Australia, although it was sold to Columbia for release in the United Kingdom. IB

Douglas Stuart, John Fernside, and George Lloyd in **The Avenger**

B

Babe (Babe, the Gallant Pig)

1995. *Director*: Chris Noonan. *Producers*: Bill Miller, Dr George Miller. *Scriptwriters*: George Miller, Chris Noonan. Based on Dick King-Smith's novel, *The Sheep-Pig*. *Director of photography*: Andrew Lesnie. *Music*: Nigel Westlake. 88 min. *Cast*: James Cromwell (Farmer Hoggett), Magda Szubanski (Mrs Hoggett), Christine Cavanaugh (the voice of Babe), Hugo Weaving (the voice of Rex), Miriam Margolyes (the voice of Fly).

Nine years after the phenomenal international success of *Crocodile Dundee, this Kennedy Miller Productions release (MCA–Universal was an overseas partner) grossed US$240 million in its first year. Nominated for six Academy Awards (Best Picture, Best Director, Best Supporting Actor, Best Adapted Screenplay, Best Editing, and Best Art Direction), it won for Best Visual Effects, as well as receiving the American National Society of Film Critics Best Film Award and the New York Film Critics Circle Award for best first film. Its Australian release was greeted with some reservations regarding its lack of Australian accents and references.

While the story brings *Charlotte's Web* to mind, the dynamics of the barnyard animal community evoke *Animal Farm* (both books became animated films). Babe, an orphaned piglet, narrowly escapes the abattoir, is adopted by Farmer Hoggett, and lives on his property. Raised by the sheepdogs on Hoggett's farm, Babe learns the ways and difficulties of the animals and of the humans as she pursues her much-ridiculed ambition to herd sheep. Helped at crucial points by the dogs and a dowager sheep, and supported by Farmer Hoggett's faith, she succeeds.

Babe's success owes a great deal to cutting-edge effects work: Karl Lewis Miller's animal training, Rhythm & Hues's special effects, sheep characters by Robotechnology, and animatronics by Jim Henson's Creature Shop together create the seamless illusion of animals talking naturally to each other in a sometimes dark, sometimes antic world inside a storybook.

RICK THOMPSON

Back of Beyond, The

1954. *Director, Producer, Editor*: John Heyer. *Script*: John Heyer, Janet Heyer, Roland Robinson. *Dialogue*: *Narration*: Douglas Stewart, John Heyer. *Photography*: Ross Wood. *Music*: Sydney John Kay. *Narrator*: Kevin Brennan. 66 min. for the Shell Film Unit. B&W. *Cast*: Tom Kruse, William Henry Butler, Jack the Dogger, Old Joe the Rainmaker, the Oldfields of Etadinna, Bejah, Malcolm Arkaringa (as themselves).

Considered by many to be one of Australia's premier films (documentary, feature or otherwise) John *Heyer's tale of the mail-run along the Birdsville track is an exemplary representation of 1950s' Australian transformational culture.

John Heyer, with valuable experience gleaned from his work as second-unit director on *The Overlanders (1946) drew the inspiration for this film from the area along the Birdsville track and, with the assistance of Douglas Stewart and over 20 technicians and actors, adapted the locations, myths, and stories of the area.

Representing the complex interrelations of the multicultural community and their environs, **The Back of Beyond** stands as a comparison piece to Robert J. Flaherty's **Louisiana Story** (1948), at the same time corresponding with Pare Lorentz's **The Plow that Broke the Plains** (1936), and Harry Watt's seminal **Night Mail** (1936). Heyer brought to the landscape an eye for poetry, storytelling, and motif that is unparalleled in Australian film.

James Cromwell and friends in **Babe**

The 'lost girls sequence' remains as one of the film's most memorable moments, obtaining a poignancy and resonance that sets it apart from many of the documentaries of the period. The film is essentially a documentary about the non-Aboriginal community's adaptation to the land. Part of this notion of adaptation is in the sense of multiculturalism presented by the film. There is an Aboriginal man revisiting a German Mission, an Afghan Muslim, and Tom Kruse as himself, representing the White bushman tradition.

The Back of Beyond received a massive distribution by the Shell company and was estimated to have been seen by over 750 000 people in the first year of its release. Since then it has become a necessary component of any appreciation of Australian cinema. DEANE WILLIAMS

Backlash

1986. *Director/Producer/Scriptwriter:* Bill Bennett. *Director of photography:* Tony Wilson. *Music:* Michael Atkinson, Michael Spicer. 89 min. *Cast:* David Argue (Trevor Darling), Gia Carides (Nikki Iceton), Lydia Miller (Kath), Brian Syron (The Executioner), Anne Smith (Publican's Wife), Don Smith (Publican).

Ten years before Bill *Bennett won critical acclaim for his improvised road movie *Kiss or Kill (1997), he was exploring the form in **Backlash**. And, while the film has its problems, it remains a watchable and at times remarkable film.

Two very different cops, jaded Trevor and diligent Nikki, are assigned to escort a murder suspect, Aboriginal Kath, from Sydney to Broken Hill. The three do not get on at all, until their car breaks down miles from anywhere, and they put aside their mutual distrust to survive. Meanwhile, there is someone on their trail, and the reason for this is not clear until the film's finale.

All three leads are dab hands at delivering Bennett's improvised script, and this gives the film its real energy. David *Argue's laconic wit lifts an otherwise unlikeable character above stereotype, and Gia *Carides demonstrates a real understanding for her role of uptight Nikki. But it is Lydia Miller as Kath—silent and passive for the first half of the film but coming into her own once it is clear that her survival skills will make all the difference—who is the most significant presence in this film. TIM HUNTER

Backroads

1977. *Director* and *Producer:* Phillip Noyce. *Scriptwriters:* John Emery, Phillip Noyce, and cast. *Director of photography:* Russell Boyd. *Music:* Robert Murphy. 61 min. *Cast:* Gary Foley (Gary), Bill Hunter (Jack), Zac Martin (Joe), Terry Camilleri (Jean-Claude), Julie McGregor (Anna).

Jack, an ockerish drifter, and Gary, a militant young Aborigine, career around western NSW in a stolen Pontiac loaded with pilfered goods, gun, and wine flagons. They visit an Aboriginal reserve and several down-at-heel country towns, collecting three fellow-travellers along the way. A larrikin escapade turns violent as it moves towards its inevitable, ugly climax.

Backroads combines elements of the road movie, *cinéma vérité* documentary, the buddy film, political polemic, and experimental film. Phil •Noyce's direction is underpinned by Russell •Boyd's accomplished cinematography, while Gary Foley's creative participation (largely through impromptu dialogue) gives a sharper edge to the film's abrasive and unsentimental representation of the plight of indigenous Australians. In a beautifully controlled performance, Bill •Hunter, chosen by Noyce for his ability to improvise, captures something of the psychic insecurities underlying white racist attitudes. **Backroads** stands up as one of the more interesting short feature films sponsored by the Australian Film Commission in the mid 1970s.

HARRY OLDMEADOW

Bad Boy Bubby

1994. *Director* and *Scriptwriter*: Rolf de Heer. *Producers*: Domenico Procacci, Giorgio Draskovic. *Director of photography*: Ian Jones. *Music*: Graham Tardif. 113 min. *Cast*: Nicholas Hope (Bubby), Claire Benito (Mom), Ralph Coterill (Pop), Carmel Johnson (Angel).

Bubby is a 35-year-old child–adult who has been incarcerated in a filthy basement room, where he has been grossly abused and degraded by his 'Mom'. Absentee 'Pop', a drunken lecher in the guise of a cleric, returns to this squalid scene to break Mom's spell over Bubby, who later suffocates the two of them with clingwrap while they lie in a drunken stupor. Bubby escapes into the world outside, where he undergoes a series of bizarre adventures and mishaps, ending up as a happily married, suburban family man.

Bad Boy Bubby is a gruelling, brutal, and often disgusting experience: incest, murder, sexual perversion, rape, sacrilege, fetishism, and violence are the order of the day, along with some vapid social 'critique'. **Bad Boy Bubby** fared well on the festival/arthouse circuit. Critics extolled Nicholas •Hope's *tour de force* performance, hailed the film as innovative and challenging, and drew comparisons with European 'wild child' films by Truffaut and Herzog. Others found the film pretentious, facile, and gross.

HARRY OLDMEADOW

Baigent, Harold ACTOR Harold Baigent had a long career as an actor in various media, including much experience with travelling companies. He made a few films in the revived Australian cinema, most memorably as the camel-driver who meets Archie (Mark •Lee) and Frank (Mel •Gib-

son) as they cross the dry lake-bed in •**Gallipoli** (1981). It was a brief but important role that reinforced the sense of Australia's isolation from world affairs, and Baigent imbued it with the sense of a lifetime of incurious self-absorption. *Other Australian films*: •**Mad Dog Morgan** (1976), •**Mad Max 2** (1981, narrator only), **Double Deal** (1981), **Slate, Wyn & Me** (1987), **Golden Braid** (1990). BMcF

Bailey, Bert (1868–1953) ACTOR This distinctively Australian actor was born in New Zealand but was raised in Sydney. Bert Bailey entered vaudeville as a tambourine player and singer. In 1905 he co-wrote the play *The Squatter's Daughter* (or *The Land of the Wattle*) with another entertainer, Edmund Duggan. The play was successful and there were two film adaptations. The first one, in 1910, starred Bailey, who also directed the film while, in 1933, Ken G. •Hall retained the title, and little else. In 1912 Bailey and Duggan wrote •**On Our Selection**, based loosely on stories by Steele Rudd. The play was popular with Australian and New Zealand audiences for the next 20 years. Raymond •Longford's 1920 film version bypassed Bailey's stage version, and its emphasis on farce, by returning to the more austere tone of the original stories. In contrast, Hall's 1932 version, scripted by Bailey and Hall and produced by Bailey, represented a return to the emphasis on farce and melodrama in the 1912 play. Bailey's interpretation of Grandad Rudd as the repository of traditional values in a changing world dominated the rest of his career in film and radio.

Other Australian films: The Christian (1911), •**Grandad Rudd** (1935, also p.), •**Dad and Dave Come to Town** (1938, also co-w.), •**Dad Rudd MP** (1940, also co-w.), **South West Pacific** (1943). GM

Baker, David (1931–) DIRECTOR/CINEMATOGRAPHER Born in Tasmania, David Baker set off for London in 1952, where he found work backstage with a theatre company, and persuaded Anthony Asquith to employ him in film. He worked his way up, from clapper loader to camera operator, to director of documentaries and then, in 1955, to Granada Television, working on current affairs, documentaries, magazine programs, and sitcoms. He returned to Melbourne in 1957 to produce a children's series for Channel 7 and, when that was axed, worked with Roger Mirams, a New Zealand producer who worked in Australia, on series such as *The Terrible Ten* and, after another short spell in the United Kingdom, *The Magic Boomerang* and *Seaspray*. More television followed (*Animal Doctor, Spyforce*), before he made his first Australian films—the final segment of •**Libido** (1973), and the powerful and disturbing short feature **Squeaker's Mate** (1974). **The Great MacArthy** (1975) was the first film to capture the ethos of Australian Rules football, but it met with a mixed reception, and Baker had difficulty finding funding for his next project. Eventually he completed **Niel Lynne** (1985), a film about personal and political commitment, with an intriguing homosexual subtext: it was screened in the Australian Film Institute Awards that year, but not commercially released, and he made no further films.   IB

Baker, Ian (1947–) CINEMATOGRAPHER After four years at the Swinburne Film and Television School, Ian Baker joined The Film House, Melbourne, in 1969 as Fred •Schepisi's cinematographer, a creative relationship that continued for 27 years. Baker photographed The Priest, Schepisi's segment of •Libido (1973), which led to Baker's first feature as director of photography, •**The Devil's Playground** (1976), again with Schepisi as director. Baker's first overseas film was Fred Schepisi's **Barbarosa** (USA, 1982) and he later worked for such international directors as Mark Goldblatt (**The Punisher**, USA, 1988) and Karel Reisz (**Everybody Wins**, USA, 1989).
Other Australian films: •The Chant of Jimmie Blacksmith (1978), •The Clinic (1983), The Lost Frontier (Australia/USA, 1986), •Evil Angels (1988).   DAVID MUIR

Baker, Reginald, L. (Snowy) (1884–1953) ACTOR Born Reginald Leslie Baker in Sydney, this actor was known as 'Snowy' because of the colour of his hair. Baker was an outstanding sportsman. He won the NSW swimming championship, represented Australia in boxing at the 1908 Olympic Games, played rugby for Australia against England, and also excelled at cricket, rowing, athletics, water polo, and diving. Baker's sporting fame translated easily into a series of films that exploited his athletic prowess. Two feature films in 1918 were followed by a partnership with E.J. and Dan •Carroll, who imported an American crew to produce action films for an international market. Although these films were not favoured by critics, they were well received by local audiences. Baker's popularity in Australian films such as •**The Man from Kangaroo** (1920) briefly rivalled American counterparts such as Tom Mix. Baker accompanied his brother Frank Baker, a stuntman, to Hollywood, where he starred in a series of action films and westerns. After his film career finished, Baker remained in Los Angeles and managed a country club.
Other Australian films: •The Enemy Within (1918), Lure of the Bush (1918), Shadow of Lighting Ridge (1920, also co.p.), The Jackeroo of Coolabong (1920, also co.p.)   GM

Ball, Vincent (1923–) ACTOR It was his swimming prowess that started Vincent Ball in films. When he arrived in the United Kingdom in 1948, his first film job was to understudy Donald Houston, the non-swimming lead in **The Blue Lagoon**. Ball did a short stint at the Royal Academy of Dramatic Art in London, then had a busy, modestly successful career in British films, with leads in small films and supporting roles (usually in robust action parts) in bigger films, including **A Town Like Alice** (1956), •**Robbery Under Arms** (1957), and **Oh! What a Lovely War** (1968). He returned to Australia in the 1970s and has been busy on stage, television, and screen ever since. He was in successful miniseries such as *Rush* and, in the cinema, has revealed a mature authority as a character player in such films as •'Breaker' Morant (1980), as an unsympathetic British colonel, as the headmaster in •**The Year My Voice Broke** (1987), and as the priest in •**Muriel's Wedding** (1994).
Other Australian films: •Summer of the Seventeenth Doll (1959), With These Hands (1972), Alison's Birthday (1979), The Highest Honor (1982), •Phar Lap (1983), Call Me Mr Brown (1986), Love in Limbo (1993), Frauds (1993), •Sirens (1994).
      BMcF

Ballantyne, Jane PRODUCER In the 1980s, Jane Ballantyne was one of a number of female producers in the Australian industry—there were considerably more women working as producers than as directors. For most of her career she has worked in a co-producer capacity, most often with Paul •Cox: on •**Man of Flowers** (1983), •**My First Wife** (1984), **Cactus** (1986), and **Lust and Revenge** (1996). She also co-produced the migrant youth drama •**Moving Out** (1983) with its director, Michael •Pattinson; the thriller, **Zoomstone** (1987), with Antony •Ginnane; and **Breakaway** (1990), with director Don McLennan.

Her co-producer credits may somewhat obscure her individual contributions, but her continuing association with Cox points to a producer's real value: the capacity to keep the films coming.   BMcF

Barrett, Franklyn (1874–1961) DIRECTOR/CINEMATOGRAPHER Franklyn Barrett (Walter Franklyn Brown), who later declared himself 'for Australia, first, last, and always', was born in England, and migrated to New Zealand about 1895, where he became a press photographer and musician. From about 1900, he made short narrative films and documentaries. In 1904 he began periodic visits to Australia and the United Kingdom, continuing to make newsreels and travelogues and, in 1908, he joined Pathé Frères in Sydney. When West's took over Pathé, he worked as both director and cinematographer on feature films, starting with **All for Gold** (1911), in which he used a split screen for dramatic effect. In 1913, when West's became part of •Australasian Films, Barrett moved to Fraser Films, working both in production and distribution. He continued to make films independently of the Combine until 1922, his prolific output including some of the most important films of the period: **The Monk and the**

"Snowy" Baker
gives an account of himself

We are in the throes of producing the greatest Motion Picture that has yet been credited to Australian brains and effort. I have jumped into this page to tell you about it. Can't stay long, as I am wanted back at Kangaroo Valley, where Mr. Wilfred Lucas is waiting to "shoot up" some more scenes.

Mr. Lucas says I am a better Stunt Actor than anyone living. He ought to know. Anyhow, he has had me leaping from crag to crag, diving hundreds of feet into roaring chasms, saving heroines—by the hundred it seems to me—fighting for my life—and these toughs Wilfred picks out are the real thing. They come at me with murder in their eyes. I have got to beat 'em up, I do! Because I know that the crank of the camera is relentlessly grinding on and on, and every punch I "get home" will be recorded on the screen for you.

And, boys! You ought to see Brownie Vernon. She is the sweetest little screen actress. As a heroine she is well worth fighting for. You will understand when you see her. This is going to be a great big winner—this first picture of ours. Mr. E. J. Carroll certainly does things right. For further particulars, get in touch with your local Theatre Manager, or

E. J. CARROLL,
BANKING HOUSE, PITT STREET, SYDNEY,

controlling world rights for Raymond Longford's production for Southern Cross Feature Films, Ltd., "The Sentimental Bloke."

Productions in preparation and for early release:—

November—A. Reg. L. Baker film, produced by Wilfred Lucas from a scenario by Bess Meredith.
December—"The Moods of Ginger Mick," by C. J. Dennis, produced by Raymond Longford.
January—"On Our Selection," by Steel Rudd.
February—A. Reg. L. Baker film.
March—"On Our New Selection," by Steel Rudd.

AGE

JOHN P. DAVIS

TWENTY-SIX

'Snowy' Baker addresses his fans, 1919

Maud Fane and Percy Marmont in Franklyn Barrett's
The Monk and the Woman (1917)

Woman (1917), •**The Enemy Within** (1918 (also co.p.),
•**The Breaking of the Drought** (1920), •**A Girl of the Bush**
(1921), and **Know Thy Child** (1921). All his films were
visually memorable, and he was prepared to tackle subject
matter that was considered 'difficult' at the time, in melodramatic stories of mixed marriage, illegitimacy, and family breakdown. Eventually, Barrett found distribution
problems insurmountable and, in 1922, he became an
exhibitor in Sydney and Canberra.

Other Australian films: as director, Struck Oil (1919); as cinematographer, The Strangler's Grip (1911), The Mystery of the
Black Pearl (1911), The Eleventh Hour (1912), Pommy Arrives
in Australia (1913), •The Joan of Arc of Loos (1916), Mutiny of
the Bounty (1916), The Murder of Captain Fryatt (1917), A
Romance of the Burke and Wills Expedition (1918), The Lure
of the Bush (1918); as director and photographer, The Christian
(1911), A Silent Witness (1911), A Blue Gum Romance (1913),
The Life of a Jackeroo (1913), •The Pioneers (1916), Australia's
Peril (1917), A Rough Passage (1922).   IB

Barrett, Ray (1926–) ACTOR   There are few more
commanding character actors in Australian cinema than
craggy-featured Ray Barrett. When he dies half-way
through •**Hotel Sorrento** (1995), the film, excellent as
much of it is, misses him badly: he is so potently alive, so
deceptively relaxed, that he appears not to be acting at all—
just slopping round a seaside house in thongs and shorts,
swearing good-humouredly. He was born in Brisbane and
worked in radio and television before going to the United
Kingdom in 1958, where he became a fixture in British
television shows such as *The Troubleshooters* (1966–71) and
appeared in a dozen films, including Lance Comfort's
clever thriller, **Touch of Death** (1962). After his return to
Australia in 1975, he worked regularly on stage, television
and screen. On the latter, he was memorably abusive in
•**Don's Party** (1976) as a failed psychiatrist venting his
spleen, as a venal policeman in •**The Chant of Jimmie
Blacksmith** (1978), and, above all, as the Chandleresque
private eye working the mean streets of Brisbane in the
sadly underrated •**Goodbye Paradise** (1983). These are but
three in a gallery of lethally exact studies: he has become
one of those actors who, whatever the quality of the film in
question, will guarantee at least an element of utter veracity as to time, place and temperament.

Other Australian films: The Australian War Memorial (1956, doc.),
Asian Students in Australia (1957, doc. nar.), Wirritt Wirritt
(1957, doc. nar.), Friend and Neighbour (1958, doc. nar.), •The
Sundowners (1960), Let the Balloon Go (1976), Brick Walls in
Blue Water (1978, doc. nar.), The Earthling (1980), A Shifting
Dreaming (1982, doc.), Where the Green Ants Dream (1984),
•The Wild Duck (1984), Relatives (1985, unreleased), Rebel
(1985), The Empty Beach (1985), Frenchman's Farm (1986), As
Time Goes By (1988), •Blood Oath (1990), Waiting (1991), •No
Worries (1993), •Dad and Dave: On Our Selection (1995),
Hotel de Love (1996), Brilliant Lies (1996), Heaven's Burning
(1997), In the Winter Dark (1998).   BMcF

Barron, Paul D. (1949–) PRODUCER   With Damien
Parer Jnr, Paul D. Barron produced •**Shame** (1988), one of
the key Australian films of the 1980s, for his own production company, Barron Films. Barron also produced, with
Gilda Baracci, the outback children's comedy •**Bush Christmas** (1983), an effective remake of the 1947 version, with
John •Ewart in the Chips •Rafferty role as a thief who,
together with John Howard, is followed by a group of children, including Nicole •Kidman, after stealing a prize race-
horse from a struggling bush family. Kidman was also the
female lead in the teenage surfing comedy **Windrider**
(1986), produced by Barron for his production company.
Less successful was the Barron-produced eccentric comedy,
Daisy and Simon (1989), based on the age difference
between Sean •Scully and Jan •Adele. This was followed by

Father (1990), a post-Holocaust drama of a young woman forced to confront the possibility that her father was a Nazi war criminal. Barron produced this film with Damien Parer Jnr, Tony Cavanaugh, and Graham Hartley for Barron Films, in conjunction with Leftbank Productions. Barron also produced a series of tele-features.

Other Australian films include: •Blackfellas (1993).   GM

Ray Barrett

Barry, Ian DIRECTOR/EDITOR   In a cinema that has tended to undervalue melodrama, Ian Barry has made one of the liveliest examples of the mode in •**Minnamurra** (1989), a story of inheritances and efforts to retain the old family home. The film is an enjoyable reworking of standard ingredients, played by a willing cast and superbly photographed, but it failed to find audiences and later appeared under several other names (**Outback, The Fighting Creed, Wrangler**) with no further success. Barry was a Sydney-based editor, working on such films as •**Stone** (1974) and a number of shorts and documentaries, before directing his first feature, the action-packed nuclear thriller, **The Chain Reaction** (1980), which he also co-wrote and which stands up better today than some of the more acclaimed entertainments of its period. His subsequent features include: **Crimebroker** (1993), a crime thriller made in the USA, with John Bach and Jacqueline Bisset; **The Seventh Floor** (1994), a melodrama of computers and blackmail in a Sydney advertising agency, released first on television; and the family comedy adventure, **Joey** (1997), about children bonding over the eponymous animal. Barry has enough feeling for the more robust genres to make one wish to see more of his work.

Other Australian films (as editor except where noted): **Waiting for Lucas** (1973, short, d., w.), **Night of Fear** (1972, sound ed.), **Zizzem Zam** (1976, short, co-ed.), **Tija: A Sikh Priest** (1978, doc.), **Clem and Faye** (1978, doc.), **Tulaw Dewata** (1978, doc.), **Ghan to Alice** (1979, doc.), **Roslyn and Blagica—Everyone Needs a Friend** (1979, doc.), **No Room at Raffles** (1981, short, d., ed.), •**Hostage** (1983, script consultant).   BMcF

Barry, Tony (1941–) ACTOR   In films good and bad, Tony Barry has established himself as a leading Australian character actor, one of those who seem incapable of striking a false note. Perhaps it is the wide range of occupations (including storeman, salesman, barman, waiter) he followed before becoming an actor that have allowed him to enter so completely into assorted roles with laconic, weather-beaten conviction. He is one of the few actors associated with the early days of new Australian cinema (see Revival, the) — for example, in •**The Mango Tree,** 1977, and •**Newsfront,** 1978 — who has worked steadily until the present, recently in •**The Road to Nhill** (1997), and television's *The Last of the Ryans* (1997). He had memorable roles in such films as •**The Irishman** (1978), as a station hand in •**We of the Never Never** (1982), and especially as the careworn father of the rape victim in •**Shame** (1988). He also had important roles in three New Zealand films: **Wild Man** (1978), **Goodbye Pork Pie** (1980), and **Beyond Reasonable Doubt** (1982).

Other Australian films: The Removalists (1975, role cut from final print), **Break of Day** (1976), •**The Picture Show Man** (1977), **Weekend of Shadows** (1978), **Mick and the Moon** (1978, doc., nar. only), **Little Boy Lost** (1978), •**The Odd Angry Shot** (1979), **Saint Therese** (1979, short), **The Good Oil** (1980), **The Earthling** (1980), **Hard Knocks** (1980), **Now and Then** (short), **With Prejudice** (1982), **Midnite Spares** (1983), **Platypus Cove** (1983), •**The Settlement** (1984), **Pallet on the Floor** (1984), **Archer** (1985), **The Coca-Cola Kid** (1985), **I Own the Racecourse** (1986), **Frog Dreaming** (1986), **Zoomstone** (1987), **The Surfer** (1988), **Never Say Die** (1988), **Man from Snowy River II** (1988), **Old Scores** (1991), •**Deadly** (1992), **Jack Be Nimble** (1993), **The Last Tattoo** (1994), •**Country Life** (1994), **Paperback Hero** (1998).   BMcF

Batterham, Kim (1955–) CINEMATOGRAPHER   Trained under Russell •Boyd, Don •McAlpine, and Brian •Probyn at the Australian Film, Television and Radio School, since 1986 Kim Batterham's career has followed two parallel paths—sometimes co-producing and/or directing as well as shooting award-winning documentaries such as **Pins And Needles** (1979) and working as director of photography on dramas for both television and the cinema, including **Black River**, (1991). Kim won a NSW Australian Cinematographers (ACS) Gold Tripod Award and a federal ACS Distinction for his cinematography of the television film *Kangaroo Palace* (1996).

Other Australian films include: Raw Nerve (1990, d.o.p.), Shotgun Wedding (1993, d.o.p.), Sample People (1998, d.o.p.).

DAVID MUIR

Bayly, Lorraine (1937–) ACTOR Best known for her three-year stint as Grace Sullivan in the long-running television serial, *The Sullivans*, and as a presenter on *Playschool*, Lorraine Bayly has, in fact, worked in all the acting media. Her film career, however, has been limited to three features: •**Ride a Wild Pony** (1975), **Fatty Finn** (1980), and •**The Man from Snowy River** (1982), the last of which gave her a substantial role as the feminist aunt of Sigrid •Thornton. Crisp in style and looking a couple of decades younger than she is, she has been largely wasted by the big screen.

Other Australian films: Heaven Help Us (1967, short).   BMcF

BeDevil

1993. *Producers*: Anthony Buckley, Carol Hughes. *Director*: Tracey Moffatt. *Scriptwriter*: Tracey Moffatt. *Director of photography*: Geoff Burton, *Production Designer*: Stephen Curtis. *Art Director*: Martin Brown. *Music*: Carl Vine. 87 min. *Cast*: Lex Marinos (Dimitri), Diana Davidson (Shelley), Dina Panozzo (Voula), Les Foxcroft (old Mickey), Cecil Parkee (Bob Malley).

Tracey •Moffatt's first feature film is a triptych of fantastic ghost stories. The film's credits are an amalgamation of the kinetic energy of the opening of a James Bond film and the graphic dynamism of Alfred Hitchcock's title sequences. Hitchcock's inspiration is manifest throughout **BeDevil**, most obviously in the generation of suspense heightened by a malevolent soundtrack. Entitled 'Mr Chuck', the first story features stylised, surreal studio sets representing exteriors. Myriad narrators, reliable and dubious, recount the story of an American soldier who haunts a bubbling swamp, disturbing developers. Moffatt abandons chronology and clear character definition in favour of a nightmarish structure. In the second story, 'Choo Choo Choo Choo', Ruby appears as a younger and as an older Aboriginal woman without clear signification of chronological time. Moffatt and her mother play the divided role. 'Lovin' The Spin I'm In' tells the tale of the haunting of a derelict building and the obstruction of redevelopment. The manifestation of the spirit accommodates the spectator's desire for resolution.   WENDY HASLEM

Behets, Briony (1951–) ACTOR British-born actor and former school teacher, Briony Behets appeared in the popular 'adult' soaps *Number 96* and *The Box* in the early

1970s, before her first feature film, the sex comedy **Alvin Rides Again** (1974). John •Duigan's low-budget domestic drama **The Trespassers** (1976) offered Behets her first serious screen role as Penny, the wife who forms a strong relationship with her husband's mistress. This was followed by the lead role in Paul •Cox's first 35mm film, **Inside Looking Out** (1977), and a continuing role in the popular television drama *Prisoner*. Behets's best role to date, however, was in her next film, the underrated Australian thriller •**Long Weekend** (1979), as Marcia, who travels with her husband (John •Hargreaves) to an isolated beach in a desperate attempt to heal their troubled marriage, only to discover the terrifying consequences of violating nature.

Other Australian films include: Nightmares (1980), Cassandra (1987).   GM

Bell, John (1940–) ACTOR John Bell, as both actor and director, is one of the major figures in Australian theatre, and was awarded an OBE for his contributions in several functions, including those of acting teacher at the National Institute of Dramatic Art and founder of the Nimrod Theatre, Sydney. To date, he has played in only two feature films: as a member of the Bohemian entourage that disturbs the rural tranquillity of **Break of Day** (1976), and as Helen •Morse's committed journalist husband in •**Far East** (1982). The latter has strong affinities with the Hollywood classic **Casablanca** (1942), with Bell standing in for Paul Henreid. The screen has clearly made little use of Bell's formidable talents.

Other Australian films: The Devil to Pay (1962, short), Clement Meadmore (1963, doc., nar.), Undefeated (1964, doc., nar.), The Luluai's Dream (1964, doc., co-nar.), A Calendar of Dreamings (1976, doc., nar.), The Magic Arts (1977, short), You're the One (1979).   BMcF

Bennett, Bill (1953–) DIRECTOR/WRITER Bill Bennett's name came to prominence when •**Kiss or Kill** (1997), which, like most of his films, he produced and wrote as well as directed, scored substantially at the 1997 Australian Film Institute awards. To admirers of his 1985 film, •**A Street to Die**, this recognition was no surprise. In **A Street to Die**, he showed a plain, uncluttered narrative style, and a flair for casting well and allowing his actors room to move. This film confronted the then-controversial issue of the effects of the defoliant, Agent Orange, on Vietnam veterans. It was an important theme, but he never allowed the film to become merely didactic at the expense of the human emotions involved. •**Backlash** (1986), a film that combines generic elements of the thriller and the road movie with serious matters relating to justice and racism, confirmed that Bennett is both proficient and committed to having something to say in cinematic terms. Set in western New South Wales, the film benefits from Bennett's having allowed his actors to improvise. Bennett was himself responsible for raising the funding for both these films; following the success of **Kiss or Kill**, he is unlikely to have to do this in future. A former journalist and documentary film-maker, he has also showed his narrative skills in the straight-to-video **Jilted** (1987), and combined elements of the odd-couple film and road movie in the comedy **Spider and Rose** (1994), in which the central relationship is between an elderly woman, Rose (Ruth •Cracknell), and the young ambulance driver, Spider (Simon Bossell), who drives her to her son's farm when she is released from hospital. He has made several further telefeatures and has filmed in the USA, where he directed Sandra Bullock and Denis Leary as a squabbling blue-collar couple in **Two if by Sea** (1996). But filming in the USA proved to be an experience he did not want to repeat. He returned to Australia to make **In A Savage Land** (1998), originally intended as an American film.

Other Australian films: Dear Cardholder (1987).   BMcF

Beresford, Bruce (1940–   ) DIRECTOR A dominant figure in the growth of the new Australian cinema (see Revival, the), Bruce Beresford has gone on to an international career that has brought him considerable acclaim, notably for the Oscar-nominated **Tender Mercies** (1983) and the Oscar-winning **Driving Miss Daisy** (1989), for which, to much astonishment, he was not nominated in the 'best director' category. He is the great craftsman of Australian cinema, able to turn his hand to a wide range of genres, and achieving a high level of success in them, certainly enough to offset the occasional flop such as **King David** (1985).

To call him a 'great craftsman' is not to damn with faint praise. His Australian films, in particular, reveal a continuing concern with certain themes and milieus. He has shown a particular interest in the way in which hierarchies work, whether within a football club's politics (•**The Club**, 1980) or in the genre structures of the heist film (•**Money Movers**, 1979), and in a peculiarly Australian resistance to authority (•**The Getting of Wisdom**, 1977; •**'Breaker' Morant**, 1980). These films further show his deftness in the establishment and observation of closed milieus: the club in **The Club**, the school in **The Getting of Wisdom**, the courthouse in **'Breaker' Morant**, the teenage surf-and-sex world of •**Puberty Blues** (1981), and the election-night tensions of a suburban house in •**Don's Party** (1976). In these confined ambiences, he has exhibited notable skill in keeping his camera fluently descriptive and discriminating, and he has invariably elicited fine performances from his actors. John •Hargreaves, Ray •Barrett and Pat •Bishop are particularly striking in the fine ensemble work on show in **Don's Party**, and Jack •Thompson and Bryan •Brown have never been

more acutely sympathetic than as bumbling outback lawyer and doomed soldier respectively in **'Breaker' Morant**. If he seems particularly alert to male vulnerabilities, it should also be noted how tenderly he has dealt with the problems of teenage girls in **Puberty Blues** and **The Getting of Wisdom**, as well as with the protagonist of •**The Fringe Dwellers** (1986), not to mention eliciting a fine award-winning performance from Jessica Tandy as matriarch in **Driving Miss Daisy**. Recently he again showed his skill in directing, and telling the stories of, women in •**Paradise Road** (1997), his first Australian film in seven years, with its superbly blended multinational cast of women.

Born in Australia, Beresford was in the United Kingdom from the mid 1960s (he was head of the production department of the British Film Institute for several years), and returned to Australia in the early 1970s, when he directed and co-wrote (with Barry •Humphries) the popular 'ocker' comedy •**The Adventures of Barry McKenzie** (1972) and its sequel, **Barry McKenzie Holds His Own** (1974). These unsubtle, but often very funny examinations of Australian male stereotypes found favour in Australia (an element of masochism here?) and in the United Kingdom, and they are important precursors of the more genteel strains of Australian film-making of the later 1970s which, in retrospect at least, seem to be reactions against Barry McKenzie and Tim •Burstall's •**Alvin Purple** films (1973, 1974). Beresford showed in these early films a vigour and feeling for the cinema that have always been characteristic of his work. With

Bruce Beresford working on 'Breaker' Morant (1980)

Burstall, Peter *Weir, and Fred *Schepisi, he must be regarded as one of the founding fathers of the renascent Australian cinema of the 1970s.

Other Australian films: Revenge of the Earwig (1958, short), **The Hunter** (1959, short), **The Devil to Pay** (1962, short), **Clement Meadmore** (1963, doc.), **It Droppeth as the Gentle Rain** (1963, short, co-d.), **Barry Humphries Stage Show Film** (1975, doc.), **Black Robe** (1991, Canadian co-prod.). BMcF

Bergen, Tushka ACTOR Tushka Bergen, who began her film career with a tiny role in *Mad Max—Beyond Thunderdome** (1985), has amassed a tidy collection of film and television credits in several countries, including the USA, the United Kingdom, and Germany. Her only two film performances of note in Australia are in George *Ogilvie's listless **The Place at the Coast** (1987) and Ian *Barry's robust melodrama, *Minnamurra** (1989). Unfortunately for Bergen, both were considerable commercial failures. In the achingly slow and atmospheric family tensions of the former, she played John *Hargreaves's daughter, resentful of his finding a new romantic interest during a long Christmas holiday. Her blonde beauty was better served in **Minnamurra** by the more spirited role of the heroine who determines to hang on to the old family home after her father's death, and she brought the appropriate zest to its full-throttled melodrama. Since then her work has been chiefly abroad, including a starring role in Whit Stillman's **Barcelona** (1994) and the title role in the little seen Australian–Canadian co-production, **Turning April** (1995). BMcF

Berryman, Ross (1954–) CINEMATOGRAPHER Born in Adelaide, Ross Berryman trained with Crawfords from 1972, working on the long-running television series *The Sullivans* and filming for Crawfords the telefeature spin-off *The John Sullivan Story* (1980). He then moved to Sydney, where he continued to work in television. He was also director of photography on the feature films **Double Deal** (1983), **Breakfast in Paris** (1982), **Melvin, Son of Alvin** (1984), and *Minamurra** (1987), and also two films not released theatrically, **A Slice of Life** (1982) and **The Sword of Bushido** (1988). Since 1988 he has worked mainly in the USA: for instance on **Keys to Freedom** (1988), **North of Chiang Mai** (1991), **Unveiled** (1992), **Above Suspicion** (1994), and **Gold Diggers** (1995). IB

Bertel, Maurice (1871–1930) CINEMATOGRAPHER Frenchman Maurice Bertel arrived in Australia in 1890, and worked as a photographer and later as a cinematographer, joining the Melbourne office of Pathé Frères in 1907 to supervise the production of their newsreel, and later to film their series of short dramas, which included **Buffalo Bill's Love Story** (1911). In 1913 he joined Australasian Films (see Greater Union Organisation), working on both features and its newsreel. He then worked on the features of Lincoln–Cass Productions, including *The Sick Stockrider** (1913), **Moondyne** (1913), **The Remittance Man** (1913), **Transported** (1913), **The Road to Ruin** (1913), **The Reprieve** (1913), and **The Crisis** (1913). For J.C. Williamson he shot **For Australia** (1915), **Within the Law** (1916), **Get-Rich-Quick Wallingford** (1916), *Officer 666** (1916), and *Seven Keys to Baldpate** (1916). He then moved to Herschells (see Documentary and Non-fiction, silent) in Melbourne, where he worked on documentaries and short films, and passed on his wealth of experience to others.

IB

Best, Peter (1941–) COMPOSER Peter Best is a highly regarded composer for film and television. He composes, orchestrates, and conducts his own scores, and has written the theme songs featured in several of his scores, among them *Tap Tap* for *The Picture Show Man** (1977). Best believes that film music adds importance to a scene and to the whole film. It can provide musical codes that function as a 'director's voice' to convey attitudes: for instance, to underscore a faint hint of unease in an otherwise 'idyllic setting'. Best thinks that, for composers, the first viewing of the film is very important. He contemplates his initial reaction to a film, then conjures up ideas that might represent the substance of the score. Sometimes these ideas may become just 'one thread in the tapestry'. The list of awards he has won for many of his scores for films and for television series and miniseries is extensive. Among them are an Australian Film Institute Best Score Award for **The Picture Show Man**, Australian Performing Rights Association (APRA) awards for *Crocodile Dundee** (1986) and *Muriel's Wedding** (1994), the Film Critics Circle and AFI Best Film Score awards for *Dad and Dave: On Our Selection** (1995) and *Doing Time for Patsy Cline** (1997). Best won APRA's Best Television Theme Award for *Wildside* drama series in 1998.

Other Australian Film: **The Sugar Factory** (1997).

DIANE NAPTHALI

Between Wars

1974. *Director* and *Producer*: Michael Thornhill. *Scriptwriter*: Frank Moorehouse. *Director of photography*: Russell Boyd. *Music*: Adrian Ford. 101 min. *Cast*: Corin Redgrave (Edward Trenbow), Judy Morris (Deborah Trenbow), Günther Meisner (Dr Schneider), Arthur Dignam (Dr Avante), Patricia Leehy (Marguerite).

While working in a hospital for shell-shocked soldiers in World War I, young Australian doctor Edward Trenbow meets a German prisoner who introduces him to Freudian psychoanalysis. Back in Australia, Trenbow, now working in a psychiatric institution, inadvertently becomes embroiled in a public controversy about Freudianism. Seeking a quiet life, Trenbow moves with his family to a country town but, again, finds himself entangled in controversy and political conflict.

Corin Redgrave's languid performance beautifully evokes the sense of a man out of kilter with the authoritarian attitudes and conservative complacencies of his time. A stylish, radical film based on a provocative and thoughtful script, **Between Wars** far outstripped the prevailing conventions of the period drama and commanded widespread critical acclaim, although only limited commercial success. The episodic structure is not without its problems, and the female characters are permitted to deliver less than they promise. Nonetheless, **Between Wars** remains one of the more ambitious achievements of the film renaissance of the 1970s (see Revival, the). HARRY OLDMEADOW

Big Steal, The

1990. *Director*: Nadia Tass. *Producers*: David Parker, Nadia Tass. *Scriptwriter*: David Parker. *Additional scriptwriting*: Max Dunn. *Director of photography*: David Parker. *Music*: Philip Judd. 99 min. *Cast*: Ben Mendelsohn (Danny Clark), Claudia Karvan (Joanna Johnson), Steve Bisley (Gordon Farkas), Marshall Napier (Mr Desmond Clark), Damon Herriman (Mark Jorgensen).

•Nadia Tass and •David Parker, the husband-and-wife team responsible for the success of •**Malcolm** (1986), have made a sweet-tempered, funny film of this tale of teenage wish-fulfilment fantasy. Seventeen-year-old Danny must buy a Jaguar to make good his boast to impress the pretty Joanna but, sadly for him, the sleazy salesman (wittily sketched by Steve •Bisley) sells him a dud. Danny's teenage obsessions—cars and girls—are made the subject of some very droll physical comedy as well as wry satire on a society that encourages macho, consumerist aspirations. When the car exhibits massive defects, Danny, with his mates, decides to take on the dealer, and revenge becomes almost as potent a motive as sexual gratification. This is a lightweight piece but its tone is not merely frivolous; it is also interested in Danny's learning processes, and •Mendelsohn gives one of his most beguiling studies of problem-beset adolescence.

BMcF

Birth Of White Australia, The

1928. *Director/Scriptwriter*: Phil K. Walsh. *Directors of photography*: Lacey Percival, Walter Sully. B&W.

The Birth of White Australia may be considered the dark, ugly side to Phil Walsh's sentimental and nostalgic •**Around the Boree Log** (1925). Unfortunately, populism, which

Damon Herriman, Ben Mendelsohn, and Angelo D'Angelo in **The Big Steal**

celebrates the power of ordinary people, is often mixed with racism, which sets out to exclude some humans from the very category of 'the people'. In many ways, **The Birth of White Australia** is a textbook of populist racism. For example, the film goes out of its way to suggest that Aboriginal people are contented subjects of White Australians, whose 'natural' enemies are the Chinese. It focuses on the racially motivated violence among the gold miners at Lambing Flat in 1861 and, by so doing, sets up a tenuous relation to the populist rebellion at the Eureka Stockade seven years before. Typically for this time period, the narrative features a father-and-daughter team who tackle the rough living of the gold diggings as mates together. Aside from its utility as a cultural document, there is little to recommend this film today.

WILLIAM D. ROUTT

Birtles, Francis, *see* **Documentary and non-fiction, silent**

Bishop, Pat (1946–) ACTOR Primarily a stage and television actor (*Dynasty, Prisoner, Ring of Scorpio, Brides of Christ*), Pat Bishop appeared in the key role of Jenny in the film version of David •Williamson's play •**Don's Party** (1976), although she had played Kath in the first Sydney theatrical production.

Other Australian films include: Human Target (1974), The Right Hand Man (1987), •Dad and Dave: On Our Selection (1995).

GM

Bisley, Steve (1951–) ACTOR Steve Bisley has been one of the busiest and most talented actors in Australian cinema and television over the past two decades. He has played in a wide range of roles but tends to specialise as flamboyant, slightly crooked hustlers (for example, the car salesman Gordon Farkas in •**The Big Steal**, 1990). He was excellent as Graeme Prowse, the exploitative news editor in the third *Frontline* television series. Bisley has also had sporadically recurring roles in the *Water Rats* and *Halifax* television series. Unfortunately, the Australian cinema has not yet provided roles with the same potential, although **The Chain Reaction** (1980) gave Bisley a rare leading role, while his performance as Redback, the bike mechanic who tries to counsel young Steve Carson (Rod •Zuanic) in the underrated realist teen drama •**Fast Talking** (1984), permitted him some dramatic depth. This cannot be said for more dubious projects such as **Summer City** (1977) and *Emma: Queen of the South Seas* (1988).

Other Australian films: •Mad Max (1979), •The Last of the Knucklemen (1979), The Little Feller (1982), Squizzy Taylor (1982), •Silver City (1984), The Winds of Jarrah (1985), Hard Knuckle (1988), The Clean Machine (1988), Over the Hill (1992), Sanctuary (1995).

GM

Bitter Springs

1950. Director: Ralph Smart. *Producer:* Michael Balcon. *Scriptwriters:* W.P. Lipscomb, Monja Danischewsky. *Story:* Ralph Smart. *Director of photography:* George Heath. *Music:* Vaughan Williams. 86 min. B&W. *Cast:* Tommy Trinder (Tommy), Chips Rafferty (Wally King), Gordon Jackson (Mac), Jean Blue (Ma King), Michael Pate (Trooper), Charles Tingwell (John King), Nonnie Piper (Emma King).

The most underrated of the Ealing Australian cycle (see Studios), **Bitter Springs** marks the first attempt at serious treatment of Aboriginal land rights in an Australian feature. Director Ralph •Smart professed himself dissatisfied with the final film, stating that the studio's instance on including Tommy Trinder as the almost obligatory comic 'new chum' undercut the essential seriousness of the film.

Set in SA at the turn of the century, the narrative follows the vicissitudes of the King Family: the father Wally (Chips •Rafferty); his wife, whom he calls 'Mother', played by Jean Blue; and son John (Charles 'Bud' •Tingwell). They and their daughter Emma (Nonnie Piper) are supported by the usual ensemble from the Commonwealth Film Unit (see Film Australia): Gordon Jackson the Scot as Mac; Tommy Trinder as the Englishman Charley; and their Aboriginal stockman Blackjack, who provides a counterpoint to Wally King's view on 'progress'. Michael •Pate, in a strong performance as mounted trooper Ransom, sketches the moral issues involved for King. There are, says Ransom, three ways of dealing with the blacks whose tribal land the King family have selected as a sheep property: 'You can hunt 'em off, you can ease 'em off, or you can take 'em in with you'. Following an uneasy truce between the selectors and the Aboriginal tribe, violence erupts in a sequence involving a kangaroo hunt, which symbolically encapsulates the issue of dispossession. The Aborigines lay siege to the King homestead, leaving Ransom to restore peace with his mounted troopers.

Chips Rafferty, in a performance as the patriarchal Wally King that is the dark side of the character he played in **The •Overlanders,** suffers a change of heart in the film's denouement, achieving a conveniently happy, although historically inaccurate, ending.

BRUCE MOLLOY

Blackfellas

1993. Director: James Ricketson. *Producer:* David Rapsey. *Executive Producers:* Penny Chapman, Paul D. Barron. *Script:* James Ricketson, Archie Weller. *Director of photography:* Jeff Malouf. 98 min. *Cast:* John Moore (Doug Dooligan), David Ngoombujarra ('Pretty Boy' Floyd Davey), Jaylene Riley (Polly), Lisa Kinchela (Valerie).

Blackfellas was the first Australian commercial film to focus on urban Aborigines. Over the three years that this film was in pre-production, it utilised the talent of Aboriginal writers, actors, musicians, film-makers, and crew. It is a social realist film that is aimed directly at an Aboriginal audience. Realism is achieved by avoiding the use of professional actors. It is based on Archie Weller's novel *Day of the Dog*, with active Aboriginal participation at every stage from script development to post-production. With contributions from White Australians, the status of **Blackfellas** as an exclusively Aboriginal film remains contentious.

Set in Western Australia among the Aborigines of the Perth area (Nyoongahs), it is the story of Aborigines caught between two laws. They struggle to exist within the constraints of White Australian law, but they are nurtured and guided by traditional custom. The narrative traces Dougie Dooligan's troubled path from incarceration to independence. Upon his release, he struggles to avoid the seductive cycle of alcohol, crime, and influential friends, all of which facilitated his previous downfall. Dougie's desire is to reclaim his ancestral property, ensuring the preservation of ancient rock paintings and the security of his elders. His nostalgic sense of responsibility is foregrounded in contrast to his girlfriend Polly's faint knowledge of her own heritage. With little clue about her ancestry, Polly's repeated claim is that Dougie's past is 'yesterday's history'. This is also reflected in the hedonistic character Floyd 'Pretty Boy' Davey, whose impetuous desire for immediate gratification is without regard for the consequences. With his resolve to forge a strong connection between his history and his future, Dougie emerges as an inspirational force.

WENDY HASLEM

Blackrock

1997. Director: Steven Vidler. *Producer*: David Elfick. *Scriptwriter*: Nick Enright, based on his own play. *Director of photography*: Martin McGrath. 90 min. *Cast*: Laurence Breuls (Jared), Linda Cropper (Diane), Simon Lyndon (Ricko) Chris Haywood (Det. Sgt Wilansky), Rebecca Smart (Cherie).

Playwright Nick •Enright based his play, *The Property of the Clan*, later called *Blackrock*, on a real-life tragedy of rape and murder, set in Newcastle. Originally conceived as therapy for those most closely involved, he adapted his play into a film that focuses sharply on the Australian credo of never 'dobbing your mates'. Teenager Jared, who lives in a state of uneasy truce with his mother Diane, one night witnesses at a surfside party the rape of a young girl and her subsequent murder at the hands of her rapist. The latter is Jared's drifter mate Ricko, whose male vanity has been wounded by the girl, and Jared's code of loyalty prevents him from helping the investigation of a crime that has shocked the community. Alongside Jared's 'secret' is his mother's: she has been diagnosed as having breast cancer, and cannot find the

means—or the occasion—to tell him. The film negotiates its two plot strands with some skill, their parallel lines converging ultimately on the issue of Jared's need to confront reality with more maturity than he has shown hitherto. It ends on a note of sober reconciliation between Jared and his mother at the graveside of the dead girl. The film rather surprisingly failed to find the youth audience that might have been supposed to respond to it but, at its best, it is unusually astute about matters of class, gender, and the generations in a realistic urban setting.

BMcF

Blake, Jon (1958–) ACTOR Jon Blake's film career was cut short in December 1986 when, after completing the last day of a starring role in the World War I military drama •**The Lighthorsemen** (1987), his car struck another car and he sustained severe injuries. It is unlikely that he will work again. The accident occurred at a time when his screen career was blossoming, following a number of leading roles (such as those in **Cool Change**, 1986, and the popular television miniseries *Anzacs*), which capitalised on his good looks. *Other Australian films include*: **Freedom** (1982), **Early Frost** (1982), **Running from the Guns** (1987).

GM

Blake, Julia (1936–) ACTOR Distinguished for her work in all the acting media, British-born actor Julia Blake came to Australia in 1953, married actor Terry Norris in 1961, and has had a busy career ever since, including a long stint in the television series *Prisoner*. Her striking features can serve causes dignified, compassionate, or sinister. In the last mode, she responded well to the melodramatic challenges of •**Patrick** (1978), as the matron of a very peculiar hospital; she was affecting as the careworn mother of the heroine in •**My Brilliant Career** (1979), made shrewish by poverty and lost hopes; and she brought warmth and dignity to the role of Frances in •**Travelling North** (1987), throwing her late-middle-aged lot in with the irascible Frank (Leo •McKern) when they make the eponymous journey. Australian films, like most others, are not rich in demanding roles for mature actresses, but Blake has made the most of what has come along, including four for director Paul •Cox: in •**Lonely Hearts** (1982), as Norman •Kaye's shrill sister; •**Man of Flowers** (1983); •**My First Wife** (1984); and **Cactus** (1989). Her performances are incisively intelligent and clearly felt.

Other Australian films: •**The Getting of Wisdom** (1977), **Snapshot** (1979), •**An Indecent Obsession** (1985), **Georgia** (1989), **Father** (1990), **Mushrooms** (1995), **Hotel de Love** (1996).   BMcF

Blakemore, Michael (1928–) DIRECTOR Long resident in the United Kingdom, where he has had a distinguished career as a theatrical director, especially with the National Theatre, Michael Blakemore has made two incursions into Australian cinema. First, in 1981 he wrote, directed and appeared in an engaging autobiographical documentary, **A Personal History of the Australian Surf**, in which he recounts his teenage preoccupation with the theatre and the surf, rather than the medical career his doctor father wants him to follow. Then, in 1994, he returned to direct •**Country Life**, a reworking of Chekhov's *Uncle Vanya* on a remote cattle station. In this, ironically, he also played the role of the expatriate celebrity whose return unsettles the hard-working family whose sacrifices have enabled his overseas success.   BMcF

Blanchett, Cate

Blanchett, Cate (1969–) ACTOR Cate Blanchett graduated from the National Institute of Dramatic Art (NIDA) in 1992 and quickly made a name on stage (voted Best Female Performer by the Sydney Critics Circle in 1994), and television (starring in, among others, the critical success *Heartland* and the under-appreciated *Bordertown*). Her first film performance was in the short feature **Parklands** (1994). She next played one of the ensemble of women in the Japanese prison camp in •**Paradise Road** (1997), followed by two starring roles. In •**Oscar and Lucinda** (1998), her delicate beauty was counterposed against the angular awkwardness of Ralph Fiennes, but her intensity and oddity matched his. In •**Thank God He Met Lizzie** (1997) she played the thankless role of the third point of the triangle, making the character convincing, even sympathetic. Her international career then burgeoned, starting with the starring role in **Elizabeth** (United Kingdom, 1998), for which she was awarded the Golden Globe and nominated for an Oscar.

Other Australian film: Dreamtime Alice (1998).   IB

Blinky Bill (Blinky Bill, The Mischievous Koala)

1992. Director: Yoram Gross. *Producer:* Yoram Gross. *Scriptwriters:* John Palmer, Leonard Lee. *Based on The Complete Adventures of Blinky Bill by* Dorothy Wall. *Music and songs:* Guy Gross. *Directors of photography:* Frank Hammond, Paul Ozerski. 80 min. *Cast:* Robyn Moore, Keith Scott, Julie Anthony.

The Yoram •Gross animation studio brought its now well-established style and formula to a very free adaptation of Dorothy Wall's 1933 classic children's stories. Working quickly (two years) and economically (A$5 million) with his preferred Australian subject matter, Gross again produced an international success. **Blinky Bill** is one of the environmental-themed feature cartoons of the early 1990s (see **Ferngully: The Last Rainforest**). The film concerns a community of bush animals, all clearly defined characters with everyday concerns, comic habits, and Australian voices. This community is threatened by the arrival of loggers intent on clear-felling the area. Blinky Bill must rescue

his mother and her companion, a frog, from the dangers arising from this destruction. Gross builds the story around songs and the images around the conjunction of animated characters and live-action bush settings. The film helped pre-sell the successful 1994 26-episode television series, also from the Gross Studios.   RICK THOMPSON

Bliss

1985. Director: Ray Lawrence. *Producer:* Anthony Buckley. *Scriptwriters:* Ray Lawrence, Peter Carey. *Based on the novel by* Peter Carey. *Director of photography:* Paul Murphy. *Music:* Peter Best. 110 min. *Cast:* Barry Otto (Harry Joy), Lynette Curran (Bettina Joy), Helen Jones (Honey Barbara), Gia Carides (Lucy Joy), Miles Buchanan (David Joy), Jeff Truman (Joel).

Peter Carey collaborated with the director to write the script for this successful film adaptation of one of his most popular and accessible novels. It is basically a family melodrama, told from the perspective of the father, Harry Joy. After a near-death experience, he abandons his former lifestyle (including his shrewish wife, objectionable children, and the business partner who has cuckolded him), finds his ideals impossible to achieve in the city, and retreats to the rainforest, where he spends eight years sending a love letter to Honey Barbara in the form of a plantation of honey-producing native trees. This was Barry •Otto's first starring role, the first of a series of inarticulate fathers with hearts of gold. The performance suits the mannered style of the film, which abandons realism long before the famous scenes of sex on a restaurant table-top, or the elephant sitting on Joy's car. Some find the style irritating and the romanticism of the plot unbearably saccharine, but others enjoy Harry Joy's unpredictable—but ultimately just—fantasy world. Peter •Best's music is particularly fine in the finale in which Harry Joy's death mirrors the opening sequence in a most satisfying closure.   IB

Blood Oath

1990. Director: Stephen Wallace. *Producers:* Charles Waterstreet, Denis Whitburn, Brian A. Williams. *Scriptwriter:* Denis Whitburn, Brian A. Williams. *Script editor:* John Clarke. *Director of photography:* Russell Boyd. *Music:* David McHugh. 108 min. *Cast:* Bryan Brown (Captain Cooper). George Takei (Vice-Admiral Baron Takahashi), Terry O'Quinn (Major Beckett), John Bach (Major Roberts), John Clarke (Sheedy), Deborah Unger (Sister Littell), John Polson (Private Jimmy Fenton).

In December 1941 the Australian Army sent the 1100-strong Gull force Battalion to the Indonesian island of Ambon, 1000 kilometres north of Darwin, to reinforce a small Dutch contingent. The Japanese, however, had selected the island as a major base to launch an invasion of

New Guinea and Australia. A 35 000 strong Japanese force invaded the island and the Gull Battalion was forced to surrender. More than 200 Australians were executed in the next few days and, by the end of the war, only 123 Australians remained alive.

The film was loosely based on the prosecution of 91 Japanese soldiers and officers. The Ambon trial was synthesised with two other trials in the script by Denis Whitburn and Brian Williams, son of the prosecutor at the Ambon trial in 1946. The film rewrites history by adding new characters and deleting some major figures. Lack of focus is a weakness of the film, which shifts between the war crimes, the trial, and an under-developed Cold War conspiracy involving American ambitions in the region. The film's virtue is that it does not restrict itself to self-righteous indignation at Japanese atrocities, but cleverly extends the narrative to universal concerns about the way in which power and privilege make victims of those that have neither.

Bryan •Brown is excellent as the Australian prosecutor with a strong supporting cast that includes John Bach as a devious officer, John •Clarke as the perceptive journalist, and Terry O'Quinn as the shadowy American liaison officer.
GM

Blue Fin

1978. *Director*: Carl Schultz. *Producer*: Hal McElroy. *Scriptwriter*: Sonia Borg. Based on the novel by Colin Thiele. *Director of photography*: Geoff Burton. *Music*: Michael Carlos. 88 min. *Cast*: Hardy Kruger (Pascoe), Greg Rowe (Snook), John Jarratt (Sam), Liddy Clark (Ruth), Hugh Keays-Byrne (Stan).

This unaffectedly pleasing children's film won less notice than the earlier •Storm Boy (1976), also adapted from a novel by Colin Thiele, but it has its own attractions. The plot centres on a boy's attempts to win his tuna-fisherman father's approval and the film's climax involves him in bringing his father's disabled boat to shore. This climax — in which the fish cease to bite, a waterspout threatens the boat, and the father breaks a leg — builds tension as the boy's resourcefulness is called into play. As well as telling this story of a boy, a man and a boat, **Blue Fin** also gives a sense of the life of the small SA coastal community in which it is set. Sequences such as those depicting a 'Miss Tuna' Ball and a funeral provide a sometimes amusing, sometimes touching context for the film's main drama.
BMcF

Blundell, Graeme (1945–) ACTOR

As Alvin Purple, the naive young man who is mysteriously irresistible to women and unable to avoid their attentions, Graeme Blundell created one of the memorable comic figures of early 1970s Australian cinema. Tim •Burstall's film, •Alvin Purple (1973), cheerfully vulgar variations on a single joke, made so much money for its production company, •Hexagon, that it quickly spawned a sequel, **Alvin Rides Again** (1974), a short-lived teleseries, *Alvin Purple*, and surfaced again ten years later in a further sequel, **Melvin: Son of Alvin** (1984), in which Blundell was reduced to playing a supporting role. In fact, his film career has been so overshadowed by Alvin that it is easy to forget that he was a regular performer in new Australian cinema (see Revival, the), as well as maintaining busy careers on the stage and, in more recent years, as a writer.

The suggestion of gormlessness that fed the character of Alvin also made itself felt in the earlier role of the shy young market researcher in •**The Naked Bunyip** (1970), in the safari-jacketed, pipe-smoking Liberal out of place among a gaggle of aggressive Laborites in •**Don's Party** (1976), of which he had directed the first stage performance, and as the pilot with a sneeze-induced impotence problem in the limp sex comedy, **Pacific Banana** (1981). In two nasty characterisations of 1987, he showed a notable broadening of his range: as the far-right Queensland butcher standing for state parliament in **Australian Dream**, and as the heroine's alcoholic stepfather in •**The Year My Voice Broke**.

Other Australian films: The Girl Friends (1968, short), •**2000 Weeks** (1969), •**Stork** (1971), **Carson's Watermelon** (1971, short), **Brake Fluid** (1971, short), **Three Old Friends** (1974, short), •**Mad Dog Morgan** (1976), **Weekend of Shadows** (1978), •**The Odd Angry Shot** (1979), •**Kostas** (1979), **Gasoline and Alcohol** (1980, doc., nar.), **The Job Interviewer** (1980, short), **Doctors and Nurses** (1981), **Getting to Know Me** (1981, short), **How to Avoid Decisions** (1981, short), **The Best of Friends** (1982), **Midnite Spares** (1983), **Those Dear Departed** (1987), **Gino** (1993, unreleased), **Idiot Box** (1996).
BMcF

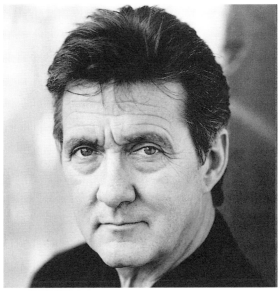

Graeme Blundell

Bluthal, John (1929–) ACTOR John Bluthal emigrated to Australia from Poland in 1938 and studied at Melbourne University. Since 1956 he has alternated between Australia and the United Kingdom, with prolonged periods in television in both countries (notably *Home Sweet Home* in Australia). A gifted comedian, Bluthal's Australian film roles have not exploited his full potential and he has often been relegated to character parts in sex films, such as Professor Jurgun Notafreud in •**Fantasm** (1976); low-budget horror films, such as the sinister guardian in **Alison's Birthday** (1981); and failed comedies, such as **Touch and Go** (1980) and **The Return of Captain Invincible** (1983). In recent years, Bluthal's acting opportunities in the Australian cinema have improved, with roles such as Paul •Chubb's eccentric father in **Stan and George's New Life** (1992) and Rufus Sewell's 'uncle' in Alex •Proyas's haunting futuristic thriller •**Dark City** (1998).   GM

Bonner, Tony (1942–) ACTOR Tony Bonner, a prolific Sydney actor since the 1960s, has not reached the same public awareness in films as he did with series roles in early television programs such as *Skippy*, *Skyways*, and, in the 1980s, the miniseries *Anzacs*. Bonner has primarily appeared as a supporting actor in most of his Australian and overseas films. Despite his good looks, Bonner has not featured in romantic films but has been more prominent in crime thrillers. He played Leo Bassett, in the tough, underrated crime thriller •**Money Movers** (1979), the pony-tailed criminal Howard Fenton in **Hurricane Smith** (1991), and the sinister Dr Jonathan Heckett in **Dead Sleep** (1989).
Other Australian films include: •They're a Weird Mob (1966), Inn of the Damned (1975), •The Mango Tree (1977), Hard Knocks (1980), •The Man from Snowy River (1982), •The Lighthorsemen (1987), •Quigley (1991).   GM

Books, *see* Select Bibliography

Borg, Sonia (1931–) ACTOR/WRITER Born in Vienna to German parents, Sonia Borg trained as an actor in Berlin, and worked with a travelling Shakespearean company in India (immortalised in the film **Shakespeare Wallah**, United Kingdom, 1965). She arrived in Australia in 1961, and obtained work as an actor for Crawfords on *Consider Your Verdict* but, as there were not many roles for women with a European accent, she was soon writing dialogue for the series as well as training less experienced actors. On later Crawford productions, such as *Matlock Police*, *Homicide*, and *Division Four*, she worked as scriptwriter, script editor, and, occasionally, producer. After ten years, she went freelance, writing mainly for television: *Rush* (1974, 1976), *Power Without Glory* (1976), *Ratbag Hero* (1991), and, most significantly, developing *Women of the Sun* (1982) with Hyllus Maris. She also wrote three films: •**Storm Boy** (1976)

was a key film of the period, playing a significant role in popularising Australian films with local audiences, •**Blue Fin** (1978) was another adaptation from a Colin Thiele children's novel, and **Dusty** (1983) was adapted from Frank Dalby Davison's classic story. All three enhanced her reputation for sensitive adaptation and for character development in naturalistic settings.   IB

Bourke, Terry (1940–) DIRECTOR Terry Bourke is a Victorian writer/producer/director who worked as a production assistant and stuntman in Hong Kong in the 1960s where he directed his first feature film **Sampan** (1968). This was followed by **Noon Sunday** in 1970, which was filmed in Guam. Bourke also wrote and directed many episodes of the World War II Australian television spy thriller *Spyforce* in 1971–72. Throughout the 1970s and early 1980s, Bourke worked extensively in the low-budget exploitation end of the Australian film industry, although his first Australian feature film, **Night of Fear,** a 54-minute horror film without dialogue that was shot in 12 days in 1972, was conceived as a pilot for a television series. After the ABC rejected the planned series, Bourke and executive producer Rod Hay released the pilot as a theatrical film. **Inn of the Damned**, another horror film starring Dame Judith Anderson and American Alex Cord, began shooting in late 1973, although it did not receive a theatrical release until 1975 following conflict between the producers, Bourke and Hay, and the Australian Film Development Corporation (see Australian Film Commission; Cultural Policy), which supplied most of the film's finance.

After directing the mystery **Murcheson Creek** (1975), a feature-length television pilot for a proposed series on Channel Nine that never eventuated, Bourke directed and scripted **Plugg** (1975), a broad sex comedy involving an incompetent private detective. In 1978 Bourke replaced John Powell as director during the filming of **Little Boy Lost**, a film that is loosely based on the true story of 4-year-old Stephen Walls who was lost in the bush in New South Wales (Walls also being the subject of a popular hit song in the 1960s). Bourke also wrote the script for the film and followed it with the script for the feature-length pilot of the children's television series *Secret Valley* (1980) for the Grundy Organisation. Two straight-to-video films, directed and scripted by Bourke followed: **Lady, Stay Dead** (1982) and **Brothers** (1982), the latter based on the story of Australian journalists who had covered the conflict in Timor (although it was filmed in The Philippines and Taihape in New Zealand).
Other Australian films include: The Tourist (1988).   GM

Boyd, Russell (1944–) CINEMATOGRAPHER A major contributor to the look of Australian films since the mid 1970s, Russell Boyd's background was newsreels (•Cinesound and HSV7, Melbourne), documentaries, and commercials (Supreme Films, Sydney), and television dramas at Robert Bruning Productions, Sydney. In 1974 he made an impressive entry into feature films with Michael •Thornhill's •Between Wars, winning the Australian Cinematographers Society 'Milli' award ('Best Cinematographer of the Year'). The following year, his overseas reputation was begun with the British Academy cinematography award and international critics' praise for his work on Peter •Weir's •Picnic at Hanging Rock. He won three Australian Film Institute Best Cinematography awards, for Break of Day (1977), •The Last Wave (1977), and •Gallipoli (1981). In 1988 he was honoured with the AFI Raymond Longford Award for his 'significant contribution to Australian filmmaking'. Other Australian films that have earned him praise include •Star Struck (1982), •The Year of Living Dangerously (1982), and Stephen •Wallace's •Blood Oath (1990). Popular successes have included •Crocodile Dundee (1986) and Crocodile Dundee II (1987). The first overseas film he photographed was Bruce •Beresford's Tender Mercies (USA, 1982), which has been followed by many international feature films for both Australian and American directors.

Other Australian films: •The Man from Hong Kong (1975), The Love Epidemic (1975), The Golden Cage (1975), Gone to Ground (1976), Summer of Secrets (1976), •Dawn! (1979), The Chain Reaction (1980), Maybe This Time (1980), •Phar Lap (1983), Stanley: Every Home Should Have One (1984), •Burke & Wills (1985), •Hightide (1987), Sweet Talker (1990), Almost An Angel (1990), Turtle Beach (1991).

DAVID MUIR

Boys, The

1998. Director: Rowan Woods. Producers: Robert Connelly and John Maynard. Scriptwriter: Stephen Sewell. Based on the play by Gordon Graham. Director of photography: Tristan Milani. Music: The Necks. 84 min. Cast: David Wenham (Brett Sprague), Toni Collette (Michelle), Lynette Curran (Sandra), John Polson (Glenn), Jeanette Cronin (Jackie), Anthony Hayes (Stevie).

This film of non-stop violence, physical and verbal, is one of the most disturbing Australian films of recent years. Brett Sprague, released from gaol, is met by his brother Steve, and goes home to a welcome from his mother, Sandra. Brett's girlfriend, Michelle, is willing to have sex, but Brett is impotent and bashes her in the laundry. Steve's pregnant girlfriend, Nola, cowers and eventually leaves. The other brother, Glenn, and his partner, Jackie, come over to celebrate, but Jackie ultimately says she will leave Glenn if he doesn't break with his brothers. This quickly turns violent, with rumpuses between the brothers, and the film has an air of real foreboding, engendered in the flash-forwards which make clear that the brothers will be involved in some dreadful crime. There is no respite from the imminence and/or reality of appalling violence, the self-perpetuating horror of which is the film's theme. The Boys is based on a play and sometimes feels and sounds like one, but the fine ensemble cast and the rigour, pace, and variety of Woods's direction maintain the tension of the piece. •David Wenham, •Toni Collette, as the tough peroxide blonde Michelle, in her best role since •Muriel's Wedding, and •Lynette Curran as Sandra, all drooping blonde curls and flowered stretch-pants, anxious not to believe the worst about 'my boys', are outstanding.   BMcF

Bradbury, David (1951–   ) DIRECTOR/PHOTOGRAPHER
Beginning as a broadcast journalist with the ABC, David Bradbury's independent and passionate political documentaries centre on struggles between ordinary people and powerful interests, with a clear sympathy for the less powerful. More interested in issues than the delineation of character, this is film-making as both political action and search for moral, humanitarian values.

Early works on political struggles outside Australia developed his style: Frontline (1979) and Public Enemy Number One (1981) presented biographies of war photographer Neil Davis and journalist Wilfred Burchett respectively, against the background of revolutionary conflict in South-east Asia. Nicaragua, No Pasaran (1984), Chile: Hasta Cuando? (1985), and South of the Border (1987) shifted the interest in revolutionary movements to Latin America.

Attention turned to Australia with State of Shock (1988), a powerful exploration of the effects of alcohol on indigenous communities; Polska (1991), and Nazi Supergrass (1993). Throughout the 1990s an increasing emphasis on environmental issues is evident in Shoalwater: Up for Grabs (1992), The Last Whale (1994), Battle for Byron (1997), and Jabiluka (1998). A common concentration on immediate, local struggles, at the expense of structural analysis, is evident in Loggerheads (1997).

In the late 1990s Bradbury began to explore digital video technologies enabling increasing centralisation of production roles, and innovative financing arrangements through the Frontline Film Foundation. Among his many awards are Academy Award nominations for both Frontline and Chile: Hasta Cuando?   PETER HUGHES

'Breaker' Morant

1980. Director: Bruce Beresford. Producer: Matthew Carroll. Scriptwriters: Jonathan Hardy, David Stevens, Bruce Beresford. Based on the play by Kenneth Ross. Director of photography: Don McAlpine. Musical arranger: Phil Cuneen. 104 min. Cast: Edward Woodward (Harry 'Breaker' Morant), Jack Thompson (Major J.F. Thomas), John Waters (Capt. Alfred Taylor), Bryan Brown (Lt Peter Handcock), Charles Tingwell (Lt Col. Denny), Lewis Fitz-Gerald (Lt George Witton).

Breaking of the Drought

This drama, based on a real-life episode of the Boer War, is centred on the court martial of three carbineers: an English adventurer, Morant, and two young Australians, Handcock and Witton. These three are being tried for the shooting of Boers who have killed and mutilated a British captain, and for the killing of a German missionary to prevent his spreading word about the carbineers holding the group of Boer prisoners. The film alternates between the courtroom, in which an Australian defence counsel fights for the lives of the accused, and the events that have led up to the trial. As the trial proceeds, the accused men realise they have been betrayed by their British superiors, including the supreme authority figure of Lord Kitchener. They have been made scapegoats to international expediency. Morant and Handcock are executed in a movingly staged sequence on a hillside at dawn; Witton is sentenced to life imprisonment.

Despite his obvious sympathy for the colonial victims of an imperial drama, director •Beresford has not sought to make a crudely anti-British polemic. As in several of his Australian films, he is concerned both to explore the nature of loyalties in a hierarchical situation and to exploit the tension to be derived from the manipulation of motives in a confined situation. Here, he is abetted by a uniformly excellent cast and by the fluid camerawork of his frequent collaborator, Don •McAlpine.   BMcF

Breaking of the Drought, The

1920. *Director/Producer/Director of photography*: Franklyn Barrett. *Scriptwriters*: Jack North, Franklyn Barrett. From the play by Bland Holt. B&W. *Cast*: Trilby Clark (Marjorie Galloway), Dunstan Webb (Tom Wattleby), Marie La Varre (Olive Lorette).

The Breaking of the Drought, most of which survives today, does not hold together as a narrative. The acting, except for Trilby Clark's quintessential portrayal of a plucky heroine, is stiff and unconvincing. Franklyn •Barrett's photography, like his direction, is only competent. Worst of all, the drought that seems intended to function metaphorically in parallel with the story of the ruin and redemption of a squatter's family winds up as shock-horror images of starving stock and parched soil brought up at arbitrary points to divert attention from the floundering logic of Barrett's scenario. And yet this film deserves its reputation as a fundamental text of early Australian cinema. The drought *is*

Lewis FitzGerald, Bryan Brown, and Edward Woodward in 'Breaker-Morant'

horrifying, Trilby Clark *is* entrancing (especially when she has set herself on the road to ruin), details of both country and city life *are* observed with documentary precision, the climactic bushfire *is* spectacular, and Sydney *is* the wickedest city in the world to the pure and upright denizens of Wallaby Station.   WILLIAM D. ROUTT

Brealey, Gil (1932–) PRODUCER/DIRECTOR This Melbourne-born film-maker has been involved in the film and television industry since the 1950s, making his first films while a student at Melbourne University. Gil Brealey worked with the ABC during the 1960s as a director, followed by four years as a producer with the Commonwealth Film Unit (see Film Australia) before taking over the leadership of the •South Australian Film Corporation during its heyday from 1972 to 1976. Brealey was made an Officer of Australia by the federal government in 1976 for his work in the Australian film industry. After directing and producing a series of short films in the 1950s and 1960s, the first feature film he produced for the Commonwealth Film Unit was **Three To Go** (1971), which comprised three youth-centred stories with a separate director for each story: Peter •Weir, Brian Hannant,

and Oliver Howes. Brealey followed this with **Flashpoint** (1972) for Film Australia, the renamed Commonwealth Film Unit, which was filmed in the Pilbara, iron ore country in WA, and released on Australian television in 1973. Brealey's next film, •**Sunday Too Far Away** (1975), was produced during his tenure at the South Australian Film Corporation, and it was the Corporation's first feature. The critical and commercial success of this film encouraged other state governments to establish similar organisations, and Brealey eventually headed the •Tasmanian Film Corporation. In 1980 Brealey was executive producer on •**Manganinnie**, and he followed this with work as the producer on •**Dusty** (1983), a moving film adaptation of Frank Dalby Davison's story of a kelpie/dingo crossbreed and his master (played by Bill •Kerr). In 1984 Brealey returned to direction with •**Annie's Coming Out**, based on the 'real-life' story of social worker Rosemary Crossley's fight against the diagnosis of a young woman, Annie McDonald, as intellectually disabled.   GM

Brennan, Richard (1943–) PRODUCER A former employee of the ABC and the Commonwealth Film Unit (see Film Australia), and a prolific producer of Australian

Intertitle from **The Breaking of the Drought**

shorts in the 1960s and 1970s, Richard Brennan produced Peter •Weir's first solo film, **Holmesdale**, in 1971. Brennan was also production manager on •**The Adventures of Barry McKenzie** (1972), **Flashpoint** (1972), and Cecil •Holmes's **Gentle Strangers** (1972), before forming B.C. Productions with director Tom •Cowan and producing Cowan's **Promised Woman** in 1975. Brennan was extremely prolific in the mid and late 1970s, and his 1980s credits include an acting role in **Going Down** (1983). Overall, Brennan's productions indicate a preference for generic and melodramatic material, including **Death-cheaters** (1976), •**Mad Dog Morgan** (1976), •**Long Week-end** (1979), •**Stir** (1980), •**Star Struck** (1982), two Mark •Joffe films—•**Grievous Bodily Harm** (1988), and •**Spotswood** (1992)—and •**Blood Oath** (1990).
Other Australian films include: The Great MacArthy (1975), The Removalists (1975), The Trespassers (1976), The Love-Letters from Teralba Road (1977), •Newsfront (1978), Molly (1983), I Can't Get Started (1985), •Cosi (1996).   GM

Briant, Shane (1946–) ACTOR British-born Shane Briant worked steadily in British films and television throughout the 1970s, including the starring role as Dorian Gray in a television remake of *The Picture of Dorian Gray*. Briant's first performance in an Australian film was a supporting role in the thriller **Run, Chrissie Run** (1984). This film established a pattern for Briant's career in the Australian cinema, where he has been largely confined to supporting roles, generally playing smooth, sinister characters, such as Stephen Enderby in •**Grievous Bodily Harm** (1988), military figures (Reichert in •**The Lighthorsemen**, 1987), or policemen (Detective Inspector Bosey in **Tunnel Vision**, 1994). Briant also appeared in the prestigious television production *Darling of the Gods* (1989), as Cecil Beaton.
Other Australian films include: Cassandra (1987), Barracuda (1988), •Minnamurra (1989), Till There Was You (1990).
                    GM

Britton, Aileen (1916–86) ACTOR After appearing in Ken G. •Hall's •**Tall Timbers** in 1937 and the 1942 short **100 000 Cobbers**, Aileen Britton made no further appearance on cinema screens until 1979, when she played Judy •Davis's grandmother in •**My Brilliant Career**. This is the screen role for which she is best known; she invested it with the imposing dignity it required. She had a long career on the stage and did a good deal of television work, including a continuing role in *The Sullivans*, but made only three further films, apart from appearing as herself in Andrée Wright and Stewart Young's documentary, •**Don't Call Me Girlie** (1985), about women in early Australian film.
Other Australian films: Fluteman (1982), Now and Forever (1983), The Place at the Coast (1987).   BMcF

Broken Highway

1994. *Director*: Laurie McInnes. *Producer*: Richard Mason. *Scriptwriter*: Laurie McInnes. *Director of photography*: Steve Mason. *Music*: David Faulkner. 98 min. *Cast*: Aden Young (Angel), David Field (Tatts), Dennis Miller (Max), Kris McQuade (Woman), Bill Hunter (Wilson), Claudia Karvan (Catherine), Norman Kaye (Kidd).

Prize-winning short film-makers don't always make prize-winning feature film-makers, and **Broken Highway** is, unfortunately, a prime example of this phenomenon. In a visually striking first feature, Laurie •McInnes concentrates heavily on atmosphere, with highly structured black-and-white images and heightened sound design (Penn Robinson is credited as Audiographer, the only known instance of this title), but she seems to have forgotten about character and plot development.

While working at sea, Angel is bequeathed dying work-mate Max's cowboy boots and a mission to Honeyfield, Queensland, but all he finds is a string of unfulfilled lives waiting for Max to return. Exactly why fellow work-mate Tatts hunts Angel down, and why they wrestle in the mud for Max's boots in the film's climax, isn't entirely clear, but then nothing really is. Moody, brooding, and displaying how good at pouting Young and Karvan are, and how ubiquitous Hunter has become in Australian films, **Broken Highway** is too indulgent and pretentious to succeed even as a 'niche market' art film.

                    TIM HUNTER

Broken Melody, The

1938. *Director*: Ken G. Hall. *Producer*: Ken G. Hall. *Scriptwriter*: Frank Harvey. Based on a novel by F.J. Thwaites. *Director of photography*: George Heath. *Music*: Horace Keats, Alfred Hill. 89 min. B&W. *Cast*: Lloyd Hughes (John Ainsworth), Diana Du Cane (Ann Brady), Frank Harvey (Jules de Latannac), Rosalind Kennerdale (Henriette Le Lange), Alec Kellaway (Joe Larkin), Harry Abdy (Sam Harris), Gough Whitlam (extra).

John Ainsworth, successful violinist, rower, and scion of a wealthy squatter is 'sent down' by Sydney University after a barroom altercation over a 'crooner'. Rejected by his family, he tramps the streets of Depression-era Sydney, eventually living 'down and out' in a Wooloomooloo cave with Joe, a petty criminal. One night, as he wanders along the new Harbour Bridge, he convinces a woman to abandon her suicide attempt. By coincidence she is ('Raggedy') Anne, the crooner for whom he risked his inheritance. Eventually fortune smiles on John, in the form of a French talent scout, and he travels to the United Kingdom to pursue a successful career as a composer, with Joe as his valet. Unimpressed by the pretentious performers he must work with, John longs for the simpler days spent in poverty with Anne and composes an opera about them, which he calls *The Broken Melody*. John returns to Australia, ostensibly to tour his opera but also secretly to rescue the family estate from foreclosure. Meanwhile, Joe conspires to reunite John with Anne, who is now a classical singer of some repute. This reunion takes place during an unbroken stage presentation of John's operatic reminiscences, which he conducts with Anne in the lead role.   DEB VERHOEVEN

Brooksbank, Anne (1940–) WRITER Widely respected as a writer and script editor, Anne Brooksbank has collaborated on several projects with her long-time partner Bob •Ellis, most notably •**Newsfront** (1978), on which she is credited with 'additional dialogue'. Her uncredited contribution to other work by Ellis has sometimes been the subject of speculation in industry circles. Her early interests in English literature led her to graduate at Masters level at Melbourne University, where she was a contemporary of writer Peter Corris. She studied painting at the National Gallery art school under John Brack. There she met Ellis,

who was researching a documentary about women at university, and she moved to Sydney to join him. Her first major credit, the children's feature **Avengers of the Reef** (1973), produced by Noel •Ferrier, marked the beginning of her scriptwriting career. **Maybe This Time** (1980) could be considered among her more personal work. She also co-wrote (with Ellis) **The Winds of Jarrah** (1985). Her many television credits include the telefeature *Archer*, the series *A Country Practice*, *GP*, *Blue Heelers*, and *Water Rats*. She is winner of several Writers Guild (Awgie) awards.

HARRY KIRCHNER

Brophy, Philip (1959–) WRITER/DIRECTOR/COMPOSER/ SOUND DESIGNER Multimedia artist Philip Brophy has said 'I always hear a film first, and I see it last'. Brophy has worked extensively in most media forms—music, performance, sound design, computer art, video, publishing— and has contributed key theoretical and critical writings in the area of sonic cinema, Japanese animation, horror, and exploitation films.

Cinesound studio set for operetta finale of **The Broken Melody**, with the ABC Symphony Orchestra

From 1979 to 1982 he created music videos, films, performances and mixed media events with an ensemble of artists known as Tsk Tsk Tsk. A significant body of short film work followed, culminating in the provocative 47-minute **Salt, Saliva, Sperm and Sweat** (1988), an 'essay film' that investigates and documents bodily functions in a loose narrative context involving an office worker. This first collaboration by director Brophy and producer Rod Bishop won the prize for best Australian short at the 1988 Melbourne International Film Festival. It was followed by the tongue-in-cheek horror-splatter film **Body Melt** (1993), which involved Brophy not only as co-writer, director, composer, and co-sound designer, but also as sound conceptualiser—a new category created specifically for this film. **Body Melt's** complex narrative structure interweaves numerous stories into a world that resembles a pop-culture museum and is populated by a panorama of characters played by popular Australian television soap icons. Brophy composed the soundtrack for Anna •Kokkinos's **Only the Brave** (1994) and Marie Craven's **Maidenhead** (1995), which won the prize for best soundtrack at the 1996 Cracow International Film Festival (Poland). From 1983 Brophy has taught soundtrack and media arts theory at the School of Art and Design at Phillip Institute of Technology in Melbourne and then in Media Arts at Royal Melbourne Institute of Technology.　　　　ANNA DZENIS

Brown, Bryan (1948–) ACTOR Bryan Brown has supplanted Jack •Thompson as the actor most epitomising the Australian male. While Thompson's career has remained static for some years, Brown has retained his star status and is as popular today as he was 18 years ago when he captured the Australian public with his portrayal of Joe Harmon in the television miniseries *A Town Like Alice* (1981).

At the age of 27 Brown left Sydney for a year's training with the National Theatre in London. Since his first significant acting role in **The Love-Letters from Teralba Road** (1977), Brown has refined his screen persona that, at its most interesting, often suggests a dark, painfully introspective streak lurking beneath his seemingly knock-about surface. Brown's entry into the Hollywood scene with the television miniseries *The Thorn Birds* (1983) did not radically alter his screen image, although there have been sporadic attempts to erase Brown's rough edges and to transform him into a more conventional (American) performer in roles such as **Dead in the Water** (1991) and **F/X 2** (1991). Brown has, on occasions, explored the dark side of his Australian stereotype, notably as the understanding but limited husband Sonny Hills in Ken •Cameron's •**The Umbrella Woman** (1987), where he played opposite his wife Rachel •Ward. Another ambitious, and underrated performance, which delved into the moral ambiguity at the heart

of this Australian archetype, came in •**Dead Heart** (1996), a special film for Brown, since he was both producer and star. The hurt that Brown suffered when the film failed to attract a large Australian audience was more than just financial. Just as Clint Eastwood managed to intersperse more personal films with commercial chores in the 1980s, Brown has maintained his international career (**Kim**, 1984, **Tai-Pan**, 1986, **F/X**, 1986, **Cocktail**, 1988, **Gorillas in the Mist**, 1988, **Blame It on the Bellboy**, 1992, **Devlin**, 1992) while developing less prestigious projects, such as his production of the television anthology *Twisted Tales* (1996), that provided a forum for Australian talent.

Other Australian films: Third Person Plural (1978), Weekend of Shadows (1978), •The Irishman (1978), •The Chant of Jimmie Blacksmith (1978), •Newsfront (1978), •Money Movers (1979), •The Odd Angry Shot (1979), •Cathy's Child (1979), •Palm Beach (1980), Blood Money (1980), •Stir (1980), •'Breaker' Morant (1980), •Winter of Our Dreams (1981), •Far East (1982), Rebel (1985), •The Empty Beach (1985), •Blood Oath (1990), Sweet Talker (1991), Two Hands (1999).　　GM

Bruce, Jack CINEMATOGRAPHER In the early 1920s two young newsreel cameramen—Jack Bruce and E.R. Jeffree—purchased Palmerston Studios from E.J. •Carroll and leased it out for feature production, for instance, to P.J. Ramster, for **The Triumph of Love** (1922) and **Should a Doctor Tell?** (1923), both of which the two enterprising camera men were employed to shoot. Bruce then went to Hollywood, where he worked as a camera technician and, when he returned to Australia in 1926, he joined Juchau Productions to photograph •**The Menace** but, in 1927, he left that company to became chief technician at the new Commonwealth Film Laboratories in Sydney. With James Grant and Jack Fletcher, he photographed •**The Devil's Playground** (1928), and he was in charge of sound on Paulette •McDonagh's production •**Two Minutes Silence** (1933). By 1937 he was managing director of Commonwealth Film Laboratories and, in that capacity, he was both production supervisor and principal backer of •**Mystery Island** (1937), and stepped in to support •**Typhoon Treasure** after Frank •Thring's death. He also did sound on **A Yank in Australia** (1942) and •**Rats of Tobruk** (1944).　　IB

Brumpton, John ACTOR John Brumpton grew up in working-class Blacktown, and became an amateur boxer and karate champion, which prepared him for the very physical roles he later played. While working as a surveyor in Canberra, he took up acting as a hobby, then moved to Melbourne to study at the Victorian College of the Arts (VCA), graduating in 1988. He played small roles in films (**Holidays on the River Yarra**, 1990; •**Romper Stomper**, 1992; **Garbo**, 1992; •**Angel Baby** 1995) and television (*Rose*

Bryan Brown

Against the Odds, 1995; *Corelli*, 1995), but he sprang to prominence with his play *Containment* ('It ain't rehabilitation, it's containment') in 1991. He and director Lawrence Johnston turned this into a script, released as *Life (1996), with Johnston directing and Brumpton playing the lead. Both won AFI nominations, and the film won the International Critics Prize at the Toronto Film Festival in 1996. After another small role (**My Forgotten Man**, 1996), he played leads in two more films: in **Dance Me to My Song** (1998) he was desired by both disabled Heather Rose and her carer, and in **Redball** (1999) he played Detective Robbie Walsh.   IB

Bruning, Robert (1928–) ACTOR/PRODUCER Robert Bruning is primarily a television producer, but his work in television drama has always had spin-offs into film. He set up Gemini Productions in 1971, to produce the television series *The Godfathers*, and then produced a series of successful telemovies, including *Is There Anybody There?* (1976), and *Mama's Gone A-Hunting*, *The Alternative*, and *Gone to Ground* (all 1977). The company was soon sold, to become a subsidiary of the Grundy Organisation; Bruning worked as an executive producer at Grundy's for some time. In the 1980s he worked as producer on the television series *Rafferty's Rules* and *Blue Heelers*, and on the under-appreciated theatrical feature *The Settlement (1984). Bruning has continued to take supporting and character roles, both in television and film. He has considerable screen presence and an evil smile. His film roles include small parts in **The Intruders** (1969), **That Lady from Peking** (1970), and **Cool Change** (1986), as well as more substantial roles as Sergeant Steele in *Ned Kelly (1970), Tom West in *Sunday Too Far Away (1975), and Elmer (the villain) in **Snapshot** (1979).   IB

Buchanan, Simone (1968–) ACTOR Simone Buchanan's main claim to fame in the Australian cinema to date has been as Lizzie Curtis, the young woman who is harassed and raped in the Australian rural melodrama *Shame (1988). Prior to her strong performance in this film, Buchanan appeared as a child in a number of films, including *My Brilliant Career (1979), **Mystery at Castle House** (1982), **High Country** (1983), **Platypus Cove** (1983), and the lead role as the young girl trapped on a lonely island in **Run Rebecca, Run!** (1982). Buchanan's most popular role, however, was as Debbie Kelly in the long-running Australian television comedy *Hey Dad*.   GM

Buckley, Anthony (1937–) PRODUCER After a long career as a film editor (of **Cinesound Review** from 1962 to 1965), and work in the United Kingdom and Canada, Sydney-born Anthony Buckley became one of the leading producers of the new Australian cinema (see Revival, the).

Before the feature revival of the 1970s got under way, he was, like many Australian film-makers, involved in the production of documentaries. He edited several films made here by overseas directors, including Michael Powell's *Age of Consent (1969), Philip Leacock's **Adam's Woman** (1970), Ted Kotcheff's *Wake in Fright (1971), and the Rudolf Nureyev– Robert Helpmann ballet version of **Don Quixote** (1973). His first feature film as producer was the well-liked *Caddie (1976), directed by Donald *Crombie, with whom Buckley formed Forest Hills Production company. Crombie was also responsible for *The Irishman (1978), *The Killing of Angel Street (1981), and **Kitty and the Bagman** (1982). Subsequently, Buckley has worked a good deal in television (including *The Heroes*), and his later films diverged from the quiet humanism of his collaborations with Crombie. They have included: Ray *Lawrence's *Bliss (1985), Tracey *Moffat's *BeDevil (1993), and George Whaley's *Dad and Dave: On Our Selection (1995).

Other Australian films: The Magic Leaf (1956, doc., ed.), **This is Rugby League** (1958, doc., ed.), **The Stowaway** (1958, asst ed.), **Magnificent Gamble** (1963, doc., ed.), **Blue Water Fever** (1963, doc., ed.), **Here Remains a Memory** (1965, doc., p., d.), **When the River was the Only Road** (1965, doc., p., d.), **They Shot Through like a Bondi Tram** (1966, doc., p., d.), **The Cave Divers** (1966, doc., ed.), **Forgotten Cinema** (1967, doc., p., d.), **That Lady from Peking** (1970, ed.), **Willy Willy** (1970, short, ed.), **Demonstrator** (1971, ed.), **Odyssey—a Journey** (1971, short, ed.), **The Choice** (1971, short, ed.), **Incredible Floridas** (1972, doc., ed.), **Sunstruck** (1972, ed.), **Whatever Happened to Green Valley** (1973, doc., p.), **Caravan Park** (1973, short, ed.), **The Fifth Facade** (1973, doc., p.), **Snow, Sand and Savages** (doc., p., d.), **A Stream Train Passes** (1974, doc., p.), **The Removalists** (1974, ed.), *The Night The Prowler (1979, p.), **Buckley's Chance** (1980, short, ex. p.), **Now You're Talking** (1983, doc., p.).   BMcF

Buday, Helen (1962–) ACTOR Most of Helen Buday's work has been on the stage, but she has appeared in three films to date, her most significant role being the lead in *For Love Alone (1986). In this version of Christina Stead's partly autobiographical tale, she played with sympathy and vivacity a young girl searching for love and independence, a search that takes her from between-wars Sydney to London, where, under the guidance of a sympathetic man (Sam *Neill), she matures and finds a vocation as a writer. The film's comparative failure probably stunted Buday's film career. She also appeared in a minor role in *Mad Max Beyond Thunderdome (1985) and as the wife of the protagonist in **Dingo** (1992).   BMcF

Buesst, Nigel (1938–) CINEMATOGRAPHER/DIRECTOR After graduating from Melbourne University in 1960, Nigel Buesst went to London, where he did a short course at the

London Film School and worked as a film editor. He returned to Melbourne in 1961, working as an editor, scriptwriter, and cinematographer on both film and television, and appearing with other members of the Carlton milieu in Peter Carmody's **Nothing like Experience** (1970). He was cinematographer on many documentaries and some features, including Antony I. •Ginnane's first feature, **Sympathy in Summer** (released 1971), and ran a photographic studio in Carlton. But he also produced and directed films himself: at first short films (**Fun Radio**, 1964; **The Twentieth**, 1966), then longer documentaries (**The Rise and Fall of Squizzy Taylor**, 1968; **Jacka, V.C.**, 1977) and part-documentaries (**Dead Easy**, 1970). He has taught film-making (1971–83 at Swinburne College of Technology and had shorter periods at the •Australian, Film, Television and Radio School (AFTRS) and Technical and Further Education (TAFE) colleges) while continuing to produce and direct his own films. **Bonjour Balwyn** (1971) and **Come Out Fighting** (1973) were important contributions to the Melbourne production revival. He also made **Jazz Scrapbook** in 1983, played a small role in James Clayden's cult thriller **With Time to Kill** (1987) and, in 1988, returned to fiction to produce and direct **Compo**. He has always been an independent film-maker, with an interest in promoting independent films, through such activities as directing the St Kilda Film Festival (1986–90) and editing the *Melbourne Film Makers Resource Book* (1991). IB

Burgomeister, The

1935. *Director*: Harry Southwell. *Producer*: Harry Southwell. *Scriptwriter*: Denzil Batchelor. Based on the adaptation by Leopold Lewis of the play *Le Juif Polonais* by Erckmann-Chatrian. *Director of photography*: George Heath. *Music*: Isadore Goodman. 56 min (?). B&W. *Cast*: Harry Southwell (Mathias), Muriel Meredith (Catherine), Janet Johnson (Annette), Ross Vernon (Christian), Stan Tolhurst (the Polish Jew). *Alternative title*: **Hypnotised**.

The stage melodrama *The Bells* had been filmed several times, in the USA and the United Kingdom, as well as in Australia in 1911 (by W.J. •Lincoln). Harry Southwell himself had produced a version, in 1925 in Belgium, but he was better known in Australia for a continuing series of Kelly gang films (for instance, •**The Kelly Gang** 1920). Throughout his long career in film-making, Southwell's reach always exceeded his grasp: this film version of the story of *The Bells* was rejected for the NSW quota, and was withdrawn from distribution, but released later in a shortened version as **Hypnotised**. In the fragment surviving in the National Film and Sound Archive (NFSA), Southwell himself can be seen as the Burgomeister, driven mad by the sound of sleigh bells that brings back to his mind the murder on which his fortune has been built. IB

Burke & Wills

1985. *Director*: Graeme Clifford. *Producers*: Graeme Clifford, John Sexton. *Scriptwriter*: Michael Thomas. *Director of photography*: Russell Boyd. *Music*: Peter Sculthorpe. 140 min. *Cast*: Jack Thompson (Robert O'Hara Burke), Nigel Havers (William John Wills), Greta Scacchi (Julia Matthews), Matthew Fargher (John King), Ralph Cotterill (Charley Gray).

Expatriate Graeme Clifford had had a great deal of experience overseas as an editor, working for such directors as Robert Altman and Nicolas Roeg, before making his début as director with **Burke & Wills**, his only Australian-directed film to date. The fateful story of the exploration party, led by the temperamental Burke, who is in love with the opera singer Julia Matthews, is a crucial element of Australian history and myth: history in the sense that the expedition did happen, myth in that its ultimate failure has come to seem symptomatic of the country's spirit in the way that the failure of Gallipoli did. Robert O'Hara Burke and the British scientist William John Wills (played by British actor Nigel Havers) set off in 1860 to cross the continent from Melbourne to the Gulf of Carpentaria: only the youthful John King returned, helped by Aborigines, to tell the tale. Russell •Boyd's cinematography ensures that the film looks resplendent, but it was over-long and lacking in the dramatic intensity it needed to sustain its legend of heroic miscalculation, and the film failed commercially. BMcF

Burke, Simon (1961–) ACTOR Simon Burke made his film début at 15 in the leading role in •**The Devil's Playground** (1976), Fred •Schepisi's semi-autobiographical account of childhood experiences in a Catholic seminary. He won much critical praise for his sensitive playing of the boy who is subject to the oppressive regime of the school and who comes to doubt that he has a vocation. A pivotal role in •**The Irishman** should have clinched his position, but the film's focus shifted in the course of the story and the part of Michael Doolan was too underdeveloped to hold it together. He has worked as actor and singer, but has made only three other Australian films, including: •**The Clinic** (1983), as a bumptious young doctor who learns from his experiences, and Slate, Wyn & Me (1987).
Other Australian films: **Passion: The Story of Percy Grainger** (1999). BMcF

Burlinson, Tom (1956–) ACTOR Tom Burlinson's most famous film performance, the title role of •**The Man from Snowy River** (1982) was also his first. Although the film featured veterans such as Kirk Douglas and Jack •Thompson, Burlinson's role as young Jim Craig was pivotal to the film's emphasis on the rite of passage to manhood of young Jim after his father's death. Burlinson

Simon Burke

Tom Burlinson

repeated the role in **The Man from Snowy River II** (1988), which duplicated the original formula with less commercial success.

Burlinson, after graduating from the National Institute of Dramatic Art in 1976, worked in theatre and television (*The Restless Years*, *Cop Shop*, *The Sullivans*, and *G.P.*) before and after his début in **The Man from Snowy River.** He followed the enormous commercial success of this film with another successful Australian film in the lead role of Tommy Woodcock, the trainer of Australia's most famous horse, •**Phar Lap** (1983). Since then Burlinson's career has not equalled the popular success of these films. He has attempted to vary his roles, beginning with an international film directed by Paul Verhoeven, **Flesh and Blood** (1985), in which Burlinson co-starred with Rutger Hauer, Jennifer Jason Leigh, and Jack Thompson in a brutal sex and swordplay fantasy set in the sixteenth century. This was followed by a starring role, with Nicole •**Kidman**, in the Australian teen movie **Windrider** (1986). **Time Guardian** (1987), an incoherent science fiction film, preceded his return to **Snowy River** in 1988. Since then Burlinson has appeared only in overseas films, including the Canadian adventure film **Kootenai Brown** (1990).   GM

Burns, Carol (1947–) ACTOR   Queensland-born, Carol Burns has had a distinguished stage career, having begun as a child performer and played with both Queens-

land and South Australian Theatre Companies. She has also done a good deal of television, notably in the series *Prisoner*, but film has scarcely begun to exploit her eloquent face and gifts for pathos and warmth. She was very touching as Maudie Plover, ill-used niece of a fanatical preacher, in •**The Mango Tree** (1977). As Aggie Doyle, the miner's wife who organises the women when the miners go on strike, in •**Strikebound** (1984), she imbues the role with strength, humour, and dignity.

Other Australian films: Bad Blood (New Zealand, 1981), •Star Struck (1982), •Dusty (1982).   BMcF

Burrowes, Geoff (1945–) PRODUCER   The partnership between Geoff Burrowes and the Scottish-born director George •Miller produced one of the most commercially successful films in Australian film history with •**The Man from Snowy River** (1982). Burrowes and Miller devised the story, based on the central characters from the famous poem, before passing it on to John Dixon to write the script. Miller and Burrowes had previously worked on television programs together at Crawfords and they were reunited in 1986 with **Cool Change.** Except for the fact that this film had a contemporary setting for its romantic story set against the Victorian high country, it was similar in many ways to the 1982 film. An official sequel, **The Man from Snowy River II**, directed and produced by Burrowes, appeared in 1988 with Tom •Burlinson and Sigrid •Thornton reprising their earlier roles and Brian Dennehy replacing Kirk Douglas as Harrison. In 1985 Burrowes also produced the highly successful miniseries *Anzacs*, with George Miller directing a substantial proportion of the production, and Burrowes was also financially involved with •Minnamurra (1989), a film that shared historical and narrative similarities with **The Man from Snowy River.**

Other Australian films include: Running from the Guns (1987), Backstage (1988).   GM

Burstall, Dan (1948–) CINEMATOGRAPHER/DIRECTOR

The son of director Tim •Burstall, Dan Burstall grew up in a film environment. After operating on several films during the early 1970s, Dan's first feature as director of photography was **High Rolling** (1977). He shot many films and miniseries for television (in Australia and the USA), winning Penguin Awards for his cinematography of *Against the Wind* (1977) and *Water Under the Bridge* (1980), the latter also earning a Sammy Award. Dan has also directed many television series, including *The Man from Snowy River* for American cable television, as well as the feature film **Beyond My Reach** (1989).

As director of photography, Dan has worked on many other films in Australia and the USA. These include: **Oz** (1976), •**Last of the Knucklemen** (1979), **Duet for Four** (1982), **Squizzy Taylor** (1982), •**The More Things Change** (1986), •**Kangaroo** (1987), **Two Brothers Running** (1988), **Kokoda Crescent** (1989), **Weekend with Kate** (1990), •**Father** (1990), **Hunting** (USA/Australia, 1991), **Ladybugs** (USA, 1992), **Ironfist** (USA, 1995).   DAVID MUIR

Burstall, Tim (1927–) DIRECTOR/WRITER/PRODUCER

Tim Burstall was born at Stockton-on-Tees, England and moved to Australia with his parents at the age of eight. He was educated at Geelong Grammar and Melbourne University where he studied English, History, and Philosophy. He taught himself film-making by making short films, beginning with **The Prize** (1960), which he wrote and directed, and which won a Bronze Medal at the Venice Film Festival (1960). He later worked in the Commonwealth Film Unit and studied at the Actors' Studio in New York on a Harkness Scholarship.

Burstall's first feature was •**Two Thousand Weeks** (1969), which he co-wrote with the film's producer Patrick Ryan. The adverse critical and box-office response to this film, together with funding and exhibition problems, caused a significant shift in the direction of Burstall's career, away from the arthouse film to more popular appeal and innovative exhibition practices with •**Stork** (1971). This part of his career culminated in the formation of the Hexagon organisation, for which Burstall directed •**Alvin Purple**

(1973), •**Petersen** (1974), **End Play** (1975), and •**Eliza Fraser** (1976); and produced or influenced the production of a number of other films. Burstall has also been a prolific writer across a number of genres including poetry, children's stories, and art criticism, in addition to writing for the screen. He has written widely about the Australian film industry, contributing to public debate about Australian film culture.

Other Australian films: 'The Child'—episode of •Libido (1973), •The Last of the Knucklemen (1979), Attack Force Z (1979), Duet for Four (1981), •The Naked Country (1985), •Kangaroo (1987), Nightmare at Bitter Creek (1988).   JOHN BENSON

Burton, Geoff (1946–) CINEMATOGRAPHER/DIRECTOR

Geoff Burton left Sydney University to work in television in Sydney, before becoming a documentary cameraman. He moved to Europe in 1969, working as a cinematographer on television dramas and documentaries, some of which he also directed. After returning to Australia in 1971, he shot documentaries and miniseries, and then his first feature, director Ken •Hannam's •**Sunday Too Far Away** (1975). This established Burton's reputation and he became a major contributor to the Australian film renaissance. His work has won six national Australian Cinematographers Society (ACS) awards, including a Golden Tripod award (Best cinematography, feature film) and the 'Milli' (Cinematographer of the Year) for •**Storm Boy** (1976). He shared with Dean •Semler an Australian Film Institute Best Cinematography Award for •**Dead Calm** (1989) and won a NSW ACS Gold award for •**Sirens** (1994). Burton was head of the Cinematography Department at the Australian Film, Television and Radio School (AFTRS) from 1981 to 1983, and has since contributed to the school's master classes.

Burton has co-directed, with anthropologist Sharon Bell, four documentaries and directed many others, including his feature-length **Flight over Equador** (USA, 1995). He also co-directed, with Kevin Dowling, the feature •**The Sum of Us** (1994), and is the director of **Aftershocks** (1999).

Other Australian films (as director of photography) *include*: •The Fourth Wish (1976), •The Picture Show Man (1977), The Sound of Love (1978), Mortimer (1978), Blue Fin (1978), Ngaw Par (The Jingle) (1979), •Stir (1980), The Winds of Jarrah (1983), Midnite Spares (1983), The Boy Who Had Everything (1984), •A Street to Die (1985), I Can't Get Started (1985), I Own the Racecourse (1986), •The Year My Voice Broke (1987), The Time Guardian (1987), Romero (USA/Australia, 1988), •Flirting (1991), Aya (1991), Garbo (1992), •The Nostradamus Kid (1993), Frauds (1993), •BeDevil (1993), The Wide Sargasso Sea (USA, 1994), •The Sum of Us (1994), •Hotel Sorrento (1995), Rough Riders (1995), Brilliant Lies (1996), Paws (1997), Wanted (1997).   DAVID MUIR

Bush Christmas

1947. *Director*: Ralph Smart. *Producer*: Ralph Smart. *Scriptwriter*: Ralph Smart. *Director of photography*: George Heath. *Music*: Sydney John Kay. 76 min B&W. *Cast*: Chips Rafferty (Long Bill), John Fernside (Jim), Stan Holhurst (Blue), Helen Grieve (Helen), Nicky Yardley (Snow), Morris Unicomb (John), Michael Yardley (Michael), Neza Saunders (Neza), Pat Penny (father), Thelma Grigg (mother), John McCallum (narrator).

The first feature film produced by J. Arthur Rank's Children's Entertainment Films, which became the Children's Film Foundation, **Bush Christmas** was a popular success in both Britain and Australia, and it established many of the characteristic features of this British series of children's films that continued for many years. **Bush Christmas** was a prototype for this series; the focus is on the activities of the children whereas the adults, aside from the villains, are largely irrelevant to the story. Also, the crooks in this film, and in subsequent films made by this organisation, are presented as comic rather than threatening figures, as these films generally avoided any sense of threat or realistic violence. Similarly, the (middle-class) parents in this film, and subsequent films, are somewhat diffident and relatively ineffectual.

In **Bush Christmas** a family of Australian rural children, and their English cousin and aboriginal friend Neza, track three thieves across the mountains (the Blue Mountains and Burragorang Valley) after they steal the family's prize mare. The children eventually recover the horse and steal the men's food and shoes while they are sleeping, and the second half of the film is primarily a cat-and-mouse game between the thieves and the children, until a search party rescues the children and arrests the men. The film has a certain 'travelogue' quality that emphasises the exotic bush setting, for British children, with close-ups of Neza relishing such local culinary delights as witchetty grubs and snake. **Bush Christmas** is a gentle comic adventure efficiently directed and scripted by Ralph •Smart, born of Australian parents in London, with superb photography by George •Heath   GM

Byrnes, Josephine (1967–) ACTOR   Red-haired Josephine Byrnes graduated from the National Institute of Dramatic Art (NIDA) in 1989, and was quickly in demand on television, playing substantial roles in the miniseries *Shadows of the Heart* (1990) and *The Other Side of Paradise* (1992). However, she was best known for her portrayal of the charismatic Sister Catherine in *Brides of Christ* (1991), for which she won a Logie award as Most Outstanding Actress. Byrnes has continued to perform in television drama; her few film roles include, most notably, Beth Wheats, who is caught up as an unwilling participant in deadly games in **Frauds** (1993), and Miriam Chadwick, who steals Lucinda's inheritance from under her nose, in •**Oscar and Lucinda** (1997). Her striking beauty and obvious talent have yet to be fully exploited on the big screen.

IB

Byron, Annie ACTOR   In 1985 Annie Byron won a well-deserved Australian Film Institute Award for her supporting role in Glenda Hambley's •**Fran**, in which she played Noni •Hazlehurst's good-hearted, put-on neighbour, also a single mother, but one who puts the needs of her children before anything else. This beautifully detailed performance should have made her one of the most sought-after actors in Australian films. However, since then, she has made few films. These include •**No Worries** (1993), •**Muriel's Wedding** (1994), and •**Doing Time for Patsy Cline**—in all of which she had small roles. Her only earlier film was •**Silver City** (1984), although she has done some television work.

BMcF

C

Caddie

1976. *Director:* Donald Crombie. *Producer:* Anthony Buckley. *Scriptwriter:* Joan Long. *Director of photography:* Peter James. *Music:* Patrick Flynn. 103 min. *Cast:* Helen Morse (Caddie), Takis Emmanuel (Peter), Jack Thompson (Ted), Jacki Weaver (Josie), Melissa Jaffer (Leslie).

This account of the true-life reminiscences of a Sydney barmaid, published anonymously in 1953, was a major success of the new Australian cinema (see Revival, the), earning $1 000 000 in its first year. It benefits greatly from the performance of Helen •Morse as Caddie, who leaves her unfaithful husband and works in a pub to support herself and her two small children. She finds love with a Greek migrant (Takis •Emmanuel) but, when he is forced to return to Greece for family reasons, she is hit hard by the Depression and suffers from malnutrition. Caddie's story largely appeals because her spirit never breaks. She is one of a number of impressive female characters in Australian films of the late 1970s. Director Donald •Crombie and scriptwriter Joan •Long not only have a good eye and ear for the lovingly recreated period; they are also strongly sympathetic to the situation of a single woman in a male-dominated society. The film is episodic in structure, and has the inconclusive ending of so many Australian films of the period, but it is undeniably touching and good-humoured. BMcF

Called Back

1911. *Director/Scriptwriter:* W.J. Lincoln. *Director of photography:* Orrie Perry. B&W.

Called Back, a film that does not survive today, seems to have been the first commercial Australian fiction film *not* to have been set in Australia. As such, it marks a significant step for the Australian fiction film industry, which had been producing recognisably 'Australian' films since before •The Story of the Kelly Gang (1906). **Called Back** is set in Italy, an indication that the company that produced it, Amalgamated Pictures, intended to compete with European and American companies on an equal basis, at least in the local market. From this point on, some of the films made in Australia were not set in Australia and the image of Australia was transformed on screen into the image of the world.

WILLIAM D. ROUTT

Cameron, Ken (1946–) DIRECTOR A prolific director, primarily of telefeatures and miniseries throughout the 1980s and 1990s, Ken Cameron's output is characterised by a 'realist' style and strong interest in social problems. A number of his telefeatures, for example, have been concerned with the shadowy world inhabited by criminals, police, and politicians, and the intricate, sometimes corrupt, relationships that form between these groups—see *The Clean Machine* (1988), *Police Crop: The Winchester Conspiracy* (1990), *Joh's Jury* (1993), and *Bangkok Hilton* (1989), the Thailand drug importation-based miniseries starring Nicole •Kidman. Cameron also directed episodes of the crimes telefeature *Cody* (1994–95), starring Gary •Sweet, together with Sweet's earlier series *Police Rescue*.

Cameron, a former NSW school teacher, was more concerned in his earlier films with the problems faced by youths at school (**Temperament Unsuited**, 1978, •**Fast Talking**, 1984) or out of school, by the unemployed and those dabbling in minor crimes (**Out Of It**, 1977, **Crime of the Decade**, 1984). A different, but related, social problem, the constrictions imposed on young women and the social

Jack *Thompson and Helen *Morse in **Caddie**

changes faced by the Catholic Church, emerged in the miniseries *Brides of Christ* (1991). •**Monkey Grip** (1982), an adaptation of Helen Garner's semi-autobiographical novel detailing a young woman's (Noni •**Hazlehurst**) romantic relationship with a drug addict (Colin •**Friels**) is consistent with the stylistic and thematic patterns of Cameron's other films. •**The Umbrella Woman** (1987), which was released overseas with the more apt ironic title **The Good Wife**, would, initially, seem to be the odd film in this overall pattern. However, on closer examination this underrated drama of a woman trapped in an emotionally, sexually, and vocationally stultifying life in a small NSW county town in the late 1930s, is perhaps Cameron's greatest film, and one that points to the structural problems in Australian society that underpin many of the more specific social issues exposed in his other films.   GM

Campion, Jane (1955–) DIRECTOR Jane Campion was born and educated in New Zealand, gaining a degree in anthropology, and travelling to London to study at the Chelsea School of Arts. Later, she moved to Sydney, gained a Diploma of Arts and attended the Australian Film, Television and Radio School (AFTRS). A rough-cut of her third short there, **Peel**, caused such a controversy that the AFTRS

chose not to finish it. It was seen, however, a few years later by film advocate Pierre Rissient, who recommended it to the Cannes Film Festival, where it won the Palme d'Or for shorts in 1986. Campion made several more shorts: **A Girl's Own Story** (1983); **After Hours** (1984); and **Passionless Moments: Recorded in Sydney, Australia, Sunday October 2nd** (1984, co-directed with Gerard Lee). The films demonstrate a surreal view of suburban life and Campion's interest in quirky material, along with the usual visuals and striking juxtapositions.

After co-directing a television series, *Dancing Daze* (1985), Campion made her first feature-length work, the telefeature **Two Friends**. It premiered the same year as **Peel** at Cannes and helped consolidate her reputation as a major director, with its tale of the break-up of two schoolgirls told via a partially time-retreating narrative. •**Sweetie** (1989), Campion's first theatrical feature, which she co-wrote with Lee, evinces a black comic edge in its story of two dysfunctional sisters, and their relationships to people and the physical world. In many ways, Campion announced herself as the most modern of Australia's directors, making much other contemporary cinema look staid and regressive. Campion's work also encouraged the view that, just as there are distinctive forms of women's writing, there may also be an

Australian women's cinema. Certainly, her collaboration with cinematographer Sally Bongers and production- and costume-designer Janet Patterson suggested a female team of remarkable skill and vision, and quite unlike anything else in cinema, although since much copied.

Campion returned to New Zealand to make •An Angel at My Table (1990), a miniseries based on the life of writer Janet Frame. It was so critically successful that it was shown throughout the world in cinemas, and has since become regarded as a feature. The only puzzling aspect of the project was Campion's replacement of Bongers, the result being that her work since has lost some of its visual edge and clarity. In 1993, again in New Zealand, Campion made her most famous work, •The Piano. This tale of a pretend-mute woman—she whispers during a love scene—who falls for the man blackmailing her for sexual gain, is the first of two films so far to play with Victorian romantic melodrama, and the passion that women readers have had for it over many decades. It was not surprising, therefore, that Campion should next choose to film Henry James' The Portrait of a Lady (1996), but the coolness of her approach, a script too unconcerned about credible motivation, and the stark inadequacies of several lead performers, make it the least-applauded of her work, although it is strongly supported by some. She worked again with her Piano star Harvey Keitel, and with fellow New Zealander Kate Winslet, in the American-made romantic drama Holy Smoke (1999).

Despite recent critical ups and downs, Campion remains by far New Zealand's most applauded and talented director, a film-maker with a particular vision and a strongly held personal style.

Other Australian films: Tissues (Super-8 short, 1980), **Mishaps: Seduction and Conquest** (short video, 1982).

SCOTT MURRAY

Cantrill, Arthur (1938–) and **Corinne** (1928–)
DIRECTORS The quarterly journal *Cantrill's Film Notes* (renamed *Cantrills Filmnotes* from No. 9, 1972), has been in continuous production since 1971, introducing ideas, nurturing talent, and stirring hornets' nests. It remains Australia's foremost journal of independent and avant-garde film and video production. Its editors, Arthur and Corinne Cantrill, began making documentary films on children's craft activities in Brisbane for the Children's Library and Crafts Movement in 1960, and followed these with simple narrative fictions such as **Kip and David** (1961–63). But the manifesto published in the journal's first issue called for films that would be more concerned with matter and form than with content, and so would 'defy analysis', and this is what they have done in most of their prolific output. A series of biographical films (on Robert Klippel 1963–65, Charles Lloyd 1966, Will Spoor 1969, and Harry Hooton 1969) challenges traditional documentary form, and culminates in the autobiographical masterpiece **In This Life's**

Arthur and Corrine Cantrill

Body (1984), which tells Corinne's personal story at the same time as it addresses issues of the writing of auto/biography through images. By then, they had made extended visits overseas: London (1965–69), New York (1973–75), and Berlin (1985), where **The Berlin Apartment** was produced. They also spent 15 months in Canberra during 1969–70 on a Fellowship in the Creative Arts at Australian National University, before settling permanently in Melbourne. Their interest in the materiality of film is evident through all their work, but becomes explicit in films such as **Three Colour Separations Studies—Landscapes** (1976), and is particularly decisive in a series of films about the film-making practice of ethnographer Walter Baldwin •Spencer; for instance, **Reflections on Three Images by Baldwin Spencer** (1974). Corinne's early training as a botanist is apparent in their many films that focus on the Australian landscape, particularly in outback regions (**At Uluru**, 1976–77, and **The Second Journey to Uluru**, 1981), but also nearer to home (**Tidal River**, 1996). They rework their earlier films, often presenting them as performance pieces, such as **Skin of Your Eye** (1971–73), **Skin of Your Eye (Seen)** (1974–76), **Edges of Meaning** (1977–79), **Fields of Vision** (1978), **Grain of the Voice** (1979–80), or **Projected Light** (1988). Although they had worked sometimes in 8 mm, most of their early work was on 16 mm, until 1990, when a visit to Indonesia convinced them to switch completely to 8 mm for films such as **The Becak Driver** (1998). In later years, Arthur taught film-making at the University of Melbourne. Over their long careers, they have been better known and more appreciated abroad than within Australia, where the lot of the independent, experimental film-maker is never easy.   IB

Captain Thunderbolt

1953. *Director:* Cecil Holmes. *Producer:* John Wiltshire. *Scriptwriter:* Creswick Jenkinson. *Director of photography:* Ross Wood. *Music:* Sydney John Kay. 69 min. B&W. *Cast:* Grant Taylor (Fred Ward), Charles Tingwell (Alan Blake), Rosemary Miller (Joan), Harp McGuire (Sergeant Mannix), John Fegan (Dalton), Jean Blue (Mrs Ward).

This striking, underrated film from left-wing film-maker Cecil •Holmes adapts the story of Fred Ward who, as Captain Thunderbolt, is driven to crime in the New England tablelands by an inequitable social and political situation. Holmes is able to exploit the generic conventions of the bushranger genre by reducing dialogue and characterisation to a minimum, so as to emphasise the visual power of his images depicting working-class resistance to capitalist exploitation.

In 1870, after Fred Ward and his best friend Alan Blake are arrested for horse-stealing, they are sentenced to breaking rocks on barren Cockatoo Island where they are victimised by the sadistic Sergeant Mannix. On a limited budget, Holmes constructs an exciting escape sequence that cross-cuts shots of the guard's feet with Ward and Blake as they carefully break their chains. After his escape, Ward becomes the notorious bushranger Captain Thunderbolt, who builds a reputation as a local Robin Hood by robbing the New England squattocracy. During this period Thunderbolt is pursued by a local policeman, Jack Dalton, a childhood friend. The government, however, becomes impatient with Dalton's lack of success and instructs Sergeant Mannix to assist the local policeman and they set a trap for the two bushrangers during which Mannix assumes that he has killed Thunderbolt only to find Blake's body with Thunderbolt seemingly free to continue his attack on wealth and privilege.

Holmes's political intentions are foregrounded during a lengthy sequence during which local officials and businessmen criticise President Lincoln's Gettysburg Address. The capitalists, dressed in black suits, smoking cigars, and drinking brandy, are robbed by Ward and Blake, and the sequence is partially filmed from beneath a glass-topped table, thereby emphasising the bloated physical traits of the men. This pejorative presentation is reinforced by their racist comments concerning the local Chinese.

Holmes's expressive, polemical style reduces character traits to the point where individual attributes are severely reduced so that the characters can be viewed as social or political signifiers. This approach to film-making demonstrates the influence of early Russian film-makers, such as Eisenstein. **Captain Thunderbolt** is one of the finest films produced during a lean period of Australian feature film-making and, although it was largely ignored by local critics, the film eventually earned a healthy profit from overseas sales.   GM

Carbasse, Louise *see* Louise Lovely

Careful He Might Hear You

1983. *Director:* Carl Schultz. *Producer:* Jill Robb. *Scriptwriter:* Michael Jenkins, from Sumner Locke-Elliott's novel. *Director of photography:* John Seale. *Music:* Ray Cook. 110 min. *Main cast:* Wendy Hughes (Vanessa), Robyn Nevin (Lila), Nicholas Gledhill (PS), Logan (John Hargreaves), Peter Whitford (George).

Not many Australian films of the last 20 years have grappled so tenaciously with such a full-throttled melodramatic scenario as **Careful He Might Hear You**. Its plot is firmly based on the custody battle between two aunts—snobbish Anglophile Vanessa and working-class Lila—for their late sister's child, PS. Their conflict, set in Sydney during the Depression, brings them to court, and is exacerbated by the return of the child's shiftless father, Logan. It is finally resolved by a ferry disaster that is the means of restoring the child to domestic warmth.

Unlike the many period films of the new Australian cinema (see Revival, the), this is not an indulgent reproduction of the recent past. Its interests are psychological and social rather than pictorial. The camera, which renders the differences between the worlds of Vanessa's chilly affluence and the warm glow of Lila's cramped suburbia, does not linger over 1930s bric-a-brac for its own sake, but conveys the child's point of view on each of these 'worlds'.

Because the melodramatic framework insists on relating everything to the child's situation, the film avoids the over-episodic treatment of the rites-of-passage theme that has been common in new Australian cinema. Its concern with the specifics of PS's problems does not, however, preclude a wider resonance: that of the Anglo-Australian schizophrenia that was once an important element in the national psyche. Vanessa's affected cosmopolitanism is shown to have no place in the growth either of PS or of her native country.

BMcF

Carides, Gia (1964–) ACTOR This prolific Sydney-born actor has worked steadily in the Australian industry since 1983, although her feature film début, at the age of 12, was in a supporting role to Bryan •Brown and Kris McQuade in **The Love-Letters from Teralba Road** (1976). Gia Carides enjoyed a diverse range of roles in the early part of her career, from the heroine Ruth in the surreal action film **Midnight Spares** (1983), to Lucy, the daughter in •**Bliss** (1985), who provides oral sex to her brother in exchange for money for drugs, to the lead role in the low-budget inter-racial drama •**Backlash** (1986). As the rookie cop Nikki Iceton, Carides, and her bigoted partner David •Argue, escort an Aboriginal woman from Sydney to Broken Hill so that she can stand trial for the murder of a publican. Directed by Bill •Bennett, **Backlash** placed a good deal of pressure on both Argue and Carides as so much of the dialogue in the film is improvised, and Carides, with her experience in Theatresports, copes extremely well with the acting demands placed on her by Bennett's distinctive style of film-making.

A key role in the popular television series Police Rescue in 1990 preceded supporting roles in **Daydream Believer** (1992), the bizarre story about a girl (Miranda •Otto) who retreats into a fantasy world in which she turns into a horse; in •**Strictly Ballroom** (1992) as Liz Holt, one of the caricatured ballroom dancers making life difficult for Paul •Mercurio; and as a waitress in a Sydney bowls club in **Greenkeeping** (1993). Ben •Lewin's romantic comedy **Lucky Break** (1994) provided Carides with the leading role of Sophie, a disabled woman who attracts Anthony •LaPaglia away from his intended bride (Rebecca •Gibney) with

her erotic prose. Carides has also appeared in Hollywood films (most notably as 'Cashmere McLeod', the 'Gennifer Flowers' prototype in **Primary Colors**, 1998) as she has been living in the USA with her partner Anthony LaPaglia. Carides also appeared as the woman who may have been sexually harassed, opposite LaPaglia, in Richard •Franklin's version of David •Williamson's play **Brilliant Lies** (1996). *Other Australian films include*: The Coca-Cola Kid (1985).

GM

Carides, Zoë (1962–) ACTOR This Sydney-born actor burst into national prominence in a popular bank commercial in the early 1990s. After a lead role in the murder drama **Kadaicha** (1988), an unreleased feature film that went straight to television, Carides appeared in television series such as *G.P.* and *Acropolis Now*. Carides then appeared in her best feature film role to date in John •Ruane's black comedy •**Death in Brunswick** (1991) as Sophie Papafogos, Sam •Neill's romantic partner, who becomes embroiled in murder in the seedy nightclub where they are employed. An appearance in the unsuccessful comedy **Mad Bomber in Love** (1992) was followed by the lead role opposite Aden •Young in **Shotgun Wedding** (1994) and Gary •Sweet's love interest, and the newest member of the rescue squad, in the feature film version of the successful television series **Police Rescue** (1994). Carides also appeared in a lead role in the unreleased, straight-to-cable, feature film **Gino** (1994) before providing support for her sister Gia in **Brilliant Lies** (1996). *Other Australian films include*: Seeing Red (1992).

GM

Carroll, Edward John (1868–1931) and **Daniel Joseph** (1886–1959) PRODUCERS/EXHIBITORS The elder brother, always known as E.J. Carroll, was a circuit showman, who screened at open-air venues in Qld in summer and ran skating rinks in the winter. In 1906, he made a fortune touring Qld with •**The Story of the Kelly Gang**, and, untypically for the time, re-invested some of his profits in production. He co-produced •**For the Term of His Natural Life** (1908) and **The Squires–Burns Fight** (1908), and brought his brother Daniel into a partnership. They profitably distributed Reginald L. (Snowy) •Baker's **The Lure of the Bush** (1918) and also Raymond •Longford's •**The Sentimental Bloke** (1919), after it had been turned down by the Combine. They next set up a production company, established the Palmerston Studios in Sydney, and contracted with both Baker and Longford to produce further films. Baker produced •**The Man from Kangaroo** (1920), **The Shadow of Lightning Ridge** (1920), and **The Jackeroo of Coolabong** (1920), all with imported American husband-and-wife team, director Wilfred Lucas and writer Bess Meredyth. Longford made •**On Our Selection** (1920), •**Rudd's New Selection** (1921), and **The Blue Mountains Mystery**

(1921). Despite their extensive exhibition interests, the Carrolls were unable to make the production venture pay and, although they offered moral support to Louise •Lovely when she returned from America to make •**Jewelled Nights** (1925), they withdrew from film-making. In 1923, the Carroll cinemas became part of Birch, Carroll and Coyle, which was later taken over by the •Greater Union Organisation. Both brothers remained important figures in the Qld film trade.　　IB

Carroll, Matt (1944–) PRODUCER Prolific filmmaker Carroll began his career as an assistant director in the late 1960s for Australian television series such as *Skippy*, and the film spin-off **The Intruders** (1969), and *Spyforce*. After serving as production manager for **Private Collection** (1972) and associate producer for **Shirley Thompson versus the Aliens** (1972), Matt Carroll, together with Gil •Brealey, produced •**Sunday Too Far Away** (1975), one of the key films of the 1970s. Carroll followed this groundbreaking film with another critical and commercial success, the poignant family film •**Storm Boy** (1976). Over the next five years, Carroll produced a number of important films, including •**The Fourth Wish** (1976), **Weekend of Shadows** (1978), •**The Money Movers** (1979), •'**Breaker' Morant** (1980), and the film adaptation of David •Williamson's play detailing the intrigue behind the scenes at Williamson's favourite Australian Rules football team (Collingwood) in •**The Club** (1980). In between these films Carroll produced *The Sound of Love* (1977) and Peter •Weir's strange drama *The Plumber* (1979) for Australian television.

Early in his career, Carroll served as project officer with the •Experimental Film and Television Fund and, between 1973 and 1982, he worked for the •South Australian Film Corporation, before taking up a position as executive producer for Network Ten. During the 1980s and early 1990s Carroll produced a number of telefeatures, including a version of David Williamson's play *The Perfectionist* (1985), *The Blue Lightning* (1986), *Frankie's House* (1992), and miniseries such as *The True Believers* (1988) and *Barlow and Chambers: A Long Way from Home* (1988). In the 1990s Carroll produced the comedy **Diana & Me** (1997) and **Passion** (1999), an interpretation of the controversial private life of Australian composer Percy Grainger.

Other Australian films include: Freedom (1982), Turtle Beach (1992).
　　GM

Cars that Ate Paris, The

1974. *Director*: Peter Weir. *Producers*: Hal McElroy, Jim McElroy. *Scriptwriter*: Peter Weir. *Director of photography*: John McLean. *Music*: Bruce Smeaton. 91 min. *Cast*: John Meillon (The Mayor), Terry Camilleri (Arthur), Kevin Miles (Doctor Midland), Rick Scully (George), Max Gillies (Metcalf).

A Volkswagen 'beetle' fitted all over with lethal-looking spikes was a key image of this dark thriller and its advertising campaign. The film revealed at once that, in Peter •Weir, a new director of more than usual promise had arrived on the Australian film scene. It was screened in the Marketplace (the unofficial screenings held continuously at all the cinemas in central Cannes) during the 1974 Cannes Film Festival, and the gimmick of the spiked car ensured that the film, if not a commercial success, was thoroughly noticed.

That image—of the absolutely quotidian, as the 'beetle' was then, suddenly made unfamiliar and frightening—epitomised Weir's output in the 1970s, when he showed a gift for suggesting how the extraordinary could at any moment upset preconceptions. The little country town of Paris is first glimpsed in long shot, nestling idyllically in the hills, as traveller Arthur (Camilleri) approaches and is suddenly distracted by a flashing light that causes him to crash. It soon becomes clear that this apparently sleepy hamlet is a death-trap for anyone who stumbles into it—or tries to get out—for the town lives on the proceeds of car accidents, and everyone, from the Mayor and the clergyman down, shares in the pickings. Weir, working from his own script and an original story of which he was co-author, makes a chilling Gothic comedy from this highly original material, and also takes satirical swipes at aspects of Australian culture and mythology.　　BMcF

Cass, Godfrey (1867–1951) ACTOR Godfrey Castieau was better known by his stage name Godfrey Cass. His father was a gaol governor, first at Beechworth, then at Melbourne Gaol, where he officiated at the hanging of Ned Kelly in 1880. As a result, Godfrey Cass had a life-long interest in Kelly, and played him on stage and in three films. He performed—his dark good looks making him a perfect villain—with the leading stage companies of the time, including J.C. Williamson, William Anderson, and Charles Holloway. In films, he may have acted in the Taits' 1910 remake of their 1906 Kelly film, but he certainly took part in several films in 1911 for Gaston Mervale's Australian Life Biograph Co.: **A Tale of the Australian Bush**, **One Hundred Years Ago**, and **A Ticket in Tatts**. Then he formed Lincoln Cass Films with W.J. •Lincoln, and played in most of their films in 1913: •**After Sundown**, •**The Sick Stockrider**, **Moondyne**, **The Remittance Man**, **Transported**, **The Road to Ruin**, and **The Reprieve**. When the company folded he returned to the stage. In 1915 Cass went to World War I. After the war, the contraction of the stock companies made his theatrical career rather more precarious but, in 1920, he was called on by Harry Southwell to once again play Ned Kelly in •**The Kelly Gang** (1920), and he continued in occasional screen roles until •**Heritage** in 1935.

Other Australian films: •The Hordern Mystery (1920), The Dingo (1923), •When the Kellys Were Out (1923), The Mystery of a Hansom Cab (1925), •Jewelled Nights (1925), The Rushing Tide (1927), Tiger Island (1930).   IB

Cassell, Alan

Cassell, Alan (1932–) ACTOR Western Australian Alan Cassell, who has had an impressive stage career, was also busy on television and as a character actor in the early years of the new Australian cinema (see Revival, the). He played the male lead in •Cathy's Child (1979), for which he won a Sammy award as the journalist who helps Cathy cut through the red tape in her efforts to have her child restored to her, and he was an imposing, opportunistic Lord Kitchener in •'Breaker' Morant (1980). These two roles hint at the kind of versatility he has shown on the stage, where his opportunities have been greater, but his film roles always carried a lived-in conviction.

Other Australian films: Plugg (1975), The Olive Tree (1976), •Money Movers (1979), Harlequin (1980), •The Club (1980), •Puberty Blues (1981), Squizzy Taylor (1982), The Dark Room (1982), •The Settlement (1984), The Big Hurt (1986), Belinda (1988).   BMcF

Castle, The

1997. *Director*: Rob Sitch. *Producer*: Debra Choate. *Scriptwriters*: Santo Cilauro, Tom Gleisner, Jane Kennedy, Rob Sitch. *Director of photography*: Miriana Marusic. *Music*: Craig Harnath. 82 min. *Cast*: Michael Caton (Daryl Kerrigan), Anne Tenney (Sal Kerrigan), Sophie Lee (Tracey Kerrigan), Stephen Curry (Dale Kerrigan), Charles 'Bud' Tingwell (Laurence Hammill), Tiriel Mora (Dennis Denuto).

Daryl Kerrigan and his devoted family are outraged when their house and others in their street are marked down to be 'compulsorily acquired' by a large corporation involved in the extension of the adjacent airport. Refusing to be intimidated by smooth-talkers in suits or by thugs in chains and leather, Daryl takes on the faceless entrepreneurs and, after an initial setback and with no help from his deeply incompetent lawyer, he has a chance meeting with a retired QC who decides to take the case to the High Court. He argues that it is impossible to compensate the Kerrigans for what is more than a mere house to them, and wins. The film's scenario smacks of old Ealing, with the little man routing big business interests, and recalls a 1950 British comedy, **The Happy Family**, on the same stay-put theme. However, good-natured although **The Castle** is, it avoids sentimentality by insisting on the idiocies of the Kerrigans as much as on their determination. Without patronising them, the script (the work of the team that produced the television series *Frontline*) finds humour in their preoccupations, however absurd, and takes satirical swipes at the processes of the law and corporations.   BMcF

Cathy's Child

1979. *Director*: Donald Crombie. *Producers*: Errol Sullivan, Pom Oliver. *Scriptwriter*: Ken Quinnell. Based on the book, *A Piece of Paper*, by Dick Wordley. *Director of photography*: Gary Hansen. *Music*: William Motzing. 90 min. *Cast*: Michele Fawdon (Cathy), Alan Cassell (Dick Wordley), Bryan Brown (Paul Nicholson), Arthur Dignam (Minister), Willie Fennell (Gordon Cooper).

This unpretentious drama, based on a real-life incident, was typical of the low-key, humanist realism that was a persistent, if not prolific strain of film-making in the new Australian cinema (see Revival, the). Cathy, a Maltese living in Australia, is helped by two journalists, Wordley and Nicholson, in her struggle to retrieve her daughter, virtually abducted to Greece by her estranged and patriarchally inclined Greek husband. Wordley sloughs off his alcoholism long enough to fall in love with Cathy and to help her overcome bureaucratic difficulties put in the way of her quest. Like so many Australian films of the period, the film runs out of momentum before the end, avoiding the emotional intensity that might have made it a more moving experience. Its great strengths lie in the performances of Michele •Fawdon as the distraught Cathy and Alan •Cassell as the disillusioned Wordley, and in director Donald •Crombie's sympathetic and unaffected handling of the film's basic situation.   BMcF

Caton, Michael

Caton, Michael ACTOR Until 1997, this Queensland-born actor was best known as Uncle Harry in the long-running television series *The Sullivans*, and he has done a good deal of other work on the small screen and the stage. His film roles have been intermittent and, with two exceptions, unremarkable. Tim •Burstall's study of men under the pressures of an isolated environment, •**The Last of the Knucklemen** (1979), saw him as part of a highly competent ensemble, playing Monk, the former teacher and seminarian, an odd man out in this setting, with quiet sensitivity. Nearly 20 years later, he was wonderfully funny and endearing in •**The Castle** (1997) as Daryl Kerrigan, determined to block the developers who want to get rid of his weatherboard house because it stands in the way of extending the adjacent airport. Caton has a major gift for portraying ordinariness without condescension.

Other Australian films: Stockade (1971), **Private Collection** (1972), Jog's Trot (1976), •**Hoodwink** (1981), Fluteman (1982), •**Monkey Grip** (1982), The Thirteenth Floor (1988), •**The Interview** (1998).   BMcF

Caught In The Net

1928. *Director*: Vaughan C. Marshall. *Producer*: Vaughan C. Marshall. *Director of photography*: Tasman Higgins. 5 reels. B&W. *Cast*: Zillah

Bateman (Phyllis Weston), John Mayer (Jack Stacey), Charles Brown (Robson).

Marshall's second feature (after •**Environment**, 1927) was a high-society love triangle, with a yacht race specially staged by the St Kilda Yacht Club. The leading lady was a visiting British actor, but she does not appear in the fragment that survives, which shows leading man John Mayer, sitting in a park reading the letter that clears his name. There is not enough in this fragment to explain the critical failure of the film, but it does show Mayer giving an engaging performance, and Tasman •**Higgins'** photography appears to advantage.   IB

Cavill, Joy (1923–) PRODUCER Joy Cavill was a prominent name in that period when Australian films were a rarity; that is, before the revival of the 1970s got under way (see Revival, the). She had worked in the United Kingdom as a film reviewer before getting her start as continuity girl on •**King of the Coral Sea** (1954) and •**Walk into Paradise** (1956), both made for Lee •**Robinson** and Chips •**Rafferty's** company, Southern International, which made several genre adventures, often in co-production with overseas companies. She worked as associate producer and co-author of the script on two more of their films, **The Stowaway** (1958) and **Dust in the Sun** (1958), and as associate producer on **The Restless and the Damned** (1959), which was not released in Australia because Southern International had failed financially by this time. With director Robinson, she co-produced **The Intruders** (1969), based on the highly successful television series *Skippy*, on which she had also worked as producer, and she produced many other popular television programs in this period. In 1970 she shared production and script credits with John •**McCallum** on the mining boom comedy, •**Nickel Queen**, which McCallum also directed. In 1964 she had directed a documentary, *The Dawn Fraser Story* and, 15 years later, she produced and wrote •**Dawn!** (1979), the feature film biography of the Australian swimming star.

Other Australian films: In Song and Dance (1964, doc., assoc. p.).
                                                                              BMcF

Celia

1989. *Director*: Ann Turner. *Producers*: Timothy White, Gordon Glenn. *Scriptwriter*: Ann Turner. *Director of photography*: Geoffrey Simpson. *Music*: Chris Neal. 102 min. *Cast*: Rebecca Smart (Celia Carmichael), Nicholas Eadie (Ray Carmichael), Mary-Anne Fahey (Pat Carmichael), Victoria Longley (Alice Tanner), Margaret Ricketts (Granny).

Ann •**Turner's** impressive début feature evokes childhood but it is not a children's film. Nine-year-old Celia Carmichael's world is full of pain, following the loss of a beloved grandmother, the threat to her pet rabbit, and the ever-present Hobbyahs, who terrorise her at night. But she is also a very ordinary little girl, whose activities and relationships resonate with the experience of all adult viewers, particularly those who can remember back to 1950s paranoia. So the comfort that Celia could have obtained from her neighbour Alice is denied, because Alice is known to be a communist, and the Hobbyahs begin to invade Celia's waking life, with disastrous results. Already a veteran actor, Rebecca •**Smart's** performance in the title role is outstanding, but it was Victoria •**Longley** who won the Australian Film Institute Award for Best Actress in a Supporting Role.
                                                                              IB

Censorship In the early years, films were screened in legitimate theatres or in temporary premises such as tents and fairgrounds: in the latter case, there was no government control over the content and, in the former case, control was exercised through the mechanisms that controlled theatrical performances, usually the local police. The film trade found the whole system irksome—even national distributors had six different state authorities to deal with, each with their own standards and procedures. Lack of uniformity meant that a film approved for one territory might be banned in another, and every decision was always tentative—reversible if the authorities received enough complaints from the public.

During World War I, national security regulations required that all films be censored by a federal agency (dependent for its authority on the Customs Regulations), and this practice continued after the war. The Commonwealth Film Censorship was located at first in Melbourne (which was the seat of the federal government), then Sydney (which was the point of entry for nearly all imported films). In Sydney, it was headed (from 1928 to 1942) by Walter Cresswell O'Reilly, whose personality was stamped on the procedures and standards adopted. Several states maintained their own censorship in addition to the federal system, covering the censorship of local productions, and also allowing the states to intervene in any decision with which they disagreed. In Vic., the *Censorship of Film Act* (1926) also established mandatory classification, preventing children between the ages of six and 16 from attending films judged unsuitable.

However, over the course of many years, each state ceded its censorship powers to the Commonwealth, by appointing the Commonwealth Censorship to act on behalf of the state: Vic. from 1926, WA, Qld, and Tas. from 1949, NSW from 1969, and SA from 1971. Even then, any state could appoint its own censors in addition, and several have done so (notably Qld and WA). Mandatory classification was abandoned, but advisory classification allowed patrons to choose not to see films that might offend and also allowed parents to protect their children from films classified as unsuitable.

Public debates about standards have ebbed and flowed over the twentieth century. In the first decade, complaints concerned fight films, which were objected to not only because of their violence, but also because they challenged social values by sometimes depicting the victory of a Black man over a White man (**Burns–Johnson Fight**, 1908). During World War I, social cohesion was protected by requiring a film of the 1917 Sydney General Strike to be held up for several weeks and then retitled, from the polemical (**The Great Strike**) to the bland (**Recent Industrial Happenings in New South Wales**). By the 1920s, the areas to which the censors were required to pay attention were more stable: they included sex, violence, and bad language, which have remained contentious to the present day, as well as some matters that are no longer considered problematic such as 'miscegenation', 'blasphemy', and, even, 'offence to a friendly nation'.

However, within the key contentious areas of sex and violence, standards have changed immensely. In 1918 it was not acceptable to depict seduction, no matter how tastefully: the NSW censors banned •**The Woman Suffers**, which includes a 'seduction scene' with the two people still fully clothed and a cutaway so discreet that modern audiences are sometimes not even sure of the sexual intent. In 1933 (•**In the Wake of the Bounty**), the naked breasts of Tahitian women were considered unacceptable for public scrutiny, and, even during, or perhaps because of, the 'permissive society', nudity was still being challenged in the 1960s, including in films (such as **The Pawnbroker**, USA, 1965) with high international reputations.

Until the 1960s, the film trade walked a fine line between not antagonising an audience that seemed in general to have faith that the system was protecting the community against evil influences, and coping with the commercial costs and inconveniences of censorship. Opposition to censorship was confined to such groups as the •Realist Film Unit, which had some of its films banned (for example, their Spanish Civil War films were banned ostensibly not on political grounds, but because they depicted real dead bodies). But, after World War II, and particularly from the 1960s onwards, public opposition to censorship grew, largely under the influence of the growing film-culture movement (film societies, film festivals, and film courses in educational institutions). This was also a time of high immigration levels, bringing to Australia waves of people with different cultural heritages, looking for films in their own languages, and with different aesthetic standards from the Anglo-Celtic mainstream. Increasingly, a film-literate public objected to bureaucratic interference in the public

exhibition of what they saw as works of art, or they simply objected to the paternalism implied in having their aesthetic and moral standards imposed by the government. There were some very public brawls about films, particularly popular films such as **Easy Rider** (USA, 1969) and **Point Blank** (USA, 1967).

Controversial cases (such as **I Love, You Love**, Sweden, 1968) sparked a major confrontation between the censors and the international film festivals of Melbourne and Sydney (and later others), leading to a compromise: festival entrance was limited to subscribers over 18, and no censorship was required for films that were imported for a single screening then re-exported. This did not quieten the anti-censorship lobby, and it antagonised the film trade, which resented special pleading by what they saw as market competitors.

The introduction of the 'R' certificate in 1971 was intended to spike the guns of the critics—henceforth, only the most extreme films would be banned entirely, and the community (particularly children) would be protected by a mandatory classification system. Exhibitors feared that the new system would ruin their businesses, and it certainly caused major changes, but not all were painful. Many of the small newsreel theatrettes, which had been struggling to find an audience since the arrival of television in 1956, found a new lease of life as specialist 'R'-houses. Drive-in audiences also began to change: one strategy was to have a session with a 'G'-rated movie for the family audience, starting as early as the light allowed, followed by a separate session with an 'R'-rated movie for couples and teenagers. In the 1980s, by the time video had swallowed up the family market, the remaining drive-ins still found 'R' movies the most viable product.

The effect of censorship on the Australian film production industry is difficult to gauge: we will never know what films were simply not made, because the existence of censorship made the risk too great. On the other hand, Australia has always had its share of sensationalist productions, again depending on what was the current interpretation of this term. Films such as **Know Thy Child** (1921) or •**The Woman Suffers** were courageous, challenging the moral certainties of their times. Other silent films simply exploited moral panics to maximise audience appeal: for example, **Satan in Sydney** (1918) and **Remorse, A Story of the Red Plague** (1917). Charles •Chauvel's run-ins with the censors were skilful marketing exercises, designed to keep his films in the public eye for many months before release. In the early days of the revival of film production in the 1960s and 1970s (see Revival, the), censorship was seen as particularly stultifying—preventing Australian producers from reaching the most lucrative section of the market. When the censors brutally cut •**The Naked Bunyip** (1970), the producer John Murray threw out an open challenge by replacing cuts to the sound with bleeps and the cut images with black film, and by running an animated bunyip along the lower edge of the screen. This was a provocative way of drawing attention to the censorship history of a film, and it was such local cases, as well as complaints from the public about the mutilation of imported films and the arguments with the festivals about importation for specialised audiences, that convinced the government of the need for a revision of censorship, leading, in 1971, to the introduction of the 'R' certificate. Although there were still plenty of films banned outright or cut, public complaints about over-zealous censors reduced considerably.

In the 1980s, the growing popularity of video led to new censorship problems: the regulations were extended to cover the new medium, but this was not enough, as classification was considered not sufficient to protect children from what might be brought into their homes by irresponsible adults. Lack of uniformity of state laws led to a lucrative market in non-violent erotica distributed out of Canberra, where the laws were the most permissive. At the same time, the censors became more strict against sexual violence, in both film and video. A key case was **Salo** (Italy, 1975), banned when its importation was first attempted, released in 1993 when community standards were judged to have changed sufficiently to warrant a change of policy, and re-banned in 1998 as part of a conservative backlash swept along by political exigencies (the lack of a government majority in the Senate).

From at least the end of O'Reilly's reign, the censors were instructed to follow community standards, and public debate frequently accused them of being out of step with the community, either by being too lenient or not lenient enough. In the late 1990s, that rhetoric was most frequently employed by conservatives, anxious to make standards more restrictive. But, to their surprise, an independent study in 1999 found that community groups assembled to check on censorship decisions agreed most of the time with the censor, and, in two of the three cases where they disagreed, they supported a more lenient classification. As Kathryn Paterson took up the position of Director of the Office of Film and Literature Classification in 1999, censorship procedures seemed reasonably stable, but standards looked set to remain contentious.   IB

Chaffey, Don (1917–) DIRECTOR   After a very busy career in British cinema, beginning with **The Secret Tent** in 1956, and encompassing a range of popular genres, Don Chaffey made three films in Australia in the 1970s. They were •**Ride a Wild Pony** (1975), **Born to Run** (1976), and •**The Fourth Wish** (1976). These were proficient and sufficiently likeable entertainments to warrant Chaffey's having a small place in Australian cinema. **Ride a Wild Pony**, like

some of Chaffey's British films, such as **The Three Lives of Thomasina** (1963), was made for the Disney organisation. It is a fast-moving adventure story, based on a children's novel by James Aldridge, about rivalry over the ownership of a pony. One of its stars was the English actor Michael •Craig, who appeared again in and wrote the script for **The Fourth Wish**, which began its life as a three-part television series, based on the dying wishes of a boy suffering from leukaemia. The film was affecting and the possibility of excessive sentimentality was kept at bay by Chaffey's brisk direction.   BMcF

Chant of Jimmie Blacksmith, The

1978. *Director:* Fred Schepisi. *Producer:* Fred Schepisi. *Scriptwriter:* Fred Schepisi. Based on the novel by Thomas Keneally. *Director of photography:* Ian Baker. *Music:* Bruce Smeaton. 120 min. *Cast:* Tommy Lewis (Jimmie), Freddy Reynolds (Mort), Ray Barrett (Farrell), Jack Thompson (Rev. Neville), Angela Punch (Gilda).

Just as Australia is approaching Federation, that symbol of national maturity, half-caste Jimmie Blacksmith declares war on the white employers who exploit him and who threaten his manhood by withholding the wages due to him. What happens to Jimmie on an individual level casts doubt on the nation's claims to respect and independence. As in Thomas •Keneally's novel, Jimmie is poignantly caught between the ways of his black forefathers and those of the white society to which he aspires, and the ending for him is inevitably tragic. Whereas Keneally dramatises Jimmie's dilemma in spare, even witty prose, Fred •Schepisi's film achieves the same thematic intensity through its imagery: Jimmie is oppressed and marginalised by the white world and estranged from the daunting landscape through which he flees.

Like many Australian films of the 1970s, **The Chant of Jimmie Blacksmith** was both based on a novel of some prestige and set in the past. Unlike many such films, it did not take refuge in nostalgia. The film's narrative, governed by Jimmie's movements from place to place in a futile search to earn a living, and thereafter hunted by white avengers, is at the service of a pressing moral issue, the relevance of which is not limited to the times in which the film is set. Despite this, and despite the passionate commitment with which it is made, the film failed at the box office. The most expensive Australian film to that time, it was perhaps too raw in its perceptions, too bleak in its outcome, for commercial success.   BMcF

Chapman, Jan (1949–) PRODUCER   Jan Chapman became a teacher after attending Sydney University, but was soon directing documentaries and short films for the ABC. She became one of the second generation of women producers, beginning with television drama in the 1980s, both series (*Sweet and Sour, Come in Spinner*) and tele-movies (*Displaced Persons* 1984, *Two Friends* 1986), then moving successfully into film in the 1990s. She has worked productively with women directors—Gillian •Armstrong (•**The Last Days of Chez Nous** 1992), Jane •Campion (•**The Piano** 1993), and Shirley Barrett (•**Love Serenade** 1996)—and her projects have a consistent interest in exploring the female psyche. She has also produced the six-part ABC series *Naked: Stories of Men* (1996). She was nominated for an Oscar for **The Piano**, and won the Australian Film Institute's Longford Award in 1997. Chapman worked in the USA on films such as **Holy Smoke** (1999).

IB

Chauvel, Charles (1897–1959) DIRECTOR/PRODUCER/WRITER

Charles Chauvel's is one of the strongest directorial voices of early Australian cinema. With the considerable help of his wife, Elsa, as credited and uncredited amanuensis and co-writer from 1933 on, Chauvel produced nine commercial features, four wartime shorts, a wartime documentary re-edited from Soviet material, and *Walkabout*, a 13-episode travel series for BBC television. The Chauvels were important in the film careers of Errol •Flynn, Chips •Rafferty, and Michael •Pate. Their work includes such films as •**Forty Thousand Horsemen** (1940), •**Sons of Matthew** (1949), and •**Jedda** (1955), which are among the very few films produced in Australia prior to the 1970s commonly regarded as screen classics today. A Chauvel film often seems better designed to move from point to point along a bush trail than to build the edifice of classical narrative. There is an air of improvisation and discovery about its structure that owes a great deal to nineteenth-century tales of heroic deeds. If this kind of epic reach often exceeded their economic grasp, the Chauvels' tenacity and their stubborn insistence on independence also resulted in a distinctive body of films in which intense emotion fuels moral stories about national identity, history, gender, and race. Charles Chauvel grew up as a privileged member of the landed gentry of south-eastern Qld; in some ways the ideas and attitudes of the squattocracy can still be found in the Chauvels' films. Sometimes celebrated or dismissed as little more than an ardent, simple nationalist, Charles Chauvel brought a great passion for Australia, its land, and peoples, to all of his work. Intermixed with the ardour of the films is a sense of history as inexorable change, moving all nations and races towards ends that cannot be foreseen, and mocking all fixed ideals.

Other Australian films: •**Robbery Under Arms** (1920, a.), **The Shadow of Lightning Ridge** (1920, a.), **A Jackeroo of Coolabong** (1920, a.), •**The Moth of Moonbi** (1926, d., w., a.), •**Greenhide** (1926, d., w.), •**In the Wake of the Bounty** (1933, d., w.), •**Heritage** (1935, d., w, •**Uncivilised** (1936, d., co-w.), •**Rangle River** (1936, co-w.), •**Rats of Tobruk** (1944, d., p., co-w.).

WILLIAM D. ROUTT

Cheaters, The

1930. *Director/Scriptwriter*: Paulette McDonagh. *Director of photography*: Jack Fletcher. *Art Director*: Phyllis McDonagh. 84 min. B&W. *Cast*: Marie Lorraine (Paula Marsh), John Faulkner (John Travers), Josef Bambach (Lee Travers), Nellie McNiven (Mrs Hugh Nash), Elaine de Chair (Louise Nash), Frank Hawthorne (Keith Manion), Leal Douglas (The Lady).

The Cheaters was the third feature produced by the McDonagh sisters. While it shared similar plotlines to their earlier work, **The Cheaters** was a more ambitious project, combining romantic tragedy and gangster elements with relative assurance. Beginning with an intricate jewellery heist, the film is essentially a tale of revenge and redemption, with two young lovers striving to overcome the bitterness of inter-family conflict. Conceived as a silent film, **The Cheaters** did not commence production until August 1929. By the time the film was ready for distribution in December that year, imported 'talkies' had made such inroads into local exhibition that silent features were already becoming outmoded. In an effort to enhance the film's commercial prospects, the McDonaghs attempted a sound version with three synchronised sound sequences and sound-on-disc recordings. However, the crude quality of the sound recording system was a great disappointment to the McDonaghs and critics alike, and plans for a general release were shelved. A second attempt to produce a sound version of **The Cheaters** was made soon after, with a new method of recording sound directly on to film strip developed by the Australian company, Standardtone. By the time this new version was ready in October 1931, the film and its fashions had dated, effectively sinking its chances of finding a market. In a post-1970 interview, Paulette •McDonagh remarked that **The Cheaters** had at the time been a bitter experience, but that they had accepted it as a 'whim of fate'. Today, **The Cheaters**—or at least the silent version—is regarded more highly, with various writers praising its dramatic unity and favourably comparing details of its set design and plot to German expressionist cinema. For all its faults, the Standardtone version survives as a fascinating hybrid. The recent discovery of four reels has provided film scholars with a rare opportunity to compare the two versions.

KEN BERRYMAN

Children of the Revolution

1996. *Director*: Peter Duncan. *Producer/Scriptwriter*: Peter Duncan. *Director of photography*: Martin McGrath. *Music*: Nigel Westlake. 104 min. *Cast*: Richard Roxburgh (Joe Welch), Sam Neill (Nine), Judy Davis (Joan Fraser), Geoffrey Rush (Zachary Welch), F. Murray Abraham (Stalin), Rachel Griffiths (Anna).

Comedy, which manages to be both good-natured and stringent, is made of diehard communism in this film, which purports to tell the story of an Australian comrade,

Joan Fraser, who idolises Stalin. She eventually meets him after much devoted correspondence, sleeps with him on the last night of his life and, nine months later, bears a son called—of course—Joe. Joe is brought up by Joan and her well-meaning fellow-traveller husband, Zachary, and grows into an agitator worthy of his likely lineage.

Director/writer Peter Duncan, in his first film, audaciously mixes moods (black humour and nostalgia) and modes (realism and fantasy, with a musical insert in which Stalin and his cronies perform to 'I Get a Kick Out of You'), and the whole is informed by the obvious affection in which he holds his characters, even at their most taxing. Judy •Davis, not a natural comedian, has exactly the right humourless dedication required of Joan and, indeed, the whole cast is excellent, entering into the quirky spirit of the project.   BMcF

Children's films Films concerning childhood have been among the most important in the Australian film industry—from •**The Kid Stakes** (1927) to •**The Shiralee** (1957), •**Walkabout** (1971), •**Storm Boy** (1976), •**Celia** (1989), •**No Worries** (1993), and •**Crackers** (1998). Some reproduce nostalgic adult memories of childhood within a realistic style (•**Smiley**, 1958). Some are designed to tear at the heartstrings, such as •**The Fourth Wish** (1976), in which a father tries desperately to fulfil his dying son's last wishes. Some acknowledge that adults and children can share fantasies (•**Babe** 1995); some depict childhood itself as fantasy—**Fatty Finn** (1980), based on the same cartoon characters as •**The Kid Stakes**, or **Ginger Meggs** (1982), based on yet another cartoon child. **Doctors and Nurses** (1981) even derives its humour from casting children in adult roles.

Such films, no matter how well received they were by children, were not produced specifically for this audience, although the line between films about children and films for children is a fine one. There have always been lobbies wishing to protect children from the harmful effects of viewing films intended for adults but, it was not until after World War II, that the pressure for better quality films to be screened at children's Saturday matinees became a push for films designed specifically for children. In the United Kingdom, this was the task of the children's entertainment film division of Gaumont-British Instructional (later known as the Children's Film Foundation): they made two films in Australia (the popular •**Bush Christmas**, 1947, and the less successful **Bungala Boys**, 1961), but their British films were also widely shown by the Australian Council for Children's Films and Television, which lobbied for better films for children and screened special children's programs of (mainly imported) films in the school holidays. After the arrival of television in 1956, the child audience was recognised as a key market segment, making it easier to sell theatrical feature films, which were sometimes based on popular television programs and, at the very least, could recoup some of their costs by later television release (**Funny Things Happen Down Under**, 1965; **The Intruders**, 1969; **Strange Holiday**, 1970; **Little Jungle Boy**, 1970; **Avengers of the Reef**, 1973).

One field of production dedicated to children was •animation, starting with Eric •Porter's **Marco Polo Junior Versus the Red Dragon** (1972). The development of animation studios from the 1970s has greatly increased the output of children's films, perhaps the most prominent being the Yoram •Gross studios, with their films based on much-loved Australian children's books (one series starting with •**Dot and the Kangaroo**, 1977, and a second starting with •**Blinky Bill**, 1992), as well as the Burbank studios, with their series of animated classics (usually distributed on video). There have also been live adaptations of children's classic novels, such as •**Playing Beatie Bow** (1986) or **The Silver Brumby** (1993).

Increasingly, the child audience is recognised to be as diverse as the adult audience. Early on, teenagers proved to be a lucrative market segment, with many •'rites of passage' films showing young people accepting more adult responsibilities: for example, **BMX Bandits** (1983), **Molly** (1983), **Tail of a Tiger** (1985), **Windrider** (1986), and •**Mull** (1989). Catering for younger children was for many years considered not financially viable. The change in this perception is directly attributable to the activities of the Australian Children's Television Foundation (ACTF), under Patricia Edgar, which, since 1981, has produced more than 150 hours of children's drama. Series such as *Kaboodle*, *Lift Off*, *Round the Twist*, *Touch the Sun*, and *Winners* have been distributed world-wide and released on both broadcast television and video. The ACTF, in the late 1990s, moved into the production of theatrical features for children.

The international success of both animated feature films and ACTF television programs has contributed to a climate in which children's films are now seen as commercially viable for theatrical release, particularly in a competitive market forced to become more specialised. The result is an increasing number of Australian film productions designed for children, and released (like their imported competitors) in school-holiday seasons. Some of these are still offshoots from television: the live-action film **Mighty Morphin Power Rangers: The Movie** (1995) was based on the successful animated television series, and the musical theatre group the Wiggles was extremely popular on television and radio (and had released audiocassettes and videos) before it made **The Wiggles Movie** (1998). But most are stand-alone productions, whether they have a child protagonist (**The Real Macaw** and **Joey**, both 1998), or are just pitched to the child audience—for instance depicting the adventures of a puppy (**Napoleon**, 1997). Australia now has an international reputation for its children's films: success in the local market has been variable, but most of these films have at least returned their costs on video or in the international market, and some have done very well indeed.

INA BERTRAND

Chilvers, Simon (1935–) ACTOR A noted Melbourne-based stage actor, Simon Chilvers has played many leading roles in the theatre and appeared often in television series. On screen, he has brought his somewhat quizzical features to a range of character roles, most often as prominent members of institutional hierarchies, such as Inspector Poole in •The Naked Country (1985) and the president of the commission of inquiry in **Ground Zero** (1987). A consummate character actor, he can be either reassuring or sinister, his face giving little away.

Other Australian films: Dartmouth (1973, doc., nar.), High Rolling (1977), Buddies (1983), •Annie's Coming Out (1984), The Big Hurt (1986), Sky Pirates (1986), Windrider (1986), Garbo (1992), Mushrooms (1995).

BMcF

Chubb, Paul (1949–) ACTOR Paul Chubb is one of the most prolific character actors in the Australian cinema with an ability to bring to the most banal film a sense of comic pathos. Chubb began his career as a comedy writer, but has appeared as an actor since his brief appearance as a policeman in •The Night The Prowler (1979). While Chubb was establishing his credentials as a character actor in Australian cinema, in films such as •**Hoodwink** (1981), •**Heatwave** (1982), **Kitty and the Bagman** (1982), and the 'standover man' Curly in •**Goodbye Paradise** (1983), television offered greater exposure in series programs such as *Daily at Dawn*. Chubb's major roles have been in low-budget films, such as Brian McKenzie's •**With Love to the Person Next to Me** (1987). Chubb, in this film, is able to infuse the role of Syd, a vicious, inept criminal, with sufficient pathos and complexity to enliven a potentially formulaic character. Chubb as 40-year-old Stanley Harris in **Stan and George's New Life** (1992) begins life anew when he takes a job with the Weather Bureau, and he followed this as private detective Dirk Trent in the comic homage to Raymond Chandler's hard-boiled world in **The Roly Poly Man** (1994).

Other Australian films include: The Coca-Cola Kid (1985), •Bliss (1985), •Robbery Under Arms (1985), Danger Down Under (1987), Bullseye (1989), Golden Braid (1991), Dead to the World (1991), Sweet Talker (1991), Mad Bomber in Love (1991), Shotgun Wedding (1994), Singapore Sling (1995), •Cosi (1996), •The Well (1997), •Road to Nhill (1997).

GM

Church and the Woman, The

1917. *Director*: Raymond Longford. *Producer*: Humbert Pugliese. *Scriptwriter*: Raymond Longford. *Director of photography*: Ernest Higgins. 7000 ft. B&W. *Cast*: Lottie Lyell (Eileen Shannon), Boyd Irwin (Dr Sidney Burton), Harry Roberts (Father Shannon), Percy Walshe (John Shannon), J.P. O'Neill (Mike Feeney), Nada Conrade (Helen Burton).

Few Australian films have tackled head-on the sectarian division within Australian society, as this film does. Eileen Shannon's father refuses consent for her to marry a Protestant. When her father is murdered, Eileen's lover (Sidney Burton) is arrested and sentenced to death. Meanwhile, the real culprit has confessed to Father Shannon, Eileen's brother. Unable to break the confidentiality of the confessional or to bear his sister's pain while an innocent man is punished, Father Shannon takes the blame himself. However, just before the priest is to be hanged, the guilty man is caught, the priest released, and the lovers are free to marry—although still 'behind the altar'.

Before the film's release, the Catholic Church was wary of it, particularly as George Marlow's •**The Monk and the Woman** was in production at the same time but, in the end, neither the Church nor the censors found anything to justify action against Raymond •Longford's film. Although none of the film survives, its enthusiastic reception suggests that it was a particularly successful example of the collaboration between director Longford and actor Lottie •Lyell.

IB

Cilento, Diane (1934–) ACTOR This striking blonde actor started and spent most of her screen career in Britain. The daughter of parents distinguished in the medical world, she was educated in Australia and the USA, and had her theatrical training in the USA and the United Kingdom. She established herself on the British stage and, in the 1950s, a discouraging decade for women in war-dominated British cinema, she was lucky and talented enough to get a range of varied leading roles in such films as **Passage Home** (1955) and **The Admirable Crichton** (1957). In the 1960s she filmed steadily, won an Oscar nomination for her role in **Tom Jones** (1963), and married little-known Scottish actor, Sean Connery. After the break-up of this marriage in the 1970s, she returned to Australia, where she has appeared in only two films: Tim •Burstall's romantic melodrama, **Duet for Four** (1982) and, with her actor son, Jason Connery, in **The Boy Who Had Everything** (1984). She also appeared in the television version of *For the Term of His Natural Life* (1982).

BMcF

Cinema and Photographic Branch, *see*
Documentary and non-fiction: silent; Film Australia

Cinemas The first cinemas, defined broadly as the premises in which films are publicly shown, were designed for purposes other than showing films: some were public

Cinemas

halls (the Melbourne Town Hall), others were legitimate theatres (the Theatre Royal in Adelaide), and others were outdoor pleasure gardens (Ye Olde Englishe Fayre in Perth).

Some communities never managed to sustain a purpose-built cinema. They relied on public halls, sometimes given a different name on picture nights: the Wagin Town Hall was called the Plaza in the 1940s, and the Albany Town Hall was called Cinema One in the 1980s. But the popularity of the new medium was such that, in more populous centres, entrepreneurs were prepared from early in the twentieth century to take the risk of adapting premises specifically for film exhibition. In 1896, there were converted shops in the Beehive Building in Adelaide, and the *Salon Perfectionne* in Collins Street, Melbourne. These were small, in contrast to the vast audiences accommodated in the early tent shows, with the projector mounted on a stand in the middle of the auditorium, where it presented as much of a novelty as the flickering image on the distant screen.

The roller-skating craze had led to the erection of rinks, at first open to the sky, later roofed over for year-round presentations. These often huge structures were adapted for use as cinemas, in both the city (West's Olympia in Adelaide) and rural areas (Bushalla's Skating Rink in Narrogin, WA, became the Amusu Theatre). They were uncomfortable, plank seating was not uncommon, and over-crowding was considered a mark of success. They were usually unlined, often constructed of corrugated iron over a timber frame, so they were furnaces in summer, ice-boxes in winter, and noisy all year around. In the cities at least, they were soon superseded by purpose-built venues: gardens (the Casino Open Air Picture Theatre in Adelaide in 1910), and hard-top cinemas (the Empire Theatre in Perth in 1909).

The first cinema-building boom produced small venues, usually not wider than two shop fronts, with the auditorium being long and narrow. These were not, strictly speaking, the 'nickelodeons' of the American industry: they were a little later than the American nickelodeons, most were purpose-built rather than converted shops, and they often survived for many years. But the American showman J.D. Williams certainly introduced some of the pizazz of his homeland's exhibition industry to Australian cinemas: in his Sydney Lyric (1911) and Crystal Palace (1912), his Melbourne Melba (1911) and Britannia (1912), and his Perth Pavilion (1914), the marquees were lit up with electric lights, the entrance foyer was thronged with patrons before and after a show, and continuous programming attracted large audiences throughout the day.

In the suburbs and country areas, purpose-built cinemas were usually smaller, but not necessarily less showy: the Barkly, built in 1915 in the Melbourne suburb of Footscray, had two ornamental towers on the facade. In many areas, the hard-top had an associated open-air venue, a descen-

dant of the 'summer pleasure gardens', where patrons reclined in canvas-covered deck chairs, under the stars. In the larger centres, open-air venues operated in summer at the same time as the hard-top (allowing patrons to choose); in smaller centres, screenings alternated between the hard-top and the open-air depending on the weather. Some open-air venues were simply a fenced area, with seating (for instance, the Semaphore Wondergraph, opened in 1910); others were true 'gardens', with deckchairs on lawn, and the perimeter fence camouflaged with trees, shrubs, trellises, and fairy lights (for instance West's Palace Gardens, in the Perth suburb of Subiaco opened in 1912).

By the 1920s, some architects had become associated with the specialised field of cinema architecture: for example, William Pitt and Charles Hollinshed in Melbourne and William Leighton in Perth. Some of the great names of architecture in Australia dabbled in the field: for example, Walter Burley Griffin designed the Melbourne Capitol in 1921. The Capitol was not completed until 1924, the year in which Sydney's Prince Edward 'Theatre Beautiful' and Brisbane's Wintergarden were built. These spectacular 'picture palaces' heralded the second major building boom, with the national exhibition and distribution companies engaged in a competitive building spree.

*Hoyts extended their already large chain by building the Regent cinemas in the major cities—Perth (1927), Sydney and Adelaide (1928), and Melbourne and Brisbane (1929)— as well as in the suburbs (South Yarra, Melbourne, 1925) and country areas (Ballarat, Vic.). Union Theatres (see Greater Union Organisation) also added to their chain, building three atmospherics: the Sydney Capitol (built in 1928 and designed by Henry White) and two designed by the architectural firm Charles Bohringer, Taylor, and Johnson—the Ambassadors (Perth, 1928) and the State (Melbourne, 1929). These cinemas pretended to be oriental palaces, with stars twinkling in the roof and classical pillars, statuary, and ornamentation all around the walls. In such places, the orchestra performed in evening dress, the organist rose from the floor playing the Wurlitzer, and patrons were seated in plush comfort.

In the 1930s, MGM constructed and remodelled showcase cinemas for their product: the Metros (Melbourne, 1934; the former Auditorium, Brisbane, 1937; Perth, 1938; and the former Regent, Adelaide, 1939). This decade saw the heyday of the *art deco* style, in, for instance, the Trocadero in Preston, Vic. (1938) or the Como, still standing in South Perth, WA (1938). Theatre musicians had disappeared with the silent film, but cinema-going was now such an established part of the social fabric that cinema buildings were often the focal point of streetscapes, as important as the town hall or the railway station: an example is Toowomba's imposing Empire Theatre (1934).

This was not so with the new phenomenon that accompanied the introduction of sound film—the newsreel theatrettes in the capital cities, such as the Times (1934) and the Mayfair (1948) in Perth. These often hid in the basement of offices or shops, with provision for only around 300 patrons. They provided a program of short films, screened continuously from about 11 a.m. to about 11 p.m., allowing patrons to enter and leave at their own convenience. But by the 1950s they were considered rather unsavoury places, and their conversion, after the introduction of the 'R' certificate in 1972, into specialist soft-porn venues seemed entirely appropriate.

By then, the cinema landscape had irretrievably altered. Daylight saving and extended hotel opening hours provided the first interruptions to the cinema boom, but it was television that seemed the main culprit. Hoyts Skyline was the first drive-in, built in 1954 in the Melbourne suburb of Burwood, and drive-ins quickly spread all round the country in both suburban and rural areas. They survived the onslaught of television better than the hard-tops, which seemed to close almost at once but, over the course of the 1960s and 1970s, even the drive-ins gradually disappeared. With the spread of domestic video, the writing seemed to be on the wall—pundits predicted the imminent end of cinema. But city cinemas survived with the building of the multiplexes, first twin cinemas, then larger and larger complexes, containing food outlets and games arcades as well as several screens.

From the late 1980s, however, audiences began to desert these city multiplexes in favour of those being built in the suburban shopping malls. These became bigger and bigger—up to ten or more screens in the one complex—screening the current Hollywood-style product. The Imax and other large-screen formats also thrived. At the same time, there was a revival of the smaller and more specialised cinema, often in one of the old-style cinema buildings that had survived the post-television demolition epidemic, such as the Rivoli (Camberwell, Vic.) and the Luna (formerly the New Oxford, Leederville, WA). Some drive-ins and picture gardens also reopened for tourists and those with a nostalgic affection for older-style venues (Peninsula Drive-in, Dromana, Vic., and Camelot Gardens, Mosman Park, Perth). In rural areas, a new version of the town-hall cinema was the municipal arts complex (such as the Matt Dann Theatre, Port Hedland, WA), screening films two or three nights a week and making enough money from the hiring of the premises to subsidise other musical and theatrical activities.

So, at the end of the twentieth century, despite the prophets of doom, film was not dead—and neither was the cinema in which it was presented.

INA BERTRAND

The New Oxford, Leederville, WA, still operating as the Luna

Cinémathèque In 1984, when it was reconfigured from the former Melbourne University Film Society (founded 1948), the Melbourne Cinémathèque represented an attempt to update and repackage the ideals of the film-society movement. By the late 1990s it was probably the largest remaining organisation of a film-society type in Australia. From 1992, its success led to the growth of the National Cinémathèque, a capital city-based touring circuit alliance, programmed by the Melbourne Cinémathèque for the •Australian Film Institute and other state-based screen culture bodies. The Cinémathèque movement has now, intentionally, taken on myriad meanings, which diverge from Henri Langlois's original conception for the original French archive and exhibitor. However, while both the Melbourne and national bodies were established with some of the cultural aims of the defunct •National Film Theatre in mind, they probably keep closer to Langlois's notion of a 'show everything' philosophy of cultural exhibition practice: this includes exploring and publicising the possibilities of cinema art through a mixed and divergent (in form and practice), although intellectually contextualised, repertory of screen classics, cult films, and archival heritage, as well as alternative and oppositional productions, screen practices, and formats. QUENTIN TURNOUR

Cinematography It is a distinguishing feature of Australian cinema that cameramen, who were central to early silent production everywhere, continued to maintain a prominent position in Australia until the television era. These cameramen, employed by a small number of production houses, maintained technical standards at a high level, despite the underdevelopment of the industry in most other respects. With a limited feature output even at the best of times, newsreels and other actuality films directed by cameramen were, along with commercials, the main source of employment within the industry. Although, technically, sound production was well established in Australia by the early 1930s, the majority of footage continued to be shot mute. Thus, it was both cheap and easy for the multiskilled cinematographers to handle many aspects of production. Indeed, until the late 1920s, Australian films were usually edited by their cameramen. Likewise, although commercial laboratories became more numerous and mechanised in that period, most veteran cameramen continued to maintain their own private processing and printing facilities. In general, laboratories were often managed and operated by men with experience as cinematographers.

It is indicative of the nature of Australian cinema that, until recently, there have been no cameramen who have been able to specialise exclusively in drama production. As a consequence, with some notable exceptions, their lighting style, even for dramas, has tended to be more functional than interpretive. Exteriors and location shooting have been their *forté*, in part because studios have usually been small, makeshift, or non-existent, with the occasional purpose-built facility that is often expensive for the prevailing low-budget work.

In the years just before World War I a number of men, often drawn from the ranks of projectionists, entered the film business and remained in cinematography and/or its associated laboratory work over the next several decades. These included Bert Cross and Maurice •Bertel in Melbourne; Al Burne in Qld; and, in Sydney, Lacey •Percival, Bert •Segerberg, and the •Higgins Brothers: Ernest, Tasman and Arthur. Arthur Higgins was, perhaps, the most widely praised cinematographer of the era, and was particularly noted for his work with director Raymond •Longford. Typically, Higgins continued producing and directing his own films, while photographing films for others, until his death in 1963. Franklyn •Barrett was another early cameraman, who directed as well as photographed some outstanding silent feature dramas. Other cameramen/labmen and film technicians included Walter •Sully, William •Trerise, Reg Edwards, Claude Carter, Jack •Bruce, and Jack Fletcher. Stills photographer Frank •Hurley also entered the cinema in the early silent era, achieving fame not only as a cinematographer and film-maker, but also as an explorer and war-correspondent.

During the 1930s, the two major employers of cameramen were •Cinesound and Fox Movietone. The Sydney headquarters and regional networks of these companies supported and trained a group of cameramen and film technicians whose influence continued through the 1960s. Focused primarily on newsreel production, these men included Jim Pearson, Ross •Wood, and Ron Horner, all of whom ultimately became producers in their own right.

In the 1930s, Cinesound's modest but consistent output of features enabled cinematographers George •Heath and George •Malcolm to make the transition to a more sophisticated drama lighting style. After World War II, they were joined by Carl •Kayser, who had learned his craft in the United Kingdom and, later, by Ross Wood. Still unable to work entirely in features, these men nevertheless provided a core of drama talent for the occasional films of the •Chauvels, the •McCreadies and the Robinson–Rafferty team (see Robinson, Lee). Ross Wood, in particular, was able to operate also on a number of the imported overseas productions that provided Australian technicians with specialised drama experience on modern equipment. In contrast, even in the 1950s, local film production relied, as it had done since the silent era, on outmoded and makeshift equipment, kept operational through the broad, multi-skilled abilities of its technicians.

An important influence on postwar cinematography was the establishment in Sydney of a Commonwealth government film unit (see Film Australia). The unit significantly increased the amount of work available for cameramen and, at the same time, introduced artistic concerns into documentary film-making, including photography. An expansion of commercial, industrial, and educational film-making at this time further enlarged the pool of cinematographers, but many still operated as cinematographer–directors. From the mid 1950s, television began to provide the opportunity for more and more complex drama and commercials production, increased specialisation, and modern equipment. These developments laid the basis for the formation, in 1958, of the Australian Cinematographers Society, which has the aim of professional and social advancement for its members.

In the 1960s, a new generation of camera assistants, schooled in the strong traditions of the past, were swept up in the economic, social, and cultural transformations that led to the government-supported feature 'renaissance' of the 1970s (the new Australian cinema; see Revival, the), and the development of a freelance model of employment. Despite—or perhaps because of—their youth, the cinematographers of this period proved to have remarkable abilities as directors of photography, contributing greatly to the critical success of the new Australian cinema. By the 1980s, Hollywood was beginning to claim the energy, high creative standards, breadth of experience, and ability for fast work of many Australian cameramen—including Don •McAlpine, Russell •Boyd, Peter •James, John •Seale, and Dean •Semmler—who were working in Hollywood, where their energy, high creative standards, breadth of experience and ability for fast work were much sought after. Working overseas, Australian cinematographers were, for the first time, able to specialise exclusively in drama production.

Australian cinematography is now as much of an art as it is a craft, and it reflects the technological changes and attendant forces of globalisation that are transforming the country. Cinematographers have access to the most up-to-date technology, which is increasingly based in digital electronics. Overseas media corporations are establishing production bases in Australia, in part because of the high output, relatively low wages, and high technical standards provided by Australian technicians. Training has moved, to some degree, from an apprenticeship system to tertiary education. And, where once cinematography was largely the preserve of Anglo-Celtic working-class men, people (including women) from a range of ethnic backgrounds are now achieving a degree of success.   MARTHA ANSARA

Cinemedia   Born from the merger of Film Victoria and the State Film Centre of Victoria in July 1997, Cinemedia encourages, promotes, and assists the production, distribution, and exhibition of screen content and culture for entertainment, education, and information.

As part of this vision, Cinemedia is building the first Australian cultural institution solely dedicated to the moving image in all its forms: the Australian Centre for the Moving Image (ACMI). Currently under construction as part of the Federation Square precinct in Melbourne, ACMI will join a handful of new media centres that make up the global family of cultural institutions devoted to the moving image.

The Centre will become a focal point for Melbourne's screen events, with facilities to enhance how Victorians and visitors relate to the screen. ACMI's distinctive features include a giant outdoor screen continuously show-casing films and special events from around the world, an interactive screen gallery featuring digital art and exhibitions, an online videotheque with 30 consoles providing touch-screen access to the Australia's largest film and video collection, three cinemas (400, 200, and 25 seats), and educational, entertaining, and informative screen programs.

Cinemedia includes: Screen Education—provides screen literacy programs for teachers and students; the Melbourne Film Office—markets the Victorian film and television production industry; Film Victoria—invests in, develops, and supports the Victorian film and television industry; Cinemedia Access Collection—provides access to Australia's largest public lending library of film, video, and multimedia; Cinemedia Production Management—provides executive-producer services for screen-based projects; Cinemedia Online—manages new media technology research projects; Venues Management—provides theatres for hire; Screen Culture—funds screen-culture events, organisations, and initiatives; Multimedia 21 Fund—invests in, develops and supports the Victorian multimedia industry; ACMI in Federation Square—a focal point for Melbourne's screen events, with facilities to enhance how Victorians and visitors relate to the screen.   JACKIE COATES

Cinesound   Despite its reputation for having deliberately killed off local film production, the 'Combine' (Union Theatres/Australasian Films; see Greater Union Organisation) financed a number of feature films, from prewar films such as **The Shepherd of the Southern Cross** (1914), to more substantial postwar productions such as •**Painted Daughters** (1925), •**The Pioneers** (1926), •**For the Term of His Natural Life** (1927), and •**The Adorable Outcast** (1928). Success was mixed, but Stuart Doyle (see Greater Union Organisation), who headed both companies, formed the opinion that it was not just the economic slump but also the monopolistic practices of the American distributors that caused the films to fail. He began to favour an Australian production industry, and argued this before the 1927 Royal Commission into the Moving Picture Industry.

Circumstance

With the coming of sound, Doyle appointed his personal assistant, Ken G. *Hall, to head a new production wing of the company, Cinesound Productions. This continued to produce the weekly newsreel **Cinesound Review** and, in 1931, Hall began work on a feature film, the box-office success *On Our Selection (1932). This was followed by a further 16 features: *The Squatter's Daughter (1933), *The Silence of Dean Maitland (1934), *Strike Me Lucky (1934), *Grandad Rudd (1935), *Orphan of the Wilderness (1936), *Thoroughbred (1936), *Lovers and Luggers (1937), *Tall Timbers (1937), *It Isn't Done (1937), *Let George Do It (1938), *The Broken Melody (1938), *Dad and Dave Come to Town (1938), *Gone to the Dogs (1939), *Mr Chedworth Steps Out (1939), *Come up Smiling (1939), and *Dad Rudd MP (1940). All except **Come Up Smiling** were directed by Hall, and all, except **Strike Me Lucky**, quickly proved profitable.

Hall was an accomplished director, with a clear vision of the kind of film he wished to make—popular and accessible films, primarily for the Australian market, but based on Hollywood models. However, the credit for the success of the enterprise must be shared with the team he put together and led so ably. In contrast to the imported sound equipment used by rival *Efftee Productions, Arthur Smith, assisted by Clive Cross, pioneered the sound equipment used by the company, saving money by using his own inventions and bypassing patents held overseas. George *Heath became the main cinematographer, although Walter *Sully and Frank *Hurley worked on some films. William Shepherd did most of the editing. Fred Finlay did the art direction for the early films, then Eric Thompson and J. Alan Kenyon took over, the latter creating magnificent special effects such as the timber drive in **Tall Timbers** or the bush glade in the opening segment of **Orphan of the Wilderness**. Hamilton *Webber wrote much of the music, and work was provided for writers such as Frank *Harvey. This was the closest we came in Australia to a 'studio', meaning not merely a building (at Bondi Junction) but a team of people working together in continuous production.

Cinesound had the prestige to attract well-known local stage actors such as Bert *Bailey, and comedians such as George *Wallace, as well as importing talent from the United Kingdom (Charlotte Francis and John Longden) and the USA (Helen Twelvetrees and Lloyd Hughes). Shirley Ann *Richards ('discovered' by Hall) and Cecil *Kellaway (already established as a stage actor and comedian) both went on from Cinesound to successful careers in Hollywood.

Until feature production ceased during the war, a Cinesound feature was a familiar and popular part of the cinema experience for Australians for a decade, and the name carried on through documentaries and **Cinesound Review**, the weekly newsreel distributed from 1931 until 1970, one full-reel (10-minute) special issue of which won Australia's first Academy Award. The company's production ceased in 1975, but Cinesound films are still fondly remembered, and draw large audiences to both cinema and television retrospectives.

INA BERTRAND

Circumstance

1922. *Director*: Lawson Harris. *Production company*: Austral Super Films. *Scriptwriter*: Lawson Harris, Yvonne Pavis. *Director of photography*: Arthur Higgins. 5 reels. B&W. *Cast*: Yvonne Pavis (Hazel Dalwood), Lawson Harris (Richard Talbot), Carlton Max (Bernard St Clare), Gordon Collingridge, Cane Arthur.

A reviewer at the time found that this story strained credulity and, indeed, it does. A young woman is seduced and abandoned; many years later, when she is living as the protégée of a rich man and her child is being cared for by others, her lover returns, but does not recognise her until they are about to be married. About 19 minutes of the film survives, enough to capture the flavour and to show that the performances are more naturalistic than the story would suggest and that Arthur *Higgins' photography is up to his usual standard. The American production team of Lawson Harris and Yvonne Pavis went on to make **A Daughter of Australia** (1922) and *Sunshine Sally (1922), before returning to the USA.

IB

City's Child, A

1972. *Director/Producer*: Brian Kavanagh. *Script*: Don Battye from a story by Brian Kavanagh. *Director of photography*: Bruce McNaughton. *Music*: Peter Pinne. 78 min. *Cast*: Monica Maughan (the woman), Sean Scully (the man), Moira Carleton (the mother).

A lonely, middle-aged spinster cares for her bed-ridden mother, uncomplainingly suffering her taunts that she had been an unwanted child. After her mother dies the woman is unable to overcome her social alienation and withdraws into a world where fantasy and reality blur. She projects her fantasies of marriage and children on to her dolls before meeting a mysterious man. They become lovers, but the man disappears when she hears the dolls discussing how ill-suited they are. While running through the streets looking for him, she collapses. A doctor tells her neighbours that she is now pregnant.

Screenings at a number of international film festivals, favourable reviews comparing it to the work of Chabrol and Bunuel, and accolades at the 1972 Australian Film Awards did not help **A City's Child** achieve wide domestic release. Shot on 16 mm for $30 000 with assistance from the Experimental Film and Television Fund, the film is notable for

Monica •Maughan's performance and as one of the first government-assisted urban-set films of the revival (see Revival, the).   BEN GOLDSMITH

Clara Gibbings

1934. Director: F.W. Thring. *Production company:* Efftee Film Productions. *Scriptwriter:* Frank Harvey. From the play by Aimée and Phillip Stuart. *Director of photography:* Arthur Higgins. 81 min. B&W. *Cast:* Dorothy Brunton (Clara Gibbings), Campbell Copelin (Errol Kerr), Harvey Adams (Justin Kerr), Noel Boyd (Yolande Probyn), Harold Meade (Earl of Drumoor), Byrl Walkely (Lady Drumoor).

Stage actor Dorothy Brunton stars as Clara Gibbings, a Limehouse pub owner who discovers that she is the legitimate heir to a fortune, but chooses to abandon her claims rather than accept the false values of 'society'. There is not a single outdoor shot, and most of the action occurs within one indoor set—Errol Kerr's apartment. However, a mobile camera, more imaginative cutting than in •Efftee's earlier productions, and strong central performances carry the film along most enjoyably. Despite approval under the NSW Quota Act, the film had limited release and was not popular with Australian audiences. Nevertheless, this last feature film released by Efftee Productions won third prize in the federal government's 1935 Commonwealth Film Awards.   IB

Clarke, John (1948–) ACTOR Film has remained a secondary medium for John Clarke, Australia's pre-eminent political satirist, who was raised in Feilding in New Zealand where he first came to fame with his rural caricature 'Fred Dagg' in the 1970s. Clarke appeared in a couple of NZ films (such as **Dead Kids**, 1981) before emigrating to Melbourne, where he has developed a strong following, initially on television and then on radio, with his weekly political 'interview' with actor Bryan Dawe. Clarke was first seen in the cinema in a small role in the •**The Adventures of Barry McKenzie** (1972). His most notable screen performance was as Sam •Neill's loyal friend, and gravedigger, in John •Ruane's black comedy •**Death in Brunswick** (1991). Clarke was also 'Script editor' for •**Blood Oath** (1990), a film that examined allegations of Japanese war crimes against Australian prisoners on the island of Ambon, part of the Dutch East Indies. Reportedly, Clarke rewrote portions of Denis Whitburn's and Brian Williams's script while on location in Qld. He also played an inquiring reporter. Clarke co-wrote the script for **Lust and Revenge** (1996), Paul •Cox's biting attack on the Australian arts establishment. Clarke wrote and directed **Man and Boy** (1986), a short film for the ABC and **A Royal Commission into the Australian Economy** (1993). He also worked on the script for the television miniseries *Anzacs* (1985).

Other Australian films: •Lonely Hearts (1982), Les Patterson Saves the World (1987), Those Dear Departed (1987), A Matter of Convenience (1987), •Spotswood (1992), Greenkeeping (1992).   GM

Clay

1965. Director: Giorgio Mangiamele. *Producer:* Giorgio Mangiamele. *Scriptwriter:* Giorgio Mangiamele. *Director of photography:* Giorgio Mangiamele. 85 min. B&W. *Cast:* Janine Lebedew (Margot), George Dixon (Nick), Chris Tsalikis (Chris), Claude Thomas (father), Robert Clarke (Charles).

Financed by the director, with contributions from the whole cast and crew, this project was always a labour of love. Giorgio •Mangiamele performed all the major technical roles; when he called the result a 'dream' he was referring to the achievement of a long-sought goal, as well as to the atmosphere of the film. The story is the old one of a criminal on the run falling in love with the girl who befriends and shelters him, and who is betrayed to the police by a jealous rival. The film was shot at Montsalvat artists' colony in the outer-Melbourne suburb of Eltham. The largely amateur cast do the best they can with the minimal dialogue, but the film's artistic pretensions constantly get in the way. Its great strength is Mangiamele's superb monochrome photography, which reveals a talent that was largely wasted in those years just before the feature film revival. The film was invited to the Cannes Film Festival, but Mangiamele had to finance this himself when the Australian government refused assistance.   IB

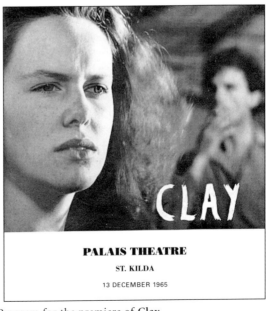

Program for the premiere of **Clay**

Clayton, John (1940–) ACTOR A familiar face on television and in films since the mid 1970s, and a regular performer in the theatre, John Clayton is one of Australia's most competent and versatile character actors. Rarely has he been allowed to occupy centre stage in the cinema for long, except for the incoherent **Cappucino** (1989) and Bob •Ellis's bitter-sweet drama, **Unfinished Business** (1986), yet his presence provides a solid backbone to any production. Clayton captured the appropriate tone of superficiality and friendship as Bill Todd, Ray •Barrett's old military colleague, who betrays him, in the underrated •**Goodbye Paradise** (1983). Other strong supporting performances include the role of Col in •**Hightide** (1987), the out-of-work football coach in •**Warm Nights on a Slow Moving Train** (1988), and the mayor in the bizarre thriller •**The Everlasting Secret Family** (1988). Since the late 1980s Clayton has worked in television, notably in the successful series *Police Rescue* and, more recently, *Heartbreak High*, and *Water Rats*.

Other Australian films include: Sidecar Racers (1975), High Rolling (1977), •The Irishman (1978), •Dawn! (1979), •Newsfront (1978), •Palm Beach (1980), Maybe This Time (1980), Freedom (1982), Ginger Meggs (1982), •Far East (1982), Midnite Spares (1983), Vicious (1987), Boundaries of the Heart (1988), Breaking Loose (1988), Out of the Body (1988), Kokoda Crescent (1988), Sebastian and the Sparrow (1989), Shotgun Wedding (1994), All Men are Liars (1995).   GM

Clifford, Colleen (1898–1996) ACTOR Somerset-born Colleen Clifford arrived in Australia in 1954, after the death of her husband, leaving behind a theatrical career that had included work with Laurence Olivier and Noel Coward. She settled in Perth, where she founded the Theatre Guild and became a theatrical director and producer, nurturing the careers of others, as well as continuing to perform herself—on stage, television, and in films. Her sweet smile and halo of soft white hair were a familiar sight on television, and in film roles such as Ettie in •**Careful, He Might Hear You** (1983), Miss Strehlow in **Where the Green Ants Dream** (1984), Mrs Haversham in **The Coca-Cola Kid** (1985), and Gran Olson in •**The Year My Voice Broke** (1987). Her last film role was as Mrs Waterson in **Frauds** (1993), at the age of 95.   IB

Clinic, The

1983. *Director*: David Stevens. *Producers*: Robert Le Tet, Bob Weis. *Scriptwriter*: Greg Millin. *Director of photography*: Ian Baker. *Music director*: Redmond Symons. 93 min. *Cast*: Chris Haywood (Dr Eric Linden), Simon Burke (Paul Armstrong), Gerda Nicolson (Linda), Rona McLeod (Dr Carol Young), Suzanne Roylance (Pattie).

This unpretentious, kindly film finds humour in the unlikely setting of a clinic for the treatment of sexually transmitted diseases. It adopts an anecdotal approach to its portrayal of a day in the life of the clinic, addressing itself matter-of-factly, and without prurience to the range of problems that confront the staff. There is some attempt to strengthen the film's narrative line by foregrounding the initial homophobia of medical student Paul and his growing respect for humane gay doctor Eric (the excellent Chris •Haywood, stalwart character player of the 1970s and 1980s film revival; see Revival, the). There is also an especially perceptive character sketch from Pat •Evison as a kind-hearted counsellor. **The Clinic** stresses the need for more sympathetic sex education, and its comedy is never at the expense of sexual difficulties or those who suffer from them. The film scarcely moves outside the clinic, but manages to suggest a large bustling city ambience.   BMcF

Club, The (aka David Williamson's The Club)

1980. *Director*: Bruce Beresford. *Producer*: Matt Carroll. *Scriptwriter*: David Williamson. Based on the play, *The Club*, by David Williamson. *Director of photography*: Don McAlpine. *Music*: Mike Brady. 96 min. *Cast*: Jack Thompson (Laurie Holden), Harold Hopkins (Danny Rowe), Graham Kennedy (Ted Parker), John Howard (Geoff Hayward), Frank Wilson (Jock Riley).

Released later in the same year as Bruce •Beresford's •'Breaker' Morant, this film shares its interest in the dynamics of men caught up in conflicting tensions in an enclosed world (a courtroom in the earlier film, a football club here) and an interest in the shifts of power in hierarchical situations. Whereas 'Breaker' Morant is set in the Boer War and leads to tragedy, **The Club** is essentially a comedy, centred on the attempts to make a highly paid recruit to a Melbourne club look foolish, and to call into question whether the coach, Laurie, should be replaced in the hope of lifting the club from its place on the bottom of the ladder. The comedy is located in the play of politics between the boardroom and the actual games, especially in the performance of Frank •Wilson as the devious president; so is the drama of loyalties and opportunism, of management versus players.   BMcF

Cluff, Jennifer (1956–) ACTOR Jennifer Cluff had appeared in two undistinguished films—**Final Cut** (1980) and **Brothers** (1982)—before giving an impressive performance as the tenacious wife of the Agent Orange victim in Bill •Bennett's •**A Street to Die** (1985), a plainly and sympathetically filmed account of what was then a major issue. She conveyed poignantly the ordinary woman who finds unexpected courage in the face of imminent personal tragedy. Since then she has shown in the telemovie *Jilted* (1987), and in •**Backlash** (1986) and **Spider and Rose** (1994), both also directed by her husband Bennett, that she has a likeable talent with which movies have done too little.

She had been on television since her teens, notably in *Seven Little Australians*.

Other Australian films: •Kiss or Kill (1997, ac, prod.). BMcF

Coard, Dennis ACTOR Slight, reflective-looking, Dennis Coard has made few films, but his performance in Ray •Argall's •**Return Home** (1990) ensures his place in the story of new Australian cinema (see Revival, the). In this well-regarded piece of lovingly observed realism, he gave a shrewd, wholly sympathetic account of the divorced Melbourne insurance broker who returns to his former home in an Adelaide seaside suburb and rediscovers the kinds of values with which he has lost touch and which, he realises, make his garage-owning brother's life more fulfilling than his. His other films include **Blowing Hot and Cold** (1989) and **Jigsaw** (1990). He had a continuing role in the popular television series, *Home and Away*. BMcF

Coleby, Robert (1947–) ACTOR This English actor has worked primarily in Australian theatre and television, and only sporadically in the Australian cinema, since 1975. Coleby's status as a leading man in television series such as *Patrol Boat* (1979) has not been matched in the cinema, except for a lead role in the romantic drama **Now and Forever** (1983). In this film, adapted from a story by Danielle Steele, Coleby plays opposite American actress Cheryl Ladd, as a man wrongfully convicted of rape. Otherwise his screen opportunities have been disappointingly few, such as that of Captain Horton in the comic book adventure **The Phantom** (1996).

Other Australian film: Real Macaw, The (1998). GM

Collette, Toni (1972–) ACTOR Few Australian actors have had so rapid an ascent to international stardom as Toni Collette, who is now in demand for films in several continents. In 1989 she won a scholarship to the Australian Theatre for Young People, and she also studied at the National Institute of Dramatic Art in 1991–92. Her stage roles include Cordelia in *King Lear* in 1994. Far from conventionally attractive, Collette has never shrunk from roles that many might have considered dangerously charmless, however dramatically meaty. After a small role as Ben •Mendelsohn's girlfriend in •**Spotswood** (1992), for which she was nominated for an AFI Supporting Actress award, and the short film, **This Marching Girl Thing** (1994), she found major success as the overweight, larcenous, ABBA-besotted heroine of •**Muriel's Wedding** (1994), for which she won the AFI Best Actress award. Muriel's coming to terms with her own identity and with her dysfunctional family, especially with her bullying father, and with the wedding-centred ideology of her patriarchal, lower middle-class Qld world, is as moving and detailed as any characterisation in 1990s cinema.

Since then, she has worked prolifically, but without finding another starring role that offered her such opportunities. However, she made a sharp impression in •**The Boys** (1998) as the (badly) dyed-blonde sex-hungry girlfriend of the newly released criminal played by David •Wenham, and she is very touching in the British film **Velvet Goldmine** (1998), as the cast-off wife of a bisexual glam-rock star. In these two films, as in **Muriel's Wedding**, she shows a real gift for defining the feelings of apparently shallow, inarticulate young women. Her gifts failed to equip her to play Harriet Smith in the British film version of **Emma** (1996), in which she seemed physically and vocally at odds with all she was given to do and say, and in the unfortunately timed Australian **Diana and Me** (1997) she showed little feeling for the romantic comedy genre, as a Woollongong girl who wins a trip to Britain to meet her namesake, Diana Spencer. Increasingly, it looks as if her work will take her overseas, and her several 1999 releases include **Eight and a Half Women** for British arthouse doyen, Peter Greenaway, and the US-based **The Sixth Sense**, with Bruce Willis.

Other Australian films: •Lillian's Story (1996, AFI Supporting Actress award), •Cosi (1996). BMcF

Robert Coleby

Colosimo, Rosa (1949–) PRODUCER/WRITER Rosa Colosimo arrived in Australia from Italy at the age of two, and grew up in the Melbourne suburb of Fitzroy. After graduation from Melbourne University, she became a teacher of Italian, and opened a bookshop to sell imported books and teaching aids. On a purchasing trip to Italy, she brought back two Italian feature films, which she distributed. She then began to produce short teaching films and, in 1982, was hired by Bob Weis as ethnic adviser on the television series *Waterfront*. This galvanised her into becoming a feature producer and, between 1985 and 1991, she wrote and/or produced eight feature films: **The Still Point** (1985, w., p.), **Hungry Heart** (1987, p.), **A Sting in the Tail** (1989, w., p.), **Closer and Closer Apart** (1989, p.), **Blowing Hot and Cold** (w., p.), **A Kink in the Picasso** (1990, ex. p.), **Jigsaw** (1990, p.), and •**On My Own** (1993, ex. p.). In 1992, she moved to Qld for a short while, then returned to Melbourne to make documentaries (**The India Connection** 1995; **Merchant of Dreams** 1994) and multimedia productions. Her stated ambition is still a high-budget, critically acclaimed feature film.   IB

Colosimo, Vince ACTOR   For a brief moment in the early 1980s, Colosimo was a name to contend with in Australian cinema. He starred as the disaffected teenage hero of Michael •Pattinson's •**Moving Out** (1983), a touching, accurately and sympathetically observed account of what it was like to be the go-between for his ethnic family in an alien community. Colosimo played with the right moodiness that seemed to derive from a sense that, whatever decisions were made, nothing would be easy for him. This film's plain, unpretentious honesty was missing from Colosimo's follow-up film, **Street Hero** (1984), made by the same director, scriptwriter (Jan •Sardi), and cameraman (Vincent •Monton). This was a much slicker production in some ways, more obviously influenced by the then-popular teen movies than by the actualities of multicultural Melbourne. Colosimo played another non-conformist hero, this time with a boxing potential that justifies the display of his well-oiled pectorals, but his performance is less interesting, less painful, than in the earlier film. He has not filmed since, but has pursued a career on the stage.   BMcF

Come Up Smiling (Ants in His Pants)

1939. Director: William Freshman. *Producer:* Ken G. Hall. *Scriptwriter:* William Freshman. Based on a story by John Addison Chandler [Ken G. Hall]. *Director of photography:* George Heath. *Music:* Henry Krips. 77 min. B&W. *Cast:* Will Mahoney (Barney O'Hara), Shirley Ann Richards (Eve Cameron), Jean Hatton (Pat), Evie Hayes (Kitty Katkin), Alec Kellaway ('The Killer'), Chips Rafferty (extra).

Come Up Smiling weaves a convoluted plot around a series of musical and comic set pieces. American vaudeville star Will Mahoney plays Barney, a two-bit circus performer whose love for his niece Pat is almost as powerful as his fear

of the boxing champ 'The Killer' and an equally urgent abhorrence of the bagpipes. Pat dreams of a successful singing career, but her moment of triumph, an appearance before the European maestro Signor Rudolpho, becomes a moment of truth when her voice suddenly gives way. An expensive operation is required and Barney resolves to help, inadvertently agreeing to fight 'The Killer' for a cash prize. It is only with the timely intervention of a bagpipe band, some carefully positioned ants, and a literal 'slate' of hand (in which Barney's gloves are dipped in concrete) that he is able to win the day. The film holds substantial interest as the only •Cinesound feature not directed by grandee Ken G. •Hall and, as such, confirms that the studio had its own 'house style'. Multiple locations, a talented but motherless heroine, distinct switching between burlesque and melodrama, heavy reliance on special effects that were dated (even for the day), and a preponderance of smutty double *entendres* mark this production as typical of Cinesound.

DEB VERHOEVEN

Comedy

Comedy   In the wake of the local and international success of •**Strictly Ballroom** (1992), •**The Adventures of Priscilla, Queen of the Desert** (1994), and •**Muriel's Wedding** (1994), Australian cinema has become synonymous with comedy. The box-office challenge of lowbrow comedy to the cultural dominance of arthouse features has been a recurring pattern in Australian cinema since the shortlived reign of 'ocker' comedies in the early 1970s was quashed by the advent of 'quality' period films in 1975. The arthouse film, inaugurated by •**Picnic at Hanging Rock** (1975), retained cultural, if not box-office, supremacy until the mid 1980s, when the unprecedented commercial success of •**Crocodile Dundee** (1986) marked a simultaneous return of comedy and audiences to Australian cinema. A shift in the industry from cultural to commercial imperatives, represented by 10BA (see Finance) tax concessions in the 1980s and Australian Film Finance Corporation (FFC) (see Finance) criteria for film funding in the 1990s, has consolidated the place of comedy as a viable category of film investment. However, comedy (with the exception of the ocker film) has yet to attract the critical attention accorded to Australian films that lend themselves readily to auteurist, social realist, or national identity agendas.

Comedy as an 'inferior', popular genre remains notoriously difficult to define. It is recognised through an interplay of visual gags and verbal jokes in either comedian-driven or ensemble-based narratives that actively deflate heroic aspirations. •**Idiot Box** (1997) offers a succinct definition of the two basic formal elements of comedy in the repeated exchange between the two male protagonists of a physical 'trick' (gag) for a verbal 'poem' (joke). In comedian films, running gags and jokes are held together by the picaresque adventures of a central comic or grotesque character (Stork, Barry McKenzie, Alvin Purple, Mick Dundee, Young Einstein, Muriel, and so on). Alternatively, a single gag can provide the structural pivot of the narrative (remote-control gadgets in •**Malcolm, 1986**; the talking pig in •**Babe, 1995**). At the other end of the spectrum, comic narratives work with an ensemble of actors and tend toward either the carnivalesque subversion of norms (**Dallas Doll**, 1993; •**Cosi** 1996), pre-oedipal wish fulfilment (•**The Castle**, 1997), or oedipal compromise and social integration (**The Best of Friends**, 1982; •**Strictly Ballroom** 1992). Since 1970, Australian comedy has been dominated by the ocker film and its mutant offspring, grotesque comedies of suburban life. Romantic comedy has been a minor strain, an infrequent and unfamiliar note in a cinema tuned into masculine myths of national identity. These myths have come under harsh scrutiny in the 1990s, in a series of comic films directed by women.

Although an irreverent, self-deprecating sense of humour has been posited as a defining characteristic of Australian identity, the incursion of women writers, producers, and directors into post-ocker comedy has produced a critical mass of films that are deeply derisive of the masculine foibles enshrined in 'Australian' humour. Jane Campion's •**Sweetie** (1989) and Monica Pellizari's **Fistful of Flies** (1997) project blackly comic visions of suburban fathers overwhelmed by their daughters' sexuality. Shirley Barrett's •**Love Serenade** (1996) and Sue Brooks's •**Road to Nhill** (1997), both set in isolated country towns, relentlessly undercut male pretensions of mastery and potency before letting their hapless victims off the hook. Emma-Kate Croghan's •**Love and Other Catastrophes** (1996), Megan Simpson-Huberman's •**Dating the Enemy** (1996), and Cherie Nowlan's •**Thank God He Met Lizzie** (1997) look to Hollywood and Europe to redefine romantic comedy, while Clara Law's •**Floating Life** (1996) deploys the icons of Australiana to subvert the basic tenets of anglo-Australian identity.

Australian film comedy since 1970 owes little to earlier comic traditions of the silent period and the studio era of the 1930s. Raymond •**Longford's** classic larrikin romance •**The Sentimental Bloke** (1919) has generated no equivalent, although the film's inner-city, working-class milieu, its mateship rituals of drinking and gambling, and its comic use of the vernacular prefigure aspects of the 1970s ocker films. The popularity of vaudeville entertainers, Roy 'Mo' •**Rene**, George •**Wallace**, and Frank •**Thring**, who translated their comic talents to film in the 1930s, established a precedent for the popular success of contemporary stand-up comedians who have made the transition from theatrical revue and television to cinema, notably Barry •**Humphries** (Dame Edna Everage, Les Patterson), Paul •**Hogan** (Mick

Dundee), the Australian Performing Group (•**Dimboola** 1979), and the Frontline team (•**The Castle**).

One reason for the lack of continuity between the early period and post-1970 comedies (apart from the thirty-year break in feature film production) is that the surviving film comedies of the early cinema championed the bush ethos. The rural Hayseeds and their close relatives, the Rudd family, featured in a series of silent and sound comedies, including three versions of •**On Our Selection** (1920, 1932, 1995). Their slapstick affirmation of the canny father, his educated daughter, and his cretinous son who manage to outwit city slickers, finds faint echoes in Barry McKenzie's colonial innocence that facilitates his triumph over swinging Londoners in •**The Adventures of Barry McKenzie** (1972). The narrative journey from the bush to the metropolis and home again in the 1920s and 1930s is reversed in the cinema of the revival period (see Revival, the). In **The Adventures of Priscilla, Queen of the Desert**, Priscilla, the converted bus, takes her reluctant Sydney drag queens on a perilous journey through the pubs and desolate landscapes of outback Australia to Alice Springs, only to affirm that there's no place like an inner-city Sydney nightclub.

A distinctive feature of the early comedies is the happy ending that affirms the family farm as the essence of Australianness (**The Sentimental Bloke**, •**The Hayseeds, On Our Selection**, •**It Isn't Done**, 1937). The comic spirit of Steele Rudd is revived in **The Castle**, whose rural idyll is a quarter-acre block next to the airport. Like **Dallas Doll** and **Babe**, **The Castle** affirms the backblock as a site of comic reversal and arcadian liberation in the face of entrepreneurial greed and manipulation.

The ocker comedies of the 1970s reacted against the bush ethos and its heroic myth, which celebrated mateship, war, and the bush as the testing grounds of masculinity. The deflation of the bush legend by the urban ocker comedy that lampoons masculinity in its grotesque forms has generated a sustained critical debate, revisited by successive writers on Australian film. The archetype of this controversial genre proved to be **The Adventures of Barry McKenzie**. The key to the appeal of the ocker film was its simultaneous parody and celebration of the rituals of mateship, updated from the bush legend of the 1890s to the urban counterculture of the 1970s. Bazza McKenzie travels to swinging London where his rise to fame begins when he masquerades as a rugged Aussie stockman in a cigarette commercial, and culminates in a clash between high and low culture on a BBC television arts program that ends in chaos as Bazza drops his pants for the cameras. The film thrives on lambasting the obnoxious colonial abroad, at the same time that it revels in its own production of a hyper-Australian vernacular.

The curiously asexual ocker cycle that began with a sex survey film, •**The Naked Bunyip** (1970), peaked with the popular sex comedy •**Alvin Purple** (1973) and declined with •**Don's Party** (1976). Tom O'Regan (*The Australian Screen*, 1989) argues that the early success of the genre owed much to its connections with the 'rough theatre' of La Mama, the Pram Factory, and the Australian Performing Group, as well as the innovative television comedy of Mavis Bramston, Norman Gunston, and Aunty Jack. Paul Hogan, who went on to make the most successful Australian blockbuster of the 1980s (**Crocodile Dundee**), created his populist ocker persona, 'Hoges', in stand-up television comedy spots and Winfield cigarette advertisements. The urban ocker comedies enabled a certain global mobility for their 'fish-out-of-water' characters, who took their audiences on a survey of different (decidedly modern) social worlds, a precedent set by the character of the Italian journalist newly arrived in Sydney in Michael Powell's comedy •**They're a Weird Mob** (1966). Even Mick Dundee, outback crocodile hunter, ends his journey in that most urban of environments, a New York subway.

If **Crocodile Dundee** can be considered a canny reprise of residual elements of the ocker comedy for an international marketplace, **Sweetie** and •**Death in Brunswick** (1991) staked out new local territory for comedy, taking it deep into the grotesque heart of Australian suburban ugliness. In her book *The Unruly Woman* (1995), Kathleen Rowe defines the grotesque in terms of 'dismemberment, horror, death, and taboo', elements that are essential to the black comedy of **Sweetie** and **Death in Brunswick**. Both films create out-of-kilter worlds where the sins of the parents are visited upon their unruly offspring, a structuring theme in **Strictly Ballroom**, **Muriel's Wedding** and **Fistful of Flies**. These are purgatorial comedies whose endings (with the notable exceptions of **Strictly Ballroom** and **Floating Life**) are barely redemptive. Key scenes in suburban grotesque films ground the genre's comic attitude in a grim recognition of death as the cost of social renewal. Graveyards figure as comic sites in **Death in Brunswick**, **Sweetie**, **Fistful of Flies**, and **Floating Life**, and the burnt-out backyard in **Muriel's Wedding** is the mother's visual suicide note satirising Australian family life.

Whereas **Sweetie** pursues a monocultural itinerary, skewed slightly by its female perspective, **Death in Brunswick** maps a multicultural suburban milieu that has not been so acutely observed since **They're a Weird Mob**. In the last film, Nino Culotta, an Italian journalist working as a builder's labourer, provides a bird's-eye view of Sydney's working class. In **Death in Brunswick** Sam Neill's character is the stranger in his own suburb who becomes embroiled in the enmities between his Greek and Turkish neighbours. **Floating Life** brings a Chinese diaspora perspective to Australian cinema, transplanting a Hong Kong family into a suburban wasteland whose hazards are deftly negotiated by the ageing parents in a rare comedy of family reunification. A truly utopian scene of social integration that embraces gender, and generational and ethnic differences is achieved in one of the most popular of the 1990s comedies, **Strictly Ballroom**. The film's happy ending, based on the formation of the heterosexual couple and resolution of the oedipal conflict, is a rarity in Australian comedy where romance is usually sidelined in favour of either mateship or women's independence.

Romantic comedy made a tentative appearance in 1982 with the release of **The Best of Friends**, •**Lonely Hearts** (1982), and •**'Norman Loves Rose'** (1982), only to disappear until •**The Big Steal** (1990) and **Green Card** (1991) paved the way for three romantic comedies directed by women making their first features: **Love and Other Catastrophes**, **Dating the Enemy**, and **Thank God He Met Lizzie**. The low-key 1982 comedies rely on the device of mismatched couples and the expectations of their respective families to create muted comic resolutions to parochial problems of sexuality, friendship, and kinship. The ending of **The Best of Friends** exemplifies the estranged ground of sexual relations in Australian cinema in a beach scene, in which the reluctant bride is publicly corralled into a marriage with her best friend, the former star of the Alvin Purple sex comedies.

A new generation of women film-makers has had some success with romantic comedy as the quintessential (American) genre of the modern woman. The films take their cues from international cinema, quoting key scenes from classic Hollywood and French films (**Love and Other Catastrophes**), borrowing the key device of the gender-switch from cross-dressing films (**Dating the Enemy**), or adding a skeptical twist to the wedding film (**Thank God He Met Lizzie**). **Love and Other Catastrophes** takes a lesson from Eric Rohmer and rematches its mismatched couples for a happy ending. In a less sanguine interpretation of the genre, the final, sombre scene from **Thank God He Met Lizzie**, of the not-so-perfect couple unloading the station wagon and two children for a beach picnic, is a wry reality-check on Hollywood's remarriage comedies where the rightness of the couple is assured.

The popular success of comedy has always been a matter of good timing in the Australian film industry. The ocker comedies of the early 1970s established an audience for a resurgent national cinema. **Crocodile Dundee** marked the success of an international perspective at a time when the industry was changing its focus from cultural to commercial imperatives. The FFC-supported industry of the 1990s has achieved popular recognition of a post-ocker Australianness through its distinctive suburban grotesque and romantic comedies, often the first features of a new, mobile generation of film-makers looking beyond the bush ethos and postwar suburbia to Hollywood, Europe, and Hong Kong for comic inspiration.

FELICITY COLLINS

Commonwealth Film Unit *see* **Film Australia**

Conferences Australia's population being largely around the edges of the continent, conferences are occasions for movement around the country and personal contact, rather than the more indirect and impersonal telephone, mail, or email. They also bind organisations together, providing an opportunity for members to exchange information and ideas, renew old friendships, and make new ones. These gatherings also represent the public face of an organisation. They are occasions for initiating or cementing business deals and professional connections, advertising new products, introducing clients to service providers, and publicising new technical or administrative developments.

For the first half of the century, to be a part of the Australian film industry usually meant to be an exhibitor, as production was limited and distribution almost entirely in the hands of foreign companies. The first film conferences were held for exhibitors, with distributors vying for custom in a brisk marketplace. Each state had its own Motion Picture Exhibitors Association (MPEA), but not all held regional conferences. Eventually the conference of the Qld MPEA became accepted as the national event. Held annually since 1945 (from 1967 always on the Gold Coast) this is now the oldest ongoing film conference in Australia, and is known as the Australian Movie Convention. It is both a conference and a trade show—bringing exhibitors from all over Australia together with national and international distributors, including those distributing local productions—for four days of film screenings, seminar discussions, and intense socialising. The convention also hosts the Australian Box-Office Achievement Awards, the Ansett Australian Star of the Year Award, the Kodak Marketing Award for an Australian film, and the Ken G. Hall Award, sponsored by the National Film and Sound Archive (see Archives) for an outstanding contribution to the Australian industry.

With the revival of feature film production since the sixties (see Revival, the), new conferences have arisen to meet the needs of the production industry. As professionals move freely between film and television production, craft guilds are often combined into 'screen' organisations, implying both film and television and, increasingly, multimedia as well. Because every screen project is the result of the combined efforts of a team of specialists, conferences are sometimes the only opportunity available for directors to speak to other directors, writers to other writers, editors to other editors, actors to other actors. So most of the screen crafts conduct regular conferences, often moving the location to encourage maximum participation. On these occasions, office bearers are elected to national associations, national policy is discussed, and lobbying programs planned. The opportunity is also taken to draw on the expertise of invited international speakers, and to listen to (and sometimes challenge) government spokespeople on the arts.

The biennial National Screen Directors' Conference, sponsored by the Australian Screen Directors Association (ASDA), is one such occasion. The second of these was held in 1995 at the •Australian Film, Television and Radio School in Sydney. In 1995 the ASDA's annual meeting took place in conjunction with a film screening on the opening night, followed by two full days of keynote addresses and panel discussions.

Another is the annual conference of the Screen Producers Association of Australia (SPAA), an organisation for producers, post-production houses and studio facilities, equipment and material suppliers to the industry, film lawyers, accountants, and completion guarantors. The eleventh conference, held in Melbourne in 1995, was a three-day feast of keynote speakers, plenary panels and discussions, and a trade show that involved members of SPAA and those who wanted to bring creative ideas and technical developments to their attention. A popular feature every year is the pitching competition, sponsored by lawyers Holding Redlich, with a first prize of a trip to the Cannes Film Festival and a hope that any good presentation will find a producer among the audience.

There are two very different biennial conferences for writers. The National Screenwriters Conference, held in odd-numbered years, is a large event, with generous private and government sponsorship. There are usually several international guest speakers, and participants include producers and industry administrators as well as professional screenwriters. The sixth was held in 1995, at Terrigal in NSW, with three and a half days comprising five major streams (adaptation, assessment, the contemporary scene, script to screen, and futures), screenings, marketplaces, plenaries, a dinner and quiz, theoretical sessions, games, and private pitches. In even-numbered years, the Australian Writers Guild (AWG) offers a more modest affair, usually held in NSW and attended by AWG members and associates: presentations are largely by Australians, and there is a particularly strong 'new writers' stream to encourage new talent.

The Society of Motion Picture and Television Engineers holds biennial conferences in Sydney for their members and other interested people. Over four days participants are offered open tutorials, technical presentations and themed discussions, as well as a large trade show: in 1997 the sessions covered television broadcasting production and post-production technology, film production, post-production, exhibition, convergence, and the Internet. It also looked forward to the Sydney Olympics in 2000.

In the early years of craft conferences, gatherings concentrated on their own craft/s but, in the 1990s, they are increasingly interacting with each other: for instance, 'Turning Potential into Performance' was held in Melbourne in 1996, jointly sponsored by ASDA and the National Performance Conference, with the intention of bringing together actors and directors in an exploration of the actor/director relationship.

Increasingly, film-industry conferences are integrating other media, and film is being integrated into the program of multimedia conferences. The Australian Interactive Multimedia Industry Association has been holding annual conferences since 1994, rotating around the state capitals: film is part of all the strands of these conferences—creative, technical, and marketing.

Bridging all the crafts is the biennial International Documentary Conference. This conference is organisationally independent of the various state bodies with a special interest in documentary, and it is also independent of the Documentary Alliance (which links all these) but, as it moves around the states, it is people most interested in documentary in that state who help to organise it. It brings together documentary producers and distributors, policy-makers, teachers, and service industry members, with conference discussions around matters of documentary principles and practice. There is a very rich parallel film program, with screenings introduced by producers and writers, and some work-in-progress presented for discussion.

These national events are supplemented by regional gatherings like QTech in Qld, or the seminars organised by the Film and Television Institute in Perth. There are also occasional conferences constructed around themes such as the centenary of cinema, celebrated at various times over the period 1994 to 1996. In addition to special sessions within some of the regular conferences (for instance 1995 ASDA), several special events recognised the centenary. 'Going to the Pictures', sponsored by the Australian Theatre Historical Society, attracted both exhibitors and academics interested in the history of cinemas and exhibition. 'The Dawn of Cinema', sponsored jointly by the Museum of Sydney and the Museum of Contemporary Art, brought together Australian and international experts on the early history of film.

The rise of film study in secondary schools and universities from the 1960s onwards has produced an academic community that occasionally contributes to industry conferences such as those run by the ASDA and the International Documentary Conference, and that also conducts its own national gatherings. The first academic organisation to sponsor conferences was the Tertiary Screen Education Association (Vic.), which held several state and national events in the late 1970s. This organisation segued into the Australian Screen Studies Association, which held national conferences in 1982 and 1984, but then faded away.

The organisation representing primary and secondary teachers of film and media studies is ATOM (Australian Teachers of Media), which holds biennial conferences, hosted in turn by its various state branches (the eighth was held in Brisbane in 1995). Australian and international keynote speakers, panel sessions, workshops designed to enhance classroom practice, and many screenings are regular highlights of these gatherings.

Harder to pigeonhole is the History and Film Conference, held biennially since 1981, rotating around the state capitals and, from 1996, including New Zealand. Initiated by tertiary screen educators, this conference is designed to bridge the professional barriers between industry practitioners, film archivists, and (secondary and tertiary) teachers of film-making, film study, and film history. Its focus is also broad—not simply the history of film, but the representation of history in film and the role of film within history.

None of these conferences could continue without the financial and moral support of film-industry bodies (television networks, equipment manufacturers, production and distribution companies, the •Australian Film Institute) and government bodies (•Australian Film Commission, state film bodies, the Australian Broadcasting Corporation), which also conduct occasional conferences themselves. The plethora of film gatherings, whether they are called 'conferences', 'seminars', 'events', or 'symposiums', can be traced through the diary pages of industry journals such as *Encore*. An enthusiast could spend his/her whole life moving from one to another—a sign, perhaps, of a vibrant film culture, or maybe of an Australian capacity to 'talk the leg off an iron pot'.   INA BERTRAND

Connell, David CINEMATOGRAPHER David Connell was director of photography on many feature films in Australia, including **Fortress** (1986), **Slate, Wyn and Me** (1987), **Bushfire Moon** (1987), **Les Patterson Saves the World** (1987), **Boulevard of Broken Dreams** (1988, for which he was nominated for the Australian Film Institute Cinematography Award), •**Heaven Tonight** (1990, for which he won the Australian Cinematographers Society (ACS) Silver Award), **What the Moon Saw** (1990), **Hunting** (1991, with Dan •Burstall), **Over the Hill** (1992), **Gross Misconduct** (1983), and **Hercules Returns** (1993). In later years he also worked overseas, on feature films such as **The Never-Ending Story II** (USA, 1989) and **Fifty Fifty** (USA 1990), and on short films such as **Secrets** (NZ, 1991). He has worked extensively in television, perhaps his best-known work being on the miniseries *All the Rivers Run* and the telemovie *Barracuda*, for which he won an ACS Silver Award.   IB

Connolly, Robert (Bob), *see* **Anderson, Robin and Connolly, Bob**

Coolangatta Gold, The

1984. *Director*: Igor Auzins. *Producer*: John Weiley. *Scriptwriter*: Peter Schreck. Developed from an idea by Max Oldfield and a story by Ted Robinson and Peter Schreck. *Director of photography*: Keith Wagstaff. *Music*: Bill Conti. 112 min. *Cast*: Joss McWilliam (Steve), Nick Tate (The father: Joe), Colin Friels (Adam), Josephine Smulders (Kerry), Robyn Nevin (The mother: Roslyn).

This family melodrama, offering a critique of aggressive male competitiveness, was unfavourably received by both critics and public, although it had at least the virtues of energy and of spectacular visual appeal. Its plot focuses on the sporting obsessions of Joe Lucas who, 20 years earlier, had been beaten in the Gold Coast Iron Man contest. Now, he is determined that his elder son, Adam, will wrest the title from reigning champion (played by real-life champion Grant Kenny), whose father had defeated Joe. Joe's relentless concentration on Adam leads to tensions as he neglects his younger son's karate ambitions and marginalises his wife's role in the family. The film does not draw the family conflicts with much psychological subtlety or detail, but the intense effort involved in the physical activities is persuasively shot, and the camera does justice to the beauty of the natural environment. BMcF

Coorab in the Island of Ghosts

1929. *Director*: Francis Birtles, Torrance McLaren. *Director of photography*: Francis Birtles. B&W.

Francis Birtles made his name as an adventurer, cycling alone around Australia, driving from London to Sydney, or travelling over the route of early explorers. He financed his adventuring with films, such as **Across Australia** (1912), **Into Australia's Unknown** (1915), and **Across Australia in the Track of Burke and Wills** (1915), as did others such as Frank •Hurley and J.E. Ward (•**Australia's Own**) in the 1920s and 1930s or, later, Keith Adams and the Leyland brothers. The last film released under Birtles's name, **Coorab** is a narrative fiction, whereas before he had produced only descriptive documentaries. This raises some questions of authenticity: there is no reason to suppose he did not operate the camera, but there is considerable doubt about how much credit should go to him (or to Torrance McLaren) for the film's present form.

The tinted print held in the National Film and Sound Archive seems to be complete, and tells the story of Coorab, a tribal Aborigine of 'the Southern Hills', and Coowangama, his childhood sweetheart, promised in marriage to an elder, Ooian. Coorab engineers the death of his rival, and spends the rest of his long life with Coowangama. The climax is an initiation ritual, in which Coorab is punished for trans-gressing tribal law — by being left overnight on the Island of Ghosts. The photography is striking, but the frequent, intrusive intertitles read rather paternalistically. The film was, nevertheless, ahead of its time in centring a narrative on indigenous people, with no White cast at all. IB

Copping, Robin (1934–) CINEMATOGRAPHER/DIREC-TOR

Robin Copping's career is inextricably wound up with that of director Tim •Burstall. Copping filmed Burstall's first feature film, •**Two Thousand Weeks** (1969), then, with his brother David Copping (production designer) and David Bilcock (editor), he formed Bilcock and Copping, to produce, with •Hexagon Productions, Burstall's next feature, •**Stork** (1971), in which he played a small role. He was director of photography on Burstall's episode of •**Libido** (**The Child**, 1973), and on Burstall's features •**Alvin Purple** (1973) and •**Petersen** (1974). He combined again with Bilcock to direct the next Alvin Purple film, **Alvin Rides Again** (1974), still for Hexagon Productions, but with Burstall now acting as producer. He went back to cinematography for **End Play** (1976) and •**Eliza Fraser** (1976) for Burstall, and **The Pirate Movie** (1982) for Ken Annakin. In a long career, he has also shot and produced several short films and documentaries. IB

Co-Respondent's Course, A

1931. *Director*: E.A. Dietrich-Derrick. *Producer*: F.W. Thring. *Scriptwriter*: Montague Grover. *Director of photography*: Arthur Higgins. *Sound*: D.J. Bloomberg. B&W. *Cast*: John D'Arcy (James Lord), Donalda Warne (Nellie O'Neill), Patricia Minchin (May Barry).

Efftee Film Production's first feature is a gentle marital farce on 'modern divorce', from an original story by former Melbourne *Sun* editor, Monty Grover. The plot revolves around the jealousy of two men for the women they love, the comic element supposedly deriving from the numerous errors made by three private detectives hired to gain evidence for one of the men who suspects his wife of adultery. There are elements of staginess, the odd plot-creak, and the obvious limitations imposed by the early sound-recording requirements, but the film is not without admirers. It has a degree of sophistication, and a sense of indifference not to be found in the later Efftee work. Its avowedly Melbourne setting, considerable period charm, and throwaway humour are equally pleasurable.

It was also the first Australian narrative film to be completed with an optical soundtrack, and part of the first all-Australian full-length unit program to be screened in this country. Yet Efftee's first modest venture into narrative film-making is now possibly the least remembered and most rarely screened of all the Studio's drama productions. The slightness of its subject, or its lack of enduring film stars or a name director, may be contributing factors but, more likely, its original billing as a support feature (to •Diggers, 1931, which doesn't stand up nearly as well) and its length (3800 ft) have not helped its cause.   KEN BERRYMAN

Cornell, John PRODUCER/DIRECTOR Cornell's career has been largely tied up with that of his mate Paul •Hogan. He had produced Hogan's very popular television show (*The Paul Hogan Show*, followed by *Hogan in London*) before producing his big-screen début, the sensationally popular •**Crocodile Dundee** in 1986. When a sequel—**Crocodile Dundee II**—was filmed two years later, Cornell took over the directing function, and, although the film failed to repeat the financial killing of the original, it was still an undoubted financial success. Cornell also directed Hogan's first American feature, **Almost an Angel** (1990), but it was the start of a box-office decline for Hogan. The Hogan persona is so idiosyncratic it is hard to detect any Cornell touches in the films he has directed.   BMcF

Cornstalks, The

1920? *Director:* Arthur Sterry. *Producer:* Humbert Pugliese. B&W.

This film, like Beaumont •Smith's **Hayseeds** series or Arthur Sterry's earlier •**The Waybacks** (1918), is a backblocks farce, this time performed by two white-faced comedians whose silly antics jar against the naturalistic locations. In the seven surviving minutes, one of these characters (presumably Cornstalk) receives an invitation to visit his nephew, so he and his friend Beano catch a steam train to the city and visit the beach before returning to the farm. It is difficult to tell how complete this fragment is, but it is clearly technically inferior to other surviving examples of the genre, which may be why it does not appear to have been released.   IB

Cosi

1996. *Director:* Mark Joffe. *Producers:* Richard Brennan, Timothy White. *Scriptwriter:* Louis Nowra. *Director of photography:* Ellery Ryan. *Music:* Stephen Endelman. 100 min. *Cast:* Ben Mendelsohn (Lewis), Barry Otto (Roy), Toni Collette (Julie), Paul Chubb (Henry), Colin Friels (Erroll).

Lewis, a young man at a loose end, lands a job directing a stage production in a psychiatric institution. One of the inmates persuades him to tackle Mozart's opera. After several mishaps, Lewis and his crew of misfits become engrossed in the clandestine production, which is paralleled by events and troubled relationships in Lewis's life.

Cosi was one of several offbeat Australian comedies of the mid 1990s. Louis •Nowra and Mark •Joffe show a deft

touch with material that might easily have lapsed into the sentimental and melodramatic. The time-honoured conventions and creative opportunities of the play-within-a-play are well handled and the three intertwined themes—the interplay of illusion and reality, the collapse of rigid madness/normality categories, and the dialectics of sexual identity and fidelity—are intelligently developed, if not in great depth. Among the film's primary satisfactions are the often touching contributions from an ensemble cast, particularly Ben •Mendelsohn's understated performance, which contrasts nicely with Barry •Otto's marvellously manic playing of the 'wise fool'.   HARRY OLDMEADOW

Country Life

1994. *Director:* Michael Blakemore. *Producer:* Robin Dalton. *Scriptwriter:* Michael Blakemore. *Director of photography:* Stephen Windon. *Music:* Peter Best. 95 min. *Cast:* Sam Neill (Dr Max Askey), Greta Scacchi (Deborah Voysey), John Hargreaves (Jack Dickens), Kerry Fox (Sally Voysey), Googie Withers (Hannah).

Michael •Blakemore's film is, according to the credits, 'suggested by' Chekhov's *Uncle Vanya* which, in plot and character-interaction, it follows closely. Alexander Voysey, a retired drama critic, returns from England with his young second wife, Deborah, to the family property that is run by his daughter, Sally, and his brother-in-law, Jack. Alexander's return, trailing clouds of an unearned reputation, precipitates a series of family crises. Jack, the Vanya character, falls in love with the selfish Deborah, and the plain Sally, in love with the local doctor, naively accepts Deborah's help in furthering her romantic cause.

The film was not well received, largely because it suggested a return of the 1970s literary period genre. However, **Country Life** builds into its texture a critique of British opportunism at work in this country. Expatriate director Blakemore addresses this theme perceptively, and gives the film a relevance that goes beyond period reconstruction or careful literary adaptation.   BMcF

Country Town

1971. *Director:* Peter Maxwell. *Producer:* Fenton Rosewarne. *Scriptwriter:* Barbara Vernon. *Director of photography:* Bruce McNaughton. *Music:* Bruce Clark. 106 min. *Cast:* Terry McDermott (Max Pearson), Gary Gray (David Emerson), Lynette Curran (Rhoda Wilson), Gerry Maguire (Philip Henderson), Sue Parsons (Jean Fowler), Carl Bleazby (Jim Emerson), Maurie Fields (John Quinney), Rosie Sturgess (Anna Maria Lini).

The small country town of Bellbird is in the grip of drought, which threatens its survival. Reporter Philip Henderson arrives as the economic crisis sharpens old tensions and jealousies. The locals eventually rally to organise a fundraising gymkhana, and a gathering at the pub breaks into celebration as the long-awaited rain arrives.

Terry •McDermott and Gary Gray were the instigators of the project, a spin-off from the ABC's popular television serial *Bellbird*. Peter •Maxwell, with a long string of success in both English and Australian television series, was recruited to direct, with a cast made up largely of the television regulars. The film was shot on 16 mm over four weeks in Yea (central Vic.) and Wentworth (NSW). It premiered in Mildura and proved popular with country audiences, but enjoyed only limited commercial release in metropolitan centres where, McDermott and Gray claimed, it was shabbily treated by the major distributors.

HARRY OLDMEADOW

Country towns The country town, uneasily situated in the Australian cultural mythos between the bush and the city, has had a magnetic attraction for post-1970 Australian film-makers. Prior to this, the country town seemed to be of little interest, save for occasional forays in the silent film period and through 'off-shore' productions such as •Smiley (1956). The new Australian cinema (see Revival, the) practically began with a country town film, •Wake in Fright (1971), and Australian film has continued to be fascinated with country towns in films such as **Break of Day** (1976), •The Mango Tree (1977), •The Settlement (1984), •Shame (1988), •The Year My Voice Broke (1987), The Crossing (1990), and •Dead Heart (1996).

The country town, like the bush that surrounds it, provides both the physical and dramatic context for particular types of narratives. It is the social and cultural as much as the physical conditions of the country town and the surrounding 'natural' environment that supply the shape, structure, and specifics of the narratives.

With rare exceptions, country towns in Australian film are represented as irredeemably awful. This awfulness may be as 'harmless' as being unrelievedly dull (**The Settlement**; •Blue Fin, 1978), or at the other end of the spectrum, it may be undeniably destructive (•The Cars that Ate Paris, 1974). The inhabitants of these towns are as much products of their subculture, circumstance, and environment as producers of it. In this, country-town films subscribe to the overall myth that Australian identity is formed chiefly by the environment. However, particular films make it clear that the environment brings out or exposes latent aspects of the specific subculture of the country town. This is usually associated with untrammelled and untroubled masculinity, which is exaggerated by the isolation, closeness, insularity, and limited size of the community (**Weekend of Shadows**, 1978).

In representing an aspect of the Australian experience, the country town in film functions, in a number of key ways, as a metaphor for Australia. This metaphorical Australia is less the Australia of the time of the film's production, especially the Australia of the time of the new Australian cinema, than it is of the Australia of the past.

Country-town films, almost always period films, tend to be based in the sort of conceptions of Australian identity that coalesced at the beginning of the twentieth century and that have retained their potency since. This nostalgia is tempered and often overturned by the routinely negative attitude such films evince towards country towns and, especially, towards the people that inhabit them (**Break of Day**). Unlike the majority of bush films, country-town films express considerable uncertainty over the dominant perceptions of Australian identity. This is not surprising given that country towns, in the Australian cultural mythos, function as sites of transition and mediation between the 'purity' of the bush and the 'corruption' (or worldliness) of the city. Thus, the country-town community can represent the last bastion of the sense of Australianness that was, allegedly, a lived experience in the past, or may represent the quintessence of that Australianness, preserved perversely by the very isolation of which it is victim.

Nearly all country-town films stress the environmental isolation of the town being portrayed. This is done through images that place the town within a *mise-en-scène* that consistently emphasises the extent to which they are small, lonely places of human origin in an otherwise barely inhabited and barely habitable landscape. This varies from the sweeping grasslands and scrub that imprison the town in **The Year My Voice Broke**, to the encompassing green of the sugar cane in **All Men are Liars** (1995), to the remote, iconographic red desert of •Razorback (1984). The effect is the same: the Australian landscape surrounds, isolates, and threatens the community uneasily inserted into it. The town may be a place of community and thus of sanctuary from the emptiness and the threat of the Australian landscape, but these recurring images are far from comforting; they imply that the communities huddle in these towns not from choice but from a need for mutual support and security. Equally importantly, the isolation is social. The community of the small country town is isolated in the sense that its attitudes, mores, and behaviours are separate from a real or implied mainstream of Australian society.

Country towns in Australian films also act metaphorically through their emphasis on, for the most part, a monocultural community. The advantage of placing so many of these films in the past is that the Anglo-Celtic make-up of the community can be justified as being somehow true to the realities of the past. The essence of Australianness is thus imagined in these films without the complicating reality of contemporary multicultural Australia. Significantly, Aborigines barely appear in these period country-town films. When they appear in contemporary narratives (**Dead**

Heart; •The Fringe Dwellers, 1986), and this is still rare, the drama is often the conflict between Australians of European descent and Aborigines, an inter-cultural clash that contrasts with the intra-cultural clashes that inform the narratives of period country-town films.

Country-town films foreground masculinity, particularly mateship, which is ruthlessly and iconoclastically attacked in more than a few country-town films (•Dimboola, 1979; Shame, 1988). Mateship and masculine behaviour generally are at the root of the aggression and the hostility that define the social relations of the country town in Wake in Fright and Weekend of Shadows.

In Break of Day and The Crossing, the 'evil' that exists in the country town is stirred from its latent state or brought to a higher level by the arrival of an outsider, setting in motion events that are attributable to the structure of social and power relations in the town. Strangers represent disturbances in, and threats to, the established order of the communities they 'invade'. In nearly every instance, that established social order is demonstrably inflexible and constricting, a mixture of narrow-mindedness and rigidly enforced limits to 'acceptable' behaviour, morals, and values. Typically, the community responds to this challenge with violence.

The country town's hostility to the outsider is often centred upon a guilty secret. The secrets, often sexual, are based on the very nature of the community and its values: sexual secrets, as in Shame and •Summerfield (1977); murder as in The Cars that Ate Paris; cowardice in war, as in Break of Day; and Aboriginal secret ritual, as in Dead Heart. Those protagonists, whether insider or outsider, who survive, then leave. Indeed, physical and psychic survival is often possible only by leaving. Often, a main character who is close to the protagonist dies (The Mango Tree, The Crossing), death or exile representing escape from the town. Only rarely is the town itself changed in ways that might be said to be better. Escape seems the only genuine option; the evil of the country town remains immutable.

The conflict that drives the narratives of country-town films is based on the incompatibility of the presence of a stranger (who may be an outsider or an estranged local) and the hidden secret, and is exacerbated by the rigid behavioural codes that the stranger does not accept or recognise (and that have served to create and maintain the secret). Frequently, these conflicts take the form of generational conflict or gender conflict. In generational conflict, the conflict occurs between the old who, whether they have a guilty secret or not, wish to maintain the status quo, and the young who find that status quo confining, depersonalising and, in some cases, personally threatening (The Mango Tree; The Delinquents, 1989; The Year My Voice Broke).

Gender conflict is usually the result of masculine dominance of the social structure of the country town and is caused by the restricting social codes of the country town that deny women their sexuality. In many cases, this conflict is caused by the oppression of 'blokedom', of patriarchy in its particular Australian country-town form. Patriarchy creates secrecy in many of these narratives, and secrets demand, in turn, complicity of silence from both men and women, a silence that is then threatened by the outsider or by a member of the younger generation (or both). It also demands conformity amongst the males, especially those who would threaten the prevailing order (Shame, Weekend of Shadows, Break of Day).

There are a few exceptions but, generally, the country town in the new Australian cinema is an unhappy place where the residue of an anachronistic set of Australian values is represented not as a dream of a simpler, golden past, but as a nightmare from which Australia may or may not have awoken.

NEIL RATTIGAN

Cowan, Tom (1942–) CINEMATOGRAPHER/DIRECTOR/EDITOR/WRITER Tom Cowan worked as a cinematographer in Melbourne for the ABC from 1960 and directed the short film **The Dancing Class** (1964) before moving to Sydney as a cinematographer with the Commonwealth Film Unit. In 1968 he left Australia to work as a cinematographer in the United Kingdom, the USA, and Asia. In India he shot **Samskara** (1971), which won several awards including the President's Award for the Best Indian Feature. On his return to Australia, he helped to establish the Sydney Film-makers' Co-operative Cinema, and was director of photography on many independent features, including the early films of John •Duigan. He directed several short films, as well as the features •The Office Picnic (1972), which he also wrote and produced; **Promised Woman** (1975), which he also produced, wrote, and photographed; **Wild Wind** (India 1975); and •Journey Among Women (1977), which he also co-wrote and photographed. His autobiographical **Sweet Dreamers** (1982) depicts the financial and aesthetic compromises required to make such personal films on restricted budgets. He was cinematographer on one of Australia's earliest Imax features, **Antarctica** (1991).

Other Australian films (as cinematographer): This Year Jerusalem (1968), Bonjour Balwyn (1971), •Pure S... (1975), The Love-Letters from Teralba Road (1977), Third Person Plural (1978), •Mouth to Mouth (1978), •Dimboola (1979), •Winter of our Dreams (1981), One Night Stand (1984), Relatives (1985), Emma's War (1988), Backsliding (1992). IB

Cox, Paul (1940–) DIRECTOR Dutch-born Paul Cox has been something of a phenomenon in Australian cinema, if for no other reason than that, for 20 years, he has persisted in making films the way he has wanted to, ignoring the lure of Hollywood and the rewards of multiplex cinemas, and doggedly expressing his creative urges in a series of films that offer a poetic perception of Australian social realities. Cox and his family endured the terrors of war and of German occupation, and the rigours of postwar adjustment, before he came to Australia in 1963 in an exchange program that enabled him to spend a year at Melbourne University. His father ran a film-production company in Holland, and photography had, from an early age, been Cox's obsession. In 1965 he formally migrated to Australia, where he made a number of short films (**Matuta**, 1965; **Time Past**, 1966) thanks to the profits of his photographic business. When he had completed a dozen or so of these, he turned to feature film-making and, with the help of a grant, made **Illuminations** (1976), a non-linear exploration of the relationship between an Australian man and a disturbed Hungarian woman. The film had only the most limited screenings and never recovered its cost. His second film, **Inside Looking Out** (1977), again focuses on a difficult relationship, but is more straightforward in its telling, while •**Kostas** (1979) marked an advance in professionalism and was critically better received than his earlier, more dauntingly subjective work. **Kostas** treats with some sensitivity an intercultural relationship, a matter of significance in Australian life, and it began Cox's productive working relationship with actor Wendy •**Hughes**, who would star for him in several films, including •**Lonely Hearts** (1982). This last film, which Cox also co-wrote, established another key relationship—with the actor Norman Kaye. In fact, a characteristic of Cox's career has been the way in which he has surrounded himself with a repertory company of actors (Tony •**Llewellyn-Jones**, Monica •**Maughan**, Sheila •**Florance**, and others) and behind-camera personnel, such as cinematographer Yuri •**Sokol** and producer Jane •**Ballantyne**.

This continuity may help to account for the striking homogeneity of Cox's output: in a cinema increasingly dominated by special effects, by a more flamboyant approach to matters of style, he has persisted in his concern for what he sees as humanly important, not showing any obvious interest in what might be commercially more advantageous. One of his later films, •**A Woman's Tale** (1991), explored the responses of an elderly woman dying of cancer—and cast the late Sheila Florance, herself in this situation, in this role. This is courageous film-making if not very likely to make its director/co-producer rich. Despite his focus on the intimate lives lived in lead-lighted suburban Melbourne, Cox has never embraced a quiet, unobtrusive linear realism, as films such as •**Man of Flowers** (1983) and •**My First Wife** (1984) attest. Stylistically, these films break with the conventions of film narration; they contain emotionally cogent images that risk breaking the narrative line. Cox's films are essentially arthouse in their orientation but, from time to time, that has proved financially reward-

ing enough to enable him to continue, and he appears to have no aspirations towards huge budgets and mass audiences, although his 1998 project, **Father Damien**, shot on Hawaiian location with an international cast, certainly extends his range. In 1998, he published a volume of autobiography entitled *Reflections: an Autobiographical Journey*. *Other Australian films*: (Shorts) Skin Deep (1968), **Marcel** (1969), Symphony (1969), **Mirka** (1970), Calcutta (1970), **Phyllis** (1971), The Journey (1972), Island (1975), All Set Backstage (1975), We're All Alone My Dear (1975), Ritual (1977), Ways of Seeing (1977). (Documentaries) **For a Child Called Michael** (1979), The Kingdom of Nek Chand (1981), Underdog (1982), Death and Destiny: A Journey into Ancient Egypt (1984), Handle with Care (1985). (Features, all co-p. and co-w., as well as d.) Cactus (1986), **Vincent: The Life and Death of Vincent Van Gogh** (1987), Island (1989), **Golden Braid** (1991), The Nun and the Bandit (1992), Exile (1994), Lust and Revenge (1996), The Hidden Dimension (1997, IMAX 3-D). BMcF

Crackers

1998. *Director*: David Swann. *Producer*: Chris Warner. *Script*: David Swann. *Director of photography*: Laszlo Baranyai. *Music*: Ricky Edwards. 93 min. *Cast*: Albert (Warren Mitchell), Bruno (Peter Rowsthorn), Hilary (Susan Lyons), Joey (Daniel Kellie), Jack (Terry Gill), Vi (Maggie King).

Swann's first feature film is a cheerfully raucous comedy about the inevitable horrors of a family Christmas reunion, given a special nudge towards mayhem by the arrival of young Joey's great-grandfather, Albert, fresh from prison. Even before this, things have been uneasy: Joey's mother, Hilary, has brought her new boyfriend Bruno and his thuggish teenage son, to share the festive season with her parents, kindly Vi, redneck bigot Jack, and dipsomanic Aunt Dotty. Sleeping quarters in Jack's Melbourne seaside home are cramped, and Joey (the source of the film's point of view) is forced to share the toolshed with smelly old Albert. However, the two form a bond and the film risks turning a little sentimental with the death of Albert. The comedy is often like a series of blackout revue sketches, some of them very funny, but underpinning it is the theme of sons in search of fathers that gives it coherence. Its ensemble cast enters into the spirit of the piece with enthusiasm, and the film has some of the appeal of the previous year's success, •**The Castle** (1997). BMcF

Cracknell, Ruth (1925–) ACTOR

Ruth Cracknell is a Sydney-based actor who has achieved great popularity and respect on the stage and who has been involved in long-running television series, notably *Mother and Son*. She has appeared in some interesting films without ever quite becoming established in the cinema as she has in the other

The family of **Crackers**

media. Her major starring role in films was as the elderly incarnation of the titular protagonist in •**Lilian's Story** (1995), as the woman who, abused in her youth by her father, and institutionalised for many years, finds the outside world alarming on her release. Had the film been better received, it might have marked a turning point in Cracknell's film career. Prior to this she had filmed sporadically, in incisive character roles such as the station owner's wife in •**The Chant of Jimmie Blacksmith** (1978), for which she won an AFI award, and as co-star in Bill •Bennett's odd-couple road movie, **Spider & Rose** (1994).

Other Australian films: The Singer and the Dancer (1977), •The Night The Prowler (1979), •The Best of Friends (1982), Molly (1983), •Emerald City (1989). BMcF

Craig, Diane (1949–) ACTOR Irish-born but in Australia since 1960, Diane Craig was a former National Institute of Dramatic Art student who made a name for herself in such television series as *Certain Women* and *Division 4*. Her first film role was that of Maggie Kelly in Tony Richardson's idiosyncratic and ill-fated •**Ned Kelly** (1970). She was

freshly charming and touching in •**The Mango Tree** (1977) as the French teacher who introduces Christopher •Pate to sex. Since then, most of her film work has been for television, but she had a good supporting role in •**Travelling North** (1987), as one of Julia •Blake's unhappy daughters, and the starring role of an aspiring politician who becomes Australia's first female prime minister in the little-seen satire **A Sting in the Tale** (1989). She is married to the actor Garry •McDonald.

Other Australian films: No Roses for Michael (1970, short), At My Age Who Cares? (1980, short), The Applicant (1981, short), Double Deal (1981), Stress (1982, doc.), The Highest Honor (1984). BMcF

Craig, Michael (1928–) ACTOR Indian-born, Canadian-educated, Michael Craig began in British films just as the industry was losing its impetus in the mid 1950s. After some stage experience, he was promoted as a handsome young leading man by the Rank Organisation in a typical genre range, including war films like **Sea of Sand** (1959), exotic adventures such as **Nor the Moon by Night** (1958), and comedies like **Doctor in Love** (1960). When given the chance, as in **The Angry Silence** (1960, about a wildcat strike) or the race-relations problem drama, **Sapphire** (1959), he showed interesting potential for character playing. After coming to Australia to appear in a play in the mid-1970s, he settled here and wrote and occasionally appeared in a number of films in the early years of the revival. He gave one of the best performances of his career in the title role of •**The Irishman** (1978), as the Qld teamster, Paddy Doolan, who cannot face the challenge of mechanised transport. He plays with real authority, and for half-a-dozen years (from 1989) he won new audiences as the senior partner in a Sydney clinic in the television series *GP*. He wrote the screenplay for and acted in •**The Fourth Wish**, the touching story of a child with leukemia, based on a television miniseries, and filmed by Galaxy, the company formed by Craig. The film starred John •Meillon and was directed by Don •Chaffey.

Other Australian films: Inn of the Damned (1974, actor), •**Ride a Wild Pony** (1975, actor), •**The Killing of Angel Street** (1981, co-w.), **Turkey Shoot** (1982, actor), **Stanley** (1983).   BMcF

Criticism and theory

Australian film criticism and theory have, at least since the 1970s, developed along two paths: the desire for a national culture on the one hand, and the appropriation of a range of imported theoretical insights—for example, poststructuralism and psychoanalysis—on the other. Although these impulses overlap significantly, it is helpful to think of them in terms of their different methods of interpreting and analysing the relationships between film form, narrative content, and the social and historical conditions of film production.

The former mode of criticism has tended to be contextualist, analysing the representation of national culture in Australian films within a range of historical contexts: for example, the silent era (John Tulloch); the period since the 1970s revival (Graeme Turner); the work of a particular director, as in Stuart Cunningham's work on •Chauvel. In contrast, film analysis informed by European poststructuralist theory has tended to have a meta-theoretical focus. It has looked to the way in which the film text itself works, in order to analyse the representation of national culture and to explore such interpretive issues as postcolonial longings for independence (Meaghan Morris), settler desires (Ross Gibson), gender politics (Annette Blonski), and the ascription of Otherness to indigenous people (Marcia Langton) and migrants.

Both these impulses in film criticism and theory have addressed the deceptively simple question of what constitutes an Australian film. In their attempt to address this issue, the editors of *The Australian Screen* (1989) observe that although •**The Sentimental Bloke** (1919) and •**Picnic at Hanging Rock** (1975) are Australian films, it is hard to see what they have in common. In what, they ask, does their Australianness reside? How should we search for it? Included in the possible approaches they suggest is a minimum definition that categorises films as Australian when any of the following criteria are met: the film is made in Australia, it is made for an Australian audience, it is made by an Australian (whether this person is working in the domestic industry or abroad). But even these apparently unproblematic criteria have proved less than useful at times, as when the Australian film industry attempted to claim the successful Jane Campion feature •**The Piano** (1993) as its own. **The Piano** is directed by the Australian-trained Campion and financed with the support of the •Australian Film Commission and the •New South Wales Film and Television Office. However, it is set in New Zealand and its narrative is so firmly rooted in the national imaginary of that country as to completely resist incorporation into any category of Australianness, particularly the category of nationalistic desires, desires that the film imputed to its New Zealand audience. The evident inadequacy of such minimal definitions and the concomitant acceptance of the need to regard Australian film as a heterogeneous category have meant that the identifying traits of Australian film have proven, on the whole, elusive. Notwithstanding this, several studies have succeeded in identifying and describing the relationship between Australian film and other forms of Australian cultural production such as literature and various other popular cultural forms. Among these are Brian McFarlane's *Words and Images: Australian Novels into Film* (1983), which emphasises the influence of the literary tradition on Australian film-making; John Tulloch's *Legends on the Screen: The Australian Narrative Film 1919–29* (1981), which examines the relationship between theatrical melodrama and Australian silent film, as well as exploring the new narrative and actorial moves against these forms by Raymond •Longford; and Graeme Turner's *National Fictions: Literature, Film and the Construction of Australian Narrative* (1986), which is influenced by the work of Lévi-Strauss and Roland Barthes in the way it construes the national culture as a fertile site of myth-making and narrative complexity. In these studies Australianness is found, if only to be deferred, at the level of the structures, of narrative. Sylvia Lawson, in her many essays and in her editorial project, the *Australian Screen* series, addresses Australian film-making in terms of its historical and institutional conditions of production; her emphasis is on the film industry as a working system.

The convergence of this contextual criticism (which both analyses and reconstitutes national film culture) with the poststructuralist work of such film critics and theorists as Morris has produced some of the most constructive and interesting recent work in Australian film studies.

Criticism and theory

A good example is Dermody and Jacka's two-volume *The Screening of Australia* (1988). A key term of this study is 'the social imaginary', a concept that has more to do with a textual mode of address and historical process, than with *Zeitgeist* and content. The notion of a social imaginary is productive as a middle term, since it belongs to a genuine middle ground between two estranged impulses in film theory. It is at once a kind of back door through which history can enter a psychoanalytic framework, and a back-door for the unconscious to enter a historical framework. Postmodern theory tells the history of the national culture, while history, in turn, determines where theory may be most usefully deployed. Dermody and Jacka are also influenced by Lawson, who has noted that the Australian film industry is affected by the fact that it operates in a nation that is postcolonial without being post-revolutionary. Australia's identification with the metropolitan centre of colonial days has remained remarkably strong, blurring and dislocating local identity. This is an effect of the fact that White settlement of Australia has never been sufficiently discomfited by its dependent status, economic or political, to develop even remotely revolutionary tendencies. And so the problem of decolonising the Australian mentality is both severe and subtle.

Two articles of film theory written by Lawson and Morris can serve as benchmarks for this survey of criticism and theory of Australian film: Lawson's 'Toward Decolonization: Film History in Australia' (in *Nellie Melba, Ginger Meggs and Friends: Essays in Cultural History*, edited by John Docker and Drusilla Modjeska, 1982) and Morris's 'Tooth and Claw: Tales of Survival and *Crocodile Dundee*' (in *The Pirate's Fiancée: Feminism, Reading, Postmodernism*, 1988). There are two main reasons for choosing these pieces. First, Lawson and Morris are unusual (both in Australia and internationally) in that they are theorists who have also been influential film critics. Second, these articles also span the moment of the new Australian cinema (see Revival, the) from the early 1970s to the 1990s, and represent the tendencies towards contextualism on the one hand, and poststructuralist theory on the other. Lawson's essay begins a volume that has its origins in 'a new phase of cultural studies . . . emerging in Australia that was trying to find new ways of negotiating the dilemma of formalism and contextualism' (*Nellie Melba, Ginger Meggs and Friends*). This volume approaches cultural analysis by taking popular culture seriously and through such starting points as feminism. Lawson's interest in the social and institutional conditions of production of Australian films was a way of defining new relationships between formalism (which held sway in English departments throughout much of the 70s) and contextualism. The books written, in the 1980s, for the Australian Screen series (Currency Press) and edited by Lawson, examined this form/context problematic. Morris's 'Tooth and Claw' combines a vision of Australian culture as syncretic, with an analysis of the various rhetorical positions that have been taken in the debate around the notion of imported culture. However, Morris's project is not only to explore the possibility of defining new speaking positions in relation to global or imported culture, but also to consider the issue of how postmodern theory, including film theory, can be politically useful for feminism. This explains the essay's concern with the position of the character of the American journalist, Sue Charlton, in •Crocodile Dundee (1986). For Morris then, formalism is undone less by contextualism than by postmodernist theories that find Australianness in the *differences* of the local from the global, and in the kinds of speaking positions available to the local critic and theorist. As an Australian film that was successful in the global marketplace, **Crocodile Dundee** provides Morris with an allegory of postcolonial survival that offers both salutary lessons and cautions.

Lawson's project of decolonising Australian film rests on the turn, or return, to history that she sees as necessary if Australian film critics and film-makers are to understand the conditions in which they work. Her article looks to the past of the Australian film industry in order to understand the conditions of its success and popularity. Lawson also celebrates this past (or at least the past of silent cinema), arguing that Australian films of 50 and 60 years ago open on to social worlds that, despite being our own in many ways, remain, at the same time, uncharted territory, no less foreign than those portrayed in Glauber Rocha's Brazilian *Cinema Novo*, and just as problematic and alive. Their vitality, the strength of their communicative links to both sources and audiences, holds clues to the puzzles of the present. Lawson 's identity as a film critic, is tied to her placement within a colonial society that cannot easily shed its colonised status. As such, she is aware of the impossibility of setting about decolonising film practice, or anything else, with the single-mindedness of, for example, the Chinese. At the same time, Australia's distance from the metropolitan centres of Europe has meant that Australian cinema has not been able to display the formal and political experimentation of Rocher's *Cinema Novo*. Lawson's target is Hollywood media and cultural imperialism. She dismisses the •Cinesound films of the 1930s as 'post-Depression . . . diversion with a kangaroo stamp on it', with Hollywood present in all of them like an 'invisible ring-master' ('Toward Decolonization'). The years from 1940 to 1971 are described as one 'long hiatus . . . punctuated by coach-party visits, from Milestone, Zinnemann, Kramer and others making bland, undistinguished mid-Pacific versions of Australian stories with, upon occasion, a local assistant editor or second unit director'. Lawson criticised those films of the 1970s that she had seen (**Picnic at Hanging Rock**; •**Caddie**, 1976; •**Sunday Too Far Away**, 1975) for baulking at their hurdles. Each, she argues, begins to explore the conflict of major oppositions—between colonial culture and the uncolonisable bush, poverty and wealth, women and patriarchal systems, the mateship ethos and capitalism—but fails to work through its conflicts, fails to make them visible through narrative indices. And the failure is like the nervousness of a speaker who is never sure of the audience and who, in midstream, senses that they might be bored, might even be leaving. The confusion, the conceptual blurrings, make the films illegible, unless due account is taken of the inheritance of silence, and the consequent groping for the lost audience: Where did the audience go when the lights went out on the old Australian picture show? Lawson seeks that lost audience and its film-makers. Her key theoretical concept in this search is her notion of Australian history as 'mediated' through the myths circulated in specific historical conditions of production and reception. For Lawson, to know Australian film history is to know these conditions. At the time of publication of Lawson's 'Toward Decolonization', this particular understanding of the history of Australian film, embodied in the Australian Screen series of books focusing on film production, was already in the process of generating what Stuart Cunningham has called the 'theoretical mode' of Australian film history, beginning with Tulloch's *Legends on the Screen* (which investigates precisely the old Australian picture show Lawson is seeking in her articles), followed by Dermody and Jacka's two-volume *Screening of Australia*.

In 'Toward Decolonization', Lawson argues that 'in late colonial and post-colonial contexts, three major theoretical necessities are efficiently exposed at once: one, that the knowledge of the conditions of production—which, importantly, include those of reception and the filmmakers' sense of an audience—is essential to any adequate reading of the products; two, that these conditions, including the biographies of the author or authors, are not simply determinants along with everything else in the sociohistorical context, but transformers; three, that methodology cannot replace history, no matter how true it is that each should inform the other'. Production and reception; film as construction and transformation; and the importance of history in revealing the relationship between, first, film and myth (understood as both narrative contradiction in Lévi-Strauss's sense, and as naturalisation of history, in Barthes's sense) and, secondly, between film and the deep structural conflicts of the time—these were Lawson's key concepts. They also permeated the books of Tulloch, Dermody, and Jacka, and others in Australian Screen series. Thus, for Lawson, the problem with Cinesound films was that they did not read Australia's deeper troubles in terms of

the structure of historical particularity, readings that she believed *were* reached in the 1919–29 period. For example, Longford's and Tal Ordell's films of this period 'acknowledged certain intractable conflicts . . . arguably imaging both the struggles of the urban working-class as the Depression loomed up, and the situation of those lone local filmmakers up against the giants' ('Toward Decolonization'). Similarly, Franklyn •Barrett's 1920s '"bush films" certainly valourised the bush, but his urban styles betrayed complexity and ambivalence; garments, decor, dancing, potent indices like the long cigarette holder and the fringed lamps and drapes all had a fascinating elegance that worked to subvert, if not quite belie, the happy endings in which men and women, severally and on horseback, headed into the outback sunsets of the "real" Australia. The patterns (as distinct from the plots) communicate conflicts within the community, which include both film-makers and audiences: conflicts between, on the one hand the given of national dreams, the masculine pioneer-mateship ethos mapped on to those intractable inland spaces, un-English, anti-English, and on the other the unarticulated suburban aspirations, spreading slowly over the hinterlands of capital cities the will to be a part of the modern, Anglo-American, urban-suburban globe, to partake in metropolitan culture, and so to be safe from that inland loneliness'. Because, for Lawson, conditions of production *spoke back* to conditions of reception, film-makers and the (now lost) picture-show audience reciprocated in a kind of authentic transparency. Film-makers could be confident in their address, and so rendered the myths back to their owners. This is not to say that Lawson believes in a naturalist transparency of 'truth' through cinema. Hers is a sophisticated realism that recognises that all film histories (not least her own) are 'narratives produced in contexts . . . The critic-historian, no less than the filmmaker, is a storyteller, reworking material from the near and further past (choosing, indeed, which past shall be of service), projecting the home society's unacknowledged conflicts, exposing, rejecting and denouncing for and on behalf of readership and audience'. She is aware that any film history and criticism 'will constitute a story that society needs to be telling itself' and, in her case, as a film critic and film-maker who had worked against the 'double colonization' of Australia and its films (first by Britain, then by the United States), the story that needed to be told at the moment of the re-invention of the new Australian cinema was the revelation (and challenge to) 'the story of Hollywood as a global force, with styles and structures which demonstrated not only colonial capitulation but also some significant colonial resistance'.

The story of Hollywood as a global force and colonial resistance to it is also Morris's theme, which is why, in 'Tooth and Claw', she focuses on **Crocodile Dundee**. But her theoretical and critical repertoire is very different from Lawson's. Morris's register is poststructuralist: she opens with Deleuze and quickly works across Lyotard, Jameson, Huyssen, and Baudrillard. In contrast, Lawson cites Gramsci early and later mentions Foucault: her intertextual register tends to be classic film-makers (D.W. Griffith, Jean Renoir, Sergi Eisenstein, Dziga Vertov, John Ford, Orson Welles, Vittorio de Sica, Roberto Rossellini) and film historians and critics (André Bazin, Kerr Jacobs, Andrew Sarris). Whereas Lawson's 'lost frontier' is that of the producers and audiences of the silent picture show, Morris's is that of the certainties and apocalypses of all grand narratives, including the feminist socialism underpinning Lawson's analysis. In Morris's article, it is precisely the tensions between these different registers that drives the agenda. Whereas Lawson's key target is a nostalgic return to the supposed transparency of relations between the conditions of production and reception in Australia's silent era, Morris theorises the relationship between postmodernism's nostalgic historicism and Jameson's (and Lawson's) 'real history'. Whereas Lawson's wager is 'resistance'—found in the 'real' interstices of 'syntagmatic structures of Australian history' and 'paradigms like farce and melodrama', a concept familiar to *Screen* theory of the 1970s—Morris is frustrated with the lack of credibility of this wager, especially the credibility of resistance theories that depend on notions of appropriation. Morris's project centres on the 'apocalyptic rhetoric pervading postmodernism', 'the problem of whether a global situation can give rise to an action capable of modifying it', which 'is also a problem of the action of a text upon the social signifying systems that make it possible, and which constitute its materials'. Lawson's assumption that the film text 'transforms' and 'subverts' is taken up in Morris's essay in the context of a discussion about theory, in which she pays particular attention to 'appropriation' as the assumed 'privileged mode of action in and by the film' **Crocodile Dundee**. Like Lawson, Morris's agenda embraces *both* resistance and British/United States imperialism, seeing **Crocodile Dundee** as a 'post-colonial comedy of survival, with remnants of the British, land-taking, appropriative regime (bushmen, Aborigines, Darwinian "natural" perils) emerging into the "multinational" cultural space of American-media modernity'. However, Morris interrogates Lawson's realist wager and all the 'nostalgic returns to a theory of cause and effect'. And, in particular, she interrogates 'appropriation' as a concept in discourses of resistance.

Lawson's criticism is certainly a celebration of a lost past (although neither a conservative nor lugubrious one), and her key loss is, indeed, a sense of impoverishment since the days of Longford, Ordell, and Barrett. Yet Morris is, finally, unable to relinquish some of Lawson's future-seeking tools:

her realism—since Morris too (among her multiple causes and effects) resorts to real causes that are 'structuring absences' of the text (in the best Althusserian fashion), as when she interprets the hostility to land rights as 'a function of the pressure of mining companies'; and Lawson's conceptual focus on conditions of reception and production, as Morris calls for a new venture into 'the gap between the politics of production, and of regimes of consumption, or rather, since that distinction is now engulfed, between the politics of culture and the politics of politics'. The meaning of 'engulfing' in this context, and its relationship to the politics of 'appropriation' that Morris analyses, is illustrated by Mick Dundee's cultural poaching of Aboriginal voices in the face of a real relation between an outback of land appropriation and an outback that 'might now also provide raw materials for global nuclear threat'. Nonetheless, this 'engulfing' of Lawson's twin projects—of production and reception analysis—does mark the major space between the two articles we have regarded here as symptomatic of Australian film criticism and theory. Lawson seeks to *retrieve* by writing a *history* of real relations, as a way past the contradictions of class, gender and racial politics. For Morris, there is no way back—neither to Australian silent film nor to the 'apocalyptic guarantees of historical determinism' that fundamentally mark Lawson's project: 'How to invent—not discover or retrieve—some connections is now a major ethical and imaginative action (and image) problem for radical politics'.

In choosing to focus on these two articles, our survey of the main tendencies and tensions in Australian film criticism and theory has, of course, overlooked other important approaches to the field. These include the film history and criticism of Scott Murray (see *The New Australian Cinema*, 1979; *Australian Cinema*, 1994), Ina Bertrand (*Cinema in Australia: A Documentary History*, 1989), Andrew Pike and Ross Cooper (*Australian Film 1900–1977*, 1980), Graham Shirley and Brian Adams (*Australian Cinema: The First Eighty Years*, 1983); the important 'film readers', including those edited by Albert Moran and Tom O'Regan (*An Australian Film Reader*, 1985; *The Australian Screen*, 1989); and work by Australian theorists that, like Morris's writings on film, draws on structuralist and poststructuralist theory in order to pose questions about the techniques and politics of film studies, but without focusing on Australian film, such as that of Barbara Creed (*The Monstrous-Feminine: Film, Feminism, Psychoanalysis*, 1993) and Laleen Jayamanne (*Kiss Me Deadly: Feminism and Cinema for the Moment*, 1995).

JOHN TULLOCH AND PAUL WASHINGTON

Crocker, Barry (1934–) ACTOR Aside from brief roles in **Squeeze a Flower** (1970) and •**Muriel's Wedding** (1994), in which he played himself, Barry Crocker's film appearances have been limited to •**The Adventures of Barry**

Barry Crocker in **Barry McKenzie Holds His Own** (1974)

McKenzie (1972) and **Barry McKenzie Holds His Own** (1974). Although Crocker has spent most of his performing career as a singer with a comedic streak in clubs, cabaret, and television, his performance as Barry McKenzie, the archetypal Australian 'ocker' abroad, was pivotal to the commercial success of the Australian film industry during the critical period of 1972–73. Budgeted at only $250 000, and funded by the •Australian Film Development Corporation, the film's strong support in Australia and, to a lesser extent, the United Kingdom, generated confidence in the Australian film industry at a crucial time. GM

Crocodile Dundee

1986. Director: Peter Faiman. Producer: John Cornell. Scriptwriter: Paul Hogan, Ken Shadie, John Cornell. Director of photography: Russell Boyd. Music: Peter Best. 102 min. Cast: Paul Hogan (Mick 'Crocodile' Dundee), Linda Kozlowski (Sue Charlton), John Meillon (Walter Reilly), David Gulpilil (Neville Bell), Ritchie Singer (Con), Mark Blum (Richard Mason).

Crocodile Dundee is the highest-grossing film in the history of the Australian cinema and its local and international appeal, especially in the USA, was primarily due to the film's ability to appear 'different' and distinctly 'Australian', especially in terms of its humour and settings, within a narrative structure that used generic conventions that were familiar to anybody with a passing knowledge of American cinema. **Crocodile Dundee** was, in fact, a film that could easily have been produced during the peak years of the classical Hollywood cinema.

The film begins with the arrival of American reporter Sue Charlton in Walkabout Creek to interview Michael J. 'Crocodile' Dundee, a man who reportedly crawled back to safety after a crocodile attack.

Having disembarked from a chartered plane, Sue is met by Dundee's business associate Walter Reilly and taken to the local hotel. When Reilly describes the crocodile attack to Charlton ('this giant crocodile came, turned him over, bit off half his leg, dragged him under . . .') and Dundee's trek back to safety through 'snake-infested swamps, on his hands and knees, right into Katherine', the barmaid takes over and readily deflates Dundee's heroic status by pointing out that Dundee went 'straight past the hospital and into the first pub for a beer.' It is this 'typically Australian' quality of attacking pretension that works so well in the film before the conventionality of the romance, and the formulaic 'fish out-of-water' sequences, in New York in the second half of the film takes over. In Manhattan the 'innocent' Dundee experiences, and triumphs over, big-city decadence (stereotypically represented by prostitutes, transvestites, muggers, and drug addicts), and corruption. Finally, the film attempts to emulate the romantic reconciliation of the odd couple, a convention that characterised so many American screwball comedies in the 1930s, as Sue and Dundee publicly declare their feelings in a crowded subway.

Paul •Hogan's desire to 'make a proper movie', as opposed to the Australian 'arty' films he so despises, predictably celebrates the superiority of Australian bush skills in any situation, thereby placing **Crocodile Dundee** within a long line of Australian films characterised by a suspicion of other cultures and 'alien' social practices.   GM

Croft, Jamie (1981–) ACTOR Child actor Jamie Croft began working at the age of nine and became a familiar face on television, particularly as Billy Lacy in *A Country Practice*, before he began to appear in film. He won the Australian Film Institute Young Actor Award for his first feature film role, as 'Ort' Flack in **That Eye, the Sky** (1994). He was the voice of the lost puppy Napoleon in the film of that name (1995), appeared in person in **Mighty Morphin Power Rangers: The Movie** (1995), and as the lead in the television series *Sun on the Stubble* (1996). He then played the lead in two more children's films: **Joey** (1997), in which he performed with a young kangaroo, and **The Real Macaw** (1998), in which his co-star was a talking macaw. He has a surprising range for a young performer, and is always appealing, even when working with animals bent on stealing the show.   IB

Crombie, Donald (1942–) DIRECTOR In the 1970s Queenslander Donald Crombie acquired a reputation for directing sympathetic, low-key, humane studies of embattled protagonists. •**Caddie** (1976), his first feature film, set this pattern, although he had had a good deal of prior television experience, notably on the highly regarded drama *Who Killed Jenny Langby?* (1974) for the •South Australian Film Corporation. Before this he trained at the National Institute of Dramatic Art (NIDA), worked for the •Commonwealth Film Unit in the 1960s, with the BBC in London from 1969 to 1971 and, in 1976, he and Anthony •Buckley formed Forest Home Films. They joined forces with experienced scriptwriter Joan •Long to make **Caddie**, which was

based on the autobiography of the eponymous barmaid. The film was made with the financial cooperation of several major sources, including the Secretariat for International Women's Year. Its heartfelt recreation of the life and hard times, from 1925 until 1932, of its Depression-hit battler protagonist was a critical and commercial success, owing much to Helen •Morse's glowing performance as the barmaid who survives personal tragedy and poverty with an unbroken spirit.

Crombie's third film, •**Cathy's Child** (1979), was similarly rooted in the real-life struggle of a woman against daunting odds. This time she is a young mother whose child is abducted by her Greek husband and who, with the help of a journalist touched by her story, wins her struggle against chilly officialdom and is reunited with her child. In the intervening film, •**The Irishman** (1978), the central character, teamster Paddy Doolan, refuses to accept the changing times, when mechanised transport in 1920s Qld threatens his traditional livelihood. All three films are short on conventional narrative organisation; all three compensate with the humane concern they persistently evince for the dogged and the put-upon, for those who rise to life's challenges instead of reacting with docile acceptance. They show Crombie's social realist strengths at their best. These are realised through an unobtrusive control of the setting and through the excellence of their performances, especially from Helen Morse, Michelle •Fawdon, and Michael •Craig as their respective stars.

Nothing has gone quite so well for Crombie since the 1970s. •**The Killing of Angel Street** (1981) was one of two films released within months of each other that were based on the death of an outspoken opponent of inner-city development. Crombie's film suffered by comparison with Phil •Noyce's •**Heatwave** (1982), which tackled the theme much more rigorously, creating the urban-thriller-with-a-conscience that Crombie seems to have aimed at. In 1985 he and Ken •Hannam, another key figure of the 1970s revival who has since lost his pre-eminence, combined to direct a television miniseries based on Rolf Boldrewood's moralising Victorian classic of bushranging life, •**Robbery Under Arms**, a two-and-a-half hour version of which was released to cinemas. Most of Crombie's subsequent work has been for television, and his career seems to have lost momentum. *Other Australian films include*: Aircraft at Work (1966, doc., w.), It's So Easy (1966, doc., w./ed.), Is Anybody Doing Anything About It? (1967, doc., w.), Canberra (1968, co-d.), Sailor (1968, doc.), Plane Mates (1969, short), Personnel or People (1970, short), Turnover (1970, short), Top End (1970, doc.), The Choice (1971, short), Australia's North West (1972, doc., p. only), A City Family (1972, doc., p. only), Our Land Australia (1972, doc., p./co-w.), Explosives—The Two-Metre Lifeline (1972, doc.), The Fifth Facade (1973, short), I Need More Staff

(1973, short), **Kilkenny Primary School**, 1973, doc.), **One Good Reason** (1973, short), **Stradbroke Infants School South Australia** (1973, doc.), **A Road in Time** (1976, doc., w. only), **Jim** (1980, doc., w.), **Kitty and the Bagman** (1982), •**Playing Beatie Bow** (1986), **Rough Diamonds** (1994).   BMcF

Cropper, Linda ACTOR A noted stage actress, Linda Cropper also scored a resounding success with her television series *Melba*, in which she played the celebrated Australian diva. Until 1997 her only roles in the cinema had been in the little-seen **Going Sane** (1986), as the secretary who has an affair with her boss (John •Waters), and the straight-to-video **The Seventh Floor** (1994). Then suddenly she gave an outstanding performance as a divorced mother with breast cancer, whose teenage son is nursing an appalling secret in •**Blackrock** (1997). Cropper played with sharp intelligence and a sympathetic feel for the constraints at work on this likeable, put-upon, tenacious woman. The film was undervalued locally and Cropper's work on screen still awaits serious attention.   BMcF

Crowe, Russell (1964–) ACTOR Following the successful release of **L.A. Confidential** (1997), there was speculation, particularly in New Zealand, as to whether Russell Crowe should be considered an Australian actor. Crowe pointed out that, although he was born in Wellington, he had spent the greater part of his life in Australia and that he is comfortable with his recognition in the USA as an Australian actor.

Crowe grew up in the entertainment industry. His maternal grandfather was Stan Wymess who received an MBE for his work as a cinematographer during World War II. Crowe's parents were caterers and he spent part of his youth on film sets in Australia. He appeared in the television series *Spyforce* at the age of six. Twenty-four years later Crowe worked with the star of the series, Jack •Thompson, as his gay son in •**The Sum of Us** (1994). Crowe graduated from an unsuccessful career as a rock singer in New Zealand to stage musicals, such as *Grease* and *The Rocky Horror Show*. The latter took him to Sydney's Kings Cross where he worked as a busker while auditioning for television and film roles. His break came when director George Oglivie selected him for the lead role in **The Crossing** (1990). Crowe's career continued in films such as •**Spotswood** (1992) and **Hammers Over the Anvil** (1991), but it was his performances as the happy-go-lucky Andy in •**Proof** (1991) and the ferocious neo-Nazi skinhead in •**Romper Stomper** (1992) that consolidated Crowe's status in Australia.

Since •**The Sum of Us** in 1994 Crowe has appeared in a succession of Hollywood films with roles ranging from the World War II pilot in **For the Moment** (1994), to the tortured protagonist in the bizarre western **Quick and the**

Dead (1995), to the composite villain who threatens Denzel Washington in **Virtuosity** (1995). However, it was his performance as Bud White, the obsessive cop in **L.A. Confidential,** that provided the breakthrough role in Hollywood. Crowe's performance as White, which tempered an explosive brutality with a redemptive search for love and affection, has synthesised many distinctive aspects of his performances since 1990. Australian producer Al Clark, who worked with Crowe in The **Crossing**, described him as possessing an 'unusual amalgam of sensitivity and strength that most actors don't have'. Crowe, on the other hand, attributes the incipient violence in his performance in **L.A. Confidential** to his experiences in the pub culture of his youth. Whatever the source, Crowe's performances in both Australian and Hollywood films have established him as the most distinctive acting talent to emerge in the Australian film industry in the 1990s. David Elphick, who directed Crowe in **Love in Limbo** (1993), suggests that Crowe will end up directing, as he is always so well prepared and because he knows that 'it is the best job on the set—you get to play every part'.

Other Australian films: •**Blood Oath** (1990), **Silver Brumby** (1993), **Heaven's Burning** (1997).   GM

Crystal Voyager

1973. Director and Producer: David Elfick. *Script*: George Greenough. *Directors of photography*: Albert Falzon, George Greenough. *Music*: G. Wayne Thomas, Bobby Gilbert, Pink Floyd. 78 min. *Cast*: George Greenough (himself), Nat Young (himself), Ritchie West (himself).

Shot over two years in California and off the Australian East Coast, **Crystal Voyager** documents American surf legend George Greenough's twin quests to find the perfect wave and to build a camera to film it. Building on the formula initiated by the hugely successful **Morning of the Earth** (on which David •Elfick, Albert Falzon, and G. Wayne Thomas also collaborated), surf footage is enhanced by synchronisation with Thomas's songs and music. The film is elevated to a level approaching the sublime in the celebrated last 23 minutes, 'Echoes', in which Greenough's own footage, shot at 10 times normal speed, takes the viewer under and down the faces of huge waves, and inside the hollow vortex tube of a wave on the verge of breaking, all to the psychedelic accompaniment of Pink Floyd. One of the most successful films of the neglected but hugely popular surf-movie genre, **Crystal Voyager** was funded in part by the •Australian Film Development Corporation, which recognised that surf movies had a large and appreciative ready-made audience on an established (independent) exhibition circuit.

BEN GOLDSMITH

Cullen, Max (1940–) ACTOR One of the great character actors in the Australian cinema, Cullen began as a stage actor in Sydney in the early 1960s and appeared on Australian television in the late 1960s. From his first screen appearance as Peeper in •**You Can't See Around Corners** (1969), Cullen developed the laconic, often slightly criminal, and always irritating character to an art form. As Tim King, the novice shearing contractor in •**Sunday Too Far Away** (1975), Cullen lures Jack •Thompson, Robert •Bruning, and Jerry Thomas away from their shearing contracts, and has a difficult time distancing himself from his former workmates in the shearing shed. When the 1956 Shearer's Strike occurs he readily sides with his working-class mates in their battle with the scab labour imported by the property owners. The dark side of this persona is evident in •**Summerfield** (1977), with Cullen as the busybody who suspects that his wife, Geraldine Turner, is sleeping with new boarder Nick •Tate. Cullen has been able to extend this character through the 1980s, particularly as Blanco White in **Boundaries of the Heart** (1988) and into the 1990s, noticeably as the sinister Stan in the award-winning •**Kiss or Kill** (1997).

Other Australian films include: Stockade (1971), •The Office Picnic (1972), •Blue Fin (1978), •Dimboola (1979), •The Odd Angry Shot (1979), •My Brilliant Career (1979), Hard Knocks (1980), •Hoodwink (1981), •Star Struck (1982), Freedom (1982), Running On Empty (1982), With Prejudice (1982), Midnight Spares (1983), The Return of Captain Invincible (1983), Stanley: Every Home Should Have One (1984), Luigi's Ladies (1989), Incident at Raven's Gate (1989), Mad Bomber in Love (1991), Garbo (1992), Greenkeeping (1993), Shotgun Wedding (1994), Rough Diamonds (1995), Spider and Rose (1994), Billy's Holiday (1995).

GM

Cult films Since the renaissance of the Australian cinema in the early 1970s (see Revival, the), some film-makers have produced works that have been embraced by certain film audiences, both in Australia and overseas, and have been transformed into cult films. These films are in some way 'on the edge'; they may be extreme works that are daring and creative, and perhaps perverse, overblown, or excessive. They are very much guilty pleasures for their audiences. In *Cult Movies* (1981), Gerald Peary describes cult films as featuring 'atypical heroes and heroines; offbeat dialogue; surprising plot resolutions; highly original storylines; brave themes, often of a political or sexual nature; definitive performances by stars who have cult status; the novel handling of popular but stale genres'.

The central factor in the determination of a cult movie is the presence of a devoted audience that frequently re-experiences the work. There is no rule pertaining to the initial audience and the film's critical reception. These pictures may have been popular at the time of their original release or failures with both critics and audiences. Cult-film fans tend to consider themselves as resurrecting or 'discovering' these movies.

In many cases, established notions of taste and standards of artistic value are directly challenged by cult films; traditional conceptions of 'good taste', do not apply as a criterion of value. Pablo Picasso's statement, 'The chief enemy of creativity is good taste', is a fitting one for films that are bizarre, offbeat, and neglected. Cult films are products of elements of popular culture that may be considered unpleasant or repellent, but that are somehow fascinating. Films such as George Romero's **Night of the Living Dead** (1968) and David Lynch's **Eraserhead** (1978) include material that at the time of original release was of an extreme nature. The cult movie may also be considered a 'bad' movie from a point of view of conventional film criticism. A key example of a film sublime in its ineptitude is Edward D. Wood Jr's **Plan Nine from Outer Space** (1959). The main point is that, as American film critic Andrew Sarris has said, cult-film audiences love a movie 'beyond all reason'.

In his influential essay on cult films ('Casablanca: Cult Movies and Intertextual Collage', in *Travels in Hyperreality*, 1984), Umberto Eco considers **Casablanca** (1942), regarded as the prototypical classical cult film, and the requirements of transforming a work into a cult object. Eco believes 'one must be able to break, dislocate, unhinge it so that one can remember only parts of it, irrespective of their original relationship with the whole'. The cult movie is memorable in its detail. Certain sequences, scenes, or shots are outstanding in their tone, style, and the emotion that is created. Eco also contends that 'a cult movie is the proof that . . . cinema comes from cinema'. This indicates that cult movies contain a high level of intertextual reference and that these films are first and foremost art works that exploit the cinematic form.

Some works gain cult status via their operation within the film-making community. Stuart Byron describes Ford's **The Searchers** (1956) as 'the Super-Cult movie of the New Hollywood' in its influence on the film-school trained Hollywood directors of the 1970s. Similarly, one could point to George •Miller's Mad Max trilogy (•**Mad Max**, 1979; •**Mad Max 2**, 1981; and •**Mad Max Beyond Thunderdome**, 1985) as providing a level of inspiration for film-makers of the 1980s and 1990s. Of all the films of the Australian cinema since the 1970s, the Mad Max trilogy has provided the greatest influence to film-makers world-wide. As Adrian Martin points out in *Australian Film 1978–1992* (1993), evidence of this is clearly seen in the work of the Coen brothers, Sam Raimi, John Carpenter, and Tsui Hark, as well as other film-makers of the Hong Kong cinema of the 1980s.

Apart from the Mad Max films, in terms of cult-film status among international audiences, Peter •Weir's •**Picnic at**

Hanging Rock (1975) and Nicolas Roeg's •Walkabout (1971) are significantly appreciated.

Perhaps the pre-eminent cult film of the early new wave of Australian cinema is Peter Weir's first feature, •The Cars that Ate Paris (1974), a multi-genre piece full of playful allusion to the horror movie, the spaghetti western, television advertising, and other cinematic forms. Weir skilfully negotiates familiar generic territory, weaving one plot convention with another to create one of the great Australian cult films. Other Australian cult films that either mix or rework well-known film styles and genres include the Chandleresque political conspiracy thriller •Goodbye Paradise (1983), the surrealistic •Bliss (1985), and Emma-Kate Croghan's campus romantic comedy •Love and Other Catastrophes (1996).

The science-fiction and horror genres contain numerous examples of the cult movie: Spirits of the Air, Gremlins of the Clouds (1989), •The Salute of the Jugger (1989), As Time Goes By (1988), Sons of Steel (1989), The Time Guardian (1986), the slasher genre piece Bloodmoon (1990), Next of Kin (1982), and Philip •Brophy's Evil Dead II-type splatter comedy Body Melt (1993).

Two underrated film-makers who are usually dismissed in discussions of Australian cinema are significant in the cult-film arena: Richard •Franklin, director of the thrillers •Patrick (1978) and •Roadgames (1981); and *metteur-en-scène* Brian •Trenchard-Smith, director of such cult pictures as Turkey Shoot (1982), described by film critic David Stratton as 'a sadistic bloodbath', •The Man from Hong Kong (1975), Dead-End Drive-In (1986), and the early Nicole Kidman teen movie BMX Bandits (1983).

Other notable films that have achieved cult status include Russell •Mulcahy's •Razorback (1984); Philippe •Mora's The Marsupials: The Howling III (1987); Richard •Lowenstein's •Dogs in Space (1987); Tim •Burstall's Attack Force Z (1982), which teamed stars Mel •Gibson and Sam •Neill; Gillian •Armstrong's musical comedy •Star Struck (1982); Rolf •De Heer's science-fiction film Incident at Raven's Gate (1989) and •Bad Boy Bubby (1994); and Geoffrey •Wright's •Romper Stomper (1992).

SCOTT J. KNIGHT

Cultural policy The Australian film industry owes its existence to government funding programs initiated in the 1960s. Funds establishing an Experimental Film Fund (see Experimental Film) and a national Film Development Corporation (see Australian Film Commission) in 1970, and a Film and Television School (see Australian Film, Television and Radio School) in 1973, went a long way toward building a skills base and guaranteeing the industry's economic viability. In the late 1990s, despite the fluctuating number of independent projects, government funding continues to underwrite screen production.

This situation contrasts with that at the beginning of the century. On 1 January 1901, the Salvation Army's Limelight Department, commissioned by the premier of NSW, filmed the parade and official ceremonies marking the inauguration of the Commonwealth of Australia. Premier Lyne's offer to assist the film-makers in any way possible boded well for future government relations with film-makers but, while several state and Commonwealth departments developed production facilities over the next few years, comprehensive programs of assistance for the production of commercial feature films were not instituted for another seven decades.

Responsibility for the regulation of cinemas and for film censorship remained with the states at Federation, but administrative costs and legislative inconsistencies, such as the banning of bushranging films in NSW from 1912, led to calls for a centralised system. The Commonwealth took responsibility for all imported films from 1918, but it was not until 1969 that the last state, NSW, appointed the Commonwealth censor to act on its behalf. In the 1920s, moralist and religious groups joined film-makers in lobbying for legislative intervention to curb the influence of American films and business practices and to assist Australian films to reach a local audience. The 1927–28 Royal Commission into the Moving Picture Industry, constituted in response to complaints of unfair business practices, recommended the introduction of a quota of empire films to offset the American influence, but the powerful distributor/exhibitor lobby was able to convince state authorities that such legislation would be unworkable. The influence of the moralist lobby declined after World War I, and a liberalisation of social attitudes, coupled with a growing acceptance of film as art, encouraged the long overdue revision of censorship regulations in the early 1970s.

In the 1930s and 1940s, policy-makers began to respond to film's educative potential by encouraging its use in schools. World War II encouraged further use of film as a medium of communication and propaganda and, in 1945, the Commonwealth created the Australian National Film Board (see Film Australia). The Board's film unit (renamed the Commonwealth Film Unit in 1956 before evolving into Film Australia in 1973) was given a brief to produce documentaries that promoted national and civic consciousness, but such encouragement to production was unusual. For a quarter of a century after World War II, nearly all the feature films made in Australia were either co-productions or foreign productions for which Australia was simply an exotic backdrop. Aspiring local film-makers were restricted to crewing on government documentaries or working in the fledging television and advertising industries, which had been boosted by the introduction of production quotas in the 1960s. No help was offered to feature film producers.

The dominant postwar political figure, Sir Robert Menzies, persistently ignored calls for assistance to film. Menzies's anglophilia was at odds with the changes in Australian society after World War II and the rising nationalism of the 1960s, but since support for the arts and local cultural expression would have implied an acknowledgment that the dominant Anglo-Australian culture was no longer sufficient for Australia's needs, a change in the official attitude toward arts funding was unforeseeable until Menzies's retirement in 1966.

It was left to John Gorton to initiate an era of cultural *dirigisme*, with the establishment of the Australian Council for the Arts (see Australian Film Commission) in 1968. Gorton was soon persuaded by advisers, including Phillip Adams and Barry Jones, that assistance to film would underscore his populist appeal and reinforce his cultural nationalist credentials. Gorton recognised film's potential to promote Australia overseas and facilitate tourism and trade. Assistance to the film industry was also consistent with Gorton's nationalist economic program for local control of industrial production and the extension of overseas markets for Australian goods.

Initially, the newly instituted Australian Film Development Corporation (AFDC) (see Australian Film Commission) was empowered to loan only the equivalent of half the budget of any project. This policy was unpopular with film-makers and, following the election of a nationalist Labor government in late 1972, the AFDC mission was amended. Heavy emphasis remained on the cultural requirement that projects demonstrate 'significant Australian content' in their crew, setting, and subject matter but, from this point, the AFDC was able to invest in productions without the expectation of financial return, as well as offer script-development assistance. The first film to benefit from these changes was •The Adventures of Barry McKenzie (1972), for which the AFDC provided the entire $250 000 budget. These policies were retained by the •Australian Film Commission (AFC), which replaced the AFDC in 1975. Pre-production assistance subsequently facilitated the development of several films that typify the so-called 'AFC genre' of arthouse and period films, including •Caddie (1976) and •Picnic at Hanging Rock (1975).

The creation of the AFC in 1975 broadened federal programs of assistance. A marketing and distribution branch was created to promote Australian films abroad, and it succeeded in initiating a strong Australian presence at the Cannes Film Festival. In 1976 a creative development branch was set up to administer funds for experimental films and to support screen culture. Film production was also boosted by the establishment of funding agencies in each of the states between 1972 and 1978. The Tasmanian Film Corporation (see Tasmania, history and images) has since been disbanded, and the other five have undergone significant revisions in their mission, but the state agencies continue to provide assistance to local film-makers.

In the early 1980s, a tax-incentive scheme (commonly known as 10BA) was introduced to encourage private investment in film. The scheme boosted film production but, as many critics argued, at the expense of cultural specificity. In 1988 the Film Finance Corporation (see Finance) was set up to invest in commercial productions, leaving the AFC to fund projects deemed culturally valuable but unlikely to return profits. In the same year, the AFC initiated a women's program to give targeted assistance to women film-makers while, in 1993, the indigenous branch was created to encourage and address the specific needs of Aboriginal and Torres Strait Islander film-makers. In addition, the National Film and Sound Archive (see Archives) was established in 1984 to promote understanding of Australia's screen heritage.

In the 1990s technological advances present new challenges for legislators and film-makers, as well as questioning the concept of a 'national cinema' upon which policy has been based. In this period, between 20 and 30 feature films were made in Australia each year, with government funding accounting for almost 50 per cent of total investment. Government funding also assisted documentary makers and the production of drama for television. Despite the success of Australian films at home and abroad, and despite the construction of new production facilities in Sydney, the infrastructure initiated in the 1970s, and built on since then, remains vitally important to the cultural health of the nation.

BEN GOLDSMITH

Cummins, Peter (1931–) ACTOR Melbourne stage and television actor Peter Cummins had one of his best screen roles in his fourth film, as Arthur Black, Jack •Thompson's shearing rival in •Sunday Too Far Away (1975). This was followed by a lead role in **The Removalists** (1975), as the cynical police sergeant who instructs a naive constable in the daily realities of police life. Since then, Cummins has maintained a steady flow of performances in supporting roles, primarily as policemen or stolid working men.

Other Australian films: •Stork (1971), •Alvin Purple (1973), •Between Wars (1974), The Firm Man (1975), The Great MacArthy (1975), •Mad Dog Morgan (1976), •Storm Boy (1976), High Rolling (1977), Blue Fire Lady (1978), Double Deal (1983), I Live With Me Dad (1985), Sky Pirates (1986), Frog Dreaming (1986), •Kangaroo (1987), •Twelfth Night (1987), Slate Wyn & Me (1987), •The Umbrella Woman (1987), Ground Zero (1987), The Man from Snowy River II (1988), Rikky and Pete (1988).   GM

Curran, Lynette (1945–) ACTOR First popular as Rhoda Wilson in the ABC's long-running serial, *Bellbird*, Lynette Curran subsequently played the role in •Country Town (1971), the film featuring the serial's characters. As well as other television and stage work (much of it for the Melbourne Theatre Company), she has since made nearly a dozen films. She showed in •**Road to Nhill** (1997) that she had developed into a considerable character actress, as one of the bowling ladies involved in a car accident. She also did incisive work in •**Bliss** (1985) as the protagonist's unfaithful wife, as the wife of local store proprietor Graeme •Blundell in •**The Year My Voice Broke** (1987) and, especially, as the mother of three dangerous sons in •**The Boys** (1998). Her talent embraces both comedy and pathos, within the bounds of an unaffected naturalism.

Other Australian films: •Alvin Purple (1973), Drift Away (1976, short), •Caddie (1976), Buckley's Chance (1980, short), A Creative Partnership—The Actor and the Director (1982, short), •Heatwave (1982), Comrades (1987), Bullseye (1987), The Delinquents (1989), Dead to the World (1991), Mushrooms (1995). BMcF

Custodian, The

1994. Director: John Dingwall. *Producer*: Adrienne Read. *Scriptwriter*: John Dingwall. *Director of photography*: Steve Mason. *Music*: Philip Houghton. 109 min. *Cast*: Anthony LaPaglia (Quinlan), Hugo Weaving (Church), Barry Otto (Ferguson), Kelly Dingwall (Reynolds), Essie Davis (Jilly), Gosia Dobrowolska (Josie), Bill Hunter (Managing Director), Norman Kaye (Judge), Steven Grives (Brennan).

One of the better Australian films released in the 1990s, with a little more care in scripting and casting The Custodian would have been outstanding. Anthony •LaPaglia is excellent as Detective Quinlan who discovers that most of his colleagues, including his superiors, and close friend Frank Church, are corrupt. The pervasiveness of the corruption threatens Quinlan's emotional stability, a problem compounded by his troubled marriage. The film links the two aspects in the opening sequence as his drunken wife humiliates herself and Quinlan in front of friends at a bar by accusing him of being a 'cold bastard'. Quinlan's moral rigidity is shown to be both a strength, in his resolve to expose police corruption, and a weakness in his personal relationships. The film never quite assimilates the two narrative strands and Quinlan's 'redemption', presented via his romance with Jilly, does not quite gel with his self-destructive professional behaviour at the end.

Quinlan infiltrates the corrupt circle of police and criminals and feeds information, including self-incriminating material, to local television reporter Reynolds. This eventually brings down everybody, including the masochistic Quinlan. This premise is effectively established in the first 45 minutes by writer-director John •Dingwall, but the film then loses its dramatic impetus by shifting the focus from Quinlan to the investigative reporter Reynolds. This also means a shift from LaPaglia, who conveys the myriad complexities of Quinlan in a superb series of understated scenes in the first half, to the less effective Kelly Dingwall, who lacks the appropriate authority to carry the film for any length of time. Nevertheless, **The Custodian** is a fine police thriller and deserved greater critical attention and a wider audience. GM

D

Dad and Dave Come to Town

1938. Director: Ken G. Hall. *Producer:* Ken G. Hall. *Scriptwriters:* Frank Harvey, Bert Bailey. *Director of photography:* George Heath. *Music:* Hamilton Webber, Maurie Gilman. 97 min. B&W. *Cast:* Bert Bailey (Dad Rudd), Shirley Ann Richards (Jill), Fred MacDonald (Dave), Billy Rayes (Jim Bradley), Alec Kellaway (Entwistle).

Dad and Dave Come to Town completes the transformation in the series that began with •**Grandad Rudd** (1935). The film begins in typical style with a broad comic sequence involving Dave's destruction of the Rudd kitchen with 'laughing gas'. After this brief sequence, the film follows a more classical narrative pattern as the Rudd family move to a large unnamed Australian city (Sydney?) when Dad inherits a female fashion store. Thereafter the film's humour emanates from incongruities of a rural life style when it is applied to city living, such as Dad and Dave's attempts to come to terms with a modern bathroom. While the humour exploits stereotypical representations of city and country, the film suggests that these differences are only shallow and that, regardless of geography, the common denominator is that they are all Australian. This inclusive approach even extends to Alec •Kellaway's relentlessly effeminate stereotype as Entwistle, the store floor-walker and fashion consultant. Entwistle's loyalty to the Rudd business is rewarded by promotion in the store and his return in the next Rudd film, •**Dad Rudd, MP** (1940).

The central plot concerns Dad's attempts to salvage the fashion store despite the attempts of rival Pierre (Sidney Wheeler) to destroy his business. The film concludes with a large-scale fashion show interspersed with slapstick comedy as Dave battles usurpers trying to repossess their furnishings. The Rudd family win out and Dad returns to the farm after leaving the store in the capable hands of daughter Jill (Shirley Ann Richards; see Richards, Ann). The film is also notable for the screen début of Peter •Finch as an earnest suitor for Sara Rudd, and he participates in one of the funniest sequences when he approaches Dad for permission to marry Sara: Dad mistakes Finch's request as an attempt to buy the family bitch. This film also changed the characterisation of Mum with the casting of Connie Martyn, and this represented a further shift in the series, as Martyn epitomised maternal middle-class values in a similar manner to comparable American actors such as Fay Holden (the Andy Hardy series) and Jane Darwell. Martyn was retained for **Dad Rudd, MP**. GM

Dad and Dave: On Our Selection

1995. Director: George Whaley. *Producers:* Anthony Buckley, Bruce Davey, Carol Hughes. *Scriptwriter:* George Whaley. Based on the stories of Steele Rudd. *Director of photography:* Martin McGrath. *Music:* Peter Best. 107 min. *Cast:* Leo McKern (Dad Rudd), Joan Sutherland (Mother Rudd), Geoffrey Rush (Dave Rudd), Essie Davis (Kate Rudd), David Field (Dan Rudd), Celie Ireland (Sarah Rudd), Noah Taylor (Joe Rudd), Cathy Campbell (Lily White), Pat Bishop (Mrs White), Ray Barrett (Mr Dwyer), Robert Menzies (Cranky Jack), Murray Bartlett (Sandy Taylor), Barry Otto (J.P. Riley), Nicholas Eadie (Cyril Riley).

The centenary of cinema coincided with the centenary of the first publication of the stories of the Rudd family on their selection: the result is this third film adaptation of the stories, an affectionate homage to early Australian film as well as to several generations of Aussie battlers on the land. It depicts the minutiae of everyday life—a dead dog in the well; the birth of Dad's first grandchild—but within a larger political and social context: for example, drought, the machinations of the banks and the squatters, and the coming of the railway. Most of the ensemble cast play these larger-than-life characters with dignity and understatement, including Leo •McKern as Dad and Joan •Sutherland (in her only film role) as Mother. The exceptions (Noah •Taylor stuttering and twitching, and an unrecognisable Robert •Menzies as the crazy Cranky Jack) provide another, broader kind of humour. Catchy music in the folk idiom and art intertitles quoting from the stories help to establish the period. The film does not please those who object to nostalgia or stereotyping, but there is much to enjoy in this gentle comedy that wears its heart on its sleeve.   IB

Dad Rudd, MP

1940. *Director:* Ken G. Hall. *Producer:* Ken G. Hall. *Scriptwriters:* Frank Harvey, Bert Bailey. *Director of photography:* George Heath, *Music:* Henry Krips. 83 min. B&W. *Cast:* Bert Bailey (Dad Rudd), Connie Martyn (Mum), Yvonne East (Ann Rudd), Fred MacDonald (Dave), Alec Kellaway (Entwhistle), Frank Harvey (Henry Webster), Grant Taylor (Jim Webster).

Dad Rudd, MP is the last, and strongest, of the four Rudd-family films directed by Ken G. •Hall. After the usual comic introduction, this time involving Dad's newly acquired fire-engine, which proceeds to run amok after Dave and company attend a small fire, the film includes a serious narrative strand that functions as an overt allegory on the state of the world in 1940. As Germany invades vulnerable countries throughout Europe, Dad Rudd is reluctantly forced to enter politics to prevent heartless politician Henry Webster (Frank •Harvey) emasculating plans to build a local dam to help the small, vulnerable farmers in the district. The film's climax is similarly less humorous than previous Rudd films: torrential rain causes the dam to collapse, vindicating Dad's opposition to changes to the dam. Dad's position on the dam leads to his political victory after the unfair tactics employed by Webster to sabotage Dad's political rallies. The film ends with Dad's stirring maiden speech to the federal parliament extolling the virtues of the man on the land and the need to combat external threats to Australian security. This political epilogue is a fitting cinematic finale to the passion for (rural) Australian values that Bert •Bailey was skilfully able to generate when given the opportunity

Dad Rudd, MP introduced Grant •Taylor as the romantic lead who courts Ann Rudd (Yvonne East) and abandons his own father in favour of Dad Rudd. Taylor's next appearance was the lead role in •**Forty Thousand Horsemen** (1940). Alec •Kellaway's effeminate character from •**Dad and Dave Come to Town** (1938) is reprised in a rural setting and is less effective than it was in the 1938 film.

GM

Dark City

1998. *Director:* Alex Proyas. *Producers:* Alex Proyas, Andrew Mason. *Scriptwriters:* Alex Proyas, Lem Dobbs, David S. Goyer. *Director of photography:* Darius Wolski. *Music:* Trevor Jones. 101 min. *Cast:* Rufus Sewell (John Murdoch), Kiefer Sutherland (Dr Daniel Schreber), Jennifer Connelly (Emma Murdoch), William Hurt (Frank Bumstead), Richard O'Brien (Mr Hand), Ian Richardson (Mr Book), Colin Friels (Walenski), Bruce Spence (Mr Wall), Melissa George (May), John Bluthal (Karl Harris), Frank Gallacher (Stromboli).

After John Murdoch wakes up in a rundown hotel with a dead body next to him the film-noir influence on Alex •Proyas's film is clearly established in this visually stunning generic hybrid that brings together a range of influences from science-fiction literature, to the work of French film-makers Jean-Pierre Jeunet and Mark Caro (**City of Lost Children**, 1995), to the obvious thematic influence of **Blade Runner** (1982) and the architectural resonances of the first two **Batman** films. Nevertheless, the cinematic nightmare that Alex Proyas creates in **Dark City** surpasses these films with its visual audacity and richness: he utilises every filmic element—from composition, sound, sets, and costume, to colour tones—to provide a stunning mosaic of meaning, sounds, and spectacle.

In **Dark City** alien visitors, the Strangers, to a perpetually dark Earth sedate Earth's inhabitants each night at midnight and remove their memories as part of their quest to see whether humans have souls. Only John Murdoch is immune to their power, and he witnesses their 'tunings', their daily re-fashioning of the city: buildings shift or disappear to be replaced by new forms as the Strangers create new architectural patterns. In these mean streets women are being killed and Murdoch, a primary suspect, is pursued by detective Bumstead, who comes complete with 1940s hat and coat, and dialogue that is consistent with this hard-boiled archetype. Murdoch's wife Emma provides support for her husband who, in turn, is threatened and protected by the scientist Dr Schreber.

These characters are deliberately stripped of any moral or narrative complexity by Proyas and fellow scriptwriters Lem Dobbs and David S. Goyer and, in keeping with the film's premise, they represent collective memories of social archetypes, alluding to a plot twist that is never fully developed. The net effect of the film's characterisations is to push the audience away from any emotional feeling of identification towards a more detached appreciation of the film's grand design so that, as the director argues, you can get a 'sense of wonder . . . where, when you perceive things, you can step back and look at the whole cosmos and get some insight into that, even fleetingly'.

GM

Dating the Enemy

1996. *Director:* Megan Simpson Huberman. *Producer:* Sue Milliken. *Scriptwriter:* Megan Simpson Huberman. *Director of photography:* Steve Arnold. *Music:* David Hirschfelder. *Cast:* Claudia Karvan (Tash), Guy Pearce (Brett), Matt Day (Rob), Lisa Hensley (Laetitia), Pippa Grandison (Collette).

This film begins in a promising manner by quickly sketching in the romantic attraction, and tensions, between studious science journalist Tash and superficial music–video–show host Brett. Then one morning they both wake up to find that they have swapped bodies, a concept used in American comedies such as **Big** (1988) and **Vice Versa** (1988). Whereas in the American films the body swap concerns the same sex, **Dating the Enemy** involves a gender switch, and the film tries to milk the situation for all its worth with jokes based on obvious gender differences. Thus, while Brett is delighted with the opportunity to wear stockings and garters, he is less impressed with his newly acquired menstrual pain. The inherent problem is that Claudia Karvan is seen coping with both of these experiences and, despite the extensive use of voice-over to try to clarify the situation, it is a little confusing trying to conceptualise Karvan as Brett and Guy Pearce as Tash for much of the film. Karvan, however, is excellent, although the film runs out of steam once it has exploited its basic premise.   GM

David Williamson's Emerald City, *see* Emerald City

David Williamson's The Club, *see* The Club

Davis, Eddie (1907–) DIRECTOR In 1968 local entrepreneur Reginald Goldsworthy set up a production company in association with the American-based Commonwealth United Corporation. The result was three modest program films all directed and written by the American Eddie Davis. Davis had some experience in American television and had directed **Panic in the City** (1967), but his trio of Australian films made scarcely a ripple in cinemas here. They are all thrillers of various kinds, shot on limited budgets, in settings that suppressed anything too specifically Antipodean, and they all star minor Hollywood names, with Australian supporting casts and technical crews. **It Takes All Kinds** (1969), starring Barry Sullivan and Vera Miles, involved art thefts and a wheat silo; **Color Me Dead** (1970), starring Carolyn Jones and Tom Tryon, was a dilute remake of the noir classic, **D.O.A.** (1950); and **That Lady from Peking** (1970), with Nancy Kwan in the title role, was a Cold War contrivance. These films gave work to some Australians in the film industry at a crucial time, but there is not much else to be said for them.   BMcF

Davis, Judy (1956–) ACTOR Although she enjoys a commanding position among stars of the new Australian cinema (see Revival, the), prolific West Australian Judy Davis has in fact made few films recently in Australia, including the little-seen •**On My Own** (1993), filmed on locations in Toronto and London, and the witty black comedy •**Children of the Revolution** (1996), in which she plays a humourless old-time communist infatuated with Stalin. Trained at the National Institute of Dramatic Art, she made her film début in **High Rolling** (1977), as a 16-year-old hitchhiker drifting around Queensland. She was then cast by Gillian •Armstrong for the central role of Sybylla in •**My Brilliant Career** (1979), based on Miles Franklin's largely autobiographical novel. She, and the film, won instant acclaim. Her performance announced a stimulating new star personality, as unpredictable as the frizzy red hair she sported in the film, full of suppressed urges and sudden rages, tender and vulnerable. Some aspects of the persona became clichés over the next few films—the aggressive twitches and switches of mood, the sly, shy smile, the mocking glance—but there was no gainsaying the rigorous interpretive intelligence she brought to the roles that followed: the tenacious prostitute with, not a heart of gold, but a conscience in •**Winter of Our Dreams** (1981); the lay preacher's sexually repressed wife in •**Hoodwink** (1981); and the urban militant on the track of corruption and murder in •**Heatwave** (1982). Not many actresses anywhere have given four such remarkable performances consecutively.

Her international career began with **Who Dares Wins** (1982), a dim political thriller based on the siege of the Iranian Embassy in London in 1981. This did little for her career, except to get her more widely noticed, but her next two international projects certainly established her reputation as a talented actor internationally. These were the television film *A Woman Called Golda* (1982), in which she played the young Golda Meir, and **A Passage to India** (1984, d. David Lean). Although she apparently crossed swords with Lean during the film's protracted shooting, she emerged with an Academy Award nomination for her perceptive delineation of the awkward, maddening, honest Adela Quested. She returned to Australian cinema for •**Kangaroo** (1987), in which she was brilliantly effective as the difficult, intelligent wife of the D.H. Lawrence character (played by her husband Colin •Friels), and for •**Hightide** (1987), a melodrama of mothers and daughters, directed again by Gillian Armstrong.

She has been described as the best film actress in the world and the hyperbole is less extravagant than such claims usually are: she has worked several times for Woody Allen; made some very off-beat projects, such as **Barton Fink** (1991) and **The Naked Lunch** (1991); rose to the high-camp challenge of **Impromptu** (1991), in which she played

Judy Davis

Dawn!

George Sand; and made the most of the costume romance conventions of **Where Angels Fear to Tread** (1992), her second brush with E.M. Forster. If she were never to film in Australia again, she would remain one of that select group who put new Australian cinema on the map.

Other Australian film: **Georgia** (1988). BMcF

Dawn!

1979. Director: Ken Hannam. *Producer:* Joy Cavill. *Executive Producer:* Jill Robb. *Scriptwriter:* Joy Cavill. *Director of photography:* Russell Boyd. *Music:* Michael Carlos. 109 min. *Cast:* Bronwyn Mackay-Payne (Dawn), Ron Haddrick (Pop), Bunney Brooke (Mum), Tom Richards (Harry), John Diedrich (Gary), Gabrielle Hartley (Kate).

This biographical drama is based on the life of Australian Olympic swimming champion Dawn Fraser. It charts the often controversial progress of her career, from her working-class roots in Sydney's Balmain area to the heights of world sporting fame and national-hero status. The film depicts Fraser as a naive, rough diamond, a female larrikin who is catapulted by her prodigious swimming ability into a variety of international and personal incidents that profoundly influence her private life and professional career. Most comfortable in the swimming pool or the public bar at the local hotel, Fraser is shown as a warm, fun-loving yet lonely woman, good-natured, but often unconventional.

This low-budget •South Australian Film Corporation production, directed by Ken •Hannam, who also directed •Sunday Too Far Away (1975) and **Break of Day** (1977), is told predominantly by flashback in a low-key style, and in an episodic narrative form that contrasts Fraser's pool success with private uncertainty. The film captures some of the harsh innocence and attitudes of the period, but it is its subject matter, the figure of Dawn Fraser, still a much venerated woman in Australia, that will ensure its survival. JOHN BENSON

Dawn, Norman (1884–1975) DIRECTOR/CINEMATOGRAPHER Born in Argentina, Norman Dawn arrived in Australia in 1926 with cameraman Len Roos, to shoot backgrounds for one of his Hollywood productions. At the time, Australasian Films were planning their most ambitious project to date—an historical epic intended to penetrate the American market. To that end, Australasian Films (see Greater Union Organisation) persuaded Raymond •Longford to give up the role of director on the project, and appointed Dawn, who became producer, director, co-editor, and co-photographer on •For the Term of His Natural Life (1927). Dawn's great talent was in special effects cinematography (glass shots, mattes, and miniatures). For this film he used paintings on glass plates to create composite images with the ruins of the convict settlement at Port Arthur,

recreating the scene as the original buildings must have appeared. His second film for Australasian Films was •**The Adorable Outcast** (1928), which he directed, produced, and wrote. Both these films were silent, made just as sound began to take over the market, and neither did as well as Australasian Films had hoped. Dawn returned to the USA, but came back to Australia in 1929 with sound-on-disc equipment, intending to make a talkie. By the time •**Showgirl's Luck** (1931) was completed, sound-on-film had become standard and, although he transferred to this system to complete the film, it was once again a commercial failure. He returned to his modest Hollywood career, making films up to 1950. His other American films include **Lasca** (1919), **The Adorable Savage** (1920), **The Lure of the Yukon** (1924), **Tundra** (1936), and **Two Lost Worlds** (1950). IB

Day, Gary (1941–) ACTOR The career of New Zealand-born actor Gary Day flourished in the 1970s with a lead role in the successful television series *Homicide* and, to a lesser extent, *The Box*. Since then Day has been a familiar face in many Australian television programs (such as *The Great Bookie Robbery*, 1986) and films, some of which were quickly relegated to video. He specialises in tough characters on either side of the law. Day had starring roles in **Crosstalk** (1982) and **The Surfer** (1988), two films deserving of more attention than they received at the time of their release. **Crosstalk**, a reworking of the dramatic premise in Alfred Hitchcock's **Rear Window** (1954), clearly suffers from a series of production problems, although the finished product effectively maintains a powerful sense of alienation emanating from a computer-dominated society. Day's authoritative performance as the ex-Vietnam drifter Sam Barlow in **The Surfer** (1988), a better film, generates a mixture of confusion and desperation, interspersed with a strong sense of survival, from a man thrust into a series of events that he does not understand and confronted by characters he cannot trust. Since these leading roles Day has been relegated to supporting performances in television series and inferior films (such as **Tunnel Vision**, 1995).

Other Australian Films: **Natural Causes** (1970), •**The Mango Tree** (1977), **Night Nurse** (1977), **Nightmares** (1980), **Duet for Four** (1982), **Body Business** (1983), **Natural Causes** (1985), **Hanging Together** (1985), **Hard Knuckle** (1988), **Sting in the Tail** (1989), **Jigsaw** (1989), **Harbour Beat** (1990), **Crimebroker** (1993).

GM

Day, Matt (1974–) ACTOR As a youngster Matt Day travelled from school to the St Martin's Theatre in Melbourne just to involve himself in the world of theatre and acting. Following two days' work as an extra on the film **Fame and Misfortune**, in 1986, his first major professional job was in 1988 in an ABC children's show *C/- The Bartons*.

Day left school at the beginning of his final year and travelled to Sydney for a two-year run on the popular television series *A Country Practice*. After a successful audition, involving the bean-bag scene from •Muriel's Wedding (1994), in front of director P.J. •Hogan, his wife and co-producer Jocelyn •Moorhouse, and lead Toni •Collette, Day was selected straight away for the role of Brice Nobes. A series of quirky comedy roles followed: •Love and Other Catastrophes (1996), the second male lead in •Dating the Enemy (1996), and the aspiring Australian country singer determined to get to Nashville in •Doing Time for Patsy Cline (1997). At this point in his career Day was determined to break away from the stereotype of naive virtuous young man. His next role as the petty criminal and potential sociopath Al, in Bill •Bennett's •Kiss or Kill (1997), brought him an Australian Film Award nomination for Best Actor.

Other Australian Films include: The Sugar Factory (1998), Muggers (1998). GM

De Groot, Andrew (1957–) CINEMATOGRAPHER

Andrew de Groot attended the Swinburne Film and Television School (see Victorian College of the Arts Film School) with Richard •Lowenstein, for whom he shot his first feature, •Strikebound (1984), which earned him an Australian Film Institute (AFI) nomination for Best Cinematography and attracted international attention for its visual treatment. He worked with the same director on the short musical drama White City (United Kingdom, 1985) and the feature •Dogs in Space (1987). De Groot has shot prize-winning shorts, documentaries, and music videos. His work on the short film Evictions (1980) won him a Kodak Award; a one-hour dramatised biography, Memories and Dreams (Czechoslovakia/Australia, 1993) won him an Australian Cinematographers Society Golden Tripod Award and an AFI Open Craft award; •To Have and to Hold (1996) won a Victorian ACS Gold Award.

Other Australian films: •Devil in the Flesh (1989).

DAVID MUIR

De Heer, Rolf (1951–) DIRECTOR/WRITER/PRODUCER

Born in the Netherlands, Rolf de Heer moved to Australia when he was eight years old. A telefeature for the ABC, *Thank You, Jack* (1985) and a children's film Tail of a Tiger (1985) established de Heer's film-making career, which has been characterised by a determination not to be constrained by classical narrative conventions and generic boundaries. Incident at Raven's Gate (1989), a generic hybrid which is part supernatural thriller, part science fiction, and part domestic drama, overcomes the limitations of its small budget with the avoidance of special effects and an effective use of sound and camera. Although the film points to the existence of aliens in the South Australian out-

back, it never shows them and restricts any sign of their existence to the effect they have on the locals. De Heer's eclectic pattern continued with Dingo (1992), with its mixture of jazz and the Australian outback, and this was followed by •Bad Boy Bubby (1994) one of the most outrageous feature films produced in Australia. This low-budget, almost surreal, presentation of incest and murder follows the picaresque adventures of an infantile adult. The film is overlaid with a strong sense of irony and black humour, which produces a strong critique of contemporary Australian society.

The Quiet Room (1996), about a child witnessing the breakdown of her parents' marriage, is, in some ways, the antithesis of the stylistic excesses of Bad Boy Bubby. Dance Me to My Song (1998), on the other hand, is a love-and-sex triangle involving Julia (Heather Rose), a woman suffering from cerebral palsy, her carer Madelaine (Joey Kennedy) and a handsome stranger, Eddie (John •Brumpton). Although the film is, characteristically for de Heer, devoid of sentimentality, with strong patches of black humour, it also displays his lack of an expressive film style with dull lighting, unimaginative sound design and routine camera work.

Other Australian films include: Epsilon (1995), •The Sound of One Hand Clapping (1998, p.). GM

De Roche, Everett (1946–) SCRIPTWRITER

After an apprenticeship spent writing popular television series for Crawford's production house, American-born Everett De Roche became one of the most proficient scriptwriters of the new Australian cinema (see Revival, the). His most notable work was in collaboration with director Richard •Franklin, for whom he wrote three witty and distinctive thrillers: •Patrick (1978), which rung clever changes on the mad-doctor theme; •Roadgames (1981), set on a Melbourne-to-Perth journey, with a bizarre assortment of characters; and the British-made horror film, Link (1986), about an overreaching scientist. The quality of the dialogue and the pacing of Patrick and Roadgames brought into the sometimes-genteel revival of Australian films a breath of invigorating, Hollywood-style fresh air, which was well matched by Franklin's genre skills. He also wrote an ecological thriller, •Long Weekend (1979), which has some genuinely alarming moments; the blackly comic •Razorback (1984), in which a wild pig memorably pulls away half a room while the television prattles on inanely; and Fortress (1986), based on the real-life kidnapping of a rural teacher and her pupils. He has been inactive in film since the late 1980s.

Other Australian films: Race to the Yankee Zephyr (1981), Frog Dreaming (1986), Windrider (1986), Heart of Midnight (1988) (co-author of story). BMcF

Dead Calm

1989. Director: Phillip Noyce. *Producers:* Terry Hayes, Doug Mitchell, Dr George Miller. *Scriptwriter:* Terry Hayes. Based on the novel by Charles Williams. *Directors of photography:* Dean Semler, Geoff Burton (opening sequence). *Music:* Graeme Revell. 95 min. *Cast:* Nicole Kidman (Rae Ingram), Sam Neill (John Ingram), Billy Zane (Hughie Warriner), Rod Mullinar (Russell Bellows), Joshua Tilden (Danny).

Following the death in a car accident of their baby son, naval officer John Ingram and his wife Rae embark on a recuperative Pacific cruise aboard their yacht *Saracen*. They rescue Hughie, a young man who comes rowing towards them with a tale of surviving a food-poisoning epidemic on the pleasure boat, *Orpheus*. John goes to investigate the deserted vessel, leaving Rae to guard Hughie. This proves no easy matter. Hughie has murdered his fellow passengers on the *Orpheus* and threatens Rae, who is forced to succumb to his sexual importunity as a way of maintaining some control in the situation of isolated menace.

Dead Calm, based on a novel that Orson Welles had long wished to film, is an exercise in skilfully sustained tension, with some effective shock moments. It is also a study of the workings of the male–female relationship. However resourceful Rae shows herself in handling the murderous Hughie, she is ultimately—as she was at the beginning, when she holds herself responsible for the child's death—dependent on John for comfort and survival. Such a need on his part is not on the film's agenda. The film works primarily as a tense reworking of the frightened-lady thriller genre, but its implied sexual politics gives it another dimension. Phil •Noyce made his name in socially aware dramas such as •Heatwave and went on to big-budget adventures such as Patriot Games (1992) in Hollywood. Dead Calm may be seen as a turning-point in his career.   BMcF

Dead Heart

1996. Director: Nick Parsons. *Producer:* Bryan Brown, Helen Watts. *Scriptwriter:* Nick Parsons. *Director of photography:* James Bartle. 104 min. *Cast:* Bryan Brown (Ray Lorkin), Ernie Dingo (David), Angie Milliken (Kate), Stanley Djanwong (Tjulpu), Lewis Fitz-Gerald (Les), Aaron Pedersen (Tony), Anne Tenney (Sarah), John Jarratt (Charlie), Lafe Charlton (Billy), David Gulpilil (Desert Man), Gnarnayarrahe Waitaire (Poppy), Marshall Napier (Sgt Oaks).

Dead Heart, based on a play of the same name by Nick Parsons and filmed at Jay Creek in the Northern Territory, is a film that refuses to present the differences between Aboriginal and White Australian cultures simplistically. The film is similar to •Deadly (1992) in that it uses a murder mystery to provide a dramatic context to explore these differences, but Dead Heart differs from the 1992 film in that Parsons and

Bryan Brown refuse to provide an easy solution. In fact Dead Heart deliberately fails to provide a rapprochement and, rather than offering a facile, optimistic resolution, it raises only questions and worries at the end. In Wala Wala, the small, remote desert settlement eight-hours drive west of Alice Springs, Kate, a married White woman, has sexual intercourse with Tony, an Aboriginal youth, in a sacred place. This violation results in Tony's death, and the drama intensifies when Senior Constable Ray Lorkin refuses to accept the local doctor's finding that the death was natural, as Lorkin suspects murder. This situation provides the context to examine a range of issues based on cultural difference and inherent distrust. When Lorkin disregards official orders to accept the medical findings of a natural death, he enters the domain of the desert Aborigines. Lorkin's decision is linked to his belief that the Aborigines must make a clean break with their past and embrace White culture, and Lorkin explains that his father was involved in taking Aboriginal children from their parents and placing them in White orphanages some years before. Nevertheless, Lorkin's position is not a clearcut one and, early in the film, he reluctantly allows Billy, his Aboriginal deputy, to be speared in the leg as retribution for his neglect in not preventing the death of an Aborigine being held in the local prison cell.

In the desert Lorkin confronts Poppy, his Aboriginal nemesis who holds views opposite to Lorkin's and rejects attempts to assimilate the two cultures. The middle ground is represented by David, the local aboriginal pastor, who works in both cultures but is ultimately shown to belong to neither. These three men, and the positions they represent, confront each other at the climax of the film. Dead Heart is ultimately a complex, confronting, topical, and dramatically satisfying film and, like other Australian films dealing with the Aboriginal community (such as •The Chant of Jimmie Blacksmith, 1978), deserved greater audience support in Australia.   GM

Deadly

1992. Director: Esben Storm. *Producer:* Richard Moir. *Scriptwriters:* Esben Storm, Richard Moir, Ranald Allan. *Director of photography:* Geoffrey Simpson. *Music:* Graeme Revell. 99 min. *Cast:* Jerome Ehlers (Tony Bourke), Frank Gallacher (Mick Thornton), Lydia Miller (Daphne), John Moore (Eddie), Alan David Lee (Constable Barry Blainey), Tony Barry (Deputy Commissioner Graham Stewart), Julie Nihill (Jenny), Martin Vaughan (Doctor Ward), Bill Hunter (Vernon Giles).

There is a sporadic pattern of films throughout the history of the Australian cinema that have reworked issues relating to Aboriginal culture into melodramatic presentations overlaid with generic conventions: for example, •The Romance of Runnibede (1928), •Bitter Springs (1950),

•The Naked Country (1985), and •Dead Heart (1996). Deadly is part of this pattern, as it uses the dramatic framework of a police investigation thriller to detail the tension and unequal distribution of power and resources among Aborigines, police, and the White community in the fictional outback town of Yabbabri (Wilcannia).

Tony Bourke, after accidentally shooting a junkie in Sydney, is sent to Yabbabri to investigate the death of an Aborigine in the local police station. Bourke is instructed to clear this matter up quickly as a favour to Deputy Commissioner Stewart and, if successful, he is promised that he will regain his detective status. After an initial welcome from the local police that indicates that Bourke will follow these orders (that is, clear the local police of any involvement in the death), Bourke gradually alienates himself from his colleagues by not following the preordained process of token investigation and clearance of police involvement. Bourke finds that a local policeman was involved in the killing, a discovery that parallels a similar event involving Deputy Commissioner Stewart when he was a junior policeman at Yabbabri many years before.

The most effective scenes in the film detail the rituals and processes of police solidarity and the subsequent breakdown in these processes as the relationship between Bourke and his colleagues deteriorates. In these scenes the film is able to assimilate its underlying social message, concerning the inequitable distribution of power in the community, into the generic framework. The film is less successful when it periodically injects an unmotivated social message concerning the plight of the local Aborigines.   GM

Death in Brunswick

1991. Director: John Ruane. Producer: Timothy White. Scriptwriters: John Ruane, Boyd Oxlade. Based on the novel by Boyd Oxlade. Director of photography: Ellery Ryan. Music: Philip Judd. 100 min. Cast: Sam Neill (Carl Fitzgerald), Zoë Carides (Sophie Papafagos), John Clarke (Dave), Yvonne Lawley (Mrs Fitzgerald), Nico Lathouris (Mustafa).

Carl is a cook in a seedy nightclub in the inner-Melbourne suburb of Brunswick. His mild, shiftless approach to life, dominated by his mother and reproached by the domestic model of his best friend Dave, begins to take on more dangerous contours when he becomes involved in the death of Mustafa, the drug-dealing Turkish kitchen-hand at the club. Carl then falls in love with Sophie, who also works at the club. These two developments complicate Carl's life in unexpected ways, including a late-night visit to a cemetery with Dave, who is also a grave-digger. The film's oddball plot is peopled with an engaging array of eccentric characters, and Zoë •Carides plays Sophie with a zesty charm that complements the shy guilelessness of Sam •Neill's Carl.

First-time director John •Ruane, who co-wrote the film with the author of the original novel, keeps the film fresh and surprising, with flashes of satirical social comedy that fuse well with the blacker humour at the film's centre.
          BMcF

Deling, Bert DIRECTOR/PRODUCER   Bert Deling dropped out of a law course to run the Melbourne University Film Society in the 1960s, and to take part enthusiastically in the Carlton 'scene'. He appeared as a pimp in Brian Davies's **Pudding Thieves** (1967), joined the ABC as an editor, then began making **Dalmas** (1973). The first half of **Dalmas** is an energetic thriller about crooked cops and the drug culture, but then the crew (including director Deling) join the cast and take over the film, so that its subject becomes filmmaking, in a way that is reminiscent of Norman Mailer's **Maidstone** (1971). It was produced on a shoestring budget and received only limited release, but paved the way for Deling's second film, •**Pure S…** (1975), which was also about drugs and was more widely screened and very controversial. In 1981 he wrote and directed the unreleased **Dead Easy**, his most conventional film, still about crime in Kings Cross, this time concerning a feud between rival gangs. He continued writing, mainly for television, including the telemovie *Matthew and Son* (1984) and the series *Sweet and Sour* (1984) and *The Last Resort* (1987–88).
          IB

Dence, Maggie ACTOR   Famous in the 1960s as the title character in television's long-running satirical revue *The Mavis Bramston Show*, Maggie Dence also did much other television and theatre work as well. Her cinema record has been only occasional and none of it has made use of her zany potential, but it deserves noting for the acid sketch of chronic boredom as a hotel receptionist in •**Wake in Fright** (1971), enervated by heat and ennui.
Other Australian films: The Best of Friends (1981), The Return of Captain Invincible (1983), Cherith (1988), Luigi's Ladies (1989).
          BMcF

Devereaux, Ed (1925–) ACTOR   Although Ed Devereaux has spent most of his career in the United Kingdom, he remains an indelibly Australian presence, partly because of his quintessentially Australian rugged looks and bearing. Beginning as a child performer, he gained wide experience in musical and straight theatre both in Australia and abroad, including a four-year touring stint with a company headed by Gladys Moncrieff in Australia and several big musicals in London, as well as a straight acting role there in *West Side Story*. He had played small roles in •**Smithy** (1946) and •**Eureka Stockade** (1949), but his film career really began with a small part in the largely Australian-made

Ealing film **The •Shiralee** (1957). His part was shot in London, and was followed by appearances in a number of popular British films, including several of the Carry On series, the Peter Sellers comedy **The Wrong Arm of the Law** (1962), and Lance Comfort's teen musical, **Live It Up** (1963) (as David Hemmings's sorely tried father).

He returned to Australia in 1964 and, as well as appearing on stage (for example, opposite Googie •Withers in *The Desire of the Moth*), he began to appear regularly on Australian television, notably in the hugely successful series *Skippy*. When Lee •Robinson filmed this as **The Intruders** in 1969, Devereaux repeated his role of national-park ranger Matt Hammond. He also appeared in Michael Powell's **•They're a Weird Mob** (1966), as the Italian hero's friendly boss; played an Aboriginal tracker in (politically incorrect) blackface in **•Journey out of Darkness** (1967); co-starred again with Googie Withers in John •McCallum's •Nickel Queen (1971), the romantic comedy centred on the mining boom; was very funny as a shorts-clad Australian diplomat in **Barry McKenzie Holds His Own** (1974); was toughly convincing as an ex-cop in Bruce •Beresford's heist thriller **•Money Movers** (1979); and was briefly authoritative as Ben Marston in the 1985 version of **•Robbery Under Arms**. Some of his best work has been for television: for example, as Lord Beaverbrook in the British miniseries *Edward and Mrs Simpson*, and as Liberal Treasurer, Phillip Lynch, in the local miniseries, *The Dismissal*. BMcF

Devil in the Flesh

1989. *Director*: Scott Murray. *Producer*: John B Murray. *Scriptwriter*: Scott Murray. Based on the novel *Le Diable au Corps*, by Raymond Radiguet. *Director of Photography*: Andrew de Groot. *Music*: Philippe Sarde. 104 min. *Cast*: Katia Caballero (Marthe Foscari), Keith Smith (Paul Hansen), John Morris (John Hansen), Jill Forster (Jill Hansen), Colin Duckworth (Pierre Fournier).

Based on a French novel that has been filmed on two other occasions (1947, 1986), and set in beautifully photographed, picturesque rural Victoria, **Devil in the Flesh** is a comparative rarity in new Australian cinema (see Revival, the) in the way in which it directly confronts issues arising from sexual love. Scott Murray, editor of *Cinema Papers*, directed his first feature with a firm focus on this central, governing idea, and this separates it somewhat from the rites-of-passage films common in the local film revival (see Rites of passage). There is an element of this in the way the schoolboy Paul falls in love with the older, more assured Marthe, but the film is just as interested in the conflict this generates for Marthe, who is married to an Italian soldier interned for the duration of the war. Unlike the novel, in which Marthe dies, Murray's script accepts a more emotionally and morally ambiguous ending. BMcF

Devil's Playground, The

1928. *Director*: Victor Bindley. *Continuity*: John Bedouin. Based on the novel *Hell's Highway* by Ashley Durham. *Directors of photography*: Jack Bruce, James Grant, Jack Fletcher. B&W. *Cast*: Elza Stenning [Elsa Jacoby] (Naneena).

The first Australian film called **The Devil's Playground** (see also **The Devil's Playground**, 1976) is pure South Seas Islands hokum. In a story vaguely reminiscent of *The Tempest*, an older man and his daughter live on a tropical island where they have to contend with two varieties of local hostility: a drunken White trader and rebellious 'natives' who work as pearl divers. With the help of a young man whose plane crashes nearby, the good White people triumph, but not before one of the most surprising surviving scenes from early Australian cinema, a scene in which the lustful trader nearly whips Naneena. The scene is surprising because of its luridly erotic character, a quality that otherwise is not manifested in the mainstream Australian footage that has been preserved from this period. WILLIAM D. ROUTT

Devil's Playground, The

1976. *Director*: Fred Schepisi. *Producer*: Fred Schepisi. *Scriptwriter*: Fred Schepisi. *Director of photography*: Ian Baker. *Music*: Bruce Smeaton. 107 min. *Cast*: Arthur Dignam (Brother Francine), Nick Tate (Brother Victor), Simon Burke (Tom Allen), Charles McCullum (Brother Sebastian), John Frawley (Brother Celian).

Fred •Schepisi's first full-length feature, from a script based on autobiographical experiences in a Catholic seminary for teenage boys, was a major critical success of the 1970s. Set in the early 1950s, it offered an unusually tough-minded approach to the coming-of-age theme so common in new Australian cinema (see Revival, the): where others of its kind were apt to be loosely episodic, this film focuses firmly on the conflicts of its young protagonist.

The seminary is a handsome building set in rural peace, but its interior is dominated by oppressive corridors, by the disciplined rituals of meals and showers, and by the spectacle of young lives being moulded in ways that threaten to deform their futures. Tom Allen is not a natural rebel. He is willing to believe he has a vocation, but he is also aware of the instinctive demands of the flesh, of the inviting freedoms of the outside world, and of a growing sense of the unnaturalness of the disciplines enjoined by the seminary.

The first Australian film to be invited to the Directors' Fortnight at the Cannes Film Festival (in 1976), **The Devil's Playground** is structured about such major oppositions as constraint and freedom, discipline and impulse, and innocence and experience. As well as offering insight into Tom's growing pains, Schepisi also provides a sympathetic picture of the life of the priests. They are not represented as ogres: some are tormented by the difficulties of their vocation, but others are clearly at peace with it. The novelist Tom *Keneally, who had written Schepisi's short film The Priest (an episode of *Libido, 1973), has the role of a jolly visiting priest who, in a sequence encapsulating the contrarieties of the life, beams at the young as he preaches hellfire.   BMcF

Dexter, Gayne Robert (?–1966) WRITER/PUBLICIST
Journalist Bob Dexter learned the film advertising business with J.D. Williams and became publicity manager of Union Theatres (see Greater Union Organisation), at its formation in 1913. In the 1920s, he spent six years in USA as director of publicity for First National Pictures, and was in charge of the American distribution of *The Sentimental Bloke (1919). He returned to Australia in 1927 and, in evidence before the 1927 Royal Commission into the Australian Film Industry, attributed the failure of the film in USA to the ugliness of its leading actors. As Bob Dexter, he became director of publicity for *Hoyts Theatres but, as Gayne Dexter he was editor and part-owner of the trade journal Everyone's: this allowed him to play an important part in shaping trade opinion about local and foreign films, and particularly about the directions that the Australian industry should be taking. Some of his predictions about the future of Australian film proved remarkably accurate. He was invited to write titles for some of Australia's major silent films, including *For the Term of His Natural Life (1927), *The Romance of Runnibede (1928), and The Grey Glove (1928). He also collaborated on the scripts for *The Squatter's Daughter (1933, with E.V. Timms) and *The Silence of Dean Maitland (1934, with Edmund Barclay). He spent some years in the United Kingdom as director of publicity for Warners, then retired to Australia, continuing for many further years to do occasional publicity, and to write on film for the popular magazine Pix.   IB

Digger Earl, The
1924. Director/Producer/Scriptwriter: Beaumont Smith. Director of photography: Lacey Percival. B&W. Cast: Arthur Tauchert (Bill Jones), Dunstan Webb (Captain Halliday).

Only the opening of **The Digger Earl** has survived, but the film begins well enough. Bill Jones, a dinkum bloke if ever there was one, heeds his country's call to arms and finds himself in the trenches at the front, where he exchanges banter with his mates and also does some fighting. The trench scenes and the battle footage are staged and photographed with something more than mere competence, and * Arthur Tauchert proves himself again the most charismatic masculine presence in early Australian cinema. Most of the film, however, concerns what happens to Bill after the

war, when he agrees to impersonate the Earl of Margate on the way home, and this footage appears to have been lost completely.   WILLIAM D. ROUTT

Diggers
1931. Director: F.W. Thring. Production company: Efftee Film Productions. Scriptwriters: Pat Hanna, Eric Donaldson. Director of photography: Arthur Higgins. 61 min. B&W. Cast: Pat Hanna (Chic Williams), George Moon (Joe Mulga), Edmund Warrington (Fatty Jones), Cecil Scott (Bluey), Norman French (Medical Officer), Guy Hastings (Quarter Master Sergeant), Joe Valli (Corporal McTavish).

Dedicated to the Australian soldiers, this was derived from the Diggers stage show, which had successfully toured Australia since World War I under the direction of Pat *Hanna. Three sketches about the Australian Imperial Forces in 1918 were loosely combined within a framing device of a returned servicemen's dinner, twelve years later: the first sketch shows malingerers Chic, Joe, and Fatty trying to stay in hospital in London; in the second, Chic, Joe, and Bluey con rum from the British Q.M. Stores; the third is a downbeat, sentimental representation of the popular song, Mademoiselle from Armentières. Hanna, who liked to end on a note of high comedy, objected to this sequence of the sketches, but Frank *Thring insisted.

The stage-related elements do not travel well to the screen, but the film remains significant as a record of an important Australian stage tradition. Presented in the first Efftee 'Unit Program' (see Efftee Film Productions), with the short feature *A Co-Respondent's Course (1931), it was moderately successful in Australia, particularly in country areas, and was released in the United Kingdom under the Quota Act.   IB

Diggers in Blighty
1933. Director/Producer/Scriptwriter: Pat Hanna. Director of photography: Arthur Higgins. 72 min. B&W. Cast: Pat Hanna (Chic Williams), Joe Valli (Joe McTavish), George Moon (Joe Mulga), Norman French (Sir Guy Gough), John D'Arcy (Captain Jack Fisher), Prudence Irving (Alison), Thelma Scott (Judy Fisher).

Pat *Hanna set up his own production company and hired the *Efftee Film Productions studio to make this second film built around the Diggers stage show. This time, episodic comedy is interwoven with narrative. There is still a trio of lazy digger mates (with Bluey of the first film replaced by Joe McTavish), but this time they unwittingly become involved with the efforts of a British spy to plant false information on an informer. Their success leads to everyone being given leave in the United Kingdom, where two romantic sub-plots reach a satisfactory conclusion, leaving the three mates with the rum.

The laboured comic tone is similar to that of the earlier film, and neither the narrative line nor the performances are strong enough to compensate. There were also technical problems, particularly with the soundtrack. The film was released in 1933 with Efftee's •Harmony Row, but was not well received.   IB

Dignam, Arthur (1939–) ACTOR

Arthur Dignam is a prolific NSW character actor who has appeared in Australian films and television programs since the early 1970s. Dignam specialises in intellectuals, scientists, religious, and other authority figures, sometimes with tortured souls. This persona crystallised in an early starring role as a priest driven insane by his celibacy in •The Devil's Playground (1976). Since then Dignam has varied this persona within certain limits: sometimes the authority figure veers towards the sinister, as with the chilling homosexual politician in the paranoid thriller •The Everlasting Secret Family (1988); sometimes it is more benign, as in the form of Pastor Anderson, one of the fundamentalist influences destined to drive Bob •Ellis's alter ego Ken Elkin towards a hedonistic, tortured life in •The Nostradamus Kid (1993); the scientist who provides the crucial advice to Claudia •Karvan and Guy •Pearce in •Dating the Enemy (1996), and as the eccentric actor Ernest Thesiger in Gods and Monsters (1999). The most notable exceptions to this casting pattern include Dignam's effective performance as Aeneas Gunn, the manager of a large cattle station in the Northern Territory at the turn of the century, in •We of the Never Never (1982), and the insensitive Gregory in the Australian adaptation of Henrik Ibsen's •The Wild Duck (1984). Dignam is the father of Nicholas Gledhill, the young actor who created such a strong impression in •Careful He Might Hear You (1983).

Other Australian films include: •Libido (1973), •Between Wars (1974), •Petersen (1974), Summer of Secrets (1976), •The Chant of Jimmie Blacksmith (1978), •Cathy's Child (1979), •Grendel, Grendel, Grendel (1981), Duet for Four (1982), The Return of Captain Invincible (1983), •Burke & Wills (1985), Those Dear Departed (1987), The Right Hand Man (1987), The Dreaming (1988), Isabelle Eberhardt (1992).   GM

Dimboola

1979. Director: John Duigan. Producer: John Weiley. Scriptwriter: Jack Hibberd. Based on the play Dimboola by Jack Hibberd. Director of photography: Tom Cowan. Music: George Dreyfus. 94 min. Cast: Bruce Spence (Morrie), Natalie Bate (Maureen), Max Gillies (Vivian Worcester-Jones), Bill Garner (Dangles), Jack Perry (Horrie).

Jack Hibberd's play Dimboola was among many Australian plays premiered at the Pram Factory in Carlton. The play, a participatory wedding reception, with the audience seated among the wedding guests, was a hit in its first season in 1969, was revived several times, toured Australia, and was successful overseas. In 1979 it was filmed by a huge cast that reads like a Pram Factory roll of honour. The film covers three days of story, with the reception as the final set piece, after the bride's kitchen tea, the groom's bucks' night, and various sub-plots. In the midst of these farcical events, Morrie and Maureen make a surprisingly convincing central couple. The narrator is the pompous English visitor Vivian Worcester-Jones. Incidental music is provided by the Dimboola brass band, a trio of singing waitresses, a versatile rock band, a pub pianist, and soulful songs to the camera by actor Chad Morgan. The citizens of the Victorian town of Dimboola cooperated in the making of the film, but the disclaimer in the final credits was probably a relief to them. It would be a pity if the only permanent record of the play is this disappointingly unfunny and stylistically incoherent adaptation.   IB

Dimitriades, Alex (1973–) ACTOR

Beginning his acting career with a stint in Neighbours (1985), Alex Dimitriades's first film role as the disillusioned and love-struck Greek teenager in Michael Jenkins's •The Heartbreak Kid (1993) took this little-known actor to the peak of stardom. As Nick, Dimitriades pounced on to the screen and immediately captivated audiences with his honesty, enthusiasm, and stunning good looks. The film's success lead to a television series, Heartbreak High, with Dimitriades starring in the first series. Moving on to roles in television in GP (1988) and Blue Murder (miniseries, 1995), then the ABC television series Wildside (1998), Dimitriades quickly established himself as an actor capable of great diversity and intensity. In 1998, he won the role of Ari in Ana •Kokkinos's Head On, his powerful performance gaining him a nomination for Best Actor at the Australian Film Institute Awards. Dimitriades's performance gained him the highest accolades and has cemented him as one of Australia's most exciting and talented performers.   KAREN FORD

Dimsey, Ross (1943–) PRODUCER/DIRECTOR/SCREENWRITER

Ross Dimsey trained and worked in the United Kingdom and the USA between 1965 and 1968, before returning to Melbourne where he worked, mainly as an assistant director, on •Stork (1971), •Libido (1973), Alvin Rides Again (1974), and End Play (1976). Dimsey wrote the script for two sex films, •Fantasm (1976) and Fantasm Comes Again (1978), before directing the successful family film Blue Fire Lady (1977), with teenage English actor Cathryn Harrison, the grand-daughter of Rex Harrison, in the leading role. Dimsey followed this with the inept thriller Final Cut (1980), for the •Queensland Film Corporation (see Queensland, history and images): it was the last film he directed. Dimsey was chief executive of the •Victorian Film Corporation in 1984 when Robert Ward, from Filmways, suggested Morris West's 1957 novel *The Naked Country* as a likely film project. The resultant film, co-scripted by director Tim •Burstall and Dimsey, was an exciting depiction of racial tension in outback Australia. Two years later, producer Dimsey clashed with writer–director Bob •Ellis during the production of •**Warm Nights on A Slow Moving Train** (1988). Each man had a different perception of the film. This was reflected in the running time: Dimsey's cut, the release version, runs 40 minutes less than Ellis's cut. Dimsey produced •**Kangaroo** in 1987, which is based on D.H. Lawrence's experiences in Australia in 1922. He also worked on a number of productions for the ABC, including the miniseries *Darling of the Gods* (1989). GM

Dingo, Ernie (1956–) ACTOR Ernie Dingo, along with Kylie Belling, was one of the few Aboriginal participants with any stage or media experience in •**The Fringe Dwellers** (1986), Bruce •Beresford's adaptation of Nene Gare's 1961 novel. Dingo's performance in the film as Phil, the young horseman who impregnates the central character, established his career in the Australian cinema and this was followed by a supporting role in the made-for-television crime thriller *The Blue Lightning* (1986). A lead role in *A Waltz Through The Hills* (1988), another telefeature that served as the pilot for a five-part series, was based on the adventures of two young children who, in 1954, walked 107 miles from their inland town to Perth. Dingo was cast in the main Aboriginal role of Charlie in **Crocodile Dundee II** (1988), Paul •Hogan's attempt to duplicate the success of •**Crocodile Dundee** (1986). Dingo's comedic function in the sequel was similar to David Gulpilil's in the 1986 film. Dingo appeared as himself in **Cappuccino** (1989), and he also had regular employment in the television series *Fast Forward* and, later, on *The Great Outdoors*. Supporting roles in **Clowning Around** (1991), which was shot as a feature but released as a miniseries, •**Blackfellas** (1993), and **Heartland** (1994) preceded Dingo's best screen role to date as David in •**Dead Heart** (1996), the local pastor in Wala Wala who is torn between two cultures in this underrated melodrama. GM

Dingwall, John (1940–) WRITER/DIRECTOR Dingwall is best known as the writer of •**Sunday Too Far Away** (1975), one of the most important films of the new Australian cinema (see Revival, the). He was born in Queensland and worked for ten years as a journalist before writing police shows for Crawford Productions, including *Homicide, Matlock Police*, and *Division 4*. The experiences of his gun-shearer brother-in-law inspired him to write a treatment about shearers but, despite four years of effort, he was unable to interest a producer. He was commissioned to write a film about Gallipoli in the early days of the •South Australian Film Corporation but, when the project was cancelled, he worked out his contract with a rewrite of *The Shearers*, which eventually became **Sunday Too Far Away.** The work of Ken •Hannam, who had been working in British television, attracted Dingwall's attention, and Hannam was hired to direct. Dingwall went on to write and produce **Buddies** (1983), which shared similar themes of mateship in an outback setting but suffered from an excessive dose of larrikin humour. With Margaret Kelly (•**Puberty Blues**), he created *Pig in a Poke* under the name of John Kelly, about a medical practice in Redfern. Dingwall also wrote and directed the low-budget **Phobia** (1990), which was well reviewed, and •**The Custodian** (1994), a film about acquiescence amid police corruption that drew on his early experiences as a police roundsman. He continues to develop his own film projects.

HARRY KIRCHNER

Dobrowolska, Gosia (1958–) ACTOR Polish-born actor who graduated from the Wroclaw Drama Studio in 1980 and appeared in a small number of Polish plays before migrating to Australia in 1982. After learning rudimentary English, Dobrowolska was cast as Nina in •**Silver City** (1984), a drama by Sophia Turkiewicz that follows the experiences of several Polish immigrants in postwar Australia. Dobrowolska was nominated for Best Actress for the Australian Film Institute awards for her performance in this film, which was followed by an entirely different role, the cool blonde on the run in Frank Shield's underrated, and very low-budget, chase film •**The Surfer,** which was shot in 1986 but not released until 1988.

Dobrowolska performed with distinction in a range of genres throughout the late 1980s and the 1990s: in comedy as nurse Ophelia Cox in **Around the World in 80 Ways** (1988); the tormented wife of Sean •Scully in the underrated marital drama **Phobia**, directed by John •Dingwall; and in a sequence of films directed by Paul •Cox (**Golden Braid**, 1990; •**A Woman's Tale**, 1991; **The Nun and the Bandit**, 1992; **Exile**, 1994; and **Lust and Revenge**, 1996). Dobrowolska played a feature role as a newspaper executive in the John Dingwall-directed police film •**The Custodian** (1994).

Other Australian films include: I've Come About the Suicide (1987), Resistance (1992), Big Ideas (1993), Cops and Robbers (1993). GM

Dobson, Agnes (1904–?) ACTOR Daughter of actor–manager Collet Dobson, Agnes Dobson appeared with the family's theatrical company from the time she was a babe in arms, and was taking speaking roles such as Little

Agnes Dobson

Lord Fauntleroy by the age of six. By the time she was 15, she was playing romantic leads, and her personal following made her a popular choice as the leading lady of two feature films: Beaumont •Smith's **Barry Butts In** (1919) was released a little earlier than Charles Villiers' **The Face at the Window** (1919). Both were light-hearted takes on established genres—the former a comedy–mystery involving a tale of long-lost relatives, the latter a farcical detective story. Both were successful financially and Agnes Dobson's work was praised. However, instead of going on to an illustrious screen career, she played only small (mostly uncredited) film parts from then on, with her main career on the stage. She also became Talks Presentation Officer for ABC radio and later a tutor with Crawfords school for actors. In her later years she was best known as Mrs Sharpshott in the ABC's long-running *Village Glee Club*, although she also made occasional brief appearances on television.

Other Australian films include: The Hayseeds' Backblocks Show (1917).   IB

Dobson, Kevin DIRECTOR   Sometimes known as Kevin James Dobson, this director began his career in television, working in several capacities for Crawford Productions, including as editor and director for such series as *Matlock Police*. He also directed Charles •Tingwell in a telemovie thriller, *Gone to Ground* in 1976, the year before he made his début as a feature film director with •**The Mango Tree**. Produced and written by Michael •Pate, with whom Dobson had worked on *Matlock Police*, this was an agreeable if somewhat ramshackle contribution to the coming-of-age genre popular in Australian cinema at the time. It was given some distinction by Brian •Probyn's camera, which lushly captured the northern Queensland locations, and by the richly felt performance of Irish-American actor, Geraldine Fitzgerald, but its episodes were too slackly linked, and actor Christopher •Pate was scarcely equal to the demands of its young protagonist. There were, however, some promising signs in Dobson's feeling for place and in his portrayal of the socially marginalised. He made only one more feature in Australia, **Squizzy Taylor** (1982), a handsomely recreated but uninvolving picture of underworld crime in Melbourne in the 1920s, with dancer David •Atkins in the role of the eponymous small-time gangster whose image was inflated by the media.

The rest of Dobson's career has been spent in television, where he has directed (or shared the direction of) such Australian miniseries as *Five Mile Creek* and *The Thorn Birds: The Missing Years* (with Richard Chamberlain reprising his role from the precursor series), the American miniseries *Survive the Savage Sea*, and the Canadian *Gold Diggers: The Secret of Bear Mountain*. If either of his features had been a commercial success, instead of mildly likeable exercises in period nostalgia, his career might have been more robust.   BMcF

Documentary and non-fiction, silent   Imported films always outnumbered local productions in Australian cinema. Australian film was almost always shown in a supportive role. More than 80 per cent of Australia's silent footage was devoted to non-fiction subjects: documentaries, actualities, newsreels, and advertisements.

Many, perhaps most, of Australia's silent-film production companies were exclusively involved in documentary and newsreel production. Documentary producers were not reliant on the expensive studio facilities required for fictional features. Consequently, individual camera operators and small companies could profitably make these films in remote parts of Australia, far from the studios and processing facilities of Sydney and Melbourne. The documentary industry was far more decentralised than Australia's feature film industry, with significant production based in Brisbane, Hobart, Adelaide, and Perth.

In the pioneer period of Australian cinema, before 1910, the predominating film fare came from the United Kingdom and France, where non-fiction films were far more popular than they were in the USA. Australia had a tradition of theatrical entertainments presenting visual records of foreign events, even before the advent of film. Cycloramas, dioramas, waxworks and paintings of current happenings served a function similar to that of the modern news films or telecast. When the Lumière Cinématographe arrived with its promise of 'placing the world within one's reach', it was tapping into a demonstrated demand for theatrical amusements in Australia.

The first few Australian producers could generally film items of only the standard one-minute length of a roll of film, usually in one continuous shot. The Lumière Cinématographe's exhibitors, Marius Sestier and Walter Barnett, shot about ten one-minute films of the 1896 **VRC Derby** and **Melbourne Cup** (see **1896 Melbourne Cup, The**), but these shots were seldom presented as a unified narrative sequence. The same could be said of Melbourne's Thwaites and Harvie (active 1897–98), who filmed a series of sporting events and specialised in processing them speedily for exhibition on the night of their filming. Sydney's Mark Blow (active 1897–98) often shot films of local schools, businesses, and events to induce participants to see themselves on the screen at his 'Polytechnic'. He made Australia's first unscheduled news film when he shot the square-rigger, the *Hereward*, aground on Maroubra beach in 1898.

In September 1898 the first 'serious' usage of Australian film took place. In Torres Strait, Professor Alfred Haddon of Cambridge University filmed Islanders and Australian Aborigines on Murray Island. His five one-minute films were the first anthropological research films shot *in situ* on a field expedition.

Documentary and non-fiction

However, all these efforts were little more than prologue for the profuse output of Australia's first corporate film producer, the Salvation Army Limelight Department (see also Historical representations). Before 1901, all the films produced by the Department were limited to one-minute's running time by their usage of the Lumière Ciné-matographe. Commencing in October 1897, they mostly filmed Salvation Army activities to illustrate the lecture on **The Salvation Army's Social Work in Australasia** (1898, 6 films and 200 slides), later known as **Social Salvation** (1899–1900, 25 films and 275 slides). This was one of the earliest examples of the documentary use of film in exposing slum conditions and social problems. The subsequent **Soldiers of the Cross** (15 one-minute films and 220 slides, first screened 13 September 1900) added costuming and elaborate settings (see also Silent film, to 1914; Historical representations). Salvation Army film activities attracted NSW government patronage. The Department was commissioned to film **The Inauguration of the (Australian) Commonwealth**, the celebrations of the swearing-in of Australia's first governor-general and federal cabinet in Sydney's Centennial Park in January 1901. More than 35 minutes of coverage were produced, six times the length of any previous Australian film. The Department followed this with **Royal Visit to Victoria** (May 1901, 20 min) for the Victorian government, and **Royal Visit to New Zealand** (June 1901, 56 min.) for the New Zealand government. The profits generated by the exhibition of these induced the Salvation Army to permit its Limelight Department to raise money by the production and exhibition of secular films. The department produced the Central Australian expedition films of Sir Walter Baldwin •Spencer (shot April–May 1901), almost 40 minutes of coverage of the customs and ceremonies of the Arrernte peoples of the area, the first major coverage of Australian Aboriginal life. Between 1900 and August 1902, Limelight Department operators (principally Joseph Perry) shot 6000 feet (100 min.) of film documenting every phase of Australian history, Aboriginal life, natural history, industry, and politics, ending with Federation. Unified by a two-hour lecture written by Salvation Army Australasian Secretary William Peart, and accompanied by 200 slides, it premiered on 10 August 1902 in Melbourne as **Under Southern Skies**, and it was by far the most elaborate Australian film presentation of its time.

From 1902 to 1904 the Limelight Department made over 50 films, ranging from three to ten minutes in length, mostly local views of Australian (and New Zealand) scenic attractions, town views (including Ballarat, Bendigo, Geelong, Mackay, Rockhampton, Mount Gambier, Broken Hill, and Adelaide) and occasional industrial documentaries such as **Port Fairy Barracouta Fishing** (1902), **Port Pirie Smelters at Work** (1903), **Sugar Cane Cutting and Planting**

at **Te Kowai, near Mackay** (1904), and **Mount Morgan Gold Mines** (1904). One of the last commissions of the Department was from the Royal Australian Ornithologist's Union, who paid them to shoot Australia's first nature film, **Voyage of the S.S. 'Manawatu' to the Islands of Bass Strait** (December 1908).

Ernest •Higgins filmed **Glimpses of Tasmania** (1905) for the Tasmanian Tourist Association, before becoming Cozens Spencer's chief camera operator in Sydney. After making a few short actualities, Higgins 'hit the big time' in December 1908 by shooting the boxing match between American Jack Johnson and Australian Tommy Burns. This *cause célèbre* was widely regarded as a symbolic racial struggle of Black against White. Its tremendous popularity meant that it was screened worldwide. Higgins then went on to shoot hundreds of Spencer actualities and scenics including **1909 Football Final**, **Marvellous Melbourne** (1910) and **Picturesque Hobart** (1911).

Johnson & Gibson, chemists from the Melbourne suburb of St Kilda, produced occasional news films and scenics from 1902 onwards. They commissioned the camera operator of the successful film •**The Story of the Kelly Gang** (1906), Charles Byers Coates, to film a series of local scenics and advertising films: for example, **Living Bendigo** (1907) and **Living Hawthorn** (1907). Johnson & Gibson went on to make hundreds of non-fiction shorts including **Opening of the Prahan–Malvern Tramway** (May 1910), **Rescue of Miner Varischetti by Diver Hughes** (1907), and a long series of travelogues made for the Victorian Railways by Johnson & Gibson's staff cameraman Orizaba Perry during 1909 and 1910.

T.J. West, the British cinema magnate, came to Australia via New Zealand where he had made a great number of local scenics. He toured Australia from March 1906, shooting such films as **Living Sydney** (April 1906), **Carlton vs Fitzroy Football Match** (June 1906), and **Australian Agricultural and Farming Pursuits** (1906). West screened Pathé's films in 1908–10, including films shot under Commonwealth government contracts. On 1 July 1909, Pathé Frères opened a film dealership in Queen Street, Melbourne, becoming the first film producers in Australia without concurrent financial interest in exhibition. By the start of 1910, Pathé Frères had the lion's share of non-fiction film production and distribution in Australia. It prepared to introduce an entirely new type of non-fiction film to the country: the regular weekly newsreel.

News films were produced in Australia from 1896, when Sestier filmed the **VRC Derby** and the Melbourne Cup (see **1896 Melbourne Cup, The**), but these were not *newsreels* by the film trade's definition of the term. The newsreel was a one-reel film of about ten minutes' duration, with several news items presented in a magazine or 'gazette' format, and released on a regular (most often weekly) basis. Newsreels were a Pathé Frères innovation. First produced in France from 1908, the London branch followed in 1910 with **Pathé's Animated Gazette**. This British newsreel was probably renamed **West's Journal of Daily Events** (1910) for occasional Australian release with local items appended.

Australia's first newsreel with wholly local content was **Pathé's Animated Gazette (Australasian Edition)**, released weekly from 28 November 1910. It initially had an average weekly length of 600 feet (10 min.), increasing by the late 1920s to almost 1000 feet (17 min.). Its colloquial name in the trade was **The Australian Gazette**, which became its official name after May 1914. Interestingly, this Australian production made its début almost a year before the first American newsreel, **Pathé's Weekly** (8 August 1911).

Pathé's Melbourne management orchestrated the birth of its local gazette by uniquely Gallic methods. Camera operators were sent to theatres with Pathé affiliation to shoot a local travelogue, often of two reels or more. Pathé films of Bendigo, Ballarat, Footscray, Broken Hill, and Parramatta made in 1910–11 survive in the National Film and Sound Archives (see Archives). The theatre owner, if he was so inclined, would subsequently be supplied with a camera and raw film by Pathé, so that he could shoot local events of interest to his patrons. Films of general interest were syndicated through Pathé for circulation around Australia in **Pathé's Animated Gazette**.

The earliest Australian newsreel items mostly covered scheduled events where coverage could be pre-planned, including processions, the laying of foundation stones, funerals, and sporting events. Pathé developed affiliations with newspapers such as the Melbourne *Argus* and Sydney *Sun* to provide tip-offs for their camera operators, and it also had commercial affiliations with fashion houses such as Melbourne's Georges, relating to the exhibition of new furs and formal wear.

Pathé's Australasian Gazette gave many local camera operators their first opportunity for regular film work. Often they went on to distinguished careers in feature production, including A.J. Moulton, Bert Cross, Franklyn •Barrett, Maurice •Bertel, Henri Herault, M. Daimon, Herbert Finlay, Al Burne, Lacey •Percival, and Walter •Sully, to name only a few.

Within two years of Pathé's introduction of the Australian weekly newsreel, at least three further Australian newsreels began. J.D. Williams introduced **Williams' Weekly** (1912–13), with camera work by the former Qld. film pioneer Bert Ive. During 1910, the Gaumont organisation started producing Australian items, including Frank •Hurley's first motion picture efforts, for their **Gaumont Graphic**. Gaumont also briefly produced a wholly Australian **G.K.L. Gazette** in 1912–13, which ceased when Gaumont was absorbed into 'the combine' (see Greater Union

Organisation; Exhibition and distribution). Adelaide's Wondergraph Theatre had its own **Wondergraph Weekly** in 1911, and Ballarat's Albert Hall ran its own **Pathé's Ballarat Gazette** in 1911–13.

As Spencers, Wests, Williams, Pathé, and Amalgamated Pictures progressively joined 'The combine', the independent reels were subsumed by **Pathé's Animated Gazette (Australian Edition)**, which became **The Australasian Gazette** in 1916. The brilliant pioneer Australian animator Harry Julius (see Animation) produced his Cartoons of the Moment as segments in **The Australasian Gazette**, many of which lampooned current developments in World War I.

Although **The Australasian Gazette**, with its guaranteed screening through Union Theatres, was the most pervasive of Australia's silent newsreels, it was not the only one. Others included the British **Topical Budget**, the independent Co-Operative Film Exchange's **Co-Operative Australian Weekly** (later **Observer Magazine**), and the Spectator Film Manufacturing Company of Sydney's **Spectator Gazette** (later **Selznick Spectator**). American film companies Fox, MGM, and Paramount produced Australian newsreel items during the 1920s. The Fox and MGM reels ran local material and used Australian camera operators only occasionally. By contrast, **Paramount's Australian Gazette** was wholly local in content, running to more than 650 weekly issues from 1918 to 1930.

By the 1920s the speed of newsreel coordination had improved. Equipment was lighter and more mobile, and film was faster and capable of performing in low interior lighting. By the end of the 1920s, panchromatic film was available for special applications. 'Ica' hand-held spring-wind cameras were first used for gazette work in Australia during 1928. Accidental, unplanned events began to be captured by newsreel camera operators. For **Paramount's Australian Gazette** Charles Herschell managed to film the collapse of a viewing platform that injured one hundred onlookers during the America Fleet's visit in 1925. In 1923, Bert Cross filmed Melbourne rioters and looters during a famous police strike, and this issue of the **Australasian Gazette** attracted an immediate export ban from the federal government.

When Fox announced that a Movietone sound newsreel truck was to be brought to Australia, **The Australasian Gazette** folded immediately in response, issuing its last edition on 27 March 1929. **Paramount's Australian Gazette** continued into 1930, by which time the number of silent picture outlets had shrunk far enough to make the **Gazette's** production uneconomic. A temporary association between Australasian Films (see Greater Union Organisation) and Vocalion Records in Melbourne briefly led to the production of a sound-on-disc **Australian Talkies Newsreel** from 1930 to 1932. By then, the first Australian sound-on-film reel, **Fox Movietone News (Australian Edition)** had begun shooting items (August 1929) and, in November 1929, released its first Australian sound newsreel, featuring incoming prime minister, James Scullin.

From the inception of cinema, Australian governments have recognised the publicity value of film. During the silent era, film was used by governments to stimulate immigration, to publicise Australian industry and tourism, and to record Australian achievements in war and peace.

In October 1898, the official artist of Qld, photographer Frederick Charles Wills, gained permission from the colony's government to make 'lantern slides . . . on the Lumière Cinématographe principle' featuring local industries, agricultural processes and town views (see also Qld, history and images). The films were intended for screening in the United Kingdom to stimulate immigration to Australia. It was the world's first in-house government film-production project. Wills and his assistant Henry Mobsby shot about 30 rolls of film, each one minute in length, between February and October 1899. Superbly composed and edited, the films vividly portray Qld colonial life and work, but they were too far ahead of their time. Without any permanent British cinemas in operation, exhibition was wholly dependent on the whim of Qld's immigration lecturer in the United Kingdom, George Randall. Lumière Cinématographes proved impossible to hire in the United Kingdom for exhibition purposes, and the project reached a dead end when Randall ultimately refused to screen the material.

During the celebrations of Federation and the subsequent royal visit for the first opening of federal parliament in 1901, the governments of NSW, Vic. and New Zealand commissioned Melbourne's Salvation Army Limelight Department to film the proceedings. In 1908 the Limelight Department received another governmental commission to record the **Visit to Australasia of the American Fleet**. However this, and work done for the Qld and NSW governments, by former Limelight Department cameraman Sidney Cook during 1906 and 1907, were all state government initiatives.

In 1903, cameraman Herbert Wyndham began filming Australian industries, scenic attractions, and sporting events for The Australian Animated Picture Syndicate, presenting their product via the touring shows of Clem Sudholz's Bio-Tableau and Entertainers during 1905, 1906, and 1907. This series, **Animated Australia**, was shot in every Australian state. It included the sheep and cattle industry in Qld and NSW, axemen's carnivals in Vic. and Tas., military scenes, and streetscapes of our major cities. Syndicate manager E.D. Tupper pressured Australia's federal government to sponsor the enterprise for its advertising value in the United Kingdom. While the series, screened in 1905 at the Hobart Premier's Conference, received verbal and written support from Prime Minister George Reid, no direct funding or concrete government support from the federal government eventuated, and the filming ceased in 1907.

In June 1908, the world's (then) largest film producer, Pathé Frères, informed the Australian government of its intention to send out a 'South Seas and Australasian Expedition', a film crew consisting of manager Leopold Sutto, with cameramen Herault and Hans Theyer. Late in 1908 this crew toured the Solomon Islands and Papua New Guinea with the famous novelist Jack London.

The time was ripe for federal government involvement in promoting the nation on film. The previous government had just been criticised for the 'piecemeal' policy of promoting the nation only to applicants for immigration. A sudden burgeoning of permanent cinema venues also gave more weight to the value of the film medium. External Affairs approved a government grant to Pathé of £2000, half of the estimated production cost of 15 one-reel Australian films. The federal government was to decide on the scenic and industrial subjects to be filmed. No local film producer was given an opportunity to tender for the production contract. This scandalous situation was deeply resented by the local industry, and probably contributed more than any other factor to the eventual termination of Pathé's commission. The Pathé crew began filming in Australia in January 1909. By September of that year they completed the job, releasing films such as **The Hop Industry in Tasmania, Harvesting in Victoria, Queensland's Wool Industry**, and **Scenes on Sydney Harbour**. Surviving fragments of these films indicate that they were proficiently shot, but lacked narrative focus and often included ludicrously misspelt titles, for example 'Adelaide and ist [sic] Environs' and 'Ponoroma [sic] of Adelaide'. Pathé's production contract was not renewed, although the company continued to produce local industrial pictures (for example, the 'Australia at Work' series) without government assistance. Films such as **The Melbourne Argus Newspaper** (1910) and **MacRobertson's Confectionery Factory** (1909) were probably made with financial support from the businesses portrayed.

In September 1911 the federal government decided to appoint its own cinematographer within the Department of External Affairs, to be more directly answerable to the wishes of the department. The successful applicant was a prize-winning art photographer, the 43-year-old James Pinkerton Campbell. During his brief and stormy 18-month appointment Campbell managed to shoot almost 20 000 feet of film for exhibition in the United Kingdom for immigration purposes, including over one hour of coverage of **Northern Territory** (1912), shot on behalf of Sir Walter Baldwin Spencer and **The Christening of the Federal Capital** (1913). Departmental conflicts over wastage of materials to achieve 'artistic effects' led to the termination of Campbell's employment in May 1913.

Campbell's replacement as Commonwealth government cinematographer was Bert Ive, the laconic Queensland cinema pioneer, who retained the position until his death in 1939. Like Campbell, Ive was initially attached to the Melbourne-based Department of External Affairs. His work continued on the same lines as Campbell's, shooting stills and promotional footage of Australian industry and scenery, chiefly for exhibition by the high commissioner (then Sir George Reid) in the United Kingdom. Ive's output was prolific, up to 1000 feet per day. Agricultural scenes, mining processes, livestock raising, naval or military manoeuvres, and sporting carnivals were his stock in trade before World War I. By March 1914 it was said that he'd shot an aggregate 100 000 feet (28 hours) of film. Few of his productions were locally exhibited, one exception being **Australian Tour of the British Association for the Advancement of Science** featuring Sir Oliver Lodge in August 1914.

During World War I new assignments were added to Ive's usual round of industrial filming. He filmed military training at Casula, Liverpool and Moore Park in 1916, and internment camps and prisoners of war at Holdsworthy, Berrima, Bourke, and Queanbeyan during 1917 and 1918. With the return of peace, Ive took the unusual step of filming the **Melbourne Peace Procession** from the air in July 1919. One of his first films to achieve wide theatrical release was **Around Australia with the Prince of Wales**, a 6000-foot (100-minute) film shot in every state of Australia during 1920.

In preparation for the 14 million visitors to Australia's pavilion at London's Wembley Empire Exhibition in 1924, the Commonwealth Cinema Branch made several special films. Director Raymond •Longford and cameraman Arthur Higgins were temporarily contracted to make two dramatised documentaries in 1923, •**Australia Calls**, showing the progress of a successful immigrant farm worker who eventually owns his own farm, and **An Australian By Marriage**.

From the start of 1925, the exhibition policy for Commonwealth Cinema Branch films was completely altered. To give them Australian exposure, they were systematically released into Australian theatres by the Famous Players-Lasky (Paramount) Exchange. This major change in policy, switching the emphasis of Commonwealth film production from stimulating immigration to boosting tourism among Australians, saw the launching of a weekly 600-foot (10-minute) film under the series title of **Know Your Own Country**. One hundred and four short films, mostly of an industrial or scenic character, were issued in this series during 1925 and 1926, each around 10 minutes in length. The Branch also made some longer films such as **Imperial Press Conference Delegates' Tour of Victoria** (42 minutes, 1925), and the two-part **Royal Australian Air Force at Work**

(1926). **Know Your Own Country** had its last release in August 1928, having run by then to over 160 issues.

In December 1928 MGM took over the regular distribution of the Commonwealth product, returning to a weekly 10-minute format under the series title of **Australia Day by Day**. **Australia Day by Day** continued well into 1930, running to over 100 issues. In 1929, Australasian Kodak began to release cut-down versions of Ive's films on 16mm 'Kodascope' reels for home-movie enthusiasts. One particularly interesting **Australia Day by Day** instalment was **Telling The World** (1929), coverage of the Commonwealth government's own cinema-production activities.

After producing over 300 silent films between 1925 and 1930, Ive shot his first talkie, **This is Australia**, a travelogue in two reels, originally with sound-on-disc (released in October 1930).

Frank Hurley, Francis Birtles, Charles Herschell, Stan Hawkins, A.C. Tinsdale, and J.E. Ward were the major players in Australian silent documentary production. Dozens of other camera operators working with feature narrative production or newsreel production also made non-fiction shorts, documentaries, and advertising film between their major projects.

Hurley was probably the most glamorous and certainly the best documented of the producers. On the basis of some newsreel work done for Gaumont in Sydney, Hurley was selected by Sir Douglas Mawson to be his official Antarctic expedition photographer and cinematographer. This was the beginning of a prolific period for Hurley, who not only shot footage in the Antarctic but also Central Australia and New Guinea, where he shot his masterwork **Pearls and Savages** (1922), which enjoyed tremendous success worldwide. Another Papuan expedition resulted in **With the Headhunters of Unknown Papua** (1923), followed by the dramas **Hound of the Deep** and **The Jungle Woman**. A stint as pictorial editor on the Sydney *Sun* and a trip to London to acquire talking-picture production skills interrupted his Australian film work until 1930, when he again joined a Mawson expedition to the Antarctic from which a sound-on-disc film, **Southward Ho! With Mawson** (August 1930) was made.

Birtles—'cyclist, explorer and Kodaker'—was probably the first producer to popularise 'feature' documentaries of outback travel. Gaumont provided a cameraman to film Birtles's 1911 bicycle trip from Sydney to Darwin, the 50-minute **Across Australia with Francis Birtles** (1912). Birtles's first solo production effort was **Across Australia in the Track of Burke and Wills** (1915). Another outback venture followed the route of a famous aerial journey on the ground, **Through Australian Wilds: Across the Track of Ross Smith** (1919), while **Australia's Lonely Lands** (1924) was his last trek film of this type. Birtles's final film, •**Coorab in the Island of Ghosts** (1929), a dramatised documentary of Aboriginal life that was co-directed by Torrence McLaren, is Birtles's only surviving film.

Herschell gave up his job as a commercial traveller in 1912 to become manager of the educational side of Pathé's business in Australia, Pathé's Home Cinemas Limited. The war stopped film supplies from Paris and, in 1914, Herschell secured a few orders to make 'shorts', possibly on the 28mm Pathé home-movie gauge. One of his first major films was **The Dried Fruits Industry** (*circa* 1915), an hour-long documentary shot in the Sunraysia district. Until 1925 Herschell and his chief camera operator Maurice •Bertel made gazettes, topicals, industrials, travelogues, and even title leaders for film distributors. Herschell had a reputation for undertaking anything to order, with the notable exception of fictional feature filming, which he abandoned after bad experiences producing Harry •Southwell's **The Kelly Gang** in 1920. In 1925, after many years of operating from cramped premises in Flinders Street, Melbourne, Herschell built commodious studios and a film laboratory in Agnes Street, Jolimont, and changed the company name to Herschell's Films. This became the centre of Melbourne's documentary production activity for the next 30 years. Cameraman Roy Driver joined the staff in 1925 and, for the last half of the 1920s, their documentary output exceeded that of any other Melbourne producer. Some of their notable films include **Round Australia with the Macrobertson Expedition** (1928, a feature-length effort) and **The Daily Doings of H.R.H. The Duke and Duchess of York** (1927, 35 min.) and **The 25 Stages In the Making of Felt Hats** (1926).

Hawkins was the managing director of the Sydney documentary-producing company of Sovereign Pictures from about 1922. Sovereign Pictures produced advertising films such as **Castrol Motor Oil: Speed** (1926), a ten-minute dramatised effort featuring a young man who flies, motorcycles, and generally relies on Castrol oil for racing success. A major documentary effort undertaken by Sovereign was **West O' Nor' West** (1927), the record of the Douglas Wylie expedition to north-west Australia, shot by Walter Sully. Early in 1927 Sovereign amalgamated with De Forest Phonofilms (Australia) Limited, importing Australia's first experimental optical sound camera. With this, Hawkins, American sound man Harry Jones, and cameraman Sully made Australia's first true sound films, most notably their sound film record of the **Visit of the Duke and Duchess of York** (May 1927), of which no copy is known to survive. In June 1928, Hawkins resigned to found his own Sydney production company, Hawkins Film Productions, producing advertising films such as **Beautiful Lines of a Woman Triumphant**, a fashion film (1928), and **Green Cloth and Maple** (1928), about the manufacture of billiard tables. He subsequently shot many advertising films and sponsored documentaries, some of which were feature length.

Two other silent advertising film companies were Topikads (Sydney and Brisbane), which employed the animator Julius after 1922; and Melbourne's Robyn Filmads, which had the distinction of being the first company to make Australian film advertisements with sound-on-disc (1929).

Australasian Films (see Greater Union Organisation; Cinesound) had an educational film division operating in Sydney from about 1924, making scenics of a similar type to the Commonwealth's **Know Your Own Country** series. In June 1925, Australasian released an interesting 10-minute film called **Australia's Films Studio**, a rare behind-the-scenes view of Australian film-making. Australasian made at least 30 one-reel scenic films between 1925 and 1930, as well as the feature-length **Tasmania at Work and Play** (1929), shot by Bert Cross.

A.C. Tinsdale, film importer and theatrical agent, made the feature **The Laugh on Dad** (1918) before embarking on an Australia-wide documentary production program, the **Mighty Australia** series (1923, 18 films totalling 100 000 feet). He took them to London but, by 1925, was reported to be bankrupt.

Many other small documentary outfits existed throughout Australia. In Brisbane there were at least four producing

Handbill advertising Francis Birtle's silent documentary **Across Australia with Francis Birtles** (1912)

topical items: Sid Cook shooting local films of schools and town scenics to the order of councils, Bert Kirwin working for Topikads, Al and George Burne working as 'stringers' for the **Australasian Gazette** and shooting occasional films for the Qld. Agriculture Department.

The Australian silent non-fiction film production industry was so diffuse, widespread and prolific that it is doubtful whether any complete account of these activities will ever be assembled. Australian feature film production was a speculative and sporadic activity, but the production of 'shorts' and newsreels was a constant outlet for Australian camera operators.   CHRIS LONG

Documentary and non-fiction, sound In some ways Australian documentary film in the sound period can be understood as a singular component of Australian film culture: there is a distinct documentary milieu comprising film practitioners, intellectuals, and writers, all of whom position themselves to one side of the film industry. There are also funding bodies that have understood documentary film as a testing ground to foster feature films. Whereas documentary cinema is traditionally seen as somehow different from feature film, the scope of Australian film production in general means that people in the film industry move between these spheres.

These ideas may also inform the curious relationship that Australian film-makers generally maintain with international cinema, one that is, at the same time, inspirational, oppositional, and adaptational. Whereas some Australian film practitioners realise their ambition in Hollywood, their training and early experience are deeply rooted in a film culture that relies on locationism as a dominant code. This can be traced back to a long history of documentary culture. It accounts for an ability to work on location with small budgets, an ability that is prized on Hollywood productions. Australia's more internationally renowned practitioners (Russell •Boyd, Dean •Semler, Peter •Weir, George •Miller, Phillip •Noyce, Chris •Noonan) began their careers making documentaries.

In the late 1940s, the burgeoning film-society movement in Australia fostered a cinema culture that enabled audiences to familiarise themselves with international cinema and to draw on it to produce documentary films that resonate with a wide range of films, movements, and cultures. The 1940s brought a multitude of documentary forms from Europe and the USA, melding a strong network of film societies and making available, for the first time, the highly influential films of the previous three decades. The most influential of these were the narrative works of Sergei Eisenstein and Vsevolod Pudovkin, Pare Lorentz's **The Plow that Broke the Plains** (1936) and **The River** (1937), Joris Ivens's **Spanish Earth** (1937), and the films of the British documentary movement, such as **Drifters** (1929), **Housing Problems** (1935), and the benchmark **Night Mail** (1936). These films established a set of compass points from which the infant Australian film community could navigate through early productions.

The film-society movement provided a network of practitioners and audiences that was influenced by the visit, in 1940, of John Grierson, progenitor of the British documentary movement, a visit crucial to documentary culture in this country. Grierson's influence is felt in Canada and New Zealand, and in Australia, where the impulse for documentary culture came from working in opposition to, while also maintaining strong connections with, a feature film industry.

The Imperial Relations Trust employed Grierson to report on the kind of documentary production that was occurring in Australia and to make projections about its future. Owing to resistance in some quarters, it was not until 1945 that Grierson's recommendations were implemented in Australia, albeit in modified form: the establishment of the National Film Board (NFB). Prior to this the Australian government had been involved in documentary film production with the cinema and photographic branch of the federal Department of Agriculture, which was effectively the first Commonwealth film-making unit and was based in Melbourne, making films primarily about the sheep, wheat and fruit industries. With the outbreak of World War II, branch personnel were diverted to the Department of Information's film division, along with Captain Frank •Hurley. It covered the war in a steady stream of newsreels with which Australian audiences became all too familiar. One member of this unit was Damien •Parer, whose penchant for filming in impossible battlefield situations led to his early death and marked him as a legend to documentary film-makers and journalists. Parer's **Kokoda Front Line** (1942) footage remains pre-eminent in Australian television culture for its visceral, masculine, nationalistic resonance. Many of the personnel involved in the propaganda efforts for the war returned to work at the NFB.

The NFB was modelled on the Grierson-inspired Canadian Film Board. It was one part of a system of sponsorship that began at this time and still exists in a modified form. The NFB evolved into the Commonwealth Film Unit and the present •Film Australia. Its legacy is felt today: for example, in a system of distribution based on Grierson's ideas about documentary as a counterweight to the emerging strength of Hollywood in the 1930s.

In Australia a major influence of Grierson's work lies in the stylistic attributes emanating from this tradition of Government-sponsored film. Australia was seen as needing unification and the NFB's charter included the representation of postwar nation-building. The NFB brought together the components of a diverse culture in an oeuvre steeped in nationalism. These films strictly followed Grierson's principles of location shooting, native actors, and documentary style.

Although the Films Division produced many ordinary films about ordinary processes, there were magnificent exceptions, including John •Heyer's **Native Earth** (1946), about Australian trusteeship of New Guinea; **Journey of a Nation** (1947), calling for the standardisation of rail gauges across all states and territories of Australia; and **The Valley is Ours** (1948), a poetic rendering of the agricultural problems, and solutions to them, in the Murray River valley. Colin Dean's film about farm mechanisation, **Capacity Smith** (1951), and Maslyn •Williams's neo-realist docudrama, •**Mike and Stefani** (1952), a veiled criticism of immigration procedures, are other examples of the achievements of creative people working within the structures of a government institution. In 1956 the Films Division became the Commonwealth Film Unit. With the Cold War and the entrenchment of an internal style, many senior people such as John Heyer, Maslyn Williams and Lee •Robinson left the Commonwealth Film Unit. The 1960s and 1970s are often seen as the low point of this institution, but there were exceptions. Expatriate New Zealander Cecil •Holmes's **The Islanders** (1968) and Richard •Mason and Jack •Lee's **From the Tropics to the Snow** (1964) are marvellous films that transcend the ideological parameters of the Commonwealth Film Unit and break new formal ground.

In addition to government-sponsored documentaries, institutional documentaries were being made. John Heyer, who had taken over the reins of the Shell Film Unit in Australia, produced possibly Australia's most memorable documentary, •**The Back of Beyond** (1954). This film distills qualities of **Night Mail** and **The Plow that Broke the Plains** in a film ostensibly about a mail run in outback Australia. It is a cyclic rumination on the rhythms, complexities, myths, and legends in a singular representation of a multicultural society in outback Australia. The Shell Film Unit stretched the boundaries of sponsored documentary with the extraordinary **The Forerunner** (1958), a film about the Snowy Mountains electricity project, which employed lilting folk-music tones and stylised composition. Adventurous sponsored films were also produced for the Australian Broadcasting Commission, the Institute of Aboriginal Studies, and the Methodist Overseas Missions, the last two in the realm of ethnographic film.

Grierson's socio-political assertions were evident in documentaries made by organisations and individuals with left-wing political agendas. The earliest proponent of this kind of film practice was Melbourne's •Realist Film Unit, whose agitation for better social and housing conditions and the maintenance of price control in postwar years resulted in the production of **A Place to Live** (1946) and **Prices and the People** (1948). The Realist Film Unit's role in stimulating film appreciation through the screening and importation of films from around the globe gave much impetus to left-wing film production and Australian documentary in general, as did the visit of Dutch maverick film-maker Joris Ivens, whose **Indonesia Calling** (1946) (made in Sydney with the clandestine aid of the film community, Australian unions, and communists) addressed the Indonesian independence struggle. The Sydney •Waterside Workers Federation Film Unit, a product of this network, extended the agitational work begun in Melbourne by the Realist Film Unit, this time with full union support. It produced epic portrayals of workers that called for better conditions on the wharves and for the working classes. **Pensions for Veterans** (1953), **The Hungry Miles** (1954), and **Bones of Building** (1956) were some of its productions.

In 1957 Cecil Holmes produced arguably the most significant document of the left in Australia, the feature-length •**Three in One**. Based on stories by Henry Lawson and Frank Hardy, it distilled a range of cinematic modes from neo-realism to social-realism and docu-drama.

More recently, the tradition of politically informed documentary has produced documentaries ranging from the directly provocative to those concerned with the archaeology of a lost film history. Pat Fiske's re-reading of the once-powerful Builders Labourers' Foundation, **Rocking the Foundations** (1985), employs archival film, interviews, and television footage in considering the positive aspects of unionism, while John •Hughes's **Menace** (1976) and **Filmwork** (1981) reveal the strong tradition of left cultural production that has been largely ignored in this country.

One of the strongest trends in Australian documentary has been in ethnographic film. Australian documentary is probably best known for its ethnographic films, emphasising the dialogue between anthropological discourses and those of creative film-making. Jerry Leach and Gary Kildea's **Trobriand Cricket: An Indigenous Response to Colonialism** (1976) remains a primary example of this dialogue. It emerged at a time when the self-representation of indigenous communities was gaining attention. Other films that attempted to open up this dialogue include Essie Coffey and Martha Ansara's **My Survival as an Aboriginal** (1979), which focused on Coffey's Aboriginal community at Brewarrina, while Alessandro Cavadini and Carolyn Strachan worked with the Borroloola Aboriginal community to produce **Two Laws** (1981), a cinematic rendition of the history of the community in relation to White colonial and, by extension, cinematic laws. Frank Rijavec's **Exile and the Kingdom** (1993) responded to media accounts of events in north-western Australian Aboriginal communities. It is an account of the community as its inhabitants saw it at the time. Like **Two Laws, Exile and the Kingdom** provides an indigenous reading of a history and culture. Perhaps the most remarkable feat in this respect is the prolonged ethnographic project of Bob Connolly (see Anderson, Robin) and Robin •Anderson's Black Harvest Trilogy, which includes **First Contact** (1982), **Joe Leahy's Neighbours** (1988) and **Black Harvest** (1992). These films examine the residue of colonialism in New Guinea as it conflicts with traditional tribal law and interpersonal relations.

Ethnographic documentary also traces the changing discourses on Aboriginality. Steve Thomas's **Black Man's Houses** (1992) redresses colonial conceptions of Aboriginality in debunking the myth of the 'last Tasmanian' and in retracing the history and presence of Tasmania's Aboriginal community, while the **Blood Brothers** (1993) series, produced by Rachael •Perkins and Ned Lander in association with the Special Broadcasting Service's (SBS) Aboriginal television unit, addresses conceptions of Aboriginality in the 1950s and 1960s and contemporary postcolonial thinking about Aboriginality.

The intersection of the personal and the ethnographic is another strong current in Australian documentary. Gary Kildea's **Celso and Cora** (1984) and Dennis •O'Rourke's •**The Good Woman of Bangkok** (1992) extend both the ethnographic and diary genres. **Celso and Cora** successfully combines the ethnographer's construction of trust while documenting the plight of an impoverished Filipino couple living in Manila. **The Good Woman of Bangkok** presents the film-maker as the structuring centre of the film, playing off the personal and the ethnographic, the subjective and objective, the represented and the representer, in a controversial study of the film-maker's relationship with Aoi, a Bangkok sex worker. As the film progresses it is less concerned with the representation of another culture than with the ethical resonances of the relationship.

O'Rourke has set himself up an international documentary framework with other films such as **Half Life** (1985) and **Yap: How Did You Know We'd Like TV?** (1974). This international aspect of documentary making characterises the work of maverick Mike Rubbo, whose Canadian production, **Solzhenitsyn's Children** (1978), and **Waiting for Fidel** (1973) are examples of international concerns being dealt with by Australian film-makers. These films represent a marked departure from the sentiments of nation-building in favour of contributing to the international stream of documentary production.

The arrival in Australia in 1982 of Chris Marker's seminal essay film **Sunless** (France, 1982) was a launching point for Australian documentary. It was almost as if Australian documentary corresponded with **Sunless's** theme: a stream of films were produced that are informed by notions of doubt, mutability, and bricolage in their documentary practices. Ross •Gibson's films **Camera Natura** (1985) and **Wild** (1993) can be seen as companion pieces, both addressing what the landscape can tell us about Australian culture, filmically and generally. Through the use of elliptical narration and rumination on the questions faced by a postcolonial White settler community, these films act as reference points for the larger Australian cinema culture. John •Hughes's **All that is Solid** (1988) draws on and recognises the work of American theorist Marshall Berman, reformulating his ideas about the impact and nature of the information age. Josko Petkovich's **Letter to Eros** (1994) grapples with the intersection of the academy, art cinema, and the will to truth in a deeply personal response to personal, academic, and international contradictions.

Helen Grace's **Serious Undertakings** (1983) draws on this stream of essay films, as well as on the strength of feminist independent film-making on an international scale. **Serious Undertakings** addresses the history of the representation of women on film, using still images and language. Adopting a strategy common to the essay film, it belongs to a moment in the early eighties that saw a flowering in the production of 'independent film', and that included the establishment of the Creative Development Fund under the Australian Film Commission's umbrella, along with the Women's Film Fund. •Tracey Moffatt's •**Nice Coloured Girls** (1987) and Laleen Jayamanne's **A Song of Ceylon** (1985) belong to this moment, addressing complex issues such as gender politics in relation to race and colonialism. Megan McMurchy, Margot Nash, Margot Oliver, and Jeni Thornley's •**For Love or Money** (1983) has some connection with these films; it employs a compilation of historical footage in a revisionist history of women's work in Australia.

Contemporary inflections of this feminist emphasis include the conflation of television current affairs, formal devices, and Brechtian elements apparent in feminist films of the early 1980s . Carole Sklan's **Guns and Roses** (1992) prefigured the attunement of radical feminist approaches in dialogue with accepted televisual technique. Jan Ruff-O'Hearne, Carole Sklan, and Ned Lander's **50 Years of Silence** (1994) is a compendium of televisual and avant-garde documentary practices, requiring the viewer to negotiate found footage, dramatic reconstruction, 16mm, High-8 and Betacam footage, public address, and personal interview in a personal account of victims of rape by Japanese armed forces in Japanese-occupied Java during World War II.

Resonating with both the British Free Cinema and American Direct Cinema movements is Brian McKenzie's singular oeuvre, in particular his **Winter's Harvest** (1980) and **I'll Be Home For Christmas** (1984). McKenzie's films represent a distinctly 'low-key' documentary form, a bleak, intimate, remarkably frank oeuvre in an ethnographic practice that represents ordinary people in everyday situations.

More recently, Australia has produced a kind of documentary that relies on high production values, including sophisticated camera work; 35mm technology; composed, artful lighting; a composed soundtrack; and deliberate and staged re-enactments—elements usually associated with a fictional narrative mode. Lynn-Marie Milburn's fanciful **Memories and Dreams** (1993), Lawrence Johnston's 'noirish' **Eternity** (1994), and Kriv Stender's anthemic **Mother Land** (1994) are recent examples of films that eschew documentary's traditional association with a grassroots film-making and the Griersonian formulation of 'the social good', in favour of an emphasis on 'cinematic' properties.

Since the earliest days of cinema, Australians have tried to make sense of the complexities of a postcolonial society. Australian documentary in the sound period has insisted on scrutinising its own practices. Australian Aboriginal and White settler cultures have produced documentary films that are remarkable in the way they draw on, reformulate, and revitalise movements, schools, and genres of documentary in an Australian context, and Australians have produced some of the world's richest documentary cultures.

DEANE WILLIAMS

Dogs in Space

1987. Director: Richard Lowenstein. *Producer*: Glenys Rowe. *Scriptwriter*: Richard Lowenstein. *Director of photography*: Andrew de Groot. *Musical director*: Ollie Olsen. 103 min. *Cast*: Michael Hutchence (Sam), Saskia Post (Anna), Nique Needles (Tim), Deanna Bond (The Girl), Tony Helou (Luchio).

After exploring a Gippsland mining community in •**Strikebound** in 1984, director–scriptwriter Richard Lowenstein turned his attention to late 1970s inner-suburban Melbourne to appraise a world of drugs, dropouts, and punk music. Once again, he is less concerned with individual stories than with recreating an ambience and, abetted again by his **Strikebound** cinematographer, Andrew •de Groot, he achieves an intense, fluid evocation of a squalid, destructive lifestyle as the camera prowls through the over-populated house where most of the action takes place. The film's incessantly pounding score insists on a kind of energy that is poignantly at odds with the lives of the affectless, stoned, despairing inhabitants of the house. In so far as there is a connecting narrative thread, it involves the love of suburban Anna for the drug-taking Sam, and her death from an overdose assumes the status of a sacrifice to the spurious romanticism of the milieu she has never fully embraced. Sam is played by the late Michael Hutchence, who became an international figure in the popular music scene.   BMcF

Doing Time for Patsy Cline

1997. Director: Chris Kennedy. *Producer*: Chris Kennedy, John Winter. *Scriptwriter*: Chris Kennedy. *Director of photography*: Andrew Lesnie. *Music*: Peter Best. 95 min. *Cast*: Matt Day (Ralph), Miranda Otto (Patsy), Richard Roxburgh (Boyd), Wayne Goodwin (Violin).

This good-natured Australian film is dependent on American country music for its inspiration, although the presentation is also consistent with the lack of narrative intensity and character complexity, combined with a fair quota of whimsy, that characterises a number of Australian films in the 1990s (see, for example, •**Love Serenade**, 1996). The film begins in a promising manner as aspiring country singer Ralph leaves the family farm in rural New South Wales for the fame of Nashville. However, on the road he falls in with drug dealer Boyd and his dippy girlfriend Patsy, and Ralph's association with these city folk leads to trouble with the police. This, of course, represents an Australian variation of the basic ingredients of the honky-tonk branch of American country music that tends to lament the inequities of life, particularly life in gaol (Johnny Cash and Merle Haggard are well-known exponents of this sub-genre of country music). Betrayal and the victimisation of innocence are other conventions that this film shares with its country-music-inspired storyline.

At this point, the film falters a little and director/scriptwriter Chris •Kennedy is only occasionally successful in balancing, on the one hand, the comic and dramatic ingredients of Ralph's wrongful imprisonment, Boyd's menace, and Ralph's dreams with, on the other, the mixed blessings of life in prison, although the musical interludes coming from the comic duo in the next cell are very welcome throughout the second part of the film. At the end the film shifts into pathos and, although this is consistent with the victimisation motif of many country songs, one suspects that its function is more likely an attempt to fulfil the comic irony inherent in the film's title. There is much to enjoy in the film, particularly the relaxed performances of Matt •Day, Miranda •Otto, and Richard •Roxburgh (who won the 1997 Australian Film Institute (AFI) Award for an actor in a lead role) and, above all, the music, which deservedly won a Best Original Score Award for Peter Best at the AFI awards in 1997.   GM

Doleman, Guy (1923–) ACTOR Guy Doleman's film career of more than four decades had its beginnings in Australia in the role of the hero's best friend in •**Always Another Dawn** (1947), a wartime melodrama that was also the starring début of Charles 'Bud' •Tingwell. Two years later, Doleman played the lead in **Strong is the Seed**, a little-seen film based on the life of William Farrer, the agricultural scientist who developed a rust-resistant wheat.

If this film had succeeded, Doleman's career might have taken off as a leading man; as it is, apart from a couple of roles overseas—**His Majesty O'Keefe** (1953) and **Dial M for Murder** (1954)—he had a run of supporting roles in Australia throughout the 1950s. These included several roles in American films made here, including •**The Kangaroo Kid** (1950, with minor Hollywood leads Jock Mahoney and Veda Ann Borg), •**Kangaroo** (1952, with Maureen O'Hara and Peter Lawford), and •**On the Beach** (1959, with Gregory Peck and Ava Gardner). He also found roles in the British-backed •**Smiley** (1956) and **Smiley Gets a Gun** (1958) and the Ealing film •**The Shiralee** (1957), starring Peter •Finch. He played a station-owner in league with rustlers in •**The Phantom Stockman** for Lee •Robinson. Doleman's career was typical of what was then available to a young film actor in Australian: slim pickings, unless you were taken up by one of the visiting overseas companies. However, he was honing his craft as a character actor, and he became something of a fixture in British films throughout the 1960s, particularly in two Bond films and in the recurring character of Colonel Ross in three films based on author Len Deighton's Harry Palmer spy thrillers, starting with **The Ipcress File** in 1963. He returned to Australian films in the early 1980s in **A Dangerous Summer** (1981), and appeared in the miniseries version of *The Shiralee* (1988).

Other Australian films: Canberra the Capital (1959, doc., nar.), Tumanu's People (1960, doc., co-nar.), Motoring—The Mother State (1960, doc., nar.), Early Frost (1982, unreleased), •Goodbye Paradise (1983). BMcF

Don's Party

1976. *Director*: Bruce Beresford. *Producer*: Phillip Adams. *Scriptwriter*: David Williamson. Based on his play. *Director of photography*: Don McAlpine. 90 min. *Cast*: John Hargreaves (Don), Ray Barrett (Mal), Clare Binney (Susan), Pat Bishop (Jenny), Graeme Blundell (Simon), Jeanie Drynan (Kath).

David •Williamson's play is transferred to the screen with little apparent 'opening out'. The party of the title is of course ambiguous: it refers both to the Labor Party, which lost the 1969 federal election, and to the election-night party given by Don in his suburban home. To this party he has invited several old friends who, in their several ways, have failed to fulfil their early promise and who, as the night wears on, settle into mutual abuse and recrimination. The evening is charged with sexual tension as the middle-aged males feel their manhood challenged by a nubile young woman, while their wives sit around viewing and discussing them with bitter cynicism. Personal failures find an analogy in the disintegration of all hopes of a Labor victory, and the presence of a Liberal-voting couple adds to the uneasy atmosphere of the evening. Neither 'party' is a success.

Bruce •Beresford directs this set-bound material with a confident sense of camera movement, so that the film avoids the trap of seeming like a filmed play. He is also served well by an experienced ensemble. BMcF

Don't Call Me Girlie

1985. *Directors*: Stewart Young, Andrèe Wright. *Producer*: Hilary Furlong. *Script*: Andrée Wright. *Directors of photography*: Erika Addis, Geoff Burton. *Music*: John Godfrey. 68 min. *Narrator*: Penne Hackforth-Jones.

The film revival of the 1970s (see Revival, the) led to a renewed interest in the history of Australian film-making, resulting in many books and several documentary films. **Don't Call Me Girlie** contributes to this, by challenging the overwhelmingly male image of the early production industry. It is a film about women in front of and behind the camera, using compilation footage from their films and interviews with and about silent film stars such as Louise •Lovely or Marie •Lorraine, or directors such as Kate Howarde or Paulette •McDonagh. Lottie •Lyell in particular is heroised , the film stopping just short of declaring her the true auteur of the films of Raymond •Longford. In the early sound period, Nancy Gurr speaks about her publicity for •Cinesound; Aileen •Britton and Ann •Richards about their roles as 'bad' and 'good' girls in Cinesound films. The film was well received by critics; it was widely shown commercially and continues to circulate on video. Andrée Wright also published a book of the same name, concluding with a chapter on Gillian •Armstrong. IB

Donovan, Jason (1968–) ACTOR The son of actor Terence Donovan. Jason, largely as a result of television exposure as Scott Robinson in the long-running Australian soap *Neighbours* from 1986 to 1989, which was also popular in the United Kingdom, established a (brief) career in the cinema. Donovan appeared in •**Blood Oath** (1990) as an Australian soldier in the courtroom drama centred on the war-crimes trial of 91 Japanese soldiers conducted in the Dutch East Indies after World War II. This was followed by the lead role in the romance **Rough Diamonds** (1993), directed by Donald •Crombie, which also starred Angie Milliken. However, Donovan's acting career, aside from *Neighbours*, has largely been confined to television, beginning with *The Heroes* (1989), a dramatisation of the raid by 14 Australians on Japanese shipping in Singapore Harbour during World War II. Donovan also had a supporting role in the miniseries *Shadows of the Heart* (1990), which was set on Gannet Island in the late 1920s, and the lead role in *The Last Bullet* (1995), a tele-feature based on the fight for survival between a Japanese and Australian soldier in one of the last battles of World War II. GM

Donovan, Terence (1939–) ACTOR Donovan, born in London, migrated to Australia in 1951 although he returned to England in 1963 where he remained until 1967 for television and theatrical roles. On his return to Australia, Donovan has been a lead actor in a number of successful television programs, including six years in *Division 4*, two years in *Cop Shop* and, more recently, a long stint in *Neighbours*. Donovan's most significant role in Australian cinema was as Eric Jackson, the security supervisor who masterminds a robbery in the tough thriller •**Money Movers** (1979). Donovan's other claim to fame was as Tom Burlinson's father in •**The Man from Snowy River** (1982). Other film roles have comprised supporting performances, except for **The Winds of Jarrah** (1985), which was the first film adaptation of a Mills & Boon novel.
Other Australian films: •The Getting of Wisdom (1977), •'Breaker' Morant (1980), A Single Life (1985), •Fortress (1986), Death of a Soldier (1986), Running from the Guns (1987), Emma's War (1988), Jigsaw (1989).

GM

Dot and the Kangaroo

1977. Director: Yoram Gross. *Producer:* Yoram Gross. *Script:* John Palmer, Yoram Gross. Based on the novel by Ethel Pedley. *Director of animation photography:* Graham Sharpe. *Director of live action photography:* Frank Hammond. *Music:* Bob Young. 86 min. *Voices:* Barbara Frawley (Dot), Joan Bruce (the Kangaroo), Spike Milligan (Mr Platypus), June Salter (Mrs Platypus), Ross Higgins (Willie Wagtail).

To launch their careers in Australian feature-length animation, Yoram and Sandra •Gross chose Ethel Pedley's 1899 environmentalist children's classic for its distinct Australian character and for its likely appeal to the international children's film market. In a bush version of *Alice in Wonderland*, young Dot wanders away from the family farm and finds herself in a world of sentient, articulate Australian animals, guided by a motherly kangaroo who has lost her own child. After several adventures, many of which stress the advantages, not superiority, of animals, the kangaroo helps Dot find her way back home. Following Disney's lead, the film has songs and cuddly characters, but features Australian icons, details, and accents; noteworthy are the animation of cave paintings and the Aboriginal dancing. The film initiates Gross's continuing stylistic hallmark: the mixing of animation and live action footage. The animated action takes place in real Australian landscapes.

RICK THOMPSON

Downer, David (1948–) ACTOR A graduate of the National Institute of Dramatic Art in 1967, David Downer has had more than 30 years of substantial success in the theatre, acquiring a résumé that would be the envy of many,

Terence Donovan

including dozens of major roles in new and classic plays. He also appeared in such well-known television series as *The Box* and *Cop Shop*, and played Liberal politician Tony Staley in the Kennedy–Miller miniseries *The Dismissal*. By contrast, he has made only a handful of films for the cinema, and only once did he show the range he has clearly achieved on the stage. This was in Henri •Safran's charming and under-valued comedy of Jewish life and anxieties, •'**Norman Loves Rose'** (1982), in which Downer found real pathos and grim comedy in the role of the young husband whose best efforts to impregnate his wife fail, while his 13-year-old brother succeeds at first try. It sounds tasteless; the fact that it wasn't is partly the result of Downer's playing of the pompous, troubled Michael. He had had a small role in **Mary, Queen of Scots** (1972) in England, where he worked for four years after finishing at NIDA but, although he made three other Australian films of more than average interest, he did not have anything very interesting to do in them.
Other Australian films: •The Killing of Angel Street (1981), •Mad Max 2 (1981), •The Settlement (1984).

BMcF

Doyle, Stuart, *see* Cinesound; Greater Union Organisation

Drynan, Jeanie ACTOR Considering that Jeanie Drynan first appeared in Australian films back in the mid 1960s with •**They're a Weird Mob** (1966), her screen output has been relatively limited. Nevertheless, Drynan has contributed effectively to two key Australian films: first, as Kath, Don's wife in •Don's Party (1976). In this role, Drynan is another victim of David •Williamson's relentless attack on the pretensions and failed desires of a group of urban middle-class people brought together at a party on the night of the 1969 federal election. The second role, Drynan's best screen performance to date, and one that deserved more recognition, was as Betty, the real victim of Bill Heslop's (Bill •Hunter) corruption and infidelity in •Muriel's Wedding (1994). As Heslop's long-suffering wife, Drynan's mixture of misplaced loyalty and frustration with her family provides a realistic figure of pathos amid the caricatures that surround her.

Other Australian films include: •Two Thousand Weeks (1969), •The Picture Show Man (1977), •Money Movers (1979), Touch and Go (1980), Fantasy Man (1984), Cappuccino (1989), Paperback Hero (1998), A Kind of Hush (1998), Soft Fruit (1999).

GM

Duigan, John (1949–) DIRECTOR/WRITER One of the bright young men of the new Australian cinema (see Revival, the) that burgeoned in the 1970s, John Duigan was born in England of an Australian father, and emigrated to Geelong, Victoria in 1961. He graduated from Melbourne University, after which he pursued his interest in theatre at La Mama and The Pram Factory, both then significant 'alternative' theatres in the Melbourne suburb of Carlton. In 1975 he published a novel, *Badge* and, in film, as both director and writer, he emerged as one of the most interesting talents. He began with low-budget excursions into urban commentary that distinguished him from, say, Peter •Weir or Gillian •Armstrong, who worked with bigger budgets and often drew on well-known literary texts. Duigan acted in several 'experimental' Carlton films—Brake Fluid (1970), **Bonjour Balwyn** (1971, co-w.), **Come Out Fighting** (1973), and **Dalmas** (1973)—before emerging as a feature director in 1975 with **The Firm Man,** which he also produced and wrote, and which offers a somewhat puzzling, surrealist account of a young man who is employed by a mysterious company and loses sense of his own direction. His next film as director (and writer), **The Trespassers** (1976), starring Briony •Behets and Judy •Morris, is a study of relationships and contemporary attitudes that moves from Melbourne to a Gippsland farm.

It was his third film as director and writer, •Mouth to Mouth (1978), that brought him serious critical attention. Compared with the gentle, decorous period pieces that were winning prestige for the burgeoning industry, this struck a note of refreshing immediacy in its representation of homeless urban youth and neglected old age. The exactness of its observation, the skill of its unpretentious story-telling, and

the sympathetic handling of its virtually unknown young starring quartet made this film an important addition to the social realism strand of the revival. Made for less than $150 000, it achieved major distribution and was financially as well as critically successful.

Duigan's next film but one, •Winter of Our Dreams (1981), again took up his interest in lives lived at the dangerous edges of a city, this time Sydney, as it traced the attempts of Lou, a prostitute, to secure the cooperation of bookshop-owning Rob, in investigating the recent suicide of a mutual friend. The film contrasts their lifestyles with sharply observed details of place and manner, and Duigan's script is sensitively attuned to temperament and milieu.

•Dimboola (1979), based on Jack Hibberd's play, and the only one of his Australian films that Duigan did not write, is a crudely unfunny account of a small-town wedding; •Far East (1982) is a romantic melodrama of the **Casablanca** school, set in The Philippines during a time of political upheaval; and •Sirens (1994) is a mildly amusing romp, based on the contrast between Norman Lindsay's sexually liberated ideals and inhibited English behaviour.

Duigan has also filmed overseas, notably on **Romero** (1989), a powerful account of the courageous Latin American archbishop; and the undervalued satirical drama of London theatrical life, **The Leading Man** (1996), starring the popular singer Jon Bon Jovi. Arguably, however, his best work has been done in Australia, notably **Mouth to Mouth, Winter of Our Dreams**, and the excellent teenage rites-of-passage movie, •The Year My Voice Broke (1987), distinguished from many of its Australian kind by the exactness of its unsentimental treatment of the pains of adolescence. The sequel, •Flirting (1991), lacked the raw truth of its predecessor, but it did introduce Thandie Newton, who has since starred for Duigan in **The Leading Man** and **The Journey of August King** (1994), the story of a runaway slave that was made in the USA.

Duigan's has been a somewhat unpredictable career, but when his sympathies are engaged he is a stimulating and risk-taking film-maker, as even a partly successful film like **Wide Sargasso Sea** (1993), a Jamaica-set version of Jean Rhys's prequel to *Jane Eyre*, attests.

Other Australian films: One Night Stand (1984, d., w.).   BMcF

Duncan, Carmen (1942–) ACTOR National Institute of Dramatic Art-trained Carmen Duncan, sister of television actor Paula Duncan, was a well-known television performer before making her screen début in •You Can't See 'round Corners (1969), the film spin-off from the television series in which she had made her name. She played leading roles in many other successful series, such as *Certain Women* and *Cop Shop*, as well as appearing in the theatre here and in the United Kingdom. For an actor of considerable style, elegance, and versatility, she ought to have had a more notable screen career than has been the case. She has had no more than moderately attractive roles in such films as **Harlequin** (1980), as the mother of the stricken child, and **Touch and Go** (1980), as one of a trio of society beauties who turn to larceny. In 1997, she appeared in the American comedy **Allie and Me**; it must be said that Australian movies have, in general, wasted her.

Other Australian films: Is Anybody Doing Anything About It? (1969, short), **A Christmas Carol** (1969, animated, voice), **Strange Holiday** (1970), **And Millions Will Die** (1973), **First Things First** (1977, short), **Obedience** (1979, short), **Turkey Shoot** (1982), **Now and Forever** (1983), **Run Chrissie Run!** (1984), **Bootleg** (1985).   BMcF

Dunlop, Ian (1927–) ETHNOGRAPHER/DIRECTOR Born in London, Ian Dunlop arrived in Sydney in 1948 and studied at Sydney University. He worked for the ABC in Sydney, then Adelaide and Canberra, before taking up a position as production assistant with the •Commonwealth Film Unit (CFU) in 1956, where he stayed until 1987. He first visited Central Australia in 1957 to complete a film on a remote weather station, **Balloons and Spinifex** (1957). After a number of early, more general, films, he began to specialise in ethnographic film, his first being the Aurukun Project in 1962, out of which came **Five Aboriginal Dances from Cape York** (1962) and **Dances at Aurukun** (1964). Then, sponsored by the Institute of Aboriginal Studies, Dunlop completed 19 archival films on **People of the Australian Western Desert** (1966/69), and a shorter, more popular version titled **Desert People** (1966). The following year he organised the CFU-sponsored UNESCO Round Table on Ethnographic Film-making in the Pacific Area. Australian ethnographic film, including Dunlop's own work, was received with great acclaim by delegates, and Australia was invited to be the featured country at the next 'Festival del Populi' in Florence. Dunlop compiled an enormous Retrospective Review of Australian Ethnographic Film 1901–1967 (including a program on Baldwin •Spencer's footage, **Aborigines of Central and Northern Australia 1902–1912**, 1966), and toured with it all around Europe for 12 weeks. After that, he was frequently invited to screen his work overseas. He made 23 films in the Yirrkala Film Project (1970–82), and two large cycles of film in the Baruya project in New Guinea, in association with Professor Maurice Godelier (**Towards Baruya Manhood**, 9 parts 1972; and **Baruya Muka Archival**, 17 parts 1991–92). His films (particularly **Desert People** and **Conversations with Dundiwuy Wanambi** 1996) have won many awards, and he himself has been awarded the Australian Film Institute's Raymond Longford Award (1968) and the Medal of the Order of

Australia (1986), and has been elected an Honorary Fellow of the Royal Anthropological Institute (1991). Since 1987 he has worked freelance at •Film Australia.   IB

Dunn, Beverley (1934–) ACTOR Beverley Dunn, long a respected and award-winning stage actor, has made only a few films. She established herself in the visual media with a long-running part in the popular ABC serial *Bellbird*, evincing the warm naturalistic approach that should have made her a certainty for a big-screen career as a character player. She has appeared in other television series such as *The Flying Doctors* but, in the cinema, she has to date played only a few roles: as one of the commissioners (along with fellow *Bellbird* colleague Alan •Hopgood) in **Ground Zero** (1987), the thriller about the aftermath of the 1950s atomic bomb tests in Central Australia; as the president of the Equal Opportunity Tribunal in **Brilliant Lies** (1996), Richard •Franklin's version of David •Williamson's play; the judge in **Gross Misconduct** (1993), another drama of sexual harassment; and, most notably, as the sympathetic Beryl Ascott, who befriends David Helfgott in •**Shine** (1996).

BMcF

Beverley Dunn

Dusty

1983. *Director*: John Richardson. *Producer*: Gil Brealey. *Scriptwriter*: Sonia Borg. *Director of photography*: Alex McPhee. *Music*: Frank Strangio. 88 min. *Cast*: Bill Kerr (Tom Lincoln), Noel Trevarthen

(Harry Morrison), Carol Burns (Clara Morrison), John Stanton (Railey Jordan), Nick Holland (Jack Morrison), Peter Aanensen (Mr Brownless).

Dusty is an excellent adaptation of Frank Dalby Davison's novel concerning an old man's special relationship with a kelpie/dingo crossbreed. Tom Lincoln, a former drover, works for Harry Morrison and he purchases a pup without knowing that it is a dingo crossbreed. The pup, Dusty, turns into a prize-winning sheep dog but, when his basic hunting instincts emerge, and he kills Morrison's sheep, Lincoln is forced to leave the property and hide out with his dog in cattle country. Within this simple tale the film perceptively explores the affinity between humans and dogs, a theme that is deepened by the inclusion of Railey Jordan who kills predatory dogs for a living but, like Tom Lincoln, has a strong awareness of the complex balance between humans, animals, and the environment.

This low-budget film deservedly produced a strong profit and it contains a finely judged performance by Bill Kerr in the central role. Similarly, John Richardson's direction avoids the obvious clichés and he manages, like Frank Dalby Davison's novel, to include the dog's point of view whenever possible.   GM

E

Eadie, Nicholas (1958–) ACTOR   Sydney actor Nicholas Eadie is a graduate of the National Institute of Dramatic Art. He is well known for his roles in the television series *Cop Shop* and in several other television dramas and series, as well as for appearing on the stage. On screen he was a handsome presence as Tom •Burlinson's rival in love and horsemanship in **The Man from Snowy River II** (1988), and he gave intelligent performances as two unsatisfactory husbands: the narrow, complacent suburbanite in •**Celia** (1989), and the racially insensitive soldier who marries the eponymous Japanese protagonist in **Aya** (1991).
Other Australian films: Undercover (1983), Reunion (1984), Jenny Kissed Me (1986), •Blood Oath (1990), •Dad and Dave: On Our Selection (1995).   BMcF

Eagels, Moneta (1924–) COMPOSER/MUSIC EDITOR   Moneta Eagles composed documentary film scores for the •Commonwealth Film Unit between 1951 and 1969, contributing some 21 scores. She served as its music editor in the period 1957–64, during which she commissioned over 65 scores from 27 composers. Her first score, **North to the Sun** (1951) was completed before she sailed for England to study composition with Matyás Seiber. There, Eagles met Ken Cameron, the musical director at the Crown Film Unit. The visit strengthened her resolve to continue to compose for film. Depending on the film's narrative, her scores can be full orchestral pictorial music, dramatic, strong, and dark, or they can be lush, sunny scores. **A Princess Comes to Australia** (1959) was composed before the Princess had arrived in the country; Eagles relied on the shot list to create a royal atmosphere. One of her finest scores was written for **Christmas in Australia** (1958), and she displayed her versatility in her descriptive score for **The Story of Diplomacy**

Nicholas Eadie

(1966). Her chilling commentary on the futility of war is heard in two films: **The Australian Airman at War** (1966) and **The Australian Seamen at War** (1969). Moneta Eagles's scores reveal a composer of considerable creative power.

DIANE NAPTHALI

Editing   As a creative craft, editing can transform films through the juxtaposition of images, variations in rhythm and pace, and the structuring of the narrative. While the concepts of editing were developed in the USA and Europe between 1896 and 1929 with the experiments of Edwin Porter, D.W. Griffith, and Vsevolod Pudovkin, its development in Australia was hampered by the size and nature of the industry. Until 1920 there were no established editors: most films were cut by the director or cinematographer. The pattern of the development of editing since then has been tied to that of the whole industry.

In the 1920s Mona Donaldson was known to work with Norman and Katherine •Dawn and was also a negative cutter for Australasian Film Laboratories; Jack Fletcher cut the films of the McDonagh sisters (see •Paulette McDonagh) who insist he was not editing, merely cutting where he was told; and Lottie •Lyell was known to edit some of Raymond •Longford's films.

The early method of editing was to project the rushes (uncut film) and then take them back to the editing room to cut over a bench that had a light box, then screen again and make changes. Timings were learnt from the length of a shot and the tempo from a sequence of joined shots. Splices were made by scraping away the film emulsion at the cut and joining the two pieces of film together with cement (glue) under pressure. Great care had to be taken when working, as the film stock, with its nitrate base, was extremely volatile.

The advent of sound on film in 1928 brought a dramatic change to film structure and film cutting. No longer did the images alone tell the story; sound could now provide vital plot details through the dialogue. Editing of picture and sound became a far more complex and specialised role, requiring synchronisation of sound with image. At •Cinesound, George •Malcolm constructed synchronisers, optical readers, and film horses that carried four reels at once and allowed any reel independent spooling from the others. It was not until 1936 that Cinesound imported Moviolas, which allowed the editor to cut image and sound at speed and in sync. Even so, many editors stuck to their manual methods.

William Shepherd is considered the first major feature film editor. He cut 19 of Ken •Hall's feature films between 1933 and 1940, including •Orphan of the Wilderness (1936) and •Dad Rudd, MP (1940). He also cut the features Cinesound took on as a production house including •Forty Thousand Horsemen (1940) for Charles •Chauvel. Frank Coffey and Mona Donaldson were also cutting for Chauvel, as was Lola Lindsay who had cut the majority of Frank •Thring's films. Shepherd had gone to Cinesound in 1930 as a newsreel editor, where George Malcolm had cut Hall's •On Our Selection in 1932 and was to cut •The Squatter's Daughter (1933). When he fell ill, Shepherd completed the film under Malcolm's guidance. Malcolm then focussed on camera work and Shepherd became the Cinesound feature-film editor.

Shepherd's assistants, called 'first cutters', were Terry Banks, Phyllis O'Reilly (Cross) and, later, Stan Moore. In World War II, Terry Banks cut the Academy Award-winning **Kokoda Frontline** and, at the end of the war, he went on to become Cinesound's chief editor, cutting •Smithy for Ken Hall in 1946 and then, in 1949, •Sons of Matthew for Chauvel. Phyllis O'Reilly edited •The Power and the Glory (1941) for Noel •Monkman, and Stan Moore became one of the few feature editors of the late 1950s and 1960s, editing The Restless and the Damned (1958), and Dust in the Sun (1960).

Newsreels, with their fast turn-around of seven days, provided a disciplined training ground for editors. To learn more sophisticated skills, editors needed to travel overseas. In 1952, film base changed from the volatile nitrate to acetate base and, in 1955, magnetic sound was introduced to replace optical sound. Flatbed editing machines were introduced, such as Intercines and Steenbecks, which made viewing easier and more accessible. In 1966, tape splicers were introduced. These major technical improvements allowed far more flexibility and experimentation in the cutting room.

However, it was the editors who came to Australia to fill the demands of television in the 1960s who had the most dramatic effect on the generation of editors to follow. Working first on television news and documentaries and, later, in television drama series, English editors such as Ernie Hilton, Arthur Southgate, Don Saunders, and Gerald Turney Smith were able to teach developed editing techniques to their assistants. When the new wave of film-makers emerged in the 1970s they found skilled editors from the various backgrounds to draw on. From newsreels came Brian Kavanagh (•The Devil's Playground, 1976) and Anthony •Buckley (•The Removalists, 1975); from commercials and television came Max Lemon (•Picnic at Hanging Rock, 1975) and John Scott (•Newsfront, 1978); and from television drama, William Anderson (•'Breaker' Morant, 1980), Sara Bennett (•The Night The Prowler, 1979), Tony Patterson (•Mad Max, 1979), David Stiven (Tim, 1978) and Tim Wellburn (•Caddie, 1976). Further opportunity for training of editors came with the opening in 1974 of the federally funded Australian Film and Television School (later the •Australian Film, Television and Radio School), which included a dedicated editing department.

The introduction of computer editing in 1991 initially caused a crisis in editing sectors. Editors were thrown into the new technology without proper training and with the added pressure that they could, with computers, shorten editing schedules and also do without assistants. Out of this dilemma in November 1995 the Australian Screen Editors Association (ASEA) was born to protect the rights and culture of screen editors in Australia. Henry Dangar became the first president of the ASEA.

The international success of Australian films in the 1980s and 1990s has drawn attention to their directors as well as their editors and some of the latter have continued to work overseas. The most noted internationally are William Anderson (•**Gallipoli**, 1981; **Fearless** 1993; **The Truman Show**, 1998); Nicholas Beauman (•**My Brilliant Career**, 1979; •**Hightide**, 1987; •**Oscar and Lucinda**, 1997); Jill Bilcock (•**Evil Angels**, 1988; •**Strictly Ballroom**, 1992; **Romeo & Juliet**, 1996; **Elizabeth**, 1998); Richard Francis Bruce (•**Careful He Might Hear You**, 1983; •**Dead Calm**, 1989; **Seven**, 1997); Veronika Jenet (•**Sweetie**, 1989; •**The Piano**, 1993; **Portrait of a Lady**, 1997).

In the late 1950s there was only a handful of editors working in Australia. By 1998 there were over 600 editors working in various parts of the industry. The explosion of images in the last half of the twentieth century, along with digital technology that can create limitless possibilities in post-production, challenge editors to keep the integrity of their craft intact.   DENISE HASLEM

Edols, Michael (1942–) CINEMATOGRAPHER Brought up in Borneo, Mike Edols began work as a photographer in Sydney in 1962 and, from 1966 to 1975, he worked for the •Commonwealth Film Unit, as cinematographer on numerous documentaries. His feature credits include: •**The Office Picnic** (1972, with Tod McSwiney and Peter Gailey) for Tom Cowan; •**27A** (1974) and •**In Search of Anna** (1979) for Esben •Storm; **The Pursuit of Happiness** (1988) for Martha Ansara; •**The Surfer** (1988) for Frank Shields; **Candy Regentag** (1989) for James Ricketson; and **Island** (1989) for Paul •Cox. In 1983 he was credited as second camera, but also as actor and co-writer on Werner Herzog's **Where the Green Ants Dream**. He has also photographed television series and documentaries and made his own films, such as the trilogy **Lalai-Dreamtime** (1976, which won several awards including the Australian Film Institute Award for Best Documentary), **Floating** (1976), and **When the Snake Bites the Sun** (1986). Since 1996, he has worked in the USA.
                    IB

Education The first moves towards film education began in the 1920s, when it was seen as an instructional tool rather than an object of study. This notion was not universally accepted and, from the 1920s to the 1950s, a number of reports questioned the instructional value of film. Fears expressed in these reports persist today in various guises, and concern the perceived harmful effects of media on children and, more substantially, confusion about the role of media in the classroom.

A symptom of this confusion is the failure to attend to practical difficulties. These have included a lack of continuity from primary to tertiary level (as exists in mathematics,

for example), the cost of equipment and its rapid obsolescence, the difficulty of timetabling feature-length films, and the need for dedicated screening and studio spaces. A lack of properly trained staff, and of a career structure for staff in media education, have meant that enthusiastic teachers move out of the field into more mainstream subject areas or out of teaching altogether. Finally, copyright again brings up the problem of costs, as individual schools and government education departments refuse to allocate sufficient funds for the purchase of films and television programs or the rights to copy them off air.

While a number of these difficulties are genuine, the failure to address them speaks of unresolved tensions and debates in relation to film education. Apart from the instructional effectiveness of twentieth-century media, debate has continued throughout the post-World War II period over the propriety of education about film and television, and its location in the curriculum. Two broad strands can be seen in this debate, both of which originate in a distrust of the effects of film and, later, television, upon audiences. In the postwar era advocates of 'film appreciation' courses were concerned with how the harmful effects of media could be countered, and how children could be taught to discriminate. In 1945, Newman Rosenthal argued for film appreciation courses as an antidote to media influence, saying that 'a good understanding by the viewer is the best single safeguard'.

In the 1960s, advocates of the teaching of 'discrimination' were influenced by the English thinker F. R. Leavis and his ideas of cultural value. However, a further strand in 'film appreciation' recognised that film-production work in schools created opportunities for developing skills in self-expression and communication. Many teachers recognised that students who performed poorly in more traditional curriculum areas were able to succeed in film-making. In the late 1960s, a number of developments aided the rise of film appreciation courses: demands for more relevant curricula; moves to school-based curriculum development and assessment (for example in the ACT and Qld); in Victoria, the existence of technical schools less fettered by the influence of the tertiary sector; and the development of senior colleges in Tas. and, later, the ACT. Federal grants in the Whitlam era helped many schools purchase equipment for film-making. This period also saw a growing awareness of television, and new debates arose concerning the place of television study in the classroom.

Film eventually achieved some degree of respectability when certain types of films were able to be appropriated into 'high culture'. Although Leavis never accepted film, others were able to construct an informal canon of films granted sufficient status to be worthy of study in schools. John C. Murray in Victoria (*10 Lessons in Film Appreciation*, 1966), and Bill Perkins in Tasmania (*Learning the Liveliest

Arts, 1972) were influential in the critical enjoyment of film and television. The recognition of more popular forms of film, and of television, challenged the comfortable assumptions prevalent in film appreciation. The influence of tertiary film and media-studies courses needs to be recognised here: auteur and genre theories, and then structuralist and poststructuralist approaches, filtered down to the secondary level. By the 1970s cinema and media-studies departments were becoming accepted at the tertiary level, and graduates were gaining employment in secondary schools, film cultural institutions such as the •Australian Film Institute (AFI), and educational associations such as Australian Teachers of Media (ATOM, a descendant of the Association of Teachers of Film Appreciation, founded in Victoria in 1963 as an outgrowth of the Victorian Association for Teachers of English), and the Australian Screen Studies Association (ASSA) at the tertiary level. Magazines and journals such as *Lumière, Cinema Papers, Filmviews, Filmnews, Metro, Continuum*, and *Cantrills Filmnotes* came and, in some cases, went.

Theory had arrived. The combination of semiotics, psychoanalysis, and ideology theory that was dominant in British screen studies became important in Australia. This theoretical ferment gave impetus to cinema studies and media studies. The place of film and media studies was now firmly established at tertiary level, and more complex and systematic studies of media were able to be undertaken at both tertiary and secondary levels.

In schools, film appreciation became media studies and encompassed the study of all the media. Central debates concerned the role of the teacher in media education. Both Leavisite and Althusserian (Louis Althusser) positions assumed that the role of the teacher was to protect students from media effects. Both views in their different ways saw the role of the teacher as moral and political guardian, responsible for protecting students against the baleful effects of popular culture.

There was a flurry of important curriculum documents in the late 1970s and the 1980s. In the ACT, media education was an established course in secondary colleges, where school-based curriculum development became the norm from 1977. In WA the draft documents 'Decoding the Mass Media' and 'Primedia Project' became 'Media Conventions' and *The Primary Media Studies Teachers' Resource Book* (1980) respectively. Shortly afterwards, Barrie McMahon and Robin Quin from WA embarked on a productive period of publishing influential text-books (beginning with *Exploring Images*, 1984). The Education Department of SA produced *Media Lab* in two volumes (pre-school–year 7, and years 8–12) in 1982, and in NSW the Mass Media Curriculum Project of 1981 became an official document, *All About Mass Media Education*, in 1984 under the patronage

of Frank Meaney. In Victoria the introduction of the Victorian Certificate of Education (VCE) for years 11 and 12, and Frameworks for pre-school–year 10, saw the introduction of a 'Media Studies Study Design' document and the inclusion of the subject of media within the 'Arts Framework' document respectively.

Film is now located in several places in the secondary curriculum. In the Victorian English *Study Design* (VCE), the emphasis is still largely on the individual, decontextualised, film-as-text, with much of the study of film being based on formalist paradigms. The study of film as text in English has been given major impetus by the regular seminars on film for students and their teachers conducted by •Cinemedia (formerly the State Film Centre, Victoria). In media studies, film is generally located among the full range of media (although often with a privileged status) and the individual text is located within the context of the media and social, economic, and political institutions. There is a recognition of the role of the audience in the production of meaning, which has led to a recognition of the role of the knowledge of students in the analysis of media. In many courses, students are actively engaged in the production of media texts of their own.

Beyond the classroom, the picture is more problematic. Most training of teachers is now carried out by secondary-teacher associations such as the Australian Association of Teachers of English and ATOM, both of which run bi-annual conferences, publish journals and study guides, and run courses and seminars. *Metro* has produced a specialist off-shoot *Metro Education*, and more academic magazines and journals such as *Continuum* and *Media International Australia* serve a vital role. The AFI, apart from the invaluable 'research and information division', has for many years been ambivalent about its educational role, and is constantly faced with the threat of cuts. In 1996, a Senate Select Committee under the chairmanship of Senator John Tierney recommended that some form of media education be compulsory at primary-school level. While media education in formal education sectors is becoming increasingly entrenched, outside these sectors it is increasingly threatened.

PETER HUGHES

Edward, Marion (1935–) ACTOR Plump and motherly in appearance, Marion Edward has spent most of her career on the stage and, for some years, was associated with the Melbourne Theatre Company. She has made only three films: **Blue Fire Lady** (1978), playing a motherly role in a dim little girl-and-horse film; •**The Wild Duck** (1984), as the housekeeper in a flavourless version of Henrik Ibsen's play of the same name; and, memorably, •**Strikebound** (1984), in which her generous reserves of warmth and wit found an outlet in the role of Meg, one of the militant women who supports the miners' strike. BMcF

Efftee Film Productions In 1930, Frank •Thring Snr sold his interests in •Hoyts and set up Efftee Productions, starting in the fire-damaged shell of His Majesty's Theatre, Melbourne, which was officially opened as a film studio on 2 June 1931. Efftee's manager, Tom Holt, was sent to purchase the latest American sound equipment, while Thring negotiated with the federal government for a reduced duty on its import. American Dan Blomberg helped to install the equipment and to train Australian staff. By the end of the year, Efftee's technical team was established: Alan Mill in charge of sound, Arthur •Higgins as cameraman, W.R. Coleman as designer, and Thring's daughter Lola as editor. Except for two early short features directed by E.A. Dietrich-Derrick (•A Co-Respondent's Course, 1931, and The Haunted Barn), Thring directed all the films, employing Raymond •Longford as uncredited assistant on some of them. As well as fiction, the company filmed vaudeville items in the Efftee Entertainers series: vocalists such as Jack O'Hagan, comics such as Ada Reeve, and musicians such as the Melbourne Chinese Orchestra. Efftee was associated with Noel •Monkman's documentaries and also produced newsreel items. Their product was distributed as 'unit programs', containing a feature and supporting films. In December 1933 Efftee moved to the refurbished and fully soundproofed Wattle Path studios in the Melbourne suburb of St Kilda, but, during 1934, release difficulties stopped production. Thring was considering moving the company to Sydney, when he died in 1936 and Efftee Productions was wound up. INA BERTRAND

Eggby, David (1950–) CINEMATOGRAPHER David Eggby began his career with Crawford Productions in Victoria on TV drama and documentaries. His first feature film as director of photography was Dr George •Miller's groundbreaking futuristic adventure •Mad Max (1979). Since then he has established a reputation, in Australia and overseas, for his action cinematography. He has won the Australian Cinematographers Society Gold Awards for •Quigley (1991) and Fortress (1993).

Other Australian films: Early Frost (1982), The Slim Dusty Movie (1984), Buddies (1983) Bullamakanka (1984), •The Naked Country (1985), •The Salute of The Jugger (1989), Lightning Jack (USA/Australia, 1994). DAVID MUIR

Eggleston, Colin (1941–) DIRECTOR Colin Eggleston had been a television story editor and director for Crawford Productions before directing his first film, the privately financed 'soft porn' Fantasm Comes Again (1977). Using the pseudonym of Eric Ram, echoing the subtlety of the film's title, Eggleston shot most of the sex scenes in Los Angeles, although the linking scenes involving a cub reporter were filmed in Australia. In 1979, under his own name, he directed the quite ingenious and disturbing ecological thriller, •Long Weekend, in which a young city couple, played by Eggleston's wife Briony •Behets and John •Hargreaves, with both of whom he would work again, creates havoc as they heedlessly and gracelessly turn a coastal paradise into a nightmare. **Nightmares** (1980) is indeed the name of the film in which Behets next appeared for Eggleston, who directed and co-produced. She also played in the horror film, **Cassandra** (1986). Eggleston wrote as well as directed these two horror-thrillers. In **Long Weekend**, which he co-produced, he showed some aptitude for creating a genuine frisson of terror, but his film career petered out in Australia. He made a further horror film called **Cattiva** in Italy in 1991.

Other Australian film: Sky Pirates (1986). BMcF

Ehlers, Jerome (1959–) ACTOR After graduating from the Australian National Institute of Dramatic Art, Jerome Ehlers made a strong impact with two miniseries released in 1989—*Bangkok Hilton* and, especially, *Darlings of the Gods*, which dramatised the 1948 Old Vic tour of Australia, headed by Laurence Olivier and Vivien Leigh. Ehlers had a key role in the four-hour production for the ABC as flamboyant Australian actor Peter Finch who developed a romantic relationship with Vivien Leigh. After supporting roles in the romance **Weekend With Kate** (1990), the Australian western •Quigley (1991), and the lead role in the low-budget crime thriller **Fatal Bond** (1992), Ehlers had his best feature-film role to date in •Deadly (1992). Ehlers, as Detective Tony Bourke, is sent to the outback town of Yabbari, after accidentally shooting a junkie in Sydney, to clear the police in the killing of an Aborigine. Bourke, however, gradually rejects police attempts to shut down the case and he forms a bond with the local Aboriginal community. This generic mixture of action and social comment provided Ehlers with a showcase for not only his striking facial features but also his considerable acting talent.

For much of the 1990s Ehlers has alternated appearances in the theatre (such as Shakespeare's *Coriolanus* in 1996 and Biff Loman in *Death of a Salesman* in 1997—both at the Sydney Opera House), with television series (such as *Heartbreak High*, 1994; *True Stories*; 1994, *Flipper*, 1995), and miniseries (such as *Frontier*, 1997; *Kangaroo Palace*, 1997).

Other Australian film: Irresistible Force (1993). GM

1896 Melbourne Cup, The

1896. Directors/producers: Marius Sestier, Walter Barnett, *Director of photography*: Marius Sestier. B&W.

The earliest surviving motion picture images shot in Australia are apparently the Lumière company footage of Derby

Day (31 October) and Melbourne Cup Day (3 November), shot by Marius Sestier in 1896 at Flemington racecourse. One film of the three taken at the Derby may have survived. It shows three attempts to put the blue riband on the winner, Newhaven, who also won the Cup that year. Probably 10 'views' were taken on Cup Day itself. Each of the surviving 'views' lasts about one minute, the length of one reel for the Lumière camera, and each has clearly been staged for maximum visual attraction.

One of the 1896 Cup films, **La Foule** or **The Crowd** is among early cinema's most perfectly evocative images. It shows the Cup Day crowd in an eternal last-days-of-the-century afternoon of parasols, glossy top hats, and fresh white linen. A handsome couple engaged in conversation, seemingly unaware of the camera, comes from the left background, moving closer and closer until they exit in the right foreground. A dandy in a white hat, who is Walter Barnett, Sestier's Australian 'co-producer', walks towards us chatting with a woman and returns later to join another group, just to keep the action flowing. An older man wearing a derby stops in the medium-close foreground to stare directly at the camera and, in the left background, a slight figure pauses and poses, hand to mouth. In the space of 76 seconds an entire way of life has dreamed itself again, privileged, beckoning, as evanescent as the November sun.

WILLIAM D. ROUTT

Elfick, David (1944–   ) PRODUCER/DIRECTOR David Elfick was the editor of the music magazine *Go-Set*, as well as a writer, director, and producer of short films and documentaries in the 1960s and 1970s, including two feature-length documentaries (**Morning of the Earth**, 1972; •**Crystal Voyager**, 1973). Elfick's first major feature film production was •**Newsfront** in 1978 and, after subsequent success with **The Chain Reaction** (1980), and •**Star Struck** (1982), he resented the loss of control imposed on 'hands-on producers' such as himself by the 10BA taxation policy in the 1980s. Nevertheless, Elfick has worked steadily in the Australian film industry in the past two decades since **Newsfront** and his output covers a number of different genres, including the musical (**Star Struck**), comedy (**Emoh Ruo**, 1985; **Around the World in 80 Ways**, 1988; **Love in Limbo**, 1993), children's film (•**No Worries**, 1993), and social drama (**The Chain Reaction**, 1980). Since the success of *Fields of Fire*, a miniseries that Elfick produced in 1987, and his subsequent co-direction of the sequel, *Fields of Fire II* (1988), and all of *Fields of Fire III* (1989), Elfick has directed most of his films, including the underrated thriller **Harbour Beat** (1990), which starred Scottish actor John Hannah.
Other Australian films include: Undercover (1984), •Blackrock (1997).

GM

Eliza Fraser

1976. Director: Tim Burstall. *Producer*: Tim Burstall. *Scriptwriter*: David Williamson. *Director of Photography*: Robin Copping. *Music*: Bruce Smeaton. 127 mins. *Cast*: Susannah York (Eliza Fraser), Trevor Howard (Captain Foster Fyans), Noel Ferrier (Captain James Fraser), John Castle (Captain Rory McBryde), John Waters (David Bracefell).

Eliza Fraser's story provided the basis for Patrick •White's novel *A Fringe of Leaves* in the same year as Tim •Burstall's film, although White changed the names and adopted a more obviously serious approach. In 1836 Eliza and her husband set out from Sydney to Singapore, calling in on the way at the Moreton Bay penal settlement run by the sadistic Captain Fyans. On leaving the colony, their ship is wrecked, and Captain Fraser and Mrs Fraser undertake a journey of survival with the help of Aborigines and of Bracefell, a convict who has escaped Moreton Bay and the unwelcome attentions of Fyans. She loses her husband along the way, but eventually makes her fortune by telling her sensational story at fairgrounds, with Eliza presented as a woman of pluck and resourcefulness in the performance by visiting British actress, Susannah York. The film displays a mixture of sexual comedy and adventure melodrama, and enjoyed modest popular success, although critics judged harshly its uncertain tone.

BMcF

Elliott, Stephan (1963–   ) DIRECTOR/WRITER As a relatively young film-maker, Stephan Elliott's work is notable for its sense of whimsy and controversy. Based in Sydney, Elliott challenges the notions of 'Australianness' and seems determined to confront audiences with his subject matter.

His first feature, **Frauds** (1993), was not well received, although it did provide a glimpse of the style to come. His next feature, •**The Adventures of Priscilla, Queen of the Desert** (1994), proved highly successful, winning the 1995 Academy Award for Costume Design, and the Best Actor award for Terence Stamp at the 1994 Seattle International Film Festival. Elliott's film about three drag queens trekking across Central Australia in an old bus, with its colourful costumes and soundtrack, grotesque characters, and study of outcasts, appealed to both homosexual and heterosexual audiences, although some critics questioned Elliott's study of women.

His most recent film, **Welcome to Woop-Woop** (1997), again saw Elliott challenging his audience with its salute to 'Ockerism' and the sardonic Australian sense of humour. Not even the inclusion of the songs of Rodgers and Hammerstein, or the return of expatriate Rod •Taylor, could save the film at the box office. Elliott's attempts to celebrate a particular period and character were not embraced.

KAREN FORD

Ellis, Bob (1942–) WRITER, DIRECTOR   Bob Ellis is a colourful New South Wales writer and, less successfully, director, who began his career in the Australian film industry by supplying additional dialogue for 'Judy', one of the case studies of three Australian youths in **Three to Go** (1971). Ellis's first notable success was his original script for •**Newsfront** (1978), a penetrating overview of Australian society in the 1950s that was dramatised through the rivalry between an Australian-based newsreel company and its American competitor. Ellis, who initially removed his name from the credits, renewed his claim to the film after its critical and commercial success. After working part-time as a film critic in the 1970s, Ellis continued his scriptwriting, and directing, throughout the 1980s with varying success. Arguably his most successful script was his collaboration with Denny Lawrence for •**Goodbye Paradise** (1983), a sad, elegiac film that combines the conventions of the hard-boiled detective genre, especially the melancholic, self-deprecating tone of Raymond Chandler, with a penetrating critique of the growing superficiality of life in Surfers Paradise. The unique, for Australia, writing style used for this film reworked generic conventions and laced them with irony and venom in a story of an over-the-hill alcoholic, magnificently performed by Ray •Barrett, who stumbles on a right-wing political and military conspiracy to allow free-market forces unbridled access to the Barrier Reef and other Queensland resources.

Ellis was less successful in adapting the characters and storyline from a Mills and Boon novel, *The House in the Timberwoods* (1959), with Anne •Brooksbank for the film **The Winds of Jarrah** (1985). Throughout the 1980s Ellis co-wrote scripts with Paul •Cox for three films directed by Cox: •**Man of Flowers** (1983), •**My First Wife** (1984), and **Cactus** (1986). Ellis also wrote scripts for films that he directed himself: **Unfinished Business** (1985), •**Warm Nights on a Slow Moving Train** (1988), the semi-autobiographical •**The Nostradamus Kid** (1993), and **Dreaming of Lords** (1993), a dramatisation of the first cricket tour of England by an Australian team that was totally composed of Aborigines. Ellis also contributed dialogue to the outback comedy **Bullseye** (1989), as well as acting in a number of Australian films: **Man of Flowers**, **Unfinished Business**, **Remember Me** (1985), **I Own the Racecourse** (1986), **Dear Cardholder** (1987), **Mortgage** (1989), **The Nostradamus Kid**, and **Down Rusty Down** (1996).

Other Australian films as scriptwriter include: …**Maybe This Time** (1980) and **Fatty Finn** (1980).   GM

Emerald City

1989. *Director*: Michael Jenkins. *Producer*: Joan Long. *Scriptwriter*: David Williamson. Based on his play. *Director of photography*: Paul

Murphy. 92 mins. *Cast*: John Hargreaves (Colin Rogers), Robyn Nevin (Kate Rogers), Chris Haywood (Mike McCord), Nicole Kidman (Helen Davey), Ruth Cracknell (Elaine Ross).

David •Williamson, arguably Australia's most successful playwright, has shown equal skill as a scriptwriter, but not particularly on the film versions of his own plays, with the exception of •**Don's Party**. There, the essential talkiness of the piece was countered by Bruce •Beresford's direction and Don •McAlpine's fluid camera work. In **Emerald City**, a very popular stage play, dependent on bold contrasts and a steady flow of one-liners, has become too static and theatrical for its own good. Its opposition of glamorous, superficial Sydney and staider, idealistic Melbourne seems simplistic in the intimacy of cinema. The film's strength is in the performances of a strong cast. John •Hargreaves and Robyn •Nevin play Colin and Kate Rogers, who migrate from Melbourne to Sydney to pursue careers in screenwriting and publishing respectively, with professional and personal results at odds with expectations. Ruth •Cracknell's film producer and Chris •Haywood's devious promoter make the most of the comedy in the film, which deals better with the surfaces than the serious issues at stake—about ambition, for instance.   BMcF

Emmanuel, Takis ACTOR   Before coming to Australia in the mid 1970s, Greek actor Emmanuel Takis had considerable experience in theatre and film. He had played in **Zorba the Greek** (1964) and **Oedipus the King** (1968), and several other films. His first Australian film was Tom •Cowan's **Promised Woman**. He followed this with two sympathetic male leads: in •**Caddie**, as the heroine's gentle migrant lover, and in Paul •Cox's •**Kostas**, again as a migrant, this time a journalist working in Melbourne as a taxi-driver who becomes infatuated with a young divorcee, played by Wendy •Hughes. He was, of course, typecast in Australian films but, within this limitation, he played with sensitivity and tact.   BMcF

Empty Beach, The

1985. *Director*: Chris Thomson. *Producers*: Timothy Read & John Edwards. *Scriptwriter*: Keith Dewhurst. *Director of photography*: John Seale. *Music*: Martin Armiger. 89 minutes. *Cast*: Bryan Brown (Cliff Hardy), Anna Maria Monticelli (Anne Winter), Ray Barrett (McLean), Belinda Giblin (Marion Singer), John Wood (Parker), Peter Collingwood (Ward).

Based on the fourth Cliff Hardy novel, and written by one of Australia's best exponents of the genre, Peter Corris, **The Empty Beach** is a mild disappointment. The film retains most of the basic ingredients of the genre but it fails to develop these conventions beyond a superficial level. The absence of voice-over, as used in •**Goodbye Paradise** (1983), for example, reduces Bryan •Brown's Cliff Hardy to an introverted observer intermittently delivering smart remarks and pseudo-tough cracks.

The film is set in and around Sydney's Bondi Beach with Hardy employed by Marion Singer to find her wealthy husband who disappeared two years ago. Marion receives anonymous information that her husband, believed dead, is still alive, and this provides the pretext for Hardy's involvement in a nightmare world that includes pensioners imprisoned in a large house where they are drugged, fed on pet food, and robbed of their pension cheques. The characteristic downbeat ending fails to provide that extra layer of poetic vulnerability found in **Goodbye Paradise**.　　　GM

Encounters

1993 Director: Murray Fahey. *Producer:* Murray Fahey. *Scriptwriter:* Murray Fahey. *Director of photography:* Peter Borosh. *Music:* Frank Strangio. 90 minutes. *Cast:* Kate Raison (Madeline Carr), Martin Sacks (Martin Carr), Martin Vaughan (Harris), Maggie Kirkpatrick (Aunt Helen), Vince Gil (Farmer), John Krummel (Miles Franklin).

Encounters is an effective low-budget thriller that displays the visual and dramatic skill of director, writer, and producer Murray Fahey who is able to generate considerable suspense out of very basic elements. Madeline Carr is a rich young woman who starts having recurring nightmares concerning her brother who died 22 years ago. Seemingly sympathetic husband Martin suggests that they return to the country estate of her youth to see if that will unlock her mental problem. When their car becomes bogged at night, Martin seeks help, leaving Madeline alone in the fog-enclosed forest. Madeline eventually finds the house of a former family employee, Harris, who, seemingly, wants to keep her prisoner.

This 'cat-and-mouse' thriller full of red herrings and periodic climaxes to keep the viewer interested relies on the filmic skills of Fahey as the plot, themes, and characterisations are very elementary. The first part of the film portrays Madeline's disturbed condition and her uneasy relationship with her husband. This provides the dramatic basis for the tension in the second half of the film, which largely takes place in an old country house owned by the sinister Harris. A skilful use of camera and sounds combines to keep the viewer engaged throughout the film and only the *dénouement*, and epilogue, which rely solely on a detective's exposition to pull the plot together, disappoint.　　　GM

Enemy Within, The

1918. Director/Scriptwriter/Producer: Roland Stavely. *Producer (?)/Director of photography:* Franklyn Barrett. B&W. *Cast:* Reginald L. 'Snowy' Baker (Jack Airlie), Sandy McVea (Jimmy Cook), Lily Molloy (Myee Drew).

The Enemy Within marked the feature début of Reginald L. 'Snowy' •Baker. Like Douglas Fairbanks before him and Jackie Chan after, Baker is best known for performing his own stunts. The surviving, near-complete print of the film gives modern viewers the chance to see for themselves some of those athletic feats. The story centres around the activities of a German spy ring in Australia in the last months of World War I. Jack Airlie is given the job of stamping the ring out, which he does with considerable help from his Black sidekick, Jimmy, played by the well-known Aboriginal boxer Sandy McVea. The movie proved an instant winner with filmgoers, but critics were generally less enthusiastic, drawing attention to the calibre of Baker's acting, the villain's motives, the excessive length (5500 ft), and some of the settings. This mattered little to contemporary audiences enthralled by the film's liveliness, but Australian producers failed to capitalise further on the national taste for action that Baker's films had revealed.

KEN BERRYMAN AND WILLIAM D. ROUTT

Enright, Nick (1950–) WRITER/ACTOR Well-known playwright Nick Enright began working professionally in theatre for J.C. Williamson at the age of 16 and was head of acting at the National Institute of Dramatic Art from 1982 to 1984. He began scriptwriting on the ABC miniseries *Come in Spinner* (1989, co-writer), but he quickly rose to international prominence with his Academy Award nomination for **Lorenzo's Oil** (1992), which he shared with co-writer and director George •Miller. •**Blackrock** (1997), from his play of the same name about a young man embroiled in circumstances surrounding a rape, attracted significant critical interest but failed to draw audiences. The teleplay *Coral Island* (1995) from the *Naked* series deals with homosexuality and personal identity, and includes semi-autobiographical references to Enright's own education at a private Catholic boys' school, and is among his best work for screen. The charming short **The Maitland and Morphet String Quartet** (1989) from his children's book of the same name included illustrations by cartoonist Victoria Roberts and became an animated film by Ann Jolliffe. Among Enright's 30 works for stage are *The Boy from OZ* (the musical based on Peter Allen's life), an adaptation for stage of Tim Winton's *Cloudstreet*, and *The Venetian Twins*.

HARRY KIRCHNER

Environment

1927. Director/Scriptwriter: Gerald M. Hayle. *Producer:* Vaughan C. Marshall. *Director of photography:* Tasman Higgins. B&W. *Cast:* Beth Darvall (Mary Garval), Hal Percy (James Denison).

Environment is one of those films that seems to have been (unconsciously) made for cultural analysis. At the same time, unhappily, it is rather tedious to watch. The film does live up to its title, championing the effects of a 'sweet and clean' environment over notions of genetic inheritance, but it is also about how much a woman must undergo before she is allowed to receive what her father has left for her in a world populated by parricides, lechers, and wowsers. Mary, whose adopted father has died, is offered a job posing in the nude. 'I have no experience as a model,' she answers, 'but I am looking for a position.' When the artist ('shall we jazz?') tries to make her 'his', she runs off, only to have the fateful painting turn up just in time to sour her best shot at true romance. This painting (*L'environnement*) actually conceals the will that makes Mary's fortune, but it must be destroyed before she finds happiness with her true love.

WILLIAM D. ROUTT

Equity, *see* Unions and Associations

Ethnic representation   The arrival in Australia of large numbers of southern and eastern European migrants after World War II dramatically altered the social composition and cultural fabric of the nation, and eventually led to the development of the notion of Australia as a multicultural society. Each new wave of migration from non-British sources has encountered a mixture of hostility and hospitality from earlier settlers. Fear of foreigners, with their potential to dilute and erode Anglo-Australian values and threaten established socioeconomic interests, is mitigated by sympathy for the underdog and the moral imperative to welcome refugees from economic and political oppression. To placate the Australian population's fear of foreigners, churches and government authorities have drawn attention to the suffering of migrants and appealed to a locally entrenched tradition of sympathy for the oppressed.

Maslyn •Williams's •**Mike and Stefani** (1952) fits into this scenario. Made by the film division of the Department of the Interior in 1952, it personalises the plight of displaced people, through the story of a Ukrainian couple who are uprooted from their homeland by the combined terror of Hitler and Stalin, confined in depressing 'displaced persons' camps, and await deliverance. The film begins with documentary footage of the interrogation and selection procedures of Australian immigration authorities, before moving on to depict the couple departing the gloom of Europe and sailing to Australia, signified in the finale as the land of hope and glory by the rising light on the horizon and the music swelling on the soundtrack.

Later government-sponsored dramatised documentaries continued to make pleas for sympathy for and understanding of the strangers in our midst. 'Toula', an episode (directed by Oliver Howe) in **Three to Go** (1971) introduces us to the social dynamics of a blue-collar Greek migrant family, through the narration of its teenage daughter, Toula, and reveals some inter-generational stresses and strains. Its final scene, an extended documentary sequence of the Easter service in a Greek Orthodox church, celebrates the 'exotic' ethnic colour of Greek religious traditions.

In the early 1960s, well before the celebrated 'renaissance' of Australian cinema (see Revival, the), an enterprising Italian migrant, a professional photographer named Giorgio •Mangiamele, set up a film studio, trained actors, and shot his own fictional narratives in the streets of Melbourne. His experimental art movie, •**Clay** (1965), was selected for Compétition at the Cannes Film Festival and received several local awards, but otherwise his work has been neglected, his contribution to Australian cinema largely unrecognised. **The Spag** (1960) and **Ninety-Nine Percent** (1963) offer especially interesting representations of the migrant experience in postwar Melbourne. The former centres on the encounters of a poor little 'dago boy', who delivers newspapers to the residents of Carlton, with do-gooding and delinquent Australians, and ends in tragedy. The latter blends comedy with pathos, telling the story of another Italian migrant, a widowed street hawker with a young son, who makes a heroic-pathetic attempt to remarry. The location-shot urban street settings, the mixture of melodrama with social realism, the meticulous miming of daily routines, and the focus on failures and fringe-dwellers suggest a debt to Italian neo-realism, but the artful camera work has Mangiamele's personal signature. The supporting cast give embarrassingly accurate performances of Australians reacting to new migrants with awkward gestures of conscientious kindness and callous cruelty.

In the 1970s, the new Australian cinema's attempt to market an image of Australia based on landscape and national character discouraged representations of ethnic minorities other than the indigenous people. Nevertheless, a few fiction films featuring the experience of non-English-speaking migrants were made. The proto-feminist Aussie battler, Caddie (Helen •Morse), in •**Caddie** (1976), was given a Greek lover. An adaptation of Theo Patrikareas's play, *Throw Away Your Harmonica*, shot in Greece and Sydney, dramatises the traumas and painful process of adjustment experienced by a Greek woman dispatched to Australia after a humiliating love affair at home (•**Promised Woman**, 1976). Turkish migrant Ayten Kuyululu directed two disturbing dramatic films (**A Handful of Dust**, 1973; **The Golden Cage**, 1975) about the devastating experiences of Turkish migrants in Sydney. Hellenophile Dutch migrant Paul Cox explored the alienation of a Greek immigrant journalist-cum-taxi-driver and his troubled relationship with an Australian woman in •**Kostas** (1979).

It is noteworthy that Takis •Emmanuel starred in three of these films (**Caddie, Promised Woman** and **Kostas**). In the 1970s, he filled a gap. As testified by director Gillian

•Armstrong and producer Margaret •Fink's efforts to cast the leading male role in •**My Brilliant Career** (1979), there was no local male actor who could convincingly play the role of a lover with appeal to women audiences. With his suave, sophisticated, mature continental manner, Takis Emmanuel supplied the necessary romantic interest, when required. (The figure of the continental lover re-emerged in Armstrong's adaptation of Helen Garner's novel •**The Last Days of Chez Nous**, 1992, when Bruno Ganz was imported for the role.)

The inadequacy of the Australian male as romantic lover was further underlined in Sophia Turkiewicz's •**Silver City** (1984), in which two migrant actors, Gosia •Dobrowolska and Ivar •Kants, performed the roles of the central romantic couple, Nina and Julian. Nina's brief encounters with Australian males are shown to be depressing. Disappointingly gauche at best, distressingly violent at worst, they offer no competition to her married Polish lover, who alone can arouse her romantically and sexually. This love story is set largely in a migrant camp in early postwar Australia, and the historically specific privations, tensions, and prejudices of the place and period are cleverly integrated into the script and the visualisation.

Also in the early 1980s, the collaborative efforts of Rosa •Colosimo (producer), Jan •Sardi (writer) and Michael •Pattinson (director) generated two teen movies with contemporary settings, starring Rosa's son, Vince Colosimo: •**Moving Out** (1983) and •**Street Hero** (1984). With popular Italian songs on the soundtrack, and its focus on an extended Italian migrant family, **Moving Out** is the more obviously 'ethnic' film. It highlights the tensions between blue-collar migrants and their Australian-educated teenage children. **Street Hero** is more of a genre movie, with its rock-music soundtrack, garish visual style, and melodramatic treatment of the teen hero's experience—in which his Italianness does not figure as a major issue.

Other Italian-Australians—Luigi Acquisto, Ettore Siracusa, and Monica Pellizzari—have actively drawn on their specific cultural experience for short fiction and experimental film productions, in various different ways. Monica Pellizzari's first feature film, **A Fistful of Flies** was released on the European film festival circuit in 1996. Her approach is broad, hard-hitting satire: she mercilessly caricatures the hysterical Italian mamma, and extravagantly mocks the developmental crises and social problems of the daughters of Italian migrants, in comic routines ranging from the burlesque to the biting. Pellizzari is not alone in making comic capital out of ethnic stereotypes. The 'typical' Greek family that polices its daughters, displays upwardly mobile ambitions, and enjoys nothing so much as a lavish wedding is lampooned in •**Death in Brunswick** (1991) and **The** •**Heartbreak Kid** (1993). Similarly, the 'sleazy Greek' male stereo-

type, popularised by television and live-theatre comedy shows such as *Wogs out of Work* and *Acropolis Now*, is also deployed to comic effect in **Death in Brunswick** and, to a lesser extent, in Aleksi Vellis's •**Nirvana Street Murder** (1991) although, in the latter two films, everyone is lampooned, irrespective of age, class, sex, age, or ethnicity.

With the entry of the second generation (the children of postwar migrants, who have been born and educated in Australia) into the film industry, there have been marked shifts in representations of ethnicity. First, as noted above, there has been a move away from social realism and melodrama towards comedy and other entertainment genres. Second, as the emphasis has shifted from the problems of the migrant generation to the concerns of the second generation, the parent generation and ethnic community values tend to be seen in a more critical light, deemed as oppressive, or as laughable as 'skip' (Anglo-Australian) values. Third, and this is especially noticeable in the case of representations of Greek women, the focus has shifted from suffering victims to active rebels, and from social oppression to sexual liberation. This last shift is pronounced, as can be seen from a comparison of the representation of, on the one hand, Toula (in **Three to Go**) and Antigone (in **Promised Woman**) with, on the other, that of Helen (the Mary Koustas character in **Nirvana Street Murder**), Sophie Papafagos (Zoë Carrides) in **Death in Brunswick**, and Christina (the Greek-Australian schoolteacher who is the heroine of **The Heartbreak Kid**, played by Claudia Karvan).

In the case of Ana •Kokkinos's **Only the Brave** (1994), and •**Head On** (1998), there is a return to the high melodramatic mode, but issues hitherto ignored in the representation of the Greek community—incest, homosexuality, and single parenthood—are taken out of the closet and made central to the narrative. **Head On**, an adaptation of Christos Tsiolkas' novel, *Loaded*, underlines the oppressive values of the Greek family and community. For the gay Greek-Australian adolescent protagonist, already confused and disturbed about his sexual and ethnic identity, the pressures to marry a girl from the Greek community and produce children are stressful.

Most of these films were made in Melbourne, where the second generation of Mediterranean migrants is well represented in local film culture. In Sydney, the home of the glitzy glamour of the Mardi Gras, a romantic view of ethnicity survives—evident in •**Strictly Ballroom** (1992). Here, Anglo-Australian dance culture is ridiculed in high-camp fashion and the hero's dysfunctional 'ocker' family is lampooned. Their phoney artificiality and cold heartlessness is contrasted to the real traditional skills (in dance and dressmaking) and natural warmth of the Spanish community and family of Fran (Tara Morice), the Cinderella heroine. The romantic couple's ultimate triumph at the ballroom dancing competition in the Latin American number is shown to be due not only to hard work and true love, but also to the hero's intimate experience of ethnicity as real nature and true culture.

If the effects of Mediterranean migration on Australian society and culture have filtered into the Australian cinema, albeit more in Melbourne than Sydney, the impact of migration from East and South-east Asia has only recently begun to be registered. This is doubtless connected to the long maintenance of restrictive (racist) immigration policies, and the relative ignorance, until recently, of Asian languages and cultures among local film-makers.

Reference to early Chinese settlers occurs, briefly and in passing, in just two Australian period films. In the prologue to Philippe •Mora's •**Mad Dog Morgan** (1976), the massacre of Chinese miners on the goldfields is graphically and elegiacally represented. Although it might be argued that this serves only to demonstrate the outlaw hero's anti-racist credentials (exemplified later in the film by his brotherhood with an indigenous Australian), it is the only occasion on which this shameful historic event, and the hostility towards Chinese settlers that engendered it, was represented in new Australian cinema. In contrast, •**We of the Never Never** (1982), which likewise focuses on White–Black relations (but features a middle-class White heroine, rather than an outcast White hero), displaces prejudice against Aboriginal Australians onto the Chinese chef on the outback station; the heroine asserts her feminist and anti-racist credentials by sacking him and replacing him with another, servile Chinese chef.

A decade later, Geoffrey •Wright's •**Romper Stomper** (1992) highlighted the racism and fascism among White working-class boys in the western suburbs of Melbourne, in graphically disturbing scenes of violent brutality against Vietnamese immigrants. However, the Vietnamese, despite retaliating as a group against their victimisers, are not developed as characters; the central dramatic triangle concerns the leader of the fascist gang, his younger brother, and his abused girlfriend. The film turns into a romantic elegy for doomed youth, rather than an attack on racism. The melodramatic climax, in which the White working-class brothers descend to fratricidal combat on the beach over the body of the girl, is performed to an audience of camera-snapping Japanese tourists, another group of 'alien invaders', who mock the trio's dramatic conflict by deeming it entertaining rather than threatening.

Hitherto, only two Australian feature films have told stories from the point of view of an Asian immigrant. **Aya** (1991), directed by Solrun •Hoaas, tells the story of a Japanese war bride, her difficult process of adjustment to life in postwar Australia, and her growth towards self-sufficiency after the disintegration of her marriage. The historical veracity and emotional truth of this first feature film derive from comprehensive research (on postwar Australian social history and occupied Japan, as well as interviews with Japanese war brides) that had formed the basis of Hoaas's earlier documentary on the subject of war brides (**Green Tea and Cherry Ripe**, 1989), from a knowledge of Japanese language and culture (although of Norwegian parentage Hoaas was born and brought up in Japan), and from Hoaas's personal experience of being a foreigner (in Japan, Norway, and Australia). The central relationship of this film, between an Australian soldier and his Japanese wife, is explored with sensitive attention to cultural differences, and the troubled ambivalent desires that attract Australian men to Asian women. Cool, distanced camera work and the subtle use of visual motifs keep the reins on the maudlin and melodramatic potential of the dramatically strong central performances, by Eri Ishida (as war bride) and Nicholas •Eadie (as the husband).

In **Floating Life** (1996), expatriate Hong Kong filmmaker Clara Law has produced the first Australian feature focusing on contemporary Chinese migrants, with dialogue in Cantonese, English, and German. **Floating Life** is a family melodrama–comedy that spans three generations, relating the stresses, strains, and antics resulting from the emigration and dispersal of the family from Hong Kong to Munich and Melbourne. Despite some problems in casting and script, due to the local shortage of bilingual actors, and a tendency to spell out points verbally, the exquisite camera work and the delicate handling of the dramatic *dénouement* expressively convey the dislocated condition of the diasporic Chinese—there is both pathos and a sense of the absurd. With the influx of talent from the Hong Kong film industry, and the emergence of a second generation of Asian-Australians, we can look forward with some eagerness to a greater number of Australian feature films focusing on the experience of migrants from Asia.　　FREDA FREIBERG

Eureka Stockade

1907 Directors: George Cornwell, Arthur Cornwell. *Production company:* Australasian Cinematograph Company. B&W.

This was the only film produced by the Cornwell brothers, and the first filmed reconstruction of the Eureka rebellion. Although its exact length is now doubtful, it was certainly presented as a full program when released at the Melbourne Atheneum in October 1907, so it was probably the second feature-length dramatised film to be produced in Australia (after •**The Story of the Kelly Gang** in 1906). The advertisements for the film list its contents, from 'Gold seekers leaving London, through scenes of life on the goldfields leading up to the rebellion, to the building and storming of the stockade, and finally an epilogue showing the city of Ballarat 55 years after'. It is some of the epilogue (the camera panning across shops in major streets, and a procession of the 7th Infantry Regiment) that survives in the National Film and Sound Archive.   IB

Eureka Stockade

1949. Director: Harry Watt. *Producer:* Michael Balcon. *Scriptwriters:* Harry Watt, Walter Greenwood. *Director of photography:* George Heath. *Music:* Ronald Whelan. 102 mins. B&W. *Cast:* Chips Rafferty (Peter Lalor), Jane Barrett (Alicia Dunne), Jack Lambert (Commissioner Rede), Peter Illing (Rafaello Carboni), Gordon Jackson (Tom Kennedy), Sydney Loder (Vern), Grant Taylor (Sergeant-Major Milne), Peter Finch (Humffray).

More ambitious in concept than •The Overlanders (1946), Ealing Studio's second Australian feature retained Chips Rafferty in the leading role of Peter Lalor, leader of the ill-fated goldminers' uprising at Ballarat in 1854. It also retained the ensemble of major characters drawn from a range of ethnic backgrounds: the Irish-Australian Lalor, the Scot Kennedy, the Italian Carboni and the German Vern, working their gold claim together, a not inappropriate theme for a nation involved in launching one of the great migration schemes of the century at the time the film was being produced.

The film's script stays close to the historical facts, yet shows a consciousness of the ambiguities of history, with several of the characters driven by the conflicting pulls of conscience and duty. As leader of the miners, Lalor is reluctant at first but is persuaded by his romantic interest, the school teacher (Jane Barrett). Similarly, goldfields commissioner Rede is not unmoved by the miners' claim that the colonial government's tax on mining is unjust, so the film avoids oversimplification of the issues involved without downplaying the excessive brutality of the police in the discharge of their duties.

Filmed on location around Singleton, and with considerable logistic support from the Australian army, Watt convincingly evokes the life of the goldfields, while the action sequences are dramatic and effective, climaxing in the attack on the miners' encampment. **Eureka Stockade** did not meet with the success of **The Overlanders**, possibly as a result of some miscasting and of the heavy-handed and obtrusive narrative devices that open and close the film.

BRUCE MOLLOY

Evans, Lindley (1895–1982) COMPOSER

Lindley Evans wrote scores for feature and documentary films. His first score for •Uncivilised (1936) does its best to underscore the bizarre scenario of a girl reporter in northern Australia who becomes enchanted with a wild White man. At the time, pioneering composers needed to search for an identity in solitary circumstances. Australia's isolation and geographic seclusion placed certain creative barriers on composing for film; composers struggled, at first, in an artistic vacuum. In 1936 Evans embarked on a study tour to Hollywood to investigate music in sound film more closely. During the recording session of a song featured in the film, he was impressed with the professional expertise displayed by an orchestra, vocalist, and technicians as they recorded a take using the playback method. (Playback equipment was installed in •Cinesound studios later that year.) Evan's next score for •Tall Timbers (1937) reveals a greater understanding of the function of film music. A score for •Forty Thousand Horsemen followed in 1940. In 1946 Evans began to write scores for the •Commonwealth Film Unit. First came **Cinderella on Strings** followed by **Capacity Smith** (1951), **Across the Frontiers** (1953), **Story of Ted Hughes** (1954), **Roof of Australia** (1957), and **About Trees** (1959).

DIANE NAPTHALI

Everlasting Secret Family, The

1988. Director: Michael Thornhill. *Producer:* Michael Thornhill. *Scriptwriter:* Frank Moorhouse. Based on Moorhouse's book of short stories, *The Everlasting Secret Family & Other Secrets. Director of photography:* Julian Penney. *Music:* Tony Bremner. 94 mins. *Cast:* Arthur Dignam (The Senator), Mark Lee (The Youth), Heather Mitchell (The Wife), Dennis Miller (Eric, the Chauffeur), Paul Goddard (The Son).

The Everlasting Secret Family begins in a visually striking fashion as The Senator (Arthur •Dignam) emerges from his chauffeur-driven car at St Michael's School for Boys and, after looking around, picks out The Youth (Mark •Lee). Soon the paranoid nature of the film becomes apparent, as the teachers in the school seem to be part of this conspiracy by which The Youth is seduced into the affluent life of The Senator. This aspect is heightened by the setting for the first scene, an athletic meeting with virile young boys dressed in their white sports clothes. The colour association reinforces the conspiratorial tone of the film: subsequent scenes show the men belonging to this group, The Rose, performing a ritualised activity dressed only in white.

After this strong opening the film's stylistic presentation weakens considerably and there is a dichotomy between style and subject matter. As the story is predicated on a lurid fantasy suggesting that many powerful groups within Australian society, especially conservative politicians, belong to an exclusive, secret, homosexual sub-society, the film calls out for an excessive dramatic style consistent with this fantasy. However, the overall presentation in terms of narrative pacing, selection of setting, colour, and performance is low-key, and the film lacks the dramatic excess necessary to bring this material to life. It belongs to a recurring genre of conspiracy thrillers (such as **The Parallax View**, 1974), but lacks an appropriate style to support its generic basis.   GM

Evil Angels

1988. *Director*: Fred Schepisi. *Producer*: Verity Lambert. *Scriptwriters*: Robert Caswell, Fred Schepisi. Based on the book *Evil Angels* by John Bryson. *Director of photography*: Ian Baker. *Music*: Bruce Smeaton. 121 mins. *Cast*: Meryl Streep (Lindy Chamberlain), Sam Neill (Michael Chamberlain), Bruce Myles (Barker), Neil Fitzpatrick (Phillips), Charles Tingwell (Justice Muirhead), Maurice Fields (Barritt). *Alternative title*: A Cry in the Dark (USA/United Kingdom).

In 1980 Azaria Chamberlain, a 10-week-old baby, was apparently killed by a dingo while she and her parents, Lindy and Michael, were holidaying at Ayers Rock, Central Australia. The case became the most widely publicised in Australian history, involving successive trials at Alice Springs and Darwin. In the latter, Lindy Chamberlain was found guilty of the murder of her baby and sentenced to life imprisonment. Her husband was found to be an accessory, his 18-month sentence being suspended in the interests of their remaining children. Subsequent evidence cleared them both, after Lindy had spent three years in gaol.

Fred *Schepisi, basing his film on John Bryson's book of the same name, makes it clear from the start that the film never doubts Lindy Chamberlain's innocence. Meryl Streep's performance, complete with an immaculate Australian accent, ensures that audience sympathy is entirely with her, as was not always so during the actual case, when Lindy's strangely affectless courtroom persona alienated many. The film is as much concerned with an indictment of a sensation-seeking media as with the central mystery of the film—how was Azaria killed? A chilly judiciary (excepting Charles *Tingwell's humane judge) and a public only too willing to pronounce its opinions, based on prejudice rather than information, come in for major criticism. In rendering these, Schepisi uses mock-documentary montage effects to create a realist background for what has the marks of a powerful melodramatic story.

BMcF

Evison, Pat (1925–) ACTOR

A New Zealand-born and partly London-trained actor who has worked in all the media, Pat Evison has long been resident in Australia, where she has won a substantial reputation as a character player. Her motherly persona can turn sour or benign as required, and she has racked up a series of memorable roles, beginning with *Caddie in 1976 and including *Tim (1979), as the loving mother of Mel *Gibson's retarded youth, and as the formidable nurse in *A Street to Die (1985).

Other Australian films: The Earthling (1980), *Star Struck (1982), *The Clinic (1983), Emma's War (1986), What the Moon Saw (1990).

BMcF

Ewart, John (1928–94) ACTOR

This Melbourne-born character actor was a familiar face in Australian films in the 1970s and 1980s. John Ewart's screen persona was encapsulated as Ugly in *Sunday Too Far Away (1975), the larrikin shearer who tells the story of the one-armed cook who specialised in rissoles and who later, without any clothes, competes with Jack *Thompson at the wash basin. This persona had begun with the role of the youngest member of the O'Riordan family struggling to settle the Lamington plateau in southern Qld in Charles *Chauvel's *Sons of Matthew (1949). Ewart's entry into the entertainment business predated even **Sons of Matthew**: he performed on radio at the age of four and later had his own long-running radio series. During the revival of the Australian cinema in the 1970s (see Revival, the), Ewart appeared in many key films between 1974 and 1978, with featured roles in *Petersen (1974), *Sunday Too Far Away, *Caddie (1976), *The Picture Show Man (1977), **Blue Fire Lady** (1978), and *Newsfront (1978). Ewart won Best Supporting Actor at the 1978 Australian Film Awards for his performance in **The Picture Show Man**. Although he worked steadily throughout the 1980s and early 1990s, many of his later films went straight to video or television.

Other Australian films: The Love Epidemic (1974), Let the Balloon Go (1976), Deadline (1981), Run, Rebecca, Run (1981), Kitty and the Bagman (1982), Crosstalk (1982), Fluteman (1982), Slice of Life (1982), *Bush Christmas (1983), *Razorback (1984), Kindred Spirits (1984), Frog Dreaming (1986), The Big Hurt (1986), Dear Cardholder (1987), Hurricane Smith (1991), Which Way Home (1991), Tracks of Glory (1992).

GM

Exhibition and distribution

In general, film supply (distribution) and film screening (exhibition) in Australia have attracted much less scholarly and community attention than indigenous film-making (production). Because the 'trade' (as distribution and exhibition are often called) has been a critical conduit for overseas control, it has frequently been depicted as essentially an agent for foreign domination. In particular, it is alleged that, in Australia, it has long operated as a duopoly that has contrived to extinguish the indigenous production industry. Because of this, it is common to view exhibition and distribution as operating in opposition to national film and film culture, and this largely explains why 'the trade' has been neglected, if not marginalised, in academic discourses.

Historically, American companies did achieve control of film distribution during and after World War I, although consolidation was a significant feature of the industry's operation prior to the arrival of American firms, and pre-war audiences already seemed to prefer American films. American control then solidified in the twenties. An influential lobby group, the Motion Picture Distributors Association of

Daybill advertising **The Face at the Window** (1919)

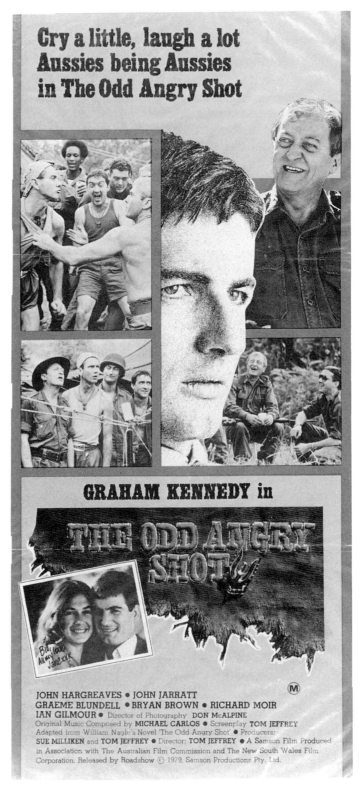

Daybill advertising **The Odd Angry Shot** (1979)

Australia (MPDA) was formed in 1924, an offshoot of the Motion Picture Producers and Distributors Association of America. Of the seven companies forming the MPDA, only one, Australasian Films (see also •Cinesound and •Greater Union Organisation), was Australian. Ironically, Australasian Films (or 'the combine' as it was often called) enjoyed a brief supremacy over exhibition and distribution. By 1920 it was alleged to have tied up 75 per cent of Australian exhibitors and to be the largest independent buyer in the New York and London exchanges. But Australasian's position as a broker was fatally undercut by the arrival of the American majors, and it subsequently declined into insignificance.

Although the same tendency towards consolidation was also apparent in exhibition, foreign interests were slower to dominate this section of the industry. Among the many independent picture shows, two Australian companies, Union Theatres (the exhibition arm of Australasian Films; see •Greater Union Organisation) and Hoyts Pictures (founded in 1909; see •Hoyts Pictures) emerged, again in the critical decade of the 1920s, as the dominant forces in film exhibition. This was achieved only after a bitter contest within the exhibition industry, which saw independents and small chains increasingly unable to resist the systematic takeover policies of the two major circuits. The growing capitalisation of exhibition was an important factor in this power struggle. The constant pressure, in the 1920s, to build more elaborate theatres and first-run picture palaces, and then, from 1928, the costs of the transfer to sound, powerfully disadvantaged smaller and independent exhibitors.

The interests of distributors and exhibitors did not wholly coincide, and it is clear that it was the distributors that occupied the dominant position within the trade. Although direct distributor-control of exhibition had yet to be achieved, foreign-owned distribution companies were already able to exercise virtual de facto control of exhibition through the operation of the infamous 'contract' system. Distributor contracts frequently compelled exhibitors to accept 'block' and 'blind' booking clauses. These clauses meant that exhibitors could be forced to hire part, or all, of a distributor's film supply for a fixed term (three, six, or twelve months), or to take films, sight unseen, often because such films had not even reached production. The system was most disadvantageous for small and independent exhibitors but, to secure a handful of top box-office films, many had no option but to assent to these provisions. The tensions inherent in the relationships between the major distribution and exhibition interests in Australia at this time were, however, at least temporarily subsumed when, in 1927, the federal government announced the appointment of a Royal Commission to enquire into the 'importation, production, distribution,

and exhibition of moving picture films' in Australia and, with this, the threat of a compulsory quota of either Australian or, more broadly, British Empire films.

The Royal Commission was part of the international politicisation of film issues at this time, and the operation of distributor and exhibitor interests lay at the heart of the inquiry—since Australian producers and independent distributors alleged that the major distribution and exhibition companies conspired to prevent the release of indigenous (and British) films. The decline in the number of British films screened in Australia (from 26.3 per cent of the total imported in 1913 to 3.4 per cent in 1923) was an important context for the possibility of state intervention in the industry in Australia: to a number of sectional interest groups, the Australian market was essentially a pawn in the struggle to rescue the disintegrating British film industry from the effects of American competition. Much of the final report represented a victory for the large distributing and exhibiting concerns, which insisted that, because exhibition was an ordinary business from which the public bought entertainment, pure and simple, the film trade no more warranted special legislative interference than did other commercial enterprises. In the absence of direct evidence of a vertically integrated trade, the report emphatically found, for example, that there 'is no American combine in existence in Australia exercising a stranglehold over the motion picture industry'. The report did recommend the introduction of an Empire exhibition quota (five per cent in the first year and 15 per cent after three years) but without any significant modifications to the contract system or to the organisation of the trade, although the report acknowledged that 90 per cent of the films screened in Australia were American in origin.

The fragile accommodation between exhibitor and distributor interests ended in the 1930s. While the Depression-induced collapse in admissions further exposed the economic vulnerability of exhibitors, the contract system insulated distributors from the severest effects of economic downturn. In 1931, the Fox film company of America acquired a controlling share in Hoyts, thus ending the freedom of local exhibition circuits from overseas ownership. In the 1930s, MGM and Paramount also acquired their own chains of first-run cinemas and, in 1945, the British Rank Organisation bought a controlling interest in Union Theatres. For more than 30 years, the two major exhibition circuits would be wholly or substantially foreign-owned. It was small consolation that the first of the small, independent distributors, such as New Dawn and Blake Films, also emerged in this period.

The near vertical integration of the Australian industry into the American film industry should not disguise the fact that exhibition continued to be a site of resistance as well as capitulation. Throughout the pre-television period, there was considerable diversity within the Australian exhibition industry. In the 1920s, palatial, first-run city cinemas on the Hollywood model were established as the crucial promotional vehicle governing a film's box-office career but, in rural and provincial Australia, crude outdoor cinemas were still routine, and many country towns depended on the visits of the peripatetic picture showman. Many suburban cinemas were similarly rough-and-ready establishments. In such locations, exhibition often diverged sharply from the increasingly omnipotent American model: film screenings were rarely continuous, intensively promoted, or an especially comfortable experience, and ownership was much more likely to remain vested in independent operators.

While independent exhibition had declined substantially by World War II, it was never extinguished, and the postwar years saw the emergence of independent distribution companies as an increasingly important force within the trade. The emergence of these companies was tied to the growth of the 'art film' market, which had existed since the 1920s when the first film societies were formed. The number of film societies increased rapidly in Australia, and internationally, from the 1950s onwards. In Australia, the first film festivals were held in Olinda in 1952, in Melbourne in 1953, and in Sydney in 1954, and they were, in turn, the product of the formation of a range of film societies during the 1940s. These societies sought to provide alternative exhibition sites for films ignored by the mainstream American- and British-dominated circuits. In drawing attention to films not distributed in Australia by the mainstream trade, film festivals served an important function in augmenting local distribution patterns. Postwar immigration, the expansion of universities, and left-wing political culture likewise fostered a new attitude to film as art, and helped create an expansion in non-mainstream exhibition and distribution organisations.

It is only since the 1970s that the mainstream trade has experienced any significant level of reorganisation prompted, to some extent, by a series of legislative inquiries that threatened much more substantial intervention than earlier government inquiries. The 1972–73 Tariff Board Inquiry, for example, found that the 'Australian distribution-exhibition network is to a great extent an integrated part of the marketing activities of foreign film producers'. In particular, the report noted that franchising arrangements between the major distributors and exhibitors made it unlikely that independent exhibitors could gain access to big box-office films and arrange suitable releases for their films. The Tariff Board Inquiry subsequently recommended massive state intervention in an industry where regulation had traditionally been restricted. The Tariff Board's recommendations aimed to break the oligopolistic

arrangements in the trade, especially through ending the big chains' monopoly of exhibition, and by severing the links between distribution and exhibition. If they had been implemented, the Tariff Board's recommendations would have radically altered the longstanding structure of exhibition and distribution. The suggestion that the big exhibition chains shed cinemas and distribution interests was not acted upon, but it did encourage a more sympathetic attitude to Australian films. Similarly, an inquiry by the New South Wales government in 1982 into distribution and exhibition in that state recommended that foreign distribution companies be compelled to handle Australian films. Although the recommendations were, again, not implemented, it was clear that distributors and exhibitors, weakened by the advent of television and video, were now operating in a changing cultural and regulatory environment. Since the Tariff Board Report, this has been most clearly seen in the new readiness of exhibition companies to invest in and distribute Australian films.

Although film distribution was, and still is, dominated by the American majors, who remain fundamentally uninterested in Australian production, there have been other highly significant changes in the distribution and exhibition environment since the 1970s. The long-standing duopoly exercised by Hoyts and Greater Union over exhibition ended in the 1960s, with the formation of the •Village cinema chain, which has since become a major player in the exhibition business, although Greater Union has subsequently acquired interests in Village. There has also been significant change in the ownership of Hoyts and Union. In 1981, Fox sold its interest in Hoyts and, after 50 years, the company was returned to Australian ownership. By the mid 1990s, ownership of Hoyts had changed again: the San Francisco investment firm, Hellman & Friedman, acquired majority ownership. In 1984 Rank divested its shares in Greater Union to its long-term partner, Amalgamated Holdings, an Australian company that retains ownership. Australian exhibitors have also established their own distribution agencies, such as the very successful local company Roadshow Film Distributors, a 50:50 venture between Village and Greater Union. Since the 1990s a number of the major exhibitors (such as Village Roadshow) have also entered partnerships with overseas companies to establish cinemas in Asian and other foreign territories.

Just as notable has been the proliferation of independent exhibitors and distributors (for example, Dendy, Ronin, and Palace) catering largely for arthouse and other specialist audiences. Although statistics are unreliable, it is thought that the independents—who have increasingly sought vertical integration in order to control the cinemas that exhibit the films they distribute—constitute about 15 per cent of the Australian film market. The greater flexibility in distribution and exhibition has meant that the Australian film trade now more closely resembles the situation prevailing in earlier periods, such as the 1920s. By the early 1990s, for example, independents accounted for more than half the cinema screens nationally. Similarities between this period and the earlier post-World War II period also include the resurgence of suburban cinema-going, which has, since 1990, accounted for more box-office admissions than city cinema-going. This reflects, in turn, the considerable boom that exhibition has enjoyed in Australia since the 1980s. Although the total number of seats has declined, the number of screens has increased under the impact of major programs of multiplex construction in the suburbs and provincial centres. This is in marked contrast to the absence of screen growth in many overseas markets. Between 1989 and 1993, Australia was one of only five countries to show an increase in cinema admissions, which have now been increasing for almost a decade. The rapid changes in exhibition and in the international distribution industry belie, however, more basic continuities. The USA remains the dominant player in the Australian market and, although its percentage of the total market has declined considerably, American films still provide the lion's share of box-office grosses.   DIANE COLLINS

Expatriates   In various artistic fields there are many examples of native-born Australians, and of people who emigrated to Australia in their childhood or adolescence, who have chosen, in later life, to live and work outside Australia, either permanently or for several years. There has also been a small but significant counter-current of artists and entrepreneurs from abroad who have chosen to base themselves in Australia for considerable periods of their lives. Both of these groups may be categorised under the general term 'expatriates'. In modern usage, this term is fluid and contestable. Whether any distinctions can be drawn between non-permanent expatriates and long-term visitors remains an open question and, with increased global 'commuting' through faster travel, the expatriate label will be a more subjective issue than ever. The complexity of this category is evident in the field of film.

From the beginnings of the film industry in Australia, people working in various branches of film have qualified as expatriates: producers, directors, scriptwriters, editors,

Foyer display, Theatre Royal, Perth, 1948

photographers, composers, set and costume designers, voice and stunt coaches, exhibitors and distributors, casting agents, and actors. Many actors have become world-famous stars, and their antipodean origins and connections have sometimes been a significant part of their fame.

In 1905, the English-born entrepreneur Cozens Spencer (1874–1930) established the main branch of his film-exhibiting business in Australia, and then based himself in Australia for nearly two decades, founding the film-production company that helped launch Raymond •Longford's career, and setting up studios in Sydney. In 1914, Frank •Harvey, a London actor, made a visit to Australia and, after staying on to direct a film, **Within Our Gates, or Deeds that Won Gallipoli** (1915), he ended up settling in Australia and pursuing a career, extending into the 1930s, as an actor and a scriptwriter.

Until the 1920s, it had looked as if an independent film industry might flourish in Australia, although there were early signs of the competing attraction of Hollywood for Australian talent in the careers of O.P. Heggie (1879–1936), Annette Kellerman (1886–1975), Clyde Cook (1891–1984), Arthur •Shirley (1886–1967), and Louise •Lovely (1895–1980). South Australian-born Heggie started his Hollywood career relatively late (1928), but he soon made his mark in character parts, most notably the blind hermit in **Bride of Frankenstein** (1935). Kellerman had already acquired legendary status as a world-champion swimmer before she left her native Sydney in 1905 to travel to the United Kingdom and Europe, and then the USA, where she was given leading roles in a string of hit films made around the time of World War I. Her life story was the subject of a Hollywood film, **Million Dollar Mermaid** (1952). She did not return permanently to Australia until 1970. Cook, Shirley, and Lovely all arrived in the USA during World War I. Cook was a vaudeville performer who was snatched up for comedy roles in about 30 films before the arrival of the talkies, and appeared in several more films after this. Tasmanian-born Shirley and Sydney-born Lovely appeared together in a Universal Studio film **Stronger than Death** (1915). They both carved out substantial Hollywood careers over the next few years, and then each decided to return to Australia to involve themselves in film production here, although with no lasting success.

Lovely's Hollywood trajectory is said to have provided a model for other aspiring Australian performers although, as early as 1917, a magazine article by the Australian entrepreneur J.H. Lipman mentioned several compatriots of his, in addition to Lovely, who already seemed launched on promising careers in American movies. They included Elsie Wilson, Enid Bennett, and Sylvia Breamer, as well as male leads such as Rupert Julian and Shirley. Early the following

year, a young Adelaide-born actress, Judith Anderson, set out for the USA on the advice of some fellow actors she had met while working for an American touring company in New Zealand.

Anderson's first stop was Hollywood, but she soon pressed on to New York when told by Cecil B. De Mille that her face, commandingly strong on the stage, was utterly unsuitable for the screen. She certainly lacked the conventional good looks of Lovely (who had hardly needed that name to underline them). However, as Lovely's loveliness faded, and with it her future in film, Anderson's grim visage, complete with a proudly sported mole just above her chin, became an asset that eventually disproved De Mille's verdict and secured her future on the screen as well as the stage, in all manner of diabolical or ferociously matriarchal parts, most notably her Academy Award-nominated role as the sinister Mrs Danvers in Alfred Hitchcock's **Rebecca** (1940). She played an Australian only towards the end of her career, in the Australian-made **Inn of the Damned** (1974), and she never came back to live in her native land.

Cecil •Kellaway, an Academy Award nominee for Best Supporting Actor in 1948, and again in 1967, was given his first Hollywood contract on the strength of his performance as an Australian squatter in the •Cinesound production of his own story, •**It Isn't Done** (1937). Kellaway's native land was South Africa, which he left for Australia as a thirty-year-old in 1921. Given that he uprooted himself again to go to the USA, he can be considered a sort of 'double' expatriate.

For many actors who hailed from countries within the British Empire, moving between its various parts provided an alternative or supplementary career path to that offered by Hollywood. Making a mark in London, the centre of the Empire and a historic theatrical capital, had long been the ambition of many colonial stage performers. Sydney-born comedian Cecily Courtneidge (1893–1980) was among the first to find an extra niche for her talents in British films, starting with **Elstree Calling** (1930). Melbourne-born stage actress, Coral Browne (1913–1991), and Adelaide-born dancer Robert •Helpmann followed a similar path. Both became notorious for their brashly irreverent tongues—easily attributable to their colonial origins—combined with an hauteur of bearing that did not so readily fit stereotypes of Australianness.

The most famous 'Australian' expatriate on the screen in this period was Merle Oberon (1911–79), whose first major appearance was as Anne Boleyn in the British production of **The Private Life of Henry VIII** (1933), and who quickly moved to Hollywood to play a dazzling succession of costume and contemporary roles over the next two decades. It was never any secret that the name 'Oberon' was a glamorisation of part of her real name (O'Brien), but few knew until quite recently that the early biographical detail provided in her publicity—notably her given birthplace of Hobart, Tasmania—was as much a fairytale concoction. It had been devised to conceal her real origins—then a possible stigma—as a Eurasian born in India. For most of the world, Tasmania was about as far away as you could get, and sufficiently obscure and exotic to account for Oberon's almost unearthly beauty. Her accent was definitely not recognisably Australian, although many antipodean performers at the time would have hoped the same was true of their own accents. Australians in general were as happy as the rest of the world to subscribe to the Oberon legend, and there are still some Tasmanians who are unwilling to relinquish it.

The Oberon legend served to connect Australia with the rest of the world, in particular a glamorous and sophisticated part of the world, and the reassurance of worth and sense of identity created by that process may be counted among the general functions of the expatriate-figure in Australian national consciousness. Australians have been happy to claim another Hollywood star of the 1930s and 1940s, Errol •Flynn, who became as famous for the sexual adventures of his own life as for his swashbuckling exploits in a string of period dramas on the screen. He also claimed Tasmania as his birthplace, although some authorities have given it as Northern Ireland. It is clear that he spent at least a good part of his childhood and schooling in Australia, and his first major role was in the Australian film •In the Wake of the Bounty (1933). Soon after completing this, he set off for the United Kingdom, where he was spotted by American talent scouts in a low-budget thriller. This led to an offer of a Hollywood contract. Around the same time, Sydney-born Alan Marshal (1909–61) rose to almost comparable prominence in Hollywood. Following his appearance in David Selznick's In the Garden of Allah (1936), he went on to play the dashing hero to a number of Hollywood's leading ladies, including Merle Oberon in Lydia (1941).

Already in decline by the late 1930s, feature-film production in Australia came to a virtual standstill once the nation committed itself to World War II. This was an added spur to ambitious actors to pack their bags for Hollywood. Sydney-born Shirley Ann •Richards, who had been lucky enough to score major parts in some of Cinesound's last feature films before the start of the war, turned up as Ann Richards in a number of Hollywood pictures from 1942, most memorably opposite Brian Donlevy in King Vidor's An American Romance (1944). Although she retired from the screen a decade later, she chose to stay on in the USA, which had been her father's native land. In a 1944 article proudly noting how 'Australians are well represented in Hollywood', a Hollywood columnist for the Australian Women's Weekly dubbed her 'Titian-haired Ann Richards'. This article also paraded the achievements of Judith Anderson, Cecil Kellaway, Alan Marshal, and some lesser-known

performers who had taken the Hollywood route, such as Constance Worth ('Jocelyn •Howarth' to Australians), Edward Ashley, and Joan Winfield.

Hollywood continued to be a strong magnet for Australians after World War II. Although the studios there, which had helped build up the big stars of the interwar years, began to decline in power after the war, it remained the film capital of the world, offering the best opportunities to performers for making an international reputation, or at least for finding reasonably regular work once their talents had been recognised. Meanwhile, Australia's own film industry, while not entirely extinguished by the war, showed only fitful signs of activity when peace returned, and hardly encouraged the youthful and the ambitious to stay in Australia.

The year after he had taken the lead part of Australia's great flying ace in •Smithy (1946), Ron •Randell signed up with Columbia Pictures, which put his good looks to work in various other heroic parts. He did not seek work in Australia again. Michael •Pate left for Hollywood in 1950, after taking prominent roles in a couple of locally made films. He did return for a brief acting tour at the end of that decade, and then more or less permanently another decade on, having chalked up a tally of over 50 films in his time away (mainly in supporting parts). He could never have matched that record of experience if he had stayed in Australia. He also worked extensively in television while in the USA. Jeanette Elphick, the Sydney model-turned-film actor, joined this generation's flight to Hollywood where, under her screen-name, Victoria Shaw, she also turned up on television shows into the 1970s. Australian television started in 1956 but, as in the case of locally made movies, it couldn't hope to match the range of opportunities provided to actors by the American, or British, equivalent. Possibly the best-known Australian-born star of this period, rugged-jawed Rod •Taylor, left for Hollywood in 1955 after playing in two Australian films. In the 1960s, he went on to appear in British films (as Randell had done earlier) and in television series. It was years before he worked in Australia again and, even then, it was only on a temporary basis, playing an American, in •The Picture Show Man (1977), and returning again in 1997 to play the tyrannical Daddy-O in Welcome to Woop Woop.

An even more famous Australian pin-up of the 1950s and 1960s was Peter •Finch, who was born in the United Kingdom and spent his early childhood there before moving to Australia. It was to the United Kingdom that he had first gravitated on leaving Australia in 1949 to continue the stage and film career he had begun over a decade earlier. His first appearance in an American-produced feature was in Elephant Walk (1954). In the 1960s, he divided his professional life fairly evenly between Hollywood and London. He played an archetypal Australian hero in A Town Like Alice

(1956), and he revisited Australia to play in •**Robbery Under Arms** and •**The Shiralee** (both 1957). He never came back again. Several lesser-known Australian film actors also moved to the United Kingdom after World War II, some of whom (such as Allan Cuthbertson, Lloyd Lamble, and Leo •McKern) could sufficiently efface their origins to play quintessentially British roles. Possibly the best-known female Australian actor in British films of the 1950s and 1960s was Queensland-born Diane •Cilento (she also played in a few Hollywood films), who was described by one pundit as like 'a lick of flame'. She re-settled in Australia in the mid 1970s.

In the early 1960s, Jack •Lee, the Englishman who made **A Town Like Alice** and **Robbery Under Arms**, set up his own production company in Australia. It was one of the first signs of the possibility of reviving a film industry in Australia. British directors Ralph •Smart (who was of Australian parentage) and Harry Watt had spent extended periods in Australia in the 1940s, attempting to establish a permanent branch of Ealing Films but, while these plans resulted in a few notable pictures, they were eventually defeated by lack of local investment. The veteran American director Clarence Badger (1880–1964), who came out to Australia to make •**Rangle River** (1936), had met with similar frustrations (he was, nevertheless, sufficiently taken with the place to retire in Australia). By the 1970s, thanks partly to increasing government interest in the local film industry (backed up by subsidies), the creative climate in Australia had become far more propitious. The scriptwriter Casey Robinson (1903–79), another Hollywood veteran, came to Australia to retire but, once in Australia, he threw his energies, both as producer and scriptwriter, into the crime thriller **Scobie Malone** (1975).

It was her marital and acting partnership with John •McCallum that brought Googie •Withers from the United Kingdom to Australia as early as 1954. This couple's travels back and forth over the years, and their professional and family commitments in each hemisphere at successive stages of their career, suggest the growing complications involved in defining or retaining the category of expatriate. The peregrinations of Barry •Humphries, since he first left his native Melbourne in 1959, suggest something similar. Such is also the case (in reverse direction to Humphries) with Michael •Craig, a British film star of the 1950s. Craig found increasing demand for his acting (and scriptwriting) talents in Australia after long-term visits in the early 1970s, but he spent the best part of the 1980s back in the United Kingdom before returning to Australia to settle.

On the other hand, the last few decades have witnessed the arrival of several actors born and trained elsewhere (such as Chris •Haywood from the United Kingdom, Alex •Menglet and Jacek Koman from Eastern Europe, and Pamela •Rabe from Canada) who have seemed content to base their work for stage and screen entirely in Australia. However, this is no guarantee that they will continue to do so. The prolific director Paul •Cox, who emigrated from Holland in the mid 1960s, has become increasingly critical in recent years of the limits (creative, financial, ideological) he continues to find in the Australian film industry, and has sought opportunities to work back in Europe.

The growing internationalisation of film production, combined with the increasing ease of travel, has meant that several native-born Australians connected with the industry have been tempted to go abroad for most of their work while maintaining their domestic base. The best-known cases are the director Peter •Weir, and the actors Judy •Davis and Geoffrey •Rush. This is not a completely new development (Frank •Thring's early film performances were all overseas, but he continued to live in Melbourne), and there is the reverse instance of Michael •Blakemore, who lives in London but returns to Australia for the bulk of his film-directing work.

Greater access overseas to financial or artistic resources has prompted various Australian directors (Phillipe •Mora, Bruce •Beresford, Fred •Schepisi and, more recently, John •Duigan) to base their work *and* lives overseas, although they revisit frequently and still make the odd picture in Australia. Mel •Gibson, who was born in the USA but had his training as an actor in Sydney and his first 'breaks' in Australian films, soon yielded to Hollywood's attractions, as it did to his, and moved back to his original homeland. For some native-born Australian actors who have recently yielded to Hollywood's call, other kinds of personal connection (such as marriage to an American, in the cases of Paul •Hogan and Nicole •Kidman) have provided additional incentives to move overseas. The expatriate trend is more moderate in extent than before, and has modified in its forms, but it is far from extinct.

IAN BRITAIN

Experimental film Experimental film-making in Australia is, as elsewhere, the result of a certain state of mind, an attitude born of personal freedom, a sense of adventure, resourcefulness, and a need to achieve something new in film. It follows that there are more varieties of experimental film than can be usefully described. Experimental film-makers reject set forms and procedures—especially those named as 'experimental' in the mass media—instead following lines of inquiry of particular interest to themselves. The films may include anything from handmade to computer-generated images, and they may be on Super-8 mm, 16 mm, or 35 mm (many practitioners work across two or more formats). Experimental films may be very short or feature-length; film loops, multi-screen, or part of mixed-media events; animated or live-action. They may be minimalist or of intense dense imagery; serious or absurd; abstract or narrative; structural or materialist; personal, erotic, anarchic, political, historical-reflexive, or postmodern; or they may resist categorisation or classification. The films may be made by artists working in other fields: for example, music, painting, dance, theatre, and writing.

It may be assumed that experimental film-making began in Australia in the early 1950s, coinciding with a number of developments: the beginning of the Melbourne and Sydney Film Festivals; the establishment of the state, national, and embassy film lending collections; the growth of film societies; greater access to tertiary education after World War II; and the arrival of artist-immigrants from Europe. In the 1950s and 1960s, 16mm film stock and processing were inexpensive, and films were self-funded. Notable among the first film-making artist-immigrants were Dušan Marek, Stan Ostoja-Kotkowski, and Ludwig Dutkiewicz (all of whom settled in Adelaide), and photographer Giorgio •Mangiamele (who settled in Melbourne). Marek, a Czech surrealist painter, arrived in Australia in 1948. While living in Papua New Guinea, he made three remarkable surreal animations: **Light of the Darkness** (1952), **Fisherman's Holiday** (1952) and **Nightmare** (1956). Several other animations made in Adelaide followed, his most celebrated being **Adam and Eve** (1962). He later made two feature-length surrealist narratives: **Cobweb on a Parachute** (1967) and **And the Word was Made Flesh** (1971).

Josef Stanislaw Ostoja-Kotkowski, a Polish artist, arrived in 1950 and made a number of films, including a significant experimental work, **Quest for Time** (1956), in collaboration with photographer Ian Davidson, who also worked with another Polish artist, Ludwik Dutkiewicz, on a strikingly photographed and finely edited experiment with metric montage, **Transfiguration** (1964).

In Melbourne from 1952 onwards, Gil •Brealey was active in film-making at the University of Melbourne, where he also encouraged others to make films, the most notable of which was the farcical **Le Bain Vorace** (1954), starring Barry •Humphries, and directed by Colin Munro. After independently making three films, two of which are now lost, Brealey made **Sunday in Melbourne** (1958), which is very much in the 'city-film' tradition, with innovative cinematography, editing, and use of sound.

The 1960s saw an explosion of experimental film-making. Contributing factors at the time included the political climate, opposition to the Vietnam War, the sense that alternative lifestyles were possible, and the new waves of film-making in Europe and North America. In Melbourne, young film-makers such as Philippe •Mora, Chris Löfvén, and Ken Shepherd were beginning, each with family encouragement. Ken Shepherd began film-making in 1963, with a 20-minute experimental portrait called **Les Gilbert:**

The Making(s) of an Artist, and followed it with **Australia** (1964), a film that grapples with the dark undertone of Australian White culture—isolation, parochialism, frustration, and desire. After his return from London to Melbourne, and painting seriously, he made his last film to date, **Disnatured** (1975), in which he experimented with a film form that does not seduce through attractive image qualities, but engages with concern for social and psychological issues—'the demise of the image', as he put it.

In 1962, Nigel •Buesst made **Fun Radio**, a dynamic celebration of commercial radio in the context of a Melbourne summer, with a complex, layered soundtrack. Among the others who produced striking experimental films in this period were Paul •Cox, with his **Time Past** (1966), a realisation of memory, and Brian Robinson, whose Marshall McLuhan-inspired **AC/DC** (1968) used constant four-frame zooms.

Sydney's experimental film-making began in the early 1960s, with the artists David Perry, Garry Shead, and Peter Kingston. In 1963, Albie •Thoms and Bruce •Beresford made **It Droppeth as the Gentle Rain**, presciently to do with global pollution, based on Jacques Prevert's surrealist ballet. Thoms followed this with **The Spurt of Blood** (1965), from a play script by Artaud. David Perry photographed and edited the film, and contributed striking animated sequences. The Thoms–Perry hand-drawn film **Poem 25** (1965) was based on a Kurt Schwitters poem of the same name. These films were integrated into theatre performances. Perry also filmed Albie Thoms's **Bolero** (1967), a formal work based on a slow tracking-shot, as well as Thoms's important feature-length experimental film **Marinetti** (1969). David Perry's **Sketch on Abigayl's Belly** (1968) and his **Album** (1970) are both finely crafted collages of personal/autobiographical material. After a period working with video, Perry returned to film with **The Refracting Glasses** (1992), an experimental narrative feature that is partly autobiographical and partly to do with the Ern Malley literary hoax.

German-born Paul •Winkler began making 8mm films in 1963 and 1964, and he made his first 16mm film in 1967. His early films were a form of experimental documentary but, by 1968, with **Red and Green**, he had embarked on the personal style of a vigorous, even visceral use of colour, texture, and formal strategies. He produced roughly one film a year from 1968. Evidence of a strong social conscience is found in many of his films, such as **Neurosis** (1970), which is about the Vietnam War, and **Scars** (1972). In 1980, he made **Sydney Bush**, which is about the encroachment of the city on the bush, and **Faint Echoes** (1988) is a meditation on Nazism.

A surprisingly strong tradition of handmade (cameraless) film-making has developed in Australia since the

Experimental film

1960s, in part due to the low cost and the appeal of working directly on the film surface. In 1967, Albie Thoms issued an important manifesto celebrating the handmade film, and he made abstract handworked films such as **Bluto** (1967), in which the optical soundtrack was also synthetically produced. Aggy Read's **Super Block High** (1968) and **Random Walk to Classical Ruin** (1971) extended the possibilities of the form. Other handmade films were produced by Lynsey Martin in Melbourne: **Approximately Water** (1972), **Inter-view** (1973), and **Whitewash** (1973). In **Inter-view**, shots of television interviewees are meticulously scraped away, leaving only tiny details—eyes, mouths, noses. **Whitewash** is even more minimal: the constantly white image shows delicate residues of abrasion and chemically induced bubbles.

Vernon Sundfors produced a series of figurative and abstract animations drawn directly on 35 mm and printed down to 16 mm, beginning with **The Space Race** and **The Fly Swatter** (both 1963). Working between Melbourne and London in the following 13 years, he made some 21 films using the same technique, as well as cut-out animation and live-action, the anarchic, absurdist qualities of which place his films in the underground film tradition of the 1960s.

Arthur and Corinne •Cantrill's work in experimental film began with a feature, **Harry Hooton** (1970), based on the work of the Sydney anarchist poet, and a series of shorter films such as **Eikon** (1969), **4000 Frames** (1970), and **Earth Message** (1970). They continued experimenting with multi-screen and 'expanded cinema' performances, and later with films such as **Island Fuse** (1971) and **Skin of Your Eye** (1973), both reworking previously shot footage to achieve movement and gesture analysis. They continued with films relating film forms to land forms (**The Second Journey to Uluru**, 1981), films exploring three-colour separation (**Waterfall**, 1984), and, starting with **Edges of Meaning** (1977), several multi-screen performance works presented at La Mama Theatre, where the projection of the film into a theatre set, and the live intervention of the film-makers, extended the meaning of the work. **The Berlin Apartment** (1987) and **Projected Light (on the Beginning and End of Cinema)** (1988) were both complex meditations on architecture and history. The Cantrills' films have been shown at the New York Museum of Modern Art, the Royal Belgian Film Archive, and the Pompidou Centre in Paris, and are held in the collections of the last two institutions.

The work of Michael Lee has influenced many film-makers. His **Black Fungus** (1971) is a disturbing commentary on society, realised through animation and found footage, collaged and superimposed in black-and-white negative and positive. In his feature-length **The Mystical Rose** (1977), one of the most widely seen experimental films in Australia, he expounded an elaborate visual critique of Catholicism in the context of mythology and popular culture, in which he effectively brought together experiments in collage, animation, and in-camera mattes, developed in his earlier short films such as **National Geographic Magazine** (1972). Lee's **Turn Around** (1983) and **Rock Heart Fire** (1986) both reflect a profound life experience he had in Central Australia.

James Clayden, an important figure in Melbourne's avant-garde, is known for his theatre work, sculpture, and painting, as well as film-making. He had begun his Super-8 film-making in 1970, and his early 16 mm work includes **Itching Comparables, From Antarctica to Ayers Rock** (1976). 'Death takes the landscape as hairpins hold the hair' is a line from Clayden's preternatural **Corpse** (1982), which is based in part on Bram Stoker's *Dracula*. The atmospheric sound for this feature-length film is by composer and film-maker Chris Knowles, who also acts in it.

Dirk de Bruyn began a large body of work in the 1970s, at first using repeated movements (often alternating negative and positive) and variations of image texture, as in **Running** and **Zoomfilm** (both 1976). Later, in films such as **Experiments** (1981), he developed reprinting and rotoscoping strategies, tightly weaving together images from home-movie footage, painting on film, and mechanical layout graphics. A period spent in his native Holland resulted in **Homecomings** (1987), and he has worked in Canada, where he shot **Rote Movie** (1994).

Marcus Bergner, a key figure in the Arf Arf sound–poetry performance group, has worked across all film gauges, making highly original animation (the 16mm **Tales From Vienna Hoods**, 1989) and using writing-on-film strategies (the 35mm **Taptap Ruin**, 1996), in which a form of animated concrete poetry is achieved. He collaborated with Marisa Stirpe, and film-makers Frank Lovece and Michael Buckley on an experimental film based on Arf Arf's work, **Thread of Voice** (1993).

There has been much significant work in Super-8. Beginning in the late 1960s and extending into the early 1980s, artists Richard and Pat Larter made many films, such as **Dreaming About the Crumbling of Your Eyes** (1975), using imagery and strategies similar to Richard Larter's paintings and Pat Larter's performances. These films comment energetically on popular culture, advertising art, fetishism, kitsch, the sex industry, political hypocrisy, and society in general. Another two working with over-the-top performance—or as theatre critic Adam Quinn has put it, 'comic-book-horror-circus'—are Maj Green and Ewan Cameron, whose outrageous films, such as **Gangster Cabaret** (1994) and **Coal Fever** (1993) (the latter shot in Berlin) extend their live work. Another artist, Tim Burns, made politically motivated Super-8 films in the USA and

Australia, such as the 100-minute **CARnage** (1977), which is about the eradication of automobiles, before moving to 16 mm production with **Against the Grain** (1980), which is realised with his usual vitality.

In the 1980s, with the rising cost of film production, Super-8 activity increased, and many film-makers engaging with the format returned to self-funded production. Melanie El Mir's Super-8 films are largely black comedies, often lightened with passages of carefully wrought, almost abstract, film-making. The expressionist camera angles and the frenetic cutting suggest obsession and neurosis, and there is often an undercurrent of eroticism. In **Embriato** (1989), **MRSOSO** (1992), and **The Treasure** (1993), she questions male/female identity by having a woman take male and female roles in the same film. Maeve Woods brings her experience as a painter to her work, displaying a sensitivity for form, colour, and texture. In **Lit Flat** (1987), she knowingly explores the spaces and light of her flat. Her more recent films, such as **Tawdry Sass** (1996), have colour and texture handworked directly onto the Super-8 film strip, overlaying photographic images. They are accompanied by poetic meditation on the process of making the film. Other film-makers, such as Marie Craven, Steven Ball, Heinz Boeck, Irene Proebsting, and John Harrison, continue the experimental film tradition in Super-8.

It is clear that, despite its small population, Australia has made a significant contribution to experimental film.

ARTHUR AND CORRINE CANTRILL

Experimental Film and Television Fund, *see*
Experimental Film, Australian Film Commission

Exploits of the Emden, The

1928. Credits for Australian material only. *Director/Producer/ Scriptwriter*: Ken G. Hall. *Directors of photography*: Claud C. Carter, Ray Vaughan. B&W. *Cast*: Members of the Royal Australian Navy.

The title **The Exploits of the Emden** covers both a 1926 German feature, **Unsere Emden**, and the Australian material produced by Ken G. •Hall to make that film about the World War I German ship more palatable to Australian viewers. The surviving footage of this movie mega-mix has a triple historical significance. First, it contains the earliest

Still from **Waterfall** (1984)

Exploits of the Emden

film work of Hall, who was to become a key figure in the next two decades of Australian film. Second, it is an example of a kind of documentary fiction production that had been a staple of the Australian feature industry since its inception. And third, it is a peculiar instance of an international co-production before such ventures were common. In this case, Australian actuality footage mixed with 'docu-drama' recreations featuring the officers and men of the Australian Navy has been edited into a complete German feature, which combined non-fiction material with an elaborate studio fiction built around the career of the *Emden*. Hall also added a certain amount of populist colour to the Australian section by featuring two sailors in a couple of mild knockabout comedy routines.   WILLIAM D. ROUTT

F

Faiman, Peter, *see* Crocodile Dundee

Faithful Narrative of the Capture, Suffering and Miraculous Escape Of Eliza Fraser, A, *see* Eliza Fraser

Fantasm

1976. Director: Richard Bruce [Richard Franklin]. *Producer:* Antony I. Ginnane. *Scriptwriter:* Ross Dimsey. *Director of photography:* Vince Monton. 90 min. *Cast:* John Bluthal (Professor Jungenot A. Freud), John Holmes (Neptune), Uschi Digart (Super Girl), Maria Welton (Iris), Al Williams (rapist).

Shot in Los Angeles, with linking scenes shot later in Australia, this send-up of popular sex-education and sex-documentary films spins a skein of scientific authority around ten 'softcore' vignettes through the frame narration of a professor of psychology. 'Re-enactments' of common female fantasies featuring American porn stars played on, and profited from, the new sexual freedoms of the 1970s. The episodes—'Barber shop' (seduction by barber, manicurist, and hairdresser), 'Card game' (strip poker leading in to group sex), 'Wearing the pants' (sado-masochism and transvestism), 'Nightmare alley' (rape), 'The girls' (lesbians in sauna), 'Fruit salad' (flavoured sex by pool), 'Mother's darling' (incest), 'Black velvet' (prostitute in control), 'After school' (teasing teacher), 'Blood orgy' (sexual sacrifice)—are as much about male titillation as female fantasy. The film was boosted by a ban in Queensland, and went on to become one of the most profitable Australian films of the decade. A sequel, **Fantasm Comes Again**, was produced in 1977. BEN GOLDSMITH

Far East

1982. Director: John Duigan. *Producer:* Richard Mason. *Scriptwriter:* John Duigan. *Director of photography:* Brian Probyn. *Music:* Sharon Calcraft. 102 min. *Cast:* Bryan Brown (Morgan Keefe), Helen Morse (Jo Reeves), John Bell (Peter Reeves), Raina McKeon (Rosita Constanza), Henry Duval (Rodolfo De Cruz).

When Jo Reeves and her journalist husband, Peter, walk into the 'Koala Klub' in an unidentified Asian country, to find it run by her former lover, Morgan Keefe, alert audiences were quick to detect cinematic echoes. Director John •Duigan acknowledged his indebtedness to **Casablanca** (1942), to Rick's bar, to the Bogart–Bergman–Henried triangle, and to the sense of a dangerous present and a past thick with memories of the same old fundamentals. As in its famous progenitor, **Far East** is fuelled by the husband's idealism as well as by the fires rekindled between Jo and Morgan (Helen •Morse and Bryan •Brown have an aptly starry gloss), and the ending involves Morgan's renewed sense of political commitment and his sacrifice in the interests of the kidnapped Peter's safety. Forty years after **Casablanca**, the enemy emerges as less clear-cut, and the film lacks political urgency; what strength it has is that of romantic melodrama, skilfully executed in the manner of classic Hollywood. BMcF

Far Paradise, The

1928. Director/Producer/Scriptwriter: Paulette McDonagh. *Director of photography:* Jack Fletcher. *Art direction:* Phyllis McDonagh. B&W. *Cast:* Marie Lorraine (Cherry Carson), Gaston Mervale (James Carson), Arthur McLaglen (Karl Rossi).

Helen Morse and Bryan Brown in **Far East**

It is unfortunate that more of **The Far Paradise** has not survived. Although we have most of the early reels and the *dénouement*, much of the plot and character development seems to be gone forever. The film tells the story of Cherry, who returns to her degenerate father, James, suffers his further abuse, and helps him to escape the justice of an outraged community. She is as blind to his deceit as she is blind to the truth of her own parenthood, which allows her to marry someone who may be her own half-brother at the end of the film. The sequence in which Cherry keeps a vigil by her dying (false) father's bed through the night is one of the most carefully realised in any Australian film of this period.

WILLIAM D. ROUTT

Farrow, John (1904–63) DIRECTOR Farrow was born in Sydney and educated in Australia and the United Kingdom before entering the royal Naval Academy. After a brief period as first mate on cargo ships, Farrow fought with the American Marine Corps in Latin America. In the late 1920s he arrived in Hollywood. His first screen credit was for co-authoring titles for the 1927 silent film **White Gold**. Farrow developed a reputation as a scriptwriter in the late 1920s and early 1930s. In 1934 he directed two short films, although his first chance to direct a major feature failed when he was removed from **Tarzan Escapes** (1936) due to censorship problems concerning the brief costume of Maureen O'Sullivan (who married Farrow in 1936). Farrow left MGM for Warner Bros in 1937 where he directed seven

films over the next two years and then moved on to RKO for a series of films including **Five Came Back** (1939), a taut melodrama, written by Dalton Trumbo, Jerry Cady, and Nathaniel West, concerning the fate of survivors of a plane crash in the South American jungle. When the plane is reconstructed there is space for only five passengers and the dramatic tension emanates from the selection of those who will live and those left behind to die. Farrow directed a remake of the film (**Back from Eternity**) in 1956.

Farrow served with Royal Canadian Navy in 1940 and 1941 until he caught a severe case of typhus. He returned to Hollywood and, in 1942, he made **Wake Island** for Paramount, a timely film that details the heroic, but ultimately doomed, defence of a small Pacific island by a combination of civilians and American marines after the Japanese attack on Pearl Harbor. It won the New York's Critics Award for Best Direction and, a first for an Australian, Farrow also received an Academy Award nomination for direction. **Commandos Strike at Dawn** (1942), a war film set in Norway, followed. Farrow returned to Paramount for the rest of the decade. He directed a range of films, many with Alan Ladd and Ray Milland, including adventures (**China**, 1943; **Calcutta**, 1947), propaganda films (**The Hitler Gang**, 1944), nautical features (**Two Years Before the Mast**, 1946), aerial films (**Blaze of Noon**, 1947), musicals (**Red Hot, and Blue**, 1949), and westerns (**California**, 1946; **Copper Canyon**, 1950). Arguably, it was Farrow's film-noir works—**The Night has a Thousand Eyes** (1948) for Paramount, **and**

Where Danger Lives (1950) for RKO—together with his bizarre hybrid of generic conventions in **His Kind of Woman** (1951, which he also made for Howard Hughes at RKO) that represent the aesthetic pinnacle of his Hollywood career. The best of these three films, **Where Danger Lives**, starring Robert Mitchum and Faith Domergue, is a harrowing film depicting Mitchum's gradual decline into paralysis, due to concussion, as he and Domergue try to reach the Mexican border ahead of the police. The rest of Farrow's 1950s output, except **Hondo** (1953) and **A Bullet is Waiting** (1954), is less distinguished, and he finished his career in 1962 directing episodes of the television series *Empire*.

Farrow won an Academy Award for Best Screenplay, with S.J. Perelman and James Poe, for **Around the World in 80 Days** (1956). Farrow converted to Roman Catholicism and wrote a number of religious books. He and his wife Maureen O'Sullivan had seven children, including Maria (Mia) Farrow. GM

Fast Talking

1984. *Director*: Ken Cameron. *Producer*: Ross Mathews. *Scriptwriter*: Ken Cameron. *Director of photography*: David Gribble. *Music*: Sharon Calcraft. *Cast*: Rod Zuanic (Steve Carson), Toni Allaysis (Vicki), Chris Trusswell (Moose), Gail Sweeny (Narelle), Steve Bisley (Redback), Peter Hehir (Ralph Carson), Tracy Mann (Sharon).

Ken •Cameron's experience as a secondary teacher is clearly evident in this low key 'realist' drama of life in the working-class suburbs of Sydney. Rod •Zuanic, as Steve Carson, provides a hard-edged acting début as the energetic protagonist from a troubled home. The episodic narrative structure details his problems at school and on the streets where he befriends Redback, an ex-con who tries to guide Steve away from a life of crime.

This atmospheric drama punctuates its overriding sense of futility and hopelessness with an underlying streak of black humour and teenage pranks, as the inhabitants of these mean streets attempt to cope with the prospect of unemployment and deprivation. A subplot involving a young teacher (Tracey •Mann) and her sexual relationship with a student anticipates the dramatic basis of •**Heartbreak High** (1993) nearly ten years later. GM

Fatal Wedding, The

1911. *Director/Scriptwriter*: Raymond Longford. *From the play*. *Director of photography*: Arthur Higgins. B&W. *Cast*: Raymond Longford (Howard Wilson), Lottie Lyell (Mabel Wilson).

The Fatal Wedding, all copies of which have vanished, was Raymond •Longford's first feature as a director. It also marked the first appearance of Lottie •Lyell on screen, and was Arthur •Higgins's first work as Director of photography on a feature film. Longford's opportunity to direct arose

when Alfred •Rolfe left Spencer's Pictures to direct •**Moora Neya** for the Australian Photo-Play Company. Longford and Lyell had been partners in the theatre and had performed in the stage version of the story, which undoubtedly recommended the project to the pioneer producer Charles Cozens Spencer. The film was shot mainly in an artist's studio converted for the purpose by removing the roof. It is said to have achieved a resounding financial success. WILLIAM D. ROUTT

Fawdon, Michele (1947–) ACTOR After a good deal of experience in radio and television, as well as some minor film work, English-born Fawdon made a striking impression in •**Cathy's Child**, as a Maltese national, a distraught young mother whose child is abducted to Greece by its father. Her playing had intensity and a strong sense of commitment. Sadly, to date the cinema has given her no other comparable opportunity, except arguably in the little-seen comedy of sexual life **Unfinished Business** (1986). There is a distinctive quality to Fawdon's screen persona that might have been better used.

Other Australian films: Stockade (1971), **The Golden Cage** (1975), **Drift Away** (1976, short), **Cradle Song** (1978, short), **Stumbling Block** (1979, short), **Maybe This Time** (1980), •**Travelling North** (1987), **The Place at the Coast** (1987). BMcF

Michele Fawdon

Fegan, Jack (1907–) ACTOR Irish-born Jack Fegan, also known as John Fegan, emigrated to Australia in the 1930s and eventually developed an acting career in radio after working on the wharves. Fegan first appeared in films in 1949 with two supporting roles, as Hayes in •**Eureka Stockade** (1949) and in the important role of Jack Farrington in •**Sons of Matthew** (1949), the man who is defeated by the Australian bush and leaves Matthew and Jane O'Riordan and their family in the valley of Cullenbenbong. In the early 1950s, Fegan appeared in the key role of Jack Dalton, who is forced to hunt down his childhood friend Fred Ward, in •**Captain Thunderbolt** (1953). However, with relatively few Australian productions during this period, Fegan was relegated to supporting roles in American and British productions filmed in Australia, such as **Kangaroo** (1952), •**Smiley** (1956), **Smiley Gets a Gun** (1958), and •**The Sundowners** (1960). Fegan's best-remembered role, however, was the gruff, craggy-faced, husky-voiced Inspector Connolly in the long-running 1960s television series *Homicide*. After Fegan left the series in 1969, he appeared in minor roles in **Moving On** (1974), •**Picnic at Hanging Rock** (1975), and •**Ride a Wild Pony** (1975).   GM

Felicity

1979. *Director*: John D. Lamond. *Producers*: Russell Hurley, John Lamond. *Scriptwriter*: not credited (assumed to be John D. Lamond). *Director of Photography*: Gary Wapshott. 90 min. *Cast*: Glory Annen (Felicity Robinson), Christopher Milne (Miles), Joni Flynn (Me Ling), Jody Hanson (Jenny), Marilyn Rodgers (Christine).

This is an intelligent example of John •Lamond's soft-porn films. It is set in Hong Kong, allowing for some sumptuous cinematography of streets, harbours, and landscapes, both in daylight and at night. But it is basically a rites-of-passage film, presenting the development of a young girl's sexuality, starting with her enjoyment of the voyeuristic attention of the gardener at her boarding school and finishing with her demanding risky sex in public places. The usual range of sexual couplings is offered, but with more narrative motivation than in many such films. In keeping with the sexual revolution of the 1970s, the voice-over constantly reminds the viewer that pleasure need not be accompanied by guilt. However, the heroine's goal, achieved by the end of the film, is a moral one—satisfying sex within a monogamous relationship.   IB

Fennell, Willie (1920–92) ACTOR   Fennell was one of Australia's best-loved comic actors, particularly in radio and cabaret, in the 1950s and 1960s. He first appeared in the cinema as the bumbling Doctor O'Hara in the family film **Little Jungle Boy** in 1970. This film was typical of Fennell's screen career over the next two decades, as he was sporadically used in supporting roles and cameo appearances to enliven proceedings in films such as •**Caddie** (1976), **Maybe This Time** (1980), **The Earthling** (1980), •**Hoodwink** (1981), and •**Reckless Kelly** (1993), but there were few roles of any substance.

Other Australian films include: The Lost Islands (1975), •Cathy's Child (1979).   GM

FernGully: The Last Rainforest

1992. *Director*: Bill Kroyer. *Producers*: Wayne Young, Peter Faiman. *Scriptwriter*: Jim Cox. Based on the stories of *FernGully* by Diana Young. *Music*: Alan Silvestri. 68 min. *Cast*: Tim Curry (Hexxus), Samantha Manthis (Crystra), Christian Slater (Pips), Robin Williams (Batty Koda), Cheech Marin (Stump), Tony Chong (Root), Tone-Loc (The Goanna).

An Australian co-production assisted by the Australian Film Finance Corporation, **FernGully** was positioned by overseas production partner Twentieth Century Fox to compete for the Disney market. This probably explains why the film lacks Australian references, despite being based on Diana Young's stories and despite being produced by the associate producer and director of the very Australian •**Crocodile Dundee** (1986). It also allows Robin Williams to compete with his role in the simultaneously released **Aladdin** (1992). As in •**Blinky Bill** (also 1992) the issue is ecological threat: in a deep rainforest, a race of fairies (humans are dimly remembered fairy stories to them) are suddenly threatened by hi-tech forest-eating machines run by huge humans. A teenage human falls into their hands and is shrunk to their size for educational and romantic purposes. This is big, rich animation ($33 million) with a debt to **The Little Mermaid** and Japanese cartoons.   RICK THOMPSON

Ferrier, Noel (1920–97) ACTOR   Ferrier hosted the first television variety show in Melbourne, *The Late Show*, and was a dominating presence throughout the first 20 years of Australian television, primarily as one of the comperes of *In Melbourne Tonight* during its golden period in the 1960s. Later he was a panelist on popular programs such as *Beauty and the Beast* and *Blankety Blanks*. Ferrier was also a fine actor and began his theatrical career as the cane-cutter Roo in 1953 in *Summer of the Seventeenth Doll*. In the cinema, Ferrier's rollicking performance as Captain James Fraser in •**Eliza Fraser** (1976) was the high point in a disappointing film. In Peter •Weir's •**The Year of Living Dangerously** (1982) Ferrier featured as the foreign correspondent Wally O'Sullivan. More recently Ferrier appeared in •**Paradise Road** (1997), and he was also the executive producer of •**The Well** (1997). Even in lesser roles, as in the popular sex comedies •**Alvin Purple** (1973) and **Alvin Rides Again** (1974), Ferrier emerged with his professional reputation intact. His rich voice and ability to disarm audiences was evident throughout his career: 'You can tell by my dignity, charm and grace that I am from Melbourne' he explained to a Sydney audience while working there in 1976.

Other Australian films: Little Jungle Boy (1970), Demonstrator (1971), **Private Collection** (1972), **Avengers of the Reef** (1973),

Scobie Malone (1975), Deathcheaters (1976), No Room to Run (1976), Turkey Shoot (1981), The Return of Captain Invincible (1983), The Perfectionist (1985), I Can't Get Started (1985), Three's Trouble (1985), Backstage (1988), Computer Ghosts (1988).   GM

Festivals   While Australian film festivals vary in magnitude, focus, and maturity, essentially they share a commitment to the patronage of Australian film culture. The Australian Council of Film Societies inaugural film festival was held in January 1952 at Olinda on the outskirts of Melbourne. The success of this festival inspired the first Melbourne Film Festival (1953). The Melbourne International Film Festival is the oldest and largest surviving festival of cinema in the southern hemisphere. It offers an annual program of international feature films, presenting the commercially viable alongside the unknown. This contemporary focus is balanced with a retrospective program: the 1996 festival was distinguished by a collection of films starring and directed by Ida Lupino. The festival also exhibits documentary, animation, and experimental programs, and it provides exposure for emerging film-makers with its annual short-film competition.

Established in 1953, hot on the heels of its Melbourne counterpart, the Sydney Film Festival has been dominated by distinctive directors who have infused the festival with variety and raised the profile of alternative cinema. Recently, the festival has been divided into a general and an alternative program, with the difference underscored by the use of different venues. In 1998 the Sydney Film Festival became the first fully to embrace the Internet by offering its program on the Internet, aiming to foster an online festival community.

The Perth International Film Festival ran annually from 1972 until 76. Its bold devotion to the exhibition of independent and avant-garde film and European art film, and to the promotion of new Australian cinema (see Revival, the), was not enough to ensure continued funding and, eventually, it was abandoned. The Festival of Perth now runs a summer 'Film Season', which is not an international film festival, at the Somerville Auditorium in the grounds of the University of Western Australia.

A comparatively recent festival, the Brisbane International Film Festival began in 1991. While it has an international program, a local focus dominates. Its 'Fast Film' competition is designed to showcase films produced locally.

The Tropicana Short Film Festival began in 1993 with a single screening at the Tropicana Cafe in Darlinghurst, Sydney. In 1998 'Tropfest' received more than 8000 patrons and was relocated outside onto Victoria Street, which was closed to traffic.

Also increasingly successful, the Sydney Mardi Gras Film Festival and the Melbourne Queer Film and Video Festival are programs devoted to the celebration of queer cinema.

Introduced in 1991, the Melbourne Festival is an annual showcase of film and video for, by, and about gay, lesbian, and queer communities. With audiences reaching 10 000, the festival introduced a national tour of program highlights.

Tasmania's Edge of the World Film Festival consists of a curated program of contemporary international short and feature films, a national short-film and video program and a Super-8 competition. Operating in a similar vein is Melbourne's White Gloves Film Festival, which limits film-makers to a weekend of shooting and editing before exhibition and the presentation of awards on Sunday night.

Among the Melbourne festivals, the St Kilda Short Film Festival eschews a temporal, thematic, generic, or stylistic agenda. Designed to encourage diversity, the festival is devoted to recognising the short film as an independent cinematic form, lifting it out of the shadows of the feature film. Melbourne's Super-8 Festival presents a program that extends this idea, exposing the diversity and creativity of the small-gauge film. The Experimental Arts Festival is a biennial festival of film, new media, video installations, performances, and sound art. Experimenta fosters innovation in the production of digital images and sound generated by new technology. This festival seeks to stretch the boundaries of media arts exhibition in Australia and is committed to the development of innovative perceptions and new concepts.   WENDY HASLEM

Fields, Maurie (1925–95) ACTOR   Well remembered by a generation of television watchers for his role as John Quinney, small-town tough-nut in Bellbird (1967–76), Fields's experience as a singer and actor in vaudeville predated this by many years. He played in several long-running television series, and his leathery, no-nonsense style informed nearly a dozen supporting roles in films, ranging from •Country Town (1971) (the film version of Bellbird, in which he repeated his original role) until his last film, •Country Life (1994). His death shortly after this was the occasion of many affectionate tributes; he had become one of the country's best character actors and an institution in Australian show business.

Other Australian films include: Alvin Purple Rides Again (1974), •In Search of Anna (1979), •Lonely Hearts (1982), Fighting Back (1982), Cactus (1986), The Bit Part (1987), •Evil Angels (1988).
                                                             BMcF

Film and Television Institute Of Western Australia (FTI)   A membership-based, non-profit organisation, the FTI actively fosters a diverse screen culture and promotes production by independent film-makers in WA. Founded in 1971 as the Perth Institute for Film and Television, it was renamed the FTI in 1982 to reflect its amalgamation with Frevideo, a video-access centre created in 1974. The FTI is one of the few organisations in Australia

Palais Theatre, St Kilda, former home of the Melbourne Film Festival

that combines film and video exhibition and production with education and the provision of resources. While most of FTI's funds are generated through its own activities, the institute receives support from both the *Australian Film Commission and *ScreenWest. The FTI's annual events include the running of the WA Film and Video Festival. In 1997 the FTI established an association with a business called Imago, with the opening of the Imago/Digital Arts Studio.   CATHERINE SIMPSON

Film Australia The Commonwealth Cinema and Photographic Branch was formally established in Melbourne in 1921 to make films to promote immigration (see Documentary and non-fiction, silent) but, over the years, its brief widened and its audiences grew, both overseas and within Australia. During World War II, the Branch became part of the newly established films division of the Department of Information: footage shot by the division's cinematographer, Damien *Parer, won Australia's first Oscar (1943). After the war, the division became the production unit for the Australian National Film Board (NFB), which was established in 1945. By 1950, the NFB had become an advisory body only, and it ceased operation in 1972. Meanwhile, the films division

moved to Sydney, operating successively out of premises in King St, Sydney; Conder St, Burwood (from 1948); and in its own new studios in Eton Rd, Lindfield from 1961. In 1956 it adopted the name the Australian Commonwealth Film Unit and, in 1973, became Film Australia. It was controlled first by the Department of Information, from 1950 by the news and information bureau of the Department of the Interior, from 1973 by the Department of the Media, then from July 1975 by the Australian Film Commission. In 1988, it was established as a company: Film Australia Pty Ltd. In 1945 Canadian Ralph Foster was appointed first Film Commissioner for one year, but no further commissioners were appointed and, in May 1946, Stanley *Hawes became Producer-in-Chief, a position he held until 1969. His successors were Denys Brown (1969–80), John Mabey (1980–84), Robyn Hughes (1985–89), Bruce Moir (1989–97), and Sharon Connolly (1997–). Over this long history, the organisation has made nearly 3000 films, some commissioned by government departments, some produced from within its own budget in the national interest. The immediate postwar period saw an Oscar nomination for **School in the Mailbox** (1947), as well as high-quality Griersonian documentaries such as **Flight Plan** (1950), and innovative work such as **Capacity Smith**

(1951) or •**Mike and Stefani** (1952). After few good films from 1954 to 1963, another rich period included **From the Tropics to the Snow** (1964), Ian •Dunlop's ethnographic films (**Desert People**, 1966), and even the occasional fiction film (**Nullarbor Hideout**, 1965). The 1970s saw a special focus on social issues and Australia's second Oscar, for Bruce •Petty's **Leisure** (1977). By this time, the Australian feature film revival (see Revival, the) had begun, and the Unit's significance in training directors, producers, and cinematographers who went on to illustrious careers in other parts of that industry cannot be overestimated. By the 1980s, Film Australia had even entered the field of fiction features, with •**Annie's Coming Out** (1984), but the majority of the output continued to be documentaries (for instance the award-winning **Mabo: Life of an Island Man** 1997).

The films have always been aimed at an education market but, since the 1970s, television has replaced commercial release in theatres as a major distribution point. In line with changing industrial trends in the commercial production industry, a re-organisation in the 1980s led to the downsizing of the permanent staff, and a policy of contracting out production, including in the 1990s increasing use of new technology. Over time, the main audience for the organisation's films has shifted: although the films are still required to present Australia's public face to the world, their function in representing Australia to Australians is increasingly recognised. INA BERTRAND AND JUDITH ADAMSON

Film Division, Department of Information (DOI), *see* Documentary and non-fiction, silent; Film Australia

Film Finance Corporation, *see* Finance

Film Queensland, *see* Pacific Film and Television Corporation

James McCarthy and Eileen Fallon laying a soundtrack at the Commonwealth Film Unit, c. 1960

Film societies Around the world, film societies were created by people interested in seeing imaginative and demanding films rather than the weekly releases of the major distributors. In Australia, this occurred after World War II, when film societies were formed in Sydney, Melbourne, Hobart, Perth, and Brisbane, at first as branches of the Australian Film Society, but soon developing independently. By 1949, attempts were made to form an overall Australian body to qualify for prints from the new British Commonwealth Federation, resulting in federations of film societies being formed in Vic. and NSW. The Australian Council of Film Societies (ACOFS) was formed in December 1949, with 40 delegates from five states and Canberra.

From the beginning, the supply of film, suitable venues, projection skills, cataloguing, and archival matters were continuing matters for concern. Prints were borrowed from the collection in the National Library of Australia, or were obtained by individuals who had overseas contacts, or who travelled abroad. The most hotly debated issue was censorship, and ACOFS lobbied unsuccessfully for an 'S' classification to enable film societies to see films in their original form. Weekend festivals were organised by state federations, the largest of these becoming the Melbourne International Film Festival (see •Festivals), which was first held at the Exhibition Buildings in 1953 and was organised by the Federation of Victorian Film Societies for the next 30 years.

In the 1960s film societies grew in numbers and membership. Some city-and university-based societies screened weekly or monthly to thousands of members. Many country towns had their own groups, and suburban societies thrived around Melbourne. In Vic., where the film-society movement had always been strong, there were well over 100 societies, but commitment and support was variable in other states. Some of the original larger societies (Melbourne, Hobart, Perth, and Darwin) had, by the mid 1970s, progressed to screening 35mm prints in large cinemas. However, the vast majority of societies used a 'core' of film study material that had been developed on 16 mm and was still screening in schools, church halls, and restaurants. ACOFS published the first catalogue of all titles available in Australia on 16mm, as it had already produced (and obtained funding for) the first proper catalogue of the film-study collection of the film division of the National Library of Australia.

Television and the establishment of arthouse cinemas began to limit the growth of the movement in the 1980s. ACOFS played a leading part in lobbying the government to provide funding to set up the National Film and Sound Archive (see •Archives) and, when the Archive was finally created as a separate body in 1984, Barrie King (the then president of ACOFS) became a member of the first Archive advisory committee. ACOFS was still importing films but, as costs rose, it became more effective to put money into the National Library's film-study collection. The number of available 16mm prints rapidly declined as the foreign embassies and consulates gradually cut back their commitment to supplying them. The Russian, Chinese, Czech, German, and, especially, the French collections, had been a staple of film-society programming. The specialist distributors who had emerged in the 1960s closed down or changed their focus.

Video, SBS television, and the ease of home viewing all worked against film societies and, for a few years, they declined. However, by the 1990s, people had begun to realise that viewing film as part of a cinema audience is a special experience. Membership numbers began to rise and are still climbing.

In 1996, the possible closure of the National Library's film-study collection presented a real threat to the continued existence of film societies in Australia. After much rallying of support around the country, and lobbying of state and federal government, this collection was moved to Vic. under the management of •Cinemedia, with sufficient funding to at least keep the collection viable and accessible. In recognition of the leading role of ACOFS in bringing about this solution, it now has a place on the advisory committee that monitors the development of the collection.

BARRIE KING AND JOHN TURNER

Film Victoria, *see* Cinemedia

Film, Television and Radio Board of the Australia Council, *see* Australian Film Commission (AFC)

Finance At the beginning of the twentieth century, film was considered to be just a business, regulation of which should be left to the market: this attitude was exemplified in the decision of Justice Pring in the case brought by producer Raymond •Longford against the distribution company Australasian Films (see Greater Union Organisation; Cinesound) in 1914. As time passed, and as Hollywood came to dominate world markets, pressure for financial protection of local film production mounted. Tariff manipulation and the imposition of entertainment taxes were primarily revenue-raising measures rather than for the benefit of Australian films. But two states introduced quotas on film exhibition to protect local films from what was considered unfair competition. Victorian quota regulations lasted from 1926 to 1940, and those in NSW from 1935 to the early 1980s but, as there was never enough product to fill the quota, enforcement was not practicable and these measures had little effect. A nation-wide quota, as recommended by the 1927–28 Royal Commission into the Moving Picture Industry, could not be implemented without support from the states, which was never given. Of the various financial recommendations of the Royal Commission, the only one that the federal government could implement on its own was the Film Awards, which were presented only twice (1930 and 1935).

It was not until the 1960s that lobbying in favour of financial assistance to film production began to make inroads into public opinion, and so into the political arena. By this time, Australian culture had been forever altered by the influx of postwar migrants, and film was at last accepted as part of that culture, with the growth of film societies, film festivals, and film appreciation in schools and universities. Financial assistance to film production was supported as a way to provide Australians with access to their own images on screen, at least as much as it was seen as promotion of an indigenous industry. The arrival of television was a catalyst for debate on screen culture, producing a Senate inquiry in 1964, under the chairmanship of Senator Vincent: the inquiry's report was accepted by both houses of parliament, but was not acted upon.

Real change began with the 1969 Interim Report of the Film and Television Committee of the Australian Council for the Arts (ACA), which recommended three initiatives: an Experimental Film Fund, a film school, and a Film Development Corporation (AFDC). These recommendations were put into effect, thus institutionalising a division between film as industry (the production of feature films for commercial distribution) and film as art (the production of shorts or experimental films for non-commercial distribution through schools and community groups, and the support of film-related cultural activities such as festivals, publications, and organisations).

Film as industry was supported by the Australian Film and Television School (later the •Australian Film, Television and Radio School—AFTRS), which would train the next generation of commercial film-makers, and by the AFDC, which would provide financial assistance in the form of subsidies and direct investment. Film as culture was supported through the Film, Television and Radio Board of the ACA (later the Australia Council), which administered the Experimental Film Fund through the •Australian Film Institute (AFI), operated a 'general production fund' (for projects not covered by the AFDC) and a 'script development fund', financed video access and resource centres in all states, and supported other cultural activities such as travelling film festivals and film-makers' cooperatives. It was, of course, never quite as simple as this suggests: there were demarcation problems, particularly over larger projects, which were still not completely supported through box-office returns, and there was constant tension over the relative merits of different kinds of projects applying for public financial support.

Following the recommendations of a 1972 Tariff Board Inquiry, the •Australian Film Commission (AFC) was established, bringing all forms of government financial assistance to film into one organisation, with four (later five) branches. The 'project development' branch of the AFC took over the funding of larger, more commercial productions, and the 'creative development branch' took over the funding of film cultural activities. Despite continuing tensions, it was the financial support of the AFDC and the AFC that underwrote the revival of Australian feature film production in the 1970s. Australian films were gaining more ready acceptance in the home market and abroad, winning acclaim in foreign film festivals and breaking into diverse markets in Asia, Europe, and America. But, the more successful they were, the more the critics questioned the need for public financial assistance to what had become a large commercial industry.

The next phase of assistance was tax relief, intended to encourage private investment in the growing film industry. It had begun in 1978, with provisions reducing the write-off period for capital investment in films from 25 years to two years. Then, from June 1981, division 10BA of the Income Tax Assessment Act delivered a tax deduction of 150 per cent of eligible film investment, and exemption from tax on the first 50 per cent of net earnings from that investment: projects had to prove their Australian credentials before the provisions could apply, and the film had to be financed, completed, and released in the year of the tax deduction. The last provision created difficulties by squeezing all production into the latter half of each financial year and, from 1983, two years were allowed for completion.

The new system was so generous that it encouraged private citizens to invest primarily to minimise their tax liabilities, with little regard to the artistic or commercial potential of the productions. Production boomed. Problems included the variable quality of the product; the unreasonably high fees paid to some participants, especially brokers and executive producers; and a general absence of budget scrutiny and the ensuing unpredictable and uncontrollable loss of government revenue through tax foregone. From August 1983, the then Labor government reduced the benefits to 133 per cent of eligible film investment, with exemption from tax on the first 33 per cent of net earnings, and introduced a 'special production fund', administered by the AFC, to cover the anticipated shortfall in investment capital. The initial grant of $5 million in 1983–84 helped in the production of 37 film and television projects, with a combined value of $74.3 million, but the cost to the government continued to rise—from $60 million in 1982–3 to $155 million in 1984–5. A tax summit in August 1985 recommended, against the advice of the AFC, that 10BA be scrapped but, instead, it was reduced again in September

1985, to 120 per cent of eligible film investment, with an exemption from tax on the first 20 per cent of net earnings, and the 'special production fund' was again increased to counterbalance this.

The stated objective in reducing the tax concession was to produce a higher quality of films by encouraging investors to be more selective but, in practice, the reverse occurred: investors sought out projects that could offer an artificially increased tax deduction. A new system was clearly necessary, and the AFC commissioned David Court to prepare a proposal, which was entitled 'Film Assistance—Future Options', and was released for discussion in November 1986. This proposal recommended a single funding agency, often referred to as a Film Bank. By July 1987, when the marginal tax rate was dropped from 60 per cent to 49 per cent, 10BA tax benefits (at that time 120/20 per cent) meant a subsidy rate to film of 38 per cent, down from the 90 per cent in the early years of 10BA. On 25 May 1988 the federal treasurer Paul Keating announced the establishment of the Australian Film Finance Corporation (FFC), with an initial budget of $70 million and a guaranteed life of four years. 10BA tax benefits were reduced to 100 per cent of eligible film investment, with no exemption from tax on earnings. 10BA projects had been declining over the previous period, in anticipation of the new scheme and, although it remained in force, it began to be used much less.

The FFC was formally established on 12 July 1988. Draft guidelines and the appointment of the first chief executive (David Pollard) were announced in August and, on 31 October, the FFC was open for business (although it was not officially opened until 3 February 1989). From January 1990 to 1998, John •Morris was chief executive officer, followed by Catriona Hughes. It quickly became the main agency for financial support of productions judged by market interest, rather than by quality-assessment panels, to have commercial potential: at first, the minimum proportion of the capital to be raised by private investment was 30 per cent; this rose to 35 per cent in 1989; and then to 40 per cent in 1991. In the first four years, nearly 200 projects were funded: 58 feature films, 47 television dramas (26 for adults, 21 for children), and 90 documentaries. Despite its overall commercial orientation, there developed, within FFC practice, a division between 'soft' deals for projects, usually with medium-to-low budgets and lacking a 'name' director; and tougher deals for projects that by reason of genre, size of budget, or the inclusion of saleable elements such as a star actor or established director, could reasonably be expected to attract a higher level of marketplace support. The FFC recouped less than half its investment overall, but was able to reinvest returns in future projects: to maintain this revolving fund, the FFC needs regularly to back winners such as •Strictly Ballroom, •Muriel's Wedding, •The Adventures of Priscilla, Queen of the Desert, and •Shine, as well as to find new talent among directors as the more established directors find other funding sources or choose to work overseas.

The first review of the FFC (in 1991) recommended its continuation, but proposed that funds be gradually reduced. The FFC budget for 1989/90 was $54.8 million; it rose to $68 million in 1991, then slowly fell each year, reaching $40 million in 1998. At the start, the major trigger for FFC investment in a project was significant marketplace support, usually by way of a pre-sale. In June 1990, the FFC established its first 'film fund', allowing the total funding of five projects (selected by a panel) without the need to attract prior marketplace support. For this initial fund a complex mechanism was put in place to attract private investment, but this soon proved cumbersome and expensive and, in 1993, the FFC won the right to fund these films directly from its budget allocation. A total of 22 films was funded this way until the Fund system was discontinued in 1997.

Meanwhile, state government bodies also provided financial assistance, and the federal government maintained financial support for the AFTRS, the National Film and Sound Archive (see Archives), •Film Australia, the Australian Children's Television Fund, and (until 1998) the Commercial Television Production Fund (scrapped in the 1998 budget) and the Australian Multimedia Enterprise (privatised in the same year). The AFC continued to administer the rest of the government assistance to film—both film cultural projects, and financial assistance to projects that could not raise the necessary pre-sale interest for FFC investment, including commercial and critical successes such as •Proof (1991), •Romper Stomper (1992), and •The Boys (1998). It also continued to negotiate, on behalf of the Australian government, with other national governments, to establish co-production treaties and near-treaty arrangements, which have their own financial benefits.

Under each of these funding arrangements (grants and subsidies, then tax relief, then the FFC), feature film production has, in general, no matter what the problems faced by individual producers and projects, continued to thrive. Smaller production projects, on the other hand have, in an era of economic rationalism and a return to the rhetoric of the market, faced a steady erosion of government financial support. A complete review of federal film funding was conducted at the end of 1997. The outcry over the recommendations of the resultant Gonski Report, from within the film industry and the general community, prevented the complete eradication of financial support for film culture. However, the pilot of the proposed 'film licensed investment companies' scheme, which aims to raise $40 million in private capital within two years, was eventually approved, albeit with its tax concession reduced from the 120 per cent recommended by the report to 100 per cent.

The FFC, AFC, and, to an almost insignificant degree, 10BA, were still providing financial support of one kind or another at the end of 1998, but there were also projects, such as •The Castle (1997), that had successfully raised their funds privately. Although encouraging private investment was the much-vaunted intention of all the government support schemes, a crackdown by the tax department on tax evasion within the film industry threatened to undermine these advances. In the world of film finance, the only thing anyone can be certain of is that nothing is certain!

INA BERTRAND

Finch, Peter (1916–77) ACTOR 'I can become anything', Peter Finch is reported as saying to a mentor at his theosophist school in Sydney in the 1920s. She had been struck with how quickly this teenager, born in London, and raised as a young boy in France and India, was developing an Australian accent. Soon after his return to England in 1949—following more than a decade as one of Australia's leading actors on stage, screen, and radio—his facial features were described by a Sydney newspaper as representing 'those of today's "typical Aussie"'.

Finch's extraordinary vocal and physical adaptability proved one of the secrets of his international renown as well as of his earlier local successes. In his first released Australian-made film, •Dad and Dave Come to Town (1938), he played a young farmer, a prototype of the several rural or outdoor 'Aussie' roles with which he became associated over the next 20 years or so. But he did not become typecast in such roles and, in other Australian-made films of the period, he could plausibly turn up as an English soldier (•The Rats of Tobruk, 1944) or as a German spy masquerading as Australian (•The Power and the Glory, 1941). When Laurence Olivier 'discovered' Finch on the Australian stage in 1948—the event that encouraged him to try his luck overseas—Finch was playing the title role in the famous French comedy by Molière, *The Imaginary Invalid*.

Conversely, while his international career saw him impersonate a wide range of national, occupational, and sexual character types, he remained, during its early phases at least, an icon of archetypal Australian maleness, bush-bred and dependably macho. He won British Film Academy awards for his portrayals of the title character in **The Trials of Oscar Wilde** (1960) and of the homosexual Jewish doctor in **Sunday Bloody Sunday** (1970), and posthumous British and American Academy Awards for his over-the-top portrayal of a frenzied American television presenter in **Network** (1976), but his first such award was the British Oscar for his performance as Joe Harmon, the gritty outback worker and Australian prisoner-of-war in **A Town Like Alice** (1956). Grittiness in different guises was the hallmark of two other characters he played in further British adapta-

tions of Australian novels: the rootless swagman Macauley in •The Shiralee (1957), and the mysterious gentleman-bushranger Captain Starlight in •Robbery Under Arms (also 1957). Shot on location, each of these films brought Finch temporarily back to Australia, but he never made another visit.

Not only a feature film actor, Finch contributed to various documentaries made for the Department of Information during World War II, supplying the voice-over, for example, in a film about Australian troops on active service, **Jungle Patrol** (1944). After the war, he served as the assistant director of a documentary on Arnhem land Aborigines, **Primitive Peoples** (1947), carrying out most of the on-location research, as well as supervising and narrating the script. He also wrote and directed **The Day** (1960), a fictionalised documentary set in Ibiza, which won him awards at the Venice and Cork film festivals.

Other Australian films: The Magic Shoes (1935, unreleased), •Mr Chedworth Steps Out (1939), Red Sky at Morning (1945), •A Son is Born (1946); •Eureka Stockade (1949), Another Threshold (1942, doc.), While There's Still Time (1942, doc.), South West Pacific (1943, doc.).   IAN BRITAIN

Fink, Margaret (1933–) PRODUCER After a varied career, including stints as clothes designer and art teacher, and after working as a technical director on several art documentaries, Margaret Fink produced her first feature film in 1975. This was the film version of David •Williamson's bleak play of police and domestic violence, **The Removalists**, on which she was also credited with production design. Although it was critically well received, it did not enjoy much popular success. Made for Fink's own production company, the film represented real creative collaboration between her and director Tom •Jeffrey, establishing her as the kind of producer who would be no mere administrator. This kind of involvement was equally true of her next film, •**My Brilliant Career** (1979), on which she invited Gillian •Armstrong, assistant art director on **The Removalists**, to direct. This gesture of faith in the 28-year-old Armstrong, the first woman director of a feature film in Australia for over 40 years, paid off. Despite difficulties with the script, originally written by Eleanor •Witcombe and, despite Fink's problems in raising finance to film Miles Franklin's semi-autobiographical novel, the film was a major success of the new Australian cinema (see Revival, the). It was shown as an official entry in the competition of the Cannes Film Festival, just days after it was finished, and was invited to several other festivals as a result. In Australia, the film was also very successful at the box office.

After this success, Fink had a long wait before getting her next project off the ground. This was •**For Love Alone** (1986), a film version of Christina Stead's novel. On the basis of the success of **My Brilliant Career**, it is easy to see that she might have been drawn to its feminist themes and attitudes. Like the earlier film, it is a period piece about a young girl's coming of age as she is torn between the conflicting demands of romance and a career. In the event, the new film enjoyed nothing like the same acclaim. While it is an accomplished piece of film-making and features intelligent performances from its leading actors (Helen •Buday, Hugo •Weaving, and Sam •Neill), the novel is an awkward, oddly unengaging piece of work, and the film cannot quite shake this off.

The film's financial failure led to the abandonment of Fink's plan to film Sumner Locke Elliott's *Edens Lost*, which she eventually (1988) made into a well-received television series. She is, like Pat •Lovell, one of the influential producers of the 1970s revival whose later careers have been sadly curtailed. Perhaps there was something too literary and decorous in her orientation for her to survive among the gaudier hues of the 1990s.   BMcF

Finney, Alan, *see* Hexagon Productions

Fitz-Gerald, Lewis (1958–) ACTOR

Youthful-looking Adelaide actor Lewis Fitz-Gerald first made his mark in •'**Breaker' Morant** (1980) as the only one of the three Bushveldt Carbineers, made scapegoats for the shooting of Boers, to escape with his life. His boyish freshness added poignancy to Bruce •Beresford's moving tale of wartime opportunism, and it is still perhaps his best role in the cinema. He graduated from the National Institute of Dramatic Art in 1978 and has since worked in theatre and television, as have most Australian actors of his generation. He has also had some substantial roles in films, including the lead in **Fighting Back** (1982), as John Embling, the dedicated remedial English teacher, on whose personal account of his real-life experiences in dealing with a disturbed and disturbing teenager the film was based.

Other Australian films: •We of the Never Never (1982), The Boy Who had Everything (1984), •The More Things Change (1986), •Warm Nights on a Slow Moving Train (1988), Rikky and Pete (1988), •Evil Angels (1988), Spider & Rose (1994), •Dead Heart (1996).   BMcF

Fitzpatrick, Kate (1948–) ACTOR

This Western Australian-born stage, television and film actor graduated from the National Institute of Dramatic Art in 1967. She was a prolific actor in the 1970s who rarely graduated to lead roles in feature films. Fitzpatrick's first feature film appearance was in Peter •Weir's début feature **Holmesdale** (1971). This was followed by a lead role as the aloof Mara in •**The Office Picnic** (1972), Tom •Cowans' caustic study of office politics and relationships, and another lead role in the

television thriller *The Night Nurse* (1977). Many directors have exploited Fitzpatrick's striking, albeit stern, facial features, particularly Carl •Schultz in •**Goodbye Paradise** (1983) and, although Fitzpatrick has only a supporting role in the film as the materialistic Mrs McCredie, her acidic interchange with the flawed 'hero' Michael Stacey (Ray •Barrett) encapsulates both her acting skill and her screen persona.

Other Australian films include: Shirley Thompson Versus the Aliens (1972), The Great MacArthy (1975), The Removalists (1975), Promised Woman (1975), Summer of Secrets (1976), The Return of Captain Invincible (1983), The Perfectionist (1985), •Heaven's Burning (1997).   GM

Lewis Fitz-Gerald

FJ Holden, The

1977. *Director*: Michael Thornhill. *Producer*: Michael Thornhill. *Scriptwriters*: Terry Larsen, Michael Thornhill. *Director of photography*: David Gribble. *Music*: Jim Manzie. 105 min. *Cast*: Paul Couzens (Kevin), Eva Dickinson (Anne), Carl Stever (Bob), Gary Waddell (Deadlegs), Graham Rouse (sergeant).

The low-key urban realism of Michael •Thornhill's film set it apart from most later 1970s Australian cinema. It is not based on a novel; nor is it set in the past or concerned to project exportable images of Australia. Instead it adopts a non-judgmental, slice-of-life approach to the problems of urban youth in Sydney's western suburbs, and Thornhill

Paul Cozens and Eva Dickinson in **The FJ Holden**

refuses to shape the film in conventional ways. Kevin, a wrecking-yard worker, begins an affair with Anne, who works in a shopping mall. The film sees them both as victims of various kinds. Kevin is locked into boorish male approaches to drinking and sex, his dreams epitomised by the eponymous yellow Holden, and is unable to appreciate Anne's hunger for real affection. She is surrogate mother in her deserted father's home, whereas Kevin's family has slightly higher aspirations (skilfully caught in the film's production design). There is poignancy in the limited horizons, which seem likely to condemn the young people to perpetuating their lifestyles, and there are beautiful performances from Eva Dickinson, pinched with cares beyond her years, and from Ray •Marshall as her kind, defeated father.

BMcF

Flaus, John (1934–) ACTOR Flaus worked as a film lecturer in Melbourne tertiary institutions, and the Australian Film and Television School, while establishing his credibility as an actor in (mainly low-budget) Australian films in the 1970s and early 1980s (including **Yaketty Yak**, 1973; **Queensland**, 1975; •**Newsfront** 1978; •**Palm Beach**, 1980; and **Plains of Heaven**, 1979). **Blood Money**, a low-budget, 63-minute film, released in 1980, offered Flaus both a lead role, as an ageing criminal with cancer, and the chance to act in the type of Hollywood movie (a low-budget 'B' crime film) that he had celebrated for so long as an academic. Bryan •Brown played Flaus's brother in this thematically dense, stylistically sparse, genre film. In the 1980s Flaus gradually reduced his academic commitments to pursue acting on a full-time basis with supporting roles in low-budget, straight-to-video, and television films such as **Archer** (1985), **Bootleg** (1985), **My Country** (1986), •**Traps** (1986), **Hungry Heart** (1987), **Stroker** (1987), **Raw Silk** (1988), **Devil's Hill** (1988), **In Too Deep** (1989), **Jigsaw** (1989), **A Kink in the Picasso** (1990), and **Breakaway** (1990). During this period Flaus also perfected his grizzled screen persona in critically celebrated films such as •**Warm**

Nights on a Slow Moving Train (1988), *Grievous Bodily Harm (1988), *Ghosts . . . of the Civil Dead (1989), *Death in Brunswick (1991), and *Spotswood (1992).

Flaus gained a strong reputation within the industry and, although some of his roles have been relatively brief in terms of screen time, they are often specially selected cameos that are crucial to the overall structure of the film. He also performed in the theatre during this period, including his one-man show **Caught** in 1989 and 1990. Flaus maintained his screen presence in the 1990s (**The Nun and the Bandit**, 1992; **Point of No Return**, 1995; *Lilian's Story, 1995; *The Castle, 1997) while establishing another career as the most recognisable voice in Australian radio and television commercials.

Other Australian films include: *Nirvana Street Murder (1991).

GM

John Flaus

Flirting

1991. Director: John Duigan. *Producers*: Dr George Miller, Terry Hayes, Doug Mitchell. *Scriptwriter*: John Duigan. *Director of photography*: Geoff Burton. 100 min. *Cast*: Noah Taylor (Danny Embling), Thandie Newton (Thandiwe Adjewa), Nicole Kidman (Nicola Radcliffe), Kym Wilson (Melissa Miles), Naomi Watts (Janet Odgers), John Dicks (Reverend Consti Nicholson).

While not as highly acclaimed as his 1987 feature *The Year My Voice Broke, *John Duigan's sequel **Flirting** offers another delicate foray into the world of adolescent rites of passage. Set in the 1960s at a private boarding school in provincial Australia, the narrative again follows the uncertain adolescent reflections of Danny Embling. Against the backdrop of an oppressive institution where he reluctantly fills the role of the school 'dag', Danny becomes fascinated with Thandiwe, a Ugandan girl boarding at the neighbouring girls' school. The film's plot centres on their struggle against barriers to their friendship and love. Before Thandiwe returns to Uganda, the couple consummate their relationship in a personal expression of physical and emotional adulthood.

While **Flirting** focuses on Danny's journey from innocence to experience, it also provides a sense of the constricted life of a boarding school during the 1960s. The place and period are depicted strongly within the *mise en scène*, adding a physical dimension to our understanding of Danny's emotional isolation.   MELINDA HILDEBRANDT

Florance, Sheila (1916–91) ACTOR

Florance, Sheila (1916–91) ACTOR Having made her first stage appearance in 1933 and starring in *A Woman's Tale in 1991 as she was dying, Sheila Florance had surely one of the longest acting careers in the annals of Australian show business. Like many Australian actors, she spent time in the United Kingdom (returning after the war with a Polish husband), acted regularly in the theatre for decades, found new and much larger audiences with television (she became famous as Lizzie Birdsworth in *Prisoner*, 1979–83), and caught the new wave of Australian cinema in the 1970s and 80s (see Revival, the). She had actually filmed as early as 1965, in Giorgio *Mangiamele's award-winning *Clay as a deaf-mute; she appeared in *Country Town (1971), the film based on the television serial *Bellbird*, and in several other films in the 1970s, but her screen career took off when she became associated with the films of Paul *Cox. She first appeared for him in his experimental feature **Illuminations** in 1976 and, as age and illness ravaged her features without diminishing their expressiveness, she made three more films for him towards the end of her life: **Cactus** (1986), **Golden Braid** (1990), and *A Woman's Tale. Under Cox's direction, she attained a new resonance that informed two other major roles she played at this time—Grandma in *The Tale of Ruby Rose (1988) and Molly, the old lady threatened with death, in *Nirvana Street Murder (1991). These films ensured that her long and honourable career ended on a high note.

Other Australian films: End Play (1976, *The Devil's Playground (1976), *Summerfield (1977), *Mad Max (1979), Hungry Heart (1987).   BMcF

Flying Doctor, The

1936. Director: Miles Mander. *Production company*: National Productions Ltd. *Scriptwriters*: J.O.C. Orton, Miles Mander. Based on the novel by Robert Waldron. *Director of photography*: Errol Hinds. *Music*: Willy Redstone, Alf J. Lawrence. 92 min. B&W. *Cast*: Charles Farrell (Sandy Nelson), Mary Maguire (Jenny Rutherford), James Raglan (Dr John Vaughan), Joe Valli (Dodger Green), Margaret Vyner (Betty Webb).

Stock plots and characters from several genres intersect in this film: the drifter who cannot settle into married life; the squatter's daughter who thinks she has found the right man; the flighty society woman who cannot love; the loss of a gold-mine in a card game and revenge of the former owner of the claim when gold is found there; the bar-room singer's doomed love for the hero; the faithful sidekick who stands by his blinded mate; the hero who dies rather than hurt his true love. The doctor comes into the story only midway through, joining the Flying Doctor service towards the end of the film, so the title does not help a viewer to navigate around this complex plot, which repeatedly fails as melodrama, despite its excess. Australian audiences gave it a lukewarm reception. Even with an imported director, writer, and star, and the presentation of Australia (from the outback to the Sydney Harbour Bridge) as exotic location, the film failed to break into the American market, and was cut before a limited release in the United Kingdom by Gaumont-British.   IB

Flynn, Errol (1909–59) ACTOR   Errol Flynn, born in Hobart, played an Australian in Warner Brothers' wartime drama **Desperate Journey** (1942), in which he fights his way out of Germany before yelling at the end of the film 'Now for Australia and a crack at the Japs'. Later, he was a sheep rancher in the western **Montana** (1950). Flynn's only real connection with the Australian film industry was his first film, in which he gave a stilted performance as Fletcher Christian in Charles •Chauvel's innovative blend of documentary and historical reconstruction •**In the Wake of the Bounty** (1933). Flynn left Australia soon after the completion of this film and, via London, where he made **Murder at Monte Carlo** (1934) at Warner's Teddington Studio, he moved to Hollywood and made **The Case of the Curious Bride** (1935), which started a long career at Warner Brothers.

Flynn's career consisted of at least three distinct periods. The first, at Warner's from the mid 1930s to the late 1940s, was his most productive, with films such as **Captain Blood** (1935), **The Charge of the Light Brigade** (1936), **The Adventures of Robin Hood** (1938), and **Gentleman Jim** (1942). In the late 1940s Flynn's career declined as his good looks faded due to an excessive lifestyle, and he suffered in a number of inferior films, such as **Adventures of Captain Fabian** (1951). After a short stint as a host on American television, Flynn's career received a boost during the two years before his death, with a number of excellent performances, mostly playing ageing alcoholics (**The Sun Also Rises**, 1957; **Too Much Too Soon**, 1958).   GM

Food   At first, food in film, including all alimentary and culinary referents accompanying it, seems unusual as a subject of film analysis and interpretation, worthy of film trivia, perhaps, but no more. Apart from extended critiques of the relatively small number of films (mostly international) in which the representation of food and eating is central to the plot—for example, **The Cook, the Thief his Wife and her Lover** (1989, d. Peter Greenaway), **Babette's Feast** (1987, d. Gabriel Axel), **La Grande Bouffe** (1973, d. Marco Ferreri), **Eat, Drink, Man, Woman** (1994, d. Ang Lee)—food in film has been, and still is, rarely explored as a meaningful subject. Food is too common an object in film, so familiar, basic, natural, real and visible that, as a meaningfully invested representational feature, paradoxically eludes the viewer's eye and is hence somewhat resistant to interpretation.

But that which in film-practitioner parlance is termed a prop becomes, in the area of film analysis and interpretation, a formal element. The difference in terms is perhaps slight, but it is nevertheless significant because it points to the processes of encoding and decoding dramatic space. *Mise en scène*, which literally means 'putting in the scene', describes the phase of film production in which the script is turned into the material world of film, the point at which ideas, themes, and emotions find expression in concrete terms, through dialogue, music, sound, camera angles and movement, character action, setting, and material objects and their arrangement within the frame. Food and its attendant referents fall within the terrain of *mise en scène*, and *mise en scène* elements are our points of entry into a film's dramatic world—but not as things that naturally happen to be in that space. Food, like any other element of *mise en scène*, is placed *there*, or arranged to *mean* and to be *read* in that space. Thus, taking a critical interest in food, an object of the material world that is already encoded and that can be re-encoded in film, is really no more nor less unusual than taking a critical interest in, say, the use and function of guns in the Western genre, trains in the films of Walter Hill, verandahs in Australian 'landscape films', or cars throughout the spectrum of Australian films from the late 1970s to the early 1980s.

The documentary film aside, in Australian cinema there is no substantive 'food film' in the vein of, for example, Marco Ferreri's **La Grande Bouffe**, in which eating, food preparation, and the rituals of dining are consistently axiomatic to the plot and theme. **La Grande Bouffe** is a film in which the abundance and luxuriousness of the food stand as counterpoint to, and final deliverance from, the bourgeois emptiness of the diners.

Food

This is not to say that the representation of food in Australian films is less significant. A few isolated Australian films thinly approximate the food film. •Don's Party (1976) and •Dimboola (1979) spring immediately to mind, but only because they centre on a ritual or festive gathering. Admittedly, in **Don's Party** and **Dimboola** alcohol plays a far more important role than food: it is the means by which various people relax their social guards, and fraternal rites are transgressed. But food still plays its part amidst, or resulting from, the histrionics of the characters. In **Dimboola**, food is one of a number of comic devices that highlight the tenuousness of social proprieties and thus the fragmentary nature of communal ties. In **Don's Party**, when a character calls attention to the low quality of the food, the fact that it is interpreted by all present as a remark about the low status of the hosts indicates the underlying tensions among supposed friends.

Food and dining scenes in Australian films tend to serve anthropological functions (What do these characters in these situations eat and how?). These scenes may also suggest a convivial atmosphere within a particular group, the reinforcement of social and familial values and, sometimes, even an expression of personal fulfilment. While such attributes are not completely unexpected or erroneous, they are not foremost. Rather, as **Don's Party** and **Dimboola** make apparent, the predominantly narrative, and visually descriptive, function of food in Australian cinema is to underscore tension, conflict, crisis, and difference. One of the best examples of this is Ken •Hannam's •Sunday Too Far Away (1975). For the first half of the film, each scene involving food (and beverage) emphasises potential conflict, in particular the working conditions of the shearers. The confluence of food and conflict occurs so often in **Sunday** that it is not surprising that the competency of the cook, and so the quality of the food provided, are major issues for the shearers. More importantly, this confluence tempers the major struggle the shearers are to face in the second half of the film: the 1955 national shearers' strike that resulted from the withdrawal of a 'prosperity entitlement' for shearers. The origins of the strike are signposted early on in the film, in a scene between Foley (Jack •Thompson) and the shearing contractor Tim King (Max •Cullen). King provides Foley's dinner, which highlights their mutual dependency: King is in need of shearers; Foley is in need of basic subsistence (food). The scene puts into relief the mutual dependency between capital and labour. But while Foley eats, King does not, or does not need to, signalling that the needs of capital go beyond a basic level. The scene also puts into relief the mutual antagonism between capital and labour, especially when provision for a basic need is withdrawn, the very reason for the shearers' strike.

In Tim •Burstall's **The •Last of the Knucklemen** (1979), food is used to mark, or carve out, the philosophical and class distinctions between characters. In the film's only food scene, the quality of the food dished out to a motley, flea-bitten, hard-edged team of drilling workers is consistent with the low end of the social scale these men occupy. But when the newly arrived Monk (Michael •Caton), a lapsed seminarian, refuses to eat the food, his place among this group in remote Central Australia is marked by a hunger less incarnate, and of a higher order, than that of the others. Similarly, a close viewing of John •Duigan's •Sirens (1994) reveals that a good many of the philosophical, aesthetic, and theological arguments between Norman Lindsay (Sam •Neill) and the visiting clergyman, Anthony Champion (Hugh Grant), take place during breakfast, lunch, and dinner.

Pointed references to food and food preparation in a diverse range of Australian films is the principal manner by which ethnicity and cultural difference are enunciated. •Crocodile Dundee (1986) uses two parallel food scenes to comment on cultural differences between the USA and Australia. In the first half of the film, Sue Charlton's (Linda Kozlowski) reluctance to partake of roasted goanna, sugar ants, and grubs ('natural' food) has its counterpart in the second half when Mick 'Crocodile' Dundee (Paul •Hogan) is offered a hotdog swimming in mustard and tomato sauce (processed food) from a New York street vendor. In both instances there is a comment that, while it is possible to survive on the food on offer, it 'tastes like shit', thereby suggesting that the cultural differences between the two countries are finally superficial and easily smoothed over.

In a film such as Teck Tan's **My Tiger's Eyes** (1988), cultural difference is not so easily resolved. A young Chinese boy growing up in Australia is struggling for identity, and this struggle is played out between his Anglo neighbours, who offer him ice-cream and wafers, and his own family, who serve up blackened fish and boiled chicken wings: 'Dim sim versus the meat pie—which is more digestible?' is a line summing up the boy's dilemma. In Jane Stevenson's Super-8 documentary **Italian Boys** (1982), Ralph Traviato's memory of homemade school lunches is of Anglo kids eagerly gathering around in fascination, and then just as quickly fleeing when he waved his lunch in front of their noses.

Perhaps the most definitive documentary examining ethnicity and the representation of food is Brian McKenzie's **Winter's Harvest** (1979). The film is an account of a custom known as 'the killing of the pig' among Italian working-class immigrants. For these immigrants, the custom is not solely one of putting a variety of salami and cured meats in store for winter; it is also a ritual with a metaphorical matrix that occasions celebration in the face of oncoming adversity. In this case, the forthcoming adversity is not only the cruelty of the winter season, but also impending legislation that, for health reasons, aims to discourage the practice of 'the killing of the pig'. When the immigrants perform their custom, there is gaiety, discussion, music, dance, and a strong sense of a group coming together. McKenzie contrasts this with the mechanised, sterile, emotionally distant butchering of pigs in an abattoir. McKenzie makes his point clear: What is to be gained by legislation and a sanitary, commercial practice that threatens a richly embroidered ritual giving these immigrants their identity in a new country?

A central motif of Gillian •Armstong's The •Last Days of Chez Nous (1992) is of cutting into food. This motif is one of the best cues to the state-of-being of particular characters, and the socio-sexual dynamics existing between them. Vicki (Kerry •Fox) arrives home to an empty house after a prolonged trip abroad. Her only welcome is a heart-shaped cake, from which she proceeds to carve a sizeable chunk. It is a gesture that signals her emotional state as well as prefiguring the film's main concerns: fractured relationships and the pain associated with them. Similarly, in another scene, when Beth (Lisa Harrow), Vicki's older and confident sister, takes a slice of Camembert, this triggers an angry outburst from her French lover, JP (Bruno Ganz), apparently because the cheese has not reached the desired maturation. The slicing of the cheese is indicative of the emotional condition existing between Beth and JP; like the cheese, their relationship is still to reach some point of maturity. Moreover, as with Vicki's cutting of the cake, cutting into the cheese signals a set of disruptive circumstances amidst the surface *bonhomie* of their emotional and domestic life.

One of the most sophisticated examples of the use of food to signal domestic and emotional turmoil is in Scott Murray's •Devil in the Flesh (1989). Adapted from Raymond Radiguet's *Le Diable au Corps*, the film re-sets the story during World War II in rural Australia, and tells of a brief love affair between a young, married French woman and an adolescent on the brink of manhood. The woman's parents, an established family in the area, host an elaborate, outdoor luncheon to which they invite the local, interned Italians. The scene gives a sense of rarefied communion despite the war in Europe, a war between the nations that are the homelands of the people sitting together at the table. And yet the scene is not without a hint of imminent doom: the fact that the lovers are seated apart, their rapture contained, prefigures their separation due to the forces (metonymically represented at the table) that brought the two together in the first place. Examples of the use of food scenes to presage impending problems within emotional relationships or domestic situations are plentiful in Australian cinema: for example, •Return Home (1990), The •Everlasting Secret Family (1988), Phobia (1990), Emoh

Ruo (1985), •The Year My Voice Broke (1987), and •The Sum of Us (1994).

Most scenes involving food are associated with communal tensions, social breakdown, cultural difference, and emotional, sexual, and marital crisis. Exceptions to this rule are rare: **Crocodile Dundee** features food as a sign of complementarity, fulfilment, co-existence, and unity; in Michael Powell's •Age of Consent (1969), food has exchange value and thus plays a central role within the characters' 'economies of desire'; in Tim Burns' **Against the Grain: More Meat than Wheat** (1981) a scene of baking bread with a revolutionary yeast parallels scenes of the making of a bomb for revolutionary purposes; and in Tracey •Moffatt's •BeDevil (1993), the combination of yabbies (indigenous food) with a creamy, white, *béchamel* sauce points to the potential for harmonious co-existence between cultures.

This small but representative sample of Australian films featuring food illustrates the dramatic uses of food in Australian cinema. Food in film can be seen as an essential feature of film language, as well as an essential cue to understanding and interpreting the values expressed.

RAFFAELE CAPUTO

For Love Alone

1986. Director: Stephen Wallace. *Producer:* Margaret Fink. *Scriptwriter:* Stephen Wallace. Based on the novel by Christina Stead. *Director of photography:* Alun Bollinger. *Music:* Nathan Waks. 104 min. B&W. *Cast:* Helen Buday (Teresa), Sam Neill (James Quick), Hugo Weaving (Jonathan Crow), Huw Williams (Harry), Hugh Keayes-Byrne (Andrew).

Christina Stead's semi-autobiographical novel of a young woman's search for love and for a niche as a writer made a disappointing film, despite an excellent central performance from Helen •Buday as the questing Teresa. Oppressed by family and unrewarding office work in 1930s Sydney, Teresa is determined not to let life pass her by. Her first mistake is to imagine that her Latin teacher, Jonathan Crow, is the answer to her dream of romance. She escapes the egotistical Crow, and Australia. In the United Kingdom she falls in love with James Quick, a gentle and gentlemanly publisher, who guides her into a new maturity.

It is easy to see the appeal of the story for Margaret •Fink, who had produced the critically acclaimed •My Brilliant Career (actor Sam •Neill and composer Nathan •Waks had also worked on the earlier film), but **For Love Alone** lacks the vivacity of the 1979 success, perhaps reflecting the differences between the two protagonists. Director Stephen •Wallace had done an impressive job with the prison drama •Stir (1980), but seemed less at home with the quieter, more reflective material at hand here.

BMcF

For Love or Money

1983. Directors: Megan McMurchy, Jeni Thornley. *Producers:* Megan McMurchy, Margot Oliver, Jeni Thornley. *Scriptwriters:* Megan McMurchy, Margot Oliver, Jeni Thornley. *Director of photography:* Erica Addis. *Music:* Elizabeth Drake. 107 min. *Cast:* Noni Hazlehurst (narrator).

This feature-length compilation film was created over a period of five years by a dedicated team who trawled through film and photographic records to locate a wide range of images about 'women and work in Australia'. This intractable material—incorporating documentary and fiction, still and moving images, silent and sound footage—was then organised into four chronological sequences: Hard labour(1780s–1914), Daughters of toil (1914–39), Working for the duration (1939–69), and Work of value (1969–83). The film also offers recurring thematic threads: the special problems of indigenous and migrant women; the struggle for equal pay for equal work; the work of women in the home; and also, repeatedly, the work of cinema as part of the process of making meaning. It is held together by a commentary, written by the production team and spoken by Noni Hazlehurst, and by an evocative music score by Elizabeth Drake. The project grew out of the women's movement of the 1960s and 1970s but, by the time it was released, it was criticised by some as rather old-fashioned, caught in the consensual politics of an earlier stage of feminism. The film remains, however, an extraordinary documentation of a complex subject: its presentation is as fresh as when it was released, and the questions it raises are still as relevant.   IB

For the Term of His Natural Life

1927. Director: Norman Dawn. *Producer:* Norman Dawn. *Scriptwriter:* Norman Dawn. Based on the novel by Marcus Clarke. *Directors of photography:* Len Roos, William Trerise, Bert Cross. 10 000 ft. B&W. *Cast:* George Fisher (Rufus Dawes/John Rex), Eva Novak (Sylvia Vickers), Dunstan Webb (Maurice Frere), Jessica Harcourt (Sarah Purfoy), Arthur McLaglen (Gabbett).

Marcus Clarke's epic novel of convict days was filmed first in 1908, but none of that version survives. In 1926 Raymond •Longford proposed to Australasian Films that a new version be produced. He was preparing this when company executives decided that the film might be promoted in the USA if American cast and crew were involved. Longford agreed to relinquish direction to visiting American Norman •Dawn, who employed his own cameraman (Len Roos). Hollywood stars George Fisher and Eva Novak were contracted for the lead roles, and some smaller roles were also taken by Americans Arthur McLaglen (the cannibal escaper Gabbett) and Dawn's wife Katherine (Mrs Vickers). The budget was the largest the company had yet provided (£60 000), permitting location shooting at Port Arthur itself (where one of Dawn's famous glass shots reconstructed derelict buildings), and huge numbers of extras.

The story of Rufus Dawes, transported for a crime he did not commit, and suffering the indignities of imprisonment, shipwreck, and misrepresentation of his role in the rescue of the heroine, proved too dark for some critics. Some also found the film overlong, jumbled, and lacking in tension, while the central performances were considered wooden. Yet, until the arrival of sound killed its market, it was a resounding financial success in Australia, and *Variety* described the film as 'grippingly dark-hued and old-worldish'. The lovingly reconstructed version now held in the National Film and Sound Archive is still very watchable, particularly for the impressive scenery and the skilful camerawork in the more gothic moments of the story (such as the gaolbreak).   IB

Forster, Jill (1936–) ACTOR Red-haired Jill Forster has to date been better known for her work in television than on the screen, in such long-running series as *The Box* in the early 1970s and, recently, as the philosophical pub-keeper in the ABC series *SeaChange*.

A player with a pleasing warmth and intelligence, she has had only minor chances in the cinema, as the mother in 'The Child', an episode of •Libido (1973); and as the watchful middle-class mother of the infatuated hero in •Devil in the Flesh (1989). She is married to the actor John •Stanton. *Other Australian films:* •Alvin Purple (1973), Crosstalk (1982), Say a Little Prayer (1993).   BMcF

Forsyth, Julie ACTOR After appearing in Feathers (1987), a short film for director John •Ruane, Forsyth made an auspicious feature début in Stan and George's New Life (1991). She played a kindly, plain country girl who has come to the city to make a new life for herself and who meets a shy bachelor, still living with his parents at 40 and desperate to break out on his own. Forsyth and Paul •Chubb, as this unlikely pair, were very sympathetic, avoiding easy comedy and easy pathos in favour of an affecting astringency. Those who had seen her on stage, for instance as Sonya in *Uncle Vanya*, would not have been surprised at the quality of her acting. She was also in the television series *Mercury*, where her unusual intensity made something memorable of a conventional role. In the cinema, she has also had a small role in Aya (1991), and, as a sheep's distinctive voice, she was heard but not seen in •Babe (1995).   BMcF

Forsythe, Drew ACTOR Forsythe, a NSW actor and graduate of the National Institute of Dramatic Art, was a

The prison escape in **For the Term of His Natural Life**

For the Term of His Natural Life

well-known figure in the early films of the 1970s revival (see Revival, the), and appeared often on television and stage. He had a bit part in the 'bikie' thriller •Stone (1974), which acquired a minor cult following, and made a popular impression in two likeable roles in well-received films: as the good-natured 'rabbit-o' who helps the ailing heroine in •Caddie (1976), and as Bruce, the film editor, in •Newsfront (1978). His easy warmth complemented Angela •Punch-MacGregor's impassioned crusader in •Annie's Coming Out (1984). He has had little to challenge him since. His last film was the stirring but unsuccessful melodrama, •Minna-murra (1989). His real gift may be for comedy, as suggested by his delightfully broad Tiger Kelly in Ginger Meggs (1982), but his friendly ordinariness is also a strength.

Other Australian films: Deathcheaters (1976), Equals Zero (1979, short), Keep Moving or They'll Get You (1979, short), Meetings (1980, short), Doctors and Nurses (1981), Dot and Santa Claus (1982, voice only), Anna (1983, short), Dot and the Bunny (1984, voice only), •Burke & Wills (1985), •Travelling North (1987).   BMcF

Forty Thousand Horsemen

1940. *Director, Producer*: Charles Chauvel. *Scriptwriters*: Charles Chauvel, Elsa Chauvel. *Director of photography*: Gerald Heath with John Heyer, Tasman Higgins, Frank Hurley, Bert Nicholas. B&W. *Cast*: Grant Taylor (Red Gallagher), Betty Bryant (Juliet Rouget), Chips Rafferty (Jim), Pat Twohill (Larry), Joe Valli (Scotty), Kenneth Brampton (German officer), Michael Pate (An Arab).

It is hard to be anything less than reverential about **Forty Thousand Horsemen**, the most-loved Australian movie for those generations who fought and died for the country in the twentieth century's wars. Its simple story of three comrades caught up in the terrible and exhilarating game of battle, its sequences of action on a scale hitherto not seen in an Australian film, its uncomplicated populist patriotism, all combine to make its viewing a defining moment for very many Australians living and dead. And indeed, the film's power is drawn from exactly that wellspring of national feeling that war uncovers, for better and for worse: the imagined community of those who face the menace. If **Forty Thousand Horsemen** convinces some viewers of the possibility of an Australian utopia where other films do not, it is because the promised land is not figured in the film, but only enacted in the deeds of people who fight for its dream. Australia is not a place, but a way of speaking and acting together against a common enemy. At the same time, the surging optimism of the film culminates in a symbolic diaspora. In covering the screen with Australians, **Forty Thousand Horsemen** also covers the Middle East—but not for the purposes of colonisation. Instead the film ultimately and triumphantly abandons its heroic couple to make an

entirely new life in the ancient land that they have watered with their blood.   WILLIAM D. ROUTT

Fourth Wish, The

1976. *Director*: Don Chaffey. *Producer*: John Morris. *Scriptwriter*: Michael Craig. *Director of photography*: Geoff Burton. *Music*: Tristram Cary. 104 min. *Cast*: John Meillon (Casey), Robert Bettles (Sean), Robyn Nevin (Connie), Michael Craig (Dr Richardson), Julie Dawson (Hannah).

Casey, a middle-aged shift worker, discovers that his twelve-year-old son is suffering from leukaemia. Casey leaves his job to spend more time with Sean, and is determined that his son's three last wishes—to own a dog, to see his mother (who had walked out eight years earlier), and to meet the Queen—should be fulfilled.

Michael •Craig reworked his successful television series for the script, which retains elements of the television 'weepie'. John •Meillon works hard in his portrayal of an ordinary battler coming to terms with his son's fatal illness, while Robert Bettles is quite convincing as the boy who knows, despite the dissimulations of the adults, that he is going to die. The wooden performances of the rest of the cast derive largely from a story that offers them little scope. The film has its poignant moments but is a rather laboured, heart-on-the-sleeve effort that is not helped by pedestrian direction.   HARRY OLDMEADOW

Fowle, Susannah (1961–) ACTOR   In 1977, Susannah Fowle, an unknown schoolgirl, was chosen for the plum leading role of Laura Tweedle Rambotham in Phillip •Adams's production of •The Getting of Wisdom, based on Henry Handel Richardson's classic autobiographical tale of schooldays at Melbourne's Presbyterian Ladies College. She played the role with raw vigour, which suited the character of a hoyden tamed by an oppressive educational system and, in the latter half of the film, she suggested the seriousness of Laura's attempt to come to terms with the 'wisdom' she has gained. She subsequently did stage and television work (including *Outbreak of Love*), and had a supporting role in •A Street to Die (1985).   BMcF

Fox, Kerry (1966–) ACTOR   Born just outside Wellington in New Zealand, Kerry Fox began her screen career with a mesmerising portrait of the victimised and tormented New Zealand author Janet Frame in Jane •Campion's **An Angel at My Table** (1990). After filming the European scenes for this film, Fox settled in Australia where she spent five frustrating years, making only three films. Fox's most substantial Australian role during this period was that of Vicki, the young woman who generates a romantic crisis when she enters the home of her older sister Beth (Lisa Harrow), in Gillian •Armstrong's **The Last Days of Chez Nous**

(1992). Fox's other significant role was the plain-looking Sally in the Chekhov-inspired •Country Life (1994), which contrasts with her striking performance the same year as the amoral doctor and flatmate in the brilliant Scottish film Shallow Grave (1994). Fox left Australia in 1993 for London where her talents have been appreciated for intense performances in films such as The Hanging Garden (1998) and Welcome to Sarajevo (1998). In 1997 Fox returned briefly to Australia for the lead role in Richard Flanagan's domestic drama set in the Tasmanian wilderness, •The Sound of One Hand Clapping (1998).   GM

Fran

1985. *Director:* Glenda Hambly. *Producer:* David Rapsey. *Scriptwriter:* Glenda Hambly. *Director of photography:* Jan Kenny. *Music:* Greg Schultz. 94 min. *Cast:* Noni Hazlehurst (Fran), Annie Byron (Marge), Alan Fletcher (Jeff), Narelle Simpson (Lisa), Travis Ward (Tom).

This touching piece of social realism, set in a characterless suburb of Perth, is perhaps as near as Australian cinema has come to sharing British film-maker Mike Leigh's compassion for life's losers and his cold anger for the systems that fail them. Fran, herself the victim of a succession of foster homes, daughter of an alcoholic mother and unknown father, has built up a fierce distrust of the social services departments whose help she should be able to claim. Her three children, whom she loves and neglects, are themselves victims of her feckless, incurably selfish behaviour, but the film, while registering this, is not judgmental about her sexual needs. With typical insouciance, she leaves the children to the care of neighbour Marge for days at a time while she takes up with barman Jeff, who abuses the oldest child Lisa and rails at the intrusiveness of the others. The film ends with the children taken into care, with Marge having had more than enough, with Jeff leaving for 'the North', and Fran alone. It does not fudge the inevitable bleakness of this closure, although this cannot have helped its commercial prospects. Noni •Hazlehurst and Annie •Byron, both of whom won Australian Film Institute awards, delivered performances of notable human veracity which make one grateful for those life-revealing details of behaviour that film can register more vividly than any other medium.
                                                        BMcF

Frances, Cornelia (1941–) ACTOR Cornelia Frances

Zulver worked in the United Kingdom on stage and in television and film before migrating to Australia in 1966. She dropped her surname, and was soon in demand on Australian television, where her commanding presence and steely voice were ideally suited to playing soap opera 'superbitches'—Barbara Hamilton in *Sons and Daughters*, Sister Scott in *The Young Doctors*, and Morag Bellingham in *Home*

and Away. Although she has played many other television roles, her film appearances are few: Mrs Darcy in The Man from Snowy River II (1988), and Tushka •Bergen's snobbish mother in •Minamurra (1989).   IB

Franklin, Richard (1948–) DIRECTOR More than

most Australian film-makers, Richard Franklin has been undervalued in his own country. He was attacked in an article by Bob •Ellis in the now-defunct *National Times* for adopting a supposedly mid-Pacific approach to production, as though any sign of Hollywood genres and narrative verve were necessarily unAustralian.

After studying at Monash University, Melbourne, Franklin trained at the Film School of the University of Southern California, during which time—the late 1960s—he was privileged to be a student observer on Alfred Hitchcock's Topaz (1969), an experience that influenced his subsequent development as a director. When he returned to Australia, he directed episodes of popular television series such as *Homicide*, as well as documentary shorts, before getting his first chance to direct a feature film, The True Story of Eskimo Nell (1975). The last was financed largely by its Australian distributor Filmways, and by the Australian Film Development Corporation, and was filmed partly in Melbourne and partly on locations at the ski resort of Falls Creek as well as, for a couple of sequences, in Montreal and Quebec. It offered a melancholy deconstruction of the myth of Eskimo Nell and of male priapism and, perhaps, would have done better financially if it had been more uncomplicatedly bawdy.

Franklin's third feature, •Patrick (1978), which he also co-produced, revealed him as a highly proficient genre director. This 'hospital thriller', with a touch of science fiction, was in the Hollywood tradition of plucky heroines and mad doctors, and it handled its conventions with flair and wit. It wears its age better than many of the more critically lauded films of the decade. Franklin confirmed its promise three years later with •Roadgames (1981), a droll and exciting road movie, involving a murder in Melbourne, a journey across the Nullarbor, and a *dénouement* in Perth. Bob Ellis's contentious article took Franklin to task for his use of American stars (Stacy Keach as the verse-quoting truck driver, and Jamie Lee Curtis as the hitchhiker he picks up), failing to do justice to the sheer professionalism of Franklin's narrative command, his penchant for Hitchcockian surprise, and the high level of visual and verbal wit. In the event, his next films took him out of Australia and, in Psycho II (1983), a more than respectable sequel to his mentor's classic, and Cloak and Dagger (1984), a very engaging exploration of a child's fantasies *and* a fast-paced and inventive thriller, he showed the sort of commercially viable skills the Australian industry could have used to advantage. His chilling British-made horror film Link (1986), which he produced as well as directed, never received theatrical release in Australia but, when he finally returned to filming here, he showed a readiness to branch out in new directions with his finely articulate version of Hannie Rayson's play •Hotel Sorrento (1995). Back in the 1970s, when Australian films were constantly preoccupied with questions of national identity and mythology, Franklin showed no interest in these themes, nor in the adaptation of indigenous literature. Now, in the cinematically more sophisticated climate of the 1990s, he brings a maturity of technique and vision to issues of what it means to be Australian in an essentially European-based and American-influenced culture.

He has not made as many films as his champions might have wished, but he has made some of the most engaging entertainments of any Australian film-maker since the revival in the 1970s (see Revival, the) got under way.

Other Australian films: •Fantasm (1976), Brilliant Lies (1996).

BMcF

Friedrich, Zbigniew (1944–) CINEMATOGRAPHER/ EDITOR Zbigniew (Peter) Friedrich was born in Poland and trained in London before settling in Melbourne, where

he worked for Crawfords as editor, sound mixer, director, and producer on television series such as *Homicide* and *Division 4*. In the 1970s he began making independent films—writing, directing, and photographing **Made in Australia** (1975) and **Apostasy** (1979) (the latter being badly mauled by the critics). In 1976, with Don McLennan, he formed Ukiyo Films, for which (as well as working on a number of documentaries) he photographed and edited the two realist dramas **Hard Knocks** (1980) and •**Mull** (1989), and edited **Slate, Wyn and Me** (1987) as well as being director of photography and editor on **Breakaway** (1990, not released theatrically). He has also worked as editor on other features—including **The Still Point** (1985), John •**Hughes's Traps** (1986), and **A Sting in the Tail** (1989)—and as both editor and director of photography on television documentaries and series.

IB

Friels, Colin (1955–) ACTOR Born in Glasgow, Colin Friels graduated from the Australian National Institute of Dramatic Art in 1976 before emerging as one of Australia's best stage actors in the late 1970s and 1980s. After a supporting role in the thriller •**Hoodwink** (1981), Friels made

Richard Franklin directing Tara Morice in **Hotel Sorrento** (1995)

Colin Friels

his first major impact on the Australian screen as Javo, the drug addict in •**Monkey Grip** (1982). This was followed by the lead role in the John •Dingwall-scripted adventure **Buddies** (1983), set in the central Queensland sapphire country around the town of Emerald. Although **Buddies** was based on an excellent concept—the romantic rivalry between Friels and Harold •Hopkins over Lisa •Peers, combined with the commercial threat posed by Dennis •Miller and his determination to destroy the Friels/Hopkins sapphire business—the execution of this concept was uneven and the film failed to attract an audience. Friels worked steadily in the Australian cinema throughout the 1980s, his most commercially successful performance being that of the simple man with a flair for devising bizarre technical contrivances in Nadia •Tass's •**Malcolm** (1986). There are, however, other less obvious highlights to his career, including his portrayal of the cynical reporter Tom Stewart in the underrated crime thriller •**Grievous Bodily Harm** (1988), and the sensitive love interest of his real-life wife Judy •Davis in •**Hightide** (1987). They also co-starred memorably as the D.H. Lawrence figure and his wife in •**Kangaroo** (1987). Friels also performed in such overseas film productions as **Darkman** (1990), in which he played the villain, and Bruce •Beresford's **A Good Man in Africa** (1993), in which he played the weak, self-centred diplomat. On Australian television, Friels appeared in the lead role as Richard Devine/Rufus Dawes in the 1983 adaptation of one of the major films of the silent period, •**For the Term of His Natural Life**. Friels also attracted a large television following in the 1990s, with the lead role in the police series *Water Rats*, for which he won the 1997 Logie award for 'Best Actor'. This followed an Australian Film Institute (AFI) Award for 'Best Actor' in **Malcolm** in 1986, and an AFI Award for 'Best Actor in a Television Drama' for *Halifax f.p.* in 1995.

GM

Fringe Dwellers, The

1986. *Director:* Bruce Beresford. *Producer:* Sue Milliken. *Scriptwriters:* Bruce Beresford, Rhoisin Beresford. *Director of photography:* Don McAlpine. *Music:* George Dreyfus. 98 min. *Cast:* Kristina Nehm (Trilby Comeaway), Justine Saunders (Mollie Comeaway), Bob Maza (Joe Comeaway), Kylie Belling (Noonah Comeaway), Ernie Dingo (Phil).

The Comeaway family live in a tumbledown river-bank settlement of Aboriginal families on the outskirts of a country town. A rebellious daughter, Trilby, persuades the family to move to a Housing Commission home, but her plans to escape after finishing school are upset when she becomes pregnant.

The Fringe Dwellers is significant as the first mainstream feature in which all the principal roles are played by indigenous actors. Aboriginal social values are positively inflected, and the contradictory social pressures felt by the Comeaways are sympathetically treated. However, the mid 1980s transposition to the screen of Nene Gare's 1960 novel and Bruce •Beresford's decision to play the narrative primarily as a family drama make for several intractable problems. The plot is formulaic and the film's inescapable socio-political dimension lacks analytical bite. Beresford's film (frequently compared with Steven Spielberg's **The Color Purple**) illustrates the limitations of the liberal 'social problem' film: well intentioned but unable to deal in any depth with the issues it raises.

HARRY OLDMEADOW

Furness, Deborra-Lee (1960–) ACTOR At 17, Deborra-Lee Furness was working as a researcher in the Channel Nine newsroom, when she was invited to join *No Man's Land*, first as a researcher, then on-air. After small parts in television, she went to New York in 1980, where she survived the fierce selection process to complete the three-year course at the American Academy of Dramatic Arts. In the late 1980s, she returned to Australia to play the lead in the television series *Kings*. Several film roles followed: the lead (Carol Grey) in **Jenny Kissed Me** (1986); Lee, the Minister for Conservation's assistant, in **Cool Change** (1986); and a small part in •**Celia** (1989). There were also several telemovies, but it was the role of Asta Cadell (•**Shame** 1988) that made her a star in Australia. In her bikie leathers, when she discards her black helmet and tosses out her long red-blonde hair, she challenges the chauvinists of Ginborak and represents hope for the women of the town. Furness returned to America to promote the film and stayed to appear in **The Last of the Finest** (1990), **Homo Faber** (1991), and **Newsies** (1992). But opportunities were opening up in Australia, so she came back for television roles in the miniseries *Act of Betrayal* (1991), the telemovie *Singapore Sling* (1993), the series *Stark* (1993), and an episode of *Halifax f.p.* (*The Feeding*) (1994). These culminated in two outstanding television performances—the blowsy and outrageous Dolores in *Fire* (1994) and the novice prison psychiatrist in *Corelli* (1995). Later film roles included fashion editor Diane in •**Waiting** (1991), Colin •Friels's wife in •**Angel Baby** (1995), and Jamie •Croft's mother in **The Real Macaw** (1998).

IB

G

Gabriel, Ben (1919–) ACTOR By comparison with his long and distinguished stage career, Ben Gabriel has merely dabbled in films but, even so, there are some authoritative supporting roles. He is one of those actors bound to be remembered on screen, even in quite small roles, whether benign (**Break of Day**, 1976) or unpleasant (•**The Mango Tree**, 1977), giving individuality to types and making acting look like life caught by a passing camera. His first film role was in the 'Joe Wilson's Mates' segment of Cecil •Holmes's 1957 •**Three in One**. Before filming again in the early 1970s, he worked with several major theatre companies and appeared in such long-running television series as *Matlock*. *Other Australian films*: Strange Holiday (1970), •The Office Picnic (1972), Flashpoint (1972), Let the Balloon Go (1976), •Hoodwink (1981), •The Killing of Angel Street (1981), Fighting Back (1982), I Can't Get Started (1985).

BMcF

Gallipoli

1981. *Director*: Peter Weir. *Producers*: Robert Stigwood, Patricia Lovell. *Scriptwriter*: David Williamson. Based on a story by Peter Weir. *Director of photography*: Russell Boyd. *Additional music*: Brian May. 110 mins. *Cast*: Mel Gibson (Frank Dunne), Mark Lee (Archy), Bill Hunter (Major Barton), Robert Grubb (Billy), Bill Kerr (Jack).

Gallipoli was one of the flagship films of the Australian film revival (see Revival, the). It not only won widespread critical acclaim for its retelling of one of the key mythic moments in the nation's history, in relation to itself and the world at large, but it was also an enormous box-office success here and was the first Australian film of the revival to achieve mainstream North American distribution. Filmed

Ben Gabriel

in South Australia, it consolidated Peter •Weir's position as the leading director of the revival, and it made a star of Mel •Gibson, American-born but long resident here.

It is, in effect, a coming-of-age film in a period setting, as were several of the *succès d'estime* films of the time, but, more explicitly than most, **Gallipoli** spells out the national reverberations of its young heroes (Gibson and Mark •Lee) who come to manhood in the fateful World War I action. Lee plays an outback lad, a runner and farmer, who is inspired by the tales of Empire read to him by his uncle and who puts his age up to enlist in the imperial cause. Gibson's character is streetwise, urban, bent on survival. They meet first at a country sports ground where they run in friendly competition, and the competition as well as the mateship is maintained as they move to Perth, to Egypt, and finally to Turkey, where one becomes the commanding officer's runner and the other, in a poignant freeze-frame, is cut down by enemy fire in a posture of heroic sacrifice. It has been described by some as a male love story; whether or not that is the case, the film undeniably enshrines the ideal of mateship. This is perhaps the heart of the film, which was criticised in some quarters for not espousing a more overtly anti-war ethos. (It was also criticised in Britain for the unflattering images it offers of the British army.) It is nevertheless moving on the level of both its personal story and its version of a nation's identity being forged in tragedy and failure.   BMcF

Gardiner, Lizzy COSTUME DESIGNER   With her partner Tim Chappell, Lizzy Gardiner won both a British and an American Academy Award for the striking costume designs on •The Adventures of Priscilla, Queen of the Desert (1994). Operating on a shoestring budget, Gardiner and Chappell produced outrageously camp costumes for the three Abba-impersonating drag queens. Gardiner's appearance at the ceremony was almost eclipsed by her costume: her evening gown comprised over 250 gold American Express credit cards painstakingly linked together—emphasising the obsession with finance in the film industry. In an ironic twist she sold the infamous dress to the credit card company for an undisclosed price. American Express planned an international travelling exhibition.

Gardiner's success led her to Hollywood where she joined the costume department on Andy and Larry Wachowski's unconventional gangster film **Bound** (1996). The focus on the manufacture of costumes and marketing at the expense of creativity contributed to Gardiner's disillusionment with the Hollywood system. After 12 difficult months there, Gardiner returned to Australia to design costumes for **Welcome to Woop Woop** (1997).

Other Australian films: Gone Fishin' (1997), **Woundings** (1998).
                                WENDY HASLEM

Garner, Alice (1971–) ACTOR   Alice Garner, the daughter of actor Bill Garner and author Helen •Garner, made her film début as a child in •Monkey Grip (1982), the film version of her mother's novel. She played Gracie, the daughter of Nora (Noni •Hazlehurst), living in a shifting inner-suburban ambience of drugs and uneasy relationships, in which the patient, clear-eyed Gracie seems wiser

than her mother. It was a startlingly truthful performance, which has so far been followed by only two further roles: as the shy Esther in •The Nostradamus Kid (1993), and as Alice in the high-spirited youth film, •Love and Other Catastrophes (1996), in which she showed an attractive sense of humour. She may well be one of the rare child actors who has successfully made the leap into adult roles.   BMcF

Garner, Helen (1942–) WRITER   One of Australia's most prominent authors, Garner worked as a teacher and journalist before rising to prominence in 1977 with her first novel *Monkey Grip*. The film version, •Monkey Grip (1982), was adapted for screen by director Ken •Cameron. Although successful critically and commercially, it failed to capture the brittle quality of the book, especially in its depiction of the heroin-dependent Javo, played by Colin •Friels. The telemovie *Two Friends* (1986), directed by Jane •Campion and produced by Jan •Chapman, marked Garner's entry into scriptwriting. Having been well received, the film was an important attempt to explore variations on traditional linear narrative structure. Garner's collaboration with Chapman continued on •The Last Days of Chez Nous (1992). Directed by Gillian •Armstrong, it is arguably one of the most underrated Australian films of recent years, exploring difficult themes such as father–daughter relationships, family loyalty, and sibling rivalry. What is especially interesting is the way in which Garner shifts our allegiances between characters throughout the film, unsettling and even confusing for mainstream audiences.

                                HARRY KIRCHNER

Garner, Nadine (1971–) ACTOR   After appearing in the popular television series *The Henderson Kids*, Garner was cast in **The Still Point** (1985) as Sarah, the troubled 14-year-old who suffers from deafness and the advent of her mother's new lover. After this low-key film, Garner returned to television and a new series of *The Henderson Kids*, followed by another children's film, **Bushfire Moon** (1987), directed by George •Miller and set in the drought-affected outback of Christmas 1891. The television series *House Rules* preceded Garner's best screen role to date in •Mull (1989) as Phoebe Mullens who, after her mother is forced into hospital with Hodgkin's disease, takes responsibility for raising her two brothers and younger sister. Garner's performance deservedly won a Best Actress Award from the Australian Film Institute.

Garner has also appeared in a range of theatrical productions, beginning with *A Day in the Death of Joe Egg* (1986), for the Melbourne Theatre Company, and others including *Amadeus* (1994), *Romeo and Juliet* (1995), *Summer of the Seventeenth Doll* (1996), *The Balcony, Three Sisters*, and *The Taming of the Shrew* (all 1997). She has also

Nadine Garner

appeared in numerous television series (including *G.P.*, 1995; *Good Guys, Bad Guys*, 1996; *Twisted Tales*, 1996; *Raw FM*, 1997).

Other Australian films include: Metal Skin (1995), for which Garner received a Film Critics Circle Award for 'Best Supporting Actor (Female)'. GM

Gavin, Agnes *see* John Gavin

Gavin, John (1875–1938) ACTOR/DIRECTOR

John (Jack) Gavin had many years experience on stage as an actor, before he embarked on a career in films, starting as an actor in **Thunderbolt** (1910) then, in 1911, as actor in, and director of, the convict and bushranging film **Moonlite**. In the same year he made **Ben Hall and his Gang**, **The Assigned Servant**, **Keane of Kalgoorlie**, **The Mark of the Lash**, and **Frank Gardiner, King of the Road**. His wife, Agnes, acted in some of these, and wrote most of them. Their working partnership continued when he established his own company and, in 1911, they made **The Drover's Sweetheart** and **Assigned to his Wife**. In 1916 they returned to film-making with two short films (**Charlie at the Sydney Show** and **An Interrupted Divorce**) and their most important and successful film of all—•**The Martyrdom of Nurse Cavell** (1916), which Agnes wrote overnight. In 1918, the couple went to Hollywood and, for seven years, John Gavin took small parts in westerns and comedies. They returned briefly

to Australia in 1922–23, and permanently in 1925, making their last film in 1928. Cooper and Pike (*Australian Film 1900–1977*) describe them as having 'more enthusiasm and stubborn persistence than talent'.

Other Australian films: The Murder of Captain Fryatt (1917, a., d.), His Convict Bride (1918, a., d.), Trooper O'Brien (1928, a., d.), A Melbourne Mystery (1913, a.), The Adorable Outcast (1928, a.)

IB

Gay cinema

The depiction of male homosexuality in mainstream Australian movies has been, at least up until the post-Stonewall early 1970s, the representation of social absence and invisibility. The only culturally sanctioned gay character type permissible on our screens prior to the years of gay liberation was the potentially peripheral pansy or limp-wristed sissy. As a re-established Australian cinema proceeds through the 1970s, 1980s, and 1990s, two other species of narrativised homosexuals begin to emerge in addition to the queenish nancy: the predatory nasty gay and the conventionally normal gay. Interpretations and representations within each of these three strands (nancies, nasties, and normals) reveal varying degrees of constrictive prejudice and constructive change in the ongoing process of moving towards a concept and reality we can call Australian gay cinema.

The pre-1970s nancy in Australian film is most notably epitomised by Alec •Kellaway's fashion salon floorwalker Entwistle in Ken G. •Hall's •**Dad and Dave Come to Town** (1938). Drawing on a Hollywood tradition already well established by such players as Franklin Pangborn and Eric Blore, Kellaway performs the supporting role of the ultra-devoted store employee to the fussy, hand-flapping hilt. However, far from functioning as just a 'silly-nelly' novelty number, Entwistle's effeminate clerk offers the emporium-inheriting Rudd clan both dedication and cooperative zeal, at one point actually engaging in fisticuffs with a commercial competitor's menacing henchmen. Entwistle's status as one of the family and part of the team is continued in Hall's •**Dad Rudd MP** (1940), in which he is invited to spend a vacation with the Rudds on their rustic estate, during which time he becomes involved in Dad's campaign to run for parliament on a 'little battler' platform. If **Dad Rudd MP** had not proved to be the last of Ken G. Hall's narrative movies before his •Cinesound outfit ceased local feature film production in 1940, who can say where and how the Entwistle character might have progressed?

It was not until after Australian cinema's protracted decrease in feature film output throughout the 1940s, 1950s, and 1960s that something like the Entwistle persona resurfaced on the big screen via the small-screen success of the commercial television soap operas *Number 96* and *The Box*. Each of these high-rating series presented amid its ensemble a prominent gay character in the 'nancy' mode: *Number 96*'s Dudley Butterfield (Chard Hayward) and *The Box*'s Lee Whiteman (Paul Karo). In Peter Benardos's 1974 film version of •**Number 96**, Dudley, a barman/waiter, cracks music-hall-style jokes ('Now I'll just have to push my sweetbreads, if you know what I mean') and relates surrounding plot events to old Hollywood movies ('For a minute there I thought it was going to be the burning of Atlanta all over again'). Meanwhile, in Paul Eddey's 1975 movie spin-off of **The Box**, Lee, a television director, positively flounces around in a garish assortment of flared trousers, jumpsuits, and platform-heeled shoes, dispensing one-liners such as 'I feel like a new man—but where am I going to find one at this time of night?'. These harmlessly humorous, 'nice nancies' seem to culminate in the Good Fairy played by Robin Ramsay, complete with bouffant hair and sparkling white suit, in **Oz**, Chris Löfven's 1976 rock-musical-Down-Under spin on **The Wizard of Oz**.

The camp-as-Christmas, *Carry On* stereotype gains some emotional dimension and plot space with the appearance of Jon Finlayson's vividly enacted George, the somewhat manic creative force behind an amateur production of Strindberg in Paul •Cox's •**Lonelyhearts** (1982). As well as delivering the standard bitchily blunt repartee ('Do something about your boobs, Kate! I can see them flapping from over here'), George also voices genuine sympathy and concern for the romance hesitantly blossoming between the movie's awkwardly matched protagonists, Patricia (Wendy •Hughes) and Peter (Norman •Kaye). It is George who gets the film's warmly optimistic final word ('Okay, Trish. This is your scene. Make a big entrance and speak your heart for a change!'), thus rounding off Finlayson's spirited portrayal of an unabashedly gay character who actually connects with, and even influences, the lives of others without being relegated to the position of amusing but irrelevant comic relief.

The theatrically gesticulating nancy reaches a sort of apotheosis in the archly glamorous persona of the drag queen, that compelling synthesis of sissy sassiness and (often) bawdily aggressive sexuality. Three drag performers, one of them a transsexual, assertively take charge of the narrative centre stage in Stephan •Elliott's widely seen, Oscar-winning (Best Costume Design) film, •**The Adventures of Priscilla, Queen of the Desert** (1994). This flamboyantly brash road-movie musical transports Mitzi (Hugo •Weaving), Felicia (Guy •Pearce), and Bernadette (Terence Stamp) from the big city to the outback in a tour bus that is initially silver, then, significantly, lavender pink . As their rowdy, rollicking journey progresses, this trio of heroically marginalised non-conformists reveal themselves to be distinct individuals by means of frank, abusive banter, stylised surreal flashbacks, and sometimes violent encounters with small-town homophobia. A highlight of the journey is the participation of Bill •Hunter's ostensibly straight and accepting Bob, who joins up with the travelling troupe, armed with a warning from Felicia: 'We may wear the frocks round here but that doesn't mean that *you* wear the pants'. Meanwhile, bus-top renditions of Verdi arias, a mid-desert cross-cultural performance of Gloria Gaynor's 'I Will Survive' (featuring gold-lamé-clad Aboriginal back-up), plus a nicely spontaneous burst of Abba's 'Mamma Mia' addressed to Mitzi's son Benji, constitute a few of the memorable musical moments in Elliott's Utopian homage to disco and 'divadom' .

The loosening- up of censorship restrictions, and the advent of the gay liberation movement and its activist politics, gave 1970s' Australian cinema a chance to explore fresh narrative options with regard to gay characters. But media attention to, and public recognition of, the existence of homosexuals seemed to lead to the proliferation of villainous, usually predatory, stereotypes in film. As historian and critic Vito Russo observes in his landmark study, *The Celluloid Closet*, 'When gays became real, they became threatening'.

So, alongside the effusively festive nancy, lurks the furtive, flesh-hunting psycho-fag: dirty, old (and younger) men moving in on innocent heroes. Such creatures dwell in the recesses of 1970s' Australian film. They loom, nasty pieces of work like Donald Pleasance's Doc Tydon in Ted Kotcheff's •**Wake in Fright** (1971), Trevor Howard's Captain Foster Fyans in Tim •Burstall's •**Eliza Fraser** (1976), John Clayton's Arnold in Igor •Auzins's **High Rolling** (1977), and Ray •Barrett's police official Farrell in Fred •Schepisi's •**The Chant of Jimmie Blacksmith** (1978). Even the principal antagonist in George •Miller's internationally popular, sci-fi action pic •**Mad Max 2** (1981), Vernon Wells's evil, leather-clad muscleman, Wez, turns out to be carnally coupled with Jimmy Brown's Golden Youth.

The only cinematically conceivable gay monster who might eclipse the malevolent psycho-fag is the bisexual bad boy. This chaos-causing chameleon is taken to melodramatic extremes in Lex •Marinos's •**An Indecent Obsession** (1985), where he's represented by Richard •Moir's Luce Daggett, a viciously spiteful inmate in the psychiatric ward of a Pacific island military hospital during World War II. On being questioned by presiding Sister Honour Langtry (Wendy Hughes) as to why he's made a pass at handsome Michael Wilson (Gary •Sweet) when he, Daggett, is not the least bit homosexual, Luce fervently responds, 'Oh, sweetie, I'm anything, anytime. Young, old, male, female. It's all meat to me'. Daggett's polymorphous rapacity predictably meets a sticky end. Much more successful at manipulating both genders, especially men, with his seductive charms is Mark •Lee as The Youth in Michael •Thornhill's solemnly mannered, darkly ironic, political fable, •**The Everlasting Secret Family** (1988).

An acclaimed attempt at a sympathetic view of the bisexual bad boy, Ana •Kokkinos's •Head On (1998), hurls us into the murky mindscape of Alex •Dimitriades's Ari, a young, unemployed, first-generation Greek-Australian whose credo is summed up in his musings on intimacy during physical intercourse: 'I've seen things, y'know. I've felt things. But then I blow and that's it. No more nice things'. Ari's tragic inability to commit or connect leads him and audiences on a spiralling descent into an all-too-real dead-end world of quick drug hits and fast anonymous sex.

As a counter-balance to narratively framing gays as either sissy or sinister, Australian movies have also fitfully sought to 'regularise' gay characters, presenting them as people who just happen to be, or, quite incidentally, turn out to be, homosexual. The very gradual history of this normalisation process can be traced to the film version of •Number 96 (1974) in which, as in the popular tele-series, Joe Hasham plays Don Finlayson, a perfectly respectable, straight-acting gay lawyer who functions as a level-headed adviser to the other much more eccentric denizens of the eponymous apartment block.

In Gillian •Armstrong's teen musical •Star Struck (1982), the revelation concerning the proclivities of cheesily charming rock-show entrepreneur Terry (John •O'May) hits the young heroine Jackie (Jo •Kennedy) not so much with the impact of shock-horror as with a shoulder-shrugging oh-well. Just as effectively, initial disapproval leading to eventual acceptance marks the reaction of youthful intern Paul Armstrong (Simon •Burke) towards his supervisor Dr Eric Linden (Chris •Haywood) in David Stevens's groundbreaking •The Clinic (1983). Throughout this genially unassuming study of the hectic comings and goings at a day clinic for sexually transmitted diseases, Haywood's incarnation of a butchly matter-of-fact professional, at world-weary ease with himself and others, absolutely shines.

The central figure, played by Nadine •Garner in Don McLennan's coming-of-age tale •Mull (1989), must not only face the fact that the object of her 17-year-old romantic crush, Guido (Juno Roxas), is gay but also that he is sleeping with her brother, Steve (Craig Morrison). Mull's stoic-spirited response, 'It's okay. It doesn't matter', suggests an open-minded attitude already eloquently demonstrated when she ushers her younger brother and sister from a church, on hearing the minister declare, 'There will be no homosexuals in heaven. Praise God'. Offering Mull slightly less orthodox counsel and comfort are her high school teacher Larry (David Cameron) and his male partner Paul (Bruce Langdon), both of whom, like Guido and Steve, are delivered straight, minus mincing mannerisms or sex-hungry tunnel vision.

Relatively straight, verging on downright ocker, is how Russell •Crowe's gay, rugby-playing plumber, Jeff, is delivered to us in •The Sum of Us (1994), scripted from his own successful theatre piece by David (The Clinic) •Stevens and co-directed by Kevin Dowling and Geoff •Burton. Jeff's domestic world is shared, indeed charismatically dominated, by his ferry-driving father, Harry (Jack •Thompson), a heterosexual widower, loudly supportive of his son's personal choices, if not himself very partial to them ('I think it was the idea of a hairy bum put me off.'). Each man is lonely and looking for love, an ideal virtually inspired by the lesbian relationship, recalled in sepia flashbacks, between Jeff's Gran (Mitch Matthews) and her long-time companion, 'Aunty' Mary (Julie Herbert). But while we watch Jeff pursue closeted landscape gardener, Greg (John •Polson), and see Harry court computer date-agency candidate Joyce (Deborah Kennedy), it becomes clear that the film's crucial emotional connection is between straight father and gay son. It is Thompson's captivating and bravura turn as a well-meaning, benignly intervening patriarch that overwhelms the movie, possibly to the detriment of Crowe's comparatively bland next of kin. Jeff's closing comments encapsulate his narrative prominence as an inoffensively 'normal', blokesy gay guy: 'I'm just gonna be me. Whoever that is.'

A side-genre of Australian cinema that employs a modulating mix of all three nancy, nasty, and normal archetypes is the prison movie. Stephen •Wallace's hard-hitting •Stir (1980) features, within its steadily boiling build-up to an inmates' riot, the tersely low-key seduction of Michael Gow's first-timer, Andrew, by Dennis Miller's seasoned older con ('What's a nice young bloke like you doin' in a nick?'). John •Hillcoat's gruesomely violent •Ghosts … of the Civil Dead (1989) introduces Dave Mason's swaggering cell-block drag queen, Lilly, who comes to a grisly finish but only after we have witnessed the character endure an enforced gang-bang ('I'm next', an off-screen voice announces). Finally, Lawrence Johnston's •Life (1996) sensitively probes the passionate complexities of masculinity from inside the HIV division of a state penitentiary where, among others, we meet Noel Jordan's fast-fading Jimmy being nursed and embraced by Robert Morgan's intensely manic Snakey. Meanwhile, David Tredinnick's vulnerable, rake-thin Ralph asks John Brumpton's newly arrived cellmate, Des, the ultimate question: 'You're not a poofter, are ya? I'm as straight as a die and that's the way it is, right?'.

PETER KEMP

Genre, post-World War II •Mad Max (1979) is a crucial film in the history of the Australian cinema. In the revival of Australian film production in the late 1960s (see Revival, the) there were two main trends. In the early 1970s the 'ocker' films, such as •The Adventures of Barry McKenzie (1972) and •Alvin Purple (1973), were influential until this cycle was replaced in the middle of the decade by period films such as •Picnic at Hanging Rock (1975), Break of Day (1976), and •Caddie (1976). The period film, with its art-cinema conventions, was the antithesis of the popular genre film, although the local and international box-office success of Mad Max had a profound effect on government film policy, notably in the Peat–Marwick and Mitchell Report, in the early 1980s, and provided the impetus for the revival of the genre film in Australia.

Following the introduction of the 10BA tax legislation (see Finance) there were numerous attempts to duplicate the overseas success of Mad Max. This was reinforced by Richard •Franklin's suggestion that internationalism of the local industry and the adaptation of American genres was, given the close cultural relationship between Australia and the USA, the correct route in the 1980s. This advice was actively opposed in some quarters and it was ultimately frustrated by the actions of Actors Equity and the federal government's desire to retain a distinctive Australian flavour. In general terms, the 1980s' output of genre films was disappointing and films such as A Dangerous Summer (1982), Turkey Shoot (1982), Now and Forever (1983), The Return of Captain Invincible (1983), Rebel (1985), The Big Hurt (1986), Sky Pirates (1986), Running from the Guns (1987), and With Time To Kill (1987) failed to locate their thematic and stylistic norms within an Australian context. Consequently, the generic elements appear sterile and devoid of the necessary social context to infuse them with any sense of contemporary relevance or thematic development.

The Australian cinema was not always antithetical to genre film production and many films produced in the sparse period between World War II and the early 1970s were influenced by the narrative and stylistic conventions of melodrama together with popular generic conventions. This was particularly noticeable in •The Phantom Stockman, (1953), •King of the Coral Sea (1954), and Walk into Paradise (1956), a series of films directed by Lee •Robinson and co-produced and written in conjunction with actor Chips •Rafferty. Perhaps the most bizarre example of this trend was the last film produced by the Australian •McCreadie brothers, an American–Australian co-production •The Kangaroo Kid (1950), which imported veteran Hollywood director Lesley Selander together with emerging cowboy star Jock Mahoney, ingenue Martha Hyer, character actors Veda Ann Borg and Douglas Dumbrille, and cinematographer Russell Harlan. These experienced Americans combined with local actors, such as Guy •Doleman and Alec Kellaway, to produce a 72-minute western that utilised many of the elements of the Hollywood series western as found in the films of Johnny Mack Brown, Gene Autry, Roy Rogers, and Tim Holt, and transposed them to an Australian goldfields setting.

The plot in The Kangaroo Kid is regularly interrupted by Australian animals, such as kangaroos and koalas, producing a generic hybrid that is primarily American in dramatic structure with an overlay of distinctively Australian icons. The pattern of transposing popular Hollywood formulas to an 'exotic' Australian setting occurred at regular intervals throughout Australian film history and has continued, sporadically, to the present day with films such as Shadow of the Boomerang (1960), It Takes All Kinds (1969), Color Me Dead (1970, a remake of the Hollywood film noir of 1950, D.O.A), The Lady From Peking (1970), Sidecar Racers (1974), •Quigley (1991), directed by Australian Simon •Wincer and starring Tom Selleck, and •Hurricane Smith (1991) with Carl Weathers. Similarly, Hollywood and British productions in Australia have continued the practice of utilising local facilities and crew for films with American or British actors situated in unspecified or alien settings—such as Harlequin (1980), Fortress (1993), No Escape (1994), and Sniper (1994), which was supposedly set in a Panamanian jungle. In these films there are no significant structural or iconographic changes to the genre so as to make them culturally specific; they could have been filmed anywhere without serious alterations to the script.

Over the past two decades, Australia's favourite aesthetic form has involved a type of 'faithfulness to reality', a form that generally refuses to recognise its generic status and differentiates itself from Hollywood, which has always been interested in refining and developing specific film genres. Instead the Australian cinema has primarily hovered in an odd zone that has been described by Adrian Martin as 'somewhere between naturalistic drama and the "tall tale", a style that's a mutation of the "poetic realism" that surges and falls away throughout international cinema history'. Even in the so-called 'suburban surreal' cycle in the early/mid 1990s, in films such as •Strictly Ballroom (1992), •Muriel's Wedding (1994), •The Adventures of Priscilla, Queen of the Desert (1994), and •Bad Boy Bubby (1994), the deviation from a mode dominated by a desire for 'naturalism' has been mostly at the surface level of setting, performance, and situation—not dramatic structure and certainly not generic innovation.

This is not to suggest that there are no Australian examples of recognisable genres over the past couple of decades. Examples include musicals •Star Struck (1982) and •Strictly Ballroom; (1992); horror and Gothic films: •Patrick (1978) and •Razorback 1984); science fiction: The Chain Reaction (1980), •The Salute of the Jugger (1989), and The Time Guardian (1987); war: Attack Force Z (1982) and •Blood Oath (1990); and variations on the thriller, including some that have utilised 'real-life' stories, (•The Killing of Angel Street, 1981; •Heatwave, 1982; •Hostage: The Christine

Maresch Story, 1983; and **Fortress**, 1986), and others that have reworked American fictional sources, such as •**Dead Calm,** the 1989 Australian version of Charles William's 1963 novel, which was being filmed as **The Deep** by Orson Welles in 1968 although it was abandoned when Laurence Harvey died. Also, two fascinating thrillers have assimilated questions of race within their generic paradigm: •**Deadly** (1992) and •**Dead Heart** (1996). It is this process, whereby specific generic forms are applied to an Australian context, that will occupy the remainder of this essay.

One of the most effective films in this regard is John •Hillcoat's underrated drama •**To Have and To Hold** (1996), which utilises the conventions of a long-established fictional tradition, the Gothic, to examine aspects of European exploitation in Papua New Guinea. This examination is not presented in a literal or documentary manner, but is mediated through the Gothic conventions of such 1940s Hollywood films as **Suspicion, Rebecca, Gaslight,** and **Dragonwyck.** Thus Gothic themes of obsession, entrapment, and victimisation based on power and privilege are revitalised and adapted to a different cultural and historical context.

The inspiration for the film emerged from a trip to Papua New Guinea by Hillcoat some years earlier and his awareness that the excessive nature of some European behaviour could be effectively assimilated into the dramatic basis of films such as **Rebecca** (1941) and **Vertigo** (1958). From this mix, Hillcoat has created a stylised film where meaning emerges less from dialogue and actions and more from the dramatic use of colour, costume (noticeably a red dress), composition, sound, and music (particularly a new arrangement of the Dylan song 'I Threw It All Away'). Each of these elements is obsessively repeated and reworked within a sequence of events that is unrelenting in its sense of fatalism and inevitability.

•**Goodbye Paradise** (1983) is another underrated Australian film. Like **To Have and To Hold**, its dramatic form is rooted in a recognisable generic tradition, in this case the hard-boiled crime fiction popularised by Raymond Chandler in the 1930s and 1940s. **Goodbye Paradise** was initially conceived by scriptwriter Denny •Lawrence and transforms, and updates, Raymond Chandler's Los Angeles of the 1940s to Queensland in the 1970s and 1980s as a way of highlighting the corrupt parallels between the cities. The film, directed by Carl •Shultz and starring Ray •Barrett as the disgraced public official Michael Francis Xavier Stacey OBE, shares Chandler's fascination and disgust with the endemic corruption and false values of big city life. Like many of Chandler's novels, it expresses its contempt for people in positions of power, particularly politicians, doctors, and police, while also subjecting the alternative lifestyles of the gullible inhabitants of the Gold Coast to the same kind of

critical scrutiny. The excellence of the writing by Lawrence and Bob •Ellis stems from its ability to build on the generic conventions while adapting them to a different historical and cultural context. For example, Ray Barrett's opening narration, as he walks along the distinctive Surfers Paradise beach with its high-rise apartments in the background, is both similar to, but also different from, the opening narration in Dick Richard's 1975 film version of Chandler's **Farewell My Lovely**. Ray Barrett, an incongruous figure on the beach in a shabby white suit, embodies the disillusionment and sense of loss that is central to Chandler's writing.

The film's underlying tone resembles the bitter-sweet quality of many of Chandler's stories, particularly *Red Wind* and *The Long Goodbye*. The film follows the structural movement in Chandler's writing as it shifts from an 'outer narrative core', the missing daughter, and the coup attempt, to an inner layer detailing Stacey's personal anxieties and relationships. Only in the final act does **Goodbye Paradise** deviate from the Chandler paradigm. In a characteristically Australian touch, Stacey is rendered dramatically impotent as he wanders in an alcoholic haze through the climactic military battle between the rebels and the Australian army.

This distrust of contemporary Australian values and the consequent longing for a golden past is a recurring characteristic of the Australian cinema. It is evident in other Australian crime films, such as •**The Surfer** (1988), directed by Frank Shields, •**The Custodian** (1994), directed by John •Dingwall and •**The Empty Beach** (1985), directed by Chris Thompson.

•**The Empty Beach** (1985), released three years after **Goodbye Paradise**, was based on the fourth Cliff Hardy novel, written by one of Australia's most successful exponents of the genre, Peter Corris. The film version is weakened by the absence of the first-person narration that performs the function of establishing a bond between the detective and his audience. As Stephen Knight points out, the detective has a public and a private voice. The public voice is expressed via the people he meets and it is aggressive and sometimes unimaginative. The private voice, on the other hand, relates directly to the audience/reader and often conveys the detective's values and sense of humanity. Without this voice-over Cliff Hardy (Bryan •Brown) is reduced to only his public voice, which often consists of smart remarks and pseudo-tough threats.

A more effective Australian crime film, capturing the amorality of contemporary life, is •**Grievous Bodily Harm** (1988), scripted by Warwick Hind and directed by Mark •Joffe. The film begins in a striking manner as schoolteacher Morris Martin (John •Waters) cries while watching a pornographic video of two women and a man. The screen goes black as loud screams are heard on the soundtrack, and a small opening appears on the right-hand corner of the screen as we gradually realise that this is a point-of-view shot from inside a car accident as the rescue workers slowly cut an opening through to a trapped man. The man gives reporter Tom Stewart (Colin •Friels) the money from a robbery to pass on to his girlfriend Susie. Stewart, however, gives Susie only $15 000 out of a total haul of $270 000, and hides the rest of the money in his ex-wife's house. The film shifts to the schoolteacher seen at the opening of the film. Martin's instability is revealed in a classroom confrontation and this is followed by reporter Stewart at a police siege where he is tricked by Sergeant Ray Birch (Bruno •Lawrence) into luring a man to his death.

This carefully scattered exposition at the start of the film raises a number of questions relating to issues that are addressed in the body of the film. Martin is crying because one of the women in the pornographic video is his wife. His discovery that she is still alive triggers a murderous sequence of events that involve both reporter Stewart and policeman Birch. These plot strands coalesce into a satisfying, if amoral, resolution as Stewart retains the $150 000. **Grievous Bodily Harm** reinforces the view expressed in both **Goodbye Paradise** and **The Empty Beach** that redemption in this world is only possible at the personal level. Social redemption or commitment to community values is shown to be foolish and irrelevant.

•**Shame** (1988) is concerned less with personal salvation than with exposing social injustice. The film begins with a leather-clad figure riding down the main street of Ginborak, a remote WA country town. The opening sequence combines the iconography of the Hollywood western, as the stranger rides into a strange town, with the distinctive imagery of the Australian outback. The twist in **Shame** is that the stranger is a woman, Asta Cadell (Deborra-Lee •Furness), and that she performs the saviour role, the usual function of the cowboy in a western. This time, however, the social problem she has to confront concerns one of Australia's most enduring myths—mateship—and the social institutions that support it. The closure of the film indicates that harassment and violence against women, which are presented as a legacy of mateship in Australia, have not been resolved. The final scene consists of a series of strident chords on the soundtrack and a freeze frame of Asta's determined face. Thus Michael Brindley and Beverley Blankenship's script, and Steve •Jodrell's direction, maintain a powerful sense of indignation as the audience is denied the traditional sense of catharsis normally offered in similar generic films. The American version of the film, with Amanda Donohue in the central role, closed on a more optimistic note.

While **Shame** effectively reworks familiar narrative conventions to emphasise its social message, Richard •Franklin's •**Roadgames** (1981) utilises a similar set of con-

ventions in a much more playful way to form a loose kind of homage to Alfred Hitchcock. The 'road games' unfold across the Nullabor Plain as Pat Quid (Stacey Keach) and 'Hitch' (Jamie Lee Curtis) follow a serial killer from Melbourne to Perth. This allows Franklin to demonstrate his mastery of the medium with a clever selection of point-of-view shots and editing devices to maintain suspense throughout the film. However, Australian critics were generally indifferent, or even hostile, and Franklin's exasperation at the treatment of **Roadgames**, and his earlier horror film •**Patrick** (1978), reveals to some extent the problems faced by Australian films that utilise popular/Hollywood generic conventions, a problem that has not disappeared as indicated by the poor audience support for two recent Australian generic films, **To Have and To Hold** and **Dead Heart** (1996), films that deserve as much attention as Australian 'non-generic' successes such as •**Shine** (1996) and •**Children of the Revolution** (1996).   GEOFF MAYER

Genre, pre-World War II

One of the commonest ways to think about a nation's cinema is in terms of the genres that characterise its film production. The western, the musical, and the gangster film are often equated with 'classical Hollywood cinema'; horror and fantasy films with the cinema of Weimar Germany; action films with late twentieth-century Hong Kong. Australia too has had its characteristic genres; and so long as one does not make the mistake of assuming that the true Australian cinema is to be found only in peculiarly Australian genres, a generic understanding of Australian cinema can be a productive one.

From the point of view of a film spectator, the genre of a film is often first discernible in publicity. The earliest Australian-made films were mainly advertised by their titles appearing in a program of films displayed on a poster; consequently those titles tended to act as lures to attract viewers, telling them, 'this is the sort of film you would like to see'. A genre of 'Australian film' that persists to this day was thus established through such titles as •**The Story of the Kelly Gang** (1906), •**Eureka Stockade** (1907), and •**The Squatter's Daughter** (1910), which advertised the Australianness of the film being shown by referring to known Australians, Australian works, or Australian events, and by using the Australian idiom.

The earliest distinct Australian film genre was the bushranger film. It seems likely that Joseph •Perry, whose work with the Salvation Army's Limelight Division continually broke new ground in the early years of the twentieth century, made the first film showing bushrangers in action, **Bushranging in Northern Queensland** (1904). **The Story of the Kelly Gang** added elements of historical specificity and of character to Perry's action. This film was about people and events well within living memory in 1906, and it concentrated on showing actions that viewers would see as displaying the character of the Kellys: their resourcefulness, chivalry, and bravery. These were the elements that John •Gavin exploited in his 1910 film, •Thunderbolt, based on popular accounts of the bushranging career of Frederick Ward, the self-styled Captain Thunderbolt. **Thunderbolt** was the first film of the production 'boom' of 1910–12. In less than seven months, at least nine more films about well-known bushrangers were made—including two remakes of **The Story of the Kelly Gang**—and bushrangers were prominently featured in several others, like Alfred •Rolfe's **The Lady Outlaw** (1911).

The police, and others in authority, regarded the bushranger genre with uneasiness. They felt that the films portrayed criminals sympathetically—and this seems to have been true in the cases of **The Story of the Kelly Gang** and **Thunderbolt**, at least. Spencer's Pictures' **Dan Morgan** (1911), on the other hand, was praised for its unsympathetic depiction of Mad Dog Morgan's violent deeds—too late to hinder a New South Wales ban on screening bushranger films. By cutting out one of the biggest markets for a film, the ban acted as a powerful disincentive to further production in the genre and, until Harry •Southwell's **The Kelly Gang** was released in 1920, no further bushranger features appeared. That film was initially passed by the New South Wales censors, although it was banned two years later, shortly before the release of Southwell's remake, **When the Kellys Were Out** (1922). At least two other films—**Robbery Under Arms** (1920) and **The Gentleman Bushranger** (1921)—also profited from the censors' brief nap in the early 1920s. Bushranger films have been made since that time, the best known of which are probably those by Cecil •Holmes (•**Captain Thunderbolt**, 1953), Tony Richardson (•**Ned Kelly**, 1970, with Mick Jagger), and Philippe •Mora (•**Mad Dog Morgan**, 1976, with Dennis Hopper). But only in the years between 1906 and 1923, and especially from 1906 until 12, did production attain the numbers and the uniformity one would associate with a popular genre (in this case, a respectable 13 per cent of the total).

Bushranging, if not banditry, is an activity specific to Australia; but the complex issues of morality, legality, and identity that the bushranger films negotiated, however indirectly, are likely to have been regularly canvassed in only one other early Australian genre: films about convicts. Prison and escape sometimes figured in bushranger films, but there is a quite separate group of films, beginning with a condensed re-telling of **For the Term of His Natural Life** (1908), which centre on the trials and tribulations of those convicted of crimes, and especially of convicts transported to Australia. The Australian interest in such stories may perhaps be presumed to have its basis in the colonial past, but the convict genre was also a staple of early film production

in other countries such as Britain and France (which, of course, the bushranger genre was not). In Australian convict films the central convict character is most often either innocent or fundamentally good, like Margaret Catchpole in •**The Romantic Story of Margaret Catchpole** (1911), who has only stolen a horse to be with her lover, and the focus of the narrative usually appears to be on enduring or transcending the sufferings of prison rather than on the brutal conditions of incarceration. The films based on the story of John Lee, 'the man they could not hang', two of which survive more or less intact today (•**The Life Story of John Lee**, 1921; •**The Man They Could Not Hang**, 1934), are among the more peculiar, but not riveting, examples of the genre.

One cluster of early films dealt with miners and the goldfields; another with the vicissitudes of establishing one's self on the land; and yet another with horse-racing, often from an owner's point of view. After the outbreak of war in Europe a new set of films was produced that intended to show the heroism of soldiers and civilians on the Allied side. Each of these groups has some claim to being called a 'genre', if only because producers, exhibitors, and customers clearly recognised each as a distinct, if sometimes overlapping, type that employed different, if sometimes overlapping, conventions and attracting different, if sometimes overlapping, audiences. Moreover, all of the genres mentioned so far seem directly connected to Australian culture. In that sense they are all subgenres of 'Australian film', even in instances where certain of the films themselves may not have been set in Australia or be about Australian characters, as is the case with some of those about convicts or war.

Australian film history, taking its cues from Australian literary history, has long recognised the polarities of 'the city' and 'the bush' as a theme of early Australian film. Films of the bush and city have a claim to be considered as genres that are of a somewhat different order from the claims of those genres we have been considering to this point. The city/bush genres have been identified as broad theoretical constructs; where the bushranger and other like genres were, in their time, pragmatic categories for making and selling movies. Within the broad theoretical genre of city/bush films, which would include such titles as •**The Breaking of the Drought** (1920) and •**The Sentimental Bloke** (1919), at least two very Australian 'pragmatic' subgenres can be identified: the 'new chum' film and the 'back-blocks farce'. Neither of these types of film is unknown elsewhere, but it is fair to say that both are more strongly represented in Australian production than they are among the films of other countries.

Cecil B. DeMille's first film, a melodrama called **The Squaw Man** (1913), and the Douglas Fairbanks' action-comedy vehicle, **The Mollycoddle** (1920), are among the

American films dealing with male members of the English aristocracy confronted and changed by the more 'natural' life of the frontier. The plot was not uncommon in late nineteenth- and early twentieth-century Anglophone popular writing and provides the basis for several Australian stories and films in which people of noble birth prove themselves in the outback. The 'new chum' variant made a (mostly) comic formula of this situation, relying on the stock character of a 'silly ass' Englishman whose upper-class affectations are undercut by the vulgar good fellowship of the station. However, by the end of the film, the 'silly ass' almost always comes good, showing himself 'a man' and a mate after all. One way of interpreting this genre's narrative movement of fitting in or reconciliation is to point out that the urban Englishman has to transform himself into something closer to the new land in order to survive. But another, equally valid, sense of what is going on lays emphasis on the aristocrat's adaptability and the narrowness of the outback community to which he has migrated. Beginning with Franklyn •Barrett's **The Life of a Jackaroo** (1913), there were at least 10 'new chum' films, including one by Raymond Longford, two starring Reginald L. (Snowy) •Baker, and no less than five made by Beaumont •Smith (two of which starred Claude Dampier), who made the last pure example, **Splendid Fellows**, in 1934.

Beaumont Smith's **Townies and Hayseeds** (1923) was advertised on a poster that featured a 'new chum' backpacker, captioned 'Made to be laughed at!', and asking 'Any chance of a job on your bally ranch, old top?'. In typical 'new chum' fashion this 'silly ass' is about to burble across the Hayseeds' paddock and into a back-blocks farce. It is no accident that this composite film was compounded by the shrewd and entrepreneurial Smith, who had made the first back-blocks farce film in 1917, and was to produce no less than seven of the 17 made to the present day. Smith's low-budget commercial success depended on an understanding of film as entirely driven by genre production. His job as a producer was to exploit the public's interest in a particular type of film as efficiently as possible and to move to the next viable topic. This is exactly what he did with the Hayseeds, his back-blocks farce family: they appeared in four films from March 1917 to January 1918; in two more films in 1923; and in **The Hayseeds**, their final effort, in December 1933.

For all Smith's ruthless commercial acumen, however, he did not invent the back-blocks farce genre. For that the credit probably belongs to Arthur Hoey Davis, writing as 'Steele Rudd' in *The Bulletin* in the year of the cinema's birth, 1895. Rudd's *On Our Selection* was something of an instant classic, and the stage version by Bert •Bailey and Edmund Duggan, in which Smith may have indeed had a hand, was extremely popular for more than 20 years. Raymond Longford directed the first two Rudd family films, **On Our Selec-**

tion (1920) and Rudd's **New Selection** (1921), which he sought to base on the stories rather than on the stage. The first one was a popular success, but it was only when the •Cinesound company transferred the Bailey–Duggan adaptation to the screen in 1932, including Bailey himself as Dad and Fred MacDonald as Dave, that 'Dad and Dave' attained an iconic status in Australian popular culture.

The principal reason for the success of Cinesound's Dad and Dave series, which extended over four films and eight years, was undoubtedly Bert Bailey, who imbued Dad Rudd's spiteful tyranny and shrill grit with his own boozy thespian charm and, one suspects, had more than a small role in shaping each of the films. 'Dad' is a central character of all of the back-blocks farces, not just the ones based on the Rudd family. He is an ageing patriarch, often beset by the profit-hungry machinations of an unscrupulous ruling class and desperately looking for someone worthy of his inheritance, a complex mixture of narrow-mindedness and generosity, tradition and innovation, oppressive and rebellious impulses. As we watch the films we recognise that his day, like the day of the bushranger, is past, but we want to see his virtues preserved in the culture that is emerging. As Beaumont Smith recognised, the 'new chum' is one possible medium of preservation but, in the later back-blocks farces, the most common inheritor of the pioneer spirit is the eldest unmarried daughter. She, rather than any of the family's inadequate males, is suited to taking Dad's battling Australian stubbornness into a modern—even a postmodern—age.

The back-blocks farce came to an abrupt stop six years after the last 'new chum' film, following the release of •**Dad Rudd, M.P.** in 1940. A well-meaning attempt to revisit **On Our Selection** in 1995 was a box-office failure. However, the broad outlines of both subgenres have continued to generate stories of migrant adaptation (**A Floating Life**, 1996) and of virtuous, if daggy, Aussie battlers (•**No Worries**, 1993; •**Love Serenade**, 1996). In this way traces of the earliest genres of Australian film can be found even in some of our very latest movies.

WILLIAM D. ROUTT

Getting of Wisdom, The

1977. Director: Bruce Beresford. *Producer:* Phillip Adams. *Scriptwriter:* Eleanor Witcombe. Based on the novel by Henry Handel Richardson. *Director of photography:* Don McAlpine. *Music:* Franz Schurmann, Sigismund Thalberg, Arthur Sullivan. 100 mins. *Cast:* Susannah Fowle (Laura), Hilary Ryan (Evelyn), Terence Donovan (Tom Macnamara), Patricia Kennedy (Miss Chapman), Sheila Helpmann (Mrs Gurley).

Like the Henry Handel Richardson novel on which it is based, Bruce •Beresford's film is an essentially episodic narrative of the efforts of its young protagonist, Laura Rambotham (Susannah •Fowle, in her début), to come to terms with a rigid system of education. The aim of the instruction offered to country-bred Laura at her Melbourne college for young ladies at the turn of the century is to instil in her a respect for rote learning, for adherence to the snobbish code of behaviour laid down by teachers and fellow students, and for the ultimate female aim of marriage. Laura rebels against these strictures, causing herself a good deal of anguish along the way. The film turns her into a budding concert pianist instead of, as in the novel, an embryo author and, in some ways, is less tough-minded than its precursor. However, in allowing that Laura's nascent lesbian sexuality may be more than just a passing phase, it is, at least in this matter, more daring than Richardson was able to be.

Beresford's other Australian films (for example, •'Breaker' Morant, 1980, •The Club, 1980, and the 'Barry MacKenzie' films) are typically marked by an anti-authoritarian strain, distrustful of institutions and of the adherence to anachronistic European modes of thinking. Laura has in common with several of his other protagonists a reluctance to conform to received wisdom and, in the end, 'gets' her own instead. The young star was supported by a strong cast of Australian character actors, including John •Waters as a petulant clergyman, Barry •Humphries (in a ripe performance as the bullying headmaster) and Sheila Helpmann (sister of Robert) in her only film role.   BMcF

Susannah Fowle and John Waters in **The Getting of Wisdom**

Ghosts . . . of the Civil Dead

1989. Director: John Hillcoat. *Producer*: Evan English. *Scriptwriters*: Nick Cave, Gene Conkie, Evan English. *Directors of photography*: Paul Goldman, Graham Wood. *Music*: Blixa Bargeld, Nick Cave, Mick Harvey. 93 minutes. *Cast*: David Field (Wenzil), Mike Bishop (David Yale), Chris DeRose (Grezner), Kevin Mackey (Glover), Dave Mason (Lilly), Nick Cave (Maynard).

Highly regarded for its brutal, futuristic portrayal of male incarceration, John •Hillcoat's **Ghosts ... of the Civil Dead** presents an environment where retribution and fortitude are futile. Self-preservation is all that matters. The inmates survive on a regime of drugs, mutilation, sodomy, and sadism. Through voice-over narration provided by various inmates, the notion of survival/damnation is articulated: not only the inmates are sentenced to a life of suffering and 'imprisonment', but prison guards, too, fall victim to the pervasive sense of subversion and futility.

The film, essentially the story of Wenzil's arrival and assimilation at the prison, traces his descent into the subversive world of imprisonment. The prisoners are kept at bay by tyrannical but equally tormented prison guards whose gradual removal of prisoners' privileges results in a barbaric revolt.

On its release, the graphic nature of the film meant that it was not overwhelmingly embraced by audiences. However the vivid, often luminous cinematography, piercing performances, and Hillcoat's chilling commentary have established **Ghosts ... of the Civil Dead** as a landmark film of the prison genre.   KAREN FORD

Giblin, Belinda (1950–) ACTOR   Belinda Giblin became popular in the continuing role of Kay Webster in *The Box*, the mid 1970s' television series about life in and around a television studio, a lounge-room breakthrough in sexual explicitness. She played the role again in the cinema spin-off in 1975, and had several other roles in the early days of the revival (see Revival, the). She co-starred with George Mallaby, her partner in *The Box*, in Tim •Burstall's thriller, **End Play**, in 1976, and had a strong supporting role in •**The Empty Beach** (1985), as the wealthy widow who employs private eye Cliff Hardy to find her missing husband. Her film career has tapered off, but she has also acted on stage and done other television work.
Other Australian films: •Petersen (1974), Say You Want Me (1977), Alison's Birthday (1981).   BMcF

Gibney, Rebecca (1965–) ACTOR   Rebecca Gibney, born in the provincial New Zealand town of Levin, began her acting career with minor roles in New Zealand films, such as **Mr. Wrong** (1985), before appearing in popular Australian television series such as *The Flying Doctors* in the mid 1980s. Lead roles in a number of low-budget Australian films, such as **Jigsaw** (1989) and **Joey** (1997), together with the unrewarding role of Anthony •LaPaglia's fiancée in the sporadically amusing **Lucky Break** (1994), have been overshadowed by Gibney's success in Australian miniseries, including *Kangaroo Palace* in 1997 (Gibney was also executive producer), and television films, such as *I Live With Me Dad* (1985). Gibney's greatest success, however, has been in the title role of the long-running *Halifax* series of tele-features, which began in 1994. GM

Gibson, Mel (1956–) ACTOR Although Australians may think of the charismatic Mel Gibson as the local boy who made good so spectacularly on the international cinema scene, he was in fact born and lived in New York State until his railroad worker father brought his family of eleven children to live in Sydney when Mel was twelve. Gibson trained at the National Institute of Dramatic Art and, on graduation in 1977, he joined the South Australian State Theatre Company. He famously played Romeo in a production of *Romeo and Juliet* at Sydney's Seymour Centre theatre, and made his film début in **Summer City** (1977), a 'road movie' with a pounding rock score. It concerned four assorted mates driving north for a surfing weekend that ends on a sober note. With likeable assurance Gibson plays Scollop, who lives for the surf. The film was modestly popular with the teenage audience at which it was aimed.

It was his chance casting in the title role of •**Mad Max** (1979) that established him as the most watchable star of the new Australian cinema (see Revival, the). He was chosen by director George •Miller to play Max Rockatansky, leader of a special law-enforcement unit, whose job is to subdue the motor-cycle gangs that are terrorising the highways of Australia. When Max's wife and son are killed by the gang, he becomes obsessed—and Gibson became an icon of local and, very soon, of international cinema. He recreated the role of Max in two sequels: •**Mad Max 2** (1981), set in an outback wasteland of the future, and made for a budget nine times that of its precursor, consolidating Gibson's heroic persona; and •**Mad Max Beyond Thunderdome** (1985), in which the character of Max has, despite the still brilliantly orchestrated moments of violence that are so memorable in the first two films, become more reflective, suggestive almost of a tragic dimension. He has become a universalised, symbolic figure of humanity as wandering survivor in a post-apocalyptic world, in which everything is for sale and only the integrity of Max stands between us and the vicious and grasping.

If the **Mad Max** films gave birth to Mel Gibson as a film star, several other appearances scattered between them did no harm to his burgeoning reputation. In Michael •Pate's adaptation of Colleen McCullough's novelette, •**Tim** (1979), Gibson showed some sensitivity as the mentally backward

son of parents worried about his future. He comes to the attention of an attractive forty-ish American businesswoman (Piper Laurie) who, after sighting him at work in her garden with his shirt off, falls in love with him. The film failed to make the melodramatic capital it might have with this material, but it gave Gibson the chance to look like a star even in inadequate material, and he won an Australian Film Institute award for his performance. His potential was confirmed in the 1980 hit, Peter •Weir's •**Gallipoli** (1981). He and Mark •Lee played two contrasting young WA athletes who go to war for different reasons. The film is movingly constructed about their abiding friendship. Good as the boyish Lee was as the more conventional Archie, it was Gibson as the street-wise Frank who dominated the film, and who is alive, a heroic survivor, at the end. He played the lead opposite American star Sigourney Weaver in Weir's next film, •**The Year of Living Dangerously** (1982), an enjoyable political melodrama set in a troubled Indonesia, derived from Christopher Koch's novel. The politics of the novel were considerably simplified in the film, which emphasised the romantic and action elements with some success. Gibson was, by now, a fully fledged star. Since this film and the last of the 'Max' trilogy, he has made no further films in Australia.

He has, however, become one of the busiest and most successful actors anywhere in the world, with major commercial successes in such films as **Lethal Weapon** (1987) and its three sequels (1989, 1992, 1998), as one of a pair of odd-couple cops pitting themselves against drug-traffickers and other low-lifes, the romantic drama, **Forever Young** (1992), and the thriller, **Conspiracy Theory** (1997). His most celebrated triumph has been **Braveheart** (1995), in which he not only played the Scottish hero William Wallace, but also produced and directed, winning the Best Director Oscar for his efforts. As an actor, he belongs in a long tradition of male stars stretching back to the likes of Clark Gable, but he appears to have ambitions that go beyond this status. *Other Australian films*: The Chain Reaction (1980, uncredited), Attack Force Z (1982). BMcF

Gibson, Ross (1956–) PRODUCER/DIRECTOR After working with Super 8 in the early 1980s, a continuing enchantment with ideas, especially with spatial representation, becomes evident in **Camera Natura** (1986); developing Gibson's published historical research (*The Diminishing Paradise*, Sirius Books, 1984) into a thoughtful, exhilarating exploration of European representations of the land in Australia. Beginning with early colonial imaginary appropriations of landscape, the film eschews conventional documentary form in favour of a more essayist style, mixing a number of modes including reconstructions and archival footage drawn from Australian cinema's obsessive search for identity through landscape.

Mel Gibson

The shamefully neglected **Wild** (1993) invokes a filmic reconciliation with the Australian landscape for non-indigenous cultures. Incorporating both archival footage (•**The Back of Beyond**, 1954) and home movies, the film uses propositional and poetic rhetorical modes weaving together a range of 'voices'. **Wild** received a Golden Gate Award at the 1994 San Francisco International Film Festival.

Also eluding recognition was the much more difficult fiction feature **Dead To The World** (1990), which was set in a postmodern urban landscape of the mind. It failed to achieve a theatrical release, challenging realist conventions of contemporary Australian narrative cinema: the setting is deliberately cartoon-like; acting, dialogue, and narrative structure are mannered; and the soundtrack is completely post-sync, creating a distancing effect at odds with audience and critical expectations.

The Bond Store (1995), continuing the analysis of spatial representation, signals a move into a multimedia spatio-narrative environment in an installation for the Museum of Sydney.   PETER HUGHES

Gillies, Max (1941–) ACTOR   To say that Melbourne High School-educated performer Max Gillies has never really found an appropriate niche in the Australian film industry is an understatement. Gillies has been associated with the industry since its revival in the early 1970s (see Revival, the). His most productive period was in the early years with featured roles in films such as •**Stork**(1971), •**Libido** (1973), **Dalmas** (1973), •**The Cars that Ate Paris** (1974), **The Great MacArthy** (1975), and •**Pure S** (1975). In 1975 Gillies had the lead role as Dead Eye Dick in Richard •Franklin's ill-fated comedy **The True Story of Eskimo Nell,** an adaptation of the bawdy ballad. Another major disappointment was the screen adaptation of Jack Hibberd's popular audience-participation play •**Dimboola** (1979), which was co-produced by Gillies (he also had a major role as the eccentric British journalist Vivian Worcester-Jones). Gillies' main claim to fame is his series of television programs in the 1980s (*The Gillies Report, The Gillies Republic,* and *The Dingo Principle*) in which he cleverly satirised well-known Australian political figures. Theatre and television seem to provide greater opportunity for Gillies' anarchic comedy style. More recently he appeared in Paul •Cox's satire on the Australian arts establishment, **Lust and Revenge** (1996).

Other Australian films: The Firm Man (1975), The Trespassers (1976), The Coca-Cola Kid (1985), As Time Goes By (1988), •A Woman's Tale (1991).   GM

Gilling, Rebecca (1953–) ACTOR   Rebecca Gilling's first film roles were as the beautiful but evil air hostess Diana in the 1974 film adaptation of the television series, •**Number 96**, and a featured role as the bikie moll in •**Stone** (1974). She then played Angelica in •**The Man from Hong Kong** (1975). Over the next few years she made her name in television, culminating in the starring role in the serial *Return to Eden* (1982, and a sequel 1985). Her first starring film role was in a similarly complex melodrama, as the troubled wife of the station owner in Tim •Burstall's •**The Naked Country** (1985). She appeared in several telemovies and television series before, in 1988, playing Johnny Dysart's wife Annie in Pino Amenta's •**Heaven Tonight**. In the 1990s she was best known as co-host of Channel 9's lifestyle program *Our House*.   IB

Rebecca Gilling

Gillmer, Caroline ACTOR   Caroline Gillmer may well be better known for her work on stage or television: she was in series such as the hugely popular *Prisoner* and *Neighbours*, and the acclaimed *Brides of Christ*. However, she has given at least one very impressive screen performance to date. This was as Hilary, the sister who has stayed at home, in Richard •Franklin's eloquent conversation piece, •**Hotel Sorrento** (1995). Concealing her own dissatisfactions under the daily demands of affection, she manages a household of tensions when her two sisters return on the occasion of their father's death. Gillmer's warmth and understanding gave the film its centre. She was a sympathetic teacher in **Fighting Back** (1982), had a small part in •**An Indecent Obsession** (1985), and played Susie in the United Kingdom–Australian co-production **Paws** (1997), a family-oriented adventure. She is an actor with generous reserves of compassion and perception who ought to be more widely used in films.   BMcF

Gilmour, Ian (1955–) ACTOR Looking younger than his actual age of 22 or 23, Ian Gilmour made his début—and a substantial impression—as the naive country boy who comes to the big city in •**Mouth to Mouth** (1978), John •Duigan's compassionate study of dispossessed youth living at the squalid metropolitan edges. Gilmour played with such persuasive and transparent sympathy that it came almost as a shock to see him in such disparate roles as one of the bored soldiers in Vietnam in Tom •Jeffrey's •**The Odd Angry Shot** (1979) and the surly country-town barman in Sophia Turkiewicz's •**Silver City** (1984), who wears his xenophobia on his sleeve. His other film roles have been comparatively small; for example, in Duigan's nuclear warning, **One Night Stand** (1984), Quentin Masters' **Dangerous Summer** (1982), during the shooting of which he broke his leg, as a spy called Marjorie in **The Coca-Cola Kid** (1985), and Fred •Schepisi's •**Evil Angels** (1988), the retelling of the Lindy Chamberlain trial. He has moved into television directing in the 1990s, in such series as *Snowy* and *Heartbreak High*, seeming for the moment to have left acting behind.

Other Australian films: •The Chant of Jimmie Blacksmith (1978), Just Out of Reach (1979), **Going Down** (1983), **The Boy Who Had Everything** (1984), Malpractice (1989).   BMcF

Ginger Mick

1920. *Director*: Raymond Longford. *Production company*: Southern Cross Feature Film Company. *Scriptwriter*: Lottie Lyell [?], Raymond Longford. Based on the verse narrative, *The Moods of Ginger Mick*, by C.J. Dennis. *Director of photography*: Arthur Higgins. 5500 ft. B&W. *Cast*: Gilbert Emery (Ginger Mick), Arthur Tauchert (the Bloke), Lottie Lyell (Doreen), Jack Tauchert (Bill), Queenie Cross (Rose), George Hartspur (Keith).

This sequel to •**The Sentimental Bloke** (1919) used the same cast and took up the story a few years later. Bill and Doreen continue to live happily on the farm, where their baby has grown into young Bill. But Ginger Mick's life in the city is still one of hard drinking and occasional run-ins with the police, until he meets Rose, marries, and joins the army. His experiences at the front are retold in letters to Bill, including his growing friendship with Keith, until Mick is killed in action. The film ends with Bill's tribute to his mate. Although none of the film survives, contemporary reports praised its understated tone (despite over-use of Dennis's verse in the intertitles), and the film was very successful, both in Australia and in the United Kingdom.   IB

Ginnane, Antony I. (1949–) PRODUCER A former lawyer and film distributor, Antony Ginnane produced films that are characterised by their adherence to generic story-lines and, for a period, imported American or British leads. These characteristics are not, however, evident in Ginnanne's first film, **Sympathy in Summer**, which he wrote, directed (on 16 mm), and produced in 1971 when he was a law student. This ambitious film, clearly influenced by the French New Wave, had little in common with his next production, the commercially successful soft-core sex film, •**Fantasm** (1976), which included footage shot in America by Richard •Franklin utilising professional porn actors. Ginnane followed this with **Blue Fire Lady** (1977), a film that targeted family audiences with its story of a country girl and her horse, and then a return to the sex film with **Fantasm Comes Again** (1977). Ginnane next co-produced (with director Richard •Franklin) one of his better films, the horror thriller •**Patrick** (1978). This preceded a dominant pattern in Ginnane's filmography of low-budget thrillers with fading or minor overseas stars. Often unreleased theatrically and going straight to video, these included **Harlequin** (1980) with Robert Powell and ageing Academy Award winner Broderick Crawford; and **The Survivor** (1981), directed by British actor-director David Hemmings, and starring Robert Powell, Jenny Agutter, and Joseph Cotton.

In the early 1980s Ginnane produced a series of similar films in New Zealand, such as the Hemmings-directed **Race For the Yankee Zephyr** (1981), with Ken Wahl, Lesley Ann Warren, George Peppard, and Donald Pleasance, **Prisoners** (1983), with Tatum O'Neal and Hemmings, and **Mesmerized** (1984), with Jodie Foster, John Lithgow, and Harry Andrews. In the late 1980s Ginnane was involved in a number of more prestigious Australian films, such as Gillian •Armstrong's •**Hightide** (1987) and Simon •Wincer's •**The Lighthorsemen** (1987), together with the underrated •**Grievous Bodily Harm** (1988), •**The Everlasting Secret Family** (1988), and •**Minnamurra** (1989).

Other Australian films include: Snapshot (1979), Thirst (1979), **Turkey Shoot** (1982), **Second Time Lucky** (1984), **The Time Guardian** (1987), **Slate, Wyn & Me** (1987), Initiation (1987), **Dark Age** (1987), The Dreaming (1988), The Seige of Firebase Gloria (1988), •Mull (1989), Incident at Raven's Gate (1989), Demonstone (1990), Fatal Sky (1990).   GM

Girl of the Bush, A

1921. *Director, Producer, Scriptwriter, Director of photography*: Franklyn Barrett. B&W. *Cast*: Vera James (Lorna Denver), Jack Martin (Tom Wilson).

Franklyn Barrett's reputation as an *auteur* of Australian authenticity rests on **A Girl of the Bush** and •**The Breaking of the Drought**, the only films of his to have been more or less fully preserved. **A Girl of the Bush** is the more unassuming of the two. In it, Lorna Denver battles to keep Kangaroo Flat out of the hands of villains, and her charitable act of caring for an abandoned baby is misinterpreted as biological motherhood by Tom, who loves her from afar (too far to ask anyone what is going on, it would seem). Matters are put right in the nick of time, and Lorna, if not the viewer, again demonstrates boundless charity by forgiving Tom's bigoted prurience. Barrett's vignettes of everyday life on the station and in the city nicely 'Australianise' this story about not seeing things clearly. Unfortunately, the film also betrays its promise in several, equally typical, sequences in which Chinese people are crudely caricatured.

WILLIAM D. ROUTT

Gone to the Dogs

1939. Director: Ken G. Hall. *Producer:* Ken G. Hall. *Scriptwriters:* George Wallace, Frank Harvey, Frank Coffey. *Director of photography:* George Heath. *Music:* Henry Krips. 83 mins. B&W. *Cast:* George Wallace (George), Lois Green (Jean MacAllister), John Dobbie (Henry Applegate), John Fleeting (Jimmy Alderson), Ronald Whelan (Willard).

George and Henry board at the greyhound kennels and work at the zoo until they are sacked for causing chaos, but not before George has produced a magical substance that gives dogs incredible energy. Jimmy the vet works hard to discover the formula, so that Black Beauty can win, while George and Henry foil the plot to switch dogs before the race. This was George •Wallace's last starring film role and features his regular partner John Dobbie. It is a typical Wallace vehicle, providing opportunity for a dance routine to the tune of the catchy theme song and plenty of slapstick, including sequences in a gorilla cage and in a haunted house. But it is a fragmented film—not quite melodrama, nor thriller, nor slapstick comedy, nor romance, and certainly not a musical, although it has elements of all of these.

IB

Good Woman of Bangkok, The

1992. Producer, Scriptwriter, Director, Director of photography: Dennis O'Rourke in association with the Australian Film Commission and Channel 4. 82 minutes. *Cast:* Yaowalak Chonchanakun (Aoi).

Theatrical releases from the USA to India have made this feature one of the most successful Australian documentaries in terms of box-office income, and it is certainly one of the most controversial. For many, Dennis •O'Rourke's use of a $100 000 award from the •Australian Film Commission to fund and film a liaison with a Thai sex worker called Aoi was beyond the pale. For others, breaking down the pretence of objectivity in documentary and simultaneously

indicting himself and western men in general was both cutting-edge film-making and an act of bravery. Contrary to many expectations, there is little, if any, material that could be considered salacious. And, although O'Rourke's presence is felt throughout, he is almost never on screen. Instead, the focus is firmly on Aoi and her story, albeit filtered through O'Rourke's lens. Whatever one's reaction to it, **The Good Woman of Bangkok** seems a logical leap in O'Rourke's career. Having made a name for himself by filming the legacy of colonial power imbalances in the Asia–Pacific region, it is only fitting that he should finally include himself within the framework of his interrogation.

CHRIS BERRY

Goodall, Caroline (1959–) ACTOR

Most of Caroline Goodall's film career has been conducted abroad, but three Australian films have showcased her slender beauty and sensitivity. They are Carl •Schultz's **Cassidy** (1989), in which she co-starred with Ivar •Kants and Peter Carroll; John Tatoulis's charming children's film, **The Silver Brumby** (1993), in which she played Elyne Mitchell, author of the novel on which the film is based and mother of the child to whom the film story is told; and, most memorably, the London-based daughter who flies home when her father dies in Richard •Franklin's •**Hotel Sorrento** (1995). In this, Goodall, Caroline •Gillmer and Tara •Morice provide a notable ensemble as they pick their ways through old conflicts towards a new understanding. In the USA, Goodall has appeared in such high-profile films as **Hook** (1991) and **Schindler's List** (1993), both for Steven Spielberg, and she starred with Jeff Bridges in Ridley Scott's shipwreck adventure, **White Squall** (1996).

BMcF

Goodbye Paradise

1983. Director: Carl Shultz. *Producer:* Jane Scott. *Scriptwriters:* Bob Ellis, Denny Lawrence. *Director of photography:* John Seale. *Music:* Peter Best. 119 minutes. *Cast:* Ray Barrett (Michael Stacey), Robyn Nevin (Kate), Don Pascoe (Les McCredie), Kris McQuade (Hooker), Paul Chubb (Curly), Guy Doleman (Quiney), Lex Marinos (Con).

This successful transformation of the Raymond Chandler school of American hard-boiled detective fiction to Surfers Paradise in Queensland was conceived by scriptwriter Denny •Lawrence and was filmed in 1981 on location for a budget of A$1.1 million. The plot concerns disgraced public official Michael Stacey's search for an ex-colleague's missing daughter. In true Chandler style, the search leads the viewer through the superficial excesses of a decadent society.

Ray •Barrett gives his finest performance as Stacey, the disillusioned alcoholic who stumbles on an army coup led by a long-time friend. Just as Chandler's Philip Marlowe is

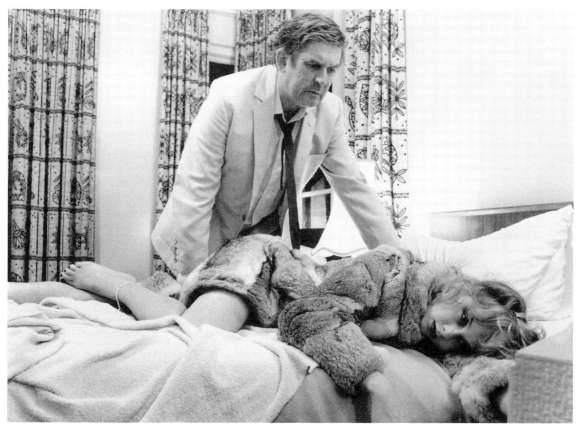

Ray Barrett and Janet Scrivener in **Goodbye Paradise**

the moral centre in a corrupt world, Stacey represents an updated perception of Marlowe's knight whose ethical and social values are shown to be distinctly old-fashioned in a rapidly changing society.

The outstanding virtue of the film resides in the quality of the writing, much of it conveyed through Barrett's wistful voice-over. The only disappointment is the ending where Stacey wanders through a military battle in an alcoholic haze after entering the conflict in a large tourist bus with the words 'Midnight Cowboy' written across the side. This shift into an absurdist mode, reminiscent of Robert Altman's **The Long Goodbye** (1973), is redeemed by the dignity of the epilogue as Stacey comes to terms with his place in the world.   GM

Gore, Sandy (1951–) ACTOR Sandy (Sandra) Gore graduated from the National Institute of Dramatic Art in 1966 and began her screen career in the quickie **That Lady from Peking** (1970), but her big breakthrough was as Kay White in the television series *Prisoner* (1978). After that, her red hair and wide smile became a familiar sight in many films, but usually in supporting or smaller roles, such as in

•'Norman Loves Rose' (1982), •**Moving Out** (1983), **I Can't Get Started** (1985), •**Evil Angels** (1988), and •**Grievous Bodily Harm** (1988). Her distinctive and faultless articulation makes her an ideal narrator in **The ABC of Love & Sex** (1978), and the voice of numerous television commercials. She had a substantial role as the music teacher who helps to turn the hero's life around in **Street Hero** (1984), and was particularly memorable as the corset designer who lives life 'brilliantly' in **Undercover** (1984). It was not her fault that the unfunny **Luigi's Ladies** (1989) is best forgotten, but she was better suited to the bohemian Aunt Maude in •**Minamurra** (1989). After that, she appeared mainly on television, her most impressive performance being Mother Ambrose in the miniseries *Brides of Christ* (1991). She returned to film in **Lorenzo's Oil** (1992), and as the dastardly Anja in the children's film **Paws** (1997).   IB

Grandad Rudd

1935. Director: Ken G. Hall. *Producers:* Bert Bailey, Ken G. Hall. *Scriptwriters:* Victor Roberts, George D. Parker. *Based on the play by Bert Bailey, adapted from the stories by Steele Rudd. Directors*

of photography: Frank Hurley, George Heath. 90 mins. B&W. *Cast*: Bert Bailey (Grandad Rudd), Fred MacDonald (Dave), George Lloyd (Dan), William McGowan (Joe), Kathleen Hamilton (Madge).

Of the four films based on the Rudd family directed by Ken G. •Hall, **Grandad Rudd** was the least successful. It represents the beginning of the transformation from the episodic celebration of rural values in •**On Our Selection** to a more classical narrative characterised by a linear structure with causal linkages between each narrative sequence that was evident in •**Dad and Dave Come To Town** (1938) and •**Dad Rudd, M.P.** (1940). **Grandad Rudd** was the second in the series and it suffered from changes to Dad's character from the 1932 film as Dad is transformed into a penny-pinching tyrant who alienates most of his family with his parsimonious behaviour. The central plot is based on Dad's determination to prevent his grand-daughter Betty's marriage to Henry Cook, a local businessman with a dubious reputation. Interspersed, there are comic interludes involving the usual broad farce favoured by Hall and his scriptwriters—such as the bizarre cricket match where there is no limit on the number of runs scored per ball that Dad exploits when the cricket ball disappears down a well and he is able to win the match with a 30-run hit. Similarly, a runaway tractor and Dad's drunken disturbance of a temperance meeting is consistent with the style of humour that characterised the four films in the 1930s and ensured their popularity in Australia and New Zealand.

GM

Grant, Jaems (1952–) CINEMATOGRAPHER Jaems Grant studied photography at Prahran College and film at Preston College before freelancing as a director of photography on television dramas, series, miniseries, docu-dramas, and documentaries, including the Peter Watkins feature-length documentary, **Resan**. A tele-feature, *The Last Of The Ryans*, won Grant a Victorian Australian Cinematographers Society (ACS) Gold and federal ACS Distinction award, and a short drama, **Only the Brave**, also won a Victorian ACS Gold award. He has won five Victorian ACS Silver awards, three Highly Commended and three Merit awards for other films. His first feature film was **To Market, To Market** (1987), followed by John •Hughes' •**Traps** (1986).
Other feature films: Hungry Heart (1987), Blowing Hot And Cold (1990), Jigsaw (1989), Kink in the Picasso (1990), •**Head On** (1998).

DAVID MUIR

Greater Union Organisation (GUO) Known as GUO, this company is one of the largest in the film trade, with a history going back to the amalgamation, over the period 1911–13, of several production, distribution, and exhibition companies into Australasian Films/Union Theatres, generally known as 'the Combine'. In 1921, its three managing directors were W.A. Gibson (also general manager of Australasian Films), Stuart Doyle (also general manager of Union Theatres), and Edwin Geach (also a Director of West's Pictures). Australasian Films was primarily a distribution company, with buyers in the major foreign film-supply capitals (including London and New York), competing with local branches of the large American distributors, as well as expanding into Asia.

Union Theatres managed the cinemas of the four holding companies, and their chain was expanded further by partnerships and mergers: for instance, with the Birch, Carroll, and Coyle circuit in Queensland in 1928. In October 1931, falling attendances convinced the controlling shareholder (the English, Scottish and Australian Bank) to force the liquidation of Union Theatres. Doyle formed a new company, Greater Union Theatres Ltd, and purchased the assets of Union Theatres for a sum equivalent to the overdraft: the new company divested itself of Australasian Films, established •Cinesound as a production subsidiary, and diversified into radio, newspapers, and importing. But the building and management of •cinemas continued to be a major focus and, in this field, it competed fiercely with •Hoyts throughout the 1920s and 1930s. As the Depression continued into the 1930s, both companies were overstretched, and the banks once again intervened, this time to force Hoyts and Greater Union Theatres into a merger as the General Film Corporation.

In 1937 Norman •Rydge took over as managing director of Greater Union Theatres, and immediately separated the company from the General Film Corporation. During World War II, the box office boomed and, in 1945, a half share in the company was purchased by the British Rank Organisation. At this time, the company showed little interest in film production, rejecting a co-production deal with Ealing in 1948 and burning its fingers with •**Sons of Matthew** (1949). After the 1973 Tariff Board Report (see •Exhibition and Distribution) criticised the exhibition giants for their lack of support of local production, Greater Union Theatres—along with Hoyts, the third national cinema chain •Village Theatres, and •Hexagon Productions—participated in the revival of Australian feature production by investing in several films, of which the most successful was •**My Brilliant Career** (1979): others were •**The Man from Hong Kong** (1975), **Oz** (1976), **Break of Day** (1976), •**Summerfield** (1977), •**The Mango Tree** (1977), **Touch and Go** (1980), and **Duet for Four** (1982).

In 1958, the four holding companies in the Greater Union Theatres group were merged into Amalgamated Holdings Ltd, with the Rydge family as the major Australian shareholders. By the 1960s, Greater Union Theatres (renamed the Greater Union Organisation in 1965, in recognition of its diverse activities) had purchased an interest in the WA Ace Group and in Village Theatres. Norman Rydge remained chairman until 1970, although he had by then been replaced by other managing directors (Keith Moremon in 1965, David Williams in 1975, and Alan Rydge in 1980). In 1984 Amalgamated Holdings bought out Rank and GUO became once again fully Australian-owned.

In 1987, Greater Union Film Distributors merged with Village Roadshow Distributors to form the distribution company Roadshow Film Distributors which, in the 1990s, was the only one of the three major distribution companies to be part Australian-owned. By then, GUO had major interests in the hospitality industry as well as in films. The company benefited from the revival in cinema attendance, expanding its chain, often in partnership with other companies: for instance, a Village Roadshow–Greater Union–Warner Bros joint venture, announced in 1995, built the Movie World theme park in Surfers Paradise and multiplexes in the major urban centres. By 1997, the success of these ventures was such that the company's activities were the subject of monopoly complaints, and the then-managing director Robert Manson estimated that by the year 2000, 20 to 30 per cent of the company's revenue would be derived from international operations.   IB

Green, Cliff (1934–) WRITER A prolific scriptwriter and occasional novelist and playwright, Cliff Green worked as a print compositor then retrained as a primary teacher, his experiences in country schools influencing much of his early work. After writing ABC children's dramas and industrial films for the •Commonwealth Film Unit, he joined Crawford Productions as a staff writer on *Homicide* (1969–70) and *Matlock Police* (1970–71). His ABC television 'play cycle' *Marion* (1973) gained attention in Melbourne Pram Factory circles and led David •Williamson to suggest him for Peter •Weir's next film. Scant critical attention has been paid to his adaptation of •Picnic at Hanging Rock (1975) alongside Weir's realisation, possibly because Joan Lindsay's 1967 novel was regarded as 'lightweight' in literary circles, Weir's evocation of mood and symbolism being considered the film's strongest elements. His work as senior writer on the ABC 26-part miniseries of Frank Hardy's *Power Without Glory* (1975–76) galvanised his reputation as a solid writer of screen adaptations. Green's two original theatrical features, **Break of Day** (1976) and •Summerfield (1977), were damned with faint praise when Australian 'nostalgia' pieces were becoming increasingly unfashionable. His ability to turn his hand to grittier material is evidenced most strongly in his television work, including the ABC crime series *Phoenix* (1991), *Janus* (1994) and, to a lesser extent, in his own television creation, the newspaper series *Mercury* (1995–96).   HARRY KIRCHNER

Greenhide

1926. *Director, Scriptwriter*: Charles Chauvel. *Director of photography*: Al Burne. B&W. *Cast*: Elsie Sylvaney [Elsa Chauvel] (Margery Paton), Bruce Gordon (Greenhide Gavin).

The footage that survives from **Greenhide**, Charles •Chauvel's second feature, repeats the powerful figure, first set in play in the film-maker's •The Moth of Moonbi, of a woman's journey into a land characterised by masculinity. As in the earlier film, the journey is ultimately quite harrowing. At first, however, Margery Paton's desire to experience the outback seems a frivolous whim and the film itself reflects that frivolity in scenes intended to be comic or titillating. It is only as the film progresses that the males in the story begin to realise the strength of character that has driven Margery to such a 'whim'. In the end it is not so much that Margery has been 'broken' by the land's violence into some kind of shape fit for a domestic bush existence, as it is that there has been a recognition of consanguinity, paralleling the lover's recognition between Margery and Greenhide, the man who incarnates the best of the land in this film. Margery belongs in the outback: its violence and passion are what she was born to know.   WILLIAM D. ROUTT

Gregg, John (1940–) ACTOR Specialising in shifty politicians, lawyers, and businessmen, stage-trained actor John Gregg has appeared as a character actor in Australian films and television programs since the late 1970s. This pattern extends through films such as •Heatwave (1982) to •Deadly (1992), and Ebbtide (1993).

Other Australian films include: Crime of the Decade (1984), •Travelling North (1987), Two Brothers Running (1988), Trouble in Paradise (1989).   GM

Grendel Grendel Grendel

1981. *Director*: Alexander Stitt. *Producer*: Phillip Adams, Alexander Stitt. *Scriptwriter*: Alexander Stitt. Based on the novel *Grendel* by John Gardner. *Director of photography*: John Pollard. *Music*: Bruce Smeaton. 88 mins. *Voices*: Peter Ustinov, Keith Michell, Arthur Dignam, Ed Rosser, Bobby Bright.

Australia's most unusual animated feature, **Grendel Grendel Grendel** takes as its basis John Gardner's retelling of the *Beowulf* legend from the monster Grendel's point of view. Set in mythic Anglo-Saxon prehistory, Grendel is a normal, well-intentioned swamp monster, none too bright but with a loving and protective (single-parent) mother. Crude, unmannerly Viking humans led by the vainglorious King Hrothgar invade their land and behave unacceptably. Nothing for it but to eat a few, reckons Grendel, as a sort of subtle hint. Back in his mead-hall, King Hrothgar misunderstands the gesture and sends his best monster-slayer, Beowulf, to kill Grendel. The first climactic epic battle in English literature ensues. This simple story is fleshed out with many characters and subplots, with comic observation of human (and monster) shortcomings, told in an extremely literate script. The most immediately striking aspect of the film is its audacious, decidedly un-Disney graphic design and colour scheme.   RICK THOMPSON

Gribble, David (1946–) CINEMATOGRAPHER After studying photography at Brisbane Technical College, David Gribble worked as a camera assistant at Supreme Studios, Sydney. His first feature as director of photography was **Private Collection** (1972), but it was Mike •Thornhill's •**FJ Holden** (1977) that attracted attention for its naturalistic lighting. His first overseas feature was **Off Limits** (USA, 1988), which led to other American films, including Gillian •Armstrong's **Fires Within** (USA, 1991). Other films: **Out of It** (1977), **The Best of Friends** (1981), •**Monkey Grip** (1982), **Running on Empty** (1982), •**Fast Talking** (1984), **Tap** (USA, 1989), **Cadillac Man** (USA, 1990), **Nowhere to Run** (USA, 1993), **The Quest** (USA, 1996).   DAVID MUIR

Grievous Bodily Harm

1988. *Director:* Mark Joffe. *Producer:* Richard Brennan. *Scriptwriter:* Warwick Hind. *Director of photography:* Ellery Ryan. *Music:* Chris Neal. 96 minutes. *Cast:* Colin Friels (Tom Stewart), John Waters (Morris Martin), Bruno Lawrence (Ray Birch), Shane Briant (Stephen Enderby), Joy Bell (Claudine).

Australia has a sad history of second-rate crime thrillers over the past 20 or so years, particularly during the •10BA period. Not so with **Grievous Bodily Harm,** a superb, if somewhat convoluted, thriller. Scripted by Warwick Hind and directed by Mark •Joffe, the film presents a series of seemingly discrete narrative strands—beginning with teacher Morris Martin crying while watching a pornographic video followed by a seemingly unrelated car accident—that only completely come together in the film's final image of a newspaper report.

Martin is a schoolteacher who commits a series of murders while obsessively pursuing his supposedly dead lover, Claudine. Meanwhile, reporter Tom Stewart, who steals stolen money from the car wreck shown at the start of the film, and ruthless cop Ray Birch, become involved in Martin's killing spree. The climax takes place in the Blue Mountains as Martin and Stewart close in on the not-so-defenseless Claudine. This film is an Australian rarity—a tough, intelligent thriller that adds a strong dose of irony to its hard-boiled view of the world.   GM

Griffiths, Rachel (1967–) ACTOR Rachel Griffiths received a deal of exposure on Australian television during the gala opening of Melbourne's Crown casino in 1996

Colin Friels in **Grievous Bodily Harm**

when she appeared topless as a protest against the Kennett Government's laissez-faire gambling policies. Prior to this Griffiths had made an impressive impact with a scene-stealing performance as Toni •Collette's free-spirited friend in •**Muriel's Wedding** (1994). This was followed by an outstanding performance in her first leading role in John •Hillcoat's underrated Gothic drama •**To Have and To Hold** (1996), in which the romantic Kate is lured up the Sepik River in PNG by Tcheky Karyo. Since then, Griffiths has appeared in a number of featured roles in Australian and overseas productions—a showy part as a leather-clad police officer in •**Children of the Revolution** (1996) preceded Michael Winterbottom's British production of **Jude** (1996), and P.J. •Hogan's Hollywood-produced romantic comedy **My Best Friend's Wedding** (1997). In a relatively short period, Rachel Griffiths has demonstrated that she is one of Australia's most versatile actors. She was nominated for an Academy Award for her role in **Hilary and Jackie** (1998).

Other Australian films: •**Cosi** (1996), **Amy** (1998), **Welcome to Woop Woop** (1997).   GM

Rachel Griffiths

Gross, Yoram (1926–) ANIMATOR/WRITER/DIRECTOR/
PRODUCER Yoram Gross has been the mainstay of Australian theatrical feature animation since 1977, when he
founded the animation studio that has provided the central
continuity for animated feature films and television series
in Australia. Born in Krakow, Poland, he studied music at
the University of Krakow, then film at the newly founded
Polish Film Institute. In 1950 he emigrated to Israel where
he made his first animated films in 1958: **Chansons Sans
Paroles** and **We Shall Never Die.** He made Israel's first feature film, the puppet animation **Ba'al Hahalomot (Joseph
the Dreamer,** 1962). The live-action slapstick comedy **Rak
Ba'Lira (A Pound Apiece,** 1963) was a commercial success.

In 1968, he emigrated to Sydney, where he made short
films (**To Nefertiti,** 1971) documentaries (**The Politicians,**
1970), commercials, proto-music videos for *Bandstand*, and
titles and graphics for films such as •**27A** (1974). In 1975, he
published *The First Animated Step,* an introduction to animation, along with a demonstration film of the same name.
His return to feature animation, •**Dot and the Kangaroo**
(1977), was carefully planned to succeed in both the domestic and the export children's film market, and to fit the
dominant Disney-feature animation format. **Dot** initiated
Gross's continuing technique of mixing live-action footage
of actors, landscapes, and animals with animated characters
in the same frame; his commitment to Australian subjects;
his facility with music and song; and his preference for stories with sentiment and messages. The film's international
success enabled him to found and maintain the Gross Film
Studios in Sydney, which has employed as many as 70 animators. Sequels have been a staple of the studio: **Around
the World with Dot** (1982), **Dot and the Bunny** (1984); **Dot
and the Koala** (1985); **Dot and the Whale** (1986); **Dot and
Keeto** (1986); **Dot Goes to Hollywood (Dot in Concert,**
1987); **Dot and the Smugglers (Dot and the Bunyip,** 1987).
In 1986, Gross began selling films to the American Disney
cable television channel. Similarly, his 1992 feature •**Blinky
Bill (Blinky Bill: The Mischievous Koala)** spun off a television series that sold to 80 countries in 1994 and, later,
became an interactive CD-ROM.

The Little Convict (1979) dramatises early European
settlement of Australia and clearly shows the Gross blend of
entertainment and didactic elements in the story of two
young convicts transported to work on a grim government
labour farm; the narrator (Rolf Harris) interrupts the animated story to comment and lead singalongs. Set in Europe,
Sarah (1980), with Mia Farrow in a live-action part, draws
on Gross's experiences as a child in World War II. **The
Camel Boy** (1984) returns to Australian subject matter: the
role of camels in outback exploration. **Epic** (1985) is a

strongly mythic story of baby twins orphaned and then raised by dingoes. In 1991, Gross made his first fully animated feature, **The Magic Riddle**, a journey through the world of fairy tales. It is a point of pride that his films are traditional, full animation, never computer animation.

In 1981, he adapted his novel *Save The Lady* into the script for the strictly live-action film of the same name, directed by Leon Thau. His awards are numerous.

RICK THOMPSON

Grubb, Robert (1950–) ACTOR The theatre and television have offered this Tasmanian-born National Institute of Dramatic Art graduate (1979) and former electrician more varied and demanding chances than the cinema has. He was placed under contract to the State Theatre Company of South Australia in the late 1970s after scoring an impressive success as a character actor in •**My Brilliant Career** (1979). In this he played Frank Hawden, the English jackeroo who pompously pays his addresses to Sybylla (Judy Davis) and has them unceremoniously rejected. He showed real comic flair in this sketch of affronted self-importance. In •**Gallipoli** (1981) he was one of the ensemble of Aussie mates who make their way from Perth to Cairo and then to battle; he had substantial but not very memorable roles in •**Phar Lap** (1983) and as Inspector Sir Frederick Moringer in •**Robbery Under Arms** (1985), and a showier opportunity as the Pig Killer in •**Mad Max Beyond Thunderdome** (1985). In Bruce •Beresford's •**Paradise Road** (1997), he appears briefly in the pre-invasion prologue in Singapore, reaffirming his capacity for authoritative command of the screen when given the slightest chance. The 1996 television series, *Mercury*, gave him a more than slight chance when he played a bullying state premier who seemed to be drawn from life. *Other Australian films*: Post-Synchronization (1981), **Remember Me** (1985), **The Pitch** (1994, short).   BMcF

Gudgeon, Mac (1949–) WRITER Well-known film and television scriptwriter, Mac Gudgeon has also been a prominent member, and president, of the Australian Writers Guild. Born in Woollongong, he studied law at Sydney University but dropped out and sought employment on Melbourne's docks, one of the few places where draft dodgers could find work. His experiences over three years as a painter and docker led to an interest in the history of the waterfront, which later found expression in his writing. While working initially as a videotape editor at Melbourne's Open Channel, he met producer Bob •Weis with whom he was to collaborate on several projects, including two miniseries *Waterfront* (1985) and *The Petrov Affair* (1986, co-written with Cliff •Green), and **Georgia** (1989), which Joanna Murray-Smith wrote from his original story-line, and which starred Judy •Davis. He also wrote **Ground Zero**

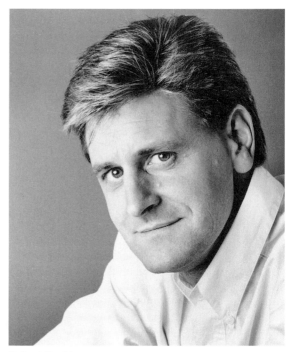
Robert Grubb

(1987, with Jan •Sardi), **The Delinquents** (1989, with Clayton Frohman), and **Wind** (1993, with Rudy Wurlitzer). Gudgeon's other television credits include *Skytrackers* (1991–93), *Snowy* (1993), *Law of the Land* (1993–94), and *Halifax f.p.* (1994–96).   HARRY KIRCHNER

Gulpilil, David (1953–) ACTOR Before making his film début in Nicolas Roeg's poetic adventure, •**Walkabout** (1971), David Gulpilil, an Aborigine from Arnhem Land, had already established himself as a dancer, had toured overseas in a dance troupe, and had taught Aboriginal dancing at a mission school. Roeg chose him to play the boy who guides the lost children, abandoned in the outback by their deranged father, back to civilisation. He invested the role of the rescuer, who is then destroyed by white disingenuousness, with dignity and poignancy. In 1976, he co-starred with Dennis Hopper in Philippe •Mora's •**Mad Dog Morgan**, as the only ally of the notorious bushranger and, in the same year, he scored a major success in •**Storm Boy**, Henri •Safran's highly popular and critically acclaimed version of Colin Thiele's children's novel. In this tale of a boy and a pelican, set in South Australia's Coorong area, he played Fingerbone Bill, the Aboriginal who teaches the boy about his environment and becomes almost a surrogate father to the boy who has little rapport with his actual father. Despite the rather self-conscious lyricism of the film as a whole, Gulpilil emerged as an actor of charismatic presence.

He confirmed this status with a compelling study in Peter •Weir's •The Last Wave (1977). Whereas in **Walkabout** and **Storm Boy** he had conveyed a striking sense of organic belonging to the strange and alluring landscapes, in **The Last Wave** Gulpilil played a tribal Aborigine living in the seedy fringes of Sydney, divorced from his true milieu, and he brought to the role a dangerous intensity that contrasted effectively with Richard Chamberlain's middle-class WASP lawyer.

Parts for Aboriginal actors were far from plentiful in Australian films. He appeared fleetingly in the American film, **The Right Stuff,** in 1983 but, since then, Gulpilil has found only a handful of roles after his very promising start in the 1970s. His best chance since then has been in **Crocodile Dundee** (1986), in which he showed some flair for comedy as the eponymous hero's slyly sophisticated mate, Neville Bell, who is bored by corroborees and tribal lore. He made a thriller called **Dark Age** (1987), which mixed crocodile-hunting thrills with environmental concerns and has never been released, and had supporting roles in Wim Wenders' Australian–French–German co-production, **Until the End of the World** (1992), and in Nick Parsons' little-seen outback murder drama, •**Dead Heart** (1996). This is an inadequate list for so arresting a performer. In 1980, he wrote a script called *Billy West*, which he hoped to co-direct as well as star in, but the project failed to materialise, and he appeared in the miniseries, *The Timeless Land*.

Other Australian films: In Song and Dance (1964, short), No Bag Limit (1973), Felix (1976, short), To Shoot a Mad Dog (1976, doc.), The Magic Arts (1977, short), Three Dances by Gulpilil (1978).   BMcF

Gyngell, Kym (1952–) ACTOR Throughout the 1980s Kym Gyngell, also known as Kim, established himself as a talented, versatile actor able to shift easily between comedy and drama. After a minor role in the nuclear thriller **The Chain Reaction** (1980), Gyngell was cast in the lead role of William John Wills in the black comedy **Wills and Burke** (1985), which was savaged by the local critics. •**With Love to the Person Next to Me** (1987), Gyngell's next film, provided his best role to date as Wallace, the alienated taxi driver who drives through the seedy areas of Melbourne at night and makes cider in his small flat during the day. Wallace, who tapes his passengers' conversation to play back to himself when he is alone, is reluctantly drawn into the lives of two neighbours and a local woman. Gyngell enlivened proceedings in two supporting roles for producer Frank •Howson, as a friend to John •Waters. Both films had a musical background: **Boulevard of Broken Dreams** (1988) and •**Heaven Tonight** (1990). In between, Gyngell provided solid support as a photographer for reporter Colin •Friels in the crime thriller •**Grievous Bodily Harm** (1988). These films, unfortunately, did not provide Gyngell with a 'breakthrough role' in the cinema and his popularity is largely due to his television work in the late 1980s and early 1990s in long-running comedies such as *The Comedy Company,* where Gyngell developed his Col'n Carpenter character, and *Full Frontal.*

Other Australian films include: Bushfire Moon (1987), Bachelor Girl (1987), •Ground Zero (1987), Backstage (1988), What the Moon Saw (1990), •Love and Other Catastrophes (1996), Amy (1998).

GM

H

Hackforth-Jones, Penne (1943–) ACTOR American-born National Institute of Dramatic Art graduate, Penne Hackforth-Jones has been long resident here and has had a busy career in all the acting media. She has done a great deal of television work, in series such as *Bellbird* and *Cash and Company*, as well as notable stage work. In films, she has become a recognisable character actor over several decades. She appeared in 'The Priest', the episode of •**Libido** (1973) directed by Fred •Schepisi, in •**Alvin Purple** (1973), as a doctor, and its sequel, **Alvin Rides Again** (1974), in Scott •Hicks and Kim McKenzie's short feature, **Down the Wind** (1975), and several other unmemorable films of the 1970s and 1980s. She surfaced again in the 1990s in several higher profile productions: •**Muriel's Wedding** (1994), •**Paradise Road** (1997), as one of the women prisoners, and the ill-timed **Diana and Me** (1997). Eloquent of face and voice, with a gift for both pathos and comedy, she is one of the many actors underused by Australian cinema.

Other Australian films: The Wanderer (1974), The Journalist (1979), Running on Empty (1982), Last Breakfast in Paradise (1982, short), Kokoda Crescent (1988).   BMcF

Penne Hackforth-Jones

Haddrick, Ron (1929–) ACTOR   Ron Haddrick, born in Adelaide, was a familiar voice in Australian documentaries from the 1950s. Haddrick also worked in England for many years. Since his return to Australia, he has provided solid performances in supporting roles in mostly undistinguished films, beginning with **Shirley Thompson versus the Aliens** (1972). Haddrick's colonialist in **Great Expectations: The Untold Story** (1987), which was shot as both a miniseries for the ABC and a feature film, was one of the few redeeming qualities in this attempt to rework Dickens's story from Magwitch's point of view after he is transported to Australia. The other major strand in Haddrick's film career has been the use of his voice in a number of animated films for Yoram •Gross, including •**Dot and the Kangaroo** (1977), **Around the World with Dot** (1982), **Sarah** (1983), **Dot and the Bunny** (1984), and **The Camel Boy** (1984).

Other Australian films include: Golden Cage (1975), The Lost Islands (1975), •Ride a Wild Pony (1975), •The Fourth Wish (1976), •Dawn! (1979), Short Changed (1986), •Quigley (1991), •Children of the Revolution (1996).   GM

Hagen, Ron (1947–) CINEMATOGRAPHER Hagen started his career with ABC TV, Melbourne, in 1971 and began freelancing in 1981. He has filmed many television dramas, series and miniseries, including *Mission Impossible* and *The Flying Doctors*. His first feature film, Geoffrey •Wright's •Romper Stomper (1992) attracted attention for its stark visual style, which the same team developed further in **Metal Skin** (1994), winning Hagen a Victorian Australian Cinematographers Society (ACS) Gold award. He has also won Victorian ACS Silver awards for a telefeature and for **Ocean Girl** (1997). Other films: **Talk** (1994), **Little Boy Blue** (USA, 1997).   DAVID MUIR

Hall, Ken G. (1901–94) DIRECTOR Forthright and energetic, Ken G. Hall was the Australian cinema's most commercially successful film-maker before the revival of the 1970s (see Revival, The). In the 1930s and 1940s he produced, directed and often wrote 18 feature films at the •Cinesound studio at Sydney's Bondi Junction. Only one of his films (•Strike Me Lucky 1934) did not return its money; •On Our Selection (1932) and •The Squatter's Daughter (1933) were the most profitable. In 1942 the **Cinesound Review** newsreel special **Kokoda Front Line**, edited under his supervision and using film shot by combat cameraman Damien •Parer, won Australia's first Academy Award.

After a start in journalism, Hall spent six months as a theatre manager for Union Theatres. He became national publicity director for it and its allied company, Australasian Films. From 1924 he was publicity director for the Australian branch of First National Pictures, travelling in 1925 to observe film production in Hollywood. Three years later he directed new sequences to replace a risible portrayal of Australians in First National's imported German film, **Unsere Emden**. The revised film, called •The Exploits of the Emden, was released in Australia with success, a fact that impressed Union Theatres' managing director Stuart F. Doyle. Hall rejoined Union Theatres in 1929 and, two years later, Doyle gave him the chance to direct **On Our Selection**. The huge success of that film led to Hall's continuous production at the newly formed Cinesound.

Hall applied the formula of 'showmanship' to all his features. This formula determined story choice, saturation publicity, and a script combining the tried-and-true with freshly exploitable ingredients. His 'Dad 'n' Dave' films—starting with **Selection**, followed by •Grandad Rudd (1935), •Dad and Dave Come to Town (1938), and •Dad Rudd M.P. (1940)—were his surest box-office earners, but he also tackled other types of comedy (•It Isn't Done, 1937; •Let George Do It, 1938), society melodramas (•The Silence of Dean Maitland, 1934; •The Broken Melody, 1938), and action films (•Orphan of the Wilderness, 1936; •Thoroughbred, 1936; •Lovers and Luggers, 1937; •Tall

Timbers, 1937), as well as musicals (•Gone to the Dogs, 1939). Although he did have a vision of Australia, he never explored it with as much passion or conscious artistry as did his closest rival, Charles •Chauvel. Hall took fewer story risks than Chauvel, remained faithful to the ideal of running a studio along Hollywood lines, and shot increasingly on the soundstage to save costs.

When all the elements in a Hall film worked, as they did in his best films—**Dad and Dave Come to Town**, •Mr Chedworth Steps Out (1939), and the Columbia-backed •Smithy (1946)—they showed a shrewd combination of story elements and Hall's talent for getting the best out of permanently employed studio technicians. Even on the one Cinesound feature that Hall did not direct, •Come up Smiling (1939), his influence as producer ensured that it looked very much like one of his own films.

Smithy followed Hall's direction of a large number of wartime propaganda films. The fact that it was his final feature would be an increasingly sore point, since he had expected Greater Union to resume regular feature production after the war. But he spent another decade making documentaries and steering the fortunes of **Cinesound Review**, the newsreel he had started in 1931 and, on which, he demonstrated time and again his instinct for story-telling and mastery of montage editing. He took his talent for news and images with him to the Sydney television station TCN-9 when he served as its chief executive between 1957 and 1966. Although not involved in 9's day-to-day output, he trained and influenced many that were, besides devising a programming policy that took the station to the top of the ratings.

In this period, Hall encouraged some independent directors (commissioning the *Project* series of documentaries, buying and screening the early work of Cecil •Holmes and Bruce •Beresford), but found himself sharply at odds with the experimental aspirations of others like Albie •Thoms and the other Sydney-based Ubu film-makers. When the industry revived, he became a vocal critic of government film-funding policies, but he did increasingly encourage the writers, producers, and directors who sent him their scripts. Among the mainstream directors whose work he applauded were George •Miller, Peter •Weir and Phillip •Noyce. He advised Noyce on the making of •Newsfront (1979) and, in 1984, Noyce had him direct a sequence of the television miniseries *Cowra Breakout*.

                                     GRAHAM SHIRLEY

Hamnett, Olivia ACTOR Born in England where she began her career in **The Spy with a Cold Nose** (1966), Olivia Hamnett gave promise as an attractive leading lady in Australian films with her first feature role as Richard Chamberlain's increasingly troubled wife in Peter •Weir's •The Last Wave (1977). Subsequently, however, she has filmed only sporadically, more often on television, as in *Prisoner*, than in the cinema. She played Jack •Thompson's wife in **The Earthling** (1980), in which she died early in the film, and was in the thriller, **Ebbtide** (1994), with John •Waters.

BMcF

Hanna, Pat (1888–1973) ACTOR New Zealand-born Pat Hanna began his career entertaining troops in World War I, during which he was in active service on the Western Front. He was a cartoonist and monologist as well as an actor, and he became famous for the three films in which he played the lanky Chic Williams, serving in the AIF: •**Diggers** (1931), •**Diggers in Blighty** (1933), and •**Waltzing Matilda** (1933). He formed a comedy troupe, 'Diggers', which toured Australia in the 1920s and, for his last two films, he formed his own production company, the first having been made for F.W. •Thring's •Efftee Productions. For a decade or so, he represented a popular 'Aussie' type. He also directed and sometimes appeared in a number of short films in the 1930s; for example, with Joe •Valli and Charlie Albert in **Long Lost Son** (1932), and in **The Gospel According to Cricket** (1932).

BMcF

Hannam, Ken (1929–) DIRECTOR Although Ken Hannam has not had a prolonged impact on the Australian film industry in terms of the number of films he has worked on, his impact has nevertheless been considerable due to the fact that he directed •**Sunday Too Far Away** (1975), one of Australia's most influential films. This film, together with Peter •Weir's •**Picnic at Hanging Rock** (1975), generated considerable international recognition at a critical time in the rebirth of feature film production in Australia. Prior to **Sunday Too Far Away** this Melbourne-born film-maker worked as an actor, writer, and director in Australian television before moving to London in 1968 where he worked on series such as *Z Cars*.

Hannam's subsequent Australian films received neither the critical nor commercial success of **Sunday Too Far Away**. **Break of Day** (1976) was a low-key study of the cultural differences in a small country town after World War I, and the critical focus on the film was more concerned with the fact that here was another dramatically subdued film concerned with Australia's rural past. The critics argued that the industry needed to move beyond this phase to contemporary problems in urban settings. Hannam's next film was the underrated Australian drama •**Summerfield** (1977) which, again, demonstrated Hannam's interest in characterisation and setting, and his film typically downplayed the melodramatic excess that was inherent in Cliff •Green's script. Hannam's last Australian feature, to date, was •**Dawn** (1979), a biography of one of Australia's best-known sporting personalities, Dawn Fraser. In the 1980s and 1990s Hannam

returned to British television series although he directed, with Donald •Crombie, the six-hour Australian television miniseries *Robbery Under Arms* in 1985, which was also released, in a shortened form, as a theatrical feature.

GM

Hannay, David (1939–) PRODUCER This prolific New Zealand-born producer has specialised in the low-budget/ exploitation side of the Australian film industry after working in radio as an actor. This pattern is evident in Hannay's first feature-film production •**The Set** (1970), with its focus on the sexual habits of a group of wealthy Sydney residents and the inclusion of a homosexual love affair and a nude bathing scene by Hazel Phillips, a daytime-television personality at that time. Further low-budget exploitation films continued in the 1970s with •**Stone** (1974) and the martial arts film •**The Man from Hong Kong** (1975). In 1982 **Early Frost** was released without a directorial credit following a dispute between the director (Brian McDuffie) and producer Hannay. In 1985 Hannay produced **Death of a Soldier** based on the Leonski killings in Melbourne during World War II. This potentially prestigious film, directed by Philippe •Mora with a budget of nearly $4 million, was virtually destroyed at the time of its release when it was blackballed by the Australian Theatrical and Amusement Employees Association (ATEA; see Unions and associations). The ATEA's action arose from a dispute over the short notice given to some crew members when the script had to be pruned due to budgetary problems.

In 1987 Hannay joined with another producer, Tom Broadbridge, to package four exploitation films for the theatrical and video market. These films (**Vicious**, 1987; **The 13th Floor**, 1988; **Out of the Body**, 1988; and **Kadaicha**, 1988), with average budgets of approximately $600 000 and short shooting schedules in Sydney, went straight to video in Australia although the most violent of the films, **Vicious** (directed by Karl Zwicky), received a brief cinema release in the USA. In 1978 Hannay returned to his native New Zealand to produce **Solo** and again in 1990 for **The Returning**. In the 1990s Hannay continued his pattern of low-budget/exploitation productions, including the 1993 erotic thriller **Gross Misconduct**, which provoked a brief controversy over its depiction of an affair between a tertiary student (Naomi Watts) and her lecturer (Jimmy Smits).

Other Australian films include: Alison's Birthday (1981), Emma's War (1988), Shotgun Wedding (1994).

GM

Hansen, Gary (1942–82) CINEMATOGRAPHER/DESIGNER In 1959 Gary Hansen formed Stasen Films with Donald B. Stanger, and began making short films and documentaries. He then worked on production design for **Night of Fear** (1973) and on art direction for **Inn of the Damned** (1975), before working as director of photography on a series of major feature films: •Cathy's Child (1979), Harlequin (1980), •Manganinnie (1980), Next of Kin (1982), and •We of the Never Never (1982). His death in a helicopter crash while on location cut short a promising career. IB

Hardy, Jonathan (1941–) ACTOR Jonathan Hardy, born in New Zealand, has also been a scriptwriter, director, and singer on occasion, as well as acquiring a reputation as a character actor. His first film was Bruce •Beresford's •The Adventures of Barry McKenzie (1972) and, thereafter, he played a string of character roles, perhaps most noticeably in Paul •Cox's •Lonely Hearts (1982). In the last, he played Norman •Kaye's pudgy brother-in-law, Bruce (of course), married to the shrewish Pamela (Julia •Blake), and with aspirations to amateur theatricals. He made the role funny and touching, resisting mere henpecked caricature. No other Australian film role has given him quite such scope, but he gave sharp individuality to Brother Arnold in Fred •Schepisi's •The Devil's Playground (1976) and, more recently, to another clerical role, the Rev. McIntyre in •Mr Reliable (1996). As well as several appearances in New Zealand productions (The Scarecrow, 1982) or Australian–New Zealand co-productions (the futuristic thriller, Death Warmed Up, 1985, and Mesmerised, 1986), Hardy wrote and directed one film, Backstage (1988), a little-seen love story with a show business background, and was co-author of the script for •'Breaker' Morant (1980).
Other Australian films: Moving On (1974, short), •The Mango Tree (1977), •Mad Max (1979), Undermining Australia (1981, short), Wipe Out the Jargon (1982, short), Wills & Burke (1985), The Delinquents (1989), Bloodmoon (1989), Tunnel Vision (1995), Down Rusty Down (1996). BMcF

Hargreaves, John (1945–96) ACTOR John Hargreaves made a great contribution to Australian theatre, television, and film in his relatively short life. A teacher in NSW, with a welding certificate under his belt, he was seduced by a travelling theatre company and went to study at the National Institute for Dramatic Art in 1969. As part of the renaissance in Australian theatre in the late 1960s and early 1970s (see Revival, the), he worked with the New Theatre group and with directors such as Jim •Sharman and George •Ogilvie.

For Thomas •Keneally, Hargreaves had 'the ultimate Australian working-class face', a fitting description for an actor who cared passionately about authenticity in Australian representations and who was keen not to lose his accent or his rhythm of speech. He believed David •Williamson to be one writer who could record Australians accurately and honestly. In his first feature, The Removalists (1975), in which he plays the innocent, wet-behind-the-ears constable who finally bashes a man to death, and in the landmark •Don's Party (1976), in which he is Don, the hopeless but lovable, emblematic Australian male, Hargreaves more than does justice to Williamson's writing and to his own belief that Australians are passionate but do not know how to talk about it. He was delighted to work with strong scripts in the television series Scales of Justice (1983), where he plays a corrupt cop, and The Dismissal (1983), where he plays the idealist Labor politician, Jim Cairns. •Careful He Might Hear You (1983) was another strong vehicle for him. Hargreaves played Logan, the seductive proletarian in the mannered bourgeois world, and showed his ability to combine the passionate and the laconic, the larrikin with the emotionally vulnerable human being.

We remember Hargreaves as Don, addressing his friend and once-upon-a-time mentor Mal (Ray •Barrett), with drunken affection as a 'weak turd'; embarrassed and silly as Colin Rogers, attracted to Helen (Nicole •Kidman) in •Emerald City (1989); and, as Bung, brightening and energising the whole army camp in •The Odd Angry Shot (1979). He did significant work until the end. So able to infuse the vernacular with charm and aggravated affection, as the White cop in •Blackfellas (1993), he tied it to racial bigotry and violence. In one of his best performances, he played Uncle Jack in •Country Life (1994), with manic intensity, full of dreams and disappointment, bursting with frustration at his fate. 'He was witty. He made people laugh. He was a dreamer, very handsome', Wendy •Hughes's Vanessa told Logan's son in Careful He Might Hear You—a fitting epitaph for a great actor.
Other Australian films: Death Cheaters (1976), •Mad Dog Morgan (1976), Little Boy Lost (1978), •Money Movers (1979), Long Weekend (1979), Beyond Reasonable Doubt (1980), •Hoodwink (1981), •The Killing of Angel Street (1981), The Great Gold Swindle (1984), •My First Wife (1984), Comrades (1987), •Malcolm (1986), The Place at the Coast (1987), Boundaries of the Heart (1988), Sweet Revenge (1990), Heroes—The Movie (1991), Rome Romeo (1991), •No Worries (1993), •Hotel Sorrento (1995), Lust and Revenge (1996).
LORRAINE MORTIMER

Harmony Row

1933. Director: F.W. Thring. *Production company*: Efftee Film Productions. *Story*: George Wallace. *Director of photography*: Arthur Higgins. 78 min. B&W. *Cast*: George Wallace (Constable Dreadnought), Phyllis Baker (Molly), Marshall Crosby (the sergeant), John Dobbie (Slogger Lee), Willie Kerr (Leonard).

This was the second of three •Efftee films featuring stage comedian George •Wallace. It was built around his vaudeville persona, with Wallace as a rookie cop on the toughest beat in town. It also introduced child star Willie Kerr, later well known to British and Australian audiences as Bill •Kerr. The rambling plot climaxes with a beautifully choreographed and very funny boxing match between Wallace as 'Dreadnought' (the police champion) and his stage foil, the huge John Dobbie. Despite the obviously painted sets and 'stagey' acting styles, including Wallace's occasional direct address to the camera, the film is enjoyable. It was successfully distributed in the United Kingdom and throughout Australia, often on a double bill with •Diggers in Blighty. IB

Harvest of Hate

1978. Director: Michael Thornhill. *Producer:* Jane Scott. *Scriptwriter:* Michael Thornhill. *Director of photography:* David Sanderson. 75 min. *Cast:* Denis Grosvenor (Peter), Kris McQuade, (Ruth), Leon Cosak (Arab Guard), Michael Aitkens (British Agent).

This low-budget film, which was released on television, is of more interest as an historical tract documenting the intensity of anti-Arab sentiments in the 1970s, at a time when the Israeli–Arab military tension was at a peak, than for any aesthetic qualities. **Harvest of Hate** is also notable for the film-makers involved: director/scriptwriter Michael •Thornhill (•**Between the Wars**), producer Jane •Scott (•**Storm Boy**) and the film's second assistant director, Scott •Hicks (•**Shine**), art director David Copping (•**Picnic At Hanging Rock**), unit manager Penny Chapman (*Police Rescue*), executive producer Matt •Carroll (•**Storm Boy**), and Gil •Brealey (**Sunday Too Far Away**), who assisted Thornhill with the script. However, all worked on better projects than this piece of exploitation.

The comic-book plot involves an adventurer (Grosvenor) and a female lawyer (McQuade) who stumble on an Arab military training exercise in the middle of the Simpson Desert and, together with British agent (Aitkens), they escape a fate worse than death to carry back this information to the authorities. The dramatic conflict in **Harvest of Hate** is based on crude national stereotypes and the film ends with a ludicrous shootout in a Barossa Valley winery.

GM

Harvey, Frank (1885–1965) ACTOR/WRITER/DIRECTOR Frank Harvey was known mainly for his association with •Cinesound between 1936 and 1940. He had arrived in Australia in 1914 to work on stage for JC Williamsons. When 'the firm' as it became known attempted to cash in on the nationalistic spirit of the time, he directed **Within Our Gates, or Deeds that Won Gallipoli** (1915), but worked mainly in theatre for the next 11 years before returning to the United Kingdom where he had considerable success with his novel and play *Cape Forlorn*, before travelling once again to Australia. In 1936 he joined Cinesound as staff writer under Ken G. •Hall, but he already had a high profile as an actor, and experience in film from his association with •Eftee Productions where he had

adapted •**Clara Gibbings** (1934), acted in **A Ticket in Tatts** (1934) and **The Secrets of London** (1934). He also acted in •Charles Chauvel's •**Heritage** (1935). He is credited as sole writer on Edwin Bowen's •**White Death** (1936), but probably with significant input from Zane Grey. •**It Isn't Done** (1937) marked the first of nine features with Cinesound, mainly as co-writer on a relatively low salary, but with the added incentive that he might earn additional money as an actor. In Hall's words, 'Needless to say, Frank wrote himself into a good fat character part in every film we made from then on.' The weight of Harvey's contribution to many of his Cinesound films is unclear. Although he is credited as sole writer on •**Tall Timbers** (1937) 'which came up as melodramatic but full of action', Hall has noted that it was from a story-line by Frank •Hurley. To further complicate matters, many of the Cinesound comedies were written by a comedy-construction team consisting of Hall, Harvey, Jim Banks (who created Ginger Meggs), Bill Maloney from Hoyts, and Hal Carleton with whom Hall had begun his career at The Film House in 1917. Harvey also shares scriptwriting credits with •George Wallace on •**Let George Do it** (1938) and •**Gone to the Dogs** (1939). Among Harvey's other scriptwriting credits can be found •**Lovers and Luggers** (1937), •**The Broken Melody** (1938), •**Dad and Dave Come to Town** (1938), •**Mr Chedsworth Steps Out** (1939), and •**Dad Rudd M.P.** (1940). After Cinesound's demise in 1940, Harvey continued acting in theatre and became a producer with ABC radio drama from 1942 to 1950.   HARRY KIRCHNER

Harwood, Alexander Roy (1897–1988) DIRECTOR/ PRODUCER While visiting Tahiti as an insurance agent, Alexander Roy Harwood (generally known as Dick, and also as A.R. Harwood) watched an American silent-film production company at work, and decided to change careers. His first film, **The Man Who Forgot** (1927), does not survive, but we know that he toured rural Victoria with it and Louise •Lovely's •**Jewelled Nights** (1925). Then he established A.R. Harwood Talkie Productions, with the intention of producing the first Australian sound features. A technical disaster on the first of these, •**Out of the Shadows** (1931), prevented its release. However, working with a camera converted to sound by an amateur mechanic and with a homemade microphone, he managed to release •**Spur of the Moment** and **Isle of Intrigue** in September 1931, just two weeks before •Eftee's first talkie program. Frank •Thring's response was to keep Harwood out of the competition by employing him as manager of the Tatler Theatre. But Harwood returned to production later, completing •**Secret of the Skies** in 1934 and forming New Era Films to produce •**The Avenger** (1937) and •**Show Business** (1938). Release problems dogged these low-budget features and, when war was declared, Harwood moved into other activities (including film exhibition), returning only briefly to direct the unsuccessful **Night Club** (1952). Harwood's importance lies in the way he publicly supported quota protection for Australian films, and in the determination with which he pursued a career in sound-film production in that difficult early period. IB

Hawes, Stanley (1905–91) DIRECTOR/PRODUCER Stanley Hawes, born in England, made his first film, **Dry Dock** (1935), at Gaumont-British Instructional Films, then transferred to Paul Rotha's Strand Films, where his best-known production was **Monkey into Man** (1937). In 1940, he was one of many young film-makers invited by John Grierson to join the newly established National Film Board of Canada. The Australian National Film Board was established in 1945 and, in May 1946, Hawes was appointed its first producer-in-chief, a position he held until he retired in 1969. He directed **School in the Mailbox** (1947), **Flight Plan** (1951), **The Queen in Australia** (1954, and Australia's first full-length colour film), and stayed on for a year after retirement to produce the films for the Australian pavilion at Expo 70 in Japan. But he was more influential in personally overseeing (as producer) hundreds of films, maintaining high production standards and the Griersonian ideals of documentary, as well as directing the policy of the Commonwealth Film Unit, including steering it through several political crises. He was a member of the Film Committee of the Australian Council for the Arts and of the Interim Council for the Film School 1970–73, and chairman of the Commonwealth Cinematograph Board of Review 1971–77. His services were also used by other governments: Malaya and Singapore in 1950, and Morocco in 1958–59. He was always active in Australian film culture organisations such as the Sydney Film Festival, the •National Film Theatre of Australia, and the •Australian Film Institute. The latter presented him with the Longford Award in 1970, the year he was also made a Member of the Order of the British Empire. In 1998, •Film Australia's inaugural Stanley Hawes Memorial Award, recognising outstanding services to documentary, was presented to the late Graham Chase. IB

Hayes, Terry (1951–) WRITER/PRODUCER One of Australia's most successful scriptwriters and producers, Terry Hayes has maintained a remarkably low public profile. Born in England, he arrived in Australia in 1953. He was a successful radio and print journalist and Derryn Hinch's producer before joining Kennedy Miller in 1980, where he became an important force in the company's growth. Throughout his film and television career, he has balanced outstanding technical ability with a keen sense of

commercial judgment. •**Dead Calm** (1989), which he co-produced and adapted for screen from Charles Williams' book, is an example of his strong belief in audience-testing. The ending, along with other sections of the film, was changed before the American release. He also co-wrote •**Mad Max 2** (1981) and •**Mad Max Beyond Thunderdome** (1985, also co-producer). Hayes shares co-writing and co-production credits on several prestigious television mini-series, including *The Dismissal* (1983), *Bodyline* (1984), *Vietnam* (1987), *The Dirtwater Dynasty* (1988), and, as sole writer, *Bangkok Hilton* (1989). His film production credits also include •**Flirting** (1991) and •**The Year My Voice Broke** (1987). •**Mr Reliable** (1996), which he co-wrote with Don Catchlove, and which was directed by Nadia •Tass, is probably his least commercially successful writing effort to date. Most recently, Hayes has worked on several large-budget film projects in America. HARRY KIRCHNER

Hayseeds, The

1933. Director, Producer, Scriptwriter: Beaumont Smith. *Director of photography:* Tasman Higgins. B&W. *Cast:* Cecil Kellaway (Dad Hayseed), Tal Ordell (Joe), Stan Tolhurst (Sam), Kenneth Brampton (Mr Townleigh).

The last of Beaumont •Smith's back-blocks films, as well as the only one to have survived, **The Hayseeds** is also likely to have been the most genteel. Following the success of Ken G. •Hall's •**On Our Selection** (1932), Smith revived the Hayseed family, who had first appeared on screen in •**Our Friends, the Hayseeds** (1917). In time-honoured entrepreneurial fashion, he also determined to tart up the production with trappings influenced by English musical films (juvenile leads with plummy accents, dancers drilled to a metronome, songs written for sopranos, tenors, and a hearty chorus). Finally, he gave Cecil Kellaway his first screen opportunity as Dad. The result is a wholesome, even cuddly, entertainment in which the simpering often totally overwhelms the vulgarity. **The Hayseeds** was also a strong performer at the box office, and its combination of 'pioneer' values and 'up-to-date' pizzaz effectively sets the tone for the complacent attitude and the warm nationalist content of much Australian film through the next several decades. WILLIAM D. ROUTT

Haywood, Chris (1949–) ACTOR Prolific British-born actor who has worked in Australian film, television, and theatre since 1970. The only real break in Chris Haywood's screen appearance was in the late 1970s when he was 'blackballed' by sections of the Australian film industry for being too outspoken in campaigning for better facilities for actors on the set. During this period he worked primarily in the theatre and in pubs. He more than made up for that absence by appearing in eight films that were released in 1982. Haywood was nominated for performances in •**Kiss Or Kill** (1997), the New Zealand film **Alex** (1993), **Aya** (1991), **Island** (1989), and he has won Australian Film Institute Awards for •**Newsfront** (1978), •**Strikebound** (1984), •**A Street to Die** (1985) and •**Emerald City** (1989).

After a lead role in •**The Tale of Ruby Rose** in 1988 Haywood was quoted as saying that he had been advised that in the future he should concentrate only on lead roles and forget about supporting roles in films such as •**Man of Flowers** (1983), •**Malcolm** (1986), and •**Dogs in Space** (1987) where he had made such a striking impression. Fortunately, Haywood rejected this suggestion by pointing out that the film comes first and it is reliant on every part, not just the lead. This is certainly true in a film such as **Kiss or Kill** where Haywood's role as the policeman on the trail of Matt •Day and Frances O'Conner could have been bland and thankless. Instead Haywood and fellow detective Andrew Gilbert, with help from Bill •Bennett's script, create separate identities for the two detectives that is not just dependent on the actions of the lead characters.

Other Australian films include: •The Cars that Ate Paris (1974), The Great McCarthy (1975), The Removalists (1975), Deathcheaters (1976), The Trespassers (1976), Out of It (1977), •Kostas (1979), In Search of Anna (1979), … Maybe This Time (1980), •'Breaker' Morant (1980), •Wrong Side of the Road (1981), With Prejudice (1982), Running on Empty (1982), •The Man from Snowy River (1982), •Lonely Hearts (1982), •Heatwave (1982), •The Clinic (1983), Attack Force Z (1982), Freedom (1982), The Return of Captain Invincible (1983), •Razorback (1984), The Great Gold Swindle (1984), The Coca-Cola Kid (1985), Wills and Burke (1985), •Burke & Wills (1985), Call Me Mr. Brown (1986), The Bit Part (1987), •Warm Nights on a Slow Moving Train (1988), Golden Braid (1990), •A Woman's Tale (1991), •Quigley (1991), Sweet Talker (1991), The Nun and the Bandit (1992), Exile (1994), •Muriel's Wedding (1994), Lust and Revenge (1996), •Shine (1996), •Blackrock (1997), •Oscar and Lucinda (1997).   GM

Hazlehurst, Noni (1953–) ACTOR   Like Helen •Morse, Noni Hazlehurst has a commanding position among Australian screen actors on the basis of a handful of films. She registered strongly with filmgoers for her performance as Nora in •**Monkey Grip** (1982), the appropriately episodic, atmospheric version of Helen •Garner's novel of drifting and drugs in inner suburban Melbourne in the 1970s. Her warmth and strength gave the film the centre it needed. In •**Fran**, three years later, she played a feckless, likeable but inherently selfish woman, who puts her own emotional needs ahead of her role as mother. No other roles have given her such interesting things to do, although she makes good comic capital from the suburban wife in **Australian Dream** (1987). Much of her work has been for stage and television, including a long commitment to the chil-

Chris Haywood

Noni Hazlehurst

dren's program, *Playschool*. The big screen could use the easy naturalness that is her stock in trade, but she has not made a feature film for several years.

Other Australian films: •**The Getting of Wisdom** (1977), **Fatty Finn** (1980), **Stations** (1983, short), •**For Love or Money** (1983, doc.), •**Waiting** (1991).　　　　　　　BMcF

Head On

1998 Director: Ana Kokkinos. *Producer*: Jane Scott. *Scriptwriters*: Andrew Bovell, Ana Kokkinos, Mira Robinson. *Director of photography*: Jaems Grant. 104 min. *Cast*: Alex Dimitriades (Ari), Paul Capsis (Johnny), Julian Garner (Sean), Tony Niko-lakopoulos (Dimitri), Elena Mandalis (Betty), Eugenia Fragos (Sophia), Damien Fotiou (Joe), Andrea Mandalis (Alex), Maria Mercedes (Tasia), Dora Kaskanis (Dina), Alex Papps (Peter), Vassili Zappa (Vassili).

As the title of this film suggests, **Head On** is full of power, aggression, antipathy, and groaning sexuality. Based on the novel, *Loaded* by Christos Tsiolkas, the film makes no apologies for its brutal portrayal of postmodern sex. It is a film that makes no moral judgment: it merely captures the ferocious excesses of Ari and his attempts to survive in a claustrophobic and alienating world. As director, Ana •Kokkinos gives the audience no opportunity for respite from the excessive and graphic nature of Ari's lifestyle; his rollercoaster ride is perpetual and we have no choice but to ride along with him.

Ari's cultural and ethnic dilemma is clearly established in the film, and the black-and-white footage of his parent's arrival to Australia serves only to highlight the enormous crevasse that exists between him and his parents. As immigrants in their new 'home', they saw Australia as a stepping stone to prosperity and success, for Ari their 'home', the place in which he exists is merely a means to an end. He has no attachment to his culture, to his home, his family, or to his friends. He is not able to connect with anyone or anything and so drifts from one episode to the next.

The representation of Ari as ineffectual and his failure to have a moral resolve has resulted in varied responses to the film: those that see it as a modern indictment of the angst experienced by most youth, Ari being just one example, and counter-criticisms that the film celebrates the hedonistic indulgences of contemporary youth. The graphic, carnal depictions of sex are confronting and, in this film, Kokkinos makes no excuses for them, for they are, after all, very real aspects of modern life. Ari's anonymous sexual encounters serve as a substitute for any real feeling in him and this is reinforced by his treatment of his 'Anglo' partner, Sean.

Kokkinos' strong direction and sympathetic reading of Tsiolkas' text has resulted in exceptional performances. The

notion that Ari is not alone in his dislocation is augmented by those around him who also seemingly fail to 'connect'. The aggression and obstinacy demonstrated by Ari's father Dimitri is effectively counterbalanced by the sensitivity displayed by Sean. Ironically, it is the character of Johnny, Ari's transvestite friend, who provides the greatest focus and hope within the film's narrative. Johnny's refusal to surrender and his embrace of the influences around him provides an effective contrast to Ari's alienation.

Kokkinos is to be commended for her attempts to enhance this through direction and editing decisions, where the audience is forced to experience Ari's displacement. Ari's emotional roller-coaster ride is conveyed using jump cuts, slow motion, and blurred images, his 'vision' becoming ours. While **Head On** has been embraced by some and rejected by others, it is a powerful account of contemporary urban living.

KAREN FORD

Heartbreak Kid, The

1993. Director: Michael Jenkins. *Producer*: Ben Gannon. *Scriptwriters*: Richard Barrett, Michael Jenkins. *Director of photography*: Nino Martinetti. *Music*: John Clifford White. 97 min. *Cast*: Claudia Karvan (Christina), Alex Dimitriades (Nick), Nico Lathouris (George), Steve Bastoni (Dimitri), Doris Younane (Evdokia), George Vidalis (Vasili), Louise Mandylor (Elani), William McInnes (Southgate), Jasper Bagg (Graham).

A dangerous fantasy or subversive melodrama? This adaptation of Richard Barrett's stage play is an elemental drama that critiques the stifling conformity of middle-class Greek culture, while having a few swings at the last vestiges of bigotry and resentment expressed by 'true Australians' towards the 'wogs'. Twenty-two-year-old teacher Christina has conformed to all of the rules set by her society—a dutiful daughter of wealthy Greek parents, Christina graduated from university and began her teaching career in the western suburbs while waiting to fulfil her chosen path as a Greek wife to Dimitri, a replica of her conservative, ambitious, father. However, Nick, a 17-year-old Greek student, offers Christina another life, a radical alternative to the pre-planned life she is living. When Christina decides to upset the school's AFL-obsessed sports teacher by coaching a soccer team, with Nick as its star footballer, her well-planned life begins to unravel.

The Heartbreak Kid cleverly attacks many of the central icons of Christina's conservative world—she rejects the house her fiancé purchased (partly with Christina's father's money) opposite her parent's house; she sleeps with Nick, her student; she rejects the advice of the family priest that she should admit her 'guilt' and humbly return to her family; and, finally, she leaves her parents to establish an independent life for herself.

Alex Dimitriades (centre) in **The Heartbreak Kid**

Ultimately, **The Heartbreak Kid** is a simple melodrama that honestly addresses a number of basic issues found in a multicultural society, such as Melbourne where the film is set, and where class, cultural, and generational values do not always sit easily together. GM

Heath, George (1901–68) CINEMATOGRAPHER Although George Heath occasionally photographed independent features (•**The Man They Could Not Hang**, with George •Malcolm, 1934; •**The Burgomeister**, 1935), he became best known for his work at •Cinesound. He first worked as a camera man on newsreels and in the laboratory, then moved to feature films as assistant to Frank •Hurley on •**Strike Me Lucky** (1934) and •**Grandad Rudd** (1935). He was credited as lighting cameraman on •**Thoroughbred** (1936), and as cinematographer on •**Orphan of the Wilderness** (1936), •**It Isn't Done** (1937), •**Tall Timbers** (1937), •**Lovers and Luggers** (1937—with Frank Hurley), •**The Broken Melody** (1938), •**Let George Do It** (1938), •**Dad and Dave Come to Town** (1938), •**Mr Chedworth Steps Out** (1939), •**Gone to the Dogs** (1939), •**Come up Smiling** (1939), •**Dad Rudd, M.P.** (1940). For Charles •Chauvel he shot •**Forty Thousand Horsemen** (1940) and •**Rats of Tobruk** (1944). He continued his association with Ken G. •Hall by filming •**Smithy** (1946), and worked on several Ealing Films (•**Bush Christmas**, 1947; •**Eureka Stockade**, 1949; •**Bitter Springs**, 1950). After **Wherever She Goes** (1951), he formed Platypus Productions with Chips •Rafferty and Lee •Robinson to make •**The Phantom Stockman**

(1953), on which he was both producer and cinematographer. Until 1962 he continued to work on numerous short films and documentaries. IB

Heatwave

1982. *Director:* Phillip Noyce. *Producer:* Hilary Linstead. *Scriptwriters:* Marc Rosenberg, Phillip Noyce. Based on an original script by Mark Stiles, Tim Gooding. *Director of photography:* Vincent Monton. *Music:* Cameron Allan. 91 min. *Cast:* Carole Skinner (Mary Ford), Judy Davis (Kate Dean), Richard Moir (Stephen West), Chris Haywood (Peter Houseman), Bill Hunter (Robert Duncan), John Gregg (Phillip Lawson).

One of two films based on the real-life disappearance of Sydney inner-suburban activist, Juanita Nielsen (the other was •**The Killing of Angel Street**), **Heatwave** established Phillip •Noyce as a highly proficient director of thrillers with a strong sense of political undertow, a reputation subsequently clinched with such high-profile Hollywood-made films as **Patriot Games** (1992). Here, Carole •Skinner plays Mary Ford (based on Nielsen), whose persistent opposition to a lavish housing development scheme, which threatens the demolition of a street of old terrace houses, costs her her life. Stephen, architect of the 'Eden' housing plan, and increasingly disillusioned with its boorish developer (Chris •Haywood in one of his many vivid character roles), becomes involved with Kate, organiser of opposition to 'Eden', and determined to find out what has happened to Mary. The film climaxes with the New Year's Eve revel in

Judy Davis and Richard Moir in **Heatwave**

King's Cross, in a cleverly shot crowd sequence. Sudden torrential rain brings an end to a heatwave—and a startling end to the film's thriller narrative. The film combines social concerns (conservation versus progress) and human dilemmas (imagination versus materialism) with the skilful manipulation of generic elements, the latter intensified by Allan's atmospheric score, cameraman Vincent •Monton's moody lighting, and Ross Major's production design. These three serve Noyce well in creating the sense of a city sweltering in heat and rotting within.   BMcF

Heaven Tonight

1990. *Director*: Pino Amenta. *Producer*: Frank Howson. *Scriptwriters*: Frank Howson, Alister Webb. *Director of photography*: David Connell. *Music*: John Capek. 95 min. *Cast*: John Waters (Johnny Dysart), Rebecca Gilling (Annie Dysart), Kym Gyngell (Baz Schultz), Sean Scully (Tim Robbins), Guy Pearce (Paul Dysart).

This has a fairly standard story-line: ageing 1970s rock star Johnny Dysart has to come to terms with the transience of fame and his own use-by date. The usual plot devices are employed: Johnny's desire to rekindle his musical career in an age in which synthesisers and drum machines rule, and the embodiment of this new musical world is his own son Paul, making a success of that same music. Even when this film was released in 1990, the idea must have seemed outdated. The relevance of the film's premise would have held weight in the mid 1980s but, by 1989–90, the disparity between 'real' rock'n'roll and that of new computerised pop had long been forgotten.

This unremarkable but competent film has some notable performers: John •Waters plays Dysart as a 'Jon English' style of entertainer; Kym •Gyngell is perfect as the burnt-out rock songwriter; and Guy •Pearce, still in his *Neighbours* days, shows some of the potential he would fulfil some years later.   TIM HUNTER

Helpmann, Robert (1909–86) ACTOR/ DANCER/CHOREOGRAPHER/DIRECTOR Known primarily for his administrative and stage work in drama and ballet in the United Kingdom and Australia, Robert Helpmann also contributed to 17 feature films, including such famous British productions as **Henry V** (1945) and **The Red Shoes** (1948), and one known documentary between 1942 and 1978.

In every one he danced or acted melodramatic character roles, and in some he was also choreographer and/or director. Only the last three, in which he plays twisted older men, and the documentary, **The Never Never Land** (1964), were Australian productions. The sight of Helpmann as a psychotic doctor eating the frogs he has sadistically killed is a focal point of the horror film •**Patrick** (1978). His well-worn face and protuberant eyes are used to sinister advantage in the role of the professor, who is also the town drunk, in the World War I drama •**The Mango Tree** (1977). Made for television, **Puzzle** (1978), a mystery melodrama, featured Helpmann as a desperate embezzler. He was made a Commander of the Order of the British Empire in 1964 and was knighted in 1968.   ANNE BITTNER

Heritage

1935. *Director*: Charles Chauvel. *Scriptwriter*: Charles Chauvel. *Director of photography*: Tasman Higgins, Arthur Higgins. B&W. *Cast*: Frank Harvey (Governor Phillip), Franklyn Bennett (James Morrison, Frank Morrison), Peggy Maguire (Biddy O'Shea, Biddy Parry), Margot Rhys (Jane Judd), Joe Valli (Short), 'Ann Wynn' [Elsa Chauvel] (Mrs Macquarie), Godfrey Cass (Harding), Rita Pauncefort (Mrs Cobbold).

Heritage sets out to actualise the links between White Australia's beginnings and its (mid 1930s) present. It does this by means of a mystical chain of being in which people of the present, such as Frank Morrison and Biddy Parry, simply figure past existences (James Morrison and Biddy O'Shea), and the present completes the failed promise of the past. History finds the fulfilment of the conflicts between ethnicities, genders, classes, localities, mother country, and colony in British Australia, and a gushing montage of plenty. Unfortunately, the film's stern solemnity mostly smothers the breathless pace and scope of its conception. The story becomes a burdensome duty in a film that wants to document comparisons and contrasts of past and present—and the creation of an Australian utopia is presented consequently as the antithesis of freedom.   WILLIAM D. ROUTT

The Hero of the Dardanelles

1915. *Director*: Alfred Rolfe. *Scriptwriter*: Phillip Gell, Loris Brown. B&W. *Cast*: Guy Hastings (William Brown).

There is a great deal for lovers of the cinema to admire in what survives of Alfred Rolfe's 1915 wartime propaganda feature, **The Hero of the Dardanelles**. In the first of what was probably four reels, the film integrates what seems to be documentary footage of training and troop departures with a simple story of a man heeding 'his country's call'. A great deal of care has been taken with the movement of characters on the screen, with lighting and positioning for maxi-

mum effect, and with cutting for effect as well, especially in the sequence covering the troops' departure for Egypt.   WILLIAM D. ROUTT

Herschell, Charles, *see* **Documentary and non-fiction: silent**

Hexagon Productions   This short-lived production company was an important player for a few years in the 1970s revival of popular Australian cinema (see Revival, the). Its main participants were Roadshow (see Village Roadshow) executive Alan Finney and director Tim •**Burstall**. The company grew out of Burstall's successful release of the broad, iconoclastic comedy, •**Stork** (1971), through Roadshow. In mid 1972 Roadshow invested substantially in Hexagon, which lasted until 1979. The films made by Hexagon were, in general, aimed at wide public support, and the first film to appear under its aegis, •**Alvin Purple** (1973), was a major commercial success, whatever the critics had to say about its ocker-style cultural aspirations. The names of many of the personnel who worked on this film and on **Stork** reappear on most of the company's later films. They include editors Edward McQueen-Mason and David Bilcock, cinematographer Robin •**Copping**, art director Leslie Binns, and sound recordist Peter Fenton. Copping and Bilcock co-directed **Alvin Rides Again** (1974), which failed to repeat the success of the earlier film, but still took more than double its budget over the next few years. Burstall directed five of the films and produced **Alvin Rides Again**, **The Love Epidemic** (1975, directed by Brian •**Trenchard-Smith**), and **High Rolling** (1977, directed by Igor •**Auzins**), while Finney's name appears on them all as associate or executive producer. The company's most ambitious enterprise, in financial terms at least, with a budget of $1 200 000, was •**Eliza Fraser** (1976), which starred Trevor Howard and Susannah York, supported by a strong local cast. In the event, the jaunty adventure story proved less popular than expected, and probably led to the winding down of Hexagon after the mild road movie, **High Rolling**, the following year. Its most ambitious products were •**Petersen** (1974), a well-observed study in thwarted aspiration, and •**The Last of the Knucklemen** (1979), a critically well regarded but commercially unsuccessful exploration of the interactions of a small group of men on a remote mining camp in South Australia. The talents and entrepreneurial zeal of Burstall and Finney provided a lively force in the first decade of the revival and their company's record shows an interesting mix of business acumen and cultural ambition.   BRIAN MCFARLANE

Heyer, John (1916–)   After an apprenticeship as a factotum in the primary feature films of the 1930s such as •**Thoroughbred** (1936), •**Heritage** (1935), and •**Forty Thou-**

sand Horsemen (1940), John Heyer's career marked him as the father of Australian documentary film. His role as second unit director and scriptwriter alongside Harry Watt on •The Overlanders (1946) began a series of films that reinvented the Australian landscape genre. With a significant role in the promulgation of the film-society movement of the 1940s and 1950s, including the setting up of the Sydney and Melbourne Film Festivals, Heyer's agitation for government involvement in film production in no small way contributed to the formation in 1945 of the •Australian National Film Board (ANFB) to which he was appointed as its first senior producer and director. For the National Film Board Heyer was to produce the award-winning **Native Earth** (1945), **Journey of a Nation** (1946), **The Canecutters**, and **Men and Mobs** (1947), and **The Valley is Ours** (1948), after which his reputation was international. He left the ANFB to head the Shell Film Unit (Australia) and, in the following year, was invited by the BBC to give the opening address with Robert Flaherty for the Edinburgh Film Festival. In 1949 he travelled to Germany on behalf of the Allied Control Commission to speak with film-makers.

The artistic licence and lack of financial impedance at Shell brought about •The Back of Beyond (1954), instantly becoming a legendary film in Australian and European film circles, winning the Grand Prix Assoluto in open competition at the 1954 Venice Biennale, and acting as a major influence on Australian film in following years. In 1956 he was appointed Executive Producer—Films and Television, Shell International, London. During the 1950s and 1960s Heyer produced or directed over 60 films for Shell, including the formally adventurous **The Forerunner** (1955), which received awards at Cannes, Venice, London, and Turin Film Festivals. He was honoured, in 1983, with retrospectives at the Sydney and Melbourne Film Festivals. The John Heyer Film Company was set up in 1967 after Heyer resigned from Shell. Here he produced and directed a series of documentaries including one on the technological achievements of the government in Dubai and **The Reef** (1978) for the Australian Conservation Foundation.

Heyer's influence on Australian film culture is enormous, both through his films and in his advocacy and agitation for film societies, festivals, and film schools. In 1970 Heyer was awarded an OBE for achievements in cinema and, in 1997, an Order of Australia. DEANE WILLIAMS

Hicks, Scott (1953–) DIRECTOR

Scott Hicks became the 'hottest' name among Australian film directors when •Shine (1996) suddenly pushed everyone associated with it into the spotlight. The film first came to notice at the American Sundance Festival early in 1996, and was snapped up by distributors. Subsequently, Hicks was nominated as Best Director for both the Oscar and the Golden Globe awards, for the Australian Film Industry awards, and for several others.

However, although this may have seemed like overnight success for Hicks, such was not the case. A drama graduate from Flinders University, Adelaide, Ugandan-born Hicks first made (produced and directed) two modest films with fellow graduate Kim McKenzie: **The Wanderer** (1974) and **Down the Wind** (1975), both dealing with idealistic young men, the former attracted to life on the road, the latter finding spiritual elation through his pursuit of a wild falcon. He then joined the •South Australian Film Corporation as an assistant director, and acted as 'runner' on such films as •**Storm Boy** (1976) and •**The Last Wave** (1977). He was first assistant on **Final Cut** (1980), an inept would-be thriller, and Bruce •Beresford's •**The Club** (1980), before getting his chance to direct a commercial feature, the road movie thriller, **Freedom** (1982), starring Jon •Blake, a film which began promisingly but lost tension and coherence as it went along. As well as acting as assistant director, he directed a number of documentaries in the 1980s, and wrote, produced, and directed the well-regarded but badly distributed children's film **Sebastian and the Sparrow** (1989), which charts the adventures of an 'odd couple' pair of kids, the sheltered one from a wealthy home and the streetwise Sparrow. In 1986, he also wrote and directed a telefeature, *Call Me Mr Brown*.

It was primarily in documentary (including the Emmy-winning **Sharks of Steel**, about submarines) that Hicks had built his reputation prior to the deserved world-wide success of the passionate and exhilarating **Shine**, which made him one of the most sought-after feature directors in the world. As his next project, he chose **Snow Falling on Cedars** (1998), a film version of David Guterman's very popular novel, starring Ethan Hawke. Whether he will ever be based in Australia again is a moot question: like so many Australian directors who have proved their mettle, he is likely to be snapped up by Hollywood where the resources for ambitious projects far outstrip what is available here. The title of his second film after **Shine** seems to state the situation boldly: **Arkansas**. Nothing equivocal about that.

Other Australian films: Ten Minutes (1973, short, actor), •Money Movers (1979, 3rd ass. d.), •Harvest of Hate (1978, 2nd ass. d.), •Dawn! (1979, 3rd ass. d.), You Can't Always Tell (1979, co.-p.), Ben Flugelman: Public Sculptor (1979, short, d., co.-p.), The First Ninety Days (1980, short, d.), Women Artists of Australia (1980, doc., d.), Attitudinal Behaviour (1980, doc., d.), The Hall of Mirrors (1982, doc., w., d.), One Last Chance (1983, short, d.). BMcF

Higgins, Arthur (1891–1963) CINEMATOGRAPHER

The most prolific and influential cinematographer in the history of Australian feature film was Arthur Higgins, the youngest of three brothers, born in Tasmania. He followed his brother Ernest •Higgins to Sydney, and embarked on a career photographing newsreels and documentaries, as well as features. He worked first for Spencer's Pictures on a series of films directed by Raymond •Longford (**The Fatal Wedding**, 1911; **The Tide of Death**, 1912; •**Australia Calls**, 1913, the last with his two brothers), and one directed by George Coates (**If the Huns Came to Melbourne**, 1916). He moved to Southern Cross Feature Films, shooting •**The Woman Suffers** (1918), •**The Sentimental Bloke** (1919), •**Ginger Mick** (1920), •**On Our Selection** (1920), •**Rudd's New Selection** (1921), and **The Blue Mountains Mystery** (1921). For Austral Super Films in 1922 he shot •**Circumstance** and •**Sunshine Sally**, and, for Beaumont •**Smith**, **Townies and Hayseeds** (1923). He rejoined Longford, filming •**Australia Calls** (1923, for the Commonwealth Immigration Office), and a series of films for Longford-Lyell Productions (**Fisher's Ghost**, 1924; **The Bushwhackers**, 1925; **Peter Vernon's Silence**, 1926), before moving with Longford to •Australasian Films to make •**The Pioneers** (1926) and **Hills of Hate** (1927). He ended the silent era by returning to his best form with •**The Kid Stakes** (1927, for Ordell–Coyle Prods), the less significant but still impressive •**Trooper O'Brien** (1928, for John •Gavin) and •**The Adorable Outcast** (1928, with Bill •Trerise). In 1928, he formed Arthur Higgins Productions, and produced and wrote **Odds On**, which was photographed by his two brothers, edited by Arthur and Sheila Moore. He also directed, with Austin Fay, **Fellers** (1931), the film that was awarded the third (and only) prize in the Commonwealth Film Awards that year. Higgins moved to Melbourne to work on Pat •Hanna's films (•**Diggers** 1931, •**Diggers in Blighty** 1933, •**Waltzing Matilda** 1933), and Frank •Thring's •Efftee films: •**The Sentimental Bloke** (1932), •**His Royal Highness** (1932), •**Harmony Row** (1933), •**A Ticket in Tatts** (1934), •**Clara Gibbings** (1934), and **The Streets of London** (1934). Although he did not work on •Cinesound features, he filmed for many directors of the early sound period, including Charles •Chauvel (•**Heritage** 1935), Zane Grey (•**White Death** 1936, with American photographer H.C. Anderson), A.R. •Harwood (•**The Avenger** 1937, with Tasman •Higgins; •**Show Business** 1938), Rupe •Kathner (**Wings of Destiny** 1940, with Tasman Higgins and Joe Stafford), Englishman Clarence Badger (**That Certain Something** 1941), Noel •Monkman (•**The Power and the Glory** 1941), and Mervyn Murphy (**Harvest Gold** 1945). His last feature film was •**A Son is Born** (1946), for which he devised a special camera boom for interiors. In the 1950s he was still working in Sydney, mainly at Avondale Studios on documentaries, and passing on his wealth of knowledge to a new generation.   IB

Higgins, Ernest (1871–1945) CINEMATOGRAPHER   Ernest was the eldest of the three Higgins brothers, and the first to start in films, projecting in Hobart in 1903 and moving to Sydney the following year. He began his cinematographic career at Spencer's Pictures, making actualities and a newsreel from 1908. He went on to make features for director Alfred •Rolfe at Spencer's: **The Life and Adventures of John Vane, the Notorious Australian Bushranger** (1910), **Captain Midnight, the Bush King** (1911), **Captain Starlight, or A Gentleman of the Road** (1911), and **The Life of Rufus Dawes** (1911). While still at Spencer's, but for Raymond •Longford, he made •**The Romantic Story of Margaret Catchpole** (1911), **Sweet Nell of Old Drury** (1911), **The Midnight Wedding** (1912), and •**Australia Calls** (1913, with his two brothers). He made one film for Australasian Films (**The Shepherd of the Southern Cross**, 1914), and formed a production company with his two brothers, mainly making documentaries and compilations. Their one feature was **A Long, Long Way to Tipperary** (1914), directed by George Dean and produced by Ernest, but this was not successful, because the company had difficulty attracting payment from Australasian Films for its distribution, and because they were the subject of litigation. Ernest Higgins continued to run the family company until his death, but the only feature films he photographed after 1914 were Longford's •**The Church and the Woman** (1917), Arthur Sterry's •**The Waybacks** (1918), Franklyn •Barrett's **Struck Oil** (1919), and Charles Hardy's **East Lynne** (1922).

IB

Higgins, Tasman (1888–1953) CINEMATOGRAPHER   As soon as Tasman Higgins moved to Sydney, he began to work with his brothers as a cinematographer, with Arthur on **The Tide of Death** (1912), and with both Arthur and Tasman on •**Australia Calls** (1913). But he was soon working on his own, starting with Raymond •Longford's •**The Silence of Dean Maitland** (1914). Most of his silent films were for minor directors: Charles Woods (**A Coo-ee From Home**, 1918), Arthur Sterry (•**The Life Story of John Lee** or **The Man They Could Not Hang**, 1921), Harry •Southwell (•**The Hordern Mystery**, 1920; •**When the Kellys Were Out**, 1923), Roy Darling (**Daughter of the East**, 1924), Gerald Hayle (•**Environment**, 1927; **The Rushing Tide**, 1927), Vaughan C. Marshall (•**Caught in the Net**, 1928). His most significant silent film was probably Louise •Lovely's •**Jewelled Nights** (1925), with Walter •Sully. He was the cinematographer on the family company's only feature film, **Fellers** (1931). After the arrival of sound, he continued to work for minor directors: Southwell again (•**When the Kellys Rode**, 1934), Rupert •Kathner (**Below the Surface**, 1938; **Wings of Destiny**, 1940; **Racing Luck**, 1942), and A.R. •Harwood (•**The Avenger**, 1937, with his brother Arthur). Although his early career was overshadowed by his brothers, he ended on a high note, working for Beaumont •Smith on •The Hayseeds (1933), and several times for Charles •Chauvel (•In the Wake of the Bounty, 1933; •Heritage, 1935, with his brother Arthur; •Uncivilised, 1936; •Forty Thousand Horsemen, 1940). IB

Hightide

1987. Director: Gillian Armstrong. *Producer*: Sandra Levy. *Scriptwriter*: Laura Jones. *Director of photography*: Russell Boyd. *Music*: Peter Best. 104 min. *Cast*: Judy Davis (Lilli), Jan Adele (Bet), Claudia Karvan (Ally), Colin Friels (Mick), Frankie J. Holden (Lester), John Clayton (Col).

Most of **Hightide** takes place in a bleak caravan park in Eden, a small coastal town on the south-east coast of NSW. The central character, Lilli, is part of a touring musical show based around Elvis impersonator Lester. The independent Lilli is fired during the tour and is stranded in Eden after her car breaks down. While living in a caravan park as the car is repaired, Lilli is found drunk in the ladies' toilet by Ally, a teenager who lives in the park with her grandmother Bet. Lilli recognises Ally as her daughter, and the remainder of the film is mostly concerned with expectations involving Ally's response when, and if, she learns that Lilli is her mother.

Director Gillian •Armstrong and scriptwriter Laura •Jones deliberately undercut the melodramatic potential of the situation and opt for ambivalence at the expense of sentiment and suspense. The ambivalence is primarily based on Lilli's response to her daughter, and the uncertainty as to whether she is capable of accepting the responsibility for the teenage girl. This tension is perfectly captured in a superb performance by Judy •Davis. GM

Hillcoat, John

(1961–) DIRECTOR John Hillcoat is a Queensland-born director who studied film-making in Melbourne where he met Evan English. Together they wrote, produced, and Hillcoat directed, •Ghosts … of the Civil Dead (1989), a searing visual onslaught that presents a disturbing picture of life inside a high-level security prison. In the stylistic basis of the film, Hillcoat and English utilise their background in rock videos with its unrelenting confrontation of images and sounds. Hillcoat and English promoted the film at the Venice Film Festival before distributing the film throughout Australia. Hillcoat followed **Ghosts … of the Civil Dead** with an equally disturbing, although totally different film, the underrated Gothic melodrama •To Have and To Hold (1996). In this visually resplendent film, Hillcoat cleverly utilises Gothic conventions to construct a terrifying adventure for a young Melbourne writer who goes to live with a disturbed Frenchman

in the remote Sepik River region of Papua New Guinea. Again, Hillcoat establishes a multi-layered film that shifts easily between an intimate personal drama involving subjugation and obsession, and the wider social context of postcolonial European exploitation in Papua New Guinea. GM

Hirschfelder, David

(1960–) COMPOSER/PERFORMER/ PRODUCER David Hirschfelder is a prolific and wellregarded composer for film. In his hometown of Ballarat, he was urged by his music teacher Sr Therese Lynch to consider music as a career, for she predicted that his talent would one day be widely recognised. Hirschfelder was always captivated by the relationships between film and music and, to comment on this musically, his film scores often adopt influences from the concert-hall repertoire, popular music, and modern styles to forge his unique compositional montage.

From the late 1970s Hirschfelder was in demand by jazz and pop groups as a keyboardist and creator of jingles and radio themes. His involvement in composing for film emerged in the late 1980s. His score for the documentary **Suzy's Story** won him the Penguin Award for Best Musical Score in 1987. Scores for miniseries include *Shadows of the Heart* (1990), nominated for Best Theme at the Australian Performing Rights Awards, and *Ratbag Hero* (1991). His film scores include •**Strictly Ballroom** (1992), a witty observation of competitive ballroom dancing that won the British Association of Film and Television Award for Best Original Score in 1993; **Dallas Doll** (1994); **The Life of Harry Dare** (1994); **Tunnel Vision** (1995); and •**Dating the Enemy** (1996). •**Shine** (1996) a biographical account of pianist David Helfgott, has a Hirschfelder score that comments on the text and visuals with dramatic intent. It won APRA's Best Film Score award in 1998 and was nominated in the 1997 Academy Awards. **The Interview** (1998) and **Sliding Doors** (1998) followed. **Elizabeth** (1998), a period score for full orchestra and choir, earned Hirschfelder his second Academy Award nomination in 1999.

DIANE NAPTHALI

His Royal Highness

1932. Producer/Director: F.W. Thring (snr). *Cinematographer*: Arthur Higgins. *Sound*: Alan Mill. *Story*: George Wallace. *Adaptations*: C.J. Dennis. 70 min. B&W. *Cast*: George Wallace (Tommy Dodds), Byrl Walkley (Yoiben), Frank Tarrant (Hozzan), Donalda Warne (Babette), Lou Vernon (Torano), Marshall Crosby (Alfam), John Fernside (Giuseppe).

Described variously as a comic fantasy, a burlesque operetta, and billed as Australia's first musical, **His Royal Highness** was the fifth feature (or near feature-length) film released by the •Efftee Studio in the early 1930s. Starring

Historical representations

vaudevillian George •Wallace in his feature film début, it was based on one of his earlier stage revues. In **His Royal Highness**, Wallace as stagehand Tommy Dodds dreams that he inherits the crown to the mid-European kingdom of Betonia. Before he is unceremoniously ejected, Tommy exercises his royal prerogative in highly unorthodox fashion: creating his own knights, prescribing his own uniforms, insisting that staff wear roller skates, teaching his footmen to play poker, and so on. Frank •Thring Snr directed the film but appears to have allowed Wallace free rein: he is rarely off the screen and the predicament of the 'Aussie battler', the innocent abroad, is milked for laughs, anticipating similar treatment in later films such as •**The Adventures of Barry McKenzie** (1972) and •**Crocodile Dundee** (1986). Made under conditions that were primitive by today's standards, the film was nevertheless the most ambitious of the Efftee feature productions. The size of the Betonian palace set alone required extensive studio floor modifications at His Majesty's Theatre in Melbourne, where Thring's early films were predominantly shot. The comparatively lavish scale of the production impressed initial audiences in Brisbane and Melbourne, but more recent assessments of the film highlight its static and stagey nature and technical deficiencies. George Wallace is generally considered to have done better work for •Cinesound in the late 1930s, although the features and shorts Wallace made for Efftee continue to have their admirers. This film was also retitled **His Loyal Highness** by Universal for distribution in the United Kingdom, to avoid offending the royal family.

KEN BERRYMAN

Historical representations   The history of cinema and the cinema of history have been coupled from birth. In several very important senses all films are historical: they turn every present into a past; every scrap of film is part of the historical record; and every film re-presents the past as present when it is projected. Only in rare instances—when the film constructs a recall that is not a full flashback, or when the film is obviously old archive stock—does our sense of watching a past override our involvement in the present that has been created by the film-makers. The traditional markers of 'historical film' are unreliable guides to what what was meant, when created, to carry weight as 'history'. When it was made, purely documentary footage was not intended as a historical representation, even if now we identify it as such, and costume drama, although set in the past, has generally been more interested in the drama, and even the costumes, than in creating historical understanding.

Moving pictures arrived at a time when Australians were intent on creating a sense of national identity, and their myth-making capacity was used to the full. Films played a special role because of their ability to move back and forth between actuality and fiction, from past to present, and even to future. The term 'screen legends' is well known as a shorthand way of referring to the combination of actor and the roles he or she has played; the larger screen legends that infuse, or confuse, a country's present with its past are an even more influential mix of fact and fantasy. Australia has no shortage of such historical mythology. All of it, even where it makes a point of being critical, is overtly or covertly nationalistic. Later audiences might laugh at the way messages were delivered to earlier audiences, but the underlying response of identification with an epic (if imperfect) history is rarely threatened. Because of socially shared expectations and a cultural consensus, the meanings communicated by screen conventions are almost always predictable. This is the importance of ideology, the system of beliefs by which people map their world. The interpretation of the past in any one film, its link to the present, and the cumulative way the past is represented in Australian films overall, are impossible to construe without a serviceable concept of ideology. While the existence and nature of ideology may be a matter of contention, it is undeniable that the whole field of historical interpretation is contested ground.

The term 'historical representation' signals this contested ground. Most people make do with the idea that anything dealing with the past is 'historical'. The signs are usually obvious. It is said that, for Sam Goldwyn, historical films were 'the ones where they write with feathers'. The story is what matters, and it becomes history if it can be supported by evidence in the documents. Take the story of the mutiny on the *Bounty*. Once it is known that Captain Bligh did, in fact, write with a quill, the whole tale of the mutiny is on the way to being believed. This is the point at which 'representation' joins the fray. Where emphasis is placed on getting the physical detail and the sequence of events 'right', have less material matters—for example, personal relations and codes of conduct (which are crucial in this particular story)—been neglected? And the story will inevitably highlight some things while omitting others. The criteria for inclusion or omission may not be made known, and would most probably not be critically considered by the authors themselves. Thus, critique that focuses on all the ways the past is represented foregrounds problems of 'representation' as fundamental to what we see as 'history'. Broadly, the shift towards problematising the construction of the past corresponds with the collapse of certainty typical of the modern world. Traditionally, historians aimed to show the past 'as it actually was'. The rise of postmodern consciousness, an awareness of multiple perspectives, means that one person's history is also another person's poison, or a feminist historian's scepticism (after all, history has been a masculine preserve), or a Koori filmgoer's outrage.

Are there ways around this minefield? Two strategies are common. We can decide to view every film within the conventions of its time and leave our present sense of history to one side, an approach that requires us to make a real effort to be conscious of history. Alternatively, we can simply continue to watch historical films without much reflection. What follows is a 'third way'. It attempts to view each historical representation as belonging to its own time, and it is aware of competing perspectives of history.

The earliest Australian films that set out to show the past were either propagandist compilations or dramas, and Australia produced some of the first such 'historical' films in the world. Most early Australian films were preceded by brief documentary movies depicting events—'actualities'. Archival work by Australian researchers has revealed that within two years of the first Edison Kinetoscope Parlour opening in Sydney—five twenty-second scenes for a shilling—the first 'actualities' were being shot and screened. Scenes of passengers alighting from the Manly ferry in October 1896 were followed by the rather more exciting first film of a Melbourne Cup. These were the first 'instant histories', precursors of today's news and current affairs. They created the historical record and celebrated it at the same time. As with all history, the choice of subject tells us something about the interests and values of the intended audience. Shorts such as **Breakers at Bondi** (1897) and **Scenes of the First Test Match, NSW Versus England** (1898) are significant historical representations, in effect ethnographies of Australian culture in the last years before Federation. Some of the world's first intentionally ethnographic films (films about indigenous customs, ceremonies, and worldviews) were made by European academics about the indigenous inhabitants of Australia. These are just as significant in terms of what they tell us about how history was viewed; they reveal as much, if not more, about the makers and the intended audiences of the films as they do about the films' subjects. From 1898 onwards, Torres Strait Islander and Central Australian Aboriginal peoples were recorded for 'scientific' purposes—and to show city audiences the 'savages' still surviving as 'civilisation' advanced.

A staple of the European civilising mission, the Christian epic, was the form taken by •**Soldiers of the Cross**, a feature-length compilation of short films and lantern slides, produced by the Salvation Army's Limelight Department. It played to an audience of 4000 at its Melbourne premiere in 1900. While the backdrops were painted, the actors playing Romans and martyrs were flesh-and-blood Salvation Army staff, and the appeal to historical authenticity was compounded by the new motion-picture medium. The next Limelight Department epic was pitched to the citizens of the new Commonwealth of Australia. **Under Southern Skies** (1902) is a two-hour history of the (then) recently united nation, with slides as well as movie segments, but without actors. There were actors in two further feature-length dramas produced by the Department before it closed in 1910: **Heroes of the Cross** (a remake of **Soldiers of the Cross**) and **The Covenanters**.

In 1906 the movie epic of the nation took a turn recognisable in the earlier and later iconography of Australian history. •**The Story of the Kelly Gang** was one of the first feature films in the world and was a huge box-office success. It brought onto the screen a counter-current to respect for King and Country: admiration of the battler, the larrikin, and the outlaw. •**Robbery Under Arms** (1907) celebrates the figure of the bushranger, and •**For the Term of His Natural Life** (1908) explores Australia's brutal convict origins. A female lead appeared for the first time in Raymond •Longford's convict drama •**The Romantic Story of Margaret Catchpole** (1911). Although not yet a 'star vehicle' for the talented Lottie •Lyell, it signalled the way in which the attractiveness and audience-following of lead players, combined with love interests, would, in the future, make such period films more involving but perhaps less significant. With this film, made at a time when modernism was not yet triumphant, we can see the beginnings of the postmodern elements that the cinema would make conventional: present actors living in a visible past, history a romantic story easily displaced by an alternative story, the experienced reality of one individual as the place where history's significance lies (•**The Woman Suffers**, a later Longford hit, was a melodrama that incorporated 'actuality' footage: scenes from the 1917 Melbourne Cup featuring parts of the race and observational shots of the crowds at Flemington Racecourse).

Before these elements became staples of films, the nascent film industry was faced with the involvement of many Australian lives in the new historical phenomenon of world war. From 1914 to 1918 and long after, Australian films dealt with individuals at war—•**Trooper Campbell** (1914), •**The Martyrdom of Nurse Cavell** (1916), •**The Hero of the Dardanelles** (1915)—and helped create the lasting historical consciousness of Australia as a nation made through trial by fire. It took a distance of more than 60 years, and involvement in another three major overseas wars, for some of the central themes to be re-processed in screen drama—notably in Peter •Weir's •**Gallipoli** (1981). The theme of a distinctive Australian male type—which we now recognise as historically formed •masculinity—was prominent in films made about World War II. Charles •Chauvel's •**Forty Thousand Horsemen** (1940) looks back to the mateship of Gallipoli and features Chips •Rafferty as the laconic Australian male archetype. He featured again in Chauvel's •**Rats of Tobruk** (1944) and •**The Overlanders** (1946), which is set during the Japanese threat to Northern Australia.

Historical representations

The **Overlanders** reintroduced another lasting theme of Australian settler history: the taming of a dangerous land. Always there as background, the landscape was not yet the star it was to become in later films. It was a locale for convicts, bushrangers, and hardworking settlers. Films about pioneers, such as the 'Dad and Dave' films (•**Dad and Dave Come to Town**, 1938; •**Dad and Dave: On Our Selection**, 1995; •**Dad Rudd, MP**, 1940) were dramas of droving, drought, and bushfire. The stories of the heroes and heroines of features such as Franklyn •Barrett's •**The Breaking of the Drought** (1920) and •**A Girl of the Bush** (1921) refer less to the audiences' own experiences (from the beginning of the century Australia was one of the most urbanised countries in the world) than to other movie images and national myths: for example, those celebrated in the Steele Rudd comedies **On Our Selection** (1920 and 1932). Later documentaries such as John •Heyer's •**The Back of Beyond** (1954) also tap into these myths.

Advances in film art and technology—cinematography that 'naturalises' its subject; 'natural' acting; and, in 1928, the addition of 'natural' sound—made the past portrayed seem more 'real'. At least as important were the conventions of continuity by which film editors disguised the constructed nature of all cinema representation. And then, only a decade after sound, came 'natural' colour. History on the screen in the 40 years after the arrival of sound was almost exclusively Hollywood history, and Hollywood's commercial preoccupations, as reflected on screen, followed the USA's historical ones: the winning of the American west; the rise of American power; American wars; and the modernisation, wealth, and poverty associated with the USA's economic revolution. While Australia was involved in some of these matters (for example, the Depression and wars), the USA's experiences and perspectives did not match Australia's. The local movie industry did not go down without a fight, and consumers did have access to British views of history, but the commercial dominance of Hollywood was impossible to challenge until more government support was again successfully argued for and won.

The film renaissance of the 1970s (see Revival, the), in which historical themes and locations played such a striking part, was not completely unheralded. In addition to the documentaries, there were foreign-funded productions such as Ken G. •Hall's •**Smithy** (1946), made for Columbia, and Ealing's •**Eureka Stockade** (1949). Chauvel's •**Sons of Matthew** (1949), a saga of three generations of the same family pioneering in the bush, set new standards of location realism, and his 1955 drama •**Jedda**, the first Australian colour feature, introduced the continent's larger history within a contemporary love story. The lovers are Aboriginal: the male star, Robert •Tudawali (Majingwanip-

ini) is depicted as exerting a 'primitive' sexual power that lures Jedda out of civilisation and into terror and death. Thus, in this early represntation of Aboriginality on screen, it appears as a threatening presence that will not survive the march of European superiority. Fred •Schepisi's •**The Chant of Jimmie Blacksmith** (1978) portrays the corrupting of uncorrupted Aboriginality, which becomes terrorising as a consequence. Powerfully revising the innocence of the White past as well as that of indigenous Australians, this film was one of the first realist representations of the otherwise largely repressed violent encounters at the centre of Australia's history.

After **The Chant of Jimmie Blacksmith**, film renditions of novels were made that were more explicit about Aboriginal–European relations, such as •**We of the Never** (1982). But the main historical contribution of the new Australian cinema was to mystify and sentimentalise the past, turning out period films featuring pretty costumes and picturesque locales, rather than historically accurate ones. The trend was set by the most famous of them: Peter •Weir's •**Picnic at Hanging Rock** (1975) and Bruce •Beresford's •**The Getting of Wisdom** (1977), both of which involve schoolmistresses and their charges in long frocks. A harder-edged nostalgia is apparent in Schepisi's •**The Devil's Playground** (1976), which portrays the more recent experience of Irish-Catholic boys' schooling. Supported by television shows such as *The Sullivans*, set before and during World War II, the new Australian cinema integrated the history of times within living memory into representations of a changing Australia of urban living and family relationships. Films such as •**Newsfront** (1978, d. Phil •Noyce) and •**My Brilliant Career** (1979, d. Gillian •Armstrong) succeed in melding social commentary with the fashion for nostalgia. In contrast, •**Strikebound** (1984, d. Richard Lowenstein) leaves little room for nostalgia in its portrayal of class realities in the Depression. It was left to the television channel SBS to squarely face the central problem of the links between White settlement and the genocide of indigenous Australians. The series *Women of the Sun* was a more confronting history of Australia than any screened in a cinema.

SBS and ABC television, with their ability to program works unlikely to be screened commercially, have been the most important exhibitors of adventurous historical films. Among those that achieved world-wide recognition are Ross •Gibson's **Camera Natura** (1985), Tracey •Moffatt's **Nice Coloured Girls** (1987) and **Night Cries** (1990), and John •Hughes's **One Way Street** (1994). Other daring works—for example, David Perry's **The Refracting Glasses** (1993), which features the fake poet Ern Malley—have yet to find a wider audience. Combinations of acted sequences with narrated ones, the recycling of older movie images, the beginnings of electronic manipulation for interpretive effect, and other strategies for making the viewer attend more closely to historical representation as convention (or question convention) will not replace narratives of adventure, family conflict, or social trauma. But the experiences of cinema audiences with the small screen of the computer, with the incessant attention-seeking of television, and with special effects on the big screen, may serve to make them more aware of the way in which everything they see is constructed.

The category of films whose historical representations we are probably least aware of— those dealing with the present or even the future—may be those that influence us most. When we watch •Sunday Too Far Away (1975, d. Ken •Hannam), we are as likely to place it in the present as in the time in which it is in fact set, 1956, because we recognise in it continuing issues and typical Australian characteristics. On the other hand, while •Puberty Blues (1981, d. Bruce Beresford) was a contemporary drama at the time it was made, we might now see the teenage girls in it as reacting in identifiable ways to historically specific circumstances. Both films are now historical source material for the study of the time in which they were produced; the historical attitudes of their origins and their audience are coded into them. That is equally true of films set in the future—most famously, the •Mad Max films of George •Miller.

Those who believe that postmodernism means the end of historical consciousness because it holds that everything, whether past or future, is mere representation are getting carried away. The relatively simple perspectives of the past presented in earlier films were already complicated by devices such as the flashback. Audiences quickly became accustomed to them. Whether films become more complicated or more simple—two equal possibilities—people will still be curious about historical specifics and about the larger stories competing to be heard.

TONY BARTA

Hoass, Solrun (1943–) DIRECTOR/PRODUCER Born in Norway, Solrun Hoass moved with her Lutheran missionary parents to Japan in 1950, where she spent much of her childhood and adolescence. In 1961, she returned to Norway to study literature and anthropology at Oslo University, but went back to Japan in 1969 to study Japanese theatre. She married and moved to Canberra in 1972, to study and teach at the Australian National University, and completed a Graduate Diploma of Film at Swinburne Institute of Technology in 1980. Most of her films have been documentaries, centring on aspects of the life and culture of Japan, such as **Sacred Vandals** (1982) concerning the women who tend the shrines on the island of Hatoma in

Okinawa. But her own experience as an immigrant shaped her perceptions of the Japanese in Australia, resulting in the feature-length documentary film **Green Tea and Cherry Ripe** (1988), in which Japanese war brides reminisce about their early life in Australia, just after World War II. Out of this oral history also came a fictional feature film, •**Aya** (1991), which was nominated for six Australian Film Industry awards that year. In 1998, her **Pyongyang Diaries,** recording her personal encounter with Communist North Korea, was officially selected for the Berlin Festival.

IB

Hogan, P.J. (1962–) DIRECTOR After a couple of commercial failures, **The Humpty Dumpty Man** (1986), as writer/director, and **Vicious** (1987) as writer, Hogan worked on his wife's (Jocelyn •Moorhouse) début feature •**Proof** (1991) as the second unit director. Hogan then struck it big with the clever Australian comedy •**Muriel's Wedding** (1994), on which he not only directed but also wrote the script from his own story. The subtle shifts in the narrative development of this film, and the knowing awareness of not only the generic conventions but also audience expectations continued in Hogan's first Hollywood film, the romantic comedy **My Best Friend's Wedding** (1997) with Julia Roberts.

GM

Hogan, Paul (1940–) ACTOR Paul Hogan, Australia's most famous television comedian of the 1970s and 1980s, became an international star with the hugely successful film •**Crocodile Dundee** (1986). Hogan preceded this film with a lead role in the popular television miniseries *Anzacs* (1985). Prior to **Crocodile Dundee**, Hogan's exposure in the USA was limited to a small number of independent television stations who screened his Australian-produced comedy *The Paul Hogan Show*. However, at the time of **Crocodile Dundee**'s release in the USA, Hogan agreed to film a series of promotions for Australian tourism ('throw a prawn on the barbie') and Hogan's presence, together with the film's popularity, was greatly increased. The film, which cleverly combined Hogan's distinctly Australian bush/larrikin response to American, and big-city, customs, with familiar (Hollywood) narrative and generic conventions, was never successfully duplicated in subsequent attempts such as **Crocodile Dundee II** (1988) and **Lightning Jack** (1994). Hogan, in between these two 'Dundee'-inspired films, starred, scripted, and executive-produced the mawkish fantasy **Almost An Angel** (1990) and he followed **Lightning Jack** with a starring role in **Flipper** (1996), a project in which he had little creative input. Despite these post-Dundee disappointments, Hogan's importance in establishing a mainstream American awareness of Australian film was very significant.

GM

Paul Hogan in Crocodile Dundee (1986)

Holden, Frankie J. (1952–) ACTOR A prominent multimedia personality, who attracted large public support in 1976 with his rock band 'Old 55', Frankie J. Holden moved from rock music to television, and to acting following the demise of his band. Holden's first film role was a cameo in •The FJ Holden (1977), followed by minor roles in •The Odd Angry Shot (1979), **The Journalist** (1979), and **The Chain Reaction** (1980). Throughout the 1980s and 1990s Holden interspersed his film roles with regular stints as a television presenter and television actor (*Cop Shop*, *The Sullivans*, *Embassy*, *The Flying Doctors*, *A Country Practice*, *Police Rescue*, and *Blue Heelers*). This included the telefeature *Police Crop* in 1989, which won him the 1991 Australian Film Institute Best Actor Award, as well as a Penguin award for Best Actor. In 1995 Holden made his theatrical début with the Melbourne Theatre Company in a 40th anniversary production of *Summer of the Seventeenth Doll*.

Holden's film work has been sporadic since 1980. Nevertheless, his touching performance in •**Return Home** as the garage owner slowly going broke, because of his inability to forego customer service and combat the large service stations, was a high point; the role earned him an AFI nomination for Best Actor. Similarly, his performance as Alexander Outhred's father in **Hammers Over the Anvil** (1994) reinforces Holden's reputation for suggesting the pain and complexity of ordinary life.

Other Australian films: •Hightide (1987), •Evil Angels (1988), •The Big Steal (1990), •Proof (1991), Ebb Tide (1993).   GM

Holland, Dulcie (1913–) COMPOSER Dulcie Holland's scores for documentary films are reflections of her enthusiastic personality. They are fresh, sunny, and optimistic. **Time Out** (1946), her first score, was premiered at Sydney's State Theatre and the musical director incorporated it into his presentation as live entertainment. This was probably the first time this approach had occurred in the sound era. Holland's repertoire of 12 scores composed for the •Commonwealth Film Unit, 1947–63, suggests that producers regarded her work as innovative yet apt musical interpretations of screen images. Over time it became possible to detect a Holland 'sound'. The casual breeziness of the score for **Paper Run** (1956) catches the informal lifestyle of Sydney's northern beaches with one of its themes, a languid *Beguine* rumba, supporting the idyllic reflections. In documentaries that describe life in the outback, Holland incorporated bush songs into her scores, adding a local flavour. One of her best scores is heard in **The Mailu Story** (1962). Her customary infectious warmth and lively organisation of sound offer sympathetic companionship to the story of New Guinea's Mailu people. Dulcie Holland is regarded as a significant contributor to the development and growth of documentary film music.

DIANE NAPTHALI

Holmes, Cecil (1921–94) A New Zealand expatriate, irascible and tenacious left-wing character who was often the victim of repressive governments, institutional constraints, and erratic economies, Cecil Holmes pursued his film-making with ingenuity and an inventiveness for bringing projects to fruition.

In 1945 Holmes returned to New Zealand from World War II and, although there were no vacancies, managed to hang around the National Film Unit long enough to get himself at first some unpaid work and later a position as newsreel editor and later director. Holmes described his film **The Coaster** (1947) as 'a bit derivative', following the Griersonian formula expressed in **Night Mail** (1936). As union representative at the Unit, Holmes, through an incident famous in New Zealand politics, instigated the first strike in the history of the public service. He eventually won public support and a years' backpay after being sacked before migrating to Australia in 1948.

Holmes first Australian film was for the Shell Film Unit. John Heyer was busy in pre-production for •**The Back of Beyond** and asked Holmes to script and direct **The Food Machine** (1952). Holmes's bushranger film, •**Captain Thunderbolt** (1953), provides a clumsy mix of po-faced political drama, rollicking yarn, and socialist realism. It also has a brashness and thorough confidence in its construction. With actors of the quality of Grant Taylor and Charles Tingwell, and a sizeable budget, the director remembered the leap from short documentaries to feature film production as being sizeable.

Holmes was approached by Frank Hardy, who was keen to realise on film an adaptation of his short story *The Load of Wood* and could provide some money derived from the sales of *Power without Glory*. On the completion of the film of Hardy's story, Holmes and Hardy decided to expand the project to include two other narratives that would frame the initial one. •**Three in One** (1957) can be seen as a movement in three parts from the overt folk mythology of •**Captain Thunderbolt** (1953) to an invocation of Italian Neo-Realism distilled through Holmes's left-wing politics.

From 1960 Holmes was involved in over 20 film productions, many as director. He worked for the ABC, making **I, the Aboriginal** (1960) and **An Airman Remembers** (1963). For Film Australia as a senior director he directed many documentaries, including the dramatised documentary **Gentle Strangers** (1973), as well as the formally innovative **The Islanders** (1968). For the Institute of Aboriginal Studies he directed **Return to the Dreaming** (1971). He made **Lotu** (1962) and **Faces in the Sun** (1965) for the Methodist Overseas Missions.

DEANE WILLIAMS

215

Hoodwink

1981. *Director*: Claude Whatham. *Producers*: Pom Oliver, Errol Sullivan. *Scriptwriter*: Ken Quinnell. Story inspired by Carl Synnerdahl. *Director of photography*: Dean Semler. *Music*: Cameron Allan. 89 min. *Cast*: John Hargreaves (Martin), Judy Davis (Sarah), Dennis Miller (Ralph), Wendy Hughes (Lucy), Max Cullen (Buster).

Before coming to Australia, English director Claude Whatham had made several quirkily interesting British films, including **That'll Be the Day** (1973), with pop star David Essex. **Hoodwink** works proficiently enough as a thriller, without fully exploiting its potential. John •Hargreaves gives an engaging performance as a criminal who escapes from prison by pretending to be blind and maintains his pretence when he meets the wife of a country lay preacher and falls in love with her. The details of his pre-prison life, his dealings with his family, and the two women with whom he has affairs, are indifferently sketched. The film succeeds in its careful construction of his prison imposture and his relationship with the repressed Sarah (a touching study from Judy •Davis), beamingly observed by well-meaning husband Ralph (Dennis •Miller, who finds compassion as well as fatuity in the role). Sarah and Ralph's middle-class life, with its pieties and decencies, is consistently well-observed, and the film gathers distinction after its commonplace opening sequences.   BMcF

Alan Hopgood

Hope, Nicholas (1958–) ACTOR   Largely unknown before his appearance in Rolf •De Heer's •**Bad Boy Bubby** (1994), Hope's performance as the socially and emotionally retarded isolate brought him instant notoriety. While the film's controversial subject matter polarised many of its viewers, Hope's performance will stand as one of the most extraordinary in the history of Australian cinema. As an actor who eschews the hype associated with the industry, he has joined the ensemble of actors used by **Paul •Cox**, appearing as MacKenzie in **Exile** (1994), and as the frustrated husband in **Lust and Revenge** (1996). In 1997 he starred as Sir George Pipps in *Frontier* (miniseries). Hope's recent work has been predominantly overseas.
Other Australian films include: Little White Lies (1996).
                                                       KAREN FORD

Hopgood, Alan (1934–) ACTOR/SCREENWRITER Melbourne-based Alan Hopgood first became known as the author of the very funny stage play *And the Big Men Fly* in the 1960s, and he has had a long career in all the media, as both writer and actor. After 10 productive years with the Melbourne Theatre Company and as a popular player in the long-running ABC television serial *Bellbird*, he became an important figure in the new Australian cinema of the 1970s (see Revival, the) as the author of Tim •Burstall's cheerful sex

farce •**Alvin Purple** (1973) and its sequel, **Alvin Rides Again** (1974). The former, with no pretensions to anything more than ribald entertainment, was a major success for its production company, •**Hexagon Productions**. Hopgood co-wrote (with director Richard •Franklin) the unsuccessful but oddly touching **The True Story of Eskimo Nell** (1975); and also wrote and acted in the sex comedy **Pacific Banana** (1981), co-authored (with Robert Guenette) **The Man Who Saw Tomorrow** (1980), based on the writings of Nostrodamus, and wrote John •Lamond's **A Slice of Life** (1983). As an actor, he has appeared in such films as •**My Brilliant Career** (1979), as Sybylla's feckless father, **The Blue Lagoon** (1980), **Ground Zero** (1987), as one of the commissioners investigating nuclear fallout in Central Australia, and small parts in **Rikky and Pete** (1988) and **Hotel de Love** (1996). His considerable acting skills have never been extended in films.
Other Australian films: The Quick Brown Fox (1980, short, w.), Mates, Martyrs and Masters (1981, short, a.), Radium (1981, short, a.), •Roadgames (1981, a.), Return to Snowy River (1988).
                                                       BMcF

Hopkins, Harold (1944–) ACTOR   Stage and television actor who began his film career in Michael Powell's •**Age of Consent** (1969) after graduating from the National Institute of Dramatic Art in 1967. Harold Hopkins followed this with a small role in the historical drama **Adam's Woman** (1970) and during the mid and late 1970s, and

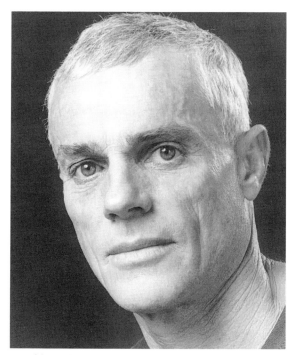

Harold Hopkins

early 1980s, Hopkins was a key performer in a number of successful Australian films, particularly as the brash Cooley in *Don's Party (1976), John Meillon's son in the nostalgic comedy *The Picture Show Man (1977), the footballer Danny Rowe in *The Club (1980), the World War I digger Les McCann in *Gallipoli (1981), and Colin Friels's partner in the South Australian opal fields in Buddies (1983). Since this period Hopkins has not had the opportunity in the Australian cinema to perform in such a rich and varied selection of film roles.

Other Australian films include: *Monkey Grip (1982), Ginger Meggs (1982), The Winds of Jarrah (1985), *The Year My Voice Broke (1987), Resistance (1992), Big Ideas (1993), *No Worries (1993), Joey (1997), *Blackrock (1997).   GM

The Hordern Mystery

1920. Director, Producer: Harry Southwell. *Scriptwriter*: M.F. Garwood. From the novel by Edward Finn. *Director of photography*: Tasman Higgins. B&W. *Cast*: Claude Turton (Gilbert Hordern), Flo Little (Midge Hordern), Godfrey Cass (Dan Yellaboyce).

The Hordern Mystery is perhaps not what one would expect from Harry Southwell, a film-maker best known for having been responsible for several dull films about the Kelly gang (*The True Story of the Kelly Gang, *When the Kellys Were Out, and *When the Kellys Rode). It is a psychopathological melodrama heavily laden with symbolism,

histrionic gestures, and meaningful looks. In spite of its slow pace and the excruciating care with which the actors mouth their lines, the film exercises a certain fascination. Every character in it, except Hordern's wronged wife Midge, is deformed by greed—not excepting the couple's annoying little child, who prays piously for presents and cannot be stopped from stealing glances at the camera. The result is a rather unpleasant viewing experience in which the obsessed Gilbert Hordern is actually *tempted* by virtue (in the person of Midge) the way protagonists in other films are tempted by vice.   WILLIAM D. ROUTT

Hostage: The Christine Maresch Story.

1983. Director: Frank Shields. *Producer*: Frank Shields. *Scriptwriters*: Frank Shields, John Lind. *Director of photography*: Vincent Monton. *Music*: Davood Tabrizi. 90 min. *Cast*: Kerry Mack (Christine Maresch), Ralph Schica (Walter Maresch), Gabriela Barraket (Mandy), Judy Nunn (Mrs. Lewis), Clare Binney (Freda Hoffman).

This is the kind of film that gives 'exploitation' a good name with its tough, breathless pacing, rapid shifts in locale (from Broken Hill to Munich), and taut control of tension and characterisation. Based on a true story, the film quickly establishes Christine Lewis as a girl out to enjoy life to the full and, after running away from home to a carnival, she meets a moody German emigrant, Walter Maresch. Maresch, obsessed by Christine's 'purity', attempts suicide after she rejects his marriage offer and Christine, believing Walter is going to die, accepts his 'death-bed' marriage proposal. Walter, however, survives and he takes Christine and their daughter Mandy to Munich where she discovers that her husband belongs to a violent neo-Nazi party. After coercing her to join in a bank robbery, Christine, Mandy, and Walter flee to Turkey where Walter places his own life at risk by refusing to abandon his wife and daughter at the Turkish border. Back in Australia, Christine realises that Walter will never change and, after being forced to participate in another robbery, Christine confronts Walter and they are arrested. Director, producer, and co-writer Frank *Shields develops the melodramatic potential of this story although he never reduces Christine to the dependent status of 'victim' as her working-class humour and desire to survive triumph even in the most extreme circumstances.   GM

Hotel Sorrento

1995. Director: Richard Franklin. *Producers*: Richard Franklin, Helen Watts. *Scriptwriters*: Richard Franklin, Peter Fitzpatrick, based on the play by Hannie Rayson. *Director of photography*: Geoff Burton. 110 min. *Cast*: Caroline Gillmer (Hilary), Caroline Goodall (Meg), Ray Barrett (Wal), Tara Morice (Pippa), Joan Plowright (Marge), John Hargreaves (Dick).

Hound of the Deep

Hannie Rayson's play, skilfully adapted to the screen, offers a sophisticated discourse on national identity while dramatising the tensions at work among a family of three daughters assembled to deal with their father's death. Hilary has stayed at home in the quiet coastal town where they grew up; Meg, married to a publisher in London, has written a novel based on her Sorrento youth, which her father sees as an act of disloyalty; and the youngest, Pippa, wants to bring Hilary's deli up to date with 'American sandwiches'. Hilary's husband, killed in an accident, has also been loved by Meg and had an affair with Pippa. The death of the father (one of Ray *Barrett's effortlessly truthful character studies) provides the occasion for the family's simmering tensions and jealousies to come to the boil, and Richard *Franklin, in a mode new to him, sustains the subtle interplay of relationships, while allowing it to ripple out suggestively into a wider cultural context.   BMcF

Hound of the Deep, The
[Pearls and Savages]

1926. *Director, Producer, Scriptwriter, Director of photography*: Frank Hurley. B&W.

The Hound of the Deep, known as **Pearls and Savages** in the United Kingdom, was the second of two fiction features made by Frank Hurley in 1926. It lacks the racial and gender twists that, today, make the first, *The Jungle Woman, of more than routine interest. Yet Hurley's cinematography is more than commendable: the 'feel' of a colonialist's vision of Thursday Island in the mid 1920s seems to have been perfectly conveyed. In the context of its photography, the film's story of pearls, inheritance, and moral character also makes a certain cultural sense. To contemporary viewers both of Hurley's 1926 films seem to be parables in which a young, manly Australia begins to assume Britain's imperial mantle in the Pacific. **The Hound of the Deep** just does not tell this story in a very engaging manner.

WILLIAM D. ROUTT

House, Lynda (1949–   ) PRODUCER   Born in Tasmania, Lynda House worked as a researcher at the Mitchell Library, Sydney, then with a television production company in London, before returning to Australia in 1980. She entered the film industry as runner on *The Year of Living Dangerously (1982), and worked on the post-production of *Careful, He Might Hear You (1983), as production manager on *Burke & Wills (1985), production coordinator on *Malcolm (1986), and production manager on *Dogs in Space (1987), Rikky and Pete (1987), Bachelor Girl (1987), and *Celia (1989), as well as line producer on Secrets (1992). Her first major credits were as producer on the unreleased Sweethearts (1989), directed by Colin Talbot, and associate producer on *Death in Brunswick (1991). In 1988 she met Jocelyn *Moorhouse and set up the production company House and Moorhouse. The company's first feature, with House as producer and Moorhouse as writer and director, was *Proof (1991), for which House won the Australian Film Industry's Best Feature Film award. The critics gave the major credit for the success of the film, justifiably, to Moorhouse, but, when House's contribution was recognised, it was usually treated as her first feature, overlooking her previous extensive experience. House went on to produce for the company *Muriel's Wedding (1994) and River Street (1996), both of which were also first features for their directors, with House's reputation as a producer growing all the time.
Other Australian film: The Missing (1998).   IB

Joan Plowright and John *Hargreaves in
Hotel Sorrento

Howard, John (1952–   ) ACTOR   John Howard, a Melbourne actor who graduated from the National Institute of Dramatic Art in 1978, has a background in all the acting media, including plays as various as *On Our Selection* and *Mourning Becomes Electra*, and television series such as *A Town like Alice*, the ABC's hard-hitting *Wildside* in 1997, and the engaging *SeaChange* in 1998. His first cinema appearance was in *Newsfront (1978). He played an argumentative Tasmanian football recruit in Bruce *Beresford's *The Club

(1980). He had a leading comic role in Henri •Safran's •Bush Christmas (1983), as one of a pair (John •Ewart was the other) of inept horse thieves who are pursued by a quartet of enterprising kids. It was an engaging remake of the popular 1947 film with Chips •Rafferty, and it benefited considerably from the drolleries of Howard and Ewart. None of his subsequent films has given him quite such scope, but there were solid supporting roles in (among others) Russell •Mulcahy's black comedy, •Razorback (1984), Fred •Schepisi's •Evil Angels (1988), and as the conventional headmaster in the under-valued •Blackrock (1997). Having missed his chance at film leading-man status, he may well be set for a sturdy career as a character actor.

Other Australian films: Gary's Story (1981), The Highest Honor (1982), September '51 (1983, short), With Time to Kill (1987), Around the World in 80 Ways (1986), •Young Einstein (1988), Singapore Sling: Road to Mandalay (1995), •Dating the Enemy (1996). BMcF

Howarth, Jocelyn (1912–63) In Ken G.•Hall's 1933 remake of •The Squatter's Daughter, Jocelyn Howarth made an impressive début as the strong-willed heroine who manages a sheep-station and survives bushfires and human skul-duggery. After one more role, in Hall's 1934 remake of Raymond •Longford's •The Silence of Dean Maitland (1934), she left for America. Beautiful and vivacious as she was, she did not, unlike Hall's other 1930s star, Ann •Richards, achieve much success in Hollywood, where she played leads in minor films (crime series for Columbia) or small roles in more ambitious projects, such as Frenchman's Creek (1945) under the name of Constance Worth. BMcF

Howlett, May ACTOR In several films, May Howlett has established a presence as one of those character players who gives such a sense of actuality to the life going on around the stars. She was the sourly censorious shop man-ageress who talks about 'girls of your type' to Eva Dickinson in Michael •Thornhill's •The FJ Holden (1977), one of the gossiping townswomen in Ken •Cameron's •The Umbrella Woman (1987), and Colin •Friels' Mum in Gillian •Arm-strong's •Hightide (1987). She has also worked in television, including the miniseries *Cowra Breakout*.

Other Australian film: Hector's Bunyip (1986). BMcF

Howson, Frank (1952–) WRITER/PRODUCER Frank Howson's long-standing interest in the stage—he was a child actor—and in the popular music industry is evident in the films with which he has been associated. In 1981 he set up Boulevard Films, named for a song he had written called 'Suicide Boulevard', and his aim was to make a film of the life of the Australian boxer Les Darcy, but he was unable to raise the necessary finance. His passion for the theatre is

seen in **Backstage** (1987), which he co-produced and co-wrote for the Burrowes Film Group, but the collaboration ended in acrimony and he wanted his name removed from the credits. In 1982 he appeared briefly in Ken Annakin's **The Pirate Movie,** as actor-singer.

Unfortunately, none of the films he has made for Boule-vard, all of them produced by himself, has had a major suc-cess, either with reviewers or at the box office, although as a body of work they are not without interest. The first three are directed by Pino Amenta. The first is **Boulevard of Bro-ken Dreams** (1988), starring John •Waters as a dying play-wright who returns from the USA to see his ex-wife and child. Shot partly in the USA and with a budget of $2 mil-lion, and drawing on Howson's musical and theatrical inter-ests, the film was successful enough commercially to enable Boulevard Films to continue production. Amenta also directed **What the Moon Saw** (1990), in which scriptwriter Howson reflects on his love of the theatre from a child's point of view, and •**Heaven Tonight** (1990), in which he uses his music background in a co-written script that pre-sents John Waters as an ageing rock singer and Guy •Pearce as his son, also aspiring to a singing career. Pearce has had major roles in the two films Howson has directed and writ-ten, as well as producing: **Hunting** (1991), a noir-ish mood piece starring American actor John •Savage as a mysterious businessman in Melbourne; and **My Forgotten Man** (1996), a biography of Tasmanian-born Errol •Flynn (the film is also known as **Flynn**), played by Pearce. The film was sev-eral years in preparation and has not had wide exhibition.

Howson's career is marked by a determined 'auteurism' that may not always work in his favour, but he has shown enough flair in several capacities to make him worth watching. BMcF

Hoyts Theatres This major exhibition company dates back to 1909, when Melbourne dentist Dr Arthur Rus-sell remodelled the old St George's Hall in Bourke St, and renamed it Hoyts De Luxe Theatre. His operating company, Hoyts Pictures, soon expanded into the suburbs and, in 1926, merged with the exhibition interests of Sir George Tallis and Frank •Thring to form Hoyts Theatres Ltd, which continued to expand nationwide. In 1932, American pro-duction/distribution giant Fox became a major shareholder, and funded further expansion. Hoyts built the palatial Regent chain in the state capitals, and in the suburbs and country areas they operated smaller, but still substantial and comfortable, cinemas with a reputation for high-quality product and service.

During the depression of the 1930s, the banks forced Hoyts into the General Film Corporation, a merger with their rival, Greater Union Theatres (see Greater Union Organisation). This split apart in 1937 and, despite repeated merger rumours in later years, the two companies continued as rivals, joined in the 1950s by the third national chain, Village Theatres (see Village Roadshow).

In 1954, Hoyts opened Australia's first drive-in, in the Melbourne suburb of Burwood, and their drive-in chain continued to expand in all states. They met the competition of television (which arrived in Australia in 1956) with an expensive program of equipping cinemas in the capital cities with Cinerama and Todd-AO. The drive-ins lasted longer than the suburban and country hardtops, which declined slowly throughout the 1960s. In 1976, the company opened the seven-screen Hoyts Entertainment Centre on the site of the old Trocadero Ballroom in Sydney, and entered the era of the multiplexes. Until then, they had remained exclusively a cinema chain but, in the late 1970s, this changed.

Hoyts was the most reluctant of the three exhibition chains to enter film production after the 1973 Tariff Board Report. In fact, in 1975 John Mostyn denied any intention to invest in the production of local features, insisting that the company already fulfilled its obligations to the industry by the exhibition of good Australian films in its cinemas. But, in 1978, Hoyts did very well out of the American blockbuster **Star Wars**, and began to invest in production after all. They put $200 000 into •**The Chant of Jimmie Blacksmith** (1978) and, after that, invested in an average of four films per year until they entered a joint venture with Edgleys in 1983. The Hoyts–Edgley films, which included **One Night Stand** (1984), •**The Coolangatta Gold** (1984), and •**Burke & Wills** (1985), were not as successful as either partner had hoped, and the joint venture formally ended in February 1987. It was, however, replaced by Hoyts Productions, which continued to invest in Australian feature productions.

Hoyts was also the last of the exhibition giants to enter distribution but, in 1979, they established Hoyts Distribution, and went on to release the two greatest box-office hits among Australian productions, •**Crocodile Dundee** (1986) and •**The Man from Snowy River** (1982). Finally, they diversified into other entertainment activities, for instance amusement machines, when they took over Goddard Industries in 1979.

Meanwhile, the structure of the company had dramatically changed. By 1979, 20th Century Fox had consolidated its control of the company, and, in 1982, they sold to Stardawn Investments (a group of four Melbourne businessmen, including Chaim Liberman and Leon Fink). In April 1985, the Fink family bought out the other partners, and consolidated all the Fink and Hoyts companies into the Hoyts Corporation: Hoyts Theatres was just one wing of this operation, managing the theatres as well as Hoyts Entertainment Ltd (which managed the film distribution interests, television interests, Val Morgan cinema advertising, and Hoyts Media Ltd—the latter had interests in other media, mainly radio). Hoyts Entertainment Ltd and Hoyts Media Ltd were both listed on the Australian Stock Exchange from 1987.

The new structure allowed for further expansion. In 1986, the Hoyts Corporation, in conjunction with the American company Cinema International Corporation (the exhibition arm of Paramount and Universal), began a further construction program, building multiplexes in all the big Australian cities, and soon after started acquiring cinemas in the north-east states of the USA and in New

Hoyts advertises **Possum Paddock** (1921)

Zealand. Despite a long-running industrial dispute with cinema workers in 1988, and large losses written off in 1990, by 1996 the Hoyts Corporation was the tenth-biggest cinema company in the world. It was no longer a family company: in 1994, 47.2 per cent of shares were held by the American investment company Hellman & Friedman, 20.7 per cent by senior management and directors, and 9.6 per cent by the Lend Lease Corporation. Since 1996, Hoyts Cinemas has been floated on the Stock Exchange and, in 1998, a joint international production venture with Village was announced, as the Corporation continued to expand.

INA BERTRAND

Hughes, John (1948–) DIRECTOR/PRODUCER/WRITER John Hughes was initially politicised by working as a cinematographer for ABC television news, then made aware of the problems of the independent film scene while taking part in the making of Bert •Deling's **Dalmas** (1970). In the 1970s he became involved in the Learning Exchange movement in Melbourne, and in video-access centres established during the Whitlam years. He won an Australian Film Institute award for his first film, the 16mm short **Nowhere Game** (1971–72), and went on to make highly regarded documentaries, always politically outspoken and usually challenging in filmic terms. In **Menace** (1977) and **Film Work** (1981), he is concerned primarily with the conjunction of film, history, and politics: in the 1980s he produced videos on industrial and cultural issues for the trade union movement. But he was always interested in form as much as in content, and in **Traps** (1986) he mixed documentary and fiction in a discussion of alternative modes of representation and the power of the media, as well as of the political events of the period between the 1983 and 1984 federal elections. The mix of documentary and fiction continued in **All That is Solid** (1988), made during an Australian Film Commission Documentary Fellowship in 1986. Still more ambitious and unsettling was **One Way Street** (1991), based on the cultural theories of Walter Benjamin. •**What I Have Written** (1996) moved completely into fiction, but continued his obsession with issues of film form.

Other Australian films: A Film About the Kinetic Work of John Hansen (1973–74), Abortion—A Woman's Decision (1973), C.F. (1982–83), Is It Working—George Seelaf, For the Record (1984–85).   IB

Hughes, Robert (1911–) COMPOSER Robert Hughes is a composer of considerable power and original voice. The 16 film scores he wrote for the •Commonwealth Film Unit between 1946 and 1965 confirm his pre-eminence among composers for film at the time. His scores can be lean and athletic, strong-willed yet melodic. At the time when royal tours stopped the nation, his scores for royal documentary films such as **Welcome Your Majesty** (1958) were of noble purpose, a quality demanded by producers for this kind of film in the 1950s and 1960s. The dark music he scored for the Unit's first full-length feature film, •**Mike and Stephanie** (1952) is aptly sombre as it charts the plight of a young Ukrainian couple in their attempt to emigrate to Australia. Two outstanding scores are for **About Horses** (1950) with its steady timpani beat under a broad theme scored with wistful string writing, and **Aborigines of Australia** (1963) a finely crafted score, tactful and supportive. Its rhythmic yet sparse orchestration signalled a new and more intimate approach in the Unit's films at the time. Hughes was chairman of the Australian Performing Rights Association from 1977 to 1984.

DIANE NAPTHALI

Hughes, Wendy (1950–) ACTOR Wendy Hughes was a key actor in the revival of Australian cinema in the 1970s and early 1980s (see Revival, the). She was educated in Melbourne and graduated from the National Institute of Dramatic Art in 1971, making a striking film début in Tim •Burstall's •**Petersen** (1974) as the university teacher who has an affair with the eponymous electrician and ditches him when she is given the chance of an overseas position. Her best early roles were: Amy, a Cinetone newsreel reporter who has affairs with two colleagues in Phillip •Noyce's •**Newsfront** (1978); the heroine's worldly, disillusioned aunt in Gillian •Armstrong's •**My Brilliant Career** (1979); the Toorak divorcee in •**Kostas** (1979), the first of several starring roles for Paul •Cox; the titular heroine in the TV series, *Lucinda Brayford* (1980), derived from Martin Boyd's novel; the shy, repressed bank clerk in her second Cox film, •**Lonely Hearts** (1982); and, most memorably, the snobbish Anglophile aunt, Vanessa, in Carl Schultz's •**Careful He Might Hear You** (1983), for which she won an Australian Film Institute award. She continued to film regularly for both television and the cinema, in both Australia and the USA (**Princess Caraboo**, 1994), but without attracting the same critical notice after the mid 1980s. Her two most recent films are for Australian directors: Paul Cox's **Lust and Revenge** (1996) and Bruce •Beresford's •**Paradise Road** (1997). Her cool beauty often suggested the repression of passions that might flare dangerously when the climate was right, and she could subdue the beauty when the role demanded it. In looks and style, she seemed potentially a great melodramatic heroine, destined for secure leading-lady status, which she may yet achieve if she gets a run of strong roles. She returned to prominence in 1998 with the leading role in the television series, *State Coroner*.

Other Australian films: Sidecar Racers (1975), High Rolling (1977), Touch and Go (1980), •Hoodwink (1981), A Dangerous Summer (1981), Partners (1982), •Duet for Four (1982), •My First Wife (1984), •An Indecent Obsession (1985), I Can't Get

Started (1985), Happy New Year (1987), Echoes of Paradise (1987), •Warm Nights on a Slow Moving Train (1988), Luigi's Ladies (1989), Wild Orchid II: Two Shades of Blue (1992).

BMcF

Humphries, Barry (1934–) ACTOR/WRITER   Best known for his stage act and television shows, this Melbourne-born actor/writer/satirist was a key figure in the commercial success of •The Adventures of Barry McKenzie (1972) as it was based on the characters Humphries developed in the comic strip that had first appeared in the British magazine *Private Eye* in the mid 1960s. Barry Humphries also played three characters in the film as well as co-writing the script with director Bruce •Beresford. Despite criticism within Australia as to the film's 'vulgar' tone and the damage it would do overseas, it was hugely popular throughout Australia and in London. Edna Everage, one of Humphries's characters in the film, had also appeared in an 'interview' in the pseudo 'documentary' •The Naked Bunyip (1970) two years earlier. In 1974 Humphries and Beresford reprised the main characters from their 1972 film in **Barry McKenzie**

Barry Humphries in **The Getting of Wisdom** (1977)

Holds His Own (1974) and they extended the setting beyond London to include Transylvania and a vampire attack on Aunt Edna from Count Plasma. The Commonwealth government did not finance the film: finance was provided by the Reg Grundy Organisation. Although **Barry McKenzie Holds His Own** had a more coherent plot and was technically superior to its predecessor, it failed to match the original film's outstanding commercial success.

Since 1974 Humphries has sporadically returned to the Australian cinema, mainly in cameo or supporting roles, in such films as **The Great McCarthy** (1975), •**The Getting of Wisdom** (1977), **Howling III: The Marsupials** (1987) and **Welcome to Woop Woop** (1997). The exception to this pattern of supporting roles is **Les Patterson Saves the World** (1987), which was written by Humphries and his wife Diane Millstead and based on one of Humphries's stage characters, the belching, chundering, womanising Sir Les Patterson, cultural attaché to the Court of St James. However, the Australian distributor, Hoyts, lost faith in the film after seeing the final cut, and Australian and British critical reaction to it was savage. **Les Patterson Saves the World** was unfavourably compared with •**Crocodile Dundee,** which had been released to glowing reviews and large audiences the year before and Humphries's film was seen as a dismal return to the 'crude excesses' of the 'ocker' comedies of the early 1970s.

GM

Hunter, Bill (1941–) ACTOR   Although Bill Hunter has spent some time overseas, primarily in the United Kingdom, his acting career parallels the revival of the Australian film industry in the early 1970s (see Revival, the). His face and voice now assume an iconic resonance through frequent appearances in key Australian films. Hunter began his film career in minor roles, such as the officer in •**Ned Kelly** (1970) and the barman in •**Stone** (1974). He seemed destined to play police officers (•**Mad Dog Morgan,** 1976), criminals or other supporting roles until Phillip •Noyce accelerated his status into leading roles with •**Backroads** (1977) and, especially, •**Newsfront** (1978). Hunter's performance in the last film as the Cinetone cameraman Len Maguire, struggling to keep his company afloat due to the competition from television, struck a nerve with Australian audiences and Hunter has been a key figure in the industry since its release. The futility of Maguire's struggle, interspersed with the ironic humour and his failed relationships, established a screen persona that was reinforced by his performance as the doomed Captain Barton in •**Gallipoli** (1981). Barton, knowing the whole military exercise is futile, chooses to accompany his men as they charge into the Turkish guns on the Gallipoli Peninsula in 1915.

Hunter has extended his range of characterisations since the early 1980s and his roles range from broad farce, the caricatured Australian Dance Federation president Barry Fife in •Strictly Ballroom (1992), to the more complex presentation of Australian entrepreneurial behaviour in •Muriel's Wedding (1994). In this film Hunter's Bill Heslop is a failed politician, adulterer, and greedy businessman—but he is also Muriel's father. The casting of Hunter, and a screen persona built up over two decades, provide a tinge of ambiguity to an essentially villainous role. This process also extends to his character (Bob) in •The Adventures of Priscilla, Queen of the Desert (1994). This paradoxical quality of moral ambiguity was epitomised by his casting as Rex Connor in the television miniseries *The Dismissal* (1983), the complex politician who contributed to the downfall of the Whitlam government.

Other Australian films include: •27A (1974), •The Man From Hong Kong (1975), •Eliza Fraser (1976), Weekend of Shadows (1978), •In Search of Anna (1979), … Maybe This Time (1980), Hard Knocks (1980), •Far East (1982), •Heatwave (1982), The Return of Captain Invincible (1983), Street Hero (1984), Rebel (1985), •An Indecent Obsession (1985), Call Me Mr. Brown (1986), Sky Pirates (1986), •Death of a Soldier (1986), Fever (1987), Rikky and Pete (1988), •Mull (1989), •The Last Days of Chez Nous (1992), •Deadly (1992), Shotgun Wedding (1993), •The Custodian (1994), •Broken Highway (1994), Every Night … Every Night (1995), •Road to Nhill (1997).   GM

Hurley, Frank (1885–1962) CINEMATOGRAPHER/PRODUCER/ DIRECTOR Frank Hurley became Australia's best-known nature photographer, with his work exhibited in galleries, in books and newspapers and magazines, and in films. His cinematographic record of the 1911 Mawson Antarctic expedition is now known as **Home of the Blizzard** (1913), his trip through tropical north Australia with Francis Birtles was released as **Into Australia's Unknown** (1915), and his most famous expedition of all, back to the Antarctic with Shackleton, as **In the Grip of the Polar Ice** (1917), re-released with sound in 1933 as **Endurance**. From June 1917 he was Australia's first official cameraman in World War I and, after the war, he returned to expeditionary photography with **The Ross Smith Flight** (1920). Further expeditions, this time to Papua New Guinea, led to two documentaries: **Pearls and Savages** (1921) and **With the Headhunters in Unknown Papua** (1923). He toured with these (as he had done with his earlier films) throughout Australia and the United Kingdom, Canada and the USA, acting as both entrepreneur and narrator. The popular success of his films on these tours, and some comments made about the potential of Papua New Guinea as an exotic location, led him to embark on the production of the dramatic features •**The Jungle Woman** (1926) and •**The Hound of the Deep (Pearl of the South Seas)** (1926). These did quite well at the box office, but Hurley still returned to documentary production, making two further trips to the Antarctic with Mawson (from which came **Siege of the South**, 1931). In the 1930s he shot several of the •Cinesound features, including •**The Squatter's Daughter** (1933, with George •Malcolm), •**The Silence of Dean Maitland** (1934), •**Strike Me Lucky** (1934, with George •Heath), •**Grandad Rudd** (1935, with George Heath), and •**Lovers and Luggers** (1937, with George Heath). He was also employed on commission by Cinesound to make documentaries for government and private sponsors: his large output during the 1930s included **Symphony in Steel** (1933), **Treasures of Katoomba** (1936), and **A Nation is Built** (1938). He did some additional shooting for Charles •Chauvel's •**Forty Thousand Horsemen** (1940), and was again an official camera man during World War II, but, after the war, he concentrated on still photography, publishing several books. His life was later the subject of a film —Anthony •Buckley's **Snow, Sand and Savages** (1973).

IB

I

In Search of Anna

1979. Director: Esben Storm. *Producer:* Esben Storm. *Scriptwriter:* Esben Storm. *Director of photography:* Mike Edols. *Music:* Michael Norton. 91 min. *Cast:* Richard Moir (Tony), Judy Morris (Sam), Bill Hunter (Peter), Alex Taifer (Tony's Father), Chris Haywood (Jerry).

Tony, a young man of Greek parentage, has just emerged from six years in gaol for armed robbery. Finding that his former girlfriend Anna has moved to Sydney, he decides to make the journey north. Prior to this, he has been beaten up by thugs employed by his former partner Jerry, who wants to know where the spoils of their robbery have been hidden. The film's procedure is to alternate between the present, as Tony hitches a lift from a liberated young woman called Sam, and the events of the past, which have contributed to Tony's sense of alienation. He and Sam are drawn to each other but, when he finds her living in Sydney with commercial photographer Peter, he decides to continue his search for Anna to Queensland—and Sam leaves Peter to drive him. Anna is one of those Rebecca-like protagonists who motivates much of the action but never appears, and finally Tony and Sam tacitly acknowledge that their future may be together. The film failed commercially at a time when such non-linear slices of contemporary reality ranked low on audience priorities; it now looks as if it would repay serious critical attention for its narrative daring and control.

BMcF

In the Wake of the Bounty

1933. Director: Charles Chauvel. *Scriptwriter:* Charles Chauvel and (uncredited) Elsa Chauvel. *Director of photography:* Tasman Higgins. B&W. *Cast:* Errol Flynn (Fletcher Christian).

Charles Chauvel's first sound feature **In the Wake of the Bounty** looks peculiar even today. At first it seems to be a travelogue about Tahiti; then it begins to look like a historical film about the mutiny on the *Bounty*; then a documentary about everyday life on Pitcairn Island; then a melodrama about the sins of the fathers being visited on their progeny even unto the present generation. Along the way the film portrays nude bathing by Tahitian women and Pitcairn boys, a decidedly uncharismatic Errol Flynn in his first screen role, and some sententious commentary about Pitcairn's inbred multiracial community as a 'utopia'. Throughout, however, there is one dominating, if naive, vision of character forged in adversity, of the challenge of unknown lands and waters, of race, destiny, and desire.

WILLIAM D. ROUTT

Indecent Obsession, An

1985. Director: Lex Marinos. *Producer:* Ian Bradley. *Scriptwriter:* Denise Morgan. *Director of photography:* Ernest Clark. *Music:* Dave Skinner. 106 min. *Cast:* Wendy Hughes (Honour Langtry), Gary Sweet (Michael Wilson), Richard Moir (Luce Daggett), Bruno Lawrence (Matt Sawyer), Jonathan Hyde (Neil Parkinson). Bill Hunter (Colonel Chinstrap).

An Indecent Obsession is a disappointing film that never fully realises the melodramatic basis of the story. Sister Honour Langtry is the chief nursing sister at Ward X in a military hospital on an unnamed Pacific island during World War II. Langtry's charges are five fragile patients. When the seemingly 'normal' Sergeant Wilson is sent to the ward, the situation rapidly deteriorates. This is compounded by Langtry's desire to release her sexual and social needs, which have been repressed by her 'indecent

Hoyt's De Luxe Theatre

For an Extended Season

Com. Sat. June 3

A Mutiny of Fools and Felons—Loving, Drinking and Fighting!

"IN THE WAKE OF THE BOUNTY"

A Charles Chauvel Production

After a Mutiny at Sea, the "Bounty," like a fabled Treasure Ship, set sail for the exotic South Sea Islands. Each sailor kidnapped a South Sea Maiden, and disappeared from civilisation for over twenty years. What became of them? Did they dwindle away to nothingness, or did some unexpected factor re-vitalise them into new activity? You must see this amazing picture to understand the true facts that lead to the mutiny and the disappearance of the mutineers.

SEE THE DANCES THE MEN OF THE "BOUNTY" SAW—TRUE TAHITIAN MEN AND WOMEN IN ALL THE GLAMOUR OF THEIR NATIVE SETTING — WHERE DRYADS ASKED NO VOWS AND KNEW NO SHAME—AND THOUGHTS OF HOME, SWEETHEARTS AND WIVES WERE BURIED UNDER THE DEMORALISING DEBRIS OF SCENTED NIGHTS AND TROPIC MADNESS!

Distributed by Universal Pictures

For General Exhibition

In the Wake of the Bounty

obsession', her sense of duty that has precluded her from forming social relationships and alienated her from nursing and military colleagues.

The film is an improvement on Colleen McCullough's novel and at least does not offer the facile ending of the novel. Nevertheless, it remains a disappointing film: director Lex •Marinos confines the emotional excess to the dialogue and rarely allows the filmic potential of melodrama to extend to other cinematic strategies such as colour, composition, and décor.   GM

International participation From the early twentieth century until the present day, there have been waves (sometimes subsiding to trickles) of overseas visitors taking part in Australian cinema. Sometimes one has felt the absolute rightness of the particular visitor for a particular role, but overwhelmingly the reasons for such appearances have been commercial. It was easier for an Australian film to reach overseas audiences, especially in English-speaking countries, if it had an established name associated with it. In Australia itself, it was also more attractive to proclaim in the film credits a name from overseas—essentially American—films. If one looks at the (in some ways comparable) history of British cinema, the same reliance on Hollywood names to bolster American distribution chances can be found, particularly in the 1930s and 1950s. As in the British situation, the 'names' imported into Australia had often lost their first lustre and were seeking to prolong their careers where the competition was less rigorous.

Commercial motives may account for most of these international visitors; it is just possible, however, that in the early days of cinema, Hollywood-trained personnel were seen as offering a level of experience and expertise that could be only beneficial to the local industry. On another level, that of exhibition and distribution, from the 1920s, the American influence began to dominate, and the encouragement of Australian production was not part of its aim. To a lesser but still significant degree, British interests were felt in the presence of cinemas in most state capitals devoted exclusively to the screening of British films, and there was a concerted effort, especially by Ealing Studios, to establish production in Australia in the decade after World War II. During those years in which indigenous features production ground almost to a halt, local distributors were of course far more interested in the screening of American and British films (including those locally produced) than in offering incentives to local production.

For more than 80 years then, the main sources of international participation have been, unsurprisingly, the USA and the United Kingdom, reflecting the two chief influences at work in determining the paths not only for Australian cinema, but also for Australian culture more broadly. The nature of these influences has been widely canvassed. As far as film is concerned, it is no exaggeration to say that, with the rest of the English-speaking (and a proportion of the non-English-speaking) world, Australia as a cinema-going nation has preferred to see American films to those of any other nation. Although there have been a few record-breaking Australian films (for example, •**The Man from Snowy River**, 1982 and •**Crocodile Dundee**, 1986), the box-office champions have tended to be, here as elsewhere, American. Nevertheless, Australia's ties with Britain, including matters of common heritage, cultural and otherwise, ensured that for at least a decade after World War II there was a substantial minority audience here for British films. British cinema declined from the mid 1960s and the growth of US-dominated television viewing in Australia no doubt helped to accelerate the Americanisation of Australian culture at a time when Australia's bonds with Britain were loosening. But, at various times, and for a network of reasons, cultural and economic, the USA and the United Kingdom were the two main sources of international participation in Australia's fitfully burgeoning cinema.

There are three main phases in this trend: the silent cinema drew on a range of talents behind and in front of the camera; the post-World War II period, in which, but for visiting American and British companies, there was virtually no feature film industry here; and the new Australian cinema since the early 1970s (see Revival, the) has witnessed a good deal of coming and going. Indeed, it may be true to say that Australia has lost more important talents, however intermittently (•Weir, •Schepisi, and •Beresford to name but three), than have been attracted from overseas to work here.

The pattern of American and British visitors was well established in the silent days, pointing perhaps to a touching faith in both the superior expertise of those from the northern hemisphere, as well as to hoped-for financial benefits. Very often, actors and directors in Australia on stage tours would be recruited to local film-making. British actors were used to treating the cinema as a source of useful income rather than as a place to hone their art, and this attitude seemed to have followed them to Australia. Among those who were, or would become, famous on stage and screen in the silent days and who filmed in Australia were: Irish Abbey Theatre actor Sara Allgood (in **Just Peggy**, 1918); Louise Hampton (imported to star in both play and film of **Driving a Girl to Destruction**, 1911); Percy Marmont (in **The Monk and the Woman**, 1917, an eighteenth-century French-set melodrama); Arthur McLaglen (brother of Victor), American boxer and vaudeville performer who had worked in British films, and made four films here, including •**For the Term of His Natural**

Life (1927) and •The Far Paradise (1928); and the vaudeville player, Barry Lupino (in The £500 Reward, 1918). American actors in Australian silent films included Eva Novak, as the daughter of a Queensland cattle station owner in •The Romance of Runnibede (1928); Hedda Barr, as a city vamp, in The Man from Snowy River (1920); Yvonne Pavis, here with her partner, Lawson Harris, who directed her in several cheap and profitable melodramas, including Daughter of Australia (1922) and •Sunshine Sally (1922); George Fisher, who played Rufus Dawes in For the Term of His Natural Life (1927); and Brownie Vernon, who made three films in 1920, the first of which was •The Man from Kangaroo.

Actors were not the only imports in Australian silent cinema. One of the most famous films of the period, For the Term of His Natural Life (from Rolf Boldrewood's classic), was directed by American Norman •Dawn, and American scriptwriter Bess Meredyth, who had a long and successful career until the 1940s, wrote The Man from Kangaroo (1920) and The Shadow of Lightning Ridge (1920), both directed by her husband, Wilfred Lucas. There were, as well, American cinematographers: for example, Robert Doerrer on The Man from Kangaroo; and Len Roos, who was co-cinematographer on For the Term of His Natural Life, Sunrise (1927), and The Romance of Runnibede. And two colourful British characters: Leonard Doogood, a vaudeville comedian, who wrote, directed, produced, starred in, financed, and distributed Algie's Romance (1918); and the author and explorer, Alexander MacDonald, who worked for several years in exhibition and distribution in Australia and, in 1929, produced, wrote, and directed The Kingdom of Twilight. It is the work of historians to assess the contribution of these overseas personnel in the pioneer days of Australian cinema, but their motives seem, essentially, to have been commercial and their contribution to strengthen the melodramatic flavour of Australian silent cinema, a flavour that was largely lost from the revived cinema of the 1970s.

Visitors in the 1930s were comparatively few. They included the American silent star, Helen Twelvetrees, whose career was in decline by the time she came to Australia to make •Thoroughbred (1936), which proved successful here; Charles Farrell, the American actor, who starred in •The Flying Doctor (1936), directed by British actor, Miles Mander; and the American husband-and-wife team of Evie Hayes and Will Mahony, who were touring Australian theatres in 1939 and starred in •Come Up Smiling (1939, later renamed Ants in His Pants), after which they spent the rest of their careers here.

In postwar Australia, apart from the work of Charles •Chauvel and Cecil •Holmes, there would have been almost no feature film industry in this country if it were not for international participation. The Americans tended to use the country as an exotic backdrop for films that might as easily have been set in Arizona: prolific B-film director Lesley Selander's •The Kangaroo Kid (1950), a western in all but location, was the first of the postwar films with American participants; and it was followed by the better credentialled but scarcely more entertaining •Kangaroo (1952, directed by Lewis Milestone, and starring Maureen O'Hara and Peter Lawford), and Long John Silver (1954), Byron Haskin's sequel to Treasure Island (1950), reuniting him with Robert Newton, the star of the earlier film, but with less successful results.

Other major American productions of the decade were: Stanley Kramer's •On the Beach (1959), based on Nevil Shute's doomsday novel set in Melbourne, and starring Gregory Peck, Ava Gardner, and Fred Astaire; the Hecht–Hill–Lancaster production of •The Summer of the Seventeenth Doll (1959), a film version of Ray Lawler's watershed Australian play directed by British Leslie Norman, emasculated by the casting of American and British stars, and a script that failed to resist the pressures of classical Hollywood closure; and, most successful with critics and public alike, Fred Zinnemann's •The Sundowners (1960), starring Robert Mitchum, Deborah Kerr, and Peter Ustinov. In all these films, supporting roles were played by local actors such as Grant •Taylor, Charles •Tingwell, John •Meillon, Rod •Taylor, and Chips •Rafferty, many of whom went on to international careers, and local technicians found experience that would otherwise have been denied them.

The British-backed films of the postwar years more deliberately sought to come to terms with the distinctiveness of Australian life. Ealing Studios, at the peak of its British prestige, made five features here between 1945 and 1959, starting with •The Overlanders (1946), Harry Watt's rousing story of a cattle-drive from Western Australia to the Queensland coast. Watt, who had a strong background in 1930s documentary film in Britain, also directed the second Ealing film, •Eureka Stockade (1949), again starring Chips •Rafferty, this time as Peter Lalor, leader of the Ballarat gold-miners in their conflict with the government over the unjust miner's licence. Rafferty also starred in Ealing's third film, •Bitter Springs (1950), directed by Ralph •Smart, a London-born Australian, who had directed the engaging children's adventure, •Bush Christmas, in 1947. Seven years later, Ealing made •The Shiralee (1957), an attractive version of D'Arcy Niland's novel, with Peter •Finch, by then an international star, as the outback drifter, and followed it with •The Siege of Pinchgut (1959), the last film made anywhere by Ealing. British director, Anthony Kimmins, made •Smiley (1956) and its sequel, Smiley Gets a Gun (1958).

Both films focused on a small boy's obsessions with owning, respectively, a bicycle and a rifle, and both used a mixture of Australian and British actors. Jack Lee, now resident in Australia, made a version of •Robbery Under Arms (1957) with Peter Finch as Captain Starlight, for the Rank Organisation, and Michael Powell, his British career in tatters after the scandal of Peeping Tom (1959), directed two likeable if unremarkable films in Australia—•They're a Weird Mob (1966), a comedy about an Italian migrant's dealing with Australian mores, and •The Age of Consent (1969), based on Norman Lindsay's novel about an artist (James Mason) and his model (Helen Mirren) in the picturesque setting of the Barrier Reef. With more fanfare and less favourable notice from critics and audiences was Tony Richardson's •Ned Kelly (1970), with Mick Jagger improbably cast in the leading role, based on a script by local Kelly authority Ian Jones. Budgeted at $2.5 million, the film was produced by Richardson's English production company, Woodfall.

At the very beginning of what is now thought of as the revival period, there was a batch of films with international credentials. American television director, Eddie •Davis made three low-budget thrillers with minor American stars—It Takes All Kinds (1969, with Vera Miles and Barry Sullivan), Colour Me Dead (1970, with Carolyn Jones and Tom Tryon), and That Lady from Peking (1970, with Nancy Kwan and Carl Betz)—and with Australians taking minor roles and technical credits. British film-maker, Philip Leacock, then living in America, directed Beau Bridges and John Mills in Adam's Woman (1970), an expensive ($2.5 million) but lacklustre convict adventure, set in the 1840s; American Marc Daniels directed Squeeze a Flower (1970), a comedy involving the secret recipe for an Italian liqueur, starring Walter Chiari; and then, in 1971, came two very notable films with overseas directors.

These were •Walkabout, directed by British Nicolas Roeg, and •Wake in Fright, directed by the Canadian Ted Kotcheff. Both had British stars (Jenny Agutter, with Aboriginal actor David •Gulpilil, in the former; Gary Bond and Donald Pleasence in the latter), and both, it might be argued, showed how freshly overseas eyes might scrutinise the Australian scene. Both were critically praised, but neither ever found substantial audiences, and were possibly too confrontational in their views of Australian life to be popular in Australia. When the 1970s revival got under way, after the release of •Picnic at Hanging Rock (1975, with British-born Rachel Roberts in the leading role) and •Sunday Too Far Away (1975), there was a renewal of attempts to lure overseas talent to this country. For the most part, the visitors were actors, some of whom, like Geraldine Fitzgerald in •The Mango Tree (1977) and Richard Chamberlain in •The Last Wave (1977), made major impressions in roles that could justify their journeys. Others, no less competent, such

as Joseph Cotten, Broderick Crawford, Sigourney Weaver, David Hemmings, Stacy Keach, Robert Powell, Jamie Lee Curtis, and Susan Penhaligan, had roles that scarcely demanded international participants. One assumes their function was to help with overseas distribution, although none of these was exactly a star of the first rank. Others in this early period of the revival included Kirk Douglas, whose name may have helped to sell •The Man from Snowy River in the USA, although its genre affiliations are likely to have been at least as influential; Jeremy Irons and Liv Ullmann in •The Wild Duck (1984), derived from Ibsen; British actor Warren Mitchell and American actor Carol Kane in the undervalued comedy, •'Norman Loves Rose' (1982); an appropriate British actor in Edward Woodward in •'Breaker' Morant (1980); British Christopher Lee and American Alan Arkin in The Return of Captain Invincible (1983), Americans James Coburn in Death of a Soldier (1984), Tina Turner, memorable as Aunty Entity in •Mad Max: Beyond Thunderdome (1985), Lee Remmick in Emma's War (1988, directed by British actor Clytie Jessop), and Meryl Streep, impressively mastering the Australian accent as Lindy Chamberlain, in •Evil Angels (1988); and Dutch Rutger Hauer in •The Salute of the Jugger (1989). Two British directors filmed here in the early 1980s: Claude Whatham made •Hoodwink (1981) and Ken Annakin made the American-financed Pirate Movie (1982, with American stars, Christopher Atkins and Kristy McNichol); and two notably idiosyncratic European directors made films of only minor interest: German Werner Herzog's Where the Green Ants Dream (1984) and Yugoslav Dusan Makavejev's The Coca-Cola Kid (1985).

The practice has continued into the 1990s, when director Wim Wenders filmed most of •Until the End of the World (1992) here, and such prominent names as Swedish Max Von Sydow (Father, 1990), American Tom Selleck in •Quigley (1991) and, from the United Kingdom, Anthony Hopkins (•Spotswood, 1992), Peter O'Toole (Isabelle Eberhardt, 1992), Hugh Grant and Tara Fitzgerald (•Sirens, 1994), and Terence Stamp (•The Adventures of Priscilla, Queen of the Desert, 1994), were lured here to play starring roles. Equity has elaborate regulations about the numbers of overseas actors who may be employed in Australian films; for one thing, the allowed number varies according to the film's budget. If such importations are to help Australian films to gain access to the rest of the world, it is hard to disapprove of them, but evidence for the efficacy of such a policy remains uncertain. Did, for example, American Linda Koslowski's name do anything for the success of •Crocodile Dundee, although the character she played was certainly American? Without wanting to encourage parochialism or xenophobia, one understands the objections of actors to the bringing in of players of no special fame or distinction but, as the local industry grows in confidence, such apprehension may diminish. Confidence will need to be a matter not only of quality but of commercial viability as well; that is, when Australian film-makers and actors are felt to be strong enough drawcards internationally, the local industry may come less to fear foreign competition in its own films and to welcome external stimulus.

Such stimulus in recent years has also taken the form of major American studios filming here, as in the cases of the **Thin Red Line** (1999), Terrence Malick's eagerly awaited return to directing, which was shot in Qld; **The Matrix** (1999), which was shot in the Fox studios in Sydney; and **Pitch Black** (1999), the Polygram horror film shot at the Warner/Roadshow studios on Qld's Gold Coast. All these involved some Australian talent, including actors Miranda •Otto (the **Thin Red Line**) and Hugo •Weaving (**The Matrix**), as well as many technicians. Further, the increasing outward traffic—director Scott •Hicks, who made •**Shine** (1996) and went on to shoot **Snow Falling on Cedars** (1998) in America is one of the most recent—may help to redress the balance and to ensure international recognition for an industry once dominated by overseas influences.

BRIAN MCFARLANE

International perceptions It made sense, of a kind, to assume that the further south European explorers went, the more grotesque life must become. What demonic freaks, what affronts to normality, might the southern continent (Australia) produce? Within its inscrutable otherness, every fantasy could be contained: it was, as Robert Hughes has said, the geographical unconscious (*The Fatal Shore: A History of the Transportation of Convicts 1787–1868*, 1987).

Australia's geographical distance and isolation from other countries, including Western ones that have been its principal cultural referents has, for most of its history, left it a seriously unknown quantity to the rest of the world. As the historian Geoffrey Blainey has noted, 'as late as the year 1961–62 only sixteen international telephone calls were made to and from Australia in the average hour' (*The Tyranny of Distance*, 2nd edn, 1966). As late as 1978 in the United Kingdom, the nation-state to which Australia has had the strongest ties, the news pages of the then paper of historical record, the *Times*, included only nine non-sports references to the Antipodean nation. That several of these were film reviews indicates the centrality of film as a cultural ambassador for Australia. In other words, the post-1970 feature film revival (see Revival, The) preceded, and sometimes paved the way for, many other cultural and trade exports that help frame overseas images of Australia, from wine and soap operas to rock music and painting. Significant overseas successes of Australian films date from 1978 in the United Kingdom, 1981 in the USA, and 1982 in France.

The international perceptions of Australian cinema and of Australia have been less than objective. The island continent's isolation from the rest of the world has, for most of its history, meant that it has acted as a *tabula rasa* on which other countries have projected their fantasies, including those of their own cultural superiority. This should not be surprising, especially in the pre-revival period. Witness a strongly French cultural snobbery in *Cahiers du Cinéma*'s dismissal of *Jedda* at its Cannes screening: '[T]he incredible childishness of the situations, the dialogue and the editing, the truly stupendous ugliness of the colours, quickly weary the most passionate of cinephiles' (André Bazin, Jacques Doniol-Valcroze, Claude Chabrol, Jean-José Richer, 'Epheméride Cannois', *Cahiers du Cinéma*, no. 48, July 1955). What may surprise is the extent to which such uninterest and projections have been sustained into the period of faster global communications and the revived feature film industry, as later citations from both *Cahiers du Cinéma* and the *New York Times* demonstrate.

International perceptions of Australian cinema conform to general principles of cultural exchange. Importing film distributors make financial calculations about how culturally assimilable the given foreign text is to their projected audience(s). And various state measures such as censorship, tariff constraints, and film subsidies similarly enact political calculations about the political, cultural, and commercial appropriateness of foreign texts. To Arjun Appadurai's description of the State as 'the arbiter of th[e] *repatriation of difference*' ('Disjuncture and Difference in the Global Cultural Economy', in Mike Featherstone, ed., *Global Culture: Nationalism, Globalisation and Modernity*, 1990), one should add the State's role as a cultural importer. Both are gatekeepers between the culturally familiar and the culturally unfamiliar, between what is increasingly shaping up to be a split, if not a hybridising, between national cultural difference and global cultural homogenisation. International cultural differences are generally acceptable in limited forms and degrees, typically in the form of projected fantasies. This is illustrated most clearly by the success in the United Kingdom of the Australian television soap opera *Neighbours*, on whose long run a much larger volume of commentary is available to researchers than that available in the form of film reviews. Perceived differences of weather (frequent sunshine in Australia) and of levels of home ownership and political egalitarianism (both supposedly higher in Australia) were assimilable as projections of relief from a grey, cramped, class-divided, Thatcherised society.

The accents of the characters in *Neighbours*, however, as heard variously in the United Kingdom and the USA, elicited responses suggesting that the unfamiliar, or the other, is acceptable provided it is not *too* different. For in the United Kingdom, the Australian accent has had sufficient exposure to become acceptable whereas, in the USA, historically less open to cultural imports, it has constantly been a sticking-point. Few films have enjoyed the circulation of *Neighbours*, and so can afford a little more difference. Thus while **Mad Max** (1979) was dubbed for its American release, few subsequent Australian films were, as the differences of accent became more accepted.

Generally, greater degrees of cultural difference are acceptable in 'high' than in 'popular' cultural circuits. In terms of global film-distribution patterns operative since the time of the Australian feature film revival, three circuits apply: mainstream cinema, art cinema, and festival (and similarly specialist) cinema (leaving aside films on cable and broadcast television). Producers and government film agencies have targeted the distribution channels of international art cinema, focusing on the Cannes Film Festival (initiated in 1974). The varying successes of export pushes into overseas territories need to be understood in terms of the pertinent international relations. Australia's film exports have been facilitated more by cultural links than by trade links, with anglophony ranking in between the two.

All three factors have been in play in relation to the principal export market, the United Kingdom, the two countries having long, shared colonial and postcolonial histories. Anglophony has been crucial to Australia's hard-won successes in the American market, well described by Tim •Burstall as 'the most lucrative, but . . . also the most insular and the most closed' ('Triumph and Disaster for Australian Films', the *Bulletin*, 24 September 1977).

Distribution deals with American major distributors, and thus mainstream releases in the USA and often elsewhere, were first secured with regularity in the early 1980s. A middle range of export markets includes those of continental Europe, notably France and (West) Germany, countries that have some cultural links to Australia, and where Australian films circulate principally in art-cinema venues. In the markets cited so far, the biggest 1990s export successes included not only •Babe (1995) and **Green Card** (1990), but also art films that have crossed over to mainstream venues, notably •**The Piano** (1993), which co-won the 1993 Cannes Palme d'Or, and •**Shine** (1996). A third range of markets is the newer ones, especially in Asia, where trade connections remain far stronger than cultural ones. In the words of Sue Murray, Director of Marketing at the Australian Film Commission (AFC), Asian territories 'are not a natural market . . . We are so culturally different that progress is slow' (1995). The Australian films known might typically consist only of •**Crocodile Dundee** (1986), possibly •**Muriel's Wedding** (1994), and probably those in a promotional festival organised by the AFC. In India and the Peoples' Republic of China in the 1980s and 1990s, neither Australia nor its cinema appeared to be well enough known

for Australian films to be identified as such. They were widely taken as coming from Hollywood (a cinema, after all, not extensively screened in either territory, but nevertheless well known as the world's major producer of anglophone films).

The choices of importers, and their distribution circuits, vitally affect international perceptions of Australian cinema. In the USA, for example, more culturally specific genres and groupings of Australian film production—social realist and ocker comedy, independent and documentary film, shorts—have received almost no theatrical distribution and, thus, limited at most to festival and similar circulation effectively form no part of American perceptions of Australian cinema. In the United Kingdom these exclusions have applied similarly, if rather less harshly. One marked difference concerns the Barry McKenzie films. In the United Kingdom the Barry McKenzie comic strips in *Private Eye* and the status of Barry Humphries as a major West End theatrical institution established a taste, of sorts, for the films ('of sorts' because of a frequent colonial 'snootiness' towards Australians and especially ockers). Meanwhile, in the USA, only the second Barry McKenzie film (**Barry McKenzie Holds His Own**, 1974) was screened, in a fugitive run in 1985, and unanimously critically drubbed, Vincent Canby describing it in the *New York Times* as 'extremely, utterly, aggressively, parochially Australian'.

Overseas distributors have focused largely on film genres or groupings that have been the most successful in Australia at the time concerned: imports of the ocker comedy of the first half of the 1970s (in the United Kingdom, if nowhere else outside Australia), the period film of the second half, the blockbusters of the 10BA period (see Finance), and a diversity of forms and genres in the 1990s. In relation to the first two of these market groupings, perceptions of Australian cinema in the late 1970s and early 1980s rested strongly on period films, whose production had been urged at home to displace the ocker comedy, for various reasons, including embarrassment about overseas perceptions of Australia. In the USA, the period film was welcomed by critics as offering fresh images of nostalgic innocence that were a welcome respite from post-Vietnam perceptions of the growing violence of Hollywood films and the sabre-rattling of the Reagan administration. In this context, American critic Pauline Kael's infamous description of •**My Brilliant Career** (1979) as 'taxidermy' is atypically tart.

In the 1980s, the two Crocodile Dundee films, the three Mad Max films, and the two Man from Snowy River films were the principal mainstream releases: they significantly raised the profile of Australian cinema in almost all markets in the two leading groupings identified above. These films yielded images of Australia and Australian cinema as dominated by the bush myth (with some generic variations in the Mad Max films). **Crocodile Dundee** was by far the most influential of these films, remaining the most successful foreign film in the USA. A crucial policy shift in the early 1990s modified such bush-myth images, which was in no small part a reaction to the 1992 Barcelona Expo, where bush images dominated the Australian pavilion and Europeans asked if there was no culture in Australia.

Where **Crocodile Dundee** succeeded in putting Australia on global maps, **The Piano** focused a reorientation of Australia's international cultural diplomacy away from what senior diplomat Richard Woolcott dubbed Australia's 'crocs and rocks' image towards the 'quality' cultural image instanced by Campion's film and, since then, actively encouraged by the Department of Foreign Affairs and Trade. Alongside the quality product of **The Piano**, other 1990s films such as •**Proof** (1991), •**Strictly Ballroom** (1992), **Muriel's Wedding**, •**The Adventures of Priscilla, Queen of the Desert** (1994) and **Shine** have been screened in all three export groupings mentioned above. Most have acquired the journalistic tag of 'quirky', a label whose vagueness perhaps marks some of the difficulty of defining the misfit characters, kitsch comedy and gaudy affront of such films. In 'More than Muriel', an article published in the United Kingdom, Australian critic Adrian Martin provides a valuable corrective to perceptions arising from these famed 1990s exports, pointing towards overlooked aesthetic strains of poetic realism, fable, and art cinema (*Sight and Sound*, vol. 5 no. 6, June 1995). The 'quirky' label also indicates the kind of script oddities that Hollywood would balk at—a blind man takes photographs (**Proof**), Holly Hunter refuses to speak (**The Piano**)—and which enable this anglophone cinema to take a place alongside American independent cinema of the kind promoted by the Sundance Festival.

One last general appraisal of Australian cinema from overseas requires mention and amply illustrates the perils of generalising on the basis of small samples. The highly influential film journal, *Cahiers du Cinéma*, commissioned a report on Australian cinema by Serge Grünberg ('Australie: du désert Hollywood', *Cahiers du Cinéma*, no. 483, September 1994). Alongside its occasional encouragements and flatteries, as Amanda Macdonald has observed, the piece is dominated by the rhetorical figure of Australia as desert, even *terra nullius*: the account thus 'participates in a long-standing French discursive habit of mythologising Australia as the vast desert island of the South Pacific' ('French Film-Crit Takes a Holiday: *Les Cahiers* Do Desert-Island Discourse', *Metro*, no. 103, 1995). This strategy allows a European, and particularly Parisian, cultural condescension to ignore blithely empirical accuracy—cavalier ignorance and mistakes abound—in favour of pre-conceived notions. In an orientalist manner, these notions of Australia and its culture and cinema reciprocally construct Paris as centre of cultural activity, and Australia as void: 'Doesn't the drama of

this semi-desert country . . . lie in its lack of a "real" history'; 'Australia, ie. nowhere'; 'a culture . . .where, it must be said, absolutely nothing happens' except for a 'fundamental Australian tendency towards *inanity*' (Grünberg).

If general perceptions of Australian cinema remain gravely impressionistic, responses to individual films sometimes tellingly and precisely reveal the cultural knowledges brought to bear in different territories in the process of reading Australian films. While the majority of both American and British critics agreed about **Crocodile Dundee's** deadpan, heartwarming humour, and the skill and charm of Hogan's acting, the two countries' different histories affected some reviewers' accounts. American cultural ethnocentrism contrasted with British cultural familiarity with its ex-colony. The British reviews gave equal attention to both the Australian and the American halves of the narrative, but six of the 13 American reviewers glossed over the Australian half in favour of the Big Apple half: 'Mick-in-New York is what **Crocodile Dundee** is all about', proclaimed Vincent Canby, the then-leading taste-broker in American film reviewing in the *New York Times* in 1986. Canby went on to appropriate Australia in thoroughly American terms: '*Crocodile Dundee* successfully creates the impression that there is something approaching a smogless, egalitarian American heaven on earth, though it's called Australia'.

Occasionally, a film can elicit sharply distinct national readings as differing sets of historical knowledges are brought to the text. '**Breaker' Morant's** (1980) tale of the Boer War triggered a belatedly colonialist response in most British critics, who read its criticism of Lord Kitchener in terms of the cheek of uppity colonials. Yet, in the USA the film's consideration of the rights of civilians in war was read in terms of the My Lai massacre in the Vietnam war. **The Piano**, by contrast, elicited remarkably similar critical responses across the four territories of France, the USA, the United Kingdom, and Australia. Given the film's central organisation around gender issues and the relative uniformity of cultural knowledges about gender in these four countries, it is unsurprising that the 77 reviews showed no substantial national variations, no specifically foreign tunes. However, had the sample been able to include New Zealand (the film is set there, it tends to represent Maoris as naive, and it was made at a time of substantial indigenous politicisation), their accounts may well have highlighted ethnic issues barely canvassed in the other four countries.

By 1997, Australia had become a significant middle-range exporter of films generating wide and positive global recognition. It may be that the better-known Australian films, and culture in general, become, the closer do overseas perceptions of Australian cinema approximate Australia's own self-image. The differential, but generally accelerating, rates of success of Australian cinema in global markets have enabled perceptions of it to advance through from ignorance, uninterest, and projections, to closer knowledge. Stereotypes such as the sunburnt country are typically more common the less the nation-state is known to the importing country. Similarly, extreme self/other constructions are more likely where there is less cultural familiarity and the perceiver feels threatened in some way. To write thus of advances, however, is not to imply a triumphal teleology celebrating Australia as advancing towards being perfectly understood around the world. The ever-increasing speed and scope of electronic communications can support such notions, but not the (almost necessarily ethnocentric) selectivity of film importing, nor indeed the cultural fragmentations within Australia itself and across other nation-states. Thus, with the 1990s weakening of national cultural and economic boundaries following the disintegration of Soviet communism and Pax Americana, international co-production arrangements of various kinds have rendered problematic the traditional assignment of a single national origin to a given film: the 'Australian origins' of **The Piano** and **Babe** have been contested inside and outside Australia.

STEPHEN CROFTS

Interview, The

1998. *Director*: Craig Monahan. *Producers*: Bill Hughes, Craig Monahan. *Scriptwriter*: Craig Monahan, Gordon Davie. *Director of photography*: Simon Duggan. *Music*: David Hirschfelder. 103 min. *Cast*: Hugo Weaving (Edward Fleming), Tony Martin (John Steele), Aaron Jeffrey (Wayne Prior), Paul Sonkkila (Det. Inspector Jackson), Laverne McDonnell (solicitor), Glynis Angel (Det. Robran), Michael Caton (Barry Walls), Peter McCauley (Det. Hudson).

Early one morning, Eddie Fleming's door is broken down by the police and he is hauled off for questioning. At first he is bewildered, and the audience is led to believe that he is innocent. Gradually this impression dissipates as he confesses to the most heinous crimes. Then he recants, blaming police brutality for extracting a false confession. By the time he is released, on the grounds that the police case has been compromised, the audience has no secure opinion left— only Eddie's final enigmatic smile to camera (innocence vindicated? guilt triumphant?).

This is a psychological thriller, with Kafkaesque pretensions, carried off by three bravura performances. Hugo •Weaving won the Australian Film Institute award for Best Actor in a Leading Role, but his performance owes a great deal also to the two angry and determined detectives against whom Eddie is pitted: one experienced and conscientious (Tony •Martin); the other brash and naive (Aaron Jeffrey). It

is a dark film, exploring the ugly side of the human condition, and paralleling this subject-matter with claustrophobic two- and three-shots in underlit interior sets, scarcely ever leaving the interrogation room. Given the popularity of the genre of 'police procedural' on television, it was surprising that this taut film was not better received by audiences.   IB

Irishman, The

1978. *Director*: Donald Crombie. *Producer*: Anthony Buckley. *Scriptwriter*: Donald Crombie. Based on the novel by Elizabeth O'Conner. *Director of photography*: Peter James. *Music*: Charles Marawood. 108 min. *Cast*: Michael Craig (Paddy Doolan), Simon Burke (Michael Doolan), Robyn Nevin (Jenny Doolan), Lou Brown (Will Doolan), Tui Bow (Granny Doolan).

This is in many ways a typical product of the new Australian cinema's (see Revival, the) first decade: it is set in the country's recent past (Peter •James's cinematography glowingly evokes early 1920s outback Qld); it is based on a novel that charts a boy's coming-of-age; it looks handsome and has a certain nostalgic appeal; and it features the episodic structure commonly found in other films of its ilk. Paddy Doolan, a teamster who refuses to accept the fact that the days of horse-drawn drays are numbered, meets opposition for his stubborn stand about his livelihood and from his sons, one of whom has left home. The other, Michael, is thrust prematurely into responsibility when Paddy is killed in an accident. The film suffers when Paddy disappears halfway through it; there is not enough interest in Michael's development to sustain the drama. Michael •Craig gives a fine performance as Paddy, winning audience sympathy as well as impatience for his futile attempt to thwart progress.

BMcF

Irving, Louis (1950–) CINEMATOGRAPHER Louis Irving trained at the Swinburne Film and Television School (see Victorian College of the Arts Film School) before joining the camera department of Crawford Productions, Melbourne, in 1971. He began freelancing in 1976, and was soon sought-after as a talented camera operator, working on films such as •**Newsfront** (1978) and •**My Brilliant Career** (1979). He has been director of photography on many television series and his first feature in this role was •**Wrong Side of the Road** (1981). His creative relationship with director Phillipe Mora began when he was a camera operator on **The Return of Captain Invincible** (1981), and this partnership continued with his work as director of photography on **Death of a Soldier** (1986), **Howling III** (1987), and **Communion** (USA, 1988).

Other Australian films: City's Edge (1982), Around the World in Eighty Ways (1986), •Twelfth Night (1987).   DAVID MUIR

It Isn't Done

1937. *Director and Producer*: Ken G. Hall. *Scriptwriter*: Frank Harvey, Carl Dudley. From a story by Cecil Kellaway. *Director of photography*: George Heath B&W. *Cast*: Cecil Kellaway (Hubert Blaydon), Shirley Ann Richards [Ann Richards] (Patricia Blaydon), John Longden (Peter Ashton), Frank Harvey (Lord Denvee), Harvey Adams (Jarms).

In **It Isn't Done**, Dad, Mum, and the eldest daughter travel to Blighty where they teach the Poms a thing or two about judging people on their merits rather than their manners. This is a comedy about 'the Australian character' in which that shadowy substance is passed from father to daughter, as is the case in some other early Australian films. To complicate matters, the conclusion of **It Isn't Done** seems to suggest that Australians are better British than the British. Dad gives up the peerage that is rightfully his so that daughter Pat can find happiness in the United Kingdom with the aristocrat who loves her. In return, Dad and Australia get the butler Jarms, a late convert to working-class brotherhood, and Dad, Mum, and Jarms all take the boat back to a sunburnt future.

WILLIAM D. ROUTT

Ive, Bert, *see* Documentary and non-fiction, silent

J

Jack and Jill: A Postscript

1970. Directors: Phillip Adams, Brian Robinson. *Producers*: Phillip Adams, Brian Robinson. *Scriptwriters*: Phillip Adams, Brian Robinson. *Directors of photography*: Phillip Adams, Brian Robinson. *Music*: Peter Best. 68 min. B&W. *Cast*: Anthony Ward (Jack), Judy Leech (Jill), Lindsay Howatt (Christopher), Stanley Randall (Stan), Rosemary Adams, Jim Berinson (Narrators).

This innovative feature, made in pseudo-documentary style over almost four years, details the lives and courtship of working-class, Protestant bikie Jack and middle-class, Catholic kindergarten teacher Jill in suburban Melbourne. The mixture of voice-of-God narration and readings of nursery rhymes both complements and acts as ironic commentary on the action on the image track. The gulf between the protagonists (symbolically represented by 'that limpid effluent' the Maribyrnong Creek, which flows between their houses) can never, the film suggests, be successfully crossed, and dooms their relationship.

BEN GOLDSMITH

Jaffer, Melissa (1940–) ACTOR Melissa Jaffer began her stage career in 1956 as Helena in *A Midsummer Night's Dream* and, the following year, made her first television appearance, on the *Barry Humphries Revues*, for the ABC. Supporting film roles began with I Own the Racecourse (1970), followed by 'Toula' (1972, an episode of **Three to Go**, produced by the Commonwealth Film Unit), **Gretel** (1973, Gillian •Armstrong's award-winning entry at the 1974 Grenoble Film Festival), •**The Cars That Ate Paris** (1974), •**Ride a Wild Pony** (1975), and •**Between Wars** (1974). A memorable performance was as Leslie, one of the barmaids in •**Caddie** (1976). In **Weekend of Shadows** (1978) she was Vi with a shady past and a desperate desire to achieve respectability at any cost. Other character roles followed, including Mrs Booth in •**Star Struck** (1982), Aunt Jenny in **Molly** (1983), the ballet teacher in •**The Coolangatta Gold** (1984), and Aunt Westbury in **The Delinquents** (1989). Although most of her career has been on stage and television (including a long run as Dr Maureen Riordan on the ABC's *GP* in 1989), her occasional ventures into film, although usually cameo or supporting performances, have been impressive.

IB

James, Brian (1923–) ACTOR Prolific actor in Australian television programs since the late 1950s, including two years as George Tippett in the Crawford's production *Skyways* which earned James a Penguin Award. James has interspersed his television commitments with frequent stage productions and less-frequent film work where he is normally cast in supporting roles as bureaucrats or patriarchal figures, such as the near-retirement schoolmaster in •**Moving Out** (1983). In 1987 he appeared as a retired English admiral in **Ground Zero** and the following year as Cliff Murchison, the father of Lindy Chamberlain, in •**Evil Angels**. James is also a familiar face, and distinctive voice, on Australian television commercials.

Other Australian films include: •Between Wars (1974), •The Fourth Wish (1976)

GM

James, Peter (1947–) CINEMATOGRAPHER At 16 Peter James began his career working for Supreme Films and Artransa Studios, Sydney, before freelancing as director of photography on short films and television series and working as camera operator on a number of films, such as Peter •Weir's •**The Cars That Ate Paris** (1974). •**Caddie** (1976), his

Brian James

John Jarratt

second feature as director of photography, instantly established James's reputation for effective visual treatment. His camera work has been recognised by ten Australian Cinematographers Society Awards (including four Golden Tripod awards and three Cinematographer of the Year Awards in 1971, 1976, and 1993) and Australian Film Institute Cinematography Awards for **Rebel** (1985), **The Right Hand Man** (1986), and **Black Robe** (Australia/Canada, 1990). His overseas career began with Bruce •Beresford's **Driving Miss Daisy** (USA, 1989) and he has worked for this director on another seven films. Much in demand in the USA, James has worked as director of photography for internationally distinguished directors such as Peter Bogdanovitch.

Other Australian films: Avengers of the Reef (1973), •The Irishman (1978), •The Killing of Angel Street (1981), •The Wild Duck (1984), Promises to Keep (Australia/USA, 1986), Echoes of Paradise (1987), •Paradise Road (1997).

DAVID MUIR

Jarratt, John (1952–) ACTOR Best known as a presenter for the *Better Homes and Gardens* television program, Jarratt first attracted attention in **The Great McCarthy** (1975) as the country hero who is kidnapped and taken to the city to play football. This lead role was followed with a more restrained supporting role as Albert in •**Picnic At Hanging Rock** (1975). Jarratt has occasionally appeared in lead roles in low-budget films, such as the road drama **Sum-

mer City** (1977), •**The Settlement** (1984), **Dark Age** (1987), and the bizarre Australian version of the Pied Piper of Hamelin, **Fluteman** (1982). However, he is more frequently seen in featured roles in more prestigious productions such as •**Blue Fin** (1978), •**The Odd Angry Shot** (1979), and •**Dead Heart** (1996) in which he plays an anthropologist who learns that his work at a small Aboriginal settlement has been in vain. Prior to this, Jarratt appeared as the ageing rock singer and Lothario in the comedy **All Men are Liars** (1994). *Other Australian films include*: Plunge into Darkness (1978), Little Boy Lost (1978), •We of the Never Never (1982), Chase Through the Night (1984), •The Naked Country (1985), Belinda (1988), Talk (1993).

GM

Jedda

1955. *Director, Producer*: Charles Chauvel. *Scriptwriters*: Charles Chauvel, Elsa Chauvel. *Director of photography*: Carl Kayser. *Music*: Isadore Goodman. *Cast*: Ngarla Kunoth (Jedda), Robert Tudawali (Marbuck), Paul Reynall (Joe).

Charles •Chauvel's last feature film **Jedda** is probably his most timely and interesting production. On one level it recounts the tragedy of Jedda, an Aboriginal woman 'raised White' and impelled to seek out her roots, who finds that death is the only possible resolution to the dilemma of her heritage. However, Jedda's motivations seem to be racial and sexual (she is driven by biology, not by ethnicity and history), and in that light the film says a great deal more about White Australia's ideas of Aboriginality than it does about the situation of Aborigines in Australia. On a somewhat different level, Jedda's journey towards death, cast out by both societies, is one that in other Chauvel films is taken only by a select few of the best humanity has to offer. Questions of interpretation aside, **Jedda** is one of the most fully mythic and dreamlike of Australian films, its excessive and melodramatic narration shaped by the Chauvels' imagination of Jedda's interior vision and Carl Keyser's colour cinematography until virtually every action and every landscape in it is saturated with feeling and mystery.

WILLIAM D. ROUTT

Jeffrey, Tom (1938–) DIRECTOR/PRODUCER Tom Jeffrey is one of a number of 1970s Australian film-makers whose careers lost momentum in succeeding decades, despite early signs of promise. He had a considerable amount of experience in radio and television before entering films, beginning with the ABC in 1957, and working on such early Australian television series as *Stormy Petrel* and, after two years with the BBC, three series of *Crackajack*. He was also active in the Producers and Directors Guild, as secretary and, in 1971, as president, and he played a significant role in the encouragement of Australian film in the 1970s. With the ABC drama department, he directed a significant amount of drama, and by the time he directed his first film he had had more experience than most.

In 1973 he was working for the Sydney-based Air Programs International, when Margaret •Fink asked him to direct **The Removalists** (1975), a film based on the play by David •Williamson (who also wrote the script). The production period was marked by disputes between director and producer over casting, costume (Jeffrey's wife Sue •Milliken, was in charge of costume and was dismissed), sets versus locations, and editing. Unlike most of the films that were winning plaudits from reviewers, **The Removalists** is set in an unattractive urban present, and involves marital bullying and police brutality. Although it has a certain power and some strong performances, it fared badly at the box office and most reviewers preferred the play.

His next film, **Weekend of Shadows** (1978), with a much larger budget and made for his own company, Samson Film Services, also failed commercially but, again, is a film of some interest. Part murder-hunt, part small-town drama, it is a sympathetically directed treatment of two kinds of outsider: a Pole suspected of murder, mainly because of his 'strangeness'; and the slow-witted Rabbit (John •Waters), who has been tricked into marriage but has contrived to make it work. Jeffrey again drew excellent performances from his cast, especially Waters and Melissa •Jaffer as his aspiring wife. Fortunately for Jeffrey, his third film, •**The**

Odd Angry Shot (1979, p. Jeffrey and Milliken) was a box-office success on its first release. Chided at the time for not taking a stronger political line, it stands up well, not so much as a film 'about the Vietnam War', but as a well-observed study of men who, for the most part, are bored by inaction. Played by a strong male ensemble cast, including Bryan •Brown, John •Hargreaves, Graham •Kennedy, and Graeme •Blundell, it catches sharply and sometimes comically the tensions felt by the combat unit 21 patrol. There are bursts of action, but the best of the film is in its study of the men's sometimes fraught camaraderie, and here Jeffrey shows his skills as scriptwriter as well as director.

Since then, Jeffrey has directed no further films, but has produced the limp comedy **The Best of Friends** (1982), co-produced with Milliken and co-written with Michael Cove; the crusading teacher drama **Fighting Back** (1983); and **Going Sane** (1987), a drama of male mid-life crisis, again starring Waters. There is a gently humane touch to Jeffrey's work that may not easily find a niche in current Australian cinema.

BMcF

Jemison, Anna, *see* Anna Maria Monticelli

Jenkins, Michael (1946–) WRITER/DIRECTOR In more recent years, Michael Jenkins has been better known for his work on the small screen than the large screen. For instance, he has been involved as director on the ABC's highly regarded series of urban crime stories *Wildside* and the moving drama *The Leaving of Liverpool*, and he was executive producer on the *Heartbreak High* series. In the early days of his career, he made a name as director on such popular series of the 1970s as *Bellbird*, *Certain Women*, and *Rush*. His first work for the cinema was as the author of the script for Carl •Schultz's •**Careful He Might Hear You** (1983), where the excellence of the writing contributed substantially to the differentiation between two conflicting lifestyles.

He wrote and directed **Rebel** (1985), which charts the romance between an American GI deserter in 1942 Sydney and the singer with an all-women band. Aspiring Hollywood actor Matt Dillon was imported to play the GI, while Debbie Byrne played the singer. They were supported by a strong cast (Bryan •Brown, Ray •Barrett, and Bill •Hunter), but it is the glitzy, stylised décor for which the film is remembered. In his film version of David •Williamson's •**Emerald City** (1989), it is again the strikingly modish décor, used to create a sense of Sydney's glamorous superficiality, that stays in the mind, along with intelligent performances by such players as Robyn •Nevin and John •Hargreaves. Perhaps if Jenkins had written the script himself, the film might have sounded less theatrical. Bryan Brown starred in his next film, the comedy **Sweet Talker**

(1991), as a Long Bay Gaol parolee who stumbles on a lucrative scam in a small coastal town and is converted to homespun values. This engaging, low-key piece was followed by •The Heartbreak Kid (1993), a bi-cultural romance about a Greek-Australian student who falls in love with his Greek-Australian teacher. The film deals honestly with the difficulties of hybrid cultures and with the particular problems relating to the teacher–pupil relationship. Jenkins has revealed a lively talent that has not yet found a major outlet in film-making.   BMcF

Jewelled Nights

1925. *Director*: Wilton Welch. *Photography*: Walter Sully, Tasman Higgins. B&W. *Cast*: Louise Lovely (Elaine Fleetwood), Gordon Collingridge (Larry Solarno), Godfrey Cass (Tiger Sam).

Only fragments remain of **Jewelled Nights**, made by Louise •Lovely Productions; it is uncertain whether these are out-takes or pieces of the film as exhibited. A young society woman (Elaine Fleetwood) flees her wedding and, dressed as a boy, roughs it at an osmiridium mine where—after some cross-gender confusion—she finds true love with a fellow miner. The film was shot in Melbourne and under difficult conditions on the Savage River in western Tas. It was intended to be the first of four films, all based on Marie Bjelke-Petersen's romance novels, that would revitalise the Australian film industry by infusing Hollywood production values.

Jewelled Nights opened to record-breaking audiences at Melbourne's Hoyts De Luxe, thanks in part to Lovely's Hollywood-style publicity, involving personal appearances and 'stunts'. The film cost approximately £8000. It did not recoup that amount because, Lovely claimed, Australian distributors and exhibitors did not support her film.

JEANNETTE DELAMOIR

Jewish Film Festival, *see* Festivals

Jewish representation
Jews have been represented in Australian films from the very beginning of Australian cinema but, from 1900 to 1996, only 14 feature films have been made that include Jewish characters or themes. Six of these films were produced before 1935, all of them by non-Jews. These pre-World War II films were followed by a hiatus of almost 50 years, until Henri •Safran made •'Norman Loves Rose' (1982). Of the eight films made in the postwar years, six were produced, directed, or written by Jews, and two were made by non-Jews. Given that Jews have been in Australia since the First Fleet and, by any criteria, the story of the Jews in Australia is a success story, the relative scarcity of Australian Jewish films and film-makers needs explaining. This is especially the case considering both the extent to which Jewish film-makers have contributed to cinema in other countries of the Diaspora, and the Jewish dominance of Hollywood, which has reinforced the perception of Jews as storytellers, entrepreneurs, and entertainers.

The most obvious explanation for the relative dearth of Jewish representation is that Jewish film production mirrored the fate of the Australian film industry, which collapsed after World War II and did not recover until the renaissance of Australian cinema in the 1970s (see Revival, the). It is no coincidence that France, with its long, distinguished history of cinema, and its artistic and commercial successes, makes more Jewish films than any other country after the USA and Israel. However, the absence of a viable postwar film industry in Australia is not a sufficient explanation for the relative lack of a Jewish presence in Australian feature films until comparatively recently. The small size of the Jewish community, Jewish immigration patterns, and the mood of the postwar Jewish community in Australia, which was reeling from the shock of the Holocaust, were also factors.

According to unofficial figures, there were 26 700 Jews in Australia in 1933. Most of them had come from the United Kingdom but, by the late 1930s, the predominantly Anglo character of Australia's Jewish community was beginning to be transformed by refugees from Nazi Europe. This change continued after World War II. Almost 35 000 Jewish refugees came from eastern Europe to Australia in the early postwar years. By the 1960s, these survivors of the Holocaust far outweighed their Anglo-Jewish counterparts. By 1971, the Australian Jewish community, which had taken almost 150 years to reach just under 30 000, had more than doubled to number 75 000. Today there are approximately 90 000 Jews in Australia, still less than half of one per cent of the total Australian population.

The small number of Jews in Australia, and the predominance of Holocaust survivors who make up the mix, is essential to understanding why Jews were slow to contribute to Australia's burgeoning film industry in the 1970s and 80s. Any comparison with the USA (or with Canada, the United Kingdom, or France), is difficult. Currently in the USA, Jews number five to six million. There are two million Jews in New York alone, and more than a million in California. Australia cannot match this concentration of Jewish activity and, over the years, has found it hard to provide the 'critical mass' of Jewish life necessary to generate a spontaneous, creative flowering.

The post-World War II Jews who did migrate to the USA encountered a large, dynamic, established Jewish community that dated back to the pre-World War I mass migrations to America from Europe. In contrast, those Holocaust Jews who fled Europe to Australia, although determined to succeed in their new country, were forced to cope with feelings of desolation and displacement, largely on their own. The Jewish writer, Morris Lurie, has described the numbing grief experienced by post-Holocaust Jews as 'shell-shock'. Today it would be called 'mass post-traumatic stress disorder'.

The impact of the Holocaust on the traumatised community was manifold, and has implications for almost all the postwar Australian films made by Jews or about Jews, from 'Norman Loves Rose', to the miniseries *The Dunera Boys* (1985, edited for video 1990), to •Shine (1996). It drove unendurable memories underground, while bringing to the fore at times obsessive love and concern for the safety and well-being of the children and grandchildren of survivors. It imported into the minds of many Jews, aspects of the victim mentality that had been created by 'eliminationist' European anti-Semitism. Fear of gentiles and shame over being Jewish led many Jews to be wary of the world: they adopted a low profile, and exhorted their children to do the same. Most longed for their children to 'do well', particularly in the professions or in business, which were seen as safe, stable, and independent of government. These attitudes were reinforced by Jewish grief at the end result of European high culture (Auschwitz), and the philistinism and materialism prevalent in the wider Australian culture of the time which, in the late 1950s and 1960s, placed a low value on both art and artists.

The collapse and slow revival of the Australian film industry, the small size of the Australian Jewish community, and its composition and psychological dysfunction after the cataclysm of the Holocaust, are all reasons for Jewish filmmakers being slow to take advantage of the cinema revival in the 1970s. When Jewish films eventually took off in the 1980s, their preoccupations were different from those evident in the six films made before 1935, which not only contained Jewish characters but, in one instance (Ken G. •Hall's •Strike Me Lucky, 1934), was also entirely built around a Jewish persona. These early films, quite apart from their intrinsic worth or otherwise, are revealing for what they tell about the nature of Australian anti-Semitism.

The first 'film' to feature Jews was the Salvation Army's •Soldiers of the Cross (1900), which included The Stoning of Stephen, a short film about 60 seconds long. Australia's attitude towards Jews was, and still is, relatively benign, if ambivalent. Populist anti-Semitism had been imported from Europe in the latter part of the nineteenth century and, again, prior to World War II. At times, this translated into crude cartoons published in the *Bulletin*, *Smith's Weekly*, and the *Melbourne Punch*. There is no way of knowing how the Jews in The Stoning of Stephen were depicted physically, as a print of the film no longer exists, but the restraint of the reviewer in the Salvationist paper the *War Cry* is noteworthy. Assiduously avoiding the value-laden word 'Jew', the author

writes that Stephen was killed 'by the fiendish fanaticism of the formal religionists of his day'.

Each of the remaining pre-World War II films offers insight into how Jews were perceived by their fellow Australians. In Raymond •Longford's •The Sentimental Bloke (1919), Steeny Isaacs, who runs a two-up school and a stall at the Victoria Market, is no imported stereotype but a short, nondescript man wearing a cloth cap. He would not have looked out of place in London's Petticoat Lane. This matter-of-fact acceptance is in sharp contrast to the pumped up fear and suspicion of Gerald Hayle's **Environment** (1927), in which Abe Halstein, the 'evil' Jewish friend of one of the characters, is depicted as a Jewish agent provocateur. He is lascivious and grasping, and single-mindedly intent on corrupting the integrity of the Australian 'body politic', represented by a pure young woman called Mary. The logo of Advance Films, which produced **Environment**, was a fluttering Australian flag but, despite the patriotism, the film failed badly.

Two films, W.J. •Lincoln's The Bells (1911) and Harry •Southwell's The Burgomeister (1935) were made from a stage play called *Le Juif Polonais* (The Polish Jew). Only a fragment remains of **The Burgomeister**, but enough of the plot is known to establish that both films pander to racial stereotypes. However, the most interesting film of this prewar era was **Strike Me Lucky**. Made at a time when anti-Semitism was on the rise everywhere, and Hollywood's Jews were turning their backs on the subject, **Strike Me Lucky** was a showcase for the Jewish comedian Roy •Rene, known to millions of Australians as simply 'Mo'. Rene made his career in vaudeville by adopting the mask of a Jewish clown. Without the feedback of a live audience, his performance became stilted, and **Strike Me Lucky** bombed. Nonetheless, 'Mo' turned prejudice on its head by transmogrifying the vicious, centuries-old European stereotype of the grasping Jew into a paradigm of the 'little Aussie battler'. In this regard the film has much to say about prewar Australian tolerance and the belief in a 'fair go'.

If these early films offer glimpses of how Jews were seen by others, the Jewish films that followed the Australian film revival are a window on how Australian Jews see themselves, and how they have attempted to come to terms with the impact of the Holocaust—the defining event of the twentieth century for Jews.

Safran, a Paris-born director who has worked extensively in television and film, came to prominence at the beginning of the Australian film revival with **Storm Boy** (1976). His 'Norman Loves Rose' owes more to the portrayal by actor Richard Benjamin of the character of Portnoy in **Goodbye Columbus** (USA, 1969) and **Portnoy's Complaint** (USA, 1972) (both based on novels by the American-Jewish author Phillip Roth) than to anything coming out of Sydney, where the film is set. Yet within the comic stereotyping—the dominating Jewish mother, the womanising father ('my-son-the-dentist who would rather have married a shiksa and become a musician')—some pertinent observations are made about the Holocaust and dysfunctional Jewish families.

Scott •Hicks's **Shine**, based on the life of concert pianist David Helfgott, is similarly illuminating. Whatever the truth about Helfgott's overbearing father whose love turned to possessiveness, the film argues, in much the same way as Sidney Lumet's **The Pawnbroker** (1965), that many Jews who survived World War II suffered debilitating psychological damage. **Shine** suggests that it is this that causes the character of Helfgott's father to behave brutally to his son.

The television miniseries *The Dunera Boys* was groundbreaking on two scores. Written and directed by Ben •Lewin and produced by Bob •Weis (both sons of Holocaust survivors), it was the first Holocaust story told in film from an Australian perspective, and the first Australian film made by Jewish film-makers to capture the unique quality and texture of the Australian Jewish experience. It was also the first film after **Strike Me Lucky** to mirror both the tolerance and the latent anti-Semitism that characterised the Australian attitude towards Jews.

Two Brothers Running (1988), directed by Ted Robinson and scripted by Morris Lurie, was unfortunately never released theatrically, although it has been screened on television. Tom Conti plays the writer Moses Borenstein, ruminating on the end of his marriage, and his existential angst. Moses's response is to tell stories, a universal Jewish solution to the human predicament. **Father** (1990), directed by John •Power, is an outsider's view of the Holocaust, and a clumsy attempt to contribute to the debate about war crimes trials, with Auschwitz being compared inappropriately with the massacre of My Lai in Vietnam.

Palace of Dreams (1985), a ten-part television series produced by Sandra •Levy for the ABC, was in its way as significant as *The Dunera Boys*. Conventional in structure, it nonetheless excelled in delineating the particularities of being religiously and culturally Jewish in Australia. Set during the Depression of the 1930s, it captured the reality for most European Jews living here: Australia, where the only real danger was assimilation, seemed an Eden far removed from institutionalised anti-Semitism.

Although Australian Jews were discouraged from pursuing careers in the arts, a number of Jews entered the film industry, and made their mark in feature films that have no Jewish content. This was the case with director Mark •Joffe (•**Grievous Bodily Harm**, 1988; •**Spotswood**, 1992; •**Cosi**, 1996), Yoram •Gross (whose animated features include •**Dot and the Kangaroo**, 1977), and producer Margaret •Fink (**The Removalists**, 1975; **My Brilliant Career**, 1979). Feature films were also made by Rivka Hartman (**Bachelor Girl**,

1987) and Monique Schwarz (**Pieta**, 1987). There was minimal Jewish content in Hartman's film, and none at all in Schwarz's, but both film-makers went on to express their Jewish identities in compelling documentaries: Hartman **in The Miniskirted Dynamo** (1996), a film about her doctor mother Dora Bialestock, and Schwarz **in Bitter Herbs and Honey** (1996), the story of the Jews of Carlton, an inner-city Melbourne suburb.

The Holocaust has determined the composition of Australia's Jewish community, coloured its thinking and, in large measure, shaped the way Jews see themselves. This is evident in the features, television dramas, and documentaries made by Jews after Australia's film revival in the 1970s and 1980s. Because Australia's survivor community was in a state of shock, Jews were unable to be confident about their identity. The fear associated with proclaiming Jewishness has now been largely dispelled by the confidence that

Roy Rene ('Mo')

Jilted

Zionism has imparted to Jewish identity. Australia's postwar Jews were too preoccupied with the camps to make movies. This was left to their children, and their grandchildren, directors such as Michael Rymer (•**Angel Baby**, 1995) and Craig Rosenberg (**Hotel de Love**, 1996), and writers such as Yael Bergman, who co-wrote and co-produced Emma-Kate Croghan's **Love and Other Catastrophes** (1996). This film about young love on a university campus in the 1990s, is only incidentally Jewish, but it vanquishes Jewish shame by the inclusion of the character Ari. His name not only conjures up the blue-eyed hero of *Exodus* (1960), it also resonates with the power conferred upon it by the Jewish state.

JAN EPSTEIN

Jilted

1987. Director: Bill Bennett. *Producers:* Bill Bennett, Jenny Day. *Scriptwriter:* Bill Bennett. *Director of photography:* Geoff Simpson. *Music:* Michael Atkinson. *Cast:* Richard Moir (Al), Steve Jacobs (Bob), Tina Bursill (Paula), Jennifer Cluff (Harry), Helen Mutkins (Cindy).

Jilted, which was filmed around the Orchid Beach resort on Fraser Island is, on the surface, a conventional romantic melodrama. Irresponsible Al is on his last chance as a reputable chef at a luxurious Fraser Island resort. Al proceeds to neglect his duties in favour of a doomed romance with a new female arrival, Harry. The inherent melodramatic basis of the film emanates from Al's attempt to romance Harry, while disentangling himself from fellow employee, and current lover, Cindy.

A notable feature of the film is the way in which Bill •Bennett transforms conventional material into a semi-improvised, depressing series of encounters, while denying any real form of catharsis and closure. Instead of the characteristic emotional climax usually found in this genre, a failed suicide attempt provides a vague, downbeat sense of resolution.

GM

'Joan of Arc' of Loos, The

1916. Director: George Willoughby. *Scriptwriter:* Herbert Ford. *Director of photography:* Franklyn Barrett. B&W. *Cast:* Jane King (Emilienne Moreau), Jean Robertson (the vision).

Footage from the last reels of The **'Joan of Arc' of Loos** was rediscovered in the mid 1990s. In this amazing cultural document, Emilienne Moreau at first masterminds her rather dull-witted lover's escape from the clutches of *les salles Boches* and then succours the unfortunates of Loos in a cellar as a battle rages above their heads in the village. When the Allies enter the town, however, Emilienne heeds a higher calling and goes to the aid of the Red Cross. Soon she is driven by the cowardly sniping of 'the Huns' to take up arms

herself. Employing a great deal of sincerity and sneaking around, she guns down two snipers and hurls bombs at others to gruesome effect. These tactics, however, are not enough to turn the tide, and the Allied troops begin to retreat. In a perfectly understandable reaction considering the circumstances, Emilienne commences singing *La Marseillaise* and waving the *tricoleur* about. This, in turn, prompts a vision of a woman in armour with her sword pointing to the sky, and all these things together inspire the Allies to retake the town. In the final scene, Emilienne is decorated for her wonderfully goofy acts of blood-letting and cheer-leading and appears on the verge of finding happiness with her one true love—a military man, of course.

WILLIAM D. ROUTT

Joddrell, Steve (1949–) ACTOR/DIRECTOR Steve

Joddrell had considerable experience as both actor and director in theatre in WA before moving into film and television. By the time he directed his first film, the short feature **The Buck's Party** (1977), he had been lecturing in the School of English at Curtin University since 1974. **The Buck's Party** was shot on 16 mm then blown up to 35 mm for theatrical distribution in Australia and New Zealand. It was well received, and won both the Best Short Film at the Sydney Film Festival and a Bronze Award at the Australian Film Institute Awards, prompting enthusiasm in WA, where it was hailed as the start of a local film industry. Joddrell left Curtin in 1984, completed his only film acting role in •**Fran** (1985), then directed the feature film •**Shame** (1988), a striking melodrama. The film had real power and, although it was not popular at the box office, it has acquired increased critical status since its release. The rest of Joddrell's substantial career has been in television, as both actor and director, particularly directing children's drama and (since his move to Melbourne in 1991) working for Simpson le Mesurier on series such as *Halifax FP* and *Good Guys, Bad Guys*. The loss to cinema is substantial, as he showed real flair in handling narrative and in articulating serious issues through well-orchestrated action.   IB

Joe

1924. Director: Beaumont Smith. *Producer:* Beaumont Smith. *Scriptwriter:* Beaumont Smith. Based on the story collections *Joe Wilson* and *Joe Wilson's Mates*, by Henry Lawson. *Director of photography:* Lacey Percival. 5000 ft. B&W. *Cast:* Arthur Tauchert (Joe Wilson), Marie Lorraine (Barbara), Constance Graham (Mary Wilson); Gordon Collingridge (Harry Black).

The surviving stills from this film show Joe and Mary working on their selection, but much of the plot concerns Harry Black's courtship of Mary's sister Barbara. The film demonstrates the virtues of rural life, requiring Harry to reform his city ways before he can become a fitting husband for Barbara. This is a strong cast, with veteran Arthur •Tauchert starring as Joe, and matinee idol Gordon Collingridge as the romantic lead opposite Isabel McDonagh in her first film role, under her stage name of Marie •Lorraine. It was filmed at Beaumont •Smith's usual speed, but was received with more critical favour than some of his other films. IB

Joffe, Mark (1956–) DIRECTOR Mark Joffe has been one of Australia's most accomplished directors over the past 15 years, but he is yet to enjoy a strong box-office hit commensurate with his talent. In the 1980s Joffe demonstrated his versatility in a range of genres, beginning with television drama (*Carson's Law*, 1983) and comedy (*The Fast Lane*, 1985), as well as telefeatures such as *Skin Deep* with Chris Langman in 1985 starring David Reyne and Briony •Behets (which focused on intrigue in the fashion industry) and *Watch the Shadows Dance* with Nicole •Kidman in 1987. Joffe's greatest break, however, was the successful six-hour miniseries *The Great Bookie Robbery* with Marcus Cole in 1986. Joffe's direction of this taut, violent, fact-based drama led to producer Richard •Brennan selecting Joffe as director for the crime thriller •**Grievous Bodily Harm** (1988). In this tough underrated film, reporter Colin •Friels becomes implicated in a complex murder plot involving stolen money and a school teacher's murderous search for his 'dead' wife. Although **Grievous Bodily Harm**, with superb cinematography by Ellery •Ryan, remained faithful to its film-noir roots, the film was ignored in the Australian Film Institute Awards and consequently received little publicity, failing to recoup its $3.4 million budget. Joffe followed this in 1989 with the four-hour television miniseries *Shadow of the Cobra*, starring Art Malik and Rachel •Ward, which was based on an American reporter's desire to get the true story of the activities of international criminal Charles Sobhraj.

Since 1990 Joffe has concentrated on feature films, beginning with the gentle comedy •**Spotswood** (1992), which presented a utopian view of employer/employee relationships in a Melbourne moccasin factory in the late 1960s, followed by the comedy •**Cosi** in 1996 and the romance **The Matchmaker** (1997), which was filmed in Ireland. GM

Jones, Gillian ACTOR Over the past 20 years, Gillian Jones has demonstrated great versatility in her Australian screen appearances. In 1987/88 she appeared, for example, in the triple roles of Viola, Cesario, and Sebastian in a film version of Shakespeare's •**Twelfth Night** (1987). Jones followed this critically applauded effort with an entirely different characterisation the following year, in the revenge melodrama •**Shame** (1988). Jones appeared in this film as Tina Farrel, a working class inhabitant of Ginborak, a small Western Australian country town, who assists Asta Cadell (Deborra-Lee •Furness) in bringing to justice a group of

young men who have been harassing the local women for some years. In a wonderfully modulated performance, Jones initially shows a mixture of suspicion (of Cadell) and fear (of the local men) but, as the film proceeds, Jones/Farrel gradually acquires the necessary courage to confront and expose the local forces shielding the rapists. Jones's first appearance on the Australian screen was in •**Heatwave** (1982) as Barbie Lee-Taylor, the prostitute who gets caught up in murder and corruption in the Sydney inner suburbs. More recently, Jones played a different sexual persona as the liberated enigmatic Catherine, a thoroughly disturbing element threatening the bland marriage of an Australian academic in •**What I Have Written** (1996).
Other Australian films include: Fighting Back (1983), I Own the Racecourse (1986), Echoes of Paradise (1988), Lover Boy (1988). GM

Jones, Ian (1931–) WRITER/PRODUCER/DIRECTOR A member of the old guard of Australian television drama, Ian Jones first became involved in films as a cinematographer on the short **Ballade** (1952), directed by Gil •Brealey. He worked mainly as a journalist with the *Herald* and *Weekly Times* before joining HSV 7 in 1956 as a director. He created the children's show *Zig and Zag*, *Meet the Press*, and a drama called *Suspect*. In 1963 he began a long association with Crawford Productions, where he became a production executive. He directed the first episodes of *Homicide* and wrote early episodes of *Division 4* (1969), *Hunter*, and *Matlock*. He was released from Crawfords to travel to the United Kingdom, where he co-wrote •**Ned Kelly** (1970), which starred Mick Jagger and was directed by Tony Richardson. He produced the feature film version of **The Box** (1975) and co-wrote •**Quigley** (1991) (for which he was credited only on the video-release version). He also wrote (and co-produced) •**The Lighthorsemen** (1987), which was unfairly derided by Australian critics at the time, but nevertheless remains memorable for its final cavalry-charge sequence. Jones created the long-running television series *The Sullivans* (1976), *The Box* (1974), and *Against the Wind* (1978). He is now retired from film-making and writes mainly historical books. HARRY KIRCHNER

Jones, Laura WRITER Enigmatic scriptwriter and daughter of prominent Australian novelist Jessica Anderson, Laura Jones has been seen as the successor to Eleanor Witcombe, as the pre-eminent writer of literary adaptations. She collaborated with director Gillian •Armstrong and producer Jan •Chapman on •**Hightide** (1987) (on which she is credited as sole writer), and this film is among her best work. Her scripts for **The Portrait of a Lady** (USA, 1995), •**The Well** (1997), **A Thousand Acres** (USA, 1997), and •**Oscar and Lucinda** (1998) are serviceable enough, but suffer nevertheless from transposition to a medium where the strengths of dense literary works are almost always likely to be diminished at the hands of even the most competent craftsperson. Not so with **An Angel at My Table** (1990), which, possibly because of its linear biographical form, translated more satisfactorily to screen, with the exception of the long period during which Janet Frame, the writer who is the subject of the film, was institutionalised, the significance of which was reduced to a few short scenes. Jones has also written for television, including two teleplays for the ABC, *Cold Comfort* (1985) and *Everyman for Herself* (1986). She has served as a board member on •The Australian Film Commission and has worked on adaptations of *Angela's Ashes* and *The Shipping News*.

HARRY KIRCHNER

Journals, *see* Magazines

Journey Among Women

1977. Director: Tom Cowan. *Producer*: John Weiley. *Scriptwriters*: Tom Cowan, John Weiley, Dorothy Hewett and cast. *Director of photography*: Tom Cowan. *Music*: Roy Ritchie. 93 min. *Cast*: Jeune Pritchard (Elizabeth Harrington), Martin Phelan (Captain McEwan), Nell Campbell (Meg), Diana Fuller (Bess), Lisa Peers (Charlotte), Jude Kuring (Grace), Robyn Moase (Moira), Rose Lilley (Emily).

Shot on 16 mm for a total cost of $150 000, **Journey Among Women** is an extremely didactic film that propagates the idea that women can live a more 'natural' existence when they are able to escape from the pressure of men and civilisation. Civilisation, in its embryonic stages, is aligned in the film with patriarchal values. The setting, the Australian colony in the late eighteenth century, functions only as a political backdrop; historical detail is not allowed to disrupt a 1970s feminist discourse. The nominal plot concerns the escape of 12 women convicts who are joined by the daughter of the judge-advocate. In the wilderness the women successfully defend themselves from wild men living in the bush and from the soldiers who try to capture them.

The film's strident message reduces all males to rapists or potential rapists. The women meanwhile never escape their status as victims, martyrs, and saviours. Much of the film is improvised and the characterisation and style are naive in the extreme.   GM

Journey Out of Darkness

1967. Director: James Trainor. *Producer*: Frank Brittain. *Scriptwriters*: Howard Koch, James Trainor. *Director of photography*: Andrew Fraser. *Music*: Bob Young. 92 min. *Cast*: Konrad Mattaei (Peterson), Ed Devereaux (Jubbal), Kamahl (prisoner), Ron Morse (Sgt Miller).

Journey Out of Darkness is of interest primarily because it was produced when there was so little Australian feature film production; it was the only Australian feature film to receive a commercial release in 1967. The story, developed by director, James Trainor, who co-scripted the film with famous Hollywood screenwriter Howard Koch (**Casablanca**, 1942), focused on a young policeman (Peterson) sent to Central Australia in 1901 to bring back an Arunta man involved in a tribal killing. Peterson, who initially cares little for the differences between European and Aboriginal systems of justice, is assisted by Jubbal, an Aboriginal policeman. During the trek back, Jubbal dies and Peterson has to rely on his prisoner to survive.

Despite the liberal sentiments inherent in the film's plot, the casting of White actor Ed Devereaux as Jubbal the Aboriginal policeman, and Sri Lankan Kamahl as the Arunta prisoner, fatally wounds the film, which is also damaged by the bland performance of American soap-opera actor Konrad Mattaei in the central role.

GM

Jungle Woman, The

1926. Director, Producer, Scriptwriter, Director of photography: Frank Hurley. B&W. *Cast*: Grace Savieri (Hurana).

In proposing **The Jungle Woman** as his first fiction feature, Frank •Hurley argued that 'the charm of Papua lies not alone in its scenery, but also in its inhabitants and their villages. We cannot parody these people in the studio'. However, even Hurley found the experience of filming in Dutch New Guinea 'well night unbearable'. The reactions of his British cast and the sole Australian cast member Grace Savieri are not known. The plot, which centres on two young prospectors captured by hostile natives and ultimately escaping separately to compete for one sweetheart, hardly redefines the South Sea romance and, despite Hurley's characteristic visual flourishes and the inclusion of much of ethnographic interest, his handling of the actors lacks assurance. At the same time, there is a certain continuity between Hurley's documentaries and his two narrative features, which probably explains the box-office appeal of both. Hurley was one of the first Australian film-makers to record a fascination with New Guinea in particular, and with the exotic in general. **The Jungle Woman** in this context is the forerunner of many later Australian films.

KEN BERRYMAN

K

Kangaroo

1952. *Director*: Lewis Milestone. *Producer*: Robert Bassler. *Scriptwriter*: Harry Kleiner. *Story*: Martin Berkeley. *Music*: Sol Kaplan. 85 min. B&W. *Cast*: Maureen O'Hara (Dell Maguire), Peter Lawford (Richard Connor), Finlay Currie (Michael Maguire), Richard Boone (Gamble), Chips Rafferty (Trooper Leonard), Clyde Combo (Aboriginal stockman), Henry Murdoch (blacktracker).

Veteran director Lewis Milestone was commissioned by Twentieth Century Fox to make a film in Australia to use accumulated exhibition funds that could not be exported due to currency restrictions. Although Milestone wanted to base his film on the novel *Landtakers* by Queensland author Brian (Con) Penton, the studio was adamant and **Kangaroo** is the quintessential American film made on location in Australia. Starring Peter Lawford, Richard Boone, and Maureen O'Sullivan, it conforms to the pattern of Hollywood foreign location films with its emphasis on American personnel in major acting and creative roles.

The plot is melodramatic and familiar. Fortune hunter Richard Conner (Peter Lawford) impersonates the son of a station owner Maguire, hoping to inherit the property after his associate, the hard-bitten Gamble (Richard Boone), murders the old man. In the tradition of Hollywood melodrama, the scheme goes awry when Connor falls for his putative sister Dell Maguire (Maureen O'Hara), raising the spectre of incest. Connor reveals all to the Maguires, earning Gamble's wrath. In a vicious confrontation with stockwhips, Connor kills Gamble, and then surrenders to the local police trooper (Chips Rafferty). Dell agrees to wait for him, effecting the narrative closure that is part of the classic Hollywood formula.

Shot in Technicolor, the film achieves authenticity through effective use of locations that enhance the starkness of the drought-affected landscape, windmills and the rain-dance ceremony of the local Aborigines. The strong cast of Australian extras including Chips •Rafferty, Charles (Bud) •Tingwell, John •Fegan and former Cinesound stalwarts Ronnie Whelan and Letty Craydon adds some Australian flavour to this 'wallaby western'.
BRUCE MOLLOY

Kangaroo

1987. *Director*: Tim Burstall. *Producer*: Ross Dimsey. *Scriptwriter*: Evan Jones. Adapted from the novel by D.H. Lawrence. *Director of photography*: Dan Burstall. *Music*: Nathan Waks. 108 min. *Cast*: Colin Friels (Richard Somers), Judy Davis (Harriet Somers), John Walton (Jack Calcott), Julie Nihill (Vicki Calcott), Hugh Keays-Byrne (Kangaroo).

Tim •Burstall's long-awaited adaptation of D.H. Lawrence's novel failed to enjoy major success with either public or critics, but is nevertheless an honourable attempt to come to terms with a difficult work. Lawrence and his wife Frieda, on whom Richard and Harriet Somers, the two main characters, are based, spent three months in Australia in 1922, and the novel, which appeared the following year, derives from his experiences there. The film focuses on the Somers' strained friendship with neighbour Jack Calcott, who tries to interest Somers in a fascist movement in Sydney. In the end Somers, although drawn to Calcott's easygoing charm, is ultimately repelled by the ideology he espouses and, following a clash between the fascist cell and the trade-union faction, sadly takes leave of Sydney. There is a certain murkiness in Lawrence's dealing with the political strife; the film merely renders this melodramatically without making it any more persuasive. More surprisingly, Burstall seems not to want to translate Lawrence's eye for the hard, bright beauty of the landscape into compelling images. He is on surer ground with the edgy relationship between Somers and Harriet, played with some emotional complexity by Colin •Friels and Judy •Davis. In general, the film succeeds best in its handling of the more personal elements.

BMcF

Kangaroo Kid, The

1950. *Director*: Lesley Selander. *Executive producer*: Beau Shiel. *Producer*: T.O. McCreadie. *Scriptwriter*: Sherman Lowe. *Director of photography*: Russell Harlan. 72 min. B&W. *Cast*: Jock O'Mahoney (Tex Kinnane), Veda Ann Borg (Stella Grey), Guy Doleman (Sergeant Jim Penrose), Martha Hyer (Mary Corbett), Douglas Dumbrille (Vincent Moller), Alec Kellaway (Baldy Muldoon), Grant Taylor (Phil Romero).

The Kangaroo Kid was produced at a time when the Hollywood series western, whereby six formulaic films would be produced each year with the same cowboy star, was coming to an end. The film was an attempt to revive the genre by grafting a familiar western plot onto a series of distinctive Australian settings, including the NSW goldfield at Sofala. American cowboy Tex Kinnane is sent to the NSW town of Gold Star to investigate a series of robberies organised by American expatriate Vincent Moller. Kinnane restores order whilst finding romance with Mary Corbett.

The cast, except for Guy •Doleman and Alec •Kellaway, is dominated by Hollywood actors such as newcomers Jock O'Mahoney (later Jock Mahoney who appeared as Tarzan in the 1960s) and Martha Hyer, together with veteran villain Douglas Dumbrille. The film was photographed by Hollywood cinematographer Russell Harlan and directed by western specialist Lesley Selander, who was responsible for many Hopalong Cassidy films at Paramount in the 1930s.

The Kangaroo Kid was financed jointly by American and Australian interests and was the last film produced by the •McCreadie brothers.

GM

Kants, Ivar (1949–) ACTOR

A graduate of the National Institute of Dramatic Art and of Latvian descent, Ivar Kants has appeared in all the acting media, including seasons with the Queensland Theatre Company and Sydney's Old Tote Theatre Company. His first impact in film was as the ambiguous and eponymous protagonist of Peter •Weir's telefeature *The Plumber*, in which he convincingly unsettles Judy •Morris's middle-class housewife as he dismantles her bathroom. Although his good looks have usually won him leading roles, he has often managed to imbue them with a slightly off-key quality that saves them from conventionality. He did what he could with the thinly written romantic lead in the 'migrant drama' •**Silver City** (1984), and, in **Jenny**

Kissed Me (1986), brought a compelling intensity to the role of the cancer-ridden partner of a woman who runs a gamut of excesses to escape the confines of country town life. This is an overcrowded and underdeveloped film, but Kants gives it moments of melodramatic power uncommon in Australian cinema.

Other Australian films: The Understudy (1975, short), •Dawn! (1979), Narcissus (1979, short), Dill Pickle (1979, short), Brothers (1982), •Moving Out (1983), •The Naked Country (1985), •Twelfth Night (1987), Gallagher's Travels (1987), Cassidy (1989).

BMcF

Karvan, Claudia (1972–) ACTOR

Claudia Karvan, together with Nicole •Kidman, was one of the promising teenage actors of the 1980s who sustained a film career in the 1990s. In •Hightide (1987), Karvan's Ally, the teenager living in a bleak caravan park on the south-east coast of Australia, comes to realise that the drunken tourist she found in the caravan park's toilet is her mother. Karvan, in a key role, is able to match the fine performances of Judy •Davis and Jan •Adele in what is essentially a melodrama centred on Ally; the film depicts an emotional tug-of-war between Ally's mother and grandmother. While •**The Big Steal** (1990) provided a comic opportunity for Karvan, a more challenging role was the young Greek-Australian teacher in •**The Heartbreak Kid** (1993) who has to confront her cultural and professional responsibilities when she falls in love with one of her students. Karvan successfully captures both the joy and anguish inherent in this situation. A cameo in •**The Nostradamus Kid** (1993) was followed by the romantic lead in •**Dating the Enemy** (1996), in which Karvan plays Tash, a character who wakes up one morning to discover that she has swapped bodies with her sexist ex-boyfriend Brett (Guy •Pearce). Karvan develops this thin comedic premise with a humorous performance as 'Brett', who discovers the joys of female clothing and the monthly pain of life as a woman.

Other Australian films include: Molly (1983), Echoes of Paradise (1988), Holidays on the River Yarra (1991), Redheads (1992), •Broken Highway (1994), Exile (1994), Lust and Revenge (1996), Flynn (1996), Paperback Hero (1998), Passion: The Story of Percy Grainger (1999).

GM

Kathner, Rupert (1904–54) ART DIRECTOR/DIRECTOR

Rupert Kathner (known as Rupe) was an artist who began his film career with Harry •Southwell, working on the set designs for •**The Burgomeister** (1935). He then tried to become a director himself, but •**Phantom Gold** (1937) was not approved for NSW quota and was distributed only in rural areas by Kathner himself, and **Below the Surface** (1938) was also rejected for quota purposes, and was withdrawn from distribution by the backers. **Wings of Destiny** (1940) was of rather more acceptable quality; it received quota approval and limited distribution, but was still not well received. His most successful venture was **Racing Luck** (1941), starring Joe •Valli and George Lloyd. He had made a number of documentaries and short films over this time, but when he did not finish **The Kellys of Tobruk** (1942), his company was taken over by Supreme Sound. He went back to working for others, photographing **Red Sky at Morning** (1944, d. Hartney Arthur), and expressed his disillusionment with the industry in a book that presented a jaundiced description of the state of film in Australia, *Let's Make a Movie* (1945). His last production, the most strife-ridden of all, was eventually completed as **The Glenrowan Affair** (1951), and he took a role in it under the pseudonym of Hunt Angels. IB

Kaye, Clarissa (1931–) ACTOR Clarissa Kaye (née Knipe) worked as a stage actor in Sydney. Her first films were the shorts **Troublemaker** (1967) and **The Drover's Wife** (1968), then the feature films •**Age of Consent** (1969) and **Adam's Woman** (1970). Her most important role was as Mrs Kelly in Tony Richardson's •**Ned Kelly** (1970); she made the character both motherly and earthily sexual. After her marriage in 1971 to James Mason she did little screen work, but there was some television (*Frankenstein: the True Story* 1973; *Salem's Lot*, 1979) and a small role in •**The Umbrella Woman** (1987). IB

Kaye, Norman (1927–) ACTOR One of the busiest and most distinguished actors in Australia, Melbourne-based Kaye has worked for virtually every notable theatre company in the country, appeared in innumerable television productions and, in the 1970s, took to the large screen as a duck to water. On the stage, he has done Chekhov, Shakespeare, Shaw, and all the major moderns; on television, he has worked for the ABC (*Ride on Stranger*) and commercial channels (*Bangkok Hilton* for Kennedy-Miller, and many Crawford series). He is a gifted musician who has held the post of director of music at several institutions.

Apart from a short in 1964, **A Beach Day**, on which he was credited as actor and composer, Kaye's screen career began in the 1970s with **Illuminations** (1976), a piece of experimental metaphysical film-making that marked the start of his association with the director Paul •Cox. Over the decades that followed, Kaye appeared in nearly a dozen further films directed by the idiosyncratic Dutch film-maker, who has so often been the abrasive and/or affectionate chronicler of Melbourne suburban lives. After a small role in the cross-cultural love story •**Kostas** (1979), Kaye starred in Cox's next film, the romantic comedy •**Lonely Hearts** (1982). He played a middle-aged piano tuner and teacher (with a toupee), who falls in love with the repressed bank clerk played by Wendy •Hughes, and his somewhat rumpled, quizzical persona was established to popular acclaim. However, he played a darker version of the middle-aged misfit in Cox's •**Man of Flowers** (1983), for which his performance as an obsessive aesthete won an Australian Film

Institute Best Actor award. He returned to a more recognisable normality in **Cactus** (1986), leaving the usual Coxian preoccupations with psychological quirkiness to others. Kaye, along with other such performers as Hughes, Chris •Haywood and Sheila •Florance, became a staple of Cox's repertory company. It is true to say that most of his best screen work has been the result of this collaboration.

This is not to undervalue the rest of his output, of which precision and versatility are trademarks. He played a swagman in •**Mad Dog Morgan** (1976), Michele •Fawdon's sterile husband in Bob •Ellis's **Unfinished Business** (1985), a washed-up sports writer in Ellis's •**Warm Nights on a Slow Moving Train** (1988), and a sinister land-owner in •**Broken Highway** (1994). He produced perhaps 20 other finely wrought character studies right up to the late 1990s in such films as **Heaven's Burning** (1996), **Paws** (1996), and •**Oscar and Lucinda** (1998). He is the sort of actor who used to be the staple of the studio system in decades past.

Other Australian films: Inside Looking Out (1977), Shadow Effects (1981), •The Killing of Angel Street (1981), Burning Man (1981), A Dangerous Summer (1982), Buddies (1982), Where the Green Ants Dream (1983), Relatives (1984, music only), I Own the Racecourse (1985), Frenchman's Farm (1986), Hungry Heart (1987), Boundaries of the Heart (1987), The Island (1988), The Golden Braid (1989), Turtle Beach (1990), •A Woman's Tale (1991), The Nun and the Bandit (1992), Exile (1993), •The Custodian (1994), •Bad Boy Bubby (1994), Shifting Sands (1994), Lust and Revenge (1995), Recycled (1997, short). BMcF

Kayser, Carl (1910–84) CINEMATOGRAPHER Carl Kayser was born in the United Kingdom, and his Australian career began as camera operator under Osmond Borradaile on •**The Overlanders** (1946). He was director of photography on •**Sons of Matthew** (1949, with Bert Nicholas), and on the dramatised documentary film **No Strangers Here** (1950) for the Australian National Film Board (see Film Australia). He was camera operator, with Ross •Wood, on **Long John Silver** (1955, d. Carl Guthrie), working on both the feature film and the television series. His outstanding work as director of photography on Australia's first colour dramatic feature film, Charles •Chauvel's •**Jedda** (1955), was one of the main reasons for the success of the film, both in Australia and overseas. Also as director of photography, he then contributed significantly to the success of the Southern International films •**Walk into Paradise** (1956, for which the colour photography was highly commended at Cannes Film Festival), **Dust in the Sun** (1958), and **The Restless and the Damned** (1959). His last Australian feature film was **Bungala Boys** (1961). After working on the television series *Riptide* (1968), he moved to Asia. IB

Keays-Byrne, Hugh (1947–) ACTOR After working on stage and in film and television in the United Kingdom, Hugh Keays-Byrne arrived in Australia in 1973. He continued his stage work with the Nimrod and Old Tote companies in Sydney, and immediately took supporting roles in film and television, winning a Sammy and a Logie for Best Single Television Performance in an episode of the television series *Rush* (1976). In film, he has specialised in despicable characters: Ambrose Kyte (•**Burke & Wills**, 1985), Kangaroo (•**Kangaroo**, 1987), and Lord Vile (•**The Salute of the Jugger**, 1989). Most memorably, he was Toecutter, the leeringly evil head of the bikie gang that exacts a cruel revenge on Jessie and the baby in •**Mad Max** (1979). In the early 1990s Keays-Byrne became involved with the independent cooperative venture Macau Light Film Co., and co-directed (with Paul Elliott) its first feature film **Resistance** (produced in 1992 but not released commercially until 1997).

Other Australian films: •**Stone** (1974), •**The Man from Hong Kong** (1975), **The Trespassers** (1976), •**Blue Fin** (1978), **Snapshot** (1979), **The Chain Reaction** (1980), **Ginger Meggs** (1982), •**Strikebound** (1984), **Where the Green Ants Dream** (1984), •**For Love Alone** (1986), **Les Patterson Saves the World** (1987).   IB

Keenan, Haydn (1951–   ) DIRECTOR   Keenan acquired a minor cult reputation for the semi-surreal **Going Down** (1983), which he produced as well as directed. Previously, he had made some award-winning short films, including nine archival films for the Australia Council (see Australian Film Commission), and had formed the company Smart St Films with director Esben •Storm, who directed •**27A** (1974), which Keenan produced and acted in. Although the film was praised by critics when it was finally seen at the Sydney Film Festival in 1974 and won several Australian Film Institute awards, it never managed to find audiences to cover its costs. **Going Down** dealt with four young women sharing a house in King's Cross, one of whom has been given money by her father for a trip to the USA. The money is stolen, and the rest of the film is concerned to find the thief—but only in a desultory way, as most of its interest lies in its exploration of the comings and goings of the communal household. The film ignores the conventions of linear realism, drawing on a fragmented approach that dared to mingle documentary and *cinéma vérité* techniques with a vestigial narrative. Keenan's only other feature to date is **Pandemonium** (1987), in which he also acted and which he co-produced, co-wrote, and directed. It is a frenetic anthology of bizarre assaults on conventional taste, and was too outré for wide distribution and perhaps not funny enough for cult status. Sadly, Keenan's once-promising career, begun when he was barely out of his twenties, seems to have petered out.   BMcF

Kellaway, Alec (1894–1973) ACTOR   Alec Kellaway had a longer career in Australian films than his more famous elder brother Cecil •Kellaway. He made his début in Ken G •Hall's •**Lovers and Luggers** in 1937 as the drunken McTavish. After a long stage career, the South African-born

Kellaway made six further films for Hall at •Cinesound, including two of the 'Rudd family' series—•**Dad and Dave Come to Town** (1938) and •**Dad Rudd MP** (1940), in both of which he played the effeminate shop floor-walker Entwhistle—and •**Smithy** (1946), as Captain Allan Hancock. A versatile character actor, he appeared in the American–Australian co-production •**The Kangaroo Kid** (1950) as Baldy Muldoon, the American hero's comic sidekick and, 20 years later, he played the Abbot in **Squeeze a Flower** (1970). *Other Australian films*: •**Let George Do It** (1938), •**The Broken Melody** (1938), •**Gone to the Dogs** (1939), •**Come Up Smiling** (1939), **South West Pacific** (1943, doc.), •**Sons of Matthew** (1949, ass. d.).   BMcF

Kellaway, Cecil (1891-1973) ACTOR   This chubby-faced South African-born British actor, who spent most of his career in America, deserves a footnote in Australian film history for the three starring roles he played in Australia in the 1930s. A godson of Cecil Rhodes and brother of Alec •Kellaway (who appeared in many of Ken G •Hall's films in the 1930s), Cecil Kellaway arrived in Australia in 1918, where he established a stage career and made his first film, •**The Hayseeds**, in 1933. In this film, a Beaumont •Smith remake of the silent comedy, he played Dad Hayseed. He also starred for Hall in likeable 'little man' roles in •**It Isn't Done** (1937) and •**Mr Chedworth Steps Out** (1939), before heading for Hollywood and enduring popularity as a character actor. Whimsical (he was Oscar-nominated for playing a leprechaun in **The Luck of the Irish**, 1948), humorous, benign, almost never sinister, he became almost too cuddly for more astringent tastes. But such tastes must have been rare because he made 80 films in his 30 years as a Hollywood institution, winning another Oscar nomination for **Guess Who's Coming to Dinner** in 1967.   BMcF

The Kelly Gang

1920. *Director, Producer, Scriptwriter*: Harry Southwell. *Director of photography*: Charles Herschell. B&W. *Cast*: Godfrey Cass (Ned Kelly), Harry Southwell (Sergeant Steele).

When the Kellys Were Out
[The True Story of the Kelly Gang]

1923. *Director, Producer, Scriptwriter*: Harry Southwell. *Director of photography*: Tasman Higgins. B&W. *Cast*: Godfrey Cass (Ned Kelly), Harry Southwell (Aaron Sherritt), Charles Villiers (Dan Kelly), Mervyn Barrington (Sergeant Kennedy), Dunstan Webb (Superintendent Nicolson).

When the Kellys Rode

1934. *Director, Scriptwriter*: Harry Southwell. *Director of photography*: Tasman Higgins. B&W. *Cast*: Hay Simpson (Ned Kelly), George Randall (Sergeant Steele).

Harry Southwell's three features about the Kelly gang have a confusing history. It is possible that for some time a film called **The Kelly Gang** may have circulated that was actually a combination of footage from the Johnson & Gibson 1906 remake of •**The Story of the Kelly Gang** and Kenneth Brampton's •**Robbery Under Arms** (1920). Harry •Southwell made a film in 1920 under this title, of which some footage survives. The film was apparently shown in Sydney without interference from the authorities. However, objections were raised to the film's portrayal of the police, and, in 1922, Southwell made what was substantially another film with the same star (Godfrey •Cass), which was released as **When the Kellys Were Out** and as **The True Story of the Kelly Gang** in the United Kingdom, where it received some favourable attention. The surviving footage from this version, which is rather disjointed but tells a more or less complete story, has certain remarkable qualities for its time, the most notable of which are the gang members' loutishness, their scruffy and unkempt appearance, and an overall sense of sordid realism that is especially pervasive in the earlier scenes and in a long close-up of Dan Kelly drinking while confronted by a snake. No matter how Southwell's first version may have shown the police (who are one and all portrayed as sterling heroes in **When the Kellys Were Out**), in this version the Kellys and their followers must have been particularly unappealing to middle-class Australian legislators. At any rate, it seems to have been banned in NSW (**The Kelly Gang** may have been banned in SA). The 1934 sound version, **When the Kellys Rode**, is disappointingly sanitised by comparison, and a repeated 'symbolic' shot of Ned and Sergeant Steele playing chess only underlines the ineptness evidenced in the rest of the film. In 1947 Southwell gave the Kelly story a final try, but eventually was forced out of the project by Rupert •Kathner, whose completed film was released four years later as **The Glenrowan Affair**.

WILLIAM D. ROUTT

Keneally, Thomas (1935–) AUTHOR One of Australia's best-known authors and winner of the 1982 Booker Prize, Thomas Keneally trained for the priesthood at St Patrick's Seminary in Sydney, but later became a teacher and academic. His first script 'The Priest', from the four-part •**Libido** (1973), marked the beginning of his association with Fred •Schepisi, which also included a convincing acting role as Father Marshall in •**The Devil's Playground** (1976). More importantly, with •**The Chant of Jimmie Blacksmith** (1978), Schepisi adapted Keneally's 1972 novel of the same name to his film. Keneally is also credited, with Sophia Turkiewicz, as co-writer on •**Silver City** (1984), although the origins of the story can be found in Turkiewicz's earlier 50-minute **Letters from Poland** (1978). *Schindler's Ark* (1982) is arguably his best known novel,

from which he wrote the film treatment and first draft for Steven Spielberg and which became **Schindler's List** (1993), winner of seven Academy Awards, including Best Picture, Best Director, and Best Screenplay Based on Material from Another Medium (Steven Zaillian). Keneally's other novels include *Confederates*, *The Playmaker*, and *Jacko*. He holds two honorary doctorates, was chair of the Australian Republican movement (1992–93), and is a fellow of the American Academy of Arts and Sciences, and the Royal Society of Literature, United Kingdom.

HARRY KIRCHNER

Kennard, Malcolm (1967–) ACTOR After graduating from the Victorian College of the Arts in 1988, Malcolm Kennard played Harley Brown in the television soap opera *E Street* from 1989 to 1991. This fitted him admirably for one of the leading roles in the teen-pic **Secrets** (1991). Since then he has appeared only in less substantial roles, in the films **Diana and Me** (1997) and **Amy** (1998). He appeared in the telemovies *The Seventh Floor* and *Joh's Jury* (1993): for the latter, he was nominated for an Australian Film Institute Award for an actor in a leading role in television drama. Although he is undoubtedly talented, he seems to have had some difficulty in moving into adult roles. IB

Kennedy, Byron (1952–83) PRODUCER In 1971 Byron Kennedy, together with George •Miller, made **Violence in the Cinema Part One**, an outrageous exercise designed to unsettle the viewer with its ability to exploit the basic kinetic effects of editing, composition, sound, and setting. This short proved to be a test run for their ground-breaking film •**Mad Max** (1979), which not only established the career of the lead actor Mel •Gibson, but also that of director Miller and producer Kennedy. Kennedy followed this with the more polished but less formally exciting •**Mad Max 2** (1981). Kennedy also produced *The Dismissal* (1983), the re-creation for television of the events leading up to the dismissal of the Whitlam Government in 1975. Kennedy's status within the Australian entertainment industry was at its height when he was killed in a helicopter crash in the Blue Mountains in 1983. Kennedy also acted in •**The Office Picnic** (1972).
Other Australian films include: Come Out Fighting (1973), •Last of the Knucklemen (1979). GM

Kennedy, Gerard (1932–) ACTOR Melbourne-based actor, primarily television and film, who excels in strong, masculine roles with a suggestion of latent violence. Gerard Kennedy received maximum exposure with lead roles in popular television programs in the late 1960s (*Hunter*, *Bellbird*, *Division 4*) and throughout the 1970s and 1980s (such as *Tandarra*, *Against the Wind*, and *Cop Shop*). Kennedy's film career began with the lead role in the Australian western **Raw Deal** (1977). This was followed with strong character parts such as Preacher Jones, who was driven to madness, in •**The Mango Tree** (1977); Chad Logan in •**The Irishman** (1978); and Frank Maguire, Bill Hunter's ambitious brother, in •**Newsfront** (1978). Two years later Kennedy played the lead character in Tim •Burstall's presentation of the John Powers' three-act play, •**The Last of the Knucklemen** (1979), a role that provided a showcase for Kennedy's special acting talent. As Tarzan, the knuckleman of the title, Kennedy was able to combine the necessary physical dimension of the character with its inherent anachronistic qualities. In recent years Kennedy has been seen on television (especially a clever performance as a cynical television executive in *Frontline*) and film in supporting roles that do not match either the quality or quantity of his late 1970s output.

Other Australian films include: •Eliza Fraser (1976), Fatty Finn (1980), The Plains of Heaven (1982), Stock Squad (1985), Running from the Guns (1987), •The Lighthorsemen (1987), The Min Min (1990), Garbo (1992), Body Melt (1994).

GM

Gerard Kennedy

Kennedy, Graham (1934–) ACTOR Famous as a Melbourne radio personality and award-winning compere of the long-running TV show, *In Melbourne Tonight* (1957–75), Kennedy went on to establish himself as a con-

siderable character actor in Australian films. He was effortlessly convincing as the sexual voyeur in •**Don's Party** (1976), with a beer tankard on a chain round his neck; as the cynical leader of a small group of the Special Air Services Regiment in •**The Odd Angry Shot** (1979), trailing a broken marriage; as the football club president who falls victim of boardroom politics in •**The Club** (1980); and as Leo McKern's aggressively friendly Queensland neighbour in •**Travelling North** (1987). The bland good humour of his small-screen image always suggested it might be fronting for something tougher and sharper, and these film performances have confirmed this: they ring changes, sometimes subtle, sometimes unnerving, on what was once perhaps the best known persona on Melbourne television.

Other Australian films: •They're a Weird Mob (1966), •The Box (1975), The Return of Captain Invincible (1982), Stanley (1983), The Killing Fields (1984). BMcF

Kennedy, Jo (1960–) ACTOR Melbourne-based Jo Kennedy had had little acting experience when Gillian •Armstrong cast her in the leading role of Jackie, the ambitious rock singer, in the charming and undervalued musical •**Star Struck** (1982). The film was wittily conceived and scripted, knowingly resuscitating several sturdy genres, and Kennedy was spirited and endearing but, for whatever reasons (and it had a troubled production), the film simply failed to take off. For one so obviously talented—as actor and singer—she has not been lucky in her screen roles. Although Ian •Pringle's **Wrong World** (1986), shot in bleakly lovely landscapes in the midwest of America and Bolivia, won Kennedy, as its junkie heroine, the Best Actress Award at the Berlin Film Festival, the film had scarcely any showings in Australia. Kennedy was again involved in a world of drugs and drifters in Mary Callaghan's punningly titled **Tender Hooks** (1989), in which her vivacity struggles to make itself felt against the prevailing inner-suburban, kitchen-sink gloom of its downbeat love story. The film had its critical supporters but did not find the youth audience at which it seemed directed. She had a tiny part in **The Boy Who had Everything** (1984), unreleased in Australia, and was peripheral to the main action in Paul •Cox's **Golden Braid** (1991). She subsequently made some short films as a student at the Victorian College of the Arts. Perhaps this will be her route back into Australian cinema, which has seen the wastage of some notable talents, but few that seemed potentially more beguiling than Kennedy's.

BMcF

Kennedy, Patricia (1917–) ACTOR In 1982 Patricia Kennedy was made an OBE for distinguished service to the performing arts, in a career that began on radio and stage in the 1930s. She appeared on television from the early Crawford series to *The Flying Doctors*, *GP*, and *A Country Practice* in the 1980s and into the 1990s. Her film performances are fewer, but memorable. She was Mrs R in •**The Office Picnic** (1972), the sympathetic Miss Chapman in •**The Getting of Wisdom** (1977), and the wise Aunt Gussie who offers moral support to Sybylla in •**My Brilliant Career** (1979). For both of the latter she was nominated as Best Supporting Actress in the Australian Film Institute Awards. In the 1980s, her screen performances were limited to leading roles in two telemovies and an unreleased film (**Departure**, 1986). In the 1990s, however, she returned to form as the aristocratic Maud Dickens in Michael Blakemore's Chekhov-inspired •**Country Life** (1994), and as Jean, the oldest of the quartet of overturned lady bowlers in •**Road to Nhill** (1997). She is regarded with great affection and respect by both audiences and her fellow actors.   IB

Patricia Kennedy

Kenny, Jan (1947–) CINEMATOGRAPHER   Jan Kenny initially worked in both film and theatre, including the •Commonwealth Film Unit (now Film Australia) and the Royal Court Theatre in London. After concentrating on camera work, Jan worked as a clapper loader on **Summer of Secrets** (1976), becoming the first woman in Australia to work on a feature film camera crew. After shooting documentaries, dramatised documentaries, television series, and dramas, in 1986 she became the first woman to be accredited by the Australian Cinematographers Society (ACS) and entitled to use the letters ACS after her name. She has won two ACS Merit awards for television dramas (1988, 1999) and one for a cinema documentary (1988), as well as a NSW ACS Gold Award and a federal ACS Distinction award for the feature film **Mary** (1994). Since 1997 she has been the head of the cinematography department at Australian Film, Television and Radio School, Sydney. Her other feature film as director of photography is •**Fran** (1985).   DAVID MUIR

Kerr, Bill (1922–) ACTOR   Having started as a child actor (as Willie Kerr) in •**Harmony Row** (1933) and •**The Silence of Dean Maitland** (1934), Bill Kerr may well lay claim to the longest acting career to date in Australian films. After stage work as a child, as well, he went to the United Kingdom in 1947, acquired fame on radio, on television (in *Hancock's Half Hour*), and in many films. Some of the most notable are **Appointment in London** (1953), **The Night My Number Came Up** (1955), and **The Dam Busters** (1955), in which he honed his characteristically sturdy, good-humoured persona. He was in Ealing's Australian-set •**The Shiralee** (1957), and returned to live here in the 1970s. He has since played memorably in Australian cinema and television. Among his best-known film roles are as the uncle who trains Mark •Lee as a runner in •**Gallipoli** (1981), as Sigourney Weaver's superior who loses her to Mel •Gibson in •**The Year of Living Dangerously**, and as the former drover who trains the eponymous dingo crossbreed in •**Dusty**. He has aged with dignity, and was much in demand throughout the 1980s.

Other Australian films: Port of Escape (1961, unreleased), **Save the Lady** (1981), The Pirate Movie (1982), •**The Settlement** (1984), Vigil (1984), •**Razorback** (1984), Relatives (1985), The Coca-Cola Kid (1985), •**The Lighthorsemen** (1987), Running from the Guns (1987), Kokoda Crescent (1987), Sweet Talker (1991), **Over the Hill** (1992).   BMcF

Kid Stakes, The

1927. Director: Tal Ordell. *Producers*: Tal Ordell, Virgil Coyle. *Scriptwriter*: Tal Ordell. Based on the comic strip characters created by Syd Nicholls. *Director of photography*: Arthur Higgins. 5000 ft. B&W. *Cast*: 'Pop' Ordell (Fatty Finn), Charles Roberts (Tiny King), Ray Salmon (Jimmy Kelly), Frank Boyd (Bruiser Murphy), Edward Stevens (Shooye Shugg), Billy Ireland ('Seasy').

Syd Nicholls, shown drawing in the film's opening credits, was a cartoonist for the Sydney *Sunday News* for decades, as well as designing art titles for many of Australia's silent films (including •**On Our Selection** 1920 and •**The Man from Kangaroo** 1920). His most popular cartoon creation was Fatty Finn but, in this film, the characters are played by live actors who are cast and dressed with remarkable faithfulness to the cartoon originals. Considering these origins, the picture of childhood presented here is surprisingly delicately observed. There is slapstick and farce (the goat eating the rich man's rose garden, or dropping from the sky into a pond, in time to be taken to win the race), but there is also the wonderfully realistic cricket match on the vacant lot, and the fight between Fatty and the rich boy from Potts Point that ends in Algie's acceptance into Fatty's gang. Tal Ordell's real name was William Ordell Raymond Buntine, and he had played many film and stage roles before making this—the only film that he directed. In a uniformly engaging ensemble of child actors, Ordell's six-year-old son Robin ('Pop') is outstanding. This is a beguiling film, which has come to be viewed as one of the great Australian films of the silent era.   IB

Kidman, Nicole (1968–) ACTOR   Tall, slender, and red-haired, Nicole Kidman has become one of the most famous products of the new Australian cinema (see Revival, the), rising rapidly to major international stardom and, in 1990, marrying one of the world's most popular film stars, Tom Cruise. Born in Hawaii, Kidman is the daughter of a distinguished Sydney psychologist. She began her film career at the age of 16 in Brian Trenchard •Smith's popular teen-cum-road movie, **BMX Bandits** (1983) and in Henri •Safran's remake of the 1940s children's adventure film •**Bush Christmas** (1983). In both she registered a cheerful, spirited presence, well attuned to the genre demands of the films. During the 1980s, she did a good deal of Australian television work, including the miniseries *Vietnam* and, perhaps most notably, *Bangkok Hilton*, which considerably extended her acting range as the young woman who is arrested in Bangkok for (unwittingly) smuggling drugs and who spends an appalling time in prison.

Her other 1980s films offered her less rewarding opportunities until Phil •Noyce gave her the role of Rae Ingram in his high-tension melodrama-at-sea, •**Dead Calm**, in 1989. She played the role of a mother traumatised by the death of her baby son in a car accident while she was driving. The film impressively focuses on her attempts to come to terms with her feelings of guilt and to reclaim a sense of her own worth during a restorative cruise with her husband (Sam •Neill). In her dealings with both her husband and the psychopath (Billy Zane), who boards their yacht with a bizarre story, Kidman revealed an emotional range and a star presence that Hollywood was quick to notice.

Subsequently, she has made only two further films in Australia, Michael •Jenkins' •**Emerald City** (1989) and John •Duigan's •**Flirting** (1991), in both of which she has subsidiary, although admittedly quite showy roles. In Hollywood she starred in a series of big-budget movies, including Tony Scott's **Days of Thunder** (1990), as a doctor, opposite Tom Cruise as an ambitious stock-car racer, and, with Cruise again, in Ron Howard's romantic adventure, **Far and Away** (1992), as an Irish immigrant. Neither of these gave her more than conventional leading-lady roles, but they brought her to widespread attention that was consolidated by her romance and marriage with Cruise. She was a gangster's moll in Robert Benton's **Billy Bathgate** (1991) opposite Dustin Hoffman, looked blondly stunning and entered into the spirit of **Batman Forever** (1995), and gave her two most complex performances to date in Gus Van Sant's **To Die For** (1995), as a television weather girl for whom the box has far more authenticity than actual life, and in Jane •Campion's uneven adaptation of Henry James, **Portrait of a Lady** (1996). In the last, Kidman seemed sometimes constrained by the motivational lacunae of Laura •Jones' script, but she worked hard to convey the Jamesean idea of 'a young woman affronting her destiny', and did so with wit, courage, and, finally, stoical resignation to her dark lot. She is now firmly established as a box-office star, which is no guarantee of good films, but which probably means she will not often film again in Australia, although she returns here regularly to visit her family. She had a major success on the London and Broadway stage in *The Blue Room* (1998).
Other Australian films: Archer's Adventure (1985), **Wills & Burke** (1985), **Windrider** (1986), **The Bit Part** (1987).   BMcF

Killing of Angel Street, The

1981. *Director*: Donald Crombie. *Producer*: Anthony Buckley. *Scriptwriters*: Evan Jones, Michael Craig. *Director of photography*: Peter James. *Music*: Brian May. *Cast*: Elizabeth Alexander (Jessica Simmonds), John Hargreaves (Elliott), Reg Lye (Riley), Alexander Archdale (B.C.Simmonds), David Downer (Alan Simmonds), Norman Kaye (Mander), Allan Bickford (Collins).

Both **The Killing of Angel Street** and •**Heatwave** (1982) were inspired by the death of reporter Juanita Nielsen and the inner-Sydney battles between residents, property developers, and the police in the mid-1970s. While there are narrative similarities between both films in terms of their content, there are stylistic difference between Phillip •Noyce's film and Donald •Crombie's. While Noyce favoured an excessive style with bold camera movements and a relentlessly oppressive atmosphere to match the enormity of the corruption, Crombie favours a more low-key presentation that only sporadically breaks out of its resolutely 'realist' surface.

Jessica Simmonds, a scientist, returns from overseas, and a failed relationship, to her inner-Sydney roots to find her father, B.C. Simmonds, leading the local residents and squatters in a fight against greedy developers who want to pull down the houses on Angel Street to make way for expensive high-rise apartments. The presentation of this

Nicole Kidman

conflict is totally polarised with innocence and virtue residing only on the side of the residents opposing the development. The developers, on the other hand, are shown to be in league with thugs, duplicitous lawyers, corrupt police, and greedy politicians. They stop at nothing to remove the residents. When B.C. is murdered Jessica's commitment to the cause strengthens and she forms an alliance with Marxist union leader Elliott. After his death she takes on the leadership of the opposition and eventually exposes the illegal actions of the major developer, Collins. The ending, however, is consistent with the conventions of the conspiracy thriller with the real villains, the politicians, police, and the judiciary escaping punishment because, unlike the residents and workers on Angel Street, they are protected by the privileges of power.

GM

King of the Coral Sea

1954. Director: Lee Robinson. *Producer:* Chips Rafferty. *Scriptwriters:* Chips Rafferty, Lee Robinson. *Director of photography:* Ross Wood. *Underwater photography:* Noel Monkman. 85 min. B&W. *Cast:* Chips Rafferty (Ted King), Charles Tingwell (Peter Merriman), Ilma Adey (Rusty King), Rod Taylor (Jack Janiero), Lloyd Berrell (Yusep), Reg Lye (Grundy).

The second feature made by the combined talents of Lee •Robinson as director and Chips •Rafferty as producer, **King of the Coral Sea** was intended, like its predecessor •**The Phantom Stockman**, for theatrical release in Australia and for sale to international television programmers. Filmed on location on Thursday Island and with underwater sequences filmed on Green Island off Cairns, the film is an adventure-romance with references to the pearling industry and to an illegal migration scam.

Performances are generally convincing, but the pace is uneven. The use of aqualungs and spearguns by the main characters was novel at the time, and the exoticism of the locations won praise from critics. Rod •Taylor's performance as the minor character Janiero attracted the attention of overseas producers and provided his entry card to Hollywood.

King of the Coral Sea was photographed by Ross •Wood. Noel •Monkman carried out the underwater photography, establishing him in a new career.

BRUCE MOLLOY

Kiss Or Kill

1997. Director: Bill Bennett. *Producers:* Bill Bennett, Jennifer Cluff & Corrie Soeterboek. *Scriptwriter:* Bill Bennett. *Director of photography:* Malcolm McCulloch. 93 min. *Cast :* Matt Day (Al), Frances O'Connor (Nikki), Chris Haywood (Detective Hummer), Andrew S. Gilbert (Detective Crean), Barry Otto (Adler Jones), Max Cullen (Stan), Barry Langrishe (Zipper Doyle).

When Nikki and Al, two young 'scam artists', accidentally kill their victim in an Adelaide motel they quickly leave town and head for Perth. However, in an unconvincing plot device, Nikki throws the victim's wallet out the car window thereby alerting the police that they are crossing the Nullabor desert. **Kiss or Kill** clearly draws on familiar film noir conventions, such as the increasing distrust that informs a relationship based on crime (**Double Indemnity**, 1944), the lovers on the run with a (slightly) disturbed female protagonist (**Gun Crazy**, 1950), the inherent eroticism emerging from the shifting patterns of dominance and submission in Nikki and Al's relationship (**Out of the Past**, 1947) and the bizarre characters, notably Stan and Adler Jones, that assist or obstruct their flight (**They Live by Night**, 1949). Although Al and Nikki are hardly the perfect, stable couple, as befits the genre, audience sympathy is strengthened by the dramatic situation (being hunted by the police and by the fact that just about everybody else in the film is more despicable, particularly Zipper Doyle, the ex-footballer child molester, who joins the hunt).

Ultimately, this is a film that should not be solely judged according to its success or otherwise in reworking the conventions as the film takes on its own momentum once the basic premise is established. For example, Bill •Bennett's style represents a radical departure to other homages to film noir or neo noir, and typically, for Bennett, it is disdainful of the formal Hollywood style as the film includes sounds but no dramatic music and most scenes are shot with continuity breaks and jump cuts reminiscent of the late-night American television series *Homicide–Life on the Streets*. Within this fluid style Matt •Day and Frances •O'Connor are excellent and the barren setting provides an effective context for Bennett to intensify the film's basic premise involving trust and distrust in relationships between men and women. The most stable relationship is between Detectives Crean and Hummer, and the film periodically pauses to add small inflections to their characterisation.

Kiss or Kill won the Best Film Award at the 1997 Australian Film Institute Awards, together with awards for Bennett for Direction and Editing while Andrew Gilbert won the Best Supporting Actor award and Wayne Pashley, Tovio Lember, and Gethin Creagh received the award for Best Achievement in Sound. Frances O'Connor won the Best Actress award at the 1997 Montreal World Film Festival.

GM

Know Your Own Country, *see* Documentary and non-fiction, silent

Kokkinos, Ana (1958–) WRITER/DIRECTOR Ana Kokkinos practised as a solicitor, a researcher, and an industrial officer before starting to make films. In 1991 she completed the Postgraduate Diploma in Film and Television at the Victorian College of the Arts School of Film and TV, writing, directing, and editing the short film **Antamosi** (1991), which depicts the relationships between three generations of women in Greek-Australian Melbourne. Following this, she directed and co-wrote, with Mira Robertson, the short film **Only the Brave** (1994), which explored the difficult lives and relationship of two friends and their respective efforts to deal with societal and cultural pressures. **Only the Brave** won the Australian Film Institute awards for Best Short Fiction and Best Screenplay in 1994, and the Erwin Rado Award for Best Australian Film at the 1994 Melbourne International Film Festival. Kokkinos's provocative début feature •**Head On** (1998) is an adaptation of the Christos Tsiolkas novel *Loaded*. The narrative is focused on 24 hours in the sex-filled, drug-riddled life of Ari (Alex •Dimitriades), a complex, passionate, tempestuous, and vulnerable young man struggling with his many demons and the pressures of his Greek heritage.

ANNA DZENIS

Kostas

1979. Director: Paul Cox. *Producer*: Bernard Eddy. *Scriptwriter*: Linda Aronson. Based on an original concept by Paul Cox. *Director of photography*: Vittorio Bernini. *Music*: Mikis Theodorakis. 94 min. *Cast*: Takis Emmanuel (Kostas), Wendy Hughes (Carol), Kris McQuade (Jenny), Sophia Harrison (Lucy), Tony Llewellyn-Jones (Tony).

Kostas is a Greek refugee journalist who lives in Melbourne and earns a living as a taxi-driver. At the airport he is transfixed by Carol—a Toorak divorcee who works in a commercial art gallery—and sets out to seduce her. Kostas and Carol become lovers: their difference forms the substance of the story. Kostas's world is one of shared rooming-houses, Greek coffee-shops, dancing, and plate-breaking in restaurants. Carol's world is alternatively élite and genteel: a world of gallery openings and polite conversations. This familiar tale is turned into a striking narration through photographer/film-maker Paul •Cox's visual style. Cox mixes film gauges incorporating home-movie footage. Characters are often framed by windows, inside looking out, or conversing in doorways, which function as borders and boundaries, metaphors for the social spaces and cultural milieus that keep the characters apart. The fact that Cox is a cultured migrant himself, born in The Netherlands, suggests that there are elements of autobiography in this tale. **Kostas** opened the 1979 Melbourne Film Festival, the first time an Australian feature received this honour.

ANNA DZENIS

Kunoth, Ngarla (1936–) ACTOR Ngarla Kunoth, also known as Rosie, was born at Utopia Station and raised in traditional Aboriginal ways. Charles •Chauvel cast her as the star of •**Jedda** (1955) when she was a young girl, living at St Mary's Hostel in Alice Springs. Her beauty and her performance are a large part of the appeal of the film: she captures brilliantly the dilemma of being caught between cultures, and the trauma of being provided no way out but death. The critical success of the film made her well known outside her own community, but she completed her education in Alice Springs and Adelaide, and then entered a convent in Melbourne for 10 years. She left in 1966, became a liaison officer with the Victorian Department of Aboriginal Affairs, and later married William Monks. In 1977 Rosie Monks returned to Alice Springs, becoming an activist on behalf of her people—standing (unsuccessfully) for the Northern Territory parliament, working for the Central Australian Aboriginal Legal Aid Service, becoming a member of the Aboriginal and Torres Strait Islander Commission, and returning to work relating to the media as a member of the governing body of the Central Australian Aboriginal Media Association. IB

Kurtz, Alwyn (1915–) ACTOR Alwyn Kurtz is a radio personality, television host (in programs such as *Beauty and the Beast*), and war correspondent who developed an acting career, primarily on television, in the long-running series *Homicide* and *Cop Shop*. Kurtz's craggy features have also contributed to films such as •**Spotswood** (1992), in which he plays the benign capitalist Mr Ball, who directs a time and motion man (Anthony Hopkins) to save his employees from unemployment, and as Mel •Gibson's father in •**Tim** (1979).

Other Australian films include: And Millions Will Die (1973), The Newman Shame (1978), The Earthling (1980), Deadline (1981), This Won't Hurt a Bit (1993), •Road to Nhill (1997).

GM

L

La Revanche (1916), *see* **The Martyrdom of Nurse Cavell**

Lambert, Anne-Louise (1956–) ACTOR Anne Lambert added Louise to her name to avoid confusion with another actor when she went to work in the United Kingdom as a result of scoring a major success in her first film role here. She played the gentle, exquisitely lovely Miranda in Peter •Weir's ground-breaking •Picnic at Hanging Rock (1975): as one of the party that is lost forever on St Valentine's Day 1900, she created an aura of beauty that overhung the whole film. Sadly, apart from scoring one of the leading parts in Peter Greenaway's first feature, the enigmatic **The Draughts-man's Contract** (1982), she has not had so memorable a film role since. She has been busy on television and the stage (she co-starred with Lauren Bacall in *Sweet Bird of Youth*), has filmed in Spain (**A los cuatro vientos,** 1987), and played in several Australian films of the 1990s, only one of which, •Lillian's Story (1996), achieved commercial distribution.
Other Australian films: Breathing Under Water (1991), Seeing Red (1992).   BMcF

Lamond, John (1947–) PRODUCER/DIRECTOR A former publicity man (on •The Naked Bunyip, 1970; and •The Adventures of Barry McKenzie, 1972) and editor, John Lamond is now best known for several soft-porn films he made in the 1970s and early 1980s. As well as producing and directing, he also wrote two of these, **ABC of Love and Sex—Australia Style** (1978) and •Felicity (1979). The former plays with the then-popular sex education format, and the latter is a paean to the joys of liberated sexuality and love. Outside this genre, he was producer and director of **Nightmares** (1980), a thriller that mixes sex, murder, and the caricature of a bitchy film critic; **Pacific Banana** (1981), a smutty comedy that stars Graeme •Blundell and seems aimed at the audience for Blundell's 1973 sex comedy success, •Alvin Purple; and **Breakfast in Paris** (1982), a thin romantic comedy. He was also producer/writer of **Sky Pirates** (1986), an action adventure-comedy, starring John •Hargreaves. In 1989, he produced the martial arts melodrama **Sword of Bushido** in the USA. For a time, he worked for •Roadshow before entering feature production.
Other Australian films: Birth of a Monster (1968, doc., ed.), A Place Called Mooroopna (1968, short, ed.), This Year Jerusalem (1969, doc., sound ed.), Devil in Evening Dress (1973, short, co-w.), Australia After Dark (1975, doc., d., p, co-w.), Slice of Life (1982, p., d.), North of Chiang Mi (1992, p., d.).   BMcF

Landscape Nationalism and cinema in Australia have always shared some basic ideological fixations. Federation and the development of cinema occurred at the same time. From the outset, Australian cinema grew within a set of themes and presumptions that were informed by a peculiar blend of modernism, racism, and idealism that shaped the new society.

By declaring itself a nation, Australia set itself apart from the rest of the world. Also, specific factions within the country made claims for true 'Australianness'. The fact that some people could now be recognised as citizens of a new civilisation meant that there had to be many people who would be denied that description. Inside and outside the geographical boundaries of Australia, the new nationalism was as much a process of exclusion as inclusion, a scheme to prioritise particular morals and peoples. For this purpose the 'White Australia' policy was legislated in the *Commonwealth Immigration Restriction Act, 1901*, and the 'exclusion laws' of 1904 demanded the deportation of all South Sea Islanders working in the sugarcane fields of northern Queensland. The new society tried to define itself by naming and ejecting the people of non-European backgrounds.

These were paradoxical times. The new nation sought to declare itself distinct from the rest of the world, but it also insisted on being defined on the image of mother England. It wanted to present itself abroad as unique and laudable but, within its own jurisdiction, it was unable to embrace the special qualities of the indigenous peoples. As nationalism and cinema were developing in Australia, the optimistic mood of the community was underscored persistently by the fearful and shameful awareness that land-grabbing had brought the new nation on to the world stage. As early photographers such as Baldwin •Spencer and the Queensland agents of the Lumière Brothers demonstrated by their fascination with indigenous cultures in Australia and the South Pacific region, the non-English aspects of this new nation were perhaps the most distinctive and arresting. Right from the start, film-makers in Australia were fascinated by the image of Aboriginal people still inhabiting their country. This is the paradox: for all their local peculiarity, the indigenous culture of colonial Australia—the people and the land that defined them—had to be categorised and negated as exotic. In this way, during the late 1980s, Lumière's agents could not resist acquiring footage of Islander sugarcane workers in tropical northern Queensland, but the exhibitors presented the 'primitives' to Australians and the rest of the world as strange images of an 'other' time, a savage past that was due for expulsion from the future that nationalism and modernity promised. The same effect occurred with Baldwin Spencer's, Francis Birtles', Charles •Chauvel's, and Frank •Hurley's images of Aboriginal and Papua New Guinean people through to the 1930s.

Within the logic of White Australian nationalism, therefore, the original people of the land could not be presented as essentially and definitely Australian. However, as so much landscape painting and photography had already suggested during the 1890s, the land itself could be offered as definitively Australian. The land was represented as the thing that sets Australia apart from the rest of the world. In all that nature, the new civilisation would locate its peculiar soul.

But European techniques of landscape portrayal tend to overlook or ignore the Aboriginal signs and meanings that have been developed and maintained. Instead, the country has usually been depicted by the newcomers as baffling and empty, as a place for alienation rather than definition. So the paradox still perplexes. The land that is supposed to define the settlers is also the place that baffles them; and the people who originally belonged to the land and know its subtleties are the people whom the new nation has rejected as alien to the great dream of the new civilisation.

At the inception of Australian national culture, as cinematic expertise developed and audiences began to grow, a deeply ambivalent relationship with the country became obvious. It was a relationship involving fascination and fear. Ever since, Australian cinema has trekked into a vast landscape of contradiction. The cameras scan and focus to find something special in the country; but the majority of characters fail to demonstrate that they are competent, at ease or at home there. As for the indigenous people who might be able to show how to identify with the country, they are overwhelmingly absent, except as insignia of adventure and moribund mysticism.

Charles Chauvel fought the paradox with a paradox. In •**Heritage** (1935) and, later, in •**Sons of Matthew** (1949), he started out celebrating the *arriving* of the first colonists and then offered a story of their *arising* from the country as a dynasty of lusty pastoralists. In the way Chauvel's narratives and settings were meant to work, the land could be shown to estrange, test and then produce native White Australians who might righteously call the country theirs. In turn, this history of pioneer toil would itself become a permanent sign of our belonging in the location. In Chauvel's visionary scheme, a national cinema would help White Australians claim a pioneer's birthright by dramatising both an awe of the land and a triumphant urge to subdue it. As if the tensions in this story-pattern were not clear enough, Chauvel went on to make •**Jedda** (1955), in which he could not resist the overwhelming dramatic power of the Aboriginal lead actors (Ngarla •Kunoth and Robert •Tudawali) at the same time as he struggled to tell what turned out to be a comparatively underwhelming story of European ascendancy in the barely civilised Northern Territory.

Not every film-maker strove to represent the country as the key to an 'essential' national character. In •**The Sentimental Bloke** (1919), Raymond •Longford concentrated on an urban-vernacular performance style as his way to define and celebrate national peculiarities in the good-hearted persona of the larrikin. In the 'jazz age' works such as •**The Far Paradise** (1928) and •**The Cheaters** (1930), the McDonagh sisters (see McDonagh, Paulette) took another tack, showing little or no interest in locally specific issues. In these films, which could have been set in any metropolis, the sisters deliberately appealed to an international popular-culture audience.

However, it is the White Australian landscape tradition that has sustained the Australian film industry. The country has persisted right up to the present as a mythic cinematic force. By portraying an awesome landscape that simultaneously defines and alienates Australians, film-makers have tried to offer an affirmative, dramatic way to live with the contradictions of our being part of a society that still remembers the estrangement of *arriving* here even at the same time as we yearn to celebrate a birthright of our *arising* here. Alienation and powerlessness might define the way we inhabit the country but, in the logic of myth, the grandeur of the setting justifies the continuation of the drama of struggling to create a new culture here.

The portrayal of the challenging, uncanny landscape and the transcendent human ordeal that it causes has always been a staple of Australian cinema, from Chauvel's geographically libidinous epics to Harry Watt's civic and dutiful •The Overlanders (1946) or Kennedy •Miller's petrol-freaked 'Mad Max' trilogy (1979 to 1985). But we need not look only at the feature films to see this tendency. Throughout the history of documentary film-making, teams of film-makers have gone into the landscape in much the same way that speculative pioneer gangs and military innovators went before them, determined to show that ingenuity, companionship, and stamina can produce profits and a kind of exhilaration in this harsh but alluring country. Consider **Among the Hardwoods** (1936) made by the Commonwealth Department of Commerce. Consider Lee •Robinson's early work for the Commonwealth Film Unit (CFU; see Film Australia)—**The Crocodile Hunters** (1946) is an arresting example. Consider, indeed, all the 'masculine films' that the executive producer, Stanley •Hawes, is reputed to have demanded from the CFU.

Although Australian cinema has been such an overwhelmingly masculine endeavour, it is no great leap to the idea that the landscape has been feminised for as long as the mysticism and challenge of the country has been dramatised. Peter •Weir's •Picnic at Hanging Rock (1975) is perhaps the most emphatic example of a film that naturalises the supposedly unreachable, ineffable, and untouchable qualities of the country within nineteenth-century clichés of feminine sexuality. And Stephan •Elliott's •The Adventures of Priscilla, Queen of the Desert (1994) shows that for all our more up-to-date consciousness about the artificiality of our cultural environment and our sexual identities, there is still little within the non-Aboriginal aesthetic—other than the sly ironic distance that 'camp' purports to offer—that might help us to re-imagine our landscape. A critique of the touristy, desert aesthetic is made beautifully in Tracey •Moffatt's **Night Cries: A Rural Tragedy** (1990), which colour-saturates its painterly settings so that all human action—Aboriginal and non-Aboriginal—is shown to be almost asphyxiated by an artificially sublime environment that presses on every aspect of human existence.

Not all landscapes from non-Aboriginal cinema conjure the drama of mysticism or heroic alienation. John •Heyer's extraordinary •The Back of Beyond (1954) is an ever-moving, ever-interconnecting set of scenes and stories about the profusion of cultures and communities that are pragmatic and which integrate along the Birdsville Track. Rather than showing the country as hazy, menacing, or unknowable, Heyer presents a landscape of clarity, depth, and integration in which a cautious kind of experimental choreography—people to country, people to people—is always being worked out through camera work, storytelling, and bushcraft. Here is a landscape that is challenging, dangerous, and demanding; but is also livable and partially comprehensible. Heyer's film has a thrilling aesthetic that is secular and 'ecological' rather that artificially sublime. **The Back of Beyond** offers a landscape of knowledge and respect rather than of terror or beautiful surrender.

This is not an Aboriginal politic or aesthetic. Nor is it the pioneer's mythic landscape. Heyer's film is one place we might inspect for an engaged rather than an alienated representation of the national setting. Another place, not surprisingly, and most excitingly, is in much of the everyday film and television work that is now coming out of the Aboriginal media corporations that produce and transmit frugally and regularly all over the country. In wise and subtle works such as **Too Many Captain Cooks** (1988, by Paddy Wainburranga and Penny McDonald), or the storytelling tapes of the Warlpiri Media Association or the Nqukurr Community School (see especially their *Weya Wi Na?*), we find films that are not interested in surrendering to the mystique of the country. Rather, they show the importance of interweaving settings and stories to create dynamic patterns of practical, custodial knowledge in the vastly complex country where our lives must take place. They are stories of diligent observation and careful, respectful toil rather than of heroism and conquest. Informed as it is by millennia of research and practice, Aboriginal cinema offers many Australians a way to know their everyday landscapes anew, as settings that can be known and loved rather than defeated, feared, or revered.

ROSS GIBSON

LaPaglia, Anthony (1959–) ACTOR

Anthony LaPaglia left Australia for the USA in the mid 1980s and since his breakthrough film as the deadpan fiancé in **Betsy's Wedding** (1990), directed by Alan Alda, he has been a fixture in Hollywood crime films. LaPaglia's work in Hollywood has largely been in featured roles, such as those in **Innocent Blood** (1992), **So I Married an Axe Murderer** (1993), and **The Client** (1994), although there has been the occasional lead performance, mainly in low-budget features such as **Empire Records** (1995) and **Killer** (1994). In the latter, LaPaglia played a hit man who changes his mind when he falls in love with his victim, played by Mimi Rogers. **Killer**, which enjoyed sporadic release through the film festival circuit in the USA, went straight to pay television in Australia. LaPaglia's Australian films have been less successful, although he gives a strong performance as the detective who blows the whistle on police corruption in •The Custodian (1994), directed by John •Dingwall. Unfortunately, the film does not match the power of LaPaglia's tormented performance as Detective Quinlan who has to confront both a marital and moral crisis. Similarly, **Brilliant Lies** (1996) fails to fulfil its strong dramatic premise despite LaPaglia's performance as the employer accused of sexual harassment, while the romantic comedy **Lucky Break** (1994) also fails to develop beyond its rudimentary premise of a man (LaPaglia) engaged to Gloria (Rebecca •Gibney) who falls in love with a disabled woman (Gia •Carides).   GM

Last Days of Chez Nous, The

1992. Director: Gillian Armstrong. *Producer*: Jan Chapman. *Script*: Helen Garner. *Director of photography*: Geoffrey Simpson. *Music*: Paul Grabowsky. 96 min. *Cast*: Lisa Harrow (Beth), Bruno Ganz (J.P.), Kerry Fox (Vicki), Miranda Otto (Annie), Kiri Paramore (Tim), Bill Hunter (Beth's father).

According to the legend in **The Last Days of Chez Nous**, rosemary grows only where a woman is head of the house. It is the desire for domestic tranquillity amid the chaos of a Glebe terrace house that informs this film. The script is sophisticated and audacious, defiantly resisting superficial solutions.

The narrative oscillates between sisters Vicki and Beth. Vicki returns from Europe disappointed, without prospects, confused, and pregnant. Her insecurity contrasts with Beth's apparent security and independence: she is disparagingly described by her husband J.P. as driven by a 'mania for resolution'. The development of a love triangle is represented without bias. Each character has a perspective, ensuring that judgments of their innocence or guilt are reserved. The consequent hostility is never quite alleviated by hints of tenderness. With the reversal of the women's roles, their relationship becomes irretrievable. Beginning with reunion and ending with discord, Gillian •Armstrong's film eschews conventional narrative form.   WENDY HASLEM

Last of the Knucklemen, The

1979. Director: Tim Burstall. *Producer*: Tim Burstall. *Scriptwriter*: Tim Burstall. Based on the play by John Powers. *Director of photography*: Dan Burstall. *Music*: Bruce Smeaton. 93 min. *Cast*: Gerard Kennedy (Tarzan), Michael Preston (Pansy), Peter Hehir (Tom), Dennis Miller (Horse), Michael Caton (Monk).

This drama, set in a mining site in Central Australia, was one of the few films of its period to offer a critique of the Australian mateship mythology. Based on John Powers' play, Tim •Burstall's script retains the focus on the interplay of character among the men who inhabit the camp and who get on each other's nerves. There are outdoor shots of the men at work, but the film's drama is essentially claustrophobic. Pansy, deliberately provocative, finally comes to blows with Tarzan, the hero of the title, although the conflicts for most of the film are enacted verbally or through poker games. The film presents a harsh picture of the effects of isolation on the group; it does not glamorise the tough outback worker and, in its honesty, it fails to provide easy

empathy for audiences. Burstall directs with abrasive vigour and there are strong performances from the ensemble cast.
                                                    BMCF

Last Wave, The

1977. Director: Peter Weir. *Producers*: Hal McElroy, Jim McElroy. *Scriptwriters*: Peter Weir, Tony Morphett, Petru Popescu. *Director of photography*: Russell Boyd. *Music*: Charles Wain. 106 min. *Cast*: Richard Chamberlain (David Burton), Olivia Hamnett (Annie Burton), David Gulpilil (Chris Lee), Fred Parslow (Reverend Burton), Vivean Gray (Dr Whitburn).

Peter •Weir's fascination with the ways in which manifestations of the extraordinary, even of the supernatural, play around the edges of the ordinary and the natural, explored in both •**The Cars that Ate Paris** (1974) and •**Picnic at Hanging Rock** (1975), is emphasised again in this film. Successful middle-class lawyer David Burton has the bases of his life and beliefs shaken by his encounter with tribal Aborigines living in Sydney. He finds that the remains of an ancient civilisation still exist under the city streets and that his own heritage is not what he thought. His dreams foretell the destruction of the city by a giant tidal wave. The film begins with hail falling out of a cloudless sky, and this image prepares us for the kinds of strangeness with which the film will confront Burton's rational intelligence. Like several of Weir's early films, **The Last Wave** develops an imagistic coherence rather than one born of linear narrative expectations. It must be conceded that the film dissipates some of the promising tension set up in its first half-hour. Despite its metaphysical pretensions, the film did well commercially both here and abroad, Richard Chamberlain's modest star power perhaps being helpful in this respect.   BMCF

Lathouris, Nick ACTOR   Billed variously as Nic, Nico, and Nicos, as well as Nick, Lathouris has played a range of ethnic roles since his début in the small role of 'Grease Rat' in •**Mad Max** in 1979. He is sometimes villainous—in John •Ruane's black comedy, •**Death in Brunswick** (1991), in which he played the droll and wicked Mustafa, who deals in drugs from his base as kitchen hand at a frowzy nightclub and who gets murdered for his pains. Sometimes his roles are more serious, as in his role as the Hot Dog man in •**Heaven Tonight** (1990), or as George in Michael •Jenkins's •**The Heartbreak Kid** (1993), in which the problems of the generations are compounded by those of conflicting ethnic ties. He has had a continuing role in the popular television series, *Heartbreak High*, and appeared in Daryl Dellora's semi-documentary drama, **Against the Innocent** (1989), a plea for moderation in counter-terrorist strategies. More recently, he has acted as dramaturge to the highly regarded ABC series *Wildside*.
Other Australian films: **Georgia** (1988), **Father** (1989), **Jigsaw** (1990), **Gino** (1994).   BMCF

Lawrence, Bruno (1954–95) ACTOR Bruno Lawrence developed a reputation in New Zealand as an actor capable of portraying confrontational characters in films such as **Utu** (1983) and especially the desperate family man in **Smash Palace** (1981). While continuing to work sporadically in New Zealand, Lawrence performed in many Australian films and television programs in the 1980s and 1990s, and he created a strong impression as the criminal Cracka Park in the television miniseries *The Great Bookie Robbery* (1986), directed by Mark •Joffe and Marcus Cole. This was preceded by the supposedly blind soldier in •**An Indecent Obsession** (1985) and Lawrence followed with a lead role as the ambitious cop in the crime thriller •**Grievous Bodily Harm** (1988), directed by Mark Joffe. Lawrence also appeared as the factory worker in another Joffe-directed film •**Spotswood** (1992). In the 1990s Lawrence was excellent as the cynical television executive in the superb comedy series *Frontline*. Lawrence returned to New Zealand in 1994 prior to his death from lung cancer in 1995.

Other Australian films include: Initiation (1987), **As Time Goes By** (1988), **Rikky and Pete** (1988), **The Delinquents** (1989), Gino (1993). GM

Lawrence, Denny (1952–) WRITER/DIRECTOR As a writer, Denny Lawrence is best known for his collaborations with Bob •Ellis, •**Goodbye Paradise** (1983) and •**Warm Nights on a Slow Moving Train** (1988), both of which are from Lawrence's original ideas. He directed the light comedy **Emoh Ruo** (1985), and his **Afraid To Dance** (1988) won the Writer's Guild Awgie for Paul Cockburn's script, but received a limited theatrical release and seems to have vanished from many of the reference books. Lawrence started out as a child actor on stage and in television, went straight to the National Institute of Dramatic Art from school, and on to the •Australian Film, Television and Radio School, where he studied writing and directing. He has worked in film as a script editor, but his main body of work can be found in television, where he enjoys a solid reputation as both a writer and director. He created the ABC television series *The Damnation of Harvey McHugh* and *Children's Hospital*, and has directed over 100 hours of series and serial television. He also directed the telemovies *Archer* (1986) and *Army Wives* (1987). HARRY KIRCHNER

Lazareff, Serge (1944–) ACTOR Born in Shanghai, of Russian–Polish parents, Serge Lazareff came to Australia in 1951 and made his first real impact in films as Mexican Pete, the womanising sidekick to Max •Gillies' Dead Eye Dick in Richard Franklin's oddly touching **The True Story of Eskimo Nell** (1975). Prior to that, he was a journalist and had trained at the National Institute of Dramatic Art before embarking on a busy career in the acting media in the 1970s.

His first film was Tony Richardson's •**Ned Kelly** (1970), followed by two larger roles in films directed by Brian Hannant—the 'Judy' episode of **Three to Go** (1971) and the short feature, **Flashpoint** (1972), in which he played the newcomer who sets off emotional turmoil in a small mining community. He became a familiar face in such popular television series as *Cash and Company*, *Young Ramsay*, and *1915*, as well as such films as •**Eliza Fraser** (1976), **The Best of Friends** (1982), and •**The Lighthorsemen** (1987), showing an engaging presence.

Other Australian films: Where We are Heading (1971, short), The Claim (1976, short), Say You Want Me (1977, short), Luigi's Ladies (1989), Departure (1994, unreleased). BMcF

Lazenby, George (1939–) ACTOR Born in Goulburn, NSW, George Lazenby worked as a car salesman before entering films in the United Kingdom in 1969. His début was accompanied by much publicity as he played the new James Bond, replacing Sean Connery, in **On Her Majesty's Secret Service**. This did more for his celebrity than for his acting career, though he has since exploited his association with the legendary agent. In Australia, he starred in the action adventure, •**The Man from Hong Kong** (1975), and several telemovies, including *Is There Anybody There?* (1976), with Wendy •Hughes, but most of his subsequent work has been in the USA, much of it on television. BMcF

Lee, Jack (1913–) DIRECTOR British-born Jack Lee was almost part of the new Australian cinema (see Revival, the) when the deal to direct •**Don's Party** (1976) fell through. His career began in documentary in the United Kingdom, where he was attached to the famed Crown Film Unit and was associated with such films as **London Can Take It** (1940) and **Children on Trial** (1946), before entering feature films with **Woman in the Hall** (1947). His greatest successes were **The Wooden Horse** (1949) and **A Town Like Alice** (1956), part of which he filmed in Australia. He then directed most of •**Robbery Under Arms** (1957). He returned to live in Australia in 1963 and co-directed the documentary **From the Tropics to the Snow** (1964). He produced several more documentaries and, in 1976, was appointed chairman of the •South Australian Film Corporation, but he never directed again.

Other Australian films: A Weekend in Australia (1964, doc., nar.), A Tradition in Wine (1968, doc., p.), Petfoods is a Serious Business (1969), Belinda (1972, doc., p.). BMcF

Lee, Margot ACTOR With a long career in radio and a television stint in Hollywood behind her, Margot Lee appeared in the first live television drama in Australia, *The Twelve Pound Look*, and in the first television series, *Stormy Petrel*, both in the early 1960s. She played a seductive nightclub singer in her first film, the racecourse melodrama •Into the Straight (1949), with Charles •Tingwell and Muriel •Steinbeck, and subsequently appeared in •Tim (1979), the romance based on Colleen McCullough's novel, *The Journalist* (1979), •Heatwave (1982), and—very enjoyably—as the pub-owning Pearl in •Star Struck (1982). She had a touch of the old-time Hollywood good-hearted blonde in her screen persona, but her real pre-eminence was on radio (she was a panel member on *Leave It to the Girls* for eight years) and television.

Other films: I Can't Get Started (1985), The Place at the Coast (1987). BMcF

Lee, Mark (1959–) ACTOR   The opening image of blonde Mark Lee preparing to sprint across the distinctive Australian landscape in •Gallipoli (1981) provides an identifiable reference point for the Australian cinema in the early 1980s. Lee is visually perfect, in terms of epitomising Australian innocence, as the sacrificial lamb slaughtered on the Gallipoli Peninsula in Peter •Weir's contemporary interpretation of the 1915 military disaster. Unfortunately, Lee has never received the opportunity to replicate the success of this film in his subsequent screen efforts, which began with the role of Bruce, who comes between Angela •Punch-MacGregor and Graeme •Blundell, in the marital comedy **The Best of Friends** (1982), followed by the young heroin addict in **City's Edge** (1982). Lee's only other significant role in the Australian cinema has been as The Youth, seduced by Arthur •Dignam into a secret homosexual society known as The Rose, in the paranoid thriller •The Ever-

lasting Secret Family (1988). Lee received an Australian Film Institute award nomination for Best Actor for his efforts in this film, which followed an earlier nomination for his performance as Archy in **Gallipoli**. He has appeared regularly on Australian television since an initial appearance in the ABC telemovie *Lindsay's Boy* in 1974.

Other Australian films include: Emma's War (1988). GM

Lee, Sophie (1968–) ACTOR   Sophie Lee's career has steadily matured from her début as a late-afternoon host in a children's cartoon show and part-time singer to screen actor with a small, albeit impressive, list of screen credits. Following experience in television drama, such as *The Flying Doctors* and *Typhon's People*, Lee received her first major feature film role as Tania, the bride with the roving husband, in •Muriel's Wedding (1994), and the film allowed her to exploit her comic potential in a number of key scenes. Following more substantial roles on television, in programs such as *Halifax, Good Guys, Bad Guys* and *Raw FM*, Lee's comic ability was foregrounded in the surprise hit •The Castle (1997).

Other Australian film: Titsiana Booberini (1997). GM

Lemon, Genevieve ACTOR   This versatile actor, comedian, and singer started out with the Rocks Players in 1977. A highlight of her stage career was her tour with *Steaming* in 1982–83 and again in 1985. She has played many roles in television, among which she was best known as Marlene

Mark Lee

Genevieve Lemon

'Rabbit' Warren in *Prisoner* in 1984. On film, she has played in a number of short films, and has had minor or supporting roles in the features **Luigi's Ladies** (1989), **•The Piano** (1993), **Billy's Holiday** (1995), and **•The Well** (1997). It is her title role in Jane **•Campion's •Sweetie** (1989) that stands out among her film performances. **Sweetie** contains echoes of her characters in both *Steaming* and *Prisoner*, in an unpredictable mixture of perversity, viciousness, and vulnerability. It earned her an Australian Film Institute nomination for Best Actress in 1989, and an Australian Film Critics Award for Best Actress in 1990.   IB

Lesbian cinema   Until recently, lesbians, as fully realised figures, were seldom seen in mainstream Australian feature films. Apart from the underlying theme of repressed adolescent lesbian desire in **•Picnic at Hanging Rock** (1975) and a brief sequence of lesbian love in **•The Getting of Wisdom** (1977), Australian films have avoided the topic. In overseas films such as **The Killing of Sister George** (1968), **Les Biches** (1968), **Walk on the Wild Side** (1962), and **The Fox** (1968), the lesbian—despite negative stereotyping—was at least present. Australian films from past decades did not even feature the stereotype of the lesbian as manhater, deviant, neurotic, or suicide. Nor has Australian cinema taken up the recent Hollywood revival of interest in the female buddy movie with a lesbian subtext as represented in **Outrageous Fortune** (1987), **Thelma and Louise** (1991), **Fried Green Tomatoes** (1991), and **Leaving Normal** (1992).

In recent years, however, three feature films have addressed the issue. They are Anne Turner's **Dallas Doll** (1993), which is still to receive a commercial release in Australia; **•The Sum of Us** (1994); and Emma-Kate Croghan's **•Love and Other Catastrophes** (1996).

Why has the Australian mainstream been so silent until now? It is a fact that until the release of **The Sum of Us** and **•The Adventures of Priscilla, Queen of the Desert** (1994), images of male homosexuals and transsexuals were largely absent from the big screen; this suggests that the silence does not represent a sexist, but, rather a homophobic bias. There is certainly a strong element of this, which may help explain why the above two films tried to appear politically correct in their representations of gay male sexuality. There is a number of possible explanations for the absence of lesbian characters in film: the domination of the Australian mainstream by straight male film-makers; the acute stigmatisation of the lesbian in Australian culture; and a general anxiety about sexual otherness, particularly queer sexual desire.

Lesbianism, however, is the subject of a number of important short fiction films made outside the mainstream by independent women film-makers—films such as Megan McMurchy's **Apartments** (1977), Ann Turner's **Flesh on Glass** (1981), Viki Dun's **Can't You Take a Joke?** (1989),

Angie Black's **State of Mind** (1990), and Leone Knight's **The Father is Nothing** (1992). Other independent films that have incorporated lesbianism cover a variety of genres: fiction, such as Sarah Gibson and Susan Lambert's **On Guard** (1983), and Tom Cowan's **•Journey Among Women** (1977), a short feature by Ana Kokkinos **Only the Brave** (1994), and documentaries such as Digby Duncan's **Witches, Faggots, Dykes and Poofters** (1979), Laura Sheedy's **Woman to Woman** (1994), and **Double Trouble** by Tony Ayres (1991).

A brief analysis of a selection of independent films from the 1970s to the 1990s reveals their main concerns as well as changes in the representation of lesbian desire. When Ann Turner's **Flesh on Glass** was screened at a Melbourne Film Festival forum in 1981 it was criticised for presenting a negative account of the lesbian experience. Adopting a conventional realistic narrative form, **Flesh on Glass** tells its story of doomed lesbian love. When the film begins, Kate, a young woman in love with her brother's wife, Aggie, has already joined a religious order. The film recalls the events that led to her decision.

Flesh on Glass is more than a story of frustrated sexual desire. Turner uses the story of Kate and Aggie to comment on the suppression of lesbian desire throughout history. This is achieved by a bold use of religious imagery, specifically a recurring Bergmanesque nightmare, in which Kate imagines herself as a nun being walled up inside a rocky outcrop. What is particularly interesting about **Flesh on Glass** is the way in which it draws on lesbianism to critique the institution of heterosexuality. Married, middle-class, respectable (he's a doctor), and self-perpetuating (she's pregnant), Aggie and Hall represent the socially sanctioned unit. Yet, ironically, the film represents the viability of their union as dependent upon the repression and exclusion of otherness—in this case, lesbianism.

Despite its uneven performances, **Flesh on Glass** presents a powerful critique of heterosexuality that functions only through the exclusion of otherness, and of masculinity that is associated with the repressive sadistic powers of the law. In a particularly powerful scene, the barely repressed attraction between Kate and Aggie finally erupts one rainy afternoon and the women make love, rolling naked in the mud of the stable floor. Compared with the stilted, passionless encounters between husband and wife, the women's love-making is represented as joyous and anarchic. The scene demonstrates the disruptive power of women's love and laughter—what Mary Russo refers to as the 'carnivalesque'.

Recent films such as Viki Dun's **Red Label** (1987) and **Can't You Take a Joke?** (1989) interrogate the nature of cinematic representation itself, specifically that of the lesbian. They base their exploration of sexual politics in the world of the lesbian detective. The opening sequence of **Red Label** comments playfully on the conventions of the hard-boiled detective genre. Letters appear on the glass door: 'Laura Hunt—Investigations'. The glugging sounds of a large volume of whisky being poured into a glass fill the sound track. A woman's voice, slow and cynical, tells us: 'It was quiet. It had been quiet for days. So quiet, I could almost hear the gold lettering of my name flake and fall to the ground.' Laura Hunt is tough, attractive, and alcoholic. She is hired by a woman to find a stolen leather jacket. Like the bird in **The Maltese Falcon** (1931), the jacket is a red herring, a device designed to justify Laura's entry into the world of lesbian leather bars where she begins her search. 'There was so much leather in the place I couldn't taste my Scotch for the smell of it.' Like many famous male detectives before her, she gets the goods and also the woman. **Red Label** is a bold, amusing film, which plays with gender as well as with the conventions of the detective film.

A more complex film that plays with the nature of humour, **Can't You Take a Joke?** also problematises gender and genre. Dun's films reflect a marked change in the representation of lesbianism; they are not concerned with lesbianism as a 'problem' or with the issue of positive images. Rather they explore the spectator/screen relationship; they seek to empower the (female) viewer by placing woman in a space traditionally occupied by a man, in which woman controls the gaze, language, and desire.

Leone Knight's two short films, **In Loving Memory** (1992) and **The Father is Nothing**, engage directly with queer theory debates; both seek to explore taboo forms of sexuality such as fetishism and sado-masochism in relation to lesbianism and androgyny. By exploring sado-masochism (also the subject of Madonna's controversial videoclip, **Erotica**), these films confront directly the debate about positive images that continues to haunt the lesbian feminist community. The former explores the nature of fetishism through the dream-like deployment of images (boots, rope, knots, uniform, the human body) and actions (cleaning boots, rolling a cigarette, smoking, masturbating). Through a careful juxtaposition of images, **In Loving Memory** confuses gender identity. In one sequence, the camera cuts from a close-up of a hand clasping what appears to be the male genital area to a woman's face. Just as the viewer is encouraged to believe that there is a male and female performer, the film ends; and the credits acknowledge only one performer—a woman, Vicki Spence. Sounds of a high-pitched 'feminine' wail, accompanied by the crack of a whip, add a suggestion of sado-masochistic desire to the already ambiguous scenario. **In Loving Memory** challenges the argument that female fetishism is not possible because woman, who does not possess a penis, has nothing to lose in the first place, nothing to fetishise.

In **The Father is Nothing**, Leone Knight adopts the same surreal, dream-like style to explore sado-masochism. The opening image of light playing on water initiates our journey through a watery tunnel leading into the world of the unconscious where a woman remembers/anticipates a scene with her lover. Their sexual encounter is eroticised through images and sounds suggesting sado-masochistic desire: an androgynous uniformed figure holding a whip; a tattooed breast; sounds of marching feet; a siren's wail. Eroticism is heightened by the repeated shot of a mouth closing on a nipple and sucking it to erection. Gender boundaries are ambiguous. Is the uniformed figure male or female? The credits acknowledge Lisa Salmon and Jasper, F2M, a 'female to male' transsexual. In a world where 'the father is nothing' gender boundaries collapse, and other/queer forms of sexual desire are made possible and powerfully appealing. In both her films, Knight employs a surreal flow of images, ambiguous gender play, and an hypnotic sound track to seduce the viewer into a mysterious erotic underworld where socially taboo forms of desire find new forms and voices.

Recent Australian feature films might have been expected to be relatively conservative in their depiction of lesbianism, given that contemporary Hollywood films, such as **Personal Best** (1982), are still dealing in stereotypes, but this is not the case. Making up for lost time, three recent Australian features appear remarkably progressive in their portrayal of gay women.

The Sum of Us (Geoff Burton and Kevin Dowling), whose main story concerns the relationship between a father and his gay son, also includes a sub-theme that documents the lesbian life of the son's grandmother. Made in 1994, **The Sum of Us** was one of the first features to attempt a positive representation of gay men and lesbians. Criticised for a tendency towards stereotyping in its representation of gay men (presented as anally fixated), the film is probably the only mainstream feature to attempt a sympathetic portrayal of older lesbians.

Emma-Kate Croghan's **Love and Other Catastrophes** (1996) is a cool but warm-hearted comedy, set on a university campus, about young love in the 1990s. There are two sets of lovers—straight and gay—but the script, with refreshing aplomb, does not draw attention to the fact that one is a lesbian couple, an approach that Hollywood still has not managed, despite decades of practice. Croghan's ability to juggle with different elements, such as comedy and satire, and to pepper the text with quotes from such odd bedfellows as Jane Austen and Doris Day, gives the film an irreverent mood. References to old movies and popular culture are deployed with intelligence and form a central part of the film's examination of the nature of 'true love'—regardless of sexual preference.

Anne Turner's **Dallas Doll** (1993) offers an amusing depiction of lesbian desire. Golf champion and New Age guru Dallas Adair, played by Sandra Bernhard, manages to seduce all members of one family (except the dog) when they invite her to Australia to improve their game. Turner effectively uses the persona of Dallas to satirise suburban life and sexual relationships. Strangely, **Dallas Doll** still awaits commercial release in Australian cinemas but, given the uneven history of the representation of lesbianism in the Australian mainstream, perhaps this omission is not so odd after all. BARBARA CREED

Lesley, Lorna (1956–) ACTOR English-born Lorna Lesley made a touching impression in the brief role of Ellie, the country town girl who gets pregnant by a newsreel cameraman during the Redex Trial in •Newsfront (1978). Her unaffected prettiness and pathos were exactly right for the part and ensured her being well remembered. A writer, as well as acting on stage, television, and radio, she is also known for her work in the cause of Actors Equity (see Unions and associations). She has appeared in several television series and in such films as **Just Out of Reach** (1979), a 60-minute film in which, starring with Sam •Neill, she played the daughter of British migrants who finds herself brought to the brink of suicide through lack of understanding from those around her; Ian •Barry's **The Chain Reaction** (1980), a thriller with a nuclear threat theme; and Howard Rubie's •**The Settlement** (1984), in which she played a barmaid and former prostitute with the eloquent directness that made Ellie so memorable.

Other Australian films: •Caddie (1976), Little Boy Lost (1978), Saint Therese (1979, short), Maybe This Time (1980), The Survivor (1981), Plain Sailing (1980, short), Stanley (1983), Resistance (1992). BMcF

Lesnie, Andrew (1956–) CINEMATOGRAPHER Lesnie trained at the •Australian Film, Television and Radio School (1976–79) and assisted directors of photography such as Don •McAlpine before he began filming current affairs, short films, documentaries, and miniseries. His first feature film as director of photography was **Emoh Ruo** (1984). Lesnie has the unique distinction of having won the Australian Cinematographers Society (ACS) 'Milli' Award (Cinematographer of the Year) two years running: 1995 and 1996. He has also won seven other ACS awards, including five Best Cinematography awards; for a miniseries, for **Spider and Rose** (1994), **Temptation of a Monk** (China 1993), and •**Babe** (1995). •**Doing Time for Patsy Cline** (1997) earned both Australian Film Institute and Film Critics' Circle cinematography awards.

Other films: Fair Game (1985), Unfinished Business (1985), Dark Age (1987), Australian Dream (1987), Boys in the Island (1988), The Delinquents (1989), Daydream Believer (1991), Fatal Past (1992), Two if by Sea (USA/Canada 1996), The Sugar Factory (1997), Babe—Pig in the City (1998). DAVID MUIR

Let George Do It

1938. Director: Ken G. Hall. *Producer*: Ken G. Hall. *Scriptwriters*: George Wallace, Frank Harvey. *Director of photography*: George Heath. *Music*: Hamilton Webber, Maurie Gilman. 79 min. B&W. *Cast*: George Wallace (Joe Blake), Letty Craydon (Clara), Joe Valli (Happy Morgan), Alec Kellaway (Mysto the Great), Gwen Munro (Molly), Harry Abdy (Elmer Zilch).

George •Wallace's first film for •Cinesound was more tightly scripted and directed than his earlier •Efftee features, so the comedy is more disciplined and the overall effect considerably funnier. Joe is so miserable that he gets drunk, intending to kill himself but, after several failed suicide attempts, he wills everything he owns to a gangster (Elmer Zilch) in return for his agreement to kill him unexpectedly. The next morning, Joe's long-expected inheritance arrives and he tries to back out of the contract, but Zilch holds him to it, and the film ends with a motor-boat chase, skilfully intercutting live action on Sydney Harbour with studio shots using back-projection. An abridged version, retitled **In the Nick of Time**, was released in the United Kingdom, where the title **Let George Do It** was applied to a George Formby feature. IB

Levy, Sandra PRODUCER Sandra Levy has been a significant producer of popular and quality television programs, particularly for the ABC, for many years. Levy's television credits include *The True Believers* (1988), *Act of Betrayal* (1988), *Edens Lost* (1989), and, especially, *Darlings of the Gods* (1989), which dramatised the 1948 tour of Australia by Laurence Olivier and Vivien Leigh. In the 1990s Levy worked on the *Police Rescue* series, and co-produced the film version (**Police Rescue**, 1994), followed by *Big Sky* (1997). Levy's film credits, although small, are equally impressive; they include •**Hightide** in 1987, **Wendy Cracked a Walnut** in 1990, and •**The Well** in 1997. GM

Lewin, Ben (1946–) DIRECTOR/WRITER Despite the bleak nature of much of his subject matter, Ben Lewin's work is almost always accompanied by a humanist, comic sensibility. Born in Poland, he moved to Australia with his parents in 1949, and practised as a barrister for three years before going to the United Kingdom to study at the National Film School. He worked mainly for the BBC, but independently produced **Welcome to Britain** (1976), a documentary about dubious immigration practices, after being unable to obtain in-house support. He created *The Migrant Experience* (1983), a six-part documentary series for •Film Australia, then wrote and directed the acclaimed miniseries *The Dunera Boys* (1985) about a wartime misadventure that found 2000 Jewish refugees stranded in the Australian desert. His first theatrical feature, **Georgia** (1989), starring Judy •Davis, was a curiously cold detective thriller about a young woman struggling to come to terms with riddles from her past. The romantic comedy **Lucky Break** (1994) drew on his own experiences with polio as a child but, ironically, was criticised for not taking this aspect of the story seriously enough. Lewin's writing credits also include the award-winning short **Plead Guilty, Get a Bond** (1990), and the popular television series *Rafferty's Rules* (1987) (series creator). He also wrote and directed **The Favour, the Watch and the Very Big Fish** (1991) (aka, 'La Montre, la croix et la maniere') in France, starring Bob Hoskins, and two telemovies: *The Case of Cruelty to Prawns* (United Kingdom, 1978), and *Matter of Convenience* (ABC TV, 1987).

HARRY KIRCHNER

Lewis, Tom E. (1957–) ACTOR   Aboriginal actor Tommy Lewis was discovered by chance at Melbourne airport by director Fred •Schepisi's wife Rhonda, as they were waiting for a plane to take them to Perth and he, then a student at Swinburne Technical College, was on his way back to Darwin. Several weeks later, Lewis was given—and passed—a rigorous test for the title role in •**The Chant of Jimmie Blacksmith** (1978), in which he gave every appearance of being a natural actor. He played the half-caste lost between two worlds who finally takes a terrible revenge on the White society he has tried to join and by which he has been exploited. It was a remarkable performance—charged with aspiration and despair—in a passionately committed film. Despite several more film and television appearances, he has never again had so exacting a role, at least in mainstream film. His second film, •**We of the Never Never** (1982), gave him a minor role as a station hand, but his third was in a film that went straight to video in Australia, **The City's Edge** (1983), although it was bought for United Kingdom distribution. Tim •Burstall's too-little-seen •**The Naked Country** (1985), based on Morris West's novel, gave him a strongly conceived character, Mundara, who has a key role in the melodramatic plot, and is allowed to speak eloquently for the rights of his people. In the lacklustre version of •**Robbery Under Arms** (1985), made in cinema and television versions, he played Warrigal, side-kick to Sam •Neill's bushranger, Captain Starlight and, although fourth-billed in Don McLennan's **Slate, Wyn and Me** (1987), his role was distinctly subordinate to the three white stars. He has done some television work (including *A Town Like Alice*), and continues to work as the town clerk of Katherine council in the NT. The total ease before the camera he showed in **Jimmie Blacksmith** should have made him a 'natural' for more prolific and demanding screen work.

BMcF

Libido

1973. *Executive producers*: Christopher Muir; John B. Murray. **The Husband**: *Director*: John B. Murray. *Scriptwriter*: Craig McGregor.

Director of photography: Eric Lomas. *Music*: Tim Healy, Billy Green. *Cast*: Bryon Williams (Jonathon), Elke Neidhardt (Penelope). **The Child**: *Director*: Tim Burstall. *Scriptwriter*: Tim Burstall from a story by Hal Porter. *Director of photography*: Robin Copping. *Music*: Peter Best. *Cast*: John Williams (Martin), Jill Forster (Mother), Judy Morris (Sybil). **The Priest**: *Director*: Fred A. Schepisi. *Scriptwriter*: Thomas Keneally. *Director of photography*: Ian Baker. *Music*: Bruce Smeaton. *Cast*: Arthur Dignam (Father Burn), Robyn Nevin (Sister Caroline). **The Family Man**: *Director*: David Baker. *Scriptwriter*: David Williamson. *Director of photography*: Bruce McNaughton. *Music*: Bruce Smeaton. *Cast*: Jack Thompson (Ken), Max Gillies (Gerald), Debbie Nankervis (Di), Suzanne Brady (Jo). 118 min.

The brainchild of a committee of members of the Producers and Directors Guild of Victoria, **Libido** utilised the talents of four established writers, two experienced feature directors (John B. •Murray and Tim •Burstall), a successful director of advertisements (Fred A. •Schepisi), and a prominent director of television series (David •Baker) to produce yet another in the series of early 1970s investigations of the male sexual impulse. Of the four stories, Schepisi's is stylistically the most interesting with its rapid intercutting of narrative threads to build the background to the story of a priest and a nun unable to reconcile personal feelings with religious commitment. David •Williamson's story of a man's celebratory infidelity on the night of his third daughter's birth was Jack •Thompson's first major starring role. Partly funded by the Australian Council for the Arts and by the distributor British Empire Films, the film was critically acclaimed, although its sexual politics may seem decidedly dated to modern audiences. In 1978, in an illuminating commentary on the writer–director relationship, the literary journal *Overland* devoted half an issue to the creative tensions between Burstall and Porter, and the genesis of their episode.

BEN GOLDSMITH

The Life Story of John Lee
[The Man They Could Not Hang]

1912. *Director*: Robert Scott. *Producer, Scriptwriter*: Phillip Lytton. *Director of photography*: Herbert Finlay. B&W. *Cast*: Mervyn Barrington (John Lee) Edna Phillips (Kate), Robert Scott, Robert Henry, Fred Cope.

The Life Story of John Lee
[The Man They Could Not Hang]

1921. *Director, Scriptwriter*: Arthur W. Sterry. *Director of photography*: Tasman Higgins. B&W. *Cast*: Rose Roonet (Kate), David Edelsten (The judge).

The Man They Could Not Hang

1934. *Director*: Raymond Longford. *Scriptwriter*: Lorrie Webb. From 'a dramatisation' by Rigby C. Tearle [J.A. Lipman]. *Directors of photography*: George Malcolm, George Heath. B&W. *Cast*: Ronald Roberts (John Lee), Arthur W. Sterry (John Lee Senior).

The story of the last years of the Englishman John Lee was filmed three times in Australia between 1912 and 1934. This suggests that Australian audiences must have found something particularly fascinating in the tale of a man who had not been killed when he was hanged but instead lived on as a condemned murderer. Only the 1921 and 1934 films survive in more or less complete form. It is their sententious, moralising tone that accounts for two decades of popularity. The first version was filmed in 1912 but not released until 1914, when Arthur Sterry and Frederick Haldane obtained the rights and began to tour country towns with a package in which the film was accompanied by a lecture, in the manner of the Salvation Army shows of a few years before. Sterry and Haldane were also responsible for the second version. The 1934 version, which was the last film directed by Raymond •Longford, maintained the heavy-handed sanctimoniousness of its predecessors and apparently surprised its backers by becoming a moderate box-office success. WILLIAM D. ROUTT

Life Story of John Lee, The (1921),
see **The Life Story of John Lee (1912)**

The Life's Romance of Adam Lindsay Gordon

1916. *Director*: W.J. Lincoln. *Producer, Scriptwriter*: W.J. Lincoln, G.H. Barnes. *Director of photography*: Bert Ive. B&W. *Cast*: Hugh McCrae (Adam Lindsay Gordon).

Three years after •**The Sick Stockrider** (1913), W.J. Lincoln directed a biography of the poet, **The Life's Romance of Adam Lindsay Gordon**, the first and last reels of which survive today. In this footage some screen time is taken up with intertitles of Adam Lindsay Gordon's verse, and even more with scenes of characters reading and writing. Hugh McCrae, a literary man himself and an Australian 'type' in the manner of Bryan •Brown, brings an undoubted charisma to the role of the older Gordon. One shot sticks in the mind long after the rest of the film has been forgotten: Gordon, a tiny silhouette with a rifle walking along the beach at dawn to the place where he will take his own life while another diminutive shadow employs the early hour to catch fish in the surf. WILLIAM D. ROUTT

Lighthorsemen, The

1987. *Director*: Simon Wincer. *Producers*: Simon Wincer, Ian Jones. *Scriptwriter*: Ian Jones. *Director of photography*: Dean Semler. *Music*: Mario Millo. 111 min. *Cast*: Jon Blake (Scotty), Peter Phelps (Dave), John Walton (Tas), Gary Sweet (Frank), Sigrid Thornton (Anne), Anthony Andrews (Maj. Meinertzhagen).

Simon •Wincer's production is set during World War I, highlighting the role the Australian Light Horse Brigade played in the 1917 cavalry charge at Beersheeba. The narrative focuses on the differing experiences of four Lighthorsemen—Scotty, Dave, Tas, and Frank—while Sigrid •Thornton plays the role of Anne, a nurse who becomes romantically linked to Dave, the pacifist caught up in a war he cannot fight. The men's personal responses to war, while unduly simplified, illustrate the types of feelings experienced by Australian soldiers at war. The film's climax comes with the charge of the Light Horse at Beersheeba, a triumph of epic proportions.

This myth-making venture from the somewhat unremarkable period of the late 1980s offers a conventional version of a legendary event. The film's lukewarm critical reception can be partly attributed to an unimaginative script, shallow characterisations, and a misplaced romantic subplot. Its most notable aspect is Dean •Semler's stunning photography. The opening horse round-up sequence is a fine example of his visually dynamic contribution to the narrative. MELINDA HILDEBRANDT

Lillian's Story

1996. *Director*: Jerzy Domaradzki. *Producer*: Marian Macgowan. *Scriptwriter*: Steve Wright (based on a novel by Kate Grenville). *Director of photography*: Slawomir Idziak. *Music*: Cezary Skubiszewski. 102 min. *Cast*: Ruth Cracknell (Lillian Singer), Barry Otto (Albion Singer/John Singer), Toni Collette (young Lillian), John Flaus (Frank), Iris Shand (Aunt Kitty).

After 40 years in a psychiatric institution, Lillian Singer (based on Sydney eccentric Bea Miles) finds herself out in the 'real world' of Sydney. She wanders the streets, busks as a Shakespearean orator, befriends hookers, has a crush on a bank manager, and meets up with former boyfriend Frank, now an alcoholic holed up in a makeshift harbour-side camp. Past and present are interwoven in a narrative that makes us feel acutely both the promise and pain of a life darkened and almost destroyed by a sadistic father, but ultimately redeemed by courage, hope, and poetry.

Lillian's Story was one of a wave of mid 1990s films exploring the problems of 'madness' and depicting the perplexities of the psychically damaged who are trying to make their way in the world of 'normality' (•**Bad Boy Bubby**, •**Angel Baby**, •**Cosi**, •**Shine**). The somewhat mannered European arthouse style, the intrusion of a ludicrous subplot, and an uneven script occasionally detract from superb and contrasting performances by Ruth •Cracknell, Barry •Otto, and Toni •Collette. HARRY OLDMEADOW

Lincoln, W. J. (1870–1917) DIRECTOR/PRODUCER/WRITER
William Joseph Lincoln first made his name in Melbourne theatre circles as a writer of successful plays, produced by the

Alfred Dampier Dramatic Company (*The Power of Wealth*, 1901; *The Bush King*, 1902; *Captain Moonlight*). He continued to write, while managing touring film and theatrical companies, including J.C. Williamsons Bio-Tableau 1904–06, and the Meynell and Gunn Dramatic Company 1906–09. In 1909 he settled in St Kilda, managing the Paradise Gardens, an open-air picture theatre on the Esplanade, but he was soon also writing and directing films. Between 1911 and early 1912 he wrote and directed, for Amalgamated Pictures: *After Sundown, It is Never Too Late to Mend, The Mystery of a Hansom Cab, The Luck of Roaring Camp, *Called Back, The Bells, The Double Event, The Lost Chord, Breaking the News, and Rip Van Winkle. After Amalgamated abandoned film production in 1912, he continued his association with the company as publicity manager, and cinema manager of both the Paradise Gardens and the Lyric Picture Gardens. But he also formed his own production company, in partnership with actor Godfrey *Cass, working from Amalgamated's former studio in St Kilda. In 1913 Lincoln-Cass Films Pty Ltd made *The Sick Stockrider, Moondyne, The Remittance Man, Transported, The Road to Ruin, The Crisis, The Reprieve, From the Wreck, and The Victory. But the venture was not financially successful, and the studio was sold to J.C.Williamsons. Lincoln's association with Amalgamated ended in 1915, but he continued to write films, some for Williamsons: in 1915 Within Our Gates and, in 1916, Within the Law, Get Rich Quick Wallingford, Edith Cavell, La Revanche, *Officer 666, and *The Life's Romance of Adam Lindsay Gordon. He also directed some of these but, in that last year, his alcoholism made him less and less reliable. Despite a certain staginess in his directing style, his prolific output over a relatively short time made him a key figure in early Australian film production.   IB

Little, Mark

Little, Mark (1960–) ACTOR Mark Little graduated from the National Institute of Dramatic Art in 1980, and made a name both on stage (as a stand-up comedian with a social conscience, and in straight roles) and on television. He was impressive in early film roles such as Carl, the keyboard player in *Star Struck (1982), or Basil, the nervous venereal disease patient in *The Clinic (1983). But he is best known for long-running television performances such as Ron in *The Flying Doctors* (1985) and Joe Mangel on the soap opera *Neighbours* (1988–91)—a good-hearted but rather foolish character, often out of work, and with a broad accent indicating he is rather further down the social scale than most inhabitants of Ramsay St. Boady O'Hagan in *Nirvana Street Murder (1991) is in a similar social position to Joe Mangel, but is a much blacker creation, subject to fits of unpredictable violence. However, Lenny, in Greenkeeping (1993), is a return to the lovable Aussie working-class battler. These leading roles all make good use of Little's

physical presence—tall and shambolic, with a mobile face and cheeky grin. He was nominated for the Australian Film Institute's Best Supporting Actor awards for both Benedict Maynard in *An Indecent Obsession (1985) and Curly in Short Changed (1986).
Other Australian films: Wills and Burke (1985), *Evil Angels (1988), Golden Braid (1991).   IB

Llewellyn-Jones, Tony

Llewellyn-Jones, Tony (1949–) ACTOR Much of the film career of this British-born actor has been associated with expatriate Dutch director Paul *Cox, who has, to a degree unusual in Australian cinema, gathered a sort of repertory company around him, including such other players as Norman *Kaye, Wendy *Hughes, and Chris *Haywood. Tony Llewellyn-Jones, the son of distinguished parents—a gynaecologist father and politician mother—became well known for his continuing role in the ABC television series *GP*. His first feature film role was in Peter *Weir's *Picnic at Hanging Rock (1975), as the gardener, Tom, who beds the maid played by Jacki *Weaver, and he had an uncredited bit part in Weir's next film, *The Last Wave (1977). He had his first role for Cox in the experimental Illuminations (1976) and, thereafter, appeared in nine films for Cox, including *Kostas (1979), *Lonely Hearts (1982), *A Woman's Tale (1991) and, perhaps most memorably, as the shy church warden in *Man of Flowers (1983). On a number of Cox's films, Llewellyn-Jones is credited as associate producer as well as acting in them. Among his films for other directors are Maurice Murphy's Fatty Finn (1980), as the 'dunny man', and Werner Herzog's Where the Green Ants Dream (1984), on which he also acted as production coordinator. He is a reliable actor who has also exerted influence behind the camera.
Other Australian films: Sacrifice (1971, short), Inside Looking Out (1977, a., assoc. p.), *My First Wife (1984, a., assoc. p.), Cactus (1986, a., assoc. p.), To Market, To Market (1987), Seeing Red (1992), The Nun and the Bandit (1992), Exile (1994), *Cosi (1996).   BMcF

Lonely Hearts

1982. *Director*: Paul Cox. *Producer*: John B. Murray. *Scriptwriters*: Paul Cox, John Clarke. *Director of photography*: Yuri Sokol. *Music arranged and performed by*: Norman Kaye. 95 min. *Cast*: Wendy Hughes (Patricia), Norman Kaye (Peter), Jon Finlayson (George), Julia Blake (Pamela), Jonathan Hardy (Bruce).

Director Paul *Cox, working on a small budget, had his first major success with this low-key study of an unlikely suburban romance. Wendy *Hughes suppresses her beauty to play Patricia, a dowdy, inhibited bank clerk who meets through a dating agency, and falls in love with, Peter, a 55-old piano tuner—and occasional shoplifter. The film charts with humour and tenderness the growth of their affection and their difficulties in dealing with the hectoring of their families. Patricia's parents require constant communiqués on the minutiae of her life; Peter's sister nags him about the need to 'do something with your life'. Cox, greatly abetted by his cinematographer Yuri •Sokol, lovingly recreates a sense of faded Edwardian suburbia, all dark panelling and lead-lighting, and of the surprising individualities of the muted lives it encloses. Hughes and Norman •Kaye each give notable performances (as they do in several Cox films), and there are sharp, wittily drawn (John •Clarke is Cox's co-scriptwriter) characterisations from Finlayson, Julia •Blake and Jonathon •Hardy.   BMcF

Long Weekend

1979. Director: Colin Eggleston. *Producer*: Colin Eggleston. *Scriptwriter*: Everett De Roche. *Director of photography*: Vincent Monton. *Music*: Michael Carlos: 92 min. Cast: John Hargreaves (Peter), Briony Behets (Marcia), Mike McEwen (Truckie), Roy Day (Old Fisherman), Michael Aitkens (Barman).

Peter and Marcia are a selfish, careless pair of suburban trendies who take their bickering to the bush for a weekend. They fetch up in an idyllic strip of coastal scrub and proceed to do their best to mess it up: they litter the camping area; Peter, in the bush, fires his new gun randomly towards the sea and kills a dugong; Marcia viciously smashes an eagle's egg against a tree. Their personal lives are in disarray, Marcia having had an abortion (the film takes a conservative view of this, as if it too were a crime against nature), and there is a growing sense of nature striking back. A possum eats their food, an eagle attacks Peter, who is later hit by a truck driver distracted by a bird. The film over-signals some of its thematic intentions but, in general, it works well as a tense thriller with a mounting sense of genuine menace in its suggestion that the natural world will tolerate only so much spoliation. Briony •Behets and John •Hargreaves are a convincingly disaffected pair, at odds with each other and with the world, and Colin •Eggleston's direction and Vincent •Monton's camerawork intelligently create the polarisations at the heart of the film.   BMcF

Long, Joan (1925–99) PRODUCER/WRITER

Before her début as a feature film producer, Joan Long had had considerable experience as a scriptwriter for the •Commonwealth Film Unit from the 1950s. She was, rarely for a woman at that time, given the opportunity to direct some short sponsored films. When she returned in the 1960s, after marriage and child-raising, she became a full-time writer and won awards from the Australian Writers' Guild for three of her scripts: two documentaries on the history of the early years of the Australian cinema, **The Pictures that Moved** (1969) and **The Passionate Industry** (1973), which she also directed, and a short fiction film, **Paddington Lace** (1971), which attracted a good deal of favourable attention just as new Australian cinema (see Revival, the) was beginning to emerge.

Her move into feature films came with •**Caddie** (1976), for which she not only wrote the script, based on the anonymous memoirs of a Sydney barmaid, but was also a partner with Anthony •Buckley and Donald •Crombie in the production company that made the film. Following the commercial and critical success of this film, Long went on to produce •**The Picture Show Man** (1977), a film about rival travelling cinema operators in outback Australia in the 1920s. She also wrote the script, drawing on the actual experiences of Lyle Penn with his travelling showman father. Long had worked hard to secure the film's funding from the •Australian Film Commission, the •New South Wales Film Corporation, and the Women's Film Fund, and the result is a modest entertainment. The film has undoubted nostalgic charm, but was perhaps too slight and meandering to find vast audiences.

She eschewed nostalgia in her next production, •**Puberty Blues** (1981), a sharply observed contemporary study of the surfing and urban subculture that was an element of the teenage scene of the time. Directed by Bruce •Beresford, the film really focuses on the rites of passage of the young girls who are marginalised by the surfing jocks and who eventually take a stand against male dominance. Long was attracted to the idea of the young women asserting themselves, and she and Margaret Kelly constructed a script based on the stories of Kathy Lette and Gabrielle Carey about their lives on the beaches of south Sydney. The film, budgeted at $800 000, was successfully distributed by •Village Roadshow. Long next produced •**Silver City** (1984), directed by Sophia Turkiewicz, a rare Australian film that deals with the important theme of postwar European immigration to Australia. It was made with script development funding from the •Australian Film Commission and the production finance was raised under the •10BA tax concession. It was screened in the Marketplace of the 1984 Cannes Film Festival, where it attracted sales and some favourable publicity, but it enjoyed only modest box-office success both here and abroad.

Long's last film, •**Emerald City** (1989), directed by Michael •Jenkins from David •Williamson's play of Melbourne–Sydney contrasts, suffered from undue verbiage. It was distinguished by some excellent performances from Robyn •Nevin and Chris •Haywood, among others, but failed to find a sufficiently fluent cinematic style to disguise its stage origins. Long, was a key figure in the history of new Australian cinema's development.

Other Australian films: Snow, Sand and Savages (1973, doc., w.).

BMcF

Longford, Raymond (1878–1959) DIRECTOR Raymond Longford is remembered as a pioneer motion-picture producer and director. Born in Hawthorn, Vic., Longford was first apprenticed to sail and later became a stage actor. He appeared in several touring productions in 1909 and 1910, often playing the villain to critical acclaim opposite his personal and professional partner, Lottie •Lyell. His first film roles were in the bushranger melodramas **Captain Midnight** (1911) and **Captain Starlight** (1911). He then directed screen adaptations of two stage successes, •**The Fatal Wedding** (1911) and **The Midnight Wedding** (1912). From 1913, until Lyell's untimely death in 1925, Longford was part of a film-making partnership that reached its peak in the 1919 production of •**The Sentimental Bloke**, regarded today as a classic. Debate continues about the real extent of Lyell's creative input in this film-making partnership. Longford's most significant contribution to the history of Australian cinema was his advocacy of a viable Australian film industry with government support. To this end, he spoke vehemently at the Royal Commission on the Moving Picture Industry in Australia (1927), and lobbied as president of the Australian Motion Picture Producers' Association. Of his more than 25 feature credits as director, only four survive today in the •National Film and Sound Archive collection: •**The Romantic Story of Margaret Catchpole** (1911), •**The Woman Suffers** (1918), **The Sentimental Bloke** (1919), and •**On Our Selection** (1920). His credits include the documentary **The Naming of the Federal Capital** (1913) and two government immigration films made in 1923.

Other Australian films include: The Life of Rufus Dawes (1911, a.), Sweet Nell of Old Drury (1911, d.), The Tide of Death (1912, d.), •Australia Calls (1913, d.), 'Neath Austral Skies (1913, d.), Pommy Arrives in Australia (1913, d.), •The Silence of Dean Maitland (1914, d.), •The Mutiny of the Bounty (1916, d.), •The Church and the Woman (1917, d.), •Ginger Mick (1920, d.), The Blue Mountains Mystery (1921, d.), •Rudd's New Selection (1921, d.), The Dinkum Bloke (1923, d.), Fisher's Ghost (1924, d.), The Bushwhackers (1925, d.), The Hills of Hate (1926, d.), Peter Vernon's Silence (1926, d.), •The Pioneers (1926, d.), •Diggers in Blighty (1933, assoc. d.), •The Hayseeds (1933, assoc. d.), •Waltzing Matilda (1933, assoc. d.), •The Man They Could Not Hang (1934, d.), •The Avenger (1937, a.), •Dad and Dave Come to Town (1938, a.), •Dad Rudd, M.P. (1940, a.), Wings of Destiny (1940, a.), •The Power and the Glory (1941, a.), Racing Luck (1941, a.), That Certain Something (1941, a.).

MARILYN DOOLEY

Longley, Victoria (1962–) ACTOR Following her roles in the television series *Mercury* and *Wildside*, Victoria Longley may well be better known for her work on the small screen than the large. In both of these she has played independent, thirtyish career women without recourse to the tough-but-warm-hearted stereotype; the roles were well written and she played them with individuating detail. In the disastrous 1997 film, **Diana and Me**, her women's magazine boss in a yellow suit, barking out orders to her minions, was one of the film's few unalloyed pleasures. In •**The More Things Change** (1986), Robyn •Nevin's sympathetic drama of role reversal and precarious relationships, she played a pregnant 19-year-old with clear plans for her future that go somewhat awry, and played her with a convincing sense of quirky refusal of what's expected. She had a rewarding secondary role in Ann •Turner's **Celia** (1989), as the communist neighbour in 1957 Melbourne suburbia; and she appeared again for Turner in the unreleased but oddly inviting **Dallas Doll** (1994), starring with American Sandra Bernhard. Longley can register warmth, wit and a not-to-be-tangled-with edge, all of which should ensure a productive career, either in leading or character roles.

Other Australian films: I Can't Get Started (1985), Turtle Beach (1991), Talk (1993), Hayride to Hell (1995, short).

BMcF

Victoria Longley

Lorraine, Marie (1899–1982) ACTOR Isabel (Isabella Mercia) McDonagh was the eldest of the three McDonagh sisters, daughters of the honorary surgeon to the J.C. Williamson theatrical company. They worked together on several feature films and a few documentaries at the end of the silent period: Paulette as director and writer, Phyllis as art director and production manager, and Isabel (under her stage name of Marie Lorraine) as leading lady. Isabel first gained film experience in two films with other directors: •Joe (1924) and •Painted Daughters (1925). Then for McDonagh Productions she played the lead in •Those Who Love (1926), •The Far Paradise (1928), •The Cheaters (1930), and •Two Minutes Silence (1933). All of these are urban melodramas, contrasting rich and poor, and allowing the heroine to move between social spheres, always retaining her charm and sophistication: in each, it is the roles that strain credulity, rather than the performances, which are restrained and often moving. In 1932 Isabel married and went to London: she refused film work there, and returned to Australia in 1935. But, in 1965, she went back to London and stayed there until she died.   IB

Lost films   It is now almost a truism to state that Australia was one of the first countries to embrace motion-picture production. What is less well known is that from 1932 Australia was also one of a growing number of countries to acknowledge, at a government level, the value and necessity of film preservation. However, the search for Australia's surviving silent films did not really begin in earnest until the 1950s and, despite some notable finds in the years that followed, the task of recovering more than a tiny proportion of the film industry's output seemed overwhelming. More than 90 per cent of Australia's silent films, and a large slice of our film production since then, has probably not survived.

While these are appalling statistics, the poor preservation rate of our archival film is similar to that of other countries. Film has traditionally been regarded as an ephemeral medium, a commodity to be discarded after use. Producers were reluctant to pay for storing their films after their commercial life had expired. In addition, much of Australia's pre-1950 film output was shot on unstable, perishable nitrate stock that required copying if it was to survive at all. Poorly processed or improperly stored acetate film also has its problems.

That much of Australia's silent and early sound film heritage survives at all is due in part to the vigilance of private collectors and former projectionists. Their passion for film helped save important components of our film history where governments or sectors of the film industry were unable or unwilling to do so. While an indeterminate amount of Australian film may still be held in private collections, over recent decades much has been lodged for long-term preservation with archival bodies, principally and initially the National Film Archive of the National Library, which became the National Film and Sound Archive (NFSA) when established as a separate institution by the federal government in 1984. While material acquired by the NFSA over this period represents only a small percentage of our missing film history, the yield—including

feature films, documentaries, newsreels, cinema and political campaign advertisements, propaganda films, and hundreds of short films (both professional and amateur)—has been both rich and varied.

Non-fiction gems that have surfaced include the earliest surviving body of government-sponsored film production, the Wills/Mobsby Collection of Queensland film actuality (1899), lodged with the National Film Archive by the Queensland Museum in 1982; William J. Jackson's silent documentary **In New Guinea Wilds** (1922); an actuality sequence from the Cornwell Brothers feature •**Eureka Stockade** (1907); items from the first Australian provincial newsreel, Pathé's **Ballarat Gazette**, filmed by Rene Tournoeur in 1911–12; part of Australia's first-known industrial documentary, filmed at the Swallow and Ariel biscuit factory at Port Melbourne in 1905 by the Salvation Army's Limelight Department; two early sound shorts produced by the •McDonagh sisters with Neville Macken for Standardtone, **How I Play Cricket** (featuring Don Bradman) and **Stranger in His Own Country** (a Kenneth Slessor-scripted film on Aboriginal race relations); a rare Spencer's Gazette item, **Hobart Carnival** (1910); home movies of state and federal politicians, including Sir Robert Menzies and Lord Casey; and **Prices and the People** (1948), an important documentary film produced for the labour movement by the •Realist Film Unit.

Important drama acquisitions include three Norman •Dawn features, **Typhoon Love** (1925), •**The Adorable Outcast** (1928), and the early talkie •**Showgirl's Luck** (1931); an incomplete print of Raymond Longford's long-lost melodrama •**The Woman Suffers** (1918); Australia's only completely sound-on-disc feature, •**Out of the Shadows** (1931); two reels of John Gavin's early bushranger feature •**Thunderbolt** (1910); three of Charles Chauvel's missing wartime propaganda shorts (**While There is Still Time**, **Soldiers Without Uniform**, and **Power to Win**); a section of the silent urban drama •**Circumstance** (1922) produced by American partners Lawson Harris and Yvonne Pavis; an incomplete copy of George Willoughby's World War I feature, •**The Joan of Arc of Loos** (1916); an optical sound version of •**The Cheaters** (1930), made originally as a silent feature in 1929 by the McDonagh sisters; a trailer of the first feature of the McDonagh sisters, •**Those Who Love** (1926); a fragment of Vaughan C. Marshall's romantic melodrama •**Caught in the Net** (1928); and the much publicised reel of •**The Story of the Kelly Gang** (1906)—about 400 feet of decaying nitrate——that was handed in to the office of *Cinema Papers* in 1982 after being salvaged from a municipal tip.

Finding 'lost' Australian films, however, is only part of the story. Before they can become freely available again, a great deal of research may be required to verify each film's identity. This is often no easy task: much pre-1930 film material survives only in fragmentary form, or in sadly deteriorated condition; title and/or production credits are often missing or inadequate; and a certain amount of early film requires unscrambling from compilation reels, assembled at one time perhaps by ex-projectionists or film handlers seeking a use for long forgotten sections or spools of 35mm film.

A perfect example of 'do-it-yourself' repackaging is evident in a reel of film acquired in 1988 and initially labelled by the NFSA as •The Kelly Gang (1920). Subsequent examination revealed tinted, red, blue, and amber sections spliced, circa 1920, into earlier footage that includes the insignia 'J&G' on intertitles. 'J&G' represents 'Johnson & Gibson'; William Johnson and Millard Gibson were the two men nominally responsible for the original version of the film, **The Story of the Kelly Gang**. But, from what we know of the 1906 production, the 'J&G' footage in this most recently acquired reel does not relate to it, nor to other surviving filmed versions of the Kelly story. The actor playing Ned is not Godfrey •Cass who featured in Harry •Southwell's 1920 and 1922 versions, nor does he resemble the Ned character from the surviving 1906 fragments. Comparison with images from a surviving poster suggests that some of the footage from this reel is from the 1910 Johnson and Gibson re-make of the Kelly film, with the crude continuity supplied by sections of Kenneth Brampton's version of •Robbery Under Arms (1920) and perhaps some material from the 1922 Kelly film.

Errors in identification may also mask the true significance of some film material. A near-complete but badly shrunken nitrate reel, initially labelled 'Melbourne Tram Ride c. 1908', was eventually copied by the NFSA after hours of painstaking repair and rejuvenation work by laboratory staff. This enabled the film to be viewed and identified by media historian Chris Long as the oldest surviving streetscape of Ballarat on film. Shot in September 1906 and entitled **Beautiful Ballarat**, it is also probably the first film taken from Ballarat's newly installed electric tramway—a primitive example of 'tram cam', as it were.

Luck can sometimes play a part in film identification too. In 1989, a six-foot piece of film spliced into a larger reel of film oddments was serendipitously matched with a movie still from the NFSA's documentation collection featuring actor Connie Martyn in a spotted dress. This tiny fragment was subsequently publicised as all that survived from Raymond Longford's 1926 adventure •The Pioneers which, in turn, prompted a call from a NSW resident who recognised the characters in the photograph and duly provided the NFSA with a mint nitrate print of a further five minutes of the missing Longford film. Given the low survival rate of the considerable Longford/Lyell output, this was an especially valuable discovery.

Another segment from a previously unknown Australian silent feature film was positively identified in 1988 by Melbourne film academic and historian, Ina Bertrand. She identified the footage—approximately 400 feet from an original 35mm nitrate print—as a segment of •After Sun-

down, after matching descriptions from a contemporary production report, published in September 1911 by the *Prahran Telegraph*. **After Sundown**, it transpired, was one of a number of features produced by Amalgamated Pictures, under the auspices of Johnson and Gibson and the theatrical entrepreneurs J. and N. Tait (at their new studio in the Melbourne bayside suburb of St Kilda). There is no record that the film was ever publicly screened, despite the ambitious nature of the project.

Valuable as such finds are, they are destined to remain as teasing glimpses of the original work. Given how little material from the silent era survives in complete form, it is not surprising that some films have been reassembled or reconstructed to approximate original release versions, or make them more comprehensible to modern audiences. For example, of almost 20 silent feature films directed by Franklyn Barrett, •The Breaking of the Drought (1920) is one of the only two surviving. It was restored by the NFSA from sections of two incomplete first-generation nitrate prints. The second of these films was discovered under a suburban house in Sydney in 1976. Some small sections have been entirely lost due to chemical decomposition.

Similar work was done on John K. Wells's •Silks and Saddles (1921), including some educated guesswork on the original narrative sequence, and on Ken •Hall's •The Silence of Dean Maitland (1934), in which some previously excised material and the original 'happy' ending were reinstated. A more celebrated example of editorial reconstruction was the 1981 re-release of Dawn's 1927 epic •For the Term of His Natural Life. With as much as 20 per cent of the original release version still missing, and a commercial cinema release beckoning, the reconstructed film was subject to a number of compromises, including projection speed, stretch printing, aspect ratio, tinting and toning, use of stills and intertitles, and soundtrack. Even the film historian who did the editing, Graham Shirley, acknowledged that the amount of interpretation required had made it almost a new film.

Reconstructing major Australian films is also a painstaking and, necessarily, expensive business. At the time of writing, the version of **The Woman Suffers** reconstructed by NFSA staffer Marilyn Dooley exists only on videotape, as does **The Inauguration of the Commonwealth**, Australia's first feature-length documentary (more than 25 of the original 35 minutes of film reassembled by Chris Long from the scattered components of the Federation coverage that still survive, an unprecedented amount for any film in Australia in 1901). For films requiring no reconstruction, there is, however, the question of whether surviving prints are the original, or most authoritative version. Early exhibitors, for example, had few qualms about re-editing the films they purchased. Nor is it widely known that many of the existing prints of Australian features from the 1930s have been copied from British release versions. Australian producers at the time had been quick to exploit sales to the United Kingdom under the favorable treatment afforded to films from empire countries as a result of the *British Quota Act* of 1927–28. Invariably, Australian films were trimmed for inclusion as one half of a double bill for release in the United Kingdom. In some cases, this practice may well have improved the films, but today's audiences should be mindful that original-release versions may have long disappeared.

There is also a feeling that some local film material ought to have survived when, in fact, it may never have existed. Filmed portrayal of the harsher aspects of the Great Depression years is a case in point. Little exists in the otherwise comprehensive local newsreel collections from the 1930s. In wishing to depict typical Depression scenes for its 1955 production **The Hungry Miles**, the •Waterside Workers Federation Film Unit was obliged to recreate the period for its own cameras. This 1950s footage has been used in many other documentaries and news programs since.

The casualty list for pre-1930s dramatic features, on the other hand, can be roughly estimated thanks to the significant efforts of Andrew Pike, Ross Cooper, Graham Shirley, and others, to document it. Recent figures suggest that only 67 of at least 259 features made in Australia from around 1910 to 1930 survive and, of these, more than half are incomplete or in fragments. The survival rate of silent fictional shorts is even worse. We still know only a little about the quantity of actuality and non-fiction footage shot in Australia or by Australians, and therefore about what amount has been lost. The fact is that the output of the documentary or newsreel sector of the local industry has always outstripped the more speculative feature film production area, and the comparative attrition rate could be as much as five or ten times higher.

The pattern of film survival in Australia also appears random at best. Marius Sestier's 1896 Melbourne Cup Carnival footage survives, but not his Manly ferry footage shot a week earlier. Cozens Spencer's **Marvellous Melbourne** (1910) survives, but not **Picturesque Sydney**, part of the same series. Similarly, an early sound film on Sydney, produced by •Efftee Film Productions as part of the Cities of the Empire series shot by Arthur •Higgins, is missing, while the companion film **Melbourne Today** survives. Much of Frank •Hurley's work is still available, but his film on the Sydney Harbour Bridge, **Symphony in Steel** (1933), seems to have disappeared. Longford's •**Sentimental Bloke** (1919) survives, but not the sequels •**Ginger Mick** (1920) or **The Dinkum Bloke** (1923); his version of •**On Our Selection** (1920) is available, but not its sequel •**Rudd's New Selection** (1921). A range of the McDonagh sisters' work is now accessible, yet no trace has been found of their last feature •**Two Minutes Silence** (1933).

For every archival gem uncovered, there are many false trails and major disappointments. Efforts to locate Louise •Lovely's sole Australian feature •**Jewelled Nights** (1925), for example, yielded only a title sequence and a few out-takes.

Excitement over the discovery of a film entitled **The Shadow of Lightning Ridge**, potentially one of Snowy •Baker's missing features, had to be modified when it turned out to be a much later in-house affair made by Union Pictures (see •Greater Union Organisation, •Village Roadshow, •Cinesound) staff, indulging in some cheap humour at the expense of their boss, Norman Rydge.

As motion-picture production enters its second century, the chances of locating further examples of our film pioneers' work grow slimmer each year. Nothing shot by Sydney photographer Mark Blow has ever been identified. Most of the Salvation Army's vast output is thought to be missing, including the majority of its most ambitious documentary-style project **Under Southern Skies** (1902). Only the opening departure sequence has been found of the first-known polar exploration film, Dr. Marshall's record of the 1907 Shackleton expedition. Even Hurley's record of the 1911–14 Mawson expedition, now incorrectly known as **Home of the Blizzard**, exists only as unsequenced and untitled camera negative and is in need of major restoration work. Similarly, Jack Percival's feature-length **The Old Bus** (1934), a detailed history of Charles Kingsford Smith and the flights of his plane *The Southern Cross*, may now only survive in small fragments via the Cinesound-Movietone library.

For all that, it is likely that some of Australia's lost films still exist in institutional or private collections. Or they may be secured in NFSA film vaults already, 'lost' only in the sense that they have yet to be formally researched or identified. But while Australian film culture and our heritage awareness have come a long way in recent decades, it is still possible for more recent films to slip through the preservation net. Without effective compulsory deposit legislation, final responsibility for lodging original negatives and release prints with the NFSA rested with producers who often lacked the time, energy, finance, or motivation to attend to the proper storage of a just-completed film.

The less high-profile the type of film, the greater the risk to its long-term survival. But even recent, seminal Australian feature films, such as **Rock'n'Roll** (1959) have been irretrievably lost, while •**Mad Max** (1979), •**Careful, He Might Hear You** (1983), •**Bliss** (1985), •**The Year My Voice Broke** (1987), and •**Evil Angels** (1988), among others, have yet to be formally archived. And for important 'Australian' feature films produced offshore—such as •**They're a Weird Mob** (1966), •**Ned Kelly** (1970), •**Wake in Fright** (1971), and **Walkabout** (1971)—the NFSA holds only used 35mm release prints as its 'preservation' material.

Even where negative material exists, the cost of striking new release prints for archival or retrospective screening purposes, as distinct from video copying for individual or small group usage, can be prohibitive. Whereas the loss of so much of our early film output seems now irreversible, it would be a pity indeed if more recent examples of our film heritage were

The Pioneers (1926), one of Australia's lost films

placed at risk simply because the generation creating this material underestimates its historical significance.

KEN BERRYMAN

Love and Other Catastrophes

1996. Director: Emma-Kate Groghan. *Producer:* Stavros Efthymiou. *Scriptwriters:* Emma-Kate Groghan, Yael Bergman, Helen Bandis. *Director of photography:* Justin Brickle. *Music:* Oleh Witer. 76 min. *Cast:* Frances O'Connor (Mia), Matt Dyktynski (Ari), Matt Day (Michael), Alice Garner (Alice), Kim Gyngell (Prof. Leach).

This film chronicles twenty-four chaotic hours of student life—university bureaucracy, money, accommodation hassles, tangled relationships of love and lust, coffee shops, drugs, sexual assignations, parties, conversations about Nietzsche and Doris Day, and plenty of cinéphile in-jokes. Shot around Melbourne University in 17 days as a collective project and on a tiny budget, the film was a big hit with critics and at Cannes, where it was snapped up for international distribution. The film director Emma-Kate Groghan commented that she wanted to catch the spirit to be found in a lot of American independent cinema. This helter-skelter, high-octane, infectious, and occasionally irritating comedy of manners is a modest but engaging work, greeted with some critical hype at the time of its release.   HARRY OLDMEADOW

Love Serenade

1996. Director: Shirley Barrett. *Producer:* Jan Chapman. *Scriptwriter:* Shirley Barrett. *Director of photography:* Mandy Walker. 97 min. *Cast:* Miranda Otto (Dimity Hurley), Rebecca Frith (Vicki-Ann Hurley), George Shevtsov (Ken Sherry), John Alansu (Albert).

Winner of the 1996 Camera D'or at Cannes, this black-humoured film received mixed reviews in its home country. Although not a perfect film, it does have a healthy sense of the absurd. Dimity and Vicki-Ann are sisters in the small country town of Sunray. When Brisbane radio personality Ken Sherry joins the local station, he moves in next door, and the sisters are soon competing for his attentions. The problem for many critics was the suggestion that Sherry was actually some sort of half-fish half-human. This touch of magic realism, it seemed, had no place in an Australian comedy. While the concept is not entirely successful, it is more 'hyper-realism' than magic realism, and deserves some commendation. First-time writer-director Shirley Barrett has an affectionately ironic sense of the town, but most notable are Rebecca Frith's underrated performance as the tightly laced hairdresser, and Miranda •Otto's performance as Dimity. She is awkward, naive, unpredictable, and gauche, and hilariously embarrassing when she offers to 'ease Ken's loneliness'.   TIM HUNTER

Lovell, Patricia (1929–) PRODUCER   Before establishing herself as one of the major producers of the new Australian cinema (see Revival, the), Patricia Lovell had spent 17 years in television as presenter, producer, and actor. She had been associated with such programs such as *Mr Squiggle*, a children's series that she hosted for 15 years, and Channel 7's *Today* as a news presenter. She saw Peter •Weir's experimental film, **Homesdale** (1971) and, when the opportunity came to film Joan Lindsay's novel, *Picnic at Hanging Rock*, the rights to which Lovell had bought in 1973, she chose him to direct, and Cliff •Green to write the script. •**Picnic at Hanging Rock** (1975) remains a landmark in the revival of cinema in Australia. Lovell's tenacity, including the raising of money privately to finance the film's first script and her dealings with distributors was, to a large extent, responsible for the film being made.

She followed **Picnic at Hanging Rock** with two more modest films, which may now be due for reappraisal. The first was **Break of Day** (1977), a small-town drama of the conflicts, romantic and ideological, of a disaffected young World War I veteran; and the second was •**Summerfield** (1977), a melodrama that combined elements of mystery story and Gothic incestuous romance, culminating in a burst of violence. Both were directed by Ken •Hannam, another key figure of the revival but, although both attracted some muted critical praise for performances and atmosphere, neither enjoyed commercial success.

Lovell's next film was a triumph with critics and audiences alike. This was the long-awaited •**Gallipoli** (1981), which she co-produced with Robert Stigwood who, with Rupert Murdoch, decided to make films for a company to be called Associated R & R Films. Although Stigwood and Lovell share the producer's credit, she is on record as saying that he did not interfere with the decisions she and director Peter Weir took. She knew from the start that this was to be an expensive project, and it could not have been realised without the participation of R & R which, incidentally, never made another film. There were production problems, but the resulting film was a powerful and moving reworking of a formative episode in Australian history and mythology. Her last cinema film to date, •**Monkey Grip** (1982), was based on Helen •Garner's novel of sexuality and drugs set in inner-suburban Melbourne. Lovell encouraged director Ken •Cameron to write the script. Again, there was trouble in raising the necessary budget and Lovell became ill during the pre-production period. In the event, following refusals from the major distribution companies, Lovell successfully distributed the film herself before it was taken up by Roadshow. It did well in Australia but failed to repeat its success overseas.

Other projects fell through for Lovell in the later 1980s, but she did produce David •Williamson's *The Perfectionist* as a telemovie. She was awarded a well-deserved MBE in 1978 for her services to Australian film and television, and it is a sad comment on the local industry, which she did so much to establish, that she has not worked more prolifically.

BMcF

Lovely, Louise (1895–1980) ACTOR   Sydney-born Louise Carbasse featured in nine Australian films during 1911–12: **A Tale of the Australian Bush** (also known as **Tales of the Australian Bush** or **Ben Hall, the Notorious Bushranger**); •**A Ticket in Tatts**; **One Hundred Years Ago**; **The Colleen Bawn**; **Hands across the Sea**; **A Daughter of Australia**; **The Ticket of Leave Man**; **Conn the Shaughran**; and **The Wreck of the Dunbar** (also known as **The Yeoman's Wedding**). By 1915 she was under contract to Hollywood's Universal Studios, her name changed to Louise Lovely, under which she achieved international recognition. Lovely's blonde curls, small stature, and pert face prompted comparisons with Mary Pickford and, almost invariably, led to roles as the melodramatic heroine. In 1918—when her contract had expired—Universal threatened legal action if Lovely, while working for another company, used the name Universal had given her. The subsequent nine-month blackban was a blow from which Lovely's career never fully recovered. Nevertheless, she made approximately 50 USA films, mainly for Universal and Fox. Lon Chaney was a frequent co-star in her Universal productions and, at Fox, she frequently partnered William Farnum, one of their major stars. Lovely traded on her star status with a vaudeville act, *A Day at the Studio*, in which she and her first husband, Wilton Welch, toured North America and Australia from 1922 to 1924.

Lovely's final film, •**Jewelled Nights** (1925), made in Tasmania, was a financial failure. The following year, Lovely testified about distribution difficulties at the Royal Commission. After marrying her second husband, cinema manager Bert Cowen, she retired from film-making.

JEANNETTE DELAMOIR

Lovers and Luggers

1937. Director: Ken G. Hall. *Producer:* Ken G. Hall. *Scriptwriter:* Frank Harvey. *Director of photography:* George Heath. *Music:* Hamilton Webber. 99 min. B&W. *Cast:* Lloyd Hughes (Daubenny Carshott), Shirley Ann Richards (Lorna Quidley), Sidney Wheeler (Captain Quidley), James Raglan (Craig Henderson), Elaine Hamill (Stella Raff), Ronald Whelan (Mendoza), Alec Kellaway (McTavish), Campbell Copelin (Archie).

Lovers and Luggers was one of •Cinesound's most profitable films in the 1930s and the reasons for its success are not difficult to find. Ken G. •Hall's production efficiently combines location footage, shot on Thursday Island by Frank •Hurley, with studio interiors and exteriors as the background to a simple melodrama based on famous pianist Daubenny Carshott's desire to prove himself a real man and find a pearl for English socialite Stella Raff. On

Louise Lovely

Thursday Island Carshott meets and falls in love with local girl Lorna Quidley as he sheds his European lifestyle and integrates himself into the local culture, which is based largely around drinking and pearling. After finding a pearl Carshott rejects Raff, who has journeyed from London to Thursday Island to claim Carshott, and settles for Lorna.

Despite the setting and the accent, **Lovers and Luggers** is similar to many Hollywood productions in the 1930s in terms of its dramatic structure and populist values—the film contrasts the rugged virtues of life on Thursday Island, and its celebration of 'masculine' activities such as pearling and drinking, with the 'soft' life of a world-famous pianist in London. The mark of Daubenny Carshott's acceptance by the inhabitants on the island comes with the line often repeated by Lorna's father, Captain Quidley, throughout the film: 'Daub's a doer'. Lloyd Hughes was imported from Hollywood for the romantic lead opposite Cinesound's favourite leading lady of the late 1930s, Shirley Ann •Richards.   GM

Lowenstein, Richard (1959–) DIRECTOR   Trained at the Swinburne Film School, Richard Lowenstein made a short film, **Evictions,** about the Depression, in 1979 after working on several other shorts, in various capacities. This proved to be the precursor of his impressive feature début in 1984, •**Strikebound,** in which he drew on research interviews conducted with Wattie and Agnes Doig and other veterans of the 1937 miners' strike at Korumburra, Victoria. Unlike most Australian films, this film (based on *Dead Men Don't Dig Coal,* a book by his mother, Wendy Lowenstein) focused on an embattled class rather than on an heroic individual. His second film, •**Dogs in Space** (1987), was similarly group-oriented, this time centred on the shifting drug-and-rock scene of inner-city Melbourne, and with the charismatic pop star Michael Hutchence as but one of the inhabitants of a scruffy household that is visited by tragedy. He made no further feature until the virtually unseen **Say a Little Prayer** in 1993. Nurtured in various capacities in short films since 1978, Lowenstein's talent is one that Australian cinema could valuably use: his direction in his first two features of actor Chris •Haywood and cameraman Andrew •De Groot shows at the very least a capacity for orchestrating notable talents.

Other Australian film: He Died with a Felafel in His Hand (1999 writer/director).   BMcF

Luhrmann, Baz (1962–) WRITER/DIRECTOR   Baz Luhrmann is a cheeky phenomenon in the Australian arts. He staged and later filmed for television a stunning, innovative production of *La Bohème.* He is clearly interested in making classic works accessible to new audiences who do not bring years of accumulated cultural baggage to their expectations, who indeed may even be wary of understanding moment to

moment what is going on. Absolute audience intelligibility seems to be one of his criteria, along with maximum enjoyment. With such apparent goals he is bound to meet his share of envenomed critical shafts—and has done so. However, with his kind of vitality ('vulgarity', to his enemies, but he would no doubt be prepared to risk—and even deserve—such an epithet), his passion for the arts, now happily including film, his riotous sense of colour and movement, and all this at the service of a rigorous sense of the integrity of the work in question, he can well afford to risk offending those who are waiting to be offended.

He appeared in two films as an actor in the early 1980s: John •Duigan's •**Winter of Our Dreams** (1981) and, in a very small role, Paul Harmon's little-seen thriller, **The Dark Room** (1982). As far as Australian cinema is concerned, his reputation rests on the surprise success of 1992, •**Strictly Ballroom**, in which he reworked and relocated the conventions of the Hollywood musical in the feverishly campy world of Sydney ballroom dancing championships. As director and writer, he made knowing fun of clichés, such as that of the heroine who takes her glasses off and unpins her hair prior to turning into a raving beauty, and satirised affectionately but sharply the whole posturing, artificial rigmarole of stylised choreography, costume, and tonsorial extravagance. The film was a major success world-wide, and paved the way for Luhrmann's next project, disingenuously titled **William Shakespeare's Romeo & Juliet** (1996). Shakespeare, however, may well have approved of this wildly updated retelling of this most famous of youth tragedies, transposed to Verona Beach, replete with television newscasts on the action, drive-by dangers, a transvestite Mercutio in silver lamé hot pants, a cast full of young tearaways, and corrupt elders and beguilingly youthful eponyms. The film may have divided the critics, but audiences, especially young ones, responded overwhelmingly, many, it seems probable, finding Shakespearean blank verse less alienatingly removed from conversation than they had feared. The Australian cinema desperately needs Luhrmann: the issues now are, can it keep him and can it afford him?   BMcF

Lye, Reg (1912–88) ACTOR   Reg Lye was one of the most successful character actors in Australian films. After a small part as a digger in •**Eureka Stockade** (1949), he became a regular in the Southern International features, produced by, and starring, Chips •Rafferty, and directed by Lee •Robinson. Lye was the chief villain in •**King of the Coral Sea** (1954), which was produced on Thursday Island in the Torres Strait. He followed this with key roles in other Southern International films such as **Walk Into Paradise** (1956), shot in New Guinea as a co-production with a French film company; **The Stowaway** (1958), filmed in Tahiti; **Dust in the**

Sun (1958), filmed near Alice Springs; and **The Restless and the Damned** (1959), filmed in Tahiti and the Tuamotu Islands. Lye was forced to work overseas in the 1960s because of the lack of opportunities in the Australian film industry, but he returned to Australia for his best screen role as the alcoholic shearer Old Garth in •**Sunday Too Far Away** (1975). Lye's effective performance in the film is crucial as it provides a vision of Jack •Thompson's likely future as a drunken shearer with no prospects and no family. Lye's best role since then was as Old Dan, the con man with the singing dog in **Molly** (1983).

Other Australian films include: •Smiley (1956), •Three in One (1957), •The Shiralee (1957), Smiley Gets a Gun (1958), •The Killing of Angel Street (1981), Freedom (1982).   GM

Lyell, Lottie Edith (Cox) (1890–1925) ACTOR/DIR-ECTOR   Born at Balmain, Sydney, Lottie Lyell studied elocution and embarked on a stage career in 1909, touring Australia and NZ with family friend Raymond •Longford. Ironically, Lyell was said to possess a beautiful speaking voice, although her entire film career was in silent films. She is celebrated today as an actor, scriptwriter, producer, director, editor, and art director; a pioneer film-maker, and an enigmatic woman. In her motion pictures, made always with Longford, she starred as characters who were demure,

defiant, and daredevil: the wronged wife in •**The Fatal Wedding** (1911), the transported heroine in •**The Romantic Story of Margaret Catchpole** (1911), the spirited princess in **The Midnight Wedding** (1912), the brave girl of the bush in '**Neath Austral Skies** (1913), and a seduced virgin in •**The Woman Suffers** (1918). Lyell's most acclaimed role was as Doreen in •**The Sentimental Bloke** (1919). Her talents as a director can only be surmised, because her credited features are lost: for example, **The Blue Mountains Mystery** (1921), and **The Dinkum Bloke** (1923). What is certain is that she was acknowledged by Longford as his partner in all their film activities. On her death from tuberculosis at age 35, the trade magazine *Everyone's* observed: 'The Australian screen has lost one of its most conspicuous figures … a distinct blow to the motion picture industry in this country and the loss of one who has left the mark of her genius on Australia's screen progress'.

Other Australian films include: The Tide of Death (1912, a.), •Australia Calls (1913, a.), Pommy Arrives in Australia (1913, a.), •The Silence of Dean Maitland (1913, a.), A Maori Maid's Love (1916, a.), •The Mutiny of the Bounty (1916, w.), •The Church and the Woman (1917, a.), •Ginger Mick (1920, a. w.), •Rudd's New Selection (1921, a.), •Australia Calls (1923, w.), The Bushwhackers (1925, w.), •The Pioneers (1926, w.).

MARILYN DOOLEY

M

Mad Dog Morgan

1976. *Director*: Philippe Mora. *Producer*: Jeremy Thomas. *Scriptwriter*: Phillipe Mora. Based on the book, *Morgan*, by Margaret Carnegie. *Director of photography*: Mike Molloy. *Music*: Patrick Flynn. 102 min. *Cast*: Dennis Hopper (Daniel Morgan), Jack Thompson (Detective Manwaring), David Gulpilil (Billy), Frank Thring (Superintendent Cobham), Michael Pate (Superintendent Winch).

Some of the films of the Australian revival of the 1970s (see Revival, the) have not worn well and their significance now derives chiefly from their context. It may well be that **Mad Dog Morgan**, less popular and less critically regarded at the time, holds up better. The story of Daniel Morgan, who turns himself into a bushranger as a lawless reaction to a brutal and brutalising society, has a free-wheeling quality, a wild disdain for constituted authority, and a surprising, unsentimental tenderness for the oppressed, that make it difficult to categorise. It is not just an action film, although the action scenes (filmed on locations frequented by Morgan) are well filmed, including the bloody attack on the Chinese mining camp; it is also an engrossing character study. Director–writer Philippe •Mora cunningly cast American renegade actor Dennis Hopper as Morgan and the associations of his image intersect resonantly with the outsider elements of Morgan. He finds—makes?—something courtly, sad, and vulnerable in this figure from Australia's dark past. BMcF

Mad Max

1979. *Director*: Dr George Miller. *Producer*: Byron Kennedy. *Scriptwriters*: James McCausland, George Miller. Based on a story by Dr George Miller and Byron Kennedy. *Director of photography*: David Eggby. *Music*: Brian May. 91 min. *Cast*: Mel Gibson (Max Rockatansky), Roger Ward (Fifi Macafee), Steve Bisley (Jim Goose), Tim Burns (Johnny), Hugh Keays-Byrne (The Toecutter), Vince Gil (Nightrider).

Mad Max roared on to cinema screens around the world depicting a futuristic world of violence and mayhem with shocking vigour, quickly provoking labels such as 'vicious' and 'degenerate', and calls for the film to be banned. Foreshadowing the men's movement in Australia by nearly 20 years, Max Rockatansky rejects and resigns from his brutal existence in the police force to enjoy life with his wife and baby son, developing an increased emotional sensitivity as he goes. But when his family is run down by a bunch of crazed bikers the ex-cop goes berserk and comes out of retirement to dispense his own version of serial rough justice.

Many critics decried the film for its excesses, and for its pandering to the American market and the international success that soon came its way. Some dismissed its comic-strip characters, effects, humour, and vitality, as well as the director's knowledge of film, evident in his manipulation of both the medium and the audience. Other writers have seen **Mad Max** as a study of masculinity in crisis, as an investigation of good versus evil, an exploration of anarchy versus authority, an analysis of gender and perversion, and a meditation on Australia's love/hate relationship with the motorcar.

Earlier films had explored the dark side of life 'down under' but, before 1979, with its post-industrial landscape, its extraordinary dynamism, its graphically implied violence, and its dreadful bleak ending, there was nothing quite like **Mad Max**. MARK MCAULIFFE

Mad Max 2

1981. Director: Dr George Miller. *Producer:* Byron Kennedy. *Scriptwriters:* Terry Hayes, Dr George Miller, Brian Hannant. *Director of photography:* Dean Semler. *Music:* Brian May. *94 min. Cast:* Mel Gibson (Max), Bruce Spence (The Gyro Captain), Mike Preston (Pappagallo), Vernon Wells (Wez).

Mad Max 2 opens with a superb montage sequence recapping the events of the first film wherein Max is devastated by the loss of his family and the self-destructive course of retribution he then exacts. Retitled **The Road Warrior** for American release, the film projects the hero into a desert wasteland where he encounters a small colony surrounded by a tribe of leather-clad barbarians hell-bent on raping and pillaging the white-clad 'settlers' and their fuel supplies. Assisted by an eccentric gyro-captain, splendidly realised by Bruce •Spence, Max becomes the community's reluctant saviour in their escape to northern climes to establish a new civilisation.

The first film sometimes exhibits a crudeness of style but the second is almost seamless in its cinematic technique, nowhere more evident than in the balletic choreography of fast-paced camera and action seen in the 20-minute chase sequence. Mel •Gibson's character is curiously passive, more the victim of others' decisions and actions than an agent in his own right. Besides pointing to a masochistic aesthetic, evident too in the film's depictions of homosexuality, the passivity suggests a mythic quality, placing the hero at the mercy of universal forces.

Whereas **Mad Max 2** is more sparse in its dialogue, it has the same high-octane energy and shock value as the first film, but the lighter touches of humour, and the life-affirming conclusion endorsing community support and action in the face of adversity, may have contributed to its greater international success. MARK MCAULIFFE

Mad Max Beyond Thunderdome

1985. Director: Dr George Miller. *Producer:* Dr George Miller. *Co-producers:* Doug Miller, Terry Hayes. *Associate producers:* Steve Amezdroz, Marcus D'Arcy. *Scriptwriters:* Terry Hayes, Dr George Miller. *Director of photography:* Dean Semler. *Music:* Maurice Jarre. *106 min. Cast:* Mel Gibson (Mad Max), Tina Turner (Aunty Entity), Helen Buday (Savannah Nix), Frank Thring (The Collector), Bruce Spence (Jedediah the Pilot), Angry Anderson (Ironbar).

An older, more mature Max follows his stolen camel-drawn vehicle to Bartertown where circumstances place him in partnership with Aunty Entity, founder and ruler of a post-holocaust junkyard society. When Max reneges on his deal to dispense with Master-Blaster who vies for control of Bartertown, Aunty casts him out into the gulag of the Australian desert. Here he is rescued by Savannah Nix a young girl who mistakes him for a long-awaited saviour figure prominent in

the storytelling of her tribe of children located at an oasis called The Crack in the Earth. Against his wishes Max leads them back to Bartertown and finally enables their escape from the desert to establish a new world.

Thunderdome gives the impression of being the most self-consciously constructed of the trilogy, reflecting on such themes as the nature of society and human endeavour, and film as modern-day mythmaking. It is also a beautiful depiction of the Australian landscape, evoking our tragic explorer history. Following their achievements in the second film, Graham Walker's production design and Norma Moriceau's creations in costuming are of particular interest, and highlight another theme evident in the film: the subversive world of the grotesque. There is a tendency to slowness, especially in the second section of the film, although the first and third still embody Dr George Miller's trademark dynamism and exuberant action pieces. MARK MCAULIFFE

Magazines In general, Australia has not been rich in high-profile film magazines and journals. All too often they have flowered briefly and vanished. At first, film was tersely noted in theatre journals, the most valuable of which from a film point of view was *Theatre* (1904–12; later known as *Theatre Magazine*, until 1924, and then as various other names until it ceased publishing in 1936). In pre-World War II days, the key journals were *Everyone's*, from 1920; and *Film Weekly*, from 1926 to 1973, which absorbed *Everyone's* in 1936. These were industry journals that became major resources for researchers of later generations. By the 1920s, then, the Australian film industry was established enough to sustain journals devoted exclusively to its interests.

As to fan magazines, in the 1940s and 1950s there were *Screen News* (begun in 1931, later renamed *New Screen News*); *Photoplayer* (begun in 1923 and lasting until 1960), which could be bought in the foyers of cinemas as well as in shops; and overseas publications (or Australian editions thereof) from the USA and the United Kingdom, such as *Movie Life* (1945–48), *Photoplay* (1945–63), *Picture Show*, and *Picturegoer*. Fan magazines provided information, of varying levels of authenticity, on new films and the lives of the stars. Then there were trade journals, which kept distributors and exhibitors informed about which films were likely to prove commercially successful, developments in cinema chains, and movement of film-industry personnel. These included two Sydney-based publications: *Movie Trader*, which offered news about production and casting, reports on box-office takings and theatre-building, 'critics' choices', reviews, and Oscar predictions and reports; and *Australasian Cinema*, described as 'The Forum of the Motion Picture Industry of Australia' and intended largely for exhibitors, distributors, and other such industry figures, and containing reports on such matters as deals relating to cinema ownership, production companies, and censorship practices. *Australasian Cinema* began its life as *Australasian Exhibitor* in 1938 and, in 1972, it amalgamated with *Showman* (begun in 1949) to form *Australasian Cinema*.

The Sydney-based *Australian Film Guide*, edited by John Howard Reid, appeared in the mid 1960s. It was pitched between the fan magazines of earlier decades and the journals that grew out of the burgeoning film-culture climate from the 1970s. The *Australian Film Guide* contained reviews and articles relating to popular cinema, including such camp esoterica as 'The Early Films of Maria Montez'. *Encore* (Sydney), billed as 'The Music and Entertainment Magazine' prior to its amalgamation in 1984 with *Australian Film Review*, described itself as 'an independent news magazine for the film, television and video industries', and included production reports and articles on such subjects as exhibitors' quotas for local films. After merging with *Encore*, the current publishing title *Encore Australia* became purely a film journal, combining trade and technology matters with production reports. In June 1970 *Lumière*, a magazine with a strong emphasis on serious reviewing and interviewing, was launched, marking a shift to Melbourne as a film-culture centre. It introduced such critics as Tom Ryan and Albert Moran, and film historian Graham Shirley. *Lumière* was concerned to promote the cause of indigenous cinema and was wide-ranging in its international coverage, offering articles on, and interviews with, film-makers, as well as reports on overseas festivals. In its third-last issue (December 1973), David Stratton praised it as 'a film magazine of international standards'.

As *Lumière* passed into oblivion, the Melbourne-based *Cinema Papers* began what must be one of the longest careers for a film journal in this country. It first appeared as a mimeographed A4 publication at La Trobe University in 1967, with Peter Beilby, Rod Bishop, and Philippe •Mora as editors. During 1969–70, it emanated from North Melbourne as a fortnightly broadsheet and ran for 11 issues. In its present form, it began as a quarterly, changed to a bi-monthly in 1978, and began publishing eight issues a year in 1998. The editors have been Scott Murray (for more than 100 issues, and the name most tenaciously associated with the journal), Beilby, Nick Roddick, and Philippa Hawker. The emphasis has been on Australian cinema, as both art form and industry, and in addition to reviews of new, mainly Australian films, production guides, and a watching brief on new technology, it contains a very valuable collection of interviews with Australian film-makers, many of whom are now international figures. In 1988 it amalgamated with *Filmviews*, then edited by Peter Tapp, who later became editor of *Metro*. *Filmviews* had grown out of *Federation News*, the organ of the Federation of Victorian Film Societies, and its content ranged eclectically over critical and theoretical issues, with interviews, book and film reviews, and longer articles. It was published from 1980 to 1988. *Cinema Papers* sought to maintain a balance between the critical and the informational, and its long life testifies to its liveliness and usefulness. It covered some of the same ground as the Sydney tabloid *Film News*, which derived from the Sydney Film-makers Co-operative. It contained incisive pieces on industrial issues as well as short reviews of variable quality, and it showed more interest than *Cinema Papers* in the theoretical debates surrounding film culture in the 1970s and 80s. It ceased publication in 1995.

Rivalling *Cinema Papers* in longevity, the Melbourne-based *Metro*, the Journal of the Association of Teachers of Film and Video (now 'of Media', leading to the acronym ATOM), has been published continuously since 1974. Its emphasis has increasingly been on scholarly criticism (it now referees its major articles), but it also includes interviews with film-makers, reviews of selected books on cinema, articles on technology, and extended analyses of important films. It is one of the rare sites in Australia for serious discussion of films and film-makers who are not necessarily buzzwords of the moment, and it also addresses itself to matters of government policy in regard to film and media issues. There is some overlap with *Cinema Papers*, but the avowed educational imperative of *Metro* ensures a significant area of difference. It also provides as an ongoing feature 'A Critical Guide to the National •Cinémathèque'. Since 1994, ATOM has also published *Metro Education*, which is directed specifically at teachers of media and English.

The Western Australian *Continuum*, founded in 1987 by Tom O'Regan and Brian Shoesmith, is an academic journal that, in its own words, 'approaches the media from a post-disciplinary cultural studies perspective'. Most issues have a special focus: for example, 'Media Education' (vol. 9, no. 2) and 'Australian Screen Comedy' (vol. 10, no 2). The academic aims of the journal are clearly reflected in the theoretical concepts its articles characteristically embrace, and in its long and imposing editorial board list. It is the nearest successor to have emerged to the short-lived but intellectually impressive *Australian Journal of Screen Theory*, which emanated sporadically between 1976 and 1984. It grew out of the burgeoning critical and theoretical debates of the 1970s, and made a significant contribution to them.

Among the many other short- and long-lived journals, the following should be noted: *Cantrill's Filmnotes* (Melbourne), a regular and handsomely produced publication edited since 1971 by documentary and experimental film-makers Arthur and Corinne •Cantrill, and reflecting their interests; the light-hearted, intelligent *Freeze Frame* (1987, Melbourne), which deserved a longer life; the Catholic-based *Annals* (Melbourne); numerous film-society and other specialist publications, including *Film Journal*, the organ of the Melbourne University Film Group, which appeared from 1956 to 1965, and *The McGuffin* (Melbourne), devoted to the films of Alfred Hitchcock; the *AFI Newsletter*, with its round-up of local film-making news and funding decisions; the electronic journal *Screening the Past*, which is based at La Trobe University, Melbourne and focuses on visual media and history; and *Media Information Australia*, a valuable record published by the •Australian Film, Television and Radio School, Sydney. What is missing is a broad-circulation, popular journal such as the British magazine *Empire*: the main journals are dominated by industrial reports and/or academic discourses, rather than being addressed to the wider cinema-going public.   BRIAN MCFARLANE

Maguire, Gerard (1945–) ACTOR

Gerard Maguire is probably best known for his work in such television series as *Luke's Kingdom* and the miniseries *The Lancaster–Miller Affair*. Nevertheless, the 1967 National Institute of Dramatic Art graduate has appeared in a number of films over 20 years, beginning with **Demonstrator** in 1971, as the student activist son of the Australian defence minister. He followed this with •**Country Town** (1971), the film version of television's *Bellbird*, with small roles in •**Mad Dog Morgan** (1976), •**Ground Zero** (1987), and •**Mull** (1989), and with a leading role as the heroine's criminal inspiration in **Kitty and the Bagman** (1983). In 1993 he co-wrote and co-produced George •Miller's enjoyably sleazy **Gross Misconduct**, in which he also played the vice-chancellor of the university at which the eponymous behaviour takes place. He has also written **Seduce Me: Pamela Principle 2** (1994), a piece of USA-based erotica, and he had a hand in the writing of the action thriller **Tunnel Vision** (1995).

Other Australian films include: •The Surfer (1988).   BMcF

Maiden's Distress, A
[The Five of Hearts, or Buffalo Bill's Love Story]

1911. From the tent show? B & W. *Cast*: E.I. Cole's Bohemian Dramatic Company.

A film featuring Edward Irham's Cole's Bohemian Dramatic Company has been preserved in the •National Film and Sound Archive bearing the title **A Maiden's Distress**. Credits on the film claim that it was produced in 1902. However, in 1902 it is likely that everything would have been shown in a single shot with the camera placed at some distance from the action. This film contains several shots, and all of them are quite close (they are medium and medium-long shots). The principal action is a standard tent-show 'turn' in which a woman is outlined by axes and knives thrown around her body, in this case with the participants dressed as Indians and cowboys. It seems likely that **A Maiden's Distress** may be part of a somewhat longer film produced by Pathé Frères in 1911, and reviewed at that time under the title of **The Five of Hearts or Buffalo Bill's Love Story**. Perhaps the most interesting thing about this film today, besides seeing the 'turn' itself, is that it is part of an early western made in Australia.

WILLIAM D. ROUTT

Malcolm

1986. *Director/Producer*: Nadia Tass. *Producer/Scriptwriter/Director of photography*: David Parker. *Music*: Simon Jeffes. 90 min. *Cast*: Colin Friels (Malcolm), John Hargreaves (Frank), Lindy Davies (Judith), Chris Haywood (Willy).

Malcolm is an *idiot savant*, incapable of 'normal' social interaction such as interviewing a prospective boarder or holding down a job in the tramways workshop, but a whiz with electronic and mechanical gadgets. When he rents his spare room to Frank, just out of gaol, Malcolm learns about a life more exciting than he had ever dreamt, and sets about convincing his new boarder that he would be an ideal partner in crime. Malcolm's gadgets are the real stars of the film: a remote-controlled toy car that can navigate the back streets of Fitzroy, a gun concealed inside a rubbish bin in a smart office building, and, most impressively of all, a getaway car that splits down the middle to allow the occupants to escape down separate passageways too narrow for pursuit. This is a caper movie, with audience sympathies firmly on the side of the criminals, who are all flawed and fallible but much too charming for their own good or ours. The three central performances are outstanding, with Lindy Davies particularly good as Frank's feisty girlfriend, who tries to explain the facts of life to Malcolm. Despite the fantastic premise of the story, this wacky comedy manages to present living-on-your-wits-in-inner-suburban Melbourne in a surprisingly realistic fashion. It won eight Australian Film Institute awards, including Best Picture, Best Direction, and Best Actor (Colin •Friels).   IB

Malcolm, George (1904–77) CINEMATOGRAPHER/EDITOR

George Malcolm began as an editor, with •**On Our Selection** (1932) and •**The Squatter's Daughter** (1933, with William Shepherd), then was credited for the special effects on •**The Silence of Dean Maitland** (1934). But he had a lifelong fascination with cinematography and also was an inventor, developing cameras in the 1920s and a colour photography system in the 1940s. He was director of photography on **The Squatter's Daughter** (1933, with Frank •Hurley), •**The Man They Could Not Hang** (1934, with George •Heath), and •**Splendid Fellows** (1934). In 1935 he began working for Mervyn Murphy's Supreme Sound on sponsored documentaries such as **Conquest** (1935, for Rural Bank), and **Eaglets** (1935, short for the •Commonwealth Film Laboratories). He went back to special effects on •**Uncivilised** (1936), then returned to cinematography as director of photography on •**Mystery Island** (1937) and •**Typhoon Treasure** (1938, with his brother Harry Malcolm). In the early 1950s he bought the film rights to the last, cut it to about 40 minutes and re-released it as **The Perils of Pakema Reef**, in newsreel theatrettes. His last features were •**Seven Little Australians** (1939—director of photography, ed.), •The Power and the Glory (1941, aerial photography, Arthur •Higgins as director of photography), and A Yank in Australia (1942—director of photography), but he continued to shoot documentaries and short films.

IB

Man from Hong Kong, The

1975. *Director:* Brian Trenchard-Smith. *Producers:* Raymond Chow, John Fraser, David Hannay, André Morgan. *Scriptwriter:* Brian Trenchard-Smith. *Director of photography:* Russell Boyd. *Music:* Noel Quinlan. 103 min. *Cast:* Jimmy Wang Yu (Inspector Fang Sing-Ling), George Lazenby (Jack Wilton), Ros Spiers (Caroline Thorne), Hugh Keays-Byrne (Morrie Grosse), Roger Ward (Bob Taylor), Rebecca Gilling (Angelica), Frank Thring (Willard).

After a spectacular opening sequence involving a car chase around, and a fight on, Uluru, this becomes a fairly standard martial-arts thriller, in which Australian locations and female actors function simply as exotic backdrops for (or distractions from) the numerous fight scenes demanded by the genre. Hong Kong Police Inspector and kung fu master Fang is summoned to Australia to interview a drug courier. When his charge is assassinated, Fang resolves to crack the drug syndicate run under the cover of a martial-arts school by Jack Wilton, played by ex-James Bond George •Lazenby (billed as 'Australia's karate champion'). Local cops Grosse and Taylor are initially flabbergasted but ultimately won over by Fang's unorthodox policing methods (beating confessions from suspects, killing large numbers of kung fu students). Execrable dialogue, casual racism, and the chauvinism of male characters (and director) are redeemed slightly by the impressive stuntwork of Grant •Page and Peter Armstrong, and by Russell •Boyd's stunning camerawork.

BEN GOLDSMITH

Man From Kangaroo, The

1920. *Director:* Wilfred Lucas. *Producers:* E.J. Carroll, Reginald L. 'Snowy' Baker. *Scriptwriter:* Bess Meredyth. *Director of photography:* Robert V. Doerrerz. 6 reels. B&W. *Cast:* Reginald L. 'Snowy' Baker (John Harland), Brownie Vernon (Muriel Hammond), Charles Villiers (Martin Giles), Walter Vincent (Ezra Peters), Wilfred Lucas (Red Jack Braggan).

Reginald L. (Snowy) •Baker was a sporting idol for his generation: a champion swimmer and rugby player who was also an outstanding boxer, sprinter, rower, and cricketer.

The Man from Kangaroo

His first two films, •The Enemy Within (1918) and The Lure of the Bush (1918), were popular successes, encouraging him to set up Carroll-Baker Australian Productions, in partnership with E.J. and Dan •Carroll. Baker then visited Hollywood and returned with an American production team—director and actor Wilfred Lucas, writer Bess Meredyth, photographer Robert Doerrerz, and actor Brownie Vernon. **The Man from Kangaroo** was the first of three features made by this team, all built around the sporting exploits of Baker as hero. In this case, he is a parson, appointed to a country town and forced to defend his church and his sweetheart against local thugs. The film, now held in the •National Film and Sound Archive, remains enjoyable—an unashamed melodrama, with spectacular scenery and action, the stunt work performed by Baker himself.   IB

Man from Snowy River, The

1982. *Director*: George Miller. *Producer*: Geoff Burrowes. *Scriptwriter*: John Dixon. From a script by Fred Cul Cullen. Based on the poem by A.B. 'Banjo' Paterson. *Director of photography*: Keith Wagstaff. *Music*: Bruce Rowland. 106 min. *Cast*: Kirk Douglas (Spur; Harrison), Jack Thompson (Clancy), Tom Burlinson (Jim Craig), Sigrid Thornton (Jessica), Lorraine Bayly (Rosemary). Alternative title: **Return to Snowy River** (USA).

George •Miller's **The Man from Snowy River**, based on Australia's much-loved poem, is an antipodean western. Jim Craig, orphaned by the death of his father, is forced to leave his 'high country' home until, as the local men tell him, he has 'earnt' the right to live there. Accepting this curiously unsubstantiated fiat, he goes to work for the American rancher, Harrison, falls for Harrison's daughter, and ends by rescuing a valuable colt, thus establishing his manhood in the eyes of the world and promising he will be back to claim his due. He recalls those heroes who went west to stake their claim in the country and tamed not only a wild landscape but a spirited woman as well.

The film reworked genre staples in ways that found popular acceptance here and abroad. Australian films had often seemed to sit uneasily between the multiplex and the arthouse, but this one went all out for commercial success and found it. A.B. 'Banjo' Paterson's poem gives the film its title and climactic action, and the photography that renders this is the film's greatest advantage. The human drama— whether Jim's rites of passage or the mysterious love triangle involving Harrison, his loquacious and sententious one-

Sigrid Thornton and Tom Burlinson in **The Man from Snowy River**

legged brother Spur, and the woman they both loved—is no match for the horses and the landscape. A melodramatic plot might have provided an enjoyable lead-up to the events in which Jim earns the right to the film's title, but the film spoils this by imposing portentous values that sit uneasily with the action rather than grow out of it. Kirk Douglas's name no doubt contributed to the film's success in the USA, but its handsome physical sheen and clear genre affiliations may have been even more responsible. BMcF

Man of Flowers

1983. *Director*: Paul Cox. *Producers*: Jane Ballantyne, Paul Cox. *Scriptwriter*: Paul Cox. *Dialogue*: Bob Ellis. *Director of photography*: Yuri Sokol. 91 min. *Cast*: Norman Kaye (Charles Bremer), Alyson Best (Lisa), Chris Haywood (David), Sarah Walker (Jane), Julia Blake (Art teacher).

One of director/writer Paul *Cox's most idiosyncratic films, **Man of Flowers** belongs to his richest period as the art-house film-maker *par excellence* of the new Australian cinema (see Revival, the). Its central character, Charles Bremer, is a wealthy recluse who pays a life-class model to undress to the accompaniment of an operatic aria, while he watches. When she is naked he goes out, crosses a busy street to a church, and begins playing the organ. And this is only how the film begins. The model, Lisa, has a crudely chauvinistic boyfriend, David, whose art is accomplished by the violent squeezing of paint over canvas, then jumping on it, and who becomes embroiled in Bremer's world.

The film is interested in Bremer's psychology: there is a nod to Michael Powell's **Peeping Tom** (1959), in the flash-backs involving a severely repressive father and over-protective mother. It is interested, too, in the relations between art and life; this element reaching a bizarre climax in which the brutal David becomes Bremer's final attempt to make art out of life—or death. Cox is surrounded by many of his favoured collaborators, including cinematographer Yuri *Sokol. He also draws notably fine performances from Norman·*Kaye as the fixated Bremer and Chris *Haywood aptly contrasted as David. It is easy to dismiss Cox in this mode as merely 'arty' and pretentious, but not many Australian films share his fascination with ideas and his cinematic fluency in rendering them. BMcF

Man They Could Not Hang, The, *see* The Life Story of John Lee (1912)

Manganinnie

1980. *Director*: John Honey. *Producer*: Gilda Baracchi. *Scriptwriter*: Ken Kelso. Based on the novel by Beth Roberts. *Director of photography*: Gary Hansen. *Music*: Peter Sculthorpe. 90 min. *Cast*: Mawuyal

Yanthalawuy (Manganinnie), Anna Ralph (Joanna), Phillip Hinton (Edward Waterman), Elaine Mangan (Margaret Waterman).

Produced by the Tasmanian Film Corporation and the *Greater Union Organisation, **Manganinnie** is one of the few films of the new Australian cinema (see Revival, the) in which an Aborigine has the central role. It is set in the context of the notorious 'black drive' of the 1830s in which the British colonial forces sought to eradicate the island's native population. The eponymous heroine, separated from her tribe, during this time meets up with Joanna, the lost daughter of a White settler, and the film records their journey together, in which the Black woman comforts the child and introduces her to the magic of the 'fire stick'. Presumably made as a children's film, **Manganinnie** is memorable for the relationship that develops between Black woman and White child, and there is pathos in Joanna's growth of confidence as Manganinnie is aware that her tribe has been wiped out. As a result, she becomes increasingly melancholy. The subject matter might have elicited a more passionate response from its makers, but the film has its own gentle virtues. BMcF

Mangiamele, Giorgio (1926–) PRODUCER/DIRECTOR/ CINEMATOGRAPHER Giorgio Mangiamele studied fine arts, film production, and journalism in Italy, before emigrating to Australia in 1952. He became a photographer in Carlton, and over the next decade made three self-financed 16mm films: the silent feature **The Contract** (1953), and two shorter films: **The Brothers** (1958) and **The Spag** (1962). All were concerned with the problems of migrants in the years immediately following World War II, as was his first 35mm film, the short feature **Ninety Nine Per Cent** (1963), about a migrant's search for a wife. His most ambitious venture was *Clay (1965), the first Australian film invited to screen at the Cannes Film Festival. He saw himself as an auteur, keeping complete control of his projects by performing all the technical roles himself, but the critics praised only the photography, and none of the films achieved wide distribution. In 1970, with **Beyond Reason**, he attempted to make a more commercial product—professionally written, shot on colour stock, and including more sex and violence than any of his earlier films. Although distributed by Columbia, this also failed. He spent three years in Papua New Guinea, making documentaries for the Papua New Guinea Office of Information, then returned to Australia in 1972, but was unable to obtain financial support for further films. IB

Mango Tree, The

1977. *Director*: Kevin Dobson. *Producer*: Michael Pate. *Scriptwriter*: Michael Pate. From the novel by Ronald McKie. *Director of photography*: Brian Probyn. *Music*: Marc Wilkinson. 104 min. *Cast*:

Christopher Pate (Jamie Carr), Geraldine Fitzgerald (Grandma Carr), Robert Helpmann (the Professor), Gerard Kennedy (Preacher Jones), Gloria Dawn (Pearl).

One of a number of Australian coming-of-age productions in the late 1970s, **The Mango Tree** benefits from the sumptuous look of Bundaberg during World War I (the work of Brian •Probyn's colour photography) but suffers from a too loosely episodic plot-line. Based on Ronald McKie's novel, it centres on the growing up of Jamie Carr, an orphan who has been raised by his indomitable grandmother. His responses to personal crises—his sexual initiation at the hands of his French teacher; his grandmother's death—and to the historical events of the period, encapsulated in a recruiting rally and the arrival of air ace Bert Hinkler, provide the rationale for the script. As Grandma Carr, visiting Irish-American actor Geraldine Fitzgerald gives a commanding performance in a film that has charm but is short on coherence. There are touching and amusing moments, but neither the script nor Christopher •Pate's central performance is assured enough to create a protagonist who would give point to the episodes. BMcF

Mann, Tracey (1957–) ACTOR Tracey Mann's early years as a performer were in her hometown of Adelaide. Then, while still a teenager, she played Tina in the television series and the film •**The Box** (1975). She has repeatedly returned to the stage, but has also done a great deal of television, including *Prisoner* (1978), *Cowra Breakout* (1984), *The Four Minute Mile* (1988), with particularly impressive performances in *Cyclone Tracy* (1986), *Janus* (1994), and *Sword of Honour* (1986), for which she won the Logie for Most Popular Actress in a miniseries. In film, she has demonstrated her versatility. Her slim build and cropped hair made her ideal for urchin roles such as Sam in **Hard Knocks** (1980), for which she won the Australian Film Institute Best Actress award and the Sammy for Best New Talent. It also suited Karli, the teenager desperate to make sense of her life in **Going Down** (1983). On the other hand, she has played a middle-class teacher in •**Fast Talking** (1984), and Miss Twisty in **Reckless Kelly** (1993). IB

Marinos, Lex (1950–) DIRECTOR/ACTOR Born in Wagga Wagga, Lex Marinos began his career as an actor, notably in the television series *Kingswood Country*, although films—as Con, the operator of the 'Midnight Cowboy' tourist bus, in •**Goodbye Paradise** (1983)—soon followed. Since the mid 1980s, however, Marinos has reduced his acting commitments in favour of direction and rugby league commentaries. Marinos's record as a director is mixed. After he co-directed the successful *Bodyline* miniseries for Australian television, his first feature film as direc-

tor was an adaptation of Colleen McCullough's •**An Indecent Obsession**, a melodrama based on the sexual tensions in a psychiatric ward on an unnamed island off the north coast of Australia at the end of World War II. The film represents an improvement on the novel, particularly the ending where Marinos' camera emphasises the inherent pathos of Wendy •Hughes's situation as she returns to the empty ward with not even the 'indecent obsession' of duty to sustain her. Marinos employed Hughes three years later in another bitter tale of unrequited love and sexual frustration in the rural melodrama **Boundaries of the Heart** (1988). **Remember Me** (1985), with Hughes as a woman pursued by her psychotic ex-husband Richard •Moir, is less successful, as the film merely heightens the clichés of the drama without providing any sense of character development or real tension. Marinos also wrote the first draft of the juvenile melodrama **The Delinquents** (1989), although he did not receive a screen credit.

Other Australian films include: •Cathy's Child (1979, actor), Perhaps Love (1987, director), Hard Knuckle (1988, director), Pandemonium (1988, actor), •Last Days of Chez Nous (1992, actor), •BeDevil (1993, actor). GM

Marshall, Ray (1920–) ACTOR For 10 years from 1975, one of the reliable pleasures of going to Australian films was the richness of its character acting. Among the many who gave our films such a look of national distinctiveness was Ray Marshall, whose craggy features and way of effortlessly inhabiting a role brought incontrovertible authenticity to a wide range of films. He made acting look like behaviour as the weary deserted father in •**The FJ Holden**, the country town mayor in •**Newsfront**, the seen-'em-come-and-go proprietor of a kids' cafe in **Street Hero**, and a shrewd-eyed backbencher in the television miniseries *The Dismissal*. There were perhaps a dozen others that made him into a local version of William Demarest, or some other such Hollywood institution. A stroke in the mid 1980s curtailed his acting career.

Other Australian films include: ABBA: The Movie (1977), Little Boy Lost (1978), •Money Movers (1979), The Journalist (1979), •The Night The Prowler (1979), •Stir (1980), On the Run (1983), Now and Forever (1983), Molly (1983), Midnite Spares (1983), BMX Bandits (1983), Where the Green Ants Dream (1984), Rebel (1985), Cactus (1986). BMcF

Martin, Tony (1955–) ACTOR Tony Martin grew up on a cattle station near Tamworth, NSW, but went on to study acting under Hayes Gordon in New York. He returned to Australia to work mainly in the theatre, with small roles in the films •**The Killing of Angel Street** (1981), •**Twelfth Night** (1987), and •**Evil Angels** (1988). Then he became an overnight star as Reverend Bob Brown in the television soap opera *E Street*, staying with the series from 1989 to 1992, and moving on to become the disciplinarian Southgate in *Heartbreak High*, and to play the lead in the moving short film **Parklands** (1994). His role as criminal Neddy Smith in the telemovie *Blue Murder* brought critical acclaim, which continued when he moved to the other side of the fence as the tortured detective Bill McCoy, seeking his lost teenage son through the Sydney underworld in the series *Wildside*. His first starring role in a feature film was as another detective, Sergeant John Steele, pitted against Hugo •Weaving's enigmatic accused in •**The Interview** (1998).   IB

Martinetti, Nino (1946–) CINEMATOGRAPHER After arriving in Australia from Italy in 1973, Nino Martinetti enrolled at Prahran College, studying art and photography. His first film was a low budget 16mm short, **Buckeye And Pinto** (1977), which earned an Australian Film Institute (AFI) Best Cinematography nomination in 1980. He worked as assistant and operator, particularly with Yuri •Sokol on films directed by Paul •Cox. He first worked as a director of photography on the ground-breaking miniseries *Women Of The Sun* (1981). His first feature as director of photography was **Wills & Burke** (1985), which won an Australian Cinematographers Society (ACS) award. His creative relationship as director of photography for Paul Cox began with **Vincent** (1986), and has continued until now, earning him much critical acclaim, another AFI nomination for **Golden Braid** (1990), ACS Gold awards for •**A Woman's Tale** (1991) and **Exile** (1994), and a Silver award for **Lust and Revenge** (1996).

Other Australian films: The Nun and the Bandit (1992), •Heartbreak Kid (1993), Hurrah (1998).   DAVID MUIR

Martyrdom of Nurse Cavell, The

1916. *Directors*: John Gavin, C. Post Mason. *Scriptwriter*: Agnes Gavin. *Director of photography*: Lacey Percival. B&W. *Cast*: Vera Pearce (Nurse Cavell), C. Post Mason (Georges Renard), John Gavin (Captain von Hoffberg).

Nurse Cavell (Edith Cavell)

1916. *Director, Producer, Scriptwriter*: W.J. Lincoln. B&W. *Cast*: Margaret Lindon (Nurse Cavell), Arthur Styan (Captain Karl), Agnes Keough (Nita), Stewart Garner (Captain Devereaux).

La Revanche

1916. *Director, Producer*: W.J. Lincoln. *Scriptwriters*: W.J. Lincoln, Fred Kehoe. B&W. *Cast*: Arthur Styan, Agnes Keough, Stewart Garner.

In the first four months of 1916 three films about Nurse Edith Cavell were released in Australia. It is a little surprising that this should have been so, since Cavell was an English-woman shot by the Germans in October 1915, and the English did not make a film about her until 1928 (**Dawn**). Apparently no footage from the Australian films survives, but they are interesting nonetheless. The first of the three is an example of a certain kind of cine-journalism. **The Martyrdom of Nurse Cavell** was in a Sydney cinema within 14 weeks of Cavell's execution. W.J. •Lincoln's version opened in Melbourne three weeks after that, probably inspired by intercity rivalry. While C. Post Mason went to the USA and United Kingdom to sell the Sydney version, steps were taken to force the withdrawal of the Melbourne film. **La Revanche**, which may have reused a great deal of material from **Nurse Cavell**, was Lincoln's compromise. It seems to have eliminated the figure of Cavell herself in order to concentrate on what happened after her death. The details of the production and distribution of these films then, are intriguing by themselves. However, there remains the question of whether this particular story about a heroic British woman martyred in a foreign land may have had a special resonance for those still trying to come to terms with what had happened to the ANZACs at Gallipoli.   WILLIAM D. ROUTT

Masculinity Sociologist Bob Connell has written of the difficulty of writing on masculinity. Working on such a topic, he suggests, is a bit like cutting your hair with a badly adjusted mechanical harvester. Writing on masculinity in Australian film is no less challenging. There is no entity, 'Australian masculinity'. One is wary of creating false unities and making generalisations that do not stand up to the evidence of films themselves. Yet masculinity definitely matters. It is so often the form in which the demand for self-respect is made, in which the assertion of human dignity is expressed—and trapped.

The very notion of the 'masculine' is, of course, relational: it is enmeshed in history, culture, and politics. Most importantly, it refers to that which is not 'feminine'; something adhering to 'the first sex'. The existential dilemmas of European art film, so frequently channelled through leading female characters or a male/female couple, are often more obliquely and less (self)consciously expressed by, and between, men in Australian films. While masculinity is neither gift nor toxin, expressive space is commonly granted, like a gift, to men. Jack •Thompson's Foley, just past his prime and uncertain of his future, is like a part of the Australian landscape in •**Sunday Too Far Away** (1975). The camera loves him as it does Mel •Gibson's Max in •**Mad Max 2** (1981). With 'the feminine' killed off, marginalised, or incorporated, Max, wounded and beautiful, vitalises the terrain.

This essay briefly explores some masculine types as created by actors whose beings and performances bring complexity and resonance to the characters, scripts, and films that they embody, voice, and inhabit. The great Australian actor John •Hargreaves provides a kind of compass for this exploration. Despite his premature death, he left us with an enormous range of work. He did not see himself as having a very strong screen persona or personal style that got in the way of presenting a character, and he was right. While there is always a strong presence, there is no greed about his performances. There is an ability to truly interact. Hargreaves believed that once an actor loses his own speech and rhythm, and adopts another language, he loses half his power. David •Williamson, he said, was a success because he could see and record who we really are, how we behave. At the same time, he suggested that by and large we do not have a camera operator who adores women; actors such as Wendy •Hughes and Judy •Davis have not really been looked at: the way women have been treated in our society is reflected in our films. In 1994, when he received his Byron •Kennedy award from fellow actor Chris •Haywood, he noted that whereas Hollywood had its screen couples—such as Rock Hudson and Doris Day, Cary Grant and Irene Dunne—we had Haywood and Hargreaves. He wasn't sure what that said about us as a culture. 'Chris is straight, anyway ... ', he quipped.

As Hargreaves said, artists such as Williamson have given us honest and accurate evocations of an Australian vernacular—from an insider's view. As outsiders to the tribe, women tend not to have language, power, or the camera's adoration. Men often appear as recessive but flawed and lovable creatures who suffer at the hands of another species: those who accuse, carp, and whinge at them, curbing their exuberance. •Don's Party (1976) is a powerful benchmark in this respect, deserving pride of place in a consideration of masculinity in Australian film. Hargreaves's Don is an emblematic figure in our culture. His wife Cath's accusations frame the film. Her way of complaining about Don makes us like him. The party's array of men is replete with occupational and marital disappointments, good lines, and crude energy. As they make (humorous) art out of their predicaments, they share a field of aggravation and an affection we can happily enter. While Cath (Jeanie •Drynan) is outside the territory, she is brought into the group to join in the laughter at the humiliated Simon (Graeme •Blundell), who cannot come close to being one of the boys. While Harold •Hopkins's ram-like and objectionable Coolie knows what he wants, Candy •Raymond's Kerry cannot acknowledge that she is a 'woman on heat', as Coolie puts it. She speaks disingenuously and is given language Williamson comes to associate with a self-serving and dishonest sexual liberation movement. Graham •Kennedy's Mack fashions humour out of his inadequacy. He brings the vulgarity and spontaneity of the variety tradition to his performance, contrasting sharply with most of the women who, while they are rightly dismissive of the men, are without their own redeeming traits.

Don's Party is a powerful film, presenting a grim picture of coupledom, outdoing more self-conscious art-cinema efforts. Jenny (Pat •Bishop), married to Mal (Ray •Barrett), Don's old mentor, cries to Don. Depressed, 'out of the human race for ten years', she recognises a corrosive resentment, even hatred in herself. Her marriage is a farce. 'Whose isn't?', Don asks her. While marriage is portrayed as a jaded battleground that sucks the life out of its contenders, the men still show signs of life, and more. Don is hopeless, but attractive and open. (Hargreaves's full expressive power lies in the way he can hold back, be central but inactive, embodying the Australian laconic.) When Jenny and Cath (before turning on each other) deliver home truths to Don and Mal, 'fifteen glasses' into their 'mutual admiration stage', and when Don and Mal resolve their talk of the sexual hypocrisy of Western society by offering each other their wives, none of this really detracts from the sweetness of their bond. With beer as the binding fluid, a physical tenderness pervades this couple's communion. What flows between the men is like courtroom evidence that can be objected to but not retracted. Love and humour are theirs, and fragments of hope lie only between the men.

There is no such hope in Colin •Eggleston's •**Long Weekend** (1978), where Hargreaves's Peter resembles Don, and his wife Marcia (Briony •Behets) outdoes Cath in carping resentfulness. In this eco-horror film with Old Testament underpinnings, a fraught malaise between the couple is embedded in the way they sin against Nature. Dialogue between the 'estranged cannibals' is harsher than in **Don's Party**, but the couple, floundering in a wasteland of dinner parties, money-making, tennis, and adultery, inhabit the same territory. To Marcia's unrelenting contempt for him, Peter replies 'Weak as you think I am, I'm all you've got'. It could be an anthem for the Australian male on film.

In his feature film début in David Williamson's **The Removalists** (1975), Hargreaves plays a neophyte cop to Peter •Cummins's taunting senior man, a sergeant who schools him in 'the law in action', the 'real law'. For the sergeant, self-control is the test of a man, and he speaks of his life with his wife in a way that invites sympathy. This comes after he has bashed mongrel-husband Carter (Martin Harris), who boasts of his sexual prowess with his wife, Marilyn (Jacki Weaver), although she is leaving him. Chris Haywood plays the removalist, pumping himself up over his ability to load a truck, defensive about his skill and his class. There is a shifting field of aggravation among the men; we cannot predict the next alliance or who the next victim will be. The critical affection Williamson will accord his men in later work is absent here; the vernacular, in the mouth of Carter, has a foul ring to it. Hargreaves's young constable Ross, a relatively recessive and innocent character, is provoked to the point where he fatally bashes Carter. The instigator of the morass of mutual destruction that ends the film is Kate (Kate •Fitzpatrick), the embodiment of Sydney's North Shore. In shades of **Streetcar Named Desire** (1951), she has a jealous, sexual hunger for her sister's working-class brute, but here it is the brute and the innocence of the young constable that is destroyed rather than the ageing belle.

Tom •Jeffrey's later male-ensemble film •**The Odd Angry Shot** (1979) deals with a group of regular Aussies who transport their humour, habits, and world-views to the war in Vietnam. Although women are not on site, they still oppress. Bill's (John •Jarratt's) girlfriend sends him a Dear John letter. (In a dream, her image and that of an Asian statue combine as the enemy.) Beer again provides the binding fluid, uniting the men, while holes in cans provoke memories of the feminine. Graham Kennedy's Harry (an older and more cynical version of Mack in **Don's Party**) provides populist commentary on the indifference and betrayal back home. And Hargreaves's Bung, in his red shorts and purple T shirt, brightens the film, energising a stagnant environment until he cries alone after the death of his mother and girlfriend, his own death providing the climax to the Vietnam events.

Another relatively undistinguished film •**Emerald City** (1989) is given a kind of earthy distinction by Hargreaves. A built-in idealism infuses his portrayal of Melbourne scriptwriter Colin Rogers, who moves with his family to Sydney to negotiate the world of money, compromise, hustlers (Haywood plays a fine 'harlot' producer) and sexual temptation (Nicole •Kidman's Helen). Ragged-looking, with a big warm style full of angst and energy, yearning and verbiage, Hargreaves is like John •Meillon, but with beauty. (Hargreaves spoke of his admiration for Meillon as a gifted actor who kept his Australianism; early in his career Hargreaves had imitated him.) Whereas Colin Rogers is given interior monologues laced with Williamson's puritanism about sexual freedom, somehow Hargreaves's openness goes against this. This openness also shaped his laconic idealist Jim Cairns in Kennedy–Miller's male-ensemble miniseries *The Dismissal* (1983). In this miniseries, Bill •Hunter, in one of his best performances, plays Rex Connor, a Labor-party saint who has sinned. And Hargreaves, too tall, too slim, and too young to portray Cairns, approximates the man in a way that is uncanny. He captures perfectly Cairns's reassessment of the relationship between politics and sexuality in a system that runs on money, lies, and power. In an act of political madness, he attempts to talk to the tabloid press honestly, about love.

In Meg Stewart's short film **Breakfast in Paradise** (1981), Hargreaves's scriptwriter character Steven Smith is a long way from such idealism. He is temporarily tied to Penne •Hackforth-Jones's Angela (coupledom drowning in ennui) and this time it is the male who harps at his consort, blaming her for the traffic jam that might make him miss his plane to Surfer's Paradise. Rangy, charming, and attractive, Hargreaves nevertheless makes us dislike him, with his sneer beneath the smile and his off-hand callousness toward Angela. Despite this, and beneath her veneer of 'suitably independent contemporary woman', Angela wants to marry him. In this film, the director, Hackforth-Jones, and Hargreaves combine forces to make us sympathise with Angela's vulnerability: we want to protect her somehow as she walks alone along the beach before finally being discarded by Steven.

In a similar way, we feel for Kris •McQuade's Jack, in Sonia Hofman's •**Australian Film, Television and Radio School** film **Morris Loves Jack** (1978). She hates her job as a cop but loves Hargreaves's Morris, whom she supports. Morris is something of a forerunner to •**Careful He Might Hear You**'s (1983) Logan: charming and hopeless. There is, of course, something fascinating about the idea of Hargreaves playing a failed actor—doing Brando/Kowalski imitations before the mirror, then mucking up an audition—when he so perfectly depicts the working-class bohemian dreaming up ways to make money, sitting nude on his Kings Cross rooftop listening to the races. Morris and Jack nicely complement each other, but the title of this little vignette has not misled us—there is a Tennessee Williams twist to their story. Almost by chance, Jack accompanies a fellow detective (played by Bill Hunter) on a raid and Morris is one of the revellers, caught kissing a man. Like **Breakfast in Paradise** in its final scenes, this short film gives an understated but powerful condolence to its female character as she walks home from the raid, alone in the street with men taunting her.

In **Careful He Might Hear You**, the seductive proletarian energy Hargreaves gives Logan suffuses and structures the whole gothic melodrama. Except for a furtive glimpse of him watching his son at his wife's grave, we do not see him until 46 minutes into the film. He is conjured up in a letter, devised in the natural sumptuousness of a Sydney locale where the repressed and icy Vanessa (Hughes), signifying all that is bourgeois and European, reigns. Logan's broad accent, his raggedly attractive being, as he stands beside the mansion's caged birds, are not assimilable to Vanessa's world. Not being able to have Logan, she perversely engulfs his son P.S. (Nicholas •Gledhill), whom he has left with solid, other-side-of-the-harbour Aunt Lila (Robyn •Nevin) and her husband George (played by Peter •Whitford, whose portrayal of the dependable worker-provider contrasts perfectly with Logan who laughs at the world 'because it's so bloody crazy'). Some of the strongest moments in this high melodrama occur naturalistically: when Logan embraces the child and when he asks him about his life and cries over the gulf between them. Although he leaves him again, the charismatic absent father gives the little boy the masculine identity he wants for himself. P.S. will no longer keep his dead mother's name for him; nor will he be William: he becomes 'Bill'.

In James •Ricketson's •**Blackfellas** (1993), David Ngoom-bujarra's 'Pretty Boy Floyd' is like a version of Logan: the charming rogue, not containable within the confines of the social. He is wild and weak. A champion at football, he 'plays deadly' but has no work ethic and will brook no assault from players or discipline from above. He is a force who draws those who love him into a turmoil of disappointment, exasperation, and anger. In a world where Floyd finally becomes 'free as a fuckin' bird' by being killed by police as he saves the lives of his friends, Hargreaves plays the White cop who strides into the poolroom with 'What's goin' on here …? Fuckin' corroboree?', tying the vernacular to full-hearted bigotry and following through with violence.

Ten years earlier, in Carl •Schultz's densely atmospheric •**Goodbye Paradise** (1983), Ray Barrett played a retired deputy police commissioner who attempts to expose corruption. Like so many Australian heroes, he fails. But in the florid localisation of the detective genre, with its weary, overripe dialogue, Barrett provided a point of decadent radiance. In Richard •Franklin's film of Hannie Rayson's play •*Hotel Sorrento* (1995), he provides an example of plain-style Australian manhood, as Wal, the father of three daughters. In this film, Hargreaves plays Dick, editor of *The Australian Voice*, a man concerned with the 'big picture' on contemporary Australia. Without losing affection for its men, **Hotel Sorrento** takes on gender issues unexcavated in Williamson, combining them with questions of local and national identity. Wal's daughters' relationships with each other and their parental home charge the drama. Yet it is hard on the audience when Barrett's patriarch drowns at sea. Like his grandson Troy (Ben Thomas), we feel comfortable with the ageing Barrett, more stooped and craggy than before, with his seaside shorts and skinny legs, the sour edge of his Mal in **Don's Party** worn away. The women's 'poor ol' mum' 'always got the rough end of the pineapple', but Dad was the one everyone loved. Their dad and his mates sat on the verandah listening to cricket, drinking, and laughing and, while their Mum ran around after them, she did not suffer in silence. She harped and whinged and nagged until in the end it killed her. Yet change has occurred. In this film we are a long way from humourless bitches in corners. When nationalistic Dick challenges expatriate writer Meg (Caroline •Goodall), it is part of a passionate round-table discussion in which the 'domestic' Hilary's (Caroline •Gillmer) calm directness can silence the company.

The year before **Sorrento**'s release, several Australian films made a great splash. •**The Adventures of Priscilla, Queen of the Desert** (1994), one of the most gynophobic male-ensemble films made in Australia, combines the Asian and the feminine in a wicked Filipina wife who oppresses Bill Hunter's salt-of-the-earth Bob. •**The Sum of Us** (1994), by contrast, is both a culmination and transformation of the vulgar, energetic 'mateyness' of earlier films, with Jack Thompson playing loving dad Harry, to Russell •Crowe's Jeff, his plain-style, rugby-playing gay son. Writer David •Stevens saw **The Sum of Us** as a kind of thank you to Australia, a 'love song' for the tolerance and 'aggressive acceptance' he found here as a gay immigrant. This love is firmly embedded in the non-toxic masculinity of the central pair.

A feature of many Australian heroes is that they do not triumph but salvage some essential part of themselves, doing so with laconic *élan*. Hargreaves, master of the laconic, jettisons it in his portrayal of Uncle Jack in •**Country Life** (1994), Michael •Blakemore's neglected free translation of *Uncle Vanya* to between-the-wars Australia. When Uncle Jack brings flowers to his brother Alex's beautiful wife Deborah (Greta •Scacchi), and finds her with the handsome Dr Askey (Sam •Neill), his disappointment floods the film. His longing is overwrought, bursting with frustration, anger, and plain bafflement at the unfairness of the world. Threatened with loss of the family property and home, Jack abuses his brother with manic intensity. Instead of working like a peasant, he too might have travelled, written books and made love to beautiful women. He retracts his words, but the passion remains as he aims his rifle at his brother from the verandah and as he despairs in the treehouse, tempted by a flask of morphia. At the end of the film, Jack sits with his niece Sally (Kerry •Fox), also disappointed in love. She comforts him in the ruins of their English garden, suggesting, radically, that they cultivate native flowers. The film cuts from the bedraggled bachelor and spinster to the rich-red bottle brush, Hargreaves's gaunt and weathered Uncle Jack looking something like Henry Lawson. Arguably, as far as masculinity is concerned, the great actor is by now no less iconically Australian.

LORRAINE MORTIMER

Mason, Richard (1926–97) PRODUCER/DIRECTOR After unsuccessfully trying his hand at acting in the Australian theatre after World War II, Richard Mason worked in the Films Division of the Australian Department of Information, a job that segued into a long career with the •Commonwealth Film Unit, later •Film Australia, where he became a prolific director/producer. Mason moved to the BBC in the mid 1960s when he made **Portrait of a Miner** (1966) before returning to the Commonwealth Film Unit. Mason's best-known film during his tenure at the Unit was **From the Tropics to the Snow** (1964), a parody of tourist travelogues, and this was indicative of his approach to documentary film-making at the Commonwealth Film Unit, where he rebelled against the dominant 'realist' approach. Mason was a lay preacher with the Presbyterian Church and a member of the Australian Labor Party, and a socially committed edge was imbued in many of his film projects. Mason's first feature film, which he directed for Film Australia, was the rural drama **Moving On** (1974). This was followed by his production of **Let the Balloon Go** (1976), a children's film for Film Australia that was sold to the American market. The bleak romance •**Winter of our Dreams** (1981) was followed by the pseudo-**Casablanca** drama •**Far East** (1982), and the absurdist nuclear comedy-drama **One Night Stand** (1984).

Other Australian films include: Room to Move (1985), Redheads (1992). GM

Mason, Steve (1954–) CINEMATOGRAPHER In 1970 Steve Mason began as an assistant in Sydney at APA and then Motion Picture Associates, later freelancing as assistant and operator for photographers such as John •Seale. He shot several documentaries, including **Kids of the Cross** (1983), which he also directed, winning the Australian Film Institute (AFI) Best Documentary award, and a docudrama, **Breaking Through** (1990), which won an Australian Cinematographers Society (ACS) Golden Tripod award. His first feature as director of photography was •**The Tale of Ruby Rose** (1988), but critical acclaim came with his adventurous work on •**Strictly Ballroom** (1992), which won an ACS Highly Commended award, and •**Broken Highway** (1994), both films being nominated for AFI Best Cinematography awards. He also won an ACS Highly Commended award for **Redheads** (1992). He has worked on the following American films: **To Wong Foo, Thanks for Everything! Julie Newmar** (USA, 1995), **That Old Feeling** (USA, 1997), **Buddy** (USA, 1997), and **Basketball** (USA, 1998).

Other Australian films: Luigi's Ladies (1989), •Waiting (1991), •The Custodian (1994). DAVID MUIR

Maternal images As a set of cultural texts, Australian cinema reflects conventions and stereotypes as well as shifts and possibilities in the representation of maternity and its relation to the construction of contemporary female subjectivity. This can be traced in a diversity of film texts throughout Australian film history, in narratives that may or may not foreground the figure of the mother but that nevertheless implicitly inscribe her within particular ideological contexts. For example, in a wide range of films that reproduces, or reflects, conventional gender images—films as diverse as •Jedda (1955, d. Charles •Chauvel), •The Getting of Wisdom (1977, d. Bruce •Beresford), •Newsfront (1978, d. Phil •Noyce), •My Brilliant Career (1979, d. Gillian •Armstrong), •Evil Angels (1988, d. Fred •Schepisi), and Little Women (1995, d. Gillian Armstrong)—mothers are subsumed in their roles of mirrors to their husbands and facilitators to their children, yet they are also perversely powerful. While the subjectivity of the mother is overwhelmed by the centrality of her children and their process of incorporation into the culturally dominant sphere of the 'Law of the Fathers', she can still influence this transition that her children make. A 'bad' mother might thus in some way disrupt this process of an appropriate relinquishing of the child into the dominant phallocentric economy. Recent Australian films such as •Fran (1985, d. Glenda Hambly), •Monkey Grip (1982, d. Ken •Cameron), •Muriel's Wedding (1994, d. P.J. •Hogan), •The Piano (1993, d. Jane •Campion), and •Lillian's Story (1996, d. Jerzy Domaradzki) offer confronting and often explicit images of the ways in which the experience and idea of maternity are perceived and produced within a phallocentric culture, detailing the difficulties involved in rethinking, let alone re-living, the dominant paradigms of both maternity and female subjectivity. Viewed as cultural texts, cinematic examples provide a mode for describing social ideas about maternity and offer possibilities for intervention, for reinscribing a status quo in which the cultural obliteration of the women who mother has been a necessary precursor for the development of individual identity.

Charles Chauvel's **Jedda** has been read as a treatise on race relations, and has been critiqued for its conventional and racist associations between ethnicity and genetically determined access to 'civilisation'. A gendered analysis of the film also not only suggests the dangers and problematic of a female sexuality that is unrestrained by association with a powerful White male but also casts a large portion of the 'blame' for the tragic events that befall Jedda (Ngarla •Kunoth) on the figure of the mother, in this case the White mistress of the station, Sarah McMann (Betty Suttor). The inherited 'sins' that beset the figure of the young Jedda in this narrative of cultural determinism are threefold: while Jedda labours under the twin negatives of her femaleness and her Aboriginality within a society structured around the dominant values of masculinity and Whiteness, she is also cursed by the irregularity of a maternal desire that the film suggests ultimately prevents her from finding a suitable role within her doubly apartheid society.

Having lost her biological baby daughter, Sarah is distraught. However, her very understandable grief, for which her husband Douglas (George Simpson-Wallis) offers her restrained comfort, is rendered suspect in the narrative by means of an 'excessiveness' that is signalled by Sarah's refusal to contemplate any further children (and presumably further sexual relations with Douglas), claiming her inability to 'die twice over' by risking another baby. The wailing of a bereft mother can be tolerated, but only in moderation, and the woman who chooses a greater measure of control over her emotional and reproductive life—and so exercises a form of independence and resistance against her husband—will, the narrative suggests, eventually pay for such inherently disruptive behaviour. Her passionate interest in her Aboriginal surrogate daughter, Jedda, is thus seen to arise from what is already coded as an irrational and potentially dangerous action on Sarah's part. The fact that all her efforts to 'civilise' the girl, to make her just like her 'own daughter', fail to protect Jedda from a fatal re-absorption into an Aboriginality that is unrestrainable by White society seems to confirm that Sarah's enterprise was, as her husband pointed out, doomed to failure.

Such concern about the illegitimate exercise of maternal power can also be seen at work in **Evil Angels**. Couched in the language of the exposé, Schepisi's film, like John Bryson's book, exonerates Lindy Chamberlain (Meryl Streep), while tracing the depth of hostility towards her, which the death and the trial engendered. A woman who is merely suspected of killing her child brings upon herself the wrath of phallocentric society and its child-centred model of subjectivity. Required to define herself so completely in relation to her child, even the *possibility* of such an aggressive act engenders a horror within the popular imagination that labels her immediately as guilty of an almost malevolent witchcraft. Supported by the sympathetic casting of Meryl Streep, **Evil Angels** asks its audience to stand back from emotive supposition and consider Lindy's subjectivity: her efforts, and her successes and failures in the suburban ordinariness of her life, and indeed the primacy of her love for her children and husband. Ironically, the Lindy we see in Schepisi's film *was* the good wife and mother of phallocentrism, albeit one with a sharp tongue and the confidence to fight back. The harsh treatment she receives at the hands of the media and popular opinion exposes the precarious position in which even the 'good mother' is held within contemporary culture—seemingly revered, yet always the first to be blamed.

In recent film narratives focusing on the emergent subjectivities of daughters, such as **Lillian's Story** and **Muriel's Wedding**, the conventional role of the mother is stultifying for the woman who mothers and ineffectual for her daughter. Lillian's mother (Anne-Louise •Lambert) may have forged a social position for herself as elegant wife, hostess, and producer of offspring, but she is powerless to curb the physical and emotional violences perpetrated by her husband Albion (Barry •Otto). Her only refuge from the horror unfurling within her family is a costly emotional disengagement. As her mother sits gazing across and beyond the park-like enclosure of her home, the needful Lillian (Toni •Collette) has to struggle to occupy a position within her kindly but distracted view. Finally Lillian's mother becomes simply absent, unable to prevent her husband's attack upon her daughter or offer any kind of positive model for Lillian to follow as the bewildered girl suffers the tyrannising authority of her father and articulates his violence through her own alienation of mind and body.

In **Muriel's Wedding,** young Muriel Heslop (Toni Collette), who struggles to gain enough self-esteem to function at all, is at least determined not to function like her mother

Betty (Jeanie •Drynan), whom she sees as a passive doormat to her obnoxious father Bill (Bill •Hunter). The character of Mrs Heslop is poignantly sketched. Bored and irrelevant to her loutish children and her blatantly unfaithful husband, her attempts at resistance are small and ineffectual: the blank cheques she passes to Muriel and the theft of sandals in the supermarket. Unrecognised by anyone, she finally makes her figurative invisibility literal by taking her own life. Ironically, it is her mother's death that snaps Muriel out of her dreams of solving all her life's problems through the possibility of a fairytale marriage. In the sombreness of the funeral and its aftermath Muriel recognises how she had contributed to her mother's sense of purposelessness, and how her own desperate efforts to get married have positioned her to replay the central error of her mother's life: the destructive and dislocating notion that a woman's identity comes entirely through her relation to husband and children.

In keeping with changing attitudes towards the role of mothering and its implications for women's subjectivity, a number of films have made mothers their protagonists, although this usually involves demonstrating the great difficulties involved in balancing the roles of mother and woman. For example, **Fran** traces the life of a young mother whose love for her children is repeatedly compromised by her need to gain self-esteem through the sexual attentions of men. Fran (Noni •Hazlehurst) is feisty and beautiful, as her friend Marge (Annie •Byron) tells her, but she does not consider herself able to function adequately without the support of a man. She is also emotionally scarred by having spent her childhood in a succession of foster homes, and her resulting animosity towards, and anxiety about, the Department of Welfare, isolates her further, blinding her to her children's needs. However, while the film does ask us to acknowledge the mistakes that Fran makes in relation to her children, it also invites our compassion through the recognition that her considerable love for them is inevitably and tragically refracted through her lack of confidence. While such a poor self-image is clearly the product of her own difficult experiences, Fran also demonstrates phallocentrism's underlying principle that while a woman may apparently be redeemed by her children, and given a role in society through her relation to them, she is literally nothing without the sexual and social significance lent to her by men. The film also implies the insidious way in which this attitude is passed on from mother to daughter. In the film's final image, the abused eldest child Lisa (Narelle Simpson) turns to her mirror to admire the face that her abuser had admired, a tentative yet inexorable movement towards a sense of self that, like her mother's, is defined almost entirely through male sexual attentions.

In Gillian Armstrong's •**Hightide** (1987), at least one aspect of the mother is also represented as limited and potentially destructive for the daughter. Grieving over the death of her husband, Lilli (Judy •Davis), who tours the Returned Services League clubs of Australia as a back-up singer, left her young daughter Ally (Claudia •Karvan) in the care of her late husband's mother Bet (Jan •Adele). Some years later, she chances across them living happily in a caravan park in a seaside town in New South Wales, and must face afresh the implications of her role as mother. Like Fran, Lilli finds it hard to contemplate herself solely in relation to her child and, even when she is re-establishing contact with her teenage daughter, she is distracted by the sexual possibilities of Mick (Colin •Friels). Thoughtful and understated, the film asks us to consider mothering as a set of behaviours that are not necessarily related to biological functions. Despite the roughness and straightened circumstances in which Bet and Ally live, Bet is able to offer the girl a loving and supportive maternal environment. Similarly, as Ally and Lilli tentatively set off on their life together, there is an implication that the teenage Ally will nurture the fragile Lilli just as much as Lilli will mother her child. In this sense, while the connections of biology are clearly emphasised, the activities of mothering are also portrayed as encompassing a diversity of forms of caring that are undertaken with varying degrees of choice and responsibility.

The Piano continues the theme of mothers and daughters in its depiction of the journey of Ada (Holly Hunter) and her daughter Flora (Anna Paquin) from the implied constraints of the Old World to the possibilities of a new life in remote colonial New Zealand. While Ada's identity, role, and social relevance are again dramatised in relation to her attachment to men—her husband Stewart (Sam •Neill) and lover Baines (Harvey Keitel)—her relationship with her daughter, with whom she has crossed the world to arrive in this mud-soaked corner of New Zealand, is clearly central to her sense of self. Exercising a limited form of power within her disempowered state by means of a 'deliberate' muteness, Ada has, with Flora, perfected a 'language' of subtle corporeality, of signs, gestures, touch, and glances, to replace the disembodied signifiers of the Law of the Fathers, the language that can arbitrarily marry her to an unknown man and shape the territorial parameters of her life. Significantly, the adult relationship that *does* work for Ada, the one that offers her possibilities for a development of self as mother, as lover, and as independent woman, is a relationship with the illiterate Baines. The communication between mother and child is thus fundamentally related to the communicative power of music, of the erotic, and of the body, which provide a crucial alternative to the decrees, measurements, and dismembering punishments of phallocentrism as characterised by Stewart. In this sense, rather than being a distraction from, or a surrogate for, the attentions of a man, Ada's role as a mother is shown to be integrally related

to her development in the multiple aspects of her subjectivity—as caregiver, as sexual, creative being, and as a female.

As women's roles change within the broad sphere of society, changes in the diversity and the possibilities for mothering are necessarily reflected in the shifting images in the cinema. In turn, a proliferation of such images in the cinema contributes to the momentum of these social changes. In Campion's film, the woman who mothers is also the woman who is sexual and independently creative, just as she is the one who survives, perhaps even triumphs, and who thus carries the moral and identificatory weight of the narrative. The 'voice' that Ada finds in the sunny warmth of her life with Baines and Flora certainly does not offer a simple solution either to her own problems or to the issues surrounding the representation of maternity. Encouraged by the love she gives and receives from her partner and child, and strengthened by the potential of a sustainable accommodation with the destructive legacies of the past, Ada both remembers and constructs a speaking voice, one that opens up a new register of cinematic and social possibilities for the complex subjectivity of the woman who mothers.

ROSE LUCAS

Mateship Although mateship, defined by the *Australian National Dictionary* (1988) as the 'bond between equal partners or close friends', is not a term of Australian origin, it is a significant symbolic concept and social practice in the Australian experience. Historian W.K. Hancock isolated significant aspects of the institution of mateship when he wrote in 1930 that 'thwarted individualism found consolation in the gospel of mateship'. Russell Ward, in his seminal account of the significance of bush attitudes in the development of the 'Australian character' in *The Australian Legend* (1958), traces the historical roots of the practice of mateship to the 'strongly egalitarian sentiment of group solidarity and loyalty … [which] was perhaps the most marked of all convict traits'. From the specific characteristics of Australia's historical development, such as the relative absence of women in rural areas and the unequal distribution of power and wealth, group solidarity among rural workers was paramount and, from this social organisation, a distinctive set of communal values developed. Mateship was at the centre of this system and was, Ward argues, the prime distinguishing mark of outback workers 50 years before Henry Lawson and others wrote so much about this practice. Ward cites Alexander Harris's 1847 tale of how he [Harris] was cared for by a mate who walked a 'full forty miles' in 24 hours carrying a pack across the mountains, and this action prompted Harris to observe the following: 'Looked at in an abstract point of view, it is quite surprising what exertions bush men of new countries, especially mates, will make for one another, beyond people of the old countries. I suppose want prevailing less in the new countries makes men less selfish, and difficulties prevailing more make them more social and mutually helpful.'

The strength of this tradition, Ward argues, was reflected in the 'free and easy hospitality that became everywhere in the interior a sort of public right'. This 'public right', however, flourished only within the 'circle of the nomad tribe', as British visitor Anthony Trollope described them in 1875. For those members of society outside this 'tribe' it was a different story. The police, the squatters, Asians and, sometimes, women, were among those groups that were subjected to ridicule, hostility and, sometimes, violence.

'Difference' provoked suspicion and distrust and, as historian Graeme Turner notes in *National Fictions* (1993), mateship, particularly in the fiction of Lawson and others, depends upon a representation of character that is ideologically opposed to the individual. Mateship, as a literary convention, was dependent upon an 'insistence that individual characteristics do not cancel out the loyalties contracted through work and association in the bush'. Just as the institution of mateship was never questioned, in literature and many films its primary attribute, Turner argues, was not the authenticity of the particular relationship but the '*negation of individuality* or even specificity of character' and this is evident in Lawson's stories such as 'Telling Mrs Baker' and 'The Union Buries its Dead'. This latter story is one of three episodes on mateship in the film •**Three in One**, directed by Cecil •Holmes in 1957. In the film, Lawson's short story is entitled 'Joe Wilson's Mates', and Rex Rienits's script emphasises the importance of the shared ideals and rituals, such as drinking and storytelling, in the outback.

The rapid growth of the union movement from the middle of the nineteenth century was, as Ward points out, due to the bushman's 'already existing ethos' and, once the idea of a trade union combination was put before them, 'it seemed to most bushmen merely a natural extension of the non-political, but cherished and familiar, sentiments associated with the concept of mateship'. William Guthrie Spence, the first president of the Amalgamated Shearers' Union acknowledged that unionism 'came to the Australian bushman as a religion. It came bringing salvation from years of tyranny. It had in it a feeling of mateship which he understood already, and which characterised the action of one "white man" to another. Unionism extended the idea, so a man's character was gauged by whether he stood true to union rules or "scabbed" it on his fellows.'

The need for worker unity, collective unionism, and class loyalty is the subject of Richard •Lowenstein's 1984 film •**Strikebound**, which focuses on the miners' strike on the South Gippsland coalfields in the 1930s. The film is told via the memory of Wattie and Agnes Doig, who lead the miners' fight against low wages and appalling conditions at the Sun-

beam Colliery. When the management brings in scab labour, the miners barricade themselves in the mine until the company agrees to negotiate. Unity, in this celebration of collective behaviour, extends to the women in the local community, who form the Korumburra Women's Auxiliary, which boycotted local shopkeepers sympathetic to the mining company.

A more traditional presentation of mateship, unionism, and the need for collective attitudes and behaviour is found in •**Sunday Too Far Away** (1975). As Turner notes, the film favourably compares the shearers' society with other groups such as the property owner, whose life is ruled by money; the scabs, who lack honour and a sense of community; and women, whose essential difference means that they have to be banned from the shearing sheds. At the end of the film, which utilises the 1956 Shearer's Strike as the background to the story, a written title informs the audience that the shearers won. Yet the emphasis in the film is not on the result, but on the fact that the men remained united in their battle with their enemy, as is evident in the film's final title: 'The Strike lasted nine months. The Shearers won. It wasn't the money so much. It was the bloody insult.'

This collective ethos was reinforced by the experience of World War I. The official Australian historian at the time, C.E.W. Bean, wrote in *The Story of Anzac* (1921) that the prevailing creed among the Australian soldiers was a 'romantic one' inherited from the gold-miner and the bushman: a 'man should at all times and at any cost stand by his mate. This was and is the law which the good Australian must never break'. Similarly, in *The Broken Years* (1974), historian Bill Gammage writes that among the soldiers "'mateship" was a particular Australian virtue, a creed, almost a religion'. This theme was reinforced by Charles •Chauvel's •**Forty Thousand Horsemen** (1940) and by the relationship among the three Anzacs Red (Grant Taylor), Larry (Pat Twohill), and Jim (Chips •Rafferty) in the film. Although Chauvel's next film, •**The Rats of Tobruk** (1944), is a more sober drama based on the exploits of the AIF in North Africa during World War II, mateship remains a central concept: the film follows another trio of mates, Bluey Donkin (Grant Taylor), Milo Trent (Chips Rafferty), and the Englishman Peter Linton (Peter •Finch).

Nearly 40 years later Peter •Weir, with help from David •Williamson's script, drew heavily upon the assumptions and values of the bush legend in •**Gallipoli** (1981). The film uses Australia's most famous military battle in an attempt to isolate the distinctive qualities of the national tradition. It begins with a series of close-ups of Archy Hamilton's (Mark •Lee) athletic training in the Western Australian bush under the watchful eye of Uncle Jack (Bill •Kerr). This opening is a calculated attempt to foreground the mythic basis of the film and its association between two integral elements of the bush legend: sport and Australia's cultural heart, the outback. The distinctive sparse, brown vegetation of the Australian land in the early-morning light provides just the right combination of beauty and harshness for a culture that demands determination and adaptability to survive. Soon the blond bushman Archy meets another Australian stereotype, the dark-haired larrikin (Frank, played by Mel •Gibson) from the city, and the two men enlist in what the recruitment officer describes as the 'greatest game of all'.

The film's central thesis is that Australian soldiers are different from, and superior to, others. The episodic narrative pattern before the suicidal charge at the Nek on the Gallipoli peninsula provides a sequence of different scenes reinforcing this myth. Yet Weir and Williamson, in their determination to perpetuate what Amanda Lohrey describes in the journal *Island* as the 'myth of rural virtue … [a] form of imaginary innocence in the cause of a fashionable and sentimental nationalism', present a one-sided view of Australian mateship that represses its dark side, particularly its underlying fear of 'difference', which sometimes erupts into a recurring pattern of violent and irrational behaviour. The Cairo sequences in the film, for example, delete all reference to the documented racist behaviour of some Australians, which included throwing Egyptian drivers off their trams and then speeding 'wildly at full speed through the darkened streets, some of them clinging boisterously to the sides and roof' (Gammage) of the vehicle, after drinking and visiting the brothels around the Haret el Wasser. The Australians also shot at the locals, assaulted railway officials, and terrorised small boys at the markets.

Drunkenness, rape, sexually transmitted disease, and general misconduct by the Australians worried authorities so much that they requested that C.E.W. Bean write an open letter to the Australian press and warn the nation that the behaviour of some of their troops was so bad that the offenders would be sent home. Although 131 disciplinary cases and 24 men with sexually transmitted disease were sent back, serious offences still occurred. On 2 April 1915, Australian and New Zealand troops behaved so badly—rioting, looting, and setting fire to the 'Wasser' district of Cairo—that the Lancashire Territorials were ordered to draw their bayonets on the Australians to prevent further damage. One Australian soldier described the riot as the 'greatest bit of fun since we have been in Egypt'. The film, on the other hand, presents the Australians in Cairo as harmless larrikins who demonstrated their difference in a relatively harmless manner by playing football, confronting local traders, and visiting brothels. Yet even here there is some indication of the Australian sense of 'superiority' in Frank's sanctimonious explanation to Snowy (David •Argue) that 'life is cheap here, Snowy, and the women have no respect for themselves. It's the same in most foreign places.' This follows Snowy's disgust at the sight of a 'dirty'

postcard showing Egyptian women. This sense of exclusion could be extended to all women in the film: females (with the exceptions of the prostitutes in Cairo, a glimpse of Archy's mother and Frank's sister, and a brief sequence on a farm in the Australian outback) are significantly absent in terms of any meaningful contribution to the war effort.

The institution of mateship provides little space for women and, as one digger wrote, women and possessions 'came in between friends'. Yet loyalty to the group was mandatory and, in **Gallipoli**, when Frank leaves his infantry mates behind to join Archy in the Light Horse, an angry Snowy taunts him with a sarcastic remark as Frank prepares to leave: 'The infantry not good enough for you, *mate*'. This remark highlights the intense level of commitment required to be a 'mate', which divides the world into a polarised state of 'us' and 'them'. Snowy's remark also invites consideration of the issue of homosexual behaviour, a facet of mateship raised by Miriam Dixson in *The Real Matilda* (1976) and Robert Hughes in *The Fatal Shore* (1986), who note that the absence of European women in the bush meant that 'mateship' found its expression in homosexuality. Thus, in **Gallipoli**, when Snowy perceives Frank's departure from his infantry 'mates' as a form of betrayal, Frank views it as the opportunity to rejoin his real mate, Archy.

•**Wake in Fright** (1971) is less subtle in its association of the mateship institution with active homosexual behaviour. The film tells the story of a young teacher John Grant (Gary Bond), who is marooned in the outback town of Bundanyabba after he loses his money in a two-up game. Grant is initially patronising towards the 'crude' behaviour of the locals, but he finds himself increasingly dependent on them as they initiate him into the joys of the local culture, including a humiliating sexual liaison, a violent, drunken kangaroo shoot, and, finally, a homosexual assault from an alcoholic doctor.

The film also reiterates Ward's argument regarding the significance of drink as a means of bonding the all-male group. He writes that, by the 1880s, mateship had become such a 'powerful institution that often one could refuse an invitation to drink only at one's own peril'. In the film, Grant initially refuses to drink when it is offered to him by men on the train from Tiboonda to 'The Yabba'. Later, when a truck driver takes offence at Grant's refusal to drink with him, Grant angrily comments that a man can commit all kinds of atrocities except refuse to have a drink. Significantly, at the end of the film, Grant accepts a drink from strangers when it is offered to him on the train journey back to Tiboonda. This pressure to conform among the 'mates' is represented in •**Sunday Too Far Away** (1975) when Barry (Sean •Scully) indicates to his fellow shearers that he would prefer to write a letter to his wife than join their evening walk to look at the sheep. Foley (Jack •Thompson) and the other men react strongly to Barry's decision; they ridicule

Barry's practice of writing to his wife ('Are ya queer or something? What the bloody hell's wrong with you?').

•Shame (1988) not only exposes this overt fear of difference but foregrounds the underlying hostility and violence that accompanies it, often presented as benign, or even affirmative, in narratives that present a positive view of the mateship tradition: for example, •The Last of the Knucklemen (1979), •'Breaker' Morant (1980), •The Man from Snowy River (1982), its sequel The Man from Snowy River II (1988), •Crocodile Dundee (1986), and its sequel Crocodile Dundee II (1988). When Asta Cadell (Deborra-Lee •Furness) rides into the Western Australian outback town of Ginborack in Shame she encounters a pervasive system of male harassment against the local women. The film effectively uses the conventions of melodrama to present a depressing view of Australian culture as a society whose central institutions—such as the police, the family, and industry—not only permit, but also implicitly encourage, conformity and prejudice: the mateship tradition is so firmly ingrained in society that it cannot be eradicated, nor is it confined to rural Australia or to one aberrant group. Its cultural and historical roots permeate Australian culture with, according to this film, devastating results.

Turner wrote in *Metro* in 1994 that it was tempting to hope that the Australian film industry 'may abandon the practice of periodically recycling nostalgic invocations of the "Australian legend" for local and foreign consumption'. Certainly there is some evidence that this system of cultural values, and its central tenet of mateship, have travelled a reasonable journey since Gallipoli in 1981. However, this tradition has been reprised so often throughout Australia's history that to write its obituary at this point is premature. Its resilience is indicated by the way it has been assimilated into such unlikely films as •The Adventures of Priscilla, Queen of the Desert (1994) and •The Sum of Us (1994). However, its presence in these films may indicate that at least mateship is finally coming out of the closet.

GEOFF MAYER

Maughan, Monica (1938–) ACTOR Like many Australian actors, Monica Maughan has made her name in all the acting media, and has won awards for appearances on stage (*The Prime of Miss Jean Brodie*) and television (*The Damnation of Harvey McHugh*), as well as the Australian Film Institute award for her delicate screen performance in •A City's Child (1972), as a fantasising spinster. She has been acting professionally since the late 1950s and made her first film in the United Kingdom in 1968—the film version of Peter Hall's production of The Winter's Tale. Her capacity for detailed, sympathetic character work has stood her in good stead in a number of films since the 1970s, including •Annie's Coming Out (1984) and in a starring role in •Road

to Nhill (1997). In the latter, she shared billing with a number of distinguished Australian actors, including Patricia •Kennedy and Tony •Barry, and her comic flair was given more scope than has usually been her lot in films. She has continued to work steadily in the theatre and on television.
Other Australian films: •The Getting of Wisdom (1977), Desolation Angels (1982) Cactus (1986), •A Woman's Tale (1991), Mrs Craddock's Complaint (1997, short).

BMcF

Monica Maughan

Maxwell, Peter (1924–) DIRECTOR With some experience in the United Kingdom as a director of 'B' films, such as The Desperate Man (1959), with William Hartnell, and Serena (1962), starring Honor Blackman, Peter Maxwell also directed most of the 34 episodes of a colonial saga, *Whiplash*, in Australia in 1961, and settled in Sydney in 1967. His first feature in Australia was •Country Town (1971), the film version of *Bellbird*, the long-running television serial. He subsequently directed several other features of which the best known is probably Touch and Go (1980), a caper comedy involving three women (Wendy •Hughes, Chantal Contouri, and Carmen •Duncan). Among other television work, he also directed 26 episodes of a children's adventure series called *The Lost Islands*.
Other Australian films: Three Workshop Films (1975, short, co.-d.), Saint Therese (1979, short, ex-p.), Fluteman (1982), The Highest Honour (1984), Platypus Cove (1983), Run, Rebecca, Run (1983).

BMcF

May, Brian (1934–97) COMPOSER Brian May became well known as a composer for film both in Australia and overseas. His reputation was such that he was offered a contract by Universal Studios (1983) and he became the first Australian composer to work in a major Hollywood production company. His conducting career began in 1968 when, for the next 14 years, he was musical director and conductor of the ABC's Melbourne Show Band. His role as musical director and conductor of the NSW Bicentennial Concert in 1988 received wide recognition. He wrote almost 50 scores for feature films, television series, and miniseries. May's first score was for **The Story of Eskimo Nell** (1975), followed by •**Patrick** (1978). His chilling scores for •**Mad Max** (1979) and its sequel, •**Mad Max 2** (1981), describe in dark, pictorial detail a dysfunctional society of the future. Awards include the Australian Television Society award for **Nowhere to Run** (1977), the Asian Film Festival award for **Harlequin** (1981), the Paris International Film Festival award for **The Survivor** (1981) and the Australian Performing Rights Association Golden award for **Mad Max** (1985). Later films include **Hurricane Smith** (1991), **Deep Sleep** (1993), and **Blind Side** (1993).   DIANE NAPTHALI

Maza, Bob (1939–) ACTOR/WRITER Bob Maza has become a role model for many younger indigenous actors. From *Bellbird* in the late 1960s, and in several other series in the 1970s, he appeared irregularly on television, but his first film role was in Esben •Storm's low-budget feature •**27A** (1974). By then he was acting and writing for the theatre, particularly Sydney's Nimrod and Redfern's Black Arts theatres. In the 1980s he won more and more substantial film roles. He was the charming but feckless Joe Comeaway, the father of the heroine, in •**The Fringe Dwellers** (1986), and again played opposite Justine •Saunders in the telemovies *Babakueria* (1986) and *No Trouble* (1987). Smaller roles followed in **Ground Zero** (1987), •**The Nostradamus Kid** (1993), and •**Lillian's Story** (1996). In Yahoo •Serious's spoof **Reckless Kelly** (1993) he played Dan Kelly, straight-faced and without any comment on his race. He wrote and acted for radio and was often seen on television; for instance, in the drama series *Heartland* (1994). In 1995 he played Gilbert, who takes his grandchildren into the bush to teach them in **The Back of Beyond**. His play *The Keepers* was on the NSW school curriculum, and he was appointed an Australian Film Commission Commissioner in 1995. He runs a media consultancy for Aborigines and Torres Strait Islanders in theatre, radio, television, and film.   IB

Maza, Rachael (1965–) ACTOR Born in Melbourne, Rachael Maza studied science at university and began to teach, before deciding that she preferred to act and, after moving first to Lismore and then to Perth, she completed a course at the Institute of Dramatic Arts. Her stage roles include starring performances in *The Aboriginal Protestors* and *Yerma*, and Miranda in the Bell Company's production of *The Tempest*. She has done small roles in many television programs, including *A Country Practice*, and larger ones in *Law of the Land* and *Heartland*. In film, her roles have gradually become bigger, from walk-ons in •**Cosi** (1996) and •**Lillian's Story** (1996) to a larger role in **Fistful of Flies** (1997). She has striking curly hair and a ready smile, and her screen performances are usually full of energy. In her first starring role, as one of the three sisters who return to the family home after their mother's death in •**Radiance** (1998), that energy is contained until its dramatic release in the closing sequences.   IB

McAlpine, Don (1934–) CINEMATOGRAPHER Don McAlpine has been one of the most influential Australian cinematographers. He started as a country 'stringer', free-lancing for the ABC, before joining their staff in Sydney. He joined the •Commonwealth Film Unit (CFU, now •Film Australia) in 1966, becoming chief cameraman in 1968 and influencing staff photographers such as Dean •Semler. McAlpine's first feature, shot while on leave from the CFU, was Bruce •Beresford's •**The Adventures of Barry McKenzie** (1972), the first internationally successful film spearheading the resurgence of Australian production. Don left the CFU to shoot the sequel, **Barry McKenzie Holds His Own** (1974), and then began freelancing, including shooting another eight films for Beresford. McAlpine's work has been acknowledged by the Australian Film Institute, with his award for Best Achievement in Cinematography for •**My Brilliant Career** (1979) and •**'Breaker' Morant** (1980), as well as five Australian Cinematographers Society (ACS) awards, including the 1980 'Milli' (Cinematographer of the Year). His contribution to the Australian industry was recognised by his induction as the first member of the ACS Hall of Fame in 1997. He was also nominated for the British Academy Best Cinematography Award for **William Shakespeare's Romeo and Juliet** (USA/Mexico, 1996).
Other Australian films: •**Don's Party** (1976), Surrender in Paradise (1976), •**The Getting of Wisdom** (1977), •**Patrick** (1978), •**The Money Movers** (1979), •**The Odd Angry Shot** (1979), The Journalist (1979), •**The Club** (1980), The Earthling (1980), •**Puberty Blues** (1981), Now and Forever (1983), •**The Fringe Dwellers** (1986).   DAVID MUIR

McCallum, John (1918–) ACTOR/PRODUCER John McCallum's career in films has been bookended by his Australian experience: it began with voice-overs for some post-war documentaries, such as **South West Pacific** and **Joe Came Back** (1946), and acting in •**A Son is Born** (1946), in which his co-stars included Peter •Finch and Ron •Randell;

and it ended with the roles of producer, director, and writer of films and television series. Born in Queensland, and trained at the Royal Academy of Dramatic Art before the war, McCallum's acting career was conducted chiefly in the United Kingdom (1947–56), where he had notable starring roles in such films as **It Always Rains on Sunday** (1948, opposite his wife Googie •Withers) and **The Long Memory** (1953). On return to Australia in the mid 1950s, he and Withers appeared frequently on the stage together, and he became managing director of J.C. Williamsons. He was executive producer on Michael Powell's •**They're a Weird Mob**, and, in collaboration with Lee •Robinson, set up Fauna Productions, which launched the successful *Skippy* series, and several others. His last film as an actor was •**Smiley** (1956), but he directed Withers in •**Nickel Queen** (1971), which he also produced and co-wrote.

Other Australian films: Australia is Like That (1947, doc.), •Bush Christmas (1947, narrator), •Three in One (1957, 'introducer'), The Intruders (1969, ex. p.), Attack Force Z (1980, exec. prod.), The Highest Honor (1984, exec prod). BMcF

John McCallum

McClements, Catherine (1965–) ACTOR Since

graduating from the National Institute of Dramatic Art in 1985, Melbourne-born Catherine McClements has had a remarkably busy stage career, including appearing in the controversial *Angels in America*, as well as classical roles and, on television, she had a continuing role in *Water Rats*. Her film career has been sporadic but has already garnered her an Australian Film Institute Best Actress Award for her performance in **Weekend with Kate** (1991), a comedy of sexual relations among (and for?) 1990s yuppies. McClements, a distinctive dark-haired, strong-jawed actor, made the most of the film's brittle dialogue and somewhat predictable situations. In •**Struck by Lightning** (1990), she brought an appropriate warmth and sexiness to the role of the social worker who visits the sheltered workshop for retarded adults and falls for the new young physical education teacher. Her other films include Di Drew's **The Right Hand Man** (1987), a strange piece of gothic costume drama set among nineteenth-century New South Wales squatters, and the unreleased **Redheads** (1992). The big screen has not yet exploited her talents as fully as the other media. BMcF

McCreadie, A.K. (?) and T.O. (?–1992) DIRECTORS/

PRODUCERS Brothers Alec and Tom McCreadie were exhibitors in suburban Sydney in the 1920s, before forming Embassy Pictures in 1940. The new company made several short films, then embarked on a program of features. •**Always Another Dawn** (1947) was the patriotic story of a young man who dies in World War II, inspired by his father's sacrifice in World War I. **Into the Straight** (1949), a conventional racing picture, did well in Perth but was less successful in the eastern states. Both were directed by Tom McCreadie but, for •**The Kangaroo Kid** (1950), the brothers hired an American director, writer, and leading players. The result is an 'Australian' western, which achieved an American release, but it was not successful enough to keep the production enterprise afloat, so the McCreadies returned to exhibition and distribution. IB

McDermott, Terry (1927–) ACTOR This South

Australian actor has performed more on the stage, radio, and television than in the cinema. Terry McDermott was a principal cast member in the popular television serial *Bellbird*. In 1971, McDermott, and another cast member, Gary Gray, formed a production company to produce the film •**Country Town**, which was based on the characters and setting of the television serial. McDermott and Gray, as well as starring in the film, also distributed it. McDermott's stolid, reliable persona was also evident as Sergeant Bronson in the long-running television series *Homicide*, and contributed to his casting as a judge in **A Single Life** (1985) and as a senator in **Against the Innocent** (1989). McDermott also appeared in one of Australia's most disappointing films, •**Dimboola** (1979).

Other Australian films include: •The Mango Tree (1977).

GM

McDonagh, Isabel, *see* Lorraine, Marie

In conversation with

JOHN McCALLUM

Did you have any experience of film before the War?

No I wasn't in any films before the War; I was at RADA [Royal Academy of Dramatic Art] then, and it was entirely focused on the stage. There was no film training at RADA in those days at all, which was surprising; we did have a little training for broadcasting but not a lot of that. We used to go down to the BBC now and then and have someone give us a bit of technique about broadcasting, but not about film.

Back in Australia after the War, what do you remember about the film scene here?

When I came out of the Army, I was approached by the •Commonwealth Film Unit, which later became •Film Australia, to make a little documentary called **Joe Comes Back**. I was a soldier coming back from the War and settling into civilian life. That was the first thing I did in films. I did another one of those, called **South West Pacific**, with Peter Finch and Grant Taylor. They were really acted documentaries with a propaganda purpose.

Jesse Lasky Jr, whose father was a big Hollywood tycoon, was out here while in the American army and he had something to do with one of those films, and it was he who said that I should go to Hollywood and he'd help me there. Well, I couldn't get to Hollywood because the ships were full of American brides going over, so I went to England instead on a troop ship going back, and I'm very glad I did. I stayed there, was lucky, and I met Googie [Withers] in my second film [**The Loves of Joanna Godden**], otherwise I'd be in Hollywood now. And I did another little film here called **A Son is Born** for Eric Porter.

What do you remember about him?

He was a very nice man, who later went into animation at the Eric Porter Studios and did very well. He died about 10 years ago [1983]. He made this film in 1945 at the end of the War, and he had a very good cast. Peter Finch was in it, Muriel Steinbeck, and Ron Randell. And there were some others in it too, who were well known: Jane Holland—she came to London and met Leo McKern. I gather they're still married.

What do remember about the film?

He made it on a shoestring of course! I remember scenes up in the house of a friend of his with a swimming pool. He used those natural locations he got for nothing. I think there were very few studio shots. He had a small office round about Bathurst Street [Sydney]; I remember being in there to say goodbye to him just before going to England when there was a fire and a lot of the film burned. Luckily he was able to put it together, but I know he lost some film while I was there! I didn't do it! I didn't set fire to it!

It's a kind of romantic melodrama stretching over two generations? Your hair is discreetly grey in it.

Oh yes, I spent most of my life when I was young greying my hair and now at Chichester two years ago I had to play a forty-year-old, believe it or not, and I had to blacken my hair.

In the postwar period in Australia was there much sense of a film industry?

No there wasn't, but there were some marvellous pioneering characters, like the Heaths. George •Heath was camera man on a film I did [•Bush Christmas]. He did documentary things too, and he and his father had a studio in North Sydney. He was a very good camera man: of course, they used old-fashioned equipment in those days, but he was very well regarded. God knows there wasn't much for him to do but there were these documentaries being made.

And there was Mervyn Murphy at Supreme. He was a pioneer in sound, another nice man. They were twice my age then, but I always had a great respect for them. Long before that, before the War, at the old Bondi Junction Studios, they had made those films with George Wallace. They went back to those days, to Ken G. •Hall's comedies. This was at •Cinesound studios.

You, like so many people, then left Australia. Did you feel that if you wanted to be an actor, particularly a film actor, there was really no choice but to leave at that stage?

Yes that's true. It was quite a decision because, at the time, just after coming out of the army, I was very lucky and got a job opposite Gladys Moncrieff in four musicals that [J.C.] Williamsons were doing. Frank Tait offered me the chance to go around New Zealand with them. Although New Zealand sounded very pleasant, I really felt I should try my luck overseas. What really changed my mind was that I saw in the paper that my old friend Trevor Howard, whom I'd been with at Stratford in 1939, had had a great success in a film called **Brief Encounter**, and I thought, well, if he can do it, perhaps I might have a chance too. I remembered Jesse Lasky Jnr: I couldn't get to America, but I could get on the *Aquitania* taking troops back to England and, indeed, they did want people there just after the War, and I was very lucky to get into films there.

You also did another voice-over in Australia as far as I know and that was for Ralph Smart's **Bush Christmas.**
I did that in London. They'd finished the film and I knew Ralph and the woman in charge, who did all the children's films—Mary Field—and she asked me if I'd do it for nothing. I was glad to because I thought it was a charming little film. I think it was made in Australia for the British Children's Entertainment Films.

And you ended up in England making A Boy, a Girl and a Bike *for Ralph Smart?*
Yes, and very pleasurable it was up in the Yorkshire Dales in summer about '47, I think. Ralph lives in Spain now.

You had almost a decade of successful film work in the United Kingdom for Ealing, Pinewood, Gainsborough, Herbert Wilcox. Why did you decide to return to Australia?
There was a recession in English film-making around the mid 1950s. RKO bought out Wilcox and I had a little bit of a contract to run with him. I was paid off because they took over everything, so that finished. [J.C.] Williamsons always wanted me to go back and do a tour, and I thought, now's the time, because I always liked the theatre better frankly, and I think Googie feels the same way. So, when Frank Tait asked us to come out and do a tour of two plays, it was very tempting. I wanted Googie to see Australia anyway, so why not on a theatrical tour? We were out here for 18 months for the two plays, *The Deep Blue Sea* and *Simon and Laura*. Generally, the tour was a big success and we loved it, and Frank Tait asked me to come back and manage [J.C.] Williamsons.

*Do you remember those two English films where you were cast as Australians—*Melba *and* Lady Godiva Rides Again?
Yes, but I never had an Australian accent you know. My mother was English and she thought, 'If he's going to be an actor, Australian parts are very limited, so he'd better speak English'. So I was sent to school in England. I find it to this day very difficult to do an absolutely genuine Australian accent, and Googie feels the same.

When you returned to Australia, you were actor, director and later managing director for J.C. Williamsons?
Yes. We were in Perth and finishing the tour before going back to England when my old father had a stroke, and so I flew over here to see him. I was in touch with Frank of course all the time and he asked me to call in at Melbourne on my way back. He asked me to join him as joint managing director of J.C.Williamsons. We talked about that on the boat home, Googie liked Australia very much and said she'd love to come out, so we did.

And were you instrumental in taking J.C. Williamsons into film-making with Michael Powell?
Yes. Michael Powell came out and said he'd bought the rights to *They're A Weird Mob*, which had been a huge success, and he wanted me to get [J.C.] Williamsons to invest in it and they hadn't made a film for decades. But I did talk them into it, and they put about £100 000 into it, which was about a quarter of the money for the film. Frank didn't like the idea. They had no experience of filming and there wasn't any filming here in those days, but I did persuade him and it was all right when they got their money back and a bit to spend.

And °They're a Weird Mob was really a very big financial success?
Yes, it did very well here, but nowhere else. It was released in England as a co-feature. I thought it would be good in Italy but it wasn't. We spent a long time trying to adapt it for Italy, but it didn't work. Micky had got the book somehow from an Australian friend and was very keen to film it. It was a low time for him frankly. He had great talent in many ways. He came up as a stills camera man, and he had a very good visual sense, but I don't think he knew very much about acting. He cast as well as he could, then left it to the actors. He knew very much how to tell the story with the camera and visually he was very good, but he was

an extremely difficult man. I remember we had a conference and Michael said he wanted another £100 000. He said, 'You've got to get it out of [J.C.] Williamsons', and I replied, 'I will not get it out of [J.C.] Williamsons. He threatened to throw a glass of water over me! In the end I did get another £120 000 from the firm, but I put money in personally, a bit too much really, and so did a friend of mine. We had the usual problems, mostly about running out of money. He spent a lot of money but I got on well with him.

You had two other film appearances in Australia. You made •Smiley for Anthony Kimmins, with whom Googie of course has worked in the United Kingdom with George Formby in Trouble Brewing. *This was a rare villain's role for you.*
I rather enjoyed that. Tony was a great friend of mine before coming out here and we saw a lot of him when we were doing *The Deep Blue Sea* at the Theatre Royal. He said, 'Do you think you could do the film as well?' Most of the locations were down at Camden Park, which was a couple of hours' drive, but we worked around the schedule and there was some studio work. It wasn't a big part. Ralph Richardson was in too; he was also out here doing a play [*Separate Tables*]: he was at the Elizabethan Theatre and we were at the Royal.

And the little boy who played Smiley, Colin Petersen, went to the United Kingdom and made a film for Wolf Rilla called The Scamp.
Did he really? He also became a drummer. He amazed us at the party at the end of a film when he did a performance on the drums. He was only a kid, 10 or 12, but he was wonderful, and then he went off with a very early pop band. I don't know what happened to him after that, but he was a very nice boy and he was brilliant on the drums.

*Your other 1950s involvement was as the 'Introducer' to the three stories in Cecil •Holmes' •*Three in One. *What do you remember about Holmes?*
I was just thinking about that the other day. Perhaps I appeared on screen; I can't remember. I remember meeting Cecil Holmes on that and he was a great [Henry] Lawson fan and some of the actors were very dedicated. Holmes was another pioneer film-maker here. He had a terribly hard time getting things going, because no one wanted to put money into films in those days. He had awful troubles. I don't know how exactly he got the money together. Wasn't it an official film again? He did

work for Film Australia later, and then he went to the NT and he did something for the Australian Institute of Aboriginal Studies up there. I never knew him well; Lee Robinson knows him much better than I do.

Where is Lee Robinson?
He's up at Blue Bay. I'm often in touch with him because we still have things to talk about to do with the old films and distribution. He's a key figure in '50s films in Australia and much later. He was making films when I was in England; he really was very important and he made some very good things too—•**The Phantom Stockman** and •**King of the Coral Sea**. He was first with the Film Division of the Department of the Interior, and then he branched out commercially with Chips •Rafferty [they set up Southern International production company in 1953] and they made about half a dozen films. •**Walk into Paradise** is still quite a remarkable film. There is a scene in that where they are making a runway; he had about a 1000 natives and it's Hollywood stuff. He gave them a handful of rice or something, and got some remarkable material. He made one later in Tahiti, a French co-production called **The Stowaway** [with Martine Carol and Arletty]. There's a new distribution company called Southern Star that is interested in taking on these films.

Most of your association with the cinema after you finished your '50s films has been as a producer. What do you see as the rewards and headaches of being a producer of films?
I wouldn't like to do any more because you spend most of the time trying to raise the money. There were tremendous difficulties in those early days when we were doing *Skippy*; nothing had been going on for ages. It wasn't easy to get equipment, casting was difficult, and the weather was against us most of the time. It was outside and there were no studios there and you had to build/arrange a headquarters and shoot inside, it was pretty much pioneer stuff. I remember the roads up here at Terry Hills just behind us. We got 40 acres on a loan from the government and of course we didn't really pay; they gave it to us for peppercorn rent. We couldn't get in, it was quite isolated, and we had a Rolls Royce in the first sequence with Frank Thring driving in, and the owner took one look at the bogged track up there and said, 'You're not having my car on that', so we had to get a Mercedes from one of the directors of the company. This was the first episode of *Skippy*, and we were rained out! And of course if you go far afield, as we did on the

Boney series, you get all sorts of difficulties of communication as you did in those days, and logistics of accommodation and getting people transported!

We had money from Germany and from England, and they were always interfering and ringing up and saying 'we don't like this, and we don't like that, and this casting isn't good,' and you've got to put up with all that.

When you're a producer do you maintain a lot of interest in the creative side of it or are you too caught up with the rest?

Oh I do. There's too much credit today given to the director of a film; critics call it *his* film, but don't forget it's the producer generally who, in the first place, has the idea of doing the film and the idea of how he wants it done, and he employs the director to do it largely his way. The public mix up the producer with tycoons who sit in offices, but a line producer is a man who's on the film. I was a line producer—the whole time on location. Certainly we were hands-on producers and the directors worked for us, and they did it the way we wanted it. If they wanted to do something different from the script, then we said of course, 'We'll listen', but by and large they were *our* films and the directors were choreographers.

How involved were you on They're a Weird Mob *in casting and locations and script?*

Very much on casting but there's was no doubt that it was Michael Powell's film. This was a little different, because he came to us with the film. It wasn't our idea to do it, so he did far more than usual. He really was producer and director on that. I was no more than executive producer. Executive producers sit in the office and get the money and employ the director and the line producer. I generally was a line producer, although sometimes I was both because I got the money and the subject together and cast it, and had a lot to do with the making of the film too. But a lot of producers don't; they get the money together, employ people and then go away. I never went away, in fact some directors thought I was a pain in the neck because I did so much!

The Intruders *was a film version of the television series, 'Skippy'. It had begun only in 1968 and this film was made in 1969; that is a very rapid spin-off. The series must have been a huge success.*

Oh it was. We got carried away with it, and we made too many. We made 91 and we didn't sell the last 39. We got into a little bit of cash-flow problem, and Packer helped us out—at a price!

This was a case of its being entirely our idea. We—the people who did **They're A Weird Mob**, except Michael Powell, principally Lee Robinson who worked on the film as production supervisor, and 'a solicitor called Bob Austin and I—decided to do a television'. **Weird Mob** had been a big success, so we thought, let's do a television of it. Then we realised there's only one idea about an Italian arriving in Australia, and you can't go on being funny about that. Lee had a friend in England, a distributor, who said, 'Why don't you do children's films?' and then we hit on the idea of a boy with a kangaroo. At least a kangaroo is different and that night we thought of the name, 'Skippy', and it all started from there. We made an episode for $18 000 and about four or five of us put money into that.

How successful was the film?

Not as successful as the TV series. We got the money back on the film but we thought it would be a bigger success in the cinema. If they could see it for nothing at home, the Mums and Dads weren't too keen to take the kids and pay at the cinema. We sold it to the Children's Film Foundation in England and they did well with it. They cut it down to a 60-minute version and played it Saturday morning in the cinemas, which had a great vogue after the War in England.

One of the names on The Intruders *was Joy Cavill. What are your recollections of her and how did you become associated with her?*

She'd been a continuity girl for me and she worked very well on *Skippy* as production manager. She was a very capable, efficient woman, wonderful in the office, very good on detail. Give her a telephone and she'd get anything. She was so good she became associate producer, and then when I did •Nickel Queen I had her as co-producer and she did a lot of the script. She's listed as co-author of the script. She was a very talented girl, a very nice girl too. I found her extremely helpful.

You set up Fauna Productions, as I understand, to make both films and television. Was that the idea?

Yes, mostly it was to be for *Skippy* and then we did use it for films. I was joint chairman with my solicitor friend Bob Austin, who was on the business side and executive producer.

In the changing climate of the 1970s did you want to be more involved in film-making or were you still very heavily committed to J.C. Williamsons at this stage?

No, I'd left J.C. Williamsons in 1967 because there were changes: Frank Tait died and I had differences with the board. I resigned in '67, then we did *Skippy* and *Barrier Reef* for a year, then *Boney* for a year. After that I went back into the theatre in London with Ingrid Bergman in the *The Constant Wife*.

•*Nickel Queen happened just as Australian cinema was getting going again. I gather it was a huge success in Western Australia.*

Wasn't it! Well it was made there and I think it ran for 20 weeks in Perth.

Was it directly inspired by the Poseidon phenomenon?

Yes it was. Our old friend, Sydney Box, had gone to live in Perth for health reasons. He suddenly sent me a script about mining. They just had the big nickel discovery and we'd finished *Barrier Reef*, when he sent me this script by a fellow called Henry James, a journalist, and of course it was very topical then. James was co-author of the script and it was certainly from his original script. Then Bob Austin raised the money and Sydney had a piece of it. And we thought it would do very well after Perth, but it never did as well anywhere else. Googie had the lead, John Laws was in it, and Ed •Devereaux, and the American Alfred Sandor whom I'd brought out here to do *Plaza Suite* on stage with Googie.

It's a cheerful good-natured film.

Yes it's only for fun. The critics took it too seriously and they didn't like it; but I liked it. I'd been doing quite a bit of direction on the TV and I thought I'd have a crack at a feature film. I quite enjoyed it. We had John •Seale as camera operator, and a very good team, with Joy Cavill, and I enjoyed it and it worked.

There seems to have been a long and somewhat troubled production history for Attack Force Z. It was directed by Tim •Burstall with a cast full of stars of tomorrow and I wondered what you recall about it. It was your own production company wasn't it?

Yes, it was John McCallum Production Centre. Again it was with Lee. We'd always thought we'd like to make films in Asia, and Lee went on a trip to Thailand, Taiwan, and The Philippines, and he came back with co-production interest in four films that we got together here. **Attack Force Z** was based loosely on fact about an attack by commandos on an island. We gave up the one we wanted to do in Thailand because we had threats. This was about dope-running, starting from the poppies and the hill factories where they distil the damned stuff and send it down to Bangkok. We had quite a good script but we weren't allowed to do it. Thailand said, 'No it's too dangerous. If you make an exposé, they'll kill you.' As a matter of fact there was an anonymous phone call saying, 'Tell McCallum if he makes that film he's a dead man'. The next one, **Attack Force Z**, was made in Taiwan with local co-production. They had a film studio but it was terrible: they didn't even have sound in this film; they looped the sound on after. You can imagine the difficulty we had; it was pioneering again. But we *did* have Sam •Neill and Mel •Gibson and John •Waters. Piper Laurie shot a film called •**Tim** in this house, and Betty Barnard, our production manager, was on **Tim**, and she said, 'I want you to meet somebody I think is going to be a star', and his name was Mel Gibson. We had a chat here in this room and I remembered him when we did this film, and we paid him $1000 a week for 10 weeks. He was very athletic, very good I thought, and, when we had another subject a year later, I rang Billy Shanahan his agent and was told he'd gone to Hollywood, and then of course after that he made the famous •**Mad Max**. I said 'We've got another script for Mel. What's his starting price?' Shanahan said, 'A million dollars'.

Am I right in thinking Phil •Noyce began the directing?

Phil was extraordinary. He was very good to start with, but he was extremely difficult up there. We were a long way from base in Taiwan and Taipei, and it was pretty cruel stuff. We were working with very difficult Chinese people, who had a general in charge of this government studio. Phil cast a man to play a tiny part—two or three lines—and he said, 'I've changed my mind about that chap, he's much too urban for a peasant', and I said, 'Look, he's got a hat on, his face is hardly seen', but Phil said, 'I won't do it'. For two days he didn't appear; it was very disruptive, so I said, 'Now come on Phil, we've got to get on with this', but he flatly refused to continue shooting with this one man. He was so incidental, he was one of the fellows they meet when they land on the island. We had six Australian actors up there and we had to get some film shot quickly, so I rang Tim •Burstall, who came up and he did virtually all of the film. Phil Noyce only did about two days. Now he's a huge success in blockbusters.

How did the film go in the end?

It was a bit too gung-ho, the whole thing. It didn't cost much because it was a television film, but it was exhibited. Roadshow put it out in Melbourne for a while but it didn't do well. We sold it abroad quite a bit and, of course, Mel Gibson's name helped.

Your next film, Highest Honour*, was directed by Peter •Maxwell who lives somewhere in the Blue Mountains.*

He did films, some in England, and then he came out here and did *Boney* and perhaps *Riptide* too. He'd done very well for us. He was very efficient. I think he again was a bit more of a visual man than an actor's director. We did a thing called *Bailey's Bird*, a television series in Penang, and he was up there quite a bit too.

Did your Highest Honour *end up having theatre screenings? I had a feeling it had been shown in cinemas as well as on television.*

Oh yes it was. We sold it to New World films who had some sort of cinema release. I don't think it ever got a release here, but it did in America, and I think it did in England too, and certainly we sold it quite well on television. Stuart Wilson was very good in it, but it got bogged down with too much Japanese dialogue, because they were co-producing, and put up half the money. They insisted on a lot of Japanese. I said, 'You're the villains in this, you beheaded the Australians.' But they thought they'd make a huge amount of money out of it; the man behind the film company was a millionaire. He took us up there, Robinson and myself and some of the actors, and we had a great jamboree of a week in Tokyo, where he had a huge launch of the damn thing in a huge cinema. He said, 'We're releasing it tomorrow all over Japan. We expect to make three million.' I think they *lost* three million.

What are your views on how Australia seems to be performing now?

Well, it went great guns for a long time, didn't it, and produced about 30 very good films, which is marvellous for this country and the Film Commission, and the Film Development Corporation, and the •10BA helped enormously. I think Australia has produced just as many films, certainly as many *good* films as England has over the last 10 years, and they've got a much bigger population. Isn't it interesting how films have come back? They're building all these complexes and more and more cinemas when we thought television would kill it.

THIS INTERVIEW WAS CONDUCTED BY BRIAN MCFARLANE

McDonagh, Paulette (1901–78) DIRECTOR Talented, extroverted, and strong in personality, Paulette McDonagh directed four features and several short films between 1926 and 1934. She was the first Australian woman fully to direct a feature film. Unique in world terms, she was also the driving force in a production collective of three sisters. While Paulette wrote and directed, Isabel, billed as Marie •Lorraine, played leads, and Phyllis (1900–82) was art director, production manager, and publicist.

Film- and stage-struck from childhood, Paulette had carefully studied American features before she entered filmmaking. The £2000 budget for her first film, •**Those Who Love** (1926), came from money willed to the family by an uncle they had never met. Although Paulette gave technical advisor P.J. Ramster the sole directorial credit for this film, she directed it virtually entirely herself. Like her second and third films, •**The Far Paradise** (1928) and •**The Cheaters** (1930), **Those Who Love** told of love triumphing in the face of parental hostility. A familiar theme, to be sure, but Paulette and her actors, especially a naturalistic Isabel, created and sustained worlds of deep emotional resonance.

The visual fluency of the first three films was helped by Paulette's collaboration with Jack Fletcher, an Australian who had trained at Hollywood's Paramount studio in the early 1920s.

Disliking the local cinema's rough bush comedies, Paulette tailored her silent films for an audience accustomed to the luxurious backgrounds, social contrasts, and enveloping melodrama of Hollywood. The publicity for **Those Who Love** claimed that it had made the NSW governor cry. It earned more money on the local market than Chaplin's **The Gold Rush** (1925). Critical response to **The Far Paradise** exceeded that for the earlier film, but financial returns were not in the same league. Today the film is the more dramatically multi-layered of their two substantially surviving silents. Money for the other, **The Cheaters**, came from a family friend, but the advent of talkies meant the film had only limited release. Paulette adapted the silent to make part- and full-talkie versions, but it is the silent that still impresses by counter-balancing a complex plot with a potent blend of romance and darker ingredients. Neville Macken, backer of **The Cheaters**, next commissioned

Paulette to make a series of short documentaries, including **Australia in the Swim** (1931), **Trail of the Roo** (1931), and **How I Play Cricket** (with Don Bradman, 1932).

In 1933, Paulette directed the feature **•Two Minutes Silence** (released 1934), based on the anti-war play by Leslie Haylen. This time, however, a limited budget so ingeniously deployed on earlier McDonagh films seems to have been stretched too thinly, and **Two Minutes** was criticised for being laboured. Paulette, however, regarded the now-lost film as her best and claimed it was 'too true' for most audiences.

After Isabel's marriage, the McDonagh film-making team came to an end. As a solo producer/director, Paulette planned one more feature but had trouble finding finance. From 1934, although still full of enthusiasm and ideas, she made no more films.   GRAHAM SHIRLEY

McDonald, Garry (1948–) ACTOR   A 1967 graduate of the National Institute of Dramatic Art, Garry McDonald is best known for his bizarre 1970s' television character Norman Gunston and later as Arthur Beare, Ruth Cracknell's exasperated, albeit tolerant, son in the long-running television series *Mother and Son*. McDonald, however, has been a character actor in the Australian cinema since the early 1970s and his greatest screen opportunity was as Ollie Rennie, the dour, compassionate director of Salt-marsh, a sheltered workshop for retarded adults in Adelaide in **•Struck by Lightning** (1990). McDonald's other major lead role in the cinema was in the ill-conceived black comedy **Wills and Burke—The Untold Story** (1985), which opened a week before a more reverent, and lavish, treatment of the same subject (**•Burke & Wills**). McDonald, one of the best comedic talents in Australia, is yet to find a suitable screen vehicle and his most productive media have been television, where he won the Silver Logie for the Most Outstanding Actor on Australian Television in 1994, and the theatre, where he has been a regular performer since 1968.
Other Australian films include: Avengers of the Reef (1973), **•Stone** (1974), **•Picnic at Hanging Rock** (1975), **•The Picture Show Man** (1977), The Pirate Movie (1982), Ginger Meggs (1982), Molly (1983), The Place at the Coast (1987), Those Dear Departed (1987).   GM

McElroy, Hal and James (1946–) PRODUCERS   These twin brothers were important figures in the revival of Australian cinema in the 1970s (see Revival, the). The two, who first worked together as assistant directors on **•Ned Kelly** (1970), were most notably associated with Peter **•Weir**'s first commercial features, as co-producers on **•The Cars that Ate Paris** (1974), **•Picnic at Hanging Rock** (1975, in association with Patricia **•Lovell**), and **•The Last Wave** (1977). In 1979, they produced the documentary **New South Wales Image**. Like a number of the influential producers of

Gary McDonald

the 1970s, the McElroys failed to sustain the momentum of their careers, at least not in comparably significant work. However, unlike some of their contemporaries, they were prepared to venture into less obviously 'prestige' territory.

Hal came into film via advertising, radio, and television, joining the **•Commonwealth Film Unit** as a production assistant in 1967. He was an assistant director on several 1970s films, such as **•Alvin Purple** (1973) and **•Caddie** (1976). Following the Weir films he went on to produce the engaging children's film, **•Blue Fin** (1978), the outback black comedy, **•Razorback** (1984), several television series, including *Blue Heelers* and *Water Rats*, and was executive producer on **•The Sum of Us** (1994), the gay love story starring Russell **•Crowe**.
Other Australian films: **•Age of Consent** (1969, ass. d.), **Adam's Woman** (1970, ass. d.), **Girl in Australia** (1971, doc., ass. d.), **Be Active—Be Attractive** (1971, doc., d.), **The Choice** (1971, short, p. ass.), **Flashpoint** (1972, ass. d.), **Sunstruck** (1972, prod. man.), **Don Quixote** (1973, prod. man.), **•Between Wars** (1974, assoc. p., prod man), **•The Man from Hong Kong** (1975, ass. d.), **The Great MacArthy** (1975, ass. d.).

Jim worked his way up in television to become floor manager and worked as second assistant director on **•Wake in Fright** (1971). He renewed his association with Weir again as producer of **•The Year of Living Dangerously** (1982), a film that had a famously troubled production history, including death threats to the company while on location in The Philippines. Subsequently, he has produced **A Dangerous Summer** (1981), a McElroy & McElroy Production, starring James Mason, and Pauline Chen's •**Traps** (1994), which was shot in Vietnam, and Nadia •Tass's •**Mr Reliable** (1996).

Other Australian films: Let the Balloon Go (1976, assoc. p.), Till There Was You (1990). BMcF

McFarlane, Andrew (1951–) ACTOR This Western Australian-born actor graduated from the National Institute of Dramatic Art in 1973, and immediately made a strong impact in television series such as *The Sullivans*, in which he played John Sullivan, and later as Lt Keating, the commander, in the excellent *Patrol Boat*. Andrew McFarlane has continued his television work with regular appearances in *The Flying Doctors* and *Rafferty's Rules*, together with a lead role in the *Halifax* telefeature series. His film career has been more sporadic, with his most prominent performance as the disturbed young World War I veteran in **Break of Day** (1976). Unfortunately, its hostile critical reaction, which lamented the lack of Australian films with contemporary settings, did little to advance McFarlane's film prospects. This was followed with the lead in *The John Sullivan Story* (1979), a feature film for Australian television. Despite another strong performance in **Boulevard of Broken Dreams** (1988), he has had few film opportunities.

Other Australian films include: Doctors & Nurses: A Story of Hopes (1981), I Can't Get Started (1985). GM

McGrath, Martin (1956–) CINEMATOGRAPHER Martin McGrath started his career in Melbourne television studios, then freelanced on documentaries, telemovies, series, and miniseries. His first feature film was **Snow—The Movie** (1982), but it was •**Proof** (1991), for director Jocelyn •Moorhouse, that established his reputation. He has won three Australian Cinematographers Society Gold awards and the 'Milli' (Cinematographer of the Year) in 1994. His work has also been nominated for the Australian Film Institute Best Cinematography award for •**Children of the Revolution** (1996) and •**Blackrock** (1997).

Other Australian films: Shark's Paradise (1986), The Humpty Dumpty Man (1986), Exchange Lifeguards (1992), Signal One (1993), •Muriel's Wedding (1994), The Seventh Floor (1994), •Dad and Dave: On Our Selection (1995), River Street (1995), Little White Lies (1996), James (1997), A Little Bit of Soul (1998), In the Winter Dark (1998), •The Sound of One Hand Clapping (1998), Passion (1999). DAVID MUIR

McInnes, Laurie (1955–) CINEMATOGRAPHER/DIRECTOR Laurie McInnes worked as camera assistant on **The Chain Reaction** (1980) and as photographer on **With Time**

to Kill (1987). Then her own second film, the 15-minute drama **Palisade**, won the Palme d'Or at Cannes in 1987, the year after Jane •Campion's **Peel** had won the same prize, and the only time that two directors from the same country had won in consecutive years. She went on to write and direct a feature film, the moody •**Broken Highway** (1994), a baroque tale of drugs and doomed relationships, set in north Queensland. IB

McKenzie, Jacqueline (1962–) ACTOR Sometimes looking waif-like, sometimes perkily tough, Jacqueline McKenzie made a vivid impact in several films of the 1990s, as well as on television in such series as *Halifax* and the miniseries *Kangaroo Palace*. Her first film was Geoffrey •Wright's controversial •**Romper Stomper** (1992), as Gabe, the middle-class incest victim who allies herself to a gang of dangerous skinhead hoodlums, becoming the lover of their leader (Russell •Crowe). She made a very strong impression as the bruised and bruising outcast. She was another sort of outcast in Michael Rymer's •**Angel Baby** (1995), in which she and John Lynch played Kate and Harry, mental patients who fall in love and whose lives hurtle out of control as a result. Warned against going through with her pregnancy, Kate ignores the advice, goes off her medication at Harry's insistence, and dies in childbirth. That the film was so painfully moving owed a good deal to McKenzie's poignant performance of a loser who suddenly and briefly finds what happiness might be. She was Colin •Friels's loyal (and funny) girlfriend in the fact-based hostage comedy-drama, **Mr Reliable** (1996). She is an actor of unusual appeal, intensity, and range.

Other Australian films: This Won't Hurt a Bit (1993), •Traps (1994), Talk (1994), Under the Lighthouse Dancing (1996), Freak Weather (1998). BMcF

McKern, Leo (1920–) ACTOR Now a household name as the claret-toping, opinionated, witty *Rumpole of the Bailey* for BBC television, Sydney-born Leo McKern, who settled in the United Kingdom after the war and turned to acting, has rarely appeared in Australian films. When he has, though, the result has been memorable, as one might have expected. He played the irascibly selfish Frank in Carl •Schultz's •**Travelling North** (1987), adapted from David •Williamson's play, and he and Julia •Blake, as Frances, with whom he 'travels north' to spend their autumn years in Queensland, struck intelligent sparks from each other. In 1995 he returned to play Dad in the latest version of the Steele Rudd stories, •**Dad and Dave: On Our Selection**, with another famous Australian, Dame Joan •Sutherland, as a majestic Mum, partner to McKern's broad-brushed rendering of Australia's best known literary hayseed. If the film had enjoyed a bigger success, perhaps McKern would have been tempted to work here more often. As it stands, his career is essentially a British one: he has made over 50 films there since his 1955 début in **All for Mary**, and the list includes such notable successes as **The Mouse that Roared** (1959), **King and Country** (1964), the Beatles' film, **Help!** (1965), **The High Commissioner** (1968), in which he played a New South Wales premier in the opening scenes, and **The French Lieutenant's Woman** (1981); and he has also done a great deal of stage and television work as well. One of the world's great character actors, he could be well used in Australian films.   BMcF

McKimmie, Jackie (1950–) DIRECTOR/WRITER   Jackie McKimmie wrote a script for a fellow student to direct in her last year at the West Australian Institute of Technology, where she studied in 1970–73. As a teacher in Sydney, she allowed her students to make Super-8 films, and continued this when she moved to the Brisbane Independent School. By then she was writing plays, short stories, and poetry. Disappointed with the telefeature made from her script *Madness of Two*, she decided to direct any further film from her own scripts, and her first was the award-winning short **Stations** (1983), distributed commercially as the support for •**Careful, He Might Hear You.** This convinced her to continue to direct her own scripts. Her first feature was **Australian Dream** (1987), an hilarious exposé of suburban life in Brisbane, with a surprising political edge, but not well received critically. She made the *Topenders* episode of the Australian Children's Television Foundation series *Touch the Sun* (1988), then moved to Sydney to make •**Waiting** (1991), which had some success with both critics and audiences, and **Gino** (1994), which was made as a feature film, but released only on television.   IB

McLean, John (1939–) CINEMATOGRAPHER   John McLean began his career with Ross •Wood at Sydney's Pagewood Studios, during the period of Ealing Film's activities in Australia, then with local companies Southern International Pictures, Artransa Park Studios, Visatone, and Ajax Films. He worked with pioneer cinematographers such as Arthur •Higgins and Carl •Kayser. As camera operator, he was in demand on local and overseas productions, including •**Age of Consent** (1969) and •**Ned Kelly** (1970). After documentaries, television specials, and miniseries, his first features as director of photography were **Demonstrator** (1971) and **The Hands of Cormac Joyce** (USA/Australia, 1972), both winning Australian Cinematographers Society (ACS) Best Cinematography awards. In 1973 he received the ACS 'Milli' as Cinematographer of the Year.

Other Australian films: •**The Cars that Ate Paris** (1974), •**Number 96** (1974), **Touch and Go** (1980), **Turkey Shoot** (1981), **Highest Honour** (1982), **Second Time Lucky** (1985), **Frog Dreaming** (1986), **Where the Outback Ends** (1989), **Wildfire** (1989).
          DAVID MUIR

McQuade, Kris (1952–) ACTOR   Kris McQuade graduated from the National Institute of Dramatic Art in 1971, and played in the ABC television series *Certain Women* (1973). She soon became one of the most familiar faces on Australian film and television, while continuing to perform on the Sydney stage. Among numerous television roles, she played the lead in the telemovie *Harvest of Hate* (1978), played Jennifer, one of the three sisters running *The Last Resort* (1988), and gave a particularly memorable performance in *Rose Against the Odds* (1991). Her most important film performances were separated by nearly 20 years of smaller roles. She and Bryan •Brown were the lovers who cannot live together, but fantasise constantly in **The Love-Letters from Teralba Road** (1977). In **Billy's Holiday** (1994), she again played half of a strained relationship, this time with Max •Cullen as Billy. Her performance is one of the charms of the film, and it seems unfortunate that she has not been given more such opportunities.

Other Australian films: **Come Out Fighting** (1973), •**Alvin Purple** (1973), **Alvin Rides Again** (1974), **The Firm Man** (1974), **The True Story of Eskimo Nell** (1975), •**Kostas** (1979), •**Lonely Hearts** (1982), **Now and Forever** (1983), **Buddies** (1983), **Fighting Back** (1983), •**Goodbye Paradise** (1983), **The Coca-Cola Kid** (1985), •**The Surfer** (1988), **Resistance** (1991), •**Strictly Ballroom** (1992), •**Broken Highway** (1994).   IB

Meagher, Ray (1944–) ACTOR   Queensland-born Ray Meagher has been a prolific character actor in Australian films, and on the stage, since the mid 1970s. Meagher epitomises the rough-hewn, knockabout Australian character: his roles reflected this persona with a fair share of villains and policemen. There have been few lead roles for Meagher, except for telefeatures such as *Mail-Order Bride* (1984) and straight-to-video features such as **Bootleg** (1985). Since 1988, however, Meagher has continued this persona in his continuing role as Alf Stewart in the long-running television soap *Home and Away*, and the popularity of this character, and of the show itself, has resulted in few screen performances during this period.

Other Australian films include: **Because He's My Friend** (1978), •**Newsfront** (1978), **The Journalist** (1979), •**Money Movers** (1979), •**The Chant of Jimmie Blacksmith** (1978), •**The Odd Angry Shot** (1979), •**My Brilliant Career** (1979), **The Earthling** (1980), •**Mystery Island** (1980), •**'Breaker' Morant** (1980), •**Hoodwink** (1981), **Mystery at Castle House** (1982), **On the Run** (1982), **The Fire in the Stone** (1983), **The Blue Lightning** (1986), **Short Changed** (1986), **Dark Age** (1987), **The Place at the Coast** (1987), **Luigi's Ladies** (1989).   GM

Media Resource Centre, Adelaide   This membership-based organisation opened on 8 June 1974, a variant in an ambitious scheme, financed by the Whitlam government through the Film, Television and Radio Board of the Australia Council (*see* Australian Film Commission), to make video-production resources available to the community. Today, only Open Channel and Metro-TV remain of this scheme. In Adelaide, where media production has been stimulated by the •South Australian Film Corporation, the centre was also a film-makers' cooperative, alternate cinema exhibitor, film school, and lobbyist. Today the centre is housed in the Lion Arts Centre, where it manages the Mercury Cinema and continues the commitment to support film, video, and new-media production and to advance screen culture.   VINCENT O'DONNELL

Media, Entertainment and Arts Alliance,
see **Unions and associations**

Meillon, John (1934–89) ACTOR
This distinguished Australian actor first appeared at the age of 11 in the ABC's radio serial *Stumpy*. John Meillon made his stage début the following year and joined the Shakespeare Touring Company when he was 16. After supporting roles in •**On the Beach** (1959) and •**The Sundowners** (1960), Meillon worked in the United Kingdom (**The Long and the Short and the Tall**, 1960; **Billy Budd**, 1962; **The Running Man**, 1963; **633 Squadron**, 1964; **Guns at Batasi**, 1964) from 1959 to 1965. After returning to Australia he appeared in •**They're a Weird Mob** (1966) and on television as McGooley's son in the celebrated series *My Name's McGooley*. Meillon specialised in comedic roles, sometimes with sinister overtones, such as that of Charlie, the all-knowing resident who greets Gary Bond on his return to the outback town in •**Wake in Fright** (1971). There were also Gothic overtones in Meillon's next two films, first as the country-town Mayor who deliberately provokes car accidents in •**The Cars that Ate Paris** (1974), followed by **Inn of the Damned** (1975), in which Judith Anderson runs amok among the residents of a rural wayside inn in 1896. These dark roles were interspersed with a lead role in the Walt Disney Production •**Ride a Wild Pony** (1975), in which Meillon's own son played his son. This was followed by •**The Fourth Wish** (1976), with Meillon as Casey, who has to come to terms with the fact that his son has leukaemia and has only a few months to live. Meillon received the 'Best Actor' award from the •Australian Film Institute for this film, which was based on a three-part television play written by Michael •Craig. Robert Bettles, who appeared with Meillon in **Ride a Wild Pony,** played his son Sean in **The Fourth Wish.** Arguably, Meillon's best Australian role was as Pym, the mildly eccentric film exhibitor traversing remote areas of Australia in the 1920s in •**The Picture Show Man** (1977), although he is now best known as Walter Reilly, the long-suffering partner to Mick Dundee in •**Crocodile Dundee** (1986).

Other Australian films include: •Walkabout (1971), Sunstruck (1972), Sidecar Racers (1975), Shimmering Light (1977), •Heatwave (1982), •The Wild Duck (1984), The Camel Boy (1984), The Blue Lightning (1986), Frenchman's Farm (1987), •The Everlasting Secret Family (1988), Crocodile Dundee II (1988), Outback Bound (1988), Bullseye (1989).   GM

Melbourne International Film Festival, *see* Festivals

Melodrama, the early years
Melodrama is at least as pervasive in Australian films prior to the renaissance (see Revival, the) of the 1970s as it is in the films of any other nation. There are few moments of intensity in any Australian film from the 1890s to the 1960s, whether in dramas, action films, or comedies, which are not instantly identifiable as melodramatic. Moreover, because Australian film was exclusively, even aggressively, a popular medium until the 1960s, there may actually have been a higher concentration of melodrama than was common in many places elsewhere in the world, specifically in the respectable middle-class cinemas of the United Kingdom and the USA.

In this understanding, melodrama is a performative 'mode', a way of acting, writing, or directing any scene. But the word has also come to be associated with a kind of 'super-genre' of films about personal suffering, often based in stories of families or of heterosexual love. Included in this super-genre are all those films that slot easily into the familiar Australian category of 'soapies', such as •**The Woman Suffers** (1918) and **The Silence of Dean Maitland** (1914, •1934), but the grouping also embraces other stories of sacrifice, such as •**The Martyrdom of Nurse Cavell** (1916) and •**Mike and Stefani** (1952). Such a super-genre for early Australian film might be extended to include almost every serious fiction film made during this period, and some analysts do tend to divide the whole of the world's output of popular movies into just two categories: comedy and melodrama. But, if there are melodramatic elements in •**The Enemy Within** (1918) or •**King of the Coral Sea** (1954), it still seems more productive to consider these 'action films' or 'adventure films' rather than 'melodramas', because the focus is on movement and excitement rather than on feeling, morality, and character. At the same time, it seems in keeping with tendencies in the films themselves to make a special place within the super-genre of filmed melodrama for melodramas of Australian character such as **The Squatter's Daughter** (•1910, 1933) and •**Sons of Matthew** (1949).

Secular, commercial, feature film production in Australia begins with •**The Story of the Kelly Gang** in 1906. Although not fiction in the usual sense of the word, what survives of the film and what we know of its presentation leaves no doubt that it was about morality, almost from beginning to end. This film's models were drawn in part from the Edwardian stage, but the film-slide-and-lecture presentations of the Salvation Army Limelight Department (see Documentary and non-fiction, silent; Historical representation) are also likely to have been an important influence. In such uplifting shows as **Social Salvation** (1898), Joseph Perry's Limelight Department successfully combined film footage, hand-coloured glass slides, music, and moral education in packages that seemed to appeal to Australian audiences. It goes without saying that the Salvation Army's dramatic entertainments employed the conventions of melodrama to drive home their social and religious messages. Melodrama is intrinsically a moral and educative mode of address: it endeavours to demonstrate what virtue and evil really are behind whatever they may have seemed to be. As was the case in the Salvation Army shows, the intense melodramatic emotions expressed in the surviving fragments of footage from **The Story of the Kelly Gang** were never intended to be experienced 'for themselves', but as vehicles for the lessons about injustice and heroism they imparted.

Moreover, the 'tableaux' type of presentation that the Salvation Army shows inherited and refined from magic-lantern slide lectures and from the conventions of stage melodrama had its own impact on the structure of filmed melodrama. **The Story of the Kelly Gang** is, like early film melodrama from other parts of the world, less a smoothly connected linear narrative than a series of striking 'moving pictures', the key moments of intensity (and instruction) from a virtual story. That is, the story of the Kellys takes second place to the privileged images that, in a certain sense, compose or generate that story and thus the feelings such images arouse and the lessons they teach: Ma Kelly holding a police officer at bay; Father Gibney pleading for the lives of the innocents in the Glenrowan Hotel; Ned in his armour gunned down by the police. Flashes of sensation are what is important to melodrama. Melodramas do not have to be 'good stories': a 'good melodrama' makes us feel in order to make us think.

Before 1911 most Australian films were ostentatiously 'Australian' in content, and the melodramas produced were more or less inevitably melodramas of Australian identity, as **The Story of the Kelly Gang** had been but, in that year, a new production firm, Amalgamated Pictures, made its début with a schedule of six features, at least three of which (**The Luck of Roaring Camp**, **Called Back** and **The Bells**) were not set in Australia. Raymond •Longford and Lottie •Lyell also began their film careers in 1911 with •**The Fatal Wedding**, a melodrama that might have been set anywhere. The popular stage was the source of these films, and of a great deal of film melodrama before and during World War I, such as Longford's 1914 version of **The Silence of Dean Maitland**. Popular history and current events provided the inspiration for such melodramatic films as **The Life Story of John Lee**, or **The Man They Could Not Hang** (1912), and the two (or perhaps three) 1916 features devoted to the underground activities of Edith Cavell during World War I in Belgium (•**The Martyrdom of Nurse Cavell** and **Nurse Cavell and La Revanche**). But there was also a certain number of melodramas written expressly for the screen, the most notable of which may have been Longford and Lyell's first original script, **The Tide of Death** (1912), which dealt with vengeance and a broken family and might have taken place anywhere but just happened to be set in Australia.

Of the surviving films made before 1920, there can be no doubt that Longford and Lyell's •**The Woman Suffers** is among the most interesting, in part because of the way in which it too makes use of its Australian setting as the backdrop for a melodramatic story that cannot be read as specifically Australian. The agents of this narrative are men who use the 'seduction' of women as a weapon in a complex game of honour and revenge. The viewing audience itself is at least partly seduced by the active narrative roles of the masculine protagonists into a certain complicity in their interplay, only to be confronted by its catastrophic results in a series of melodramatic images of the feminine protagonists' suffering that shatter the formal strictures of the conflict and point unmistakably to the oppressive mores that prompted it.

In the 1920s, as a response to what American and European businessmen believed to be a core cinema audience of women, women increasingly became the foci of American and European melodramatic films. Something similar seems to have happened in Australia where, between the wars, many of the most notable melodramas were centred on women. •**A Girl of the Bush** (1921), •**Sunshine Sally** (1922) and Charles •**Chauvel's** first feature, •**The Moth of Moonbi** (1926), adopted the Longford and Lyell convention of staging common melodramatic stories about women in clearly identifiable Australian settings. Other films with kindred plots, such as •**Environment** (1927) and the •McDonagh sisters' •**The Far Paradise** (1928), deliberately avoid showing a specifically Australian landscape, thus 'internationalising' the stories and their settings. There were also some traditional melodramas about masculine protagonists made during the 1920s. These included another version of **The Life Story of John Lee** (1921), which emphasised the tragedy of the protagonist's life—spared only to be lived out, like Job's, in suffering—and **The Dinkum Bloke** (1923), the last of the Longford and Lyell 'Bloke trilogy'.

In the 1930s it became even more common for Australian melodramatic films to be traditional melodramas 'with an Australian accent', or to virtually ignore local settings. •**The Cheaters** (1930) and •**Two Minutes Silence**

(1933), produced by the McDonagh sisters, were deliberately made in an 'international style', as was •Efftee's filmed version of the play, •Clara Gibbings (1934). A third film version of John Lee's story, set in the United Kingdom, was made in 1934, as •The Man They Could Not Hang, by none other than Raymond Longford. The Silence of Dean Maitland was also filmed again in that year, by Ken •Hall, as •Cinesound's second feature. This old-fashioned theatrical melodrama proved popular at the box office, partly because of some astutely up-to-date and prurient publicity about scenes of partial nudity. Indeed, the melodramatic mode coloured almost all the features that Cinesound produced in the 1930s, many of which, like •Lovers and Luggers (1937) and •The Broken Melody (1938), used 'international' settings, stars, and accents. However, even such obviously Australian films as Cinesound's •Orphan of the Wilderness (1936) or the independently produced •Seven Little Australians (1939) were less concerned with articulating national character than with telling a moving story in an Australian setting. One of the most appealing of these films is •Mr Chedworth Steps Out (1939), which is surprisingly delicate in its blend of sentimental comedy and socially inflected melodrama. Cecil •Kellaway gave one of his most tactfully nuanced performances in the title role.

World War II, and the cultural crisis it brought in its wake, also apparently reshaped notions of melodrama to the point that the incidence of 'universal' or traditional stories went into steep decline. Certainly, the melodramatic mode was prominently employed in wartime spy thrillers such as •The Power and the Glory (1941), in the Smiley films (•Smiley, 1956; Smiley Gets a Gun, 1958), and in the Lee •Robinson–Chips •Rafferty adventure films of the 1950s. But, apart from •A Son is Born (1946) and Into the Straight (1949), it is hard to find any all-Australian production that fits obviously into the category of the traditional 'weepie'—from the beginning of the war right up to Giorgio Mangiamele's •Clay (1965). On the other hand, L'Ambitieuse [The Restless and the Damned] (1959), •The Summer of the Seventeenth Doll (1959) and •On the Beach (1959) were among the overtly melodramatic films made in Australia by foreign production companies during this period. Clay itself has a strong claim to being the first example of an 'art cinema' feature made in Australia, based on its languid pace, visual style, and elliptical narrative. As such, it may be said to have heralded a new era of self-consciously artistic film-making, but it did so in the time-honoured tradition of German Expressionism: on the back of a luridly melodramatic plot about menace and a forbidden passion that can be fulfilled only in death.

The success of The Story of the Kelly Gang and the bushranger films appears to have inspired dramas of Australian identity. These films depicted the assertion of noble character in the face of specifically Australian conditions of land and law. That fact that the Australian so identified was often an outlaw tied the nascent bushranger genre all the more securely to the conventions of traditional melodrama as practised by the likes of the Irish playwright Dion Boucicault (1820–90), four of whose plays had been adapted for the Australian screen before the end of 1912.

Other genres of the period 1910–20 melodramatically identified Australians with convicts, miners, bushmen (•The Sick Stockrider, 1913), Anzacs (•The Hero of the Dardanelles, 1915), and pioneer settlers (•The Pioneers, 1916). Unexpectedly, most of these Australian identities were masculine. Still, there were a few, such as the Longford and Lyell collaboration •The Romantic Story of Margaret Catchpole (1911) and John •Gavin's His Convict Bride (1918), that brought together ideas of Australianness and melodramatic ideals in the character of a noble woman.

Although many of the melodramatic films of the decades that followed were Australian in setting but 'universal' in plot, it would not do to downplay the significance of their local specificity. Films such as A Girl of the Bush flaunt their nationalism in the archetypal resonance of their titles, as well as in the touches of local colour and the countryside that frame their stories, and Sunshine Sally shows that she is proudly Australian in the urban dialect that she and her mates speak in the film that bears her name. The melodramas were not about those tests of character that make Australians, but the films asserted an unmistakable Australian identity.

During the 1920s, in films such as •The Breaking of the Drought (1920), •Ginger Mick (1920), and •The Birth of White Australia (1928), melodramatic stories were told about what it means to be truly Australian. In them 'Australian' character was challenged and defined by the land, by war, and by other racial/ethnic groups. Of this cluster of films, one of the most interesting is •For the Term of His Natural Life (1927), in part because it displays many of the melodramatic qualities of films made 10 and 20 years before, and also because its story of noble and ignoble doubles, of saintly suffering at the ends of the earth, and of what is monstrous in the human, seems to demand to be read as an allegory of the forging of Australian character that the other films translate into more explicit terms.

Of course it is possible to read some of the traditional melodramas filmed in Australia as allegories of national character. The Man They Could Not Hang and The Story (or Life) of John Lee, filmed three times from 1912 to 1934, lends itself to such an interpretation. In 1885, because of a quirk in British law, Lee escaped the death penalty when the machinery intended to hang him thrice failed to do its job. At the same time, he had to live out his life (more than 23 years of it) in an English gaol, as a condemned murderer.

Melodrama

Like many other convicts, Lee insisted he had never committed the crime attributed to him, and apparently, near the end of his life, after he had been released into the custody of his nearest family, his protestations of innocence were upheld in the dying confession of another. Although Lee was British and lived out his life in the United Kingdom, there do not seem to have been any British films about him (the 1939 film **The Man They Could Not Hang** is an American horror film unrelated to Lee's story). The melodramatic Australian films about him deal primarily with the years after his miraculous escape from the retribution of the law. Like a transported convict or a migrant, Lee had, in effect, been granted a new life. But, in spite of the clear judgment of heaven (and his own tediously exemplary behaviour), his true worth remained unrecognised: the United Kingdom deemed him something less than a person when, in fact, he may have been something more. The appeal of this tale from popular history to Australians, a population often stigmatised as the castoffs of the mother country, may well have been very deep and strong. Lee's fortitude and virtue, presented hagiographically in the films, arguably provided a model of character for two generations of Australians convinced of their own value but conscious of where they stood in British eyes.

In the 1930s the incidence of overt melodramas of Australian character declined steadily. In part this may have been because of the revival of the backblocks farce in the Dad and Dave series (1932–40). These films, with their melodramatic speeches about pioneer spirit, may have filled some sort of unconscious need for films about the formation of national character. Whatever the cause, **The Squatter's Daughter** (1933) and •**Heritage** (1935) stand out among the melodramas of the 1930s because they are explicitly about Australianness. Both are also, and not coincidentally, about the inheritance of character: that is, about breeding and race. From its first appearance, melodrama tended to see fundamental or essential character as the result of biological heritage, in the sense of 'blood will tell', and it is precisely this tendency that lent itself to exploitation in melodramas of national character all over the world during the years up to World War II.

The Squatter's Daughter is a particularly rich example of this kind of biological variant of the melodrama of Australian character. Like **For the Term of His Natural Life**, made five years before, **The Squatter's Daughter** is a 'remake' of an earlier film that was already a remake of a text in another medium. But where Marcus Clarke's novel was recognised as a classic of Australian literature, the source of the 'original' 1910 **The Squatter's Daughter** was a popular stage melodrama by Edmund Duggan and Bert •Bailey that has apparently seen print only in a 'novel of the play' by Hilda Duggan (1923). Ken Hall's 1933 film eliminated a sig-

nificant bushranging element in the original and, today, the film seems almost obsessively preoccupied with breeding. 'Old Ironbark', the owner of Waratah, is an advocate of all the old-fashioned virtues, including the raising of pure merino sheep. He is apparently struck blind on his journey back to Waratah from abroad, but his blindness is contrived to allow him the better to discern good breeding from bad. The main plot hinges on attempts to dilute Waratah's pure merino stock as part of a scheme by vengeful and misguided representatives of the lower orders to upset the established balance of power, melodramatically equated with the powers of nature in a sensational bushfire sequence. A key subplot focuses on Jimmie Enderby, who is well bred, disabled, and loves Zena, an 'Afghan' (read 'gypsy'—that is, she is of a different 'race'), and the film seems to suggest that there is a correlation between Jimmie's disability and the direction of his passion. In the end, the film refuses either to kill off Jimmie and Zena or to show the consummation of their true love: it simply forgets them and, in their stead, gives us a scene in which Clive Sherrington learns that he is not the pure-bred heir of 'Old Ironbark' that he imagined himself to be, but someone whose past was a lie and whose future is uncertain. To postmodern eyes, Clive, and the couple Jimmie and Zena, appear as strangely prophetic metaphors for the convolutions of contemporary Australian identity, but it is clear that **The Squatter's Daughter** finds that identity more traditionally, in its pure merino sheep and the human pure-breeds whose steadfast character emerges in the trials to which they are subjected: Old Ironbark, Joan Enderby (who owns and manages a rival estate) and Wayne Ridgeway, Ironbark's true son.

World War II, its aftermath, and the concomitant direct exposure to American culture, sparked an increase in the production of films in which the virtues of Australian character were extolled. •**Forty Thousand Horsemen** (1940) and •**The Overlanders** (1946) are undoubtedly the best known of these, but all Chauvel's later films, all the Ealing Films' (see Studios) productions in Australia, as well as at least one Hollywood film, •**The Sundowners** (1960), can be classed among the melodramas of Australia character. At the same time, a film of the 1950s attempted to deal seriously with Australianness somewhat outside of the conventions of melodrama. Cecil •Holmes's •**Three in One** (1957) was resolutely populist in its orientation, but, like its Italian neorealist models, it seemed destined for an 'art-house' audience, as **Clay** would be some eight years later. Holmes's laconic and distanced view of intense feeling has some claim to the status of a 'typically Australian' attitude and, in its own way, **Three in One** is as necessary for the 'cooler' films of the Australian •revival, as anything produced by the New Wave or Hollywood.

WILLIAM D. ROUTT

The villain still pursues her . . . **Joe** (1924)

The hero to the rescue . . . **The Hills of Hate** (1926)

Melodrama

Melodrama, the later years   The rise of the new Australian cinema (see Revival, the) in the 1970s coincided roughly with the rehabilitation of melodrama as a mode as deserving of serious critical discussion and discrimination as any other. There were several important studies from the late 1960s on, including Robert Heilman's *Tragedy and Melodrama: Versions of Experience* (1968), Thomas Elsaesser's article, 'Tales of Sound and Fury' (in *Monogram*, 1972), and Peter Brooks's ground-breaking study of melodrama in relation to the nineteenth-century novel, *The Melodramatic Imagination* (1976). These and other works in the field undertook to theorise the play of melodramatic themes and structures in literature, drama, and film. It is at least arguable that film benefited most from this interest, the word 'melodramatic' most often having been employed as a dismissive pejorative.

Critical and theoretical work on melodrama as a genre argues for an approach to the rendering of human experience in terms of how its protagonist is characteristically seen in conflict with external forces, rather than, as in tragedy, torn between warring inner urges. It is concerned with identifying the Manichean view of the world that underlay so much melodramatic plotting: good and evil are clear and separate opposites, whatever blurring may obscure this dichotomy during the course of the narrative; guilt and innocence will be unequivocally established by the story's end; and reward and punishment will be justly apportioned. Procedurally, melodramatic narrative has been seen as a series of 'blockages' or frustrations delaying an outcome in which the good are vindicated and innocence rewarded, in cathartic release for the audience. It is clear that the classical Hollywood narrative cinema, from the time of D.W. Griffith in the second decade of the twentieth century, through the heyday of the studio system and, most notably, in the 1940s and 1950s, was powerfully allied to the paradigms of melodrama. Theorists describe film melodrama as an 'excessive' mode, as a way of registering the film-makers' attempts to bridge the gap between what is represented on the screen and what it is intended to connote.

Other writing about the melodramatic mode seeks to widen the application of the term. For some time the term was restricted to family melodrama, often derisively referred to as 'women's pictures' but, more recently, melodramatic impulses and structures have been shown to underpin other kinds of film-making. These include action melodramas, in which characterisation is minimal and the protagonist's conflict is wholly external; films in the Gothic horror tradition; small-town melodramas; and thrillers of various kinds; as well as the romantic dramas more widely associated with the term. It might be argued that melodrama, in its stylistic, structural, and thematic interests, is so pervasive that it is less helpful to consider it as a genre than as a mode whose influence is felt across a number of genres.

In the new Australian cinema, melodrama has only rarely been allowed to have its head. In several of his 1970s films, Peter •Weir showed a penchant for melodramatic plotting—and a refusal to carry this through. •The Cars that Ate Paris (1974), •Picnic at Hanging Rock (1975), and •The Last Wave all reveal an essentially melodramatic basis to their plotting, but none actually exploits this for its full worth. In each case, the basic conflict is clearly posited: between small town and stranger; between the College and the Rock (or nurture and nature, or Europe and Australia); and between civilised urban living and threatening primal forces. All three, in their different ways, opt for something arbitrary, unsettling, with apocalyptic overtones, rather than pursuing the impulses that initiate the narratives to their 'logical' conclusions, thereby denying audiences the kind of gratification mentioned earlier. There is, of course, no reason a film-maker should not choose to deflect genre expectations or create a hybrid genre, except that commercial success, one of the imperatives for so expensive a medium, has usually been allied to such satisfaction; a satisfaction that, one might add, Weir embraced in American films such as **Witness** (1985) and **Dead Poets Society** (1989).

Carl •Schultz's •**Careful He Might Hear You** (1983) is still perhaps the most successful Australian venture into the field of family melodrama. At its heart is a struggle for the custody of an orphaned small boy, P.S., a conflict between two aunts who represent opposing principles and opposing views of Australia. Lila (Robyn •Nevin) is the 'Aussie battler' who is motivated by warm-hearted concern for P.S. and has, with her husband George, given him a secure home in a Sydney suburban weatherboard, with street cricket for games and 'common' neighbours. The other aunt, Vanessa (Wendy •Hughes), offers him a far grander house, the prospect of European tours, private education, and an Anglophile view of what is valuable in life. The film eschews a simplistic perspective in the working out of these conflicting influences, and arrives, very satisfyingly, at the only possible conclusion. In the 'excessive' form of melodrama, the two impulses at work in the life of P.S. are reinforced at every level in contrasts of *mise en scène*, soundtrack, and editing. Within the framework of melodrama, the film offers a commentary on what has been described (by novelist Martin Boyd) as the 'geographical schizophrenia' that underlies the Australian experience for so many of its population: the New World–Old World conflict that is at the heart of many American films finds its Australian equivalent in several films of this period (for example, **Picnic at Hanging Rock**; •**My Brilliant Career**, 1979; and •**Gallipoli**, 1981), but nowhere is it developed with such melodramatic vigour—and rigour—as in **Careful He Might Hear You**.

Among the other films in which melodrama is allowed its head, two of the most interesting are Steve •Jodrell's

•Shame (1988) and Ian •Barry's •Minnamurra (1989), neither of which achieved any commercial success, although Shame has since attracted a good deal of discussion, including a book-length study by Stephen Crofts. The film's title is double-edged: it points to the thematic agenda of the film, in which a small-town is made to feel shame by the actions of a disinterested outsider; and it also alludes to its famous American ancestor, the classic Western Shane (1952), in which an outsider rides into a vulnerable community and stays to help it deal with a threat to its safety. Asta Cadell (Deborra-Lee •Furness), a city barrister, rides into the small Western Australian township of Ginborak and into a web of class- and gender-driven prejudices, brought to a head by the rape of a young girl by the son of the town's wealthiest citizen. Its strength lies in the melodramatic clarity with which the polarities are established: innocence and guilt are in no doubt; all that is in doubt is how justice, which comes to be personified in Asta, will bring about the protection of the former and the punishment of the latter. Despite the classic simplicity with which the issues are laid before the viewer, the film resonates beyond its particular setting to mount a critique of Australian patriarchal brutalities, the hypocrisies of mateship, and the power of wealth in a society where other means of social demarcation are less clear. Another small-town melodrama that has acquired a critical reputation since the time of its release in 1987 is Ken •Cameron's •The Umbrella Woman, in which a justifiably bored young wife (Rachel •Ward) is led by frustration to pursue the sexual attentions of the new barman in town (Sam •Neill), who brings a superficial whiff of city sophistication to the arid rituals of her life. This film, like Shame, also questions the mores of a male-dominated community and is very sympathetic in its depiction of a woman's sexual and emotional needs, although it offers, in terms of melodrama, only a very muted sense of closure, implying that those needs remain unmet.

The family has been characteristically the site of many notable melodramatic fictions, although in new Australian cinema it more often provided the occasion for episodic rites-of-passage narratives (see Rites of passage). Three films that, in their different ways, find their centres in family matters are Minnamurra, Gillian •Armstrong's •Hightide (1987), and Scott •Hicks's •Shine (1996). Of these, Minnamurra (a critical and commercial failure) exhibits the most conventional trappings of melodrama: a spirited heroine determined to save the family home when her father dies; a scheming neighbour; two contrasted suitors; faithful family retainers; and a preoccupation with wills and inheritances. (It shares some of these characteristics with the hugely successful action adventure •The Man from Snowy River, 1982.) It is not a subtle film, but its melodramatic vigour and visual and kinetic excitement give it a narrative drive not often found in the Australian cinema of the period. Hightide is a low-key account of a singer, Lilli (Judy •Davis), stranded in a Victorian seaside resort where she is found drunk by a teenage girl who she realises is the daughter she has deserted. Instead of opting for the kind of mother–daughter melodrama of, say, King Vidor's classic Stella Dallas (1937), Armstrong instead dissipates such potential by settling for a more ambiguous morality and for the kind of 'realism' that was more to the contemporary critical taste—and which seems an obdurate refusal of emotional possibilities. Shine, loaded with honours and awards, and based on the real-life story of the pianist David Helfgott (played with dazzling skill and charisma by Geoffrey •Rush), fuses the 'excessive' and exalting aspects of melodrama with the panache of an old-time Hollywood biopic. It does so with an intelligence and passion rare in Australian cinema, as it charts the efforts of the piano-playing child prodigy to surmount the pressures imposed on him by his Holocaust-victim father, to climb out of the mental breakdown into which this pushes him, and to rehabilitate himself with the loving care of the astrologer who loves and marries him. It is, in itself, an inspiring story and it is made into an inspiring cinematic occasion by the film's awareness of the seductive power of melodrama, of conflicts clearly articulated, and of an emotionally charged *dénouement*.

Among the rest of the films that show at least an awareness of melodramatic procedures are two films based on novels by Colleen McCullough: Michael •Pate's •Tim (1979), in which a middle-aged woman gambles on happiness with a handsome but intellectually handicapped young man (Mel •Gibson); and Lex •Marinos's •An Indecent Obsession (1985), in which tensions—romantic and otherwise—run high in the psychiatric ward of a military hospital on a Pacific island at the end of World War II. In An Indecent Obsession, the sister-in-charge (Wendy •Hughes) provides the focus for assorted passions and resentments that are heightened by the arrival of a handsome young sergeant (Gary •Sweet). Neither of these films (popular with neither critics nor audiences) fully capitalised on their emotional potential: the script in each was full of underdeveloped motivation and barely serviceable dialogue, and the relationships seemed consequently *jejune*: great film melodramas have, however, evolved from less promising origins. The sub-genre of romantic melodrama was better served by John •Duigan's •Far East and Peter Weir's •The Year of Living Dangerously (both 1982), films that combine love stories with political events in the volatile climates of the Philippines and Indonesia respectively. If neither film works the love-and-politics combination as eloquently as, say, Casablanca so famously did, this may be because the polarities of the 1982 films are less clearcut than they were in 1942 and the changes in sexual mores make the 'love vs duty' dichotomy less decisive.

The films mentioned above could all essentially be contained in the traditional melodramatic categories that stress romantic relationships, family and small-town conflicts, and stories of passionate commitment. Another batch of films should be included in this survey because they also make use of the structuring distinctions discussed so far. These are thrillers and action films, in which forces of good are pitted against those of evil, most notably Dr George *Miller's *Mad Max (1979) and *Mad Max 2 (1981). These combine brilliantly filmed action with moral allegory. Further examples include Richard *Franklin's cinematically knowing, Gothic science-fiction thriller, *Patrick (1978), in which a plucky nurse thwarts the sinister machinations of a strange hospital; and *Roadgames (1981), which plays wittily with many melodramatic conventions, such as the missing corpse, and mistaken identity and purpose. Two films that combine such conventions with an awareness of the kinds of corruption possible in big-city developments, Donald *Crombie's *The Killing of Angel Street (1981) and Phil *Noyce's *Heatwave (1982), both recall a Sydney journalist who protested against such developments and subsequently disappeared. Noyce's *Dead Calm (1989) is set in the enclosed world of a yacht at sea, a thriller in which a woman traumatised by the death of her child is sexually challenged when a psychotic young killer boards the yacht. Even Baz *Luhrman's musical *Strictly Ballroom (1992), works some melodramatic elements (youthful rebellion, generational conflict, romantic and professional contrasts) to popular effect. There are other titles one might adduce, but these are enough to suggest the range of films in which melodramatic impulses are at work, although not often carried through with the full-throttled approach that characterises such Hollywood exemplars of the genre as It's a Wonderful Life (1946), Laura (1944), and Random Harvest (1942). The literary and theatrical taste of the 1970s was not likely to applaud melodrama, and the new Australian cinema won critical attention largely for gentle literary *adaptations and quiet social realism. What is more surprising is that film-makers were, for the most part, ready to acquiesce in an aesthetic that might have seemed to be at odds with proven commercial success.   BRIAN McFARLANE

The Menace

1928. *Director:* Cyril J. Sharpe. *Producer:* Percy Juchau. *Scriptwriter:* Louise Miller (?). *Director of photography:* Jack Bruce. B&W.

The very little that remains of **The Menace** contains quite a bit of fun. There are two 'impenetrable' disguises, two resourceful heroines, and some improbable action. Many better-known Australian films from this period offer the viewer a great deal less. Apparently, the plot involved drug-smuggling and, as was unfortunately all too common at the time, may have held the Chinese community partly to blame.   WILLIAM D. ROUTT

Mendelsohn, Ben (1969–) ACTOR   The gangly, good-natured persona that Ben Mendelsohn honed in a batch of films at the start of the 1990s can give way to darker possibilities, as he showed in True Love and Chaos in 1996, in the role of the dangerous Jerry. Indeed, he first made a strong impression as the unstable Trevor in John *Duigan's *The Year My Voice Broke (1987), a rites-of-passage drama set in rural New South Wales, in which, in contrast to the gentle Danny (Noah *Taylor), he is the destructive member of a teenage triangle, lawless, and undisciplined. It was his next three films that established him as the engaging, somewhat inarticulate young man who wins audience sympathy: as Gary, the apprentice mechanic, in Ray *Argall's *Return Home (1990), having trouble with his girlfriend and finding a surrogate father in the garage owner's brother who is also trying to sort out his life; as the nervous teenager, Danny, who buys a dud Jaguar to impress a girl in Nadia *Tass's *The Big Steal (1990), and takes on the sleazy salesman (Steve *Bisley); and as Carey, the factory assistant in Mark *Joffe's *Spotswood (1992), an amiable comedy of industrial relations in a Melbourne suburban moccasin factory. In all three, Mendelsohn brought a sharp intelligence to the playing of the none-too-bright young man, in pursuit of girls who seem just a step ahead and above him, fundamentally honest, and in reaction against insensitive or opportunist elders. In Aleksi Vellis's *Nirvana Street Murder (1991), he had a variant on this role as Luke, the elder brother of the dysfunctional, wildly unpredictable Boadey, who provides further ongoing problems for Luke who already has another set with his Greek-Australian girlfriend and her family.

For a few years, it seemed difficult to avoid Mendelsohn in Australian films, and his authority in discriminating among these late teenagers/twenty-somethings grew with each exposure. Since then, he has worked again for three of his earliest directors: for Duigan in *Sirens (1994), for Joffe in the touching, multi-star *Cosi (1996), and for Tass in Amy (1998). He has also done a good deal of television work, in the ABC's *GP*, for instance. It will be interesting to see how fluidly he negotiates the transition into fully mature roles; he has been an attractively ingenuous figure as the young man on the brink of serious adulthood.

Other Australian films: The Still Point (1985), *Quigley (1991), Say a Little Prayer (1992), Map of the Human Heart (1993), Metal Skin (1993), Idiot Box (1996), Sample People (1999).

BMcF

Menglet, Alex (1956–) ACTOR   Alexei Menglet was born in Moscow, of theatrical parents, and arrived in Australia via West Germany in 1980. He found work under Jean-Pierre Mignon at Anthill Theatre in Melbourne, and took small television roles such as a Russian defector in

Ben Mendelsohn

Mercurio

Skyways and a KGB agent in *Holiday Island*, and later played a film director in *Carson's Law* (1983). His television career culminated in the title role in the miniseries *The Petrov Affair* (1987) but, in film, he has played only smaller roles: Paul in **The Still Point** (1985), William Brahe in **Wills and Burke** (1985), Sullivan in **Sky Pirates** (1986), a Telecom man in •**The More Things Change** (1986), Laszlo in **Georgia** (1988), Karl Heinmann in **Against the Innocent** (1989), Mr Goldman in •**Celia** (1989), Big Mac in **Holidays on the River Yarra** (1991), Con 2 in •**A Woman's Tale** (1991), and Tito in **Zone 39** (1997). Kim Trengrove (*Out of Character*, 1991) describes him as 'a highly passionate man with a great sense of mischief, charm and mock diffidence'. His accent limits the roles available to him, but his reputation continues to grow.

IB

Mercurio, Gus (1928–) ACTOR Australia's highest-ranking boxing referee, marine, chiropractor, cake-decorator and television host, this Milwaukee-born actor came to Australia for the 1956 Olympics and a job as a chiropractor at Ballarat, and has resided in Australia since the 1970s. With his gravelly voice, strong physique, and outgoing personality, Gus Mercurio was a natural for the 1970s action television series *Cash and Company* and its sequel, *Tandarra*. The western elements of the series, including the distinctive iconography of guns, costumes, horses, and setting, and narrative elements, similar, in a much less complex way, to Sam Peckinpah's **The Wild Bunch** (1969), were extended into a feature film, **Raw Deal** (1977). After the series concluded, Mercurio worked extensively in the Australian industry as a character actor in films that range from the dreadful **Turkey Shoot** (1982) to the more respectable •**The Man from Snowy River** (1982,) and •**Doing Time for Patsy Cline** (1997), together with a good deal of television work.
Other Australian films include: Alvin Rides Again (1974), •Eliza Fraser (1976), High Rolling (1977), Harlequin (1980), The Return of Captain Invincible (1983), Running from the Guns (1987), Crocodile Dundee II (1988), Official Denial (1993), Lightning Jack (1994).

GM

Mercurio, Paul (1963–) ACTOR Paul Mercurio, a dancer, began his film career in a stunning manner as Scott Hastings, the 'rebel' in •**Strictly Ballroom** (1992) who simultaneously threatens the conservative dance establishment while romancing and training his novice dancing partner, Fran (Tara •Morice). The film was a spectacular début for Mercurio, who was able to combine his expertise in dance with a role designed to enhance his romantic appeal. The film was successful on both counts. Mercurio's next film role was a strange choice: the masochistic Elliot Slater, who pays to live on a fantasy resort island of bondage and S&M devotees in the film adaptation of Anne Rice's 'underground' novel **Exit to Eden** (1994). In this limp comedy, directed by Hollywood veteran Gary Marshall, Mercurio has no opportunity to dance and his romantic interludes consist mainly of floggings from Dana Delany. The failure of the film represented a significant setback to Mercurio's film aspirations. A supporting role in another Hollywood film, **Red Ribbon Blues** (1995), was followed by the lead role in the independently produced American science-fiction film **Dark Planet** (1995). Mercurio returned to the Australian cinema in the outback thriller •**The Back of Beyond** (1995) and the Mark •Joffe-directed comedy •**Cosi** (1996).
Other Australian films: Welcome to Woop Woop (1997), James (1997).

GM

Mike and Stefani

1952. Film Division, Dept of Interior for the Department of Information. *Producer, Scriptwriter*: R. Maslyn Williams. *Photography*: Reg Pearse. *Music*: Robert Hughes. *Narration*: Martin Royal, Josephine O'Neill. 64 min. B&W. *Cast*: Mycola, Stefanie, Ginga, Ladu, Valerie Paling (as themselves).

Mike and Stefani, one of the finest achievements of the film division of the Australian government's Department of Information, eschews the conventions of institutional documentary in favour of a romantic-realist drama of displaced persons in postwar Europe. The story of a Ukrainian couple separated by war, the film traces their separate stories of labour camps and months of chaos and loneliness in the resettlement camps of postwar Europe, and their struggle to relocate themselves, eventually in Australia. Designed to address perceptions that immigration selection procedures were inadequate, the film emerges as a paean to the human spirit such as that found in the Italian neo-realist films in the postwar years.

Ron Maslyn •Williams and cameraman Reg Pearse made this beautiful unfolding film of a family's struggle with the forces of history on a shoestring in war-ravaged Europe, only to see the film caught uncomfortably between a commercial film trade unwilling to accept the film's gritty realism and a government institution incapable of comprehending its scope and length. The reunion and selection interview scenes in **Mike and Stefani** are two of the best narrative moments in Australian documentary.

DEANE WILLIAMS

Miller, Dennis (1937–) ACTOR Dennis Miller's career as a stage actor stretches back to 1959, and he has had seasons with most of Australia's leading theatre companies, as well as much television experience, in such long-running series as *Bellbird* (as Constable Des Davies), *Homicide*, and *A Country Practice*. His first feature film was Tim •Burstall's •**Stork** (1971) and, since then, he has become a regular and enjoyable character actor in Australian films. He conveys a pervasively Australian essence in whatever part he plays, whether comic (as in the popular stage play *And the Big Men Fly*) or sinister (the chauffeur in Michael •Thornhill's •**The Everlasting Secret Family**, 1988) or simply a sturdy good bloke (as in Philip •Noyce's •**Heatwave**, 1982). Like many of the best screen actors, he works with economy to sketch the outlines of his character, filling these in with convincing detail. One of the best film illustrations of his approach, as it seems to a viewer, is as Ralph, the beaming lay preacher, in Claude Whatham's underrated thriller, •**Hoodwink** (1981), in which his basic good nature is increasingly at odds with his suspicions about his wife's (Judy •Davis) relationship with the 'blind' prisoner (John •Hargreaves), whom he takes into his home. It was a shrewdly observed piece of character work. He gave excellent performances as Horse, a miner on a Central Australian drilling site, in Burstall's •**The Last of the Knucklemen** (1979), and as Redford, a good-humoured crim, in Stephen •Wallace's •**Stir** (1980). In more recent years, he has been seen more often on the small screen rather than the large.

Other Australian films: Neville Mendham, Agronomist (1968, doc., co-n.), The Hot Centre of the World (1970, short), •Alvin Purple (1973), The Great MacArthy (1975), •Eliza Fraser (1976), •Mad Dog Morgan (1976), The Journalist (1979), •Star Struck (1982), A Most Attractive Man (1982, short), Platypus Cove (1983), Buddies (1983), •Silver City (1984), Shark's

Dennis Miller

Paradise (1986), Frog Dreaming (1986), •Evil Angels (1988), •Emerald City (1989), This Won't Hurt a Bit (1993), •Broken Highway (1994).   BMcF

Miller, Dr George (1945–) DIRECTOR

Queensland-born George Miller graduated as a doctor and practised in Sydney for 18 months before forming a partnership with producer Byron •Kennedy. Their first film, a 1972 short called **Violence in the Cinema Part 1** (there never was a part 2), displayed their impressive film-making skills, particularly editing, in this cutting satire directed at those critics who were attacking violence in the cinema in the early 1970s, particularly those voices raised against Sam Peckinpah's **Straw Dogs** (1971) and Stanley Kubrick's **A Clockwork Orange** (1972). Miller's ability to generate maximum tension and emotion from the *mise-en-scène* continued in his first feature, the ground-breaking action film •**Mad Max** (1979) and the international success of this film resulted in offers from the Hollywood studios. Miller, after spending some time in the USA, returned to Australia with Kennedy to direct •**Mad Max 2** (1981), which was followed by the television miniseries *The Dismissal* (1983). Miller co-directed this with Phillip •Noyce, George •Ogilvie, Carl Shultz, and John •Power.

After accepting an offer from Steven Spielberg to direct the final segment in **The Twilight Zone: The Movie** (1983) in Hollywood, Miller returned to Australia to direct, with George Ogilivie, the final film in the Mad Max trilogy, •**Mad Max Beyond Thunderdome** (1985). Except for an unhappy experience in Hollywood directing **The Witches of Eastwick** (1987), starring Jack Nicholson, Cher, Susan Sarandon, and Michelle Pfeiffer, Miller spent the rest of the 1980s and 1990s producing films for the production company Kennedy–Miller (•**The Year My Voice Broke**, 1987; •**Dead Calm**, 1989; •**Flirting**, 1991; •**Babe**, 1995) and television miniseries (*Vietnam*, 1987; *Bangkok Hilton*, 1989). Miller's only directorial credit during this period was the Hollywood-based drama, **Lorenzo's Oil** (1992), the powerful, true-life story of Michaela and Augusto Odone who overcame medical conservatism to keep their son alive after he is diagnosed with adrenoleukodystrophy, a degenerative disease. Miller also wrote, produced, and directed his personal overview of Australian cinema, **40,000 Years of Dreaming** (1996).

Other Australian films include: Babe: Pig in the City (1998).
                                                                GM

Miller, George (1943–) DIRECTOR

Scottish-born director who migrated to Melbourne with his parents when he was a child. George Miller began directing series, such as *Division 4, Matlock Police, Cash and Company, The Sullivans, Bluey,* and *Young Ramsay* for television in the late 1960s and 1970s before graduating to popular miniseries such as *Against The Wind* (1978), *The Last Outlaw* (1980), *All The Rivers Run* (1983), *Anzacs* (1985) and *The Far Country* (1986). Miller's first feature film, the commercially successful •**The Man from Snowy River** (1982), was produced by Geoff •**Burrowes** who worked with Miller at Crawford's in the 1970s. Since **The Man from Snowy River**, Miller has been a prolific director of Australian (**Cool Change**, 1986; **Bushfire Moon**, 1987; **Over the Hill**, 1992; **Gross Misconduct**, 1993) and overseas productions (**The Aviator**, 1984; **The Neverending Story 2: The Next Chapter**, 1991; **Andre**, 1994) that resist strict auterist classification and generic consistency, and are characterised mainly by their commercial basis—although there is a relatively high quotient of 'family' or children's films in his output, such as **Zeus and Roxanne** (1997).

Other Australian films include: •**In Search of Anna** (1979, ass. d.), The Chain Reaction (1980, ass. p.), Les Patterson Saves the World (1987).   GM

Miller, Natalie, *see* In conversation with Natalie Miller (p. 317) *and* Sharmill Films

Natalie Miller

Milliken, Sue (1940–) PRODUCER Sue Milliken was a journalist before working on continuity for ABC television and then on the television series *Skippy*. Her first production credit was as production manager on the Disney telefeature *Born to Run* (1976). Samson Films was set up with the profits from this, making **Weekend of Shadows**

(1978), on which Milliken was associate producer. Her first full credits as producer were with Tom •**Jeffrey** on •**The Odd Angry Shot** (1979) and **Fighting Back** (1982). In 1980, she began to manage the Australian branch of the completion bond company, Film Finances. She continued to do this successfully while producing in her own right •**The Fringe Dwellers** (1986), **Les Patterson Saves the World** (1987), **Black Robe** (1991, the first official co-production between Australia and Canada), •**Sirens** (1994), •**Dating the Enemy** (1996), and •**Paradise Road** (1997). She conducted a major review of the •South Australian Film Corporation in 1988, and chaired a review of the Western Australian film industry in 1992. In 1993 the •Australian Film Institute presented her with the Raymond Longford Award and, in December that year, she became chair of the •Australian Film Commission, a position she held until June 1997.   IB

Miner's Luck, A

1911. Production Company: Photo Vista, sponsored by Pathé Frères B & W. *Length*: 1000 ft.

Miner's Luck is an example of an 'undocumented' film from the early years of Australian production. Apparently mentioned nowhere in contemporary accounts, this complete one-reel film survived by accident. Today it is the earliest complete Australian fiction film known to exist. It tells a simple story of money and gender. A banker from the city buys a successful miner's claim. A drunken, lustful labourer steals the money and imprisons the miner in his own shaft. A sundowner then steals the swag from the fleeing labourer. Meanwhile, the miner's two daughters have discovered the terrible deed and set about putting things right. The true hero of the piece is Vera, the youngest daughter, who is one of those serious little girls who appears to have been born permanently attached to a pony. It is she, at any rate, who trots in from the back of the frame and scoops up the money from the sundowner's stash in a lightning strike from the saddle. It is not difficult to discern in **Miner's Luck** a perfect fable in miniature about certain economic and cultural forces at work in twentieth-century Australia.

WILLIAM D. ROUTT

Minnamurra

1989. Director: Ian Barry. *Producer*: John Sexton. *Scriptwriter*: John Sexton. *Director of photography*: Ross Berryman. *Music*: Mario Millo. 92 min. *Cast*: Jeff Fahey (Ben Creed), Tushka Bergen (Alice May Richards), Steven Vidler (Jack Donaghue), Richard Moir (Bill Thompson), Shane Briant (Allenby). *Alternative title*: **The Fighting Creed** (video).

Although this film neither won favour with reviewers nor found substantial audiences, it is an enjoyable fling at

In conversation with
NATALIE MILLER

Did anything in your background or education incline you to an interest in film?

It came from a childhood of just going to the movies. My parents lived in St Kilda and every Saturday night they had permanent seats at the Palais Theatre, and I would often get taken. That probably introduced me to the world of film. I was absolutely besotted with the MGM musicals and that's what started it all. I had a teenage crush on Peter Lawford, would go to any lengths to find out fragments of information about him; he even came to Australia to film *Kangaroo and I went with a girlfriend to where he was shooting. I guess a lot of people had this experience of loving Hollywood. But, no, none of my family was involved in the business; my father had a drapery store in Bourke Street, so I suppose we were very urban people.

As I understand it, you came to film work via PR.

When I finished my Bachelor of Arts course at Melbourne University, where I'd majored in English, I knocked on doors and got a job in a small public relations company. I was always very interested in writing and I got trained in journalism and public relations, and was a jack-of-all-trades in this small company. I learnt hands-on business skills and, when I left after a number of years, I looked for a freelance journalist job, and got a position at the ABC in the publicity department, and then in television publicity. I did Channel 2 publicity for a number of years.

How useful has that PR experience been to you in film distribution and exhibition?

It's very useful really. After I left the ABC, and I had a child by then and was looking for freelance work, I got a job at the Melbourne Film Festival. I did the public relations work there with Erwin Rado. I worked very closely with him for years and years. I think it was that combination of the public relations work with the Festival and my interest in film that led to my buying my first film, **The Exterminating Angel**. So it was the combination of my interest and skills that probably led to distribution. As a distributor, apart from buying the film, you're getting it out there to the public and that involves public relations.

What is a distributor and what is an exhibitor?

A distributor is a person who takes on a film, buys the rights to it for a certain period, usually pays a royalty for those rights, and is then responsible for looking after that film in their territory. If I buy the Australasian rights, I'm responsible for bringing that film to the public in our territory and, to do this, I've got to negotiate to get it into a cinema. I've got to market the film, design the ads, make sure trailers, posters, and materials are ready; there's a multitude of things a distributor does. The biggest film I've ever handled as a distributor is the Australian film *Crackers, which went out nationally and in all the multiplexes. Having an Australian film, we had all the stars here, so it was a question of getting them interviewed by the television and the press, and running press previews. All those jobs come under the banner of the distributor, whereas an exhibitor owns the cinema and, if you own the cinema, you're responsible for planning what films you want to put in it, booking them, negotiating the terms with the distributor. The distributor gets a percentage of the box office when a film plays in a cinema, and the exhibitor negotiates this. It's the exhibitor's responsibility to bring that film to their particular audience and good exhibitors will do an extra lot of promotional work to promote the films they have on in their cinema. So it's a joint effort.

As distributor, you're making money for yourself and for the company from whom you bought it?

You pay the company in advance. The first part of your earning goes back to pay for the prints and the trailers, and very often you might do a lot of work and not even recoup what you've outlayed. Once you have recouped that, then they take half of it again, so unless you have a real hit it's not easy to do that well as a distributor.

Why did you want to be an exhibitor as well?

When I was buying films, I thought it would be good to have a cinema to place my own films in, but the industry changed and, after a few years, I actually couldn't afford to buy the sort of films that I used to buy, like **The Tree of the Wooden Clogs**. Suddenly all this arthouse fare became the darling of everybody—

not like the days when I bought my first films and prices were low. There were more buyers in the market, with people outbidding each other.

You set up Sharmill in 1967. How did it come about and where does the name come from?

The name Sharmill was just hastily thought up when I bought **The Exterminating Angel** and I had to register a company name to make my purchase. It came from my maiden name Sharpe, the 'shar' of Sharpe and the 'mill' of Miller, my married name.

And it came about because you wanted to buy **The Exterminating Angel?**

It occurred to me that there were films in the Melbourne Film Festival that were never bought, and never seen by the public other than at the Festival. I mean a film like **The Exterminating Angel,** a masterpiece, had already been in a festival some years prior, and I thought, let's see if we can bring it into the country. So I hired the Palais St Kilda and put it on and was amazed how people queued round the block for it.

Was the logical order of things to go into distribution first; then, when you had a film you wanted to show, it became a matter of exhibition?

I think you could go either way. If you're an exhibitor and you're finding it hard to get product from somebody else, if you're in a competitive area, then the logic would be to buy your own to supply your own cinema. So it can go either way, they're very interlinked.

When did you buy into or lease the Longford Cinema?

That's leasing. Fourteen years ago. It was a 50/50 partnership between Michael Walsh and Andrew Pike and me. I went into partnership with them in the Longford and some years later we bought Michael out and still later Andrew moved out. So at the moment, I'm the sole leaseholder of the Longford, but things in our business can change every week. At the time, I thought I'd like a cinema, but I wouldn't go into one unless it was one I had a real feeling for. The Longford had the •Australian Film Institute [AFI] as a tenant for some years but it was very difficult in a high-cost cinema area to make a go of it. I said to the owner that, if the AFI left, I'd be interested in going in, and that's what happened. I was very lucky to have that opportunity because, at that stage, people were going out of cinemas. Video had just started and people were

closing cinemas. I knew the area, I used to work and live here, and I knew it would have potential.

How close an eye do you keep personally on its working?

I do all my own ads and programming but once your business grows you can't be as hands-on as you were in the days when you had your distribution in only one cinema. Six years ago Barry Peak of the Valhalla [repertory cinema] asked me would I be interested in looking at a cinema in Carlton, and I said yes because that's another area I knew, from when I'd been to Melbourne University. Carlton and South Yarra are two of the best areas for the cosmopolitan-type operations we want to run, so this unlikely partnership of Longford and Valhalla started up at the Nova with two screens and we wondered at the time how we'd fill them. A couple of years later we had four and then five screens, and we plan to have eight. We then went on, two years ago, to develop a Nova in Adelaide and I'm a shareholder in that.

Is choosing the films for the Longford wholly your decision?

I'd discuss it with my staff because I'm like that, but basically it's my decision.

And what kind of working relations do you have with the major distributors whose films you quite often screen?

Oh very close. Having a single screen these days is very difficult because you have to be free at the time you have a chance to get a film and, not only that, but also I'm competing now with three other arthouses in the area. We're talking at one of the toughest times that I've had. We had big plans to triple the Longford and we shelved them for the time being; it was a bit expensive and then we revised the plans, but we're just waiting to see what happens in the area rather than commit ourselves.

Do you have an over-all policy about programming at the Longford?

I do have a policy but I can't always uphold it because films I want mightn't be available at the time. If I'd been able to fit in **The Thief,** I would have to keep it as an arthouse film, but these days even the subtitled films are very difficult to get the returns on.

Sometimes you have to go commercial. I ran **Crackers** because it was my passion. It might have been too commercial for the Longford; it's probably as commercial as I'd ever get but, in the name of Australian films, you can go a bit commercial. The ideal films that have worked there are things like •**Shine, Like Water for Chocolate, Once Were Warriors,** and •**The Piano.** These have been some of the big successes over the years, along with **Mona Lisa** and **Ju Dou.** We played films like **The Sacrifice** and I like to think they were a success; because they were great films, they didn't have to do so well. **The Sacrifice** was disappointing, it was a wonderful film, and you think, why aren't people coming to see it? Another big success was **Angel at My Table.** For about 10 years I had a dream run and hardly anything was disappointing. In more recent times, when I haven't always had the pick of the bunch to run, I've had some disappointments.

You're sticking your neck out more than distributors who just have antennas alert for commercial success.
I was always sticking my neck out but there is a niche audience, and I think the niche audience knows what it wants to see. It doesn't necessarily want to support a film just because it's an arthouse film, but it seems to have an antenna about the ones it wants to support or know about.

How important was your attendance at overseas festivals in determining what Sharmill would buy?
The first time I went to Cannes, and I've been going there for more than 20 years, was a very big experience for me, and I think it gave me a panorama of world cinema. I think it's very important to have that panorama; in learning the trade I found that going to Cannes gave me that concentrated time to do it. It's wildly competitive and hard work these days, but it has its moments of enjoyment. In the old days, they used to stop for two hours for lunch and go to the beach; there's none of that any more. You're up and out early in the morning because (a) the festival's grown, it's huge, and (b) there is so much more product and so many more competitors.

Has the arthouse market grown a lot?
I think it has and that's why I think the major exhibitors are looking to us. The major companies are picking up world rights to these films, and it makes it much more difficult to buy. So you run around trying to find that extra little gem that nobody else has got and half the time you find it's either been sold already or one of your competitors is eyeing it.

In this highly competitive market have you missed out on any films you particularly wanted to get?
I miss out on them all the time as a distributor. My latest pride and joy, apart from this experience of doing a national comedy, is that I've just bought at Cannes this year a film called **Love is the Devil** directed by John Maybury starring Sir Derek Jacobi; it's about the life of Francis Bacon. It's really brilliantly made and that gives me a lot of pleasure, so I don't stop to think, will I make money? I know I'm responsible for the producer and the company but, if you put your passion into exhibiting it, the rest will follow—hopefully.

Do you detect any differences between the ethos of the Longford and that of the Nova?
The Nova can service an across-the-board audience very easily whereas I find the Longford probably will verge more to an older audience these days, and I think a lot of that's to do with the fact the older audience doesn't like going into multiplexes. I think it likes coming to a boutique cinema. That's why I think this movement of arthouse in multiplexes will have its place but it will never replace a boutique cinema. I think we give the personal service at both our boutique cinemas but, for South Yarra, we have a fairly loyal audience. Most of the films we play at both the Longford and the Nova come from other distributors, say, from Polygram or NewVision or Roadshow. There's a whole lot of distributors out there and we deal with all of them all the time. We do a mix of all their product.

What do you think is the importance of the arthouse cinema in the overall pattern of distribution and exhibition in Australia?
It's extremely important because the arthouse distributor pioneers new directors. I mean, you buy a film like Jim Jarmusch's **Strangers in Paradise,** and the next time round a bigger distributor will pick it up, and then the next time round you see one of the majors has got that film. Take Steven Soderbergh's **Sex, Lies and Videotape,** which NewVision bought as a distributor; now the new Soderbergh is owned by UIP, and has bigger stars in it. We put a lot of work into establishing the names of directors and then it's a fact of business life that next time round you mightn't get that film, you certainly wouldn't as a distributor, and so you move on and try to pioneer somebody else.

You had some producing experience in the 1970s, with In Search of Anna *and* The Great MacArthy. *How did you get into that?*

I distributed [director] Esben Storm's film •27A (1974) and we went on to make **In Search of Anna** and I had a bit of experience on the production side. I'm not sure how I got into **The Great MacArthy**, but that's where I learnt about film-making, talking to the producer and director along the way, finding locations, all sorts of things. This could easily have taken me on a career as producer. I went on to do a half-hour short with Malcolm Robertson and Alan •Hopgood; we were going to make a feature together and bring Tom Conti out to star in it; and we were in pre-production when the money fell away. It was around the time I took over the Longford. I just felt, I don't know if I've got the temperament for a producer. I'm sure I could do the job, but you need a lot of patience when the money and the projects fall away. Also, I like to know what I'm doing when I get up in the morning. You've got to be so tenacious about it all. Anyway, I had this opportunity of exhibition so my career veered away from producing, but I let out that sort of interest by being on the Board of Film Victoria for many years. It involved a lot of script-reading and giving money to films.

In the 30 odd years since you established Sharmill have you been able to identify any major trends in exhibition and distribution?

When I took over the Longford in November 1984, there wasn't even a multiplex. I opened my Longford when cinemas were closing down, and, then a few years later, suddenly I saw this multiplex explosion at the same time as all these individual sites were closing down and, as the years went by, I saw multiplexes growing from six, to eight, to 30 screens in Marion in South Australia. So I've seen this enormous explosion of screens across Australia and, in addition, I've seen a lot of the smaller cinemas that closed down re-open.

In this period have you been aware of a growth of something you might call a film culture in Melbourne?

Absolutely, because of the media taught in schools, SBS television, all that sort of thing … I'm not sure that the culture of the young people is the culture that you and I knew, that purist European cinema culture.

What do you think about the level of writing on the cinema in Australia? Do you feel cinema is now taken as seriously as the other arts?

It's hard to generalise. I think we have a number of film critics who actually write extremely well, but who I don't think are as in touch with the audience that they write for as they should be. That's an argument about what is a critic, but I still think a critic of a particular outlet or paper has a duty to be in touch with their audience. I think we have some who write really well and are a little out of touch with the audience, some who are in touch with the audience but don't write so well, and I guess we have a few who both write well and are in touch with their audience.

Do they contribute to this film culture we're talking about?

They do. In the earlier days, newspapers like the *Age* used to contribute—Colin Bennett contributed to our film culture because he involved himself with the AFI and with the Film Festival and the film schools, and he wrote a lot of very solid articles about all these institutions, with a lot of involvement. I'm not sure we have as many critics today who are as involved in all that.

He helped create a climate that made us want to have our own cinema.

This is really what I'm suggesting we don't have today. I think that there are still many issues you could write about: the •VCA [Victorian College of the Arts] film school, funding problems. You could do major pieces on that. I reckon you could find a topic every Saturday to write a major piece on, like Colin Bennett used to do. Film culture is an expanding thing; it doesn't keep still. We don't read major pieces in the newspaper about what the AFI is doing any more.

Are there any major changes you plan in the running of either Sharmill or your exhibition business?

You can't stand still in this climate. The business has changed and a number of independents have sadly gone to the wall. They may rise up again as something else but it's sad to see independents sell out. So, one has to make a business plan; you can't just go on from year to year without looking into the future, and saying, 'Where am I going to be in five years time?' You have to plan now for that.

THIS INTERVIEW WAS CONDUCTED BY BRIAN MCFARLANE

melodrama in full cry, rare in new Australian cinema (see Reveival, The). It rehearses many of the typical elements of the genre, including the saving of the family home when the father dies. Its protagonist is a young woman of the 1890s, who is determined not to let the neighbouring robber baron take over the old place, and who is also being romantically pursued by two men. One is a suave type who knows how to wear a dinner jacket and conduct himself in a drawing room; the other is a man of the people who signals his affiliations by dropping his 'g's. The outcome of these interrelated plots is not always predictable, and the glimpses of bohemian life in Melbourne contrast well with the sweeping depiction of wide rural acres and the kinetic vividness of the scenes involving the moving of horses (to be sold to Lord Kitchener in South Africa). **Minnamurra**'s real star may be cinematographer Ross •Berryman, who matches its hectic action with an aptly florid visual style. BMcF

Minogue, Kylie (1968–) ACTOR Kylie Minogue, probably one of the most internationally famous Australians of recent decades, began her career in 1976 as a child performer in the long-running television series *The Sullivans*. She became a household name for her stint, from 1985 to 1988, as Charlene in the series *Neighbours* which, inexplicably to many, caught the voracious attention of several continents. Her big screen début was in Chris •Thomson's **The Delinquents** (1989), a film version of Criena Rohan's novel that disappointed both critics and audiences. Minogue performed capably enough as the pretty teenager rebelling against the strictures of her life, but the film never opted boldly for the all-out melodramatic approach that might have made it more engrossing. Her subsequent film roles, including two in the USA—a comedy, **Bio-Dome** (1996), and an action thriller, **Street Fighter** (1994), with Jean-Claude Van Damme—and the Australian **Hayride to Hell** (1995), with Richard •Roxburgh, have not given her a secure film base. She has had a very successful recording career and has always commanded a remarkable amount of press coverage. Her sister, Dannii Minogue, is also pursuing a career in show business. BMcF

Mitchell, Heather ACTOR After small roles in **I Can't Get Started** (1985), and •**Malcolm** (1986), Heather Mitchell played Margot Ryan in **The Place at the Coast** (1987), a major supporting role as the love interest of the father of the teenage heroine. She can be elegantly beautiful

Jeff Fahey in **Minnamurra**

(the senator's wife in *The Everlasting Secret Family 1988), distantly loving (Martin's mother in *Proof 1991), or absolutely professional (Simmo, Gary Sweet's superior officer in the television series *Cody* 1996). But her most complex character was the disturbed satanist wife of the treasurer in the black comedy A Little Bit of Soul (1998).

Other Australian films: *Children of the Revolution (1996), *Thank God He Met Lizzie (1997). IB

Mitchell, Warren (1926–) ACTOR

Warren Mitchell, London-born but long based in Australia, which he first visited in the late 1960s, has spent his late middle age very busily in the acting media here. He had appeared in nearly 30 films in Britain before achieving real fame as the right-wing bigot Alf Garnett in the BBC comedy series, *Till Death Us Do Part*, starting in 1966. After training at Royal Academy of Dramatic Art after the war, he had some uninviting jobs before landing a string of small parts in 1950s television and films, the latter including Manuela (1957), The Pure Hell of St Trinian's (1961), and The Spy Who Came in from the Cold (1965). Post-Garnett success brought larger roles and, in the early 1970s, he was invited to star in the Queensland Theatre Company's production of *The Merchant of Venice*. His main screen work in Australia has been for television, especially in prestigious miniseries such as *The Dunera Boys* (1985), but he has also appeared in several films made for the big screen, including the touching comedy of Jewish life, *'Norman Loves Rose'* (1982). As the father with prostate

Warren Mitchell

trouble and an over-anxious wife, he skilfully avoided cliché and stereotype. Since then, he has filmed again in Britain (for example, Jack Gold's The Chain, 1985) and twice more in Australia—in Kokoda Crescent (1989), with Ruth *Cracknell, and *Crackers (1998). BMcF

Mo, *see* Rene, Roy

Moffatt, Tracey (1960–) PHOTOGRAPHER/DIRECTOR

Tracey Moffatt is an internationally renowned photographer, famous for her intricately composed and innovative imagery. Her images give prominence to Aboriginality, and are informed by an extensive cinematic literacy. Placing herself in the picture, Moffatt is often compared with the American photographer Cindy Sherman. She is successful as an independent photographer, but does not limit herself to still images, producing documentaries, fiction films, or television. Moffatt's art reflects her desire to complicate the stereotypical representation of Australian Aboriginals.

Her first fiction film, Nice Coloured Girls (1987), is a tale of survival in an urban ghetto. Moffatt combines documentary conventions with irony to counter the White male anthropological perspective. Subtitled throughout, the female Aboriginal voice is transferred into text elevating it to the status of the written accounts.

Night Cries: A Rural Tragedy (1990) has a more contrived, artificial, but stunning visual style. Shot entirely on a studio set, this short, intense film is set amid an illusory surreal landscape intensifying the colours of an Albert Namatjira landscape. There are few spoken words to propel the narrative, but disembodied noises combine to build a relentless soundscape. Sources include animal noises, baby cries, the sound of a woman choking in an Haitian voodoo ceremony, and industrial noise. Inspired by Charles *Chauvel's film *Jedda (1955), Moffatt resurrects the two primary characters and propels them 30 years into the future, transforming the relationship between child and mother into carer and invalid.

Moffatt's first feature film *BeDevil (1993) received an ambivalent critical response. This triptych of ghost stories continues the stylistic experiments of Night Cries: A Rural Tragedy. Moffatt presents a complex series of narratives concerned with the mystification of the dead, emphasising the presence of death in life. Only the second feature film to be directed by an indigenous Australian, and the first to be released commercially, BeDevil represents a dynamic, significant, but undervalued element of Australian film history.

Other Australian films: Watch Out (1987), A Change of Face (1988). WENDY HASLEM

Moir, Richard (1950–) ACTOR

A familiar face on the Australian screen, particularly in the late 1970s and especially the early 1980s, Richard Moir also worked as an editor in Sydney from the mid 1960s and he edited feature films such as •27A, (1974) and short films such as A Handful of Dust (1974). Moir was assistant film editor for the 1975 television special *Hogan in London*. He also produced, and co-scripted with Esben •Storm, the outback crime story •Deadly (1992), and he appears in the film in a minor role as Willie the pathologist.

Moir's principal contribution to the Australian cinema has been as a lead actor who specialises in men with troubled backgrounds. This persona ranges from the excessive and bizarre Howard, who stalks Wendy •Hughes in Remember Me (1985), to the irresponsible chef in Bill •Bennett's •Jilted (1987), the morphine-addicted doctor in Wrong World (1986), and the disturbed World War II soldier Luce Daggett under Wendy •Hughes's care in •An Indecent Obsession (1985). Moir's performance in the film resulted in a nomination for 'Best Actor' Award at the 1985 Australian Film Institute (AFI) Awards. However, the most impressive performance by Moir in this vein was in Phillip •Noyce's excellent environmental thriller •Heatwave (1982). Moir's obsessive architect Stephen West is forced to confront radical activist Kate Dean (Judy •Davis) who opposes his plan to provide high-density housing in the inner suburbs of Sydney. The film, which obliquely draws on the real-life drama involving the disappearance of Sydney journalist Juanita Nielson, provides a complex examination of the West–Dean relationship that is threatened by the extent of the political and business corruption. Moir also had the lead role in Esben Storm's impressive •In Search of Anna (1979) as the ex-convict travelling the east coast of Australia with Judy •Morris in a 1938 Buick in search of an old girlfriend. Moir was nominated for 'Best Actor' at the 1979 AFI Awards for his performance in this film. Throughout the 1970s and 1980s Moir also appeared in popular Australian television series, such as *Cop Shop*, *The Sullivans*, *A Country Practice*, *Carson's Law*, and *G.P.* He has also had lead roles in miniseries such as *The Bodysurfers* and telefeatures such as the impressive post-Vietnam drama *The Long Way Home* (1985).

Other Australian films include: Flashpoint (1972, prod. ass.), •The Odd Angry Shot (1979), The Chain Reaction (1980), With Prejudice (1982), Sweet Dreamers (1982), Running on Empty (1982), The Plains of Heaven (1982), Going Down (1983), Hard Knuckle (1988), •Minnamurra (1989), Isabelle Eberhardt (1992), Welcome to Woop Woop (1997), Joey (1997).　　　GM

Molloy, Mike (1940–) CINEMATOGRAPHER　Mike Molloy trained at •Cinesound, Sydney, on newsreels, documentaries, and commercials, before freelancing in the same areas. He moved to the United Kingdom in 1967 and was camera operator for such visually oriented directors as Nicolas Roeg and Stanley Kubrick. He returned to Australia

Richard Moir

to shoot his first feature as director of photography, Phillipe •Mora's •Mad Dog Morgan (1976). Beginning with Jerzy Skolimowsky's The Shout (UK, 1978), he went on to establish a strong international reputation. He has received much critical acclaim for his photography of such films as Ken •Hannam's •Summerfield (1977). He has worked on the following films, among others: Hardcore (UK, 1977), The Kidnapping of the President (Canada, 1980), The Human Factor (UK, 1980), Shock Treatment (UK, 1981), Dead Easy (1982), The Return of Captain Invincible (1983), Reflections (UK, 1984), The Hit (UK, 1984), Link (UK, 1986), Scandal (UK, 1989), Bethune (Canada, 1990), Bliss (USA, 1997), Welcome to Woop Woop (1997), All the Little Animals (UK, 1998).　　　DAVID MUIR

Money Movers

1979. *Director*: Bruce Beresford. *Producer*: Matt Carroll. *Scriptwriter*: Bruce Beresford. *Director of photography*: Don McAlpine. 92 min. *Cast*: Terence Donovan (Eric Jackson), Tony Bonner (Leo Bassett), Ed Devereaux (Dick Martin), Bryan Brown (Brian Jackson), Alan Cassell (Sammy Rose), Ray Marshall (Ed Gallagher).

Money Movers is a tough thriller with a strong nihilistic streak; it assumes that all levels of Australian society are corrupt. Eric Jackson, a security supervisor at Darcy's Security Services, plans to rob the business of $20 million.

Jackson's gang includes his brother Brian and union official Ed Gallagher, whose ability to call a stoppage at the appropriate moment is an integral part of the plan. Corrupt cop Sammy Rose and greedy businessman Jack Henderson also learn of the heist and complicate Jackson's execution of the robbery, which is ultimately frustrated by ex-cop Dick Martin.

Bruce •Beresford's clever script gradually shifts sympathy from Jackson to the ex-cop Martin, who admits he was on the take while he was a member of the police force. The violent climax is well staged. This is an underrated film with strong performances and a fast-moving story that sustains its cynicism until the end.   GM

Monkey Grip

1982. *Director:* Ken Cameron. *Producer:* Patricia Lovell. *Scriptwriter:* Ken Cameron, in association with Helen Garner. Based on the novel by Helen Garner. *Director of photography:* David Gribble. *Music:* Bruce Smeaton. 99 min. *Cast:* Noni Hazlehurst (Nora), Colin Friels (Javo), Alice Garner (Gracie), Harold Hopkins (Willie), Candy Raymond (Lillian).

Nora's final voice-over comments on her life as 'a complicated dance to which the steps hadn't been quite learnt', and the film, based on Helen •Garner's taxingly episodic novel, bears out this sense of what the preceding summer has been like for her. The two main figures in her dance are her daughter Gracie (Alice •Garner, Helen's daughter, who won an Australian Film Institute award for this début role), who sometimes already seems more clear-sighted than her drifting mother, and her junkie lover Javo, whose addiction makes him emotionally unreliable. The film reproduces the novel's episodic habits but gains considerably from its sensuous evocation of inner-suburban Melbourne in the late 1970s (bars, coffee shops, experimental theatre, clubs, swimming baths) and from Noni •Hazlehurst's central performance. She brings warmth and poignancy to the protagonist, who seems happy with an apparently shapeless lifestyle but inherently longs for a commitment that such a milieu is unlikely to provide.

BMcF

Monkman, Noel (1896–1969) CINEMATOGRAPHER/ DIRECTOR/PRODUCER Noel Monkman was born in New Zealand, but arrived in Australia in 1920 as a musician. He was also a keen amateur still photographer and cinematographer and, in the 1930s, took this up as a profession, working on **Movietone News**. His special interest in natural history led him to experiment with photomicrography, and to become expert in underwater cinematography. With Frank •Thring Snr, he formed Australian Educational Films and, for that company, produced five short films on the

Great Barrier Reef and several other short nature films, which were distributed through •Efftee Film Productions. Both his feature films—•**Typhoon Treasure** (1938) and •**The Power and the Glory** (1941)—are held in almost complete form in the National Film and Sound Archive. The former is interesting without being exciting, the latter is an excellent example of a spy thriller of the period. Monkman did the underwater photography on •**King of the Coral Sea** (1954), but most of his later life was spent producing and photographing his own documentaries, the last of which was **Invisible Wonders of the Great Barrier Reef** (1961). His career in film, in which his wife Kitty played a continuing important role, is described in two autobiographical books: *Escape to Adventure* (1956) and *Quest of the Curly-Tailed Horses* (1962).   IB

Monticelli, Anna Maria ACTOR In her early films this Tangiers-born actor was known as Anna Jemison. Her background is exotic: her mother was Spanish, her father Italian, and she was raised in Rome and spent a good deal of time in various European countries before settling in Australia. She has worked on stage and television (notably in the series *The Restless Years*), as well as film, making her screen début in the New Zealand film **Smash Palace** in 1981. She had several secondary but rewarding roles in the 1980s, in •**Heatwave** (1982), as Richard •**Moir**'s wife, •**Silver City** (1984), as the heroine's friend, and part of the film's romantic triangle, and •**My First Wife** (1984). Monticelli was in Jane •Campion's drama of sexual harassment, **After Hours** (1984). She still awaits a major film opportunity.

Other Australian films: The Dark Room (1982), Archer (1985), •The Empty Beach (1985), Nomads (1986).

BMcF

Monton, Vincent (1949–) CINEMATOGRAPHER/DIRECTOR Vincent Monton's career began when he was a teenager and made a short film that won a silver medal in Milan. Monton started at Crawford Productions, Melbourne, in 1967 and graduated to shooting the television series **Homicide**, which earned him a Sammy award for Best Cinematography. He began freelancing in 1972 and his first feature film as director of photography, **The True Story of Eskimo Nell** (1974), won the Australian Film Institute Best Cinematography award. In later years he was to earn four other nominations. Monton travelled to Europe to study new techniques, such as Super 16, which he used on •**Moving Out** (1983). His next film, •**Hostage: The Christine Maresch Story** (1983), was shot in Australia and Germany, and helped establish his international reputation, leading to such overseas films as **Voyeur** (USA, 1983) and **Second Sight** (Canada, 1993). His photography of Australian films such as •**Newsfront** (1978) attracted much critical acclaim.

The first feature film Monton directed was **Windrider** (1985), followed by second-unit directing on films such as **Bodily Harm** (1987) •**Dead Calm** (1989) and **Return to the Blue Lagoon** (USA, 1991).

Other Australian films include: The Trespassers (1975, d.o.p.), •Fantasm (1976, d.o.p.), Raw Deal (1977, d.o.p.), Fantasm Comes Again (1977, d.o.p.), Blue Fire Lady (1978, d.o.p.), Snapshot (1978, d.o.p.), Thirst (1979, d.o.p.), •Long Weekend (1979, d.o.p.), Race for the Yankee Zephyr (Australia/NZ, 1981, d.o.p.), •Roadgames (1981, d.o.p.), Crosstalk (1982, d.o.p.), •Heatwave (1982, d.o.p.), •'Norman Loves Rose' (1982, d.o.p.), Molly (1983, d.o.p.), Street Hero (1984, d.o.p.), Double Sculls (1986, d.o.p.), Seige of the Achille Lauro (1989, d.o.p.), Fatal Bond (1992, d.) Lucky Break (1994, d.o.p.), Point of no Return (1995, d.o.p., w.)

DAVID MUIR

Moora Neya,
or The Message of the Spear

1911. Director: Alfred Rolfe. B & W.

Alfred •Rolfe, who had begun his film directing career earlier in 1911 for Spencer's Pictures, joined The Australian Photo-Play Company in June to helm their first release, **Moora Neya**. This film, now lost, appears to have been the first fiction feature to have given a prominent role to actual Aboriginal people rather than to White actors in black-face. Publicity claimed that the group involved was situated near Brewarrina on the Darling River of central northern NSW. On its release, **Moora Neya** was praised for its authentic Australian bush atmosphere.

WILLIAM D. ROUTT

Moore, John ACTOR John Moore's career includes some of the more innovative and politically conscious film projects, but also some B-grade Australian films. He was nominated for an Australian Film Institute award in 1993 for his starring role as Dougie Dooligan in •**Blackfellas**. Moore's character is a young Aboriginal man caught between two cultures. Part-European, part-Aboriginal, Dooligan's dual identity situates him at the periphery of both the White and indigenous communities. Improvised dialogue and a lack of resolution contribute to his portrayal of a quietly charismatic but troubled character.

In 1991 Moore participated in the ground-breaking production of **Bran Nue Dae**, an experimental Aboriginal musical. In the following year he played Eddie in Esben •Storm's •**Deadly**, a timely film about an inquest into the death of an Aboriginal man in custody. Moore has also starred in **The Life of Harry Dare** (1995), a comedy about a father and son who head off in search of a car. One of his more outlandish projects is **Zombie Brigade** (1988), a vampire film set in Toodyay, Western Australia. Moore's character is involved in the raising of the dead to contend with the

spirits of Vietnam veterans who are haunting the town in a deathly protest against redevelopment.

Other Australian films: Natural Justice Heat (1996), The Missing (1998).

WENDY HASLEM

Moorhouse, Frank (1940–) WRITER Former journalist and one of Australia's most prominent authors, Frank Moorhouse's entry into scriptwriting was marked by two shorts, **The Girl from the Family of Man** (1970) and **The Machine Gun** (1971), both directed by Michael •Thornhill, with whom he has collaborated on several projects. His first feature, •**Between Wars** (1974), drew consistent arthouse audiences but failed to gain acceptance at a popular level, possibly due to its courageous but cynical portrayal of Australian society of the period and its deliberately detached and understated treatment of character. With the exception of *The Disappearance of Azaria Chamberlain* (1984), a television potboiler docudrama in which he appeared as 'host', his other films have their origins in his literary work. **The Girl Who Met Simone de Beauvoir in Paris** (1984), a short directed by Richard Wherrett, is arguably closest in style to the journalistic prose for which he gained attention early in his career. **The Coca-Cola Kid** (1984), a feature from a short story by the same name, promised more than it delivered and, in addition to Dusan Makavejev's uneven direction, the script itself is fraught with moral contradictions. Its notions of public versus private morality nevertheless have some links to •**Between Wars**, and through to •**The Everlasting Secret Family** (1988), the latter sometimes at odds with his apparently libertarian views, which go back to the Sydney 'Push' of the 1960s. Moorhouse also co-wrote the telemovie *Time's Raging* (1984) with his one-time partner Sophia Turkiewicz (•**Silver City**) and Keith Dewhurst.

HARRY KIRCHNER

Moorhouse, Jocelyn (1960–) DIRECTOR Jocelyn Moorhouse graduated from the •**Australian Film, Television and Radio School** in 1984, and worked for network television as a script editor. Her short film, **The Seige of Barton's Bathroom**, was developed into a 12-part television series and, during her spare time, Moorhouse wrote the script for •**Proof** (1991), her stunning directorial début. The budget for **Proof** was $1.1 million, funded entirely from government sources, and it was selected because of its coherent and tight script, a result of the years Moorhouse spent in developing her unusual concept of a blind man who takes photographs in a futile attempt to vindicate his perception of the world around him. The film's complex interplay involving three main characters refuses to sentimentalise them and retains its strong dramatic edge to the end. **Proof** is one of the key contemporary Australian films. Moorhouse also produced •**Muriel's Wedding** (1994) for her husband, •P.J. Hogan, while also contributing to its script, which was initially called 'Rowena's Wedding'. Moorhouse's next two films were large-budget domestic dramas produced in Hollywood, **How to Make an American Quilt** (1995) and **A Thousand Acres** (1998).　　　GM

Mora, Philippe (1949–) DIRECTOR The son of a well-known Melbourne restaurateur and art dealer father and an artist mother, Paris-born Philippe Mora began as a painter before directing (and writing) his first film, the 70-minute **Trouble in Megalopolis**, made in London in 1969. The film was shot in four weeks, with glimpses of such luminaries as Germaine Greer and Richard Neville but, despite its trendy credentials and considerable publicity, it was scarcely seen. He also made two full-length compilation documentaries overseas: **Swastika** (1974), a savagely ironic account of Hitler's rise, and **Brother Can You Spare a Dime** (1975), in which he drew on newsreel footage and old movies to evoke the Depression of the 1930s. Both did surprisingly well at the box office, revealing Mora as a film-maker of flair and feeling. In Australia he was co-founder (with Peter Beilby) of the journal *Cinema Papers* at La Trobe University.

His Australian film-making career began ambitiously with •**Mad Dog Morgan** (1976), the sympathetic and idiosyncratic portrait of the Irish bushranger Dan Morgan, played by American cult actor Dennis Hopper as the victim of a repressive regime. In spite of success with critics and an award at Cannes as the best western, the film found only modest audience support. Its bursts of violence put it at odds with the other Australian period pieces popular at the time, with the exception of •**The Chant of Jimmie Blacksmith** (1978), which also failed commercially. Today, **Morgan's** passionate commitment to its subject makes it seem more vivid than its more decorous contemporaries.

Mora's has been a strange, even wayward, career, much of it conducted overseas. The Australian fantasy-adventure **The Return of Captain Invincible** (1983) was a spectacular failure with audiences, although it had some satirical edge in its depiction of an American super hero who is victimised by McCarthyism in the early 1950s and ends up in the Australian outback. Overseas stars Alan Arkin and Christopher Lee suggest the film's international aspirations, but its uncertainty of tone doomed it with audiences. **Death of a Soldier** (1987) uses the true-life 'Leonski murders' of the 1940s as a starting-point for a rumination on Australian–American relations, both reflective and boldly stylish, in ways that recall **Mad Dog Morgan**. Its strong cast is headed by the American actor James Coburn as Major Dannenberg who defends Leonski, the American soldier charged with strangling three Melbourne women, and Bill •Hunter, as the Australian policeman in charge of the investigation. The film ran into serious industrial problems from

the Australian Theatrical and Amusement Employees Association and, over a year later, achieved only the most limited independent distribution.

Mora's subsequent work, across a range of American genres, has not been widely seen in Australia. It includes science fiction (**Precious Find**, 1996), a dinosaur comedy (**Pterodactyl Woman from Beverly Hills**, 1994), and action adventure (**Back in Business**, 1997), all starring Brion James, one of the replicants in **Blade Runner** (1982). Australian cinema arguably needs Mora's quirky, flamboyant talent more than the USA does; one would have thought 1990s film-making in Australia a likelier context for his style than earlier decades.

Other Australian films: To Shoot a Mad Dog (1976, doc., co-w., nar.), The Howling III: The Marsupials (1987).　　　BMcF

More Things Change, The

1986. Director: Robyn Nevin. *Producer*: Jill Robb. *Scriptwriter*: Moya Wood. *Director of photography*: Dan Burstall. *Music*: Peter Best. 94 min. *Cast*: Judy Morris (Connie), Barry Otto (Lex), Victoria Longley (Geraldine), Lewis Fitz-Gerald (Barry), Peter Carroll (Roley).

This drama of role-reversal raises some pertinent issues about Western life towards the end of the twentieth century. A couple with a young daughter lives on a farm in the hills beyond Melbourne, the wife, Connie, commuting to the city to carry out her high-powered job with a publishing firm. The husband, Lex, has the daily responsibility for their child and for getting the run-down farm into order. Increasingly, Connie feels she is 'just the one who brings home the pay packet', and the gender resentments are aired in surprising ways. There is a parallel story involving the pregnant household help, Geraldine, who goes ahead with a marriage to a man who is not the father of her child.

The film was actor Robyn •Nevin's first directorial effort, and it was a largely female-centred production: in addition to Nevin, the producer, scriptwriter, designer, and editor are all women. Despite some dissipation of its narrative tensions, it is a sympathetically conceived film, written and acted with sensitivity for the fraught relationships it depicts.　　　BMcF

Morice, Tara (1965–) ACTOR The surprise hit of Australian cinema in 1992 was Baz •Luhrman's •**Strictly Ballroom**. Part of the reason for its success was that everyone involved seemed to understand the conventions on which it was based. Tara Morice certainly did as the 'plain' girl with glasses and an ethnic background, who removes the former and capitalises on the latter to win the hero (Paul •Mercurio) and the ballroom dancing championship in which they compete. Busy in the theatre as well, Morice has since made only two further films: **Metal Skin** (1994), a further study in urban violence from Geoffrey •Wright, who made •Romper Stomper (1992) and, in quite different vein, Richard •Franklin's reflective •Hotel Sorrento (1995), in which she plays one of Ray •Barrett's returning daughters.

BMcF

Tara Morice

Morris, John (1933–) PRODUCER John Morris has spent much of his career in shaping policy in key administrative positions. After dropping out of medicine at Sydney University, he joined the •Commonwealth Film Unit (CFU) in 1952, first as a production assistant then as a producer/director, for instance, on The Road to the Clouds (1958), made in New Guinea. He spent 18 months in the United Kingdom working freelance before returning to the CFU in 1964, eventually becoming head of production of •Film Australia. In 1973 he joined the •South Australian Film Corporation and, in 1976, he was appointed managing director, overseeing, in a long career there, productions such as •Storm Boy (1976), •'Breaker' Morant (1980), and The Shiralee. He was executive producer on •Robbery Under Arms (1985) and •Playing Beatie Bow (1986). In 1988 he became founding director of the •NSW Film and Television Office, then chief executive of the Film Finance Corporation from January 1990 until his resignation in mid 1997. Other positions he has held are council member and deputy chairman of the •Australian Film, Television and Radio School, chairman of the Australian Education Council's Enquiry into Children's Television, and inaugural member of the Board of the Australian Commercial Television Fund. He has been an outspoken advocate of government financial support for the film industry for many years.

IB

Morris, Judy (1947–) ACTOR Judy Morris was, like so many other Australian film actors, trained for the stage, at the National Institute of Dramatic Art, and was a well-known figure on local television before the film revival of the 1970s (see Revival, the) gave another string to her bow. Her interesting and somewhat febrile delicacy had made itself felt in such television series as Over There and Certain Women. She mined elements of neurotic sexuality in such early films as 'The Child', an episode of •Libido (1973), with echoes of Joseph Losey's The Go-Between (1971), and the tense telefeature, The Plumber (1979), directed by Peter •Weir, as a middle-class suburban housewife threatened by the eponymous and ambivalent tradesman. She had a substantial starring role in Chris McGill's romantic drama **Maybe This Time** (1980), in which the title refers to her aspirations in relation to men. •Phar Lap (1983) offered her a conventional role as the wife of the American magnate (Ron Leibman), but she played it with grace and charm. In general, it must be said, films have not really exploited her idiosyncratic appeal very intelligently. Her most striking performance is, arguably, as Nicole •Kidman's domineering mother (a 1989 version of Gladys Cooper in **Now, Voyager**, 1942) in the television miniseries Bangkok Hilton. Most of her recent work has been for television.

Other Australian films: Australia, the Biggest Island in the World (1969, short), Stirring the Pool (1970, short), Three to Go (1971, 'Judy' episode), Avengers of the Reef (1973), •Between Wars (1974), The Great MacArthy (1975), Scobie Malone (1975), Master of the World (1976, voice only), The Trespassers (1976), •The Picture Show Man (1977), The Making of Anna (1978, doc) •In Search of Anna (1979), The Girl Who Met Simone de Beauvoir in Paris (1980, short), •Razorback (1984), Going Sane (1986), •The More Things Change (1986).

BMcF

Morse, Helen (1946–) ACTOR Born in the United Kingdom, but living in Australia since the age of four, Helen Morse has, it seems, preferred the stage to films, thereby robbing Australian cinema of a potential star. Despite the relative rarity of her film appearances, and there has been none since the mid 1980s, she established a firm place for herself in the first decade of the Australian film revival (see Revival, the) with three contrasting images of women: as the sympathetic Ma'mselle de Poitiers in •Picnic at Hanging Rock (1975), as the Depression-hit Sydney barmaid in •Caddie (1976), and as the sophisticated, sexually liberated Jo in •Far East (1982). In each of these, her delicate beauty seemed to belie an inner toughness, variously at the service of bringing comfort to distraught schoolgirls, desperately fighting poverty and weariness without losing humour behind a Sydney bar, and renewing an old love affair without betraying her husband's cause in the volatile Philippines. She studied at the National Institute for Dramatic Art, played an impressive variety of classical and modern roles on stage, did voice-over for several animated shorts, and came to notice in the 1974 television series, *Marion*. There were small roles in several films, most notably in •Stone and •Petersen (both 1974), plaudits for a charming but tiny role in the British film, **Agatha** (1979), based on the disappearance in 1926 of Agatha Christie, and much praise for her prisoner-of-war heroine in the television miniseries, *A Town like Alice* (1981), opposite her **Far East** co-star, Bryan •Brown.

Other Australian films: **Great Barrier Reef** (1968, doc., co-nar.), **Adam's Woman** (1969).   BMcF

The Moth of Moonbi

1926. Director, Scriptwriter: Charles Chauvel. From the novel, *The Wild Moth*, by Mabel Forrest. *Director of photography*: Al Burne. B&W. *Cast*: Doris Ashwin (Dell Ferris), Arthur Tauchert (Black Bronson).

The surviving footage from Charles Chauvel's first feature, **The Moth of Moonbi**, is striking evidence of the director's figural ambition. It marks the first time a Chauvel film tells the story of a woman's odyssey: Dell Ferris's physical and spiritual journey from the outback to the city and home again. Like his masculine protagonists, Chauvel's female voyagers are impelled towards the unknown by forces within and beyond themselves that they do not comprehend. The recurring, stereotyped figure of Dell as a 'moth' attracted by the unattainable light of the moon generates the forward-and-back story of her journey and inflects its conventional opposition of country and city towards another kind of structure that transcends the dichotomy, mythologising Woman and Australia in the process. In the end Dell confronts the past from which she has attempted to escape, learning that the man she loves killed the father who hated her—which is to say that the land that grants her refuge from the betrayal and pain she has met with in the city is itself inextricably grounded in violence and desire, just as it is, inescapably, her future.

WILLIAM D. ROUTT

Mothers, *see* **Maternal images**

Motion Picture Distributors Association of Australia, *see* Exhibition and distribution

Motion Picture Exhibitors Association of Australia, *see* Exhibition and distribution

Motzing, William (1937–) COMPOSER American-born composer William Motzing came to Australia in 1972. He has contributed to the Australian film and television industries, composing over 12 scores for feature films, many scores for television and miniseries, and documentary films. Motzing's love of jazz found him teaching Jazz Studies and film scoring at the NSW State Conservatorium of Music and tutoring in film scoring at the •Australian Film, Television and Radio School. His first film score was for •Newsfront (1978). Its director, Phillip •Noyce, has said that Motzing's composing style possesses the ability to decode the director's sometimes confused responses to his own film. Further, Motzing has the ability to deliver exactly what was asked for, along with adding something of his own imprint to the score. Joan •Long, producer of the feature film •Silver City (1984), commented that Motzing's score helped give her film a bittersweet quality which complemented the mood of the film. Television producer, Terry Hayes, found that the score which Motzing composed for his miniseries *Vietnam* (1986) delivered the maximum dramatic effect while capturing the intimacy necessary in writing for the small screen.

Other film scores include •**Cathy's Child** (1979), and •**Young Einstein** (1988) with Martin Arminger and Tommy Tycho.   DIANE NAPTHALI

Mouth To Mouth

1978. Director: John Duigan. *Producer*: John Sainken. *Scriptwriter*: John Duigan. *Director of photography*: Tom Cowan. *Music*: Roy Ritchie. 96 min. *Cast*: Kim Krejus (Carrie), Sonia Peat (Jeanie), Ian Gilmour (Tim), Sergio Frazetto (Serge), Walter Pym (Fred).

John •Duigan had already shown a willingness, not too common in the late 1970s, to confront the problems of contemporary life in a cinema whose prestige lay chiefly in its graceful recreations of the past. Carlton-based, he had been involved in low-budget film-making for some years, winning critical notice but little commercial success. **Mouth to Mouth** was his first to win mainstream theatrical release. There was widespread praise for its sympathetic, rigorous treatment of the dramas of drifting lives among the unemployed young. Two girls, recently released from a correction centre, take up with two boys, the shy country boy Tim, and the more streetwise Serge. They pair off sexually in the less-expected combinations and set themselves up in an old loft, which they share with an elderly derelict, who dies after being beaten by suspicious police. The film has a sense of humour which ensures that, despite the grim social facts it dramatises, it is not just a depressing experience, and Duigan gets engaging performances from his young cast, two of whom (Sonia Peat and Sergio Frazetto) were non-professionals and the other two scarcely known.   BMcF

Moving Out

1983. Director: Michael Pattinson. Producers: Jane Ballantyne, Michael Pattinson. Scriptwriter: Jan Sardi. Director of photography: Vincent Monton. Music: Danny Beckerman. 91 min. Cast: Vince Colosimo (Gino), Maurice Devincentis (Renato), Tibor Gyapjas (Allan), Sally Cooper (Sandy), Desiree Smith (Helen).

This heartfelt little film focuses sympathetically on a real problem in Australian society. Gino feels himself growing further away from his parents who still speak scarcely any English, preferring what he angrily calls 'Wog' language. He thinks of himself as Australian rather than Italian, only once letting his dimly remembered feeling for Italy break through his usual facade of hostility to the country he left as a small child. His resentments flare when relations from Italy come to stay at the family's inner-suburban house, and are fanned by his schoolmates who do not share his parents' aspirations and who bring him into trouble with the police. The title refers to Gino's parents' decision to move to outer-suburban Doncaster, leaving the new arrivals in their Fitzroy house to repeat the cycle of mobility. It also suggests that Gino will soon need to move out from under the parental roof. The young people are well contrasted and there is an incisive study from Brian James as a sorely tried teacher. In the following year the same director/writer/star team produced the slicker but less affecting **Street Hero**.

BMcF

Mr Chedworth Steps Out

1939. Director: Ken G. Hall. Producer: Ken G. Hall. Scriptwriter: Frank Harvey. Based on a novel by Francis Morton Howard. Director of photography: George Heath. Music: Hamilton Webber. 92 min. B&W. Cast: Cecil Kellaway (George Chedworth), James Raglan (Brian Carford), Joan Deering (Gwen Chedworth), Rita Paunce-fort (Mrs Chedworth), Jean Hatton (Susie Chedworth).

In 1938 Cecil •Kellaway interrupted his busy career at RKO in Hollywood to return briefly to Australia for **Mr Chedworth Steps Out**. It is easy to see why Kellaway returned for this role as it was perfectly suited to his screen persona, a persona that he maintained in the American cinema for the next three decades. As the likeable family man victimised by a pretentious wife, ungrateful employers, and a gambling son (Peter •Finch), Kellaway, as George Chedworth, dominates the film. When his employers demote him after 24 years to the position of caretaker, Chedworth is able to escape the relentless nagging by his wife and embark on a new lifestyle after he finds a bag of (counterfeit) money. His good fortune continues when a racing bet succeeds and his seemingly worthless gold-mining shares return a large dividend. However, when the counterfeiters track him down and try to beat him into submission, Chedworth resists

them until the police arrive. At the close of the film, Chedworth's personal and economic confidence now allows him to establish himself within his family. This position is reinforced by an elaborate hoax devised by George to humiliate his wife in front of her elitist friends.

On the surface **Mr Chedworth Steps Out** appears to be merely a routine melodrama, interspersed with comic moments, and dominated by a polished performance from Kellaway. However, the film's depiction of family life, particularly in the presentation of his wife (Rita Pauncefort) as socially ambitious and lacking any affection for her husband, together with the arbitrary treatment inflicted on him by his employers, renders this film as one of the more critical depictions of Australian middle-class family life in the late 1930s. The relatively bleak presentation is interrupted a couple of times with musical performances from Jean Hatton (Susie Chedworth), a 15-year-old soprano who was briefly promoted by •Cinesound as 'Australia's Deanna Durbin'.

GM

Mr Reliable

1996. Director: Nadia Tass. Producers: Jim McElroy, Terry Hayes. Scriptwriters: Don Catchlove, Terry Hayes. Director of photography: David Parker. Music: Philip Judd. 113 min. Cast: Colin Friels (Wally), Jacqueline McKenzie (Beryl), Paul Sonkkila (Allan), Frank Gallacher (Fergusson), Barry Otto (the Premier).

In the long hot summer of 1968 small-time criminal Wally Mellish, armed with a sawn-off shotgun, holed up in a suburban Sydney house with girlfriend Beryl and her infant son. An eight-day siege during which the police commissioner was taken hostage, and Wally and Beryl were married, turned into a media circus with the house encircled by police, reporters, and carnivalesque crowd of onlookers barracking for the 'little battler' inside. **Mr Reliable** blends elements of drama, romance, farce, satire, and social comment in reconstructing this bizarre episode, using it as an emblem for a period of lost innocence. There are moments of high comedy and pathos but, as a whole, this box-office fizzer is an uneven achievement: it lacks narrative drive and sustained dramatic tension, the comedy is intermittent and the social criticism (concerning attitudes to migrants, the Vietnam war, police bungling, political chicanery) rarely rises above a clichéd treatment of its targets.

HARRY OLDMEADOW

Mulcahy, Russell (1953–) DIRECTOR This Melbourne-born director began his career directing the television rock program *Countdown* at the ABC and made a number of award-winning shorts (**Delicious Dreams Despite Depression**, 1976). Russell Mulcahy established an international reputation with his video-clips for artists such as Duran Duran, Air Supply, Rod Stewart, and Elton John. His first feature film, •Razorback (1984), illustrates his strong visual style and, together with cinematographer Dean •Semler, Mulcahy produced a visually striking horror film that has a strong vein of black humour running through its outrageous premise of a giant feral pig terrorising people in outback Australia. After the international commercial success of the hybrid science-fiction/historical drama **Highlander** (1986), starring Christopher Lambert and Sean Connery, and the less successful sequel **Highlander II: The Quickening** (1991), also with Lambert and Connery, Mulcahy directed the American urban thriller **Ricochet** (1991), which is arguably his best film to date. Subsequent films included the British crime film **Blue Ice** (1992), the caper film **The Real McCoy** (1993), and the big-budget Hollywood thriller **The Shadow** (1994), based on the 1930s and 1940s radio and pulp character.   GM

Mull

1989. Director: Don McLennan. *Producer:* D. Howard Grigsby. *Scriptwriter:* Jon Stephens. Based on the novel *Mullaway* by Bron Nicholls. *Director of photography:* Zbigniew Friedrich. *Music:* Michael Atkinson. 90 min. *Cast:* Nadine Garner (Phoebe Mullens), Bill Hunter (Frank Mullens), Sue Jones (Deborah Mullens), Craig Morrison (Steve Mullens), Bradley Kilpatrick (Alan Mullens).

Nadine •Garner won an Australian Film Institute Best Actress award for playing the title role in this coming-of-age drama set in the Melbourne seaside suburb of St Kilda. Phoebe Mullens, known as Mull, suddenly finds the long Christmas holidays shattered by the collapse of her mother with terminal Hodgkin's disease. Now, added to her adolescent problems, she finds herself shouldering the burdens of her family. These include nursing her bedridden mother, coping with the drug addiction of her gay brother, Steve, and the problems of her younger brother and sister, for whom life is made more difficult by the tensions created by their father, Frank. The last is a precariously reformed alcoholic and fundamentalist religious zealot, with little understanding of his children. Mull is pushed into awareness of the truth of the relationships around her, and tentatively tests the waters of approaching adulthood. Director Don McLennan treats the pains enjoined by generation gap, gender, and sexual preference with sensitivity and vivacity, avoiding the sentimental pitfalls of the rites-of-passage genre.   BMcF

Mullinar, Liz (1945–) CASTING
British actor Liz Mullinar migrated to Sydney with her then husband Rod •Mullinar in 1966. Despite her stage experience, she was unable to find work, so began giving acting workshops for children, and eventually joined an advertising agency as a casting director. When the marriage broke up, she decided, in 1969, to go out on her own, coining the term 'casting consultant' to add prestige and justify charging adequately for the service. Although there had been other influential casting directors (for instance, Bunny Brooke at Crawfords and Jan Russ at Grundys, in the 1970s), Mullinar's was Australia's first independent screen-casting agency, casting for both film and television (including commercials). Against all predictions it was immediately successful and, after two years, she went into partnership with Hilary Linstead, renaming the company M & L Casting. It continued to grow until, in 1985, the two partners split the company, each continuing with the kind of work they had done before. The new Mullinar Casting also continued to grow, becoming Australia's most influential casting agency, with 20 000 people on their file and a staff of 16 in 1994. Greg Apps operated a franchise in Melbourne from 1985 to 1992, then Mullinar opened her own Melbourne office, with a computer link to the Sydney office and the capacity to view show-reels in both locations. By then, Mullinar had given some of our greatest actors their first roles (for instance, Wendy •Hughes, Colin •Friels, Judy •Davis), and had also 'discovered' talent in unlikely places, such as Jo •Kennedy, or the two leading children in the television series *The Leaving of Liverpool* (Christine Tremarco and Kevin Jones). She had also chaired the syndicate that set up the Belvoir Theatre in Sydney, and been a member of the •Australian Film Commission and the board of the National Institute of Dramatic Art. The company continued its successful operation after Liz Mullinar ceased her personal involvement in 1996. By then, screen casting was recognised as a specialist field, and the industry directory (*Encore Directory*) listed more than 50 casting companies.   IB

Mullinar, Rod (1943–) ACTOR
This British actor has worked in Australia since the mid 1960s. Rod Mullinar's screen career in Australia began in 1969 with the role of a policeman in the international co-production **It Takes All Kinds** (1969), followed by the gay lover in the controversial drama •**The Set** (1970). However, with a few exceptions, such as the lead role of Peter Lalor in **Stockade** (1971), a rarely seen re-creation of the events at the Eureka Stockade, a key role in the excellent thriller •**Patrick** (1978), and the lead in the pedestrian romance **Breakfast in Paris** (1982), he has mostly been cast in supporting roles that exploit his looks. The exception to this pattern is his effective performance as Hagan, the villain in the excellent low-budget thriller •**The Surfer** (1988). Mullinar has also appeared in Australian television drama.

Other Australian films include: **Down the Wind** (1975), **Raw Deal** (1977), **…Maybe This Time** (1980), •**'Breaker' Morant** (1980), **Thirst** (1981), **Duet For Four** (1982), **Now and Forever** (1983), **The Humpty Dumpty Man** (1986), **Echoes of Paradise** (1988), •**Dead Calm** (1989).   GM

Muriel's Wedding

1994. *Director*: P.J. Hogan. *Producers*: Lynda House, Jocelyn Moorhouse. *Scriptwriter*: P.J. Hogan. *Director of photography*: Martin McGrath. *Music*: Peter Best. 101 min. *Cast*: Toni Collette (Muriel), Bill Hunter (Bill), Rachel Griffiths (Rhonda), Sophie Lee (Tania), Rosalind Hammond (Cheryl), Belinda Jarrett (Janine), Pippa Grandison (Nicole), Jeanie Drynan (Betty), Daniel Wylie (Perry), Gabby Millgate (Joanie), Gennie Nevinson (Deidre), Matt Day (Brice), Chris Haywood (Ken Blundell), Daniel LaPine (David Van Arkle).

This assured film shifts rapidly from a surreal depiction of suburban life to pathos and comedy and back again. Muriel Heslop's life in Porpoise Spit is an unhappy one, largely due to her overbearing father and bitchy school friends. Ostracised because of her weight and lack of 'style', Muriel escapes into Abba songs and an obsessive desire to marry. She steals money from her father and heads to a beach resort off the Qld coast where she meets Rhonda, an old school friend. At this point Muriel begins the transformation that is marked in the final scene by a change in her priorities. Instead of a false marriage, Muriel commits herself to Rhonda, her cancer-stricken friend, and the film concludes with their escape from Porpoise Spit.

Muriel's Wedding demonstrates writer/director P.J. •Hogan's ability to blend seemingly discrete elements into moving comedy. The film contains a series of strong performances from Toni •Collette, Bill •Hunter, Rachel •Griffiths, and especially from Jeanie •Drynan as Muriel's mother, the sad housewife who is highly protective of her corrupt and unfaithful husband. Her death provides the catalyst for Muriel's development. **Muriel's Wedding** was a commercial success in the USA, and prompted Julia Roberts to select P.J. Hogan as the director for her romantic comedy **My Best Friend's Wedding** (USA, 1997). GM

Murphy, Paul (1954–) CINEMATOGRAPHER Paul Murphy started in 1972 as a camera assistant with Martin Williams Productions, Brisbane. He moved to Sydney in 1976, freelancing as focus-puller on films such as •**The FJ Holden** (1977) and •**In Search of Anna** (1979). He became a director of photography in 1979, attracting critical attention with his first feature, director Ray •Lawrence's •**Bliss** (1985) and •**Emerald City** (1989), both of which were

Rachel Griffiths and Toni Collette in **Muriel's Wedding**

nominated for Australian Film Institute cinematography awards. He won an award at Atlantic City for **Under the Lighthouse Dancing** (1997). Much of his work has been on miniseries, such as *Harp in the South* and *The Heroes*. He began working in the USA in 1990, shooting both cinema and television features.

Other Australian films include: **Dead End Drive In** (1986), **Dallas Doll** (Australia/UK, 1994), **TunnelVision** (1995), **Mighty Morphin Power Rangers—The Movie** (Australia/USA, 1995).

DAVID MUIR

Murray, John B. (1931–) PRODUCER/DIRECTOR/WRITER
John B. Murray has been active in the industry as a writer, director, and producer. He worked with the ABC as a director prior to entering into independent production of shorts, sponsored documentaries, and commercials. Murray was active in the rebirth of the Australian film industry (see Revival, the): his semi-documentary film •**The Naked Bunyip** (1970) was a landmark film in demonstrating that there was a substantial local audience for Australian films. Murray's film combined interviews about various aspects of sexuality within a fictional framework. He bypassed the traditional exhibitors by exhibiting the film himself on 16 mm. When the Commonwealth censors insisted on a number of deletions from the film, he blacked out the designated images and inserted a caricature of a bunyip. Murray's actions during this period contributed to the liberalisation of film censorship in Australia. Murray was associate producer on •**Two Thousand Weeks** (1969) and executive producer, and one of the four directors, of •**Libido** (1973). He was co-producer for •**We of the Never Never** (1982) and producer for •**Lonely Hearts** (1982). He also acted as producer for his son Scott Murray's, •**Devil in the Flesh** (1989).

GM

Music A great number of musicians compiled scores, and some composers contributed mood music and short episodic pieces, for motion pictures during the silent era. Many composers have also written scores for sound films: these artists were largely overlooked until the resurgence of Australian cinema after 1970 (see Revival, the). By the 1980s, the industry had gained international prominence and, as a result, so did Australian composers and their film scores. Today, more than a dozen composers have made careers in composing for film.

In Australia, music and film became companions in 1894 when five electric-powered Edison kinetoscopes (also known as cinematographs), machines for showing motion-pictures, were exhibited in a converted shop in Pitt Street, Sydney; patrons viewed the show, a 30-second looped film, through an eyepiece. Musical accompaniment was provided by a wax cylinder phonograph. In 1895, three Edison kinetophones were exhibited in Charters Towers, then Queens-

land's thriving gold-mining centre. Kinetophones (kinetoscopes with phonographs fitted internally) supplied, through stethoscope tubes plugged to patrons' ears, two and a half minutes of music unsynchronised with the film. The exhibitor chose the musical program from a playlist of popular pieces found in the Edison catalogue. In August 1896, American illusionist Carl Hertz demonstrated the cinematograph in Harry Rickard's New Minstrels and Specialty Company at the Melbourne Opera House. The short films were accompanied by music from a pit orchestra. Patrons were dazzled by this exceptional novelty and came to realise, after the initial shock of viewing the realism of the action, that the basic difference between moving pictures and live acts was that moving pictures created an artful illusion of real life on the screen in a theatrical manner. Public endorsement of this new entertainment caused screen novelties with musical accompaniment to become an essential component in variety-hall entertainment. On occasions, patrons were invited to sing along to the musical accompaniment, and lantern slides were provided by music publishers. There was little attempt to synchronise mood music with projected images. In September 1896, Marius Sestier, the agent of the Lumière brothers, pioneer French filmmakers and inventors of the cinematograph, arrived in Sydney and established the Salon Lumière in Pitt Street. A program presented in Paris ten months previously was the one screened on opening night. The Salon was furnished with Austrian chairs and a large decoratively framed screen. During the films, music was provided by a small ensemble led by one of Sydney's foremost conductors and arrangers, Roberto Hazon and, on occasions, by the Lyceum Theatre Orchestra. The Lumière enterprise signalled the introduction in Australia of all-film programs with musical accompaniment, as public entertainment.

The Salvation Army was the largest producer of silent films between 1897 and 1909, exhibiting over 300 films, hundreds of slides, and sound recordings, many of which formed part of lecture presentations promoting the social work of the Salvation Army. Its multimedia lectures, which lasted up to three hours, were always accompanied by music. The film-making activities of the Salvation Army had their genesis in the Army's Limelight Department, which began when pioneer film-maker Joseph Perry and his wife toured Australia in 1891 with a slide projector (local corps officers providing suitable hymn accompaniment to the shows). In 1897, the Limelight Department acquired a movie projector and began producing secular as well as religious films. By 1900 the Army had established the Biorama Company, whose bands toured Australia, Batavia and New Zealand with the Limelight Department. At its peak, there were 21 Salvation Army units touring, each with its own films and orchestras, the largest with 20 musicians.

After the turn of the century, 'the pictures' were established in converted shops, halls, under canvas, and in open-air auditoriums. In these all-film venues the projector was placed to the rear of the audience and, as the program commenced, musicians seated near the stage took up their instruments and began to play. What was heard was the music they knew, with little thought of synchronising appropriate music to action on the screen. On occasions, a lecturer on stage would deliver a discursive account of the plot, while actors, singers, and sound effects provided additional commentary backstage. From about 1913 onwards, professional musicians began to make artistic musical statements to support images unfolding on the screen. Different arrangements of musicians provided musical sound: sometimes it was supplied by orchestras or small ensembles; in other instances it was provided by a pianist or a theatre organist; and occasionally by someone operating a player-piano or Fotoplayer. Eventually, musical directors in cinemas started to use cue sheets, which prescribed the tempo, duration, and title of the music, and the opening dialogue or action for each sequence in the film. Some musical directors compiled their own cue sheets. Others preferred the cue sheet devised by the motion-picture companies. Many musical directors across Australia borrowed scores from music libraries: the standard fare was concert music, 'gems' from popular classics, salon music, hit tunes from Tin-Pan Alley and, later, 'hot' jazz arrangements. Australian compositions were rare, almost buried in music libraries beneath the weight of music from abroad. In the opulent city picture-palaces that emerged in the early 1920s, music created a 'highbrow' ambience; the musical director's carefully compiled score was played by the cinema's resident 'symphony' orchestra.

Of the 259 silent feature films produced in the era, only 67 survive. The •National Film and Sound Archive (NFSA) has released several of these on video recordings, complete with restoration work, colour tints, and musical accompaniment. Music-making is often essential to the plot and includes (silent) bush dances, soirées, musicians accompanying formal balls and, in the 1920s, enthusiasts dancing the latest jazz craze. Original scores held in the National Library include those composed by Herbert de Pinna and Frederick Hall. Allan & Co. and Paling & Co. were the major publishers of Australian film music. Their published music consisted of short, episodic pieces of sentimental charm and illustrative music intended to augment the appropriate emotional moments in the film. Originally scored for piano, these pieces could easily be modified (often marked with cues) for ensembles or orchestras. However, local composers and compilers of film music were largely unknown to reviewers of films or to audiences. Although film-industry journals such as *Everyones* and *The Film Weekly* reported in detail on musical accomplishment in cinemas, little information or publicity about this extensive musical activity found its way into newspapers of the day, apart from reviews of grandiose live stage presentations in city cinemas.

During the sound era, limited resources available for film-making meant that music was the lowest priority in Australian film production. To keep within budgets, works by composers of the past (Beethoven, Mendelssohn, Tchaikovsky, Wagner, Elgar) were used as background music. Between 1930 and 1970, 35 composers were commissioned to write scores for feature films. The sporadic nature of film production restricted opportunities for composers in film. Generally, film music was disregarded by critics and the public, although some theme songs caught the attention of film audiences. The perception was that locally composed film music was an art form outside the existing musical heritage of Australia. That it did not arouse interest suggests it may have been dismissed as unimaginative or lacking originality or verve, with the inference that it was neither technically accomplished nor artistic enough to flourish. Where film music was written about, there was insufficient rigour when referring to composers. Their names were frequently misspelt and, too often, production companies omitted the names of composers from screen credits. Further, books and articles that refer to the history of Australian film in this period tend to ignore composers. Within the industry, visionaries such as Raymond •Longford, Ken •Hall, and Frank •Thring Snr were outspoken supporters of the value of music and film as artistic partners. In the 16 feature films produced by Cinesound Productions (1932–40; see •Cinesound), Hall made increasing use of film music, encouraging his musical directors to experiment and become more practised at delivering what was required. The films he made in the 1930s comment substantially on connections between Australian musical and social life. For example, the sophisticated homestead house party in •The Squatter's Daughter (1933) includes first-rate dance music played (on screen) by the Jim Coates Orchestra; themes from Wagner's *Träume* are employed as a *leitmotif* to depict Alma, the seductress of a willing clergyman in •The Silence of Dean Maitland (1934); and the musical drama •The Broken Melody (1938) features an operetta climax composed by Alfred Hill and featuring tenor Lionello Cecil, the Richard McLelland Choir, and members of the ABC Symphony Orchestra. •Efftee Productions (1931–34) made shorts using a diversity of musical talent, including singer Kathleen Goodall accompanying herself at the piano, the Sundowners male quartet, instrumentalists, vaudevillian George Wallace, the Melbourne Chinese Orchestra, and Jack O'Hagan singing and providing piano accompaniment for some of the 13 theme songs he composed for films.

The largest employer of composers after World War II was the Department of the Interior's film unit (later, the

Music

Commonwealth Film Unit, now •Film Australia), which has commissioned over 400 scores from 100 composers, creating the largest collection of manuscripts in Australia (deposited in the Australian Archives). One of the earliest was composed by John Antill for **School in the Mailbox** (1947), a film nominated for an Academy Award in 1948. Many of these scores exhibit stirrings of innovation and imagination, and many embody resolutely personal visions, becoming as much reflections of Australian life and customs as are the images provided on the screen.

In the 1950s and 1960s, the film industry was in the doldrums. Few feature films, and even fewer scores, were produced. Foreign production companies using Australia as a location offered some work to Australian film-makers, but the scores for these films were commissioned from overseas composers with international reputations, including Ralph Vaughan Williams, John Ireland, Alfred Newman, Matyás Seiber, Ernest Gold, and Dimitri Tiomkin. The exclusion of local composers from such projects caused hurt and bewilderment. Some, notably John Henry Antill, Esther Rofe, Robert •Hughes, and Dulcie •Holland, had been composing documentary film scores since the mid 1940s, and their work was acknowledged by innovative producers at the time as a big step forward for film music in Australia. Others, such as Willy Redstone, Lindley •Evans, Raymond Hanson, Peter Sculthorpe, and Don Burrows, had contributed scores for feature and documentary films. During this period, only three Australian composers were engaged for international projects: Alfred Hill and Henry Krips for Columbia Pictures' •Smithy (1946) and Sydney John Kay for the Rank Organisation's •Bush Christmas (1947). Sculthorpe wrote a score for Michael Powell's production •Age of Consent (1969) but, after technical problems in the recording session, it was replaced by a score by the English composer Stanley Myers.

With the re-birth of the film industry after 1970, composers exhibited a renewed energy in their creativity. Bruce •Smeaton, Brian •May, and Peter •Best led the way and were followed by others who were similarly driven to produce scores that portray Australia's history as well as its contemporary (and increasingly) diverse social profile. Sculthorpe's scores for •Manganinnie (1980) and •Burke & Wills (1985), Patrick Flynn's score for •Caddie (1976), Best's score for •The Picture Show Man (1977), and Bruce •Rowland's score for •The Man from Snowy River (1982) paint musical montages of the past. Best's quintessential musical description of home-spun, laconic folk hero Mick Dundee in •Crocodile Dundee (1986), John Clifford White's realisation of a dysfunctional social group in •Romper Stomper (1992), and David •Hirschfelder's amusing characterisation of internal politics within the competitive ballroom dancing scene in •Strictly Ballroom (1992) are examples of the talented soundtracks of this period. Similarly, •Mad Max (1979) and •Mad Max 2 (1981), with May's scores of chilling percussive impulses, are cinematic musical codes describing a terminally ill society of the future. Scores for films with child-centred scenarios, popular throughout the history of Australian film, are numerous: for example, George Dreyfus's score for **Let the Balloon Go** (1976) and Michael Carlos's score for •Storm Boy (1976). In the 1980s and 1990s, despite the increased output of Australian composers for film, many local producers continued to approach overseas composers. The Australian Guild of Screen Composers, established in 1984, went some way towards representing composers' interests, promoting awareness of locally composed music, and lobbying the •Australian Film Institute, the Australasian Performing Rights Association, and television's Logie awards to include categories of composition for film and television. In the past, with the exception of Sculthorpe and Dreyfus, composers tended to specialise, composing either for the concert hall, or for film and television. Today, composers of concert music are more likely than previously also to compose for film. Nigel •Westlake has achieved critical acclaim for his scores for **Antarctica** (1992), **The Edge** (1996), and •Children of the Revolution (1996), as has Ross Edwards for his dramatic score for •Paradise Road (1997). The practice of including previously composed (and well-known) music in scores to underpin plot developments has continued. Peter •Weir's productions •The Cars that Ate Paris (1974) and •Picnic at Hanging Rock (1975) employ previously composed music, with Smeaton's original music named as 'additional original music' in the screen credits. Weir used music from the past in his other Australian-directed films: •The Last Wave (1977, score by Charles Wain), **The Plumber** (1979, score by Rory O'Donohue), •Gallipoli (1981, score by May), and •The Year of Living Dangerously (1982, score by Maurice Jarre). Hirschfelder's **Strictly Ballroom** employs *Rumba de Burros*, *Tequila*, and *La Cumparsita* to create the Latin flavour in ballroom dancing; Guy Gross's score for •The Adventures of Priscilla, Queen of the Desert (1994) peppers the film with enduring rock songs and Abba classics; Best's score for •Muriel's Wedding (1994) also uses Abba; Westlake's score for •Babe (1995) acknowledges Saint-Saëns's *Symphony No. 3, 'Organ'*; Hirschfelder's 1997 Academy Award nomination score for •Shine (1996) celebrates the piano repertoire, in particular Rachmaninov's *Piano Concerto No. 3*; and Edwards's score for **Paradise Road** incorporates traditional airs and excerpts from the standard repertoire that was arranged as choral music by Margaret Dryburgh and Norah Chambers in a Sumatran prison camp during World War II. The efforts of pioneering musicians of the past forged pathways for contemporary composers, who have produced screen scores of creative distinction. For the first time, Australian scores are being noted and commented on by critics and audiences.

DIANE NAPTHALI

WILL PRIOR.

Interior of Theatre Beautiful.

LESLIE V. HARVEY.

PRINCE EDWARD
THEATRE BEAUTIFUL · CASTLEREAGH ST. OPP. HOTEL AUST.
Mng. Dirs. E. J. CARROLL · DAN CARROLL · E. J. TAIT
NOW PLAYING 2·30 AND 8

PROGRAM

Unit One (at 2.30 and 8)
"The Iron Trail Around the World."
Musical Accompaniment by Will Prior's Orchestra.

Unit Two (at 2.38 and 8.8)
LESLIE V. HARVEY, The Brilliant American Organist
at the £10,000 Orchestral Organ, playing
1. "The World is Waiting for the Sunrise."   2. "Yearning."

Unit Three (at 2.45 and 8.15)
WILL PRIOR, The celebrated Musical Director and his
Concert Orchestra, in
1. "Light Cavalry" (Suppé).
2. "Melodies of Other Days."
with Leslie V. Harvey assisting at the Orchestral Organ.

Unit Four (at 2.55 and 8.25)
WILL PRIOR'S Presentation to "The Iron Horse"
in Three Scenes :
1. "The Invasion." 2. "Introducing Judge Haller."
3. "Haller's Saloon."
Featuring Max and Babette, Leslie V. Harvey, Norman White,
Ernest Fellowes, James C. Bain, Edmund Duggan,
Babs Duggan, Stella Macpherson, Beryl Jollife,
Thomas Dowling and Marsh Little.

Unit Five (at 3.5 and 8.35)
William Fox's Theatrical Production
"THE IRON HORSE."

For Cast see last two pages of this Souvenir.

Will Prior conducting his Concert Orchestra on the special hydraulic-raised platform.

Section of Main Court.

The Hands of Harvey on the Organ Keyboard.

Music and live presentations were integrated into early film programs, as here at the Prince Edward Theatre, Sydney, 1924

Song-sheet cover for Jack O'Hagan's theme song for **Saturday Night** (1922)

Mutiny of the Bounty, The *see* **In the Wake of the Bounty**

My Brilliant Career

1979. Director: Gillian Armstrong. *Producer:* Margaret Fink. *Scriptwriter:* Eleanor Witcombe. Based on the novel by Miles Franklin. *Director of photography:* Don McAlpine. *Music:* Nathan Waks. 100 min. *Cast:* Judy Davis (Sybylla Melvyn), Sam Neill (Harry Beecham), Wendy Hughes (Aunt Helen), Robert Grubb (Frank Hawden), Max Cullen (Mr McSwat).

Gillian •Armstrong's film is archetypal 1970s 'prestige' Australian cinema. Adapted from literature (Franklin's classic, essentially autobiographical tale), concerned with rites-of-passage dramas in the life of an outback girl on the brink of womanhood, it is set at a time when Australia may be said to have been on the brink of nationhood. The fine detail of the period setting discriminates carefully among a number of class levels in both settings and costumes.

My Brilliant Career stands superior in this rather decorous genre because of the rigour with which it pursues Sybylla's growth and intentions, not lingering over the picturesque past for its own sake. The film follows her 'career' from her hapless father's rundown farm to the affluence of her grandmother's home, where she falls under the influence of her aunt Helen, whose broken marriage has made her wary of men, and to the relative grandeur of Five Bob Downs, the property of Harry Beecham, with whom she very nearly falls in love. Her brief time as governess with the filthy but not unlikeable McSwat family stiffens her resolve to belong to no one, at least not until she is certain of her own capacities and identity.

Armstrong develops the feminist thinking of the novel. That Harry is presented so attractively gives Sybylla's decision a more single-minded ideological cast: she resists what must have seemed an alluring offer of marriage and settles for trying a career as a writer. Judy •Davis and Sam •Neill came to international attention for their performances as Sybylla and Harry and, although the film may now seem a little naive (so is the novel), it remains a high-watermark of its genre, with Armstrong orchestrating some notable talents (writing, acting, cinematography, music) of the early days of new Australian cinema (see Revival, the).

BMcF

Judy Davis and Carole Skinner in **My Brilliant Career**

My First Wife

1984. Director: Paul Cox. *Producers:* Jane Ballantyne, Paul Cox. *Scenario:* Paul Cox. *Scriptwriters:* Paul Cox, Bob Ellis. *Director of photography:* Yuri Sokol. 95 min. *Cast:* John Hargreaves (John), Wendy Hughes (Helen), Lucy Charlotte Angwin (Lucy), David Cameron (Tom), Anna Jemison (Hilary).

In the 1980s, expatriate Dutch film-maker Paul •Cox was the prime chronicler of the emotional lives of suburban Melbourne. This film is based, he claims, on the break-up of his own marriage, and he has allied himself sympathetically with the character of John, who is nonplussed when his wife, Helen, announces that she wants to leave him. Cox is less interested in motivating the break-up than in charting its aftermath. One of its effects is to make John aware of the fragility of all human relationships: the marriage of Helen's parents exists as an unexamined complacency; and his own parents have survived an early infidelity by the mother. The film's strength is in the way it tests bonds that have previously been taken for granted and in Cox's readiness to go beyond linear realism in the process. An unexplained train racing across the screen at intervals has an oddly unsettling effect: it draws our attention to the film as an artifice at the same time as it adds to the sense of unease.   BMcF

Myles, Bruce (1940–   ) ACTOR/DIRECTOR   Bruce Myles began his acting career in 1959 with the Independent Theatre in Sydney. He worked in the United Kingdom from 1965 to 1971, and returned to Australia, where he became primarily associated with the Melbourne Theatre Company, as both actor and (from 1978) director. He played Chief Prosecutor Barker in •**Evil Angels** 1988, and Reginald, the accountant taken hostage in the unreleased **Breakaway** (1989). He has had small roles in several other feature films (including **The Road Builder,** 1971; **Sweet Talker,** 1991; •**A Woman's Tale** 1991). He directed two short films (one of which, **Ruthven,** won the 1989 Australian Teachers of Media Award for Short Fiction) and co-directed (with Michael •**Pattinson**) the feature film •**Ground Zero** (1986).

IB

Lucy Charlotte Angwin and Wendy Hughes in **My First Wife**

Mystery Island

1937. *Director:* J.A. Lipman. *Producer:* Jack Bruce, George Malcolm. *Scriptwriter:* Harry Lauder II. *Director of photography:* George Malcolm. *Music:* Rex Shaw. 56 min. B&W. *Cast:* Brian Abbott (Morris Carthew), Jean Laidley (Audrey Challoner), William Lane-Bayliff (Captain Druce), William Carroll (Chief Officer Vowels), George Doran (Reverend Abel/Detective Flynn), Moncrieff Macallum (Green/Arnold), Desmond Hay (Packer).

A murderer (Arnold) is one of 10 people shipwrecked on a Pacific island, but only the captain knows which one is the murderer, and the captain has lost his memory. This plot premise is convincingly established, except for some creaking model work as the ship goes down, but the mystery generates little tension. There was more drama among the cast: Brian Abbott and Leslie Hay-Simpson (who acted under the name Desmond Hay) were lost at sea while attempting to return to Sydney in an open boat from location on Lord Howe Island. The film was modestly successful, but only as a supporting feature.　　　　　　IB

N

Naked Bunyip, The

1970. *Director*: John B. Murray. *Producer*: John B. Murray. *Scriptwriters*: Ray Taylor, John B. Murray. *Director of photography*: Bruce McNaughton. *Music*: Janet Laurie (composer), Gerald Lester (music), John Romeril (lyrics). 136 min. *Cast*: Graeme Blundell (market researcher), Gordon Rumph (Computer Chief), Barry Humphries (Edna Everage).

The Naked Bunyip holds a special place in Australian film history for helping dispel the long-held view that Australians had no desire to see locally produced films. Producer-director John B. •Murray bravely took on the foreign-owned distribution–exhibition chains by making a film that could be shown in independently hired halls and cinemas. As his subject, he chose an 'if it doesn't work, nothing will' topic: sex. Murray artfully fashioned a 136-minute feature on varied aspects of Australian sexuality. The often-confronting documentary material is humorously laced by a dramatic narrative starring Graeme •Blundell as an inept market researcher, foreshadowing his •**Alvin Purple** persona a few years later. Humour is also found in the brief cameo of Barry •Humphries as the housewife, not-yet superstar, Edna Everage.

The Commonwealth censor (see Censorship) considered it too risqué at the time and tried to cut the film. Murray chose to render 'inoffensive' the saucier bits with a superimposed graphic of a bunyip. Murray's defiant political stand created massive publicity and helped the film become a hit. However, the censorship and distribution battles should not overshadow the film's importance as a clearheaded chronicle of Australia's sex attitudes at a time of massive personal and societal change.

BMcF

Naked Country, The

1985. *Director*: Tim Burstall. *Producer*: Ross Dimsey. *Scriptwriters*: Ross Dimsey, Tim Burstall. *Director of photography*: David Eggby. *Music*: Bruce Smeaton. 92 min. *Cast*: John Stanton (Lance Dillon), Rebecca Gilling (Mary Dillon), Ivar Kants (Sergeant Neil Adams), Tommy Lewis (Mundara), Simon Chilvers (Inspector Poole), John Jarratt (Mick Conrad), Neela Dey (Menyan).

Set in northern Qld in 1955, **The Naked Country** is a strident melodrama that dramatises the long-running issue of land rights between pastoralists and Aborigines in northern Australia. Based on Morris West's novel, written in the 1950s, the film uses stereotypes from that period and proceeds to interrogate their underlying values and assumptions. Lance Dillon is established in the opening scenes as a patronising and uncompromising White farmer with little regard for Aboriginal rights or concern for his wife Mary. Dillon's point of view is vehemently opposed by young Mundara, who resents Dillon's disregard for Aboriginal land rights. Mundara tells Dillon that Dillon would not survive three days living off the land, a challenge that changes both men and eventually becomes the dramatic centre of the film. Dillon's 'potency' and power, with regard to both the Aborigines and Mary, is symbolised by his importation of a pedigree bull to service his cows. When Mundara and fellow Aboriginal youths kill the bull, the political and social issue of land rights moves from a rhetorical level into the physical realm: Dillon is forced to take up Mundara's 'challenge' and fight a prolonged battle for his life as the Aboriginal youths pursue him across the outback.

The uncompromising position expressed by Dillon is contrasted in the film by the liberal attitudes of Sergeant Neil Adams. Adams is established, in the early sections of the film, as a potential 'hero' and a romantic partner for Mary. This is conveyed not only through the casting (good-looking Ivar •Kants compared with the austere-looking John •Stanton), but also in the way the film establishes an exotic history for Adams as a basis for understanding his sympathy for the Aboriginal point of view. He is also 'endorsed' through Mary's attraction to him (they have a brief affair). Interestingly, however, the film eventually reveals Adams to be weak, symbolised by his alcoholism, thereby shifting the audience's attention and sympathy back to Dillon and his primal conflict with Mundara. Mary's return to her husband reinforces this.

The film closes with Dillon expressing his respect for Mundara and Aboriginal culture: this is symbolically expressed by Dillon swinging the dead man's tribal implement in the same manner as Mundara did throughout the film. In terms of the political balance between pastoralist and Aborigine, the film's ending represents a progressive shift that can be compared with the viewpoint endorsed at the close of •Bitter Springs (1950), a film that addressed similar issues 35 years earlier.   GM

Narrative paradigms

Australian film conforms to a number of clearly defined narrative paradigms, notably the domestic melodrama and the epic tale of survival. Together they raise an interesting model for national analysis—the city dramas reinforcing commonality of European origins, and the bush dramas proposing 'difference' and the ennobling effects of a pioneering attitude. Often the two were combined to create a dialogue. Early models drew on early literary 'examples' and also reflected domestic preferences in theatre. Quality innovations by Raymond •Longford (•The Sentimental Bloke, 1919) and Franklyn •Barrett (•The Breaking of the Drought, 1920), found a local response, but costs and distance failed to ensure a return from international markets. Other experiments with realistic urban narratives, such as •The Kid Stakes (1927), did not lead to the establishment of an enduring genre. The national epic found a natural home, beginning with •For the Term of His Natural Life (1927) and later In the Wake of the Bounty (1933) and •Heritage (1935). Frank •Hurley attempted to adapt his documentary approach to the adventure silent •The Jungle Woman (1926), but the story-line floundered in melodrama as the characters floundered in New Guinea swamps.

The banning in NSW of bushranger films in the 1920s, allegedly because of the rise in crime they inspired, curtailed a promising line of development. The rural comedy based on or inspired by the novels of Steele Rudd (On Our Selection, 1920; The Hayseeds series) used knockabout humour and contrived story-lines. Adventure star Reginald L. (Snowy) •Baker made a few successful films, including

•The Man from Kangaroo (1920) but continued his career in the USA. Limited home-grown narrative models served the industry well until the arrival of sound, by which time local audiences were favouring American studio productions. Competing studios of the 1930s, such as Melbourne's •Efftee Productions and Sydney's •Cinesound, attempted to modify their modes of production to suit local consumption. The Pat •Hanna series at Efftee—•Diggers (1931) and •Diggers in Blighty (1933)—created an enduring Australian stereotype—the larrikin bushman soldier, but productions were hampered by inadequate finance.

Cinesound in Sydney revived the pioneering epic with •Tall Timbers (1937), and domestic melodrama with Ken G. •Hall's •The Silence of Dean Maitland (1934). Tales of mistaken identity and long-lost heirs to fortunes appeared as a sub-genre, which may have related to an emerging national preoccupation with estrangement from the United Kingdom. The effects of the Depression, competition by American studios, and the cost of conversion to sound had almost stifled feature film production by the end of the 1930s. Hall later produced the key national epic •Smithy (1946), the story of Australia's most famous aviator Charles Kingsford Smith, released in the USA as Pacific Adventure. Charles •Chauvel, Australia's most prolific producer/director, began his most significant output in the 1930s. His innovative •Uncivilised (1936) probed the perils of the outback, as a female investigative journalist pursued a wild white man, perhaps inspiring •Crocodile Dundee (1986). Two wartime productions — •Forty Thousand Horsemen (1940), followed by •The Rats of Tobruk (1944) — mixed quirky melodramatic plots with dry digger humour. •Jedda (1955) made full use of the Australian landscape but, as in most of Chauvel's work, an over-melodramatic script marred the achievement. Postwar activity relied almost entirely on imported productions, including Ealing films of the 1950s based on documentary events (•The Overlanders, 1946; •Bitter Springs, 1950). A short-lived partnership among director Lee •Robinson, actor Chips •Rafferty, and a French company produced exotica such as Walk into Paradise (1956), which failed in all markets. Only Cecil •Holmes' fine compendium of stories by Henry Lawson, Frank Hardy, and Ralf Peterson—•Three in One (1957)— displayed a commitment to social analysis, but Holmes' leftist politics contributed to the film's distribution problems. The import On the Beach (1959) aptly depicted Melbourne as the last city left at the end of a nuclear war.

The 1970s and 1980s revival (see Revival, the) responded to a brief influx of quality 'imported' productions such as •Walkabout and •Wake in Fright, both produced in 1971. The new industry was a stridently home-grown phenomenon, its talents drawn from television and the theatre, using local directors who had learnt their craft in those areas or at the fledgling film and TV school. Story-telling skills had to be developed by writers and directors, and a whole range of personnel, from the producer down, refined production skills. While government support released film-makers from international feature film financing models, it also led to narrative innovations that did not conform to mainstream American paradigms.

The lack of writers with feature film expertise was a major problem. From the outset the industry resisted importing scriptwriters, and Terence Rattigan's adaptation of Patrick White's *Voss* remains unproduced to this day. Experiments with 'ocker' comedies—•**Stork** (1971), **Barry McKenzie** (1972), and •**Alvin Purple** (1973)—were inspired by the British sex comedies of the 1960s and, while popular with local audiences, did not set an appropriate tone for a national film industry. The substantial financial successes of the ocker films did not guarantee their survival.

The following stage saw the development of locally positioned film stories, usually in period settings. •**Sunday Too Far Away** (1975) and •**Picnic at Hanging Rock** (1975) set the style for loose narratives that neither promised nor delivered formal closure although, in terms of the development of Australian film, a significant industrial achievement had been registered by the making of both films. **Sunday's** narrative simply ended, rather than being concluded, although there is considerable evidence that John •Dingwall's original story-line contained more formal dramatic elements. **Picnic**, derived from Joan Lindsay's purposely enigmatic novel, inspired many successors with the benefits of period settings. Other period films followed in quick succession—•**The Getting of Wisdom** (1977), •**Between Wars** (1974), **Break of Day** (1976), and even tongue-in-cheek spoofs such as •**Eliza Fraser** (1976).

The characteristic films of the early revival stage affected a poetic film style heavily reliant on visual qualities and art direction. Elements of plot, characterisation, and formal closure were not given a high priority. The emphasis on art direction and calculated photographic effects may have been designed to deflect viewers from problems of story and plot. These period films, while they avoided analytical development of characters, and generally avoided psychological exploration altogether, opened ongoing debates on representations of Australian life and identity.

The narratives were situated on the canvases of epic painting, mixed with domestic realism and modified melodrama. After Fred •Schepisi's promising début feature •**The Devil's Playground** (1976), which dealt with sexual and religious tensions in a Catholic boys' school, his •**The Chant of Jimmie Blacksmith** (1978) attempted to move the period genre into the depiction of racism and dispossession of the Aborigines, but its violent scenes elicited a muted critical and commercial response.

Critics noted narrative defects in the period drama: unmotivated action and dialogue, weak or inconsistent characterisation, lack of formal closure, recessive heroes and heroines, and the general omission of formalised character goals and aims. •**My Brilliant Career** (1979), •**Newsfront** (1978), •**'Breaker' Morant** (1980), and •**Gallipoli** (1981) attempted to break this straitjacket by building in elements of formal closure, but failed to make the outcomes character-driven. Writers and directors would not circumvent these problems until well into the 1980s.

The adaptations of successful plays such as •**Dimboola** (1979), and the consistently popular dramas of David Williamson—**The Removalists** (1975), •**Don's Party** (1976), and •**The Club** (1980)— began a tradition of films sourced from plays. Like the melodramas of the 1920s they posed other problems. Literalistic attempts at social realism often made the films endlessly talkative and the issues seem, in retrospect, less than consequential. Hannie Rayson's **Hotel Sorrento** (1995) raised a similar response in the 1990s. The personal narratives of Paul •Cox were more authentic—•**Lonely Hearts** (1982), •**Man of Flowers** (1983), and •**My First Wife** (1984) used their grounding in the lives of the Melbourne middle class to present emotional conflicts of real intensity. The first approach was literary, the second more filmic.

Genre experiments included telemovies such as *The Plumber* (1979) and •**Petersen** (1974), an urban comedy of manners starring Jack •Thompson and Wendy •Hughes, and the **Casablanca**-inspired •**Far East** (1982), starring Bryan •Brown and Helen •Morse. These linked emerging stars into localised versions of British and American genres, although the main characters lacked identification with the milieu depicted and often came across as spectators to the working out of their own destinies. Michael •Thornhill's •**The FJ Holden** (1977) essayed a gritty Ken Loach-like realism, but the intention was misread by the public and critics alike. When dedicated genre-thrillers were attempted, such as •**Patrick** (1978), they often did better overseas than on the local market which, it seemed, was not ready for genre production.

Even established television genres such as the crime film provided little inspiration. Perhaps the weight of cultural baggage films were required to carry precluded stories based on conventional oppositions of good and evil. Choice of narrative styles attempted, with varying success, to present a world view, and to depict characters and events that were 'Australian', although the controlling motivations were, in the final analysis, commercial. By the late 1970s these strategies were beginning to wear thin and film-makers and producers were looking for new ways of attracting audiences and, hopefully, making their films more 'commercial' in the Australian context. This meant the revival of the period film for one last big-budget fling, as well as launching a search for 'foreign' genres that could be located in the Australian context. A rush of films attempting to claim the status of national epic followed, with •**Gallipoli** at one end of the spectrum and •**The Man from Snowy River** (1982) and •**Phar Lap** (1983) at the other. The sporting epic •**The Coolangatta Gold** (1984) marked the nadir of this nationalistically motivated endeavour, its mediocre story-line mirroring the social conservatism of the times.

Experimental narratives had had an even briefer efflorescence, and the work of Bert •Deling (**Pure S…**, 1975), Albie •Thoms (**Palm Beach Story**, 1980), Esben •Storm (•**In Search of Anna**, 1979), and Haydn •Keenan (**Going Down**, 1982), while gaining renewed critical attention at the present time, did not lead to further innovation. Jim •Sharman's realisation of the Patrick White script •**The Night The Prowler** (1979) left local audiences and some critics baffled. Lower-budget films such as •**Winter of Our Dreams** (1981) and •**Heatwave** (1982) examined contemporary themes of love and betrayal, but even these modestly experimental narratives were eclipsed by the spate of conventional films spawned by the 10BA tax-based system of film funding (see Finance).

In this overheated period, the quality of scripts declined as the industry became driven by shoddy financial imperatives. A glut of inferior films was produced and quality productions such as •**Monkey Grip** (1982), based on the Helen •Garner novel of the same name, had difficulty finding a market. The loose apparently unstructured narrative confused most filmgoers and critics. Gillian Armstrong's direction of •**The Last Days of Chez Nous** (1992) put Garner's style in firmer focus. Peter •Weir's major Hollywood-style drama set in Indonesia •**The Year of Living Dangerously** (1982), appeared somewhat dated, and the talents of Mel •Gibson and Sigourney Weaver did not ensure a viable American release.

Films stripped of the period underpinning them were filmed in cities that were not so different from cities in the USA and Europe. They had their narrative weaknesses exposed to a more penetrating critical gaze. Measured against foreign productions, contemporary Australian subjects began to appear risky ventures. Gillian Armstrong, after her début success with the •**My Brilliant Career** (1979), took on the music film genre in •**Star Struck** (1982), which adapted the tried and true formula of an unknown band making good against all odds, but the dramatic oppositions were weak. The music theme was to surface again in her •**Hightide** (1987). Ken Cameron's •**Fast Talking** (1984) also failed to engage general audiences. •**Razorback** (1984) a dedicated horror film with a terrifying special-effects pig, was dismissed by local critics and generally rejected by the Australian movie public, yet was quite well received by American audiences.

Optimism still ran high, but the relative commercial and critical failure of many films showed that something was wrong with the industry. The conventional wisdom was that many of the failed films were too understated to be promoted successfully, or that the films would only appeal to specific audiences, or that Australian distributors did not know how to promote innovative product. But even when films appeared to be aimed and pitched directly to a specific audience, the real problems lay in the story development processes.

The praise that Australian feature films had previously garnered from overseas and local critics rapidly diminished. The early 1980s saw the industry struggling to survive. This was a crisis period during which production values took precedence over story structure and characterisation. Producers and directors were pre-eminent and the writers' possible contributions were marginalised. Ultimately, the industry's two resounding successes succeeded through their reliance on durable stereotypes. **Mad Max** (1979) was inspired by both the Australian cult film **Stone** (1974) and **The Wild One** (1954). Firmly defined in the action genre, the significant gestures of the protagonist are mainly physical, and any self- or social-analysis is excluded. Good and bad social forces are clearly opposed, with the good characters being forced into more desperate acts of violence to counteract the bad. Mel •Gibson's character follows the Brando model, remaining speechless for long sections of the film. **Mad Max** had two sequels—•**Mad Max II** (1981) (in the USA it was called **The Road Warrior**) and •**Mad Max: Beyond Thunderdome** (1985)—a sure indicator of a successful genre innovation.

Television comedian Paul Hogan made his screen début with •**Crocodile Dundee** (1986), the apotheosis of the larrikin hero transposed into an exotic bush epic. Its success was due to an astute integration of cultural clichés with the carefully reconstructed 'ocker' hero. The Paul Hogan persona of **Crocodile Dundee** owes something to Pat •Hanna, and the story-line has some similarities with Charles •Chauvel's •**Uncivilised**, where a woman journalist goes in search of a wild white man. By applying a success-driven paradigm in which the hero achieves all his goals, **Dundee** created the perfect cultural bridgehead into the American marketplace. The sequels seemed unable to repeat this formula. The story-lines were notably weaker and the social canvas less finely observed.

•**Shame** (1988) applied the conventions of the classic American western, translating the setting to country-town Australia, and substituting a woman lawyer on a motorcycle for Alan Ladd on a horse. Like the Ladd character in the classic **Shane** (1953), the protagonist Asta arrives in a town where evil is rampant in the form of gang rape. She uses her mental and physical skills to punish the wrongdoers and continues on her way. **Shame**, while attracting favourable critical comment in Australia and the USA, did not achieve success in the cinema, but is a reliable performer with TV audiences.

Australian film-makers revitalised the futuristic action movie laced with violence. Like the Mad Max series, •**Romper Stomper** (1992) and **Metal Skin** (1995) draw on the tradition of American exploitation films. The makers of •**Mad Max** took on the American thriller genre with •**Dead Calm** (1989), although the story is the standard piece of survival against all odds, as Billy Zane pursues Nicole •Kidman around a drifting yacht. The ending was reshot after extensive audience-testing of the finale indicated that the Zane character had to be convincingly terminated by the heroine. •**Dead Calm** was a calculated genre thriller rewarding the production company's attentions by going to blanket American release.

Intensive script-editing by applying the standard Hollywood paradigms codified by Syd Field and Lynda Segar became a primary development tool of the 1990s. Its application by writers and directors demonstrated a resurgence of interest in the power of the narrative, and confidence in the use of two key elements of film construction—the endearing character construct and the use of developed social-realist observation. Nadia •Tass and David •Parker's •**Malcolm** (1986) employed intensive script development strategies, and their subsequent films —Rikky and Pete (1988), •**The Big Steal** (1990), and •**Mr Reliable** (1996) — used off-beat narratives combined with street realism and special effects to create a resurgence of the urban comedy.

These street-wise comedies, retaining strong elements of social-realism, showed that lower budgets did not reduce the chances of box-office success if the story-lines were sufficiently well honed. Owing something to the content, if not the style, of British social realism of the 1950s and 1960s, these films gave fresh inspiration to the development of contemporary themes. The low-budget success •**Proof** (1991) from the writer/producer/director team of Lynda •House and Jocelyn •Moorhouse triggered a flow of films based on social observation and well-honed narrative skills.

While the story-line of •**Strictly Ballroom** (1992) may be thin in the extreme, its energy of characterisation and interaction, and the mastery of cinematic technique signalled a new era in Australian narratives. The resurgence was validated by the Cannes Palm D'Or for •**The Piano** in 1993. During the 1980s and 1990s Australian film developed a number of enduring paradigms: the story of worth and survival, the larrikin hero or sometimes heroine, the likeable loser, the family melodrama, often incorporating the dialogue and dialectic between city and country—the city being tough and corrupting, the country being empowering and purifying. These are the prevailing myths of the Australian film industry reborn into the 1990s.

More recent box-office successes, including •**The Adventures of Priscilla, Queen of the Desert** (1994), •**Muriel's Wedding** (1994), and •**Babe** (1995), used intensive script development to refine their appeal. As Australian product assumes a higher profile in world markets, the stakes are raised in terms of film story-telling. Australian films have become international films. This fundamental acceptance sums up the industry's new-found maturity and confidence. •**Shine** (1996), •**Love and Other Catastrophes** (1996), •**What I have Written** (1996), and •**Love Serenade** (1996) signal a return to the 'personal' film model so often proposed but rarely produced during the 1970s, allied with a much more hard-headed approach to story construction and character goal realisation. The successes of the period 1984 to 1996 have been achieved through a better understanding of the rules of film story-telling, and also a growing ability to tailor stories to satisfy audience expectations.

The current range of Australian film production demonstrates an improved understanding of genre rules and preferences, illustrating an effective, if sometimes uncomfortable, welding of commercial and cultural imperatives. Current Australian production must, however, continue to struggle with the potentially divergent demands of cultural relevance and economic viability.   IAN STOCKS

National cinema   As critics, film directors, policy-makers, and audiences, we routinely situate Australian cinema as a national cinema in our commentary, film-making, lobbying, policy-making, and appreciation. This enables us to place Australian cinema internationally in relation to other national cinemas and Hollywood. And it enables us to tie the local cinema to the international through a model of the cinema: the national cinema model.

The national cinema model evolved to create a modest space nationally and internationally for local film-making activity alongside the dominant Hollywood cinema. National cinemas make sense, as film historian Thomas Elsaesser once observed, 'only as a relation, not as an essence'. For its part, Australian national cinema was shaped by the competition provided by the North American film-production and distribution industry, and in its role as a subsidiary component of runaway productions of that industry: for example, Stanley Kramer's classic film on the coming of a nuclear holocaust •**On the Beach** (1959).

In their own domestic markets, as well as internationally, national cinemas are often structurally dispensable. Exhibitors, distributors, and audiences can make do without their product. Of the 238 theatrical releases in Australia in 1991, 60 per cent were from the USA, 10 per cent from the United Kingdom, 14 per cent from continental Europe, and nine per cent from Australia; of the remainder, three per cent were from other territories. Such marginalisation makes them dependent. National cinemas are mostly mixed commercial and public enterprises, sustained by a high degree of formative government assistance. Australian cinema is what it is today because of ongoing government assistance since 1969, which has helped Australian features in the 1980s to make up between five and 21 per cent of the local cinema box office.

As a national cinema, Australian cinema has responded to Hollywood's pre-eminence through local film production, film policy, and critical strategies designed to compete with, imitate, oppose, complement, and supplement international cinema. Australian film producers often tackle the competition head on at home and abroad, with titles such as •**Crocodile Dundee** (1986), •**The Piano** (1993), and •**Babe** (1995), which circulate in the same way as Hollywood major product. Such films are, if not imitative, then interchangeable with the international product, as the prevailing international styles, techniques, concepts, and sensibilities are used, adjusted and transformed in their local enactment in national productions.

Film-makers counter Hollywood competition by seeking 'complementarities': local specificities in domestic social events, issues, stories, and myths, which foreground the coherence of the national cultural system. Fred •Schepisi drew on a dramatic Australian incident in •**Evil Angels** (1988), the story of a baby taken by a dingo at Uluru (Ayers Rock) and the ensuing court case, which made world news; Ken •Hannam told the story of a famous shearers' strike in •**Sunday Too Far Away** (1975); Simon •Wincer used the story of a legendary race horse of the Great Depression in •**Phar Lap** (1983); and Peter •Weir focused on the Gallipoli campaign of World War I in •**Gallipoli** (1981), a film whose distribution enlisted the educational apparatus, with schools around the country organising matinee visits. Film-makers also drew on more localised approaches by foregrounding the Australian speech in the work of scriptwriter and playwright David •Williamson (•**Don's Party**, 1976; •**Stork**, 1971; The Removalists, 1975; •**The Club**, 1980).

Almost every national cinema at some stage goes local in order to go international. Without a strong and continuous tradition of film-making, Australian cinema has marketed its national history as spectacle: for example, in •**We of the Never Never** (1982). The humanist values, individuality, black humour, and quirkiness of contemporary Australian films are often said to establish the international appeal of films such as •**Sweetie** (1989), •**Lonely Hearts** (1982), •**The Adventures of Priscilla: Queen of the Desert** (1994), and •**Proof** (1991). Going local holds out the prospect of a culturally authentic, medium-to-low budget cinema recouping its money from the domestic market and being attractive to international audiences. This can be seen in 1970s classics such as Fred •Schepisi's •**The Devil's Playground** (1976) and

Phil •Noyce's •**Newsfront** (1978), and in 1990s titles such as Baz •Luhrmann's •**Strictly Ballroom** (1992) and P.J. •Hogan's •**Muriel's Wedding** (1994). There is also room here for a commercially oriented exploitation cinema: for example, the 1970s sex comedy •**Alvin Purple** (1973) and the low-budget exploitation film •**Mad Max** (1979).

Film-makers can also seek an aesthetic distinction by promoting cinema art. Since the 1970s film revival (see Revival, the), there has been a handful of internationally recognised Australian cinema auteurs—notably Weir, Bruce •Beresford, and Schepisi from the 1970s; Gillian •Armstrong, •Noyce, and George •Miller of the 1980s; and, lately, the Australian-trained Jane •Campion. There is also no shortage of avant-garde cinema stylists (Albie •Thoms in the 1970s; Tracey •Moffatt in the 1990s), internationally renowned documentary and ethnographic film-makers (David •Bradbury, Denis •O'Rourke, David and Judith MacDougall, Bob •Connolly and Robin •Anderson), feminist experimental film-makers (Helen Grace, Layleen Jayamenne) and indigenous filmmakers (Moffatt). There is also a group of recognisable actors used by art cinema and mainstream directors alike (Judy •Davis, Jack •Thompson, Sam •Neill, Russell •Crowe).

One function of auteur cinema has always been to take a nation's cultural tradition as expressed in its novels, theatre, and opera and to present them in the cinema. Australian cinema is rich in such adaptations: Raymond •Longford's adaptation of C.J. Dennis's •*The Sentimental Bloke* (1919), Armstrong's take on Miles Franklin's •*My Brilliant Career* (1979), Weir's version of Joan Lindsay's •*Picnic at Hanging Rock* (1975) and Christopher Koch's •*The Year of Living Dangerously* (1982), Schepisi's rendition of Thomas Kenneally's •*The Chant of Jimmie Blacksmith* (1978), Beresford's adaptation of Henry Handel Richardson's •*The Getting of Wisdom* (1977), and Richard Franklin's version of Hannie Rayson's •*Hotel Sorrento* (1995). It was not until Picnic at Hanging Rock that art and national identity were brought together in film: for the first time, a nation's character seemed publicly embodied in a personally idiosyncratic and poetic cinema that critics and audiences alike could contrast to slick Hollywood commercial entertainment.

The largely European-derived art-film model had an impact on Australian production. Australian cinema has, since the 1970s, been a cinema created for the representation of modernist cultural themes (existentialism, the absurd, alienation and loneliness, 'boundary situations') and modern political issues (class, gender, race), providing the doubling of aesthetics and politics. The best representatives of this tendency in Australian cinema usually combine fragments of all of these: from Picnic at Hanging Rock (1975) to Paul •Cox's •**Man of Flowers** (1983); from Beresford's **Don's Party** to Armstrong's •**The Last Days of Chez Nous** (1992). Many of Australian cinema's narrative resolutions and thematic preoccupations—although not necessarily their means of realisation—are classically those of the international art cinema. Witness **Mad Max**, •**Caddie** (1976), •**'Breaker' Morant** (1980), and •**Monkey Grip** (1982). In such films, localising becomes the means of internationalising; internationalising the means of localising.

National cinemas work to be local while streamlining themselves to be of interest to audiences outside Australia. To be 'wholly local' in a pure form, in front of and behind the camera, is not the natural condition of a national cinema. Beresford's •**The Adventures of Barry McKenzie** (1972), a classic comedy of an 'ocker' in the United Kingdom, was made at a time when film policy and criticism gave near exclusive priority to representing Australia to itself. But this film was self-consciously made for the British and Australian market, and was successful in both (the Barry Humphries comic strip on which the film was based was more popular in the United Kingdom than in Australia). Its hero, the monstrous Barry McKenzie, must visit the 'old country', England, in order to acquire his inheritance.

This process of streamlining has a bearing on what is selected from the cultural archive in the making of films. British involvement in the colonial and postcolonial periods is foregrounded in many Australian films, including notable successes such as **Gallipoli** and **'Breaker' Morant**. When Michael •Blakemore adapted Chekhov's play *Uncle Vanya* for his •**Country Life** (1994), he set it in turn-of-the-century Australia. The play's metropole–province relation was reconfigured as a British/Australian relation within an Australian family. Sometimes this divide is updated, as in Mark •Joffe's evocation of the Ealing comedies of the 1940s and 1950s in •**Spotswood** (1992). In this film, an English efficiency expert, played by Anthony Hopkins, is contracted to restructure an Australian moccasin factory where the workers are more interested in racing slot cars than working. He eventually 'bends' towards his eccentric workers.

Most national cinemas involve players (actors, directors, distributors, festival organisers, composers, and so on) in the creation, financing, and circulation of the national cinema. One manifestation of this is the on-screen figure of the 'American in Australia'. Stacy Keach and Jamie Lee Curtis in •**Roadgames** (1981) do battle across the Nullabor plains with an odd assortment of 'weirdos', including a sex murderer, unfriendly police officers, and cranky drivers. In Australian films, Americans are often problematic figures with whom Australians need to come to terms, as in •**The Man from Snowy River** (1982) and **Dallas Doll** (1993). In the latter film, Sandra Bernhard plays a morally questionable character who seduces, and is simultaneously desired and eventually repelled by, nearly every other character. American actors sometimes play Australian characters, most notably Meryl Streep in •**Evil Angels**, Robert Mitchum and Deborah Kerr in •**The Sundowners** (1960), and Richard Chamberlain in •**The Last Wave** (1977) (in which the Chamberlain character is given a South American heritage).

Many smaller national cinemas are—in product, orientation, industry, and language—part of each other. For Australia and New Zealand, the close cultural, language, and historical links forge an Australasian film-making identity. Vincent Ward, Jane Campion and Cecil •Holmes (regarded by some as a film-maker whose promise, evident in •**Three in One** (1957) and •**Captain Thunderbolt** (1953), was tragically unable to be fulfilled) are all New Zealanders. There is a long history of Australian directors making New Zealand films, including Longford's **A Maori Maid's Love** (1916). New Zealand actors have always had a strong presence in Australian films, from Vera James in Franklyn •Barrett's 1921 classic **Girl of the Bush** (1921), to Neill in •**Dead Calm** (1989) and •**Death in Brunswick** (1991).

Smaller national cinemas are often part of larger national cinemas. The Australian cinema of the 1930s consciously foregrounded its links to the United Kingdom, using it as a means both to create product suitable for sale there and to express a dominant cultural ideal that projected Australia as a British-derived society. In •**Broken Melody** (1938), the talented musician denied opportunity within Australia goes to the United Kingdom to claim his destiny as a composer of merit, and later returns to Australia to reclaim his lover, retrieve his place in his father's affections, and bail out the family farm. For its part, the postwar Australian feature cinema up until the 1970s was, in large part, a consequence of the outreaching of other national cinemas—British, American, and even French and Japanese cinemas.

There can, at times, be a happy mutuality between, on the one hand, Australia being the location for other imaginings and, on the other, Australians claiming these imaginings as theirs. The most obvious examples here are Harry Watt's •**The Overlanders** (1946), Jack •Lee's •**A Town Like Alice** (1956), Fred Zinnemann's **The Sundowners**, Robert Powell's •**They're a Weird Mob** (1966), Nicholas Roeg's •**Walkabout** (1971), and Ted Kotcheff's •**Wake in Fright** (1971). These directors took Australian cultural artifacts—literature for Powell, Zinnemann, and Kotcheff; and previous 'images' of Australia for Roeg—and transformed them into films. **Wake in Fright**'s middle-class school teacher experiencing a vernacular working-class male regional culture fashioned the male ensemble film. With its dystopic view of mateship, and its construction of the Australian male as dysfunctional and misogynist, it introduced the idea of endemic and structural evil to Australian cinema. These rhetorical figures have persisted through to the present, from **Don's Party** to •**Romper Stomper** (1992). **Walkabout**'s emphasis on the uncanny and the other-worldly, the mundane and the spiritual, and the tragic clash of Aboriginal and non-Aboriginal peoples in the Australian continent, opened directly onto Weir's **The Last Wave**, Schepisi's **The Chant of Jimmie Blacksmith**, Moffatt's **Night Cries: A Rural Tragedy** (1989), and the children's films •**Storm Boy** (1976) and •**Manganinnie** (1980).

At some time or other, most national cinemas are not coterminous with their nation states. Weir's romantic comedy **Green Card** (1991) is typical of the high-budget strand of Australian film-making in the 1990s: it has an Australian director, it is funded by French and Australian investors, and its post-production was carried out in Australia. It is a French–Australian co-production set and shot in New York. **Green Card** tells the story of a 'marriage of convenience' between a French man, played by Gerard Depardieu, and an American woman, played by Andie MacDowell. The comedy and the developing romance between these two characters evolves once they are subject to an official investigation over the status of their 'marriage'.

There are also the various diasporic cinemas that sometimes have the stature of a cohesive 'national' cinema: for example, the 'overseas Chinese' cinema of Clara Law (**Floating Life**, 1996) and the Jewish cinema that is Henri •Safran's comedy '**Norman Loves Rose**' (1982) and the Jackie Farkas short film **The Illustrated Auschwitz** (1992). Farkas's film recounts a survivor's experience of the Holocaust and how her memory of it is connected to her first post-Holocaust cultural experience of watching the children's classic **The Wizard of Oz**. Monica Pellizari's short films, such as **Just Desserts** (1993), contribute to both the Italian and Australian cinema. By the same token, there also appears to be an Aboriginal and Torres Strait Islander cinema in, for example, Tracey Moffatt's **Night Cries**; the touring season of films **Hidden Pictures** (sponsored by the Australian Film Commission); and films that promote an indigenous cinema whose beginnings are located in collaborations between non-Aboriginal film-makers and Aboriginal actors and individuals, such as Ned Lander's tale of an Aboriginal band on the road in •**Wrong Side of the Road** (1981) and Noyce's low-budget road movie •**Backroads** (1977).

Despite the promise of the festival circuit and the national cinema ideal of international cultural exchange, most national cinemas are language cinemas relying substantially on fellow language speakers for profit. As an English-language cinema, Australian cinema is oriented in the first instance towards English-language audiences and the diverse pathways of English-language cinema. Without language barriers, British, Australian, New Zealand, and Canadian film-makers have a chance of breaching the huge North American market and so producing major international films. Some Australian films—**Crocodile Dundee**, **The Man from Snowy River**, the **Mad Max** (1979, 1981, 1985) trilogy, and **Babe**—can claim their place as dominant

entertainment forces. **Crocodile Dundee** was the most successful film internationally in its year of release and the most successful foreign film ever in the American market: it made $174.6 million in its American theatrical release. By virtue of its size, wealth, and international dominance, English-language cinema is the most internally differentiated and diverse of all language cinemas. This makes it notoriously difficult to describe the Australasian, British, and Canadian cinemas: their significant internal diversity and fragmentation are partly explicable in terms of the enormous diversity of the Hollywood cinema as the vernacular English-language cinema.

Australia's social and cultural proximity to the USA also means that local films feel Hollywood competition intensely. Sharing a common language and many common cultural infrastructures, there is no large gap between locally produced cinema and the dominant Hollywood cinema. Like the USA, Australia is a new-world society, a former British colony, and a society formed by ethnically diverse migration. Like their Canadian counterparts, Australian film-makers are often seen as lesser versions of American film-makers. Producing in English also encourages a sense amongst audiences, distributors, and exhibitors that Australian cinema is interchangeable with American cinema and, to a lesser extent, British films. Making distinctions among the various cultures in English is undercut by the coherence of the English-language cinema and cultural system and its domination by Hollywood cinema.

If this carries with it the problem of distinguishing what is Australian from what is American and British, it also makes for a local advantage. Schepisi maintains that it is 'easier for Australians to go and work in that area [universal film]' than it is for many other nationals. He maintains that 'it's part of us, it's just as much a part of us as being Australian. So it's not like we're going over and working in some strange area entirely'. This quality—which makes distinguishing American, British and Australian components to the culture so difficult, as they are always shifting inter-generationally and historically—leads to an unsettling quality in local product, in part because, at the same time that Australian product can look like Hollywood and British films, it is also different from it.

Australian film-makers do not have either the huge cinema market of the USA or the large cinema market of the United Kingdom, France, Italy, and Germany to work from. Because national cinemas are, as a rule, more solidly commercially grounded in larger than in smaller countries, a medium-sized national cinema such as Australia's has a more difficult time of it. In 1993 France released 133 local features, while Australia released only 18 of its own. Servicing 17 million people, Australia is not large enough to support an extensive film-production industry, nor the scale of local production necessary for higher-budget film-making. As a medium-sized producer, it cannot as easily differentiate itself by occupying a market niche, as can the larger French, Italian, and British cinemas.

In international circulation, Australian cinema is known through a limited number of auteurs and actors. As with Ingmar Bergman and Liv Ullman in the Swedish cinema of the 1960s, Australia was known in the late 1970s for its directors (Armstrong and Miller) and their actors (Davis and Gibson): the literary drama, **My Brilliant Career** and the dystopic road movie **Mad Max** were held to express a distinctive Australian voice. Because Australia is necessarily at the margins of the international trade in national images, it becomes known internationally for a narrow range of features: peoples, stereotypes, myths, and settings. At the height of **Crocodile Dundee**'s extraordinary world-wide success in 1986–87, Australian tourists were reported as resenting the film's outback yokel version of the Australian type. Ways of knowing Australia by its flora, fauna, and landscape privilege the countryside and the wilderness. Australian cinema's penchant for producing 'oddballs' such as Bubby (•**Bad Boy Bubby**, 1994), Barry McKenzie, Muriel (**Muriel's Wedding**), and David Helfgott (•**Shine**, 1996), or monsters such as the roo-shooters in •**Razorback** (1984) and the misogynist men in **Wake in Fright**, intersects with the representation of Australian 'freakishness' in news items on international screens. Such estimations have wider relevance in structuring the interpretation of Australian cinema generally. Serge Grunberg's major 1994 essay on Australian cinema for *Les Cahiers du Cinéma* (September, 1994; see also International Perceptions) is part of a long-standing French habit of mythologising Australia as the desert island of the South Pacific.

National cinemas legitimate and keep alive a variety of film-making and critical options. They provide multifaceted ways of valuing, knowing, acting, and believing in an Australia cinema. They enable powerful distinctions to be made between Australian cinema and other national cinemas; between Australian cinema and the Hollywood cinema; and between different kinds of Australian cinema. The national cinema idea has so shaped and defined the public understanding of Australian cinema that it is almost impossible to think of any other way of knowing it.   TOM O'REGAN

National Film and Sound Archive, *see* Archives

National Film Theatre of Australia (NFTA)

Founded in 1966 'to bring the best of world cinema to as wide an Australian audience as possible', the NFTA aimed to complement the roles of film festivals and film societies through the year-round presentation of seasons of related films.

The first national season in August 1967 was a partially imported selection of films by Josef von Sternberg, who had been a guest of the Sydney Film Festival two months earlier. The first fully imported season—the films of Japanese director Kon Ichikawa—was screened nationally in April 1968. By 1972, branches had been established in all states and the ACT, showing both imported prints and films selected from the 16mm libraries of Australian television networks. The films and programs were wide-ranging, including 'Hitchcock's British Films', 'Surrealism in the Cinema', 'Sixties New Cinema', the musicals of Astaire and Rogers, films featuring Humphrey Bogart, and films directed by Mizoguchi and Ozu.

Attendances peaked in 1974, with more than 51 000 admissions to around 720 screenings, and a membership of 9800. This rapid growth taxed an organisation that relied on enthusiasm and voluntary effort. Although funding from the newly established Film, Radio and Television Board of the Australia Council (see Australian Film Commission) made possible the employment of full-time staff in the national office in Sydney, resources were thinly spread. In 1979 the national committee agreed to a merger with the •Australian Film Institute (AFI), as required by the then funding authority, the •Australian Film Commission.

For several years the AFI injected substantially increased funds into the NFTA, but membership and attendances declined to a level that the AFI considered financially unsustainable, and the last NFTA screenings were held early in 1982. The founding director of the NFTA was Robert Gowland (1968–75), who was succeeded by Bruce Hodsdon (1975–77) and Rod Webb (1977–79).   BRUCE HODSDON

Neal, Chris COMPOSER   Chris Neal is a prolific composer for film. Since 1978, he has composed many scores for feature films (for example, the thriller **13 Gantry Row**, 1998); for 18 documentaries (**The Disappearance of Azaria Chamberlain**, 1982); for telemovies, including films that target a younger audience (the *Winners* series and the *Touch the Sun* series); and for television miniseries (*Bodyline*, 1984). When composing for film, Neal prefers to read the script as early as possible to allow his subconscious to start working on some aspect of what may become music in the film. When he becomes 'in synch' with the images, he targets a particular emotional line and elevates it with the music chosen. He works with as many orchestral colours as are at his disposal. Even though he may construct orchestrations at the piano, he maintains 'a feel' for the rhythm of the sequence, which will not vary from one viewing to the next. He then extrapolates orchestrations from this process if the score is to be recorded acoustically. Neal regards his score for **Turtle Beach** (1991) fondly; its East-meets-West philosophy gave him personal satisfaction. His favourite television works include *The Shiralee* (1987), and he is also proud of the film •**The Nostradamus Kid** (1993).   DIANE NAPTHALI

Ned Kelly

1970. *Director*: Tony Richardson. *Producer*: Neil Hartley. *Scriptwriter*: Tony Richardson, Ian Jones. *Director of photography*: Gerry Fisher. *Music*: Shel Silverstein. 103 min. *Cast*: Mick Jagger (Ned), Clarissa Kaye (Mrs Kelly), Mark McManus (Joe Byrne), Allen Bickford (Dan Kelly), Ken Goodlet (Superintendent Nicholson), Frank Thring (Judge Barry).

In the 1960s, many film-makers planned movies based on the story of Australia's best-known bushranger and folk hero, anticipating local appeal, but only this version by celebrated British director Tony Richardson reached the screen. The result, despite Richardson's record and Jagger's 'Kellyesque' anti-establishment reputation, is enormously disappointing. Jagger's star quality is negated by a catatonic performance and an appalling accent; he stumbles through the film with his mind obviously elsewhere (Marianne Faithfull, who accompanied Jagger to Australia for the shoot, attempted suicide during filming and lay in a coma for several days). The legend (both Jagger's and Kelly's) suffers as a result. Unlike earlier film versions of the story, **Ned Kelly** emphasises the treatment meted out to poor Irish-Catholic farmers by the Protestant establishment as a motivation for Ned's actions, and characterises Ned as a class warrior and a proto-republican. The innovative device of linking the gang's exploits through the use of anti-authoritarian ballads, never quite comes off.   BEN GOLDSMITH

Neill, Sam (1948–   ) ACTOR

Of the stars who emerged from the new Australian cinema (see Revival, the) of the 1970s, Sam Neill was perhaps the first to take off internationally, preceding Mel •Gibson and Judy •Davis, who both went on, a year or so later, to major successes overseas. Neill was born in New Zealand, where he had five years experience as a director of the National Film Unit. He appeared in several films there, including the popular **Sleeping Dogs,** before coming to Australia in the year of its release, 1977. His darkly brooding good looks, recalling the young James Mason, made him an instant star when he played Harry Beecham in •**My Brilliant Career** (1979). He had to wait nearly a decade for another comparably rewarding role in Australian films.

By 1981, he was appearing in films overseas, including **The Final Conflict: Omen III.** He returned to Australia to star as Captain Starlight in an overlong remake of •**Robbery Under Arms** (1985), cut down from the miniseries of the same name, in which Neill's performance had style but not quite the panache of Peter •Finch's earlier incarnation of the role. He plays the heroine's gentlemanly mentor and lover in •**For Love Alone** (1986). In •**The Umbrella Woman** (1987) he played a ladies' man, who drifts into a country town to work as a bartender, and unsettles the female protagonist.

Both these were reasonably rewarding roles, but his next offered him several rigorous challenges: in •**Evil Angels** (1988), he played a real-life figure, Michael Chamberlain, co-starring with Meryl Streep (as Chamberlain's wife Lindy, accused of murdering her own baby—an incident that had led to a much-publicised court case). Under the direction of Fred •Schepisi for the second time—the first was in **Plenty** (1985), filmed in the United Kingdom and also starring Streep—Neill gave a subtle performance as a man under great pressure. In 1989 he co-starred with Nicole •Kidman in Phil •Noyce's tense thriller •**Dead Calm** (1989).

He showed an unexpected gift for comedy in John •Ruane's off-beat •**Death in Brunswick** (1991), as the scruffy cook of an even scruffier restaurant, who gets involved with crooks. He played Holly Hunter's tormented husband in •**The Piano** (1993), and the disillusioned doctor in •**Country Life** (1994), Michael •Blakemore's undervalued outback version of Chekhov's *Uncle Vanya*. In •**Sirens** (1994) he played the Australian painter Norman Lindsay, and he was a Russian agent in the dark comedy •**Children of the Revolution** (1996), which also starred Judy Davis. Between visits to Australia and his native New Zealand, he has been persistently in demand overseas—in, for instance, **The Hunt for Red October** (1990), **Jurassic Park** (1993), and **The Horse Whisperer** (1998)—without becoming a top star. Perhaps this is the result of a versatility that shies away from imprinting each role with his own signature; perhaps his persona is too quiet, too reflective, for top male stardom in

Sam Neill

an international cinema dominated for over a decade by movies that value action over acting; perhaps, simply, he is more interested in being an actor than a star. If that is the case, he has had as good a range of opportunities, in both cinema and television, as most actors of his generation.

Other Australian films: Just Out of Reach (1979), The Journalist (1979), Attack Force Z (1982), The Magic Pudding (forthcoming, anim.).　　　　　　　　　　　　　　　　　　BMcF

Nevin, Robyn (1942–　) ACTOR　A dominant figure in Australian theatre, Nevin, now director of the Sydney Theatre Company, has also racked up a string of impressive cinema performances, without becoming the major film star her talents might have led one to expect. After graduating from the National Institute of Dramatic Art in 1960, she concentrated on the stage, where she won a reputation for versatility, and she also had a four-year run as a television announcer in Tasmania. Her first film role was as a nun in •Libido (1973, 'The Priest' episode). She had good character roles in •Caddie (1976), •The Irishman (1978), and •The Chant of Jimmie Blacksmith (1978), and she played a worried social worker in Fighting Back (1982). Her best film roles to date are in two films released in 1983, both directed by Carl •Schultz: Kate, the erstwhile lover of Ray •Barrett's private eye in •Goodbye Paradise; and the working-class aunt fighting her snobbish sister for custody of their orphaned nephew in •Careful He Might Hear You (1983). She invests the former with a beguiling autumn glamour; the latter with a detailed understanding of the quotidian demands of a battler's life. In 1997 she showed a subtle sense of comedy in her cameo as the High Court judge in •The Castle. In 1986, she directed her first film, •The More Things Change, a drama of relationships and role reversals.

Other Australian films: •The Fourth Wish (1976), •The Coolangatta Gold (1984), •Emerald City (1989), Resistance (1992), Greenkeeping (1992), Lucky Break (1994), •Angel Baby (1995).　　　　　　　　　　　　　　　　　　BMcF

New Australian cinema, *see* Revival, the

New South Wales Film Corporation, *see* New South Wales Film and Television Office

New South Wales Film and Television Office (NSWFTO)　Based in Sydney, NSWFTO was established to extend the work of the New South Wales Film Corporation (NSWFC). The latter, which commenced operation in July 1977, was created to assist the development of feature films and, through its Government Documentary Division, to make, promote, and distribute documentary films for NSW government departments. Having accumulated a sizeable deficit, the NSWFC was disbanded in 1988.

That year the FTO was established as a statutory authority with responsibility to provide financial and other assistance to the film and television industries in NSW. Unlike the NSWFC, however, the FTO was originally not permitted to invest in production. During the 1992–93 financial year, the FTO was allocated $1 000 000 by the state government for strategic production investments. Healthy financial returns on the investments subsequently convinced the state government to include annual allocations for equity investments in film and television productions as part of the FTO's recurrent funding. In 1996–97 total expenditure by the FTO on production investment amounted to $2 257 000. Approximately 80 per cent of that sum went to fiction features, 12.2 per cent to documentary, 4.4 per cent to television series, and 3.2 per cent to animation.

Among its many ongoing activities, the FTO actively seeks to attract offshore production to NSW, and to encourage local producers to develop projects in association with overseas partners. As with the NSWFC, the Government Documentary Unit of the FTO is the executive producer of film and video programs for NSW government departments. Initiatives include support for projects by indigenous film-makers, the Young Filmmakers' Fund, and contributions to the development of the 'new media' industry in NSW. The FTO also functions to extend and inform screen culture within the state. To this end, the FTO makes funds available for the support of a range of activities, including film and television festivals and seminars, and a number of locally based screen-studies newsletters and journals.　　　　　　　　　　　　　KEITH BEATTIE

New South Wales, history and images
The first motion-picture footage produced in Australia was shot in NSW, then still a self-governing colony of the United Kingdom, on a Sunday afternoon in October 1896. Passengers were filmed disembarking at Manly pier from a Sydney Harbour ferry, and this short film was exhibited at the Tivoli Theatre in Pitt Street in central Sydney a few days later. On the modest scale that then pertained throughout the world, the shooting and exhibition of one-minute 'actualities' (see Documentary and non-fiction, silent), Australian film production had commenced. However, NSW was not to keep its pioneer status for long.

Except for that very first film, in the ever-changing, cyclical history of the Australian film industry, NSW, for all its dominance of film production in Australia throughout the following century, has never led those changes. A week or two after the Manly ferry film, the French camera operator Maurice Sestier, and his Sydney-based partner Walter Barrett, filmed the •1896 Melbourne Cup, a horse race that had already achieved a position as the as-yet unfederated Australia's premiere sporting event. For the next decade and a

In conversation with

ROBYN NEVIN

Let's start with your early life …

I was born in 1942 in Melbourne, lived in the suburb of Canterbury till I was 11, and went to school at Genazzano Convent in Kew—a very conventional and quiet life as a child, very conventional family, no hint of what was to come. Then we moved to Hobart and I went to a school called Fahan in Sandy Bay, run by two dedicated women, the Misses Morphett and Travers, who had a lasting effect on me and who provided a good argument for single-sex schools. It was a small school, and one of the headmistresses—Audrey Morphett—had a passion for the annual school play. She was also the senior English teacher. She used to take a famous story—a fairy tale or a children's story, usually a classic tale—and turn it into a school play each year. She spotted me one year—I think she thought, because I was small and pretty and had black hair and white skin, that I would make a good Snow White. That was how my career began—my love of theatre. She took it very seriously, and she convinced me of the seriousness of the pursuit. I was about 11.

I used to do the lead in the school play every year, which got me out of hockey practice and things like that … I was completely absorbed by the way in which you created a world: that imaginative process I found very persuasive. And I was a great reader. I lived in a world of books: I was one of those conventional children with a book under the bedclothes … But acting was the thing at school that I did very well—I knew that I did it very well. And so it seemed logical to proceed from there to NIDA [National Institute of Dramatic Art]. I remember the morning at assembly when a green prospectus was held up and it was described, and any interested students were invited to come to the headmistress's study and get a copy of it. And so I did, and I ended up going to NIDA in 1959, leaving school too early, before I had finished, but in order to be there as one of the original students. And that passion was supported by my parents with some nervousness, but the support was so great from the school that my parents were convinced by that and also it was on campus at the university … So I was just 17 when I went to NIDA.

Do you think your parents would have been worried if it had not been respectable?

Oh yes, I don't think they would have agreed. I can remember going up to have an evening with my mother and I think my father was there and Miss Morphett and Miss Travers, and we discussed it, and they really gave it their blessing, because it was part of an educational institution. And we did English 1 then and my English lecturer was Leonie Kramer, so it was all right … and we did Theatre History. There was a reasonably strong academic strain through the course—not that I cared about that. It all seemed proper, and it was partly supported or subsidised by the ABC.

Did you have a scholarship?

No, my parents supported me. And I worked in Woolworths. If I hadn't chosen acting I may well have had a career in management in Woolworths, because I remember they tried to snaffle me and promote me.

I'm glad they failed.

Well, I might have been heading a corporation by now, who knows?

What about the major shifts in your life.

Well, I had a long career as an actor. One of the most important times in my life as an actor was working for Rex Crampthorne in the 1970s. That opened up a new way of working in the theatre. Before that I had only experienced it as hierarchical, a system where the director held secrets that were imparted one at a time to a group of lowly powerless actors. Rex worked in a democratic manner and over an extended period of time. We would have three to four months of rehearsal. And it was all completely poverty-stricken, and unnoticed by the rest of the community. But it was serious research, laboratory work. That was the era of Grotowski, when theatre was considered a laboratory for research. Rex was a serious academic who just had a great sense of theatre, and so he opened a lot of doors for me. I began to understand the importance of the whole, as opposed to the alternative—which was the only way that I had known—which was always a mystery to me, and I was never comfortable. Suddenly I became comfortable: it was the whole that we should all be concerned with, and that suited my sensibility.

What do you mean by democratic?

Well, we worked at the pace of the slowest member of the group. Every member of the group's opinion was valued. And we all embarked on the journey together, and at the end of the journey—on opening night— we all knew as much as everybody else, everybody had contributed equally, because we waited for the slowest people. And I found that a wonderful discipline.

Where was this?

A little theatre called Jane Street in Sydney, which is no longer there. It was a little converted church hall in Randwick, owned, I think, by the University of NSW, under the umbrella of NIDA: it was NIDA sponsorship that enabled this to happen. I was there right at the beginning with Rex and then he developed the group and went on to other things. He was the single greatest influence … This was in the 1970s. I had graduated in 1961, so I had a lot of time in between.

And then I suppose the next most important thing would be my progression from being an actor to being a director, which was enabled by International Women's Year. There was a Women's Festival to celebrate that year, and they approached the Sydney Theatre Company [STC] and asked them if they would contribute, so the STC asked me (I think I was playing Lady Macbeth at the time). They asked me to chose a play to direct, and I chose a play called *The Butterflies of Kalimantan* by Jennifer Clare. And I directed that and it was very successful, and that was an extremely important move. The next most important thing was becoming an associate director of a state theatre company, so then I was in senior management at a time when there was a certain concentration on raising consciousness in the community to equalise the number of women in senior positions, so I was part of applying the affirmative action policies within the company. And I was associate director at the Sydney Theatre Company for three or four years and again at the Melbourne Theatre Company. The next most important thing was becoming CEO of a state theatre company (Queensland Theatre Company).

When was your first film?

•Libido with Fred (•Schepisi): it was his first film. He was making commercials and was very successful. And he wanted to make this little film—my part was called 'The Priest', and it was put into that parcel, given that ridiculous title of **Libido**, sold on its sexual merits, which was silly. I remember first meeting Fred at his house in Hawthorn, and it was a white room with a white piano, and *Trois Gymnopedie*, that Erik Satie piece, was playing when I was ushered into the room and was waiting for him. He approached the story very seriously, as a serious piece of writing. It was semi-autobiographical work by Thomas •Kenneally, who had married a nun. And I worked with a great friend and colleague, Arthur •Dignam. He and I were working actors in the theatre together. That's probably why Fred gave me the role. I think he was very attracted to Arthur in the role and then Arthur, I suspect, said, 'She's really good and interesting. Why don't you meet her?' And I remember meeting Fred and Rhonda who was then his casting agent, in a hotel room in Sydney—I think it was my first interview for a film, but I'm not sure—I have a very bad memory for all this history. But it was an extraordinary experience. I remember the technique that Fred used for doing 360-degree camera work for one particular scene between Arthur and me, and the cable just being wound around our legs till we virtually couldn't move. And the conditions were really tough—it was very low-budget. It is reminiscent of making one of the graduating student films now—everyone very new to it, very enthusiastic, but the conditions are really tough. I also remember Rhonda holding up an onion to make me weep and me saying, 'Oh no, I don't need the onion, take it away thank you'.

Had there been any attention paid to screen acting in your NIDA course?

I don't remember any. I don't think so.

Did you find any difficulty with it?

No. I do remember somebody coming up to me at the première and saying, 'I just want to give you this piece of advice—never, ever appear on screen again without makeup'. She was a make-up artist as it turned out—but I remember being shocked at that extraordinary response, because I believed absolutely in the importance of being real and I couldn't see any need to try and enhance my appearance, when I was playing a part.

The camera gets so much closer than an audience does—does that make a difference to your acting? Do you find the camera intrusive or do you just forget about it?

No, I don't forget about it. I don't work to a camera. I don't know how to, and I've never been encouraged to do so by a director. I think many directors I've worked with have been slightly in awe of the weight of my experience, because I've usually had more experience as an actor than they have had as a director. I can feel that they are often a bit intimidated, but I would welcome any advice about how to improve my film technique. I don't have a film technique. I just do it as truthfully as I know how, and I just know how to adjust from being in a large space to being in a small space. It seems obvious to me—it is just like life. If you are on stage, you try to reach people at the back of the auditorium, but if you are in a room you just try to reach those people. I don't work to a camera, if that is what you mean: I don't even know the jargon.

I don't either, but it just seemed to me that the technology and the people operating it would intrude into your performance.

Well, a theatre audience intrudes too. Of course, you can hear them, just as well as they can hear you—they forget that sometimes. You hear the coughing, the shuffling, the whispering, whatever sounds they make. And you have a sensor that takes into account whatever's happening out there. And there is a symbiotic relationship between an audience and an actor on stage—you affect each other, undoubtedly, as in any relationship between human beings in a live situation. Maybe on a film set some actors have that relationship with the camera—the camera is their audience, or the cinematographer behind it, or the crew. Some people I know work to the crew, and I have been on some sets where that makes a difference, where you can feel the attention of the crew. And then I've been on others where they just wait till a shot is complete, or they are just watching their particular area of work. But I have been in situations where crews really lock into the moment. And maybe that gives some actors something to work with.

What do you consider the key films of your career?

•Careful, He Might Hear You was a key film. It was interesting for me because I really wanted to play Vanessa (the Wendy •Hughes character), and the producer wouldn't even consider me because I wasn't a tall, beautiful blonde. And I could see exactly why they chose Wendy, of course, and she is a wonderful actor. But I really wanted to do it, and I knew it was absolutely within my range. I knew I could play Vanessa—I know that character very well, and I wanted to do that kind of obsession. It was one of the few times in my life when I've actually had an ambition and verbalised it, and been rejected. And I *love* Sumner Locke Elliott's work, and I did have a relationship with him, and I think he finally regarded me as one of his family because I had played two of his 'aunts', who were significant people in his life and significant works of literature in his life. I recorded a talking book of *Water Under the Bridge*, and I played Carrie, and he wrote this wonderful letter saying that he thought that was the ideal Carrie. So, I have that kind of range, because of my theatrical training, which I believe *is* the training ground for all actors in any medium. Because when I was young, working in companies, I was required to play a whole range of roles that, as a freelance actor working outside of the company, you would never have the opportunity to play—old, young, working-class, upper-class, a king, a servant, the whole range … But in films it is very unusual to play that kind of range, because people have an idea of the sort of persona that you project, and if you have projected it once that is what they expect. That is my impression of the film industry, but I am sure people would argue with that.

Lila is a wonderful role: the film has two great women's parts. And I also enjoyed Shasta in Water under the Bridge.

Yes, I think that was an important piece of Australian television—it was ahead of its time, because the miniseries was just beginning to be popular, and people had not yet got into that pattern of staying home three nights in a row. But I did get that enormous response, and people still come up to me and say, 'I love Shasta in *Water Under the Bridge*'. I hold that one very dear to my heart. It was a wonderful piece and wonderfully realised by the director.

How is the preparation for a stage role different from the preparation for a film?

In the theatre you rehearse towards presenting the whole story, and as I usually play large roles I am often on stage the whole way through, so what I work towards is developing the shape of the character in a two-hour period. In film you often have no rehearsal. So, by the time I come to the first day rehearsal in the theatre I have to have a thorough sense of the whole, and I find that two and half weeks in I have the whole in my head—you know that finally the whole of you will be seen, the audience has the whole of you in sight for the whole of the time you are on stage, and everything you express with your body for the whole of the time is meaningful. That is the major difference between film and stage—that you have that much control over the role and the audience's perception of it, and you control where the focus goes. In film, of course, the director controls where the focus goes. And in film you arrive and you just do three minutes a day, or three lines or a page, and you have to keep that graph of the whole journey in your head. And that is tricky.

Do you watch rushes and does that affect what you do the next day?
Not really—unless, in consultation with the director, there is some kind of concern about some aspect of the performance.

So, what is coming from inside your head is the determining factor?
Absolutely.

How did you prepare particularly for Shasta?
It was extraordinary, and I must salute the producers and the director of that because of their approach. They gave us four weeks of rehearsal. And, I remember Sam •Neill coming in (he was going to play Neil) to do a day of rehearsal, and instead of rehearsing we just sat around and talked about it, and a couple of days later he withdrew and went to Hollywood and that was the end of Sam Neill in Australia—we just missed him! So David Cameron and I played the central roles, and we had both read the novel. During that three-week rehearsal period, we had all our costumes for the whole series in our dressing rooms, and we were allowed to choose what our characters would wear that day (within a limited range), and we wandered in and out of wardrobe, makeup, administration, the producer's office, we talked and talked to the director, David and I did scenes together, and we just absorbed the whole, and by the time we came to do it I knew it backwards. It was a remarkable absorption process, which is exactly the process you have in the theatre, because you have four weeks during which the stuff is absorbed into the

muscles. And you feel the spirit of it—it is a mysterious process, and people have written theses on it, and sometimes it is not helpful to analyse too deeply, but there is something mystical, spiritual about it. I believe in the importance of the Gift—not that I think about it all day, but I believe fundamentally in it. So, we would come in to the set at 5 o'clock, in that studio in South Melbourne, with Igor [•Auzins) the director, and we just knew it, we did it, and Igor would say, 'That's terrific!'. Then the producer and the crew would come in and we would just do it. I couldn't do it now—my brain is so overloaded. The most extraordinary sequences—I had to cook, with amazing chunks of dialogue, emotional range, very complex moves, and I'd do the master and it would be perfect. Then we'd chop it up, and I'd have to remember the enormously complex sequence of moves in unison with the dialogue. It was very hard to do, but we just knew the material inside out—all of us, the director and the leads, and so on. There was something special about that one.

How was that different in terms of preparation from Careful He Might Hear You?
Well, I don't think we had any rehearsal period: I think we just got there on the day and got into costume and rehearsed. We would have had some time in discussion, reading I think, but no real rehearsal. So you have to bring it all with you on the day. It was very difficult filming with the little boy [Nicholas Gledhill]. He'd have a line of dialogue, and I think his mother had rehearsed it with him the night before, so it sounded very stilted. It didn't sound like a response to what I had just said, so I discovered this technique one day of saying, 'What, darling?' and he'd repeat it, so I'd say, 'What, darling?' as if I didn't understand it, and his natural need to communicate and help me to understand gave the lines the expression … I discovered it a bit too late in the filming, but once I did it was a great help.

It's an extraordinary performance from a little boy.
Well, he was an extraordinary child, and exquisitely beautiful. I grew very, very fond of him.

What about •Emerald City?
Emerald City was a flawed film. But it was important for me to do a work of David Williamson on screen. It was a play that I had loved doing and I felt very thankful to be in the movie version. I didn't expect to

be, because I thought I was probably too old, and not gorgeous enough, because that's the way producers tend to look at female actors. And I know there was a difficult moment over my hair because I fought to retain my grey hair, and the producers found that difficult, but finally they accepted it. It was difficult to do: it wasn't stylistically clear in terms of its direction or the way we approached it.

Was that in the writing?
No. The script had really (necessarily) reduced the play down, and John •Hargreaves was keen to get back a lot of the material from the original stage play, because he thought passionately—and I agreed with him—that some of the scenes had lost the wonderful structure that David had created for the stage play. And so some material was brought back, and there was a discussion about a stylistic approach that was based on those heavily dialogued Hollywood movies, of that marvellous period when they had a lot of dense dialogue spoken with great speed, but I don't think that it was stylistically consistent throughout the film.
   •The Castle I just completely adored doing! I am such a complete fan of the Working Dog people! When I was asked if I would be happy to do some work on **The Castle** for a very low amount of money, I said I would do anything for them—anything, because I think they are so brilliant. And I would be thrilled and excited to be part of anything that came out of that creative pool. I thought it was a wonderful movie.

How did you come to direct a film?
Jill •Robb rang up and asked me if I would direct •**The More Things Change**. And I was completely astonished, and very unconfident and she was persuasive and enthusiastic. She said she wanted a director with acting experience because she felt it was such a strong performance piece, and so she finally convinced me. I was very nervous until I started doing it, and then I just did it. I didn't understand what all the fuss was about concerning the transition from acting, because it is all story-telling and knowing where to put the focus. And directing actors—that I know how to do! It was the most wonderfully positive experience, because I knew how to do it without knowing how I knew. I didn't really do it any differently from directing a play. I learned so much from it that the next time the lead-up to the shoot will be very different—but I probably won't ever do it again. I haven't felt the need, the desire.

But I had a very supportive producer who set it up for me so that my cinematographer would help me in designing shots, and he'd just wheel me around as if I were the camera, and I'd say, 'Travelling two-shot' (and there were lots of travelling two-shots, because I adore them), and 'singles' and that's the coverage we did.

Did you ever think of acting in it yourself?
Oh god, no—I have no interest in doing both. They're two completely separate responses. I use different parts of my brain and my personality and character. I'm much more selfish as an actress. As a director I am enormously generous and loving and patient, and I adore the actors, but as an actor I have to have all that given to me.

Did you cast it?
Yes. But Jill Robb was in at every step of the way. I found it very difficult to cast the central role—a woman of that age and type. I was mad about Victoria •Longley: I saw her at NIDA and put her straight into a stage play, then into a film, then into another stage play, and then I said, 'I'll leave you alone now to get on with your own career'. I thought it was getting to the point where I had to find someone else to encourage.

Do you have any plans of filming anything the Queensland Theatre Company are doing?
I am very interested in the principle of preserving theatre works and when I first applied for the position up there I told the board I was very interested in approaching the ABC or SBS to look into the possibility of covering some of our productions. What with one thing and 40 000 others I haven't done it, but I must put it on the agenda again.

Are you thinking of it as an archival process or as a screen production in its own right?
Well, something between the two, though not a screen production. That's the tricky area—because something designed for the stage is another sort of beast.

Have you seen the South Australian Twelfth Night?
No, is that a good example?

No, I don't think it really works, but I understand why they wanted to do it.
So, I would be doing it with television cameras, and then close-up coverage, but not pretending that it is a film.

Perhaps something like American Film Theatre back in the 1970s?

Yes. Also it is a wonderful way of serving the regions, with stuff they would not get otherwise, and no-one's ever going to do on television. I'm very interested in that, and I think it would be wonderful if someone somewhere would develop a policy. For instance we are just about to go into development on *The Marriage of Figaro*: I've got Geoffrey Rush coming back to Queensland (the first thing he's done on stage since his Oscar), and we are opening a new theatre up there—brand new, state of the art, opening during the Brisbane International Festival. Queensland Theatre Company is opening it, and that will be an extraordinary production, and only Brisbane will see it. Already I've got the possibility of an *Australian Story*, following the process. The problem is, you don't want cameras in your rehearsal room, you don't want that kind of tension. But I think some productions are worth preserving.

Has there ever been an occasion when being a woman has made things difficult for you? Do you feel some sort of responsibility to other women?

I do, but not to the point where I will promote women over men for the sake of increasing the female quota. Actually we have an imbalance at the Queensland Theatre Company: I want more men. I think it is unhealthily unbalanced towards women. I do have a sense of responsibility towards woman—but I have greater sense of responsibility to nurture people in the way I was nurtured, and I was nurtured because there was a wonderful system in place and that's the system of the State Theatre Companies. It was actually a company that gave me the foundation on which I was able to build: that gave me opportunities as a freelance actor and director that I would never otherwise have had. I think there is something really wonderful about those arts organisations when they look to providing career paths for individual artists. It is changing, but as long as I've got any influence I will make sure there are career paths because I think it is important to build for the future. I think all funded bodies have a responsibility to the culture and to the state: we must look to both promoting and preserving and exploring the art form, and really taking care of individual artists. So, that's my greatest responsibility.

You mentioned the 'Gift' earlier…

It is talent. You can subsidise companies, and subsidise films, and subsidise writers—and finally what emerges is talent. All the support in the world—and I acknowledge that is important for infrastructure and policy-building—is not enough unless you allow talented people to come through, make opportunities available.

THIS INTERVIEW WAS CONDUCTED BY INA BERTRAND

---

half, Vic. was the centre of film production in Australia, a fact signalled by the Melbourne-based Limelight Division of the Salvation Army (see Documentary and non-fiction, silent; Historical representations), Australia's first film-production house, filming the elaborate parades and ceremonies surrounding the proclamation of the Commonwealth of Australia on 26 January 1901 in Sydney.

As the story film took over from actualities (again, the first Australian story films were produced in Melbourne), NSW began to assert itself as the dominant site for such productions. By 1910, the majority of such films being produced in Australia was being shot in NSW. Following the success of •The Story of the Kelly Gang (1906, produced in Melbourne), a cycle of bushranger films set the pattern for narrative feature films to be produced in NSW. Even after bushranger films were banned by the NSW police department and other story-lines were found to replace bushranging, feature film production continued to be located, for the most part, in NSW, with a plethora of production companies and producers, including subsidiaries of overseas companies such as Pathé (see also Documentary and non-fiction, silent), basing themselves in Sydney at different times.

In the period of silent-film production in Australia, which lasted until 1930, no less than two-thirds of all films produced in Australia were made in NSW and, in many other years, this proportion was higher. So dominant was NSW that the classic Australian film of the period, •The Sentimental Bloke (1919), was shot almost entirely in Sydney, despite the fact that the well-known narrative poem on which it is based, by C.J. Dennis, is clearly located in Melbourne. The other justly famous film of the period, •On Our Selection (1920), was also shot on location near Sydney, even though its literary origins located the stories in Qld. Although the first film studio in Australia was built in Melbourne, it was the studio opened in September 1912 at Rushcutters Bay in Sydney that, throughout the silent period, was Australia's most complete film-producing facility, firmly establishing NSW's dominance. After being suitably renovated, it continued to be used after the coming of sound.

Paradoxically, as film production dwindled throughout the 1920s, the position of NSW as the site of feature film production strengthened. By the mid 1920s, there was an increasing tendency for Sydney-based film-makers to seek exotic locations such as the Barrier Reef, the rainforests of Qld, and further afield in the Pacific and New Guinea. Urban-based stories tended to be shot in Sydney, often in studios rather than on location. The arrival of American and (later) British sound films threatened to smother an increasingly moribund Australian film-production industry.

The economic demands of conversion to sound technology reduced an already diminished film-production industry. Once again, Victorian-based producers took the initiative in sound-film production and, for a short while, it seemed as if Sydney and Melbourne might become equally important sites of film production. However, by the mid 1930s, film production had largely ceased in Melbourne, and Sydney was more than ever the centre of Australian feature film production. Throughout the rest of the 1930s, with the exception of one or two independent producers, home-grown feature films were almost entirely the products of the Sydney-based •Cinesound Productions, controlled by producer–director Ken G. •Hall. In 1934 a new sound studio was built at Pagewood in Sydney by the newly formed National Studios (see Studios). This company provided facilities for its sister company National Productions, as well as for independent producers. Although it was linked with Gaumont-British Picture Corporation, and through Gaumont-British to its USA owner Twentieth-Century Fox, both the production and studio arms of the company folded after two productions.

From the mid 1930s, the Australian feature film industry was almost synonymous with Cinesound Productions. Cinesound's main studio (number one) was in Bondi, Sydney, and the old Rushcutters Bay Studio was Cinesound number two. A small studio was maintained in Melbourne. All 16 Cinesound features produced between 1932 and 1940 were shot in NSW, in many cases using a mixture of bush exteriors and studio interiors. Even Charles •Chauvel, the most persistent of the independent producers, who had favoured Qld for many of his earlier films, shot his masterpiece •Forty Thousand Horsemen (1940) in Cinesound's Bondi studio and on the sandhills of Cronulla.

During and immediately after World War II, feature film-making became even more sporadic, and even more centralised in NSW. Other parts of Australia occasionally supplied exotic locations, but Sydney was where the producers and directors who were able to make films at all had their offices and facilities. Cinesound ceased feature film

production in 1940, and concentrated on newsreel production until the 1970s. Throughout the barren 1950s and 1960s, NSW was also the usual (but not invariable) location for the few overseas and co-productions made in Australia.

Despite its previous dominance and the slender thread of film production there in the three postwar decades, NSW was not in the vanguard of the largely government-led revival of the Australian film industry in the 1970s (see Revival, the). The earliest developments took place in Melbourne, and the first box-office successes were Melbourne-produced films. South Australia provided both the finance and the location for the first critical success of the new Australian cinema, •Sunday Too Far Away (1975), and Vic. was the location for the even more acclaimed Picnic at Hanging Rock (1975). It was not until 1977 that NSW followed the lead of the Commonwealth and other states and created its own film organisation, the New South Wales Film Corporation (NSWFC; see the New South Wales Film and Television Office).

While, like other state corporations or commissions, the NSWFC was given responsibility for all aspects of NSW government short- and documentary-film production, its most public responsibility was to encourage the production of feature films in an overall Australian context, rather than in the narrow context of NSW alone. The main form of this encouragement was financial assistance by way of script and project development, but direct investment in feature film productions was also undertaken. The NSWFC took a strong role in marketing of Australian films, especially those with which it had some financial connection. A key initiative was the opening of an office for this purpose in Los Angeles. Within two years, the NSWFC had invested nearly $3 million in a range of films, a number of which were notable successes, such as •My Brilliant Career (1979) and •Newsfront (1978).

In the decade following its creation, the NSWFC, like all such bodies, attempted to stay in touch with the dynamics of film production in Australia. It shifted its emphasis as demands required (from direct financing and investment to script development), supported a short-lived professional training program, sent some scriptwriters to the USA for further training, and even distributed films itself (as in the case of •Bliss, 1985). Despite the NSWFC, the fact that the offices of the •Australian Film Commission were in Sydney, and the fact that most of the producers in Australia were located in Sydney, NSW did not fully regain its prewar dominance of film production with the revival of film-making in Australia. While still the most productive state, its share of the overall production of films seldom rose above 50 per cent from the mid 1970s onwards and frequently fell below that figure. Changes in film-making practices and technology meant that films such as •Mad Max (1979), •Crocodile Dundee (1986), and many others were shot on locations outside NSW, while their production companies were based in Sydney. Important as the NSWFC was, private investment, especially during the 10BA period (see Finance), was responsible for the greater proportion of films produced in NSW.

In 1988 the NSWFC was replaced by the •New South Wales Film and Television Office (NSWFTO), which was initially under the direct supervision of the Minister for the Arts. A Board of Management was appointed in 1996. At its inception, the main aim of the NSWFTO was to encourage film production to take place in NSW. This was done by providing financial assistance for script and project development, but not by investing directly in films. In 1992, however, the financial reins were loosened, a Production Investment Fund was created, and the NSWFTO became an investor in some productions. Investment was made in several spectacularly successful films, including •The Adventures of Priscilla, Queen of the Desert (1994), and •Muriel's Wedding (1994).

The main role of the NSWFTO was to be a 'supporter' of the industry rather than a 'player', at a time when economic considerations forced states—particularly NSW, Vic., and Qld—into competition for film-production dollars. The source of production budgets was no longer state treasuries but the Commonwealth (through the National Film Finance Corporation and, as previously, the Australian Film Commission) and off-shore production companies. Qld, with a fully equipped modern film-studio complex, attracted most of the off-shore investment during the 1990s. This situation changed following the development, in the late 1990s, of a major studio complex in central Sydney by Twentieth-Century Fox.

The image of NSW is almost synonymous with the image of Australia in film. While this Australian image has been a shifting and dynamic one over the century of film production in Australia, NSW has provided the core and the diversity of that image. At the same time, films shot in NSW have tended to deny specificity of location. City and bush in 'NSW films' are more likely to be generically Australian than they are to be identifiably NSW. Sydney serves as *the* generic city in many films made there, and no particular recognition, or narrative and dramatic significance, is derived from the Sydney location, even when use is made of recognisable Sydney landmarks and features such as Sydney Harbour. As early as 1919, Sydney served this function: The Sentimental Bloke was shot in the streets of Woolloomooloo and on the sands of Manly Beach. The NSW bush has also served as both generic anywhere-in-Australia and acceptable substitute for other designated places in Australia. The •Dad and Dave series of films, up to the most recent (•Dad and Dave: On Our Selection, 1995), used bush locations close to Sydney instead of the 'genuine' locations

of Steele Rudd's stories, southern Qld. Forced by circumstances beyond his control, Chauvel reshot his climactic conclusion to •Jedda (1955) in the Blue Mountains near Sydney, as substitute for Northern Territory locations. In films such as •The FJ Holden (1977), Emoh Ruo (1985), •Idiot Box (1997), and Floating Life (1997), Sydney's outer suburbs stand for Australian suburbs everywhere. The western suburbs of Sydney serve as an index of an essential and geographically anonymous Australianness to a greater extent than does Sydney represent 'city' and the NSW countryside, the 'bush'. Certain locations are favoured by filmmakers. Braidwood in southern NSW has been used as a country-town setting in films as diverse as •The Year My Voice Broke (1987) and Dad and Dave: On Our Selection. The inner-city suburb Balmain has been used as location for numerous films including •Monkey Grip (1982), •The Sum of Us (1994), and •Children of the Revolution (1996). From as early as •Wake in Fright (1971), Broken Hill and its environs have been used to portray the harsher aspects of the Australian environment in films such as The Adventures of Priscilla, Queen of the Desert and a suitably post-apocalyptic setting for Mad Max 2 (1981). Through continued use, these locations become generic rather than specific. Although, in total, a considerable diversity of locations in NSW has been used for different films, these locations are often selected by film-makers and thus perceived by local and overseas audiences as distinctly Australian, rather than as specific and distinct images of NSW.

Few films celebrate any quintessential 'Sydneyness', or denigrate it for that matter. An exception is •Starstruck (1982), in which the Sydney Harbour Bridge is omnipresent in reality: the pub in which most of the action takes place is almost underneath the Bridge itself and, iconically, the pub and the stage of the Opera House in the final sequence of the New Year's Eve concert are replete with replicas and representations. Few films are quite as self-conscious in their use of Sydney icons, although there may be a certain ironic appropriateness that One Night Stand (1984) locates its nuclear-war scenario in and around the Opera House. The Sum of Us uses Sydney Harbour, at least to the extent that one of its main characters is a ferry captain. Occasional films have taken specific Sydney incidents as the inspiration for, or substance of, their narratives. •The Killing of Angel Street (1981) and •Heatwave (1982) take well-known events from Sydney in the 1970s as their basic plots. A historical ferry accident serves as a *deux ex machina* resolution to •Careful He Might Hear You (1983), a film that uses Sydney Harbour as both a literal and metaphoric divide between classes. More broadly, NSW is identified in some bush films. Little Boy Lost (1978), a film located in the bush, takes a true and widely publicised story as its narrative; and •The Chant of Jimmie Blacksmith (1978) uses some of the locations of the historical events upon which its narrative, from a Thomas Keneally novel, is based.

There is a clear dichotomy in the image of NSW created and maintained by the distinct images of bush and city. Bush locations, aided by the frequency with which the narratives that use them are placed in the past, almost inevitably reflect images of more essential Australianness: simplicity and demonstrable Australian 'values'. The city, whether specifically designated as Sydney or not, is a much more anonymous image of modernity and thus of essential 'city-ness' that overrides the specifics of geographic and cultural location. In contrast, the overall image of NSW is metonymic for Australia of the past and the present—outback, city, and suburb—an Australia in which the actuality and the specificity of NSW is submerged, ignored, or assumed to be unproblematically identical with Australia.

NEIL RATTIGAN

Newsfront

1978. Director: Phillip Noyce. *Producer:* David Elfick. *Scriptwriter:* Phillip Noyce. Based on an original script by Bob Ellis. *Director of photography:* Vincent Monton. *Music:* William Motzing. 110 min. *Cast:* Bill Hunter (Len Maguire), Wendy Hughes (Amy McKenzie), Gerard Kennedy (Frank Maguire), Chris Haywood (Chris Hewitt), John Ewart (Charlie Henderson).

Director-writer Phillip •Noyce has gone on to a very successful international career as the maker of such expensive action hits as **Patriot Games** (1994) and **Clear and Present Danger** (1994), but it is arguable that he has never made a more likeable film than **Newsfront**, which, of all the Australian films of the 1970s, remains perhaps the most attractive. Although it is set in the decade after World War II, it is not a softly nostalgic exercise; it is heartfelt in its sympathy for the decent man trying to hold on to ideals, but it is also astringent about the inevitable changes in postwar Australian life, with, on the one hand the attempts of the Menzies government to maintain British ties and, on the other hand, the irresistible lure of the USA.

From a story by Bob •Ellis (who subsequently disowned then reclaimed it), **Newsfront** skilfully balances and interweaves the private and the public. It has real historical value as a representation of key events of the period: postwar migration, Menzies's failed attempt to outlaw the Australian Communist Party, the Redex motor trials, and the 1956 Olympic Games in Melbourne. These events are foregrounded as they impinge on the lives of two rival newsreel cameramen: Len Maguire, who works for Cinetone, the all-Australian company; and Charlie Henderson, who works for the rival, American-owned Nesco, for whom Len's brother also works. The film traces

the parting of the ways for the brothers; the breakdown of Len's marriage to Fay, who is unyielding in her puritanical version of Catholicism; Frank's return—Americanised—to Australia; and Len and his sidekick's coverage of the Redex trial and the floods in and around Maitland in country NSW.

The public events are recreated partly from the use of actual newsreel footage, partly from specially staged action, and the melding of the two sorts of representation is a *tour de force*. This balancing act is reflected in the public–private interaction, and the sense of this dichotomy is reinforced (although not schematically) by the film's movement between colour and black-and-white. At its centre, providing a focus for the film's discourses on tradition versus progress, sexual freedom versus fidelity, and nationalism versus internationalism, is a towering performance from Bill •Hunter as the determined, compassionate Len. It has few rivals in new Australian cinema (see Revival, the).

BMcF

Newsreels, silent, *see* Documentary and non-fiction, silent

Newsreels, sound   By the sound period, the weekly newsreel form was well established, generally consisting of a number of unrelated short items on current events. It was shown in the first half of the cinema program, after the cartoon and before the second feature. Sound made a difference: it allowed greater realism and more cohesion by replacing intertitles with music and a spoken commentary, potentially creating the commentator as 'star'.

The first sound newsreel produced in Australia was **Australian Talkies Newsreel**, which was made in Melbourne from June 1930 to March 1931 by Australasian Films (see Greater Union Organisation; Cinesound) in association with Vocalion Records. This was short lived, as its sound-on-disc system was soon superseded.

A silent newsreel was distributed by Fox from 1919, with occasional Australian items contributed by Fox's representative in Australia, Claude Carter. In the mid 1920s, Carter established Filmcraft Laboratories with Ray Vaughan, to shoot and process items for Fox Movietone in America and, in 1929, Fox Movietone (Australia) was established to produce items for Fox's international newsreel and to establish an Australian edition. On 2 November 1929, the first Fox Movietone Australian issue was produced, presenting a speech by Prime Minister Scullin. From January 1931 a weekly Australian Fox **Movietone News** was issued, heralded by two laughing kookaburras.

At this time, Stuart Doyle (see Cinesound; Greater Union Organisation) of Australasian Films/Union Theatres, concerned that Fox seemed to be stealing a march on his company, and resentful at having to pay high prices to screen the Fox newsreel in Union Theatres, required Ken G. *Hall, who was working to a busy location schedule on *Cinesound's first feature, to find time to establish a newsreel. Hall put Bert Cross on the job and the result was **Cinesound Review**, a much more frugal operation than **Movietone News**, but one that served Doyle's purpose admirably. The first issue was exhibited in Union Theatres on 7 November 1931; it claimed to be 'The voice of Australia' and it used a kangaroo on its masthead (as had the **Australasian Gazette** and before that **Spencer's Gazette**).

In Melbourne, Herschell's (see Documentary and non-fiction, silent) and the *Herald* newspaper collaborated to produce the **Herald Newsreel** from 21 September 1931. In September 1932, this was absorbed into **Cinesound Review**, which was then screened in Victoria under the name of **Herald Cinesound News Review**. Thus, by the end of 1932, only two Australian newsreels survived. As these developed, so did the rivalry between them, nicely dramatised in Phil *Noyce's feature film *Newsfront (1978). Movietone was always better equipped: although their first studio was destroyed by fire in June 1933, it was completely rebuilt and reopened in February 1934, with the best of imported equipment. Cinesound, on the other hand, shared studio facilities with feature production and made do with equipment often constructed in-house, although still with great ingenuity, by brilliant technicians such as Arthur Smith.

The stuff of newsreels was current events, but the primary function of the newsreel was still that of any film—to entertain. Sustaining audience interest required that news stories cover intrinsically important subjects and appear to be capturing the news as it happened. Competition over stories was intense: there was an annual battle to bring the Melbourne Cup to the screen first, and each of the newsreels occasionally managed to scoop the other. **Movietone News** covered the arrival of Amy Johnson in Brisbane from the United Kingdom in 1930, and Cross captured for **Cinesound Review** the moment of Captain de Groot slashing the ribbon to open the Sydney Harbour Bridge in March 1932. But most news was not so dramatic, and still had to be presented economically and with editorial flair. **Movietone News** was edited first by American Harry Lawrenson, then by several others, but it came to be associated particularly with Harry Guinness who, when he thought the subject warranted it, presented the commentary himself in his most portentous manner. Wherever possible, Hall closely supervised the editing of **Cinesound Review**, and his expert team included editor Terry Banks and such writers as Tom Gurr and Ralph Peterson.

At first, **Movietone News** used location sound linked by intertitles, but it was not long before voice-over commentary became the standard practice. Much depended on this commentary: it not only linked disparate items, but also established the tone of items and positioned the audience within them. Particularly in the 'magazine' items—the reports of fashion parades, pet shows, and other such 'fillers'—the often racist and sexist humour is, from the perspective of the 1990s, offensive, but it was greatly enjoyed at the time. The colloquial voice of Charles Lawrence delivered the jokey, blokey commentary of **Cinesound Review** from the beginning, and he had a loyal following, including many women. From 1935 until shortly before his death 20 years later, Jack Davey did the same for **Movietone News**.

Because they continued to send items to Fox in the USA, Movietone selected material with an international audience in mind. Cinesound did not do this, but occasionally it used the newsreel to advertise its feature films, constructing news items around the arrival of a foreign star such as Helen Twelvetrees, and usually reporting the premiere of a Cinesound feature. Movietone advertised other local productions such as *Kangaroo (1952), and constructed news items around events such as screen testing for the **Smiley** (*1956, 1958) films. The stylistic differences between the two newsreels are most apparent during World War II, when they were provided with the same footage by the Department of Information (see Documentary and non-fiction, silent; Film Australia): Cinesound's **Kokoda Front Line** (1942), edited by Terry Banks, won Australia's first Oscar, while Movietone's **Road to Kokoda** (1942), from the same footage shot by Damien *Parer, is entirely unmemorable. During the war, the editorial stance of both newsreels became stronger; both made more full-reel 'specials' such as the Kokoda films and **Assault on Salamaua** (1943).

After the war, newsreels recorded some of the problems of postwar reconstruction (such as the housing shortage) as well as political events such as the defection of the Petrovs and the campaigns to ban the Communist Party. They even became a part of the political process when the Australian Security Intelligence Organisation visited Cinesound repeatedly to watch footage of protest rallies and marches, in order to identify participants.

After the war, there was one brief attempt to challenge the duopoly. In 1947, Joel Moss wanted to open the Mayfair newsreel theatrette in Perth, but was refused access to both the established newsreels. He went into partnership with John Macauley, employed Leith Goodall on camera, and produced **Westralian News**. For the first time, Perth citizens could see a newsreel with predominantly Western Australian content. But production was uneconomical, as all processing had to be sent to Herschell's in Melbourne. In October, Moss accepted Cinesound's offer of supply of **Cinesound Review**, and the **Westralian News** ceased production.

Television arrived in Australia late in 1956. Cinesound studios made the television news for Channel 9 in Sydney for some years, but the television stations soon preferred to develop their own news sections. Television finally killed the newsreel in two ways. A weekly cinema newsreel could never compete with daily television news so, as television spread through Australian homes, both film newsreels shifted to more magazine-style items. At the same time, the smaller suburban and rural cinemas gradually disappeared, taking with them the major newsreel market, until the two newsreels were combined into **Australian Movie Magazine** in October 1970. Even this could not survive the further contraction of the market: its final issue was in November 1975. But, in the 1970s, the newsreel libraries of both companies were lodged with the National Film and Sound Archive (see Archives), forming the nucleus of an invaluable historical collection recording Australian history and values over more than half a century.

IB, Graham Shirley and Neil McDonald

Newton, Bert (1938–) ACTOR After a career as a radio announcer, Newton went on to become an institution on Australian television culminating, in 1992, with *Good Morning Australia*, on which he plays, with consummate professionalism, genial host to a wide range of guests. To date, he has appeared only twice on cinema screens, with leading roles in two children's films directed by Maurice Murphy: **Fatty Finn** (1980), in which he played the father of the comic-strip hero; and **Doctors and Nurses: A Story of Hopes** (1981), in which he played a derelict patient in a hospital run by children. BMcF

Ngoombujarra, David (1967–) ACTOR/DANCER/ MUSICIAN David Ngoombujarra is a member of the Ngaia Wanga tribe from Meekatharra in WA. Before becoming an actor, he worked in his family's orange grove, but also presented tribal music and dance and told Dreamtime stories in primary schools. In 1988, he hitch-hiked and walked to Sydney, earning his living from busking. Almost immediately he obtained a major role in Philip •Avalon's **Breaking Loose** (1988). A small part as a dancer in •**Young Einstein** (1988) followed. He then returned to WA for his most important role, as 'Pretty Boy' Floyd Davey in •**Blackfellas** (1993). For this he won an Australian Film Institute Best Supporting Actor Award, as well as a Sydney Film Critics Award. With his height, dancer's grace, and highly mobile face, he was ideally cast as the cheeky and charming best mate and nemesis of hero Doug Dooligan. His television roles include the series *Heartland*, *The Man from Snowy River*, *Janus*, and *Corelli*. In 1998, he played Willie in **The Missing**. IB

Nickel Queen

1971. *Director*: John McCallum. *Producer*: John McCallum. *Scriptwriters*: Henry C. James, John McCallum, Joy Cavill. *Director*

of photography: John J. Williams. *Music*: Sven Libaek. 89 min. *Cast*: Googie Withers (Meg Blake), John Laws (Claude Fitzherbert), Alfred Sandor (Ed Benson), Ed Devereaux (Harry Phillips), Peter Gwynne (Andy Kyle).

This was John •McCallum's début as a director, although he had been involved previously in Australian cinema as both actor and producer. (Here, he is also co-scriptwriter.) **Nickel Queen** cashes in on the mining boom of the late 1960s, notably the Poseidon eruption, and casts McCallum's wife, celebrated British actor Googie •Withers, in her first Australian film role. She plays Meg, proprietress of a pub, who hears a rumour of a nickel strike near her small WA desert town and promptly stakes the first claim. Subsequently, she is exploited financially and romantically by an American mining executive and by an ambitious hippie, before settling for a more dependable old admirer. Withers plays Meg with style and good humour. The film has some amusing comedy at the expense of social aspiration, but it achieved real commercial success only in WA, where the subject matter was of most pressing interest. BMcF

Night The Prowler, The

1979. *Director*: Jim Sharman. *Producer*: Anthony Buckley. *Scriptwriter*: Patrick White. Based on the play by Patrick White. *Director of photography*: David Sanderson. *Music*: Cameron Allan. 90 min. *Cast*: Ruth Cracknell (Doris Bannister), John Frawley (Humphrey Bannister), Kerry Walker (Felicity Bannister), John Derum (John Galbraith), Maggie Kirkpatrick (Madge Hopkirk).

Jim •Sharman's version of Patrick •White's novella is predictable in its uncritical adoption of White's almost formulaic anti-middle-class bias, but it is also an often fascinating walk on the wild side of family relations and repressions. Released to a chorus of critical abuse and to a public that showed no interest in it, the film has withstood the years surprisingly well. It certainly did not belong to the discreet, decorative school of literary adaptation that won critical acclaim in the latter 1970s; it was too odd, too confronting for that. Like much of White's fiction, it impugns urban bourgeois culture. It has no sympathy for anyone except its lumpish heroine, who may or may not have been raped by an intrusive prowler. In any case, she becomes a liberated prowler of the night, invading homes such as those of her affluent, blinkered parents and exploring the more dangerous possibilities of Centennial Park, with its human flotsam. Kerry •Walker gives the heroine a certain presence that distracts from the lacunae of the plot, and Ruth •Cracknell and John Frawley are lethally accurate as her parents, whose own preoccupations with levels of respectability hint at major repressions. BMcF

Nihill, Julie (1957–) ACTOR Unfortunately, Nihill's best performance to date occurred in a film that has been seen by few people. **Boundaries of the Heart** (1988), directed by Lex •Marinos, was an unreleased theatrical feature that went straight to video in Australia. Nihill played June Thompson, the young romantic companion for ageing Billy Marsden (Norman •Kaye), the owner of the only hotel in Olwyn's Boundary, a remote outback town in the 1950s. Thompson's arrival at Olwyn's Boundary provokes tension within the hotel, particularly with Marsden's daughter Stella (Wendy •Hughes). Nihill's performance in the film resulted in an Australian Film Institute nomination for Best Supporting Actress in 1988. With the exception of **Rebel** (1985), Nihill's other screen appearances have been in supporting roles, although she plays an important continuing role in the popular television series *Blue Heelers*.

Other Australian films include: A Slice of Life (1980), •We of the Never Never (1982), •Careful, He Might Hear You (1983), Undercover (1983), •Kangaroo (1987), •Deadly (1992).

GM

Julie Nihill

Nirvana Street Murder

1991. *Director*: Aleksi Vellis. *Producer*: Fiona Cochrane. *Scriptwriter*: Aleksi Vellis. *Director of photography*: Mark Lane. 75 min. *Cast*: Mark Little (Boadey), Ben Mendelsohn (Luke), Mary Coustas (Helen), Sheila Florance (Molly), Tamara Saulwick (Penny).

This is one of the comparatively rare films that acknowledge Australia's now intensely multicultural society—and the sometimes violent results of the ethnic mix. The film is short, modest in scope, and informed by a sense of social commitment and a free-wheeling approach to film-making. First-time director Aleksi •Vellis, drawing on his own experiences, observes with the insight of the cognoscenti but maintains enough distance to make a statement that impugns neither Greek nor Anglo-Celtic culture while, at the same time, seeing potential for emotional disruption in each. Luke, with a Greek-Australian girlfriend (whose mixed mores cause problems for her), has a dim, criminally inclined brother, Boadey, whose dizzy girlfriend Penny is pregnant. The other important character is the elderly Molly who trusts Luke and allows him to bring his friends to her grand old house, where they and she play strip-poker with Boadey. Boadey repays her trust by trying to drown her in her own water-bed. This is an original piece of work: its characters are not merely 'representative' of one culture or another: they are quirkily individual, benign or dangerous in varying degrees, and the cast is uniformly responsive to the freshness of the writing and the direction.

BMcF

No Worries

1993. *Director*: David Elfick. *Producers*: David Elfick, Eric Fellner. *Scriptwriter*: David Holman, based on his play *No Worries*. *Director of Photography*: Steven F. Windon. *Music*: David A. Stewart, Patrick Seymour. 92 min. *Cast*: Amy Terelinck (Matilda Bell), Geoff Morell (Ben Bell), Susan Lyons (Ellen Bell), Geraldine James (Ann Marie O'Dwyer), John Hargreaves (Clive Ryan).

Although this film was finished in 1992, it did not receive a theatrical release until 1994 because distributors were not sure of its appeal in metropolitan areas. **No Worries** is a simple story, but its straightforwardness gives it emotional power.

Matilda Bell is an 11-year-old girl living with her parents on a central NSW sheep farm in the grip of a severe drought. They try to keep themselves solvent and cheerful, but a fierce dust storm destroys any hope the Bell family had left. The only time the film falters is when they move to Sydney: it becomes too heavy-handed and didactic. The rest of the time, however, it is an affecting and well-made portrait of outback farmers and their lot in life.

TIM HUNTER

Non-fiction: silent, *see* Documentary and non-fiction, silent

Non-fiction, sound, *see* Documentary and non-fiction, sound

'Norman Loves Rose'

1982. *Director*: Henri Safran. *Producers*: Henri Safran, Basil Appleby. *Scriptwriter*: Henri Safran. *Director of photography*: Vince

Monton. *Music*: Mike Perjanik. 98 min. *Cast*: Carol Kane (Rose), Tony Owen (Norman), Myra De Groot (Mother), David Downer (Michael), Barry Otto (Charles).

Given that successful comedy was not common in 1980s Australian cinema, it is surprising that **'Norman Loves Rose'** was so easily dismissed by both reviewers and audiences. Until this film, Australian films centred on the family tended to emphasise the pains and frustrations of growing up, charting the rites of passage of their protagonists. Henri •Safran's film, on the other hand, set firmly—and unusually—in a Jewish middle-class family, has fun with the demands of family life. Michael is having trouble impregnating his wife Rose (the American actor Carol Kane), a matter for concern in a culture preoccupied with this evidence of virility and fertility. His adolescent brother Tony, who adores Rose, has no trouble whatsoever. The Jewish parents are played by Myra De Groot and Warren •Mitchell with a sensitivity that keeps stereotypes at bay and, in the rendering of Michael's humiliation and of the emptiness of his randy dental partner's sexual boasting, the film gives weight to its essentially comic mode.   BMcF

Northbound Ltd, The

1926. *Director*: George Palmer. *Producer*: George Palmer. *Scriptwriter*: George Palmer. *Directors of photography*: Reg Edwards, Albert Drysdale. 43 min. B&W. *Cast*: George Palmer (George Webb), Phyllis Blake (Helen Webb), Robert Williams (Mr Brooks), Thelma Nelson (Hazel Brooks).

The National Film and Sound Archive (see Archives) holds several silent short fiction films, of which this film is one of the best and most complete. The story is unconvincing: it develops as a tale of betrayal and revenge, until the final few minutes when all is explained as misunderstanding and coincidence. But effective use is made of the contrast between, on the one hand, the isolation of the house and the mill in the timber country and, on the other, the office and busy street scenes in Sydney, and there are engaging performances from the four lead players, including the young director playing the main role. There is also skilful inter-cutting to build tension as the car races the runaway train (the Northbound Limited) towards a dangerous bridge. The art titles (attributed to 'Tootles') are attractive, if occasionally too long.   IB

Nostradamus Kid, The

1993. *Director*: Bob Ellis. *Producer*: Terry Jennings. *Scriptwriter*: Bob Ellis. *Director of photography*: Geoff Burton. *Music*: Chris Neal. 120 min. *Cast*: Noah Taylor (Ken Elkin), Miranda Otto (Jennie O'Brien), Arthur Dignam (Pastor Anderson), Jack Campbell (McAlister), Loene Carmen (Meryl).

The virtue of this film is the script, which is similar in tone to other scripts by Bob •Ellis (especially •**Goodbye Paradise**,

1983), with its stinging one-liners and bitter-sweet observations on Australia. Unfortunately, Ellis (scriptwriter and director) shows little interest in transforming his script on to the screen. Ken Elkin is the 'Nostradamus Kid': twice in his life he is certain that an apocalypse is about to devastate the world, or at least his world. The first time occurs while Elkin is a rebellious participant at a Seventh Day Adventist camp in 1956, and the second happens in 1962 during the Cuban missile crisis, when he is a university student in Sydney.

The Nostradamus Kid seems to wallow in self-pity. Women, in Elkin's world, are a source of pain and mystery. However, this is mitigated by a self-deprecating tone that exposes Elkin's inability to see beyond his own needs and desires. Even during intercourse with his university lover Jennie, his self-absorption causes him to be oblivious to the fact that she has experienced her first orgasm.   GM

Novelisations   Novelisations are books that have been adapted from the scripts of feature films, for the novel format. Novelisations have often been considered substandard works of literature, but the writing quality varies, as it does in any type of literature. Some are half-novelisation and half-original, such as Steele Rudd's •*The Romance of Runnibede* (1928) and John Powers's •*The Last of the Knucklemen* (1979), which were written simultaneously with the scripts and released at the same time as the feature films.

Novelisations can be profitable for writers; the immediacy of the film 'tie-in' can lead to large sales of the book if the film becomes popular. Usually a novelisation will ride on the film's success; the publicity of the latter will be used to promote sales of the book, a film poster or a still from the film is often used on the cover, and a number of coloured or black-and-white stills may be placed throughout the text.

In the 1920s and 1930s, novelisations of silent films appeared on the American market. Although it was not exactly a novelisation, a small booklet was released by the producers of the •**The True Story of the Kelly Gang** (1906), outlining the film's story with a number of black-and-white stills from the film. The novelisation as a commercial product emerged from the mass paperback phenomenon of the 1950s. Film-producers discovered that, if a new film was based on an existing book, the sales of that book could be hitched to the initial publicity and success of the film. On the other hand, if a film did not derive from a published literary source, a novelisation of the script could also promote the film. There has been a tremendous increase in the popularity and output of film novelisations since the 1970s. The public discovered that a means of extending its enjoyment of the film was to go back and read the book, which could be kept on its bookshelves as a 'memento' of the film.

After World War II, Ealing, a British company, made •**The Overlanders** (1946) in Australia. Dora Birtles wrote a novelisation from the script by Harry Watt. The book has a superb front cover with a sepia photograph of Daphne Campbell and Peter Pagan, and the back cover is a montage of stills from the film. The novelisation was extremely popular and, in the first year of the film's release, it ran to three editions, including a World Film edition with 48 black-and-white stills. As late as 1987, the book was reprinted in 'Virago Modern Classics'. •Eureka Stockade (1949), another Ealing production, also directed by Harry Watt, was promoted by a novelisation written by Rex Rienits. The front cover shows a photograph of Chips •Rafferty and the book contains 32 stills from the film. From •Bitter Springs (1950), an Australian-backed Ealing film, came a novelisation by J. Clifford King, with a front cover photograph of Nonnie Piper; it includes 29 photographs throughout the text.

There have been many novelisations to promote a number of small-budget Australian features. •Two Thousand Weeks (1969) gave rise to a lavish book with many photographs and read like a photo-novel. Raw Deal (1976), Summer City (1978), Little Boy Lost (1978), •Newsfront (1978), Thirst (1979), •In Search of Anna (1979), •The Odd Angry Shot (1979), The Journalist (1979), The Earthling (1980), A Dangerous Summer (1982), Kitty and the Bagman (1983), Run Rebecca Run (1983), and Bushfire Moon (1989) are but a few of the others. An unusual novelisation is Crocodile (1978), as it derives from an uncompleted film. The book was written by Carl Ruhen from the script by Terry •Bourke, but the film was never made. The film The Pyjama Girl Case (1978), with a novelisation by Hugh Geddes and an excellent still of American actor Ray Milland on the front cover, has never been released in Australia.

Novelisations of films such as •Alvin Purple (1973), •Eliza Fraser (1976), •Mad Dog Morgan (1976), •The Last Wave (1977), •Patrick (1978), •Mad Max (1979), Snapshot (1979), Touch and Go (1980), Harlequin (1980), The Chain Reaction (1980), •The Man from Snowy River (1982, adult and children's versions), •Phar Lap (1983), •Silver City (1984), Undercover (1984), •Romper Stomper (1992), •The Piano (1993), •Muriel's Wedding (1994), Lover Boy (1994), and Metal Skin (1995) have all been published with excellent cover photographs that promote the film.

The novelisation of •Strictly Ballroom (1992) was ghost-written without an author credit. However, sometimes the scriptwriters or film directors prefer to write their own novelisations in order to protect the story-line. Esben Storm's •In Search of Anna (1979), Rob George's Captain Johnno (1987) and You & Me & Uncle Bob (1993), John Duigan's Room to Move (1984) Denis Whitburn's Billy's Holiday (1995), and Jane •Campion's •The Piano (1993) are examples of this practice.

Many novelisations are written quickly to exploit the popularity of the film, but some novelisations complement and elucidate the film, as was the case with •Muriel's Wedding (1994), Alison's Birthday (1979), Squizzy Taylor (1982), The Man from Snowy River (1982), Summer City (1977), and •Bush Christmas (1947). Some publishers—such as Horwitz, Penguin/Puffin, Sun, Rigby, Collins, and Ashton Scholastic—have been active in publishing novelisations, while authors such as Keith Hetherington, Carl Ruhen, Richard Butler, Roger McDonald, Maureen McCarthy, and Jocelyn Harewood have written a number of film novelisations.

WAYNE LEVY

Nowra, Louis (1950–) WRITER/PLAYWRIGHT Known mostly for his work in the theatre (including *Inner Voices*, *Visions*, and *Summer of the Aliens*), Nowra has also produced a significant body of work for the screen. His first feature script **Map of the Human Heart** (1993), based on a story by the film's New Zealand director Vincent Ward, remains one of the most underrated Australian films in recent years. Epic in conception and execution, its complex but unambiguous narrative structure combines sophisticated and accessible symbolism with a grounded exploration of important cross-cultural themes of identity and place. •Cosi (1996) was faithful to the spirit of the original stage production but, possibly because of this, along with its overly theatrical performances from a cast of Australian luminaries, it failed in its transition to the screen. The well-crafted **Heaven's Burning** (1997), starring Russell •Crowe, about the kidnapping of a Japanese bride, had difficulty finding its theatrical niche, while **The Matchmaker** (1996) (co-written by Nowra) was poorly received by critics and at the box office. •Radiance (1998), the first feature of Aboriginal director Rachael •Perkins, was a hit with festival audiences, and one of its three leads (Debra Mailman) won the 1998 Australian Film Institute Award for Best Actress in a Leading Role. Nowra has also written for television.

HARRY KIRCHNER

Noyce, Phillip (1950–) DIRECTOR Phillip Noyce was included in the first intake of the Australian Film and Television School (see Australian Film, Television and Radio School) in 1973, after managing the Sydney Film-makers' Co-op from 1970 to 1972. After writing, directing, and producing an extensive number of short films, which were celebrated for their subject matter and stylistic innovations, during the 1970s and early 1980s, Noyce directed his first feature film, •Backroads, in 1977. This was followed by •Newsfront (1978) and a clever reworking of the disappearance of Sydney activist and journalist Juanita Nielson in the environmental thriller •Heatwave (1982). These three films are instructive in their efforts to critique aspects of Australian society (past and present): they represent formal attempts to wed stylistic innovation to ideologically progressive perspectives. This pattern continued in Noyce's next two

productions for Australian television: an episode of the miniseries *The Dismissal* (1983), which focuses on the events leading up to the ejection of the Whitlam Government from office in 1975; and *The Cowra Breakout* (1985), which details the mass breakout at the Japanese internment camp at Cowra in NSW in August 1944, an event that culminated in the death of 231 Japanese. After the commercial and critical failure of his next feature film, **Echoes of Paradise** (1988), Noyce shifted to more commercially oriented films and a more conventional film style, beginning with •**Dead Calm** (1989). **Dead Calm**, based on Charles Williams's 1963 novel of the same name and previously filmed by Orson Welles in 1968 (a version that was never commercially released) was a simple, effective exercise in suspense. It featured Sam •Neill and Nicole •Kidman as a husband and wife threatened by a crazy stranger (played by the American actor Billy Zane) on the Pacific Ocean. The film's critical and commercial success provided the opportunity for both Noyce and Kidman to move to Hollywood. Whereas Noyce's Hollywood output has always been technically proficient, it has varied in quality and commercial acceptance. It is ironic to see one of Australia's most socially committed film-makers direct (successfully) two adaptations of novels by the conservative author Tom Clancy: **Patriot Games** (1992) and **Clear and Present Danger** (1994).
GM

Number 96

1974. *Director:* Peter Benardos. *Producer:* Bill Harmon. *Scriptwriters:* David Sale, Johnny Whyte. *Director of photography:* John McLean. *Music:* Tommy Tycho. 113 min. *Cast:* Johnny Lockwood (Aldo), Phillipa Baker (Roma), Gordon McDougall (Les), Sheila Kennelly (Norma), Pat McDonald (Dorrie), Ron Shand (Herb), Bunney Brooke (Flo), Joe Hasham (Don), Tom Oliver (Jack), Rebecca Gilling (Diana), Lynn Rainbow (Sonia), Alistair Smart (Duncan), James Elliott (Alf), Elisabeth Kirkby (Lucy), Jeff Kevin (Arnold), Elaine Lee (Vera), Chard Hayward (Dudley), Bettina Welch (Maggie), John Orcsik (Simon).

The television serial *Number 96* ran from 1972 to 1977. The story is built around the residents of an apartment building, and the tone constantly shifts between exploitation (the serial contained much nudity and Australia's first openly homosexual television characters) and broad comedy. The feature film used the same cast and characters, and much the same episodic soap-opera style. One narrative line follows Vera's rape and romance; another the plans for the ruby-wedding celebrations of Dorrie and Herb; another the plot to drive Sonia to suicide so that Duncan can inherit her fortune. There are also several sub-plots, including Simon and Don realising true love. By the final fancy-dress party, all these narrative threads have drawn to some sort of conclusion, although the writing still allows for most characters to continue occupying the same apartments in the ongoing television saga.

The budget was so low that the producers would not disclose it, and the critics savaged the result: but the loyal television audience flocked to the film. It remains an entertaining, bawdy romp, demonstrating a sexual openness surprising for its time.
IB

Nurse Cavell, *see* **Martyrdom of Nurse Cavell, The**

O

O'Connor, Frances ACTOR   After appearing in several popular television series, including *Blue Heelers* and *Frontline*, Frances O'Connor suddenly appeared in several high-profile roles in films in 1996–97. The first was in the engaging student-oriented romp, •**Love and Other Catastrophes** (1996), as the lesbian Mia, involved in a precarious relationship. This was followed by winning the Australian Film Institute Best Actress award for Bill •Bennett's road movie thriller, •**Kiss or Kill** (1997), winner of the Best Film award and co-starring Matt •Day; and then the romantic comedy, •**Thank God He Met Lizzie** (1997), opposite Richard •Roxburgh, as the sprightly former lover he didn't marry, and whose memory haunts him on his wedding day. In other words, she has been seen in good company and has had exposure across a genre range. The failure of **A Little Bit of Soul** (1998), a black political satire that misfired, has probably been only a minor setback in a career that has gained remarkable momentum in a couple of years. She also appears regularly on stage, scoring a notable success in *The Herbal Bed* and starring in *Mansfield Park* in the United Kingdom in 1999.

BMCF

O'May, John (1947–) ACTOR   Raised in Baltimore, USA, actor–singer John O'May came to Australia in 1972, and quickly established an enviable stage reputation in both straight plays and musicals, including the role of Che in the national tour of *Evita*. He has appeared in several television series, such as *The Sullivans*, but to date has merely flirted with films. His best role was as the rock-show host in Gillian •Armstrong's charming and underrated musical, •**Star Struck** (1982). He had minor roles in the semi-musical, •**Rebel** (1985), and the sub-Hitchcockian thriller, **Georgia** (1989). Perhaps to his disadvantage, Australian cinema has not had a notable history in the musical genre in which he might have starred.

BMCF

O'Rourke, Dennis (1945–) PRODUCER/DIRECTOR/CINEMATOGRAPHER   Active since the 1970s, Dennis O'Rourke is a major figure in the Australian documentary scene. Together with peers such as Robert •Connelly, Robin •Anderson, Chris Owen, and Gary Kildea, with all of whom he has worked, O'Rourke shares a commitment to a regional focus on the Asia–Pacific area and the impact of European culture on it. Australia's foray into colonialism, in Papua New Guinea, has been an important focus in this work. O'Rourke's films there range from his 1977 film on the 1975 independence day, **Yumi Yet**, to his caustic 1987 observation of European and American tourists on a trip up the Sepik River, **Cannibal Tours**. He has also covered Aboriginal land rights issues in **Couldn't Be Fairer** (1984), American cultural imperialism in Micronesia in **Yap—How Did You Know We'd Like TV?** (1980), and the impact of the atomic bomb tests in the Marshall Islands in **Half Life** (1985). Never one to shy away from controversy, O'Rourke attained a new level of notoriety in 1992 with his box-office hit, •**The Good Woman of Bangkok**, in which he took the abiding interests of his career to new levels by both filming and participating in the Thai sex tourist trade.

CHRIS BERRY

Odd Angry Shot, The

1979. Director: Tom Jeffrey. *Producers:* Sue Milliken, Tom Jeffrey. *Scriptwriter:* Tom Jeffrey. Based on the novel by William Nagle. *Director of photography:* Don McAlpine. *Music:* Michael Carlos. 92 min. *Cast:* Graham Kennedy (Harry), John Hargreaves (Bung), John Jarratt (Bill), Bryan Brown (Rogers), Graeme Blundell (Dawson).

William Nagle's autobiographical novel tells an episodic rites-of-passage story, following Bill's first tour of duty, from the party given by his family before he leaves for Vietnam to his return to Australia a year later: the film still presents events from Bill's point of view, although he is no longer explicitly the narrator. It was promoted with the slogan 'Cry a little, laugh a lot … Aussies being Aussies in **The odd angry shot**'. This encapsulates the film's determinedly cheerful mood, despite its vivid depiction of the discomforts of camp life and the dangers of combat. Harry acts as mentor for the younger men and as the mouthpiece for the film-makers' anti-war sentiments. The soldiers' sense of isolation from the people 'back home' strengthens their dependence on each other, on 'mateship', with all its homoerotic overtones, and basic insecurity about sexuality. All the performances are outstanding.   IB

Office of Film and Literature Classification,
see Censorship

Office Picnic, The

1972. *Director*: Tom Cowan. *Producer*: Tom Cowan. *Scriptwriter*: Tom Cowan. *Director of photography*: Michael Edols. *Music*: Don Mori, the Eclipse Alley Five. 83 min. B&W. *Cast*: John Wood (Clyde Wood), Kate Fitzpatrick (Mara), Philip Deemer (Peter), Gaye Steele (Elly), Patricia Kennedy (Mrs Rourke), Ben Gabriel (Mr Johnson), Max Cullen (Jim Cullen).

Amid the monotony of office work in an unnamed government department, where gossip, innuendo, and sexual frustration are rife, Peter, a young mail clerk, and Elly, a new telephone operator, are drawn together by their common sense of alienation from the lives and interests of their older colleagues. At the annual office picnic in the country, a year's repressed tensions, lubricated by alcohol and desire, are released with devastating consequences. After a fight with the drunken Clyde, Peter and Elly disappear into the night. Subsequent attempts to find them come to nothing. Shot in black and white for $30 000, part funded by the •Experimental Film and Television Fund, **The Office Picnic** is a compelling study of gender relations in a claustrophobic environment. The enigmatic ending is typical of the absence of narrative closure, which would become a feature of many Australian films of the 1970s.   BEN GOLDSMITH

Officer 666

1916. *Director*: Fred Niblo. *Scriptwriter*: W.J. Lincoln. From the play by Augustin McHugh adapted by George M. Cohan. *Director of photography*: Maurice Bertel. B&W. *Cast*: Fred Niblo (Travers Gladwin), Enid Bennett (Helen Burton).

The American theatrical personality, George M. Cohan, wrote **Officer 666**, a farce in which an Irish policeman uncovers criminal secrets among the upper classes. The Australian film version was one of four features released by J.C. Williamson Ltd during 1915 and 1916 to cash in on the firm's stock of theatrical productions. It was the first film directed by Fred Niblo (Cohan's son-in-law and the actor/manager of his Australian touring company), who went on to make a name for himself as one of the most tactile Hollywood directors of the 1920s. The surviving reels suggest that **Officer 666** was a competent adaptation for 1916. The film makes good use of cross-cutting between locations and even employs cinematic trickery in at least one shot. Presumably these modest virtues are due to Niblo, who also manages to keep the action moving right up to the climactic scene, when the one-scene one-shot style, which was then the norm, seriously slows the pace.

WILLIAM D. ROUTT

Ogilvie, George (1931–) DIRECTOR   One of Australia's leading stage directors, George Ogilvie has had an enormous amount of experience, both here and abroad, with classic and modern plays, much of his best work having been for the Melbourne Theatre Company, which he had joined in the late 1950s when it was called the Union Theatre Repertory Company. He has also done a good deal of drama teaching, both at London's Central School of Speech and Drama and at various Australian institutions, including the Theatre of the Deaf in Sydney. His career as a film director has been more limited, but he collaborated notably with Dr George •Miller to direct •**Mad Max Beyond Thunderdrome** (1985). Miller had been impressed with Ogilvie's work on the Kennedy–Miller miniseries *The Dismissal* and wanted him to direct the third of the 'Mad Max' films. Ogilvie undertook workshops with the actors on the film, while Miller had responsibility for the actual shooting.

Ogilvie claimed to enjoy smaller projects more and his other film work bears this out. **Short Changed** (1986) confronted problems of injustice in the lives of black Australians. Its script was by Aboriginal activist Robert Merritt and focuses on a custody battle for the child of a white middle-class woman divorced from an Aboriginal man. It received only minor release, and Ogilvie's next film, **The Place at the Coast** (1987), an intimate family drama, fared no better. **The Place at the Coast**, although strongly acted by John •Hargreaves as the widowed father of a teenage girl (Tushka •Bergen), was achingly slow and over-emphatic in making its points about jealousy and relationship and the environment. In 1990 he made **The Crossing** (1990), a small-town drama of teenage anxieties and inter-generational failures of understanding, starring Russell •Crowe. Some of Ogilvie's best work is undoubtedly for television: not only *The Dismissal*, but also other major productions such as *The Shiralee* (the miniseries version starring Bryan •Brown), and *The Last of the Ryans*, the true-life drama based on Ronald Ryan, who was hanged in the 1960s. Unsurprisingly in view of his background, Ogilvie is essentially an actor's director. BMcF

Oliver, Pom PRODUCER Pom Oliver, born in the United Kingdom but long based in Sydney, was very much involved in the first decade of the Australian film revival of the 1970s (see Revival, the). Her first work in Australia was on the television series *Catch Kandy* in 1972. Thereafter, she was credited as production manager, production coordinator, production secretary or assistant, unit manager on 10 films before winning the full producer or associate producer credit on half a dozen or so features. The early films include such significant titles as •**Alvin Purple** (1973), •**Petersen** (1974), •**Between Wars** (1974), •**The Cars that Ate Paris** (1974), •**Picnic at Hanging Rock** (1975), •**Caddie** (1976), •**The FJ Holden** (1977), and •**The Night The Prowler** (1979). After serving as associate producer on Ken •Hannam's unusual melodrama, •**Summerfield** (1977), she produced **The Journalist** (1979), •**Cathy's Child** (1979, again with Hannam), •**Hoodwink** (1981), **Running on Empty** (1982), and **The City's Edge** (1983). For some years, she and Errol •Sullivan ran a production company in Sydney, CB Films, often operating with the assistance of the New South Wales Film Corporation, and often she and Sullivan are listed as co-producers. In 1986, she produced **Biggles: Adventures in Time** in the United Kingdom.
Other Australian films: Don Quixote (1973, p. sec.), •**The Man from Hong Kong** (1975, p. sec.), •**Ride a Wild Pony** (1975), **Break of Day** (1976). BMcF

Oliver, Tom (1937–) ACTOR Tom Oliver is best known for his long runs in television series: *You Can't See Round Corners* (1967), *Number 96* (1972–74, and the film in 1974), *Bellbird*, *Prisoner* (1978–80), and *Neighbours* (1987–). He has also played in other television series (Reg Withers in *The Dismissal* 1983) and telemovies, as well as in films, including **Colour Me Dead** (1970), **That Lady from Peking** (1970), •**Nickel Queen** (1971), and **ABBA: The Movie** (1977). His cheery smile makes him a plausible but likeable rogue—Jack Sellars in *Number 96* or Lou Carpenter in *Neighbours*. He was also one of the producers of the melodrama **The Right Hand Man** (1987). IB

On My Own

1993. *Director*: Antonio Tibaldi. *Producers*: Leo Pescarolo, Elisa Resegotti. *Scriptwriters*: Gill Dennis, Antonio Tibaldi, John Frizzell. *Directors of photography*: Vic Sarin, Ian Owles (London). *Music*: Franco Piersanti. *Cast*: Mathew Ferguson (Simon Henderson), Judy Davis (his mother), David McIlwraith (his father), Jan Rubes (the Colonel), Nicholas Van Burek (Max Cobb), Rachel Blanchard (Tania).

This quiet, gentle film follows the confusion and anger schoolboy Simon Henderson feels when he learns that his estranged mother is schizophrenic. This discovery compounds his profound sense of loneliness: Simon spends most of his year in an expensive boarding-school in Toronto while his father lives in Hong Kong with a younger woman, and his mother resides in London.

After a two-year absence, Simon's mother spends one night with her son in a hotel and a mixture of ecstasy, confusion, and pain marks the reunion. Later she dies in a train accident in the United Kingdom and Simon briefly joins his father for the funeral. The bulk of the film, however, chronicles Simon's essential loneliness as schoolmates, parents, teachers, and girls briefly pass through his life without any real sense of personal connection. Although mother and son reunite in a dream near the end, the film scrupulously avoids sentiment, melodrama, suspense, and romance. Mathew Ferguson is excellent as the confused, alienated student, while Judy •Davis captures the confusion and complexity of Simon's mother. GM

On Our Selection

1920. *Director*: Raymond Longford. *Producer*: E.J. Carroll. *Scriptwriter*: Raymond Longford. Based on the stories by Steele Rudd. *Director of photography*: Arthur Higgins. 6890 ft. B&W. *Cast*: Percy Walshe (Dad Rudd), Beatrice Esmond (Mrs Rudd), Tal Ordell (Dave), Arthur Greenaway (Sandy Taylor), Evelyn Johnson (Kate).

This film survives almost complete (76 min.) in the •National Film and Sound Archive, and is one of the films on which rests Raymond •Longford's reputation as the greatest Australian film director of the silent period. Although stage plays about the Rudd family living and working on their selection were already popular, Longford went back to the original stories for his inspiration, producing characters who retain their humanity and are never patronised, no matter what happens to them. There are farcical moments (like the possum in the bed), but most of the film is gently humorous, laughing with the characters rather than at them, and always aware of the hardships that such families endured. Tal Ordell (who later directed •**The Kid Stakes**) is an inspired Dave, and it is a high moment of the film when he 'goes through the First Set' with an imaginary partner in the middle of a ploughed paddock. The naturalness of the acting and the starkness of the life proved too much for some critics, but Longford was vindicated by the popular success of the film. IB

On Our Selection

1932. *Director*: Ken G. Hall. *Producer*: Bert Bailey. *Scriptwriters*: Bert Bailey, Ken G. Hall. Based on the works of Steele Rudd. *Director of photography:* Walter Sully. 99 min. B&W. *Cast:* Bert Bailey (Dad Rudd), Fred MacDonald (Dave), Alfreda Bevan (Mum), John McGowan (Maloney), Molly Raynor (Kate).

The first Steele Rudd stories were published in the *Bulletin* in 1895. In 1912 Bert •Bailey first played the stage role with which he would be associated for the rest of his life—Dad Rudd. Bailey's Dad is rotund, jovial, and constantly at odds with his foolish children: he has lost the wiry aggressiveness of the Percy Walshe character in the Raymond •Longford film. Fred McDonald's Dave is completely gormless, and the other children all appear to be little short of idiotic, with the exception of Kate, the romantic lead, who marries Sandy, the owner of the neighbouring property. This is altogether a broader and more farcical version of the story than Longford's, but it retains the determination and optimism of the farming family in the face of constant adversity, encapsulated in Dad's powerful speech about never losing heart. Shot as an •Australasian Films Production, it was released as •Cinesound's first feature, the film's popular success launching the company into feature production, and Ken •Hall into a career as a director. IB

On the Beach

1959. Director/Producer: Stanley Kramer. *Scriptwriters:* John Paxton, James Lee Barrett. From the novel by Nevil Shute. *Director of photography:* Giuseppe Rotunno. *Music:* Ernest Gold. 134 min. *Cast:* Gregory Peck (Dwight Towers), Ava Gardner (Moira Davidson), Fred Astaire (Julian Osborne), Anthony Perkins (Peter Holmes), Donna Anderson (Mary Holmes).

The most expensive and the longest, by just one minute, of the American location films made in Australia in the 1950s, **On the Beach** is also the bleakest. The story concerns a group of people awaiting death in Melbourne, the last surviving city in the world as a radioactive cloud drifts south after a nuclear cataclysm has wiped out the northern hemisphere. Based on a novel by Nevil Shute, Stanley Kramer's film shifts the emphasis from technology to human drama in its depiction of a group of American and Australian characters deciding how to spend their final weeks.

With Gregory Peck, as the captain of the visiting American submarine, and Ava Gardner, as his dissolute Australian lover who is redeemed by the relationship, in the major roles, and with support from Fred Astaire, as a remorseful scientist, and Tony Perkins, as an uxorious naval officer, this film probably had the most distinguished cast of American actors ever assembled in Australia until **The Thin Red Line** in 1998. Predictably, the production was accompanied by much hype and publicity, including the notorious gibe, attributed to Ava Gardner, about Melbourne being a perfect setting for a film about the end of the world.

Released in 17 cities throughout the world at the same time, it met with a mixed response, some critics praising its serious themes while a few found it excessively and stridently emotional.

BRUCE MOLLOY

Orphan of the Wilderness

1936. Director: Ken G. Hall. *Producer:* Ken G. Hall. *Scriptwriter:* Edmond Seward. *Director of photography:* George Heath. *Music:* Hamilton Webber. 85 min. B&W. *Cast:* Brian Abbot (Tom Henton), Gwen Munro (Margot), Ethel Saker (Mrs Henton), Harry Abdy (Shorty McGee), Ronald Whelan (Mel), Joe Valli (Andrew McMeeker).

The importation of kangaroos, koalas, an emu, a snake, and a bullfrog into a carefully recreated studio exterior, consisting of ferns, grass, shrubs, small pool, and a waterfall at the •Cinesound Studio provides a beautifully photographed 12-minute prologue. This is an appropriate recreation of a fantasy bushland setting for the highly sentimentalised tale of the adventures of Chut, a bush kangaroo, who loses his mother to hunters at the start of the film. Chut is adopted by pastoralist Tom Henton who is persuaded to place the young kangaroo with a travelling circus managed by Shorty McGee. McGee, however, trains Chut as a boxing kangaroo for the amusement of his circus customers by whipping him. When Tom's friend Margot, a circus performer, discovers McGee's cruelty, she confronts the circus manager and, eventually, Tom and Margot are reunited with Chut after he attacks McGee and runs away from the circus.

Orphan of the Wilderness was voted the best Australian film of 1936 by the Film Critics Guild of Australia and was a popular success with holiday audiences in Australia. Chut became a favourite in much the same way that Skippy the bush kangaroo was embraced by children three decades later. The simplicity of the narrative structure and the filmic presentation, which exploits a basic tenet of theatrical melodrama with regard to the inherent innocence of wild animals, provides another commercial vindication of the Ken G. •Hall/Cinesound policy of generic stories overlaid with a thin veneer of 'Australianness' in terms of setting and speech.

GM

Oscar and Lucinda

1998. Director: Gillian Armstrong. *Producers:* Robin Dalton, Timothy White. *Scriptwriter:* Laura Jones. Based on the novel by Peter Carey. *Director of photography:* Geoffrey Simpson. *Music:* Thomas Newman. 132 min. *Cast:* Ralph Fiennes (Oscar Hopkins), Cate Blanchette (Lucinda Leplastrier), Ciaran Hinds (Rev. Lindsay Hasset), Tom Wilkinson (Hugh Stratton), Richard Roxburgh (Mr Jeffris), Josephine Byrne (Miriam Chadwick), Clive Russell (Theophilus).

A USA–Australian co-production, with a mixed British and Australian cast, Gillian •Armstrong's film **Oscar and Lucinda** has won plaudits for its respect for Peter Carey's award-winning novel, but it was always going to be an unlikely starter for mainstream box-office success. It follows the narrative lines of Carey's somewhat bizarre story. He was reputed to be pleased with the result, although wisely absolving himself from how that result was reached.

In the late nineteenth century, Oscar Hopkins, a compulsive gambler, migrates from the United Kingdom to Australia to escape his addiction. On the ship, he meets Lucinda Leplastrier, a rich young Australian woman who owns a glass factory. In Sydney, Oscar, loving Lucinda but believing her to be in love with the Reverend Hasset, parson in an outback NSW parish, undertakes to build a glass church and to transport it by river to Hasset's township. The events that follow are narrated in the voice-over of Oscar's great-grandson (Geoffrey •Rush); they are neither expected nor very credible by ordinary realist criteria.

The film is no more committed to realism than the novel is, and its strange story needs to be told with a conviction of its poetic truth. Laura •Jones's script is perhaps too concerned with fidelity to the novel, so that the film is intermittently breathtaking, as in the visualisation of the church afloat, but the sheer oddity of the eponymous characters, vividly played by Ralph Fiennes and Cate •Blanchett respectively, somehow avoids a narrow preoccupation with realism, without quite aspiring to the poetic. Certainly, though, the film, in Geoffrey •Simpson's cinematography and Luciana •Arrighi's production design, is always sumptuous to look at. BMcF

Oscars The Awards of the American Academy of Motion Pictures Arts and Sciences, now commonly known as 'Oscars', are still the most coveted in the Western world. Longevity no doubt helps to explain this—they have been in operation since 1927—and they command a world-wide attention that is probably the envy of, say, the British Academy of Film and Television Arts (founded as the British Film Academy in 1947) or the •Australian Film Institute (founded in 1958). Australia was scarcely represented among Oscar nominations, let alone wins, until 1980. In fact, before that date, the only Oscars won for Australian film-making were for the Best Documentary Feature, **Kokoda Front Line** (1942, Ken G. •Hall and Damien •Parer), and by Bruce •Petty for Best Animated Short Film, **Leisure** (1976). The following Australians had won awards for their work in films made elsewhere: Robert Krasker, Best Cinematography, for **The Third Man** (1950); Orry-Kelly, Best Costume Design, for **An American in Paris** (1951, with Walter Plunkett and Irene Sharaff), for **Les Girls** (1957),

and for **Some Like It Hot** (1959), and nominated for **Gypsy** (1962); John •Farrow for Best Screenplay (Adaptation—shared with James Poe and S.J. Perelman) for **Around the World in 80 Days** (1956); John Truscott, for Best Art Direction (shared with Edward Carrere and John W. Brown), and Best Costume Design for **Camelot** (1967); Peter •Finch, for Best Actor (posthumous) in **Network** (1976). There has not been a flood of awards since 1980 but, on several occasions, Australians and/or Australian cinema (they are not always the same thing) have enjoyed a high profile at the ceremony. Perhaps the most jubilantly received at home was Geoffrey •Rush's Best Actor award for •**Shine** (1996): an Australian actor in a much-admired Australian film. It received several other nominations, including those for Best Film and Best Direction, both of which were won by **The English Patient**, which also won the Best Cinematography award for Australian John •Seale. There was high excitement at the 1993 Oscars when •**The Piano**, directed by Oscar-nominated New Zealand director Jane •Campion, won the Best Film award, and American Holly Hunter and Anna Paquin won the Best Actress and Best Supporting Actress awards respectively for their performances in it. In 1994, Lizzie •Gardiner and Tim Chappel won the Best Costume Design award for the extravagances of •**The Adventures of Priscilla, Queen of the Desert**, and in 1995 a team of four won for Best Visual Effects for their work on •**Babe**. In 1983, diminutive American actor Linda Hunt won the Best Supporting Actress award for her playing of the male Chinese dwarf in Peter •Weir's •**The Year of Living Dangerously**. Recent Oscars won by Australians for non-Australian films include: Dean •Semler, Best Cinematographer for **Dances with Wolves** (1980), Luciana •Arrighi, Best Art Direction for **Howard's End** (1992), and Mel •Gibson (actually American-born) co-produced, directed and starred in **Braveheart** (1995), which won Best Picture award, and the award for Best Achievement in Makeup for Paul Pattinson. Throughout the 1980s and 1990s there has been a stream of nominations that, however sceptical one may be about awards, indicates that internationally Australia's is no longer an unknown cinema. BMcF

Otto, Barry (1941–) ACTOR Barry Otto was born in Brisbane, where he established himself as a theatre actor in several companies. In 1981 he did a season with Sydney's Nimrod Theatre and, in 1999, he scored a major success on stage in *Showboat*. His television experience includes *The Dismissal* (1983), but he is probably best known now as a major character actor in Australian films. His first film role was as the protagonist's randy dentist friend in the comedy of Jewish life, •'**Norman Loves Rose**' (1982), in which he caught vividly the pain beneath the bravado. He starred in the adaptation of Peter Carey's novel •**Bliss** (1985), as Harry Joy, who gets a second chance at life, and he has a small role in the film version of Carey's later novel •**Oscar and Lucinda** (1998), as Lucinda's gambling associate. In between these brushes with Carey, he was credibly serious as the role-reversing husband in •**The More Things Change** (1986), touchingly self-effacing as the henpecked husband until his big moment comes in •**Strictly Ballroom** (1992), and never less than an authentic and authoritative presence in such varied films as •**Lilian's Story** (1995), •**Dad and Dave: On Our Selection** (1995), and •**Kiss or Kill** (1997). He has also acted in films made in Hong Kong, the USA, and Germany. Never a conventional leading man on the screen, either in looks or in the roles he has played, Otto's contribution to the wealth of Australian screen character acting has been striking. He is the father of the popular screen actor Miranda •Otto.

Other Australian films: About Time (1983, short), Undercover (1984), Howling III: The Marsupials (1987), •The Custodian (1994), •Cosi (1996), •Mr Reliable (1996), Dead Letter Office (1998). BMcF

Barry Otto

Otto, Miranda (1967–) ACTOR Miranda Otto's first
film, **Emma's War,** was released in 1988 (and made two years earlier), but she became a major presence in Australian cinema in the latter half of the 1990s. Trained at the National Institute of Dramatic Art, she played Lee Rem-

mick's daughter in **Emma's War**, a child on the brink of womanhood; had the leading role in the little-seen comedy, **Daydream Believer** (1991), as a young woman who retreats into fantasy when reality becomes too demanding; and played Lisa Harrow's daughter in •**The Last Days of Chez Nous** (1992), one of Gillian •Armstrong's least popular films. Otto, vivid, auburn-haired and drawing on reserves of idiosyncrasy, came into her own in 1996 in two films: **True Love and Chaos,** in which a bizarrely assorted carload of people (Hugo •Weaving, Naveen Andrews, Noah •Taylor, and Otto) make an erratic but exhilarating journey across the Nullarbor, during which she has an engaging dance sequence in an outback pub; and •**Love Serenade,** in which she plays one of two country-town sisters besotted by a lugubrious disc jockey, and shows a subtle grasp of film comedy. The film version of Elizabeth Jolley's novel •**The Well** (1997) was not very well received, but Otto and Pamela •Rabe won critical acclaim for their playing of the two women locked in a strange relationship on a Western Australian farm. In the same year she was funny and touching in •**Doing Time for Patsy Cline,** another outback road movie, in which she played an aspiring country singer, named for her idol, and, in the following year, she brought gentleness and charm to the otherwise thin romance, **Dead Letter Office.** Her range is considerable and she imbues all her roles with an intensity of conviction that

Miranda Otto

has sometimes carried the films over rough spots. She is the daughter of actor Barry *Otto.

Other Australian films: Zoomstone (1987), Initiation (1987), The 13th Floor (1988), *The Nostradamus Kid (1993), In the Winter Dark (1998), The Thin Red Line (1999).   BMcF

Our Friends, The Hayseeds
[The Hayseeds]

1917. Director, Producer, Scriptwriter: Beaumont Smith. *Director of photography*: Harry Krischock. B&W.

Few Australian 'lost' films are more culturally significant than **Our Friends, The Hayseeds**, for this was the first film of the 'back-blocks farce' genre, which was to be a mainstay of the Australian film industry until World War II and *Dad Rudd, M.P. (1940). Beaumont *Smith, the film's producer, scriptwriter, and director had learned the genre by helping to invent it—having collaborated with Bert *Bailey and Edmund Duggan on the 1912 stage version of *On Our Selection*. From this broad, popular show, Smith took the idea of a bumbling, but noble, 'Dad' whose stubborn attachment to the land and his family articulated an image of the rural battler that remains potent in Australian politics even today. Smith made films swiftly, cheaply and with an eye to what people wanted to see: four Hayseeds' films were released between March 1917 and February 1918, each set in a different Eastern capital (Adelaide, Sydney, Brisbane, and Melbourne). He was also canny about market saturation: the fifth Hayseeds' film was not made until 1923, and *The Hayseeds—the last and the only to survive—in 1933, after the success of *Cinesound's *On Our Selection the year before. Elements of the 'farce bucolic' that Smith introduced to the cinema can still be found in suburban Australian comedies such as *The Castle (1997).

WILLIAM D. ROUTT

Out of the Shadows

1931. Producer/Director: A.R. (Dick) Harwood. *Cinematographer*: Reg Edwards. *Sound*: Bert Goody. 47 min. B&W. *Cast*: William Greene (Robert Graham), Edna Lyall (Nita Rolls), Paul Plunkett (Bob Graham), Sefton Winder (Harry), Syd Hollister (Bubbles).

The complete seven-reel 35mm nitrate picture print of Australia's first completed full talkie was presented to the National Film and Sound Archives by Victorian film collector Jim Ness in 1989. **Out of the Shadows** was the only completely sound-on-disc feature film made in Australia, and the only talkie drama to be produced entirely at *Australasian Films (later *Cinesound's) studio in St Kilda. Completed in 1931, the film was never officially released, after a series of technical problems with the primitive disc-

recording business, although producer–director Dick Harwood maintained that the acting and camerawork were more than adequate. Sound-on-disc production, however, was not continued in Melbourne after the importation of RCA sound-on-film cameras by Frank *Thring Snr. In spite of its sound deficiencies, the film has great technical and historical significance. The soundtrack was cut on the first disc recorder used by the Bellbird Record Company at the old World Record plant in Brighton. Everything about the production was highly experimental, from the incandescent lighting used on the sets to the disc and film editing technique, which had to suit a soundtrack system that could not be edited in any way.

Some of the disc soundtrack has also survived, featuring many of the acting personnel on the film (established stage and radio performers who were not otherwise recorded or filmed, including local jazz musicians Ern Pettifer and Lionel Corrick, who perform one of the musical interludes), and enabling Archives staff to match the image and sound components for at least part of the film for the first time since 1931.

KEN BERRYMAN

Overlanders, The

1946. Director: Harry Watt. *Producer*: Michael Balcon. *Scriptwriter*: Harry Watt. *Director of photography*: Osmond Borradaile. *Music*: John Ireland. 91 min. B&W. *Cast*: Chips Rafferty (Dan McAlpine), John Nugent Hayward (Bill Parsons), Daphne Campbell (Mary Parsons), Jean Blue (Mrs Parsons), Helen Grieve (Helen Parsons), John Fernside (Corky), Peter Pagan (Sinbad).

Harry Watt's first feature following a distinguished career in documentary was also the first Australian film of a planned cycle of 10 by the English company, Ealing Studios. Intended as a tribute to the Australian contribution to the Allied war effort, Watt decided to avoid the conventional war propaganda genre in favour of a celebration of the efforts of ordinary people. This tribute took the form of an episodic narrative about a disparate group of characters droving a vast herd of cattle from the threatened Kimberleys 'clear across Australia' to central Queensland.

These characters—drawn from Aboriginal, white Australian, British, and Scottish backgrounds—are welded into an effective team as they confront and surmount a series of natural and cultural obstacles: crocodile-infested rivers, dry wells, internal politicking, and a climactic cattle stampede. The style throughout is realistic with the ending decidedly downbeat, possibly a legacy of Watt's training in the Grierson school of documentary.

The performances are strong, especially that of Chips *Rafferty as the boss of the drove, who manages to combine personal force with laconic self-deprecation in a role that was to establish him as an international star. He is effectively supported by John Nugent Hayward as the station owner Parsons, who is accustomed to being in charge, and Jean Blue as Parson' resilient if long-suffering wife.

Widely released and well received overseas, **The Overlanders** contained a strain of social criticism unfamiliar in Australian films to this time, and clearly influences the style and structure of the 1948 Howard Hawks' western, **Red River**, although the differences in the narrative structure between the two films provide some interesting insights into the differing characteristics of Australian and American films.

Ealing Studios, incidentally, never completed their planned 10 Australian films, managing only five between 1945 and 1959.

BRUCE MOLLOY

P

Pacific Film and Television Commission (PFTC)

First mooted as part of Queensland's bid for the Multi-Function Polis (MFP), the development of a Film–Television–Multimedia precinct was retained as an initiative by the newly elected Goss Labor Government when the MFP was lost to South Australia in 1990. In 1991, after a couple of years in administrative limbo, the PFTC, which had as its primary objective economic benefit to Queensland through attracting interstate and overseas productions, was placed under the aegis of the Queensland Film Development Office (QFDO) to act as its marketing and locations arm.

The state government's major motivation was to ensure that it recouped more than $20 million invested in the studio complex at Coomera in the Gold Coast hinterland. This studio was established by Dino de Laurentiis in 1988, then purchased by *Village Roadshow, which soon after entered a partnership with Warner Brothers and expanded the facility. The PFTC was instrumental in attracting ancillary services to the Warner Roadshow Studios (WRS), and introduced various incentive schemes to attract production, mainly from the USA, to Queensland generally and WRS in particular. Starting with *Mission Impossible*, a number of features, 'movies of the week', and television series were attracted to Queensland during the 1990s.

When the value of film and television production in Queensland increased from under $20 million in 1990 annually to over $50 million in 1992, the state government established the PFTC as a semi-autonomous state-owned company, but with its own board of directors and a chief executive officer.

The PFTC continued in this role of attracting foreign and interstate production to Queensland until late 1997. At that time, the short-lived National-Liberal coalition government restructured government film agencies, combining the PFTC and Film Queensland (formerly Queensland Film Development Office), under the PFTC title. As a result of this restructuring, the PFTC now has responsibility for developing local (Queensland-based) production, as well as marketing Queensland locations. The restructured PFTC experienced pressure from recently established studio facilities in Sydney and Melbourne, but in the late 1990s, its policies of aggressive and effective marketing were maintaining production levels in Queensland of around $120 million annually.   Bruce Molloy

Page, Grant (1939–) STUNTMAN

The doyen of Australian stunt artists, a university graduate, and former journalist, married to stuntwoman Zenda Graves, Grant Page is one of the few in his branch of the profession to become well known. In the 1970s he was a major contributor to the action movies directed by Brian *Trenchard-Smith, such as *The Man from Hong Kong (1975) and The Deathcheaters (1976), in which he also acted, but his acting talents were far more limited than his stuntman's skills. He led the team that provided the brilliant stunts for *Mad Max (1979) and *Mad Max Beyond Thunderdome (1985), and for *Roadgames (1981), in which he also played the villain. He is the head of the Sydney company, 'Cunning Stunts', and has coordinated the stunts for many television series, such as *All the Rivers Run* and *Boy from the Bush*.

Other Australian films (as stunt coordinator) *include*: The Stuntmen (1974, doc.), The Love Epidemic (1975, a. only), *Mad Dog Morgan (1976, a. only), *Eliza Fraser (1976), Let the Balloon Go (1976), *Don's Party (1976), *The Picture Show Man (1977), *The Last Wave (1977), *The Irishman (1978), Thirst (1979),

•The Year of Living Dangerously (1982), •Phar Lap (1983), •The Lighthorsemen (1987), Tender Hooks (1989, a. only), Till There Was You (1990).   BMcF

Painted Daughters

1925. Director: F. Stuart-Whyte. Director of photography: Lacey Percival. B&W. Cast: Marie Lorraine (Evelyn Shaw), Phyllis du Barry (Saharab).

Although what survives of **Painted Daughters** is woefully incomplete, the film appears to have been one of the most interesting Australian productions of the 1920s. In the first place, **Painted Daughters** was explicitly intended to have 'international' appeal, just as many Australian films are today. This meant that the in-your-face Australian qualities of other 1920s' features were subordinated to 'background' for a 'sophisticated' high-society story about reuniting the women from a slightly saucy chorus-line of years before. It also meant that style entirely dominated substance, leading to at least three intriguing sets of images: the highly symbolic (and conceptually incoherent) opening credit image featuring Father Time as a beautician, the rhythmic 'Floradora' montage, and a vivid avant-garde evocation of the 'D.T.'s' in which a drunk is assailed by phantom birds. The existing footage presents a kind of avant-garde narrative as well, for the story unfolds with seemingly nothing of significance to resolve. The title **Painted Daughters** bears no relation whatever to any element of the film and, finally, there is a really dull fire that seems to have been tossed in only to get the proper couples together before the production crew ran out of film.   WILLIAM D. ROUTT

Palm Beach

1980. Director, Producer, Scriptwriter: Albie Thoms. Director of photography: Oscar Scherl. Music: Terry Hannigan. 88 min. Cast: Nat Young (Nick Naylor), Ken Brown (Joe Ryan), Amanda Berry (Leilani Adams), Bryan Brown (Paul Kite), John Flaus (Larry Kent).

Surf, sex, drugs, and rock'n'roll on Sydney's northern beaches are at the heart of this film. Palm Beach provides the locale for three individual searches: Joe, surfer, pusher, and police informer, is looking for a drug deal; Paul, unemployed and in an unhappy relationship, is searching for a job but eventually resorts to a supermarket robbery; private detective Larry Kent is trying to track down a missing teenager. The three never meet, but their paths criss-cross through the favoured haunts of the beach subculture, much of the action being played out against the ubiquitous sounds of commercial radio.

The fractured narrative structure, the absence of psychologically developed motivation, long takes, minimal editing within scenes, overlapping sound, hand-held cameras, improvised dialogue, and an analytical approach to the social milieu all announce an 'experimental' or 'alternative' aesthetic, which inhibits the usual patterns of identification and participation while retaining aspects of commercial narratives. **Palm Beach** is a bold but only partially successful attempt to bridge the gap between 'experimental' and mainstream cinema.   HARRY OLDMEADOW

Paradise Road

1997. Director: Bruce Beresford. Producers: Sue Milliken, Greg Coote. Scriptwriter: Bruce Beresford. Director of photography: Peter James. Music: Margareth Dryburgh, Ross Edwards. 114 min. Cast: Glenn Close (Adrienne Partiger), Pauline Collins (Margaret Drummond), Frances McDormand (Dr Verstak), Elizabeth Spriggs (Mrs Roberts), Wendy Hughes (Mrs Dickson), Pamela Rabe (Mrs Tippler), Jennifer Ehle (Rosemary Leighton-Jones).

Bruce •Beresford's first Australian film for 10 years recalls such 1950s' British wartime films of suffering and atrocity as Jack Lee's **A Town Like Alice**, in which a group of women are held prisoner by the Japanese. Some have said that it is undesirable to recall old enmities and to represent former enemies as brutal torturers. Equally, there may be something salutary in reminding viewers, anaesthetised by the spectacle of special effects-created violence in modern cinema, that there are some kinds of dehumanising activity that form part of our recent history and ought, in no circumstances, be allowed to occur again.

Following the fall of Singapore, a group of assorted women (played by a very accomplished ensemble of Australian and overseas actors) find themselves in a Japanese prisoner-of-war camp and the film portrays the extraordinary events that take place there. Under the leadership of the musically gifted Adrienne and the missionary Margaret Drummond, and to sustain their spirit and morale, the women are welded into a choral orchestra. Among the film's most moving moments (inspirational is not too strong a word) are those in which they perform the 'Going Home' theme from Dvorak's *New World Symphony*. It stops the bullying Japanese guards in their tracks, and the skill of Beresford, one of Australian cinema's most notable storytellers, and his cast makes this remarkable story convincing. It is based on events that actually happened, but it acquires a persuasive emotional truth that goes beyond mere historical authenticity.   BMcF

Parer, Damien (1912–44) CINEMATOGRAPHER Damien Parer began his cinematographic career as camera assistant on •**The Flying Doctor** (1936) and •**Rangle River** (1936). Stan Tolhurst and George Hughes collaborated, with Parer on camera, for a series of film 'poems' based on Henry Lawson and A.B. 'Banjo' Paterson, called **This Place Australia** (1938). Parer was working for the Department of

Information (DOI) when World War II broke out, so he was employed on newsreels at home in Australia. In February 1940 he was the first camera man sent overseas by the DOI. His footage was among that sent back to Australia for distribution to the two newsreel companies: **Cinesound Review** and **Movietone News**. Parer was in Sydney when Ken G. •Hall was preparing the newsreel containing the Kokoda footage, and Hall invited him to record some opening remarks: the result was **Kokoda Front Line**, the episode of **Cinesound Review** that shared (with three others) an American Academy Award for documentary in 1942. However, within the DOI his skills and experience were not appreciated and he became increasingly disillusioned. In 1943 he resigned to accept a position with Paramount, still as a war cameraman. He was killed while filming, walking backwards in front of advancing American troops on Peleliu. Some of his war footage was used after his death in the feature films •**A Son is Born** (1946) and •**Mike and Stefani** (1952).   IB

Parker, David (1947–) CINEMATOGRAPHER/PRODUCER David Parker has writing credits and directed two films, but is perhaps best known to date as the producer and cinematographer on several successful films directed by his wife Nadia •Tass. Their successful collaboration first came to notice when they made •**Malcolm** (1986), the popular comedy of crooks, a mechanical genius, and an unusual getaway vehicle. The film scooped the pool at the 1986 Australian Film Institute awards, winning in eight categories, as well as the Byron Kennedy Award for Parker and Tass. They followed this with **Rikky and Pete** (1988), a story of a runaway brother and sister, which did reasonably well without repeating the earlier film's success. Both critics and audiences responded more warmly to their third film, •**The Big Steal** (1990), an engaging comedy of kids, a Jaguar, and a crooked car salesman, which, like **Malcolm** and •**Mr Reliable** (1996), a quirky hostage comedy-drama based on a real-life occurrence, recalled some of the feeling of the Ealing comedies of several decades earlier. They made the USA-based **Pure Luck** (1991) for Universal, and **Amy** (1998), again starring Ben •Mendelsohn, who came to prominence in **The Big Steal**. Parker was cinematographer on these six films, wrote all but **Pure Luck** and **Mr Reliable**, and produced all but **Mr Reliable**. The films he has directed are **Hercules Returns** (1993), a film-within-a-film satire, starring David •Argue, and **Diana and Me** (1998), which concerned a Woollongong girl (Toni •Colette) with the same name as the Princess of Wales. The death of Princess Diana before the film's release necessitated the shooting of a new prologue and epilogue. In 1983, the film **Thunder Warning**, a crime thriller, was based on a novel of Parker's. He and Tass have been a significant team in the history of 1990s' film-making in Australia.

Other Australian film: Hotel de Love (1996, p.).   BMcF

Parslow, Frederick (1932–) ACTOR Although he had two significant roles in the 1970s, as Alvin Purple's father in •**Alvin Purple** (1973) and as the Reverend Burton in •**The Last Wave** (1977), as well as narrating several documentaries, this talented Melbourne actor was primarily a stage and television player with only a couple of screen credits in the 1980s, including the historical melodrama •**Minnamurra** (1989), and the television drama *Deadly Decision* (1988).   GM

Pate, Christopher (1952–) ACTOR The son of Michael •Pate, Christopher Pate made his first acting impression as a regular on the television serial *Bellbird* in the early 1970s. After a minor role in the bushranging drama •**Mad Dog Morgan** (1976), and a supporting role in the Australian western **Raw Deal** (1977), Pate had the best role of his screen career in •**The Mango Tree** (1977) as the young man working his way through adolescence with the help of an assortment of eccentric characters in his small north Queensland town. **The Mango Tree** was scripted and produced by Michael Pate. After this high point, Christopher Pate's career rapidly declined and his subsequent screen performances consisted of minor roles in **Howling III: The Marsupials** (1987), *Frankie's House* (1992), **Official Denial** (1993), and the dismal comedy **Exchange Lifeguards** (1993).   GM

Pate, Michael (1920–) ACTOR A multitalented film, television, and radio actor, Michael Pate has also produced, scripted, and directed films in Australia and the USA. After working in radio and on the stage in Sydney in the 1940s, Pate created a strong impression as Shane O'Riordan, the dominant son in Charles •Chauvel's pioneering melodrama •**Sons of Matthew** (1949). After appearing as a trooper in •**Bitter Springs** (1950), Pate left Australia for Hollywood, where he worked consistently for the next 17 years. During this period he became one of Hollywood's most striking character actors, with a particular penchant for playing brash gunmen (**Lawless Street**, 1955; **Reprisal** 1956; **Westbound**, 1959; **Walk Like a Dragon**, 1960) or Indian chiefs, such as Vittorio in **Hondo** (1953), the superb John Wayne western, directed by expatriate Australian John •Farrow. Pate reprised this role in the 1960s television series that produced one film **Hondo and the Apaches** (1967), an inferior version of the 1953 film. Also notable in this regard was a key role as Sierra Charriba in Sam Peckinpah's **Major Dundee** (1965). Pate's other Hollywood roles included most genres, from horror (**The Black Castle**, 1952; **Curse of the Undead**, 1959), adventure (**Congo Crossing**, 1956; **Desert Hell**, 1958), science fiction (**The Amazing Colossal Man**, 1957), war (**PT 109**, 1963) plus historical dramas such as the Roger Corman-directed **Tower of London** (1962) and **King Richard**

and the Crusaders (1954). Alongside his prolific film roles, Pate regularly appeared as a guest artist in the top-rating television series of the 1950s and 1960s, such as *Gunsmoke*, *Zorro*, *Maverick*, *Rawhide*, *Wagon Train*, *Batman*, *Voyage to the Bottom of the Sea*, and *Mission Impossible*. He also wrote the story for two Hollywood films, **Escape from Fort Bravo** (1953), the large-budget western starring William Holden and Eleanor Parker, and the Allan Dwan-directed science-fiction film **The Most Dangerous Man Alive** (1961) starring expatriate Australian actor Ron •Randell.

Pate returned to Australia in 1968 and spent some time as a television executive. He also produced the Michael Powell-directed film •**Age of Consent** (1969), from the Norman Lindsay story. In 1977 Pate scripted and produced •**The Mango Tree**, which starred his son Christopher •Pate. The film was directed by Kevin Dobson who had worked in television with Pate in the early 1970s at Crawford Productions in Melbourne where Pate was starring in the long-running series *Matlock Police*. Pate also directed, scripted, and produced the romantic film •**Tim** (1979), starring Mel •Gibson and Piper Laurie.

Other Australian films include: Little Jungle Boy (1970), •Mad Dog Morgan (1976), Duet for Four (1982), The Return of Captain Invincible (1983), •The Wild Duck (1984), The Camel Boy (1984), Death of a Soldier (1986), Howling III: The Marsupials (1987), Official Denial (1993).   GM

Patrick

1978. *Director*: Richard Franklin. *Producers*: Antony I. Ginnane, Richard Franklin. *Scriptwriter*: Everett de Roche. *Director of photography*: Don McAlpine. *Music*: Brian May. 115 min. *Cast*: Susan Penhaligon (Kathy Jacquard), Robert Helpmann (Dr Roget), Rod Mullinar (Ed Jacquard), Julia Blake (Matron Cassidy), Helen Hemingway (Sister Williams).

Patrick is diagnosed as suffering from psychokinesis, a condition that confines him, comatose, to a hospital bed, from which, however, he is able to bring about the unexpected movement of objects and people at a distance from himself. On this premise, scriptwriter Everett •de Roche and director Richard •Franklin have fashioned a film that plays impudently with the conventions of several Hollywood genres: there are, for instance, the plucky-woman-in-danger role, the hospital thriller, complete with mad doctor and sinister matron (played with relish, respectively, by Robert •Helpmann and Julia •Blake), and touches of romantic melodrama. However, the film is more than just a sum of its engaging parts. Franklin, particularly in his collaboration with de Roche, shows a delight in the story-telling capacity of film, trusting his images as much as the often witty dialogue ('I won it in a card game', snaps Dr Roget when asked where he got a piece of crucial technology). It was not the kind of film typically offered by the new Australian cinema of the 1970s (see Revival, the), but it was more fun than many taken more seriously and it announced in Franklin a talent worth watching and cherishing.   BMcF

Pattinson, Michael (1957–) DIRECTOR After directing episodes of the television soaps *Young Doctors* and *Prisoner* in the late 1970s, together with a number of shorts (such as **The Importance of Keeping Still**), this Melbourne film-maker directed his first feature, the critically acclaimed •**Moving Out**, which was released in 1983. **Moving Out**, with a script by Jan •Sardi, and its penetrating focus on cross-cultural confusion and alienation, was followed by another Jan Sardi-scripted film, **Street Hero** (1984), with the same lead actor, Vince •Colosimo and, although it retained some similarities with the previous film, notably the problems facing a working-class youth, the blending of music and drama resulted in a less 'realistic' style. In 1987 Michael Pattinson co-directed, with Bruce •Myles, the anti-nuclear conspiracy thriller •**Ground Zero**, based on the aftermath of the Maralinga nuclear tests. This was followed by the quirky romance between Rosanna Arquette and Bruce •Spence in **Wendy Cracked a Walnut** (1990), and a teen film, **Secrets** (1992), featuring the reaction of five Australian teenagers to the Beatles' arrival in Melbourne in 1964 that reunited Pattinson with Jan Sardi.

Other Australian films include: The Last Bullet (1995).   GM

Peak, Barry (1951–) EXHIBITOR/DIRECTOR Known mainly as a film exhibitor, Barry Peak began screening repertory films in Sydney and later at the Palais in St Kilda, before starting the Valhalla cinemas in Sydney and Melbourne with his friend and business partner Chris Kiely, with whom he had worked since their Sydney University days. The Valhalla cinemas became well known for their **Blues Brothers** seasons from 1984 to 1996, and attracted large late-night audiences, many of whom dressed up as characters from the film, spoke in unison with the dialogue, and participated in the musical sequences. Peak and Kiely collaborated on four features, with Peak mainly directing and Kiely mainly producing, including **Future Schlock** (1984), **The Big Hurt** (1986), and **As Time Goes By** (1988). All four films fall loosely into the schlock-comedy genre, **As Time Goes By** being the most successful, supported by good-natured performances from a cast that included Nique Needles, Ray •Barrett, and Bruno •Lawrence. The little-known **Channel Chaos** (1985), set in a television station, later became available on video, but was considered so bad that Peak and Kiely never bothered to show it in their own cinemas. The Valhalla partnership lasted from 1976 to 1987. Kiely and Peak may have decided that their affection for cinema was best expressed through exhibition. Kiely

Patrick

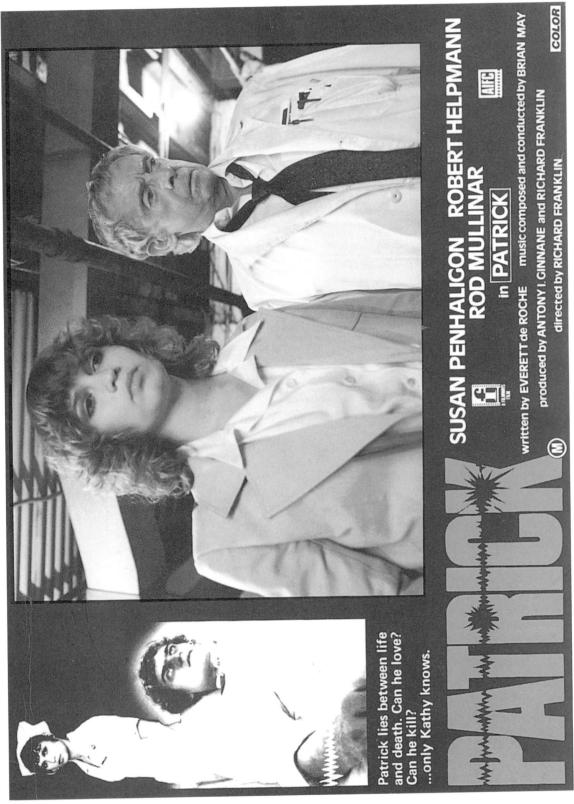

Poster for Patrick

continues to run the Valhalla in Sydney and Peak is a partner in the Nova arthouse chain across three states.

HARRY KIRCHNER

Pearce, Guy (1967–) ACTOR There is little in Guy Pearce's Australian filmography prior to 1996 to prepare one for his skilful performance as the ambitious, repressed Los Angeles cop Ed Exley in Curtis Hanson's superb film noir **L.A. Confidential** (1996). Up to this point Pearce's screen career had not matched the popularity generated by his role of Mike Young from 1986 to 1990 in the long-running Australian soap opera *Neighbours*. A significant role as John •Waters's son in •**Heaven Tonight** (1990) was followed by the disappointment of a minor role, and static performance, in the uneven thriller **Hunting** (1991). The state of Pearce's screen career in the early 1990s was summed up by the working title, and fate, of the much-heralded film version of Errol •Flynn's early life, **My Forgotten Man** (also known as **Young Flynn** and **Flynn**), with Pearce in the lead role. Although this film, which began production in 1989, was largely remade in the early 1990s, it never received a theatrical release. During this barren period, Pearce appeared on the stage in the United Kingdom in *Cinderella* and toured Sydney, Adelaide, and Brisbane in *Grease*. He also returned to television from 1993 to 1996 in the series *The Man From Snowy River*. Valuable exposure for Pearce in America in 1994 followed the popularity of •**The Adventures of Priscilla, Queen of the Desert**, with Pearce as Adam, one of the drag queens. Comedy derived from cross-gender complications was also at the centre of his next film, •**Dating the Enemy** (1996), where Pearce was forced reluctantly to inhabit Claudia •Karvan's body. GM

Pearls and Savages, *see* **The Hound of the Deep**

Peers, Lisa (1956–) ACTOR Lisa Peers, a prominent Sydney-born actor, especially in the 1970s, when she appeared in the popular television serial *Bellbird* and in the title role of the series *Andra*, first appeared on the big screen as Sheila, the 'cocky's' daughter in •**Sunday Too Far Away** (1975). She shares a key scene in the film away from the shearing sheds when Foley (Jack •Thompson) breaks down and discusses his past as a gun shearer and, implicitly, his doubts about the future—something he is unable to do with his male mates in the shed. Sheila also strikes a blow against the all-male shearing shed when she successfully bargains with Foley to watch the men at work—much to the disgust of some of the other shearers ('ducks on the pond'). After a key role in the strident historical drama •**Journey Among Women** (1977), Peers had a lead role in **Solo,** (1978), an Australian–New Zealand co-production filmed at Waimarana, which examines differing romantic aspira-

tions during an aerial journey across New Zealand's north island. The lead role of Jennifer, who comes between Colin •Friels and Harold •Hopkins, in **Buddies** (1983) followed a featured role in •**Monkey Grip** (1982). Peers's only other screen performance of note was the romantic lead in the straight-to-video thriller **Glass** (1989).
Other Australian films include: **Going Down** (1982), **This Won't Hurt a Bit** (1993). GM

Percival, Lacey (?–1969) CINEMATOGRAPHER Percival was a photographer in rural New South Wales before becoming a projectionist in Sydney in 1908. His first camera work on features was for the Australian Film Syndicate (**The Golden West**, 1911). He then moved to Australian Photo-Play Company and worked with John •Gavin on films for Australian Famous Features (•**The Martyrdom of Nurse Cavell**, 1916; **His Convict Bride**, 1918). In 1918 he moved to West's Pictures, working on their newsreel and later on Australasian Films' **Australasian Gazette**. He filmed other productions for Australasian (**Cupid Camouflaged**, 1918) but also worked freelance for Beaumont •Smith (**Desert Gold**, 1919; **The Man from Snowy River**, 1920, with Al Burne; **The Betrayer**, 1921; **Prehistoric Hayseeds**, 1923; •**The Digger Earl**, 1924; •**Joe**, 1924; •**The Adventures of Algy**, 1925) and other producers (**£500 Reward**, 1918; **The Face at the Window**, 1919; •**Robbery Under Arms**, 1920; •**Possum Paddock**, 1921; **The Dinkum Bloke**, 1923; **The Dingo**, 1923; **Dope**, 1924; **The Mystery of a Hansom Cab**, 1925; •**Painted Daughters**, 1925; •**Around the Boree Log**, 1925; **The Sealed Room**, 1926; **Down Under**, 1927; •**The Birth of White Australia**, 1928, with Walter •Sully; **The Kingdom of Twilight**, 1929, with Walter Sully), including on one occasion Australasian Films (**Tall Timber**, 1926). He joined Automatic Film Laboratories in 1927 and set up his own company (Percival Film Laboratories) in 1935, where he worked until he retired in 1948. ROSS COOPER AND ANDREW PIKE

Perkins, Rachel (1970–) DIRECTOR Over her 10-year career Rachel Perkins has made a distinctive impression across the Australian film and television industries. As a film-maker and television producer, she works towards a reconsideration of the concept of the essence of Australian iconography by encouraging Aboriginal access to the film-making practice. Perkins is productive in establishing schemes to promote the advancement and continuation of Aboriginal film-making.

In association with Ned Lander, Perkins developed a series of documentaries for SBS that shed light on what would otherwise be concealed moments of Aboriginal history. The series *Blood Brothers* was awarded the inaugural 'Tudawali' award for excellence in indigenous film and television. Perkins' directorial contribution to the series was called

Guy Pearce

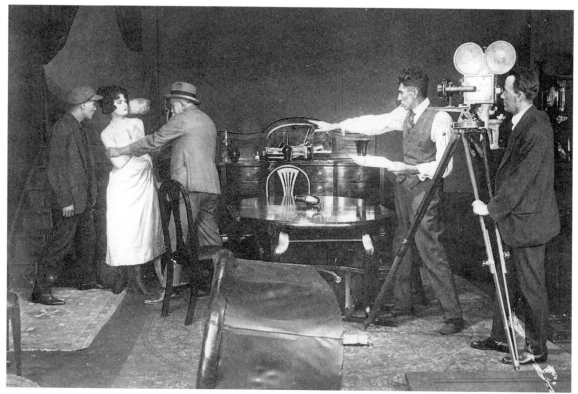

Lacey Percival behind the camera as Dunstan Webb directs **Dope** (1924)

Freedom Ride. This is an historical account of an Aboriginal civil rights movement led by her father, Charles Perkins.

As the executive producer of the ABC's Indigenous Program Unit, Perkins initiated *Songlines*, a series exploring a range of Aboriginal music. Most recently she has been involved with the establishment of the National Indigenous Documentary Fund.

Released in 1998, •**Radiance** is Perkins' début film, introducing her uncompromising, eclectic vision to the big screen. **Radiance** formed part of a national travelling exhibition of Aboriginal short films under the title 'Shifting Sands: From Sand to Celluloid'. In the creation, production, and dissemination of images, Rachel Perkins perpetuates her father's commitment to dissolving racial disparity and promoting positive, diverse images of indigenous Australians.   WENDY HASLEM

Perry, Joseph, *see* Documentary and non-fiction, silent

Perry, Orrie, *see* Silent film, to 1914

Perth Institute of Film and Television, *see* Film and Television Institute of Western Australia

Peter Kenna's The Umbrella Woman, *see* Umbrella Woman, The

Petersen

1974. Director: Tim Burstall. *Producer:* Tim Burstall. *Scriptwriter:* David Williamson. *Director of photography:* Robin Copping. *Music:* Peter Best. *107 min. Cast:* Jack Thompson (Tony Petersen), Jacki Weaver (Susie Petersen), Wendy Hughes (Trish Kent), Belinda Giblin (Moira), Arthur Dignam (Charles Kent).

Tony Petersen, electrician and former football star, is taking an arts course at Melbourne University where he has an affair with married English tutor Trish Kent. Caught between loyalty to his nice but dim wife, Susie, and the prospect of education, he finds himself up against social and intellectual pressures with which he is ill-equipped to deal. Trish wants a child from him, but rejects him when she is offered a job at Oxford, and her effete husband Charles fails him in his examinations. He rapes Trish and returns bitterly to his electrician's work and casual infidelity.

Tim •Burstall, pioneer of the reviving Australian cinema, had commercial successes with his 'ocker' comedies, •**Stork** (1971) and •**Alvin Purple** (1973), which critics denounced as exploitative in their frank sexuality. **Petersen** received rough critical treatment, as if it were more of the same, whereas it is, in fact, a serious study of inarticulate aspiration. The gap between Petersen's home life and the radicalism of the 1970s university campus is for him unbridgeable except in sexual terms, and •Thompson's performance, part cheeky charm, part nascent awareness, creates a touching figure. There are the nudity and sex scenes that characterised the comedies, but the effect here is essentially not prurient but painful. The film has its crudities of dialogue and characterisation (Arthur •Dignam's caricatured pipe-smoking academic is one), and some dated bursts of 'lyrical' photography (on beaches and country roads), but at its centre is a story worth telling, energetically played out against acutely observed social backgrounds, which makes the film a valuable document of its times.   BMcF

Petty, Bruce (1929–) ANIMATOR/DIRECTOR   Best known for his sharply anti-establishment cartoons, which appeared from the 1950s in *Punch*, the *New Yorker*, the *Australian*, and the *Age*, Bruce Petty brought his distinctive, sprawling, spiky line-drawing style to his first short film, **Hearts and Minds** (1967), directed by Phillip •Adams, an anti-Vietnam war statement. **Leisure** (1976), with contributions from David Denneen's Film Graphics, is a witty observation of people at rest and at play; in 1977, the film won Australia's second Academy Award. In **Karl Marx** (1977), he mixed animation and live actors (as did Yoram •Gross). Typically, his leftist political stance does not stand in the way of his irreverence in this biography of Marx. He again mixes actors and animation in **The Movers** (1986), an overview of history. His images and thinking are busy, reflecting intricate inter-relations in a style that is snarly in attitude and line.

Other Australian films: The Money Game (1972), A Big Hand for Everyone (1971), Australian History (1971), Megalomedia (1981), The Clever Country (1992).   RICK THOMPSON

Phantom Gold

1937. *Director*: Rupert Kathner. *Producer*: Rupert Kathner. *Scriptwriter*: Rupert Kathner. *Director of photography*: Rupert Kathner. *Music*: Rex Shaw. 64 min. B&W. *Cast*: Captain A.C. Stevens (narrator), Stan Tolhurst (Harry Lasseter), Bryce Russell (Paul Johns), Captain W.L. Pittendrigh (Himself), Bob Buck (Himself), Old Warts (Himself).

As a film-maker, Rupert •Kathner's ambition always exceeded his capacity. In his book, *Let's Make a Movie* (1945), he was scathing about the work of others but, as he directed, produced, wrote, and photographed this feature film himself, he must also take responsibility for its failings. He was not adequately equipped for location sound, so most of the film is presented as images accompanied by a voice-over, in dead-pan style, often casually offensive and racist. The style shifts,

from documentary (following one of the many expeditions that went out in search of Lasseter's lost reef) to re-enactment (of Bob Buck's version of Lasseter's disappearance and death, and of Captain Pittendrigh's account of his plane crash and near death during the search). An increasingly over-wrought tone in the voice-over attempts to produce the drama lacking in the images. It is not surprising that the film was refused quota registration in NSW, or that distributors were reluctant to handle it.   IB

Phantom Stockman, The

1953. *Director*: Lee Robinson. *Producer*: Chips Rafferty, George Heath. *Scriptwriter*: Lee Robinson. *Director of photography*: George Heath. *Music*: William Lovelock. 67 min. B&W. *Cast*: Chips Rafferty (the Sundowner), Jeanette Elphick (Kim Marsden), Max Osbiston (McLeod), Guy Doleman (Stapleton), Henry Murdoch (Dancer), Bob Darken (Roxey), Joe Scully (Moth), Albert Namatjira (himself).

This was the first collaboration between Chips •Rafferty and Lee •Robinson and, because of financial restrictions imposed by the Commonwealth government that limited the amount of capital they could raise, Rafferty and Robinson decided to shoot an Australian western around Alice Springs. Robinson's script stays strictly within the conventions of the American series western involving the plight of the rancher's daughter who, after inheriting a large property when her father is murdered, is threatened by a greedy neighbour who covets her land. With the assistance of her loyal foreman (McLeod) and the mysterious Sundowner, and his trusty Aboriginal companion, the ranch is saved and the villain (Stapleton) defeated.

This story shares more than a passing resemblance to the staple plot of the Lone Ranger series, which was popular on American television at that time, together with countless other series westerns. Some critics have pointed to the Sundowner's supernatural power of mental telepathy in his ability to summon the Dancer and other Aborigines as a unique touch, but this was a relatively conventional element in many Hollywood series films, including westerns. **The Phantom Stockman** is distinguished only by the spectacular setting, the languid pace of the film, and the brief inclusion of Aboriginal artist Albert Namatjira, who had been the subject of a 1947 documentary by Robinson. The film earned a healthy profit in Australia and overseas.   GM

Phar Lap

1983. *Director*: Simon Wincer. *Producer*: John Sexton. *Scriptwriter*: David Williamson. *Director of photography*: Russell Boyd. *Music*: Bruce Rowland. 118 min. *Cast*: Tom Burlinson (Tommy Woodcock), Martin Vaughan (Harry Telford), Judy Morris (Bea Davis), Celia de Burgh (Vi Telford), Ron Leibman (Dave Davis).

Any story of the brief, tumultuous career of Australia's most famous race-horse must suffer from the fact that everyone knows how it ends. After an unparalleled series of wins in Australia, in the face of opposition from snobbish racing club dignitaries, its owner, American magnate Davis, insists on taking it to America, where it wins but dies shortly after, in what remain mysterious circumstances. David *Williamson's script begins with the death, thus setting itself the task of finding other interests to impel the film. How Phar Lap rose from being an equine Aussie battler (although it came from New Zealand) to an icon of national aspiration and achievement proves nearly adequate to the film's narrative, even if director Simon *Wincer relies too much on slow-motion effects to record the horse's triumphs. In a strong cast, Martin *Vaughan as the trainer and Ron Leibman as the horse's owner, are especially convincing as they delineate different perceptions of what Phar Lap stands for, and Tom *Burlinson plays the legendary strapper, Tommy Woodcock, who, in his old age, plays a small role in the film.

BMcF

Phelps, Peter (1960–) ACTOR Since starting in Australian television in the soap opera *The Restless Years*, Peter Phelps's career has taken him to New Zealand (the lead, Patrick, in **Starlight Hotel** 1987), the USA (a small part as an Australian surfer in **Point Break** 1991, and the continuing role of Trevor Cole in the television series *Baywatch* 1989–90, and a spin-off movie) and the United Kingdom (John Pope, in **Merlin** 1992). His Australian film career began with a small role in **Undercover** (1984), then he impressed with the dual role of Judah/Robert opposite Imogen Annesley in *Playing Beatie Bow (1986), and Dave, the crack shot who refuses to kill a man in *The Lighthorsemen (1987). Three films in which he played leading roles did not secure a theatrical release: **Breaking Loose** (1988), **Justified Action** (1993), and **Rough Diamonds** (1994). He played in television series and telemovies before returning to film as Leo Megaw in the science fiction thriller **Zone 39** (1997). He then completed a film-making course at New York University, and returned to Australia with the intention of directing films from his own scripts. Meanwhile, he accepted the lead in the television series *Stingers*, having finally thrown off the male bimbo image of his early years.

IB

Phipps, Max (1939–) ACTOR This flamboyant Melbourne actor is best known for his role in the 1970s as the transvestite Dr Frank N. Furter in one of the most successful stage versions of *The Rocky Horror Show*. Max Phipps's other key acting role was as Gough Whitlam in the groundbreaking miniseries *The Dismissal* (1983). He has been less successful in capturing key roles on the big screen, although his screen career extends back to 1969 and the film adaptation of the popular television series *You Can't See Round

Corners. This was followed by supporting roles in a number of horror films: first, the Gothic drama *The Cars that Ate Paris** (1974) and then two inferior films, the vampire tale **Thirst** (1979) and **Nightmares** (1980). A featured role as the sadistic warder in *Stir (1980) reinforced Phipps's screen image as a villain, which was confirmed by roles in *Mad Max 2 (1981), **The Return of Captain Invincible** (1983), and as the quasi Nazi-villain Savage in **Sky Pirates** (1986). In the 1990s Phipps appeared mainly on television.

Other Australian films include: Polly Me Love (1976), Emoh Ruo (1985), **Dark Age** (1987), What the Moon Saw (1990).　　GM

Photography, *see* Cinematography

Piano, The

1993. *Director*: Jane Campion. *Producer*: Jan Chapman. *Scriptwriter*: Jane Campion. Based on the novel, *The Story of a New Zealand River*, by Jane Maunder; uncredited. *Director of photography*: Stuart Dryburgh. *Music*: Michael Nyman. 115 min. *Cast*: Holly Hunter (Ada), Harvey Keitel (Baines), Sam Neill (Stewart), Anna Paquin (Flora), Kerry Walker (Aunt Morag).

One of the most honoured films of the new Australian cinema, **The Piano**, in fact, raised some controversy about its nationality: it is a French-financed Australia–New Zealand co-production, with a New Zealand director and two American stars. Perhaps its mixed parentage helps to account for its touch of the 'marvellous': how many films in the realist tradition, Australian, American, or whatever, dare to excite their viewers with an image as rare as that of a grand piano on the deserted beach of a largely untamed frontier? And the rest of the film lives up to the suggestiveness of this image that, one gathers, was director Jane *Campion's starting point on the film.

The mute Scottish woman, Ada, and her daughter Flora, who communicates for her, are in nineteenth-century New Zealand, where Ada is due to enter into an arranged marriage with landowner Stewart. The piano at once becomes a bone of contention when Stewart refuses to transport it to his home, and his agent, Baines, makes a bizarre sexual deal with Ada for the restoration of the piano. Before the curious resolution two hours later, Ada has been shockingly mutilated by the enraged Stewart and nearly loses her life as the piano sinks into the sea.

Merely to outline the plot can give little idea of the strangeness of the film, of its refusal of the conventional, not merely in plot development but also in the oddly muted palate in which cinematographer Stuart Dryburgh works, and in the dangerous gaps between the spoken and the unspeakable, between Ada's yearnings and Stewart's obtuse demands. It may well be a film whose aspirations exceed its achievements, Oscars notwithstanding, but there is something breathtaking about its sheer daring.

BMcF

Holly Hunter and Anna Paquin in **The Piano**

Pickering, Joseph CINEMATOGRAPHER Joseph Pickering was director of photography with Brian •Probyn on the short feature **Gary's Story** (1980), then on a number of major theatrical features, including **Queen of the Road** (1984), **Windrider** (1985), **•Warming Up** (1985), **•Shame** (1988), and **Sons of Steel** (1989). In the 1990s he worked mainly on television series (including *The Flying Doctors*, 1992; *Heartbreak High*, 1995–96; *Wildside*, 1997–99), but was also director of photography on **Idiot Box** (1996). IB

Picnic at Hanging Rock

1975. Director: Peter Weir. *Producers:* Hal and Jim McElroy. *Scriptwriter:* Cliff Green. Based on the novel by Joan Lindsay. *Director of photography:* Russell Boyd. *Music:* Bruce Smeaton. 115 min. *Cast:* Rachel Roberts (Mrs Appleyard), Dominic Guard (Michael Fitzhubert), Helen Morse (Diane de Poitiers), Jackie Weaver (Minnie), Vivean Gray (Miss McCraw).

This was the film that brought new Australian cinema (see Revival, the) to national and international attention. It constituted a serious departure from both the realist strain and from the 'Ocker' comedies that had accounted for most of the Australian film-making in the first half of the 1970s. Derived from Joan Lindsay's novel about a party of school-girls who, with one of their mistresses, disappear on Hanging Rock on St Valentine's Day 1900, the film offers a poetic treatment of the nature–nurture dichotomy. Nurture, in the form of an anachronistic and repressive system of middle-class education, based on European tenets, proves inadequate to the lure of nature in the form of the forbidding rock faces and crevices.

The film's coherence derives less from taut narrative than from the interactive imagistic power of these two monoliths—the Rock and the School—arbitrarily set down in the Australian bush. Shimmering summer gives way to bleak autumn as the mystery deepens, and its consequences ripple out in ways that are not always convincing in conventional narrative terms. However, it signified a directorial talent that could organise aural and visual imagery of a kind new to Australian cinema. BMcF

Picot, Genevieve (1956–) ACTOR This Tasmanian stage, television, and film actor appeared in the popular television series *The Sullivans* before graduating from the National Institute of Dramatic Art in 1979. After a supporting role in the ABC eight-part historical series *The Timeless Land* (1980), Genevieve Picot won the lead role as the fashion novice Libby in '**Undercover**' (1984), David •Stevens'

Picnic at Hanging Rock

whimsical account of the early history of the Australian underwear company Berlei. A supporting role in the family drama **To Market To Market** (1987) preceded Picot's best role to date as Celia, the bitter, love-stricken housekeeper to Hugo •Weaving's Martin in the celebrated 1991 film •**Proof.** Picot's multi-layered performance is a crucial element in Jocelyn •Moorhouse's film; the role, in the hands of a lesser actor, could easily have degenerated into a stereotypical portrait of sexual repression. Picot generates sympathy for Celia's inability to ignore Martin's indifference to her feelings, thereby providing a moral context to understand the petty, and not so petty, actions directed against her employer. A brief appearance as a store detective in •**Muriel's Wedding** (1994) and a guest spot in the *Halifax f.p.* series were followed by another critically acclaimed performance tracing the early life of New Zealand socialist Sonya Davies in **Bread and Roses** (1994), which was released as both a two-part miniseries and as a film.

Other Australian films include: True Love and Chaos (1996).   GM

Picture Show Man, The

1977. Director: John Power. *Producer:* Joan Long. *Scriptwriter:* Joan Long. *Director of photography:* Geoff Burton. *Music:* Peter Best. 98 min. *Cast:* Rod Taylor (Palmer), John Meillon (Mr Pym), John Ewart (Freddie Graves), Harold Hopkins (Larry Pym), Patrick Cargill (Fitzwilliam).

Lyle Penn's autobiographical account of a travelling picture show was the inspiration for this light-hearted story of showman Maurice Pym, his son Larry, and pianist Freddie, on the road in NSW in the 1920s. Their rival, the 'damn Yankee' Palmer, is much more canny—always ahead of them with better transport and more up-to-date equipment. But Pym's Pictures survives, even making the transition to sound, with the help of Freddie's savings.

John •Meillon and John •Ewart make a great team, including performing together as a supporting vaudeville act (the song 'Tap, tap' became a minor hit). The dapper Freddie, in his straw boater, is a particularly engaging character, interceding where necessary between father and son, while also following his own agenda (his courtship of a beautiful widow as he tunes her piano is a gem). Lucy, who wins Larry's heart, is a modern version of the earlier 'squatter's daughter' character.

The film was Joan •Long's second feature production (after •**Caddie**, 1976) and John •Power's first feature. Production difficulties led both to retire temporarily from feature films, but the result was well received by audiences, and by overseas critics and film festivals, although less popular with Australian reviewers.   IB

Pike, Andrew, *see* Ronin Films

Pioneers, The

1916. Director: Franklyn Barrett. *Producers:* Franklyn Barrett, Leopold A. Nettheim. *Scriptwriter:* Franklyn Barrett. From the novel by Katharine Susannah Prichard. *Director of photography:* Franklyn Barrett. 6 acts. B&W. *Cast:* Winter Hall (Dan Farrel), Alma Rock Phillips (Deirdre), Lily Rochefort (Mary Cameron), Charles Knight (Donald Cameron), Fred St Clair (Davey Cameron).

1926. Director: Raymond Longford. *Production company:* Australasian Films. *Scriptwriter:* Lottie Lyell. From the novel by Katharine Susannah Prichard. *Director of photography:* Arthur Higgins. 8000 ft. B&W. *Cast:* Virginia Beresford, William Thornton, Augustus Neville, Geoerge Chalmers, W. Dummitt, Robert Purdie.

Katherine Susannah Pritchard's classic novel of outback life tells the story of a pioneer couple, Donald and Mary Cameron, their son Davey, and their neighbours, Dan Farrel and his daughter Deidre. The hotel owner, McNab, blackmails Deidre with knowledge of her father's convict past, but McNab is accidentally killed, enabling Deidre and Davey to marry. Franklyn •Barrett's film was produced within a year of the novel winning £1000 in a literary competition run by the publishers Hodder & Stoughton. Only stills remain of this version, which was not successful at the box office. The second version was one of only three films that Raymond •Longford made for •Australasian Films before his relationship with the company broke down into the acrimony that was so apparent in his evidence before the 1928 Royal Commission. The fragments surviving in the •National Film and Sound Archive support the judgment of reviewers at the time that the treatment of the locations and characters was comparable to Longford's naturalistic style in city films such as •**The Sentimental Bloke**. Some reviewers objected to the melodramatic events of the story, but the film was a success with audiences.   IB

Playing Beatie Bow

1986. Director: Donald Crombie. *Producer:* Jock Blair. *Scriptwriter:* Peter Gawler. Based on the novel by Ruth Park. *Director of photography:* Geoffrey Simpson. *Music:* Garry McDonald, Laurie Stone. 93 min. *Cast:* Imogen Annesley (Abigail), Peter Phelps (Judah, Robert), Mouche Phillips (Beatie), Nikki Coghill (Dovey), Moya O'Sullivan (Granny), Don Barker (Samuel), Damien Janko (Gibbie), Su Cruikshank (Madam).

Sixteen-year-old Abigail is unhappy and out of place in the 1980s. When she follows Beatie Bow back 100 years into the Rocks area of old Sydney, she discovers a world where she can fit in. She falls in love for the first time, but Judah is promised to Dovey. Abigail must grow up enough to admit this and to let him go. In this fairytale, rather than the hero rescuing the heroine, it is she who must perform the rescue task, which frees her and allows her to be rewarded with the hero.

There are strong performances from all the young people and some wicked cameos from the older cast, particularly the drunken Samuel who roars through the streets brandishing a sabre, and the immensely bulky madame who leers evilly at the captive Abigail. The set piece of the film is a fight in the brothel, with a cage of snakes overturned in the middle of the brawling men. But this very moral world is not simplistic: the dilemmas of growing up are treated seriously, sexist stereotyping is avoided, and the past is not seen only through rose-coloured glasses.   IB

Imogen Annesley and Peter Phelps in
Playing Beatie Bow

Polson, John ACTOR Polson is a prolific young actor who has steadily gained recognition, particularly after his edgy performance as Glenn Sprague in •**The Boys** (1998). John Polson's acting career began with a supporting role in the telefeature *Call Me Mr. Brown* (1986), directed by Scott •Hicks and based on the true-life 1971 extortion attempt of Qantas airlines. Polson next appeared in the popular miniseries *Vietnam* (1987) before acquiring a leading role in the

low-budget teenage drama **Raw Nerve** (1990). This was followed by the pivotal role of Private Jimmy Fenton in •**Blood Oath** (1990), and his testimony in the film recalling his brother's death is a crucial moment during the trial of Japanese soldiers accused of war crimes against Australian prisoners of war. Polson's acting career gained momentum throughout the 1990s with key roles, such as Russell Crowe's potential lover in •**The Sum of Us** (1994), and films such as •**Sirens** (1994), •**The Back of Beyond** (1995), and **Idiot Box** (1996).
Other Australian films include: •**For Love Alone** (1986), **Tender Hooks** (1989), **Candy Regentag** (1989), **Dangerous Game** (1991), **Gino** (1993), **Siam Sunset** (1999, d.).   GM

Porter, Eric (1911–83) ANIMATOR/DIRECTOR/PRODUCER
Eric Porter trained in commercial art at East Sydney Technical School, and his first paid job was for Ken G. •Hall, making an animated advertising film for an Adelaide butcher. As he learned more about animation, he established an ongoing correspondence with Walt Disney, who was generous with technical advice. In 1930 Porter set up his own company, producing mainly advertising: even his Willie the Wombat character, intended as the hero of a cartoon series, was converted into a sales pitch for a bank, in the animated short **Waste Not, Want Not** (1939). After his only live-action feature film was released, •**A Son is Born** (1946), he returned to animation and documentaries. In the early 1950s, Columbia Pictures invited Porter to produce two 10-minute colour cartoons, so he used the wombat character in a less Australian-specific incarnation in **Rabbit Stew** (1952) and **Bimbo's Auto** (1954). However, when this did not lead to further work for Columbia, he turned to television, creating some of the best-known characters on the box (Louie the Fly for Mortein, Friar Tuck for McWilliams Wines, and Mr Sheen), as well as the *Yellow House* children's television series, and contract animation for other American companies. His workforce grew to nearly 300—the largest production company in the country. In 1972 he produced and directed Australia's first animated feature film, **Marco Polo Junior Versus the Red Dragon** and, in 1976, he produced the telemovie **Polly My Love**. He was presented with the AFI's Raymond Longford Award in 1982.   IB

'Possum Paddock

1921. *Director*. Charles Villiers, Kate Howarde. *Producer, Scriptwriter*. Kate Howarde. From her play. B&W. *Cast*: John Cosgrove (Andrew McQuade), James Martin (Dan Martin), Leslie Adrien (Nancy McQuade), Jack Kirby (Hugh Bracken).

'Possum Paddock, Kate Howarde's popular play, seems to have made a rather dull transition to the screen on the evidence of the reels that survive. The film is of most interest today because of the roles that Howarde took in the film's

production (director credits are shared with veteran actor, Charles Villiers, who appears at the time to have been attempting to break into feature directing). There is also a shot that makes telling use of empty space and the map of Australia, a brief, climactic auction sequence that is nicely observed, and a subplot involving a dastard who impregnates one woman, attempts to rape another, and somehow atones for it all by writing a letter offering to marry his first victim.

WILLIAM D. ROUTT

Power and the Glory, The

1941. *Director*: Noel Monkman. *Scriptwriters*: Noel Monkman, Harry Lauder 2nd. *Director of photography*: Arthur Higgins. *Music*: Henry Krips. 93 min. B&W. *Cast*: Katrin Rosselle (Elsa Marnelle), Eric Bush (Ted Jackson), Lou Vernon (Professor Marnelle), Eric Reiman (Von Schweig), Peter Finch (Frank Miller).

Noel •Monkman's second and last feature was a thriller, visually reminiscent of the 'mad scientist' genre, with laboratories full of bubbling retorts and strange gases rising. But this scientist is a Czech pacifist (Professor Marnelle), working in Germany on a new fuel, and trying to keep the secret of its poisonous gas by-product from the Nazis. He and his daughter (Elsa) escape to Australia, but von Schweig follows and captures them, assisted by Australian fifth-columnists, until they are rescued by an Australian aviator (Ted), who loves Elsa. Despite some stereotypical Nazi villains and the racist depiction of a Chinese cook, this is an enjoyable film: the scenes of planes being tested and of aerial combat (provided by the RAAF) are exciting, and the action moves briskly.   IB

Power, John (1930–) DIRECTOR   After an initial period as a journalist, John Power shifted across to television news, working as a current affairs and documentary producer, and as director at the ABC. In this capacity he produced the award-winning documentary **Like a Summer Storm** (1972) and directed **Billy and Percy** (1973), a dramatisation of the relationship between former Australian prime minister Billy Hughes and his secretary Percy Deane. In 1975 Power won 'Best Director' at the Australian Film Awards for **Billy and Percy**. Power's first feature film was •**The Picture Show Man** (1977), a leisurely, elegiac celebration of an early independent film exhibitor, superbly played by John •Meillon, who travelled the remote areas of NSW in the 1920s. While the tone of the film was light-hearted, it also reinforced the prevailing Australian ethos of survival against powerful obstacles that, in the film, took many forms, including flammable film, the new sound equipment, and the threat from American domination of the industry, represented in the film by the rivalry between Meillon and Rod •Taylor. In the 1980s Power worked exten-

sively in television where he directed miniseries such as episode five of *The Dismissal* (1983), *Alice to Nowhere* (1986), *Tanamera: Lion of Singapore* (1989), and *All The Rivers Run II* (1990), together with television pilot programs such as *Sky Trackers* (1990). During this busy period Power also directed a feature film, **Father** (1990), a study of the aftermath of the Holocaust as it affected a daughter's faith in her German father many years later in Australia with regard to the extent of his participation in atrocities during World War II.

Other Australian films include: The Sound of Love (1977), The Great Gold Swindle (1984), A Single Life (1985).   GM

Preston, Mike (1940–) ACTOR   British-born Mike Preston had established himself as a singer before coming to Australia in 1967. His rugged build (perhaps the result of an early career as a boxer?) made him an imposing presence in Australian television, as a talk-show host, and in several early films of the revival (see Revival, the). He was strikingly good as the miner Pansy, whose ruthlessness triggers much of the drama in Tim •Burstall's •**The Last of the Knucklemen** (1979), a then-rare film critique of Australian male values. There were further strong roles in •**Mad Max 2** (1981), as Pappagallo, and for Burstall again in the romantic drama **Duet for Four** (1982), in which he played the rough-hewn toy manufacturer caught in a network of bourgeois deceit. Since then, his work has been mainly for television.

Other Australian films: Barney (1976), …Maybe This Time (1980).
BMcF

Pringle, Ian DIRECTOR   One of the more innovative Australian directorial talents, Ian Pringle has persistently had trouble in getting his films seen. He worked in television before making a series of short films including **Flights** (1977) and the 50-minute featurette **Wronsky** (1979), and directed his first feature, **The Plains of Heaven**, in 1982. Set in the Victorian Alps and sumptuously shot by Ray •Argall, this film makes no concession to popular taste. It is an essentially 'interior' drama of the relationship between two men employed on a remote relay transmission station and, with diametrically opposed views on life, getting on each other's nerves, as their isolated situation pushes them towards loss of sanity. Richard •Moir, who played the younger of the two men, also starred in Pringle's next film, **Wrong World** (1986), again photographed by Argall, and again obdurately arthouse in its orientation, as it unfolds the developing relationship between a morphine-addicted doctor (Moir) and a street junkie (Jo •Kennedy). The film is set in Bolivia, the American mid-west, Melbourne, and the north-western Victorian town of Nhill, and its episodes are linked by the doctor's voice-over. Despite winning a Best

Actress award for Kennedy at the Berlin Film Festival, the film has scarcely been seen here.

By the time he made his third feature, Pringle had settled in Berlin, under the informal tutelage of Wim Wenders. **The Prisoner of St Petersburg** (1988) is an Australian–German co-production, set in Berlin, that is luminously evoked in Argall's black-and-white cinematography. It charts the wanderings of a young man (Noah •Taylor), who is obsessed with Russian literature, and the two drugged young women he meets, one of whom, Elena (Solveig Dommartin), he believes he has known in the remote past. This can never have looked like commercial material and it had only very limited screening in specialist cinemas. His next, **Isabelle Eberhardt** (1992), has been similarly elusive. With locations in Algiers, Geneva, and Paris, a fascinating protagonist in the eponymous traveller, and a cast that includes Peter O'Toole, the film suffers from the pretention that is always a danger in Pringle's films but, like his others, it also aims to do things less obvious, and to do them in less obvious ways.

He acted as associate producer on **The Tale of Ruby Rose** (1988), •**Celia** (1989), and co-producer on Geoffrey •Wright's successful but controversial, •**Romper Stomper** (1992); perhaps his instincts as a producer are more commercial than those that guide him as a director.

Other Australian films include: The Cartographer and the Waiter (1977, short), Bare Is His Back Who Has No Brother (1979, doc.), Jack and the Soldier (1979, short), Lover Boy (1988, assoc. p).

BMcF

Probyn, Brian (1921–82) CINEMATOGRAPHER British cinematographer Brian Probyn made his first feature film in 1962. By the time he arrived in Australia in 1973 he had already worked as director of photography in the United Kingdom (for instance on **Poor Cow,** 1967; and three Hammer horror films in 1972–73) and in the USA (for instance, on **Downhill Racer,** 1969; and **Badlands,** 1973). He came to Australia as cinematographer on **Inn of the Damned** (1975) becoming the first overseas director of photography to be given permission, at a time when the film industry was booming and resources were stretched. He stayed on to film the disastrous **Plugg** (1975) and to make a better impression on Kevin •Dobson's first feature film, •**The Mango Tree** (1977), and on Yoram •Gross's **The Little Convict** (1979). He photographed a number of documentaries and short features (including **Jog's Trot** 1976 and **Gary's Story** 1980, with Joseph •Pickering), and tutored in cinematography at •Australian Film, Television and Radio School in 1979, before returning to the United Kingdom as a visiting lecturer at the National Film School. •**Far East** and **Sweet Dreamers** (both 1982) were his last features in Australia.

IB

Proof

1991. *Director*: Jocelyn Moorhouse. *Producer*: Lynda House. *Scriptwriter*: Jocelyn Moorhouse. *Director of photography*: Martin McGrath. *Music*: Not Drowning, Waving. 86 min. *Cast*: Hugo Weaving (Martin), Genevieve Picot (Celia), Russell Crowe (Andy), Heather Mitchell (Mother), Jeffrey Walker (Young Martin).

This is an innovative film and a striking début by director Jocelyn •Moorhouse. Based on the unlikely premise of a blind man (Martin) using photography to validate his understanding of the world, the film continually selects the most perverse narrative option. Martin, in an attempt to prove that his mother lied to him when he was a young boy, enlists the assistance of Andy, a laconic restaurant worker, as his 'eyes'. Martin is particularly interested in the contents of a photograph of his garden that was taken when he was a young boy. This photograph, he believes, will confirm his suspicions concerning his mother's lies. He also has a bizarre relationship with his housekeeper, Celia. Martin, as he explains to Andy, keeps Celia in his employment because she desires him. By denying her what she wants she cannot, he reasons, pity him.

This is a perfectly formed film, based on carefully modulated shifts in power among the three characters. Celia emerges as the least sympathetic character and Moorhouse, despite proclaiming her affection for the character, foreshadows Celia's dark side early in the film—particularly in a shot of Celia's disembodied face in a mirror as she applies lipstick prior to Martin's arrival. Moorhouse's assured direction cuts through any hint of sentiment or pretension and leaves the audience with an ambivalent projection of Martin's tortured world. The film's critical acclaim at Cannes was, for once, well deserved and established a major figure in the Australian film industry.

GM

Proyas, Alex (1965–) DIRECTOR Born in Egypt to Greek–Egyptian parents, Alex Proyas and his family emigrated to Sydney when he was three years old. After graduating from the Australian Film and Television School, Proyas earned his living making rock clips and commercials for his production company, Meaningful Eye Contact. Proyas composed the score for the Jane •Campion short **A Girl's Own Story** (1984) before directing his first feature, **Spirits of the Air, Gremlins of the Clouds**, in 1988. This languid, post-apocalyptic story involving a futuristic aviator and his desire to assemble a light plane to take him over mountains and away from his mysterious pursuers, was characterised by Proyas's rich visual imagination, a characteristic that extends through all of his feature films.

After industry and critical acclaim for his video clip for the Crowded House song 'Don't Dream It's Over', Proyas established a reputation in Los Angeles directing rock clips and commercials. After signing with the influential CAA agency, Proyas directed **The Crow** (1994), a revenge tale based on James O'Barr's comic book. Although the film was a commercial success, due largely to support from young audiences, the film was a painful experience for Proyas as the film's lead actor, Brandon Lee, was accidentally killed towards the end of the production. After rejecting offers to direct sequels to **Batman** (1989) and **Alien** (1986), Proyas developed the script for •**Dark City** (1998) with scriptwriters Lem Dobbs and David S. Goyer, and it was directed by Proyas at the new Fox Studios in Sydney.

Dark City is a futuristic thriller that combines Proyas's interest in exploiting, and extending, those film-noir visual conventions that convey a sense of urban alienation with the narrative possibilities inherent in science-fiction literature. Literary science fiction, Proyas argues, contains a 'sense of wonder … where, when you perceive things, you can step back and look at the whole cosmos and get some insight into that, even fleetingly'. GM

Puberty Blues

1981. *Director:* Bruce Beresford. *Producers:* Joan Long, Margaret Kelly. *Scriptwriter:* Margaret Kelly. Based on the novel by Kathy Lette and Gabrielle Carey. *Director of photography:* Don McAlpine. *Music:* Les Gock. 86 min. *Cast:* Nell Schofield (Debbie), Jad Capelja (Sue), Geoff Rhoe (Garry), Tony Hughes (Danny), Alan Cassell (Vickers), Kirrily Nolan (Mrs Vickers), Rowena Wallace (Mrs Knight), Charles Tingwell (Headmaster).

Bruce •Beresford's suburban variation on the rites-of-passage theme prevalent throughout the late 1970s is notable for its female view of a male subculture. Two adolescent girls, Debbie and Sue, set out to gain admission to the popular local 'surfie' crowd. Initially, they are content to conform to a lifestyle dominated by chauvinistic and sometimes misogynistic males. However, the girls become disillusioned and reject the passivity that is required of them. In a triumphant scene that details their reclamation of self-respect, and their coming of age, the girls subvert the status quo, and surf the waves themselves.

Beresford's choice of a contemporary setting for his subject matter marks a significant departure from the New Wave trend of harking back to the past with features based on period-set texts. Strong performances by Jad Capelja and Nell Schofield reinforce the sense of vibrancy and freshness achieved within the narrative. MELINDA HILDEBRANDT

Punch-McGregor, Angela (1953–) ACTOR Although

she has had some leading roles since, Angela Punch (she added the '-McGregor' when she married her agent) arguably gave her finest performances in supporting/character roles

before reaching the age of 30. As Gilda, the wife of the half-caste protagonist in •**The Chant of Jimmie Blacksmith** (1978), she was very affecting as the hapless girl, adrift from her own people as Jimmie is from his, and she is brilliantly effective in •**Newsfront** (1978) as Fay, the tight-lipped, puritanical wife of the liberal news-cameraman Len (Bill •Hunter). Her instincts carefully reined in, her religion an unquestioning acceptance of dogma, she is nevertheless a figure of real pathos when her marriage falls apart.

In starring roles, she seemed never quite to have the command of the screen she so effortlessly established in her first two films. There was a bad career move in going to the USA to co-star with Michael Caine in **The Island** (1980), possibly the worst film in his long list of credits. In her two major Australian leading roles—in •**We of the Never Never** (1982), as Mrs Aeneas Gunn, and •**Annie's Coming Out** (1984), as the crusading social worker—she has not the star charisma that would lift the films above the descriptive and into the realm of the emotionally charged. She *acts* well enough, but she remains obdurately unexciting. Still young, she may yet find her métier as an incisive character actor, the niche in which she began. NIDA-trained, she has been active in all the performance media.

Other Australian films: D'Arcy (1979, short), **The Survivor** (1981), **The Best of Friends** (1982), **Double Deal** (1983), **The Delinquents** (1989), •**Spotswood** (1992), **Terra Nova** (1998).

BMcF

Pure S…

1975. *Director:* Bert Deling. *Producer:* Bob Weiss. *Scripwriter:* Bert Deling, John Hooper, David Shepherd, John Tulip, Bob Weiss, John Laurie, Alison Hill, Ann Heatherington. *Director of photography:* Tom Cowan. *Music:* Spo-de-o-dee, Toads, Red Symons, Martin Armiger. 83 min. *Cast:* Ann Heatherington (Sandy), John Laurie (John), Carol Porter (Gerry), Gary Waddell (Lou), Max Gillies (Dr Wulf).

Pure S…'s comedic, confrontational but determinedly non-judgmental treatment of 48 hours in the lives of four small-time drug users divided critical opinion on its release in 1976, with one reviewer describing the film as the 'most evil' he had ever seen. The film had previously been refused classification by the Commonwealth Film Censor, R.J. Prowse, but was granted an 'R' certificate and screened at the 1975 Perth Film Festival, when the title was changed from **Pure Shit** (the high-grade heroin that is the object of the characters' frenetic quest) to the more innocuous **Pure S…** With the $28 000 budget partially provided by the Film, Radio and Television Board of the •Australia Council, and the Buoyancy Foundation, a drug-users' support agency, the film was designed as a corrective to government anti-drugs films and as a critique of institutional approaches to drug use, in particular the fledgling methadone program. Cast and crew were predominantly clients, staff and associates of the Foundation. Leavening its uncompromising depiction of the rituals and results of heroin addiction with incisive dialogue, innovative editing, and camerawork that gave a junkie's-eye view of the world, together with scenes of high comedy (including a farcical attempt to rob a pharmacy), **Pure S...** was a welcome antidote to the recently formed •Australian Film Commission's preference for period drama and helped establish social realism as one of the core concerns of the revived feature industry.

BEN GOLDSMITH

Pym, Walter (?–1980) ACTOR   After a long career on the Australian stage and radio, with a television series, *Whiplash*, in the early 1960s, Walter Pym appeared in half a dozen films during the 1970s revival (see Revival, the), up to the time of his death. He had a film background as narrator of many documentaries of the war period and after, and had a small role in Charles •Chauvel's •**The Rats of Tobruk** (1944) but, by the time he returned to films, he was very elderly. His two most striking roles were as the old derelict in •**Mouth to Mouth** (1978), whose plight offers a bleak prognosis for the four young people living on the city's edge, and in •**Patrick** (1978), as Captain Fraser, one of the patients in the hospital presided over by the sinister Dr Roget (Sir Robert •Helpmann).

Other Australian films South West Pacific (1943, doc.), End Play (1976), Snapshot (1979), Thirst (1979), The Earthling (1980).

BMcF

Q

Queensland Film Corporation, *see* Queensland,
history and images; Pacific Film and Television
Corporation

Queensland, history and images

Accidents of history and geography have played a significant part in shaping the development of the film industry in
Qld, and the images of the state that have found their way
into film. Historically, Qld was settled later than most Australian states and this, coupled with its large indigenous
population and the dramatic and often tragic events of its
exploration, have contributed to its image as a frontier state.
Geographically, Qld is a large state with an area one-fifth of
the continent and a coastline that extends from near the
equator to the subtropics, paralleled for much of its length
by the Great Barrier Reef. This range and diversity of exotic
locations has attracted a large number of Australian and
foreign location films.

The major settlement of Qld took place in the latter half
of the nineteenth century, at a time of expansion of settlement through land selection and gold rushes. A pearling
industry developed, centred on Thursday Island in the
Coral Sea; gemfields were discovered west of Rockhampton;
and extensive deposits of other valuable minerals were
located in the far west and north. Qld became the site of
Australia's most extensive use of indentured labour,
imported from South Sea islands by large landholders to
work on the sugarcane fields. This supply of 'Kanakas' was
often the result of kidnapping by so-called 'blackbirders',
and the system approximated the plantation slavery of
North America and the Caribbean.

Repressive conditions on the waterfront and in the
shearing sheds led to the great strikes of the 1890s, and

the Australian Labor Party (ALP) was formed in the western Qld town of Barcaldine following a confrontation
between striking shearers and a force of Qld militia. For
most of the first half of the twentieth century, the ALP
was the dominant force in state politics but, following the
ALP split of the 1950s, the state came under the control of
conservative politicians.

The sharply drawn oppositional political patterns of Qld
political history have provided a mythic cast to Qld life.
Together with the exotic locations and the presence of great
agricultural and mineral wealth, the frontier aspects of Qld
life made it often seem to other Australians a land of
promise, a mythic destination. These elements have helped
to shape the representation of Qld and Queenslanders in
Australian feature films. Although comparatively little film
production occurred in Qld until recent times, a surprisingly large number of films contain allusions to the state.

As Pat Laughren and Chris Long have shown in their
documentary **Cinema in Colonial Queensland** (1996), film
exhibition and film production commenced early in
Qld. Kinetoscope viewing occurred in Brisbane in August
1895. It was followed in the same month by a Kinetophone
demonstration, which synchronised image with music
and dialogue, in the thriving goldmining town of Charters
Towers.

Shooting of film in Qld commenced in 1898, when the
Haddon anthropological expedition recorded native
dancers on Murray Island in Torres Strait, foreshadowing a
recurrent thematic pattern. The Queensland Agricultural
Department established a moving picture unit in 1899, possibly the first in-house government film unit in the world.
As well as agricultural activities, its camera operators Wills
and Mobsby recorded significant political and social events

such as the departure of the steamer 'White Star', which carried a government mission to investigate sexual abuse of native women by Torres Strait pearlers.

The Salvation Army's Limelight unit (see Documentary and non-fiction, silent) commenced its Qld operations in 1899 under Herbert Booth. Booth's camera operators Joseph •Perry and Sidney Cook filmed activities at the boys' hostel at Riverview near Ipswich, as well as scenes of Aboriginal life at Deebing Creek, and the visit of the Duke of York to Qld in 1900.

The first record of a fiction film shot in Qld is a newspaper report of a bushranging story filmed at Winton, western Qld, in 1904. Feature film production in Qld in the silent period was sporadic. *Australian Film 1900–1977* (1998) lists only 11 silent films shot there between 1913 (Raymond •Longford's 'Neath Southern Skies) and 1929 (Alexander Macdonald's **The Kingdom of Twilight**).

Of the silent films shot in Qld, the most notable are probably Charles •Chauvel's two films: •**The Moth of Moonbi** and •**Greenhide**, both released in 1926. The first of these films foreshadows his later work with its examination of the impact on a central female character of transposition from one cultural milieu to a diametrically opposed one. In both films, Chauvel handles location shooting and the activities of farm and station life with a keen eye for realism.

Frank •Hurley's •**The Hound of the Deep** (1926) uses Thursday Island locations and the pearling industry as backdrop for a dramatic quest for a valuable pearl. American director Scott R. Dunlap, used Murgon, near Ipswich, as a location for a formulaic Hollywood version of a Steele Rudd story, •**The Romance of Runnibede** (1928). The plot involves the abduction of Sydney-educated Dorothy Winchester (American actor Eva Novak) by an Aboriginal tribe who want her as their 'White Queen'. Despite its fanciful story, the film is well produced and makes effective use of bush landscape and station life. Two other silent films worth comment are **Retribution** (1921) and •**The Kid Stakes** (1927). **Retribution**, with a cast of Brisbane stage actors, contains an interesting twist to its plot of jewel theft on the gemfields around Anakie: its principal character is a female detective. Although **The Kid Stakes** is Sydney based, the goat-cart race sequence was shot in Rockhampton, since the Royal Society for the Prevention of Cruelty to Animals would not permit such activities in NSW.

The patterns of representation of Qld established in these silent films have continued into the sound period, which falls into two clear divisions in terms of production. Before 1977, when the Queensland Film Corporation (QFC) was established, with its objective 'to encourage the development of the film industry in the state', few feature films originated in Qld (before 1977 only 18 sound films were shot in whole or in part in the state). Three of these were the work of Charles and Elsa Chauvel: •**Heritage** (1935), •**Uncivilised** (1936), and •**Sons of Matthew** (1949). **Heritage**, Chauvel's tribute to the twin themes of development and pioneering, contains scenes of an Aboriginal attack filmed near Canungra in the Gold Coast hinterland. Although most of **Uncivilised** was shot on Palm Island, off Townsville, the setting is a remote part of the NT. **Sons of Matthew** shows Chauvel's cinematic powers at their peak: he uses the natural environment in powerful counterpoint to human passions. Set and photographed on the Lamington plateau, the film justifies Stuart Cunningham's description of it as 'the great Queensland film'.

Tropical Barrier Reef islands provide the setting and location for •**White Death** (1936), and •**King of the Coral Sea** (1954). In **White Death**, American author Zane Grey plays himself as he hunts a great white shark that has terrorised the Aborigines on the island he visits. **King of the Coral Sea** revisits the dramatic potential of the pearling industry, using the familiar formula of exotic locations spiced with larger-than-life characters. The Barrier Reef is also the setting for Michael Powell's •**Age of Consent** (1969). Set in Brisbane and on the Coral Coast (although most prints have the Brisbane sequences deleted), **Age of Consent** transposes the Norman Lindsay novel to a contemporary time, and to an exotic island location (Dunk Island). Once again, the story is replete with eccentric characters, as Powell captures the lushness of the tropical island setting.

Melbourne producer/director Tim •Burstall continued the tradition of locating fantastic adventure in exotic Qld with his version of the Eliza Fraser story, •**Eliza Fraser** (1976). The sequences involving life among the Aborigines were shot in the actual locations on Fraser Island, although the Aborigines themselves had to be brought to the island from the far north, since no indigenous people remain there. Burstall's next Queensland film, **High Rolling** (1977), also has an imported star (Timothy Bottoms) and is set amid the sunshine and glitz of Surfers Paradise.

The first Qld-initiated feature for many years was John Cox's **Surrender in Paradise** (1976), a low-budget 16mm film set on the Gold Coast, with turn-of-the-century bushrangers transferred via a time warp to present-day Surfers Paradise.

The late 1970s also saw a number of literary adaptations of works by Queensland authors, many of which explore the theme of growing up in country towns. Kevin •Dobson's version of Ronald McKie's •**The Mango Tree** (1977) is set in and around Bundaberg. Donald •Crombie's •**The Irishman** (1978), based on Elizabeth O'Conner's book, makes effective use of landscape and an old mining plant around Charters Towers.

A recurrent location, often with shadowy connotations, is the Gold Coast. Eddie •Davis's **Colour Me Dead** (1970), **High Rolling**, Ross •Dimsey's **Final Cut** (1980), and Frank Shield's

Queensland

•The Surfer (1988) all emphasise the meretricious aspects of Australia's most popular holiday destination. Carl •Schultz's •Goodbye Paradise (1983) most effectively encapsulates this trend: corrupt politicians, new-age charlatans, and avaricious developers emphasise the moral bankruptcy that the film's protagonist, the ex-cop Stacey (played by Ray •Barrett), sees behind the glamour. Igor •Auzins's •The Coolangatta Gold (1984) presents a more wholesome version of life on the Gold Coast, highlighting the influence of the physical environment on the lives of its athletic protagonists.

The QFC provided backing for a range of forgettable or occasionally embarrassing films such as Touch and Go (1981) and Turkey Shoot (1982), which were misconceived as likely to be 'popular' and consequently profitable. It also supported several films that have not received the critical recognition they deserve. Buddies (1984), scripted and produced by John •Dingwall, was shot on location on the sapphire fields around Emerald and Rubyvale in central Qld, with the harsh red soil and sparse forest providing an effective backdrop for a powerful story of mateship. •The Settlement, (1984) celebrates the right of characters to choose their own lifestyle and to fight free of the crushingly respectable conventions of small-town life. What Goodbye Paradise did partially for the Gold Coast, Jackie •McKimmie's Australian Dream (1987) does more completely for Brisbane. Australian Dream is a savage attack on suburban conformity and pretension and the hypocrisy of politicians. McKimmie's shotgun approach to social parody punctures most of her targets in a film that teeters between hilarity and loss of control.

During the final years before its demise in 1987, the QFC supported several other serious projects. Three of these were literary adaptations. Morris West's •The Naked Country (1985) explores the Aboriginal land rights issue; •The Fringe Dwellers (1986) relocates Nene Gare's story of the fortunes and misfortunes of an Aboriginal extended family, the Comeaways, from WA to south-east Qld; and •Travelling North (1987), adapted from the play by David •Williamson, offers a contrast between the bleak Melbourne cityscape and the tropical vegetation and dazzling sweep of the coast line around Port Douglas.

The theme of journeying to Qld emerges repeatedly in Australian feature films, sometimes directly, sometimes obliquely. Most directly, it occurs in films such as The Overlanders and Sons of Matthew, (in the latter Qld becomes the site of security or potential wealth). More obliquely, it occurs in films such as •Picnic at Hanging Rock (1975), •Mad Max 2 (1981), and Rikky and Pete (1988). The most subtle evocation of this idea is John •Ruane's Queensland (1976), with its two main characters continually planning, but never achieving, their escape north.

The strong tradition of location film-making has continued with Chris •Thompson's adaptation of Criena Rohan's novel, The Delinquents (1989), and Carl Schultz's update of the Captain Starlight story in Bullseye (1989). Jackie McKimmie's insightful •Waiting (1991), although set on the Darling Downs, was actually shot in (and funded by) NSW. In recent years the distinctive use of Queensland locations has been made by emerging Queensland filmmakers. Laurie •McInnes graphically evokes the texture and seediness of the port of Brisbane in her black-and-white first feature •Broken Highway. Novelist Gerard Lee effectively catches the tempo of life in a small north Qld town in All Men are Liars (1995). Pauline Chan substitutes the rainforest and wetlands scrub around Innisfail for Vietnam in •Traps (1994).

When the QFC was wound up in 1987 amid scandal and acrimony, its decade of production had produced few memorable films. Its replacement, the Queensland Film Development Office (QFDO), later restyled Film Queensland (FQ; see Pacific Film and Television Corporation (PFTC)), undertook to stimulate local production and develop local film-making talent. QFDO played a key role in revitalising film culture through the 1989 'Queensland Images' Film Retrospective, the forerunner of the Brisbane International Film Festival, which was to be established in 1992. QFDO was also important in planning the integration of Dino de Laurentiis's Oxenford film studio, established in 1988, into the Qld production scene. The large, modern studio complex produced a series of low-budget genre films, such as Blood Moon (1990), before it was taken over by •Village Roadshow, which later entered into a partnership in studio operation with Warner Brothers.

The PFTC was established under QFDO auspices to oversee the marketing of Qld as a location and to attract production here. In 1992 PFTC became a semi-autonomous government company. It has been a significant economic success, helping attract a succession of film and television productions. Most have been movies of the week for American television networks, but some have been big-budget features such as Fortress (1993), No Escape (1994—AKA Escape from Absolon), Streetfighter (1995), The Phantom (1996), and The Thin Red Line (1999). While these films make an economic contribution and provide experience and employment for locals, they have no direct cultural relevance to Qld or Australia.

The existence of two film agencies in the state—FQ with responsibilities for developing local film-making and PFTC with a mandate to market Qld as a location—has caused tension within the state's film-making community, particularly in Brisbane. In 1998 the government announced that these two organisations would be merged. Whatever the final outcome of this merger, and despite unprecedented levels of production that made Qld the premier state in Australia for film and television drama production in 1995, **Sons of Matthew** remains unchallenged as the pre-eminent Queensland film.

BRUCE MOLLOY

Queer Film and Video Festival, *see* Festivals

Quigley

1991. *Director*: Simon Wincer. *Producers*: Stanley O'Toole, Alexandra Rose. *Scriptwriter*: John Hill. *Director of photography*: David Eggby. *Music*: Basil Poledouris. 119 min. *Cast*: Tom Selleck (Matthew Quigley), Laura San Giacomo (Crazy Cora), Alan Rickman (Elliott Marston), Chris Haywood (Major Ashley Pitt), Ron Haddrick (Grimmelman). *Alternative title*: **Quigley Down Under** (USA).

In 1987, Simon •Wincer, director of three modest features, left Australia for the USA, returning four years later as the acclaimed director of the American miniseries *Lonesome Dove*. His homecoming was not a happy one. **Quigley** was instantly and unanimously dismissed as a tenth-rate western, and the cultural purists complained loudly about its foreign lead actors. However, **Quigley** is one of the most visually impressive films made in Australia, Wincer and director of photography David •Eggby capturing with a rich and subtle palette figures artfully positioned in a dramatic landscape.

Matthew Quigley is an American bounty hunter brought to Australia by the evil Elliott Marston to wipe out 'vermin'. That turns out to be Aborigines who rightfully want use of their own land. Quigley is not only seduced to the Aboriginal cause, but into the arms of Crazy Cora.

In •**The Lighthorsemen** and *Lonesome Dove*, Wincer showed himself to be without equal in filming men on horseback, and in this respect **Quigley** bristles with visceral excitement. The action scenes are brisk and well-shot, leading to a dramatically convincing showdown between Quigley and Marston, which revolves round a line of dialogue oft-repeated in a fashion found in many a John Wayne western. Wincer's film is stunning to look at and listen to, is amiable fun, and the notion of an American rescuing Aborigines is delightfully subversive in a film culture too often vengefully correct politically.

SCOTT MURRAY

Quinnell, Ken (1939–) WRITER Originally from a background in publishing and freelance journalism, including assignments for *Screen International* and *Rolling Stone*, Ken Quinnell frequently combines contemporary social issues with an understated dramatic approach. His adaptation of •**Cathy's Child** (1979) marked an important point in the expression of cross-cultural conflict in Australian cinema, while the underrated **Short Changed** (1986) failed to gain the attention it deserved in a year of large-budget taxation-incentive-assisted movies. Directed by George •Ogilvie and co-written with Robert J. Merritt, it follows the story of a young Aborigine's attempts to re-establish his relationship with his son by a white middle-class woman, and successfully addresses complex issues of race and class without sentimentality or melodrama. Not without humour, Quinnell provided John •Hargreaves with an excellent vehicle for his comedic talents in •**Hoodwink** (1981). He has worked extensively as a script editor (for example, on material by Frank Hardy and Dennis •Whiteburn), and he co-wrote and directed the telemovie *City's Edge* (1986). He is now mainly involved in educational and corporate film and video production, both as a director and writer, and has also worked as script editor for SBS.

HARRY KIRCHNER

R

Rabe, Pamela (1959–) ACTOR Pamela Rabe was born in Canada, where she graduated in 1981 from the Playhouse Acting School in Vancouver, and came to Australia two years later. Since arrival, she has become one of the dominant actors in this country, widely acclaimed in all the acting media. On stage, she has played both classic and new roles, as in *Much Ado About Nothing* and *Three Tall Women*, working extensively for both the Sydney and Melbourne Theatre Companies. On television, she gave a commanding performance in *Mercury* as an influential politician who tangles, sexually and otherwise, with the press. To date the highlight of her screen career is probably her Australian Film Institute award-winning performance in •**The Well** (1997), as the land-owning protagonist in the film version of Elizabeth Jolley's novel, but she has also had strong roles in Paul •Cox's •**Lust and Revenge** (1995), Mark •Joffe's •**Cosi** (1996), and Bruce •Beresford's •**Paradise Road** (1997). She is an actor of great potential, range, and power.

Other Australian films: Against the Innocent (1989), •Sirens (1994), **Vacant Possession** (1995). BMcF

Radiance

1998 Director: Rachel Perkins. *Producers*: Ned Lander, Andrew Myer. *Co-producer*: Jenny Day. *Scriptwriter*: Louis Nowra. *Director of photographer*: Warwick Thornton. 80 min. *Cast*: Rachael Maza (Cressy), Deborah Mailman (Nona), Trisha Morton-Thomas (Mae).

Resisting the desire for historical categorisation, Rachel •Perkins describes her début feature film **Radiance** as the first Aboriginal film with jokes. Jokes aside, **Radiance** is only the third feature film to be directed by an indigenous Australian. This reveals a surprising dearth of Aboriginal participation in a cinema that so recently celebrated its centenary.

Set in an elevated Queensland home bound by sugarcane plantations behind and an expanse of ocean in the foreground, **Radiance** explores the fantasy of returning home, dispelling utopian ideals of the family with a combination of comedy and tragedy. Although the narrative is initiated with the death of the maternal figure Mary, Mary's spirit remains and is incarnated by each of her three daughters in disparate ways.

Louis •Nowra's script is constructed around an indigenous point of view where issues of reconciliation, land rights, and the stolen generation shape the sisters' lives, resulting in a dynamic narrative full of collisions and driven by a triad of richly drawn female characters. Deborah Mailman won an Australian Film Institute award for best actress as the youngest sister Nona. Her character is acutely represented, enduring a rite of passage that results in a reconsideration of her origins, allowing her transition from child to adult.

WENDY HASLEM

Rafferty, Chips (1909–71) ACTOR Chips Rafferty was Australia's most prominent and significant actor during the barren Australian feature film period of the 1940s, 1950s, and 1960s. Born John William Pilbean Goffage, Rafferty worked in a number of outdoor jobs before entering the film industry in Sydney in the late 1930s. After two uncredited parts, Rafferty won a key role in •**Forty Thousand Horsemen** (1940) as Jim, one of the three Anzacs highlighted in Charles •Chauvel's popular account of the Sinai Desert campaign during World War I. This film, together with his next two films, the war drama •**The Rats of Tobruk** (1944), also directed by Chauvel, and •**The Overlanders** (1946), established the Rafferty screen persona for the next three decades. Australian, and overseas, acceptance of

Pamela Rabe

In conversation with

PAMELA RABE

How did you come to Australia?

I grew up in Canada. My father was a senior civil engineer in the public service, my mother was a homemaker. We travelled around Canada quite a bit, but I spent most of my teenage years, my early years at University, and my acting training in Vancouver. That's where I met Roger Hodgman, an Australian visiting director who was running a theatre company. And we were together when he was offered a job back here in Melbourne and, in 1983, I followed him here, and we were married.

Can you remember the first time you saw a stage performance and the first time you saw a film?

At three I was taken by the next-door neighbour to see **Snow White**. I spent most of the time under the seat, but I will always remember that queen!—not because she was terrifying, but because she was much more interesting. We had no tradition in my family of going to see live performance, other than concerts. Film was much more a part of my life than theatre: I would have been 16 or 17 before I saw a stage performance. In fact, I expected that I would be involved in film in some way: I was obsessed with film, not necessarily acting.

You didn't run away to Hollywood?

No. I ran away from Hollywood, as I think a lot of Canadians do. You are forced into a position, as you mature in Canada in the arts: you know that you either give in and go south, or you burrow down and create your own little sense of self, or else you take a political stance and run away as far as you can. So it was the serendipity of meeting my husband at the same time as the boom of late 1970s Australian film-making that meant there were a lot of retrospectives going on. I'd just graduated from acting school. I was going to have to move east to Toronto to try to pursue a stage career, or go off and try my hand in New York, or go south to Hollywood, and just at that time Roger introduced me to Australian films, and then he was offered a job and he said, 'Do you want to come?'

He wooed me with Australian films—I remember some of them quite strongly. The first one to make a very strong impact was probably •**'Breaker' Morant**. It was at a time when I was drawn to foreign cinema, seeing a lot of French and German films, all subtitled, and there wasn't much happening in the English film industry. So, with **'Breaker' Morant** for the first time I was seeing something in the English language, that came from a perspective that I could recognise, and it surprised me how much I could identify with it.

How did the ending appear to you? Barry Jones and Phillip Adams suggest that Australian recessive heroes are always defeated in the end…

I was a sucker for it—it touched something in me, and I was very willing to go on that journey. Also my greatest love was Hollywood musicals: so I think it appealed to the romantic in me, the notion of how we, as Canadians, had been hard-done-by. But I can remember that by the time •**Gallipoli** came round I was pissed off at how obvious the manipulation was. I remember saying at the time that the Australian films that I was seeing relied too heavily on very noisy scores—I wished they'd back off. We didn't need that much prodding of our buttons.

You have mentioned two very male films…

Well, that was all there was really. The last one we saw, two days before we left, was •**Don's Party**, which just about made me cash in the ticket. Then there was •**The Cars that Ate Paris**, but also •**Picnic at Hanging Rock**— by coincidence they were showing a huge retrospective of Australian films at one of the cinemas.

So, when you came to Australia did you feel you were coming to the place where the films came from?

Oh, yes, and I was very excited about it, and very upset when I started to meet people who worked in the industry who were cynical. And of course I could feel as the years passed that for me too that beautiful gloss was gone: something had been corrupted by getting too close to it. So I find I am much more critical now of Australian films than I was when I arrived. I was in love then—in all senses of the word. I still am—but it is a matured relationship.

But, when you did get here you didn't go into film—you went onto the stage first.

Yes, but by the time I'd been spat out the other end of an actor's training in Canada (and I think it is pretty similar around the Western world), I'd been custom-built for stage work. I had also come to believe that my assets as a performer were better suited to the stage, so I was quite happy to pursue that. I think there's a feeling—rightly or wrongly—that there are certain things an actor can be taught that will prepare them for any medium, whether it be film, stage, television, radio, whatever … and then there are a few extra specific skills to be added for stage performance, skills that are of absolutely no use whatsoever on film. You're trained by people who work in live performance: they train you for what they know—as well as trying to make you the most composite performer possible—so you end up with a bias towards stage.

Are there other performers who have been your idols or models?

Lots of them. Everything you see has an impact on shaping your standards and your goals and values. I don't consciously try to be *like* someone else: I try to be as *good* as someone I admire.

How do you prepare for a role?

It has been my experience that the ways you are offered roles on film and offered roles on stage are very different. Frequently on stage you have a lot of warning—you are told months, sometimes a year or more—ahead of time. Most of the films I have done I have found out as little as the day before it started, so I don't think I have yet got the knack of what's required for preparing for a film role. It always has to do with having some connection to what has been written in a script, and if it doesn't tweak something, make something go flutter inside, make me think, 'I understand what that is, and I think I can go there' —if it doesn't have that little tweak, I'm in trouble. Very often, the stage roles I play are old, what would be defined as classics, with a lot of material written about them. If I have a lot of lead time, I can read around the script and get myself prepared. With film, it is often an unknown entity, and a liquid one—the script is changing all the time, is perhaps not even in its final draft. Sometimes it is not as good as you would like it to be in script form, but you go on a wing and a prayer, on the potential. And sometimes I am not really sure

how well suited to it I am, whereas on stage I don't do it unless I feel that I am suited to that role. My experience always with film has been that the text is a floating thing.

Do you have much input into that process?

Sometimes yes, but not in a major way. If you have the luxury of a little bit of preparation time in pre-production with the director and some fellow-actors, and occasionally the writer, invariably that time is spent on text adjustments—on making the dialogue sit a little easier. In the case of **Vacant Possession** we actually had a two-week workshop, with some funding from the •Australian Film Commission. And yes—I think the actors did have quite a bit of input, sometimes just in the words, sometimes a little bit in the structure of the story-telling—scene order or things like that.

I would think that you would have more control and therefore more responsibility on stage.

I wouldn't say that—the responsibility is just different. With stage work you have a kind of nursery in the rehearsal room, for anything from three to six weeks and sometimes longer, with just you and the director and fellow-actors, in relative safety, where you are allowed to fail. At the end of it there is just you and your fellow-actors on stage, with some help from lighting and costuming and design, so you and the audience come together to create something electric, in a live situation. All the things that you do to make sure that what happens on stage is real is to do with having experimented and failed in a rehearsal room, having in effect done your own editing. On film, your responsibilities are so much more difficult to describe … You have no control over how what you do is going to be used, so you have to work with everything in your being to make sure that what you produce—perhaps 15 seconds a day when you need to be absolutely on—that what you do is utterly truthful, even if you are lying through your teeth. You have to be sure that that connection, from you right through the lens down onto the film, is just so true that the director and the editor can take advantage of it in the editing room, because it is real, it is working for them.

What was your first screen performance?

A student film at university in Canada. It was called **The Woman for Me**, and it won a short film prize. After that—a little television, I think, the ABC probably:

I have done my stints in *A Country Practice* and things like that. In Australia, my first feature film was •Sirens. The experience of being inside the making of a film was so utterly different from standing outside and watching it! I had a lot of time to think about the nature of what was required of me as an actor in that process. I've been quite lucky in the films I've been involved with: a lot of them have been ensemble pieces, which meant that even though my own input might have been minor, I was involved for the entire shoot. Sirens was the first like that. We spent seven or eight weeks up in the Blue Mountains, all together as a cast, so I had a lot of time on my hands. Although I was present, doing a lot of work in the background (with and without my clothes), I had a lot of time to think about how to serve the process.

As usual, I'd been given 24 hours' notice to come up and do a screen test, and I spent all that time swotting, trying to learn the text. My strongest memory of going to the screen test was realising, from looking at the drawings, that I had to keep my tits up. And how much that hurt! The whole stance of the Lindsay girls, the models, was that completely different contortion of one's body! Who knows why I was cast. I assume something to do with the look—Rose was pretty robust, and I think because of my look, my size, my colouring, I seemed appropriate.

Vacant Possession was quite soon after—I did a couple of plays in between, but Margot [Nash] had approached me before **Sirens** with a first draft of **Vacant Possession**, and when we were getting closer to the making of it I think I had just finished the shoot for **Sirens**.

Have you worked for other women directors?
Margot, then I did a film with Samantha Lang—•The Well. I've worked with a lot more men than women … This is a question you are asked a lot, especially if you are going to film with a female director—more so than with a stage piece. I don't know why, but, as journalists clamber to get an angle on something when they are writing a piece, that's usually the first one they get hold of: 'What do you think of being directed by a female?' Especially as the two films that I've worked on that have been directed by a woman have also had a pretty major female component—the writer, the technical crew. I find it really hard to make sweeping generalisations about it: every director I work with is very different. I am not quite sure what I mean by this, but there are directors—both male and female—who have feminine qualities, and there are directors—both female and male—who have male qualities. I can't say that female directors speak a language I understand more clearly, or are nicer, or are more egalitarian, or any other of the clichés that people expect you to say, or that I perhaps expect myself to think. I can't make any sweeping generalisations like that. I have found just as many sexual tensions on a set with a female director as with a male. Partly because I think the relationship between a performer and a director is often a sexualised one—in the same way that a parent–child relationship is sexual. It is a very vulnerable relationship, that involves a great neediness from the actor in that process, a great dependence and trust, that is quite similar to a sexual relationship, especially as you go into quite raw places.

Does this make you want to become a director?
So that *I* can be the one who parents, abuses, exploits, manipulates, nurtures? I don't know. I've been privileged to work with some very good directors, and that's daunting. I feel the same way about teaching—I've had such wonderful teachers, that strike the fear of God in me and then I think 'I couldn't begin to do that!'. I have marvelled at the skills of many different directors. Watching Bruce •Beresford deal with the chaos of film-making was a fascinating experience. Watching Paul •Cox put things together (and I had only a little bit to do in **Lust and Revenge**) … Watching Sam Lang, straight out of Film School, dealing with all that … What links them all for me is something to do with creating an atmosphere where the performers feel safe and yet still are able to deal with the mayhem, the battle zone.

Is it easier filming something you have already done on the stage?
Yes. The only time I've done that was with •Cosi, and it was one of the few times where I felt free during the filming process. I needed the rehearsal of a stage season to get to know that character. The actual text of the film was quite different from the stage play, but I think I knew who *she* was. I came from a base of understanding and trust that I knew who she was, in a different way from other films I've done. That says to me that I've got to understand, I've got to do more preparation.

Cosi was another ensemble, very different from The Well.

The Well was an ensemble of two, with a few other characters coming in and out. I had very little preparation. I got the phone call just four days before the shoot started and I was right into wig fittings and costume fittings, and a couple of days going over text with the director and Laura •Jones and Miranda •Otto. I was working with a built-up shoe, and that was a nightmare as well, because that kept changing: the shoe was being made, and when it arrived it was exactly the opposite to the rehearsal shoe. And that was a metaphor for the whole process of filming, because you were just working on the balls of your feet, going with the flow … That was fantastic as an experience—very unusual for me—and it happened so quickly that I didn't have time to panic.

It was a very intense performance.

Yes, and I don't know that I am quite comforted by that remark. I worry sometimes that that's the quality that I'm used for—my intensity. It's an adjective often used to describe my performances on stage, and I see it as a kind of flaw. I think it is great to be committed, but in the end if you see the cogs working too much it's a problem. But, that said, it was a very intense story—full on, but also kind of passive. Elizabeth Jolley had created this gothic tale, where the visuals were so strong … This woman with the long plait down her back, and a stick and a built-up shoe and a limp. That creates such a strong graphic statement within a frame on a screen that when you start layering things on top of that as a performer it can get too intense. I knew that a lot of my job was just to watch Miranda—and thank God she was so wonderful to watch. I knew that so long as I was true to Hester Harper's obsession with young Katherine—that as long as I watched Miranda, for the most part I would be okay. Then there were certain points when I had to do a bit more than that, and I got myself into a bit of trouble sometimes … But it was an extraordinary process—a really interesting process to go through. Very little preparation time.

Miranda and I were in everything and often the rushes were being screened in places we couldn't get to, and we were in make-up at 5 o'clock in the morning when they were often being screened. I love watching rushes but, as I hadn't seen them this time, I had a very strong reaction when I saw a work print. It was pre-final grading and pre-soundtrack (so no

score added). I don't think I am bad at making the leap of imagination to the finished product, but I still think this is a very naked, even frightening, way to watch a performance. I really thought that I had let the storytelling down in the final stages of the film. That was also another lesson, because the next time I saw it I was in the Palais at Cannes, party frocks and all. And I was amazed at how much music and sound *can* correct little flaws. I was really thrilled once more editing had been done. I felt less bad about my performance then.

Other people can't have felt bad about the performance: it won several awards.

I think lots of things contribute to why you win awards. I feel very privileged to be singled out, but often the most important component is the role you are playing.

Do you think of yourself as Australian now?

Yes, I was naturalised and became a citizen in the mid 1980s.

Because the inevitable question that is asked of Australian actors is, 'Don't you want to go overseas? Don't you want to get to Hollywood?'

I don't really see myself anywhere—I either don't have time, or I don't find it a constructive exercise. I probably *should* take a bit more responsibility at seeing myself in places, in positions, and then working towards getting there. I certainly do not see myself going to Hollywood—it was never an objective. But probably if somebody offered me a job in Hollywood, something I wanted to do, I'd do it. I'd have to wrestle with my beliefs and take that cheque! But it has never been important to me, and I don't think it is to many Australian actors. There are a few, and good luck to them—it is a terrible journey to put yourself on. It's the same with stage performers, who just pack their bags and go off to New York because they want to be on Broadway. I've never thought that achievement was to do with a pot of gold at the end of a rainbow: to me achievement was to do with working and getting better. As a migrant to Australia, I am so grateful and pleased with the kind of career I've enjoyed in Australia, which is just slow and steady. I have worked a lot, and I hope I am getting better. You don't get better by being unemployed.

THIS INTERVIEW WAS CONDUCTED BY INA BERTRAND.

these qualities as 'typically Australian' parallels, on a smaller scale, the process that enshrined John Wayne in the USA. In both cases, the screen mystique was conflated not only with the actual person, but also with the national character. Rafferty epitomised the lanky, tanned, easygoing bush stereotype—ready to drink, fight, and generally 'hop in' and tackle any problem. This stereotype was also characterised by a laconic sense of humour and by a quiet disdain for intellectuals and authority. Just as John Ford was able to exploit this persona and reveal its dark underside by extending its defining features (for example, Wayne's obsessed performance in **The Searchers**, 1956), so the Canadian director Ted Kotcheff was able to expose the dark underbelly of this Australian stereotype in Rafferty's last film •**Wake in Fright** (1971), in which Rafferty played Jock Crawford, the seemingly affable policeman from the 'Yabba'.

With Lee •Robinson and George •Heath, Rafferty formed Platypus Productions in 1952–53 and, in 1953 with Robinson, he formed Southern International, which was active in trying to keep the Australian film industry alive during the 1950s. The financial and production history of Southern International during the 1950s is fascinating in itself. During this period, Rafferty starred in and produced the outback 'western' •**The Phantom Stockman** (1953), a pearling melodrama set on Thursday Island co-starring Charles •Tingwell and a young Rod •Taylor; •**King of the Coral Sea** (1954); and •**Walk into Paradise** (1956), another exotic melodrama filmed in colour in New Guinea as a co-production between Southern International and the French company Discifilm. These films were directed by Lee Robinson (with Marcel Pagliero sharing the credit for the final film) and were financially successful. The American rights for **Walk into Paradise** were bought by Hollywood producer Joseph E. Levine, who retitled the film **Walk into Hell** and successfully released it in the USA with additional jungle footage.

As local feature film production dwindled in the 1960s, Rafferty worked overseas in character parts in both film (**The Wackiest Ship in the Army**, 1961; **Mutiny on the Bounty**, 1962; **Kona Coast**, 1968; **Skulduggery**, 1969), and American television series (*Gunsmoke*, *The Monkees*, *Big Valley*, and *Tarzan*). However, he kept Australia as his home base and returned to the local screen whenever the opportunity arose in international films produced in Australia (**Smiley Gets a Gun**, 1958; •**The Sundowners**; 1960, •**They're a Weird Mob**, 1966). Sadly, Rafferty died of a heart attack in Sydney in 1971 at the age of 62, just as the Australian film industry was about to enter a new, relatively prolific stage of production. He was awarded an MBE in 1970.

Other Australian films include: •**Come Up Smiling** (1939), •**Dad Rudd** (1940), •**Bush Christmas** (1947), •**Eureka Stockade** (1949), •**Bitter Springs** (1950), •**Kangaroo** (1952), •**Smiley** (1956).   GM

Randell, Ron (1918–) ACTOR This Broken Hill-born actor had a long and modestly successful career in American and, later, international films, as well as on British television, but it is arguable that his most memorable screen role was as Sir Charles Kingsford Smith in Ken G. •Hall's Australian 'biopic' •**Smithy** in 1946. This made him a star locally, and he played the aviator-hero with engaging charm and cheerfulness. He followed it with a role in Eric •Porter's •**A Son is Born** (1946), which reunited him with Muriel •Steinbeck, his co-star in **Smithy**, and in which two future stars, John •McCallum and Peter •Finch, had featured roles. Prior to **Smithy** he had worked in radio and wartime documentaries. In late 1946 he signed a contract with Columbia, with whom he stayed until 1951. Among his best-known films overseas were **Kiss Me Kate** (USA, 1953, as Cole Porter) and **I am a Camera** (United Kingdom, 1955).   BMcF

Rangle River

1936. *Director*: Clarence Badger. *Scriptwriters*: Charles and Elsa Chauvel. Based on a story by Zane Grey. *Director of photography*: Errol Hinds. *Music*: Alfred Lawrence. 86 min. B&W. *Cast*: Victor Jory (Dick Drake), Margaret Dare (Marion Hastings), Robert Coote (Reggie Mannister), Cecil Perry (Donald Lawton), George Bryant (Dan Hastings).

The story was written by American western writer Zane Grey during a fishing trip to Australia, and was adapted by Elsa and Charles •Chauvel. The plot of **Rangle River** is consistent with the narrative conventions of the Hollywood series western of the 1930s, with a passing nod to the emerging singing cowboys such as Gene Autry. Dan Hastings, with daughter Marion and foreman Dick Drake, try to save the family ranch from the machinations of villainous neighbour Donald Lawton. Lawton, in an attempt to destroy the competition from Hastings's beef, secretly blocks the flow of the Rangle River, thereby denying water to Hastings' cattle. However, Drake, with the assistance of British visitor Reggie Mannister, forces Lawton to release the water, thereby saving the ranch and the beef contract.

While the plot is strictly formulaic, and the romance between Drake and Marion totally predictable, this is a slick film with an effective use of close-ups and dramatic compositions. Similarly, the action sequences, particularly the climactic battle between Drake and Lawton, which takes the form of a prolonged and, for the period, explicitly violent battle with whips, is expertly done. Much of the credit for the quality of the production must go to veteran American director Clarence Badger who was imported from Hollywood for the film, and **Rangle River** was well received by Australian critics and audiences. The casting of American actor Victor Jory in the lead role as the hero Dick Drake was unusual: Jory, who appeared in Hollywood films from the early 1930s to the late 1970s (including **Gone With the Wind**, 1939; **The Man from the Alamo**, 1953), was a villain in most of his American films, whereas in **Rangle River** he is a rugged hero with a slightly sinister smile. British actor Robert Coote and Australian radio, stage and film performer Rita Pauncefort supply the comedy relief.

GM

Rats of Tobruk, The

1944. *Director, Producer*: Charles Chauvel. *Scriptwriters*: Charles Chauvel, Elsa Chauvel with Maxwell Dunn. *Director of photography*: George Heath. B&W. *Cast*: Grant Taylor (Bluey Donkin), Peter Finch (Peter Linton), Chips Rafferty (Milo Trent), George Wallace (Sergeant George Wallace), Joe Valli (the Northumberland Fusilier).

The Rats of Tobruk is a more melancholy film than its much-loved predecessor, •**Forty Thousand Horsemen** (1940). War in this film is not so much an adventure as an initiation, a passage from the golden dreams of childhood to the bleak, dull morning of an adult awakening. In keeping with this change of emphasis, Peter, a lonely 'doomed-warrior as boy–poet' figure, continually usurps our attention from the plodding variants of the 'dinkum Aussie bloke' that surround him. Linton's longing, an ache so strong one can almost touch it, is not assuaged by the brief love he finds with a woman. He is tormented by a desire that has no name and that survives him in the film, incarnate in his voice in the scene of the death of the character Milo as he glimpses paradise, and also in our strange certainty that this story can have no end.

WILLIAM D. ROUTT

Raymond, Candy

(1950–) ACTOR Candy (Candice) Raymond trained at the National Institute of Dramatic Art and began her acting career on the stage. She became a familiar face on television in series such as *Skippy*, *Prisoner* and *Number 96*, as well as in telemovies and miniseries. She has also written for television and magazines. Her first film performance was a minor role in **Shirley Thompson Versus the Aliens** (1972). With a reputation as a sex symbol, she was too often cast simply for her looks; for instance, as Miss Willing in **Alvin Rides Again** (1974) and in •**Money Movers** (1979). She had little to do as Alex's mother in **Ginger Meggs** (1982), and only slightly more as Annie, the older woman who owns the white Porsche and whose insensitivity sets off the events of **Freedom** (1982). But she had an opportunity to demonstrate her performance skill as Lillian in •**Monkey Grip** (1982), Kerry in •**Don's Party** (1976), and Miss Zielinski in •**The Getting of Wisdom** (1977).

IB

Razorback

1984. *Director*: Russell Mulcahy. *Producer*: Hal McElroy. *Scriptwriter*: Everett de Roche. *Director of Photography*: Dean Semler. *Music*: Iva Davies. 95 min. *Cast*: Gregory Harrison (Carl Winters), Arkie Whiteley (Sarah Cameron), Bill Kerr (Jake Cullen), Chris Haywood (Benny Baker), David Argue (Dicko Baker), Judy Morris (Beth Winters), John Ewart (Turner).

Director Russell •Mulcahy's surreal horror film mixes a number of contemporary horror conventions, largely from the 'revenge-of-the-animals' cycle popularised by **Jaws** (USA, 1975), with a distinctive blend of bizarre characters reminiscent of •**Mad Max 2** (1981). Mulcahy combines these elements with the stylistic characteristics developed from his years working on rock video clips.

The poor excuse for a plot involves American Carl Winters, who travels to the Australian inland to investigate the death of his wife Beth. In a highly stylised setting of spectacular sunsets and barren salt plains, Winters encounters a range of Australian atrocities involving brothers Benny and Dicko Baker and the monstrous razorback, a feral pig. The sheer madness of **Razorback** is fun for a while, particularly when the film seems to be using its odd setting to satirise a range of contemporary issues, including the dingo baby case and environmental protests.

GM

Realist Film Unit and Association (1945–62)

Formed initially by New Theatre actor and producer Bob Matthews and freelance cinematographer Ted Cranstone to screen the **Why We Fight** series, the Realist Film Unit was joined by Ken Coldicutt, whose experience with the Friends of the Soviet Union in the importation and projection of films expanded the Unit's repertoire. With the aid of Gerhard Harant, the Unit embarked on a production program under an umbrella organisation, the Realist Film Association, which maintained a regular screening program of films not available at commercial cinemas. The Unit's productions include **A Place to Live** (1946), a film delineating housing contrasts in Melbourne, **In My Beginning** (1947), about an attempt to establish a progressive school at Warrandyte, Victoria, and **Prices and the People** (1948) an argument for a 'Yes' vote in the 1948 federal referendum on whether to continue war-time price controls.

The Association's legacy is its contribution to and promulgation of the network of film societies that emerged in the late 1940s in all Australian capital cities. The Association regularly screened films on Sundays or over a weekend when the New Theatre was not performing. Its repertoire encompassed a huge variety of films, from **Battleship Potemkin** (1925), **Grass** (1925), and **Earth** (1930) to **Metropolis** (1926), **The Blue Angel** (1930), Chaplin shorts, Hammid's **The Valley of the Tennessee** (1944), Van Dyke's

Religion

The City (1939), and Cecil •Holmes's **Fighting Back** (1948). The Realists lent equipment and films, as well as giving advice on how to handle film, promote a screening, and form a society. Alongside the state government Film Library, the Association contributed to an 'alternative' film culture that has its resonances in the vibrant repertory clubs and societies that exist in contemporary Australia.

DEANE WILLIAMS

Religion The Salvation Army's Limelight Company (see Documentary and non-fiction, silent; Historical representations) went into film production in 1899, screening their Biblical film clips with slides and a lecture in 1900 as •Soldiers of the Cross. Their work, both religious and secular, continued for a decade. Australian cinema has strong religious origins. Despite Australia's White settlers not holding religion in high esteem (or recognising Aboriginal worship, lore, and dreaming as religious) and later generations seeing themselves as overtly secular, Australians have tended to have a basic respect for religion, a substantial tradition of church attendance and, in the latter part of the twentieth century as church attendance declined, a more comfortable attitude towards spirituality. It is helpful to use the distinctions among religion, church, and spirituality to interpret the place of 'religion' in Australian cinema.

Aboriginal religion, sometimes in contrast to Christianity, but especially in relation to Aborigines caught between two religions and two cultures, is portrayed in such films as •Jedda (1955), •Journey out of Darkness (1967), •Walkabout (1971), •The Last Wave (1977), •The Chant of Jimmie Blacksmith (1978), Where the Green Ants Dream (1984), and •Dead Heart (1996).

As migration from Asian countries and the practice of Islam, Buddhism, and Hinduism increases, it is to be expected that these major world religions will feature more heavily in Australian films. Documentaries have probed these religions but, in feature films, their presence has been minimal: Islam in Sydney-based Turkish director Ayten Kuyululu's **Handful of Dust** (1973), a film about a blood vendetta, and **Golden Cage** (1975), highlighting the tensions when a Turkish migrant wants to marry a local girl (an 'infidel'); and Buddhism in **Island** (1989), in which a Sri Lankan woman with Buddhist background is marooned in Greece.

There is a more limited presence than might be expected of Judaism and •Jewish representation in Australian cinema. Several prominent Australian directors did not explore religious themes in their films made at home but were comfortable in dramatising them in their first American films. Examples are Bruce •Beresford with **Tender Mercies** (USA, 1983) and **King David** (USA, 1985), Peter •Weir (**Witness**, USA, 1985), Gillian •Armstrong (**Mrs Soffel**, USA, 1985), Carl •Schultz (**Seventh Sign**, USA, 1988), and George

•Miller (**The Witches of Eastwick**, USA, 1986, and **Lorenzo's Oil**, USA, 1992).

Religion and God, apart from the churches, do not feature strongly in Australian films. Two exceptions, both of which received critical acclaim, are John •Ruane's adaptation of Tim Winton's **That Eye the Sky** (1994), in which a young boy sees an aura over his bush home where his father lies in coma, and Lawrence Johnston's **Eternity** (1994). In the former, a wandering American evangelist who is struggling with his own sinfulness transforms the lives of the family. A 'miracle' healing of the father may be from the faith of the evangelist, but is likely to be from the faith of the boy, who frequently goes out into the night to gaze at the stars and God's presence in that eye, the sky.

Lawrence Johnston's **Eternity** is one of the more profound treatments of religion, the more so, perhaps, because it was not intended as a 'religious' film. In a striking visual style that includes talking-head 'witnesses', archival footage, and dramatic re-enactments in black-and-white photography, Johnston re-creates the story of vagrant Arthur Stace, who, after a conversion experience (with Anglican and Baptist influences) discovered his vocation—to write the word 'Eternity' in copperplate on the streets of Sydney, half a million times over 30 years.

But it is through church stories that religion is most strongly present in Australian cinema. During the silent era there is comparatively little. There are some pre-*Thorn Birds* dramas with clergy and sex: Catholics in •The Church and the Woman (1917) and Anglicans in •The Silence of Dean Maitland (1914). There are the expected parsons, often stereotypes, although the veteran stuntman Snowy •Baker was an athletic Reverend in •The Man from Kangaroo (1920). And some were villains, especially the hypocritical Meekin and North in •For the Term of His Natural Life (1927). The Irish Catholic tradition received the rugged sentimental treatment in •Around the Boree Log (1925), a film based on the ballads of 'John O'Brien'.

The churches were even more absent from the films of the 1930s, especially those of Ken G. •Hall. The exception is a remake of **The Silence of Dean Maitland** (1934). This absence continued during the lean years of Australian production—the 1950s to the early 1970s—although the Billy Graham organisation produced a 'Christian Western', in which a bigoted and racist young man is converted after listening to Dr Graham (Shadow of the Boomerang, 1960).

Religion and the churches have provided a substantial amount of material for our cinema. Anglicans tend to have been presented in a more stereotypical mode: the parson is seen as the one who baptises, marries, and buries. During the 1970s a number of them appeared as tormented in their beliefs: for instance, Frederick •Parslow in •The Last Wave (1977) and Charles •Tingwell, anguished from a pulpit, in •Petersen (1974). Clergy and 'wowserism' in connection with the paintings of Norman Lindsay was the subject of •Sirens (1994). This was perhaps the closest Australian cinema has come to an analysis of the role of the Anglican Church in Australia until Gillian •Armstrong's version of Peter Carey's •Oscar and Lucinda (1998). Ralph Fiennes's Oscar is a tormented priest, a convert to Anglicanism from the Plymouth Brethren, a compulsive gambler whose dream of transporting a glass church cross-country provides striking religious imagery. His confession within the church provides a dramatic religious climax.

The Salvation Army has usually been used to indicate the compassionate face of Christianity. However, a number of directors have highlighted the Army and its beliefs. •Strikebound (1984) dramatises the Gippsland coal strikes of the 1930s: Mrs Doig, wife of one of the leaders, is a sincere Salvationist. Paul •Cox uses an Army couple in his adaptation of the Guy de Maupassant story 'Golden Braid' (1990), in which the husband is a devout caricature and his wife turns away from her religion as she becomes involved in an affair. The grandmother in •The Sum of Us (1994) is devout, as is her lesbian partner, although an Army commentator sees this long-term relationship as unrealistic for elderly Salvationists. Far more positive is the representation of the Army in •Bad Boy Bubby (1994), in which the street singing of the Salvation Army members while they feed Bubby is the first music heard by the vagrant, mentally handicapped Bubby. One of the young women also offers him sexual experience, singing hymns of praise all the while. Barry •Otto plays a Salvationist in •Lillian's Story (1996), in which the Army serves as a refuge from a tyrannical father who has driven his daughter Lillian (based on Sydney's Bea Miles) into an asylum. These images offer a more complex picture of the Salvation Army.

Seventh Day Adventism is the central subject of only two films, both of which are substantial. Fred •Schepisi's •Evil Angels (1988) explores the Lindy Chamberlain case and gives considerable attention to the Chamberlains' belief in this religion, seeing it as deeply sustaining during the trials. A truckie at the opening of the film laughs and swears at the Adventists, but the film opens up to its audience the church and its place in 'ordinary' Australian society. The other film is Bob •Ellis's autobiographical tale •The Nostradamus Kid (1993), in which 1950s Adventists are seen as religious eccentrics, sometimes fanatics, who isolate their adherents from society with apocalyptic beliefs and fears. Such religious grounding proves inadequate for life in Australia and has to be rejected or changed.

In recent years there has been an increasing number of references to the Orthodox churches in films, especially the Greek Orthodox Church: for example, •Caddie (1976), •Kostas (1979), •Cathy's Child (1979), and Island (1989). Melbourne, which has the largest number of Greeks outside Athens, provides the setting for •Mull (1989); •Death in Brunswick (1991), which ends with an Orthodox wedding;

and •The Heartbreak Kid (1993), which dramatises the conflicts between the generations, a theme also suggested in Only the Brave (1994) and Head On (1998). There is a Russian Orthodox wedding in •My First Wife (1984) and, pessimistically, a Rumanian orthodox migrant (complete with an icon collection) who has gone mad in Melbourne's western suburbs and has a destructive influence on his son in Metal Skin (1995). The number of 1990s films that touch on Orthodox themes indicates that Australian audiences can expect more Orthodox stories.

The church that has received most attention in Australian cinema is the Roman Catholic Church: many prominent Australian stars, writers, and directors were raised as Catholics. In the early and mid 1970s Fred •Schepisi conducted serious explorations of Catholic issues in 'The Priest' (scripted by Thomas Kenneally), a short study of a priest in vocational crisis, in one of the stories in •Libido (1973); and in his acclaimed autobiographical portrait of a teenager in a Marist Brothers' Juniorate, •The Devil's Playground (1976). The Devil's Playground, a knowing re-creation of a rather more ignorant 1950s, raises serious issues of religion, training, commitment, and, especially, sexuality. These issues were received with great interest by the Australian public and have continued to fascinate, as was attested by the high ratings for several screenings of Brides of Christ (1991), a television miniseries that focused on nuns in the 1960s and on changes in the Catholic Church that were occurring around this time.

Films that explore different facets of Catholic life in Australia include •They're a Weird Mob (1966), a film that gives an old-fashioned portrait of this church; •Newsfront (1978), which looks at moral stances and behaviour in the context of newsreel photographers; •The Settlement (1984), a thoughtful and satiric picture of repressed, respectable Catholics (women, in this case) and the alarming surfacing of their passion; •Far East (1982), a film that offers sympathetic glimpses of social activists in The Philippines. Far East was directed by John •Duigan, who also made Fragments of War (1988), a telemovie about Damien •Parer, an Oscar-winning war cinematographer and devout Catholic; Romero (1989), a film about the assassinated archbishop of San Salvador; and Pieta (1987), which shows a middle-aged woman, an art teacher, confronting her narrow Catholic education. A nun (fictional), abducted to secure the release of her niece and facing celibacy vow dilemmas, is the subject of The Nun and the Bandit (1992); and a nun (factual), Mary MacKillop, is the chief character of Mary (1994). Since 1972, there have been a considerable number of films that treat Catholic issues to a lesser extent.

Many ministers of religion in Australian films are not specified as belonging to a particular church. They fulfil the expected role of clergy, although they are often used to make points about the ineffectuality of churches. Examples range from a priest speaking insensitively about Aboriginal issues at a graveside in •**Deadly** (1992) to the irreverent spoof of Barry McKenzie's cousin, Kev the Rev, giving a lecture in Paris on 'Christ and the Orgasm' in **Barry McKenzie Holds His Own** (1974).

Methodist and Presbyterian clergy are represented critically in **The Chant of Jimmie Blacksmith**, in which Jack •**Thompson** gives a complex performance as a Methodist who means well but feels he has contributed to Jimmie's violence by imposing Christian ways; and in •**The Getting of Wisdom** (1977), in which Barry •**Humphries** and John •**Waters** play self-important chaplains. Ernie •**Dingo** plays a Lutheran minister caught between government officialdom and tribal religious customs in •**Dead Heart** (1996).

The majority of other churches represented are evangelical or Pentecostal, with some films featuring lay preachers (most of whom are portrayed as bizarre or ineffectual), as in •**Hoodwink** (1981), **Mull, Backsliding** (1991), and **Dallas Doll** (1994),.

A majority of Australians may see members of these churches as 'odd', even 'mad'. This perception, and the issue of the sometimes violent consequences of fanaticism, is a strong theme in a number of films, especially those that represent ordinary citizens who 'get' religion: in **Backsliding** a religious fanatic's beliefs lead to violence; a born-again lighthouse keeper kills his children in **Madness of Two** (no date); another born-again father murders in **Fatal Bond** (1992); and a young soldier in •**An Indecent Obsession** (1985) is rendered 'berserk' by his religion.

It seems that many Australians who are not affiliated with religion or a particular church are nevertheless not reluctant to speak about their spirituality. While they may not 'believe in' or be committed to a particular deity or deities, they still have a sense of the transcendent that leads to meditation or prayer, and that is embodied in principles and values that guide life. This is the language that many writers and directors used in the 1990s.

Period films such as •**Picnic at Hanging Rock** (1975) embody the origins of this spirituality, its mystery and its association with the land. The •**Mad Max** trilogy sees the hero, who is Australian and intercultural, as saviour and liberator. The resilience of the human spirit shines through in Australian films, even when Australians look at life 'de profundis' ('out of the depths', as Psalm 130 puts it).

PETER MALONE

Rene, Roy (1891–1954) ACTOR With his spluttering speech, leering white face, and painted black beard, Roy Rene was the king of comedy in Australia for 40 years. Known to millions as 'Mo', his blue humour, larrikin behaviour, and impeccable timing entertained Depression audiences. Born Henry (Harry) Van der Sluice in Adelaide, he was the son of a Dutch-Jewish cigar-maker and an Anglo-Jewish mother. He first performed at Adelaide's Theatre Royal as Little Roy, the boy soprano and, at the age of 13, moved to Melbourne with his family. When his voice broke he changed his name to Boy Roy and appeared in blackface as a 'corner man' in suburban minstrel shows. At 19 he moved to Sydney (with J.C. Williamson), performed in vaudeville, and adopted his trademark Jewish mask after the Australian tours of Julian Rose and other American 'Hebrew' comics. He later changed his name to Roy Rene after a famous French clown, and teamed up with Nat Phillips in 1916, as 'Stiffy and Mo'. After World War II, he became known as 'Mo McCackie' after his phenomenally popular radio show, *McCackie Mansions*.

Rene's only film appearance was in Ken G. •**Hall's** •**Strike Me Lucky** (1934), made for •**Cinesound**. Written by Victor Roberts and George D. Parker, the film was intended to showcase Rene's comic genius, but the script was inconsequential, and Rene was at sea in a medium that did not enable him to work an audience. **Strike Me Lucky** has been accused of being anti-Semitic but, although Rene played the grotesque Jewish caricature for laughs, his inspired clowning made Depression audiences identify with the Jew as underdog. Mo's antecedents came from turn-of-the-century vaudeville, where minstrel shows, featuring black-faced whites, diffused hostility by exploiting and inverting ethnic stereotyping. In **Strike Me Lucky**, in contrast to what was happening in Germany at the time, the Jewish clown became 'our mate Mo', and the quintessential Aussie battler.

JAN EPSTEIN

Return Home

1990. Director: Ray Argall. Producer: Cristina Pozzan. Scriptwriter: Ray Argall. Director of photography: Mandy Walker. 87 min. Cast: Dennis Coard (Noel), Frankie J. Holden (Steve), Ben Mendelsohn (Gary), Micki Camilleri (Judy), Rachel Rains (Wendy).

With considerable experience as an editor and director of photography, Ray •**Argall** made an auspicious debut as director with this affectionate but astringent piece of low-key realism. The film stands firmly by such old-fashioned virtues as family feeling and individual integrity in the face of threats from some of the more dubious benefits of progress. Noel is a successful Melbourne insurance broker in his late thirties who returns one summer to the Adelaide suburb of his youth to stay with his brother Steve, who runs a garage that is failing commercially because of competition from the larger service-station franchises. The film doesn't sentimentalise Steve's attitude: it applauds the personal service he still provides, but makes it clear that he also needs to keep more firmly abreast of customer needs. His loyal wife Judy, and his apprentice Gary, are also aware of this, and Noel is increasingly drawn back into the family circle and into a surrogate father role with Gary. The return home has proved more than merely geographical: it has led Noel to question the values by which he has lived. This simple story is directed and acted with rare delicacy of feeling, and the overall effect is of a species of urban pastoral, rare in a cinema that has more generally located such virtues in a rural setting. It is in the vein of quiet naturalism that was largely displaced in the 1990s by a flashier, less obviously indigenous mode, and it may be said to exhibit the failings of the mode as well as its strengths. Certainly, it sometimes loses its narrative tension, lingering too long when it should move on, but more often it strikes one with the truth of its observation and the aptness of its unaffected cinematic style.   BMcF

Reviewing   When moving pictures were first screened for Australians in 1896, reviewers, like their foreign counterparts wrote rapturously of the intensity of the cinematic experience. The reviewer for the *Age* in Melbourne was especially impressed by a short film shot at the seaside. 'The rhythmic motion of the waves, the spray and foam and broken waters where the waves were reft by boulders were so

intensely natural', he wrote, 'that the audience, which had been growing enthusiastic over the display, broke into a storm of applause'. But would the visceral power of film be a force for good or evil? Australian reviewers would go on debating this question for years to come, as would the rest of the community.

The most optimistic view in those early years was put forward by the Salvation Army. In its magazine *The War Cry*, it welcomed the new medium as a brilliant invention for spreading God's word for 'the salvation and blessing of mankind', then went on to put theory into practice by forming its own production company (see Documentary and non-fiction, silent; Historical representation) and producing the Biblical epic **Soldiers of the Cross** (1900; see Silent film to 1914). *The Bulletin* took a more cynical and snobbish view. As far as its reviewers were concerned, moving pictures were entertainments designed to appeal to 'the lower orders' and it was only appropriate that the first footage to be shot in Australia should be a horse race—the

Roy Rene (right) in **Strike Me Lucky** (1934)

Reviewing

Melbourne Cup— and that the first narrative film—**•The Story of the Kelly Gang** (1906)—should be a 'twopenny-coloured melodrama' glorifying a bushranger.

Was this the light in which Australians wanted the national character portrayed? Already the main themes of popular critical debate were emerging. Was the establishment of a national cinema a good thing? If so, what should it be like? Did moving pictures have a particular potency in their ability to corrupt the innocent and inflame the criminal classes? Should special rules of censorship apply?

In the minds of most reviewers, the release in 1919 of Raymond •Longford's endearing film of C.J. Dennis's **•The Sentimental Bloke** seemed to clinch the argument about the value of having a national cinema. Longford gave articulate interviews about eliciting understated performances from his actors and achieving a naturalistic style, and most reviewers were duly appreciative. The discussions provoked by **The Sentimental Bloke** touched, for the first time, on the qualities that distinguished film from other art forms, but only briefly. The reviews of this period showed none of the sophistication of film writing in the USA, for example; critics writing for the *Nation, New Republic* and the *Motion Picture World* were defining film as an art with a language of its own as they pondered the power of D.W. Griffith's close-ups and analysed camera movement, composition, and the role of lighting in the creation of mood. Newspaper reviews, while shorter, were often just as thoughtful, particularly when it came to the moral contradictions posed by the emotive power of the filmed image. Reviewing Griffith's **Intolerance** in the *New York Herald Tribune* in 1916, Heywood Broun declared him 'an immature philosopher, a wrongheaded sociologist, a hazy theologian, a flamboyant historian, but a great movie man'. The director's grasp of historical fact may have been tenuous but his passion for the past was undeniable. Broun continued: 'Griffith is tickled to death to learn that there was once a town called Babylon full of folk who loved and laughed and fought, with never a thought that they were ancients'.

In Australia, meanwhile, critics remained generally distrustful of film's capacity for straying from the truth. Some, conversely, were just as unhappy when it struck, as they saw it, too closely to reality. In 1919, the *Sydney Sun* reviewer found Longford's **•On Our Selection** (1920) altogether too realistic in its depiction of the harshness of bush life: 'This "holding a mirror up to nature" needs discretion'. Nonetheless, by the time talkies arrived, all but destroying the local industry with Hollywood imports, Australian reviewers had made up their minds that indigenous cinema was something worth having. The films of Ken G. •Hall and Charles •Chauvel in the 1930s and 1940s were hailed for the vividness with which they crystallised the Australian identity. Highlights were heralded as national triumphs, imperfections viewed with indulgence. Kenneth Wilkinson's *Sydney*

Morning Herald review of Hall's 1932 re-make of **•On Our Selection** reflected the critical climate. The film had flaws, he said, but it was possible to regard them with a genial and affectionate eye, just as one looked on the amiable weaknesses in the character of one's friends.

It was also hoped—and this, too would become an enduring theme—that film would help raise Australia's profile in the world at large. This hope certainly conditioned the local response to Chauvel's **•Jedda** (1955), one of the few Australian films made during the 1950s. The story of a tragic love affair between an Aboriginal girl brought up by White station owners and an Aborigine from a distant part of the NT, **Jedda** was released by Columbia Pictures after a protracted, complicated, and expensive shoot, and became a notable example of the phenomenon we now know as the 'well-hyped' film. The trade paper *Film Weekly* set the tone, declaring that it would be of 'long-range importance' in selling Australia to the rest of the world.

This sanguine forecast proved wide of the mark. France's influential *Cahiers du Cinema* disliked everything about the film, and the *New York Times* expressed bafflement that a well-brought up girl such as Jedda would run off 'with a weird-looking tribal barbarian from the hills'. While the United Kingdom's *Monthly Film Bulletin* was relatively kind, its faint praise suggested that the film was both dull and paternalistic. This paternalism was condemned at home in a review in the literary journal *Overland*, which judged **Jedda** 'a thoroughly bad film. It peddles the worst kind of racist nonsense'. But most Australian reviewers were once again inclined to be indulgent, glossing over the film's artistic failures to concentrate on the effort and boldness that had gone into the making of something 'truly Australian' in difficult times.

The revival of Australian cinema in the early 1970s (see Revival, the) was part of a renewal of interest in all the arts. The Menzies government had come to an end, bringing about a surge of intellectual energy. The community that had coalesced around film festivals, film societies, and the underground movement had campaigned throughout the 1960s for the subsidisation of local industry. As a result of this activity, specialist journals began to appear. By 1974 *Cinema Papers* was being published regularly and independent film-makers who had joined together to start the Sydney Filmmakers' Co-operative had begun publishing a newsletter, which, in 1975, was transformed into *Filmnews*, a newsprint magazine of news, reviews and discussion. There was renewed interest in film in the mainstream press; critics included Sylvia Lawson (see Criticism and theory), Michael •Thornhill, P.P. McGuinness, and Bob •Ellis—all of whom had long been involved in film-making or film culture.

Internationally, it was an exciting time for film criticism. The 'auteur' theory was being expounded and debated in the pages of *Cahiers du Cinema, Positif, Movie, Sight and*

Sound, and other film journals in France, the United Kingdom, and the USA. Several Australian critics did their best to air these issues, but to the Australian reader it often seemed as if he or she were viewing the drama from a distant seat in the back circle.

More immediate and persuasive were the arguments championing the need for an Australian cinema. The idea of film as a potent means of expressing national identity had become so exalted by the time the industry's renaissance finally arrived that many of the films themselves were judged a sad disappointment. •**Two Thousand Weeks** (1969), Melbourne director Tim •Burstall's film about a journalist in the midst of crucial decisions about love, marriage, and his future career prospects, received such a critical battering that its run in the cinemas was disastrously short. The 'ocker' comedies that followed also failed to impress. Burstall's •**Stork** (1971), written by David •Williamson, was liked for its lack of pretension and the naturalness of its dialogue, but •**Alvin Purple** (1973) and •**The Adventures of Barry McKenzie** (1972) were both criticised for portraying Australians and Australian culture as unsophisticated and uncouth. The London success of **The Adventures of Barry McKenzie** was written off as an example of the British taste for tales of the barbarism of their colonial cousins.

Critics and other guardians of the concept of Australian national identity were satisfied with the arrival of Peter •Weir's •**Picnic at Hanging Rock** (1975). Here was the Australian landscape, lit by Russell Boyd (director of photography), looking like a painting from the celebrated Heidelberg School of artists, and portrayed as part of an ambiguous narrative, full of mysterious, pantheistic allusions that encourage comparisons with the techniques of European art films. Helen Frizell's review in the *Sydney Morning Herald* typified the response to **Picnic at Hanging Rock**: ' . . . the best Australian film I have ever seen—and the most unusual in its distillation of youth, summer and tragedy'.

This success was repeated with the release of •**The Getting of Wisdom** (1977), •**The Chant of Jimmie Blacksmith** (1978), •**My Brilliant Career** (1979), •**'Breaker' Morant** (1980), and •**Gallipoli** (1981)—films that established Australian cinema so firmly in the eyes of critics both at home and abroad that when the trend eventually started to play itself out in the mid 1980s it left behind the discomfiting suspicion that period pictures might turn out to be the only thing that Australian film-makers could do. There were isolated successes in other genres, the most exhilarating being George •Miller's •**Mad Max** in 1979, which managed, on a budget of $4 000 000, to become the most commercially successful Australian film made to that point. Most critics were impressed, although some had reservations about the ferocity of its action scenes. Phillip Adams, writing for the *Bulletin*, attacked it as an example of 'the dangerous pornography of death'.

As the 1980s continued, a spate of bad and mediocre films financed under the federal Government's 10BA tax concession scheme (see Finance) emerged, and much of what was written about Australian cinema struck an increasingly despairing note. By the end of the decade, the tone began to change, inspired by the success of Paul •Hogan's •**Crocodile Dundee** (1986); the arrival of new talents such as Nadia •Tass, David •Parker (•**Malcolm**, 1986), Jane •Campion (•**Sweetie**, 1989), and Jocelyn •Moorhouse (•**Proof**, 1991); and by increasingly mature and personal work from established figures such as Gillian •Armstrong, Paul •Cox, and John •Duigan. Reviewers acclaimed the downbeat charms of 'the Melbourne film' and, with the arrival of •**Strictly Ballroom** (1992), •**The Adventure of Priscilla, Queen of the Desert** (1994) and •**Muriel's Wedding** (1994), found they could at last embrace the raucously vulgar strain in the national character that they had denied so strenuously 20 years before in their reactions to **The Adventures of Barry McKenzie**. So enthusiastic was the response to the exuberance and outrageousness of films such as **The Adventures of Priscilla** that the attitudes of 15 years before were effectively reversed, and the genres promoted by reviewers during the 1970s and early 1980s were treated less than generously. Richard •Franklin's adaptation of Hannie Rayson's play •**Hotel Sorrento** (1995)—distinguished by strong performances from Caroline •Gillmer and Caroline •Goodall—received mixed notices, and Michael •Blakemore's •**Country Life** (1994), a retelling of Chekhov's *Uncle Vanya* in an outback setting, was roundly criticised as stagey and old-fashioned.

Most reviewers welcomed as new and innovative this resurgence of the contemporary film with an urban or suburban setting. One of the most controversial films of the 1990s—Geoffrey •Wright's stark and sometimes brutal story of the racist exploits of a gang of Melbourne skinheads, •**Romper Stomper** (1992)—was generally admired by reviewers for the power and assurance of Wright's direction. The criticism it attracted because of the violence of its images and the alleged ambivalence of its portrayal of racism, came mainly from columnists and commentators in other sections of the media. Their reaction was typical of a tendency to blame the influence of film for all kinds of social ills. The suspicions first voiced about the psychological effects of the new medium on its audiences back in 1896 had hardened, a century on, into an urge to make film a scapegoat for everything from poor literacy to incitement to crime.

Australian reviewers have generally argued against this view and against censorship, but the larger questions about the nature of film and its effect on its audiences are not discussed as fully or as deeply as is possible. Although individual films themselves are widely discussed in the press and on radio and television, there has been no growth in specialist journals: *Cinema Papers* continues, but lack of adequate funding forced *Filmnews* to cease publication in 1995. Meanwhile, film has become a more ubiquitous and powerful medium than was envisaged a century ago, and the marketing of new features has become so sophisticated that the size of a film's promotional budget can rival the cost of production. As a result, the prevailing film climate is saturated with hype and marketing, making the business of review and analysis more important than ever. SANDRA HALL

Revival, the In writing about Australian cinema since the late 1970s, it has been common to use terms like 'revival', 'renaissance', and 'new Australian cinema' as a way to contextualise the burgeoning of the local feature film industry in that decade. There is disagreement about which films really ushered in the revival: some might locate its beginnings in two notable films made by overseas directors, •**Wake in Fright** and •**Walkabout** (both 1971); some might incline to the commercial success of the 'ocker' comedies •**Stork** (1971), •**The Adventures of Barry McKenzie** (1972), and •**Alvin Purple** (1973); and many would agree that the 'prestige' arm of new Australian cinema got underway with •**Picnic at Hanging Rock** and •**Sunday Too Far Away** (both 1975). These last two brought Australian cinema to serious international attention after what can only be seen as a long drought in the postwar period, during which most of the few feature films made here were the products of overseas production companies, especially American and British. There was a sustained campaign throughout the 1960s from commentators such as Colin Bennett and Michael •Thornhill for government intervention to help foster the local industry. The upsurge of production in the 1970s, loosely dubbed the revival, is at least partly the result of the untiring efforts of such apologists. BRIAN MCFARLANE

Richards, Ann (1918–) ACTOR In the latter half of the 1930s, Ann Richards (then billed as Shirley Ann) was Australia's leading female film star. After a little stage work, she was built up as a star by Ken G. •Hall's •Cinesound company, perhaps Australia's nearest approach to Hollywood-style studio grooming. She first appeared in Hall's •**It Isn't Done** (1937), opposite South African-born Cecil •Kellaway, who went on to a long career as a character player in Hollywood, and John Longden, who shortly after returned to the United Kingdom, after making several films here. Three more films for Hall followed swiftly: •**Tall Timbers** (1937), a forest-set romance; •**Lovers and Luggers** (1937), an adventure melodrama, set on and around Thursday Island; and •**Dad and Dave Come to Town** (1938), one of the films based on the characters created by Steele Rudd; and she starred with Will Mahoney and Evie Hayes in •**Come Up Smiling** (1939), the only Cinesound feature not directed by Hall. She had a notably fresh, natural appeal, appearing well at home in outdoor tales, and she became popular enough to

attract Hollywood's attention. She was signed by MGM, first appearing in **Random Harvest** (1942), and had substantial roles in a dozen films (including the female lead in King Vidor's steel-making saga, **An American Romance** (1944), and several 'heroine's best friend' roles), before retiring in 1952 to live in California with her American husband. She reappeared in Australian cinema as herself in Andrée Wright and Stewart Young's documentary about women in early Australian cinema, •**Don't Call Me Girlie** (1985). BMcF

Ricketson, James (1949–) DIRECTOR/WRITER/ACTOR Primarily a director of documentary and social-realist narratives, James Ricketson has also acted, most notably playing Phillip Adams in Werner Herzog's **Where the Green Ants Dream** (1987). Ricketson's provocative oeuvre includes the acclaimed television documentary *It Wasn't Going to Happen to Me* (1974), an account of a businessman's final days as he succumbs to cancer. With **Third Person Plural** (1978) Ricketson experimented with improvised dialogue and a disjointed narrative. Together with Archie Weller, Ricketson received an Australian Film Institute award for the best adapted script for •**Blackfellas**, which he also directed, in 1983. This collaborative project offered film-making experience for Aboriginal casts and crews. As a reciprocal gesture, Ricketson was granted rare access to the Western Australian Nyoongah community. His films reveal an interest in representing Aboriginal issues with integrity. This is evident in his direction of the first episode of the groundbreaking television series *Women of the Sun* (1981).

Ricketson's voice has been prominent in debating the constitution of the Australian film industry. He advocates a 'poor cinema', one that is contemporary, intelligent, challenging, original, low in budget, and rich in creativity. Ricketson's criticism and film projects express the desire to create a uniquely Australian film industry.
Other Australian films: Reflections (1973), Joker (1974), Drifting (1975), The Seventh Age (1975), Jacob's Ladder (1979), A Wall of Silence (1981), Everyday Challenge (1981), Candy Regentag (1989). WENDY HASLEM

Ride A Wild Pony

1975. *Director*: Don Chaffey. *Producer*: Jerome Courtland. *Scriptwriter*: Rosemary Anne Sissons. *Director of photography*: Jack Cardiff. *Music*: John Addison. 88 min. *Cast*: Michael Craig (James Ellison), John Meillon (Mr Quayle), Robert Bettles (Scotty Pirie), Eva Griffith (Josie Ellison), Graham Rouse (Bluey Waters).

The story of this outdoors children's adventure film, based on *A Sporting Proposition* by James Aldridge and set in the 1920s, centres on the rivalry between two children for ownership of a Welsh pony. Scott (well played by Robert Bettles) is the son of poor migrant farmers and Josie is the crippled, pampered daughter of a well-to-do horse-breeder. After

Scott plays truant from school to ride the pony, the police get involved: legal complications and social tensions follow—but all ends well when Scott and Josie become close friends.

Ride a Wild Pony was the first feature made in Australia by the Walt Disney organisation, for which British director Don *Chaffey had already made several features. It was shot, with a predominantly Australian crew, in Chiltern in northern Vic., with a budget of $1 million. It did well throughout Australia and was widely applauded as a stylish children's feature.   HARRY OLDMEADOW

Rites of passage   There has been an abundance of Australian films with rites-of-passage narratives. These comprise a serious genre of films, often adaptations of literary texts rendering a protagonist's journey to adulthood. Various teen movies delve into contemporary adolescent milieus. In other films, adolescent rites of passage are remembered and, to some extent, resolved by adult characters while, in some, teenage characters undergo their coming of age on the fringes of some dramatic event in their parents' or employers' lives.

The first colour feature film made by an Australian in Australia was Charles *Chauvel's *Jedda (1955). On a cattle station in the Northern Territory Jedda (Ngarla *Kunoth) becomes the surrogate daughter of the owner's wife. Jedda's coming of age is complicated by her desire to experience her tribal rituals, walkabouts, and the songs and dances of the corroboree. Declining the prospect of assimilation and integration offered by her adoptive mother and father, respectively, Jedda develops a fatal attraction for a virile, renegade, loin-clothed tribal Aborigine. The film implies that problems of identity are tragically insoluble for those who have been removed from the world of their birth parents.

*The Chant of Jimmie Blacksmith (1978), an adaptation of Thomas *Keneally's novel and directed by Fred *Schepisi, delivers a similar scenario being played out a century earlier. Again, the result is violent and tragic: Jimmie (Tommy *Lewis) erupts when his Aboriginal and European identities converge and when the thwarted prospects they create become too much to bear. An adaptation of a novel of the same name by Nene Gare, *The Fringe Dwellers (1986), directed by Bruce *Beresford, is the story of Trilby (Kristina Nehm) who urges her family to move into a township where she hopes to have a 'normal' life. The experiment fails: she packs her suitcase and leaves to seek a life of her own in the city.

Some recent films have narratives about Aboriginal characters who endeavour to step outside their allotted place on the edge of White Australian culture with varying degrees of success. *Wrong Side of the Road (1981) directed by Ned Lander, is the story of a group of rock musicians who travel the outback to make a living at various venues in the face of prejudice and harassment. *Blackfellas (1993), directed by James *Ricketson, is the story of Doug Doolihan (John *Moore), who, on his release from prison, attempts to

break with his endearing but incorrigible childhood mate, Floyd (David *Ngoombujarra), upon his release from prison. Doug's coming of age, delayed by the demise of tribal customs and ceremonies as well as by his petty criminal activity, is difficult and precarious.

Adaptation films in this genre about the rites of passage of adolescents are usually set in rural or outback settings and are almost always set in the past at a time when Australia was struggling to achieve nationhood or experiencing its first optimistic independent flourish. *The Man from Snowy River (1982), directed by George *Miller, is an adaptation of A.B. (Banjo) Paterson's poem of the same name. The film reveals how men form relationships with each other and how, in communities where traditional roles prosper, this mateship is often the most important aspect of a young man's journey to adulthood.

Peter *Weir's *Gallipoli (1981), with its penetrating script by David *Williamson, is an influential contribution to the mythology of mateship and identity. It is a potent blending of the heroic legends of the bush worker and the digger, or infantry soldier. Archie (Mark *Lee), the eldest son of an outback station owner, is a fervent believer in the Empire and behaves altruistically, running on command into the fire of the Turks' machine guns, whereas Frank (Mel *Gibson), a wandering city-born labourer of Irish descent, who is not enamoured of the British, acts out of a self-interest that is nonetheless heroic. *The Lighthorsemen (1987), directed by Simon *Wincer, includes a rites-of-passage motif about a young Melbourne lad (Peter *Phelps) who, despite having never ridden a horse, enlists in the elite cavalry unit of the Australian army in World War I and, in the heroic charge of the fortress of Beersheba in Palestine, shows the necessary verve and intelligence required of its members.

Film adaptations of coming-of-age novels also include female stories. Peter Weir's *Picnic at Hanging Rock (1975), based on a book by Joan Lindsay, is the story of the disappearance of a handful of virginal schoolgirls climbing the rocky labyrinth of Hanging Rock in Victoria on a St Valentine's Day picnic in 1900. The survivors fear that some sordid sexual ordeal has occurred, and there is a latent message that sensuality, like the mysterious rocks and luxuriant bush, is menacing and therefore frightening. *The Getting of Wisdom (1977), directed by Bruce *Beresford, was adapted for the screen by Eleanor *Witcombe from the novel of the same name by Henry Handel Richardson. *My Brilliant Career (1979), directed by Gillian *Armstrong, was another Eleanor Witcombe adaptation, this time of a novel by Miles Franklin. The protagonists of these films—Laura (Susannah *Fowle) in The Getting of Wisdom; Sybylla (Judy *Davies) in My Brilliant Career; and, to some extent, Jessica (Sigrid *Thornton) in The Man from Snowy River—attempt to overthrow traditional, passive feminine roles, seeking to define their own identities. Often, the agents by which patriarchal constructions of sexuality and power are perpetuated are female elders entrusted with the task of nurturing young women. These older women prove to be favourably disposed to such traditional womanly roles and attributes as marriage and modesty. Laura and Sybylla experience desire that lies outside the sort of social behaviour expected of women. Each is tolerated, however, as an eccentric nonconformist. These films demonstrate the paradox that this complicated and fraught process generally gives young women a better preparation for early adult life than the limited rites of passage of young males.

•The Mango Tree (1977) is concerned with the influence of a grandmother (Geraldine Fitzgerald) on a boy's social and psychological development. Set in a small sugarcane town during World War I, the film dramatises the boy's sexual initiation with his French teacher. •The Irishman, another adaptation set in the bush, is the story of a boy, Michael Doolan (Simon •Burke), who works with his irascible father (Michael •Craig) and his bullock team in an era when the threat of motorised transport looms and is taken as a personal affront by the father. After his father dies in an accident, Michael accepts his premature coming of age and assumes his father's position as breadwinner.

There are numerous contemporary coming-of-age films. They deal with subjects such as family and friendship, education, loss of innocence, sexual discovery and sexual initiation, the vicissitudes of urban life, and competitive sport. A category has emerged in which rites of passage are denied to adolescents by malevolent intervention or psychological imbalance. In •Mull, a teenage girl (Nadine •Garner) takes on the role of domestic manager of her home and family when her mother becomes sick and dies. She battles with her father (Bill •Hunter) for her rights and those of her siblings, especially the right to reject their father's evangelical religion. In •Muriel's Wedding, Muriel (Toni •Collette) is despised by her peers in Porpoise Spit for her naivety and dowdiness. However, a new friend, a move to Sydney, a job, and a social life allow her to become a 'changed' person whose antics dismay her dreadful father (Bill •Hunter) and delight and alarm her dole-queue sister. Muriel's dreamt-of rite of passage is a white wedding, but her real coming of age occurs when she admits to herself that she has made a mistake in becoming a bought bride and disengages herself from the sham.

In •The Big Steal (1990), Danny Clark (Ben •Mendelsohn) celebrates his eighteenth birthday. His delightfully 'daggy' father (Marshall Napier) proudly presents him with his lovingly restored early-model small sedan that in no way compares with the car of Danny's dreams. Danny engages in a humorous oedipal tussle with his girlfriend's father, as well as with a shifty car salesman, and in the process changes from hapless victim to young man of some consequence.

Other films based on family dynamics show an adolescent character coming of age on the fringes of other goings-on. In •Return Home (1990) Garry (Ben Mendelsohn) is employed by one of two brothers who are going over old ground, particularly their own adolescent strife with their father, as each performs the role of Garry's surrogate father in their particular field of expertise. •Spotswood (1992) is driven by a narrative about a very old-fashioned factory undergoing the scrutiny of an economic rationalist. Carey (Ben Mendelsohn) eventually relinquishes his infatuation with the boss's daughter and begins to value his friendship with Wendy (Toni Collette), his neighbour and co-worker. In •The Last Days of Chez Nous (1992), Annie (Miranda •Otto) develops a friendship with a student lodger while domestic chaos reigns at home: her mother (Lisa Harrow) is attempting to resolve her problematic relationship with her own father (Bill •Hunter), and her aunt is having an affair with her mother's husband.

While many of the characters in coming-of-age films are preoccupied with school and with acquiring some sort of knowledge to equip them for adult life, it is often their informal learning that has the most immediate value. •The Heartbreak Kid (1993) portrays a teacher–pupil romance that is underscored by the difficulty of being different in a supposedly multicultural school where mainstream values predominate and even dictate which sports may be played. Street Hero (1984) makes a case for the redeeming power, in the lives of alienated migrant students, of a good teacher, music, and group bonding in the school orchestra. Fighting Back (1983) tells the story of the difficulties faced by a highly strung, violent, and apparently unteachable boy, and by his mother and his committed remedial teacher. In •Flirting (1991) and •Fast Talking (1984) schools from different ends of the social spectrum are represented and, in both, teenagers are exposed to incompetent and bullying teachers, outmoded rules, and corporal punishment, all of which inspire the students to find very creative ways to circumvent them.

Loss of innocence, sexual discovery, and sexual initiation are, of course, constant themes in coming-of-age narratives. In •The Year My Voice Broke (1987) Danny Embling (Noah •Taylor) is an amiable loner who receives a puzzling lesson in the obscure ways of men through his infatuation for brave Freya (Leone Carmen), and her mistreatment by her adoptive father, her boyfriend, and the gossiping men of the town. Flirting, the next episode in Danny's life, depicts his assertion of a unique independence for himself while at boarding school.

In •Puberty Blues (1981), two girls try to find a place for themselves among a group of young surfing enthusiasts on the beaches at Cronulla beach in Sydney. They refuse to submit to the domestic and sexual roles to which the boys would relegate them. Coming of age begins when they realise that their gender need not condemn them to vicarious enjoyment of life through the feats of boyfriends. In The Deliquents (1989) Lola (Kylie •Minogue) plays a pregnant schoolgirl in a 1950s Queensland town whose marriage to her merchant-seaman sweetheart enables her to become the surrogate mother of her deceased friend's daughter. Lola's story reveals the newness and energy of the youth revolution in the rock 'n' roll subculture of the time.

Bizarre and erratic religious interpretations and practice feature prominently in some coming-of-age films. In •The Devil's Playground (1976) Tom Allen's (Simon Burke) rite of passage entails walking out of the seminary he has chosen to enter and possibly out of the devout religiosity that initially led him there. He especially rejects the seminary's celibate atmosphere, the presence of which is represented by a repressed yet predatory, authoritarian brother, and the equally macabre deluded fanaticism of some of his peers. In •The Nostradamus Kid (1993) a Sydney writer looks back, on his fortieth birthday, over his chaotic, egocentric, deluded, adolescence as a 1960s university student, a role played with a detached air of chaos by Noah Taylor. The writer explains that his coming of age was difficult to achieve because he was unable to cast aside his commitment to 'fulness of response' and his apocalyptic view of the world, attitudes acquired through his participation, as an adolescent, in Seventh Day Adventist summer camps.

The milieu depicted in many contemporary coming-of-age films is that of urban adolescent life. •Moving Out (1983), which centres on the concern that the central character Gino (Vince •Colosimo) feels about leaving his inner-suburban life for the void of the outer suburbs, explores the dilemma of being both an adolescent and a migrant. In •Mouth to Mouth (1978), two female escapees from a juvenile institution team up with two country boys looking for work in Melbourne. The narrative follows their attempts to set up 'house' in a squat, find jobs, and keep out of trouble and one step ahead of the police. •Romper Stomper (1992), another contribution to the 'barren-urban-wasteland' genre of Australian cinema, has a powerful, shocking narrative about a group of racist skinheads. Individuals in the group must submit to the group's interests, as decreed by their manipulative leader, Hando (Russell •Crowe). Davey (Daniel Pollock), his right-hand man, finds love with Kate (Jacqueline •McKenzie), a homeless girl and, in a struggle to the death with Hando, achieves his rite of passage to a life outside the raggle-taggle group of violent misfits.

Considering the widespread obsession with spectator sports and sporting champions in Australia, it is unusual that the feature film industry has not yet plundered or mastered this aspect of teenage life. •The Coolangatta Gold (1984) focuses on two Queensland brothers and their father. Steve (Joss McWilliam) is successfully establishing a life of his own. Adam (Colin •Friels), on the other hand, has superior athletic ability, and is coached by their fanatical

and hysterical father for victory in an iron-man race. Steve overcomes his burning desire for revenge at being relegated to mere training partner, nuisance, and ne'er-do-well and, in a benevolent coming-of-age gesture, allows his father to have his day. •Dawn! (1979) follows the life of Olympic swimmer, Dawn Fraser (Bronwyn Mackay-Payne). Her life is one of lackadaisical acceptance of her talent and of controversies with officials and journalists caused by her spontaneous, gregarious nature, daredevil antics, and her popularity. Her prodigious athletic ability cannot protect her from the censure of the rigid enforcers of rules, discipline, and decorum. In •Strictly Ballroom (1992), aspirant ballroom-dancing champion (Paul •Mercurio) also falls foul of rule-makers. Individuality and creativity are not readily rewarded, as they undermine the power of those who regulate and teach ballroom dancing as a competitive sport.

The emergence of a group of films about the unavailability of a conventional coming of age for some adolescents illustrates dark aspects of Australian life, including sexual predatoriness, banishment of the radically different, and perversely inadequate parenting. In •Shame (1988), Lizzie (Simone •Buchanan), who is encouraged by a yuppie city lawyer (Deborra-Lee •Furness) to press charges for rape, is tormented and abducted by her rapists. The film may be interpreted as a portrayal of the annihilation of the dignity and safety of adolescent females in a small rural township, usually the heartland of traditional Australian family values, where male predatory behaviour is not curtailed by social or legal means.

•Bad Boy Bubby (1994) is the story of a male child kept in infantile dependency and social isolation by his mother. It is a narrative about the ultimate denial of rites of passage, although Bubby (Nicholas •Hope) does eventually wander into the world outside his mother's room. His ramblings are appreciated as rap lyrics by a rock band and its audience, and his unique sensitivity allows him to communicate with the severely speech-impaired. One of the protagonists in •Angel Baby (1995) is a schizophrenic girl, Kate (Jacqueline McKenzie), who decides, aided by group therapy and counselling, to have a relationship with another patient. Things go awry when Kate becomes pregnant and ceases taking her medication. The tragedy highlights how a conventional coming of age is unobtainable for some clients of the psychiatric industry.

As depicted in Australian films, teenage years may be a bit of a romp interspersed with moments of insight, revelation, pleasure, and joy—accompanied by various social disasters, emotional traumas, and psychological dilemmas. They may, however, also be an unhappy or melancholy time when the young are overwhelmed by rules and the persistence with which they are enforced by parents, teachers, the police, and other officials. Adolescents may be affected, spasmodically or persistently, by emotional and psychological turmoil, social isolation, alienation, frustration, and anger, all of which can degenerate into violent incidents or a generalised rampage against the world.

There is a lot of death in coming-of-age films. It may be symbolic of the decline of childhood security, dreams, and fantasies, and of the demise of childhood attachments to parents. All adolescents find it necessary to deal with problems in achieving independence and personal sovereignty. Australian coming-of-age films explore how young people meet or fall short of their own, and everyone else's, expectations.   FELICITY COGAN

Road Games

1981. *Director*: Richard Franklin. *Producer*: Richard Franklin. *Scriptwriter*: Everett De Roche. *Director of photography*: Vincent Monton. *Music*: Brian May. 101 min. *Cast*: Stacy Keach (Pat Quid), Jamie Lee Curtis (Hitch), Marion Edward (Frita), Grant Page (Smith or Jones), Thaddeus Smith (policeman).

Director Richard •Franklin's acknowledged indebtedness to Alfred Hitchcock is everywhere apparent in this engaging comedy thriller: in the impudence of the cutting that catches the viewer between laughter and shock, in its love of making the ordinary seem strange, and most obviously in a heroine called Hitch. The film begins teasingly with a report about a corpse found in a garbage dump, and follows this with the garroting of a girl in a motel room. The report has been heard by truck driver Quid, who has a literary bent and who later sees his dog Boswell sniffing around a garbage bin. Quid's trucking assignment is to transport a load of refrigerated carcasses across the Nullarbor Plain to Perth, and most of the film is taken up with this journey, photographed for stylish menace by Vincent •Monton. Quid meets a variety of oddball characters, including Hitch, the American diplomat's daughter, to whom, against orders, he gives a lift, and another of those sparring partnerships so reminiscent of Franklin's mentor is created with zest and wit. There are jokes and red herrings along the way, but there is a real psychopath at large too, and real danger outside the comparative safety of Quid's truck; and the film emerges as a satisfying mix of thriller and romantic comedy, reaching a climax in the backstreets of Perth. It is not often that these two strands have been so neatly interwoven in Australian cinema, but Franklin's Hollywood-style narrative skills, drawing on Everett •De Roche's inventive script, create a genre delight.   BMcF

Road to Nhill

1997. *Director*: Sue Brooks. *Producer*: Sue Maslin. *Scriptwriter*: Alison Tilson. *Director of photography*: Nicolette Freeman. *Music*: Elizabeth Drake. 100 min. *Cast*: Monica Maughan (Nell), Tony Barry (Jim), Lynette Curran (Margot), Bill Hunter (Bob), Patricia Kennedy (Jean), Lois Ramsay (Carmel), Terry Norris (Ted), Alwyn Kurts (Jack), Paul Chubb (Maurie), Matthew Dyktynski (Brett), Denise Roberts (Gwen), Kerry Walker (Alison), Bill Young (Brian).

Lynette Curran, Monica Maughan, Lois Ramsay and Patricia Kennedy in **Road to Nhill**

The truck driver plays games... The hitchhiker plays games. And the killer is playing the deadliest game of all!

ROAD GAMES

Starring STACY KEACH as "Quid" and JAMIE LEE CURTIS as "Hitch" in ROAD GAMES
Produced & Directed by RICHARD FRANKLIN Co-Producer BARBI TAYLOR Executive Producer BERNARD SCHWARTZ
Screenplay by EVERETT DE ROCHE A QUEST FILMS PRODUCTION
AVCO EMBASSY PICTURES Release

PG PARENTAL GUIDANCE SUGGESTED
SOME MATERIAL MAY NOT BE SUITABLE FOR CHILDREN
© 1981 AVCO EMBASSY PICTURES CORP.

Road Games

415

A car containing four women bowlers (Nell, Jean, Margot, and Carmel) overturns on the road home from Nhill. When they do not arrive at the appointed time, the town begins to mobilise. As the fire brigade truck, the ambulance, and various cars pass and miss each other on the roads; as the policeman (Brett) tries to find out what happened well after it is all over; as the stock agent's wife (Gwen) spreads the news over the phone; and as other drivers and people working in surrounding farms stand around debating what should be done next, we gradually come to understand the dynamics of this small community. Although it is often very funny, we seldom laugh. Although there is constant activity, nothing happens. But the long silences, the camera's fondness for vistas, and the slow pace of the narrative provide opportunities for the large ensemble cast, in which the four central performances are outstanding. The only disappointment is Phillip •Adams's redundant 'voice of God' in the opening and closing minutes of the film.　　　IB

Road Warrior, The, *see* **Mad Max 2**

Roadshow, *see* **Village Roadshow; Hexagon Productions**

Robb, Jill (1935–) PRODUCER London-born but long resident in Australia, Jill Robb has had a varied association with the local film industry. At first, she was a continuity girl for Lee •Robinson's Southern International Pictures, where she also worked as a production secretary. She worked on the television series *Skippy*, ultimately as associate producer, and became executive producer for the •South Australian Film Corporation (SAFC) (for which she made several documentaries) in 1972 and commissioner of the •Victorian Film Corporation in 1975. In 1976 she acted as associate producer on •**The Fourth Wish**, based on Michael •Craig's touching story of a dying child and his father. Back with the SAFC as acting head of production, she encouraged producer Joy •Cavill, who brought forward a script based on the life of swimming star Dawn Fraser, and the SAFC backed this (•**Dawn!**, 1979) with Ken •Hannam as director and Robb as executive producer. In her subsequent career she has produced some popular television series, including *Embassy* and *Snowy River: the McGregor Saga*, but to date only two further films. •**Careful He Might Hear You** (1983), based on a Sumner Locke-Elliott novel she had long admired, remains one of the most accomplished melodramas of the Australian revival, notable for Carl •Schultz's sensitive but full-throttled direction, an ensemble of fine performances, and a production design that contributes a great deal to the film's meaning and impact. In 1986, she made •**The More Things Change**, a curiously undervalued drama of a modern marriage in which role reversal causes problems. This latter film was very much a female enter-prise: not only was it produced by Robb, but also it was directed by actor Robyn •Nevin, and written by Moya Wood. Like all Robb's films, it is characterised by strong concern for intimate human values.
Other Australian films: •**They're a Weird Mob** (1966, production secretary).　　　BMcF

Robbery Under Arms

1920. *Director, Scriptwriter*: Kenneth Brampton. From the novel by Rolfe Boldrewood. *Director of photography*: Lacey Percival. B&W. *Cast*: Kenneth Brampton (Captain Starlight).

The 1920 film adaptation of **Robbery Under Arms** is among the most under-appreciated early Australian feature films. Kenneth Brampton's scenario exploits the 'social odyssey' aspects of the novel to the detriment of its Victorian melodramatics and its incipient social criticism. The acting, with the exception of Brampton's own 'blacksheep' characterisation of Captain Starlight, stays firmly within the adequate range. Perhaps most unfortunately and most trivially, there is an embarrassing moustache on the face of Hilda Dorrington in the role of the spurned and vindictive Kate Morrison. However, the fact that the Marsden boys spend time droving cattle, shearing sheep, panning for gold, and watching country horse-racing, as well as bailing up coaches, escaping from prison, and fleeing from troopers, adds a great deal of specific visual and cultural interest to a story whose characters and plot mechanisms are perhaps a mite well-worn. If the actors tend to underplay, at least most of them are neither wooden nor hysterical. Brampton's direction combines sound figure grouping, economical action, and a good sense of what will work in a film. But what makes the film really worth looking at is Lacey •Percival's cinematography, which includes some of the most sensitive, inventive, and appropriate work of its kind in early Australian cinema.　　　WILLIAM D. ROUTT

Robbery Under Arms

1957. *Director*: Jack Lee. *Producer*: Joseph Janni. *Scriptwriters*: Alexander Baron, W.P. Lipscomb. From the novel by Rolf Boldrewood. *Director of photography*: Harry Waxman. *Music*: Ronald Whelan. 104 min. *Cast*: Peter Finch (Captain Starlight), Ronald Lewis (Dick Marston), Maureen Swanson (Kate Morrison), David McCallum (Jim Marston), Jill Ireland (Jean).

So many bushranging films had been made during the silent and early sound period that the NSW government had banned them. Consequently, Australian film-makers had avoided the genre for some years before Jack •Lee made this version of the classic bushranging novel.

The story has its origins in fact as it documents the involvement of the Marston brothers with the gentleman bushranger Captain Starlight, played with considerable charm by Peter •Finch. The narrative follows his scheme to steal a very valuable herd of cattle from Central Australia and sell them at the markets in Adelaide in one of the largest cattle-stealing exploits in Australian history. The romantic involvement of the older brother Dick with the fiery Kate Morrison eventually leads to the failure of the Marstons' attempts to go straight, and to the death of their father and Starlight.

Shot on location in the Flinders Ranges, and near the town of Bourke in NSW, the film catches the colour and beauty of the stark landscape, but the dramatic intensity is variable with even the closing climax lacking the close-ups that might have given the film more impact.

BRUCE MOLLOY

Robbery Under Arms

1985. *Directors*: Donald Crombie, Ken Hannam. *Producer*: Jock Blair. *Scriptwriters*: Graeme Koetsveld, Tony Morphett. *Director of photography*: Ernest Clark. *Music*: Garry McDonald, Laurie Stone. 141 min. *Cast*: Sam Neill (Starlight), Steven Vidler (Dick), Christopher Cummins (Jim), Liz Newman (Gracey), Jane Menelaus (Aileen).

This lavishly mounted film was the fifth screen adaptation of Rolf Boldrewood's classic bushranging story, its immediate predecessor being Jack •Lee's British-made version of 1957, with Peter •Finch. The narrative traces the exploits of Captain Starlight, a British aristocrat turned bushranger, and a gang of Australian larrikins in the 1880s: cattle rustling, stage hold-ups, bank robberies, shoot-outs, and chases are interleaved with several romantic sub-plots.

Robbery Under Arms is not without its attractions: Sam •Neill's panache as Starlight, an engaging performance from Steven •Vidler, Paul •Chubb's hilarious cameo, and Ernest Clark's intermittently impressive photography of the Flinders Ranges. However, the film's provenance in a projected miniseries is altogether too evident in its sprawling and disjointed plot, its superficial treatment of the colonial themes, the stereotypical female roles, and its confused use of disparate generic elements drawn from the Boys' Own matinee serials, the western, the Victorian melodrama, TV miniseries soap, and Marlboro commercials.

HARRY OLDMEADOW

Roberts, Wyn

ACTOR Long a respected stage actor, Wyn Roberts has made only a handful of films. His most memorable role is still that of the slow-thinking Sergeant Bumpher in •Picnic at Hanging Rock (1975), who was out of his depth in the investigations of the disappearance of the school party, although **Listen to the Lion** (1977), a little-seen short film, gave him a major role as a Sydney derelict. In other films such as **Weekend of Shadows**, he brings to quite small roles an easy authority and conviction born of

years of experience in character-creation, and the camera seems to catch his quiet watchfulness unawares. He has also played in several television series, including the long-running *Prisoner*.

Other Australian films: At the Land's End (1961, doc., nar.), **With Gentle Majesty** (1962, doc., nar.), **The New China** (1965, doc., nar.), Flashpoint (1972), Fighting Back (1982), **Return to Snowy River** (1988). BMcF

Robertson, Tim

(1944–) ACTOR A Melbourne-based stage and television actor, Tim Robertson has made occasional forays into the cinema, sometimes in low-budget straight-to-video crime thrillers such as **With Time to Kill** (1987) and **Ebbtide** (1993), and more often in supporting roles in prestigious productions such as •Bliss (1985), •Kangaroo (1987), and •The Big Steal (1990). One of Robertson's more off-beat performances was as Owen Owen, a homicidal Welsh storekeeper visited by John •Waters in the outback in **Going Sane** (1987). Robertson was also associated with the La Mama and Pram Factory theatrical group in the 1970s. He performed in its dismal film adaptation of the successful play •Dimboola (1979).

Other Australian films include: •The Cars that Ate Paris (1974), •Petersen (1974), The Great MacArthy (1975), •Pure S... (1975), •The Chant of Jimmie Blacksmith (1978), •The Last of the Knucklemen (1979), •Phar Lap (1983), Jenny Kissed Me (1986), Bachelor Girl (1987), •The Year My Voice Broke (1987), The Time Guardian (1987), •Evil Angels (1988), Father (1990), Aya (1991), Amy (1998). GM

Robinson, Lee

(1923–) DIRECTOR A key figure in the Australian film and television industry for more than 50 years, Lee Robinson has not, until recently, received recognition commensurate with his accomplishments. Raised in a Mormon family, Robinson began as a short-story writer before he was employed as a scriptwriter by the newly created Department of Information (DOI) Film Unit (which became •Film Australia). Robinson scripted and directed **Namatjira the Painter** in central Australia in 1947, and during this period he was assisted by British director Harry Watt who was shooting •Eureka Stockade (1949) in Sydney. Robinson also worked on other documentaries for DOI, including **Outback Patrol** (1947) and **Crocodile Hunters** (1949) in the NT, and **The Pearlers** (1949) in Broome, WA.

Robinson and Chips •Rafferty formed Platypus Pictures in 1952 to develop feature films at a time when the local feature industry was dormant and government obstacles, in terms of raising capital in Australia, were considerable. There was, for example, a £10 000 budget limitation on Australian films. During this period Robinson was unable to finance a crime thriller that he wrote and it was eventually filmed as the •Seige of Pinchgut (1959), the last film ever produced under the Ealing name.

Robinson's first feature, •The Phantom Stockman (1953), was a dramatic hybrid that combined the narrative conventions of the Hollywood series western with distinctive Central Australian settings, and the film included a brief appearance by Aboriginal painter Albert Namatjira. The film's financial success, from local and overseas sales, provided the basis for the establishment of Southern International, the company Robinson formed with Rafferty to develop a larger budget film, •King of the Coral Sea. This film was directed by Robinson on location on Thursday Island in 1954, with underwater sequences shot on Green Island off the north Qld coast. An adventure melodrama, involving illegal immigrants and a kidnapping, the film was commercially successful.

Southern International's next film, •Walk Into Paradise (1956), had nearly finished pre-production when French producer Paul-Edmond Decharme suggested a co-production with his film company, Discifilm. A French dialogue director, Marcel Pagliero, was added to the production team to help with the two French stars and the 12-week shoot in the New Guinea Highlands. This colour film, costing £65 000, was also commercially successful, particularly when Hollywood entrepreneur Joseph E. Levine bought it for the American market for $60 000 and, after being retitled as Walk into Hell, the film made a substantial profit for Levine's Embassy Films. The other French co-productions between Discifilm and Southern International, The Stowaway (1958) and The Restless and the Damned (1959), were less successful, as was Robinson's return to Alice Springs for Dust in the Sun (1958), which starred British actor Jill Adams.

After working on •They're a Weird Mob (1966) as production supervisor, Robinson continued to write and direct documentaries throughout the 1960s. Robinson also developed, with John •McCallum, the enormously popular Skippy television series for Fauna Films and this led to a spin-off film The Intruders (1969). Robinson's Fauna Company also produced Barrier Reef, Boney and Shannon's Mob for television before he became interested in the Asian market. He shot Bailey's Bird in Malaysia before producing the feature film co-productions, Attack Force Z (1982) in Taiwan, and Southern Cross (1982) in Japan.

Other Australian films include: •Nickel Queen (1971, ex. p.).

GM

Rolfe, Alfred (1862–1943) DIRECTOR/ACTOR Son-in-law of actor/manager Alfred Dampier, and an actor himself (including in his first three films), Alfred Rolfe became one of the most prolific and influential film producers of the early silent period. He made at least 13 films in 1911 (Captain Midnight, the Bush King; Captain Starlight—A Gentleman of the Road; •Moora Neeya; The Lady Outlaw; Dan Morgan; In the Nick of Time; Mates of the Murrumbidgee;

Way Outback; What Women Suffer; The Cup Winner; Caloola; The Miner's Curse; and King of the Coiners), and at least eight in 1912 (Do Men Love Women?, The Sin of a Woman, Crime and the Criminal, Cooee and the Echo, The Love Tyrant, The Cheat, Won on the Post, Moira or The Mystery of the Bush). Most of these were outdoor action stories, filmed on location and acknowledged particularly for their naturalistic performance style. During World War I he specialised in patriotic films, such as The Day (1914), Sunny South or The Whirlwind of Fate (1914), How We Beat the Emden (1915), •The Hero of the Dardanelles (1915), and the short film Will They Never Come? (1915). Even his The Loyal Rebel or Eureka Stockade (1915) was interpreted as a war allegory, expressing the Australian fighting spirit, and Cupid Camouflaged (1918) was a romance produced as a fundraiser for the war effort. He also directed short films of industrial processes and some for cinema 'singalongs', before leaving show business in the 1920s. IB

Romance of Runnibede, The

1928. Director: Scott R. Dunlap [and William Reed and perhaps Wallace Worsley, uncredited]. Producer: Frederick Phillips. Scriptwriter: John M. Giles. From the novel by Steele Rudd. Titles: Gayne Dexter. Director of photography: Len Roos. B&W. Cast: Eva Novak (Dorothy Winchester), Gordon Collingridge (Tom Linton), Claude Saunders (Sub-Inspector Dale), Dunstan Webb (Goondai).

At the very end of The Romance of Runnibede it appears very much as though Tom Linton and Sub-Inspector Dale have found true love, but too late. Their rivalry for Dorothy Winchester has led to Dale's sacrificing himself to rampaging Aboriginal people who, for some unknown reason, think that Dorothy is a reincarnation of an important tribal figure. However, when Dale dies in Tom's arms, the latter's grief is so 'over the top' that one cannot help thinking that Dorothy must have occupied second place in their affections. This moment is definitely the high point in what is otherwise an all-too typical example of colonial pop fiction, in which educated and sophisticated Dorothy from the city incarnates both a Dionysiac primordial past and an ordered imperial future, while the rural 'squattocracy' jousts with government authority for her favour. WILLIAM D. ROUTT

Romance of the Burke and Wills Expedition of 1860, A

1918. Director: Charles Byers Coates. Directors of photography: George Louis Gouday, Franklyn Barrett, A.O. Segerberg, Walter Sully. B&W.

Viewers of the surviving few minutes of A Romance of the Burke and Wills Expedition of 1860 may be nonplussed that those minutes are so abundantly feminine. Women are in virtually every shot of a film we might suppose would have been solely about men adventuring. There is even a rather lengthy minuet sequence in which women are dancing dressed as men. The explanation probably lies in the film's title. It seems at least partly to have been intended as a *romance*, a tale of loves won and lost, of what women do in the real world while men are being historical. If this is so, **A Romance** belongs to a line of 'sophisticated' deconstructions of history, the best-known early exponent of which was Ernst Lubitsch, who did not begin to make films in this vein until 1919.

WILLIAM D. ROUTT

Romantic Story of Margaret Catchpole, The

1911. *Director*: Raymond Longford. *Director of photography*: Ernest Higgins. B&W. *Cast*: Lottie Lyell (Margaret Catchpole), Raymond Longford (Will Laud), Sybil Wilde (Little Kitty), Arno (the horse).

About two reels of **The Romantic Story of Margaret Catchpole**, Raymond •Longford's second feature, have escaped the ravages of time. The story centres on Margaret Catchpole who steals a horse to join her escaping lover. She is arrested and transported to Australia where, after many years, she finds happiness. In the surviving footage, the coast of NSW stands in for the south coast of the United Kingdom, and our courageous heroine dresses in man's attire to effect the appropriation of the horse. She is captured and eventually arranges for her lover's escape. Perhaps the most appealing performance in the film is Sybil Wilde's as 'Little Kitty', Margaret's equally plucky sister. Longford's direction is disappointingly pedestrian, and Lottie •Lyell and Sybil Wilde put their hands to their brows so often that one is driven to speculate that they have both inherited some kind of bizarre behavioural tick.

WILLIAM D. ROUTT

Romeril, John

(1951–) WRITER/PLAYWRIGHT Once described as a great survivor of Australian theatre, John Romeril has not received the same critical attention for his film work as for his plays. Of his 60 plays in various styles, the expressionistic *Floating World* (1974) is his best known, having gained attention for its surreal dialogue and stage imagery. Romeril became involved in theatre at Monash University, Melbourne, during the early days of La Mama Theatre, and was a seminal member of the Australian Performing Group (Pram Factory), which included John •Duigan, David •Williamson, Bruce •Spence, and Peter •Cummins. His first feature, **Bonjour Balwyn** (1969), was directed by Nigel •Buesst and starred John Duigan (also co-writer) in one of his rare screen roles. A Milos Forman-style sociopolitical satire, which derived its name from the final predicament of a magazine editor on a downward slide who

ends up door-knocking in a middle-class suburb, it was considered fringe at the time and played mostly in small art houses. **The Great MacArthy** (1975), from the novel by Barry Oakley, is about an 'innocent from the bush', a talented young footballer who finds himself in an unintelligible world of sex, club politics, and the contradictions of the city. It is a curious mixture of social satire and existential rights of passage. Romeril has also written for television, including *Best of Mates* (1972), *Charlie the Chequer Cab Kid* (1973), *Everything's a Hustle* (Inside Running series) (1989), and the education series *Six of the Best* (1981–82). His most recent play is *Kate and Shiner* (1998).

HARRY KIRCHNER

Romper Stomper

1992. *Director*: Geoffrey Wright. *Producers*: Phil Jones, Ian Pringle, Daniel Scharf. *Writer*: Geoffrey Wright. *Director of photography*: Ron Hagen. *Music*: John Clifford White. 94 min. *Cast*: Russell Crowe (Hando), Daniel Pollock (Davey), Jacqueline McKenzie (Gabe), Alex Scott (Martin).

It could be argued that **Romper Stomper** was perhaps the most controversial and confronting mainstream Australian film of the early 1990s. Public debate focused around its themes of blatant anti-Asian racism and right-wing skinhead fascism (*Mein Kampf*-inspired) and its stylistic realism. The style of presentation included a complex combination of such techniques as hand-held documentary-style camera work, relentless action sequences, rapid cutting, strong heavy metal music, and extremely creative use of film sound

Set in Melbourne's multicultural western suburbs, this R-rated film's dark narrative weaves a complex path through a number of dramatic but ultimately flawed relationships as it attempts to explore the subcultural lifestyle and values of those on the edge of the society. The film concentrates on the emerging romantic relationships between Gabe (Jacqueline •McKenzie), a wealthy incest victim and sufferer of epilepsy, Hando (Russell •Crowe), unemployed skinhead leader, and Davey (Daniel Pollock), his second in command, as they attempt to confront with violence their perceptions of the Asianisation of their suburb and country. Any hope for their relationships and the skinheads' quest ultimately fails in a closing scene of ironic tragedy.

Romper Stomper gained three Australian Film Industry awards, including Best Actor for Russell Crowe and consolidated Geoffrey •Wright's reputation as a director. However, its positioning in the marketplace as similar to Kubrick's **A Clockwork Orange**, the **Mad Max** trilogy, and the films of Sam Peckinpah probably limited its appeal across the broader Australian film-going public on release, although subsequent video sales proved very successful.

JOHN BENSON

Ronin Films   This company, founded by Andrew Pike and Merrilyn Fitzpatrick, has played an important role in exhibition and distribution since it was founded in 1974. It has distributed over 120 feature films from such diverse countries as China, the USA, the United Kingdom, Japan, France, Russia, Thailand, Spain, Germany, Papua New Guinea, and New Zealand. Ronin commenced with, and has maintained, a special interest in the cinemas of China and Japan, and was one of the first distributors in Australia to recognise the importance of the 'fifth generation' of Chinese film directors.

Ronin has also championed the work of independent Australian film-makers, having long-term relationships with Jane •Campion, Vincent •Ward, David Caesar, Baz •Luhrmann, Scott •Hicks, and Tracey •Moffatt. Material support has taken the form of active investment or production guarantees for films, including: •Waiting and **Holidays On the River Yarra** (1990), **Aya** (1990), and •**Strictly Ballroom** (1992). Ronin also distributed •**Shine** (1996) and •**Road to Nhill** (1997).

Distribution of documentaries has been a major strength; Ronin has developed a strong market for non-fiction films in the education sector. In the late 1990s the Ronin Education collection comprised over 250 titles, including a large number of significant Australian documentaries. Ronin has had a strong presence in exhibition of both features and documentaries. In the late 1980s it formed strategic partnerships with other distributors to run cinemas in Sydney and Melbourne. In Canberra, Ronin continues to own and operate the Electric Shadows Cinema, which began repertory in 1979, and the Center Cinema.

Managing director Andrew Pike began his career in distribution and exhibition at the Center Cinema, where he introduced a number of innovations to Canberra cultural life, including late Friday night supper shows. He has experience in almost every field of the Australian film industry. After completing an MA on the history of Australian cinema at the Australian National University he co-authored, with Ross Cooper, *Australian Film, 1900–1977: A Guide to Feature Film Production* (Oxford University Press, 1980), and he has published a number of articles in journals and newspapers. He served for three years as consultant to the National Library's Film Lending Collection, and as a research fellow in the Department of Pacific History at the Australian National University.

He has made several films, directing **My University**, which won the short film prize at the Sydney Film Festival in 1974. He co-directed **Angels of War** (1982) and co-produced and recorded sound on **Man Without Pigs** (1990). He served as a member of the Board of the •Australian Film Commission from 1989 to 1992, was awarded the Australian Film Institute's Byron Kennedy Award for services to the Australian film community in 1986 and a Special Award by the Australian Film Critics Circle in 1992 for his contributions to the film industry.   PETER HUGHES

Rosenberg, Marc (1950–) WRITER/PRODUCER   In 1975 Marc Rosenberg moved from Texas to Australia, where his interest in playwriting turned to film. He took the one-year scriptwriting course at the Australian Film, Television and Radio School, where he wrote **Gary's Story** (1980), starring John •Howard and directed by Richard Michalak. This film won best short film at the Sydney Film Festival. His reputation for comedy and snappy dialogue led producer Hillary Linstead to commission him to rewrite •**Heatwave** (1982), after eight earlier drafts by original writers Tim Gooding and Mark Stiles remained too much in the social-realist mode for director Phillip •Noyce's sensibilities. Rosenberg managed to interest Antony I. •Ginnane in **Incident at Raven's Gate** (1989), for which Rolf •De Heer and James M. Vernon had been attempting unsuccessfully to raise money, and subsequently shared writing and producing credits with De Heer. Despite the film's admirably ambitious but somewhat muddled narrative, the collaboration continued, this time on **Dingo** (1992), from Rosenberg's original script, which had been 10 years in development. The script won Rosenberg a New South Wales Premier's Literary Award and a Writers Guild Awgie, but **Dingo** had a disappointing theatrical season and is probably best remembered for its overly long music sequences featuring Miles Davis and a performance so approaching catalepsy as to render Colin •Friels's acting efforts alongside him heroic. Rosenberg's other credits include the Australia–Belgium co-production **Australie** (1989, co-w.), and **The Serpent's Lair** (AKA **The Nesting**, 1995, also assoc. p.), for American Home Box Office. He now lives in America.

HARRY KIRCHNER

Rouse, Graham (1934–) ACTOR   Although Graham Rouse has been working in the entertainment industry since 1954, and in films since 1970 with **That Lady from Peking**, he has been seen only in supporting performances. However, there have been a number of key roles in films such as •**Ride a Wild Pony** (1975) and •**The Odd Angry Shot** (1979). Rouse was also effective as General Sutherland in the television miniseries *The Last Bastion* (1984).

Other Australian films include: •The FJ Holden (1977), Weekend of Shadows (1978), •Blue Fin (1978), The Best of Friends (1982), •Heatwave (1982), Dead End Drive-In (1986), Rikky and Pete (1988), •Mr. Reliable (1966).   GM

Rowland, Bruce (1942–) COMPOSER   Bruce Rowland is a self-taught musician and composer. In 1962 he began writing songs for the children's television program, *The Magic Circle* (later, *Adventure Island*). By 1969 he had moved into jingle writing, and now has over 2000 jingles to his credit. In 1981, 10 composers were invited to audition for the feature film, •**The Man from Snowy River** (1982). His audio tape of *Jessica's Theme* convinced the producer that this was what he required. Rowland produced a rich and haunting score that vividly describes the rugged beauty of the Snowy region of south-eastern Australia. The popularly acclaimed score found Rowland producing scores for big-budget feature films. Rowland's approach to writing for film rarely varies. He talks to the director and the actors to ascertain their approach to a particular scene. Next, he watches the scene on video, then sits at the piano with a click track and bases the melody on what the scene is saying until the musical sequence 'feels right'.

Rowland has won a number of awards, including the Australian Film Institute's Best Film Score awards for **The Man from Snowy River** (1982), •**Phar Lap,** and **Rebel** (1985); and a Penguin award for the television series *All the Rivers Run* (1984)   DIANE NAPTHALI

Roxburgh, Richard (1962–) ACTOR   Richard Roxburgh built an enviable reputation as a stage actor, perhaps above all for his notable interpretation of *Hamlet* at Sydney's Belvoir Street Theatre, before busying himself with films. Having embarked on a screen career in the mid 1990s, he appeared in a rapid succession of high-profile roles in which he made it clear that a major new film actor had arrived on the scene. Whether he will remain an interesting film actor rather than a star is debatable, although his major roles to date have all been slightly off-centre, not allowing him to get by on star charisma but requiring careful character delineation. The first film in which he drew serious attention was •**Children of the Revolution** (1996), in which he played Joe Welch, agitator son of fervent communist Joan Fraser (Judy •Davis) and Joe Stalin (F. Murray Abraham): like the rest of the cast, he entered into the black, somewhat zany comedy of the enterprise, in what was certainly not a conventional leading-man role. In •**Doing Time for Patsy Cline** (1997) he was again an idiosyncratic figure, as the dangerous Boyd, boyfriend of Miranda •Otto's aspiring country-and-western singer—this time he was an abrasive loud-mouth, an inventive liar who regards truth as 'a malleable construct', and pulls a gun on the naive country boy who hitches a lift with him. He had the romantic lead in •**Thank God He Met Lizzie** (1997), but the intelligence of his playing and the strangely morose, watchful quality of the character of Guy, in the act of marrying one woman while remembering another, seemed to put him at a distance from the sort of involvement one expects of a romantic comedy lead. His fourth role in just over a year was as the strident, potentially brutal government clerk in •**Oscar and Lucinda** (1998), a role secondary to those of Ralph Fiennes

and Cate •Blanchett. Variety of character interest appears to be his priority, and, as well as these very disparate film roles, he also won acclaim for his television performance as Ronald Ryan in *The Last of the Ryans* (1997). Co-starring again with Miranda Otto in **In the Winter Dark** (1998), he seems certain to be a major contender in the future of new Australian cinema—if he wants to be.

Other Australian films: Tracks of Glory (1991), **Talk** (1994), **Hayride to Hell** (1995), **Passion: The Story of Percy Grainger** (1999).   BMcF

Richard Roxburgh

Ruane, John (1952–) DIRECTOR/WRITER   John Ruane's sporadic career began as co-scriptwriter on Chris Fitchett's **Blood Money** (1980), an unusually reflective reworking of the crime-thriller genre. He also co-wrote **Cassandra** (1986), Colin •Eggleston's psychological horror film, before making his directing bow with the short film **Feathers** (1987), a 49-minute drama adapted by Ruane from a Raymond Carver story and starring Julie •Forsyth. Ruane suddenly came to prominence with •**Death in Brunswick** (1991), a curiously low-key and unique black comedy romance. How a shiftless cook (Sam •Neill) in a seedy nightclub in the Melbourne inner suburb of the title finds himself mixed up with drug-trafficking, a midnight burial, and an inter-cultural romance, as well as warding off a dominating mother, made for one of the most attractive entertainment packages of its year. It is sly, witty, alert, and ought to have ensured Ruane a busier subsequent career—should he have wanted one. In the event, he wrote and directed **That Eye the Sky** (1994), an adaptation of Tim Winton's fantasy, which won an Australian Film Institute Young Actor Award for its child star, Jamie Crofts, but which slipped in and out of cinemas without attracting much attention. Then, in 1998, the over-whimsical romance, **Dead Letter Office** (1998) appeared, written and co-produced by Deborah Cox, and starring the ubiquitous Miranda •Otto. Among the bolder successes of the 1990s, there ought to be a place for the gentler humours of films such as **Death in Brunswick**. BMcF

Rudd's New Selection

1921. Director: Raymond Longford. *Producer:* E.J. Carroll. *Scriptwriter:* Raymond Longford. Based on the stories by Steele Rudd. *Director of photography:* Arthur Higgins. 6000 ft. B&W. *Cast:* J.P. O'Neill (Dad Rudd), Ada Clyde (Mum), Tal Ordell (Dave), Lottie Lyell (Nell), Charlotte Beaumont (Sarah), Louis Fors (Joe), Gilbert Emery (Mr Dandelion).

Less than a year after •**On Our Selection,** Raymond •Longford released his second feature film about the Rudd family, with only one member of the cast of the first film—Tal Ordell as Dave. The family even has different children now, with Lottie •Lyell playing Nell, who replaces Kate as the more refined daughter. Her romance is one plot-thread, while another concerns Mr Dandelion's attempts to persuade the family to support his parliamentary candidature on a prohibition ticket. The broad comedy and the realistic setting are similar to **On Our Selection** and the film was popular, although none of it survives. IB

Rural life   Literary and visual representations of Australian rural life—of 'outback' life or life in 'the bush'—go back to the early nineteenth century. In due course, the bush became to Australians what the West had become to Americans, 'a major shaping instrument of the Australian national spirit and outlook' (*The Oxford Companion to Australian Literature*, 1994). By the turn of the century, the bush was well established as a glorified legend, a social, cultural, and national myth that ever since has inspired political thinking, the arts, and debates over national identity. Whatever the real determinants of rural life in Australia—an agricultural industry scattered about the country and a population that consists of a wide spread of social groupings (rich Whites, poor Whites, Aborigines, manual labourers of all types, miners, drovers, squatters, small farmers, settlers, shopkeepers, outback shearers, and others)—the bush myth was a simpler view of it all. The myth of bush life ignored the inherent conflicts of rural society and invented a different sort of conflict, that between the country and the

city. It put the emphasis on family-based social organisation and on efforts to fight off the hardships caused by an uncompromising environment and by such natural catastrophes as periodic droughts. From the point of view of the legend, rural life had less to do with social rankings, conflicts, forced mobility, and mixed fortunes, than with such virtues as stability, egalitarian mateship, and allround existential competence. Seen in this way, the bush was not so much a place as a state of mind.

However, the bush myth, which was above all a city legend, had a complexity of its own. As John Tulloch writes, 'the squatters emphasised the manly independence and fortitude which had transformed a wasteland into a pastoral paradise … The farmers epitomised their status as the moral as well as the economic backbone of a country fast expanding away from the eastern city vices. The selectors emphasised the purifying ritual of seasonal hardships' (*Legends on the Screen*, 1981). The bush myth relied on a belief in the redemptive and purifying quality of bush life and the corrupting and soul-destroying nature of city life. The bush legend incorporated these beliefs in a variety of social and thematic structures—the hero as pastoralist, farmer, jackeroo, drover, station worker, shearer, swagman, villainous overseer, bushranger—and in the enduring antithesis of city and bush. Adherence to the bush myth reinforced, throughout the arts and in cultural politics, the Romantic and modernist habit of thinking, writing, and filming in opposites.

Bushranging was the topic of both the first Australian drama to be performed on the stage (*The Bushrangers*, 1828, by David Burn) and the first Australian full-length feature film, •**The Story of the Kelly Gang** (1906), of which six other versions were made in subsequent years. Films on bushrangers drew on a rich body of nineteenth-century literature in which the bushranger often figures as an ambiguous character caught between criminality and social protest against corrupt government action and excessive forms of authoritarianism. Many bushrangers (for example, John Donohoe, Matthew Brady, Ben Hall, Frank Gardiner, Captain Thunderbolt, and Ned Kelly) have entered the pantheon of Australian folklore and have thus become essential components of the bush legend. Most films about bushranging (•**Robbery Under Arms**, 1907, based on Australia's most famous bushranging novel; **The Life and Adventures of John Vane**, 1910; •**Thunderbolt**, 1910; **Captain Midnight**, 1911) were made between 1906 and 1912; in 1912 the NSW Police Department banned bushranging films. The ban was not lifted until the 1940s and had a powerful influence on Australian popular culture: 'The entire folklore relating to bushrangers was effectively removed from the most popular form of cultural expression' (Pike and Cooper, *Australian Film: 1900–1977*, 1998). The Australians had lost their West. The remakes of these early bushranging films (in the 1950s, 1960s, and 1970s) benefitted from the improved technical capabilities of cinema but, on the whole, lagged behind the originals in thematic urgency and melodramatic power.

The years between 1906 and 1914, the most productive and nationalistic period for the Australian cinema, witnessed the screening of outback Australia. Anything from stories of the convict days (**For the Term of His Natural Life**, 1908) to fantasies of station life in the outback (•**The Squatter's Daughter**, 1910 and **The Land of the Wattle**, 1910), to romantic bush yarns (•**The Romantic Story of Margaret Catchpole**, 1911), and, of course bushranging adventures, became subject matter for films. But it was not until after World War I, when talented film-makers such as Raymond •Longford, Franklyn •Barrett, and Beaumont •Smith appeared on the scene, that the rural film came into its own and established a thematic and narrative tradition that has remained resilient until today.

The agile film-maker/showman Beaumont Smith cashed in on the surge in comedy (after the waning of war stories) and a renewed interest in nationalism (which more often than not goes hand in hand with revivals of the bush legend) just before, and immediately after, the end of World War I, when he initiated the Hayseeds film series (•**Our Friends the Hayseeds**, 1917; **The Hayseeds Come to Town**, 1917; **The Hayseeds' Melbourne Cup**, 1918; **Townies and Hayseeds**, 1923), adaptations of the rural stories of Steele Rudd. The Hayseeds series seems to be driven by an appreciation of the popular qualities of the story. Most of his other feature films, such as **The Man from Snowy River** (1920) and **While the Billy Boils** (1921) have a similarly calculated and formulaic quality about them. But it was Raymond Longford's •**On Our Selection** (1920) that brought about real changes in adaptations of bush narratives: a new sincerity (a relaxation of the moralising aspect of the bush/city antithesis), the strenghtening of the realistic mode ('The true art of acting is not to act' is a typical Longford statement), and thematic purpose (with the emphasis on the tough conditions and experiences of rural life, as against farce and comedy). **On Our Selection** and its sequel •**Rudd's New Selection** (1921) were based on, and contributed to, the enduring success of Steele Rudd's 'Dad and Dave' stories (originally written for the *Bulletin* and collectively published in 1899). Future adaptations of Rudd's 'Dad and Dave' stories benefited from Longford's approach.

The two complete surviving feature films by Franklyn Barrett became, like many of Longford's films, something like blueprints for subsequent films. •**The Breaking of the Drought** (1920) works with an impressively naturalistic concept of human existence and is now valued not only as a documentary record of the harsh conditions of life in the country, but also as an authentic record of the slum-like nature of much city life at the time. The drought scenes were filmed with such naturalism that the whole film was thought to be too harmful to Australia's image for export, and it led to a tightening of Commonwealth censorship laws (see •Censorship).

•**A Girl of the Bush** (1921) also stands in the tradition of films that hold that rural life embodies the indomitable Australian spirit at its best. Once more there is the persistent contrast between sanctioned country values and urban evil, and the tightly packed plot is entirely determined by the principles of documentary realism. The film has been criticised for the melodramatic posturing of its stage-trained actors, and for its all-too-obvious commitment to the ideals of Australian nationalism. A more positive assessment would recognise the way in which naturalistic plot details modify idealised notions of bush life.

With the arrival of sound in 1930–31 and the establishment of •Cinesound in 1932, Australian film entered, despite the Depression, a new era of successful and profitable film-making. The rural film once more came into prominence. The first production of Cinesound, under the management of Ken G. •Hall, was yet another version of •**On Our Selection** (1932). The film, a record success at the box office, was a clever mix of bucolic themes presented in the comic and melodramatic mode, and it once and for all established Dad Rudd as the inimitable grass-roots folk hero. Longford's naturalistic version had found a modern, sophisticated, ideologically less-oppressive counterpart. Hall's commitment to a method of film-making that does not neglect entertainment, audience expectations, and commercial viability, and his unashamed flirtation with familiar Hollywood models, is also a hallmark of his other films on rural topics: •**The Squatter's Daughter** (1933), •**Grandad Rudd** (1935), •**Dad and Dave Come to Town** (1938) and the carefully structured and dramatic •**Dad Rudd, MP** (1940). The 'Dad and Dave' series might easily have continued for another decade but for the intervention of World War II.

The war years were a busy period for the Australian film industry (propaganda films, newsreel coverage of the war), but feature production was all but halted. Of the two major directors of this period, Ken Hall and Charles •Chauvel, it was the latter who, true to his belief that 'the only way in which we can give a film an international appeal is to make it Australian', contributed two narratives to the lean postwar years. •**Sons of Matthew** (1949) is a rural drama on a large scale, an epic story of heroic men pitted against natural catastrophes, such as bushfires and cyclones, and firmly tied to a landscape that becomes an integral part of the plot. •**Jedda** (1955), Chauvel's last film and the first feature in colour by an Australian company, is a similar attempt to give structural prominence to Australian landscapes—the rainforests of south-east Queensland and the Central Australian desert—and to allow geographical features to achieve the status of actors in the narrative. Jedda is, above all, a landmark in the portrayal of Aborigines on the screen, subtly depicting the dilemma in the relationship between uprooted Aborigines and liberal Whites, and was an inspiring influence on films as diverse as Nicolas Roeg's •Walkabout (1971), Peter •Weir's •The Last Wave (1977), Fred •Schepisi's •The Chant of Jimmie Blacksmith (1978), Tim •Burstall's •The Naked Country (1985), and Bruce •Beresford's •The Fringe Dwellers (1986).

When feature production in Australia reached an all-time low in the 20 years after World War II, it was British and American companies that maintained the interest in the Australian outback and bush themes. Although many of their products (such as •Kangaroo, 1952; Long John Silver, 1954; and Strong is the Seed, 1955) were hardly more than commercial exercises, at least one of them, Harry Watt's •The Overlanders (1946) reflected a genuine desire to come to terms with Australian realities and to present an Australian story—the overland drive in 1942 of 100 000 head of cattle from the NT to the Queensland coast—to foreign audiences. Two other films, Jack •Lee's •Robbery Under Arms (1957) and Tony Richardson's •Ned Kelly (1970), further testify to the ongoing interest, on the part of foreign film-makers, in the bush myth.

With the revival of the Australian film industry during the 1970s (see Revival, the), the rural film virtually disappeared as a specific film genre, with the exception of such films as •The Man from Snowy River (1982), but the new Australian cinema soon discovered an unparalleled sense of the symbolic power of Australian landscape features. It made sophisticated use of the ambiguous quality of essentialist geographical myths in films as different as the period film (•Picnic at Hanging Rock, 1975), the social realist film (•Sunday Too Far Away, 1975), and the 'social problem' film (•Shame, 1988). Much contemporary Australian cinema is, in fact, landscape cinema. The notion of a powerful, mysterious, and archaic nature is a fact of Australian culture, as it may be a fact of American (popular) culture, and as it is no longer a fact of European culture. In Europe this possibility has long been destroyed by the way Europeans have defused and familiarised concepts of nature and by sentimental cultural forms such as the Heimatfilm.

The new Australian cinema has, above all, exploited the duality of menace and redeeming sublimity, the 'terrible beauty' so characteristic of the landscape myth: for example, in films such as •Wake in Fright (1971), •Long Weekend (1977), The Chant of Jimmie Blacksmith (1978), •Gallipoli (1981), •We of the Never Never (1982), and even in lesser films such as The Winds of Jarrah (1983), •Travelling North

(1987), and the satire-cum-fairy-tale-adventure romance •Crocodile Dundee (1986).

More direct continuations of the old-style rural film, such as •Dad and Dave: On Our Selection (1995) tended to be more critical successes than crowd pleasers. The 1990s, however, also ushered in a new brand of outback film that was not so much interested in foregrounding or celebrating a time-honoured formula, as in using the formula as a framework for the exploration of contemporary issues. Although David •Elfick's •No Worries (one of the best Australian films of 1993) comes nearest to the old rural film blueprint—complete with droughts, floods, and dust storms—it nevertheless puts the emphasis squarely on a modern theme: for the stricken family, life in the city occurs in the midst of a multicultural community. •Road to Nhill (1997) explores the idiosyncracies of life in a small country town: a road accident shocks the townspeople into a new awareness of the hidden traps and dangers of their self-absorbed ways of living, depicting the head-in-the-sand complacency of small-town people everywhere. There is ample reason to believe that there will always be film-makers and audiences in Australia who like it 'outback'.

FRANZ KUNA

Rural myth   The cultural importance of myths of rural existence is evident in the central role they play within Australian narrative traditions. Australian film has foregrounded rural settings, exploited the distinctiveness of the Australian landscape, and represented country communities as models of social organisation just as enthusiastically as has Australian fiction. While the influence of the myths associated with the bush and country life does vary over the history of the industry, they are visible in a wide range of Australian films, from •The Squatter's Daughter (1910) to •The Adventures of Priscilla, Queen of the Desert (1994). Like many other settler societies, White Australia has been avid in its attention to the landscape it has appropriated, working hard to generate a mythological depth that will give it meaning and secure it as a marker of national identity. Throughout the first three decades of the film industry's history in Australia, and again in the first decade of its revival during the 1970s (see Revival, the), the representation of rural life has been a key strategy for proposing Australia's distinctiveness. More recently, we have seen the rural myths challenged by a new focus on urban and suburban life. This too has been in response to new influences motivating a process of redefinition of the Australian identity.

The beginning of the Australian film industry was dominated by films dealing with rural subjects. Many of these films drew on the so-called 'bush myth' of the 1890s, the subjects and values associated with the fiction of Henry

Lawson, Joseph Furphy, and Steele Rudd. Like other rural myths, the bush myth presents a particular form of experience as natural and authentic, and it enabled rural existence to be broadly accepted as quintessentially Australian from the 1890s to at least the 1970s. According to *The Australian Legend* (1958), Russell Ward's account of this strain of Australian social history, life in the Australian bush nurtured a distinctive brand of egalitarianism and a code of cooperation that became fundamental to the Australian national character. Typically, it was a way of life built on surviving the encounter with a landscape that was alien and inhospitable but, nevertheless, more productive as a source of personal and spiritual opportunities than was early Australian society. It was a way of life, too, that was characterised as masculine. As some of the writers of the 1890s describe it, colonial society provided a place for women, whereas those charged with negotiating some accommodation between the demands of society and the dangers of the landscape were laconic, resourceful, and stoical men. This is a mythology that grew out of communities of rural, itinerant workers, and had the effect of privileging a model of social organisation based almost entirely on masculine work—the famous system of •mateship.

Compared with analogous myths from the USA or the United Kingdom, the Australian rural myth is distinctive. Whereas the structure of the confrontation with the landscape for the American individual is encapsulated in the western—the intrepid individual prevails over the landscape and the society; and whereas the British individual may tame the landscape but succumb to the society; the Australian individual is stranded in the middle of the nature–culture divide, alienated from a banal society and hostile nature, forced to accept survival on terms determined by the land. From this fundamental dilemma much Australian narrative flows, resulting in a set of mythologies that establish the national type of the bushman and an idealised version of the bush as Australian icons.

Early Australian silent films such as •**The Sentimental Bloke** (1919), •**On Our Selection** (1920), and •**Rudd's New Selection** (1921) drew directly on the literary sources identified with this new national type and their classic locations. In *Legends on the Screen: The Narrative Film in Australia 1919–29* (1981), John Tulloch demonstrates the centrality of the bush myth to such early Australian films as •**The Breaking of the Drought** (1920), •**A Girl of the Bush** (1921), and •**The Man from Snowy River** (1920). He shows how they employ the myths and reinforce the value systems Russell Ward was to identify in *The Australian Legend*. Similarly, Bruce Molloy's *Before the Interval* (1990) traces these influences into early Australian talkies of the 1930s and 1940s. From the 1940s to the end of the 1960s, a period when Australian film production almost halted while Hol-

lywood or British films were shot here, most films made in Australia were based on definitions of the Australian experience that were almost uniformly rural. Whether they were produced primarily for an Australian audience, such as •**Smiley** (1956) and •**The Back of Beyond** (1954), or by foreign studios for an international audience, such as •**The Shiralee** (1957) and •**The Sundowners** (1960), Australian films during this period foreground the landscape and the communal myths of rural existence. It's not surprising then, that this influence continued, and was probably even enhanced initially, during the first years of the revival.

The Australian experience represented through these myths was often grim: bush life was hard, elemental, and unforgiving. However, we can see a change in the mode of their representation in our films over time. The early films, such as the **Dad and Dave** comedies or •**A Girl of the Bush**, adopt a cheerfully celebratory perspective on the hardships depicted as fundamental to the Australian way of life. Testing as these hardships were, they built character that in turn helped build a resourceful and resilient nature. By the time of the revival of the 1970s, however, the bush legend was regarded with a little more ambivalence. •**Sunday Too Far Away** (1975) recognises the authenticity and value of the male-dominated world of rural work, but it also views it nostalgically, as an anachronistic way of life soon to disappear. Similarly, colonial period dramas such as •**The Irishman** (1978) or •**The Picture Show Man** (1977) nostalgically depict rural occupations embedded in a way of life that has now gone.

Notwithstanding such ambivalence, the foregrounding of the landscape in these revival films was an essential element in their attempt to address an Australian audience. Indeed, the revival of Australian film derived a great deal of its credibility for Australian audiences, and its distinctive appeal for foreign audiences, from the way it looked and what it looked at. Foreign co-productions had, in the past, failed to get 'the look' of the Australian landscape right, primarily because the film stock used had never been able to handle the harshness of the Australian light. Partly as a result of technological developments in film stock, Australian films of the revival were able to represent the landscape, the light, and the physical location accurately—exciting recognition from Australian audiences and generating a strong sense of the exotic for foreign audiences. It became clear, very quickly, that the Australian bush offered new images for audiences to consume. Further, the Australian bush already contained a store of Australian fictions to put on the screen. Adaptations of novels and stories set in the bush and period dramas offering stories of pioneering or convict society dominated the first decade of the revival as contemporary subjects—despite the initial burst of 'ocker' comedies that delighted audiences but alarmed the funding bodies—routinely failed to attract funding.

Cruel as such a proposition may seem, there is a standard opening for Australian films of the 1970s. We first see a vista of bush, often empty and flat. Against this background, the main character is immediately positioned in terms of conflict, the vulnerability of their tenure or that of human society. Dominated by this challenge, but still undeterred, the individual moves into the tide of the story. Films that commence this way include •Picnic at Hanging Rock (1975), **Sunday Too Far Away** (1975), •**Wake in Fright** (1971), •**My Brilliant Career** (1979), and one could name many more. Criticism of the repetitiousness of this genre (what Dermody and Jacka (1988) call the Australian Film Commission genre) increased during the decade as audiences tired too. The dominance of the period drama declined from the early 1980s, moving to television in the first wave of miniseries and informing many successful primetime drama series thereafter (*A Country Practice* and *Blue Heelers* for instance) as a testament to the tenacity of the rural myth's continuing hold on the popular imagination.

Some variation in the narrative and ideological function of the rural myth, however, developed in Australian film during the 1980s. Traditional bush myths influence the **Mad Max** trilogy but without the nationalist overtones or the nostalgic complacency found in some of the earlier period dramas. •**The Man from Snowy River** (1982) breaks with the tradition of cool, cultured, and enigmatic cinematography typical of such respected films as **Picnic at Hanging Rock** as it sends the camera hurtling around the mountains in an exuberant and unequivocal celebration of the landscape. •**Crocodile Dundee** (1986) exploits the potential for self-parody within the bush myth by simultaneously offering up rural models of behaviour for nationalist admiration and comic appreciation, while spreading the spectacular landscape of Kakadu all over the screen. Some films have told stories that develop sharply explicit critiques of the Australian legend and referred knowingly to the visual conventions associated with it. Steve •Jodrell's •**Shame** (1988) examines the regressive side of one rural community and its entrapment within the value system of mateship, while •**The Umbrella Woman** (1987) investigates what the rural community offers to the women stranded within it. Alternatively, **The Adventures of Priscilla, Queen of the Desert**, definitely urban and contemporary in the detail of its subject matter, offers a surprisingly traditional account of the encounter between the individual and the Australian landscape that indicates the ready currency of the myths of rural existence for even the most urban of film-makers.

The key variation, however, lay in the increasing attention the 1990s directed towards Australian suburban life—so much that it seemed as if myths of suburban existence were now competing with the rural myths for centrality in the representational repertoire of Australian film. Representations of contemporary suburban existence excited the kind of recognition and affection Australian audiences once offered to representations of country life. **The Heartbreak Kid** (1993), •**Muriel's Wedding** (1994), •**Mr Reliable** (1996) and •**The Castle** (1997) are all examples of this. Far from desiring only complacent renditions of suburban existence, however, audiences also turned out to see such confronting films as •**Romper Stomper** (1992) and **Idiot Box** (1997).

The rural myths have helped Australian films to structure their narratives and to address their local audiences. However, their function in the 1980s and 1990s became conservative and even anachronistic. By looking backwards to an idealised rendition of the national past that could not help denying black histories, many Australian films of the 1970s found it quite difficult to offer critical appraisals either of Australian colonial history or its outcomes. The conservatism was evident in a stylistic complacency, too, a reliance on tasteful art direction and visual conventions that squandered some of the opportunities of popular feature films. While these myths retain their meaning and their cultural potential, it is significant that they no longer dominate Australian films, now giving way to narratives eager to reflect, and reflect on, a wider range of contemporary locations.

GRAEME TURNER

Rush, Geoffrey (1951–) ACTOR When Geoffrey Rush won the Best Actor Oscar for 1996, this was a triumphant moment not only for one of Australia's most respected actors but also for Australian cinema. It vindicated the film-makers' faith in an *actor* rather than a star, suggesting that the film industry can sometimes be guided by its most intelligent perceptions rather than mere box-office considerations. Born in Qld, Rush began as an amateur actor in Brisbane; he went to an acting school in Paris in the 1960s, and returned to work with the Queensland Theatre Company. He had acquired a high reputation as a theatre actor, in everything from Shakespeare to Wilde, before beginning in films with the tiny role of a detective in the underrated thriller, •**Hoodwink** (1981). He repeated his stage role as Aguecheek in the filmed version of Neil Armfield's production of •**Twelfth Night** (1987). Rush played a fine role as the foolish Dave in the surprisingly unsuccessful •**Dad and Dave: On Our Selection** (1995), its bizarre physicality recalling his stage performance as one of the funniest Jack Worthings ever in *The Importance of Being Earnest*; and his talent for comedy was tapped again in a very different role in •**Children of the Revolution** (1996).

In the latter, he played Zachary Welch, the long-suffering, gently ineffectual husband of committed, humourless (and very funny) Joan, played by Judy •Davis. It was fascinating to watch Rush make so much of his seemingly

Geoffrey Rush

self-effacing role, coming so soon after the pyrotechnics of *Shine. In **Shine**, he played the controversial pianist David Helfgott, whose career has also been reactivated by the film. Profoundly disturbed, scarred by his relations with his taskmaster-father, talking incessantly and smoking wildly, Rush played Helfgott with a passionate intensity perhaps unique in Australian cinema. Again, though, he showed glimpses of the humour that never seems far from the surface of any Rush performance or, indeed, from his off-screen persona, as evidenced in the interviews he conducts with rare articulateness. And following the worldwide success of **Shine**, with all manner of awards for Rush's performance, he became an unusual celebrity, able to talk intelligently and wittily about his work and his own surprising stardom.

Geoffrey Rush's *annus mirabilis* came in 1996, with **Shine**, **Children of the Revolution** and the excellent, lowkey television series *Mercury*, which is set in a city newspaper office. Rush (and the writers) carefully avoided noisy stereotypes in the character of the chief editor, Bill Wyatt. It is of course unlikely that Australian cinema can hope to contain a star of Rush's magnitude; he has starring roles in big-budget international films such as **Elizabeth** (1998), **Shakespeare in Love** (1998), and **Les Misérables** (1999). He provided the voice-over in Gillian *Armstrong's *Oscar and Lucinda** (1998), as Oscar's great-grandson. He is married to the actor Jane Menalaus, so family ties may ensure that Australian cinema will have a place in his future.

Other Australian films: *Star Struck (1982), Call Me Sal (1996, short), A Little Bit of Soul (1997). BMcF

Ryan, Ellery (1946–) CINEMATOGRAPHER After graduating with Honours from the Swinburne School of Film and Television (see Victorian College of the Arts School of Film and Television) in 1975, Ellery Ryan worked as camera assistant and then director of photography at Fred *Schepisi's Film House before freelancing from 1982, mainly on films and miniseries for television. The high quality of his work was first recognised when his second feature film, *Grievous Bodily Harm (1988) was nominated for an Australia Film Institute (AFI) cinematography award, as was *Death in Brunswick (1991) and That Eye The Sky (1994), which won the Critics Circle award for best cinematography. He has twice won the AFI Best Cinematography Award, for *Spotswood (1992) and *Angel Baby (1995), which also won him an Australian Cinematographers Society Gold award for best cinematography on a feature film.

Ryan has worked on many other films. These include **Desolation Angels** (1982), **Bit Part** (1987), **Harbour Beat** (1990), **Gino** (1994),*Cosi (1996), **Wishful Thinking** (USA, 1997), **The Matchmaker** (UK, 1997), and **Dead Letter Office** (1998).

DAVID MUIR

Rydge, Norman, *see* Greater Union Organisation; Village Roadshow; Cinesound

In conversation with

GEOFFREY RUSH

You've become one of the most famous film stars in the world since •Shine. Has this kind of status come as a shock, been difficult to cope with?

It's funny to hear you say the word 'film star'. I still deep down feel I'm a character actor, and I would probably like to call myself a film *actor*, because the word 'star' seems to associate itself with other cultures and different eras of commercial movie-making that I've never really been part of.

I'm aware of the recognition factor, of a kind of profile that is in contrast to having been a stage actor for so many years. There you do feel, particularly in Australia, in terms of the public knowing that you or your profession exists, that you're hiding under a very dark rock. So by contrast it feels to a degree exposed, but there's an aspect of it that I quite enjoy because it gives me a chance to pump up the image of the industry a bit.

And it presumably gives you a lot more choice?

Yes. I've facetiously said in an interview that I feel as though I've been offered every Australian film that's about to be made. But I can't say that I've ever had lean years because I was very happy with the direction my theatrical life always took. I found my niche in the theatre in marginalised eccentric character parts, and that seemed to be developing at quite a good rate for me. But when films got offered they tended to be for one scene in something and I'd think, well, I *could* do that but I'd be turning down Autolycus in *The Winter's Tale* over in Adelaide or Thersites with a company in Brisbane, and I thought these were much more interesting.

As a character actor, the choice may always be wider to you…

I don't know how I'm seen. I think at the moment there's probably a saturation of too many offers in Australia that I have to sift through and think, 'That's a rather silly choice. I'm not right for that and there's a much better actor to play that part', but, yes, the choice is great and I'm really glad now. In the 1980s there was a general feel that the kind of screen persona that was most dominant was for those kinds of roles that were

played by Mel [•Gibson] or Colin •Friels or Bryan •Brown, you know what I mean …

Very obvious 'leading-man roles'?

Yes, there was a particular genre. And when •Shine came along people were a bit taken aback, thinking, 'We just didn't expect to see a major drama with that kind of central figure'. Take a character like David Helfgott: you don't often have a character with such an aberrant personality at the very centre of the film. I would say for me it was an extension of the kind of things I've done on stage because the characters at the centre of all the great classical plays are strange, kind of pushed to an extreme, and I don't think in movies that it generally is the case that the hero is absolutely that far outside of society. A lot of the sponsoring people, when they first saw the film, didn't know about David. They weren't too sure if they were going to feel comfortable spending the whole film with this person.

How did you first get involved with Shine?

They were casting in 1992. The first I heard of it was when Brenda Lister, my agent, rang me up and said, 'You've got to come down to the office. I've just read the most extraordinary script. I cried'. Agents don't cry when they read scripts, they're too busy. So I went down and read it and it was a great read. Every other time I've read a script, to me it always seemed like such a recipe book. I was used to plays with chunky dialogue and big scenes or weighty ideas or whatever, and I would read the script and think it will really depend on what the director does with this, because I'm not getting the tone of the film on the page. Shine had that. It was terribly well written, so that you could get a glimpse of what the power of the film might be. Then I went along to meet Scott •Hicks, and I think I might have done something for the camera, I can't recall. What I found out later was that they were always determined to offer me the role. I just didn't expect in those days that people offered you things.

Had they seen you on the stage?

Yes, Scott was from Adelaide and he'd seen quite a few things from the early to mid 1980s that I'd done on stage, and I found out later that Liz •Mullinar [agent] had said to him when she'd read the script that there was only one actor in the country that could play this, which was very flattering, and that was me. There was uncertainty at that stage of the script whether there would be two Davids or three Davids, or the turnover point from who played what age group. I think ultimately that they were looking for an eight-year-old boy, an adolescent, and then probably someone around 30 who could play 20 and 40 with a bit of make-up. I was far too old at that point to convincingly play 20, but Scott got so excited by the test that we did and then Noah [•Taylor] came on board. I'm always amazed when I see the film; Noah was something like 26 or 27 when we shot the movie, but he's a very convincing pubescent Jewish boy undergoing his bar-mitzvah at 13. So, once that combination happened, the script was adjusted in some ways to tell the story in that way. Because everyone was aware of the pitfalls of the 'biopic'—you get used to a character for 20 minutes' screentime, and then he gets dumped and somebody else comes along, and you just have to accept that we're now into the next phase of the life, and so on.

The biopic was a very unusual genre to find in Australian film-making.
Yes. I think it is a biopic, but everyone was aware of wanting to avoid what had become the cliché of that particular genre. Sometimes you need some of the building blocks of storytelling to take an audience with you and you've just got to find fresh ways of doing that. I think the real germ of the script was layering with that series of flashbacks and having me appear at the beginning and then through strange kinds of jumps. David's life does just jump around in his mind.

In the original script, there was another layer of the film that involved David and Gillian making a journey back to London. That was what was triggering all of the memories within memories and the last scene had a shot of me going back ultimately to visit Sir John Gielgud, who would have been 111 at the time—20 years later! Actually, I think he had his 91st birthday on the set.

How did you find Scott Hicks as a director? Did he in fact give you a lot of direction?
It was a curious procedure really. We got on terribly well, and in some ways he gave me a lot of leeway, because it was three years before we actually got in

front of the cameras. I signed on at the end of 1992 and met David, and we'd done camera tests. We were due to start filming in early 1993, but then the finance kept falling through and we didn't actually get in front of the cameras until early 1995. In that time we would just keep meeting up: I'd get a phone call every six months saying, 'It's been pushed further down the track'. And in that time Scott and I developed this understanding of each other. He could see that I liked to pore over research material. I listened to lots of tapes of David, watched lots of videos of him, met him a few times. There was some great material there at my disposal, David having been a fairly popular current affairs item in the mid 1980s when he made the comeback at the wine bars. There was a lot of coverage on *Willesee* and *Nationwide*, and so on. It was better for me to look at David as he was then 10 years ago, rather than as he was when we were making the film.

There is presumably a major challenge in playing a living celebrity?
Yes, I didn't really want to assault his personal life too much. I didn't want him to feel as though I was spying on him or digging my way into him. I mean, just for himself and for Gillian and his immediate family, I felt I had to be truthful enough and honest enough to honour him for the kind of personality that he was.

I'd spent about four months with a tutor because I knew for myself that to really persuade an audience that I was a prodigiously talented concert pianist I couldn't bluff my way through that too much, and I knew for myself as an actor that I wanted to have shots in the film that were wide enough to show my hands, my elbows, my shoulders, my head, and the keyboard all within the one frame where I was actually—presumably—doing it. Of course it is David playing and I'm miming, but I didn't want any close-ups of eyes, cut away to the hands, whatever. I knew that was sort of an aspect of the character that had to be nailed and it took some research, just as attuning myself to David's speech patterns took some work. Scott was very impressed and pleased with the kind of commitment that I made to it, but there came a point when he said, 'You must also realise that David exists in this script as a certain character to serve the nature of this particular narrative. We're not doing a documentary of his whole life so there's also got to be aspects of you in there to make this character live.' So to a degree I had to make it my own and not feel as though I was just doing an impression of David, or taking on a few of his more noticeable attributes. When you meet David at first most people feel as though they're thrown into a bit of a social deep end and they're not sure how they're going to manage this extraordinary generosity of contact, and invasion of space and barrage of dialogue and thoughts, but you kind of jump into the stream and go with it and that's how the film attempts to operate.

What about the other challenge—I mean chronologically in story time you have to give the impression that you've grown out of Noah Taylor. Were you conscious of this?
Oh very much so. People generally wanted to hear an answer that suggested there was some sort of symbiotic para-psychological experience for us, but the sort of things we talked about were just tiny details like: how do you hold your cigarettes? how do you push your glasses? when do we first begin to see the beginnings of some breakdown in the speech patterns? I think Noah is a bit of an unsung hero in this film because he had to completely invent an adolescence that he couldn't observe or could only draw from the script and certainly couldn't see in the existing David, the man who was in his late 40s when we shot the film. So he had to invent that and he just had to work backwards and join up some of those dots between childhood and maturity. People say to me now they recall scenes from the film that I actually wasn't in, which is a great compliment. It was actually the other actor.

How do you account for the extraordinary international success of the film?
I don't know, it certainly did make a big splash. I think a little bit of it is to do with what I was talking about earlier in terms of its freshness and how disarming and unexpected the central character of the film was. There's an intrinsic fascination for most people in confronting a personality like David's, to be seduced by it, in the same way that he does so wonderfully when he performs. There's a curious magnetic appeal there that digs deep into people and they don't expect that from cinema any more. And this was a mainstream movie; it didn't get tucked away in art cinemas where you think we're going to have a kind of difficult experience.

Did that success surprise you?
No, because everyone handled it so well. Fineline in America and •Ronin Films here were exemplary after the buzz that emerged from Sundance. They kept it under wraps here for about seven months I think. They just let enough little bits out to the press to tease everyone, so that when it opened people were very keen and it had a 'must see' aura to it. It had done a few festivals, and there was talk in the industry about 'this extraordinary film **Shine**'. And then we got some nominations and some awards, from the New York Film Critics' Circle and the LA Film Critics' Circle, and then there was a Golden Globe nomination, and the film started to play in a few more cinemas. Then we won a Golden Globe and an Oscar nomination, and it was playing in more cinemas. By the time it was Oscar-nominated, it was playing in 800 or 1000 cinemas in the USA, which is a fair cultural impact.

What the Awards did in terms of raising the profile of the all the people involved with the film from the makers to the technicians to the cast, and in its role as a representative for that moment in time of the Australian film industry, was fantastic. I don't think it hurts on a marketplace level to know that people have a real interest in the films that we're making here.

You had a long and respected career as a stage actor before being involved in films and I wondered in general how useful you found this stage training when it came to making films?
Up until **Shine** I'd made one major film, •**Dad and Dave: On Our Selection**, which was shot at the end of 1994, so it was about three months before **Shine**. I'd been in the stage version of *On Our Selection* that George Whaley had directed back in 1979 and George had been talking about putting it on screen for years. Prior to that we'd done a film version of a very successful stage production of •*Twelfth Night* which Neil Armfield directed in South Australia.

It's a quite interesting film but it's not completely a film; there's something still a bit stagey about it. And before that I'd done a spit and a cough in •**Star Struck** and a bit in •**Hoodwink**. I think that's all, so I wasn't really in tune with the medium at all. I've heard this about me: 'Oh I don't know if we can use Geoffrey Rush for a film, it'll be too big, he's from the theatre'. And there's a degree of truth in that because the sort of technique you use on the stage where you might be playing to 2000 people at the Comedy Theatre in Melbourne is certainly going to be different to what you use in front of a camera that's two feet away. I just think it's a question of degree and knowing where your audience is placed. And the great myth I grew up with is that on film you've got to pull it all back in, and not show anything, let the camera seek it out, let the camera discover it in you, and just 'be' on screen. Now, David Helfgott is not the sort of character you can just 'be'! The guy's spilling out all over the place, he's physically and verbally very extravagant, and Scott Hicks was great in that respect. He just said, 'Know where the audience is, I'm only three feet away and I'm right next to you, you don't have to project it, play it truthfully for me'. Now that I've seen myself on screen a few times, I'm starting to toy with how little you can do in certain scenes and how *much* you can do because I love seeing big passionate performances on film.

I agree but you can also have the rewards of very small effects on screen, and I thought you came nearest to that in Mercury *on television where it seemed to me you were very deliberately resisting being a stereotypical loud newspaperman …*
Sure, and that was part of the reason for doing it: the chance for me to train myself in front of a camera, because I did that series for something like six months. It was just wonderful to do that on a daily basis for 26 weeks or something.

I'd still like to think I'm at school on this one. After all of the public success of **Shine**, I had the good fortune of being offered the role of Javert in **Les Misérables**. Now that performance is by my standards so minimalist I hope it registered; it's had a wonderful response from people which is fantastic. That was a deliberate actorial choice to grab something where I could test myself to see how still, how rich a definition and rhythm you could give to a character while externalising hardly any of it.

Is it true that the first thing you did in Shine *was in fact the comeback performance?*
No, it was second. The first day we shot the wedding, which was great to do. It was a big group scene and it was very joyous—it was a good one to warm up with. And then the second day we shot literally the second-last scene of the film, which is where he breaks down at the final concert. That was an extraordinary day for me, it was one of those days that I would probably always think of as a great career moment. We had 300 extras being shifted around to fill the screen and create this impression of the auditorium being packed. We didn't particularly want David or Gillian on set when we were

filming scenes about them because we just felt a little too difficult. I didn't want to feel judged; I wanted to be the only David Helfgott on set so that people got used to the character I was creating without making comparisons. And also just a practical thing: David on the floor would be having such a wonderful time, going round embracing and talking to everyone, so that you'd get nothing done. But on this particular day Gillian turned up because it was a special thing for her as she'd been at the equivalent of that 10 years earlier. I knew that I had to go on and play a fairly momentous scene and I wasn't quite sure what to do with it. And there were maybe two or three lines of dialogue only at the edge of the stage where Lynn [Redgrave] is crying and there's a standing ovation. Lynn came to me and said, 'Don't be upset but Gillian's here—she wants to sit in with the crowd. She's crying. She just saw you in the shirt.' And I was at my most David Helfgott, because I had one of David's concert shirts on, and the glasses. Lynn said, 'She just saw you warming up backstage and went "Oh my God it's David"'. For me it was just a fantastic endorsement. It was the best review I think I could ever get, and that put a certain emotional wash over the whole day.

They shot all the other stuff: the crowd standing up, clapping, and the dialogue. Then, they finally swung the camera around and came to do my close-up: I felt a bit blocked and a bit self-conscious. The trigger for me was Marta Kaczmarek, who played my mother in the film, a Polish actress from Perth. Suddenly, I'm looking out at all these people clapping and cheering and stomping, and they were so genuine for each take, and among all that I saw what Marta was doing off camera. She could have had a stand-in there if she wanted but she was sitting there and quietly setting off this bombshell, this emotional powder keg of something so deeply European, and I thought, my God, you're offering me all that off-camera and I thought that's what this scene's about: the fact that everyone is there. Ben Rosen's come back, the sisters are there, the mother's there, Gillian's there, all the people who've had such an impact on his life—but his father isn't! And it played, and Scott kept filming beyond what the planned sequence was. When he said, 'Cut!', everyone went very quiet; it was a nice actorial moment.

To go back, how did you come to be in those earlier films? Had you been wanting to get into films anyway?
I'd studied in Paris at the LeCoq School and came back to fulfil a kind of a bond I suppose because the

Queensland Theatre Company had given me some money to pay for my fees in the last year of school and I had to come back and work for them on salary for 6 months at some point before 1980. I think that was the agreement. Anyway I came back in early 1978 to do *King Lear* with Warren Mitchell and that took me to Sydney. In 1979 and 1981 I was living and working in Sydney and that's when I did *On Our Selection* on the stage.

It was the Jane Street Company and that's where I first met Kerry •Walker, Mel •Gibson, Robert Menzies and all those people, and I'd had three years of a quite good profile for someone new to the town. Quite a few films were happening. And Gillian •Armstrong was a buddy in a way: I can't remember auditioning, so I think she must have offered me the **Star Struck** role. It was quite good because I had about eight days when they were filming the big Opera House sequence at the end with the concert. I had very little to do but it was nice to get to see the film being made. And I just went along to meet Claude Whatham, who directed **Hoodwink,** and I quite liked the fact that he was casting me as a detective because no-one else was going to do that in Australia!

I haven't looked at **Hoodwink** for years, but I remember when we made it it was right out of whack with the kinds of films that generally were being made, as was **Star Struck**—it was a musical comedy. They've both got extraordinary qualities to them.

Why do you think Dad and Dave *didn't go on to be a big success?*
I don't know. It was of those *Zeitgeist* things. My memory of doing it on stage back in 1979 was when there was a certain retro quality about doing that kind of play. We were doing it in tandem with *Waiting for Godot* and it was interesting to see such a crack company—Kerry Walker, Barry •Otto, Don Crosbie and Mel Gibson—all brought together for the Jane Street Season doing a fairly hoary old piece of melodrama about pioneering life on the land. It was quaint but very funny and the raw, almost physical slapstick of the performance on stage used to have people just screaming! It became very successful and you couldn't get a ticket. It just tapped a nerve and people had a great time with it. I think some of that quality had gone by the time the film came out although not totally. Most of the audiences I saw it with thought it's a different world now but there's still something there because

George Whaley the director had very consciously tried to anchor it in a kind of social reality. He wanted to give it a genuine social context and credibility, but still keep the book's mad, absurd slapstick. Somehow I think they marketed the film in an odd way. They tried to make it happen as a love story, that's how the poster shaped it, and we had shocking press.

Were you pleased with your own performance as Dave? I thought it had that antic quality that I keep finding in your work.
That role was my first major splash on the Sydney stage I think. I have a very good recall of the tone of the performance live with an audience, and I don't feel the film performance captures the edge that was there on stage, where you could have the house roaring at some of the stuff. That's an example of when a screen performance is not 100 per cent in your hands. George shot a lot of group scenes, and because 'Dave' doesn't have a lot of dialogue, in the frame with a lot of characters you had to glean what Dave was thinking, feeling, or responding to. So I felt maybe he faded into the background a bit too much. 'Dad and Dave' is a pretty comic relationship; we maybe could have got more mileage out of that cinematically.

I also enjoyed the first comedy you did for Peter Duncan, •Children of the Revolution, *a low-key film performance. Were you happy with that?*
I was very lucky because, having done nothing in films, suddenly in an 18-month period I ended up doing **On Our Selection**, **Shine** early in 1995, and straight off that and literally on to the set of **Children of the Revolution**. I was in high heaven because suddenly I'd done three films—one was a really good ratbag country clown, one was David Helfgott, which was like a gift of a part for a character actor, and then came **Children of the Revolution**. Peter Duncan had seen my work in the theatre and said, 'I've written this part for you', and it was a very modest character. Peter kept saying he's the human glue that's going to hold it together. Everyone else is erratic, or a hothead, basically, and Welch is this sort of simple carpenter/cabinet maker who doesn't want to make waves, and just wants to have a happy quiet life and love this woman. And that was perfect for me because I've always tried to look for contrasts from role to role. I think that's what I was trained in when I joined the Queensland Theatre Company in my early 20s and did eight plays a year.

On **Shakespeare in Love**, which I recently finished in England and which was my sixth or seventh film, I felt the apprenticeship was over. I felt that I knew the rhythm, I had the basic building blocks of how to go to a set every day, and have an idea about how to approach a character and how it might all happen. I knew, for instance, that my instincts were telling me what the framing was and that's very important to me. That is like me knowing how close the audience is.

Children of the Revolution *is an interesting film to find in Australia where political satire hasn't been a common genre. Were you taken with the script?*
Yes, very much. I was just about to film **Shine** in England when I got the script for **Children of the Revolution.** How lucky I was being offered these two scripts in a row! Again, it was a great read and I liked the intensity of its imagination, and the danger and bravery with which it cut across what everyone else was doing. I wondered, Why does this happen in Australia? People come out of film school, their first films are often devastatingly brilliant with a unique voice that seems assured and confident and mature. I would think the nearest film that would come to it would be something like *Goodbye Paradise. Now whether that had a direct influence on Peter I don't know.

Among the films you've made since are several international productions: Elizabeth, Les Misérables *and* Shakespeare in Love. *Is it still crucial for Australian actors to appear in international films? Could you have a film career here if you wanted to?*
I don't know, I really don't know. Everyone's circumstances are so different. I'm very much in it for the long term, always have been in terms of the theatre. I always saw myself as a long-distance runner, not a sprinter. I want to be around in my 70s doing it, and I want it to be consistent and regular and developmental. Fortunately up until now that generally, to my own level of satisfaction, has been the case.

THIS INTERVIEW WAS CONDUCTED BY BRIAN MCFARLANE.

S

Safran, Henri (1932–) DIRECTOR   Born in France, Henri Safran cut his teeth in television in the United Kingdom in the late 1950s before coming to Australia to work with the ABC (1960–66) as a drama and documentary director (he became an Australian citizen in 1963). He followed this with another stint in British television before returning to Australia in 1975. He had a major critical success with the 1976 children's film •**Storm Boy**, about the devotion of a small boy to a pet pelican. The film was given more substance by the interaction of the boy with his Aboriginal friend, Fingerbone (David •**Gulpilil**), and the difficulties in dealing with his reclusive father (Peter •**Cummins**). The •**South Australian Film Corporation** produced the film, which gained considerably from the beauty of its Coorong settings and from its simple narrative lines, derived from the popular children's novel by Colin Thiele. It was much praised both locally and abroad.

Safran has not had a comparable success since then. His comedy of Jewish life, •**'Norman Loves Rose'** (1982), which he also wrote, had its supporters, but not enough for commercial viability. As a study of the pressures of marriage in a patriarchal society, it found veins of real warmth and sympathy, and its central premise—a 13-year-old boy impregnates his sister-in-law as his brother has signally failed to do—was handled with a delicacy that suggested Safran's otherwise untapped flair for comedy. •**The Wild Duck** (1984), an antipodean version of Ibsen, never looked like being popular, despite starring Jeremy Irons and Liv Ullman, and •**Bush Christmas** (1983) was an agreeable enough children's film, without erasing the memory of Ralph •**Smart**'s 1947 film of the same name. Since then, Safran's work has been confined to television series, the most notable of which was *A Fortunate Life* (1985), derived from A.B. Facey's celebrated autobiography. Safran's seems a gentle humanist talent that has had trouble finding projects in the more garish, brash Australian cinema of the 1990s.

Other Australian films include: **River of Life** (1962, doc., p.), **Democracy** (1976, short), **Listen to the Lion** (1977).   BMcF

Salute of the Jugger, The

1989. Director: David Peoples. *Producer:* Charles Roven. *Scriptwriter:* David Peoples. *Director of photography:* David Eggby. *Music:* Todd Boekelheide. 100 min. *Cast:* Rutger Hauer (Sallow), Joan Chen (Kidda), Vincent Phillip D'Onofrio (Young Gar), Anna Katarina (Big Cimber), Delroy Lindo (Mbulu).

David Peoples won an Academy Award for his screenplay for Clint Eastwood's **Unforgiven** (1992), but perhaps his finest work has been as writer–director of his sole Australian feature, **The Salute of the Jugger**. Set in an apocalyptic future, it tells of an itinerant band of players skilled in The Game. They wander across the desert wasteland to the Red City, the underground world where the rulers live on one luxurious level, while everyone else is in the bowels. At Red City, they are pitted against the best and cruellest team in The League. Inspired by the once-great but now excommunicated Sallow, the motley team wins a heroic struggle.

Brilliantly shot by David •**Eggby**, and directed with a pulsating energy by Peoples, this remarkable film remains little seen—perhaps it was a victim of the anti-10BA (see Finance) sentiment and preoccupation with international films that sometimes blinded commentators. With its mythic elements, reminiscent of Matsuhira Kawabata's 'life game' novel *The Master of Go*, this is a true gem of 1980s Australian cinema.   SCOTT MURRAY

Salvation Army, *see* Documentary and non-fiction, silent

Sardi, Jan (1953–) WRITER   Jan Sardi has worked consistently in film and television since the production of his first original script •**Moving Out** (1983), which drew on his experiences as a teacher in inner-city schools. A welcome departure from the increasingly glossy Australian films of the time, its authenticity of setting, dialogue, and story resulted in a convincing depiction of contemporary urban youth culture. Perhaps just as importantly, it contributed to a confidence in the ability of low-budget contemporary films to draw wider audiences. Sardi's collaboration with Michael •Pattinson continued on the more lavishly budgeted **Street Hero** (1984), and on **Ground Zero** (1987) and **Secrets** (1992). **Street Hero** might have been more successful had it stuck with the modest production values and straightforward narrative structure of **Moving Out**, while the solid dramatic premise of **Ground Zero**, which Sardi co-wrote with Mac •Gudgeon, became tangled in an uncomfortable mixture of generic film styles. He is best known for •**Shine** (1996), based on a story by Scott •Hicks, and he was nominated for an Academy Award in the Best Original Screenplay category. Sardi has been actively involved in the Australian Writers Guild, and has written extensively for television. He also worked on a project for Columbia Pictures about the life of Don Eldon, a photojournalist and artist who was killed in Somalia in 1993 at the age of twenty-two.   HARRY KIRCHNER

Saunders, Justine (1953–) ACTOR   Justine Saunders moved from Qld to Sydney to work for a fashion house. She entered acting in 1975 as Ruby in *The Cake Man* at Redfern's Black Theatre, and repeated the role many times over the years, including, to great acclaim, in 1982 at the World Theatre Festival in Denver, Colorado. She attended the National Institute of Dramatic Art in 1980, but seemed to be asked mainly to play stereotypes of Black women—in her own words 'bashed, shot, raped, burnt and drunk', or 'the naked aboriginal girl of the outback'. These were the roles she tended to play on television (*Bellbird*, *Against the Wind*, *Ben Hall*, *Rush*, *Luke's Kingdom*) and even in her first major film •**The Chant of Jimmie Blacksmith** (1978). But she has played less stereotypical roles: from the air hostess in *Skyways*, to her most important television role as feisty Nerida Anderson in *Women of the Sun* (1982). She was named National Aboriginal Artist of the Year in 1985, played the lead in the Belvoir Theatre Company's *Capricornia* in 1988, and toured the USA with a one-woman show. On screen she has often played opposite Bob •Maza: •**The Fringe Dwellers**, 1986), the telemovies *Babakueria* (1986) and *No Trouble* (1987), and the miniseries *Heartland* (1994).
Other Australian films: •Until the End of the World (1992).   IB

Scacchi, Greta (1960–) ACTOR   Greta Scacchi, born in Milan and raised in London, moved to Australia with her parents in 1975, although she returned to London and lessons at the Old Vic in 1978. After a major role in **Heat and Dust** (United Kingdom, 1982), Scacchi returned to Australia for a lead role in the miniseries *Waterfront* (1983), and she alternated between the United Kingdom and Australia for many roles in the early and mid 1980s. Following her steamy performance as the seductress to Harrison Ford's victim in **Presumed Innocent** (USA, 1990), Scacchi added Hollywood to Australia, France, Germany, Italy, the United Kingdom, and West Germany, as countries in which she had made films. **Presumed Innocent** was followed by a key role in Robert Altman's humorous attack on the superficialities of the Hollywood film industry in **The Player** (USA, 1992). While her early roles were tailored to her overt screen sexuality (**White Mischief**, United Kingdom, 1988; **A Man in Love**, France, 1987), maturity in the 1990s has provided her with a range of roles that allow characteristics other than just her sexuality to emerge. These roles include Tom Berenger's scheming 'wife' in Wolfgang Peterson's **Shattered** (USA, 1991); the repressed Deborah Voysey, the wife of an elderly drama critic returning to his family property in Australia, in •**Country Life** (1994), and the Australian photojournalist Judith who becomes involved in the plight of the boat people in Malaysia in the 1970s in **Turtle Beach** (1992). The disappointment of this film, together with her underdeveloped character in Gillian •Armstrong's drama about Cuban refugees, **Fires Within** (1991), was more than rectified by Scacchi's subtle performance as Albert Finney's alienated wife in Mike Figgis's splendid film version of the Terence Rattigan play **The Browning Version** (United Kingdom, 1993). In 1996 Scacchi won an Emmy for Outstanding Supporting Actress for the HBO production of *Rasputin*.
Other Australian films include: The Coca-Cola Kid (1985), •Burke & Wills (1985), •Cosi (1996).   GM

Schepisi, Fred (1939–) DIRECTOR   A key figure of the rebirth of Australian cinema in the 1970s, Fred Schepisi has since become a sought-after director of international films. He was educated at Assumption College, in Kilmore in country Vic., and he drew on his Roman Catholic background for his first two feature films: 'The Priest', an episode of the four-part film •**Libido** (1973), and •**The Devil's Playground** (1976). He worked for some years in advertising and in 1963 he joined the Melbourne branch of •Cinesound, whose manager he later became and whose production facility he bought in 1966. He renamed it The Film House, and it has been associated with him ever since. At this stage of his career he produced many documentaries and other short films, including television commercials.

Greta Scacchi

Schepisi

Libido grew out of workshops organised in Melbourne by the Producers and Directors Guild of Australia with a view to training writers for the screen. All four of the short films were on the theme of love, and each was written by a professional writer with an established reputation in another medium. Novelist Thomas •Keneally was the author of 'The Priest', a film that charts the tormented course of a doomed liaison between a priest (Arthur •Dignam) and a nun (Robyn •Nevin).

Keneally played the role of a jolly, hellfire-preaching visiting priest in the Catholic seminary that provides the setting for Schepisi's first full-length feature film, **The Devil's Playground**. Schepisi, as director and scriptwriter, drew substantially on recollections of his own Catholic upbringing for this film, which portrays the growing conflict between young Tom Allen (Simon •Burke) and the rigid disciplines of the order, an incompatibility that is mirrored in the experiences of some of the Brothers. While this film enjoyed considerable success with critics and public alike, his next film, •**The Chant of Jimmie Blacksmith** (1978), the most expensive Australian film to that date, failed at the box office, find-

ing greater critical favour abroad. The American reviewer Pauline Kael, no great fan of Australian cinema, found it 'magnificent', and the film was invited into the official Competition at the Cannes Film Festival. Based on Keneally's novel of the tragic plight of a part-Aboriginal man (the film was set in the late nineteenth to early twentieth century, around the time of Federation), the film is made with passion and commitment, and has a great visual sweep.

It took eight years for Schepisi to direct another Australian film, •**Evil Angels** (1988, called **Cry in the Dark** in the USA). In this period he had made four films abroad, including the Western **Barbarosa** (1982), the film version of David Hare's play **Plenty** (1985) (starring Meryl Streep and Sir John Gielgud), and the box-office success **Roxanne** (1987), based on the play *Cyrano de Bergerac*. **Evil Angels** cast the media as the enemy in its telling of the trial of Lindy Chamberlain for the death of her daughter at Uluru, an Australian landmark and sacred Aboriginal site. His subsequent films have all been made overseas, including a fine adaptation of the play *Six Degrees of Separation*. His films in Australia have been fewer than one might have wished, but

Fred Schepisi on set of **The Chant of Jimmie Blacksmith** (1978)

his contribution to the growing prestige of new Australian cinema (see Revival, the), both stylistically and in terms of content, is undeniably important.

Other Australian films include: Breaking the Language Barrier (1965, short), **The Shape of Quality** (1965, doc.), **People Make Papers** (1967, doc., w.), **And One Was Gold** (1966, doc., w.), **Up and Over Down Under** (1966, doc.), **Switch On** (1967, doc.), **The Plus Factor** (1967, doc.), **Tomorrow's Canberra** (1972, p.).

BMcF

Schultz, Carl (1939–) DIRECTOR Carl Schultz's career trajectory is like those of several other directors of the early days of the new Australian cinema (see Revival, the): several attractive features in the late 1970s and early 1980s, a tapering off, the odd American film, and then television. Born in Hungary, he became a long-term resident of Sydney, where he worked for the ABC from 1972 to 1978. He made his feature début with •**Blue Fin** in 1978. Although this was, like the earlier film •**Storm Boy** (1976), supported by the •South Australian Film Corporation and employed many of the same personnel (scriptwriter, cinematographer, child star, composer, and art director), it enjoyed nothing like the same success. However, it is an engaging piece of entertainment, with enough exciting action (involving a crippled tuna-fishing boat) and astutely observed small-town life to ensure its appeal to a wide age range.

Schultz's two best films—•**Goodbye Paradise** (1983) and •**Careful He Might Hear You** (1983)—were released in 1983. The former, one of the neglected films of the Australian revival, is a reworking, set in Qld, of the genre of the hard-boiled private-eye thriller, full of felicitous echoes of Raymond Chandler; Ray •Barrett's alcoholic Stacey, tracking purveyors of corruption of many kinds, is one of the most impressive characterisations in Australian cinema. **Careful He Might Hear You** is another genre triumph, this time of the family melodrama kind. The 'He' of the title is a small boy who, in immaculately re-created Depression-hit Sydney, becomes the centre of a custody battle between two aunts, neither of whom can answer all his needs. The film ends with his insisting on his own identity as an individual and not as a mere appendage to someone else's life. Everything in the film—narrative control, *mise en scène*, editing, and music—works towards developing this central theme (and there are larger, national echoes), doing so through the full panoply of melodramatic procedures.

Following these genre pieces, Schultz made two highly regarded television series, *The Dismissal* (1983) and *Bodyline* (1984), and has since filmed sporadically, for cinema and television, in the USA, Canada, and Australia, but without attracting as much attention as he did with his earlier films.

Other Australian films: Earth Patrol (1978, short), **Bullseye** (1987), •**Travelling North** (1987).

BMcF

Scott, Jane (1945–) PRODUCER Jane Scott's name has appeared, in one or other capacity, on some of the most important productions of the new Australian cinema (see Revival, the). Born in the United Kingdom but permanently resident in Australia since 1975, she produced the honours-laden •**Shine** (1996), and can trace her involvement back to the popular 'ocker' comedies •**The Adventures of Barry McKenzie** (1972) (on which she worked as production secretary) and its sequel, **Barry McKenzie Holds His Own** (1974) (as associate producer). She was again associate producer on •**Storm Boy** (1976) and •**My Brilliant Career** (1979), and on two films for producer Antony I. •Ginnane, **Harlequin** (1980) and **The Survivor** (1981), both of which are thrillers with supernatural elements and star minor overseas luminaries. Her first film as solo producer was Carl •Schultz's underrated private eye pastiche •**Goodbye Paradise** (1983), a film of style and wit. She and Schultz were briefly reunited in 1989 on **Boys in the Island**, an ill-fated version of Christopher Koch's novel; their association on this film was brief because when shooting was due to begin Schultz was still tied up with post-production work on his first Hollywood film **The Seventh Sign** (1988), and was replaced by first-time director Geoffrey Bennett. The film had great trouble finding distribution and has scarcely been seen. In 1987, Scott took over production (from Jan Sharp) of the intercultural love story **Echoes of Paradise**, directed by Phil •Noyce, a film that suffered another of those troubled production histories that were endemic in the new Australian cinema. Having been line producer on •**Crocodile Dundee** (1986), she co-produced **Crocodile Dundee II** (1988), the sequel to Australia's top money-making film; **Crocodile Dundee II** made money but was not in the blockbuster league of the first film. Since then, Scott has produced **Shine**, which won audiences as well as critical plaudits wherever it was shown, and •**Head On** (1998) for upcoming director Ana •Kokkinos. Unlike other women producers who launched their careers in the euphoric 1970s, Scott has persisted with mainly high-profile projects, and has also worked in television: for example, the series *Boys from the Bush* (United Kingdom).

Other films: Oz (1976, assoc. p.), •**Harvest of Hate** (1978, p., telemovie, some cinema screenings), **The Making of Anna** (1978, doc.; Scott made a cameo appearance in this), •**In Search of Anna** (1979, p.), **Dangerous Summer** (1980, doc., p.).

BMcF

ScreenSound Australia, *see* **Archives**

ScreenWest ScreenWest, a service agency of the Western Australian Ministry for Culture and the Arts, exists to promote WA as a culturally distinctive centre for competitive and creative screen production. Founded as the

West Australian Film Council (WAFC) by Brian Williams from the Producers Guild of Western Australia, the organisation was set up in response to local film-makers' efforts to establish a viable film industry in WA and to attract some of the government funding (and subsequent commercial investment) granted to similar organisations in other states. The WAFC held its first meeting in 1978 and was renamed ScreenWest in 1994 to reflect substantial restructuring of the organisation, which included the implementation of a more commercially aggressive approach in the marketing of the industry, and to represent the inclusion of television production into its charter.

ScreenWest's funding program is designed to foster the development and production of quality marketable film and television projects and to promote WA screen culture. The funding program gives advisory assistance to priority projects through the script office, which assists telemovies, low-budget feature films, documentaries, and animation. ScreenWest's industry-services program supports infrastructure and commercial developments, and promotes WA as a production location as well as focusing on policy development and industry promotion.

ScreenWest's annual events include the running of the 'Small Screen, BIG PICTURE' television conference, which attracts international delegates, encourages debate about issues affecting the industry, and provides networking opportunities for industry personnel in WA. A few notable projects in which ScreenWest has been involved include **Exile and the Kingdom** (1994), voted Best Documentary at the Australian Film Institute (AFI) Awards in 1994, and •**Blackfellas** (1993), which received AFI awards for Best Screenplay and Best Supporting Actor. ScreenWest's support of children's and youth television programming has led to series such as *Ship to Shore* (1993–98) and *Sweat* (1996) being screened in over 40 countries worldwide. The Lotteries Commission of Western Australia currently provides $2 million annually in support of the ScreenWest funding program.   CATHERINE SIMPSON

Scully, Sean (1947–) ACTOR   In the early 1960s Sean Scully appeared in three films for Disney (**The Prince and the Pauper**, 1962; **Dr Syn, Alias the Scarecrow**, 1962; and **Almost Angels**, 1962), and in films for other companies in the United Kingdom and Europe (for example, he played the lead role in **Hunted in Holland**, United Kingdom, 1960). Scully's first major role in Australia was a lengthy appearance in a romantic role in the popular television serial *Bellbird* in the early 1970s. His television work continued with prominent roles in a number of miniseries in the 1970s and 1980s (*Power Without Glory*, *Sara Dane*, *Against The Wind*, and *The Dismissal*). After playing the lead role in the rarely seen •**A City's Child** (1972), Scully's best film role

in the 1970s (although it was relatively brief) was in •**Sunday Too Far Away** (1975), as the shearer Beresford who is always writing to his wife, much to the disgust of Jack •Thompson and the other shearers. Minor roles in •**Eliza Fraser** (1976) and the comedy **High Rolling** (1977) followed. At the end of the 1980s Scully had leading roles in two films that failed commercially: **Daisy and Simon** (1989) and **Phobia** (1990). Scully was excellent in both. In the first, he plays a troubled accountant who seeks a break from the pressures of the big city and forms an odd partnership with middle-aged Daisy (Jan •Adele) on a remote farm. He has a more demanding role in **Phobia** (1990) as the husband participating in the final hours of a failed marriage.

Other Australian films include: Smiley Gets a Gun (1958), Departure (1986), **Cactus** (1986), **Kadaicha** (1988), •**Heaven Tonight** (1990), **Turtle Beach** (1992), Shotgun Wedding (1994).   GM

Sean Scully

Seale, John (1942–) CINEMATOGRAPHER/DIRECTOR   One of Australia's world-class cinematographers, John Seale started as an assistant with the ABC in Qld in 1962. He soon established a reputation for camera-operating that enabled him to freelance from 1968, working on seminal films such as •**Picnic at Hanging Rock** (1975). Seale's third film as director of photography, **The Survivor** (1981), was nominated for both Australian Film Institute (AFI) and Sammy awards for cinematography. Seale's AFI nominations continued with •**Careful, He Might Hear You** (1983) and •**Silver**

City (1984). He won an Australian Cinematographers Society (ACS) Golden Tripod (Best Cinematography Award) and the ACS 'Milli' (Cinematographer of the Year) for •Goodbye Paradise (1983), and he received both honours again for his first overseas film, Peter •Weir's Witness (USA, 1985), which also earned him nominations for both the American and the British Academy Awards. Children of a Lesser God (USA, 1986) won the ACS Golden Tripod, and Rainman (USA, 1988) received the American Society of Cinematographers Outstanding Achievement Award, as well as nomination for the American Academy Awards. Premier Magazine named him Cinematographer of the Year for his work on Gorillas in the Mist (USA/Africa, 1988), which was also nominated for a British Academy Award. In 1990 he received a tribute from the Australian Film Critics Circle, and a program of his work was screened at the Hong Kong Film Festival. Seale's biggest success to date, The English Patient (USA, 1996), won American and British Academy Awards; Best Cinematography awards from film critics societies in Los Angeles, Boston, Chicago, and Florida; and an award from the American Society of Cinematographers. He was also named Cinematographer of the Year in the European Film Awards. Since then he has been inducted into the ACS Hall of Fame (1997) and won the Chauvel Award at the Brisbane Film Festival, as well as a Kodak Vision award in Hawaii. In 1998 he received a Rotary award for 'Vocational Excellence' and, unique among Australian cinematographers, had an honorary doctorate conferred upon him by Griffith University. Among his other American films are The Mosquito Coast (1986), Dead Poets Society (1989), and Lorenzo's Oil (USA/Australia 1992). Seale has also directed one feature, Till There was You (USA, 1990).

Other Australian films: Deathcheaters (1976), Fatty Fin (1980), Doctors and Nurses (1981), Fighting Back (1982), Ginger Meggs (1982), BMX Bandits (1983), •The Empty Beach (1985).

DAVID MUIR

Secret Of The Skies

1934. *Director*: A.R. Harwood. *Scriptwriter*: Laurence Brewer. *Director of photography*: Stan Pentreath. *Music*: The Early Victorians. 56 min. B&W. *Cast*: John D'Arcy (Captain Sinclair), Norman Shepherd (Hal Wayne), Ella Bromley (Anne Walters), Fred Patey (Frederick Holtz), James Dee (Monty Wright).

Despite the disclaimer at the beginning of the film, declaring it entirely fiction, the story of Secret of the Skies was inspired by the disappearance of a plane called Southern Cloud in 1931, one of the great mysteries of Australian aviation history. In this film, the plane is never found because a bank robber (Hal Wayne) highjacks it, and when the crew try to return to course he breaks vital instruments, forcing a crash-landing so far off course that rescuers never reach it.

Filmed mainly on location in spectacular mountainous timber country, the acting and direction are rather stiff and formal. However, in a time of great enthusiasm and curiosity about aviation, this was given a better reception than other A.R. •Harwood films.

IB

Segerberg, Albert Oscar CINEMATOGRAPHER A.O. Segerberg (known as Bert) started filming actuality as early as 1896, worked on *Pathé Frères* gazette (see Documentary and non-fiction, silent), became manager of the laboratory of Stanley Crick's Australian Photo-Play Company, and acted as camera operator on several of their feature films, including Cooee and the Echo (1912), Whose Was the Hand? (1912), and Moira or The Mystery of the Bush (1912). He went on to make newsreels for the Fraser Film Co., and worked freelance as a cinematographer on short films and documentaries, including a series of short educational films (Australia at Work), and films on commission for Paramount. He photographed the feature films The Rebel (1915), •The Mutiny of the Bounty (1916 with Franklyn •Barrett; see In the Wake of the Bounty), The Hayseeds Come to Sydney (1917), The Hayseeds' Backblocks Show (1917), The Hayseeds Melbourne Cup (1918), and •A Romance of the Burke and Wills Expedition of 1860 (1918, with G.L. Gouday, Barrett, and Walter •Sully). He gave evidence to the 1927–28 Royal Commission into the Moving Picture Industry, supporting government contracting out of production to private companies.

IB

Semler, Dean (1943–) PHOTOGRAPHER/DIRECTOR The first Australian to win an Academy Award (Oscar) for cinematography, Dean Semler's career began, aged 16, at Channel 9, Adelaide, where he soon became a television camera operator. His passion for film led to work with ABC television news in Adelaide and then Sydney (1968), where he was also camera operator on the current affairs program *This Day Tonight*. During eight years with Film Australia (1971–79), he benefited from the experience of chief cameraman Don •McAlpine and earned respect for his own cinematography of documentaries, cinema shorts, and ethnographic films. Dean Semler shot his first feature, Let The Balloon Go (1976), while at •Film Australia. After going freelance, he shot documentaries, television series, and feature films, starting with •Hoodwink (1981). The quality of Semler's camera work was recognised with an Australian Cinematographer Society (ACS) Distinction and Golden Tripod Award in 1981 and another Distinction for •The LightHorsemen (1987). He shared with Geoffrey •Burton an Australian Film Institute Best Cinematography Award for •Dead Calm (1989). The first of many overseas features was Cocktail (USA, 1988), before he won the coveted American Academy Award for his cinematography of Dances

Sentimental Bloke

with Wolves (USA, 1990). In addition to his work as director of photography on Australian and international films—including •**Razorback** (1984), •**Mad Max: Beyond Thunderdome** (1985), **Young Guns** (USA, 1988), **City Slickers** (USA, 1991), and **Waterworld** (USA, 1995)—Semler has also directed two feature films: **Firestorm** (USA, 1998) and **The Patriot** (USA, 1998).

Other Australian films include: Kitty and the Bagman (1981, d.o.p.), •Mad Max II: The Road Warrior (1981, d.o.p.), Undercover (1983, d.o.p.), •Razorback (1984, d.o.p.), Coca-Cola Kid (1985, d.o.p.), Mad Max: Beyond Thunderdome (1985, d.o.p.), Going Sane (1986, d.o.p.), Bullseye (1987, d.o.p.).

DAVID MUIR

Sentimental Bloke, The

1919. Director: Raymond Longford. *Producer*: Raymond Longford. *Scriptwriter*: Raymond Longford. Based on the verse narrative, *The Songs of a Sentimental Bloke*, by C. J. Dennis. *Director of photography*: Arthur Higgins. 6700 ft. B&W. *Cast*: Arthur Tauchert (Bill, the Bloke), Lottie Lyell (Doreen), Gilbert Emery (Ginger Mick), Harry Young (The Stror'at Coot), Margaret Reid (Doreen's mother).

This is the most important Australian production of the silent era: if there were better films produced during this period they have not survived. It was the pinnacle of achievement of the Longford–Lyell creative team, and, although it was his first feature film, it was also the best performance of Arthur •Tauchert's long career.

The success begins with the choice of subject: Dennis's long verse narrative, first published in 1914, telling of the transformation of the 'Bloke' from urban larrikin to rural married bliss, under the influence of love for Doreen, for whom he promises to give up the rough habits of 'the Push'. It is to Longford and Lyell's credit that they recognised the dramatic potential of this episodic and rhapsodic narrative, without feeling the need to pad it with incident. They even use the verses, skilfully but selectively, as intertitles, thus drawing on popular knowledge. They move the location from the back streets of Melbourne to the slums of Wooloomooloo, but they carry this off too, creating (with the help of Arthur •Higgins's outstanding photography) a milieu of unromanticised poverty in which lives are enriched by genuine comradeship. Gilbert Emery's lean and cocky 'Ginger Mick' is a wonderful foil for Tauchert's stocky and pugnacious 'Bloke'. Even the smaller roles fill in this picture with warmth and conviction, especially the 'Stror'at Coot' (who manages to retain audience sympathy) and 'Mar', whose reduced gentility is both painful and touching. This is an often funny film, but it never makes us laugh at the expense of its characters. It is, in fact, a national treasure. IB

Sentimental Bloke, The

1932. Director: F.W. Thring. *Production company*: Efftee Productions. *Scriptwriter*: C.J. Dennis. Based on his narrative verse *The Songs of a Sentimental Bloke. Director of photography*: Arthur Higgins. 92 min. B&W. *Cast*: Cecil Scott (The Bloke), Ray Fisher (Doreen), Tal Ordell (Ginger Mick), Athol Tier (Artie), Edna Morecombe (Effie), Keith Desmond (Uncle), Dora Mostyn (Ma), William Carroll (the 'Stror'at Coot').

Dennis wrote the script for this adaptation of his verses. Still centred on the Bloke's transformation, it adds new characters with the broadly drawn Artie and Effie, and a secondary plot of the Bloke protecting 'Uncle' from city swindlers. Since Raymond •Longford's version, the verses had moved from being a contemporary, if rather contrived, picture of larrikin life, to a still-loved but more remote and quaint piece of history. Frank •Thring Snr's combination of sound with silence and intertitles (using Hal Gye's cigar-smoking cherubs from the published verses) captures this ambivalence well. But the narrative structure is less successful. The story has lost its episodic and rhapsodic quality: instead of an apostrophe to the dawn, we have 'Erb's missing gold teeth; instead of a realistic enactment of an embarrassing encounter with the 'Stror'at Coot' in the milk bar, we have a farcical comedy of entrances and exits involving the crooks, the Bloke, and a flower-pot.

Nevertheless, this is one of Thring's more successful films, retaining much of the charm of the original story. Although the critics ignored it, the public made it one of the few •Efftee Productions to recover its costs. IB

Serious, Yahoo (1953–) ACTOR/DIRECTOR To say that Newcastle-born Greg Pead 'changed' his name seems an understatement. Now known as Yahoo Serious, he has made two films that may have appealed to yahoos but which have clearly either reached much wider audiences or revealed that there are more yahoos around than one might have expected. Before his enormous commercial success with •**Young Einstein** (1988), he had been, among other things, an art student and a maker of commercials. If the term 'auteur' still has any authority, it must be attached to him if for no other reason than that he not only directs and stars in his two films, but also co-produces and co-writes them; he was also supervising editor and stunts coordinator on **Young Einstein** and fulfilled all these functions except stunts on his second film **Reckless Kelly** (1993).

As a consequence, the two films entirely reflect his zany, iconoclastic approach to historical events. Each proceeds through a series of wild, often comically inventive episodes rather than a coherent plot. **Young Einstein**, made in 1986 but re-released two years later after an inauspicious first release, posits the Tasmanian birth of Albert Einstein and attributes to him a range of achievements, including the invention of rock 'n' roll. **Reckless Kelly**, made with American backing but less successful than its predecessor, sticks to the outline of the Kelly myth of robbing the rich to help the poor, but relocates it in a world of corrupt business practice, the myth-making function of the Hollywood machine, and the Australian republican movement.   BMcF

Set, The

1970. *Director*: Frank Brittain. *Producer*: Frank Brittain. *Scriptwriters*: Diane Brittain, Roger Ward. Based on the novel by Roger Ward. *Director of photography*: Sandor Siro. *Music*: Sven Libaek. 102 min. B&W. *Cast*: Sean McEuan (Paul Lawrence), Rod Mullinar (Tony Brown), Denis Doonan (Mark Bronoski), Hazel Phillips (Peg Sylvester), Julie Rodgers (Cara), Brenda Senders (Marie Rosefield).

This film paved the way for the sexual openness of television series and films such as •**Number 96** and •**The Box**. It has a similar episodic and rambling narrative, centring on the sexual insecurities of the bisexual hero, Paul. His artistic aspirations are even more problematic: he uses Marie's contacts to break into Sydney's upper-class art world, then bluffs his way into a job designing a theatrical set.

Camera work, editing, and music are all competent, but the dialogue is excruciating, and the only actor who can rise above it is Rod •Mullinar, beautiful, brooding, and delivering his lines convincingly. Advertised as an exposé of Sydney high society, it caused a furore because of its nudity, particularly that of Hazel Philips, a presenter of women's daytime television. After a brief popular success, it did not do well at the box office, but it remains important as, in Mike •Thornhill's words, 'Australia's first professional sexploitation movie'.   IB

Settlement, The

1984. *Director*: Howard Rubie. *Producer*: Robert Bruning. *Scriptwriter*: Ted Roberts. *Director of photography*: Ernest Clark. *Music*: Sven Libaek. 98 min. *Cast*: Bill Kerr (Kearney), John Jarratt (Martin), Lorna Lesley (Joycie), Tony Barry (Crowe), Katy Wild (Mrs Crowe).

In this underappreciated film, Martin and Kearney are mates who work the fairgrounds as a boxer and a conman respectively. Joycie is an ex-prostitute and temporary barmaid in a conservative country town, where the mates end up when Kearney is taken ill on the road. She comforts them with rum bought from the pub and with her body when Kearney is shivering in the hut that the mates have occupied on the outskirts of town. It turns into an unlikely threesome, to the horror of the conservative women of the town: the outrage is led by the town policeman's wife, who

eventually burns the hut down. Because the moral of this unconventional love story is that sticking by your mates and your principles is more important than considering what others may think, the trio leave the town to face an uncertain future together. Naturalistic performances and a deceptively simple directorial style make this modern fairytale surprisingly convincing.   IB

Seven Keys to Baldpate

1916. *Director*: Monte Luke. *Scriptwriter*: Alex C. Butler. From the play by George M. Cohan, based on the novel by Earl Derr Biggers. *Director of photography*: Maurice Bertel. B&W. *Cast*: Dorothy Brunton (Mary Norton), Alex C. Butler (Jim Cargan), George Villiers (Thomas Hayden).

The stage version of **Seven Keys to Baldpate** was a very popular 'old dark house' comedy thriller, which, like •**Officer 666**, was written by the American showbusiness celebrity George M. Cohan. Although it has been adapted for the screen several times, the Australian film version, made along with several other features in order to cash in on the stock of theatrical productions held by the company J.C. Williamson (see Wartime film-making), seems to have been the first. **Seven Keys to Baldpate** was directed by Monte Luke, a man apparently overwhelmed by the movies. The result is an uninteresting adaptation of really good original material, acted without flair, and seriously marred by inept scripting as well as some very badly worded intertitles, including such queasy sentences as 'Disbelieving Mary had lost the bribe-money, the gang accuses her of stealing it'.

WILLIAM D. ROUTT

Seven Little Australians

1939. *Director*: Arthur Greville Collins. *Production company*: O.B. Pictures. *Scriptwriter*: Patrick V. Ryan. Based on the novel by Ethel Turner. *Director of photography*: George Malcolm. *Music*: Nellie Weatherill. 63 min. B&W. *Cast*: Charles McCallum (Captain Woolcot), Patricia McDonald (Esther), Sandra Jaques (Meg), Robert Gray (Pip), Mary McGowan (Judy).

Seven Little Australians, Ethel Turner's classic of Australian children's literature, published in 1894, was extremely popular. It is therefore rather surprising that it was not filmed until 1939. Perhaps the problem was finding enough competent juvenile actors for the seven children of Captain Woolcot. Nevertheless, the young cast do surprisingly well, considering the staginess of the dialogue and the woodenness of the direction. Little tension is generated, even by what should have been the climax of the film—the sacrificial death of Judy to save her baby brother and restore family harmony. The film feels anachronistic, with a narrative style that would have been more at home in the mid 1920s.

Shame

Although Arthur Collins had worked earlier in the United Kingdom and had, in the 1930s, directed several minor Hollywood films, **Seven Little Australians** was a failure both critically and at the box office, and Collins did not make another feature until 1947 (**Strong is the Seed**).   IB

Shame

1988. Director: Steve Jodrell. *Producers:* Damien Parer, Paul D. Barron. *Scriptwriters:* Beverly Blankenship, Michael Brindley. *Director of photography:* Joseph Pickering. *Music:* Mario Millo. 94 min. *Cast:* Deborra-Lee Furness (Asta Cadell), Tony Barry (Tim Curtis), Simone Buchanan (Lizzie Curtis), Gillian Jones (Tina Farrel), Peter Aanensen (Sergeant Wal Cuddy).

When a leather-clad figure on a motorcycle rides into a small town in outback WA in the opening sequence of **Shame**, the audience is alerted in narrative and iconographic terms to the western movie genre. Here, the stranger proves to be Asta Cadell, a lawyer from the city. Like the hero of many a western, including George Stevens's classic, **Shane** (1953), on which the Australian film seems clearly modelled, Asta becomes involved with elements of the community that are under threat, and prolongs her stay to help out.

Specifically, she is shocked to find that gang rape is an accepted part of the male-dominated ethos of the town, and she persuades one of its latest victims, Lizzie, to stand up against the powerful forces in the town that seek to keep her quiet. Asta offers a different, more aggressive role model for Lizzie and those like her. The outcome of her efforts on their behalf is both tragic and vestigially hopeful: Lizzie has died, but Asta has mobilised a spirit of protest that will be harder for the authorities to ignore. Much of the film's strength is the result of a compelling central performance from Deborra-Lee •Furness as Asta, and of its taut reworking of genre conventions.   BMcF

Sharman, Jim

Sharman, Jim (1945–) PRODUCER While very young, Jim Sharman travelled around Australia with his father's boxing troupe. As an adult, he worked first for an advertising agency, then the ABC, before completing the theatre direction course at the National Institute of Dramatic Art. After graduating, he made his name as a theatrical producer and entrepreneur, mounting Australian productions of the blockbusters *Hair, Jesus Christ Superstar*, and *The Rocky Horror Show*. His first film was the short **Arcade** (1968), and in 1972 he wrote, produced, and directed his first feature, **Shirley Thompson Versus the Aliens** (1972). The film critic David Stratton described this as 'a crazy mixture of psychological thriller, science fiction, fantasy and fifties rock musical'. While the critics did not like it, it later became something of a cult success. Sharman then went to London to stage *The Rocky Horror Show*, and made a film of this in 1974 that became a cult classic and was screened for many years in midnight shows, to enthusiastic audiences. He returned to Australia to produce **Summer of Secrets** (1976) and •**The Night The Prowler** (1979), two films featuring bizarre events and characters. Both films were savaged by the critics, often for the same audacity and originality that brought him such praise for his stage presentations. He returned to the United Kingdom, where he made one more film, **Shock Treatment** (1981), before coming back to Australia where he continued to push the boundaries of theatrical presentation (for instance, in staging *The Eighth Wonder* at the Sydney Opera House in 1995).   IB

Sharmill Films

Sharmill Films This independent distribution and exhibition company takes its name from the single and married names—Sharp and Miller—of its founder (in 1967) and driving force, Natalie Miller. Educated at the University of Melbourne, Miller worked first for a public relations firm before transferring to the Australian Broadcasting Corporation (ABC). After three years she took a PR job with the •Melbourne International Film Festival, which she held for the next 16 years. Although film was her first love, there is no doubt that her experience of promotion helps to account for the longevity of Sharmill in a fiercely competitive industry. Miller has chosen films with care, and Sharmill has come to be associated with the best of 'arthouse' quality. Through regular attendance of the Cannes Film Festival, Sharmill has acquired exhibition rights of such successes (critical and often commercial as well) as **Truly Madly Deeply** (1992), **An Angel at My Table** (1990), and **Ju Dou** (1990). Sharmill distributes nation-wide, and exhibits in Melbourne at two cinemas: the Longford in South Yarra and the Nova in Carlton. It has maintained an important presence in Victorian cinema, as a reliable outlet for alternative film-making, which would have difficulty finding a place in the multiplexes regularly used by the major distributors.   BMcF

Shattered Illusion, The

1928. Director, Scriptwriter: A.G. Harbrow. *Director of photography:* Reg. Robinson. B&W. *Cast:* J. Robertson Aiken (Lewis Alden), Gret. Wiseman (Joyce Hilton), Clare Dight (Mrs Elsworth), Norman Arthur (John Elsworth).

The Shattered Illusion is a laboured 'movie with a message'. Lewis Alden is a financier and workaholic control freak whose overtaxed mind finally snaps him into amnesia. He takes a job as a stoker and is shipwrecked with the Elsworths and their niece Joyce. The Elsworths own a plantation, and

Mrs Elsworth knows exactly what to do in a shipwreck. Joyce finds some trousers. Alden gets his memory back and discovers his companies have got along perfectly well without him. Alden is soft, self-involved, and convinced of his indispensibility: he learns to be different in the regenerative atmosphere of the desert island. On the other hand, the Elsworths and Joyce are all that is straightforward and pure in the new land. Having found out what real life is about on the island, Alden determines to throw in financiering for the simple existence of a primary producer with Joyce.

WILLIAM D. ROUTT

Shine

1996. *Director*: Scott Hicks. *Producer*: Jane Scott. *Scriptwriter*: Jan Sardi. *Director of photography*: Geoffrey Simpson. *Music*: David Hirschfelder. 105 min. *Cast*: Geoffrey Rush (David Helfgott, adult), Noah Taylor (David, adolescent), Armin Mueller-Stahl (Peter Helfgott), Googie Withers (Katharine Susannah Pritchard), Lynn Redgrave (Gillian), John Gielgud (Professor Cecil Parkes).

First screened to acclaim at the Sundance Film Festival in January 1996, **Shine** has since become one of the most widely praised and honoured of all Australian films. It is based on the story of the musical prodigy David Helfgott, whose career has been reactivated in tandem with the film's success. **Shine** works on a number of levels. It is a powerful story of the pain that families can generate: as a child, Helfgott is dominated by his overprotective father's ambitions for his musical career, and suffers a breakdown, from which he is rescued by Gillian, the astrologist who marries him and nurses him back to health. It is also in the tradition of the 'biopic', in which aspiring artists overcome obstacles as they pursue their art to the point of personal gratification and public acknowledgment. And it combines both these strands with a passionate melodramatic flair that is rare in Australian cinema. It is a genuinely inspirational story that achieves a convincingly upbeat ending.

The film's major triumph is Geoffey •Rush's performance as the tormented adult Helfgott, profoundly disturbed, endlessly talking, vulnerable, and obsessive. Among the many awards Rush won for the role was the American Academy Award for Best Actor of 1996. Noah •Taylor convincingly suggests the boy's increasing trauma and his wild talent, and there are luminous cameos from John Gielgud as the London-based music teacher and Googie •Withers as the Australian author who encourages his talent. The film has been a major commercial as well as critical success, and has shown that Australian films need not be tied to overtly 'national' themes to find international acceptance.

BMcF

Shiralee, The

1957. *Director*: Leslie Norman. *Producer*: Michael Balcon. *Scriptwriters*: Neil Paterson, Leslie Norman. From the novel by D'Arcy Niland. *Director of photography*: Paul Beeson. *Music*: John Addison. 103 min. *Cast*: Peter Finch (Macauley), Dana Wilson (Buster), Elizabeth Sellars (Marge), George Rose (Donny), Rosemary Harris (Lily Parker), Russell Napier (Parker), Sidney James (Luke).

Peter Finch marked his return to films made in Australia with a fine performance in Ealing Studio's **The Shiralee**, based on the novel by D'Arcy Niland. As Macauley, the itinerant bush worker who returns to his home in Sydney to find his wife and small daughter living with another man, Finch gives a modulated and controlled performance that suggests inner strength and volcanic violence. Macauley takes his daughter Buster and heads back to the bush where Buster becomes his 'Shiralee' or burden.

On the road they encounter many adventures as Macauley attempts unsuccessfully to unload a reluctant Buster on friends and acquaintances. His wife Marg, effectively played by Elizabeth Sellars, sues for divorce and custody, and Macauley discovers some of the consequences of his former relationship with Lily Parker. The film highlights the developing love between father and daughter, and ends with Macauley facing the prospect of settling down with Lily.

Effectively combining footage shot on location in Sydney and country NSW with studio footage in the United Kingdom, the film features a strong supporting cast, including Sid James, Charles •Tingwell, Bill •Kerr and Ed •Devereaux.

BRUCE MOLLOY

Shirley, Arthur (1887–1967) ACTOR/PRODUCER/DIRECTOR Born in Hobart, Arthur Shirley became a stage actor before starring in two films in 1914: **The Shepherd of the Southern Cross** and the first version of **The Silence of Dean Maitland**. Then he went to Hollywood, where he worked for Kalem and Universal, playing major roles in **Stronger than Death** (1916, with Louise •Lovely), **The Fall of a Nation** (1916) and **Modern Love** (1918). In 1920 he returned to Australia, proposing to build a studio in Sydney and set up a Hollywood-style production house. His matinee-idol looks and undoubted acting experience were countered by his litigiousness and poor business sense: his new company began production on **The Throwback**, of which some out-takes are held in the National Film and Sound Archive (see Archives), but the film was not completed, and the company was disbanded. Shirley tried again with **The Mystery of a Hansom Cab** (1925), which he wrote, produced and directed, as well as taking the lead role. This made enough money for him to be able to start **The**

Shine

Noah Taylor in Shine

Sealed Room (1926), which he again wrote, produced, and directed, as well as starring as the detective. But his success was short-lived. He did not have enough money to continue in production in Australia. He tried unsuccessfully to distribute his films in the United Kingdom, and to establish a production house in Rhodesia, and was prevented by immigration rules from returning to work in Hollywood. He returned to Australia in 1934, but was never again able to mount a film production.   IB

Short film   Whenever we hear about a renaissance of Australian cinema, whenever 'Australian cinema' is celebrated, it is almost always 'the feature' that is the focus and reason for the celebration. When declarations are made that Australian cinema has finally found its voice, it is the internationally praised features that are held up as evidence. The success stories are the familiar ones of •**Shine** (1996), •**The Piano** (1993), •**Proof** (1991), •**Muriel's Wedding** (1994), and •**The Adventures of Priscilla, Queen of the Desert** (1994). When short films are remarked upon, they are most likely to be short films that have served as calling cards or *entrées* to the world of the feature. The mainstream commercial press has reported the story of Colin Mowbray whose •Victorian College of the Arts School of Film and Television (VCA) graduating film **Happy Little Vegemites (unauthorised by Kraft)** (1995) so impressed American B-film svengali Roger Corman, on his visit to our shores, that Corman invested in the feature-length remake. Similarly lauded was Robert Luketic's VCA short **Titsiana Booberini** (1996). Following its screening at the Telluride Film Festival in Colorado, Luketic was offered the prestigious gig of directing the Hollywood remake of **The Trouble with Angels.**

This tendency to consider features as the definition of cinema is widespread. Several years ago, as part of the Centenary of Cinema in Australia, the National Film and Sound Archive (NFSA; see Archives) conducted a poll in which a select group of people were invited to nominate the hundred 'key' Australian films most deserving of preservation on the strength of their historic and cultural significance. Summarising the results of this survey in 1996, in *Cinema Papers* (issue no. 108) Ken Berryman found the sample to be dominated by narrative features—so much so that only one non-feature (Damien •Parer's documentary **Kokoda Front Line**, 1942) made it into the top 100. The first shorts to be mentioned were **Passionless Moments: Recorded in Sydney Australia Sunday October 2** (Jane •Campion and Gerard Lee) and **Night Cries: A Rural Tragedy** (Tracey •Moffatt, 1990), which were equally placed at 142. It should be noted that these two shorts are the early works of film-makers who have subsequently become feature directors. Scanning the pages of *Cinema Papers* over the past decade also reveals that shorts are rarely the subject of individual reviews.

But not every critical voice is so fixated on the feature. Addressing the issue of film history in one of the •Australian Film Institute's 'Conversations on Film' sessions, John •Flaus invoked a compelling ecological metaphor. He suggested that when you look at a landscape from a plane what you see are the tallest trees, giving you one perspective on that part of the world. But what you do not see from this height is the undergrowth: the moss, the shrubs, the scrub, and the smaller bushes that make the larger ones possible. Similar sentiments were at play when Adrian Martin, one of the most prolific and consistently interesting writers on the history and aesthetics of the Australian short-film form, was asked to speculate on an 'Australian new wave'. For Martin, this 'new wave' is to be found particularly in works that come from the short film/independent 'underbelly', 'delirious works full of cinematic memory', such as Philip •Brophy's **Salt, Saliva, Sperm and Sweat** (1988) and Ross •Gibson's **Camera Natura** (1986), as well as the dialogue between form, styles, and ideas that takes place in the works of Super-8 practitioners—a rich tradition indeed. Is it possible to communicate some sense of its richness?

Short-film activity in Australia begins to be documented as early as the 1940s. In 1944–51 the •Realist Film Unit, which was allied to the Communist Party, exhibited and distributed progressive films. It also produced a number of shorts, documentaries, and newsreels. In 1945, the radical film-maker Joris Ivens came to Australia and made, for the Waterside Workers Federation, **Indonesia Calling** (1946), a provocative call to action. In the 1950s the Waterside Workers Federation established their own film unit (see •Waterside Workers Federation Film Unit), and between 1953 and 1959 this unit produced a number of films relating to specific union campaigns. The Australian Council of Film Societies (see Film societies) was founded in 1950; one of its strongest centres was in Victoria. Between 1950 and 1958 Gil •Brealey was president of the Melbourne University Film Society and also formed his own group, Experimental Film Productions. Brealey and his fellow students made a number of short films as well as a weekly newsreel recording university events and related activities. Brealey's short films are playful and irreverent, particularly three spy spoofs he made, the last of which was **Le Bain Vorace** (1954).

The 1960s were heady times during which there was an exponential growth in film production. This was the time when New Wave movements in France, the USA, the United Kingdom, and Italy, among other centres, were reconceiving the possibilities of cinema, and the dreams and manifestos of the films associated with these movements resonated as inspirational shockwaves all over the world. In Sydney in 1965, Albie •Thoms, David Perry, Aggy Read, and John Clark formed UBU, Australia's first 'consciously avant-garde film-making group'. Dedicated to creating, exhibiting, and discussing experimental films, UBU took its name from Thoms's first stage production, Alfred Jarry's *Ubu Roi* (1962). UBU organised screenings of their own work, films as varied as Thoms's **Bluto** (1967), a handmade scratch film described as 'kinetic art'; and David Perry's poetic, diaristic **A Sketch on Abigayl's Belly** (1968), a film that provoked the ire of the censor because it showed a naked pregnant woman. They also organised screenings of the works of the international avant-garde. As well as this, they produced a newsletter *UBU News*, which provided a forum for issues pertinent to the activities of underground film-makers. Meanwhile, in Melbourne in 1966 a diploma of art (film and television) was introduced at Swinburne Technical College (later to become part of the VCA). This was the first course of its kind in Australia.

Two aesthetic traditions have been noted as very influential on the burgeoning short-film activity of the 1960s. The first is the romantic fascination with the power and the potentiality of the image that can be found in the American avant-garde, such as Stan Brakhage's 'cinema eye' abstractions and Maya Deren's trance-like psychodramas. The second is the formal and conceptual interrogation of the materiality of the cinema itself and its means of production, preoccupations that can be said to define the work of the British structural-materialists. It is said that the work of Arthur and Corinne •Cantrill, key figures in the Australian independent film scene, is influenced by these twin traditions. The Cantrills began their prolific production in the early 1960s, making abstract shorts and some narrative and documentary work. A fascination with film form has dominated their cinematic investigations. This has also extended to installations in performance spaces, events that endeavour to expand the cinema experience beyond the conventional theatre. A series of such presentations employed three screens, split screens, photographed and real objects, and translucent screens that were intended to create an awareness of the relation between screen surface and projected image.

The early culture of Australian short film, in which the Cantrills were so pivotal, was rich and productive. Experiment in form is a common feature of the films produced: for example, Thoms's **Bolero** (1967), a fifteen-minute tracking shot down the length of an Australian back street; John Dunkley-Smith's **Train Fixation** (1977), with its obsessive structural repetition of blurred trains; Lynsey Martin's handmade scratch film **Whitewash** (1969–73) and his wry and playful **Leading Ladies** (1973), which inventively uses found test footage from film leaders; and Dirk De Bruyn's trance-like **Zoom Film** (1978), in which a face flickers from being a positive to a negative image, and the representational and the abstract are juxtaposed, in mesmeric ways.

Another key film of this early period, Michael Lee's **Mystical Rose** (1975), has acquired its own cult status. Its racy, provocative montage, replete with sexual and religious iconography, seems as contemporary now as it did for the film-maker who, at the time, was expressing an intensely personal, cathartic vision.

The 1970s were also the times of the Sydney and Melbourne Film-makers Co-ops. The Sydney Film-makers Co-Op was born in 1970. It regarded itself as a distributor and exhibitor of films, it housed a significant collection of independent work, and it published and distributed a monthly film journal, *Filmnews*, which was dedicated to writing about Australian film culture, particularly the work of the independent sector. Screenings of the work of local film-makers in Melbourne moved from gallery spaces to the Maze in Spring Street until, in 1971, it found a centre in Lygon Street, Carlton, which became the newly constituted Melbourne Film-makers Co-op. During this time, experimental practice encompassed a diverse range of feminist, documentary, political, and social concerns, in films as varied and distinctive as George •Miller's send-up of the way academics analyse violence in the cinema (**Violence in the Cinema: Part 1**, 1972); Margot Nash and Robin Laurie's **We Aim to Please** (1976) with its provocative look at female sexuality; Jeni Thornley's compilation image repertoire **Maidens** (1978); John •Hughes's agitprop films **Menace** (1978) and **Filmwork** (1981); and Richard •Lowenstein's **Evictions** (1979), which cuts together dramatic re-enactments of evictions with personal reminiscences. .

Also beginning in 1970 was the Australian government's policy of assistance to the film and television industry. This was one of the first steps in the government's efforts to encourage film as cultural expression through direct sponsorship of production. Its strategy, in part, was to identify and support project proposals from talented individuals who would then, through the educative process of undertaking their own production, develop skills that would enable them to move into the commercial mainstream. The fund established to assist low-budget films was variously called the Experimental Film and Television Fund, Basic Production Fund, the Creative Development Fund, and The No Frills Fund (see Experimental film and Australian Film Commission), and continues to go through many incarnations.

In the 1980s, writing on short films, the film critic and theorist Adrian Martin described a cultural milieu fuelled by 'factional disputes', where 'early Super-8 film-makers rejected political statement and art-world aestheticism' while the later wave 'developed a more refined aesthetic approach to the medium'. Factional disputes extended to felt differences between self-trained film-makers and those who gained their craft at film schools such as Swinburne (VCA) and the •Australian Film, Television and Radio School (AFTRS). This perceived difference was further compounded in the late 1980s when video artists were making claims for the specificity of their own medium. Yet, Martin argues, for all of these differences, there was more that connected the films than separated them. Writing in a catalogue essay on the occasion of a 1994 retrospective of Australian experimental film artists, Martin observed that when aesthetic concerns were foregrounded, 'Family resemblances of style and content form across different generations and social groups'. The differences that seemed to separate film-makers across decades, generations, gauges, and cities almost disappear.

In 1982 Super 8 came to prominence in public art and film spaces. There was the first-ever program of Super 8 at the Melbourne Film Festival (see Festivals); a series of regular screenings at the Royal Melbourne Institute of Technology; a season curated by the NFSA called 'The Super-8 Phenomenon', which was promoted as 'home movies leave home'; and the 'Popism' exhibition at the National Gallery of Victoria, for some the most significant event of all, which featured a key film component. Many of the films screened at these events were the work of film-makers and artists who had gathered at the Clifton Hill Community Music Centre, an exhibition and performance space that for several years was the creative home in Melbourne for some truly innovative new work. Many of these film-makers had come from the visual and performing arts and worked across music, sculpture, photography, painting, video, theatre, and critical/theoretical practice. The performance group Tsk-Tsk-Tsk were emblematic multimedia artists. Their work includes **Texts** (1979), an event that sought to analyse the narrative organisation of popular forms of culture; **Phantom** (1980), which re-tells the famous Phantom comic strip in the style of French New Wave Cinema; and **The 1980 Moscow Olympics as Televised by HSV Channel** 7 (1980), which appropriates and re-edits a range of television texts.

Super 8 was embraced by people who saw it as a way to quickly and cheaply produce films that could cross over a wide range of film-making practices. The register of films is testament to their variety of form, style, and experiment: from Stephen Harrop's transgressive **Square Bashing** (1982); Andrew Frost's televisual dreamscape **S.S.S.** (1986); Anne-Marie Crawford's reverie **Underground** (1986); Jayne Stevenson's study of **Italian Boys** (1982); Bill Mousoulis's reflective **Love Letter** (1985); Chris Windmill's ethereal **Congratulations Gazelle Head** (1987); Nick Ostrovskis's grainy, evocative **West Gate Bridge** (1984); and Catherine Lowing's provocative **Knife in the Head, Spooky** (1985); to Steven Ball's poetic speculation **Periscope 180** (1992). The

mutations vary from Bill Mousoulis's narrated document of the writing of a love letter—with its memories very much focused on the ordinary, the everyday, and the banal—to Chris Windmill's story which begins in an ordinary way, with girls working in a suburban fashion boutique, and then suddenly transforms magically.

For some 1980s film-makers, postmodern experimentation becomes a playful engagement with images from popular culture such as can be found in Jo Bogdanov's **Private and Confidential** (1983), a vibrant, witty, humorous look at True Romance Comics. In contrast, other films have been concerned with the personal, subjective, diaristic, and autobiographical. This is true in different ways of Merilee Bennett's **A Song of Air** (1987), in which the film-maker reflects on her relationship with her Methodist, High Court judge father, incorporating his 16mm home-movie footage of family life in 1950s Qld; Gillian Leahy's **My Life Without Steve** (1986), which documents a contemplative and reflective year in a room; and David Perry's **Love and Work** (1986), which reanimates, reflects on, and 'narrativises' Perry's early experimental film work and video diaries. Other film-makers have sought to create incisive documents of their cultural, social, and historical moment. For some, this has taken the form of experimental narratives combined with theoretical investigations, such as Laleen Jayamanne's **Song of Ceylon** (1985), which enacts feminist debates on psychoanalysis, hysteria, and the body, by exploring the body in many incarnations. Other shorts also represent and analyse the experiences of ethnic and indigenous film-makers. Tracey Moffatt's •**Nice Coloured Girls** (1987) and **Night Cries: A Rural Tragedy** (1990) examine the history of White–Aboriginal relations and dramatise issues of loneliness and oppression. In different ways Monica Pellizzari's **Rabbit on the Moon** (1988), Luigi Acquisto's **Spaventapasseri** (1986), and Ana •Kokkinos's **Antamosi** (1991) and **Only the Brave** (1994) excavate and analyse the problems of growing up in a Greek family in Greek–Australian Melbourne.

Increasingly, since the late 1980s many short films that are stylised and narratively experimental tackle pressing contemporary issues and questions. Lawrence Johnson's striking **Night Out** (1989) foregrounds complicated questions about gay relationships and commitment. Richard Franklin's **No Way to Forget** (1996) is a sombre and disturbing film about black deaths in custody. Irving Sen's **Tears** (1996) poetically and searingly dramatises a teenage couple leaving their mission home but finding themselves taking separate paths. There are now also many inventive instances of that very marketable type of short—the 'gag' film. In this category is Kriv Stenders's **Two/Out** (1998), a fast-moving comedy–drama about the strange relationships and longings that form between two men sharing a prison cell. Lynn-Maree Danzey's **Fetch** (1998) takes as its subject a 'first date', which proves to be the catalyst for the many unfortunate and surprising incidents that follow.

The 1990s was a time of marked pluralism. With the possibilities for image-making significantly changed, and with an exponential growth in new digital technologies, increasingly sophisticated production was available to all those with access to a decent computer. But is this newly democratised culture everything that it seems to be? What are the current issues for those making short films? These questions were addressed at a forum at the St Kilda Short Film festival in 1998, and the discussion was predominantly focused on the questions 'How film-makers can get their films made?', 'Where can these films be screened?', and 'Who will see them?' Exhibition and distribution has always been a problem for makers of short films. In the 1980s, mainstream cinema chains conducted a campaign with the contentious motto 'No More Boring Shorts'. The success of this campaign reduced the opportunities for shorts to be seen on the big screen. There is some sense that this situation is now changing. An increasing number of film festivals are dedicated exclusively to short films, including the St Kilda Short Film Festival, Tropicana, Matinaze, the Café Provincial Comedy Festival, Flickerfest, Watch My Shorts, and the White Gloves Festival (see Festivals). Many of the boutique cinemas regularly schedule packages of shorts and screen them as individual programs. Television is also expanding its role as an exhibitor of short films: both the government broadcasters have undertaken a number of initiatives. SBS hosts local and international shorts in the avant-garde 'Eat Carpet' program. The ABC has been involved in commissioning several packages of short films (*Microdocs*, *Microdance*, *Loud*, *Race Around the World*) as well as films for the Short Wave series, a half-hour program showcasing new work.

While the number of spaces and places where Australian short films can be seen is increasing, the appropriateness of their screening locations is sometimes questionable. For example, in 1998 a local cable station screened Kathryn Millard's **Parklands** (1996), an inventive, passionate, emotional short film about a daughter's efforts to excavate something of her father's life, after being confronted by pieces of the past at his funeral. There is also the problem of archiving and access. The National Library's decision to jettison the infrequently borrowed films in its collection (mainly short films, documentaries, and educational and instructional pieces) is a blow to research on short films. The richness and variety of our short-film heritage will only be understood if we have a chance to do the research. Unfortunately, this is becoming a more compro-

mised task: many short films remain in jeopardy, waiting for more enlightened cultural attitudes to prevail. (See also Experimental film.)
ANNA DZENIS

Shorter, Ken (1945–) ACTOR In 1967 and 1968 Ken Shorter appeared as perennial loser Frankie McCoy in the television adaptation of John Cleary's 1947 novel *You Can't See 'round Corners*. At the end of the series, the television production team completed a film version that was released in 1969, to great popularity in Perth and to a more moderate reception in the eastern states. A featured part in the international co-production •**Ned Kelly** (1970), was followed by the lead role as an undercover policeman sent to infiltrate a motorcycle gang in •**Stone** (1974). This preceded a key role as Frankie, the scab who confronts the striking shearers at the climax of •**Sunday Too Far Away** (1975). Except for a featured role as a wealthy man who has a brief affair with a former (married) girlfriend (Judy •Morris) in **Maybe This Time** (1980), Shorter's acting career after the mid 1970s was away from Australia—mainly in the United Kingdom (for example, he played Lady Dalrymple's butler in **Persuasion**, 1995).
GM

Show Business

1938. *Director:* A.R. Harwood. *Producer:* A.R. Harwood. *Scriptwriter:* Frank Chapple. *Director of photography:* Arthur Higgins. *Music:* Frank Chapple. 90 min. B&W. *Cast:* Bert Matthews (Cogs), Joyce Hunt (Nina Bellamy), Fred Tupper (Fred Hamilton), Chick Arnold (Red), Bonnie Dunn (Tap Dancer), Betty Matear (Jean), Jimmy McMahon (Wally Winter), John Barrington (Bill Winter), Guy Hastings (Sir James Winter).

This musical was A.R. •Harwood's most expensive production, and was a twist on the traditional story of the young people who 'put on a show' and succeed despite their inexperience. Here the entrepreneurs are brothers—Bill Winter (who produces a stage musical) and Wally Winter (who produces a film). The twist is that the leading lady, Nina, is a conniving self-promoter who is exposed as a fraud. After a false start in Melbourne, the film was produced in Sydney, and was accepted for NSW quota, receiving some favourable reviews. But it managed only limited release, and Harwood made no more films until 1952, when he used part of the story of **Show Business** in the even less successful film **Night Club** (1952).
IB

Showgirl's Luck

1931. *Director:* Norman Dawn. *Producer:* Norman Dawn. *Scriptwriter:* Martyn Keith. *Directors of photography:* Norman Dawn, Jack Fletcher, Walter Sully. *Music:* Jack O'Hagan, Ormond

Bulners. 55 min. B&W. *Cast*: Susan Dennis (Peggy Morton), Sadie Bedford (Mona), Arthur Tauchert (Hap), Arthur Clark (Barry), Fred Bluett (Hollis), Paul Longue (Dud Grey), Olga McCann (Chummy).

Several companies competed during 1931 to produce Australia's first talkie feature. In the end, A.R. •Harwood's •**Spur of the Moment** and Frank •Thring's (Snr) •**Diggers** were screened before **Showgirl's Luck**, but the last remains of great interest historically, as it builds a story around the film industry itself, and contains several shots of movie cameras and new sound gear in action. The story tells how Peggy (played by Dawn's wife Katherine, working under the pseudonym of Susan Dennis) is given a job on the first Australian talkie, but Mona tricks her into believing the job is withdrawn, and takes Peggy's place. Peggy eventually gets her revenge—the leading man's attentions—and her chance to star. The sound quality is poor and the film was not widely distributed, but it contains several examples of Norman •Dawn's camera talents, particularly a scene in which Peggy's nausea at smoking her first cigar is represented by optical tricks that distort the image of her face until her bug-like eyes fill the screen. IB

Sick Stockrider, The

1913. *Director*: W.J. Lincoln, from the poem by Adam Lindsay Gordon. *Director of photography*: Maurice Bertel. B&W. *Cast*: George Bryant (The Stockrider), Godfrey Cass (his mate).

The **Sick Stockrider**, W.J. •Lincoln's film version of Adam Lindsay Gordon's poem, survives in a complete one-reel print. The film seems strange to audiences today. Much of it consists of very long takes of the title character mouthing Gordon's verse, which then appears on the screen in the form of intertitles. As the highlights of the stockrider's life are recalled in the poem, we see their illustration on the screen. At the time, filmed poetry constituted a popular genre in the United Kingdom, the USA, and Australia. The **Sick Stockrider** may be the first filmed Australian poem; other survivals of the genre include •**Trooper Campbell** (1914) •**The Sentimental Bloke** (1919), and •**Around the Boree Log** (1925). WILLIAM D. ROUTT

Siege of Pinchgut, The

1959. *Director*: Harry Watt. *Producer*: Michael Balcon. *Scriptwriters*: Harry Watt, Jon Cleary. *Story*: Inman Hunter, Lee Robinson. *Director of photography*: Gordon Dines. *Music*: Kenneth V. Jones. 104 min. *Cast*: Aldo Ray (Matt Kirk), Heather Sears (Anne Fulton), Neil McCallum (Johnny Kirk), Victor Maddern (Bert), Carlo Justini (Luke), Alan Tilvern (Superintendent Hanna), Gerry Duggan (Pat Fulton), Grant Taylor (Constable Macey).

The last of the Ealing (see Studios) Australian cycle of features, **The Siege of Pinchgut** closed the cycle, as •**The Overlanders** (1946) had opened it, with Harry Watt as director. Thematically, **The Siege of Pinchgut**, which depicts the fracturing of family solidarity and the submerging of community benefit in private gain, is the polar opposite of **The Overlanders**. Matt Kirk (played by American actor Aldo Ray), convicted of a crime he did not commit, is 'sprung' from prison in a very effective pre-title sequence that reflects the structural influence of television on feature film-making. Matt's escape is organised by his brother Johnny, played by Canadian actor Neil McCallum. No attempt is made to account for the American accents of these two actors, even though they both allude to the rituals of Australian boyhood.

The attempt to flee Sydney at night using a fishing boat goes wrong when the propeller is fouled, and the escapees land on Pinchgut, the convict nickname (in colonial times) for the rock island on which Fort Denison, a former military establishment, was built. No longer an active military establishment, the fort is supervised by an Irish caretaker (a strong performance by Gerry Duggan) and his family. The fort's magazine contains shells for a still-functional five-inch naval gun mounted on its ramparts, a relic of World War II. Turning a misfortune to advantage, the desparate group, which includes an Italian and a cockney (former criminal colleagues of Matt), seize the caretaker's family as hostages and train the naval gun on an explosives ship moored nearby. Matt issues an ultimatum by telephone: he wants the guarantee of a new trial or he will destroy the ship, threatening much of harbourside Sydney with destruction.

Matt's nemesis, the police inspector Madden, stalls for time while the senior bureaucrats seek a politically expedient end to the crisis. Meanwhile, Johnny has become romantically entangled with the caretaker's daughter, and the solidarity of the escapees is shattered as they begin to take casualties from police snipers. The final storming of the island provides a violent narrative closure, but does not resolve any of the deeper issues of the film.

BRUCE MOLLOY

Silence of Dean Maitland, The

1934. *Director*: Ken G. Hall. *Producer*: Ken G. Hall. *Scriptwriters*: Gayne Dexter, Edmund Barclay. *Director of photography*: Frank Hurley. *Music*: Hamilton Webber. 97 min. B&W. *Cast*: John Longden (Cyril Maitland), Charlotte Francis (Alma Lee), Jocelyn Howarth (Alma Gray), John Warwick (Henry Everard), John Pickard (Tommy Everard), Patricia Minchin (Marion Everard), Audrey Nicolson (Lilian Maitland), Bill Kerr (Cyril Maitland Jnr).

Silent film

Although there was a concerted effort in this 1934 *Cinesound production to update aspects of the 1914 version, **The Silence of Dean Maitland** remains a prime example of Victorian melodrama transferred to the screen. This morality play of guilt, betrayal, and redemption extends over more than a 20-year period, beginning when a young woman, Alma Lee, seduces Cyril Maitland, the Anglican curate of the small coastal town of Grenville. Alma's pregnancy, and Maitland's refusal to marry her, together with the fact that he is engaged to another woman, eventually leads to the death of Alma's father when Maitland accidentally strikes him. Maitland, however, refuses to take responsibility for his actions, letting his best friend Henry Everard take the blame, and Henry is gaoled for 20 years.

During this period, Maitland marries Everard's sister Marion, and rises to the position of bishop of the neighbouring city of Bellminster. Everyone except Maitland is punished for Maitland's transgressions: Maitland's son is born blind; Henry's fiancée refuses to marry; Alma arrives in Bellminster suffering from a terminal illness; her daughter, also named Alma, is prevented from marrying the man she loves (Tommy Everard) because he is wrongly thought to be her uncle. Henry Everard's release from prison provides the dramatic catalyst for the truth to emerge, and Maitland finally confesses his guilt to his church congregation. Maitland suffers a heart attack, and a kind of moral equilibrium is restored at the end the film: on his deathbed he marries his illegitimate daughter Alma to Tommy Everard. This intricate, interlocking story is matched in melodramatic intensity by the excessive acting styles and the way in which everyone connected with Maitland is punished excessively. The final scene in the film has Maitland lying on a couch, his wife nearby, and his blind son singing 'Abide With Me'. The boy's voice is supplemented by a church choir and, as Maitland dies, the windows open to show that he has achieved a degree of spiritual peace and his ascent to heaven is indicated by a final montage of clouds. This melodrama, with British actor John Longden in the lead role, was one of Cinesound's most popular films.   GM

Silent film, to 1914

On 30 November 1894, just five weeks after their London premiere, Edison's 'kinetoscope' 35mm film-viewers introduced movies to Sydney. Twenty-five thousand Australians saw the machines in their first month of exhibition. Under the management of the MacMahon brothers, a successful nationwide kinetoscope tour followed. The films were all shot in Edison's New Jersey 'Black Maria' studio.

Sound films made their Australian début when the MacMahons exhibited three of Edison's phonograph-equipped 'kinetophone' viewers at Charters Towers in Qld on 16 September 1895. They had soundtracks with full dialogue, made by synchronising locally recorded wax cylinders with the kinetoscope's American films. Standard cylinder phonographs did not have enough volume and clarity to fill a theatre, so these sound experiments did not survive the advent of film projection.

On 17 August at the Melbourne Opera House, the magician Carl Hertz gave Australia's first private preview of film projection on to a screen. His film exhibitions to the paying public began as an interlude for his magic act five days later. Hertz introduced R.W. Paul's films of familiar British locales, all less than a minute in length.

Australia's antipodean isolation from the hub of British-colonial culture saw this type of film appealing to local audiences. Furthermore, Australians were prepared to pay sixpence or a shilling for admission—considerably more than their American counterparts were paying at the time. Local taste for films of European places and events lasted until World War I, when closer links with Hollywood modified the composition of Australian cinematic fare. New films, actualities, and illustrated lectures were Australia's cinematic staple before 1910.

There were several early and abortive attempts to establish Australian venues exclusively dedicated to film projection. The first was opened by the MacMahon brothers at Brisbane's Royal Arcade on 26 September 1896. Two days later, Marius Sestier (the Lumière Cinematographe's local concessionaire) opened Sydney's 'Salon Lumière' in a former Pitt Street shop. A similar Melbourne shop exhibited Gustave Neymark's *Cinematographe Perfectionne* [sic] in October 1896. In March 1897, Sydney's Mark Blow opened a movie show integrated with amusement arcade machines, eventually known as 'The Polytechnic'. However, by late 1898, the vogue for these embryonic 'cinemas' had passed. Their programs of unrelated minute-long films could not sustain interest.

Before the advent of Australia's first permanent city cinemas around 1906, there were no Australian film libraries or exchanges. Show people had to purchase their films outright. Regardless of their country of origin, the films were usually imported from British film dealers, or were bought from Australian photographic warehouses such as Baker & Rouse, Osborn & Jerdan, and Harrington's. The producers prominently represented before 1905 included R.W. Paul, the Warwick Trading Company, Williamson, Bamforth and (after 1903) Urban—all British firms. Next in popularity came the French product: Lumière, Star (Melies), and later Gaumont and Pathé. French film dealerships (Pathé and Gaumont) did not open Australian branch offices until 1909. Only a few American films slipped through the net before 1905, chiefly the Edison product.

Each Australian capital had a few specialist 'lanternists' (slide and film showmen). In Melbourne, both Alex Gunn and the St Kilda chemists Johnson & Gibson offered operators on hire (with films, slides, and a projection plant) to assist fundraisers and theatrical performances. A few Australian city music halls offered a brief assortment of films as a 'chaser' on their otherwise 'live' programs. In summer, film was also shown at continentals—outdoor shows of film and live performance held at night in suburban parks.

However, Australia's dominant form of film exhibition in this pioneer period was the travelling picture show. Portable and inexpensive, it was an ideal entertainment for Australia's widely dispersed middle-class population. Each showman spent a few nights showing his stock of film in a theatre, hall, or Mechanic's Institute before moving on to the next locality on his itinerary. They used Australia's extensive railway and coastal steamer network to travel, rarely straying from that network before the introduction of the motor car. Such shows were more common here than in the United Kingdom or the USA.

From the start, Australian producers could only supplement and complement the vastly more numerous film imports. On 25 October 1896, Australia's first film was made by Sestier, **Passengers Alighting from the Paddle Steamer 'Brighton' at Manly**. Straight after this test, he took the Lumière Cinematographe to Melbourne where he filmed the VRC Derby and Melbourne Cup (**•1896 Melbourne Cup**), both at Flemington Racecourse. A few street and military scenes were filmed on his return to Sydney, but the effort ceased in December 1896.

The Sydney photographer Mark Blow shot about 40 one-minute actualities through 1897 and 1898. Like Sestier, Blow had his own exhibition venue, 'The Polytechnic', to recoup his production costs. Other potential Australian film-makers were impeded by the lack of permanent exhibition venues. Melbourne's E.J. Thwaites and R.W. Harvie built a movie camera in March 1897, shooting several horse races soon afterwards, and made the first film of an Australian Rules football match in July 1898. Their interest was chiefly technical, and production ceased within 18 months.

Specialist applications of film were pioneered in Qld. Professor Alfred Haddon of Cambridge University filmed Torres Strait Islanders and Australian Aborigines on Murray Island during an anthropological expedition to the Torres Strait. These films, shot in September 1898, were the first anthropological research films shot on location. Haddon urged Walter Baldwin Spencer to film the central Australian Aborigines. As a result, Spencer shot over 40 minutes of Arrente ceremonies and customs during April and May 1901, and gave the world's first major screening of ethnographic film at the Melbourne Town Hall on 7 July, 1902.

Soon after Haddon's seminal effort, Qld's official artist and photographer F.C. Wills shot about 30 Qld films to promote emigration from the United Kingdom. The films give a vivid picture of Australian life in 1899, relics of the world's first in-house government film production project.

Some travelling shows used film only as an interlude in their 'live' performances. Carl Hertz, Cogill's Minstrels, Colonel Lumare's Company, the Corrick Family Entertainers, the Hellers, the Newbury–Spada Company, Delroy and Bell, Brisbane's Ted Holland Company, Hobart's J.C. Bain Company, and the Cunard Family Entertainers all gave shows of this type. Their films tended to be brief, lightweight material—comedies, trick films, travel scenes, and news items, presented on the 'sandwich principle'. Many of their early projectors (Lumière, R.W. Paul, Watson's, and Demeny's) could run no more than one-minute rolls of film without reloading.

Other touring companies relied solely on film exhibition, having longer and more sophisticated film programs to compensate for the lack of 'live' support. These all-film companies frequently offered serious fare, almost invariably with guiding narration provided by a lecturer. As early as 1897, films dealing with a single subject or event were assembled by these exhibitors to make a full program or 'feature' presentation. **Queen Victoria's Diamond Jubilee Procession in London** (1897) was one of the earliest 'feature' subjects shown in colonial Australia. Its many local exhibitors included Brisbane's G. Boivin, Melbourne's Alex Gunn, and Adelaide's G. Bull. They could select from the jubilee coverage of at least 18 British and continental film-producers, some offering versions 35 minutes in length. Australian exhibitors could combine the several versions to make a very long show, or they could just use highlights from one or more. At this stage, the exhibitor usually acted as the editor and compiler of his feature-length actualities as an assembled 'package'. Projectors having 1000 feet (17 minutes) of film-load capacity became available from several manufacturers, notably Edison, Warwick, and Gaumont.

Australian audiences' enthusiasm for these lengthy nonfiction programs and films set Australia on a fundamentally different evolutionary path from that of the USA. Edifying and educational films found a more ready audience with Australia's middle class than they did in the 'nickelodeons' and dime museums of urban working-class USA. Many early American films were locally regarded as vulgar. Sydney exhibitions of the American Veriscope Company's 90-minute film of the **Corbett–Fitzsimmons Boxing Contest** (1897) were reviewed in September 1897 as 'an hour of gory carnage'. In spite of the fact that it was the first feature-length film shown in Australia, it did poor business and was soon withdrawn. The same applied to a 50-minute film of the

Corbett–Jeffries Fight (producer unknown, 1900). In 1904, Australia's first major film obscenity charge was laid against risqué American movies shown in Mutoscope flip-card peepshows. 'It was a matter for regret', said the Magistrate, 'that any company should have thought that such an exhibition would be tolerated in Melbourne.' An exception to the general standard of the American product was the Hollaman & Eaves 1897 film of **The Oberammergau Passion Play**, depicting the life of Christ. This 50-minute (2900-foot) film had its Australian début in Hobart on 14 August, 1899, supporting the appearance of Orpheus McAdoo's Afro-American 'Jubilee Singers'. The film was a logical development of the religious slide shows presented by Australian clerics in pre-cinema days.

More often, Australian show people were exhibiting films such as Méliès' **Cinderella** (seven minutes, 1899), **Little Red Riding Hood** (nine minutes, 1900), **Joan of Arc** (14 minutes, 1900), and **A Trip to the Moon** (14 minutes, 1901). Typical long non-fiction films shown in Australia included **Funeral of Gladstone** (in versions by Chard, Lumière, R.W. Paul, G.A. Smith, and Warwick), **The Great Spanish Bullfight** (15 minutes, Lumière, 1898) **and Funeral of Queen Victoria** (various producers, circa 45 minutes, 1901).

Several outstanding British exhibition companies toured Australia with single-subject film programs, exploiting the jingoistic sentiment stimulated by the Boer War and Federation. Wyld and Freedman's British Biograph used 70mm unsprocketed film running at 30 pictures per second, giving huge images of superb clarity. Their Boer War films taken on the battlefield by W.K.L. Dickson created a sensation. Commencing at the Melbourne Athenaeum at the time of the relief of Mafeking (May 1990), the show toured Australia for two years. Another patriotic manifestation was the visiting Our Navy Company, which showed 10 000 feet (170 minutes) of film on every aspect of British navy life, shot by Alfred J. West of Southsea near Portsmouth. This unique entertainment, managed by the MacMahon brothers, brought celebrity narrator G.H. Snazelle and projectionist (later local-production pioneer) Herbert Wyndham to Australia. It raised the social standard of Australian cinema by aiding naval recruitment and attracting Royal patronage. When the Duke and Duchess of Cornwall and York visited Australia for the first opening of federal parliament in 1901, one of West's cameramen (Chief Petty Officer MacGregor) accompanied them and shot a 90-minute film of the tour. Other Melbourne and Sydney royal-visit coverage totalling 45 minutes was shot by the British Warwick Trading Company's visiting camera operator Joseph Rosenthal. Local cameramen Stephen Bond and Mark Blow also took feature-length records of Australia's 1901 royal tour. However, the outstanding pioneer producer of Australian feature-length films was the Salvation Army Limelight Department (see Documentary and non-fiction, silent).

The Limelight Department, based in Melbourne, gave slide shows descriptive of its social and religious work from 1891, and in 1897 it added motion pictures to its outfit. Chief technician Joseph Perry was filming Salvation Army activities late in 1897 and, by the start of the following year, had completed Australia's first film studio at the rear of the Bourke Street headquarters in Melbourne. For the next six years, about 80 per cent of all Australasian film was shot by the Limelight Department.

Australasian Salvation Army Commandant Herbert Booth wrote, directed, and narrated their first 'feature length' screen presentations. The first of these lectures was **The Salvation Army's Social Work in Australasia**, initially illustrated by six one-minute films and 20 slides, and presented at the Sydney Town Hall on 11 July, 1898. By 30 October 1899 it was called **Social Salvation**, and was expanded to include 275 slides and 25 one-minute films in a 150-minute lecture presentation. By then, it had been delivered in hundreds of Australian venues by Limelight Department operators.

Booth and Perry followed this effort with their well-known **Soldiers of the Cross**, a lecture on the early Christian martyrs illustrated by 15 one-minute films and 220 slides. It was first shown on 13 September 1900. Having the nation's only film studio and several touring 'Biorama' film shows, the Limelight Department took on Salvation Army fundraising more directly. It began to shoot and exhibit non-religious films, often under government contracts. For the NSW government it filmed **The Inauguration of the Australian Commonwealth** (1901) in Sydney. Thirty-five minutes in length, it was the nation's first film to approach 'feature length', and was six times the duration of the then-longest Australian film. It made so much profit that the Salvation Army had to register Australia's first production company, 'The Australian Kinematographic Company'. Commissions followed from the Victorian government to film the **Royal Visit to Victoria** (20 minutes, 1901) and from the New Zealand government with **Royal Visit to New Zealand** (56 minutes, 1901) (the first major film made abroad by an Australian crew).

Shooting film prolifically during 'Biorama' exhibition tours of Australia, the Salvation Army's Joseph Perry and Sidney Cook assembled a lavishly illustrated two-and-a-half hour lecture that traced Australian history from exploration to Federation. **Under Southern Skies** (first screened on 10 August 1902) featured 6000 feet (100 minutes) of film and 200 slides, and was by far the longest and most elaborate Australian film presentation of the period. Its successful 'roadshow' through Vic. and NSW was followed by a host of Australian production milestones. The Army made short narrative fictional efforts such as **Sensational Rescue from Drowning at Queenscliff** (July 1903), **The Adventures of an Australian Stock Rider** (July 1903), and even the nation's first bushranging film, **Bushranging in North Queensland** (March 1904).

By 1904 Melbourne's Limelight Department had attracted the attention of the Salvation Army's British command. Joseph Perry and James Dutton took a complete production and exhibition outfit to London's International Salvation Army Congress, demonstrating their product and shooting film extensively there and in Europe. On 10 October 1904 they presented this **Salvation Army International Congress Cosmorama** coverage at the Melbourne Town Hall, with 10 000 feet (two and a half hours) of film. Having established contacts with British film companies in London, the Limelight Department subsequently decided to screen the foreign product, and Australian production was greatly curtailed for three years. Others took the lead, and the Limelight Department never regained its dominance of Australian production.

The Australian film business slumped during 1902–04, and revived with the advent of several important show people from abroad. Cozens Spencer and his projectionist wife Eleanor brought their 'Great American Wonderscope' (later 'Theatrescope') company to Australia from New York in 1903. His profits were ploughed back into multiplying the number of his touring shows. By July 1905 he had a long lease on the Sydney Lyceum, which became his exhibition base. After commissioning several short actualities, he joined Hugh D. McIntosh in producing a film of Sydney's Burns–Johnson Fight (December 1908), by far the highest grossing Australian film of the decade. Four months after its production, 20 prints were continually booked up in the United Kingdom alone. Spencer produced his first fictional feature film in 1910, **The Life and Adventures of John Vane** (SA. Fitzgerald) and, in 1912, built Australia's largest film studio in Rushcutter's Bay.

The British showman Thomas J. West, a slide exhibitor since 1878, had taken up film exhibition in the United Kingdom by 1899. His initial Australasian foray was to New Zealand late in 1904, showing films on tour with The Brescians, a musical troupe lured to Australia by the entrepreneur Edwin Geach. He continued his New Zealand practice of shooting and showing local films after taking a long lease on Sydney's Palace Theatre from March 1906. West's main exhibition interest was in non-fiction film. By late 1909 he appeared to have signed the world's (then) largest producing concern, Pathé Frères, to what we would now call a 'city first-run' agreement for Australia. West thus became the first Australian exhibitor to feature Pathé's films of Australian industries made for the Commonwealth government (1909).

His outlets also pioneered the screening of Australia's first newsreel made in the customary multi-item 'magazine' format: **Pathé's Animated Gazette—Australasian Edition** (released weekly from 28 November 1910).

The St Kilda chemists Millard Johnson and W.A. Gibson screened films at various Melbourne venues from 1902. Their first big exhibition 'hit' was with shows undertaken in association with Messrs J. & N. Tait, the theatrical entrepreneurs, screening the hour-long **Living London** (Urban, 1904). Their tour of Australasia and India induced the Taits to ask Johnson and Gibson to make a long film of •**The Story of the Kelly Gang** (1906). Charles Byers Coates, a British camera operator with almost a decade of film-making experience, was employed to undertake camera work and direct the photographic composition. The Cullinan–Grist dramatic company provided the acting talent, filmed over a series of weekends in the bush around Melbourne under the direction of the Taits. When the film was released on 26 December 1906, at the Melbourne Athenaeum, its running time was said to be 40 minutes, although advertisements claimed the length to be 4000 feet (67 minutes). It was the first long and fully integrated fictional narrative film made in Australia. However, **The Story of the Kelly Gang** was preceded by many Australian and foreign films of similar length, and could only be defined as 'the world's first feature film' in narrow and conditional terms. What is not in doubt is its huge financial success, which almost immediately induced the MacMahon brothers in Sydney to make two similar films, **Robbery Under Arms** (1907) and •**For the Term of His Natural Life** (1908), for both of which Charles Byers Coates was again hired as camera operator and director. By then he worked under the Sydney management of Osborn & Jerdan.

Australia experienced an early flowering of feature film production between 1906 and 1912, pre-dating similar activity in the United Kingdom and America. Australian production rapidly declined afterwards, as a result of the formation of a monopolistic exhibition 'combine' integrating West's, Spencer's, Pathé, Tait's, Johnson & Gibson, and J.D. Williams. The combine's policy favoured import over local production on the grounds of cost, thus terminating Australia's first vigorous period of production.

CHRIS LONG

Silks and Saddles

1921. *Director, Producer, Scriptwriter, Editor:* John K. Wells. *Story:* John Cosgrove. *Director of photography:* Al Burne. B&W. *Cast:* Brownie Vernon ('Bobbie' Morton), John Cosgrove (Dennis O'Hara), John Faulkner (Richard Morton, Snr), Tal Ordell (Phillip Droone), Kennaquhair (Alert).

Silks and Saddles is the only surviving Australian feature of several during the silent era to deal with what the American scenarist Bess Meredyth saw as our only truly national subject: horse racing. The racing theme was picked up by John K. Wells, a young American, through the medium of the Australian writer John Cosgrove, who also supplied the storyline for •**Sunshine Sally** (1922), which is another Sydney-based feature directed by an American. In essence, **Silks and Saddles** is a routine melodrama centred around Bobbie Morton, the daughter of a stud farm owner, and her efforts to train her prized horse Alert to win the Spring Cup. In the process she has to contend with racetrack intrigue, the gambling debts and cruel maiming of her brother, and the attentions of rival suitors. Circumstances ultimately force her to don the scarlet colours of a jockey. Brownie Vernon, yet another American, plays Bobbie with considerable charm.

KEN BERRYMAN

Silver City

1984. *Director:* Sophia Turkiewicz. *Producer:* Joan Long. *Scriptwriters:* Sophia Turkiewicz, Thomas Keneally. *Director of photography:* John Seale. *Music:* William Motzing. 101 min. *Cast:* Gosia Dobrowolska (Nina), Ivar Kants (Julian), Anna Jemison (Anna), Steve Bisley (Viktor), Debra Lawrance (Helena).

Xenophobic attitudes to the postwar wave of European migrants are dramatised in Sophia Turkiewicz's first feature film, extending concerns first explored in her 1978 short, **Letters from Poland**. A Polish migrant herself, she uses a flashback to trace the experiences of a group of compatriots who arrive in Australia in 1950, and who are herded into a migrant hostel of corrugated-iron dormitories before making their ways to the city. The protagonist, Nina, falls in love with Julian, who is married to Anna, and runs a gamut of intolerance as she confronts the challenge of her new country. The film begins with a chance reunion between Nina and Julian, before plunging back into the events of an earlier decade. It has value as a document recalling an era in which the more sophisticated multiculturalism of today was preceded by an unwelcoming suspicion of those from different backgrounds, but the romance between the principals is written and played without much depth of feeling.

BMcF

Simpson, Geoffrey (1947–) CINEMATOGRAPHER Geoffrey Simpson attended the South Australian School of Art and then the London Film School. He commenced freelancing in Adelaide in 1973. Two documentaries won him Australian Cinematographers Society (ACS) Gold Awards, as did Australia's first Super-16mm feature, **Centrespread** (1980), but his feature film reputation began with •**Playing Beatie Bow** (1986), which won the ACS Golden Tripod and

'Milli' award (Cinematographer of the Year). He has also won one gold and two silver ACS awards for television films. **The Navigator** (New Zealand/Australia, 1988) won cinematography awards from the Australian Film Institute (AFI) and the New Zealand film industry; •**The Last Days of Chez Nous** (1992) was nominated for an AFI award; •**Shine** (1996) won both the AFI and Cameraimage (Prague) cinematography awards; and •**Oscar and Lucinda** (1998) won the Best Cinematography Award at San Diego. Other American films he has worked on include **Till There Was You** (1990), **Green Card** (1990), **Fried Green Tomatoes** (1991), and **Little Women** (1994).

Other Australian films: **Call Me Mr Brown** (1986), **Initiation** (1987), •**Celia** (1989), •**Deadly** (1992). DAVID MUIR

Sirens

1994. *Director:* John Duigan. *Producer:* Sue Milliken. *Scriptwriter:* John Duigan. *Director of photography:* Geoff Burton. *Music:* Rachel Portman. 90 min. *Cast:* Hugh Grant (Anthony Campion), Tara Fitzgerald (Estella Campion), Sam Neill (Norman Lindsay), Elle Macpherson (Sheela), Portia de Rossi (Giddy).

Writer-director John •Duigan's career has had a wayward look since his realist films of the 1970s. Socially committed films such as •**Mouth to Mouth** (1978) could scarcely have anticipated this softly nostalgic romp in which an uptight British couple (endearingly played by Grant and Fitzgerald) loosen their sexual and emotional stays under the liberating influence of Norman Lindsay and the freewheeling 'community' with which he has surrounded himself. Lindsay's sexual mores scandalised the 1920s, but now they tend to look merely like opportunities for well-proportioned young women to remove their clothes. Campion, a shy Anglican clergyman, is charged by his bishop to report on a rumour that Lindsay has painted a blasphemous picture, but potential censure gives way before the seductions on offer. The motif of British stiffness melted by Australian freedom is treated with undemanding good humour. A newsworthy element of the film was the film début of the model Elle MacPherson, although it made little demand on her acting ability.

BMcF

Skinner, Carole ACTOR With no more than a few minutes of screen time, Carole Skinner's short-order cook in •**Monkey Grip** (1982) suggests a lifetime of dealing with tiresome customers. Following her début as the Mother Superior in •**Alvin Purple** (1973), she quickly established herself as one of the best character players in Australian cinema; in the old days of the American studio system, she would have made scores of films by now and become an instantly recognisable face. She was Mrs McSwat, good-natured slattern and loving mother to a filthy litter, in •**My**

Brilliant Career (1979). In •Heatwave (1982), she played Mary Ford, a fictionalised version of Sydney journalist Juanita Nielson, who disappears following a series of outspoken articles criticising urban development in a militant news-sheet. Most of her roles were less substantial, less likely to motivate narrative moves than to provide the pleasures of felt life. She did this with effortless authority.

Other Australian films include: •Eliza Fraser (1976), A Most Attractive Man (1981), •Goodbye Paradise (1983), The Marsupials: Howling III (1987), •The Good Wife (1987).   BMcF

Smart, Ralph (1908–) DIRECTOR/PRODUCER/WRITER A British-born film-maker with Australian parents, Ralph Smart entered the British film industry in the late 1920s as a scriptwriter. In 1940 he came to Australia where he directed shorts for the Department of Information (see Documentary and non-fiction, silent; Film Australia). After the end of World War II, Smart was the associate-producer of •The Overlanders (1946) and he directed •Bush Christmas (1947) the following year, before returning to the United Kingdom. Smart returned to Australia in 1949 to direct one of Australia's best films of the period, •Bitter Springs (1950), for Ealing Studios, a film featuring Chips •Rafferty, Tommy Trinder, Michael •Pate and Charles •Tingwell. Smart returned to the United Kingdom after this film and directed the award-winning Never Take No for an Answer (1951), and he followed this up with the script for the melodrama Where No Vultures Fly (1951). In the 1950s and 1960s Smart worked extensively in British television, as the producer of the *Danger Man* series, for example, before returning to Australia in 1970 where he worked on the *Riptide* television series. Smart now lives in retirement in Spain.   GM

Smart, Rebecca (1976–) ACTOR Flaxen-haired child actor Rebecca Smart made a major impression in the title role of Ann •Turner's Celia (1989), as the eight-year-old who finds her grandmother dead, is oppressed by her fervidly anti-communist parents, and is agitated by the Victorian government's determination to stamp out the rabbit plague (the film is set in 1957). Smart, under Turner's sensitive direction, ensured that the child's point of view governs the audience's response to this semi-Gothic tale of suburban repression. Before Celia, she had been seen in small roles in •The Empty Beach (1985), The Coca-Cola Kid (1985), and Echoes of Paradise (1987). She followed Celia with the plum role of Buster in the television miniseries *The Shiralee*, in which she played opposite Bryan •Brown. More television work followed, along with roles in several little-seen films, such as Richard •Lowenstein's Say a Little Prayer (1993) and the telemovie *Doom Runners* (1996), until she surfaced again in Steven •Vidler's undervalued •Blackrock, the savage 1997 critique of male surfside bonding. It will be interesting to see if the intense, talented Smart successfully makes the transition to adult roles.

Other Australian films: Violet's Visit (1995), Tom's Funeral (1999).
BMcF

Smeaton, Bruce (1938–) COMPOSER Bruce Smeaton is a prolific composer for film. He orchestrates and conducts the majority of his scores written for feature films and television series. Smeaton plays most instruments and his music is solidly based in a knowledge of the mechanics of the instruments. His craft skills extend to the integration of ethnic and ancient instrument in his scores: the inclusion of the koto in *A Town Like Alice* (1981) prompted him to learn Japanese musical notation. Smeaton's prodigious output of film music began with scores for Peter •Weir's The Cars that Ate Paris (1974). The haunting music he composed for Weir's •Picnic at Hanging Rock (1975) includes Gheorghe Zamphir's unearthly sounding pan pipes. The versatility in Smeaton's repertoire is evident: for example, the historical television series *The Timeless Land* (1980); the animated feature •Grendel, Grendel, Grendel (1981); the crime drama Squizzy Taylor (1981), with its jazz-inspired score; and the hard rock soundtrack he produced for Street Hero (1984). In 1984 Smeaton founded the Australian Guild of Screen Composers (AGSC). He has received five Australian Film Institute awards (including Best Original Film Score Award for Street Hero), Penguin and Sammy awards, and the AGSC Special Award for Outstanding Contribution to Film Composition (1994).   DIANE NAPTHALI

Smiley

1956. *Producer:* Anthony Kimmins. *Scriptwriters:* Moore Raymond, Anthony Kimmins. From the novel by Moore Raymond. *Director of photography:* Edward Scaife. *Music:* William Alwyn. 97 min. *Cast:* Colin Petersen (Smiley), Bruce Archer (Joey), Ralph Richardson (Reverend Lambeth), John McCallum (Jim Rankin), Chips Rafferty (Sergeant Flaxman).

Despite its multinational origins in terms of development and funding (it was funded by British and American companies and had a British director), this film has an authentic Australian feel. This is largely due to the fine Australian cast (Ralph Richardson is the only British actor) and to its effective evocation of small town life. Son of a poor and dysfunctional family, nine-year-old Smiley is determined to earn enough through odd jobs to buy himself a racing bike. His efforts involve him in various misadventures, including drug-dealing by the unscrupulous local publican, played by John •McCallum in his return to Australian films after a decade in the United Kingdom. When his shiftless father, one of many in Australian films, steals his savings, Smiley accidentally knocks him out. He then flees into the bush where a swagman saves his life after he is bitten by a snake. The locals acknowledge his efforts and bravery by raising money to buy the long-desired bike. Colin Petersen is effective as Smiley and, following some other appearances in British films, he went on to fame and fortune as drummer with the Bee Gees.

BRUCE MOLLOY

Smith, Beaumont (1881–1950) DIRECTOR

Like Ken G. •Hall, Beaumont Smith's background was in publicity and journalism. Again like Hall, his feature films combined nationalistic ingredients with novelty and demonstrated an ability to capture audience taste without any pretensions to 'art'. Both directors were consistently successful in financial terms, and both turned repeatedly to bucolic comedy.

Smith's enduring rural family were the Hayseeds, inspired (like Hall's later series) by the family created by the Australian writer Steele Rudd in his collection *On Our Selection* (1899). After Smith's directorial début with •**Our Friends the Hayseeds** (1917) came six more films in the series, ending with his first talkie: **The Hayseeds Come to Sydney** (1917), **The Hayseeds' Back-blocks Show** (1917), **The Hayseeds' Melbourne Cup** (1917), **Townies and Hayseeds** (1923), **Prehistoric Hayseeds** (1923), and •**The Hayseeds** (1933). Although Smith also made films partly in New Zealand (for example, **The Betrayer**, 1921), most of his 19 features tapped a vein in Australian nationalism, which was on the rise in the years after World War I. Perhaps the most nationalistic were adaptations from poems and stories by Banjo Paterson and Henry Lawson: **The Man from Snowy River** (1920), **While the Billy Boils** (1921), and •**Joe** (1924).

The sole survivors of Smith's output are his two talkies, as well as fragments from •**The Digger Earl** (1924) and the complete •**The Adventures of Algy** (1925). Known as 'One take Beau' or 'That'll do Beau', Smith worked as his own producer, director, writer, editor, distributor, and publicist, and each of his films came in on budget and schedule. Despite continued audience support for his films, diminishing returns forced him to retire from continuous production in 1925. He returned to make two sound features—**The Hayseeds** and •**Splendid Fellows** (1934)—but spent the rest of his career in film exhibition and distribution.

Other Australian films: Satan in Sydney (1918), Desert Gold (1919), **Barry Butts In** (1919), The Gentleman Bushranger (1922), Hello Marmaduke (1924).

GRAHAM SHIRLEY

Smithy

1946. *Director*: Ken G. Hall. *Producer*: N.P. Perry. *Scriptwriters*: John Chandler [Ken G. Hall], Alec Coppel. *Director of photography*: George Heath. *Music*: Henry Krips. 119 min. B&W. *Cast*: Ron Randell (Sir Charles Kingsford Smith), Muriel Steinbeck (Mary Powell), John Tate (Charles Ulm), Joy Nichols (Kay Sutton), Nan Taylor (Nan Kingsford Smith).

'Who's Smithy?' an American pilot asks a group of flying officers sitting in a services' bar during World War II. The pilot is told by a senior officer, 'Smithy started the job you boys are finishing'. The film flashes back to 1916 in London, where wounded flier Charles Kingsford Smith is being awarded the Military Cross. The rest of the film shows how his wartime courage and enterprise are devoted to the challenges of early trans-ocean flight. The first half, neatly and swiftly told, chronicles his determination to fly from California to Sydney, punctuated by six years of setbacks. The ultimately successful flight is accompanied by tense reporting of potential hazards and euphoric landings along the way. The second half, dealing with his marriage to Mary and with attempts to establish airmail routes, leading to the fatal last flight from the United Kingdom when he is too ill for the task, is less compelling. However, director Ken G.•Hall, in his last full-length feature, is still able to create real suspense in a mid-air attempt to transfer oil from one engine to another, and he manages a moving finale that places Smithy's achievements in the context of the postwar world of 1946. Ron •Randell plays Smithy with an engaging charisma that does much to weld the essentially episodic structure together, and there are appearances from 'real-life' participants such as Billy Hughes and Captain P.G. Taylor. Despite the film's box-office and critical success, Columbia Pictures did not fund any more films in Australia.

BMcF

Sokol, Yuri (1937–) CINEMATOGRAPHER

Yuri Sokol trained at the National Institute of Cinema in Russia (1954–61), taught cinematography in Moscow (1974–78) and was a well-established director of photography before reaching Australia at the end of 1979. The first feature he shot in Australia, director Paul •Cox's •**Lonely Hearts** (1982), won the Australian Cinematographers Society (ACS) Silver Award and critical acclaim. Sokol's other films have earned the following awards from the ACS: three silver, four gold, two Golden Tripod (best cinematography), and one 'Milli' (cinematographer of the year—for **Georgia**, 1988). His films have also attracted three best-cinematography nominations from the Australian Film Institute. He has worked on the following Russian films: **Desert Heat** (1961), **Djura** (1964), **Roll Call** (1965), **Nobody Else** (1967), **Shine Brightly My Star** (1969), **Residence Permit** (1970), and **Dr Evans' Silence** (1972).

Other Australian films: •Man of Flowers (1983), •My First Wife (1984), Cactus (1986), •Warm Nights on a Slow Moving Train (1988), Struck By Lightning (1990).

DAVID MUIR

Soldiers of the Cross, *see* Silent film, to 1914;
Documentary and non-fiction, silent; Historical representations

Son is Born, A

1946. *Director*: Eric Porter. *Producer*: Eric Porter. *Scriptwriter*: Gloria Bourner. *Director of photography*: Arthur Higgins. *War photography*: Damien Parer. *Music*: Sydney John Kay. 85 min. B&W. *Cast*: Muriel Steinbeck (Laurette Graham), Peter Finch (Paul Graham), John McCallum (John Seldon), Ron Randell (David Graham), Jane Holland (Kay Seldon).

In 1920, heavy-drinking womaniser Paul Graham marries Laurette against her family's wishes. He neglects her and spoils their son David, turning him against Laurette, who finally leaves Paul. David stays with his father and refuses all contact with his mother, who marries her employer Seldon, who has helped to arrange her divorce. When Paul dies, David, now grown up, goes to live with his remarried mother, and to revenge himself on her 'desertion' of his father, he woos Seldon's daughter Kay and deserts her immediately after their marriage. In wartime New Guinea, the drama of David's regeneration takes place: he is reunited with Kay and vows to repair the damage done to their parents. The film is awash with entertainingly developed Oedipal variations, and the production values are of a quality to stand comparison with similar Hollywood family melodramas of the period. It is interesting as Eric •Porter's only excursion into live-action feature film—and for the number of future stars in its cast. BMcF

Sonkkila, Paul ACTOR

Trained in London, Paul Sonkkila has had a career that spans more than 20 years, on both stage and screen. In film he has always been a reliable character actor, without becoming a star. His performance as Detective Inspector Jackson in •The Interview (1998) is typical: he is impressive, forceful, and memorable, in a comparatively small role.
Other Australian films: •Stir (1980), •Hoodwink (1981), •Gallipoli (1981), With Prejudice (1982), Freedom (1982), •The Year of Living Dangerously (1982), Gross Misconduct (1993), That Eye, the Sky (1994), •Mr Reliable (1996). IB

Sons of Matthew

1949. *Director*: Charles Chauvel. *Producer*: Charles Chauvel. *Scriptwriters*: Charles and Elsa Chauvel. *Director of photography*: Bert Nicholas, Carl Kayser. *Music*: Henry Kripps. 107 min. B&W. *Cast*: Michael Pate (Shane), Ken Wayne (Barney), Tommy Burns (Luke), John Unicomb (Terry), John Ewart (Mickey), Wendy Gibb (Cathy McAllister), John O'Malley (Matthew O'Riordan), Thelma Scott (Jane O'Riordan), John Fegan ((Jack Farrington).

Sons of Matthew is one of the great Australian melodramas. The film's thematic celebration of endurance and survival was matched by its troubled production history, which lasted more than two-and-a-half years. At one point the production nearly closed. The epic story traces the first three generations of the O'Riordan family and their determination to succeed, first in the valley of Cullenbenbong in NSW and, later, on the Lamington plateau in the mountainous rainforest of southern Qld.

In the first part, Matthew and Jane O'Riordan, and their family of five sons and two daughters, struggle to establish themselves. The film opens in spectacular fashion as Matthew fights the wild stallions to save his mares just as Jane gives birth to their first son Shane, the 'first Australian O'Riordan'. This powerful sequence, depicting the elemental drives emanating from the combination of nature, sex, and fertility, is essential and provides an appropriate thematic context for Charles •Chauvel's excessive, melodramatic style.

In the second half, Matthew and Jane's sons, together with a neighbour's daughter, Cathy McAllister (the repository of 'nature'), travel 600 miles north to the 'Green Kingdom', a mountainous plateau in southern Qld. After the spectacular felling of the huge trees and the establishment of a tentative base on the Lamington plateau, the dramatic focus foregrounds the sexual rivalry between Shane and his brother Barney for Cathy. While the film provides numerous cues that Shane is the 'natural' partner for Cathy, it takes a fierce storm, and a superb feat of location film-making, for Shane's passion to boil over in the declaration of his true feelings for Cathy ('You think I'm going to let Barney marry you and spend a lifetime of nights thinking of you in his arms? You're going to be my wife and bear my sons because that's the way it was meant to be and neither you, nor I, nor Barney can do anything about it . . . You and the earth, Cathy, that's all I want').

Sons of Matthew is formally, and thematically, one of the most significant films in the history of the Australian film industry, and is the high point of the Chauvel's career. The Chauvel's knowledge of classical conventions, combined with melodramatic devices and a heartfelt concern for the film's protagonists and their desires, blend more easily in this film than in any other in their long career. GM

Sound

Sound shorts synchronised with cylinder or disc were screened in Australia at various times during the silent era. For four years from 1921, Ray Allsop, Ronald Davis, and George •Malcolm were the earliest known Australians to experiment with short films synchronised to sound-on-disc and (in Allsop's case) cylinder. While perfecting his Raycophone sound projector in late 1928 and early 1929, Allsop filmed four sound-on-disc musical shorts.

By 1923, Dr Lee De Forest, American founder of De Forest Phonofilms, had perfected an amplification process that enabled a mass audience to experience sound-on-film, a system first developed in the United Kingdom in 1906 by Eugene Lauste. In early 1927 De Forest Phonofilms (Australia) filmed synchronised shorts, including coverage of the visit to Sydney and Canberra by the Duke and Duchess of York. On 9 May the highlight was their sound-on-film coverage of the Duke's opening of Canberra's first federal parliament.

Feature-length sound films arrived in Australia with the Sydney opening of the American films **The Jazz Singer** (1927) and **The Red Dance** (1928) in December 1928. In 1929 talkies achieved global acceptance. From mid 1929, spurred by the huge cost of overseas technology, Australian film technicians stepped up their experiments in disc and optical (sound-on-film). The inventors included Jack Fletcher, whose Standardtone sound-on-film system covered the Sydney arrival of aviatrix Amy Johnson in June 1930, and Sid Guest, who, at Vocalion Records in Melbourne, invented a synchroniser to link a movie camera with an imported 33-revolutions-per-minute disc recorder. **Fellers** (1930), the first Australian talkie feature, used the Vocalion equipment to musically accompany most of the film and add dialogue to the final reel. The silent version of •**The Cheaters** (1930) was initially modified with three disc scenes shot at Vocalion, then re-worked as a full talkie using Standardtone equipment to re-shoot the closeups and dub the wide shots.

Some of the experiments were linked to •newsreel ambitions. An Australian edition of the previously imported **Movietone News** began in November 1929. For nine months from June 1930, Movietone's first Australian sound rival, **Australian Talkies Newsreel**, used Melbourne-based disc technology. After Movietone had put the long-running silent newsreel **Australasian Gazette** out of business, Australasian Films' (see Greater Union Organisation; Cinesound) Sydney laboratory superintendent Bert Cross was determined to have his reel return to production with sound. By mid 1930, former radio engineer Arthur Smith, assisted by Clive Cross, had developed a viable optical recorder at Australasian's Bondi Junction studio. After being tested on a series of short films, the system was used on a feature, Ken G. •Hall's •**On Our Selection** (1932), the huge success of which provided the basis for ongoing feature production at the •Cinesound studio. From November 1931 the Smith and Cross system was also used on the weekly newsreel **Cinesound Review**.

From 1930 sound-on-film achieved dominance over sound-on-disc. The first all-talking Australian features to be released—A.R. Harwood's **Isle of Intrigue** and •**Spur of the Moment** (1931)—both used a locally developed sound-on-film system. For the next 20 years, optical sound recording remained the industry standard around the world. For release prints, there were two distinct types of optical sound: variable density and variable area. The latter took over completely after 1970.

During World War II, Germany perfected a quality quarter-inch recorder called the Magnetophon, which used a quarter-inch tape coated with iron oxide. A prototype was taken to the USA and, in 1948, Ampex released the USA's first quarter-inch recorder. Four years later, Arthur Smith completed the Australian film industry's first magnetic sound recorder using 35mm perforated film that was coated with iron oxide, then split down the middle to provide a more cost-effective 17.5 gauge. Smith's recorder was first used on the short film **I Found Joe Barton** (1953), before Smith achieved industry-wide sales that kept him busy until the early 1970s.

Magnetic recording was not only cheaper (stock could be re-used if a mistake was made), but it also improved fidelity and delivered the three-channel stereo that was a feature of CinemaScope, which was used in Australia on **Long John Silver** (1954). Just as magnetic recording phased out optical, the arrival in the early 1960s of imported quarter-inch recorders, such as the Nagra III and Perfectone, phased out magnetic perforated film as a recording medium. Not only were the new machines easily portable, but they also used a 'pilot tone' to accurately synchronise the camera with the recorder. In the 1960s the major 16mm camera makers also produced models that recorded sound on a magnetic stripe down the edge of the film.

Vast changes to film and television sound occurred in 1970–1990. Foremost among these were the move to digital recording, greatly improved noise reduction, and the use of timecode in post-production synchronisation. Introduced in the early 1970s, timecode synch allowed multi-track sound and a video image to be run back and forth during a sound mix, 20 times faster than the old film system. From the mid 1970s, Dolby A noise reduction brought a new way of reducing the noise from recording media without affecting recorded sound. Further advances in noise reduction were Dolby SR (or Spectral Recording) introduced in 1986 and first applied to an Australian film print with **The Crossing** (1990); Dolby SR.D, introduced in 1994 and first used in Australia on **Lightning Jack**; SDDS, introduced in 1994 and first used on the locally mixed **Little Women** (1994); and the best-known system, the CD-based DTS, introduced in 1995, with •**Babe** being the first Australian film on which it was used.

The change from analogue recording to recording on DAT (digital audio tape) took place between 1990–91. Providing much higher quality, digital sound was resistant to wear and tear. By 1992, two particular types of DAT recorders, the ADAT and DA88, were widely used by recordists and post-production studios. Australian invention again had a role in the new technology. In 1978, Graham Thirkell and Roger Savage, commissioned by the post-production house Soundfirm, developed a world first, the Editron, a multiple-format synchroniser for film,

Raycophone challenges imported sound systems, 1935

multi-track sound, and video. In 1985 another Soundfirm innovation, a computerised console (the Harrison Series 10) for the mixing and replaying of sound, was used for the first time in the world on the television miniseries *Vietnam*. Other milestones in Australian film sound were •**Mad Max** (1979), the first film mixed completely in 24-track sound; •**Mad Max 2** (1981), the first film mixed in Dolby Surround using Stereo Variable Area; and •**Dead Calm** (1989), the first movie to use Dolby SR at every stage from on-set recording to release print.

GRAHAM SHIRLEY

Sound of One Hand Clapping, The

1998. *Director*: Richard Flanagan. *Producer*: Rolf De Heer. *Scriptwriter*: Richard Flanagan, based on his novel. *Director of photography*: Martin McGrath. *Music*: Cezary Skubiszewski. 93 min. *Cast*: Kerry Fox (Sonja Buloh), Kristof Kaczmarek (Bojan Buloh), Rosie Flanagan (Sonja, aged 8), Jacek Koman (Picotti), Evelyn Krape (Jenja), Melita Jurisic (Maria).

Richard Flanagan's film, structured in a non-linear fashion, explores Sonja Buloh's return to the Tasmanian highlands where she grew up. She is pregnant and has had a dauntingly difficult life: 20 years after leaving home, with grim realism but without undue self-pity, she wants to try to fit together the pieces of her past. These include her mother's desertion of her father and herself at the age of three, her father's descent into bullying alcoholism, the abuse she has suffered, and the human warmth she has been offered by Jenja, an old family friend.

The film moves between past and present, and between Australia and Slovenia, in its search for answers for Sonja, the roots of much of her unhappiness, and that of her parents, being located in dreadful events of World War II and in the painfulness of the subsequent migrant experience in insular Tasmania. The core of the film is in the relationship that Sonja tries to re-form with her father, and the overall grimness is relieved by a moment of reconciliation between father and daughter and by touches of cultural-clash humour. It is held firmly together by Kerry Fox's eloquent, detailed performance as the mature Sonja.   BMcF

South Australia, history and images

Like the people of the eastern states, South Australians enjoyed their first vision of cinematic images through the Lumière cinematographe (1896) and the Edison Vitascope (1897) (see •Silent film, to 1914). Lacking famous attractions such as the Melbourne Cup or Sydney Harbour, South Australians had to wait until Federation, and the establishment of an exhibition circuit that included SA's ports and mining towns, to see their geography and population on screen. For ethnographers such as Baldwin •Spencer, Adelaide was the gateway to the Central Desert and the NT. Setting out from Oodnadatta in 1901 with 3000 feet of film, he made unique records of the Dieri, Urabunna, and Arrernte peoples en route to Charlotte Waters in the Northern Territory.

Otherwise, early shorts were a mixture of documentaries, civic propaganda, and commercial advertising (much of which cannot be reliably dated). The agricultural display of the Adelaide Show was an obvious choice. Its bustle was captured by Cozens Spencer and his wife in 1906. The Adelaide City Council watched the construction of barn-like cinemas in hot, dry Adelaide with apprehension. The Spencers responded with a celebration of the prowess of Adelaide's firemen, **Fire Service**. Audiences could also see their growing urban presence in the Tait brothers' **Animated Adelaide**, a series of tracking shots that proceeded from the Town Hall to Rundle St, centre of the city's commerce and entertainment. One enterprising businessman made sure he and his logo were featured by planting himself in front of the camera-van during its trip down King William Street.

As these shorts developed into newsreels, the images continued to be of such things as sporting events, provincial celebrations, disasters, and local industry, following the patterns established in Paris, London, Melbourne, and Sydney.

Besides the Adelaide Show, which was filmed again in 1912, 1917, and 1918, images of the renowned South Australian wine industry were shown: **The Wine Industry in SA** (1915), **Penfold Winery at Magill** (1916), and **Wine Industries of South Australia** (1921). Electric trams were another mark of modernity and were the subject of newsreels made in 1915 and 1917. The tourist potential of the planned parkland city emerged in Pathé Frère's **Glorious Adelaide** (1910), in the vignettes of **Adelaide in a Hurry** (1911), and in **Wattle Day** (1914) and the Commonwealth-sponsored **Adelaide and Environs** (1925). Typical of the desire to see country and city bonded, **From Pasture to Table** (1913) charts the progress of meat from cattle to beefsteak, and was filmed to celebrate the opening of the new abattoirs.

Films reflected the popular interest in sports: swimming (**Port Adelaide Aquatic Carnival**, 1911), rowing (**Henley on Torrens**, 1912), pageants (**Australia Day Pageant**, 1918), football (**Interstate Football**, 1923), and cycling (**Adelaide to Melbourne Motor Cycle Reliability Test**, 1923). Horseracing then took over: The Adelaide Cup and Oakbank racemeets were chronicled continuously from 1912 to 1922. Even vice-regal events (**Anniversary Day at Glenelg**, 1910; **The Governor at the Children's Hospital**, 1923) were put at the service of the film industry. By 1922 **Who's Who in Australia—Governor of SA** was a reminder to those lobbying for more censorship of film that this august figure had himself attended the cinema and pronounced it respectable.

The filming of the opening of new cinemas such as the Regent in 1928 and the Pavilion in 1912 was self-advertisement of an even more blatant kind. **The Construction of the Pav** (1912) was speeded up by the projectionist, who would hand crank the projection reel faster and faster until the audience roared at the sight of workmen flicking together planks and mortar at frantic speed: South Australian film-makers had discovered comedy. In 1914 they also discovered fictional narrative. **Nice Goings on at Henley Beach**, described as 'the first story picture ever taken in SA', combined these two forms and paved the way for satires on art snobbery such as **Distributing the Old Wild Oats**, and 'flapper flics' featuring 'Adelaide's girliest girls'. **Why Men Go Wrong** laid them in the aisles with its shocking images of 'Adelaide's gay life', which did not, of course, mean Mardi Gras .

What Happened to Jean (1918) was another in-joke, this time featuring recognisable high-society figures: Adelaide, the city of churches, had also discovered sex. In 1918, Raymond •Longford's •**The Woman Suffers** was produced. This melodrama is informed by Lottie •Lyell's intelligent performance and the cinematographer's eye for locations: wild cliffs, flooded rivers, and lush pastures. Inhabited by stock bush characters—'cads', 'swaggies', and parsons—and moving freely from the country to the streets of Adelaide, it sums up SA's picture of itself during the silent era.

The second phase of the state as a location for film is marked, as it is elsewhere in Australia, by essentially foreign interests in Antipodean 'difference'. The first notable images of SA were of its indigenous people, the Aborigines. Simplistic as its resolution is, •Bitter Springs (1950) does attempt to show the state's occupation by a people to whom the Whites are not only colonists but oppressors, and who must convince them to share its resources, in this case water. Shot around the town of Quorn, it is also a wry example of the way in which a climate does not always behave as it should. The film's story has Quorn in the grip of a drought but the normally arid town obliged with a downpour during filming. For the American production of •The Sundowners (1960), the scrub north of Port Augusta was more cooperative, providing Robert Mitchum, Deborah Kerr, and Chips •Rafferty with the expected imagery of the continent's centre: bluffs and saltbush, candlebark, cliffs, and gullies.

The third and greatest phase in the state's vision of itself was launched in 1972 with the foundation of the •South Australian Film Corporation (SAFC). Premier Don Dunstan's concept of Adelaide as a city of the arts was matched by the decision of SAFC's chief executive officer, Gil •Brealey, to use the National Film Board of Canada, with its links to television production and education, as a model. With co-producer John •Morris the SAFC found immediate and far-reaching success, encouraging similar bodies in other states and establishing a new model for national filmmaking. While it moved through many genres, directors and producers, it had three broad effects: the fostering of confident 'auteurs' such as Peter •Weir; a style of cinematography that matched Hollywood and rivalled Europe in its painterly definition of colour; and the extraordinary contrast between the cultural oasis of Adelaide and the rest of the state. The industry did eventually realise the full beatitude of its locations. The Murray and the old river towns along it, from Mannum to the expanses of the Coorong, the German hamlets and vineyards of the Barossa, the Flinders Ranges, and the Desert now came into their own.

This was a period of great invention. Port Augusta again served as the canvas for the blue and yellow palette of shearers in •Sunday Too Far Away (1975). Martindale Hall near Clare was transformed into the girls' school of •Picnic at Hanging Rock (1975), and Peter Weir returned to Adelaide's affluent suburbs for pictures of eerie domestic life in The Plumber (1978) and •The Last Wave (1977). •Gallipoli (1981) was recreated on the cliffs of the Eyre Peninsula. Further west towards the Nullarbor, the wild waves of Cactus beach served as adventure's end for the children of Scott •Hicks's Sebastian and the Sparrow (1989), while Streaky Bay perfectly captured the tuna fisheries of •Blue Fin (1978). Thunder-laden skies at Goolwa and the sandy stretches of the Coorong featured in Russell •Boyd's unforgettable cinematography in • Storm Boy, which launched the careers of young Greg Rowe and David •Gulpilil. SA's subtle beauty and atmosphere were becoming national landmarks without the established fame of the eastern seaboard, cities and bush. Producer Jock Blair took another direction in a series of period television melodramas such as Sara Dane (1982), Robbery Under Arms (1985), Under Capricorn (1982), and the time-travelling film •Playing Beatie Bow (1986).

This period earned the SAFC the sarcastic nickname Eighteenth Century Fox. But it was also a time of intense training for local technicians, who learned to transform mundane reservoirs into historic settlements, create Universal Studio-style street facades, and transform buildings into perfect colonial Georgian structures. With some close ups and crew work impossible on location, sound-stages in the Adelaide suburbs of Norwood and later Hendon facilitated the completion of coherent continuity editing.

Road movies such as Ned Lander's •Wrong Side of the Road (1981) explored stretches of the state where opportunities for the unemployed young people and Aborigines were few and far between. Other disadvantaged groups such as the intellectually disabled were foregrounded in Jerzy •Domaradzki's •Struck by Lightning (1990). By the late 1980s, Adelaide had all the best and worst elements of a metropolis: a dolce vita café society (Mario Andreacchio's affectionate Al Fresco), organised crime (Bruce •Beresford's •Money Movers, 1979) and a rebellious youth culture (Hicks's Freedom, 1981).

At this stage there could be no doubt about SA's visibility throughout the cinematic world. Struck by the lunar landscape round the opal town of Coober Pedy, George •Miller and George •Ogilvie created visions of the apocalypse in •Mad Max: Beyond Thunderdome (1985). This science fiction raised the historical implications of the nuclear testing that had actually taken place at Maralinga, and formed the starting point for Michael •Pattinson's Ground Zero (1986). •Burke & Wills (1985, d. Graeme Clifford) depicted the doomed explorers of 1860 traversing the same beautiful desolation as these films, a route followed with a more deliberate sense of the fantastical by the three drag queens of Stephan •Elliot's •The Adventures of Priscilla, Queen of the Desert in 1994. When European directors of the stature of Werner Herzog and Wim Wenders (•Until the End of the World, 1992), also seized on this desert iconography of shard mounds, stars, dunes, and mysterious underground clefts, the state was firmly on the map of the international imaginary.

Another kind of imaginary world was being fashioned on much smaller budgets by the independents. Their experimental shorts also had a surrealist tinge, sharpened by satire and more directly political approaches. Among the earliest and best examples of the concern with the position of women and cultural minorities was Margaret Dodd's **This Woman is Not a Car** (1982), which mixes images of mothers, ceramics, and cars until they assume each other's qualities as vehicles, ornaments, and receptacles. An even more anarchic body of work was produced by the artist Tim Burns, whose underground politics permeate the Trans-Pacific journey of **Against the Grain** (1985). Harry Bardwell rubs the Government's nose in the state's uranium industry in **Backs to the Blast** (1981). This growth in cutting-edge work was nurtured first by the Film Co-op and, from 1974, by the South Australian Media Resource Centre (MRC; see Media Resource Centre, Adelaide), together with Adelaide's tertiary institutions, especially Flinders University, which provided the state and the nation with hundreds of graduates trained as actors, theorists, and practitioners of film-making. These included the actors Syd Brisbane, Ulli Birve, Peter Douglas, Nicholas •Hope; inventive scripter and cinematographer Gerald Thompson; Joya Stevens, whose shorts have won international prizes; Shane McNeil, whose ingeniously devised locations subvert established genres; Kay Pavlou, who makes documentaries and features; and Jenni Robinson and Patricia Balfour, who use postmodern theory in their film essays.

The most recent phase of SA cinema has continued the push of the 1980s. Andreacchio moved into features with the exploitation 'flick' **Fair Game** (1985) and the rival to •**Babe** (1995), **Napoleon** (1993), which amusingly sends its animal characters out on the road. •**Bad Boy Bubby** (1994) earned director Rolf •De Heer and actor Nicholas Hope instant acclaim for its hyper-real cinematography of a weird Port Adelaide setting, a method that he used with less success in the science-fiction **Epsilon** (1994), perhaps because of the gap between the stunning motion-control technology and the overshadowed actors. **The Quiet Room** (1995) touched raw nerves about family and disability and marked a return to naturalism.

An even darker side of Adelaide has been tracked by Craig Lahiff. With 'noir' scripts by Peter Goldsworthy, Terry Jennings, and John Emery (who also wrote **Freedom**), films such as **Strangers** (1982), **Coda** (1986), **Fever** (1987), and **Ebbtide** (1993) move through a sophisticated, murderous and toxic society with style. Like Lahiff, co-producer Wayne Groom has also scripted and directed an Adelaide milieu that might easily take its place on the other side of the Pacific or the Mediterranean. **Centrespread** (1980) outraged the city's puritans with what was seen as pornography. But **Maslin's** (1996), shot on the Fleurieu Peninsula's nudist haven of the same name, reveals a more mellow aesthetic: an innocent delight in sexuality. Paul •Cox's troubling preoccupations are evident in **Lust and Revenge** (1995), a veiled satire on film-funding: even after the SAFC came loyally to his support, the satire remained. This film presents Adelaide at its most gracious, showcasing the elegant State Gallery and Carrick Hill, and including idyllic visions of the swans and gulls on the Torrens River. James Currie's impeccable sound mixing on this film is a reminder of the contributions made by ever more skilful technicians throughout this period.

Another outstanding success from SA is Scott Hicks. After making features and documentaries, he finally achieved international success with •**Shine** (1996), which first caught the attention of the Hollywood pantheon at the Sundance festival in the USA. Its portrayal of the breakdown and return to fame of concert pianist David Helfgott won fame for all involved. The SAFC astutely lent assistance early in the project.

Judith McCann, chief executive officer of the SAFC until 1999, was a consistent champion of the local industry. The SAFC, the MRC, and the involvement of the universities are reminders of how vital the state has been to the nation's filmic renaissance. With former SAFC board member Jane Scott as producer, **Shine** won both AFI and Golden Globe prizes and was nominated for seven Academy Awards. The list reflects in microcosm the experience of SA cinema.

Writer Jan •Sardi is the author of the great screenplay for **Ground Zero** (see above). The director of photography Geoffrey •Simpson was cinematographer for **Playing Beattie Bow**. Pip Karmel has edited two of Hicks's previous South Australian features, the telemovie *Call Me Mr Brown* (1985) and **Sebastian and the Sparrow**. Geoffrey •Rush established his reputation as a powerful actor and a brilliant comedian in Jim Sharman's Lighthouse Ensemble at the South Australian State Theatre Company. Rush won the Academy Award for Best Actor for his performance in **Shine**. Hicks, himself a product of Flinders University in SA (where the teaching programs were initiated by Wal Cherry, George Anderson, and Brearley), is an example of the innovation that the Dunstan era began. Since the end of that epoch, SA's documentary film-makers, independents, 'tyros', and auteurs have shown themselves capable of tackling the wildest landscapes with the deepest emotion.

NOEL PURDON

South Australia Media Resource Centre,
see Media Resource Centre, Adelaide

South Australian Film Corporation

The creation of this state corporation in 1972, the first of its kind, defined a role for state governments in the resurgent Australian film industry. The initiative of Labor premier Don Dunstan, the corporation was part of a visionary plan to move SA away from a dependence on manufacturing and to nurture a civil society in Adelaide through cultural enterprise.

The new corporation ran the film library, had a monopoly of all government film production, and had the authority to borrow (initially) $400 000 per year to develop what Dunstan called 'an area of influence and activity of its own'. The choice of Gil •Brealey as chairman/director made it inevitable that the 'area of influence' would be feature film. •Sunday Too Far Away (1975), •Storm Boy (1976), •Picnic at Hanging Rock (1975), •Money Movers (1979), and •'Breaker' Morant (1980), were all produced while the corporation was located in the Adelaide inner suburb of Norwood, during the time of Brealey's directorship (he left in 1976).

The consolidation of production, studio, and library functions on an industrial site in Hendon in 1981, and the departure of Matthew •Carroll, signalled a move to television miniseries production, which continued into the 1990s, initially fuelled by the 10BA tax concessions (see Finance). In many ways, the corporation set up to establish a viable film industry in SA had become that industry.

In 1993, after a government review, the present, more narrowly focused corporation emerged. The film and video library was closed and the collection redistributed. The corporation no longer acts as a producer. Instead it invests in project development and production, is a facilities house, and helps promote SA as a production venue and warehouse of talent. Recent productions associated with the corporation include •Shine (1996), Heaven's Burning (1997), and Dance Me to My Song (1998).   VINCENT O'DONNELL

Southwell, Harry ACTOR/DIRECTOR

Born in Wales, Harry Southwell worked as a scenarist for minor American studios from 1917, before marrying an Australian and moving to Australia in 1919. By overstating his Hollywood experience, he managed to raise money for a series of films that he directed and produced. He directed, produced, wrote, and acted in his first Kelly film (•The Kelly Gang, 1920). He then made a society melodrama (•The Hordern Mystery, 1920) and his second Kelly film (When the Kellys Were Out, 1923; see Kelly Gang, The), before going overseas, where he made two films in France (David, 1924, and Le Juif Polonais, 1925). He returned to Australia and completed Down Under (1927) and his third Kelly film, When the Kellys Rode (1934; see Kelly Gang, The). Although his directorial career was a succession of disasters and the films he produced were never more than third-rate, by some strange coincidence most of his Australian productions survive, if only in fragments. We can even see him performing, in •The Burgomeister (1935). His last film (A Message to Kelly, 1947) was left unfinished, but formed the basis of Rupert •Kathner's Glenrowan Affair (1951). Southwell remains a strange and colourful figure whose reach always exceeded his grasp.   IB

Spence, Bruce (1945–) ACTOR

This tall, gangly New Zealand-born actor has worked in Melbourne theatre since the 1960s. Spence was a prominent member of the Australian Performing Group at the experimental theatre La Mama and, later, at the Pram Factory. He became one of the most distinctive personalities on the Australian screen in the 1970s, largely as a result of the relative success of his first major feature film, •Stork (1971). This broad comedy, which featured Spence as an urban anarchist with a variety of social and sexual hang-ups, established his screen persona for many years, during which it was recycled as the Redex driver in •Newsfront (1978), the hapless groom in the disappointing comedy •Dimboola (1979), the Gyro Captain in •Mad Max 2 (1981), Jedediah the Pilot in •Mad Max: Beyond Thunderdome (1985), and Ronnie (Rosanna Arquette's husband) in Wendy Cracked a Walnut (1990). Among Spence's attempts to move beyond this image was his role as Jonah, the recluse who counsels young Danny (Noah •Taylor) and Freya (Loene Carmen) in •The Year My Voice Broke (1987), together with his supporting role in the gentle comedy Sweet Talker (1991).

Other Australian films include: Dead Easy (1970), Moving On (1974), •The Cars that Ate Paris (1974), The Firm Man (1975), The Great McCarthy (1975), •Mad Dog Morgan (1976), Let the Balloon Go (1976), •Eliza Fraser (1976), Oz (1976), Deadline (1981), Double Deal (1983), Midnight Spares (1983), Buddies (1983), Bachelor Girl (1987), Rikky and Pete (1988), Bullseye (1989), •Dark City (1998).   GM

Spencer, Walter Baldwin (1860–1929) ETHNOGRAPHER

Englishman Walter Baldwin Spencer was professor of biology at Melbourne University from 1887 to 1919, an internationally recognised anthropologist (he was elected a Fellow of the Royal Society of Anthropologists in 1900), and was knighted (1916). In July 1894 he met Francis James Gillen (1855–1912), an Australian who, while working for the postal service on the 'overland telegraph line' from Adelaide, had acquired an immense knowledge of Aboriginal culture and language. In 1901 these two took a Warwick Cinematograph camera, an Edison phonograph, and two still cameras into the NT to record the life of the indigenous Australians—producing Australia's second moving picture and sound anthropological record (see Silent film, to 1914). Spencer conducted a second expedition without Gillen in 1912, and substantial silent-film footage from both expeditions survives (it is held in the Museum of Victoria and in the National Film and Sound Archive). The footage from both these trips shows camp life (families around the campfire, women grinding seeds and cooking, young boys being taught by warriors, camp dogs), ceremonies (totem ceremonies, burials, corroborees), and hunting expeditions (through the bush, as well as in small boats on waterways).

Viewing these records now is an eerie and dreamlike experience. They follow none of the conventions we have come to expect of films (including films of record): in disconcerting silence, people move to and fro across the line of sight of the immobile camera, or recede so far into the distance that they become indistinct. At the time, the films and sound recordings were presented as accompaniment to Spencer's popular and profitable public lectures, in Australia and overseas.

IB

Spirit of Gallipoli, The

1928. *Director, Producer:* Keith Gategood, William Green. *Scriptwriter:* Hal Carleton. *Director of photography:* Jack Fletcher. B&W. *Cast:* Leo Meagher (young Billy Austin), Keith Gategood (Billy Austin), Marie Miller (Gladys Merton), William Green (Jack Thomas), Gwen Sherwood (Mrs Austin), Samuel Harris (William Austin).

Scarcely mentioned in histories of Australian film, **The Spirit of Gallipoli** can nonetheless tell us a great deal about the horizons of most Australians during the late 1920s. It is practically an amateur production, made by two army trainees with no previous film experience, but the roughness of its technique proves an exact match for the mundane suburban life it depicts. The story, such as it is, follows Billy Austin's metamorphosis from larrikin to responsible landholder through the spine-stiffening effects of peacetime military training. But the film unfolds as a series of awkward re-enactments of an everyday life in which all drama and danger have been relocated to the past of World War I. Billy's apotheosis occurs at the finals of the regimental boxing championship, in which a subjectively weaving camera vividly conveys his near defeat. One cannot but recognise that this battering is really the only way in which Billy can demonstrate that he is worthy of all the death and maiming he has envisioned in his reading about the war.

WILLIAM D. ROUTT

Splendid Fellows

1934. *Director:* Beaumont Smith. *Producer:* Beaumont Smith. *Scriptwriter:* Beaumont Smith. *Director of photography:* George Malcolm. 84 min. B&W. *Cast:* Frank Leighton (The Hon. Hubert Montmorency Ralston), Leo Franklyn (Thompson), Frank Bradley (Jim McBride), Eric Colman (Reverend Arthur Stanhope), Isabelle Mahon (Eileen McBride).

Beaumont •Smith's films had been built around 'silly-ass' Englishmen and hayseed Australians: in this, his last film, he incorporates both, but in a more mellow way. Monty, the aristocratic English 'black sheep' is transformed by his Australian experience into a mature, resourceful young man, able to recognise his manservant Tommy as a 'cobber'. The value and inevitability of links between Australia and the United Kingdom are also demonstrated: Monty and Tommy take part in the London-to-Melbourne centenary air race in

a plane designed and built in Australia, financed by an Englishman, and inspired by the romance between Monty and Eileen. Newsreel footage of the actual race and of the centenary celebrations in Melbourne is incorporated into the film, and Sir Charles Kingsford Smith takes the cast on an aerial tour of Sydney. Despite this topicality, and the optimistic tone of the film, it did not do well at the box office.

IB

Sport   It is not surprising that film provides a complex and often inconsistent representation of sport in Australia. Film in Australia began with sport: the •**1896 Melbourne Cup** carnival produced one of the first films made in Australia. This actuality footage of local popular culture is now a valued historical artefact, while the race itself was the focus of concentrated newsreel attention in the years before television and was central to several films, including Ken G. •Hall's •**Thoroughbred** (1936) and Simon •Wincer's •**Phar Lap** (1983). The silent-film era in Australia also put sporting stars on the big screen in American films: swimmer Annette Kellerman and athlete Reginald 'Snowy' •Baker established careers in Hollywood based on their sporting skills and appearance.

While newsreels emphasised the sport of the day, especially racing and cricket, it is surprising that sport has not been as significant an aspect of mainstream commercial film-making as it has in the general culture. Perhaps the largest single sub-genre of sports films is associated with the sport of surfing and the alternative culture of the 1960s and 1970s. Often using innovative exhibition and financing techniques, these films, such as **Morning of the Earth** (1972) and •**Crystal Voyager** (1973), proved lucrative in Australia and overseas, and they launched the career of David •Elfick, who moved into producing fiction features.

Mainstream features have, however, tended to avoid sport as a central concern, preferring instead to use its metaphoric dimension as a narrative device to investigate other issues. Peter •Weir's •**Gallipoli** (1981), with its emphasis on athletics, football, and an ideal notion of sportsmanship, is a case in point, as is Bruce •Beresford's •**The Club** (1980), which explores power politics within the setting of a football organisation. Both these films were written by David •Williamson (the latter is based on his successful play of the same name). Ken •Hannam's **Break of Day** (1977) uses a small post-World War I country-town cricket match to isolate key story elements, but the emphasis is never directly on the game. Rather, it is on what the game says about the hero and the town's attitude toward him. Other mainstream films that have emphasised sport with varying degrees of success include •**The Coolangatta Gold** (1984), •**Warming Up** (1985), and •**Dawn!** (1979). A vast range of films give an almost cameo role to sport, or locate a character within a sporting context: for example, the South African swimmer seeking a marriage partner in •**Muriel's Wedding** (1994) and the football champion and paedophile villain Zipper Doyle in •**Kiss or Kill** (1997). Less mainstream, but of importance in a country with a number of Aboriginal boxing champions, is **Come Out Fighting** (1973), Nigel •Buesst's documentary-style drama funded by the Experimental Film Fund (see Experimental film), a movie about a young Aboriginal boxer forced to choose between his promising sporting career and campaigning for Aboriginal rights. Similarly, the Australian National Film and Sound Archive's (see Archives) series on sport, in the recent two-volume compilation on the Victorian Football League, not only caters for an emerging niche market, but, through sensitive and informed analysis, locates sport, its fans, and its competitors in a popular culture that has a long social history in Australia. The same organisation has also produced **The Game is Up** (1989), which documents the contribution that Australian women have made to sport from 1896 to the 1956 Olympics.

This confidence in the legitimacy of sport as a fit subject for documentary film-making achieves a complex expression in Mike Cordell's •**The Year of the Dogs** (1997), which undertakes a *cinéma vérité* documentary analysis of the Western Bulldogs, an Australian Rules football team, following the team throughout an entire season. This investigation portrays the emotional intrigues from the point of view of players and spectators, and speaks clearly to anyone who has ever been a contender or a fan. In this, it echoes that flickering image of a horse and a finishing line in Melbourne in 1896.   JOHN BENSON

Spotswood

1992. *Director*: Mark Joffe. *Producers*: Richard Brennan, Timothy White. *Scriptwriters*: Max Dann, Andrew Knight. *Director of photography*: Ellery Ryan. *Music*: Ricky Fataar. 90 min. *Cast*: Anthony Hopkins (Wallace), Ben Mendelsohn (Carey), Alwyn Kurts (Mr Ball), Bruno Lawrence (Robert), John Walton (Finn).

Evoking, as many reviewers noted, memories of old Ealing-style films in which the 'little man' eventually triumphs over attempts by experts to bring him up-to-date, **Spotswood** (named for the Melbourne industrial suburb in which it is set) is an affectionate but not soft-centred comedy. Visiting star Anthony Hopkins plays Wallace, the efficiency expert (the film was titled **The Efficiency Expert** in the USA), who is brought in to modernise Mr Ball's moccasin factory, a business run on family lines and operating at a huge loss. The outcome, in general terms, is clearly posted: Wallace will have to learn that there is more to life than productivity, a fact that is brought home to him by the massive job loss that results from his 'success' in the restructuring of another company.

The fact that his marriage to Caroline (Angela •Punch-Mac-Gregor) is none too happy is another indication of the human lessons he needs to learn, and the sense of communal solidarity he finds at Ball's factory offers further instruction. The film is peppered with engaging performances (especially from Alwyn •Kurts as the factory owner and Ben •Mendelsohn as the boy whose cooperation Wallace tries to win) and it argues its way through to a more humanely based set of labour relations. Set in the late 1960s, the film may perhaps seem remote from the harsher industrial climate of the end of the century, but it works as a story of oppositions being forced to find a workable middle ground.   BMcF

Spur of the Moment

1931. *Director*: A.R. Harwood. *Production company*: A.R. Harwood Talkie Productions. *Scriptwriter*: A.R. Harwood. *Directors of photography*: Leslie McCallum, Ed Wintle. 50 min(?). B&W. *Cast*: James Alexander (Anthony Iredale), Beatrice Touzeau (Claire Rutherford), William Green (Inspector Perry).

Betty Davies, credited with writing the story of this film, became better known as the playwright, novelist, and radio writer Betty Roland. The story is a rather creaky murder mystery, with an innocent man (James Alexander) refusing to compromise a woman who could clear his name (Claire Rutherford), and a detective (William Green) forcing a confession from the real murderer by a re-enactment of the crime. The sound quality is poor, because of exaggerated diction and inadequate equipment. The film is significant, however, as a survival from a brave production enterprise that tried to challenge the better-equipped and more highly capitalised •Efftee Film Productions and did, with its companion production **Isle of Intrigue** (1931), reach screens earlier than Efftee's first sound feature, •**Diggers** (1931).   IB

Squatter's Daughter, The

1910. *Director*: Bert Bailey. *Producer*: William Anderson. From the play by Bert Bailey and Edmund Duggan. *Director of photography*: Orrie Perry. B&W. *Cast*: Olive Wilton (Violet Enderby), Bert Bailey (Archie McPherson), Edmund Duggan (Ben Hall).

The first version of **The Squatter's Daughter** is one of Australia's most important 'lost' films. Although the film apparently does not exist in any form today, it is supposed to have been 6000 feet long when it was released (that is, it lasted from 60 to 90 minutes). Films of this length did not become common for another five years. More significantly for Australian popular culture, this version of **The Squatter's Daughter**, which employed the talents of Bert •Bailey and Edmund Duggan, seems likely to have been a fairly faithful reproduction of that team's immensely popular stage production. This was a melodrama 'with the lot': a spirited girl of the bush, a 'new chum', rival sheep stations, nasty bushrangers, wood-chopping and shearing contests, horse stunts, and acres of native fauna. More than two decades later, Ken •Hall, with Bailey's help, produced a new version of •The Squatter's Daughter (1933) that is today recognised as one of the richest documents of interwar Australian culture. There is every reason to believe that the earlier version would merit at least equal attention.

WILLIAM D. ROUTT

Squatter's Daughter, The

1933. *Director*: Ken G. Hall. *Producer*: Ken G. Hall. *Scriptwriters*: Gayne Dexter, E.V. Timms. Based on the play by Bert Bailey and Edmund Duggan. *Directors of photography*: Frank Hurley, George Malcom. *Music*: Frank Chappel, Tom King. 104 min. B&W. *Cast*: Jocelyn Howarth (Joan Enderby), Grant Lyndsay (Wayne Ridgeway), John Warwick (Clive Sherrington), Fred MacDonald (Shearer), W. Lane Bayliff ('Old Ironbark').

Ken G. •Hall followed the success of •On Our Selection (1932) with another film based on a Bert •Bailey play that had been filmed in 1910. However, Hall and scriptwriters Gayne Dexter and E.V. Timms altered many of the plot elements, especially the references to bushranging. What Hall and the scriptwriters retained was the strong nineteenth-century theatrical dramatic structure—including traditional melodramatic elements such as sudden blindness, 'forbidden' inter-racial romance, stolen babies, and powerful obstacles to true romance—and an expansive acting style that has much in common with both nineteenth-century theatre and silent cinema. The film even includes a last-minute rescue by a dog.

The plot centres on the battle between two sheep stations: Enderby and Waratah. Enderby is controlled by young Joan Enderby, who struggles to combat the machinations of her rival, Clive Sherrington, the manager of Waratah station. As foreclosure nears, a mysterious stranger, Wayne Ridgeway, appears. He secretly purchases a sufficient number of Joan's sheep to forestall Sherrington. However, a climactic bush fire threatens not only Joan's sheep, but also the lives of the principals, with the fire performing its traditional melodramatic function of punishing the villains and removing obstacles to the union between the couple, Joan and Wayne. A last-minute disclosure involving babies switched at birth reveals Wayne as the true heir to Waratah station, and thus the two stations come together in the epilogue.

The film also functions as a paean to the ideological, as well as economic, significance of the sheep industry to Australia's development: the film opens with a prologue consisting of twelve lengthy shots of a sheep muster combined with the stirring song 'Land of Hope and Glory' on the soundtrack. This aspect is reinforced by a number of speeches throughout the film. Not surprisingly, the film was a major commercial success in New Zealand as well as in Australia. This formula for audience acceptance—strong melodramatic structure combined with visual beauty (photographed by Frank •Hurley and George •Malcolm) and easily recognisable stereotypes celebrating traditional pioneering qualities—was duplicated 50 years later in •The Man From Snowy River (1982).

GM

Stanton, John (1945–) ACTOR A performer of charismatic presence, John Stanton has been inadequately used by Australian cinema. He has worked for some of the country's most acclaimed theatre companies and made an imposing Ralph Nickleby in the marathon stage version of *Nicholas Nickleby*. On television, he had continuing roles in such popular series as *Bellbird*, *The Box*, and (in the title role) *Bellamy*, but his crowning achievement was his extraordinary incarnation of Malcolm Fraser in the much-lauded miniseries *The Dismissal* (1983). Perhaps a shade sombre for conventional leading-man roles, Stanton has made the best of what has come his way in films, including the lead opposite Liddy Clark in **Kitty and the Bagman** (1983); the role of the professional dog-hunter in •**Dusty** (1983), the film version of Frank Dalby Davison's novel; and the starring role of Lance, the troubled landowner, in Tim •Burstall's •**The Naked Country** (1985), a stirring melodrama based on Morris West's bestseller. He co-starred with Pamela •Rabe in the little-seen **Vacant Possession** (1995), a story of racial and family conflict. Featuring two of the most potent actors in local films, this ought to have won a wider audience. Stanton has also appeared in the American-made **Tai-Pan** (1986) and **Rent-a-Cop** (1988), and in a pair of martial-arts action films for director Brian •Trenchard-Smith—**Day of the Panther** (1988) and **Strike of the Panther** (1988). Most of his films to date have asked too little of him.

Other Australian films: **Three to Go** (1971), •**Libido** (1973), **The Great MacArthy** (1975), **Run Rebecca Run** (1982), **Tomorrow's Child** (1982, doc., nar.).

BMcF

Star Struck

1982. *Director*: Gillian Armstrong. *Producers*: David Elfick, Richard Brennan. *Scriptwriter*: Stephen MacLean. *Director of photography*: Russell Boyd. *Music*: Mark Moffatt. *Choreographer*: David Atkins. 105 min. *Cast*: Jo Kennedy (Jackie), Ross O'Donovan (Angus), Margo Lee (Pearl), Pat Evison (Nana), John O'May (Terry).

The musical is a film genre that the USA has made peculiarly its own. Until the flamboyant examples of the 1990s (•**Strictly Ballroom**, 1992, •**The Adventures of Priscilla, Queen of the Desert**, 1994), the most attractive of the meagre pickings in

Australian cinema, although it was not a box-office favourite, was **Star Struck**. It rehearses some of the clichés of the genre and imbues them with a likeable, distinctly Australian flavour. The 'kids putting on a show' convention meets that of 'saving the old home from the receivers'. Along the way, 18-year-old Eve, a punk rock singer, and her band, The Wombats, win a New Year's Eve contest at the Sydney Opera House. This win takes care of the former two conventions, ensuring success on every plot level. The musical score is largely unmemorable, but there is enough exuberance and wit in the film as a whole for this not to matter greatly. There are also engaging performances from the young leads: Jo •Kennedy as Eve and Ross O'Donovan as Angus, her 14-year-old cousin with an entrepreneurial flair.　　　　BMcF

State Film Centre of Victoria, *see* **Cinemedia**

Steinbeck, Muriel (1920–82) ACTOR A distinguished performer on radio and stage, Muriel Steinbeck had her most famous film role as Mary Powell, the woman who married Sir Charles Kingsford Smith, in •**Smithy** (1946), Ken G. •Hall's 'biopic' and the last feature made by Hall's •Cinesound company. She had already appeared in wartime documentaries such as **South West Pacific** (1943), but **Smithy** proved to be a popular success and brought her to the attention of a larger audience. She appeared in the leading role of the put-upon heroine in Eric •Porter's •**A Son is Born** (1946), a film now notable for showcasing three stars of the future: Ron •Randell (who played the title role in **Smithy**), John •McCallum, and Peter •Finch (these last two left Australia shortly after filming **A Son is Born**, to pursue careers in the United Kingdom). An attractive brunette, Steinbeck, who could be gentle-mannered or tensely interesting, made only four other films: **Into the Straight** (1948), a horse-racing melodrama with Charles •Tingwell; **Wherever She Goes** (1953), a naive biography of the early life of pianist Eileen Joyce, in which Steinbeck played Joyce's mother; **Long John Silver** (1954) (a sequel to Walt Disney's production of **Treasure Island**, 1950), in which she played Lady Strong; and Michael Powell's •**They're a Weird Mob** (1966), in which she took the role of the heroine's mother. **They're a Weird Mob** was her last cinema film, but she appeared in Australia's first television soap opera, *Autumn Affair*.　　　　BMcF

Stephenson, Pamela (1950–) ACTOR Born in New Zealand and a graduate, in 1970, of Australia's National Institute of Dramatic Art, Pamela Stephenson worked mainly in the USA and the United Kingdom in the 1970s, playing roles in popular British television programs such as *The Professionals* (1977), *The New Avengers* (1976), and *Tales of the Unexpected* (1979). Stephenson's most famous television appearance during this period was in the

British satirical comedy *Not the Nine O'Clock News* (1980). Her screen persona has varied little from her comedic television roles, except that the sexual aspect, with a dangerous edge, has gradually overwhelmed her screen roles at the expense of her other comic attributes. This mixture of sexual fantasy and danger was evident in her first screen role as Mary Ann Phillips in **Private Collection** (1972), a fantasy woman in a 'Harlow' wig with murderous intentions towards her husband, a role that was reprised in a much broader manner in **Those Dear Departed** (1987). Since the 1970s Stephenson's roles have tended towards the obvious, as an increasingly larger-than-life parody of the aggressive blond sexpot, an image that was strengthened by her appearance as Loreli Ambrosia in **Superman III** (1983) and as Veronique Crudite in **Les Patterson Saves the World** (1987).

Other Australian films include: Doctors and Nurses: A Story of Hopes (1981).　　　　GM

Stevens, David (1940–) DIRECTOR It was his television reputation, honed in such series as *Young Ramsay* and *The Sullivans* and clinched by the successful *A Town Like Alice* (starring Bryan •Brown and Helen •Morse) that led to Stevens's début as a film director. Born in Palestine to Anglo-Dutch parents, and educated in the United Kingdom (including drama training at the Royal Academy of Dramatic Art), he came to Australia as a television director in 1970 after wide-ranging experience in theatre and radio.

Stevens made two engaging films in the 1980s. The first was •**The Clinic** (1983), a 'serious comedy' set during one day in a Melbourne clinic for sexually transmitted diseases. Its essentially episodic structure was given some shape by the focus on a prejudiced young intern (Simon •Burke) as he gradually adopts a more tolerant attitude through to his exposure to the non-judgmental approach of the gay doctor (Chris •Haywood) who runs the clinic. Stevens, working from a sensitive script that shows a fine ear for the nuances of anxiety, maintains exemplary control over his material: he takes a genuine problem and treats it in such a way as to give both pathos and humour their proper innings. It is pleasing to note that so unpretentious and decently intentioned a work enjoyed a prosperous box-office season. Stevens's second film, **Undercover** (1983), focuses on the career of a young country girl (Genevieve •Picot) who enters the fashion world of 1920s Sydney and becomes part of fashion entrepreneur Fred Burley's campaign to promote Australian merchandise, starting with his own lines in women's underwear. As an Australian film in which women were not marginalised, this good-natured, somewhat under-powered film was mildly unusual in the early 1980s, and there is an especially enjoyable performance from Sandy •Gore as the waspish Burley's chief designer. The film's commercial failure brought Stevens's directing career to a halt, although in 1988 he made an American crime thriller, **Kansas**, starring Andrew McCarthy and Matt Dillon. On the basis of his two Australian features, his is a gently endearing talent, spiked by a saving sharpness in tone.   BMcF

Stir

1980. Director: Stephen Wallace. *Producer:* Richard Brennan. *Scriptwriter:* Bob Jewson. *Director of photography:* Geoff Burton. *Music:* Cameron Allan. 101 min. *Cast:* Bryan Brown (China Jackson), Max Phipps (Norton), Dennis Miller (Redford), Gary Waddell (Dave), Phil Motherwell (Alby).

In 1980, **Stir** seemed a decent and serious attempt to understand how tensions escalate in prison, between and among 'crims' and 'screws', to the point where violence inevitably erupts. The protagonist, China Jackson, who has spoken out on television about prison bashings, and who, three years later, is on his way back to prison, acts as a catalyst for the simmering resentments, not just between prisoners and warders, but also between warders and an ineffectual administration (epitomised by the humane, but weak, warden Norton and the absurd governor, who appears at a moment of crisis in his bowling costume). By comparison with later films, such as John •Hillcoat's •**Ghosts . . . of the Civil Dead** (1989) and Laurence Johnston's **Life** (1996), **Stir** may seem unsophisticated in its even-handed disposition of blame among those on either side of the bars, but Stephen •Wallace's first feature is still a valid film response to a socially important matter.   BMcF

Stitt, Alexander

(1937–) DESIGNER/WRITER/DIRECTOR/ANIMATOR   Stitt's multifarious career is emblematic of the profiles of animators in industries that are not large enough to support continuous specialisation. A graphic artist, he joined Fanfare Films as art director in 1958 and worked on the **Freddo the Frog** series. In 1962 he opened his own studio, Al et al, providing film and graphic services. In 1965 he was at Eric •Porter Productions as a designer on children's television variety projects. He directed his own shorts **Film Film** (1975) and **One Designer, Two Designers** (produced by Phillip •Adams, 1978). For Adams, he created the Norm cartoon character for Life: Be In It, a long running public-health campaign. He also created ICPOTA, the animated character for the *Age*, a Melbourne newspaper. He provided graphics and title sequences for such films as •**The Devil's Playground** (1976), •**The Chant of Jimmie Blacksmith** (1978), **Next of Kin** (1982), •**Evil Angels** (1988), **The Russia House** (USA, 1990), **Six Degrees of Separation** (USA, 1993), and **I.Q.** (USA, 1994).

His major film-industry accomplishment is the direction of two animated features: •**Grendel, Grendel, Grendel** (1981) and **Abra Cadabra** (1982). **Grendel, Grendel, Gren-**

del, a rowdy, gaudy, sophisticated retelling of the story of Beowulf, via a novel by John Gardner, combines a working knowledge of Anglo-Saxon poetry with audacious work with colour and form. As the first Australian animated feature aimed at adults, it has become an unjustly overlooked milestone of Australian cinema. **Abra Cadabra** is another retelling, this time of the story of the Pied Piper of Hamelin. For this film, Stitt had access to more sophisticated technology, particularly multiplane camera stands and Dolby Stereo sound, which the film uses to explore the possibilities of three-dimensional effects.   RICK THOMPSON

Stone

1974. Director: Sandy Harbutt. *Producer:* Sandy Harbutt. *Scriptwriters:* Sandy Harbutt, Michael Robinson. *Director of photography:* Graham Lind. *Music:* Billy Green. 126 min. *Cast:* Sandy Harbutt (Undertaker), Ken Shorter (Stone), Hugh Keays-Byrne (Toad), Rebecca Gilling (Vanessa), Helen Morse (Madison Vincent).

An environmentalist is assassinated at a rally, and the murder is witnessed by a drug-addled member of the Gravediggers biker gang. When three Gravediggers are murdered in an attempt to cover up the property development scam behind the assassination, a clean-living undercover cop, Stone, is reluctantly allowed to ride with the gang, but they never forget that he is not a true biker. Sandy Harbutt's visually and technically impressive first (and only) feature is a gem. **Stone** is clearly influenced by the visual style of **Easy Rider** (USA, 1969), particularly the scenes in the gang's hideout, where editing gives the impression of a stoned or hallucinating camera, and unfamiliar camera set-ups and radical point-of-view shots manage to conceal flaws in the storyline. Extended sequences of bike convoys and races through Sydney streets are lovingly shot and backed by a mesmerising score by Billy Green, recalling the surf films of American cinematographer, actor, and writer George Greenough (for example, •**Crystal Voyager**, 1973). Despite its 'R' rating for violence and language, the film was a major success for its main backer, the Australian Film Development Corporation (see Australian Film Commission; Cultural policy).   BEN GOLDSMITH

Stork

1971. Director: Tim Burstall. *Producer:* Tim Burstall. *Scriptwriter:* David Williamson, from his play *The Coming of Stork*. *Director of photography:* Robin Copping. *Music:* Hans Poulsen. 90 min. *Cast:* Bruce Spence (Graham 'Stork' Wallace), Graeme Blundell (Westy), Sean McEuan (Tony), Helmut Bakaitis (Clyde), Jacki Weaver (Anna).

Tim •Burstall's second feature was one of the first major commercial successes of the new Australian cinema (see Revival, the) and is the originator of the 'ocker' comedy, the first original and distinctively Australian genre of the revival. **Stork** was also David •Williamson's first film script; Williamson would later script some of the defining films of the Australian 1970s and 1980s (for example, **The Removalists**, 1975, and •**Don's Party**, 1976). The story of a reed-thin, aspiring-anarchist hypochondriac takes (and sends) up •**Two Thousand Weeks's** (1969) theme of Australia's intellectual, political, and cultural cringe. **Stork** evolved from the groundbreaking Melbourne theatre company La Mama. In an effort to get around the reluctance of local distributors to handle Australian features, Burstall and his associates initially showed the film at the St Kilda Palais, Melbourne, on 27 December 1971, where it ran for a highly rewarding six-week season. As a result of its success in Melbourne, **Stork** was picked up by Roadshow (see •Village Roadshow) and distributed nationally. The first film of Burstall's production company •Hexagon Productions, an enterprise that arose from this association with Roadshow, was the seminal ocker text •**Alvin Purple** (1973). BEN GOLDSMITH

Storm Boy

1976. *Director*: Henri Safran. *Producer*: Matt Carroll. *Scriptwriter*: Sonia Borg, from the novel by Colin Thiele. *Director of photography*: Geoff Burton. *Music*: Michael Carlos. 86 min. *Cast*: Greg Rowe (Mike Kingley or 'Storm Boy'), Peter Cummins (Tom Kingley or `Hide-Away'), David Gulpilil ('Fingerbone' Bill), Judy Dick (Miss Walker), Tony Allison (Ranger).

Mike lives on the edge of an isolated wildlife reserve with his father who, wounded by his wife's unfaithfulness, has shunned the materialism and duplicity of modern society. Mike's life changes when he meets 'Fingerbone' Bill, who has been banished by his people, the Kunai, and now lives on the reserve. They rescue three pelican chicks orphaned by hunters. The overlapping stories of alienation, marginalisation, and loss that connect Storm Boy, the outcast 'Fingerbone' Bill, and the pelicans that the boy raises are powerful allegories for potential relations between Blacks and Whites in Australia. They also impart valuable lessons about the use of and respect for the natural environment, lessons that have considerable resonance beyond the school-age target audience. The film benefited from the •South Australian Film Corporation's strategic marketing of the film to schools and from the provision of ancillary study material by the state's Education Department, which set Colin Thiele's novel for study in schools. BEN GOLDSMITH

Storm, Esben

Storm, Esben (1950–) DIRECTOR/ACTOR Danish-born, and long based in Australia, Esben Storm studied film at Melbourne's Swinburne Institute (now University) of Technology. He worked for a time as a production assistant for the Commonwealth Film Unit, before he and Haydn •Keenan formed the production company Smart Films in 1971. The company's first feature film (they made several shorts, including Storm's **In His Prime**, 1972, which he wrote, edited, directed, and co-produced) was •**27A** (1974), which was directed and written by Storm and produced by Keenan. The film, shot on a budget of $13 000, won a cult following for its uncompromising portrayal of an alcoholic who finds himself trapped, under section 27A of Qld's Mental Health Act, in a hospital for the criminally insane. Despite his final release, the film was too downbeat to attract major distributors, but it was praised for its bitter reflection of a society that can cause such disorders and perpetuate them, and for a remarkable central performance from Robert McDarra as Bill, a character who is treated brutally for his refusal to 'knuckle under'.

It is at least arguable that Storm has yet to surpass this feature début, although his 1979 film •**In Search of Anna** was at least interesting in its non-linear treatment of its 'quest' theme. It engages in a process of alternation between, on the one hand, the journey north of its hero (Richard •Moir) with a liberated young woman called Sam (Judy •Morris) and, on the other, the big-city menace that has led to the hero serving a five-year jail sentence. At a time when gentle literary pieces were winning most of the critical plaudits, this film was adventurous enough in ambience and narrative procedures to warrant more attention than it received. Since then, Storm has acted in a number of short films, as well as several features, including **The Coca-Cola Kid** (1985), **Wrong World** (1986), and •**Young Einstein** (1988), and has acted in and/or directed several television films and series. As a director of feature films, however, he has made only three more: **With Prejudice** (1982), based on the trial of three members of a sect called the Ananda Marga, who were accused of conspiracy to kill; the over-long comedy **Stanley** (1983), which he also wrote; and •**Deadly** (1992), which he also co-wrote and which is based on an inquest into an Aboriginal death in custody. Although there are merits in each of these, none received wide distribution, and Storm has spent most of the 1980s and 1990s either in television or acting in other people's films. After a promising start, his career looks disappointing.

Other Australian films: **Doors** (1969, short, w., d., ed., co-p.), **Dangling Conversations** (1970, short, w., ph.), **One Man Bike** (1970, a.), **Water for a City** (1971, doc., assoc. p.), **Teaching a Language Structure by the Australian Situational Method** (1972, two short docs, assoc. p.), **Flashpoint** (1972, assoc. p.), **Gentle Strangers** (1972, assoc. p.), **A Motion Picture** (1973, doc., p.), **Avengers of the Reef** (1973, unit manager), **Floating** (1975, doc., ed.), **The Making of Anna** (1978, doc.), **Hanging About** (1980, short, a.), **Last Breakfast in Paradise** (1982, a.), **Greetings from Woollongong** (1982, short, a.), •**Monkey Grip** (1982, a.), **Going Down** (1983, a.), **I Live with Me Dad** (1985, 'a.), **Pandemonium** (1988, a.). BMcF

Storm Boy

Greg Rowe in **Storm Boy**

Story of the Kelly Gang, The

1906. *Director*: Charles Tait(?), Charles Byers Coates(?) *Producers*: John Tait, Nevin Tait, Millard Johnson, William Gibson. *Scriptwriter*: Charles Tait. *Directors of photography*: Millard Johnson, Orrie Perry, Reg Perry. B&W.

The Story of the Kelly Gang was Australia's first secular narrative feature, one of the first films, if not *the* first, in the world to resemble what we would call a 'feature film' today. At a time when the norm was a program of one-reel shorts, **The Story of the Kelly Gang** was initially released in four reels, and it alone occupied the entire evening's program. The film chronicled the career of Ned Kelly and his gang from the time that Kelly was supposed to have wounded Constable Fitzpatrick to Kelly's capture by police after the bloody siege of the Glenrowan Hotel. It seems to have been a box-office success in both Australia and the United Kingdom (where it was promoted as 'the longest film ever made'). The film was remade and re-released in 1910.

Stage shows about the Kellys had been produced since before Ned's death by hanging in 1880. One or more of these popular productions may have furnished the dramatic incidents, and some of the cast, of the film, which was backed by members of the Tait theatrical dynasty. However, since the production of **The Story of the Kelly Gang** was preceded by shorter films about bushranging, it can be seen to have arisen from a specifically Australian *cinematic* tradition within the wider context of Australian popular culture. Globally, bushranger stories and ballads are related to an international tradition of outlaw legends that also found a place in American western movies around 1907–08, although the first western feature was still many years away when **The Story of the Kelly Gang** was produced.

About nine minutes currently survive out of the film, which may have initially run to 40 or more minutes (and subsequently seems to have been increased to at least an hour). Footage from the both the 1906 and 1910 version survives and, to complicate matters, portions of another film on the Kelly gang that is currently dated as having been produced in 1906 have been found. The visual composition and dramatic staging of **The Story of the Kelly Gang** are not especially adventurous for the time. However, the image of Ned in his armour staggering from side to side as he is gunned down is an instantly recognisable Australian cinematic icon.

The Story of the Kelly Gang can be said to have set a pattern for early commercial film production in Australia. Until the rest of the world caught up, Australian fiction films tended to be rather longer than was usual in the USA and Europe—that is, they were produced to be

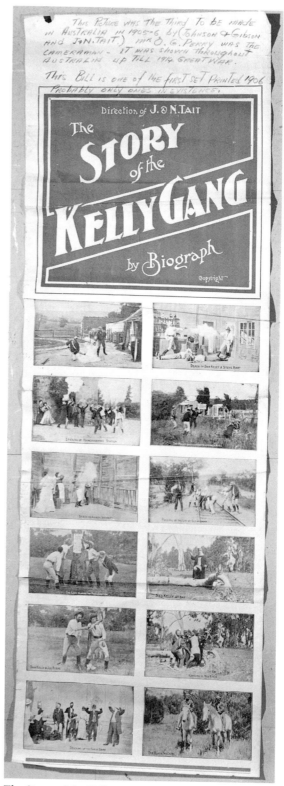

The Story of the Kelly Gang (1906)

The Story of the Kelly Gang (1910)

featured on the program. Their content was aggressively Australian, creating a self-consciously national cinema drawn from popular history, literature, and drama that celebrated the achievements of bushrangers, convicts, and other 'common folk'.

WILLIAM D. ROUTT

Street to Die, A

1985. *Director*: Bill Bennett. *Producer*: Bill Bennett. *Scriptwriter*: Bill Bennett. *Director of photography*: Geoff Burton. *Music*: Michael Atkinson, Michael Spicer. 91 min. *Cast*: Chris Haywood (Colin Turner), Jennifer Cluff (Lorraine Turner), Peter Hehir (Peter Townley), Andrew Chirgwin (Paul Turner), Peter Chirgwin (Jason Turner).

Based on the true story of Colin Simpson (here called Turner), this is a modestly effective piece of social realism with a didactic purpose. Bill •Bennett (director, producer, and scriptwriter) has fashioned drama from the resistance of personal determination in the face of obstructive bureaucracy. When Col and Lorraine Turner come to live in a war veterans' housing estate in outer-suburban Sydney, they find that all the people who have served in Vietnam during the Vietnam war are suffering various forms of malfunction. Col traces his declining physical condition to the effects of Agent Orange, a defoliant used in the war by the Americans, but has difficulty in getting his case considered seriously by medical and other authorities. After his death, Lorraine continues the battle and eventually is able to confide to the backyard tree under which Col's ashes are buried, 'We've won!' There are performances of touching authenticity from Chris •Hayward and Jennifer •Cluff, and production design and camerawork strengthen this sense of the actual.

BMcF

Strictly Ballroom

1992. *Director*: Baz Luhrmann. *Producer*: Tristram Miall. *Scriptwriters*: Baz Luhrmann, Craig Pearce, based on the National Institute of Dramatic Art stage production devised and developed by the original cast. *Director of photography*: Steve Mason. *Music*: David Hirshfelder. 94 min. *Cast*: Paul Mercurio (Scott Hastings), Tara Morice (Fran), Bill Hunter (Barry Fife), Pat Thomson (Shirley Hastings), Gia Carides (Liz Holt), Barry Otto (Doug Hastings).

One of the successes of 1992 was this Australian reworking of the old Hollywood staple of the young couple who overcome obstacles prior to a musical triumph in the last reel. In its story of young people asserting their individuality, breaking from the conventions of their elders, and finding romance as well as professional success, the film skifully reassembles some familiar ingredients.

Scott, the young hero, rebels against the rules of the ballroom dancing competitions, even though he is expected to be the next champion. In doing so, he causes outrage all

Frame enlargement from surviving footage of **The Story of the Kelly Gang**— possibly an out-take from the 1906 version

around. He breaks with his former partner Liz, and takes a new one in the homely Fran (who becomes more attractive when she removes her glasses). They win the championship by dancing the *pasadoble*, taught to them by Fran's Spanish father and grandmother. The film works variations on a series of oppositions—gender, generations, and ethnic origin—and stresses Paul's youthful triumph by the parallel of his docile father's failure, in similar circumstances, to follow his instincts.

There may be nothing new about the film except its setting, but it is persistently good-natured and assured as it moves towards its upbeat ending. The musical numbers, which are chiefly concerned with Scott and Fran's secret preparations, are interspersed with the reactions to his original act of rebellion and speculations within his family and the dancing studio about his intentions. The charm of the young stars is sturdily supported by some of Australia's best character actors. BMcF

Strike Me Lucky, *see* **Rene, Roy**

Strikebound

1984. *Director:* Richard Lowenstein. *Producers:* Miranda Bain, Timothy White. *Scriptwriter:* Richard Lowenstein, adapted from the book *Dead Men Don't Dig Coal,* by Wendy Lowenstein. *Director of photography:* Andrew De Groot. *Music:* Declan Affley. 101 min. *Cast:* Chris Haywood (Wattie Doig), Carol Burns (Agnes Doig), Hugh Keays-Byrne (Idris Williams), Rob Steele (Charlie Nelson), Nik Foster (Harry Bell).

Richard •Lowenstein's first feature, based on his mother's book, is unusual in Australian cinema. First, it deals with a serious socio-political issue—the miners' strike in South Gippsland in the 1930s—and makes this its central subject, not just the basis for a fictional drama. Second, its concern is with a class (a group of people) and a movement, rather than, as is usually the case in commercial cinema, with individuals. Sadly, it must be conceded that the film's pursuit of a neglected subject—the working class and its principles and problems—and its refusal to settle for more traditional narrative modes did not work in its commercial favour.

Paul Mercurio and Gia Carrides in Strictly Ballroom

It has an honourable place in recent Australian film, not merely for its good intentions, but also for the skill with which it makes cinematic capital of these. In using interviews with the real-life figures of Wattie and Agnes Doig to comment on the action of the strike, to recall what was endured and achieved, Lowenstein daringly challenges the usual suspension-of-disbelief procedures of film-making. Although these two figures are used as a critical focus for the film's events, their personal stories are subordinated throughout to the privations of a class, in its protest against appalling conditions of work and inadequate pay. The film is laced with humour and, although it caricatures the villainy of the mining manager, it provides a moving experience through its depiction of the mining community's solidarity. BMcF

Struck By Lightning

1990. *Director:* Jerzy Domaradzki. *Producers:* Terry J. Charatsis, Trevor Farrant. *Scriptwriter:* Trevor Farrant. *Director of photography:* Yuri Sokol. *Music:* Paul Smyth. 105 min. *Cast:* Garry McDonald (Ollie Rennie), Brian Vriends (Pat Cannizzaro), Catherine McClements (Jill McHugh), Henry Salter (Noel), Denis Moore (Foster).

Two rejects from conventional education form an odd-couple team who overcome obstacles to run a sheltered workshop for retarded adults in an old seaside Adelaide house. Pat Cannizzaro trains the inmates to play soccer, quickly winning their trust as a result of his charismatic, sympathetic approach, and Ollie Rennie, cynical and semi-alcoholic, is nevertheless committed to the task of doing his best for those in his care, battling opportunism on the board of management. He and Cannizzaro inevitably clash in their methods, but the film convincingly shows them moving towards a position of mutual respect for each other. An attractive social worker, Jill, provides another basis for tension between them, but the film's real success is the casting of Down Syndrome adults who ensure that the film is genuinely affecting and without sentimentality. They repay Cannizzaro's belief in their capacity for human achievement and make one hope that the film goes beyond mere entertainment and broadens community understanding.

BMcF

Studios   The history of film studios in Australia is marked by remission and resurgence. Studios, companies that produce films, and the buildings and stages in which films are produced, have, over 90 years, been subjected to a variety of local and global forces in their attempts to secure a place for their products on the Australian and international markets.

While a number of entrepreneurs produced actuality shorts at the end of the nineteenth century, the leading producer, distributor, and exhibitor of films at the time was the Limelight Department of the Salvation Army (see Documentary and non-fiction, silent; Historical representations). Established in 1892, the Department sought to spread the Christian message through public lectures accompanied by hand-tinted lantern slides, and dramatised sequences. Production of the multimedia presentations was subsequently broadened to include filmed sequences, as in the ambitious **Soldiers of the Cross** (1900) (see Silent film, to 1914; Documentary and non-fiction, silent; Historical representations). In 1908 the Department constructed a studio in the Melbourne suburb of Malvern, where it produced further religious epics for another two years before being disbanded.

A brief 'golden period' of Australian film production was inaugurated on 4 March 1911, when John and Nevin Tait who, in 1906, produced **The True Story of the Kelly Gang** (see **Kelly Gang, The**), joined with producers Millard Johnson and William Gibson to form Amalgamated Pictures. The company opened a studio in the Melbourne suburb of St Kilda in May 1911 and made nine films by early 1912. At the same time, in Sydney, the Australian Life Biograph Company, with a studio near Manly, produced a number of films, and the Australian Photo-Play Company filmed 20 features in and around Sydney. In August 1912, producer–distributor Cozens Spencer opened Sydney's first purpose-built studio at Rushcutter's Bay. The three-storey structure included state-of-the-art equipment and was used by Raymond •Longford, among others, who made three films in the studio, including •**Australia Calls** (1913).

In 1913, the end of the early golden era of studio-based production was hastened through the merger of various companies involved in production, distribution, and exhibition. The new company, Greater Union Theatres and the associated Australasian Films (see Greater Union Organisation), together known derisively as 'the combine', preceded by a few years the system of vertical integration that developed in Hollywood. The company stressed the distribution and exhibition of American films over Australian film production, while actively seeking to marginalise and then bankrupt local studios. It was not until the 1930s that a number of Australian studios returned to feature production.

In 1931 Frank •Thring (Snr) commenced film production after selling his share in •Hoyts Theatres. Thring's company, •Efftee Film Productions, leased the fire-damaged His Majesty's Theatre in Melbourne and converted it into a sound stage. Thring produced several features and numerous shorts at the site before moving his RCA sound recording equipment to St Kilda in mid 1934 and to Lane Cove in Sydney the next year. The company produced nine features, one unreleased, before Thring's death in 1936, when the company ceased production. Efftee's equipment was purchased by the Mastercraft Film Corporation in an unsuccessful attempt to open a new studio in Sydney. The consortium behind the venture included Longford and Jack •Bruce, managing director of Commonwealth Film Laboratories (CFL). CFL was formed in 1927 and, by the late 1930s, the company had produced a number of features at its Sydney studio. The CFL sound stage was used throughout the 1940s for a variety of productions, including scenes for Charles •Chauvel's •**The Rats of Tobruk** (1944), and by 1951 the company was producing films in its new studio at Turrella in Sydney.

In 1935 Australia's National Studios made an ambitious attempt to compete with Hollywood's heavily capitalised studios when it opened a facility in the Sydney suburb of Pagewood. The modern sound stage, modelled on the London studio facilities of the British company Gaumont-British, was to be used to make films featuring international stars, while the resemblance to Gaumont-British was intended to secure British distribution and exhibition rights for National films. A heavy investment of capital in the project was squandered through poor management, which, together, with the economic failure of the studio's one film, •**The Flying Doctor** (1936), forced the company into early bankruptcy.

In 1932 •Cinesound Productions established a vertically integrated studio system based on Hollywood models. Production took place at one of three Cinesound sound stages—two in Sydney and one in Melbourne—and the studio employed a group of technicians and maintained a troupe of actors. Between 1932 and 1939, the studio produced 16 profitable features, most of which were directed by Ken G. •Hall for executive producer Stuart Doyle (see Cinesound), and a continuous stream of documentary footage for its news magazine program **Cinesound Review**. In 1940 Cinesound ceased production for the duration of the war and its new managing director Norman •Rydge, unconvinced by the cost-effectiveness of production over exhibition, failed to revive feature production after the war. World War II saw a marked decline in studio output. During the late 1940s, studio-based production rested on government-sponsored documentaries produced by the Commonwealth Film Unit (see Film Australia), and on features produced by Ealing Studios of the United Kingdom. Ealing planned to upgrade the National Studios at Pagewood as its permanent production facility in Australia, but the plan was thwarted in 1950 by a lack of local financial investment necessary to ensure its success.

Throughout the 1960s, a number of small commercial production companies maintained themselves by shooting television programs, advertisements, and documentaries. Documentary film production was led by the Commonwealth Film Unit, later Film Australia which, in 1963, opened new studios at Lindfield in Sydney. By 1969 no Australian studio was committed to the production of feature films. In the early 1970s, initiatives taken by the Commonwealth government, among them financial support of feature film-making, resulted in renewed financial investments in the feature film industry. The changes were exemplified by •Hexagon Productions, which, after the success of its first production •Alvin Purple (1973), was able to maintain feature production until 1977. That year the Yoram •Gross studios, which commenced production in 1968, released •Dot and the Kangaroo. Yoram Gross studios continued to produce animated features for the Australian and American markets throughout the 1980s and 1990s, making it the longest continually running studio in Australia's film history.

During the 1980s and 1990s, a number of American companies constructed new sound stages in Australia for local and American productions. The trend was initiated in 1986 when the American independent producer Dino De Laurentiis built a studio at Coomera in Qld. Distribution difficulties forced De Laurentiis to withdraw from the project and the studio was purchased jointly by the •Village Roadshow group of companies and Warner Bros. The Warner Roadshow venture resulted in the creation of Australia's only fully integrated entertainment company. The studios at Warner Roadshow Movie World commenced production in 1988–89. Since that time, the studio has produced a number of Australian features and various 'offshore' Hollywood productions. In 1998, following the lead of Warner Roadshow, Fox Studios Australia opened a new production facility on its Sydney Showground site, primarily for Hollywood co-productions such as •**Dark City** (1998) and **Matrix** (1999).   Keith Beattie

Sullivan, Errol (1943–) producer Before forming a production company with Pom •Oliver in 1977, Sydney-based Sullivan had been involved in several films as, variously, unit manager, assistant director, and location manager. Thus his name is to be found on the credits of such films as **Promised Woman** (1975, unit manager, ass. d.), **The Removalists** (1975, ass. d.), **The Great MacArthy** (1975), •**The Man from Hong Kong** (1975), •**Caddie** (1976, location and unit manager). Sullivan was also first assistant director and co-associate producer on Michael •Thornhill's eloquent study of Sydney's western-suburbs youth, •**The FJ Holden** (1977). He and Oliver formed CB Films, often operating with the assistance of the New South Wales Film Corporation (see New South Wales Film and Television Office). Their first feature was •**Cathy's Child** (1979), based on journalist Dick Wordley's account of the real-life attempts of a Maltese woman to retrieve her child whose father has taken her back to his home in Greece. The film received excellent notices and was favourably viewed at the Cannes Festival, but, sadly, it failed to find substantial audiences.

He and Oliver co-produced the ingenious thriller •**Hoodwink** (1981), and **The City's Edge** (1983) for CB Films. Sullivan alone produced **Crosstalk** (1982), a thriller with echoes of Hitchcock's **Rear Window**, and a film with one of the most troubled and acrimonious production histories in Australian cinema, including the dismissal of its original director. Perhaps his experiences on this film discouraged Sullivan; for whatever reason, he did not work on another feature film until the 1994 'father-and-gay-son' drama, •**The Sum of Us**, on which he was executive producer, a function he repeated on •**The Well**, the 1997 version of Elizabeth Jolley's novel. In the interim, he was either producer or executive producer on some popular television series, including *The Four Minute Mile* and *Water Rats*.   BMcF

Sully, Walter cinematographer Wally Sully was a cinematographer on •newsreels and shorts before working on the feature film •**A Romance of the Burke and Wills Expedition of 1860** (1918). Working with De Forest Phonofilms in 1927, he was sent to record silent footage of the declaration of Canberra as the national capital, footage that was later linked with radio broadcasts of the speeches into a sound 'featurette'. He worked with Tasman •Higgins on •**Jewelled Nights** (1925); was assistant to Frank •Hurley on •**The Jungle Woman** (1926) and •**The Hound of the Deep** (1926); and worked with Lacey •Percival on •**The Birth of White Australia** (1928) and **The Kingdom of Twilight** (1929), and with Norman •Dawn and Jack Fletcher on •**Showgirl's Luck** (1931). This last was his only experience of sound film before his most famous work—cinematography on •Cinesound's first feature film, •**On Our Selection** (1932).   IB

COMMONWEALTH FILM LABORATORIES PTY. LTD.

Announce the Formation of Australia's Premier Film Organisation

AVONDALE STUDIOS PTY. LTD.

Avondale Studios, situated at Turrella near Arncliffe, and formerly Commonwealth Film Laboratories Production Studios, have now been established as an independent production organisation.

These studios, which contributed towards the technical excellence of such major Australian productions as "The Overlanders," "Sons of Matthew," "Eureka Stockade" and "Bush Christmas," are now geared for large scale production of feature films, documentary, travelogue, instructional and advertising films. They embrace the allied branches of 35 mm. processing laboratories, 16 mm. laboratories and short subject facilities through Australian Instructional Films. The most modern overseas techniques and equipment have been adopted, including the largest Western Electric Sound Recording System in the Southern Hemisphere. Mr. Charles Chauvel, renowned Australian Producer/Director, is on the board of Avondale Studios to advise on all stages of production. Enquiries are welcomed from Government Departments, Industrialists, Advertising Service Agents, and other organisations interested in a professional film service complete from scripting to distribution and embracing the most modern black and white and colour processes in 35 mm. and 16 mm. film.

AVONDALE STUDIOS PTY. LTD.

Henderson St., Turrella, N.S.W.

With which is associated

**Commonwealth Film Laboratories Pty. Ltd. ● Charles Chauvel
Australian Instructional Films ● Associated Film Printers**

CHARLES CHAUVEL
Advisor to Production

Australian producer/director and writer. Famous for "Forty Thousand Horsemen," "Sons of Matthew," etc. His professional advice is available to all seeking production services from Avondale Studios.

J. A. BRUCE
Technical Director

Leading technical film personality for over 25 years; founder and designer of Commonwealth Film Laboratories Pty. Ltd. and Avondale Studios.

LLOYD RAVENSCROFT
Business Manager

Well known in the production industry for over 12 years; has served on many feature films, including "Smithy" and "Bush Christmas," as production unit manager.

LEX HALLIDAY
Producer of Short Subjects

Experienced publicity executive; director of advertising, industrial, educational films; authority on 16mm. distribution. Has created such popular series as "Australians at Work," "Wild Life," etc.

Publicity for Avondale Studios

Sum of Us, The

1994. Directors: Kevin Dowling and Geoff Burton. *Producer*: Hal McElroy. *Scriptwriter*: David Stevens. *Director of photography*: Geoff Burton. *Music*: Dave Faulkner. 92 min. *Cast*: Jack Thompson (Harry Mitchell), Russell Crowe (Jeff Mitchell), John Polson (Greg), Deborah Kennedy (Joyce Johnson).

The Sum of Us is a deeply felt humanist film, adapted by David Stevens from his play, which was originally performed off-Broadway. This comedy-drama concerns Harry Mitchell's desire for his gay son Jeff to find a partner for life, a desire that widower Harry also expresses for himself. Jeff, in turn, experiences difficulties in developing a relationship with gardener Greg, who confronts the reverse problem with his homophobic father.

Stevens's play was originally set in the western suburbs of Melbourne and the film, unfortunately, transposes the setting to Sydney to, ostensibly, exploit internationally recognised visual symbols such as the Harbour Bridge , the Opera House, and the gay Mardi Gras. Basically a paean to sexual tolerance, the film seemingly reworks the 'ocker' stereotype in an unfamiliar way, although Harry is anything but your classic 'ocker', despite the superficial trappings of clothes, speech, and a love of beer and football. A sub-plot concerning Harry's mother's lesbian relationship serves to reinforce the film's central discourse of the affirmation of sexual choice, and its exploration of the difficulties faced by those who choose an alternative life style.

Although there are a number of touching moments, as well as some truly funny scenes and strong performances from Jack •Thompson and Russell •Crowe, the film never quite shakes off a stilted theatrical quality that largely derives from the dialogue, which, while suitable for the theatre, sounds mannered on film. This perception is reinforced by Harry's direct address to camera, which becomes increasingly intrusive as the film progresses. GM

Summer of the Seventeenth Doll

1959. Director: Leslie Norman. *Producer*: Leslie Norman. *Scriptwriter*: John Dighton, from the play by Ray Lawler. *Director of photography*: Paul Beeson. *Music*: Benjamin Frankel. 97 min. *Cast*: Ernest Borgnine (Roo), Anne Baxter (Olive), John Mills (Barney), Angela Lansbury (Pearl), Ethel Gabriel (Emma), Vincent Ball (Dowd), Janette Craig (Bubba), Deryck Barnes (Bluey), Frank Wilson (Vince), Al Garcia (Dino), Jessica Noad (Nancy), Al Thomas (Spruiker), Tom Lurich (the Atom Bomber), Dana Wilson (little girl).

The decision of the American company Hecht-Hill-Lancaster to film Lawler's ground-breaking play met with a mixed response in Australia, especially when the location was moved from Melbourne to Sydney, non-Australian were cast in the four major roles, and the ending was altered to make it more commercially attractive. The change in location was clearly an attempt to open the action to avoid the staginess that is the inherent cinematic problem in adaptations of stage plays, and to use locations set around Sydney Harbour that would be recognisably Australian to overseas audiences.

For 16 years, Roo and Barney, two canecutters from north Qld, have spent their lay-off season in Sydney with their barmaid girlfriends. This year is to be different: Barney's girl has married and moved on, and Roo, troubled by a bad back, has had an indifferent season and is consequently strapped for funds. Roo's girl Olive has found Pearl as a replacement playmate for Barney, but the old magic isn't there for a range of reasons that are progressively revealed as the plot unfolds. The title derives from Roo's custom of bringing a kewpie doll each year to mark his return.

Although the leading players are strong character actors, none has the real star quality that might have made the foreign casting work as it does in, for example, •**The Sundowners** (1960). At the heart of the play lies an allegory about the changing face of Australian culture and society and, although the non-Australian actors may convey this theme in terms of the structure of the film, they do not achieve it effectively in narrative terms. Ernest Borgnine is the best of the four. Ethel Gabriel, from the original stage production, suggests how much better the film might have been, and receives strong support from the other Australians in the cast. BRUCE MOLLOY

Summerfield

1977. Director: Ken Hannam. *Producer*: Pat Lovell. *Scriptwriter*: Cliff Green. *Director of photography*: Mike Molloy. *Music*: Bruce Smeaton. 91 min. *Cast*: Nick Tate (Simon Robinson), John Waters (David Abbott), Elizabeth Alexander (Jenny Abbott), Charles Tingwell (Dr Miller), Geraldine Turner (Betty), Max Cullen (Jim), Michelle Jarman (Sally Abbott).

Simon Robinson, the new schoolteacher in the small seaside community of Bannings Beach in south-eastern Vic., becomes curious about the mysterious disappearance of his predecessor, Peter Flynn. Robinson also becomes involved with the reclusive Abbotts, particularly Jenny, the mother of one of his pupils. These two narrative strands seem to merge when Robinson finds Flynn's car in a shed behind a house owned by the Abbotts; the film up to this point is atmospheric and mysterious. The ending, however, is a disappointment, as the 'guilty' secret that Robinson discovers, involving Jenny and her brother David, is foreshadowed in a number of ways throughout the film.

Angela Lansbury, Anne Baxter, Ernest Borgnine, Ethel Gabriel, and John Mills in **The Summer of the Seventeenth Doll**

Summerfield is representative of the virtues and faults found in many Australian films produced in the late 1970s. Visually the film is striking and generates a brooding atmosphere consistent with its generic conventions, and the high production values belie its relatively small budget ($560 000). The script, on the other hand, does not totally justify these achievements: the double murder and suicide late in the film seem pointless, leaving the audience with a sense of disappointment.   GM

Sunday Too Far Away

1975. *Director*: Ken Hannam. *Producers*: Gil Brealey, Matt Carroll. *Scriptwriter*: John Dingwall. *Director of photography*: Geoff Burton. *Music*: Patrick Flynn. 94 min. *Cast*: Jack Thompson (Foley), Max Cullen (Tim King), Robert Bruning (Tom West), Jerry Thomas ('Basher'), Peter Cummins (Arthur Black), John Ewart ('Ugly'), Sean Scully (Beresford), Reg Lye (Old Garth).

'Shearers', John •Dingwall's original title for his script, drew attention to an occupation that has contributed to the male-dominated mythology of Australian outback life (see Mateship). The film sets out less to espouse such a mythology than to understand it. It offers a compassionate treatment of the pressures exerted by such a life, in which the long periods of separation from the ordinary comforts of home and relationships are filled by the rough-and-ready camaraderie of mateship and the male urge to competitiveness; it portrays a culture where serious emotions are almost never revealed. While **Sunday Too Far Away**, a study in maleness and vulnerability, is essentially a milieu piece, the character of Foley is allowed centre stage. This is partly the result of the

Nick Tate, John Waters, and Elizabeth Alexander in **Summerfield**

charisma of the young Jack •Thompson in the role, partly because of Foley's role in leading his mates in the shearers' strike that abruptly ends the film, and partly because he is given a scene in which he breaks down and weeps. Foley encapsulates Australian male competitive urges and laconic good humour and, at the same time, makes us aware of what such accepted behaviour may suppress.

Along with •**Picnic at Hanging Rock**, released in the same year, it was influential in 'launching' the new Australian cinema and in defining one of its crucial paths. Whereas **Picnic at Hanging Rock** ushered in the vogue for decorous period pieces, **Sunday Too Far Away** won critical acclaim for its understated realism, its refusal of conventional plot tidiness and, in doing so, it helped to shape the idea of Australian national cinema as being in opposition to the dominant Hollywood paradigms.   BMcF

Sundowners, The

1960. *Director.* Fred Zinnemann. *Producer.* Gerry Blattner. *Scriptwriter.* Isobel Lennart, from the novel by Jon Cleary. *Director of photography.* Jack Hilyard. *Music.* Dimitri Tiomkin. 133 min. *Cast:*

Deborah Kerr (Ida Carmody), Robert Mitchum (Paddy Carmody), Peter Ustinov (Venneker), Glynis Johns (Mrs Firth), Dina Merrill (Jean Halstead), Chips Rafferty (Quinlan), Michael Anderson Jr (Sean Carmody), Lola Brooks (Liz).

An outstanding cast of imported and local actors makes this film arguably the most successful Hollywood film made on location in Australia. Fred Zinnemann evokes an authentic sense of land and people, starting with Robert Mitchum's portrayal of the nomadic drover Paddy Carmody, who is as charming as he is shiftless and as ready with his smile as he is with his fists. Mitchum receives strong support from Deborah Kerr as his long-suffering wife Ida who loves him dearly but is frustrated by his unwillingness to settle down. Peter Ustinov as the remittance man Venneker, and Glenys Johns as the wryly humorous publican, play their parts with admirable conviction and vitality. These imported actors are backed up by a fine collection of Australian actors, including Chips •Rafferty, John •Meillon and Dick Bentley in a rare film appearance.

All the bush rituals are included, from picnic races and a shearing contest to a two-up game and a 'blue' between rival

Peter Cummins and Jack Thompson in **Sunday Too Far Away**

shearing gangs. Much of the action is viewed through the eyes of Paddy and Ida's son Dean, who is struggling with the problems of impending adulthood. With photography by Jack Hildyard that captures the sweep and beauty of the Australian landscape, **The Sundowners** is a genuine pleasure to watch. The score by Dmitri Tiomkin makes clever use of traditional bush tunes to establish a tone that is good-humoured and evocative of the Australian character.

BRUCE MOLLOY

Sunshine Sally

1922. *Director*: Lawson Harris. *Producer*: Lawson Harris, Yvonne Pavis. *Scriptwriter*: John Cosgrove. *Director of photography*: Arthur Higgins. B&W. *Cast*: Yvonne Pavis (Sal), Joy Revelle (Tottie Faye), John Cosgrove (Spud Murphy), Dinks Patterson ('Skinny Smith'), Lionel Lunn (Basil Stanton).

Sunshine Sally begins as one of the most charming Australian films of the 1920s, as well as one of the few to have continued the tradition of 'working-class slice-of-life-comedy' so auspiciously begun with •**The Sentimental Bloke** (1919). Yvonne Pavis and Joy Revelle play 'straight-up' working girls with great panache and John Cosgrove's script seems content to let them have their heads, stringing incident upon incident, and heading nowhere in particular. Once the real story starts, however, a lot of the charm disappears. Although the film survives only in incomplete form, it seems clear that Sally's courage and her desire to better herself are bred into her genes. She thinks she is just a working-class kid, but she was actually born a 'toff'. When upper-class Basil Stanton saves her at the beach, all the fun is over and the serious business of eugenic matchmaking begins in melodramatic earnest.

WILLIAM D. ROUTT

Surfer, The

1988. *Director*: Frank Shields. *Producers*: James M. Vernon, Frank Shields. *Scriptwriter*: David Marsh. *Director of photography*: Michael Edols. *Music*: Davood Tabrizi. 90 min. *Cast*: Gary Day (Sam Barlow), Gosia Dobrowolska (Gina), Rod Mullinar (Hagan), Tony Barry (Calhoun), Gerard Maguire (Jack), Kris McQuade (Trish).

This tough action thriller concerns Vietnam veteran Barlow, who leads a simple life renting surfboards at Surfers Paradise. The film is consistent with the conventions of the genre: Barlow becomes involved with a mysterious woman (Gina), who asks him to take a letter to an old friend. When the friend is murdered, Barlow and Gina are chased along the coastal fringe of Qld by a corrupt cop and a ruthless casino operator. The film never slows down to allow intricacies of characterisation to intrude on the generic plot, which is based on a series of betrayals culminating in a violent climax.

While this is familiar territory in Hollywood, it is relatively rare in the Australian cinema. The film remains faithful to its generic roots, despite a minuscule budget. Frank Shields's direction is impressive and covers the implausibilities in the story with a fast-moving narrative and a no-nonsense style that was rewarded by the film's selection for the Director's Fortnight at the Cannes Film Festival in 1987.

GM

Sutherland, Joan (1926–) ACTOR Although Joan Sutherland is designated here as 'actor', this is not the profession for which one of Australia's two most famous sopranos is likely to be remembered. In her dazzling operatic career, much of it master-minded by her conductor-husband Richard Bonynge, she was so vocally thrilling that her limited acting capacities were overlooked. In her one film to date, •**Dad and Dave: On Our Selection** (1995), she is idiosyncratically cast as Mum, and is given the film's most platitudinous and nationalistic dialogue. Her performance remains a stately curiosity; it would not be hard to think of a dozen character actors who could have played the role with more ease and warmth, and it doesn't seem likely that her screen career will take off. No doubt it is not a priority with her.

BMcF

Sweet, Gary (1957–) ACTOR This former school teacher has made a greater impact on television than in the cinema, beginning with *The Sullivans* (1976) and continuing through successful series such as *Police Rescue* (1990–94) and *Blue Sky* (1997). Sweet had lead roles in popular miniseries such as *Bodyline* (1984—as Donald Bradman) and *Tanamera—Lion of Singapore* (1989). Sweet's role in •**An Indecent Obsession** (1985)—as the new arrival in the psychiatric ward of a military hospital during World War II who upsets the finely balanced equilibrium established by nurse Honour Langtry (Wendy •Hughes)—is a rare highlight in a screen career that does not seem to have given him the chance to make full use of his talents.

Other Australian films include: **Nightmares** (1980), •**The Lighthorsemen** (1987), **Fever** (1987), **The Dreaming** (1988), **What the Moon Saw** (1990), **Love in Ambush** (1997). GM

Sweetie

1989. *Director*: Jane Campion, *Producer*: John Maynard, *Screenplay*: Jane Campion, Gerard Lee. *Director of photography*: Sally Bongers. *Cast*: Genevieve Lemon (Sweetie), Karen Colston (Kay), Tom Lycos (Louis), Jon Darling (Gordon), Dorothy Barry (Flo).

With **Sweetie**, Jane •Campion made her mark as a stylistically innovative, original film-maker. Campion's selection of Sally Bongers to photograph **Sweetie** made Bongers the first woman in Australia to shoot a 35mm feature film. In this film Campion rekindles her fascination with the tenuous divide between civilisation and barbarism. The first sequence belongs to the introverted Kay, who visits a psychic, desperate for a clue to help her find love. Interpreting the formation of tea leaves, the psychic informs Kay that she will recognise her soulmate by a question mark on his head. When she encounters Louis, Kay notices that a twist of his hair couples with a freckle on his forehead to form the distinguishing feature. She disregards his fiancée and seduces him beneath a car in an underground car park. Kay's phobia about trees emerges when Louis replaces their Hill's hoist with an elder tree to mark their first anniversary. The clothes line lies prostrate in the backyard, a tired reminder of suburban upheaval. Campion includes speedy black-and-white images of ferocious subterranean roots rupturing surfaces to reflect Kay's psychosis. Like the elder tree, Kay's family tree suffers from 'disease'.

Kay's life is hijacked when her graceless sister invades her home. Sweetie (Dawn) is diametrically opposed to Kay. Irresponsible, erratic, and an exhibitionist, she is prone to tantrums. Louis politely declines Sweetie's voracious sexual appetite. The level of intimacy between Sweetie and her father hints at an incestuous relationship. Kay is forced to contend with her ravenous uncivilised 'other'. Beginning as a bizarre black comedy, **Sweetie** illuminates the dark side of the family and reveals profound desecration.

WENDY HASLEM

Swinburne Film School, *see* Victorian College of the Arts School of Film and Television

Sydney Film Festival, *see* Festivals

Szeps, Henri (1943–) ACTOR Now best known as the unsympathetic dentist son of Ruth •Cracknell in the ABC sitcom *Mother and Son*, the heavily moustachioed Henri Szeps has a long and varied background on stage and screen as well. Born in Lausanne, Switzerland, he came to Australia when he was eight and was educated at Sydney University while studying acting at the Ensemble Theatre. In the United Kingdom in the early 1970s, he appeared on stage and television (for example, *Colditz*) before returning to Australia where he as acted in plays such as *Travelling North* (repeating his role in the film version of this in 1987), appeared in television series such as *Number 96* and *Ride on Stranger*, and played a part in *The Plumber*, a telemovie directed by Peter •Weir (1979). In general, his film roles have given him less scope than those in the other media, but he did have a leading role in •**Warming Up** (1985).
Other Australian films: •**You Can't See Round Corners** (1969), **God Knows Why But It Works** (1975, short), **The Claim** (1975, short), **Say You Want Me** (1977, short), **Low Flying** (1979, short), **Fatty Finn** (1980), **Buying Blues** (1980, short), **Meetings** (1980), **Firm Foundations** (1981, short), **Mystery at Castle House** (1982), **The Best of Friends** (1982), **Run, Rebecca, Run** (1983), **Now and Forever** (1983), **Edge of Power** (1987), **Les Patterson Saves the World** (1987), **Seeing Red** (1992).   BMcF

T

Tale of Ruby Rose, The

1988. Director: Roger Scholes. *Producers:* Bryce Menzies, Andrew Wiseman. *Scriptwriter:* Roger Scholes. *Director of photography:* Steve Mason. *Music:* Paul Schutze. 100 min. *Cast:* Melita Jurisic (Ruby Rose), Chris Haywood (Henry Rose), Rod Zuanic (Gem), Martyn Sanderson (Bennett), Sheila Florance (Grandma).

The location of this film, on the snow-covered slopes of the Tasmanian highlands, dwarfs the characters—Ruby Rose, her husband Henry, and her adopted son Gem, who live a spartan existence in a slab hut under the Walls of Jerusalem. Filled with unreasoning terror, Ruby makes a pilgrimage through the snow to find her grandmother and the explanation that will make life once again bearable. The small cast makes the most of its opportunities, with particular credit to Melita Jurisic in the title role. This is a starkly beautiful film, with a story so intense that it was apparently too strong for the major distributors: the film was eventually shown in arthouse cinemas and overseas, where it was well received. It was nominated for best film and best direction in the 1987 Australian Film Institute awards, and won the award for music.   IB

Tall Timbers

1937. Director: Ken G. Hall. *Producer:* Ken G. Hall. *Scriptwriter:* Frank Harvey. Based on an original story by Frank Hurley. *Director of photography:* George Heath. *Music:* Lindley Evans. 89 min. B&W. *Cast:* Frank Leighton (Jim Thornton), Shirley Ann Richards (Joan Burbridge), Campbell Copelin (Charles Blake), Frank Harvey (Darley), Aileen Britton (Claire Darley), Joe Valli (Scotty).

Although at one point declaiming that, 'trees are like humans' this film devotes itself to the unsentimental pur-

suit of large-scale deforestation. And this is the least of its contradictions. **Tall Timbers** revolves around a series of complicated rivalries between individual characters and timber companies. Two opposing timber firms (one exemplary, the other unscrupulous) agree to a 'race' in order to secure a lucrative contract. The upstanding Burbridge team are thwarted by saboteurs, including the shadowy Darley and the caddish Blake, who seduces Darley's sister Claire with promises of marriage while courting Burbridge's adopted daughter Joan with a view to her inheritance. Staving off what appears to be imminent defeat, Burbridge employee Jim Thornton devises a 'timber drive' in which trees at the top of a ridge are felled, taking the lower reaches of the forest before them. Meanwhile, the pregnant Claire unites with Joan to expose the duplicitous Blake who is subsequently killed by Darley. Darley then imprisons Joan and Jim in the midst of the oncoming drive. After a narrow escape, Jim is revealed as the long-lost son of Burbridge and the scene is set for his marriage to Joan. Despite placing great narrative stock in the success of the timber drive, Ken G. •Hall found effecting the event to be more elusive. After failing at several efforts to create an actual timber drive, he employed resident effects specialist J. Alan Kenyon to reproduce the scenes in miniature.   DEB VERHOEVEN

Tasmania, history and images

Tas. is an island state with a tiny population, fickle weather, and terrain that is, for the most part, wild. These factors have had an important bearing on its representation in film. Geographic isolation and bad weather make film production in Tas. more difficult and expensive than in other states: tales set in Tas. have frequently been shot on the mainland. The Tasmanian landscape, however, remains a serious cinematic temptation. Mountainous, wooded, and shrouded with rain, it is picturesque and sombre. A knowledge of Tasmanian history deepens this impression: key sites of European settlement include shipwrecks, prisons, prison camps, work camps, and dams. Local legends populate the rainforests with extinct life forms and the degenerate descendants of escaped convicts. Caricatures such as Disney's 'Tasmanian Devil' and Yahoo •Serious's 'Young Einstein' exploit these back-woods legends. Merle Oberon banked on the marginality of Tas., by concealing her mixed-race parentage falsely claiming to have been born in Zeehan, a remote Tasmanian mining town. The Tasmanian wildness contributed to the public persona of Errol •Flynn, who grew up in Hobart, the capital city.

Many Tasmanian tales are stories of entrapment and escape. The penal settlement at Port Arthur was used for shooting elements of •**For the Term of His Natural Life** (1927). Cinematographer Len H. Roos visually reconstructed the ruined buildings by shooting through images painted on glass. Louise •Lovely apparently fell in love with the landscape of Tas.; she went there to make part of •**Jewelled Nights** (1925), an adaptation of Marie Bjelke-Petersen's 'mining romance'. The story concerns an escaped bride who hides out in a north-west coast mining camp under cover of male dress. The film failed, and Lovely retired from production to marry a local exhibitor and settle in Hobart.

In some cases, the fantasy is of escape from the island itself, as it is for Christopher Koch in **The Boys in the Island** (1989), a semi-autobiographical film about the pleasures, and perils, of leaving Tas. for the 'Otherland' (the mainland). Indeed, the Tasmanian contribution to Australian film has frequently taken the form of exported (or escaped) talent. The •Higgins brothers (Ernest, Arthur, and Tasman) grew up in Hobart before developing important careers as cinematographers. Arthur Higgins worked with Raymond •Longford on •**The Sentimental Bloke** (1919) and •**On Our Selection** (1920), among many other films. Tasman Higgins worked with Charles and Elsa •Chauvel on •**In the Wake of the Bounty** (1933), the film that gave Errol Flynn his first break. Both the Higgins brothers worked with Frank •Thring Snr, and both contributed to the impact of Damien •Parer's war footage for the documentary **Kokoda Front Line** (1942), which won the 1942 documentary •Oscar.

One of the few films made almost entirely in Tas. is the children's film **They Found a Cave** (1962), an adaptation of a Nan Chauncy story. A local boy called 'Tas' helps four British orphans defeat their evil guardians. This film showcased Tas. and its talented people. Peter Sculthorpe (born in Tas.) wrote the musical score. Andrew Steane, the director, had previously worked in the Tasmanian State Government's department of film production. The physical resources of

this department, and some of its personnel, were used to establish the Tasmanian Film Corporation (TFC) in September 1977. Malcolm Smith, the first director of the TFC, came from the South Australian Film Corporation, and established the TFC in the image of that successful entity. While the bulk of the TFC's production was non-theatrical, it did produce two feature films during its period of public ownership: •**Manganinnie** (1980) (also scored by Sculthorpe) and **Save the Lady** (1981). **Manganinnie** fictionalises a key incident in the history of European settlement of Tas.: the attempt to corral the Aboriginal population. Set in 1830, the film opens with the rout of an Aboriginal encampment by White soldiers. Manganinnie, an Aboriginal woman, finds herself dispossessed. Joanna, a White child, leaves her own family to follow Manganinnie into the bush. The pair form a bond, but Manganinnie returns Joanna to her White family before dying of despair. **Save the Lady** is a children's film in which the saviours are a group of school children and the 'lady' is a condemned ferry (ferries became important after Hobart was split by the collapse of the Tasman Bridge). After a change of state government, the TFC was sold to a private owner in February 1983, despite trenchant criticism from Gil •Brealey, among others. Malcolm Smith became the inaugural general manager of the Australian Film Commission's film development branch. TFC Pty Ltd subsequently produced **Departure** (1986), a drama about a family losing its reputation, before changing hands again in 1988, becoming Tricom Audio-Video.

Subsequently, two feature films, both independently financed, have been made by directors who deliberately defied obstacles to filming in Tas. •**The Tale of Ruby Rose** (1988) is about a woman who responds to isolation by producing a baroque mythology connected to the mountainous landscape. Writing in *Back of Beyond* (1988), Ross Gibson says this 'landscape-story' depicts types and habitats that challenge the dominant mythology of Australian film: 'Either you deny them their classification as "Australian", or you refigure the epithet "Australian"'. •**The Sound of One Hand Clapping** (1998) continues the Tasmanian challenge to a sunny national mythology. The bright, optimistic images of Hydro-electric dams (and workers' camps) produced by government documentaries are inverted and darkened by **The Sound of One Hand Clapping**. It tells the story of a migrant family that is all but destroyed by an unforgiving social environment. These two films exploit the Tasmanian landscape to tell gothic tales that emphasise difficult emotional and spiritual connections to a place that can be as terrible as it is beautiful.

There has recently been renewed enthusiasm for film production in Tas. Emerging electronic production formats promise to be less constrained by weather and distance than older technologies. In 1998, a school of animation was established in Hobart.   JOY McENTEE

Tasmanian Film Corporation, *see* Tasmania, history and images

Tass, Nadia (1955–) DIRECTOR Born in Lofi, a Macedonian village in northern Greece, Nadia Tass arrived with her family in Australia in 1966, and settled in Melbourne. She started acting as a schoolgirl in an episode of *Homicide*, and was heavily involved in the Melbourne theatre scene as well as television acting while studying psychology at Melbourne University, and theatre at the Victorian College of the Arts, and while training as a secondary teacher. She entered film after visiting her husband David •Parker, who was working as a stills photographer on the set of •The Coolangatta Gold (1984). She and Parker became partners in Cascade Films, and co-producers, with Tass directing and Parker as cinematographer, on a number of successful films, beginning with •Malcolm (1986). Though Parker later moved into direction, the couple continued as a team, producing **Rikky and Pete** (1988), •The Big Steal (1990), •Mr Reliable (1996), and Amy (1998), as well as the television miniseries *Stark* (1993). Their work together is always entertaining, often funny, and usually has an underlying seriousness. In 1991, they opened the Melbourne Film Studio in Port Melbourne, refurbished with the money they had made from their first Hollywood film, **Pure Luck** (1991), starring Danny Glover and Martin Short. In 1986 the AFI presented them with the Byron Kennedy Award. Tass returned occasionally to the theatre, directing *Summer of the Aliens* (1992) and *Miss Bosnia* (1996). IB

Tate, Nick (1942–) ACTOR Prominent in Australia in the 1970s and early 1980s, Tate concentrated on American films and television in the 1990s, including two episodes of *Star Trek*. The son of Australian actors John Tate and Neva Carr-Glyn, Tate moved to the United Kingdom in the 1960s and achieved some prominence in the television series *Space 1999*. His first Australian film role was a lead performance as Brother Victor in •The Devil's Playground (1976), the critically acclaimed study of life in a Catholic seminary in the 1950s. This was followed by the mystery thriller •Summerfield (1977), with Tate in the role of the new schoolteacher in a small Westernport Victorian town who is intrigued by the disappearance of his predecessor, while also becoming involved with the isolated family of a young pupil. Tate performed in a number of Australian television series in the early 1980s, including *Holiday Island* and *Scales of Justice*, while also appearing as the father in •The Coolangatta Gold (1984) and the reporter Henneberry in the detective thriller •The Empty Beach (1985), based on the novel by Peter Corris. However, his screen appearances since the mid 1980s have been reduced to supporting roles in films such as •The Year My Voice Broke (1987) and •Evil Angels (1988), and a brief role in the British production Cry Freedom (1988), in which he played an Australian journalist who assists Donald Woods's escape from South Africa. GM

Tauchert, Arthur (1877–1933) ACTOR Arthur Tauchert worked the vaudeville circuits, first in Sydney, then nationally, before taking his first screen role in 1916, in the short film **Charlie at the Sydney Show**. He was already over forty, paunchy, and decidedly not handsome, when he played the romantic lead in Raymond •Longford's •The Sentimental Bloke (1919). Publicist Gayne •Dexter attributed the failure of the film in USA to the ugliness of its central characters, but the Australian public loved the film, and took Tauchert's character to heart, as they had its literary precursor in C.J. Dennis's verses. The continuance of the character of the Bloke (in •Ginger Mick, 1920; and later in radio performances), and similar characters in other films (The Dinkum Bloke, 1923; •Joe, 1924; or even •The Digger Earl 1924), sustained Tauchert's reputation. However, he also played other types (**Odds On**, 1928), and smaller roles in other silent films (**The Jackeroo of Coolabong**, 1920; •The Moth of Moonbi, 1926, •For the Term of His Natural Life, 1927; •The Adorable Outcast, 1928). In the early days of sound film, he played one of the leads in **Fellers** (1930), and a supporting role in •Showgirl's Luck (1931), before he became too ill to continue working. Of the films in which he played leading roles, only one survives—fortunately it is •The Sentimental Bloke. IB

Taylor, Barbi PRODUCER One of an impressive number of women producers who emerged in the 1970s, Barbi Taylor began her career in films as production manager on Ross •Dimsey's **Blue Fire Lady** (1977), an unpretentious film aimed at teenage girls who love horses. She was associate producer on Simon •Wincer's thriller, **Snapshot** (1979) and on Rod Hardy's minor horror film, **Thirst** (1979). She co-produced Richard •Franklin's teasing •Roadgames (1981) and Ken Annakin's ill-fated **The Pirate Movie** (1982), and was line producer on Brian •Trenchard-Smith's **Frog Dreaming** (1986), **Heaven Tonight** (1990), and on the scarcely seen biopic, **My Forgotten Man** (1996), based on the life of Errol •Flynn. Apart from **Roadgames**, Taylor has not been as lucky as some of the other women producers of the revival (see Revival, the). BMcF

Taylor, Grant (1917–71) ACTOR Although Grant Taylor was born in the United Kingdom, he became one of Australia's most popular screen, radio, and stage performers in the 1940s and the early 1950s. Taylor began his film career as the romantic lead courting Dad Rudd's daughter in •Dad Rudd, M.P. (1940). This was followed by his most important role: Red Gallagher, an Anzac fighting in the Sinai campaign in World War I, in Charles •Chauvel's inspirational •Forty Thousand Horsemen (1940). Taylor had the opportunity to move to Hollywood after the success of this film, but he stayed in Australia at a time when the local film industry was moribund. Taylor worked in films whenever possible, including support roles in transplanted westerns such as •The Kangaroo Kid (1950) and other international co-productions such as Long John Silver (1953), directed by Hollywood veteran Byron Haskin, in which Taylor appeared with his son Kit. Kit •Taylor, as Jim Hawkins, had a more substantial role than his father in this film. Other international co-productions included the South Seas adventure His Majesty O'Keefe (1953), also directed by Byron Haskin, in which Taylor had a featured role in this Burt Lancaster vehicle. This was followed by supporting roles in co-productions such as Smiley Gets a Gun (1959), •On the Beach (1959), and •The Siege of Pinchgut (1959). Taylor finished his career in the United Kingdom in small character parts in films such as Quatermass and the Pit (1967) and British television series.

Other Australian films include: •The Rats of Tobruk (1944).   GM

Taylor, Kit (1942–) ACTOR   After the key role of Jim Hawkins in the international co-production Long John Silver (1953), child actor Kit Taylor accompanied his father Grant •Taylor to the United Kingdom in the late 1950s, where he eventually appeared in the British thriller In the Devil's Garden (1971). Kit's return to the Australian screen was as the quick-tempered dentist who loses his girlfriend to Cooley in David •Williamson's acerbic comedy •Don's Party (1976). Although Taylor has worked steadily in Australian films and television since then, he has been largely confined to supporting roles.

Other Australian films include: •Ride a Wild Pony (1975), Weekend of Shadows (1978), Early Frost (1982), Cassandra (1987), Innocent Prey (1988), Rough Diamonds (1994).   GM

Taylor, Noah (1969–) ACTOR   Noah Taylor is one of Australia's most distinctive actors with particular expertise in delivering self-deprecating dialogue, a skill that was brilliantly exploited in his first film as Danny Embling in •The Year My Voice Broke (1987), as well as its sequel •Flirting (1991) and, particularly, the Bob •Ellis quasi-biographical film •The Nostradamus Kid (1993). Taylor, largely as a result of his age, hang-dog looks and screen mannerisms, has been predominantly stereotyped in 'rites-of-passage' films as he has been able to effectively convey adolescent torment and alienation. A key role for Taylor's career was the adolescent David Helgott in •Shine (1996), a role for which he was nominated by the Screen Actors Guild for Outstanding Performance in a Supporting Role, and he

won Best Actor at the Fort Lauderdale International Film Festival for his performance in this film.

Other Australian films include: The Prisoner of St. Petersburg (1990), Dead to the World (1990), Secrets (1992), •Dad and Dave: On Our Selection (1995), True Love and Chaos (1996), He Died With a Felafel in His Hand (1999).   GM

Taylor, Rod (1929–) ACTOR   Roughly every 20 years, it seems, Rod Taylor appears in Australian films. Born and educated in Sydney, the ruggedly handsome actor began his career in radio before appearing in his first film, a short, The Stuart Expedition (1951). His feature début was in Lee •Robinson's Southern International production, •King of the Coral Sea (1954), followed by Long John Silver (1954), the sequel to Disney's Treasure Island (1950). He then went on to establish a successful international career in such films as Separate Tables (1958), The V.I.Ps (1963), and Hotel (1967), co-starring with Merle Oberon, then believed to be Australian). He returned to Australia in 1976 to shoot •The Picture Show Man (1977) in northern NSW, as the pushy American rival to John •Meillon's travelling cinema operator in the 1920s. He made no further film here until 1997, when he appeared in Stephan •Elliott's The Big Red, with Albert Finney, and again for Elliott, in Welcome to Woop Woop (1998). Not a notably subtle actor, he has nevertheless always had a strong presence in leading-man roles. In 1968 he played the Australian detective in the British-made version of a Jon Cleary novel, The High Commissioner.   BMcF

Teale, Leonard (1922–94) ACTOR   Born in Brisbane, Leonard Teale, also known as Leonard Thiele, had a distinctive, authoritative voice that was utilised in Sydney radio and on the stage for many years. Teale's show business career began in the 1940s as Australian feature film production went into a sharp decline and his screen appearances were limited to locally filmed international co-productions such as •Smiley (1956), Smiley Gets a Gun (1958), •The Sundowners (1960), and Bungala Boys (1961). The only Australian-financed film that Teale appeared in during this period was 'The Load of Wood' segment in the Cecil •Holmes-directed trilogy about mateship, •Three in One (1957). Later in his media career Teale's popularity soared with his recordings of traditional Australian stories. In the 1960s he was the lead actor in the Australian television police series Homicide.

Other Australian films include: …Maybe This Time (1980), Stanley: Every Home Should Have One (1984).   GM

Telefeatures   The telefeature, in its strictest sense, is a narrative drama of at least 60 minutes duration, produced and shot (on film or video) specifically for television programming. In the Australian context, however, the telefeature category has tended to be defined expansively, so as to also include theatrical features that have debuted on television, 'features' edited from a television miniseries (*Act of Betrayal*, 1987), or double-episode pilots for serials or series (*Boney*, 1990), including serials that have not been developed beyond the pilot. A particular category of telefeatures has been responsible for blurring the definition: features that for one reason or another have bypassed cinemas and débuted on television (such films invariably undergo a cosmetic re-classification to remove the straight-to-television stigma). It is not uncommon, for instance, to find Australian feature films that have been financed, produced, and marketed specifically for their premieres on domestic television, some having enjoyed a release in foreign territories but not on local shores (for example, *Alex*).

Scott Murray's *Australia on the Small Screen 1970–1995* (Oxford University Press, 1996) is the first study aimed at reclaiming this not insignificant although poorly documented and even more poorly regarded category of Australian screen production. Murray assiduously avoids the blurry demarcation between the telefeature and its various clones by distinguishing telefeatures from unreleased theatrical features, television pilots, and so on. The 25-year period of his research identifies 420 such programs in all.

Get The Picture (Australian Film Commission, 3rd edition, 1994) lists *Crisis* (d. Bill Hughes), shot in 1971 and subsequently screened on Channel Nine (GTV9), as the first Australian telefeature. The mid 1970s saw a flurry of telefeature production, with 50 produced in the three years between 1975/76 and 1977/78. Many of these were ABC productions, with a smattering of independent productions by the Grundy Organization and others. The name of veteran television actor Robert Bruning crops up in the producer and executive producer credits of many of these films.

Mirroring the boom in film and television production in Australia in the mid 1980s, a record number of 111 telefeatures were completed between 1983/84 and 1987/88, coinciding with the peak concessions under the 10BA film financing arrangements (see •Film finance), an average of 22 per year over a five-year period.

Several interesting factors help explain this onslaught of activity, above and beyond the impetus provided by tax-driven private investment in the local film and television industries. In the early 1980s, television offered film producers modest, less-risky opportunities than the then volatile film market. Despite the successes of such films as •Mad Max 2 (1981) and •The Man from Snowy River (1982), record numbers of homegrown features were finding it difficult, if not impossible, to gain releases in local cin-

emas. Coupled with this problem of gaining access to local screens, the costs of staging release campaigns in a market dominated by studio blockbusters were out of reach for the bulk of the more modestly budgeted and conceived Australian productions. In addition, with the arrival of video, cinema admissions slumped from their peak in 1982, and regained strength only at the end of the 1980s.

Investment by television networks minimised the financial risk to producers, and eliminated the make-or-break nature of cinema ventures. Television offered a huge potential audience, and low-cost, cross-promotional opportunities. Most importantly, however, the runaway successes of pioneer television miniseries such as *A Town Like Alice* (1981) and *The Dismissal* (1983) placed a premium on quality, locally made dramas based on national histories and culturally specific issues. This was the context in which Australian miniseries production flourished and, with it, the telefeature.

These conditions, together with the generic conventions of the standard narrative drama (that is, the feature length of such productions), determined the scale and concerns of telefeatures of this period. Among the better known are *Archer* (1985), which told the true story of the first winner of the Melbourne Cup; *Call Me Mr Brown* (1986), a thriller based on the true story of Peter Macari, who extorted A$500 000 from Qantas Airways; the romantic comedy *A Matter of Convenience* (1987), which derives its humour from the clash of ethnic cultures in Melbourne's colourful and easily recognisable bayside suburb of St Kilda. From the prestigious Kennedy Miller group came 1987's *Fragments of War: The Story of Damien Parer*, based on the biography of the acclaimed World War II cameraman. Easily the best known telefeature of this era is the ABC-produced *Two Friends*, directed by Jane •Campion from an original screenplay by the novelist Helen •Garner.

Like most made-for-television programs, actors identifiable by a television audience and story matters take precedence over directors and authors. It is worth noting that the television star system pre-dates the emergence of a recognisable star system in Australian cinema.

As in other areas of Australian screen production, federal government funding mechanisms and policy have largely determined the parameters of the telefeature. While the Film Finance Corporation (FFC—see •Finance) is precluded from funding the production of television serials and series, miniseries and telefeatures remain within its ambit. FFC-funded productions include *Cody*, *Halifax FP*, and *The Feds*. While these bear the distinctive characteristics of long-running television drama (principal characters who reappear in every episode, lack of narrative closure, and continuity of context and place), they are nonetheless self-contained, feature-length narratives capable of being programmed in any order, and able to be marketed, promoted, and sold singly or collectively. These Australian police thrillers offer the flexibility of filling a single two-hour television programming block (that is, a standard movie-on-television slot), rather than the two 2-hour blocks of prestige television miniseries, such as *Prime Suspect*.

Market forces have also renewed the interest of television networks in telefeature production. The advent of rival cable-TV networks in Australia in the mid 1990s has ushered in heated competition between cable and free-to-air networks for the broadcast rights to latest, first-release movies, the first round of which has been clearly won by the cable operators. Having lost (or ceded, given the cross-ownership interests between free-to-air and cable) the rights to this staple of television programming, movie slots on free-to-air schedules have become increasingly filled with second- and third-rate American telefeatures. In this arena of fierce competition and bids to establish dominance within select genres and formats (sport, current affairs, movies, gameshows, comedy serials, and so on), the network-supported telefeature is a guarantee of exclusive, and so far at least, high-quality, movie-slot programming. With a cable-TV network co-funding the production of a local telefeature and free-to-air networks continuing to make investments, the continuation of telefeature production has never looked more assured.

PAUL KALINA

10BA, *see* Finance

Tenth Straw, The

1926. *Director*: Robert McAnderson. *Director of photography*: Claud C. Carter. B&W. *Cast*: Ernest Lauri (Bruce Lowe), Peggy Paul (Marie Lowe).

Although at least one reel of **The Tenth Straw** is missing, and although the rest is marred by ham acting, dull direction, and inept montage, there is still much of interest in the film. In the first place, top-billed Ernest Lauri actually disappears approximately halfway through the film and never returns in a kind of antipodean anticipation of Janet Leigh in **Psycho** (1960). At the same time, the narrative seems to be transmuting from convict drama to a tale of Lasseter's gold. But neither of these strands holds the film's interest. Action shifts to the penal settlement and to a complicated drama of right and wrong couples. Migration appears to be the issue here. None of the major characters is initially located in Australia, and it is the arrival of the convict's sister, Marie, that finally precipitates the actions that tie up the narrative threads and create an ideal couple. Most remarkable of all is the way the film

figures Tommy, a black tracker played by an unidentified young Aboriginal man, whose many close-ups make of him an amazed spy in the White world of deceit, murder, and greed. It is Tommy who is vouchsafed the film's most violent moment, when he re-enacts one White man's story of the murder of another, looking up at the camera to tell those who are looking that this is how it was done.

WILLIAM D. ROUTT

Tester, Desmond (1919–) ACTOR After several very successful years as a clever and versatile teenage player in such notable British films as **Tudor Rose** (1936), Hitchcock's **Sabotage** (1936), and Carol Reed's **The Stars Look Down** (1939), Tester shortened his career by declaring himself a conscientious objector at the outbreak of war. He made only one more film in the United Kingdom, turned to the stage, and came to Australia to play in *Sailor Beware* in 1956 and settled here. He had two long-running television series (*Channel Ninepins* and *The Kaper Kops*) and appeared in character roles in four films: **Barry MacKenzie Holds His Own** (1974, as Marcel Escargot), **Save the Lady** (1981, as a ferry-boat captain), **Brothers** (1982, unreleased), and an antipodean version of Ibsen, •**The Wild Duck** (1984).

BMcF

Thank God He Met Lizzie

1997. *Director*: Cherie Nowlan. *Producers*: Carole Hughes, Jonathan Shteinman. *Scriptwriter*: Alexandra Long. *Director of photography*: Kathryn Milliss. *Music*: Martin Armiger. 91 min. *Cast*: Richard Roxburgh (Guy Jamieson), Cate Blanchett (Lizzie), Frances O'Connor (Jenny), Linden Wilkinson (Poppy), John Gaden (Dr O'Hara).

On his wedding day, Guy cannot stop thinking about his former girlfriend, Jenny. Images of their past together continually distract him from the affair of the moment; that is, the reception following his marriage to Lizzie. The film is structured about a series of flashbacks that contrast the charming upper-class Lizzie with the zanier Jenny. Romantic comedy has not been a significant genre in recent Australian cinema and this is one of the better ones. One of its strengths is in the way it makes Guy's choice between the two women a difficult one: neither is cast in the mould of 'other woman'; and its originality lies in starting where romantic comedy has most often ended: with decisions made that have to be lived with. Director Nowlan (in her first feature film) and writer Long keep the sympathies fairly distributed between the women, but Richard •Roxburgh's intelligent performance lacks the charisma of, say, a Cary Grant to make the audience understand what the fuss is about.

BMcF

They're a Weird Mob

1966. Director: Michael Powell. *Producer:* Michael Powell. *Scriptwriter:* Richard Imrie [Emeric Pressburger]. Based on the novel by Nino Culotta [John O'Grady]. *Director of photography:* Arthur Grant. *Music:* Lawrence Leonard, Alan Boustead. 112 min. *Cast:* Walter Chiari (Nino Culotta), Clare Dunne (Kay Kelly), Chips Rafferty (Harry Kelly), Alida Chelli (Giuliana), Ed Devereaux (Joe).

John O'Grady's hugely popular account (written under the pseudonym of Nino Culotta) of an Italian migrant's experiences in coming to terms with Australian life provided the basis for this film, which marked theatrical company J.C. Williamson's re-entry into film-making after a very long break. At the time, actor–producer John •McCallum was its managing director, and he arranged the agreement between the firm and British director Michael Powell, to make the film on a budget of $600 000. The resulting film was a great commercial success in Australia, although it did less well elsewhere.

It remains a good-humoured celebration of national stereotypes, as sportswriter Nino, on arrival in Australia, finds the journalist's job he had expected has vanished and he takes work as a builder's labourer. In the fairytale manner of the plot, he falls in love with (and of course wins) a rich girl whose father (Chips •Rafferty), in best democratic manner, had also begun as a bricklayer. Along the way, and through a series of more or less discrete episodes, he is initiated into Australian pub mores, the sun-and-sex culture of Bondi beach, the skill in not working too hard on the building site, mild xenophobia, and a lamington afternoon tea, which, to everyone's relief, gives way to alfresco beer-drinking.

There are not many traces of Michael Powell's once-dazzling directorial skills, but there is a pleasingly relaxed approach that allows the episodes to build, and he is not above taking a naive pleasure in the beauty of Sydney Harbour. There is a moment of focus-distortion to signify Nino's exhaustion that recalls how imaginative Powell once was, but mostly he is content to trust the material. Audiences were more than happy to collude with the film's view of 'a big country', which is reinforced in its theme song. For all its light-heartedness, it is an important film in the re-emergence of the country's film industry.   BMcF

Thompson, Jack (1940–) ACTOR   It is not easy to associate the suited, plummily toned Jack Thompson who has become familiar for his television advertisements with the dominant, iconic presence of the first decade or more of the new Australian cinema (see Revival, the). In the 1970s, from his role as the kangaroo-shooting yahoo in •**Wake in Fright** (1971) onwards, his was a quintessentially Australian persona: outgoing, boorish with women, hard-drinking, good-natured, and with more than a touch of the larrikin.

His background—he was adopted at the age of eight by the Sydney actor John Thompson, he worked as a jackeroo before joining the army for six years, and he began acting while a university student—suggests a range of experiences that may be unusual for an actor. It may also suggest why the persona is more complex than at first appears. There is something very disturbing about the mindless, overbearing matiness in **Wake in Fright**; the eponymous electrician in Tim •Burstall's abrasive 1974 film •**Petersen** is frustrated in his attempts to further his education, is humiliated by his intellectual superiors, reveals his vulnerability on several occasions, and shows that the 'ocker' facade is no more than that. This facade is affectingly pierced in •**Sunday Too Far Away** (1975), in which the apparently competitive macho shearer breaks down when confronted with the lacunae of his life. There is a touch of the 'lair' in his good-natured SP bookie who gives the heroine and the film a name in •**Caddie** (1976); and he gives real weight to the role of the about-to-be-replaced football coach in •**The Club** (1980).

The element of the authority-defying iconoclast dominated these earlier films, but even then he showed himself willing to extend his range in character roles, making demands at odds with those of conventional leading-man parts, such as he had in two poor films: Scobie Malone (1975) and **The Journalist** (1979). Perhaps he was always, at heart, a character actor, and he performs distinguished work in this vein as the conscientious, limited parson who tries doggedly to help the half-caste protagonist in •**The Chant of Jimmie Blacksmith** (1978), and as the somewhat hapless lawyer from outback NSW who tries to save the condemned men in •**'Breaker' Morant** (1980) and grows in moral dignity as he does so. He could do little for the legendary figure of Clancy (of the Overflow) in •**The Man from Snowy River** (1982), and, although he has continued to work steadily on both large and small screens, it is at least arguable that he has not surpassed the film performances he gave in the first decade of his screen career. He has filmed internationally since the NZ-made **Bad Blood** (1981), the telemovie, *A Woman Called Golda* (1982) with Ingrid Bergman, and Nagisa Oshima's **Merry Christmas, Mr Lawrence** (1983). In 1997 he had a major role in the American **Midnight in the Garden of Good and Evil**.

Thompson's real importance in the revival of Australian cinema in the 1970s is that he offered variations on what was conceived as a recognisable and popular Australian 'type', and in the re-establishing of a national cinema in this country one should not underestimate the significance of such images. He struck chords to make him one of the stars of the new Australian cinema and, if the image now appears somewhat jaded in a film such as •The Sum of Us (1994), this may be the result either of Thompson's having outlasted its viability or of Australian cinema's having worked its way past such archetypes. Making him the devoted father of a gay son was a plot device that seemed at odds with the recycled 1970s persona of the actor.

Other Australian films: That Lady from Peking (1970), No Roses for Michael (1970, short), Personnel or People (1970, short), By-Pass (1970, short), Where Dead Men Lie (1972, short), •Libido (1973, 'Family Man' episode), •Mad Dog Morgan (1976), Stallion of the Sea (1979, doc., nar.), The Earthling (1980), Give Trees a Chance (1980, doc., nar.), A Shifting Dreaming (1982, doc., nar.), •Burke & Wills (1985), •Ground Zero (1987), •Turtle Beach (1991), Wind (1992), Resistance (1992), Under the Lighthouse Dancing (1996), The Magic Pudding (anim. 2000-voice). BMcF

Thoms, Albie (1941–) DIRECTOR/WRITER Albie Thoms's interest in film began at the University of Sydney, where he produced films as elements within theatrical works, in a similar fashion to the French avant-garde classic Entr'acte (produced in 1924 by Rene Clair for screening within a ballet performance). Thoms produced the short experimental films It Droppeth as the Gentle Rain (1963, presented within *A Revue of the Absurd*), Spurt of Blood (1965, inspired by Antonin Artaud's Theatre of Cruelty), and Poem 25 (1965, inspired by a poem by Kurt Schwitters). While working in television (for example, *Contrabandits*), Thoms also became a film activist—writing, lobbying (particularly against censorship), and (with others, including John •Clarke, Aggy Read and David Perry) founding Ubu Films and the Sydney Film-makers Co-operative. Screenings of his parody of James Bond (Blunderball 1968) raised funds for Ubu, and Ubu published his *Handmade Film Manifesto* (1967), which proclaimed the virtues of eliminating sound and drawing directly on to the film stock. He followed these principles in Poem 25, Bluto (1966) and David Perry (1968). However, in other films he did use a camera—playing with and distorting what it recorded in films such as the controversial feature Marinetti (1967–69, based on the aesthetic principles of Italian futurist F.T. Marinetti), and the shorter films Man and his World (1966–69) and Rita and Dundi (1966–67), and making it an actor in the long tracking shot that comprises almost all of Bolero (1968). His later live action feature films, Sunshine City (1970–74) and Palm Beach (1980) construct a unique sense of place while avoiding or subverting traditional narrative structures. His *Polemics for a New Cinema* (Wild & Woolley, 1978) remains an important collection of writing on local and international avant-garde film. IB

Thomson, Brian PRODUCTION DESIGNER This art director has influenced the look of Australian theatre and cinema with his experimentation in innovative design. Characterised by the production of artificial, surreal worlds, his designs subvert the conventional notions of time and space, eschewing veracity and embracing surrealism. He has designed sets for the theatre, musicals, operas, television miniseries, rock videos, and exhibitions. Thomson's first feature film was Shirley Thompson Versus the Aliens in 1971 for Jim •Sharman. He continued his collaboration with Sharman in 1975, designing the production of The Rocky Horror Picture Show in the United Kingdom. In 1985 he won an Australian Film Institute (AFI) award for best production design on Rebel. The script required the reproduction of Kings Cross during World War II, but Thomson produced a surreal set by decorating the interior of the Air-Raid Club with corrugated iron and pink neon lights to provide a distinctive, artificial world. The use of litter as props continued the surrealist fascination with the repressed underside of society.

Thomson directed Night of Shadows in 1984. This short black-and-white film experimented with alternatives to editing and was shot by Russell •Boyd.

Other Australian films: Shock Treatment (1981), •Star Struck (1982), Street Hero (1984), Ground Zero (1987), Turtle Beach (1991), Frauds (1993). WENDY HASLEM

Thomson, Chris (1945–) DIRECTOR Prolific director who moves readily between television miniseries and features and theatrical films. Chris Thomson began his career with a number of telefeatures and miniseries in the late 1970s and early 1980s for the ABC: *Top Mates* (1979); *A Place in the World* (1979); *Big Toys* (1980), scripted by Patrick White from his play; *1915* (1982); and *Man of Letters* (1984). Thomson during this period also directed the depression-based union drama *Waterfront* (1984) with Jack •Thompson and Greta •Scacchi, followed by the large-budget ($3.6 million), critically acclaimed miniseries *The Last Bastion* (1984), which detailed General Douglas MacArthur's Melbourne-based campaign against Japanese expansion in the Pacific in 1941, and his turbulent relationships with Winston Churchill and President Roosevelt.

Thomson's first feature was the detective film •The Empty Beach (1985), based on the Peter Corris novel. Corris also worked on the script but the finished film, which retained some of the hard-boiled characteristics of its source, did not live up to the commercial expectations of the producers or distributors. As a result, plans for future films based on Corris's Cliff Hardy, starring Bryan •Brown, were shelved. Similarly, The Delinquents (1989) did not fulfil expectations, although the casting of Kylie •Minogue in the lead role ensured copious publicity for the film. Thomson worked mainly on television productions in the late 1980s and 1990s, including *The Perfectionist* (1985), *Cody* (1994–95) and *Betrayal* (1995) for *The Feds* series of telefeatures, together with *The Morrison Murders* (1996), based on the true-life American husband/wife murder, which was filmed in Hollywood for American television.

GM

Thornhill, Michael (1941–) DIRECTOR In his capacity as film critic (three years with the *Australian*) and lecturer, Michael Thornhill was one of the key figures in the promotion of the new Australian cinema (see Revival, the) and continued his political function in the industry's reformation as a director of the •New South Wales Film Corporation after 1977. His actual output as a feature film director has been meagre, but three of his films reveal him to be an unusually observant film-maker who is willing to take risks.

After making several documentaries and two short films (**The American Poet's Visit**, 1969, and **The Girl from the Family of Man**, 1970) based on stories by Frank •Moorhouse, a regular collaborator, he made his feature début with •**Between Wars** (1974). Scripted by Moorhouse and starring British actor Corin Redgrave, the film concerned a doctor who struggles to maintain idealism in the face of a repressive authority. The film quite daringly deals with notions of Freudian psychiatry: 'daringly' in the sense that it does not subordinate its conceptual framework to the purely personal, although the latter aspect is played with intelligence and feeling. **Between Wars**, for which Thornhill arranged distribution himself, was essentially arthouse fare, winning more critical plaudits than box-office success, and his next feature, •**The FJ Holden** (1977), was in three states given an 'R' censorship rating, thereby denying admission to the very group that might most have appreciated it—the under-18s, who could have been expected to revel in its rock music score. This is an uncompromisingly bleak study of the limited vistas and masculinist ethos of working-class culture in Sydney's western suburbs. This is represented as a society with little to offer its young beyond boozing and affectless sex. Thornhill does not fudge his harsh vision, drawing beautiful performances from non-professional Eva Dickinson, as the prematurely careworn daughter of a deserted father, and Ray •Marshall, effortlessly inhabiting the latter role.

Resuming his association with Moorhouse in 1988, Thornhill made •**The Everlasting Secret Family**, a bizarre version of Moorhouse's long short story about a kind of homosexual society that acts as a source of political power and leadership. Implications relating to the nature of conservative Australian political life and its conspiratorial underpinnings meant that the film was not without interest, but its appeal was too obscure for anything but arthouse exhibition.

It is perhaps a reflection on the state of the local industry that someone as articulate and venturesome as Thornhill has not been able to work more prolifically. His three most interesting films make little concession to popular taste and are, in their different modes, distinguished by their uncompromising attitudes.

Other Australian films include: The Explorer (1963, short, ed.), The Esperance Story (1969, doc.), Leonard French's Stained Glass Screens (1969), The Machine Gun, 1971, short, p.), Mr Fixit My Dad (1971, doc. co-w.), Kevin and Cheryl (1972), Summer of Secrets (1976, p.), •Harvest of Hate (1978), The Journalist (1979, + co-w.), Greed (1982, doc., ex-p.).

BMcF

Thornton, Sigrid (1959–) ACTOR Born in Canberra, but based in Melbourne, Sigrid Thornton has become one of the best-known actors in Australian film and television. She had already been seen in such television series as *Certain Women* and *Homicide* when she made her film début as one of the bitchier schoolgirls in Bruce •Beresford's •**The Getting of Wisdom** (1977), one of the period films that enjoyed a vogue at the time, and she followed this with a role in the social realism of Michael •Thornhill's •**The FJ Holden** in the same year. Her first starring role in films was in Simon •Wincer's **Snapshot** (1979), as the young hairdresser who gets lured into sleazy and dangerous situations that threaten her life. Thornton responded well in this minor thriller to the demands of the woman-in-danger role; she introduced the spunky, determined persona that she honed in subsequent roles, most popularly in •**The Man from Snowy River** (1982) and its sequel **The Man from Snowy River II** (1988), as Jessica, the squatter's high-spirited daughter who is won to the high country by the eponymous hero. She was similarly full of high-spirited independence in the minor up-country road movie, **Slate Wyn & Me** (1987), but she was given a chance to be affecting in a more low-key role in Wincer's •**The Lighthorsemen** (1987). Some of her more recent films have not enjoyed major release: **Over the Hill** (1992), as an unfeeling daughter dealing with an elderly mother; the American sci-fi thriller, **Trapped in Space** (1993); and Carl •Schultz's political romance, **Love in Ambush** (1997). She has had some high-profile television work, especially in *The Far Country*, a 1986 version of Nevil Shute's novel, and the ABC series *SeaChange*. She has also been a spokesperson for the industry on a number of occasions, and a member of the Australian Film Institute board since 1993.

Other Australian films: King of the Two Day Wonder (1979), Duet for Four (1982), Street Hero (1984), Niel Lynne (1985).

BMcF

Thoroughbred

1936. Director: Ken G. Hall. *Producer:* Ken G. Hall. *Scriptwriter:* Edmond Seward. *Director of photography:* George Heath. *Musical director:* Hamilton Webber. 89 min. B&W. *Cast:* Helen Twelvetrees (Joan), Frank Leighton (Tommy Dawson), John Longden (Bill Peel), Nellie Ferguson (Ma Dawson), Edmond Seward (Mr Terry).

A plethora of international accents, startling special effects, potted social commentary, and a British exhibition deal mark **Thoroughbred** as one of the most ambitious films to emerge from the •Cinesound stable. This unbridled equine romance begins with an almost exact reproduction of the opening sequence of an earlier Ken G. •Hall film, •**The Squatter's Daughter** (1933), although most contemporary comparisons were to its Hollywood antecedent, **Broadway Bill** (1934). Joan, a Canadian adopted by the kindly Ma Dawson, is a horse-breeder who dreams of training a Cup winner. Luck seems to favour Joan when she acquires a sickly thoroughbred, Stormalong which, under her care, recovers well enough to become a Melbourne Cup favourite and the envy of international gangsters. Several attempts to assassinate 'Stormy' are foiled and the stage is set for a climactic Cup race in which the horse literally falls over the line (it has been fatally shot), and Joan's braggart boyfriend Tommy (son of Ma) Dawson is simultaneously paralysed after plunging from a balcony. Joan's conclusive devotion to the now invalid Tommy apparently demonstrates her belief that although eugenics is useful for understanding horses it has little relevance to humans. Her conviction appears less concerted in light of the fact that two endings to the film were originally shot, including an unreleased finale that would have Tommy dead and Joan paired with his romantic rival, the blue-blooded Bill Peel.

Thoroughbred is also notable for the first use of what was to become a signature Cinesound effect—rear-projection. Indeed, the film's deployment of this technology was so effective that 21 minutes of footage were cut in the United Kingdom in the misguided belief that the horses had been subject to cruelty.   DEB VERHOEVEN

Those Who Love

1926. Directors: P.J. Ramster, Paulette McDonagh. *Producer:* Paulette McDonagh. *Scriptwriter:* Paulette McDonagh. *Director of photography:* Jack Fletcher. 6000ft. B&W. *Cast:* Marie Lorraine (Lola Quayle), William Carter (Barry Manton), Robert Purdie (Sir James Manton), Sylvia Newland (Bébé Dorée), George Dean (Parker).

This was the first of four features produced by the •McDonagh sisters—Paulette as director/producer/writer,

Phyllis as production manager and art director, and Isabel as the star (under her stage-name Marie •Lorraine). For this first feature they employed P.J.Ramster as director, but found his work not acceptable, and relegated him to technical support.

This is a typical Hollywood story—a family romance, built around class distinction and requiring noble sacrifice from both lovers. Barry Manton leaves his wealthy family, meets Lola in a dance-hall, and marries her. But she runs away from him, believing she is standing in the way of a family reconciliation. Some time later he is taken ill, and rushed to the hospital where she now works. In order to secure money for his treatment, she approaches his family, and his parents are won over by their charming grandson. All that survives in the •National Film and Sound Archive is an extended trailer, with beautiful art intertitles.   IB

Three in One

1957. Director: Cecil Holmes. *Producer:* Cecil Holmes. *Director of photography:* Ross Wood. *Music:* Raymond Hanson. 89 min. B&W. **Joe Wilson's Mates**: *Scriptwriter:* Rex Rienits. Based on the story 'The Union Buries its Dead' by Henry Lawson. *Cast:* Edmund Allison (Tom Stevens), Reg Lye (the swaggie), Alexander Archdale (Firbank), Charles Tasman (the undertaker), Don McNiven (Patrick Rooney). **The Load of Wood**: *Scriptwriter:* Rex Rienits. Based on a story by Frank Hardy. *Cast:* Jock Levy (Darkie), Leonard Teale (Ernie), Ossie Wenban (Sniffy), John Armstrong (Chilla), Jim Doone (Joe). **The City**: *Scriptwriter:* Ralph Peterson. *Cast:* Joan Landor (Kathie), Brian Vicary (Ted), Betty Lucas (Freda).

Australian feature film production was in the doldrums in the 1950s, when Cecil •Holmes persuaded Frank Hardy to back him in the production of a film from Hardy's short story 'The Load of Wood'. In this story, the men on the sustenance gang complain of lack of firewood, so Darkie promises a shed full of wood to whomever will accompany him on an expedition to steal it from the hated landowner. Ernie is the only one who agrees, and we hear the story told through his voice-over. Two more short films were then produced: **Joe Wilson's Mates** (about the funeral of a transient in an outback town, where all that is known about him is that he was a member of the union), and **The City** (about the stresses in a relationship when the young couple cannot marry because of the postwar housing shortage). A link was then provided by the narration of John •McCallum, but the reluctance of the distributors to handle Australian product, and the left-wing sympathies of the film, prevented its commercial distribution. In Australia, each story was occasionally shown as a supporting featurette, but overseas the film was well received in festivals and on the art-house circuit, and it still stands up well against realist films of its time.   IB

Thring, Frank W. (1883–1936) DIRECTOR/PRODUCER
Frank W. Thring joined the film trade as a touring exhibitor in Tasmania becoming, in 1915, part-owner of the Melbourne cinema chain Electric Theatres. In 1918 he became managing director of the distribution company J.C. Williamson Films Ltd and, in 1926, he became joint managing director of •Hoyts Theatres Ltd. In 1930 he sold his interests in Hoyts and set up •Efftee Productions, both managing the company and producing and directing most of its films, including seven features (•**Diggers**, 1931; •**The Sentimental Bloke**, 1932; •**His Royal Highness**, 1932; •**Harmony Row**, 1933; •**A Ticket in Tatts**, 1934; •**Clara Gibbings**, 1934; **The Streets of London**, 1934). From August 1933 he became increasingly active in theatrical promotion, aiming to develop a stable of talent that could move easily among film and stage, and—after his 1935 purchase of Melbourne station 3XY—also radio.

Release difficulties led him to become an advocate of quota protection for Australian films and, as the Victorian government was refusing to amend its legislation to cover features, Thring decided to move Efftee to Sydney, where he established links with the Mastercraft Film Corporation and began production on **Collitt's Inn**. In March 1936 he left for the USA to engage directors, technicians, and actors for the Sydney operation. He returned to Melbourne on the Mariposa in May, already critically ill, and died on 1 July 1936. With his experience in exhibition and distribution, he was greatly missed as the production industry continued lobbying for government assistance. His son was the actor Frank •Thring.   IB

Thring, Frank (1926–94) ACTOR The son of Frank W. •Thring, Frank Thring was predominantly a stage actor who ventured into films (and television) primarily for money and amusement: it was not a medium he took seriously. This is reflected in the larger-than-life comic roles he accepted in films such as **Alvin Purple Rides Again** (1974), •**The Man from Hong Kong** (1975), and **Howling III: The Marsupials** (1987). Even Thring's screen performances overseas, as Pontius Pilate in **Ben Hur** (1959) or Herod in **King of Kings** (1961), tended towards the grotesque and the excessive. On occasion, when sufficiently motivated, Thring could convey a strong sense of terror and persecution, as Superintendent Cobham in •**Mad Dog Morgan** (1976) or Judge Barry in •**Ned Kelly** (1970). Overall, his dramatic skills were mostly reserved for the stage. The rest of the time Thring was content to convey his larger-than-life personality in other facets of the media, including populist journalism as 'Veritas', the most 'feared' critic of television standards in the 1960s.
Other Australian films include: •**Age of Consent** (1969), •**Mad Max Beyond Thunderdome** (1985), •**Death of a Soldier** (1986).   GM

Thunderbolt

1910. *Director*: John Gavin. *Producer*: H.A. Forsyth. From the novel *Three Years with Thunderbolt* by Ambrose Pratt. *Director of photography*: A.J. Moulton. B&W. *Cast*: John Gavin (Thunderbolt).

John Gavin's first feature film as director and star was also the first film of a short-lived production 'boom' that saw 81 commercial narrative films released between November 1910 and July 1912. Two reels of **Thunderbolt** survive. They show early incidents from the career of Frederick Ward, 'Captain Thunderbolt', based on a highly fictionalised account written by Ambrose Pratt with the help of William Monckton, who rode for a time with Thunderbolt. Gavin, a generous figure of a man with a rather limited acting range, plays Thunderbolt earnestly. Much of the action is filmed in a style that was old-fashioned even in 1910: long, unbroken takes with the camera positioned at some distance from the meandering activity it is intended to record. Nonetheless, **Thunderbolt** is an important film for its role in setting the pace of the 'boom', which included the production of so many films sympathetic to bushrangers that the New South Wales police banned the genre in 1912.

WILLIAM D. ROUTT

Ticket in Tatts, A

1934. *Director*: F.W. Thring. *Production company*: Efftee Film Productions. *Story*: George Wallace, John P. McLeod. *Director of photography*: Arthur Higgins. 88 min. B&W. *Cast*: George Wallace (George), Frank Harvey (Brian Winters), Campbell Copelin (Harvey Walls), Thelma Scott (Dorothy Fleming), Harold Meade (Mr. Fleming).

This was the last •Efftee feature film to star vaudevillean George •Wallace. Its theatrical ancestry is evident in the detours of the plot through George's disastrous career, first as a grocer's assistant, then as a stable hand, and a tedious series of song-and-dance routines at the Cup Eve party. The main narrative focus, however, is on preparations for the Melbourne Cup, with George whistling at the right moment during the race to encourage Hotspur to win despite a crooked jockey. In addition to George's story, complicated still further by his dalliance with the maid from the racing stables, there is a high society romance, the resolution also hinging on Hotspur winning the Cup.

Despite its vaudeville associations, this is a more complex narrative than earlier Wallace vehicles, and F.W. •Thring consistently made use of location shooting, including intercutting footage of a Flemington race meeting. The film was distributed by Universal in Australia, with modest success.   IB

Tim

1979. Director, Producer, Scriptwriter: Michael Pate (based on the novel by Colleen McCullough). *Director of photography:* Paul Onorato. *Music:* Eric Jupp. 109 min. *Cast:* Piper Laurie (Mary Horton), Mel Gibson (Tim Melville), Alwyn Kurts (Ron Melville), Pat Evison (Em Melville), Deborah Kennedy (Dawnie Melville).

Tim is an intellectually retarded 24-year-old labourer hired as a gardener by Mary Horton, a wealthy, cultured, middle-aged American businesswoman. The relationship moves through friendship, dependency, and troubled romance towards a fairy-tale marriage. We learn about Tim's simple, good-hearted, working-class family, which has to come to terms with the death of mother Em and with sister Dawnie's suspicions of Mary's motives.

The film's best moments derive from creditable performances from Mel •Gibson, Alwyn •Kurts, and Pat •Evison. It also has a sympathetic depiction of the working-class milieu, but these are by no means enough to rescue the film from an implausible and often silly narrative that carries the stamp of melodrama. It fails to engage the potentially interesting issues implicit in the central relationship. Piper Laurie's performance, Eric Jupp's score, and Michael •Pate's direction are all redolent of the television soaps.

HARRY OLDMEADOW

Time In Summer

1968. Director: Ludwik Dutkiewicz. *Production company:* Arkaba Films. *Director of photography:* Ian Davidson. *Music:* Richard Meale. 64 min. B&W. *Cast:* Christina O'Brien (Anne), Peter Ross (her brother), Rory Hume (Shawn), Andrena Gwynn-Jones (Mrs Harper).

This enchanting film dispenses with anything but the barest narrative elements, which may have contributed to the distributors' unwillingness to handle a film clearly ahead of its time, yet unlikely to find a broad local audience. The film purportedly interlaces the stories of Anne's holiday romance with a boy she meets while skinny-dipping, and her brother's scattered memories leading up to the car crash that opens the film. However, there is no indication in the film that the two are related. Mysterious, mad women; beachside trysts; wild drunken parties; furious games of table tennis; tragedy at a horse race; the consummation of first love; and sunsets over the ocean swirl around and dissolve in this richly rewarding and visually delightful film. Cinematographer Ian Davidson utilises a range of camera techniques to masterful effect in this film, which was screened at the Berlin Film Festival in 1968, but was neither widely seen nor reviewed in Australia.

BEN GOLDSMITH

Tingwell, Charles

Tingwell, Charles (1923–) ACTOR One of Australia's most affectionately regarded actors, Charles Tingwell, known as 'Bud', has had a career that virtually tells the story of the postwar Australian film industry. In the years immediately following the war he did what could be done here: secured major roles in several of the more ambitious indigenous productions, appeared in American and British films made here, and starred in one of Lee •Robinson's Southern International productions. He went to the United Kingdom in the late 1950s, where he maintained a busy career for over a decade, before returning to become a fixture in Australian television and in the burgeoning local film industry of the 1970s. It is arguable that no Australian actor has had so sustained a film career, or so convincingly made the transition from young leading man to reliable character actor.

Tingwell began as a professional actor while still at school in Sydney in 1940, became a radio announcer before war service with the RAAF from 1941 to 1945, and subsequently had experience as a theatre director, as well as continuing regular radio work, including a stint as Bob Dyer's assistant. After a small role in Ken G •Hall's •Smithy (1946), he played the lead in T.O. •McCreadie's •Always Another Dawn (1947), a sentimental melodrama of love and war, as an heroic young naval officer; and starred again for McCreadie in Into the Straight (1949), this time in a decidedly non-heroic role and in a film that performed better commercially. He played the son of a pioneering family in the Ealing-made outback saga, •Bitter Springs (1950), with Chips •Rafferty and Gordon Jackson; and supported Hollywood stars Maureen O'Hara and Peter Lawford in the Twentieth Century Fox adventure •Kangaroo (1952), a western in all but name. Fox gave him a supporting role in the American war drama, The Desert Fox (1953), and offered him a contract that he declined. Tingwell co-starred with Grant •Taylor in Cecil •Holmes' first feature film, •Captain Thunderbolt (1953); and had the lead in Lee Robinson's •King of the Coral Sea (1954), with another future star, Rod •Taylor.

During his prolific career in the United Kingdom, he worked for several studios, including Hammer and Rank, but his biggest success was as Inspector Craddock in the four Miss Marple mysteries made by MGM-British, with Craddock maintaining his patience in the face of the eccentric methods of Margaret Rutherford's Miss Marple. His final film in the United Kingdom was as Jacko in Ralph Thomas's thriller, Nobody Runs Forever (1968), which reunited him with Rod Taylor. He also did television there, including Emergency Ward 10, before returning to Australia in 1972, when he immediately began to appear in local television. In 1974, on the big screen, he played Jack •Thompson's sympathetic clergyman father in •Petersen. Since then, he has been almost constantly in work in film, television, or theatre. His films have involved him in some notable character roles, such as Lieutenant Colonel Denny in •'Breaker' Morant (1980), the headmaster in •Puberty Blues (1981), the estranged wife's middle-class father in •My First Wife (1984), the understanding judge in •Annie's Coming Out (1984), and the humane retired barrister who decides to emerge to defend the beleaguered householder in •The Castle (1997). It hardly matters what role Tingwell turns his attention to: he imbues everything with such an unobtrusive sense of respect for the role that he is effortlessly convincing. In fact, his *persona*, off-screen as well as on-screen (to judge from interviews), seems so instinctively humane that it might be more difficult for him to convince audiences of serious villainy; then again, his technical mastery is now so complete, that he could pull it off without our noticing the effort. In 1998, he was asked to direct the feature film **Second Drills**, and throughout the 1990s he has been busy as actor, producer and director on television, and as an actor on stage. Tingwell was made a member of the Order of Australia in 1999 for services to the performing arts.

Other Australian films: The Glenrowan Affair (1951, nar.), Stealthy (1953, doc., nar.), Jungle Warfare Training (1955, doc., nar.), •Smiley (1956), The Snowy Mountains Scheme: Showing the Guthega Project (1956, doc., nar.), •The Shiralee (1957, nar.), The Unitisers (1968, doc., nar.), The Australian Flight 1919 (1969, doc., co-nar.), End Play (1975), •Eliza Fraser (1976), •Summerfield (1977), •Money Movers (1979), The Journalist (1979), Gold Mines of Australia (1981, doc., nar.), Freedom (1982), •Malcolm (1986), Windrider (1986), •Evil Angels (1988), Amy (1998), The Craic (1999).   BMcF

To Have and To Hold

1996. Director: John Hillcoat. *Producer*: Denise Patience. *Scriptwriter*: Gene Conkie. *Director of photography*: Andrew de Groot. *Music*: Nick Cave, Blixa Bargeld and Mick Harvey. 100 min. *Cast*: Tcheky Karyo (Jack), Rachel Griffiths (Kate), Steve Jacobs (Sal), Anni Finsterer (Rose), David Field (Stevie), Robert Kunsa (Luther).

The credits at the end of John •Hillcoat's gothic drama acknowledge the 'storm footage by Simon Kerwin Carroll', which was specifically commissioned for insertion at a key moment to enhance the film's dramatic fabric and the recurring reference to the 'pure and polar concepts of darkness and light, salvation and damnation'. It is this knowledge and the careful reworking of gothic conventions that makes this film special in the history of the Australian cinema. Unlike the 'excess' in films such as •The Adventures of Priscilla, Queen of the Desert (1994), where 'excess' remains at the superficial level of costume, or setting, the excess that is inherent in To Have and To Hold is restrained by gothic conventions as the film follows a disciplined pattern of dramatic escalation.

To Have and To Hold was inspired by a trip Hillcoat took with his sister to Papua New Guinea. The desire to dramatise the extremes of life that he witnessed was integrated with conventions of melodrama and the 'gothic', reinforced by reference to two Hitchcock films: **Rebecca** (1940) and **Vertigo** (1958). The basic story combines elements of these films as Jack (French actor Tcheky Karyo), an expatriate living in New Guinea, is distressed by the death of his wife, Rose. Two years later he visits Melbourne, where he is attracted to Kate, a writer of romantic fiction. After a brief romance he persuades her to return to his remote house on the Sepik River. Kate, however, soon realises that Jack is obsessed by the memory of Rose. Gradually, her fantasy of living in a 'tropical paradise' with a sensuous Frenchman is destroyed by his aberrant, erratic behaviour. The situation is heightened by the mysterious presence of Luther, a Papuan who was seemingly involved in Rose's death.

To Have and To Hold subsumes a postcolonial critique into this dramatic structure as European exploitation is dramatised not only through the commercial activities of Jack and Sal, but also via Luther, the youth who is imprisoned and loses his left eye. Whereas Kate is able to escape Jack's obsession and madness, the film highlights the fact that the economically subservient locals are not so lucky. In the closing images of the film, its recurring formal

Charles ('Bud') Tingwell

In conversation with

CHARLES TINGWELL

Your film career divides chronologically into three main sections: Australia–United Kingdom–Australia. Did it seem necessary to leave the country in the 1950s if you wanted to pursue a career as a film actor?

No, not only did I not leave it but I turned down a contract in Hollywood to come back. The only reason I went to England was to finish a very small role I had in •The Shiralee. It was mainly shot here but there were some studio scenes including one back projection scene of me in a truck with Peter •Finch. The production manager said, 'If you could get to London it would help us a lot. We can't really afford to give you the big first-class trip but we'll give you enough days to pay for the trip if you and Audrey [Mrs Tingwell] want to go over there.' So I went to England and did the shots for The Shiralee, and Audrey and I were just going to stay in London, watch as much telly as possible, come back, and shoot the usual line, 'I have been studying television' when someone mentioned this new experimental show called *Emergency Ward 10*. It was only scheduled to run for a few weeks but it took off. We were sort of trapped. My agent said, 'Stay on if they offer you any more episodes', and they did. The show became an immediate hit and then I discovered Australia House was rather keen for me to stay on because I was playing a surgeon that was a different image for Australians. So we accidentally stayed in London for 16 years with our stuff still in storage in Sydney. But I never intended to stay!

What did the film scene seem like in Australia after the War?

It went through surges. There was a lot of promise in the 1940s with Tom and Alec •McCreadie doing •Always Another Dawn and Into the Straight, Charlie •Chauvel of course had •Sons of Matthew coming along … I was offered a part in that, but, by the time they made up their minds about when they were going to shoot, I was offered the lead in Always Another Dawn, so I took that instead. There was Arthur Collins making Strong is the Seed, a story about William Farrer that starred Guy Doleman, who worked with us in Always Another Dawn; Eric •Porter was doing •A Son is Born

about that time; there was Ralph •Smart's •Bush Christmas in preparation; and then of course •Eureka Stockade in 1949, and I had a tiny part in that. It was a very busy period, but it seemed to start tailing off in the early 1950s again.

What do you remember about working for the McCreadies?

Tom was the director and Alec was the producer. I remember them being enormously efficient. Tom wasn't an experienced film-maker, although he and Alec had made some interesting documentaries before that. What they did was to work things out to the nth degree. Their shooting scripts had every shot listed, which was a little bit more detailed than was practised then or now. They offered me a contract to do a second film, which was Into the Straight, with a retainer, and one of my tasks was to do a shooting script in the style that Tom liked from a dialogue script again written by Zelma Roberts, who wrote the original script of •Always Another Dawn, and that was almost like converting a radio script into shooting script form. I don't mean Tom necessarily stuck to all my suggested shots but it was a wonderful learning experience.

Where did they make their films?

We used, as most people have been doing over the years, the Showgrounds in Sydney. They're doing it again now. We had the Poultry Pavilion, which was actually on Lang Road, which runs around the back of the Showgrounds, so they had street access. The studio scenes for •The Overlanders were done there. Jack •Bruce and a colleague of his who ran the Commonwealth Film Laboratories also used the Poultry Pavilion, and an excellent studio it was too.

How were those two films you did for the McCreadies received by the public and critics at the time?

One of my worst ever crits was for Always Another Dawn, and the tag was 'Tingwell, Tingwell, little star, must you wonder why you are?' This was actually clever because I did spend a lot of the film looking off into the horizon, thinking, rather bravely too! The first length I think was about 95 minutes and it was a bit slow, but the British version was trimmed down to 73 minutes and it really moved along! Had they released the 73-minute version we might have got less rude notices. On the other hand, people like Robert Dunstan in Melbourne gave it a real rave, and there were probably a few in between. **Into the Straight** got 'fairly good', 'straightforward', 'well done', etc. **Always Another Dawn** had a premiere at the Embassy Theatre in Sydney, which was one of the nice posh houses, a nice one as I remember. I think •Greater Union may have come aboard with **Into the Straight**. Had the crits been a little bit more encouraging they'd have had longer runs. They were respected movies and I was surprised how well made they were when I saw them again recently.

Is it true that you had a small part in •Smithy?
Yes, thanks to my mother. I was a pilot in the Air Force in the war and I arrived home just before the European War ended. My mother said, 'Go out to •Cinesound; they're making **Smithy** and you'd be a very good "Smithy"'. I remember saying, 'No, Ron •Randell's playing "Smithy"'. But I went out and the casting director Frank Brooks saw me in uniform and said 'Can you read lines?' 'Yes', I replied. 'Good, you're in, providing you bring your own uniform.' I played the part of a control tower officer right at the beginning of **Smithy**. It's the first sequence, of an American-liberated aircraft landing in Australia during World War II, and it cuts to the interior of the control tower and the young bloke, me, says 'Control to commanding officer, 12 liberators ex-Oakland California all down Sir'. Tom McCreadie gave me the lead in **Always Another Dawn** because of that one line.

What do you remember about those films you made for overseas companies in Australia and of the general feeling about them coming here to make films like •Bitter Springs for Ealing or •Kangaroo for Fox, for instance?
We just thought, that's a bit of a turn up, someone's coming out to make a movie. There was no sort of resentment that I remember. **Bitter Springs** was a wonderful one to be involved in because we worked with the Ooldea tribal people, and we were among the very few people who'd ever worked alongside Aboriginal tribal people on more or less equal terms. Once someone says 'action', you're all equal. Ooldea used to be a stop on the Nullarbor Railway line. The Ooldea people were helped by a couple of marvellous Methodist missionaries, who just stayed in the background making sure they were OK. The director, Ralph •Smart, was Australian and he had a bit to do with the planning of the story though I think Bill Lipscomb, one of Ealing's respected writers, wrote the script, and Leslie Norman was associate producer. He came out to see why we were so far behind schedule— we broke the drought in South Australia, but we caught up quickly when Les came out. **Kangaroo** was interesting because we saw the full American production team come out. They sent out one of the top crews, and a big star like Maureen O'Hara. What impressed me with them, and later when I worked in Hollywood and watched other films being made, was that everybody's just so very efficient and the difference is whatever happens with great inspirational directors and/or actors and/or script. It was all on a bigger scale, I suppose, but, looking back I thought Harry Malcolm [cinematographer] and his team did a fabulous job on **Always Another Dawn**. Budget was limited but we had all we needed to make the film.

Am I right in thinking you turned down the offer of a contract with Fox when you made Desert Rats?
Yes, and years later Chips •Rafferty said, 'I did too, but I didn't talk about it as much as you did!' I was the very last in the casting, I flew in on a Sunday, it was all very quick, they zoomed me out to the studio, I had my return ticket in my hand but no deal, there hadn't been time for any of that, and Billy Gordon, the head of Fox, offered me a seven-year contract. I said 'I've just got here! I'd better not, not yet anyway. Can I just do one for the film?' He said, 'All right, but it's there if you want to sign it.' They didn't pester me about it, but my new chums in Hollywood told me not to get too excited about it, because, if they've paid a return airfare, they always offer a contract, so that if you take off and become great they've already invested the cost of the airfare and if it doesn't work out they can sack you every six months anyway. I'd had the lead in the first telemovie made in Australia about six months before, and had I signed the contract with Fox I couldn't have done any more. There were all sorts of reasons why it didn't seem like a good idea at the time: it seemed to us that, back in Australia, a lot of what we'd been working for could have been about to happen and Chips's company was starting and we were planning to do •King of the Coral Sea.

How did you become involved with that company—Southern International?

I can't remember exactly how we started. I'd met Chips in the Air Force and then in **Bitter Springs**. In 1949 he played my father which I don't think pleased him all that much because he was actually only 14 years older than me! That became a close association. Chips was very good about trying to get better financial conditions for a couple of the Aboriginal actors from Queensland. We often talked about getting together to make films, and then we were in the same hotel in Hollywood on **Desert Rats**. By then we were talking about doing **King of the Coral Sea**. He'd already made **The Phantom Stockman** with Lee [•Robinson], a very low-budget film that was well and truly in profit by the time he got back. So that made the likelihood of doing **King of the Coral Sea** very much firmer.

Was it an original script?

Yes with a few small things of mine thrown in. Chips and I had discussed it a lot while sitting around the swimming pool in Hollywood, and it was going to be a very simple adventure story. Later, I thought they'd over-complicated it, so I sat down and I wrote a lot of suggestions. Chips rang and said, 'I've got your letter', and I thought, 'Here comes the blast', but he said, 'You're right. We want to buy it.' I thought that said a lot for his integrity because it really was their idea. I'd beaten them up five pounds a week, from 50 to 55 pounds a week to play one of the main roles, so I said, 'What's the airfare to Thursday Island and full board?' and it was about seven pounds a week. I said, 'Good, you can take my wife at your expense'. I went back to the 50 pounds a week and it was one of the happiest deals I've ever done. We were two weeks on Green Island doing the underwater scenes, as well as Thursday Island for the first five weeks. I like to think that some of the ideas in it were mine, here and there. It was a popular film at the time.

Chips Rafferty at his best seems like one of those great screen actors who look as if they're doing nothing at all.

I learnt a great deal from him. One of the most valuable things I learnt from him was in his last years. Chips flew over to do a round of episodes in *Emergency Ward 10*, playing an Australian journalist who was getting a bit past it, and was over there freelancing to cover a test series. I saw him looking at some handwritten notes just before a take and afterwards I asked, 'What's that?'

He said, 'Oh, I've been doing this for years. I write out all my lines on a separate piece of paper so I don't have to carry the script. That becomes part of the learning process and I've always got it there to refer to'. I've been doing that ever since. Wonderful tip! He played an Irish sea captain in an historical film on TV in Britain, and one of the producers said after, 'We always thought he was a good actor but we didn't know he was a great actor until then'. You'd have been laughed at in Australia by the cynics out here. In Hollywood, they gave him a permanent Green Card as a mark of respect for his standing in the international industry. He was held in very high esteem around the world but it was hard to get Aussies to accept it.

You worked with another hero of Australian films in the 1950: Cecil •Holmes. What do you recall of working with him on •Captain Thunderbolt?

A lot of Aussie film-makers miss out one very essential element of film-making that I saw in action in America. There they took a lot of time out to prepare a scene before they rolled any footage of it, and I think a lot of directors in Australia back in those days didn't know what to do if they did that. They didn't know about rehearsing; very few of them had ever done any theatre work of any kind, and Holmes seemed to be reluctant to commit himself to the rehearsal idea. But there was some lovely stuff in **Thunderbolt**; it was good to be involved in it. Every film I saw being made at Fox, every time I watched a take, the take was the result of a lot of very meticulous preparation. It took me a while to talk Lee Robinson into doing that when we were making **Coral Sea**. Chips and I had a long scene that I thought had been over-scheduled, and I said, 'If we rehearse this we could shoot it much faster'. We rehearsed it on the front verandah that night and sure enough we got about two-and-a-half days ahead of schedule because there was nothing more to shoot. We were very well prepared, Chips and I. Ross Wood saw the rehearsals and knew exactly the way he wanted to shoot it.

*Was **Thunderbolt** filmed in New England?*

Yes, we went up to Thunderbolt country in northern New South Wales, Glen Innes, round that territory. I think there's a small town called Yooralla. I know there is a cemetery in the town that has got Thunderbolt's grave. There were some claims that they shot the wrong man, and the police had buried him as Thunderbolt, but Thunderbolt actually survived. There were a lot of stories around the district, some were on the police side, some on the bushranger's side, of course. Fred Ward, known as Thunderbolt (played by Grant •Taylor), and Alan Blake, the guy I played, dressed alike, and both rode similar horses, so when they split up the police weren't sure in the distance which one to chase. We followed that line, and it gave a quite interesting point to the story. You could still buy an argument up there when we shot it in the early 1950s because there would always be somebody who'd say, 'My great-grandfather was in that round-up and they got him'— or they didn't get him. It was officially being made as a television film, years before telly started here of course; their idea, I think, was to go for what seemed to be an expanding market with film material for television, but it was good enough to release as a feature film. I suppose it ran a bit shorter than the average feature. I'm pretty sure it was on British telly when I was over there. Again some fine work by Ross •Wood [cinematographer], great stuff.

The last two films you did here before going to the United Kingdom were Smiley *and* The Shiralee. *Was* Smiley *affiliated with some British company?*
It was Anthony Kimmins. That rings bells but I can't remember which company [London Films].

Where was it filmed?
That was in New South Wales, I was playing in Sydney in the theatre then with Googie •Withers and John •McCallum's first company in Australia in *Simon and Laura* and *The Deep Blue Sea*, and it was a bit 'old palsy' but I loved it and of course John and I had a matinee, and we had to get back to Sydney to do it. I'm pretty sure we were shooting around one of the traditional places like Scone or somewhere out of Sydney.

The little boy was marvellous. He was Colin Petersen and he went on to England and became a drummer. When they did a sequel, called **Smiley Gets a Gun**, Tony Kimmins said, 'If I can get Colin Petersen you must come out and be the headmaster again'. Anyhow they couldn't get Colin for the sequel, and Len Teale played the headmaster.

A number of London-based Australian actors had parts in The Shiralee, *but you'd done your work mostly in Australia?*
Oh yes, sure. Finchy and I in our early scenes were out again in one of the nice country towns and we just

shot around there. I remember Finchy being very impressed by a couple of blokes who came into the pub one day and started chatting to us. They were a couple of kangaroo shooters and they were saying things like, 'You can tell my mate's done more kangaroo-shooting than I have because he's only got half a finger there and he's worn his trigger finger down'. Finchy loved this; he'd been in England for quite a while and to bump into these amazing characters, for real, was fascinating! He and I had been rough old radio actors together but, by the time he came back for **Shiralee**, he was very much known as a London actor. That doesn't mean he spoke posh or anything like that, he was just a well-employed actor. He hadn't changed at all.

Though this interview is really about your Australian career I can't resist asking you about playing Inspector Craddock to Margaret Rutherford's 'Miss Marple'.
That's was fabulous and it was so ordinary too. I've still got a mental picture of me standing in the hallway of our London house when the phone rang. 'Hello it's George Pollock here, I'm a film director and I've been asked to direct a film with Margaret Rutherford based on the Agatha Christie's Miss Marple stories. I wondered if you'd be interested in playing the Inspector?' I was doing *Emergency Ward 10* and replied, 'Oh yes, as long as I give them notice they'll write me out and say I've gone to another hospital'. And this lovely script arrived and we did the first one early 1961. It wasn't till we did the fourth one that George found out I was Australian. They did wonderfully well with those films. Margaret, who was then 70, was, at one stage, the top female box-office star in the USA. She was a lovely woman, a great pleasure to work with. She and Stringer [Davis], her husband, as a couple, were great. She insisted on sharing the cost of the wrap party with MGM on the fourth one, on condition she provided the music and everybody's partners were invited, which was unusual. She'd formed some kids who'd been in trouble into a pop group and she acted as an unpaid, unofficial agent for them. We think that she organised this whole thing just to give these chaps a go.

You came back to Australia in the 1970s. What specifically brought you back?
Oh we'd saved the fare. I had the lead in a play in London called *A Girl in My Soup* for two years. I

took over in 1970 and when we discovered we'd saved the airfare we decided to just do a quick trip home to see my mother. Just before I left London I got a letter from Hector Crawford saying, if you're in Australia, could you do something for us while you're here? Lots of offers came in and then Alwyn •Kurtz resigned from *Homicide* so Hector asked if I'd take over for about a year. So, very like going to England, we didn't intend to stay, but I then got involved as a director with Crawford's so it worked out quite well.

You've been busy every since. Have you been pleased with the range of things that have come your way?
Oh yes. I did three years on *Homicide*, then they made me a director on such things *as The Sullivans*. I produced other shows like *The Flying Doctor* miniseries and found I could do it. I got some nominations as best director, but I loved seeing the development of all the skills. And I loved working for people like Tim •Burstall. We'd heard about the new film-makers in London; Tim was one of them and he put me into •Petersen.

You have very good scenes with Jack •Thomson in that.
Jack and I had done an episode of *Homicide* together. I'd seen Jack doing some very, very good work, and then I discovered he was the foster son of John Thompson who was an old radio colleague of mine. When they asked me to play his Dad in **Petersen** it was great. I loved doing that and it fitted in nicely in one of the production breaks in *Homicide*.

You got some very good character roles, one with Jack Thompson again in •'Breaker' Morant?
We were all in the court, I don't know whether we exchanged any words except 'objection sustained' or something like that but it was good to be there to watch Jack at work because he did a wonderful job. They all did. To me that was as good as anything I'd ever seen in Hollywood, that kind of working atmosphere. When those guys were at work, they are those characters for those however many seconds of the take and/or rehearsals. It was like that on •The Castle too; it was an extraordinarily involving feeling on the set, and with Margaret Rutherford you couldn't but believe this was really happening. In a way I suppose it's a bit childlike: you're pretending to be those people, which is what kids do.

All those parts I've been mentioning, along with say Helen's father in •My First Wife and the judge in •Annie's Coming Out, are all on the whole very sympathetic parts aren't they?
I suppose so yes, but I love playing the baddies. I got some wonderful baddie roles in England on telly, in one-off dramas. Everybody wanted to shoot me after 'Breaker' Morant, I think! One of the best films I ever had was a sort of Hitler parallel in a brilliantly written piece about an advertising agency for one of the commercial channels, and I loved doing that. I remember saying to the director, 'Why me? But thanks'. He said, 'You're always playing nice guys; it would be interesting to see what you do with this guy'. As long as you do it with absolute involvement in the scene and you try to be as real and as believable and truthful as possible then it doesn't much matter. I suppose I've always tried not just to be the nice fellow, but to try to find the weaknesses in the character. One of the characters I liked most in Australia was the nasty businessman in Bruce •Beresford's •Money Movers.

You've worked with some of the most prominent directors in new Australian cinema—Burstall, Fred •Schepisi, Beresford, Paul •Cox. I'd be interested in any recollections you have about working with any of those.
I must say they were all very good. I could see very little difference between the best of our directors and the best of the ones I worked with overseas. Fred, Paul, and Bruce worked very delicately up close with actors. Some of the best directing I've ever seen an actor get was to a nice chap who was sitting beside me in 'Breaker' Morant. He was really an extra and Bruce would take plenty of time to talk about his thought processes. To see him take that much trouble with 'just an extra' was marvellous, and he treated this man as if he was a highly intelligent actor. I don't remember doing any takes with Bruce where I felt unprepared, so we must have rehearsed well. Tim too, but I thought for a while he was almost treating me with too much respect. In **Petersen** I revelled in the fact that he let me have my head a little bit. I loved doing that part; I saw a cynical side to the man of the cloth and I think that was in the script too. Fred, I found just marvellous. We'd known each other for a long time, but we'd never really worked together. When we started working together on •Evil Angels, I thought this will be interesting and he was all I expected.

Do you like a director who gives you quite a lot of interpretive direction?

No, again the good ones respect your version of it if it's along the right lines. I had scenes in **The Castle** that were so delicately written you could very clumsily muck up lovely little gags like the one when I first meet the bloke and he says, 'Will your son get off?' I have to say, 'It's his first appearance, it's embarrassing'. I had to very gently work out a way that it could be misinterpreted so that it wouldn't make him look an idiot. I love those sorts of actors' problems and that's where you need a fine director in case you go off on the wrong foot.

Having a stage background as well, do you like a lot of rehearsal?

I like to get very comfortable with what I'm doing and, as a director, I like to rehearse until the actors are absolutely comfortable. I've never been in a position where directors have really instructed us. Cecil Holmes, whom we all had great respect for, was often a bit daunted by actors and I remember him coming to Grant [Taylor] and me once and saying, 'Can't you do it better?' We just said, 'Well, all right, whatever!'

The Castle *has recently had a very big success. How did you find working with the Frontline team?*

Great. Again it was like the best of the Hollywood things—so well prepared. We had this very short shooting schedule. I had worked with them in some sketches in *The Late Show* and I was so charmed by the fact that they had a hand-held camera, I said 'I'd like to do a series like this, it's fantastic'. Little did I know they were planning to do *Frontline* and I used to love going occasionally to watch them shoot it, though I was never in it as an actor. I'd see guest actors do work in *Frontline* better than I'd seen them do, and there was one bloke who said he'd always been daunted by the camera until he did an episode of *Frontline*. I put that down to the fact that they prepare well and rehearse comfortably but in a very concentrated way. And for **The Castle** we rehearsed in four marvellous sessions of about four hours each, exactly the way we rehearsed the Lux Radio Theatre— just sitting around reading, and by the time we started shooting we felt totally saturated in those characters, and the work got better and better and nobody changed a word.

Why do you think it's taken off and been such a success?

I think it must have just struck a chord. The script was fantastic; it was a great read. That's not always the sign of a good script but it was in this case. When I came to the role itself and just after half-way through, with this marvellous writing round the sentiments of the house, Rob said, 'What do you think?' I said, 'The script is so good the danger may be that we may feel an urge to make it even better. Don't let us.' And he didn't, in the nicest way, and nobody wanted to either. It became a sort of mutual admiration thing for us and Rob. It was a very, very good experience the whole thing.

It could so easily have toppled into caricature or patronage.

I found out later that one or two people did think they were getting at the working man, but it was very much from their own backgrounds. And Rob always said that at every meal he can remember while growing up his father said something complimentary about the food. So there was a lot of love going on behind that.

Your latest film is **Amy** *…*

It's a good, interesting script. It's got a pop music background, it's a very strong serious story about a child who can't speak, and it turns out that there's a very traumatic experience she had. It's a bit hard to say too much about it without giving the plot away.

Talking about actors directing, I read lately that you're directing a film shortly.

I'm supposed to be. It's a very strong story about a father and son situation, and we've got Bill •Hunter and Paul •Mercurio very keen to do it. The script didn't quite match the strength of the story and, after a lot of suggestion from me, they got a very good, competent writer with a great track record, Roger Dunn, who's coming aboard to iron out the problems in it. It's powerful stuff, a bit violent here and there. And out of the blue this young producer asked me if I'd direct it. It will certainly depend on very strong performances by the actors. It's to be called **Second Drills**, because it's about an army man. All being well, we're supposed to shoot in October [1998].

Then I've got another one to act in after that, a brilliant story to be directed by Geoffrey Nottage, about three chaps who flew in the same aircraft in World War II. Its title is **The Edge of the Stream**, which is a term sometimes used on bomber command for the aircraft outside the main group or on the edge, which is a very vulnerable spot and this is about three chaps who survived being shot down in war, and they get together again when they're in their 70s. Vince Ball, Bill Kerr, and I play the three survivors. That's a nice one to look forward to in the new year.

In your long career, what sort of changes do you feel you've seen in Australian cinema?
Probably the most important thing for me is now the general acceptance out in the community that we make good movies and to me that's very important. There was a time when there seemed to be a policy of 'Why bother?' because we had all these wonderful films coming in from overseas. People I think are accepting the fact that it is very good to see yourselves up there on the screen. I'm astonished at the standards. The good films don't have to parade being Australian; they could be from anywhere, they are just great movies.

THIS INTERVIEW WAS CONDUCTED BY BRIAN MCFARLANE.

---

elements involving music, colour, costume, and composition coalesce into a powerful anti-colonial image of European exploitation and entrapment.　　　　GM

Traps

1994. *Director*: Pauline Chan. *Producer*: Jim McElroy. *Scriptwriters*: Robert Carter, Pauline Chan. Based on characters from the novel, *Dreamhouse*, by Kate Grenville. *Director of photography*: Kevin Hayward. *Music*: Douglas Stephen Rae. 100 min. *Cast*: Saskia Reeves (Louise Duffield), Robert Reynolds (Michael Duffield), Sami Frey (Daniel Renouard), Jacqueline McKenzie (Viola Renouard), Kiet Lam (Tuan).

Pauline Chan was born in Saigon, went to school in Hong Kong, and studied film-making at UCLA. Then she came to Australia, where she appeared as an actor in several television productions before completing the directing course at the •Australian Film, Television and Radio School. Her short films, **Hangup** and **The Space between the Door and the Floor** were screened in *Un Certain Regard* at Cannes. **Traps** is her first feature. The novel on which it is based is a contemporary story of a British couple visiting Tuscany; however, this adaptation turns them into an Australian couple (Michael and Louise) visiting Vietnam in the 1950s. There are sexual tensions within this marriage, exacerbated and complicated when the couple stay with a French landowner (Daniel) and his feisty daughter (Viola). The political and personal principles of all four European characters and of the Vietnamese servant Tuan are finally tested when the Vietminh overrun the house and the decision has to be made to kill or be killed. The early days of the conflict that was to become the Vietnam war are powerfully drawn: the title of the film comes from the way Chan sees the French trapped in their colonial responsibilities and attitudes, just as the Duffields are trapped within their marriage.　　　　IB

Travelling North

1987. *Director*: Carl Schultz. *Producer*: Ben Gannon. *Scriptwriter*: David Williamson. Based on the play by David Williamson. *Director of photography*: Julian Penney. *Music*: Alan John. 96 min. *Cast*: Leo McKern (Frank), Julia Blake (Frances), Henri Szeps (Saul), Graham Kennedy (Freddie), Michele Fawdon (Helen), Diane Craig (Sophie).

This love story about two people in their late middle-age proved one of the most attractive films of the late 1980s, uniting the talents of David •Williamson, in a less abrasive mood than usual, adapting his own play to the screen, of Carl •Schultz, who had shown himself a master of mood and character in •**Careful He Might Hear You** (1983), and of a superbly chosen cast. Frank, irascible music-lover, and his partner, Frances, divorced mother of grown-up daughters, decide to leave Melbourne to spend their last years in Queensland. Frances experiences guilt in leaving her daughters, but Frank's demands on her are all-consuming, and, as his heart condition deteriorates, he becomes increasingly difficult to live with. Although the film represents an obvious 'opening out' of the play, it remains very much a conversation piece but, in the expert hands of Leo •McKern and Julia •Blake, along with a touching and funny performance from Graham •Kennedy as a lonely neighbour, this is not a serious problem.　　　　BMcF

Trenchard-Smith, Brian (1946–) DIRECTOR A British-born film-maker who moved to Australia in the 1960s, Brian Trenchard-Smith wrote, produced, and directed *The Stuntmen* for television in 1973; and this documentary capitalised on his work in this area. Trenchard-Smith also produced trailers for feature films, and he has been a prolific director of action films since the commercial success of his second feature film, •**The Man from Hong Kong** (1975). This co-production between the •Greater

Union Organisation and the Hong Kong film company Golden Harvest starred popular Hong Kong martial arts actor Jimmy Wang Yu. A similar comic book action film, **Deathcheaters** (1976) followed, featuring Australia's best-known stunt man Grant •Page.

Trenchard-Smith's films are usually marked by fast-moving plots, dramatically effective action sequences, economy of effort, and a lack of pretension. This mixture often produces entertaining films, such as the 1983 teen movie **BMX Bandits**, which starred Nicole •Kidman and David •Argue; and **Dead-End Drive-In** (1986), which was based on a story by Peter Carey. However, sometimes, when the script fails to capture the appropriate light-hearted sense of action and violence, the comic-book plots can easily lapse into absurdity, as with the 1982 disaster **Turkey Shoot**. Nevertheless, Trenchard-Smith's undoubted skill in this genre of film-making has produced a substantial body of work that, occasionally, deviates from the action thriller; for example, the 1986 domestic melodrama **Jenny Kissed Me**. *Other Australian films include*: The Love Epidemic (1974), Frog Dreaming (1986), Day of the Panther (1987), Strike of the Panther (1987), The Siege of Firebase Gloria (1988), Out of the Body (1988), Official Denial (1993).   GM

Trerise, J. William (1898–1982) CINEMATOGRAPHER

William ('Bill') J. Trerise entered the film industry in 1913 as assistant projectionist at Sydney's Lyceum Theatre. He then started as a camera assistant and became a cameraman for •Australasian Films, particularly on the **Australasian Gazette**. He was second cameraman to Len Roos on •**For the Term of His Natural Life** (1927) and to Arthur •Higgins on •**The Adorable Outcast** (1928). He also shared credits on **The Grey Glove** (1928) and •**Tall Timbers** (1937), and was the sole cinematographer on **The Russell Affair** (1928). In 1930, after the coming of sound, Trerise worked for Fox's **Movietone News**, achieving fame for such technical feats as simultaneously varying camera speed and shutter opening (changing from normal to slow motion) at the finish of the Melbourne Cup. He became Movietone's senior local cameraman and one of their two cameramen on the wartime documentary **Jungle Patrol**, shot in New Guinea. In 1945 Trerise joined the government's Department of Information Film Unit (which became •Film Australia), where he shot many documentaries, including Stanley •Hawes's Oscar-nominated **School in the Mailbox** (1947). He was chief cameraman there until his retirement, and spent some time training film cameramen at ABC television.   DAVID MUIR

Trooper Campbell

1914. *Director*: Raymond Longford. From the poem by Henry Lawson. B&W. *Cast*: Lottie Lyell.

Surviving footage from **Trooper Campbell**, an early one-reel film directed by Raymond •Longford and based on Henry Lawson's poem, was only discovered in the late 1980s. The footage gives some indication that the film may have been originally designed to be accompanied by a 'live' recitation of the poem synchronised to the actors' lip movements—a mode of exhibition that has been documented in other countries, including Russia, in the years before the start of World War I. Apparently Longford made another Lawson film, **Taking His Chance**, as well.

WILLIAM D. ROUTT

Trooper O'Brien

1928. *Director*: John Gavin. *Producer*: Herbert Finlay. *Scriptwriter*: Agnes Gavin. *Director of photography*: Arthur Higgins. B&W. *Cast*: John Gavin (Sergeant O'Brien), Gordon Collingridge (Glen O'Brien).

In the autumn and winter of 1928, **Trooper O'Brien** was apparently a box-office success in rural areas, where movie goers may have been expecting an action film about bushrangers. Although there were some scenes featuring bushrangers, these were pirated from •**The Kelly Gang** and •**Robbery Under Arms** (1920) and, in order to get them in the film at all, John and Agnes Gavin had to make it clear that their story was a paean of praise for the police. Otherwise **Trooper O'Brien** tells a tale familiar to Australian audiences of the day, in which an orphaned girl raised by common (Irish) people turns out to be the inheritor of (British) wealth and position.   WILLIAM D. ROUTT

Trop Fest (Sydney), *see* Festivals

True Story of the Kelly Gang, The, *see* Kelly Gang, The

Tudawali, Robert [Majingwanipini] (?–1967)

ACTOR Majingwanipini, who worked in two Australian films under the name Robert Tudawali, is a rare presence in the world cinema of the 1950s—a black masculine figure of violence and sexuality. In •**Jedda** (1955), Majingwanipini's performance makes Marbuck, both the hero and the villain of the film, a proud figure of mystery whose sensuality and power enthrals Jedda and awakens her to the realities of her heritage. Marbuck is the outlaw counterpart of Jedda, who has been brought up within a White family and finds herself between two worlds. Marbuck is also a killer, outcast by Aboriginal people and Whites alike. Jedda and Marbuck's romance, and their flight from both ways of life, ends tragically and seems to warn the viewer of tragedies to come for Aboriginal people. Majingwanipini's impact is somewhat blunted in **Dust in the Sun** (1958), in which he plays Emu

Foot, another killer who lives outside of both societies according to a code of his own. The three years between films tell another tale about the lack of opportunities for even the most charismatic of Aboriginal performers in Australian films at mid century. After **Dust in the Sun** there were no more films. 'Robert Tudawali' found himself, even as Jedda, Marbuck, and Emu Foot, between cultures, lacking the support of either. By 1961 his 'troubles with the law' had become material for journalists and, by 1967, his physical life was over.

WILLIAM D. ROUTT

Turner, Ann (1960–) DIRECTOR/WRITER Ann Turner's first feature as director and writer, •**Celia**, is one of the defining films of the 1990s revival in Australian film-making. Released in 1989, it nonetheless foreshadowed the quirky and unpredictable blends of comedy and melodrama, sentiment, and irony that were to characterise the best Australian work of the 1990s, and it includes a knockout performance by Rebecca •Smart. Derek Malcolm's favourable review of the film in the *Guardian* brought Turner international recognition almost before she had been noticed in Australia. Yet it was three years before her second feature as director would be released. In the interim she wrote for the television series *Embassy* and *Police Rescue* (directing an episode of the latter as well), and adapted Blanche d'Alpuget's *Turtle Beach* for the screen, eventually writing a rewrite of D'Alpuget's original adaptation. Her second feature, **Hammers over the Anvil** (1992), a film intended to herald the •South Australian Film Corporation's re-entry into production, did not find a wide audience. Turner directed and co-wrote the script from Alan Marshall's well-known memoir *I Can Jump Puddles* and the film starred Russell •Crowe and Charlotte Rampling. She continued to act as both writer and director on **Dallas Doll** (1994), a film she also co-produced. Despite, or perhaps because of, the presence of Sandra Bernhardt in the title role, **Dallas Doll** virtually disappeared on release. Distributors may have found its cool blend of the bland and the surreal a little too hard to sell. At the time of writing, her last work has been the four-minute *Bathing Boxes* episode of the BBC television series *Picture House*, first shown in 1995.

WILLIAM D. ROUTT

Twelfth Night

1987. *Director*: Neil Armfield. *Producer*: Don Catchlove. *Executive producer*: Tom Stacey. *Scriptwriter*: Neil Armfield. Based on the play by William Shakespeare. *Director of photography*: Louis Irving. *Music*: Alan John. 117 min. *Cast*: Gillian Jones (Viola; Sebastian; Cesario), Ivar Kants (Orsino, Duke of Illyria), Jacqy Phillips (Countess Olivia), Peter Cummins (Malvolio), Kerry Walker (Feste).

In a decade that has seen some of the boldest and most successful attempts to bring Shakespeare to the screen, this film, directed by Neil Armfield and based on his critically regarded stage production, is Australia's one contribution to recent cinematic bardolatry. It unfortunately had only the most limited release, but it is a notable production, with some fine performances from such actors as Geoffrey •Rush as Aguecheek, John •Wood as Sir Toby Belch, and Peter •Cummins as Malvolio. Perhaps the insistent artifice of this most touching and delicate of Shakespearean comedies resists screen success; Trevor Nunn's attractive 1996 version was scarcely more popular with film audience.

BMcF

27A

1974. *Director, Scriptwriter*: Esben Storm. *Producer*: Haydn Keenan. *Director of photography*: Michael Edols. *Music*: Winsome Evans, Michael Norton. 86 min. *Cast*: Robert McDarra (Bill), Bill Hunter (Cornish), Graham Corry (Peter Newman), T. Richard Moir (Richard), James Kemp (Slats).

After being sentenced for a petty offence, Bill, a middle-aged derelict, volunteers for one week's psychiatric treatment for alcoholism. Once inside the psychiatric institution, he discovers he can be detained indefinitely. Bill rebels against his confinement and treatment by a bullying nurse (Bill •Hunter in his first major film role). He escapes several times—once on a futile visit to his estranged and dying wife—only to end up back on the bottle and back inside.

A low-budget feature shot on 16 mm, **27A** was acclaimed for its realistic treatment of the harsh conditions inside psychiatric institutions, and critics drew comparisons with Ken Loach's **Family Life** (United Kingdom, 1972). Robert McDarra, a real-life alcoholic who died two years later, gives a strong performance that was nevertheless unable to hide the gap between the film's ambitions and their rather uneven realisation, hampered by mannered cinematography and weak dramatic development. Nonetheless, **27A** remains a landmark in the cinema's attempt to confront the bleaker realities of contemporary Australian life.

HARRY OLDMEADOW

Two Minutes Silence

1933. *Director*: Paulette McDonagh. *Production company*: McDonagh Productions. Based on the play by Leslie Haylen. *Director of photography*: James Grant. 75 min. B&W. *Cast*: Marie Lorraine (Denise), Campbell Copelin (Pierre), Leo Franklyn (Private Simpson), Frank Leighton (Captain Lessups), Ethel Gabriel (Mrs Trott).

This was the last film of the •McDonagh sisters—Paulette as director, Phyllis as writer and art director, and Isabel as star (under her stage name of Marie •Lorraine). The play on which it was based had been first performed in 1930, and was set on Armistice Day some time after the end of World War I. As the clock strikes 11, four members of the household of General Gresham remember how the war affected each of them: the colonel himself, his charlady Mrs Trott, the French governess of the colonel's children, and the butler. Despite its bleak tone, it was universally praised by the critics, and well supported by the public. However, the McDonagh team broke up after this and made no more films.   IB

Two Thousand Weeks

1969. *Director*: Tim Burstall. *Producer*: Patrick Ryan. *Scriptwriter*: Tim Burstall/Patrick Ryan. *Director of photography*: Robin Copping. *Music*: Don Burrrows. 85 min. *Cast*: Mark McManus (Will), Jeanie Drynan (Jacky), Eileen Chapman (Sarah).

This is perhaps the most significant Australian film of the late 1960s. Its story concerns Will, a writer/journalist whose personal life is torn between his wife (Sarah) and girlfriend (Jacky), and the demands of a dying and critical father, while his professional life as a writer is at the crossroads, limited by his 'Australian' rather than British experience.

The expectations held by the film community for **Two Thousand Weeks** in 1969 were high. Billed as an art film, Tim •Burstall likened its form to Fellini's **8 1/2** (Italy, 1963) in that the action revolved around one man and the relationship between his problems and the problems of an emerging generation of Australians. While the film is often visually striking, it was savaged by the critics of the period, who found its script and performances inconsistent and its concerns at times pretentious. Despite its limitations, **Two Thousand Weeks** remains a sensitive cultural indicator of the transition in both the Australian film industry of the period and of Burstall's career; many of its primary concerns are given greater social voice in the political reforms of the early 1970s.   JOHN BENSON

Typhoon Treasure
[The Perils of Pakema Reef]

1938. *Director*: Noel Monkman. *Production company*: Commonwealth Film Productions. *Scriptwriter*: John P. McLeod. *Directors of photography*: George Malcolm, Harry Malcolm. 89 min. B&W. *Cast*: Campbell Copelin (Alan Richards), Gwen Munro (Jean Roberts), Joe Valli (Scotty Macleod), Douglas Herald (Buck Thompson), Kenneth Brampton (Alfred Webb).

Noel •Monkman had an established reputation for nature films, including a series filmed on the Great Barrier Reef. His first feature film uses the reef as location, standing in for the South Sea islands. It tells the story of two drug smugglers (Buck Thompson and Alfred Webb) who are trying to find some pearls on a wreck. The rightful owner (Alan Richards) and his sidekick (Scotty Macleod) must struggle through the jungle, pursued by cannibals and crocodiles, to reach the wreck site in time to foil the plot, allowing the villains to be apprehended and Richards to be reunited with his sweetheart, Jean. There are some well-choreographed action sequences (both fights and chases), and some spectacular jungle scenery and underwater photography on the reef, but the film did not do well. It was later cut to 40 minutes and released in newsreel theatrettes as **The Perils of Pakema Reef**.   IB

U

Umbrella Woman, The

1987. *Director*: Ken Cameron. *Scriptwriter*: Peter Kenna. *Director of photography*: James Bartle. *Music*: Cameron Allan. 95 min. *Cast*: Rachel Ward (Marge Hills), Bryan Brown (Sonny Hills), Sam Neill (Neville Gifford), Steven Vidler (Sugar Hills).

The British title of this film, **The Good Wife,** captures the inherent irony that permeates the film, set in the small Australian town of Corrimandel in 1939. The film's opening images, which borrow from the Heidelberg School of Australian painting, point to the centrality of the bush ethos in the film. The film then proceeds to expose the limitations of this ethos. Marge Hills is married to Sonny, a timber worker. Bryan •Brown's Sonny, with his beard and laconic speech, is a clear manifestation of the Australian bush worker. Instead of the usual celebration of this stereotype, the film reveals its constrictions. He loves Marge but it is not enough, and the story details her entrapment in this shallow world. Marge's sense of desperation, which she cannot articulate or understand, forces her into a series of roles from dutiful wife to Sonny, sexual teacher to Sonny's brother, and obsessive stalker to lecherous barman Neville Gifford.

The Umbrella Woman was marketed as a late example of the soft-centred period films. Nothing could be further from the truth; it is one of the most subversive films to emerge in the past 20 years. The final sequence of images, showing Marge's face trapped within the ubiquitous blinds as she looks out on a barren future, represents one of the most intelligent, and moving, epilogues in the history of the Australian film industry.   GM

Uncivilised

1936. *Director*: Charles Chauvel. *Scriptwriters*: Charles Chauvel, E.V. Timms. *Director of photography*: Tasman Higgins. B&W. *Cast*: Dennis Hoey (Mara), Margot Rhys (Beatrice Lynn). Ashton Jarry (Akbar Jan/Peter Radcliffe), Kenneth Brampton (Trask).

In **Uncivilised**, Charles •Chauvel returned to the story of a woman's journey that had structured his silent features, •**The Moth of Moonbi** (1926) and •**Greenhide** (1926). The result is the finale of a trio of miscegenated forms (•**In the Wake of the Bounty**, 1933, and •**Heritage**, 1935, had preceded this film). Here, however, the parentage is narrative and commercial: colonial adventure, *Tarzan of the Apes*, and exotic operetta. Beatrice Lynn, a quintessential representative of urban civilisation (not least because she is an adventurous woman), travels to the heart of an Aboriginal jungle and is violently transformed by it and by its White king, Mara. As happens so often in Chauvel's films, the voyager determines to stay out and away from civilisation, in a place where life is more tempestuous and honest—making a choice in some sense against Whiteness at the same time as she is choosing to be 'White'. No film of Chauvel's is more crossed by race and desire than this one, and none is more absurd, excessive, and clumsy. This is a 'bad' movie, but it is a lot more interesting than most 'good' movies of the period.   WILLIAM D. ROUTT

Unger, Deborah Kara (1964–) ACTOR
Deborah Kara Unger was the first Canadian accepted by the Australian National Institute of Dramatic Art. After a supporting role in the Australian television drama *Bangkok Hilton* (1989),

Union Theatres

Unger appeared in two failed Australian films, **Breakaway** (1990) and the relatively high-budget **Till There Was You** (1990), directed by John •Seale. The latter was shot largely in Port Vila in Vanuatu. She then appeared in •**Blood Oath** (1990) as Sister Littell, a nurse who assists the war crimes trials held at the end of World War II. Unfortunately, Unger's role in this film, which focuses on Japanese behaviour towards Australian prisoners on the Dutch East Indies island of Ambon, was not fully developed. Moreover, the romantic relationship between Littell and Captain Cooper (Bryan •Brown), which was signalled initially in the script, fails to eventuate, and her role dissipates as the film progresses. She left Australia for Hollywood after **Blood Oath**. Her subsequent performances in films such as the British-financed romantic drama **No Way Home** (1996) and the American film **Crash** (1996), David Cronenberg's controversial study of the link between sexual arousal and car injuries, have dramatic intensity. GM

Union Theatres, *see* Greater Union Organisation

Unions and associations Before the mid 1940s most screen unions and associations represented picture-theatre employees. From 1902 an association of stage employees in Brisbane included live-theatre workers, some of whom projected film as part of a mixed theatrical repertoire. The Sydney Stage Employees Association, formed in 1908, had projectionist members and, by the following year, there were similar bodies in all states.

By the late 1930s the various stage-employee organisations had become the Australian Theatrical and Amusement Employees Association (AT&AEA). In a twist that left many members bemused, Bill Harrop, secretary of the NSW branch, was also the honorary business manager of the 'bosses' organisation, the New South Wales Motion Picture Exhibitors Association. (A Motion Picture Distributors Association, formed in 1926, ran separately.) By 1970, moves were being made to replace Harrop, initiated by AT&AEA's largely cinema-employee membership, who were dissatisfied with Harrop, and by production activists who were keen for the union to represent their interests. Joining as organiser in 1970, John McQuaid took over as AT&AEA secretary six months later. As well as affiliating the body with the New South Wales Trades and Labor Council, the Australian Council of Trade Unions, and the Australian Labor Party, McQuaid organised the strike that led to cinema employees' achieving a five-day working week and penalty rates for weekend work.

The earliest-known producer organisation was the Motion Picture Association, whose members, including Raymond •Longford and Arthur •Shirley, lobbied the NSW government for a local film quota in 1926. In the 1930s, the Talking Picture Producers Associations of Victoria and New South Wales continued to press for workable quotas in both states. These groups, however, were short-lived and without proper organisational bases. Around 1946, the Film Producers Association of Australia (FPAA) was formed. Its members included Charles Chauvel Enterprises, •Cinesound Productions, and Embassy Pictures. Until at least 1952, the FPAA lobbied Canberra to terminate the production activity of the film division of the federal Department of the Interior and allow FPAA members to resume the high level of Commonwealth production they had enjoyed during World War II. In 1956 a new body, the Australian Film Producers Association (AFPA), was formed 'to promote, foster and encourage the Australian film industry and to undertake all necessary steps to achieve these objects'.

In 1946, film-production technicians formed the Motion Picture Technicians Association (MPTA), and Bill Harrop was its secretary by 1954. The fact that MPTA was solely a NSW body for a number of years was highlighted by the case of John Leake, a Movietone camera operator who filmed the Royal Tour of 1954. Although Leake filmed all over Australia, Movietone was prepared to pay him overtime only when he filmed in NSW. MPTA was officially absorbed into AT&AEA in the early 1970s.

The Actors Federation, formed in 1921, began pressing for a film actors' award in 1936. Three years later, the newly formed Actors Equity absorbed the federation. For the next 32 years, general secretary Hal Alexander ran an organisation that was unified despite a membership drawn from diverse political backgrounds. Equity signed film-award agreements with producers in 1947, 1954, and 1957 and, in 1955, expressed concern about television arriving in Australia 'without adequate safeguards for the protection of local artistic talent and cultural values'. In 1960, as a result of campaigning by Equity and AFPA, a federal ministerial order decreed that all television commercials locally transmitted be of Australian origin.

In 1962–63, at the urging of AFPA, the federal government conducted the Nimmo and Vincent inquiries into the local television and film industries. In March 1965, almost a year after the government had adjourned inconclusive debate on the wide-ranging Vincent report, the lobby group the Australian National Television Council (later the Australian Mass Communication Council) organised a National Television Congress in Sydney that called for the debate to be resumed. The congress provided a springboard for increased agitation for government support by a host of existing and new organisations: Actors Equity, AFPA, the Australian Cinematographers Society (ACS, formed in

1958), the Australian Writers Guild (AWG, formed in 1962), the Film Editors Guild of Australia (formed 1962), AT&AEA, and the Producers and Directors Guild of Australia (active since the early 1960s and incorporated in 1966). The combined effort of this lobby helped ensure federal support for the film and television industries after 1969. Employer and employee groups also joined forces on the highly effective Australian Film Council from 1968, and on the Television: Make it Australian Committee in the early 1970s.

If there was unanimity between the production unions and associations over government support, other issues divided them. The success and the increased professionalism of the film industry in the mid 1970s brought a growth of unionism, higher wages, and new awards to regulate work conditions. In 1978, when fewer films were showing profit and private investment was more elusive, Actors Equity found itself increasingly at odds with the Film Producers Association of Australia (FPAA), which had formed in 1972 to link AFPA with the Australian Motion Picture Studio Association.

Whereas producers wanted to enhance their market appeal by importing overseas 'name' actors, Actors Equity opposed this trend, hoping to safeguard the employment of its members and ensure the survival of a national cinema through the appearance of recognisably Australian actors. In 1979 an Actors Equity/FPAA Feature Film Award restricted imported actors to those of 'international merit' and, in 1980, Actors Equity's 'defence of employment policy' limited the number of imported actors. As revised in 1982, the policy demanded 'no imported artists at all for films based on sources considered part of Australia's heritage or based on historical fact'. Actors Equity and AT&AEA also successfully pushed for residual agreements, health and safety coverage, and childcare, while AT&AEA opposed the indiscriminate importation of film technicians. In 1992 both bodies merged with the Australian Journalists Association to form the Media Entertainment and Arts Alliance (MEAA). The employer agency, FPAA, underwent three more name changes: Film and Television Production Association of Australia in 1976, Screen Production Association of Australia in 1985, and Screen Producers Association of Australia (SPAA) in 1994. Around 1980 it merged with the Independent Feature Film Producers Association, which had formed in 1977.

The late 1990s brought an industry-wide campaign against a High Court decision to count New Zealand television programs as Australian television quota content. But there was also debate over legislation to introduce 'moral rights'—the means by which a film's creator or author can have redress in the event of their film' being significantly changed after its release. Presenting different views of the moral rights debate were the AWG, SPAA, the Australian Screen Directors Association (ASDA, formed in 1980), and broadcasters. Tackling other issues, SPAA, MEAA, ASDA, and AWG evolved a strategic plan for script and project development. SPAA and ASDA formed a joint documentary council that, among other activities, lobbied on the issue of Australian content on pay television. Negotiations between the various bodies continued over rates of pay, working conditions, and repeat and residual agreements.

Other groups were also formed: •Women in Film and Television (WIFT) in 1982, to support and advance the status of women working in the screen industries; the Australian Guild of Screen Composers in 1985, to represent the interests of composers working in these same industries; the Australian Screen Sound Guild in 1988, to recognise, promote, and facilitate original and creative work in screen sound; and the Australian Screen Editors in 1995, to represent editors at a time of dramatic change in computerised technology. Like the Australian Screen Sound Guild, both the ACS and the AWG run annual awards to recognise excellence in their fields.

GRAHAM SHIRLEY

Until the End of the World

1992. Director: Wim Wenders. *Producers:* Jonathan Taplin, Kim Vercera. *Scriptwriters:* Peter Carey, Wim Wenders. Based on an original idea by Wim Wenders and Solveig Dommartin. *Director of photography:* Robby Müller. *Music:* Graeme Revell. 151 min. *Cast:* Solveig Dommartin (Claire Tourneur), William Hurt (Sam Farber, alias Trevor McPhee), Sam Neill (Eugene Fitzpatrick), Ernie Dingo (Burt), Rüdiger Vogler (Phillip Winter), Max Von Sydow (Henry Farber), Jeanne Moreau (Edith Farber).

Director Wim Wenders may well have over-extended himself with this film, but he still managed to make an intellectually challenging and speculative film about the near future. It is 1999, a rogue nuclear satellite threatens to end the world, and Claire Tourneur, through a series of random occurrences, finds herself chasing Trevor McPhee, a man she hardly knows, around the world.

In many ways, this is two films packaged as one. The first half is a well-paced and visually stimulating global road movie. Unfortunately, it slows right down in the second half. Set in the Central Australian outback, it becomes a much more contemplative, issue-based science-fiction film. As a many-handed co-production, it is a slick, good-looking film with an exciting contemporary soundtrack, but it did not capture the imaginations of audiences or critics.

TIM HUNTER

Urban life

Urban life In the opening scenes of •Crocodile Dundee (1986), the camera swoops in over the skyline of a big metropolis to find Sue (Linda Kozlowski), a journalist in her Manhattan office, teeing up the job of a lifetime to travel to the Australian outback. The view of the city that is fleetingly evoked—as the vibrant epitome of Western society, the point of centrality from which all subsequent culture emanates—is one that rarely appears so unequivocally in Australian cinema. Even in the **Crocodile Dundee** films, despite their strong appeal to American audiences, this glittering urban promise is finally revealed as suspect, a dubious prize for endeavour, a potentially treacherous mirage. If cinema can be interpreted as representing certain aspects of cultural imagery, reflecting, by virtue of repetition, the undercurrents of value, anxiety, and preoccupation that thread their way through the diversities of a historically and geographically specific society, an examination of the urban within Australian cinema would suggest that the city is regarded with far more suspicion and ambivalence in the Australian psyche than it might be in the American. With its bright lights, bustling people, marked socioeconomic differences, suburban expanses, and anonymity, the city has never seemed to offer the Australian imagination the same possibilities for individuation or self-knowledge as could be found in the open territory of the bush, the proving ground of the outback. The mythologised 'call' of the open spaces persistently haunts and informs the multitude of narratives of self and national culture that constitute recent Australian cinema. However, the image of the city—in both its hyper-urban and its sub-urban manifestations, and as it directly abuts or contrasts with its seeming antithesis, the bush—also exerts a significant, albeit ambivalent, pressure on cinematic constructions of the subjective and of what might constitute Australian culture.

In some representations, the city is depicted forcibly as a source of corruption and constraint for both individual and community. In a film such as •Mouth to Mouth (1978), young unemployed people, coded as 'innocent' due to their lack of experience, drift into the city from the outlying areas of country and suburb. Attracted by the city's possibilities of work, love, and excitement, they soon become caught by poverty, homelessness, alienation, violence, and addiction. The final scenes of the film show the character of Carrie (Kim Krejus) wandering down a city street, finally isolated from her small group of friends and lost in the obliterating anonymity of the next pick-up, the next fix. This city is malevolent in its indifference to her plight; its fast pace, colour and consumerism offer only momentary distraction from the far-ranging social ills that have produced Carrie's predicament.

•Mad Max (1979) also features the city as the root of the corruption that permeates all aspects of its quasi-apocalyptic society. The city is equated with a dissolute lifestyle of artificial stimulants, fast cars, and mindless aggression. While the messianic Toe-Cutter (Hugh •Keays-Byrne) and his gang range across the roads in and out of the city, pursued by the almost equally corrupt and corrupting police, the violence that they enact is seen to emanate from the city as centre of an industrialised and mechanised social structure, reaching out like tentacles to the surrounding countryside. By contrast, the humanity that is glimpsed through Max's (Mel •Gibson) relationship with his wife and child at their remote house by the beach is seen to be morally superior to the competitive values represented by the city, but also as crucially vulnerable to being overtaken and crushed by them. Tragically, the city, and the rampant selfishness and amorality that it represents, is a poison that even Max, the family man and reluctant hero, carries with him, contaminating the privileged rural retreat in which he and his family are seen to love and play.

In •Romper Stomper (1992) catastrophic eruptions of anger and racial violence take as their backdrop the streets, tunnels, and laneways of Melbourne's inner west. The actions of Hando's (Russell •Crowe) neo-Nazi gang seem to be the product of an unhappy urban blend: socioeconomic factors of unemployment, aggressive sexism, ignorance, and bitter hostility and a sense of grievance focused on a racialised 'other' (who is perceived as taking sustenance away from 'real'—that is, Anglo-celtic—Australians). The hatred and self-centredness that permeates this society is not, however, limited to the so-called working class. The sexual abuse perpetrated on Gabe (Jacqueline •McKenzie) by her father, within the confines of a wealthy home, suggests a moral rot that transcends socioeconomic status, or the descriptor of 'what suburb you come from'. As in the **Mad Max** narrative, the social ills depicted so graphically and controversially in **Romper Stomper** are seen as synonymous with urban life, if not directly caused by it. Although the young protagonists attempt to leave the city behind in search of something better that is imagined to lie in a geographical 'elsewhere', their attempts prove futile because, like Max, they take their urban malaise with them. As a consequence, an otherwise idyllic beach becomes the site of a deadly re-enactment of the values that they are ostensibly fleeing. In particular, these include the vicious competition between males symptomatic of a fundamental objectification of 'the other', and a wild resort to violence in a desperate attempt to protect the self, or even more tragically, to break the grip of the polarities of victims and victimisers, of those who survive and those whose 'expendability' ensures that survival.

However, the city is not always portrayed so negatively in Australian cinema. In •**Lillian's Story** (1996), for instance, the city, with its potential to incorporate a wide range of diversity and eccentricity is, for the character of the mature Lillian (Ruth •Cracknell), a kind of haven, at least in comparison with the oppressions of her elegant suburban home and the disciplinary regime of the asylum. While the city is in part figured as a place of drifters and callous indifference, it does, in its size and multivalency, also retain a capacity for kindness and moments of connection amid the flux of self-involvement. At least on the city street, in the anonymity of the taxi or the bus, Lillian is free to speak the poetry forbidden her at home, free to call attention dramatically to the heart-felt intensity of her 'stories'. However, there are limits to the sense of community, even of family, that she is able to construct for herself in the city, as she discovers in the 'humpy' under the bridge, and the film's closing image sees her taking her final taxi right out of town, off the made roads of urbanisation and into an outback that is figured as a site of almost spiritual homecoming—a return that is significantly *not* to the bourgeois home of her childhood. This structural movement also implicitly characterises the experience of 'death' as one of being no longer 'in the city', thus foregrounding the paradox of the non-urban as either a state of exile from the centre, or an escape from the 'false' into the 'real'.

Similarly, the overall narrative structure of •**The Adventures of Priscilla, Queen of the Desert** (1994) is concerned with movements away from and towards the city. The journey of two gay men and a transsexual out from Sydney and through the remoteness of Australia to Alice Springs is, in some ways, represented as liberating. This literalised 'coming-out' narrative culminates in the fantastical 'drag' to the top of Uluru where the image of the 'cock in a frock on a rock' signals an attempt to position the non-macho male within a landscape and an economy dominated by conventional myths of the bush. However, this journey away from the city and its ideological territories also has its oppressive aspects. Although welcomed by a group of Aborigines along the road, the travelling troupe also meet with sexism and xenophobia, and their show does not take the heart of Australia by storm as they might have hoped. At least for Tick (Hugo •Weaving) and Adam (Guy •Pearce), it is the return to the city, with its night clubs and greater diversity of people and attitudes, that constitutes the most significant freedom. It's in the city that they can perform their versions of Abba songs with impunity, displaying an exhibitionism, an open sexuality and a radical exploration of masculinities that the rural ethos of a hegemonic and singular masculinity characterised as disruptive, illegitimate, and dismissively feminine. The myth of the outback, and of the bushman

who inhabits it, has only ever been a fit for the myth of the 'real man'—White, heterosexual, laconic. In this sense, **Priscilla** points to the tensions as well as the distinctions, that might exist between rural and urban Australia and, while offering no simple dichotomies, its narrative does present the city as at least the place with greater options and flexibility, especially for those who do not conform to dominant behavioural expectations.

Cinema's representation of the suburbs, as both a subset of the urban and, at times, as something quite distinct, even oppositional, is similarly equivocal, yet it also carries with it a greater weight of nostalgia and sense of potential, perhaps because the suburbs are so often depicted as the locus of family and community life. In a film such as •**Spotswood** (1992), for example, despite the economic and social hardships that confront the community of workers and management at Ball's moccasin factory, the image of the working-class suburb of the 1960s (significantly the period of the childhood and youth of many who now make and watch films) is idealised as the heartland of family and community, the geographical and historical place where a straightforward kindness and generosity is valued over the cut and thrust of economic rationalism. It is in the relative simplicity of the life of the family, who have always worked at the factory, that a richness of connection is experienced. The budding relationship between the young man, Carey (Ben •Mendelsohn), and Wendy (Toni •Collette), the proverbial girl-next-door, is seen to be far more rewarding than emotionally sterile relationships predicated upon class and opportunism. After their love for each other has matured, Carey and Wendy clamber to the top of a building in the film's closing image; in this moment of intimacy and commitment, they look out over the industrial suburbs spread below them—from Spotswood, to Yarraville, to Seddon, this is the landscape of a future in which love and domesticity are privileged over wealth and individual status.

This idealisation of the suburb is also very evident in •**Return Home** (1990), where the 'big city'—figured as the high-rise of Melbourne in comparison with the flatter, 'suburban' Adelaide—is seen as the place where marriages fall apart, where sons and brothers lose the vital connection with their families, and where individuals can be alienated from themselves and their communities in the quest for money and prestige. The 'return' to the suburbs is seen as the prodigal son's return from the false gods of the city, a return to the continuities of family, and also to reactionary notions of what it means to be masculine and Australian. The suburb here is figured almost as a frontier—one that is fought for and celebrated as a proving ground of masculinity, at the same time as it is seen to be overtaken by the economic pressures of urbanisation and is thus nostalgically mourned.

Urban life

The other side of the suburban coin is of course a profound sense of the suburbs as an emotional and cultural wasteland. In films such as •The FJ Holden (1977) and •A Street to Die (1985), the suburbs are experienced as crushingly constrictive to the individual, where the pressures of homogeneity and lack of opportunity conspire to create a claustrophobic, dead-end street. Even films that explore notions of lifestyle experiments in the suburbs—such as •Monkey Grip (1982), •Dogs in Space (1987), and even •Love, and Other Catastrophes (1996)—depict old patterns and despairs reasserting themselves irrespective of apparent efforts at radical change. This is also apparent in •The Last Days of Chez Nous (1992), where, despite more bourgeois efforts at rethinking concepts of monogamy and what constitutes the household or 'family', old narrative paradigms of jealousy and betrayal re-emerge, and the final scene shows the rebellious, radical sister Vicky (Kerry •Fox) caught 'in a home of her own', and in the very same patterns of housework and domestic monogamy that she thought she had been working to resist.

The city is an ambivalently represented icon within Australian cinema. It can glitter like a jewel of opportunity, as in •Emerald City (1989), only to appear as hollow and corrupt; it can be something to escape from, as in Return Home, privileging instead the family and community values of the suburbs. Conversely, the suburbs themselves can be seen as oppressive, forcing the protagonist who survives such pressure towards either the proving territory of the bush, or immersion in the play of possibilities available in the flux of the hyper-urban. In this sense, the city stands as the marker of a transition in Australian culture between, on the one hand, the masculinist and nationalist ethos of the bush and the bushman as the site of authenticity and, on the other, the postmodern sphere of change, movement, difference, and inter- and intra-nationalisms. Perhaps the **Crocodile Dundee** narrative is prescient in this respect. Although the culmination of its adventure and romance occurs in the city—and being situated in New York, the film implicitly suggests that the city is always imagined as foreign and American—Mick's (Paul •Hogan) masculinity and legitimacy is still figured visually as being that of the bushman. In fact, the city is a source of potential de-masculinisation for this macho hero forged by the outback, who must keep his Akubra hat and bush trappings around him in order to survive. Events in both **Dundee** films oscillate between New York and Australia, or more archetypally between the city and the bush, and this is indicative of a closed dialectic in which ideas about what is urban and what is not, what is Australian and what is not, are locked into a tortured and ambivalent interdependence. As it is represented in recent Australian cinema, the city, both as trope and as image, is our inheritance from, and our link to Western industrialised culture. Poisoned chalice or bridge to the future, the shimmering phantasmagoria of the city stands awkwardly at the cusp of how we think about ourselves as Australian, its grid of connections a maze that must be continually renegotiated in the cinematic products that both reflect and produce Australian culture.

ROSE LUCAS

514

V

Valli, Joe (1886–1967) ACTOR Joe McParlane, better known by his stage name of Joe Valli, was a vaudeville artist before he became one of the most familiar faces in Australian films of the 1930s and 1940s, appearing not only in most of the *Cinesound films but also in many other productions. He was short and slightly built, with a pronounced Scottish accent, and all these features were used as the subject of humour. After a small role in the first *Diggers (1931), he co-starred with Pat *Hanna in *Diggers in Blighty (1933), and again in *Waltzing Matilda (1933). After that, although he was a consummate comedian, he was more often cast as the 'comic relief' in film dramas such as *The Flying Doctor (1936), or *Rats of Tobruk (1944), and his starring roles were limited to less expensive productions like **Racing Luck** (1941).

Other Australian films: *Heritage (1935), *Orphan of the Wilderness (1936), *Tall Timbers (1937), *Let George Do It (1938), *Typhoon Treasure (1938), *Dad Rudd, M.P. (1940), *Forty Thousand Horsemen (1940), *The Power and the Glory (1941), Harvest Gold (1945), *Smithy (1946)   IB

Vaughan, Martin (1931–) ACTOR A respected character actor, Brisbane-born Martin Vaughan has had wide experience on the stage, starting in Melbourne in 1964, and on television, where he won much acclaim for his performance as John West in the ABC's *Power Without Glory* in 1976. On screen, his intense features have most often represented deprivation or single-minded determination in a range of films. His most notable role was in Simon *Wincer's *Phar Lap (1983), as trainer Harry Telford, who buys the legendary horse for his American businessman employer. Vaughan brought the right tenacity and obsessiveness to the role and, in the same year, showed a nice comic touch as a hapless Qld senator in the television miniseries *The Dismissal*. He had a small part in Michael *Thornhill's *Between Wars (1974) and a larger one as Mr Hussey, the lugubrious drag-driver in *Picnic at Hanging Rock (1975). Apart from a major role as an ageing urban vigilante in the scarcely seen **Kokoda Crescent** (1989), his film work has been mainly confined to minor supporting roles in such films as *Ride a Wild Pony (1975), *Hoodwink (1981), *We of the Never Never (1982) (in which he plays a station hand), the Western Australian-made **The Winds of Jarrah** (1985), *Deadly (1992) (a drama about Black deaths in custody), and the Spanish-made thriller **Beso del Sueño** (1992).

Other Australian films: Can We Have Assurance? (1978, short), Letters from Poland (1978, short), Low Flying (1979, short), Just Out of Reach (1979), Downwardly Mobile (1979, short), Matilda (1979, short), Alison's Birthday (1980), Backs to the Blast (1981, short, nar.), Run, Rebecca, Run (1982), A Shifting Dreaming (1982, doc.), Fluteman (1982), September 1951 (1983, short), Constance (1984, short), The Phantom Horseman (1990), *Encounters (1993), Cops and Robbers (1994).   BMcF

Victorian Film Corporation, *see* Victoria, history and images; Cinemedia

Victoria, history and images The peepshow kinematograph appeared first in Sydney in November 1894, before being shown in Melbourne and, later, in country areas. However, the first public performance in Australia of projected moving pictures was by magician Carl Hertz at the Melbourne Opera House on 22 August 1896. Soon after, Vic. was featuring in Australian-made films, such as those of the Melbourne Cup carnival in November 1896 (see **1896**

515

Martin Vaughan

Melbourne Cup, The). By the beginning of the new century, the most prolific film producer in Australia was the Limelight Department of the Salvation Army (see Documentary and non-fiction, silent), which built Australia's first specialist film studio under the roof of the Salvation Army Citadel in Bourke Street, Melbourne. Under Joseph Perry's direction, the Department produced and exhibited films on religious subjects (for example, the multimedia presentation *Soldiers of the Cross*, 1900) and social subjects (such as the work of the Army with newly released prisoners), as well as commissioned documentaries, including some not filmed in Vic. itself (for example, **Inauguration of the Commonwealth**, 1901).

In these early years, camera operators travelled all over the state, recording the ordinary life of the people as much as big events such as Australian Rules football finals, and producing films such as **Living Hawthorn** (1906), **Marvellous Melbourne** (1910), and **Living Bendigo** (1911). Some of these films have survived and have been reissued by the National Film and Sound Archive (see Archives) in compilations such as **Living Melbourne 1896–1910** (1988) and **Living Ballarat 1901–1941** (1990).

Before World War I, Johnson & Gibson became the largest exhibitor/distributor in the state. They worked with theatrical entrepreneurs John and Nevin Tait to produce what may well be the first feature-length fiction film in the world, *The Story of the Kelly Gang* (1906). Johnson and Gibson formed Amalgamated Pictures, which became the leading producer of fiction films in the state until 1913, when the company joined with T.J. West, Cozens Spencer, and, finally, J.D. Williams to become Australasian Films (see Greater Union Organisation), the notorious 'Combine'. The Combine was based in Sydney at Spencer's studio at Rushcutters Bay, leaving Amalgamated's St Kilda studio to be leased by independents such as W.J. *Lincoln (who had produced films for Amalgamated before forming Lincoln-Cass Productions with actor Godfrey *Cass) and J.C. Williamson Films (a subsidiary of the theatrical firm, for whom Lincoln continued to direct). From World War I to the early 1920s, therefore, more fiction films were being made in Sydney than in Melbourne. However, non-fiction film continued to thrive in Vic. in this period. From 1921 to 1939 the Cinema and Photographic Branch, the federal government's official film unit, responsible for representing the nation on film, was based there.

In the late 1920s, the drought of fiction features was broken by independent producers such as Gerald Hayle, A.R. *Harwood, Leo Forbert, A.G. Harbrow, and Vaughan Marshall, some of whom continued to make films into the 1930s, when production—despite the added costs and technical problems of sound—was booming in Melbourne. The most successful Victorian producer of the early sound period was Frank *Thring (Snr), who formed *Efftee Film Productions in 1930 and made seven features and many short films before his untimely death in 1936. Like Williamson's work, Efftee's output was often based on successful stage presentations: dramas such as *A Co-Respondent's Course (1931) and variety performances from artists such as Pat *Hanna's 'Diggers' company and those whose stage acts were recorded on the short film series **Efftee Entertainers**. There was nothing particularly local to Vic. in these productions: indeed, the producers made conscious efforts to avoid parochialism, and to imitate (not always successfully) what they considered to be the international (Hollywood) style.

From the outbreak of World War II to the 1960s, few features were produced in Melbourne; non-fiction again became the mainstay of film production. On the commercial end of this spectrum was Charles Herschell, a prolific producer of documentaries and promotional films: at the radical activist end was the *Realist Film Unit, and the related Realist Film Association, which provided an alternative to commercial film exhibition in its programs at the New Theatre in Flinders Street. The Realist Film Association was part of the blossoming of film culture in Vic. in the postwar period.

Australia's first film festival was held at Olinda, in the Dandenong Ranges just outside Melbourne, in 1952. The following year, the Melbourne Film Festival was born (see

Festivals). The success of this venture was assured by the healthy growth of •film societies throughout Vic. after World War II. The Federation of Victorian Film Societies imported films for hire by member societies and published a journal, *Federation News*. Both the •National Film Theatre and the •Australian Film Institute were founded in Melbourne, and both grew out of the film-society movement.

Film-industry journals and film-fan publications existed before this, but the first mainstream national publications (see Magazines) aimed at what was becoming known as the 'film-buff' audience also started in Melbourne: *Lumière* (published from 1971 to 1974) and •*Cinema Papers* (after a short false start, in continuous publication since 1974). Film appreciation began to be taught in secondary schools, and the Association of Teachers of Media formed in Vic. in the 1960s and distributed their journal, *Metro*, to teachers all over the country, eventually becoming a national organisation (see Education). Similarly, the Tertiary Screen Education Association of Victoria became the basis for the shortlived Australian Screen Studies Association. Coburg Teachers College was the first tertiary institution, followed by the Centre for the Study of Educational Communication and Media at La Trobe University in the Melbourne suburb of Bundoora, to specialise in film and media, although film studies are now taught at most of the major tertiary institutions in Vic.. The first film school in Australia (that is, the first recognised tertiary organisation for the training of industry professionals), was at Swinburne Institute of Technology. This unit is now the Department of Film and Television at the •Victorian College of the Arts.

Alternative film practice has also flourished in Vic.. The Melbourne Film-makers Co-op operated in Carlton from

Rivoli Theatre, Camberwell, Vic.

the 1960s to 1977 and, since 1986, the Modern Image Makers Association has been serving a similar function. Since 1971, a feature of the alternative film-making scene has been the outstanding journal *Cantrills Filmnotes*, published by film-makers Arthur and Corinne •Cantrill.

In the postwar period, the vibrant Victorian film culture, centred in Melbourne, kept debate about film alive, even in periods when production languished. Some of the earliest films of the •revival arose directly out of this culture, including Tim •Burstall's **The Prize** (1960), Brian Davies's **Pudding Thieves** (1967), and Phillip •Adams and Brian Robinson's •**Jack and Jill: A Postscript** (1970).

In 1976, the Victorian Film Corporation (which was later called the Victorian Film Commission, then Film Victoria and, in 1996, amalgamated with the State Film Centre to become •Cinemedia) was established. In 1975 •**Picnic at Hanging Rock**, which features a Victorian geographical landmark, was funded by the •South Australian Film Corporation and, except for those exteriors of the rock that could not be filmed anywhere else, was shot mainly in South Australia: the establishment of the Victorian Film Commission meant that this was less likely to happen for subsequent films with a significant Victorian content or talent. The Commission provided Victorian film-makers with government funding and infrastructure support, and they used it enthusiastically.

Vic. has been home to writers such as Cliff •Green and Sonia •Borg; actors such as Bruce •Spence, John •Clarke, and Elspeth Ballantyne; producers such as Lynda •House and Timothy White; and directors such as Richard •Franklin, Lawrence Johnson, Ana •Kokkinos, and Richard •Lowenstein. Paul •Cox made a reputation as an arthouse movie maker, with films such as •**Lonely Hearts** (1982), •**Man of Flowers** (1983), and •**A Woman's Tale** (1991) although, in the 1990s, he has been increasingly working outside Australia. Fred •Schepisi made commercials between features such as •**The Chant of Jimmie Blacksmith** (1978) and •**Evil Angels** (1988), and the latter earned him an international career and reputation. Nadia •Tass has specialised in unconventional comedies such as •**Malcolm** (1986) and •**The Big Steal** (1990).

During the 1980s and 1990s, Vic. acquired a reputation for what has been called 'urban fringe' movies—comedies or dramas, often with comparatively low budgets and small casts, set in sometimes bleak inner-suburban locales, with unpredictable story-lines and oddball characters. Early examples can be seen in the films of Tass and Cox mentioned above. Among the best-known recent examples are •**Death in Brunswick** (1991), **Holidays on the River Yarra** (1991), •**Proof** (1991), •**Spotswood** (1992), •**Romper Stomper** (1992), and •**Head On** (1998). One feature of these films is their recognition of Melbourne's ethnic mix and social

tensions; another is their precise sense of urban landscape and of the relation between people and their environment.

It would be a mistake to pigeonhole Victorian film-making as serious social comment or 'quirky' comedy. It is not easy to label any one of the films mentioned above, and the output from Vic. also includes productions as varied as Corinne Cantrill's autobiographical epic **In This Life's Body** (1983), Solrun •Hoass's lyrical and disturbing portrait of an interracial marriage in •**Aya** (1991), Philip •Brophy's filmically literate splatter-spoof **Body Melt** (1994), and Dean Murphy's rural 'teen pic' **Lex and Rory** (1994).

In the 1990s film-making went through a technological revolution. Victorian film-makers were in an excellent position to take advantage of this, as they were superbly served by companies such as Cinevex, AAV, and Soundfirm (which did the post-production for the American film **Romeo & Juliet**, 1996).

In Vic., as elsewhere, there has never been agreement about the merits of individual films. Perhaps this should be seen as evidence of the health of both film culture and film production in this state.

Ina Bertrand

Victorian College of the Arts School of Film and Television
Previously known as the Swinburne Film and Television School, the Victorian College of the Arts (VCA) School of Film and Television had its genesis as Australia's first film school at Swinburne Institute of Technology in 1966. Brian Robinson, its first head, was closely associated with the School for 25 years: it was founded on his philosophy, which emphasised creativity, generalist training, and the writer/director combination. The School has also produced an array of art directors, cinematographers, and animators. Although a small institution, it has had a disproportionate influence on the Australian film industry through its talented graduates. Jenny Sabine succeeded Robinson in 1988, and the School joined the VCA in 1992. Barbara Paterson

Victorian Film Corporation, *see* Victoria, history and images; Cinemedia

Vidler, Steven
(1960–) Actor Until 1996, Steven Vidler was known as an actor with a promising string of credits in film and television (*The Dunera Boys*); then, he directed his first film, •**Blackrock**, based on Nick •Enright's play about a rape and murder that was covered up by the Australian custom of not 'dobbing' your mates. The film failed to find the audience it deserved, but it revealed Vidler as a new director with a firm grasp of narrative and the power of *mise en scène* in evoking the criss-crossing strands of a community. Prior to this, he had given likeable perfor-

mances in: •**Robbery Under Arms** (1985), as Dick Marston, who falls under the lawless influence of Captain Starlight; as a bleached-headed prison parolee stirring up hostilities in Rolf •De Heer's **Encounter at Raven's Gate** (1988); and as the heroine's proletarian suitor in the undervalued melodrama •**Minnamurra** (1989). He brings a disarming and deceptive casualness to these roles that makes him a performer to watch.

Other Australian films: •The Umbrella Woman (1987), Harbour Beat (1990), •No Worries (1993), Napoleon (1995, voice only), The Thin Red Line (1998, USA). BMcF

Steven Vidler

Village Roadshow

The third national exhibition chain had its origins in a small group of hard-top cinemas opened by Roc Kirby in Melbourne suburbs in the 1940s. The Kirby group joined with Bill Spencer and Ted Alexander to form Village Theatres, which opened its first drive-in in Croydon in 1954, and expanded to the suburbs (Rowville, Essendon) and country areas (Hamilton, Wangaratta, Stawell, and Launceston, Tasmania). The company survived the introduction of television, despite the contraction of profits and the closure of some of its venues. In the early 1960s Village went into partnership with •Greater Union Organisation (GUO) to build a drive-in in Geelong and eventually GUO bought a one-third interest in Village.

The company was soon operating hard-tops as well as drive-ins, and also became involved in distribution and production. Roadshow Distributors was formed in 1968, one-third owned by Village: its profits on the re-issue rights of **South Pacific** (USA, 1958) were so large that it expanded, obtained the American International Pictures franchise, and invested more money in cinema building. Village Roadshow also formed the production company •Hexagon Productions and, in the late 1970s, diversified, opening car-racing tracks in Sydney, and Village Family Entertainment Centres in Melbourne. In 1987 Greater Union Film Distributors merged with Village Roadshow Distributors to form the distribution company Roadshow Film Distributors which, in the 1990s, was the only one of the three major distribution companies to be part Australian-owned.

Meanwhile, the company was ideally placed to take advantage of the cinema revival of the 1980s. In 1985 Cinema City opened in Bourke St, Melbourne and, in 1987, Village entered a joint venture with GUO to put multiplexes in Westfield shopping complexes in most states. The group continued to expand and diversify. By 1991 managing director Graham Burke explained that they had four main interests: Warner Bros Movie World (theme park), Warner Roadshow Studios (opened 1989 on the Gold Coast), Roadshow distribution and Village cinemas (which continued to expand multiplexes), and production of films (such as **Turtle Beach**, 1991) and television (such as the series *GP*).

In the 1990s they expanded production, distribution, and exhibition interests in the United Kingdom, Europe and the USA, and moved into Asia, as well as continuing to build multiplexes, and plan megaplexes, in Australia (in a joint venture with Warners/GUO). The expansion brought the group into diverse entertainment activities: they owned the Daydream Island resort, operated cinemas around the world, operated radio stations in Malaysia, and formed a production company with American actor Dustin Hoffman. In 1998 they entered a joint venture with their other cinema chain rival, •Hoyts Theatres, to produce films (including Australian films) for the international market. From being the youngest and smallest of the national chains, by 1996 Roadshow Distributors was Australia's largest distribution company, and Village claimed to be the largest cinema chain in the world. INA BERTRAND

W

Wagstaff, Keith (1936–) CINEMATOGRAPHER The son of pioneer producer Vern Wagstaff, Keith Wagstaff studied at Swinburne Film School (see Victorian College of the Arts School of Film and Television) and started work at his father's Cineservice laboratories. He has shot many international documentaries and his first feature, •**The Man from Snowy River** (1982) established his reputation for sympathetically portraying the Australian environment. He won the Australian Cinematographers Society Golden Tripod award in 1998 and a Penguin award in 1985 for his cinematography of television miniseries.

Other films: •**The Coolangatta Gold** (1984), **Running from the Guns** (1987), **Wild Horses** (USA, 1985), **The Man from Snowy River II** (1988), **Backstage** (1988), **Diana and Me** (1997).

DAVID MUIR

Waiting

1991. *Director*: Jackie McKimmie. *Producer*: Ross Matthews. *Scriptwriter*: Jackie McKimmie. *Director of photography*: Steve Mason. *Music*: Martin Armiger. 95 min. *Cast*: Noni Hazlehurst (Clare), Deborra-Lee Furness (Diane), Frank Whitten (Michael), Helen Jones (Sandy), Denis Moore (Bill), Fiona Press (Therese), Ray Barrett (Frank).

This was Jackie •McKimmie's second feature, after **Australian Dream** (1987). From the opening moments, in which Clare (Noni •Hazlehurst) stands up in the river to reveal she is heavily pregnant, it is clear that this is a film about what have been called 'women's issues'—childbirth, motherhood, relationships. When the arrival of the baby is imminent, Clare's three friends and their various partners and children converge on her home in rural Queensland: Therese to complete her documentary film on the preg-

nancy, professional Diane to simply lend moral support, and earth-mother Sandy to claim the baby, for this is a surrogate pregnancy. The house is crowded and chaotic, the characters all pursuing their own agendas, and the strained atmosphere is convincingly captured. The performances of the ensemble cast mesh beautifully, and Fiona Press deserved her Australian Film Institute Award for Best Actress in a Supporting Role. IB

Wake In Fright

1971. *Director*: Ted Kotcheff. *Producer*: George Willoughby. *Scriptwriter*: Evan Jones. Based on the novel by Kenneth Cook. *Director of photography*: Brian West. *Music*: John Scott. 109 min. *Cast*: Gary Bond (John Grant), Donald Pleasence (Doc Tydon), Chips Rafferty (Jock Crawford), Sylvia Kay (Janette Hynes), Jack Thompson (Dick).

Outback schoolteacher John Grant, on his way to Sydney for the holidays, loses his money in a two-up game during an overnight stop in the mining town of Bundunyabba. He falls in with two miners who take him on a spotlighting expedition to shoot kangaroos. Grant's time in this unpleasant locality assumes for him the significance of a descent into a personal hell, from which he barely emerges to make his way back, a little older and a good deal wiser, to his railway siding school.

Canadian director Ted Kotcheff has submitted some of the national myths to rare cinematic scrutiny. Outback hospitality is seen as potentially oppressive in its insistence, the image of the heroic outdoorsman is qualified by the mindless brutality of his proclivities, and the sacred notion of mateship is for once queried rather than merely celebrated. A symptom of the film's approach is in the performance of

Chips •Rafferty, icon of laconic Australian maleness, as a venal policeman, at least partly responsible for Grant's troubles. The film's perceptions were perhaps too harsh for the popular acceptance that greeted such myth-espousing films as •Gallipoli (1981) and •The Man from Snowy River (1982). Its picture of a place, urban and rural, which is hostile to sensitivity and individuality, and which equates manhood with careless camaraderie and violence, is almost uniquely unsettling in the history of new Australian cinema (see Revival, the).   BMcF

Walkabout

1971. *Director*: Nicolas Roeg. *Producer*: Si Litvinoff. *Scriptwriter*: Edward Bond. Based on the novel by James Vance Marshall. *Director of photography*: Nicolas Roeg. *Music*: John Barry. 100 min. *Cast*: Jenny Agutter (Girl), Lucien John (Brother), David Gulpilil (Aboriginal), John Meillon (Father), John Illingsworth (Husband).

James Marshall's novel is essentially a children's story, albeit a rather alarming one, but the film version created by the British writer Edward Bond and director Nicolas Roeg, has a sophisticated sense of danger and intercultural tension that places it at a distance from its original intended audience. Several decades later it remains one of the most imaginative films ever made in this country and one of the most potent distillations of the threat of its landscape.

A mentally disturbed city businessman drives his 14-year-old daughter and his six-year-old son, both clad in the school uniforms that symbolise their White, middle-class backgrounds, into the Australian desert, ostensibly for a picnic. He goes abruptly berserk, tries to shoot them, sets fire to the car, and kills himself. The children begin the long trek home, helped by a young Aborigine who, as they near civilisation, hangs himself when the girl deliberately ignores his courtship rituals.

Merely to outline the plot can give little sense of the film's power to disturb. The journey itself is both physically arduous *and* exhilarating; the terrain both awesomely beautiful *and* alarming; and these contrasts underline the conflict between primal impulse and 'civilised' inhibition, between two cultures, one at home, the other adrift, in the poetically rendered version of 'Australia'. Although it was critically well received, the film did not do well commercially; its insights were too unsettling for comfort. This is, perhaps, not surprising when one considers that Roeg was the co-director of the nightmarish **Performance** (1970), and Bond the author of the play *Saved*, which began with a baby being stoned to death in its pram.   BMcF

Walker, Kerry

Walker, Kerry (1948–) ACTOR Kerry Walker graduated from the National Institute of Dramatic Art in 1974, and performed with the Marion Street Theatre in Sydney, the Hunter Valley Theatre Company in Newcastle, and the Melbourne Theatre Company's 'Theatre in Education' program, before winning the leading role of Felicity Bannister, in •The Night The Prowler (1979). This introduced her to Patrick •White, whose protégée she became: White's biographer, David Marr, describes her as 'a superb dead-pan clown offstage and on'. At the same time she has a reputation for seriousness and stillness in her performances. She continued to be seen more on stage than screen, but took small parts in many films: The Singer and the Dancer (1975), Double Deal (1981), •Bliss (1985), Bullseye (1987), Wendy Cracked a Walnut (1990), Daydream Believer (1991), •The Piano (1993, as Aunt Morag), •Cosi (1996), and A Little Bit of Soul (1998, in which she played the voracious Eugenie Mason). Her voice was used in Talk (1994) and •Babe (1995), but her most impressive screen performances were two larger roles: Feste in the disappointing •Twelfth Night (1987), and Alison, Lynette Curran's lesbian partner struggling to keep the relationship private in a small country town on the •Road to Nhill (1997). In 1989 she won a three-year Australian Artists Creative Fellowship, and studied Asian drama, mounting a production of Nano Rantiarno's play *The Cockroach Opera*. Her reputation continues to grow.   IB

Walker, Mandy (1963–) CINEMATOGRAPHER Mandy Walker was a camera assistant for seven years before gaining the opportunity to shoot documentaries and short films, including **As the Mirror Burns** (1990), which was nominated for an Australian Film Institute (AFI) cinematography award and won an Australian Cinematographers Society (ACS) award. A short drama, **Parklands** (1996), won an ACS award and the AFI Best Cinematography, Non-Feature Award. Her second feature film, **Eight Ball** (1991) won her an ACS award and •The Well (1997) was nominated for the AFI Best Feature Film Cinematography Award and won a Victorian ACS Silver Award.

Other Australian films include: •Return Home (1990), •Life (1996), •Love Serenade (1996).   DAVID MUIR

Wallace, George (1895–1960) ACTOR George Wallace was a very physical comedian, who had only to walk on to obtain a laugh: he was short and stocky, with a habit of staring straight at the audience, on stage or screen, with a cheeky grin. His trademark costume was a check shirt not quite tucked into trousers that constantly threatened to escape their moorings. His skill as a singer and dancer was disguised behind slapstick, including another trademark—falling on his left ear. He first made his name as Onkus in the stage duo Dinks and Onkus, and was already popular in Australian vaudeville when he joined •Efftee Film Productions, performing both in the **Efftee Entertainers** series, and in feature films: •His Royal Highness (1932), •Harmony Row (1933), and •A Ticket in Tatts (1934). All these simply transfer the stage persona to the screen, including his stage partner John Dobbie, whose height, bulk, and deep voice were a perfect foil. Wallace then made two films for •Cinesound: •Let George Do It (1938), partnered with Joe •Valli, and •Gone to the Dogs (1939), back with John Dobbie. For Charles •Chauvel he played comic relief (again with Joe Valli) in •The Rats of Tobruk (1944), and his last screen appearance was a bit part in Wherever She Goes (1951).

IB

Wallace, Stephen (1943–) DIRECTOR Stephen Wallace began his career as a production assistant, documentary writer, and director at •Film Australia before embarking on an uneven series of feature films, along with television work, including the award-winning telemovie Olive (1987). The lead-up of nearly a decade of documentary and short fiction work preceded the perceptive low-budget film novella The Love-Letters from Teralba Road (1977), which introduced Bryan •Brown to the screen. The story was based on some actual love letters, which Wallace had found in an old house. He set the film in urban wastelands and tenderly charted the difficulties of a marriage that keeps foundering on the husband's violent and drunken outbursts. Made for $25 000, it won three prizes at the Australian Film Awards in 1977, and garnered praise for the sensitivity of Brown and Kris •McQuade in the leading roles.

Despite the film's warm critical reception, it was three years before Wallace made his first full-length film, the powerful prison drama •Stir (1980), again starring Bryan Brown, who had come to prominence in 10 films since his Teralba Road debut, including Wallace's short film Conman Harry and the Others (1979). Wallace skilfully orchestrates the tensions of men herded together in prison, and understands that prison life brutalises screws as well as crims. The climactic outbreak of violence is filmed with kinetic power and control, derived from Wallace's skill in suggesting a claustrophobic system bursting apart, and the framing and lighting of cameraman Geoffrey •Burton.

Wallace's subsequent films have been uneven. The Boy Who Had Everything (1984) was set in affluent harbourside Sydney, with Diane •Cilento as the rich alcoholic mother of Jason Connery (her real-life son from her marriage to Sean Connery), a public-school boy who fails to come to terms with university in the troubled 1960s, and finally cuts loose from it and from his mother. The film, which failed to exploit its potential for family melodrama, was finally released in the United Kingdom but not in Australia, except on video. •For Love Alone (1986), the film version of Christina Stead's novel of a young girl's rites of passage from an oppressive 1930s' Australian background to

her ultimate liberation, both sexually and professionally (as a writer) in London, was intelligently written (by Wallace) and acted (especially by Helen •Buday as Teresa and Sam •Neill as her British lover), but failed to repeat producer Margaret •Fink's success with a not-dissimilar project in •My Brilliant Career (1979).

Wallace had a return to form with the war crimes melodrama •Blood Oath (1990), which was based on the trial following the atrocities committed on the Japanese-held island of Ambon during World War II. However, it is not in the end a bitter attack on the Japanese so much as a philosophical treatment of the brutalising effects of war. In this dividedness, it recalls the depiction of both crims and screws as victims of the system in Stir. Acts of brutality between one race and another are also central to Turtle Beach (1992), based on Blanche d'Alpuget's novel about a reporter (Greta •Scacchi) pursuing horrific stories of the treatment of Vietnamese refugees in Malaysia in the 1970s. It was reported that some scenes were re-shot in post-production by Bruce •Beresford. Wallace has never had a major box-office hit but, flaws and all, his work has been persistently more interesting than the Australian average. He became president of the Australian Screen Directors' Association in 1993.

Other Australian films: Just Below Par (1968, doc.), Balmain (1969, doc., co.-ed.), The Look (1970, short), Patterns of Time and Distance (1972, doc., co-w.), Brittle Weather Journey (1973, short, w.), Break-Up (1975, short, w.), Zizzem Zam (1976, short, ass. d.), Captives of Care (1981, doc.), So You're Getting a Divorce (1981).

BMcF

Walton, John (1953–) ACTOR Trained at the National Institute of Dramatic Art, John Walton had worked for Sydney's Old Tote Theatre Company and the South Australian Theatre Company, and he had become a familiar face on television before making his screen début in Undercover in 1983. On television he had continuing roles in such series as Cop Shop and The Young Doctors, and the miniseries, Bodyline. In the punningly entitled Undercover, he played Fred Burley, pioneer of women's foundation garments and of the slogan 'Buy Australian'. The film was engaging enough, but enjoyed only modest success. He had perhaps his best role in •Kangaroo (1987), Tim •Burstall's unfairly neglected adaptation of D.H. Lawrence, as the sinisterly friendly Jack Calcott, playing interestingly against his blonde good looks but, again, the film failed to find large audiences. Walton seemed fated to appear in commercially unsuccessful films: he next gave a fine, moving performance as Tas, one of the mates who gets killed, in Simon •Wincer's lavish but generally uninvolving epic, •The Lighthorsemen (1987). Since then, apart from excellent work in Shotgun Wedding (1994), his roles have become smaller and fewer, although television and the theatre have offered some consolation.

Other Australian films: Luigi's Ladies (1989), •Spotswood (1992), •Muriel's Wedding (1994).   BMcF

Waltzing Matilda

1933. Director: Pat Hanna. *Production company*: Pat Hanna Productions. *Scriptwriter*: Pat Hanna. *Director of photography*: Arthur Higgins. 77 min. B&W. *Cast*: Pat Hanna (Chic Williams), Joe Valli (Joe McTavish), Norman French (James Brown), Dorothy Parnham (Dorothy).

Pat •Hanna's third production has a mix of narrative and sketches similar to •**Diggers in Blighty** (1933), and relies on comic stage 'business' similar to both that and the earlier •**Diggers** (1931). The characters of Joe and Chic continue but, in peacetime, their camaraderie is strained when Joe gives Chic and his new mate James Brown jobs at the station where he is foreman. Chic and James are running from the law after a misunderstanding (in fact, the private detective who is following them is trying to notify Brown of an inheritance). The comedy (such as it is) lies in their attempts to evade the detective, and in Chic's bumbling about in the world of the squattocracy. Leaving James to marry the boss's daughter (Dorothy), and Joe with marital and economic prospects on the station, Chic humps his bluey alone into an unknown future. The character, now pathetic in spite of the cheeky smile to the camera in the final frames, could not sustain further films: Hanna, whose whole career was built around that character, made no more.   IB

Ward, Rachel (1957–) ACTOR

Daughter of the Earl of Dudley, and former model, Rachel Ward made her first screen impact in the Burt Reynolds-directed crime thriller **Sharky's Machine** (1981), although she had already appeared in two low-budget horror films: **The Final Terror** (1981) and **Night School** (1981). In 1983 Ward appeared opposite Bryan •Brown in the popular American miniseries *The Thorn Birds* and followed this in **Against All Odds** (1994), the dismal remake of **Out of the Past** (1947). Ward's acting career slowed down for a period after marrying Brown and moving to Australia in the early 1980s. In 1987 she appeared with Brown and Sam •Neill in •**The Umbrella Woman** as Marge Hills, the confused, lonely wife who betrays husband Brown by lusting after villainous Sam Neill. Ward was excellent in this difficult role that required her to communicate abject humiliation and rebellion, together with a sense of entrapment within the narrow social and economic opportunities available to a married woman in a small pre-World War II Australian country town. In the late 1980s and 1990s Ward resumed her international career in films such as **After Dark My Sweet** (1990), based on a Jim Thompson novel, and as

Queen Isabella in **Christopher Columbus: The Discovery** (1992). During this period Ward had a featured role in the John •Duigan-directed film, **Wide Sargasso Sea** (1992), based on the Jean Rhys novel, which, in effect, was a prequel to the story of *Jane Eyre*.

Other Australian films include: Fortress (1986).   GM

Ward, Roger (1936–) ACTOR

Roger Ward, with his height and characteristically shaved head, has been a distinctive character actor in many Australian crime and adventure films over several decades. Ward appeared in minor roles in overseas films such as **Mutiny on the Bounty** (1962), before entering the moribund Australian film industry in the 1960s in films such as •**They're a Weird Mob** (1966) and the American co-production **It Takes all Kinds** (1969). He also wrote the story for the controversial film that exposed the sex lives of the Sydney elite in •**The Set** (1970). Ward, however, has largely been typecast as the chief villain or aggressive policeman in most films, epitomised by his role as the sadistic guard in **Turkey Shoot** (1981), with occasional glimpses of other facets of his acting talent, such as in his role as Mel •Gibson's superior officer, Fifi Macaffee, in •**Mad Max** (1979).

Other Australian films include: Squeeze a Flower (1970), Dalmas (1973), •**Stone** (1974), Moving On (1974), The Love Epidemic (1975), •**The Man from Hong Kong** (1975), •**Mad Dog Morgan** (1976), Deathcheaters (1976), No Room to Run (1976), High Rolling (1977), •**The Irishman** (1978), Touch and Go (1980), The Chain Reaction (1980), Lady Stay Dead (1982), Brothers (1982), The Pirate Movie (1982), •**Robbery Under Arms** (1985), •**Young Einstein** (1988), •**Quigley** (1991), Fatal Bond (1992), Rough Diamonds (1993).   GM

Warm Nights on a Slow Moving Train

1988. Director: Bob Ellis. *Producers*: Ross Dimsey, Patric Juillet. *Scriptwriters*: Bob Ellis, Denny Lawrence. *Director of photography*: Yuri Sokol. *Music*: Peter Sullivan. 91 min. *Cast*: Wendy Hughes (Girl), Colin Friels (Man), Lewis Fitz-Gerald (Brian), Norman Kaye (Salesman), John Clayton (Football Coach), Rod Zuanic (Young Soldier), Grant Tilly (Politician), Peter Whitford (Steward).

Director and co-writer Bob Ellis disowned this film when it was commercially released 35 minutes shorter than his final cut. What did those missing 35 minutes contain? Would they have given the film some much-needed genuine depth and insight, or would they have been more of the same pseudo-philosophical one-liners?

The film, produced with the belief that brooding obscurity, unnamed characters, and pretentious aphorisms were considered meaningful, is about an art teacher who works as a prostitute on an overnight train to finance her disabled brother Brian's morphine habit. She assumes a different identity each time, seduces a likely lonely target and stings them for payment. But then she meets the Man, falls in love with him, and plans on trading her train ticket in. Ten years on, alongside some embarrassing fashions from Wendy •Hughes, and Colin •Friels's shocking accent, Ellis's attempt to present whoring and journeys as philosophical metaphors for life appears superficial, affected, and very dated.   TIM HUNTER

Warming Up

1985. Director: Bruce Best. *Producer:* James Davern. *Scriptwriter:* James Davern. *Director of photography:* Joseph Pickering. *Music:* Mike Perjanik. 94 min. *Cast:* Barbara Stephens (Juliet Cavanagh-Forbes), Henri Szeps (Peter Sullivan), Queenie Ashton (Mrs Marsh), Adam Fernance (Randolph Cavanagh-Forbes), Lloyd Morris (Ox).

Juliet, with her son Randolph (known as Andy), leaves her latest macho boyfriend and buys a country ballet school in the one-horse town of Wilgunyah. The venture seems doomed as she falls foul of the local football team, the policeman who trains them, and the publican. After the hall in which her classes are to be held is burned down, Juliet, undeterred, convinces the football team that ballet training wins matches, and mobilises the town's women to demand the right to drink in the public bar. But she also confronts her own sexism, learning that Peter plays a mean violin, and allowing Andy to start football training. This is broad comedy, with such set-pieces as the footballers and the dancers training (loudly) on either side of a portable screen in the hall. But, despite moments of farce, it has a solid core in which Juliet and Peter pair off without either being forced to compromise their principles.   IB

Wartime film-making

Imported films of the Boer War were shown in Australia, but the first war in which Australian cinematographers took moving-picture footage was World War I. Bert •Ive filmed on one of the troop-ships travelling from Melbourne to Albany to join the first convoy to Europe in November 1914: he showed the regimen for keeping fit, as well as the cheerful demeanour of the troops before they continued on to training camps in Egypt. Later, in his capacity as official cinematographer for the Commonwealth government, he recorded military training camps and internment camps. Many of the activities on the homefront were filmed for the silent •newsreels: marches and processions, patriotic rallies, recruitment drives, and Red Cross working bees. Australasian Films (see Greater Union Organisation) employed cartoonist Harry Julius (see Animation) to make short animated propaganda films for inclusion in the **Australasian Gazette**: these films, some of which survive, depicted inspiring images such as a German spurred boot crushing the homes of the Belgians, and a Turkish chicken cringing between the Allied forces and the Germans, who have trained their guns on the Turkish rear

to prevent retreat. Propaganda shorts urging a 'Yes' vote in the conscription referenda of 1916 and 1917, were shown, by government regulation, in every Australian cinema, even in areas where such government interference in the democratic process was bitterly resented. But it was not until June 1917 that Australia officially had cinematographers at the front: Frank •Hurley, assisted by Hubert Wilkins (both were formally attached to the British forces, although they were permitted to film the Australians on the battlefields of France and the Middle East). Some of this newsreel and actuality footage is held in the collection of the Australian War Memorial, and some is held in the •National Film and Sound Archive (NFSA; see Archives), which has issued a videotape compilation, making what has survived accessible to the general public.

There is very little left, however, of the many feature films made in Australia during the war. In 1913 the major Australian film companies had merged into what was known as the 'Combine'—with distribution through •Australasian Films and exhibition through Union Theatres (see Greater Union Organisation; Exhibition and distribution). Although several of its member companies were also producers, the Combine decided to withdraw from feature production (while still maintaining their weekly newsreel), leaving the Australian market wide open to the product of Hollywood which, during World War I, expanded its worldwide influence. It may well have been the impetus of the war that slowed the Hollywood takeover of Australian markets: in the early stages in particular transport difficulties limited the supply of foreign films and a nationalistic fervour encouraged local productions on patriotic themes. It has been said that the entry of the theatrical company J.C Williamson Ltd into feature production was prompted by a fear that Hollywood intended to film its stage repertoire. During the war it made several films of plays, including (all in 1916) •**Officer 666**, **Get-Rich-Quick Wallingford**, **Within the Law**, and •**Seven Keys to Baldpate**. But the company also catered to the patriotic mood with films such as **Within Our Gates** (1915) and **For Australia** (1915). Meanwhile, Australasian Films had also re-entered feature production, some said in order to support their case to the government against film import duties. They, too, concentrated on patriotic war stories, producing **How We Beat the Emden** (1915) and •**A Hero of the Dardanelles** (1915), and advertising their goldfields picture **The Loyal Rebel** (1915) as an allegory of the Australian fighting spirit. In these early years, the films expressed the popular myths of the brave Australian soldier, the dangers of spies and saboteurs, and the inferiority of the enemy. However, among the numerous depictions of the heroic sacrifices being made by soldiers, were a few that recognised the role of women: three film versions were made of (British nurse) Edith Cavell's story (including •**The Martyrdom of Nurse Cavell**, 1916) and the romantic potential of the image of the (Australian) nurse at the front was milked in **Scars of Love** (1918). Later, as enthusiasm for the war waned, the proportion of war stories declined, and those that were produced either did not succeed with the public (**The Murder of Captain Fryatt**, 1917) or were advertised as not being war films at all (**•The Enemy Within**, 1918). The sexually transmitted disease scare, largely fuelled by the epidemic among the troops, produced only one feature film, which did not mention the war at all—**Remorse, or The Red Plague** (1917). Two feature films made in 1918 to raise funds for patriotic causes similarly avoided all reference to the war: **Cupid Camouflaged** and **What Happened to Jean**.

But the war had enshrined the image of the Anzac in the national mythology, and that image persisted in films between the wars—heroically in **•Ginger Mick** (1920), **•The Spirit of Gallipoli**, (1928), **•The Exploits of the Emden** (1928), and **Fellers** (1930); and less heroically in **•The Digger Earl** (1924) and **•Diggers** (1931). It carried over into two films by Charles **•Chauvel** released during World War II: **•Forty Thousand Horsemen** (1940), which celebrated the Australian desert campaigns of World War I, and **•The Rats of Tobruk** (1944), which showed the continuity of the Anzac spirit into the new conflict.

In other ways, World War II was very different. First, Australian cinematographers were appointed from the start by the Australian government to work with the war correspondents, to keep the nation informed and morale high for the duration of the war, and to record the war for posterity. The Department of Information's (DOI) Film Division (see Film Australia) sent a unit overseas, including cinematographers Damien **•Parer** and Frank **•Hurley**, Ron Maslyn **•Williams** as script-writer/producer, Alan Anderson as sound engineer, and George Silk as stills photographer. They recorded Australian participation in all theatres of war, often at great personal risk, and much of this footage survives in the Australian War Memorial. Two compilation tapes have been made by the NFSA (see Archives)—one of the home front and one of the various war fronts. Sometimes this footage was the best way to counter the inaccuracies and anti-Australian bias of official communiques issued by MacArthur's staff in the Pacific. The footage was returned to the DOI, which distributed it to both of the competing newsreels, **Cinesound Review** and **Movietone News** (see newsreels). The government's control over the footage (including rights of embargo) made 'scooping' of rivals difficult: still, on at least one occasion, Movietone managed it by incorporating the footage into the international issue of their newsreel, then showing the international version in Australian cinemas. The newsreels provided the same sort of morale-boosting as they had done in World War I, but added new forms to the old repertoire, particularly in the form of longer, more documentary-style reports on particular campaigns. The DOI also commissioned short films (both semi-dramatised and documentary) from the major commercial companies, **•Cinesound**, Chauvel, Movietone, Herschells, Commonwealth Laboratories, Mervyn Murphy, George **•Malcolm**, John **•Heyer**, and the Arthur **•Higgins**–Neville Bletcher team. The Australian War Memorial commissioned Mervyn Scales and Arthur Higgins to make **Sons of the Anzacs** (1944), an outstanding compilation film scripted and partly narrated by Chester Wilmot.

Australian production of feature film had almost dried up, a victim first of confusion over the application of the government guarantees applicable under the 1937 NSW Theatres and Public Halls Act, then of wartime rationing of electricity and film stock, and loss of key personnel to the services. Cinesound released three feature films in 1939: **•Come Up Smiling**, **•Mr Chedworth Steps Out** and **•Gone to the Dogs** and, in 1940, made **•Dad Rudd M.P.** before formally abandoning feature production in June, continuing only with **Cinesound Review**. Chauvel's two wartime epics (**Forty Thousand Horsemen** and **The Rats of Tobruk**) did well with audiences and, by the end of the war, several features were in production (including Ealing's **•The Overlanders**, Ken G. **•Hall's •Smithy**, and Eric **•Porter's •A Son is Born**), all of which were eventually released in 1946.

After the revival of Australian feature film-making in the 1960s and 1970s (see Revival), both world wars continued to attract the attention of film-makers sporadically. World War I was revisited in films such as **•Gallipoli** (1981) and **•The Lighthorsemen** (1987), and in many television series, including *Anzacs* (1985) and *1915* (1982). World War II appeared in films such as **•Blood Oath** (1990) and **•Paradise Road** (1997), as well as in television miniseries such as *A Town Like Alice* (1981) and *The Heroes* (1989). The Anzac myth was prominent in these representations, but not always quite so heroically and unquestioningly as it once was: Australian soldiers were shown to have visited prostitutes and to have behaved badly in the Wazza riots in Cairo in 1915 (**Gallipoli**) (see Mateship), the existence of shirkers was hinted at (**Break of Day**, 1976), women were permitted a larger role in the drama (*1915*, **Paradise Road**), and some soldiers were even shown paralysed with inaction in combat (*Anzacs*, **The Lighthorsemen**).

By the time of the Korean War, the Australian feature film industry was in the doldrums, and the newsreels were struggling, so little attention was paid to that war on film. But, in 1956, television arrived in Australia. The Vietnam War became the first 'television war', with reports being presented in the living-rooms of the nation only a day or so after events occurred. The cinema newsreels were outclassed, and paid little attention to that war, particularly after it began to divide the nation: heroic images seemed increasingly out of place. Feature film production, on the other hand, was beginning to struggle back, so it is perhaps surprising that during the war only one feature film concerned the war itself—**Demonstrator** (1971), a story of political intrigue set in Canberra and depicting the protest movement as manipulated by sinister foreign forces—but it was not widely released. In later years, however, the Vietnam war was represented in several films and television miniseries. •**The Odd Angry Shot** (1979) was unusual in depicting the war itself: it was more usual for films to deal with the home front, and particularly with the figure of the Vietnam veteran (for example, •**A Street to Die** 1985, **Slate, Wyn and Me** 1987).

Film-making during wars is often logistically more difficult than in peacetime, but its function in reflecting society's values continues, making films (both fiction and non-fiction) a useful barometer of public attitudes—recording the swelling or waning in support for particular conflicts and reflecting changes in nationalist myths that underpin participation in wars. Wartime film-making, as well as the representation of war at other times in a nation's history, is therefore a rich—and still under-explored—resource for the historian.

INA BERTRAND AND NEIL MCDONALD

Waters, John (1945–) ACTOR English-born John Waters (his father was actor Russell Waters) first made his mark in Australia in the stage production of *Hair*. He has also been a folk singer and recording artist, and has had success on the stage (especially in *They're Playing Our Song*) and in popular television series such as *Rush*. His screen career got off to a promising start in the 1970s, with good roles in •**Eliza Fraser** (1976), •**The Getting of Wisdom** (1977), and as the dim-witted protagonist of **Weekend of Shadows** (1978). Waters, through a watchful, subtle approach to his roles, seemed to have major potential but the films that should have capitalised on this have not been forthcoming. It may be that, for a conventional leading man

Ken G. Hall directs Grant Taylor and Ron Randell in a wartime propaganda short

status, there was always too melancholy a cast to his persona, but this certainly suited several of his films. He has made the most of what was offering, particularly in •'Breaker' Morant (1980) and as the disturbed teacher in •Grievous Bodily Harm (1988), but such parts have not been frequent enough for him to sustain the promise of screen stardom he suggested in the 1970s.

Other Australian films: And Millions Will Die (1973), End Play (1976), •Summerfield (1977), Attack Force Z (1982), Going Sane (1986), Boulevard of Broken Dreams (1988), •Heaven Tonight (1990), Ebbtide (1994), The Real Macaw (1998).

BMcF

Waterside Workers Federation Film Unit

(1953–58) One of the few trade-union film groups in Australia, this Sydney-based unit was formed by waterside workers Keith Gow and Jerome 'Jock' Levy, who were joined in 1954 by Norma Disher. They produced eight films for the Federation, and eight other commissioned works, including three for the Building Workers Industrial Union. These short works included documentaries and animation, and they focused on industrial disputes, safety, housing shortages, and other social and labor issues, interpreted from a working-class viewpoint. Stylistically, the film-makers employed the Griersonian documentary style (see •Documentary), the newsreel format, and the realism of Soviet and European film-makers such as Sergei Eisenstein. They were supported by left-wing unionists, writers, artists, and theatre workers, especially those involved in the New Theatre. The unit members worked collectively and often involved other waterside workers in the production process, as extras or helpers. They employed a grassroots distribution and exhibition system, showing their films at union and community meetings, and from their Kombi van, which doubled as a production vehicle and screening platform. Their films were bought by unions, libraries, and government departments, won awards locally and overseas, and were seen in film-society and festival screenings. Their best known work is The Hungry Miles (1955), which was produced to give a history of the waterfront industry from the workers' perspective. Scenes from this film depicting living conditions during the Depression have often been used in later works, especially television documentaries.

LISA MILNER

The Waybacks

1918. Director: Arthur W. Sterry. Producer: Humbert Pugliese. From the play by Phillip Lytton, based on the novels by Henry Fletcher. B&W. Cast: Vincent White (Dads Wayback).

The surviving footage from The Waybacks, a 1918 backblocks farce, shows a creditable attempt to convert the popular stage production into a constantly moving, Mack Sennett type of slapstick burlesque. The action is often staged in the middle distance and almost every shot contains roiling movement of characters from background to foreground. Most of the expected stereotypes of the genre are represented in exuberant caricature: white-bearded, comic Dad, dumpy, good-hearted Mum, attractive and grotesque daughters, hopeless and hapless suitors, assorted bumpkin neighbours—and heaps of grubby children, entranced by the camera. Not without charm, the most coherent narrative segment in what survives covers part of the Wayback family's trip to the city where they run foul of a hotel manager who does not like their pet cockatoos, and make friends with a tipsy impersonator of Charlie Chaplin who is working outside a cinema.

WILLIAM D. ROUTT

We of the Never Never

1982. Director: Igor Auzins. Producer: Greg Tepper. Co-producer: John B. Murray. Scriptwriter: Peter Schreck. Based on the book by Mrs Aeneas Gunn. Director of photography: Gary Hansen. Music: Peter Best. 134 min. Cast: Angela Punch-McGregor (Jeannie), Arthur Dignam (Aeneas Gunn), Tony Barry (Mac), Tommy Lewis (Jackeroo), Lewis Fitz-Gerald (Jack), Sibina Willy (Bett Bett).

When Jeannie Gunn joins her husband on Elsey Station in the Northern Territory in 1901, she is the first White woman to set foot on the property. She faces not only physical deprivation, but also the limitations imposed by the mateship culture that dominates life on the station, all of which is captured naturalistically and movingly in the film. The cinematography, outstanding both in wide vistas and in intimate moments, won Gary •Hansen an Australian Film Institute award. In Mrs Gunn's book, her husband is known as the Manuka, and remains rather distant and enigmatic. In the film, Aeneas Gunn is a central figure, maintaining his view of Aborigines as children who need to be led, while Jeannie defends their right to make their own choices. It is a major ideological change, and one which, despite the careful period re-creation, makes the film a film of the 1980s, a time when Australia was rethinking racial issues. IB

Weaver, Jacki

(1947–) ACTOR One of the most engaging moments in the new Australian cinema (see Revival, the) occurs when the spunky, diminutive Jacki Weaver pokes her tongue out at a disapproving passenger on a tram in •Caddie (1976). She plays one of barmaid Caddie's friends and brings an irrepressible spontaneity to the small role that is characteristic of her work in all the acting media. She began her stage career at Sydney's Phillip Street Theatre while still a schoolgirl, and appeared in a diversity of plays at the Nimrod Theatre and the Old Tote Theatre Company, also becoming well known on television before starting in films. She played herself in •The Naked Bunyip (1970), as one of the 'interviewees' whose opinions were sought by the shy young man conducting a survey of Australian sexual mores; was the virginal hero's first love in •Stork (1971); was one of several nubile young women in •Alvin Purple (1973); and then moved into more substantial roles.

She was affectingly honest in •Petersen (1974), as the dim young wife whose plumber husband outgrows her when he takes to university studies, and her scenes with Jack •Thompson in the title role are among the most natural and touching in the film. In •Picnic at Hanging Rock (1975) she plays Minnie the housemaid and brings a note of uncomplicated good-nature and sexuality to the film's hothouse atmosphere, and she had her strongest role to date in The Removalists (1975), as the naive young wife whose husband treats her brutally. These excellent performances ought to have led to a richer career in films; perhaps the failure of Squizzy Taylor (1982), in which she played the female lead opposite David Atkins as the famous Melbourne gangster, stalled her progress. She has done a good deal of stage and television since, but no further feature films until •Cosi (1996). Hers is too enjoyable a talent for Australian cinema to waste.

Other Australian films: •They're a Weird Mob (1966), Abra Cadabra (1983, short, voice). BMcF

Weaving, Hugo (1960–) ACTOR Hugo Weaving

attracted attention in 1984 with his role as English cricket captain Douglas Jardine, the villain who plotted Don Bradman's downfall, in the Australian miniseries *Bodyline*. In 1988 he had the lead role in another popular miniseries *The Dirtwater Dynasty*. Weaving's major screen break was in the award-winning film •Proof. His multilayered performance as Martin, the blind man who takes photographs of the world around him so as to prove that it exists, won him the Australian Film Institute Award for 'Best Performance by an actor in a Leading Role' in 1991. The film's intense exploration of Martin's destructive relationship with his housekeeper Celia (Genevieve •Picot) provided an ideal showcase for these two skilled actors. Since **Proof**, Weaving's screen roles have been diverse. They include the crooked cop out to stop whistle-blowing Anthony •LaPaglia in the uneven police thriller •The Custodian (1994), a drag queen in •The Adventures of Priscilla, Queen of the Desert (1994), and an appearance in the youthful comedy True Love and Chaos (1996). Weaving has interspersed these roles with television work, including the 'lust' episode in *Seven Deadly Sins* (1992), *The Bangkok Hilton* (1990), and *Halifax f.p.* (1997), and with frequent stage work.

Other Australian films include: The City's Edge (1983), •For Love Alone (1986), The Right Hand Man (1987), Wendy Cracked a Walnut (1990), Reckless Kelly (1993), Exile (1994), Frauds

(1994), •Babe (1995), •The Interview (1998), Babe: Pig in the City (1998), Matrix (1999, USA), The Magic Pudding (anim. 2000-voice). GM

Webber, Hamilton COMPOSER British-born com-

poser and conductor, Hamilton Webber was one of the few musical directors in the film industry in the 1920s and 1930s who was classically trained. In 1929 Stuart •Doyle appointed him as conductor of the Melbourne State Theatre Orchestra; Webber was unique among musical directors in Australia, for he wrote his own column in the State Theatre's in-house magazine, *The State Review*. In April 1930 Webber announced that his orchestra would be renamed the Australian National Orchestra. His vision was that it would be Australia's largest permanent orchestra, giving concerts and making broadcasts of concert music. In 1934 he became musical director of •Cinesound Productions. Ken G. •Hall had a personal regard for Webber and he considered that his score for •The Silence of Dean Maitland (in which Webber employed a *leitmotiv* device from Wagner's *Träume* to depict Alma, the seductress of a willing clergyman) gave music its rightful place in an Australian sound film for the first time. Other Webber scores followed: •Thoroughbred (1936), •It Isn't Done and •Lovers and Luggers (1937), •Mr Chedworth Steps Out (1938) (in which he made his only on-screen appearance, conducting the Cinesound orchestra) and his crowning achievement, •The Broken Melody (1938). DIANE NAPTHALI

Weir, Peter (1944–) One of the most influential

films associated with the rebirth of Australian cinema in the 1970s was Peter Weir's •Picnic at Hanging Rock (1975). Derived from Joan Lindsay's novel of the same name, Weir's film was characterised by a languorous visual style, a concern for period detail, an imagistic unity rather than a tightly constructed narrative, and an interest in youthful rites of passage. In these ways it ushered in a whole spate of such films that helped to define the nature of the new Australian cinema (see Revival, the). If the influence was not wholly beneficent, sometimes encouraging an indulgent form of film-making, there is no denying that it established the new Australian cinema as a force to be reckoned with, both in Australia and abroad. And it established Weir as a major new director.

Prior to **Picnic at Hanging Rock**, Weir had made several short films and documentaries, beginning in 1967 with **Count Vim's Last Exercise**. He won some notice for a lively if undisciplined talent in such films as 'Michael', part of a trilogy on the theme of youthful rebellion, **Three to Go** (1969), and **Homesdale** (1971), a black comedy in which the mentally disturbed are given the opportunity, in the eponymous institution, to act out their private fantasies.

Hugo Weaving

Peter Weir working on **The Cars that Ate Paris**

Weir's first film to achieve wide distribution was •**The Cars that Ate Paris** (1974), a film that undermines the apparent realism of its setting by calling its idyllic small-town setting into question, for the peaceful-seeming country town of Paris maintains its prosperity by the deliberate orchestration of motor accidents. The film's premises was audacious and it alerted moviegoers for the first time to Weir's fascination with the way the extraordinary hovers at the edges of the quotidian, threatening various kinds of status quo.

In **Picnic at Hanging Rock** this theme is pursued through attention to two monolithic images: those of Hanging Rock which, on St Valentine's Day 1900, simply swallows up several members of a picnic party, and of Appleyard College, the school for young ladies from which the party has come. The Rock offers an invitation to a loosening of the mores kept under strict (and strictly European) restraint at the College. A carefree excursion becomes an ongoing nightmare. In •**The Last Wave** (1977), torrential

rain appears out of a clear blue sky, foreshadowing the disruption of the ordinary in the life of the film's protagonist, a company lawyer, who increasingly finds the certainties on which he has built his life are losing their authority. He is forced to make allowance for non-rational forces at work in his middle-class Anglo-Saxon life when he comes to believe he is descended from an ancient race that inhabited Australia in prehistoric times. The telemovie which followed, *The Plumber* (1979), is a minor but neatly worked out piece in which, again, middle-class education proves unequal to invasion by basic urges and fears.

Weir's next film, •**Gallipoli** (1981), a re-telling of the famous Australian coming-of-age exploit, which made a star of Mel •Gibson, was an enormous critical and commercial success in Australia, and achieved mainstream release in the USA where it was distributed by Paramount. Weir now seemed poised to make the international transition, and his 1982 film, •**The Year of Living Dangerously**, a melodrama of political and sexual loyalties, was set wholly in strife-torn Indonesia. It starred Gibson again, supported by the American actors Sigourney Weaver and Linda Hunt (bizarrely cast as a male dwarf), was distributed by Metro-Goldwyn-Mayer, and had the gloss of international film-making.

Since then, Weir has filmed entirely in the USA; although **Green Card** is an Australian co-production, it is to all intents and purposes an American film, with American and French stars, and a plot that owes something to the American tradition of screwball comedy. Of his other American films, **Witness** (1985) and **Dead Poets Society** (1989), set respectively in an Amish community and a private school for boys, cleverly embrace the procedures of classical American cinema to produce melodramas based on a clash of cultural viewpoints.

Of the first generation of 'new Australian film-makers', Weir is probably the one with the most distinguished record. When one recalls that his peers included Fred •Schepisi, Gillian •Armstrong, and Bruce •Beresford, all of whom went on to solid international success, it must be allowed that this was a very remarkable efflorescence in Australian film history.   BMcF

Weir, Wendy PRODUCTION DESIGNER/COSTUME DESIGNER/ PRODUCER   For more than two decades Wendy Weir has actively collaborated on husband Peter •Weir's films. She has designed costumes and sets, produced, and acted as a consultant. She assisted in the development of the luminous appearance of •**Picnic at Hanging Rock** (1975), designing layers of enmeshing, restrictive costumes that presented a pristine facade. These crisp, white costumes were designed to contrast with the monumental landscape of Hanging Rock. Her fascination with the presentation of characters in imposing Australian landscapes continued with her coordination of the design of •**Gallipoli** (1981).

With •**The Year of Living Dangerously** (1982), Weir was forced to create sets representing Indonesian streets in a studio in Sydney when production was abandoned due to threats to their safety while filming in Indonesia. In the USA, Wendy Weir produced the critically acclaimed film **Witness** (1985). Under the name Wendy Stites she designed **Dead Poets Society** (1989), and the Australian/French co-production **Green Card** (1990). On **The Truman Show** (1998), Stites is credited with the role of special design consultant in creating the parallel diegetic worlds of the film, and the serial within a Hollywood biosphere, one that was designed for maximum voyeurism.   WENDY HASLEM

Weis, Bob (1947–) PRODUCER   In 1983 Bob Weis co-produced, with Robert Le Tet, •**The Clinic**, the story of one day in a clinic for the treatment of sexually transmitted disease and other sexual problems. The episodic structure

of the film, which includes a suicide within its overall comic tone, is essentially non-moralistic in its attitude to the range of sexual issues confronted by the medical staff. Both the subject matter and treatment of this film are indicative of the idiosyncratic film projects favoured by Weis. His more mainstream films include •**The Empty Beach** (1985), as executive producer, **Georgia** (1989), as producer and co-scriptwriter, and **Lucky Break** (1994). It is here that Weis, who worked with director Ben •Lewin in these last two film, favours quirky characters and non-formulaic stories with a socially progressive bias. This characteristic is even more pronounced in Weis's low-budget films, which include the rarely seen •**Pure S...** (1975), an episodic story of four young heroin addicts searching for their next hit, and **Wills & Burke** (1985), an absurd spoof perversely released the week before the mainstream epic •**Burke & Wills**. It also describes Weis's successful television productions such as *The Dunera Boys* (1985), *Women of the Sun* (1982), *Waterfront* (1984), and *'Raw FM'* (1997/98).   GM

Well, The

1997. Director: Samantha Lang. *Producer*: Sandra Levy. *Scriptwriter*: Laura Jones. *Director of photography*: Mandy Walker. *Music*: Stephen Rae. 102 min. *Cast*: Pamela Rabe (Hester Harper), Miranda Otto (Katherine), Paul Chubb (Harry Bird), Frank Wilson (Francis Harper), Steve Jacobs (Rod Borden), Genevieve Lemon (Jen Borden), Simon Lydon (Jock).

This impressive film is saturated with a strong sense of gothic repression. The blue tinge that pervades virtually all exteriors in the film is combined with the chilly, barren Cooma landscape to mirror the sexual and social repressions of middle-aged Hester Harper, who lives on a remote farming property with her sick father Francis. Into this sterile context comes young Katherine, and Hester's plans for her are transparent in her retort to her father's reaction to Katherine's arrival. Francis asks, 'What have you brought me, Hester?' to which she replies 'I've brought Katherine, father. But she's for me.'

In a dramatic context similar to Joseph Losey's British film **The Servant** (1963), Katherine exploits Hester's inhibitions and an early scene shows Katherine dancing in the passage-way of the family home as the deprived Hester watches the young woman's body movements. Although Lang emphasises Hester's desire, and suggests the repressed fetishistic basis of the relationship with lingering shots of fabrics, clothes, and boots, she carefully avoids confirmation of physical consummation. While Hester hovers near Katherine's bed in one scene, she is not shown entering it.

The film opens with a scene of Katherine dancing at a party as the crippled Hester watches her younger partner.

Katherine then insists on driving back to their cottage and the vehicle hits a man sitting in the road. For the next hour the film reverts in time to the period leading up to this incident, beginning with Katherine's arrival at the farm and the death of Hester's father. Hester's decision to sell the property provides her with ample money and she leaves Katherine in a cottage as a prelude to their European trip. During this pre-accident period, Hester spends a deal of money on Katherine and, for possibly the first time in her life, seems to be enjoying herself. However, the overall structure of the film is affected by placing the accident at the start so that even during this seemingly idyllic period the audience is aware that darkness and death are ahead.

After the death on the road, Hester disposes of the body by placing the man in a well near their cottage. At the same time Hester discovers that a large amount of money has been stolen from the cottage. Katherine, on the other hand, starts 'communicating' with the dead man and her relationship with Hester disintegrates to a point at which the relationship is beyond repair. She leaves the cottage as Hester learns that the police are going to examine her motor vehicle. An insert near the end of the film reveals the fate of Hester's money.

This is a measured and rather precise film that often reverts to a range of filmic devices, such as clothes, composition, colour, body language, and editing, rather than dialogue, to convey meaning. Samantha Lang was nominated for the Golden Camera and Golden Palm awards at the 1997 Cannes Film Festival, and Pamela Rabe won the Best Performance award by an Actress in a Leading Role at the 1997 Australian Film Institute Awards. Also, Laura Jones won the award for Best Screenplay Adapted from Another Source and Michael Phillips for Best Achievement in Production Design.   GM

Wenham, David ACTOR   Stage-experienced David Wenham, whose theatre successes include *Hamlet* for the Belvoir Street Theatre, Sydney, and *Tartuffe* for the Sydney Theatre Company, suddenly became a very recognisable film actor in 1998. This was on the strength of his appearance as the quietly iconoclastic Diver Dan in the miniseries *SeaChange*, and of his riveting performance as Brett Sprague in •**The Boys**. Directed by Rowan Woods, the latter proved to be one of the most demanding Australian films of 1998, with its pervasive aura of something appalling about to happen, and much of this tension was generated by Wenham's watchful, dangerously implosive rendering of the just-released prisoner with new violence in mind. He had played the role in the award-winning stage production of *The Boys* at Sydney's Griffin Street Theatre in 1991, and was associate producer on the film. Wenham has appeared in two American films, **No Escape** (1994) and **Dark City** (1998). He has become an actor to watch: his command of a minimalistic screen style seems to link him to some of the most famous of all screen actors.

Other Australian films include: Greenkeeping (1993), •Cosi (1996), A Little Bit of Soul (1998).   BMcF

Western Australia, history and images   In WA, moves in the 1890s towards nationhood and Federation occurred quickly, as a result of the 'Great Rush' for gold. The discovery of gold prompted a fivefold increase in the population of WA in a decade, including a large influx from the eastern colonies, and it transformed an economically and politically backward—and socially conservative—British colony, into a dynamic frontier Australian state. Amid this ebullience, the first motion pictures were shown in the colony on a bright moonlit Saturday night, 21 November 1896, to an excitable crowd of 3000 at an outdoor theatre in Perth.

The impact of motion pictures on this isolated but vigorous community was immediate. Within 10 years, the first motion pictures were being made and shown locally to a burgeoning audience. As well as exhibiting motion pictures depicting scenes from abroad, visiting and local film-makers placed cameras at advertised places or events and simply filmed the assembled crowds. This assured a paying audience: people loved to see themselves and familiar things.

By World War I, as a small film-production industry developed, many outdoor and indoor venues were exhibiting motion pictures, a few of which were produced locally (especially newsreels and promotional films). More and more 'picture theatres' were built throughout WA, and this continued despite the privations of war.

The 1920s brought economic prosperity and further immigration to WA. Local film-makers began to appear: for example, Fred Murphy, who, after serving in World War I, stopped over in Hollywood before returning home to produce numerous films that promoted WA. These included **The Land of Opportunity** (1920), and narrative films such as **Dreams and Screams** (1923) (a film in the slapstick genre of Charles Chaplin). 'Picture palaces' were opened in WA by the larger Australian film exhibition and distribution chains; in the late 1920s, Perth audiences were seated in such 'atmospheric' surrounds as the Ambassadors Theatre with its 'Florentine garden, above which stars twinkled and clouds wafted under an azure dome' (see Cinemas).

The immediate effect of the Depression was an evaporation of motion-picture production and a decline in cinema audiences but, by the end of the 1930s, locally owned cinema chains, such as the Grand Theatre Company, were successfully competing with nationally operated chains, such as Hoyts. Audiences were larger than ever. Most motion picture production in WA in the 1930s and during World War II was for newsreel companies such as **Australian Sound Films**, **Western Mail Newsreel**, **Cinesound Review**, and **Fox Movietone News** (see newsreels).

After World War II, the government itself became a filmmaker, with the creation of the Western Australian Government Film Unit and the commissioning of films promoting WA by commercial film-making companies such as Southern Cross Newsreels/ Films. The economic, industrial, and social development of WA in the late 1940s, 1950s, and early 1960s is well documented in these films: hundreds were produced covering such diverse topics as immigration, banana-growing in Carnarvon, bee-keeping methods, forecasting bushfires, and the whaling industry. The vast major-

ity of these films featured the cinematographic work of Leith Goodall and, later, Alex McPhee.

In October 1959 television commenced in WA, and its success soon caused many cinemas to close, especially in suburban Perth and the country. Drive-in theatres, catering to the continuing popularity of summer outdoor theatre, commenced in the 1950s and continued to be well attended until the 1970s, when the rise in popularity of home video players lessened their appeal.

In the 1960s a wave of prosperity swept over WA: development projects occurred in iron ore, bauxite, oil, gas, and nickel; and dramatic changes to the economy and society, documented by film-makers, took place. Government again provided the impetus for motion-picture production, utilising the efforts of local film-makers such as Bryan Lobascher, David Moore, Brian Williams, Michael Baker,

The Capitol Theatre, Perth, WA

and Don Shepherd. One type of film that comes close to a Western Australian film genre is the •short mining film such as **The Mineral Wealth of Western Australia** (1963), **Western Australia Wins Key Industries** (1965), and **Moving Mountains** (1966). At the end of the mining boom, •**Nickel Queen** (1971) was made. It starred Googie •Withers, was supported by the premier and the state's minister for Industrial Development (Sir Charles Court), and was billed as the first feature film in WA. The mining boom caused a transformation of WA's built environment, resulting in the destruction of many 'picture palaces'. In the main, they have been replaced by cinema complexes that house a number of screens under one roof, reducing the seating available for one film from well over a thousand to a few hundred.

The 1960s saw the beginnings, and the 1970s the consolidation, of movements to entrench WA's film-making culture in the mainstream. This is evidenced by the commencement of technical, followed by tertiary, media studies and motion-picture production courses, as well as by the establishment of film festivals, support for local film-production, and funding bodies such as the Perth Institute of Film and Television (now the •Film and Television Institute of Western Australia) and later the Western Australian Film Council (now •ScreenWest). As a result of the accidental destruction of most of the films of Fred Murphy, the State Film Archives was begun, albeit in embryonic form. Australia's only regional film archive, it is now part of the J.S. Battye Library of West Australian History, and has extensive holdings of WA's motion picture heritage.

Local television production also provided a stimulus for the Western Australian film industry. Local television stations produced material such as nature documentaries, some of which ended up on the world market. Importantly, many film-makers, such as Guy Baskin and John Izzard, began to produce motion pictures that focused in new ways on subjects such as WA's unique wildlife, and environment, and social issues such as the life of the local Aboriginal people. As a local film-making culture developed, and Australia embarked on an investment boom in the 1980s, WA made

The Grand Theatre, Perth, WA

more narrative feature films, including •**Fran** (1985), **Tudawali** (1987), and •**Shame** (1988). These were produced by Barron Films; Paul D. •Barron, Glenda Hambly, and David Rapsey were involved in writing and production, and leading actors Noni •Hazlehurst, Ernie •Dingo, and Deborra-Lee •Furness were featured.

In the 1990s there has been considerable activity in motion-picture production and screen culture in WA, with steady funding from bodies such as ScreenWest, and through the Lotteries Commission, accompanied by a significant amount of private investment in local production. Some documentary films empathetically allow the subjects ownership of their own stories; for instance, **The Joys of the Women** (1993), **The Coolbaroo Club** (1995), and **No Milk, No Honey** (1997), which represent, respectively, the communities of Italian immigrant women, Nyungar Aborigines, and British group-settlers. Barron Entertainment continues its prodigious output, alongside other film-making companies such as Electric Pictures, CM Film Productions, RT Films, ICA Productions, Storyteller Productions, and Wildfire Films International, making for an active WA film-making community. In the 1990s, after a gap of several years, narrative feature film returned with **Justice** (1998), made by West Coast Pictures.

National and international backing, and demand for Western Australian films does seem to be gaining ground, and emerging film-makers are encouraged by the Western Australian Screen Awards. GERARD FOLEY

Western Australian Film Council, *see* ScreenWest

Westlake, Nigel (1958–) COMPOSER/PERFORMER
Nigel Westlake composes for the concert hall and theatre. He has also written scores for feature films, documentary films, television series, and numerous themes for ABC and SBS television programs. After initial studies with William •Motzing at the •Australian Film Television and Radio School in 1982, his first film score for **The Bus Trip** was produced under Motzing's tutorage. James McCarthy, then music editor of •Film Australia, was at the screening and he invited the composer to write scores for documentary films, a moment Westlake considers his 'first break' in film composition. Westlake is largely self-taught as a composer. His intuitive process was enhanced with the award of an Australia Council grant in 1993 to study orchestration. His film work includes scores for •**Children of the Revolution** (1996) and **A Little Bit of Soul** (1997). IMAX scores include **Antarctica** (1991), **The Edge** (1995), and a trailer for **Sydney—Story of a City** (1998), His score for **Imagine** (1993, 3D IMAX) won the Best Exhibit award at the Taejon Expo

'93 in Korea. •**Babe** (1995), directed by Chris Noonan, produced by Bill and George •Miller, and accompanied by a Westlake score, won the Golden Globe Award for best picture/musical comedy in that year.
Other Australian film: Babe: Pig in the City (1998).

DIANE NAPTHALI

Westmore, Joy (1932–) ACTOR
Although she has had a long and distinguished career in the theatre, it was the continuing role of Joyce Barry in the popular television series, *Prisoner* that made Joy Westmore a household name for several years. She also appeared in other series such as *Embassy* and *Cluedo*. Given her range, wit, and incisiveness, it is surprising she has not made more films: she had brief roles in Ken •Hannam's •**Summerfield** (1977) as a coastal resort artist, in Tom •Jeffrey's •**The Odd Angry Shot** (1979), and as the Matron in John •Lamond's lamentable **Nightmares** (1980); and bigger ones in Robyn •Nevin's •**The More Things Change** (1986), her most developed role, as the heroine's mother. Her comic flair had some scope as the eponymous Les's good lady in George •Miller's **Les Patterson Saves the World** (1987), which proved a box-office flop.

BMcF

What I Have Written

1996. Director: John Hughes. *Producers*: Peter Sainsbury, John Hughes. *Scriptwriter*: John A. Scott. *Director of photography*: Dion Beebe. *Music*: John Phillips, David Bride, Helen Mountfort. *Cast*: Martin Jacobs (Christopher Houghton/Avery), Gillian Jones (Frances Bourin/Catherine), Jacek Koman (Jeremy Fliszar), Angie Milliken (Sorel Houghton/Gillian).

At the narrative core of **What I Have Written** is a domestic melodrama involving betrayal, desire, lust, and retribution. In the hands of director John •Hughes this material is transformed into a fragmented, cool film that utilises many techniques associated with art cinema, particularly frequent shifts in temporality, designed to both disorient and engage the viewer in a game of character and narrational duplicity. The story begins with Christopher's affair with Frances Bourin in Paris while he is on sabbatical leave with his wife, Sorel. The relationship between Christopher and Bourin intensifies after Christopher's return to Melbourne via a regular exchange of sexually explicit letters and after Christopher suffers a cerebral haemorrhage. His colleague Jeremy sends a semi-autobiographical novella, supposedly written by Christopher, to Sorel who tries to piece together the exact nature of her husband's relationship with Bourin.

Sorel's search for the 'truth' regarding her husband is only one layer in the film that, at different times, invokes aspects of similar films concerned with the reliability of the image and play between meaning and cinematic form (such as **La Jetée**, 1962; **Poison**, 1991; **Bad Timing**, 1980; and especially **Blow Up**, 1966). **What I Have Written** is an impressive film that provides many entry points for the viewer by supplying just enough character development and narrative motivation to engage on an emotional level while also providing a formal mosaic that allows those who are interested to seek connections involving repetition, placement, and composition of the carefully selected still and moving images. GM

When the Kellys Rode, *see* The Story of the Kelly Gang

When the Kellys Were Out, *see* The Story of the Kelly Gang

White Death

1936. *Director*: Edwin G. Bowen. *Producer*: Edwin G. Bowen. *Scriptwriter*: Frank Harvey. *Directors of photography*: H.C. Anderson, Arthur Higgins. *Music*: Isadore Goodman. 81 min. B&W. *Cast*: Zane Grey (Himself), Alfred Frith (Newton Smith), Nola Warren (Nola Murchinson), John Weston (John Lollard), Harold Colonna (David Murchinson), James Coleman (Prof. Lollard).

Zane Grey arrived in Australia in 1935 for a highly publicised deep-sea fishing expedition, and was greeted warmly by the many fans of his paperback western novels. In addition to a film record of the trip, Grey produced this feature film, employing his general manager as director and one of the photographers he brought out from the USA. He also borrowed Frank •Harvey and Arthur •Higgins from •Cinesound, and used the Cinesound studios. Set on a Great Barrier Reef island, the main story of the film is Grey's attempts to catch a killer shark known to the local Aborigines as White Death. Sub-plots concern the romance between Nola and John, and the comic antics of Mr Smith, protector of fish (Grey's revenge on the Royal Society for the Prevention of Cruelty to Animals, which had complained about his fishing venture). After uniformly bad reviews, the box-office success of the film was brief. IB

White, Patrick (1912–90) WRITER One of Australia's
best-known authors, Patrick White is most famous for his 1973 Nobel Prize for literature. •**The Night The Prowler** (1979) is his only produced script. Its genesis came from an alleged rape in Martin Road, Sydney, where he lived. From the incident, he developed a fictional scenario that suited his own sensibilities and used it as a springboard to attack the bourgeois values of Felicity's (Kerry •Walker's) parents, and to foreground her 'liberation' from her own

claustrophobic world. This premise originally manifested itself in a short story that White commenced in London in 1969, and which was first published in 1974 amid several abortive attempts by Harry Miller to organise production of a film version of White's novel *Voss*. The suburban gothic elements of the film, which border on slapstick, might reasonably be ascribed to director Jim •Sharman, if it were not for evidence of these in the script itself: 'Shot of Mrs Burstall's open mouth, if possible down to the uvula'. It was White's intention from the outset that Sharman should direct the film. When it opened the Sydney Film Festival in 1978, those expecting something approaching the metaphysical gravity of White's literary work must have been disappointed. Overall, it was unfavourably received. Possibly anticipating a different reaction or, as David Marr believes, 'as a shield against the nervous hopes raised by the film', White had already commenced work on another script, *Monkey Puzzle*, in which he hoped to interest Barry •Humphries. The fact that *Monkey Puzzle* was never produced may well have been an important loss, as it was White's first attempt in fiction to explore the process of writing. HARRY KIRCHNER

Whitford, Peter (1939–) ACTOR Perhaps best
remembered as PS's Depression-defeated uncle George in Carl •Schultz's •**Careful He Might Hear You** (1983), Peter Whitford is one of those effortlessly convincing character actors who are a major strength of Australian cinema. He invested this role with a fine blend of sturdy socialist decency and the pathos of a man with nothing to cling to but the heart's affections, contrasting strikingly with John •Hargreaves' eloquent sketch of the dashing wastrel, Logan. Whitford had already a range of classic and modern stage roles to his credit, and appearances in such television series as *Cop Shop* and *The Sullivans*, before his first screen role in Gillian •Armstrong's •**My Brilliant Career** (1979), as the heroine's expansive and bibulous Uncle JJ. Some of his best work has been on television, where he played Dr Evatt in *The Last Bastion*, but there were telling, if brief, character parts in •**Strictly Ballroom** (1992), where he was touching as the gay dance partner of the hero's mother, and as Mr Ahearn, unheeded adviser to the heroine, again for Armstrong in •**Oscar and Lucinda** (1998).
Other Australian films: With Prejudice (1982), •Phar Lap (1983), Dead-End Drive-In (1986), Running from the Guns (1987), •Warm Nights on a Slow Moving Train (1988). BMcF

Wild Duck, The

1984. *Director*: Henri Safran. *Producer*: Phillip Emanuel. *Scriptwriters*: Tutte Lemkow, Dido Merwin, Henri Safran. *Additional mater-*

ial by Peter Smalley. Based on the play by Henrik Ibsen. *Director of photography*: Peter James. *Music*: Simon Walker. 92 min. *Cast*: Liv Ullman (Gina Ackland), Jeremy Irons (Harold Ackland), Lucinda Jones (Henriette), John Meillon (Old Ackland), Arthur Dignam (Gregory Wardle), Michael Pate (Mr Wardle).

Set in turn-of-the-century Australia, this version of Henrik Ibsen's tragedy is little more than a curiosity. Worth noting as an honourable attempt by Australian cinema to adapt a classic work from another culture, it fails to catch fire or make much of the transplant. Henri •Safran had shown skill in directing children in •**Storm Boy** (1976) and •**'Norman Loves Rose'** (1982), and does so here with Lucinda Jones as Henriette, the child who is sacrificed to her foolish father Harold's quest for the ideal at the instigation of his well-meaning, dangerous friend Gregory. Gregory suggests that Henriette is really the daughter of his father and Gina, the father's ex-housekeeper, now Harold's wife. Strongly acted by international and local stars, the film does not flinch from Ibsen's insights into the nature of truth and illusion but, not surprisingly, the film reached only the most limited audiences.   BMcF

Williams, Kim EXECUTIVE Kim Williams's name appeared as producer (*Police State*) or executive producer (*Good Vibrations*, *Police Rescue*) on television programs in the late 1990s. However, his career as an influential executive in Australian cinema dates back to 1984, when he entered the industry as chief executive of the •Australian Film Commission. He stayed in this position for four years. As chairman of the •Australian Film Finance Corporation (AFC), which he helped to set up, he had strong views on the need for the industry to achieve financial credibility. He believed that the AFC provided the 'framework' for the industry and that it was the responsibility of the film-makers to attend to the matter of quality, a belief honed during the period of the •10BA tax concession when, he contended, many films were made that should not have seen the light of day. He later ran the production arm of the Southern Star Group, joined the ABC to form Australian Information Media, and, in 1995, became the chief executive of Fox Studios Australia. The Fox Studios cover a 28-hectare site that was once the Sydney Showgrounds. One of its first productions under Williams's management was Gillian •Armstrong's •*Oscar and Lucinda*.   BMcF

Williams, Ron Maslyn (1911–) Like those of John •Heyer, Maslyn Williams's first experiences were as a factotum on feature films of the 1930s such as Charles •Chauvel's •*Uncivilised* (1936). Williams's training in music enabled him to quickly pick up on ideas of editing and continuity,

and the experience of being on the Pagewood studio lot proved invaluable. As a staff member at National Studios, Williams also worked on the British Gaumont production of Miles Mander's •**The Flying Doctor** (1936) on which Damien •Parer also worked as a camera assistant. Clarence Badger's •**Rangle River** (1936) was also made at National and added to Williams's experience.

Williams later became editor with the Commonwealth government's Cinema and Photographic Branch of the Department of Agriculture, which was effectively the first Commonwealth film-making unit and was based in Melbourne. He joined the officer-in-charge, Lyn Maplestone, who was to write and direct the work of two cameramen, Bert Ive and Reg Pearse, from which Williams then constructed the finished product. In 1940 Williams joined Parer, Alan Anderson and George Silk under Frank •Hurley as a director–editor in North Africa, Greece, Yugoslavia, Syria, Crete, and the Pacific in the Department of Information's film unit, which supplied footage to •Cinesound and Movietone for newsreel production. After the war he joined the •Australian National Film Board (ANFB) as senior producer responsible for such films as **Goldtown** (1948), **Music Camp** (1958), **The Music Makers** (1945), and **This is the ABC** (1955). These films all displayed his interest in music and sound in film with an emphasis on dialogue and the assertion of the music score over image. Williams's earlier films can be understood as testing grounds for the singular romantic realist film •**Mike and Stefani** (1952), which combines elements of newsreel technique with those of melodrama and documentary. Along with Colin Dean he took on the ambitious documentary experiment **Melbourne Wedding Belle** (1953), utilising Ferraria colour and multiple overlapping sung narrations. Towards the end of his stint at the •Commonwealth Film Unit, Williams produced a series of films dealing with political, economic, and social developments in the territory of Papua New Guinea. These include **New Guinea Patrol** (1958), **Way to a New World** (1959), **An Agricultural Officer in Papua and New Guinea** (1961), and **The Cruise of the Magi** (1962). Since leaving the ANFB he has carved a larger persona for himself as an author of many fiction and non-fiction books.

DEANE WILLIAMS

Williamson, David (1942–) WRITER Australia's most popular playwright, David Williamson has written more than 20 plays, 15 feature films, five radio plays, and has also directed for theatre. He has adapted many of his plays for film, including •**The Removalists** (1974), •**Don's Party** (1976), •**The Club** (1980), •**Travelling North** (1987), **Sanctuary** (1995), and **Brilliant Lies** (1996). His

David Williamson

Wilson, Frank (1924–) ACTOR   This radio and television personality was a dominant figure in Melbourne television in the 1960s and 1970s. Frank Wilson compered a number of extremely popular programs, including *In Melbourne Tonight* and *New Faces*. Prior to his work in television, Wilson had a supporting role in 1959 in the Hecht–Hill–Lancaster film production of •**Summer of the Seventeenth Doll**, which was shot at the Artransa and Pagewood studios in NSW after the setting of Ray Lawler's play was shifted from Carlton to Sydney. After a minor role in **Alvin Rides Again** (1974), he had a prominent role in the underrated crime thriller •**Money Movers** (1979). This was followed in the 1980s and 1990s with sporadic appearances in supporting roles. Wilson's most important film performance in his post-television period was as the dying Father Jerome who greets Lothaire Bluteau at a remote outpost after Bluteau's 2500-km journey across seventeenth-century North America in **Black Robe** (1992), Bruce •Beresford's elegaic story of religious redemption and futility. Wilson also appeared briefly as Pamela •Rabe's father in the Gothic drama •**The Well** (1997).
Other Australian films include: •*Patrick* (1978), The Journalist (1979), **Fatty Finn** (1980), •'Breaker' Morant (1980), •The Club (1980), **Going Sane** (1987).   GM

Wincer, Simon (1943–) DIRECTOR   Like so many Australian directors, Sydney-born Simon Wincer was snapped up by Hollywood after his first major success. This was •**Phar Lap** (1983), a subject no Australian film-maker could afford to mess up, but it had actually been quite a long time arriving for Wincer. His career had begun at the ABC, and he worked for three years as a director and stage manager in British television in the latter half of the 1960s, returning to Australia in 1970 to join the Melbourne television production company, Crawfords, working on some of its biggest successes, such as *Matlock Police* and *The Box*.

He made his first feature film, **Snapshot**, in 1979 and, in the following year, was appointed chief executive for film and television for the Michael Edgely Organisation. **Snapshot** is a neat enough if generally unremarkable thriller. It begins well with the camera conducting a teasing pursuit of a girl through city streets but, once the suspense is revealed to be anti-climactic, the film never recovers its tension. The 1980 political thriller-cum-fantasy, **Harlequin**, is firmly aimed at international audiences, in its diction (politicians are all 'senators' or 'governors'), and in its casting (Robert Powell as the Rasputin-like figure, Broderick Crawford and David Hemmings as politicians of varying degrees of corruption). The domestic melodrama at the film's heart, involving a seduced wife and gravely ill son, remains underdeveloped.

original scripts include •**Eliza Frazer** (1976), •**Gallipoli** (1981), **Partners** (1981), and he re-wrote •**The Year of Living Dangerously** (1982, from the novel by C.J. Koch) after attempts to raise money on earlier drafts had been unsuccessful. (Koch, who is uncredited, claims a substantial contribution to the final script.) After training and working as an engineer and lecturer, Williamson was an early member of the Australian Performers Group (Pram Factory). However, his plays, which might broadly be described as naturalistic, were seen as distinct from the group's more experimental approach to theatre, and he was considered something of an outsider. Sometimes accused of being overly sensitive to criticism, Williamson has a capacity to lampoon his own world, as can be seen in •**Emerald City** (1989), in which a serious screenwriter sells out to commercial values. Williamson was also co-producer and co-writer on the television miniseries *The Last Bastion* (1984). Among his other television credits are *Certain Women* (1975), *The Perfectionist* (1985), and *The Four-Minute Mile* (1988). He is emeritus president of the Australian Writers' Guild and holds honorary doctorates from Monash University and the University of New South Wales.   HARRY KIRCHNER

In conversation with

DAVID WILLIAMSON

When did you first decide that you wanted to be a writer, and was drama always your preferred métier?
Writing stories fascinated me from an early age. I wrote very simple little stories not long after learning to write. In my late teens I wanted to write novels and tried to do so at great length, but soon found out that shaping deathless prose was probably not my métier. It was during the performance of a play at the MTC in my early twenties that I first felt that drama was what I wanted to write. There was a connection between actor and audience that grabbed me, an immediacy and an excitement that enthralled me and, for no good reason, I felt that this was what I could do. I can't remember what the play was, but I remember vividly the experience of being 'called'.

What sort of movies and directors made an impression on you when you were a young man?
In my late teens and early twenties the director who made the greatest impact on me was Ingmar Bergman. **Wild Strawberries**, **Through a Glass Darkly**, **The Virgin Spring**, and **Cries and Whispers** were among those that had great impact. I could raise no interest in the then fashionable Italian directors, finding movies like **L'Avventura** pretentious, and **La Dolce Vita** a boring cry of pain from the over-privileged. The angst of Italian boredom was not as compelling to me as Bergman's ferocious honesty in facing the dark side of human nature and facing the fact that happiness is a rare human achievement. I think I also like the dramatic intensity of Bergman. It felt nearer to theatre in the best sort of way. I did like Truffaut's **400 Blows**, but found **Jules and Jim** less than honest. I also remember being blown away by Sergei Bondarchuk's **War and Peace** for its sheer epic sweep. I saw American movies but can't remember one that left much of an impression except **High Noon**, directed by Zinnemann. I lie. **In the Heat of the Night**, written by Stirling Silliphant (I often used to take more notice of writing credits than directing credits in American movies), had an impact, as did **Little**

Big Man and of course **The Graduate**. Again, the dialogue was of more interest in the American movies than the visual style. ('One word young man—plastics.'). But it was definitely the European cinema that left the greatest impression in those early years.

Now I'm asking you to be very subjective, but what's the greatest difference for you between watching a great play and a great film?
I've come to the conclusion that drama is character driven to a greater degree than film, which tends to be narrative driven. Drama of course has a story structure, but that story is often driven by the unfolding of character and can cope easily with many characters being equally important. In a sense it's the clash of character, each trying to push their own agenda, which excites me about drama. The often-quoted disadvantage of drama, that it's a story told in long shot, is actually an advantage in this respect. Film, with its camera directing our attention remorselessly, virtually makes it imperative that we tell either one person's story (Joseph Campbell's hero narrative being the most popular structure), or the story of a two-person relationship. ('They hate each other at the start and eventually fall in love' structure, or the buddy structure.) Once the camera has singled out a face in close-up, we know that's whose story we'll be watching. On stage we're watching everyone's story, or more broadly the story of how conflict is inevitable given that we all have our own agendas. On film we are watching an arc of development as the hero survives, tests, and learns from them, and emerges a wiser and better person at the end. In this sense there is always an element of myth and fairy tale. We are told that if we learn from our trials we can overcome. Drama at its best does not share this naive optimism. It says that a lot of our behaviour is neurotic and instinctive, and that many of us learn very little; that this makes life difficult rather than a mythic hero's self-improvement journey. Of course, not all film is genre driven and mythic. I guess that's why I was attracted to Bergman.

You were involved with La Mama in the 1970s when it famously provided the context for the cinema revival. What was it like?

I was at the first meeting Betty Burstall called to found La Mama, but was an almost totally unknown revue writer and didn't have the confidence to push myself. I sneaked away, and the work of Jack Hibberd and John •Romeril was done. I sent scripts to Betty some years later. She got two short plays produced, then Al Finney asked me to write the end of a play that the actors could improvise up to. That became *The Coming of Stork* in 1970, which was written backwards. How was it? Intimidating I guess. I was an engineering graduate studying psychology as a second degree, and a married man with a small child living in suburbia. The student actors tended to be arts graduates with a much greater theoretical knowledge of the current trends in film and theatre than I had, and much greater confidence in articulating their ideas than I had. They did spot the potential of *The Removalists* (Bruce •Spence and Peter •Cummins) and *Don's Party* (Graeme •Blundell), and gave them good gritty productions, for which I'm grateful. I owe them my career. But I have to say I never felt at ease, because I didn't find the theories in the *Tulane Drama Review* as compelling as they did. In particular, I didn't think the dreaded 'naturalism' was dead or ever would be. I thought an approximate depiction of reality, albeit with a satiric edge, was effective theatre. Still do.

You have both written original scripts and adapted your own plays. What are the relative problems of both roles?

Scripts as scripts seem to have fewer problems in the sense that they can be told in the appropriate narrative fashion, which I outlined before. •Gallipoli was essentially a buddy narrative structure—Archie and Frank facing the horrors of the bloodiest war ever fought. Not that it didn't take Peter •Weir and me a long time to settle on this kind of essential simplicity. It started as an epic documentary but we finally realised that the laws of film narrative had to be obeyed. •Phar Lap was a hero story with the strapper Tommy Woodcock as the human hero, learning to overcome obstacles, and train his beloved horse himself. Play adaptations present the problem that my plays, being essentially character-interaction

pieces with many important characters, are difficult to fit into the single-person narrative structure. There was pressure to do so. There was a lot of debate about 'whose story' •Don's Party was. Bruce •Beresford was smart enough to realise that it had to be an ensemble piece and with the fluid and expert camera work of Don •McAlpine, the ensemble nature of the piece did, I think, make effective cinema. •The Club and •Travelling North did bend further towards the 'whose story is it?' imperative. The filmed **Club** tended to become the recruit Geoff Hayward's story, and Carl •Schultz, the director of **Travelling North** firmly believed that it had to be Frank's story.

Further to my last question, what was your experience with three of your works, The Removalists, Don's Party, *and* Brilliant Lies?

The Removalists did attempt to retain the ensemble nature of the stage play, but it didn't have the visual layering of **Don's Party**, in which Beresford and McAlpine had something going on in the foreground, middle ground, and background most of the time. It had more of the feel of a filmed play. I didn't write the script of **Brilliant Lies** but I think that Richard •Franklin, the director, and Peter Fitzpatrick, the co-writer, evolved an effective flashback style to allow the tension of the final incident to be present from an early stage in the narrative, and hence effectively built narrative tension into an essentially character-driven piece. I thought it was a very well-made movie.

What is it like to adapt someone else's work, as you did with Christopher Koch's novel •The Year of Living Dangerously?

Peter Weir and Koch fell out while trying to develop the script. Peter then used another writer whose work he didn't like, then asked me to help. I was pleased to do so as I admired Peter and the book. We went through many drafts with Peter providing important input. Peter finally felt he couldn't really tell the story without Billy Kwan's voice-overs, and I agreed with this decision. It does result in the unusual convention that we hear the voice-overs of a character who dies before the film ends. The main work of adaptation was spareness, both of dialogue and story structure. The story structure had to be simplified in order to compress it into film length. The voice-overs in effect mean that it is Billy Kwan's story, as well as

Hamilton's and Jill's. So it could never conform to the classic film narrative hero structure, which is probably why it was not a huge box-office hit, but much admired.

Can you talk about the gestation of Gallipoli?

As I hinted at earlier the gestation took some time. Peter Weir called me up and gave me a bullet he'd picked up on the beaches of Gallipoli, and asked me to write it with him. Having rather foolishly turned down the offer to write •Picnic at Hanging Rock I wasn't about to do it again. We started out wanting to do a huge story with many characters in order to do justice to a great Australian mythic event. Kristin (my wife) found many old veterans, and she and I interviewed them. My attitude changed from the condescending disdain of someone who found the old diggers on Anzac Day embarrassing to an attitude of respect for the horror they had gone through, and the courage with which they had faced it. I think Peter had always had that attitude, so the effect of the research was that we both wanted to make the same picture. Eventually after many drafts, as indicated earlier, we found the most effective way to tell the story was to utilise an age-old narrative structure of power and simplicity, with two young men who initially were rivals bonding in the horror of battle. Phillip •Adams proclaimed the film to be homoerotic (in a tone of praise— 'the first Australian gay love story'), and suggested that the two lead characters were projections of Peter and myself. While I admired Peter, and I hope he did me, I think the explanation for any such overtones that were evident was perhaps more prosaic. In our research Kristin and I certainly did detect homoerotic overtones in the way wartime relationships were described. Most of the diggers had a special 'pal' who they shared a foxhole with behind the lines. And the roles did tend to be split between the domestic and the foraging role. I don't think much, if any, sex went on in the foxholes, but the closeness of the relationships was evident in the way they were described to us.

Which of your scripts are you most satisfied with, and why?

Gallipoli. I think it was an opportune blending of Peter's and my talent, and remains for me a vividly powerful story about the horror that ensues when tribalism is allowed to run amok.

In the 1990s you spent some time in Hollywood. How different are the two film cultures?

Hollywood is a bustling heady culture where everything seems possible but isn't. Australia is a pessimistic film culture where they tell you nothing is possible but sometimes it is. In America I was typically asked to write films with a critical edge to them, films that suggested that all was not well with America. I was asked to do this on the basis of **Gallipoli** and **The Year of Living Dangerously**, which a lot of producers sincerely admired. But they admired them precisely because they were pessimistic and said that the world is often very unjust and cruel. They were not straight genre pieces radiating optimism about the ability of the individual to overcome all obstacles. Hollywood makes genre movies because genre movies tell reassuring myths and hence make money. The pressure all the time was to make the characters 'likeable'. ('David, I've got to feel that I want to spend two hours of my life with the characters you write.') And to make the endings upbeat. None of the scripts I wrote were made. In hindsight I'm not surprised, but I'm still saddened as I think I did some good writing in those years.

Finally, lofty claims are often made for Australian cinema as a mirror of the national life. Is film more important in this respect than any other of the arts?

No, I don't think it is. In fact, given the fact that the competition is so unequal in dollar terms between Australian and American films, both in terms of production and marketing budgets, I don't think we can expect our films to have the same audience reach as Australian television, which competes on more even budgetary terms, or Australian drama, which competes with identical budgets in the state theatre companies. The occasional Australian film will hit a nerve and say something that's important to our sense of who we are, but the fact that only four per cent of the audience last year went to Australian films indicates that the power of the Australian film industry as a mirror of national life has been somewhat oversold. Australian novels and poetry, competing on more equal terms than film, also get a much greater market share than film.

THIS INTERVIEW WAS CONDUCTED BY PETER ROSE.

Australia's most famous racehorse may have seemed a natural for screen treatment, but the fact that everyone knows its sad, if mysterious, ending perhaps robs it of some of its dramatic potential. Nevertheless, Wincer has given the film a peculiarly Australian appeal, as a result of which Phar Lap becomes identified with the myth of the 'Aussie battler', as does his trainer, Harry Telford. The film was popular here but, despite a sympathetic script by David •Williamson, beautifully muted camera work from Russell •Boyd, and a strong cast (Ron Liebman is especially astute as a sceptical American magnate), the film failed to repeat this success overseas.

Most of Wincer's subsequent work has been in the USA, where he has directed a range of genre movies with no special distinction: for example, **D.A.R.Y.L.** (1985), a science-fiction comedy; the agreeable boy-and-animal film, **Free Willy** (1993); and **The Phantom** (1996), based on the famous action comic-strip and shot largely in Australia. In Australia he made the visually striking but too leisurely •**The Lighthorsemen** (1987), in which he allowed too many disparate plot strands to divert attention from the central military action; and •**Quigley** (1991), an outback adventure with overseas stars Tom Selleck and Alan Rickman. The unsuccessful western **Lightning Jack** (1994) is another attempt to capitalise on Paul •Hogan's charisma, and is now remembered, if at all, as the first film financed by the floating of a public company on the stock exchange. Investors are unlikely to grow rich. BMcF

Winkler, Paul (1939–) DIRECTOR

Paul Winkler was born in Hamburg and migrated to Australia in 1959. He was a bricklayer, who continued with his craft, specialising in brick arches and cellars for trendy homes in inner Sydney, where he attended screenings and discussions at the Film-makers Co-operative Cinema. He made his first film in 1962, starting with 8mm silent film, then adding sound in 1964, moving to 16mm in 1967, and settling on his standard 16mm colour film from 1968. He employs the full range of avant-garde techniques, but is particularly noted for his use of mattes. His work is held in collections in the USA, Canada, Germany, and Belgium, as well as Australia, and has been frequently exhibited overseas, where audiences seem more attuned to its formal qualities, disorienting rhythmic compositions, and confrontational poetics. Among his better-known works are **Dark** (1973–74), **Brickwall** (1975), **Sydney Harbour Bridge** (1977), **Glitter** (1990), and **Green Canopy** (1994). A filmography to 1994 was included in the volume published for the retrospective presented by the Museum of Contemporary Art, Sydney 1994 (*Paul Winkler, Films 1964–94*).

Other Australian films include: Capillary Action (1998). IB

Winter of Our Dreams

1981. *Director*: John Duigan. *Producer*: Richard Mason. *Scriptwriter*: John Duigan. *Director of photography*: Tom Cowan. *Music*: Sharon Calcraft. 89 min. *Cast*: Judy Davis (Lou), Bryan Brown (Rob), Cathy Downes (Gretel), Baz Luhrmann (Pete), Peter Mochrie (Tim).

Early in his career, director–writer John •Duigan made several small-scale realist dramas of urban life, including •**Mouth to Mouth** (1978) and this film, set in inner-suburban Sydney, moving between the sophisticated, liberal middle-classes and those whose world is closer to the edge. Lou, a Kings Cross prostitute and drug-taker, forces bookshop-owner Rob to reconsider the premises on which his life functions when she enters his life after the suicide of Lisa, a mutual friend. Rob has long put behind him his days as a university militant, the context in which he knew Lisa, but Lou's uncompromising directness gets under the skin of his complacency. The film is not schematic in its approach to these two characters; its view of them is complex enough to resist this. Rob's 'open marriage' to Gretel is not pilloried for its agreeable comforts and Lou's street life is not sentimentalised, but the film is humanely concerned about the brutal divisions of such a society, and has finely detailed performances from Judy •Davis and Bryan •Brown in the leading roles. BMcF

Witcombe, Eleanor (1923–) WRITER

In an era that produced several unremarkable films from literary works, Eleanor Witcombe's adaptations of Henry Handel Richardson's •**The Getting of Wisdom** (1977) and Miles Franklin's •**My Brilliant Career** (1979) were arguably not only the most important but also the most successful. The narrative coherence of **My Brilliant Career** arguably exceeds that of the book, but perhaps more importantly its portrayal of Sybylla managed to combine the spirit of the original character with twentieth-century feminist sensibilities. While remaining faithful to the novels, both films achieved the rare quality of working equally on both a cinematic and dramatic level.

Born in South Australia, Witcome attended the National Art School in Sydney. Her interest in theatre led to early commissions to write children's plays, after which she moved to London, where she worked for the BBC. After returning to Australia, where she founded the Australian Theatre for Young People, she became a leading writer of radio drama, which she continued alongside her work in television. This included *Number 96* and *The Mavis Bramston Show*, but more memorably her adaptations of *Pastures of the Blue Crane* and *Seven Little Australians*. She also co-wrote the miniseries *Water Under the Bridge*. Witcombe has been involved in various projects in the USA, including a film about Daisy Bates (with Katharine Hepburn), which was abandoned because of Hepburn's ill-health, and a Paramount commission on a miniseries about the life of Baby Doe. She precedes Laura •Jones as the pre-eminent Australian scriptwriter of adaptations.   HARRY KIRCHNER

With Love to the Person Next to Me

1987. Director: Brian McKenzie. *Producer:* John Cruthers. *Scriptwriter:* Brian McKenzie. *Director of photography:* Ray Argall. 98 min. *Cast:* Kim Gyngell (Wallace), Sally McKenzie (Gail), Paul Chubb (Syd), Barry Dickins (Bodger), Terry Gill (Security Guard).

Wallace drives taxis at night and makes apple cider during the day in his run-down flat in the bayside Melbourne suburb of St Kilda in this low-key 'slice of life' from documentary film-maker Brian McKenzie. Wallace, estranged from his country girlfriend, is a repressed voyeur who experiences life mainly through the people who hire his taxi. During the day Wallace listens to their conversations, which he has secretly taped. Life, however, starts to impinge directly on him when neighbours Syd and Bodger, a couple of inept thieves, force him to participate in one of their robberies. After Syd and Bodger are arrested Wallace forms a tentative relationship with Gail, Syd's ex-girlfriend.

This is an intriguing, low-budget film, with skilful performances from Kim •Gyngell, Sally McKenzie and Paul •Chubb. It captures the futility and squalor of Wallace's world without sentimentality or condescension. McKenzie plays with the temporal presentation of the events to emphasise both the monotony and the significance of the customers, and their lives, to Wallace. There is, however, no dramatic pay-off in the film as McKenzie, unlike Scorsese in **Taxi Driver** (1976), steadfastly refuses to provide a resolution to any of the film's narrative strands.   GM

Withers, Googie (1917–) ACTOR

One of the great stars of British cinema in its heyday of the 1940s and 1950s, Indian-born Googie Withers has had a long connection with Australia following her marriage to John •McCallum. They have worked together in Australian theatre since the mid 1950s, alternating with stage and television appearances in the United Kingdom. Her most notable British films include **On Approval** (1944), **Pink String and Sealing Wax** (1945), and **It Always Rains on Sunday** (1948), in which she showed a remarkable sensual boldness, unusual in the cinema of the time. Sadly, she has made only three films in Australia: •**Nickel Queen** (1971, d. McCallum), as a Western Australian pub proprietor at the time of the mining boom of the late 1960s; •**Country Life** (1994), Michael •Blakemore's underrated reworking of Chekhov's *Uncle Vanya* set on an outback cattle station; and Scott Hicks's

Googie Withers in **Nickel Queen** (1971)

•**Shine** (1996), in which she gave a warmly sympathetic account of Katharine Susannah Prichard, mentor to the young David Helfgott.   BMcF

Woman Suffers—While the Man Goes Free, The

1918. Director: Raymond Longford. *Cinematographer:* Arthur Higgins. *Script, Art direction, Editor:* Lottie Lyell. 76 min. B&W. Reconstruction circa 1991. *Reconstruction:* Marilyn Dooley, *Video:* Erik Liepins, *Conductor:* Donald Hollier, *Sound recording:* Wanda Lazar. *Cast:* Boyd Irwin (Phillip Masters), Connie Martyn (Marion Masters), Paul Baxter (Little Phillip), C.R. Stanford (John Stockdale), Ida Gresham (his wife), Evelyn Black (Joan), Chas H. Francis (Stephen Manton), Roland Conway (Ralph), Lottie Lyell (Marjory).

This film was inspired by scandalous newspaper accounts of pregnant single women committing suicide to avoid dishonour. The story focuses on Phillip Masters's desire to avenge his sister's suicide by involving her lover's sister in a similar scenario of seduction and betrayal. This convoluted melodrama relies on coincidence and unfolds in cycles of seduction and revenge where marriage represents the ultimate resolution. These melodramatic excesses are counterpoised with 'actuality' footage. Raymond •Longford incorporates scenes from the 1917 Melbourne Cup,

In conversation with

GOOGIE WITHERS

John McCallum participates in this interview: his contributions are given in square brackets.

Why have you made only three films in Australia when there were so many more you could have made?

No, there were no more I could have made. There wasn't one film when I thought, 'My God! I should have played that part, or I would have been good in that', because they're all intensely Australian, and I'm not an Australian and I find it very difficult to act one. I stand out as an English woman, and they don't think of me as being an Australian. I've only played one Australian part and it was a desperate flop. It was a play that I did for John [•McCallum] when he was with Williamsons, and they had been badgering him to put on an Australian play. Then one came along that seemed not bad, but we had to juggle it a bit so that I was the English wife of an Australian man who owned a big property, and when he died I had to run it. It was called *Desire of the Moth* and it was absolutely slated, and I realised then I really can't play an Australian woman.

But you did Katherine Susannah Pritchard with, not a strong, but a very convincing Australian accent in •Shine.

I worked very hard at it but I had very little to do. I had a voice coach who helped me with my accent. I was forced into it because, when I took the part, the idea that I was going to do the accent never occurred to me. Everybody knows her by her work and her name, but I doubt if many people had ever heard her speak, except maybe at a meeting or something like that. Therefore I said, 'Does it matter if I have an English voice?' and the producers didn't seem to think it mattered. But Mr Ric Throssell did. I phoned him and said, 'Do you know I'm playing your mother?' and he said, 'Yes and you're absolutely miscast. I don't mean you yourself; I'm a great admirer of your work. But you don't sound like an Australian woman, you sound like an English woman'. I said, 'With all due respect to your mother I very much doubt if anybody knows what her voice sounded like, so it doesn't really matter'. Then I said, 'Let's forget that for the moment, and let me just get from you a little bit of her history, the way she dressed, and how she behaved and all the rest of it', and he gave

me the most wonderful clues. He had no idea he was doing it but for me it was tremendous. He said she always wore black velvet trousers, high red-heeled shoes, and smoked constantly out of a short cigarette holder—and, I mean, there she was in front of me and he didn't know that he'd given me this, because he was only nine or 10 when she died. Anyway, having heard all of this, I asked the producer and the director, 'Do you think I should try an Australian accent, I'm really not awfully good at it?', and they said, 'We'll get somebody down on the set to go through the lines with you'. And so we did. I tried it out and it was all right, but I don't think I could really support a large part playing an Australian woman.

What was your experience of working with director Scott •Hicks and with Noah •Taylor?

I liked Scott very much; I thought he was an excellent director. I did very little with him but I was extremely impressed. I haven't really often come across directors that I think are marvellous; I think most directors leave it up to you and are much more interested in the shot and how they're going to shoot it, but Scott Hicks wasn't like this. I was fascinated. I knew that I was playing a well-known woman, not just a character written in, but this woman meant nothing to me, I'd never heard of her. In fact, in the scene where she first appears, I think they might have said something like, 'I want you to meet a very famous writer', because I don't think it's clear who she is at that point, and a lot of people wouldn't have heard of her.

What about •Country Life which I like, but I think you don't?

I did quite like it, but I hated going from having played up until then the rather glamorous parts to suddenly playing this old crow! The first time I saw the rushes, I said, 'God Almighty I'm never going to look at another one again!', and I could hardly watch myself on that screen. Michael •Blakemore [director] and Robin Dalton [producer] phoned me in England and said, 'You've got to be brave!'. I replied, 'What do you mean "brave"?'. I think I've seen that play [*Uncle Vanya*] a hundred times and the old nurse is quite a pleasant little old woman, she's not this grotesque creature that they made me in to. It was the first time I'd seen myself looking 148 on the screen and that threw me.

Where was it filmed?
Just outside Maitland. It was dreadfully hot, it was very unpleasant, but I was living in a very nice comfortable motel. Michael Blakemore was incommunicado with all of us the whole time. He just came home and went straight upstairs to his room. He did much too much: he directed, he played the main part, and he'd written it! That's too much for any one man to do.

Working backwards through your Australian film career what do you remember of •Nickel Queen?
I loved **Nickel Queen**, I loved the location, and I thought the part was fun. I didn't have to look an old

bag in that. She'd made a fortune and she had John Laws as her lover, and it was all frightfully flash. [John McCallum—It is a museum piece because of having John Laws' only film appearance.] He played the hippie who was living on the station with all these little hippie girls, and then suddenly he picked me up, or I picked him up, and we go off together, and he suddenly arrives shaved and looking like John Laws looked 30 years ago.

[John McCallum—You know that that film was just made for entertainment and fun, and the critics took it too seriously, as though it should be a very dramatic piece of work. It's not meant to be; it's just about some hippies who come into a mining town in WA, and it was quite funny.]

THIS INTERVIEW WAS CONDUCTED BY BRIAN MCFARLANE.

featuring parts of the race and observational shots of the enormous crowds at Flemington Racecourse.

Controversy followed the film's 1918 premiere. It was banned after only two weeks of exhibition. Some suggest that this was due to a veiled reference to abortion, a scene that remained in the script and was never shot, but Longford suspected forces in the industry of conspiring to undermine his career.

Longford and Lottie •Lyell's film was rediscovered in 1983 during the Australian Film and Sound Archive's drive to recover early Australian films. Sixty-five years of neglect resulted in severe damage to the nitrate film stock. To contend with this degeneration, archive staff made some changes to the video version. Intertitles were added for narrative cohesion and sequences were tinted with food colouring to resemble original tints. The recovery and reconstruction of **The Woman Suffers** fills a gap in our understanding of Longford's place in Australian film history.   WENDY HASLEM

Woman's Tale, A

1991. Director: Paul Cox. *Producers:* Paul Cox, Santhana Naidu. *Scriptwriters:* Paul Cox, Barry Dickins. *Director of photography:* Nino Martinelli. *Music:* Paul Grabowsky. 93 min. *Cast:* Sheila Florance (Martha), Gosia Dobrowolska (Anna), Norman Kaye (Billy), Chris Haywood (Jonathan), Ernest Gray (Peter), Myrtle Woods (Miss Inchley).

A Woman's Tale is the story of Martha, a dying woman who is passionate about life. While we are made aware of her physical decay, Paul •Cox foregrounds her determination to remain independent. Martha must contend with her son

Jonathan's desire to remove her to a nursing home, and the constant evidence of familial neglect that affects her invalid neighbour, Billy. She adores her nurse, Anna, encouraging her affair with a married man, and welcoming their expression of love within her home. While the film concludes with Martha's death, one gains a distinct sense of the dignified way she lived her life.

This portrayal of a woman's tenacious resistance to assumptions about the aged is beautifully directed. Cox's use of slow motion during points of crisis or contemplation creates a remarkable atmosphere. The surreal dream-vision of Martha's pale face staring through bare trees is hauntingly evocative. Sheila •Florance herself died a few months after the film's completion.   MELINDA HILDEBRANDT

Women in Film and Television

This community-based organisation aims to promote the profile and participation of women in screen-based media industries. Women in Film and Television (WIFT) primarily functions as a networking organisation, facilitating the exchange of information between members working in film, television, video, and new-media technologies. WIFT further aims to improve the status and representation of women on the screen as part of encouraging a diverse screen culture.

State WIFT organisations first emerged in NSW in 1982, in Vic. in 1982 (although it was incorporated and formally launched in 1988), in WA in 1983, and in SA and Qld in 1992. The original focus was on providing networking opportunities for women in the film and television industry by way of seminars, screenings, and newsletters. By 1990, this focus was broadened to include professional-development training, job referral services, career forums, and national conferences.

In September 1993, WIFT Australia was launched with the intention that state organisations would collaborate on issues of national importance. Representing over 1000 women, WIFT Australia comprised two member-delegates from each of the state bodies. Before winding up in 1998, it was responsible for national initiatives focusing on the impact of new-media technologies on women in film, television, video, and related media industries. State-based WIFT organisations continue to operate with the support of member volunteers, industry sponsorship, and intermittent federal- and state-government funding.

SUE MASLIN

Wood, John (1946–) ACTOR   John Wood's career in film has been largely peripheral to his success as a television performer (*Rafferty's Rules, Blue Heelers*) and stage actor. Only a lead role in his first film, •**The Office Picnic** (1972), and supporting roles in the crime thriller •**The Empty Beach** (1985) and the outback comedy **Bullseye** (1986), together with an energetic performance as Sir Toby Belch in the adaptation of •**Twelfth Night** (1987), have offered Wood screen opportunities of any substance.

Other Australian films include: Blue Fire Lady (1977), Ginger Meggs (1982), Displaced Persons (1985).   GM

Wood, Ross (1916–80) CINEMATOGRAPHER   Ross Wood edited **Red Sky at Morning** (1945), then acted as director of photography on **Strong is the Seed** (1949), and as camera operator on •**Bitter Springs** (1950). In the 1950s he was the most prolific Australian cinematographer, producing what Graham Shirley has called 'vivid, adventurous' camera work on •**Captain Thunderbolt** (1953), and continuing with •**King of the Coral Sea** (1954, with J. Jackson), •**The Back of Beyond** (1954), and •**Three in One** (1957). But this was a lean period for indigenous production, and, on the co-produced features, Australian technicians were required to take a back seat, as Wood did on **Long John Silver** (1954, camera operator with Carl •Kayser, under Carl Guthrie), •**Smiley** and **Smiley Gets a Gun** (1956 and 1958, both camera operator under Edward Scaife), and •**On the Beach** (1959, camera operator under Giuseppe Rotunno). He founded the Sydney-based company Ross Wood Productions, which made many documentaries in the 1950s and 1960s, some for the Shell Film Unit. He was one of the army of cameramen on the •Commonwealth Film Unit's **The Queen in Australia** (1954) and won the Kodak Award in 1969 for the short film **And Then There Was Glass**. Ross Wood's brother Syd (1914–1983) was a newsreel cameraman with **Movietone News** from 1931 to 1965: Ross and Syd were the

models for the two brothers in Phillip •Noyce's feature film •**Newsfront** (1978). Ross Wood Productions invested in the feature film •**Stone** (1974) and, after Wood's death, an annual Australian Cinematographers Society Ross Wood Award for cinematographic innovation was instituted in his honour. The company continued after 1980, under the direction of Ross Wood Jnr.   IB

Worth, Constance *see* Howarth, Jocelyn

Wright, Geoffrey (1959–)   A product of Melbourne's •Swinburne Film School, Geoffrey Wright, despite only having completed three features to date, has forged a strong reputation in the Australian film industry for both his films and public persona. Wright's public comments have largely been directed at the critics of his films and the film industry more generally, especially on the release of his second film: the confronting and problematic •**Romper Stomper** (1992). As with **Romper Stomper,** Wright's other feature releases in Australia—**Lover Boy** (1988) and **Metal Skin** (1994)—are set in Melbourne's western suburbs, and feature torrid, gritty narratives that focus on young working-class men caught in impossible relationships with little hope of escaping their nihilistic futures.

These films, especially **Romper Stomper** and **Metal Skin,** are rendered in a confronting amalgam of cinematic styles ranging from the 'in your face' social realism of docudrama to the excesses of the modern video clip. This combination of fatalistic unrelenting narrative and Wright's aesthetic dexterity aims to present a psychologically authentic view of Australian culture as it is experienced by those who are marginalised by or alternatively trade in the social dislocation of unemployment, youth alienation, violence, and blatant racism. These concerns in Wright's films are often compounded by his outspoken public persona when he takes on public advocacy of his films and their concerns, as both a product of a working-class background himself and commentator on the social environment portrayed in his films.

Wright's success with **Romper Stomper,** particularly, established his credibility as a writer and director both here and overseas, and has been his passport to the international film industry.   JOHN BENSON

Wrong Side of the Road

1981. *Director*: Ned Lander, *Producers and Writers*: Ned Lander, Graeme Isaac, *Director of photography*: Louis Irving. *Art director*: Jan Mackay, *Cast*: Bart Willoughby (Bart), Chris Jones (Ricky), John Miller (John), Leslie Graham (Les), Veronica Rankine (Vonnie). 79 min.

Wrong Side of the Road focuses on the members and crew of No Fixed Address and Us Mob, bands that originated at the Centre for Aboriginal Studies in Music. The film is essentially a social-realist drama. It also contains elements of the documentary, road movie, and musical. Ned Lander's allegorical narrative is drawn from life stories. Scripted lines and improvised dialogue produce an episodic chronicle that is distinguished by non-actors and a polyphony of voices.

With polemical lyrics and a rhythmic reggae background, the music of both bands is the dominant force in the film, often providing respite from aggressive verbal collisions. The performance of music symbolises unity; this is best represented in Aunty Veronica's kitchen, where sweet voices sing nostalgic harmonies as she taps out the rhythm with a pair of spoons. This contrasts with the cold, obstructive language of White authority figures. The drama concludes without resolution; issues raised have currency long after the credits roll. **Wrong Side of the Road** was awarded the Jury Prize at the 1981 Australian Film Institute Awards.

WENDY HASLEM

Year My Voice Broke, The

1987. Director: John Duigan. *Producers*: Terry Hayes, Doug Mitchell, Dr George Miller. *Scriptwriter*: John Duigan. *Director of photography*: Geoff Burton. 105 min. *Cast*: Noah Taylor (Danny), Loene Carmen (Freya), Ben Mendelsohn (Trevor), Graeme Blundell (Nils Olson), Lynette Curran (Anne Olson).

New Australian cinema (see Revival, The) established the coming-of-age film (see Rites of passage) as a sub-genre in the 1970s and 1980s, but the effect was usually more nostalgic in tone than is the case in **The Year My Voice Broke**. Director-writer John •Duigan's film is a more abrasive experience than most, beginning with its austere setting in the harshly beautiful southern tablelands of NSW, signalling that this will be a less cosy experience than most of the films set in the recent past, and focusing on more seriously painful teenage emotions than many other such films. Danny (the compelling, idiosyncratic Noah •Taylor) dotes on his childhood friend Freya (newcomer Loene Carmen), but must face the truth that she has fallen in love with the older local tearaway Trevor (Ben •Mendelsohn, ubiquitous star of Australian cinema since the late 1980s). Danny attaches himself to the pair in ways that can only bring heartache, and the film does not flinch from this. The rawness of adolescence is intensified by the constraints of the small town and by the metaphysical significance of the deserted house on the hill, once the home, it transpires, of Freya's prostitute mother. In 1991, Duigan wrote and directed •**Flirting**, a sequel to the film; three years later, Danny is now in the confines of a boarding school and in the grip of another adolescent passion, this time with the daughter of a black African nationalist who, for different reasons, is also an outsider.   BMcF

Year of Living Dangerously, The

1982. Director: Peter Weir. *Producer*: Jim McElroy. *Scriptwriters*: David Williamson, Peter Weir, C.J. Koch. Based on the novel by C.J. Koch. *Director of photography*: Russell Boyd. *Music*: Maurice Jarre. 117 min. *Cast*: Mel Gibson (Guy Hamilton), Sigourney Weaver (Jill Bryant), Linda Hunt (Billy Kwan), Bill Kerr (Colonel Henderson), Noel Ferrier (Wally O'Sullivan).

This was a watershed film for Peter •Weir: he had been perhaps the most striking talent of the new Australian cinema in the 1970s, and this thriller, set in the politically turbulent Indonesia of the 1960s, marks his transition to international film-making. His subsequent career has been based in the USA, and this film, distributed by MGM, looks forward to a new phase of glossier, more assured, often melodramatic film-making by Weir. C.J. Koch's novel makes much more of the political turmoil in post-colonial Indonesia than does the film, charting an aborted left-wing coup that is followed, in turn, by the installation of a new right-wing leader, Suharto. In Weir's film, based mainly on a screenplay by David •Williamson (an earlier version by Koch himself had been found unsatisfactory), the love story between Guy, an Australian journalist, and Jill, a British Embassy official, is given greater prominence, partly through the sheer star power of the actors, but also partly through the deliberate subduing of the political events to the level of exotic background. The affair is also highlighted through the performance of Bill Kerr as Jill's superior, who is in love with her, and that of diminutive American actor Linda Hunt, in the Oscar-winning role of Billy Kwan, the Chinese dwarf who is infatuated with Jill. As a love story, the film is appealing: the relationships are vividly portrayed, set against the backdrop of a world in turmoil, and the tale rises to a strong, romantic closure that had not previously been characteristic of Weir's films.   BMcF

Mel Gibson in **The Year of Living Dangerously**

Year of the Dogs

1997. Director: Michael Cordell. *Producer*: Michael Cordell. *Director of photography*: Michael Cordell. *Music*: Scott Saunders. 89 min.

This documentary is a behind-the-scenes look at the misfortunes of the Footscray Football Club, a battling Australian Rules football team based in the western suburbs of Melbourne. The film follows the fortunes of the club throughout the 1996 season. Michael Cordell was provided with access to areas of a football club that are normally hidden from the media, and the documentary provides a moving, penetrating examination of the pressures imposed on players, administrators, coaches, and even supporters. These pressures are epitomised in a scene in the coaching box early in the season: coach Alan Joyce makes repeated attempts to wipe the sweat from his forehead as his team commits mistake after mistake. Except for excerpts from a handful of key games, Cordell concentrates on the internal workings of the club, punctuated by scenes depicting the reaction of two ardent supporters, a mother and daughter, who attend every game and most training sessions.

Unlike media reporting of Australian Rules football, Cordell is able to capture the real pain and emotion that is the intangible quality of football clubs. Each group portrayed in the film has a slightly different motivation for wanting the club to succeed. For the players, it is their feelings for each other: for example, in the final game of the season they play well beyond expectations as a tribute to their retiring captain, Steve Wallis. The level of physical stress is also carefully documented: the film shows, mainly through the recurring injuries suffered by the player Danny Southern, the physical price that the game exacts.

In a revealing sequence near the end of the film, coach Wallace and his staff plan for the next season: highlighting the fact that everybody is ultimately disposable in this industry, and that individual players only have limited tenure at the club, it is decided the player Tony Liberatore, who epitomises the tenacity of this battling club, will be dropped from the team. Liberatore's playing life is extended at the end of the season when he agrees to sacrifice 50 per cent of his salary. As Australian Rules football continues to lose its Victorian suburban roots and moves relentlessly into the world of network-television sport, corporate money, draft selections and interstate loyalties, Cordell's documentary captures the final moments of a club that represented the dreams of a specific geographical socio-economic group for nearly 100 years. At the end of the season, in keeping with a corporate decision to change the image of the club, the name of the team is lost forever, replaced by the more marketable 'Western Bulldogs'.

GM

You Can't See Around Corners

1969. Director: David Cahill. *Producer*: Peter Summerton. *Scriptwriter*: Richard Lane. Based on the novel by Jon Cleary. *Director of photography*: Graham Lind. *Music*: Tommy Tycho. 98 min. *Cast*: Ken Shorter (Frankie McCoy), Rowena Wallace (Margie Harris), Carmen Duncan (Myra Neilson), Judith Fisher (Peg Clancy), Lyndall Barbour (Mrs McCoy), Slim de Grey (Mick Patterson).

Jon Cleary's novel was first published in 1947. Although the film updates the story to the 1960s, it avoids politics, and is basically a somewhat naive and naturalistic rites-of-passage film. Frankie McCoy is conscripted, then deserts: he is a loser, whose problems escalate from owing money, to petty crime, to accidentally killing a woman he has picked up in Kings Cross, to being himself accidentally killed. The story was first produced as a 26-episode serial by the Seven television network in 1967, then as a cinema feature by the same team. The cost of $60 000 was modest even for the time. The film broke box-office records in Perth and went on to be modestly successful in the eastern states and on Australian television, although critics called it conventional and predictable.   IB

Young, Aden (1973–) ACTOR   Canadian-born Aden Young's Australian film credits are quite prolific. His role as a seventeenth-century Jesuit priest in Bruce •Beresford's **Black Robe** (1991) introduced Australian audiences to this brooding actor with classic good looks. Young's film credits are noted for their diversity: his performances have ranged from the tormented exile in Paul •Cox's **Exile** (1994) to the man obsessed with his machine in Geoffrey •Wright's bizarre **Metal Skin** (1994). Young's repertoire has also included the comedies **River Street** (1996), in which he plays a spoilt and desensitised real-estate agent forced to work at a halfway house for troubled youth, and the ill-fated **Hotel de Love** (1996), opposite Simon Bossell: as twins, they compete to win the heart of the same girl.
Other Australian films include: **Over the Hill** (1992), **Shotgun Wedding** (1992), **Love in Limbo** (1993), •**Broken Highway** (1994), •**Cosi** (1996), •**Paradise Road** (1997).

KAREN FORD

Young, Bob (1923–) COMPOSER   Bob Young, (known as 'Beetles') has been a prolific composer for television shows and has also written scores for feature films, the Commonwealth Film Unit (see Film Australia), animated features, telemovies, and television series. He has enjoyed a long association with the film and television industries. Young became interested in television after its inception in 1956, and was musical director and arranger with Sydney's Channel 9 program *Bandstand* for 13 years. Later, Young worked on three Channel 7 programs: *The Dave Allen*

Aden Young in **Black Robe** (1991)

Young Einstein

Show, The True Blue Show, and *The Mike Willesee Show.*
Between 1967 and 1971, when production of Australian feature films had virtually ceased, Young worked on a number of American co-productions that had little box-office appeal: •**Journey Out of Darkness** (1967), **Adam's Woman** (1970) (also featuring his theme song), and **It Takes all Kinds** (1969) (which included a song sung by John Farnham). His animated feature films, which target young audiences, have been more recognised, and some of these Yoram Gross productions remain in video stores today. They include •**Dot and the Kangaroo** (1977), **The Little Convict** (1979), and **Dot and the Koala** (1985). Among Young's awards is the 1976 Sammy Award for the telemovie *Is There Anybody There?*   DIANE NAPTHALI

Young Einstein

1988. *Director:* Yahoo Serious. *Producers:* Yahoo Serious, Warwick Ross, David Roach. *Scriptwriters:* Yahoo Serious, David Roach. *Director of photography:* Jeff 'Ace' Darling. *Music:* William Motzing, Martin Armiger, Tommy Tycho. 91 min. *Cast:* Yahoo Serious (Albert Einstein), Odile Le Clezio (Marie Curie) John Howard (Preston Preston), Peewee Wilson (Mr Einstein), Su Cruickshank (Mrs Einstein).

Like the best science fiction, this story asks 'What if . . . ?' But this is broad comedy, so that question is complicated by outrageous anachronisms: What if Albert Einstein had been born on an apple orchard in Tasmania? And what if he put the bubbles in beer and invented rock 'n' roll and made the first surfboard? And what if his companion in saving the world from nuclear disaster was Marie Curie? The result is an enjoyable romp, as chaotic and unpredictable as its main character. Odile le Clezio as Marie is a delightful foil, wise and feisty, unfazed by Albert's electrified hair or his anti-social habits. This was Yahoo Serious's first feature film, and he directs with a verve and passion that is matched by his central performance: it does not always work, but at its best it sings. The critics were divided, but the public loved it.

IB

Z

Zuanic, Rod (1968–) ACTOR   Rod Zuanic was born in France and came to Australia at the age of five with his Slavic parents. In 1984 Australian director Ken •Cameron was searching schools in the western suburbs of Sydney looking for a feisty teenager for his social realist drama •**Fast Talking** (1984). Zuanic was selected for the lead role of Stephen George Carson, the doomed youth whose mechanic friend (Steve •Bisley) tries unsuccessfully to steer Carson away from a criminal career. After this eye-catching acting debut, Zuanic alternated between supporting roles in Australian feature films (such as •**Mad Max: Beyond Thunderdome**, 1985; **The Place at the Coast**, 1987; •**Warm Nights on a Slow Moving Train**, 1988; and •**The Tale of Ruby Rose**, 1988) and television programs such as *Special Squad, Fast Lane, Cody, Water Rats*, and *Big Sky*. Zuanic also had a featured part in Cameron's telemovie *Crime of the Decade* (1984), which also focused on romance and unemployment as it affects youths in the outer suburbs.   GM

APPENDIX 1: AUSTRALIAN FILM INSTITUTE (AFI) AWARD WINNERS (FIRST PRIZE ONLY)

AFI Award Winners: Feature Films

GRAND PRIX* (1958–75)

Year	Film	Producer/Co-producers	Director
1963	Adam and Eve	Dusan Marek	Dusan Marek
1970	Three to Go: Michael	Gil Brealey	Peter Weir
1971	Homesdale	Richard Brennan, Grahame Bond	Peter Weir

* Note that the Grand Prix prize was awarded not every year, but on a discretionary basis.

BEST FILM

Year	Film	Producer/Co-producers	Director
1976	The Devil's Playground	Fred Schepisi	Fred Schepisi
1977	Storm Boy	Matt Carroll	Henri Safran
1978	Newsfront	David Elfick	Philip Noyce
1979	My Brilliant Career	Margaret Fink	Gillian Armstrong
1980	'Breaker' Morant	Matt Carroll	Bruce Beresford
1981	Gallipoli	Pat Lovell, Robert Stigwood	Peter Weir
1982	Lonely Hearts	John B. Murray	Paul Cox
1983	Careful, He Might Hear You	Jill Robb	Carl Schultz
1984	Annie's Coming Out	Don Murray	Gil Brealey
1985	Bliss	Tony Buckley	Ray Lawrence
1986	Malcolm	David Parker	Nadia Tass
1987	The Year My Voice Broke	Terry Hayes, George Miller, Doug Mitchell	John Duigan
1988	The Navigator	John Maynard	Vincent Ward
1989	Evil Angels	Verity Lambert	Fred Schepisi
1990	Flirting	George Miller, Doug Mitchell, Terry Hayes	John Duigan
1991	Proof	Lynda House	Jocelyn Moorehouse
1992	Strictly Ballroom	Tristram Miall	Baz Luhrmann
1993	The Piano	Jan Chapman	Jane Campion
1994	Muriel's Wedding	Lynda House, Jocelyn Moorhouse	P.J. Hogan
1995	Angel Baby	Timothy White, Jonathan Shteinman	Michael Rymer

1996	Shine	Jane Scott	Scott Hicks
1997	Kiss or Kill	Bill Bennett, Jennifer Bennett	Bill Bennett
1998	The Interview	Bill Hughes	Craig Monahan

BEST ACHIEVEMENT IN DIRECTION

Year	Director	Film
1971	Peter Weir	Homesdale
1972	Tim Burstall	Stork
1973	Eric Porter	Marco Polo Junior Versus the Red Dragon
1974/5	John Power	Billy and Percy
1976	Fred Schepisi	The Devil's Playground
1977	Bruce Beresford	Don's Party
1978	Philip Noyce	Newsfront
1979	Gillian Armstrong	My Brilliant Career
1980	Bruce Beresford	'Breaker' Morant
1981	Peter Weir	Gallipoli
1982	George Miller	Mad Max 2
1983	Carl Schultz	Careful, He Might Hear You
1984	Paul Cox	My First Wife
1985	Ray Lawrence	Bliss
1986	Nadia Tass	Malcolm
1987	John Duigan	The Year My Voice Broke
1988	Vincent Ward	The Navigator
1989	Fred Schepisi	Evil Angels
1990	Ray Argall	Return Home
1991	Jocelyn Moorhouse	Proof
1992	Baz Luhrmann	Strictly Ballroom
1993	Jane Campion	The Piano
1994	P.J. Hogan	Muriel's Wedding
1995	Michael Rymer	Angel Baby
1996	Scott Hicks	Shine
1997	Bill Bennett	Kiss or Kill
1998	Rowan Woods	The Boys

BEST PERFORMANCE BY AN ACTOR IN A LEADING ROLE

Year	Actor	Film
1972	Bruce Spence	Stork
1973	Robert McDarra	27A
1974/5	Jack Thompson	Petersen
	Jack Thompson	Sunday Too Far Away
	Martin Vaughn	Billy and Percy
1976	Simon Burke	The Devil's Playground
	Nick Tate	The Devil's Playground
1977	John Meillon	The Fourth Wish
1978	Bill Hunter	Newsfront
1979	Mel Gibson	Tim
1980	Jack Thompson	'Breaker' Morant

1981	Mel Gibson	Gallipoli
1982	Ray Barrett	Goodbye Paradise
1983	Norman Kaye	Man of Flowers
1984	John Hargreaves	My First Wife
1985	Chris Haywood	A Street to Die
1986	Colin Friels	Malcolm
1987	Leo McKern	Travelling North
1988	John Waters	Boulevard of Broken Dreams
1989	Sam Neil	Evil Angels
1990	Max von Sydow	Father
1991	Hugo Weaving	Proof
1992	Russell Crowe	Romper Stomper
1993	Harvey Keitel	The Piano
1994	Nicholas Hope	Bad Boy Baby
1995	John Lynch	Angel Baby
1996	Geoffrey Rush	Shine
1997	Richard Roxburgh	Doing Time for Patsy Cline
1998	Hugo Weaving	The Interview

BEST PERFORMANCE BY AN ACTRESS IN A LEADING ROLE

Year	Actress	Film
1971	Monica Maughan	A City's Child
1972	Jacki Weaver	Stork
1973	Judy Morris	Libido: The Child
1974/5	Julie Dawson	Who Killed Jenny Langby?
1976	Helen Morse	Caddie
1977	Pat Bishop	Don's Party
1978	Angela Punch McGregor	The Chant of Jimmie Blacksmith
1979	Michelle Fawdon	Cathy's Child
1980	Tracy Mann	Hard Knocks
1981	Judy Davis	Winter of Our Dreams
1982	Noni Hazlehurst	Monkey Grip
1983	Wendy Hughes	Careful, he Might Hear You
1984	Angela Punch-McGregor	Annie's Coming Out
1985	Noni Hazlehurst	Fran
1986	Judy Davis	Kangaroo
1987	Judy Davis	High Tide
1988	Nadine Garner	Mullaway
1989	Meryl Streep	Evil Angels
1990	Catherine McClements	Weekend With Kate
1991	Sheila Florance	A Woman's Tale
1992	Lisa Harrow	The Last Days Of Chez Nous
1993	Holly Hunter	The Piano
1994	Toni Collette	Muriel's Wedding
1995	Jacqueline McKenzie	Angel Baby
1996	Judy Davis	Children of the Revolution
1997	Pamela Rabe	The Well
1998	Deborah Mailman	Radiance

BEST PERFORMANCE BY AN ACTOR IN A SUPPORTING ROLE

Year	Actor	Film
1974/5	Barry Humphries	The Great McCarthy
	Reg Lye	Sunday Too Far Away
1976	Drew Forsythe	Caddie
1977	John Ewart	The Picture Show Man
1978	Ray Barrett	The Chant of Jimmie Blacksmith
1979	Alwyn Kurts	Tim
1980	Bryan Brown	'Breaker' Morant
1981	Bill Hunter	Gallipoli
1982	Warren Mitchell	'Norman Loves Rose'
1983	John Hargreaves	Careful, He Might Hear You
1984	Steve Bisley	Silver City
1985	Nique Needles	The Boy Who Had Everything
1986	John Hargreaves	Malcolm
1987	Ben Mendelsohn	The Year My Voice Broke
1988	Kim Gyngell	Boulevard of Broken Dreams
1989	Chris Haywood	Emerald City
1990	Steve Bisley	The Big Steal
1991	Russell Crowe	Proof
1992	Barry Otto	Strictly Ballroom
1993	David Ngoombujarra	Blackfellas
1995	Ray Barrett	Hotel Sorrento
1996	Armin Mueller-Stahl	Shine
1997	Andrew S. Gilbert	Kiss or Kill
1998	John Polson	The Boys

BEST PERFORMANCE BY AN ACTRESS IN A SUPPORTING ROLE

Year	Actress	Film
1976	Melissa Jaffer	Caddie
	Jacki Weaver	Caddie
1977	Veronica Lang	Don's Party
1978	Angela Punch McGregor	Newsfront
1979	Pat Evison	Tim
1980	Jill Perryman	Maybe This Time
1981	Judy Davis	Hoodwink
1982	Kris McQuade	Fighting Back
1983	Linda Hunt	The Year of Living Dangerously
1984	Anna Jemison [Anna Maria Monticelli]	Silver City
1985	Annie Byron	Fran
1986	Lindy Davies	Malcolm
1987	Jan Adele	High Tide
1988	Tina Bursill	Jilted
1989	Victoria Longley	Celia
1990	Julia Blake	Father
1991	Fiona Press	Waiting
1992	Pat Thomson	Strictly Ballroom
1993	Judy Davis	On My Own

1994	Rachel Griffiths	Muriel's Wedding
1995	Amanda Douge	That Eye The Sky
1996	Toni Collette	Lillian's Story
1997	Cate Blanchett	Thank God He Met Lizzie
1998	Toni Collette	The Boys

BEST ACHIEVEMENT IN CINEMATOGRAPHY

Year	Cinematographer	Film
1976	Ian Baker	The Devil's Playground
1977	Russell Boyd	Break of Day
1978	Russell Boyd	The Last Wave
1979	Don McAlpine	My Brilliant Career
1980	Don McAlpine	'Breaker' Morant
1981	Russell Boyd	Gallipoli
1982	Gary Hansen	We of the Never Never
1983	John Seale	Careful, He Might Hear You
1984	Dean Semler	Razorback
1985	Peter James	Rebel
1986	Peter James	The Right Hand Man
1987	Steve Dobson	Ground Zero
1988	Geoffrey Simpson	The Navigator
1989	Dean Semler	Dead Calm
1990	Jeff Darling	The Crossing
1991	Ellery Ryan	Spotswood
1992	Peter James	Black Robe
1993	Stuart Dryburgh	The Piano
1994	Nino Martinetti	Exile
1995	Ellery Ryan	Angel Baby
1996	Geoffrey Simpson	Shine
1997	Andrew Lesnie	Doing Time for Patsy Cline
1998	Geoffrey Simpson	Oscar and Lucinda

BEST ORIGINAL SCREENPLAY

Year	Screenwriter/s	Film
1974/5	David Williamson	Petersen
1976	Fred Schepisi	The Devil's Playground
1977	David Williamson	Don's Party
1978	Anne Brooksbank, Bob Ellis, Philip Noyce	Newsfront
1979	Esben Storm	In Search of Anna
1980	Jonathan Hardy, David Stevens, Bruce Beresford	'Breaker' Morant
1981	David Williamson	Gallipoli
1982	Bob Ellis, Denny Lawrence	Goodbye Paradise
1983	John Dingwall	Buddies
1984	Bob Ellis, Paul Cox	My First Wife
1985	Glenda Hambly	Fran
1986	David Parker	Malcolm

1987	John Duigan	The Year My Voice Broke
1988	No nominations	
1989	Gerard Lee, Jane Campion	Sweetie
1990–92	No nominations	
1993	Jane Campion	The Piano
1994	Rolf de Heer	Bad Boy Bubby
1995	Michael Rymer	Angel Baby
1996	Jan Sardi	Shine
1997	Santo Cilauro, Tom Gleisner, Jane Kennedy, Rob Sitch	The Castle
1998	Craig Monahan, Gordon Davie	The Interview

BEST SCREENPLAY ADAPTED FROM ANOTHER SOURCE

Year	Screenwriter	Film
1978	Eleanor Witcombe	The Getting of Wisdom
1979	Eleanor Witcombe	My Brilliant Career
1980–82	No nominations	
1983	Michael Jenkins	Careful, He Might Hear You
1984	John Patterson, Chris Borthwick	Annie's Coming Out
1985	Peter Carey, Ray Lawrence	Bliss
1986	Bruce and Rhoisin Beresford	The Fringe Dwellers
1987	David Williamson	Travelling North
1988	No nominations	
1989	Robert Caswell, Fred Schepisi	Evil Angels
1990–92	No nominations	
1993	James Ricketson	Blackfellas
1994	David Stevens	The Sum of Us
1995	Richard Franklin, Peter Fitzpatrick	Hotel Sorrento
1996	Louis Nowra	Cosi
1997	Laura Jones	The Well
1998	Stephen Sewell	The Boys

BEST ACHIEVEMENT IN EDITING*

Year	Editor/s	Film
1967		Cardin in Australia
1968	Stefan Sargent	The Change at Groote
1969	Peter Tammer	And Then There Was Glass
1970	Rod Adamson	Big Island
1971	No nominations	
1972	Award withheld	
1973	David Stiven	One Hundred a Day
1974/5	No nominations	
1976	Edward McQueen-Mason	End Play
1977	William Anderson	Don's Party
1978	John Scott	Newsfront
1979	Tony Paterson and Clifford Hayes	Mad Max
1980	William Anderson	'Breaker' Morant
1981	William Anderson	Gallipoli

1982	David Stiven, Tim Wellburn, Michael Balson and Chris Plowright	Mad Max 2
1983	Tony Paterson	Phar Lap
1984	William Anderson	Razorback
1985	Brian Kavanagh	Frog Dreaming
1986	Ken Sallows	Malcolm
1987	David Pulbrook	Ground Zero
1988	John Scott	The Navigator
1989	Richard Francis-Bruce	Dead Calm
1990	Robert Gibson	Flirting
1991	Ken Sallows	Proof
1992	Jill Bilcock	Strictly Ballroom
1993	Veronika Jenet	The Piano
1994	Suresh Ayyar	Bad Boy Bubby
1995	Dany Cooper	Angel Baby
1996	Pip Karmel	Shine
1997	Henry Dangar	Kiss or Kill
1998	Jill Bilcock	Head On

*From 1967–73 this award was known as the Film Editors Guild of Australia Award.

BEST ORIGINAL MUSIC SCORE

Year	Composer/s	Film
1974/5	Bruce Smeaton	The Cars that Ate Paris
	Bruce Smeaton	The Great McCarthy
1976	No nominations	
1977	Peter Best	The Picture Show Man
1978	Bruce Smeaton	The Chant of Jimmie Blacksmith
1979	Brian May	Mad Max
1980	Peter Sculthorpe	Manganinnie
1981	Rory O'Donoghue, Grahame Bond	Fatty Finn
1982	Bruce Rowland	The Man from Snowy River
1983	Bruce Rowland	Phar Lap
1984	Garth Porter, Bruce Smeaton	Street Hero
1985	Ray Cook, Chris Neal, Peter Best, Bruce Rowland, Bill Byers	Rebel
1986	William Motzing, Martin Armiger	Malcolm
1987	Paul Schutze	The Tale of Ruby Rose
1988	Mario Millo	The Lighthorsemen
1989	Graeme Revell	Dead Calm
1990	Phil Judd	The Big Steel
1991	Michel Legrand, Miles Davis	Dingo
1992	John Clifford White	Romper Stomper
1993	Michael Nyman	The Piano
1994	Douglas Stephen Rae	Traps
1995	Peter Best	Dad And Dave: On Our Selection
1996	David Hirschfelder	Shine
1997	Peter Best	Doing Time for Patsy Cline
1998	Thomas Newman	Oscar and Lucinda

BEST ACHIEVEMENT IN SOUND

Year	Sound department	Film
1977	William Anderson	Don's Party
1978	Don Connelly, Greg Bell, Phil Judd	The Last Wave
1979	Gary Wilkins, Byron Kennedy, Roger Savage, Ned Dawson	Mad Max
1980	Gary Wilkins, William Anderson, Jeanine Chialvo, Phil Judd	'Breaker' Morant
1981	Don Connelly, Greg Bell, Peter Fenton	Gallipoli
1982	Penn Robinson, M. van Buuren, Bruce Lamshed, Roger Savage, Byron Kennedy, A. Steward, Lloyd Carrick	Mad Max 2
1983	Peter Burgess, Peter Fenton, Phil Heywood, Ron Purvis, Terry Rodman, Gary Wilkins	Phar Lap
1984	Gary Wilkins, Mark Wusiutak, Roger Savage, Bruce Lamshed, Terry Rodman, David Harrison	Street Hero
1985	Mark Lewis, Penn Robinson, Julian Ellingworth, Jim Taig	Rebel
1986	Roger Savage, Dean Gawan, Craig Carter, Paul Clark	Malcolm
1987	Gary Wilkins, Mark Wasiutak, Craig Carter, Liva Ruzic, Roger Savage	Ground Zero
1988	Lloyd Carrick, Craig Carter, Peter Burgess, James Currie, Phil Heywood, Peter D.Smith, Livia Ruzic	The Lighthorsemen
1989	Ben Osmo, Lee Smith, Roger Savage	Dead Calm
1990	Ben Osmo, Gethin Creagh, Roger Savage	Blood Oath
1991	Henri Morelle, Ashley Grenville, Jamie Currie	Dingo
1992	Steve Burgess, David Lee, Frank Lipson	Romper Stomper
1993	Lee Smith, Tony Johnson, Gethin Creagh, Peter Townend, Annabelle Sheehan	The Piano
1994	David Lee, Glenn Newnham, Livia Ruzic, Roger Savage	Muriel's Wedding
1995	Frank Lipson, David Lee, Steve Burgess, Peter Burgess, Glenn Newnham	Metal Skin
1996	Toivo Lember, Roger Savage, Livia Ruzic, Gareth Vanderhope	Shine
1997	Gethin Creagh, Toivo Lember, Wayne Pashley	Kiss or Kill

| 1998 | Andrew Plain, Ben Osmo, Gethin Creagh | Oscar and Lucinda |

BEST ACHIEVEMENT IN PRODUCTION DESIGN

Year	Art director/s	Film
1977	David Copping	The Picture Show Man
1978	Lisa Coote	Newsfront
1979	Luciana Arrighi	My Brilliant Career
1980	David Copping	'Breaker' Morant
1981	Herbert Pinter & Wendy Weir	Gallipoli
1982	Graham Walker	Mad Max 2
1983	John Stoddart	Careful, He Might Hear You
1984	Tracy Watt, Harry Zettel, McGregor Knox, Neil Angwin	Strikebound
1985	Brian Thompson	Rebel
1986	George Liddle	Playing Beatie Bow
1987	Brian Thompson	Ground Zero
1988	Sally Campbell	The Navigator
1989	Chris Kennedy	…Ghosts of the Civil Dead
1990	Roger Ford	Flirting
1991	Chris Kennedy	Spotswood
1992	Catherine Martin	Strictly Ballroom
1993	Andrew McAlpine	The Piano
1994	Owen Patterson	The Adventures of Priscilla, Queen of the Desert
1995	Steven Jones-Evans	Metal Skin
1996	Roger Ford	Children of the Revolution
1997	Michael Philips	The Well
1998	Luciana Arrighi	Oscar and Lucinda

BEST ACHIEVEMENT IN COSTUME DESIGN

Year	Costume designer/s	Film
1977	Judith Dorsman	The Picture Show Man
1978	Norma Moriceau	Newsfront
1979	Anna Senior	My Brilliant Career
1980	Anna Senior	'Breaker' Morant
1981	Norma Moriceau	Fatty Finn
1982	Norma Moriceau	Mad Max 2
1983	Bruce Finlayson	Careful, He Might Hear You
1984	Jan Hurley	Silver City
1985	Roger Kirk	Rebel
1986	Terry Ryan	Kangaroo
1987	Jennie Tate	The Umbrella Woman
1988	Glenys Jackson	The Navigator
1989	Rose Chong	What the Moon Saw
1990	Roger Kirk	Blood Oath
1991	Tess Schofield	Spotswood
1992	Angus Strathie	Strictly Ballroom

1993	Janet Patterson	The Piano
1994	Lizzy Gardiner, Tim Chappel	The Adventures of Priscilla, Queen of the Desert
1995	Terry Ryan	Billy's Holiday
1996	Terry Ryan	Children of the Revolution
1997	Louise Wakefield	Doing Time For Patsy Cline
1998	Janet Patterson	Oscar and Lucinda

RAYMOND LONGFORD AWARD

This award is given to individuals who have made outstanding contributions to Australian film-making.

Year	Winner
1968	Ian Dunlop
1969	Not awarded
1970	Stanley Hawes
1971	Not awarded
1972–5	Not awarded
1976	Ken G. Hall
1977	Charles Chauvel (posthumous)
1978	The McDonagh sisters
1979	Jerzy Toeplitz
1980	Tim Burstall
1981	Phillip Adams
1982	Eric Porter
1983	Bill Gooley
1984	David Williams
1985	Donald Crosby
1986	Barry Jones MP
1987	Paul Riomfalvy
1988	Russell Boyd
1989	John Meillon (posthumous)
1990	Peter Weir
1991	Fred Schepisi
1992	Lee Robinson
1993	Sue Milliken
1994	John Hargreaves
1995	Dr George Miller
1996	Not awarded
1997	Jan Chapman
1998	Charles 'Bud' Tingwell

BYRON KENNEDY AWARD

This award is given to encourage unorthodox and visionary approaches to achieving excellence in film-making.

Year	Winner/s
1986	Roger Savage
1985	Andrew Pike
1986	Not awarded
1987	Martha Ansara
1988	George Ogilvie

1989	Jane Campion
1990	Denis O'Rourke
1991	John Duigan
1992	Robin Anderson, Bob Connelly
1993	Mat Butler, Evanne Chesson, Adrian Martin, Garry Warner
1994	John Hargreaves
1995	Jill Bilcock
1996	Laura Jones
1997	John Polson
1998	Arthur Cambridge, Alison Barrett

THE JURY PRIZE

This prize was introduced in 1976 along with changes to the voting procedures. It is awarded by the AFI jury to a feature film of outstanding merit, with particular emphasis on creativity.

Year	Film	Winner/s
1976	The Devil's Playground	Fred Schepisi
1977	Storm Boy	Henri Safran
1978	Mouth to Mouth	John Duigan
1979	Mad Max	George Miller, Byron Kennedy
1980	Hard Knocks	Don McLennan
1981	Wrong Side of the Road	Ned Lander, Graeme Isaac
1982	Journey to the End of Night	Peter Tammer
1983	The Year of Living Dangerously	Linda Hunt, Peter Weir

SPECIAL ACHIEVEMENT AWARD

| 1986 | Crocodile Dundee |

YOUNG ACTOR AWARD

Year	Actor	Film
1991	Lauren Hewett	Act of Necessity
1992	Alexander Outhred	Hammers Over The Anvil
1993	Robert Joamie	The Piano
1994	Zybch Trofimiuk	Sky Trackers
1995	Jamie Croft	That Eye The Sky
1996	Petra Jared	Mirror, Mirror
1997	Jeffrey Walker	The Wayne Manifesto
1998	Paul Pantano	Water Rats

BEST FOREIGN FILM

Year	Producer	Film
1976	Robert Altman	Nashville
1978	Charles H. Joffe	Annie Hall
1979–91	Not awarded	
1992	Robert Cooper	Truly Madly Deeply

Australian Film Institute Awards

1993	Stephen Woolley	The Crying Game
1994	Duncan Kenworthy	Four Weddings and a Funeral
1995	Robin Scholes	Once Were Warriors
1996	Joel Coen	Fargo
1997	Simon Channing-Williams	Secrets and Lies
1998	Arnon Milchan, Curtis Hanson, Michael Nathanson	LA Confidential

AFI Award Winners: Non Features

GOLD AWARD AND GOLDEN REEL AWARD (1963–79)*

Year	Film	Director/s
1963	The Land that Waited (*Gold Award*)	Gil Brealey
1964	The Dancing Class (*Gold Award*)	Tom Cowan
	I the Aboriginal (*Gold Award*)	Cecil Holmes
1966	Concerto for Orchestra (*Golden Reel Award*)	Robert Parker
1967	Cardin in Australia (*Golden Reel Award*)	Peter Thompson
1968	The Change at Groote (*Golden Reel Award*)	Stefan Sargent
	The Talgai Skull (*Golden Reel Award*)	Tom Haydon
1969	Bullocky (*Golden Reel Award*)	Richard Mitchell
1969	The Die Hard: The Legend of Lasseter's Reef (*Golden Reel Award*)	David Crocker
1970	The Gallery (*Golden Reel Award*)	Philip Mark Law
1971	A Big Hand for Everyone (*Golden Reel Award*)	Michael Pearce
1972	Jackpot Town (*Gold Award*)	Roger Whittaker
1973	Tidikawa and Friends (*Gold Award*)	J. and S. Doring
1974/5	Mr Symbol Man (*Golden Reel Award*)	Bruce Moir, Bob Kingsbury

* Note that the the Golden Reel and Gold Awards were awarded on a discretionary basis (thus, for example, between 1976 and 1979 only Bronze or Silver awards were handed out).

BEST DOCUMENTARY*

Year	Film	Director/s
1980	Frontline	David Bradbury
1981	Stepping Out	Chris Noonan
1982	Angels of War	Andrew Pike, Hank Nelson, Gavin Daws
1983	First Contact	Bob Connolly, Robin Anderson
1984	Kemira: Diary of a Strike	Tom Zubrycki
1985	Raoul Wallenburg: Between the Lines	Bob Weis
1986	Chile: Hasta Cuando?	David Bradbury
1987	Painting the Town	Trevor Graham
1988	Cane Toads: An Unnatural History	Mark Lews
1989	Joe Leahy's Neighbours	Robin Anderson, Bob Connolly
1990	Handmaidens and Battleaxes	Rosaline Gillespie
1991	Canto A La Vida	Lucia Salinas Briones
1992	Black Harvest	Robin Anderson, Bob Connolly
1993	Exile and the Kingdom	Frank Rijavec
	For All the World To See	Pat Fiske
1994	50 Years of Silence	Ned Lander, Carol Ruff
1995	The Good Looker	Claire Jager
1996	Not Fourteen Again	Gillian Armstrong
1997	Mabo: Life of an Island Man	Trevor Graham
1998	The Dragons of Galapagos	David Parer, Elizabeth Parer-Cook

*From 1980 this award replaced the Gold Awards and Golden Reel Awards.

BEST ACHIEVEMENT IN DIRECTION IN A DOCUMENTARY

Year	Film	Director
1998	Big House	David Goldie

SHORT FICTION CATEGORY: GOLD AWARDS

Year	Film	Director
1977	Love Letters from Teralba Road	Stephen Wallace
1978	Temperament Unsuited	Ken Cameron

BEST SHORT FICTION FILM

Year	Film	Director/s
1980	Gary's Story	Richard Michalak
1981	Captives of Care	Stephen Wallace
1982	A Most Attractive Man	Rivka Hartman
1983	A Town Like This	John Prescott
1984	Getting Wet	Paul Hogan
1985	The Cellist	Robert Marchand
1986	The Mooncalf	Ian Rochford
1987	Feathers	John Ruane

1988	Cherith	Shirley Barrett
1989	Bonza	David Swann
1990	Sparks	Prue Adams, Robert Klemner
1991	The Tennis Ball	John Dobson
1992	Road To Alice	Stavros Efthymiou
1993	Mr Electric	Stuart McDonald
1994	Only the Brave	Ana Kokkinos
1995	The Beat Manifesto	Daniel Nettheim
1996	No Way To Forget	Richard Frankland
1997	The Beneficiary	Graeme Burfoot
1998	Two/Out	Kriv Stenders

BEST SHORT ANIMATION FILM

Year	Film	Director/s
1980	Pussy Pumps Up	Antoinette Starkiewicz
1981	No award	
1982	Flank Breeder	Bruce Currie
1983	Dance of Death	Dennis Tupicoff
1984	Ned Wethered	Lee Whitmore
1985	Waltzing Matilda	Michael Cusak, Richard Chataway
1986	The Huge Adventures of Trevor, A Cat	John Taylor
1987	Crust	John E. Hughes
1988	Where The Forest Meets the Sea	Jeannie Baker
1989	Still Flying	Robert Stephenson
1990	Picture Start	David Atkinson, John Bird
1991	Union Street	Wendy Chandler
1992	Shelf Life	Andrew Horne
1993	The Darra Dogs	Denis Tupicoff
1994	Gorgeous	Kaz Cooke
1995	Small Treasures	Sarah Watt
1996	Lovely Day	Chris Backhouse
1997	Uncle	Adam Benjamin Elliot
1998	Vengeance	Wendy Chandler

BEST EXPERIMENTAL FILM (1960–90)

Year	Film	Director/s
1960	The Blackman and his Bride	Tim Burstall
1962	Conference Room	B. Porter
1963	Adam and Eve	Dusan Marek
1964	Say Bow Wow	Gil Brealey
1965	Sound and Image	B. Phillips
1966	Portrait of a Girl	John N. Bale
1967	Hearts and Minds	Bruce Petty
1967	Man and His World	Albie Thoms
1968	Run I'm After Me	Julian Gibson
1969	After Proust	Christopher McGill

1970	Earth Message	Arthur Cantrill
1971	Some Regrets	Brian Robinson
1972	Magic Camera Film 2	Victor Kay
1973	Scars	Paul Winkler
1974–78	Not awarded	
1979	Sydney Harbour Bridge	Paul Winkler
1980	Self Portrait Blood Red	Ivan Durrant
1981	Drink the Moon	Mark Foster
1982	The Bridge	Mark Foster
1983	Serious Undertakings	Helen Grace
1984	Passionless Moments	Jane Campion, Gerard Lee
1985	The Lead Dress	Virginia Murray
1986	My Life Without Steve	Gillian Leahy, Digby Duncan
1987	Palisade	Laurie McInnes
1988	A Song Of Air	Merilee Bennett
1989	Soul Mate	Linc Hiatt

BEST ACHIEVEMENT IN CINEMATOGRAPHY IN A NON-FEATURE FILM

Year	Film	Cinematographer/s
1981	Desire	Louis Irving
1982	Greetings From Wollongong	Louis Irving
1983	The Lion in the Doorway	Paul Elliot
1984	A Girl's Own Story	Sally Bongers
1985	Hunters of the Skies: The Fishing Hunters	Lindsay Cupper, Jack Cupper, Roger Whittaker
1986	Flight of the Windhorse	Paul Tait, Michael Dillon
1987	Palisade	Laurie McInnes
1988	South of the Border	Phillip Bull
1989	Shadow Panic	Sally Bongers
1990	The Space Between the Floor and the Door	Dion Beebe
1991	And a Fire Engine To Go With the Dog	Brendan Lavelle
1992	Not awarded	
1993	Kangaroos: Faces in the Mob	Glen Carruthers
1994	Eternity	Dion Beebe
1995	Twelve Moons	Jin Li
1996	Parklands	Mandy Walker
1997	The Human Race	Ulrich Krafzik, Wade Fairley, Ian Pugsley
1998	Dragons of Galapagos	David Parer

BEST SCREENPLAY IN A NON-FEATURE FILM

Year	Film	Screenwriter/s
1983	Marbles	Wendy Thompson
1984	A Girl's Own Story	Jane Campion
1985	Not awarded	
1986	Rocking the Foundations	Pat Fiske
1987	Witch Hunt	Barbara Chobocky, Jeffrey Bruer, Sue Castique
1988	Not awarded	

Australian Film Institute Awards

1989	Bonza	David Swann
1990	Sparks	Catherine Zimdahl
1991	Plead Guilty, Get a Bond	Ben Lewin
1992	Not awarded	
1993	Just Desserts	Monica Pellizzari
1994	Only the Brave	Ana Kokkinos, Mira Robinson
1995	The Beat Manifesto	Tony MacNamara, Daniel Nettheim, Matthew Schultz
1996	Cabbie of the Year	Mick Connolly
1997	My Second Car	Stuart McDonald
1998	Mate	Evan Clarry

BEST ACHIEVEMENT IN EDITING IN A NON-FEATURE FILM

Year	Film	Editor/s
1967	Cardin in Australia	
1968	The Change at Groote	Stefan Sargent
1969	And Then There Was Glass	Peter Tammer
1970	Big Island	Rod Adamson
1971–72	Not awarded	
1973	One Hundred a Day	David Stiven
1974–82	Not awarded	
1983	Double Concerto	Suresh Ayyar
1984	Getting Wet	Paul J. Hogan
1985	Nicaragua: No Pasaran	Stewart Young
1986	Rocking the Foundations	Stewart Young, Jim Stevens, Paul Hogan
1987	Kick Start	Nubar Ghazarian
1988	Cane Toads, An Unnatural History	Lindsay Frazer
1989	Australia Daze	Denise Haslem, Tim Litchfield
1990	The Wonderful World of Dogs	Lindsay Frazer
1991	Donald Friend: The Prodigal Australian	Tim Lewis
1992	Not awarded	
1993	Gumshoe	Suresh Ayyar
1994	Watch the Watch	Suresh Ayyar
1995	Code Blue	Belinda Hall
1996	Rats in the Ranks	Ray Thomas
1997	Year of the Dogs	Stewart Young
1998	Box	Cath Chase

BEST ACHIEVEMENT IN SOUND IN A NON-FEATURE FILM

Year	Film	Sound department
1983	Birdmen of Kilimanjaro	Max Hensser
1984	Every Day, Every Night	Neil Bell, Kathy Mueller
1985	The Lead Dress	George Worontcshak, Rex Watts, Peter Watson Jnr, Stuart Beatty
1986	Flight of the Windhorse	Hugo Devries, Alasdair MacFarlane
1987	The Musical Mariner (Part One)	David Fanshawe, Alasdair MacFarlane
1988	South of the Border	John Patterson, Annie Cocksedge, David Bradbury

1989	Bodywork	Liam Egan, Greg Bell, Robert Sullivan
1990	Land Bilong Islanders	Bronwyn Murphy, Rex Watts
1991	Chainsaw	Victor Gentile
1992	Not awarded	
1993	Exile and the Kingdom	Noeline Harrison, Lawrie Silverstrin, Kim Lord
1994	Universal Appliance Company	James Currie
1995	The Beat Manifesto	John Willsteed
1996	No Way To Forget	Mark Tarpey, Neil McGrath
1997	The Drip	Vladimir Divlijan
1998	Urban Clan	Michael Gissing

OPEN CRAFT AWARD

Year	Film	Winner/s
1993	Memories and Dreams *(for innovation in form)*	Lynne-Maree Milburn
1994	Only The Brave *(for performance)*	Elena Mandalis
1995	The Good Looker *(for music score)*	Paul Grabowsky
1996	Rhythms of Life *(for special effects)*	Andrew Davies-Coward, Mark Lamble, Mike Carroll, Simon Kerwin-Carroll
1997	Frontier: Worse Than Slavery Itself *(for research and script)*	Bruce Belsham, Victoria Pitt
1998	After Mabo *(for visual design)*	John Hughes, Uri Mizrahi

APPENDIX 2:
HISTORY OF THE AUSTRALIAN
FILM INSTITUTE AWARDS

In 1958 the small indigenous Australian film industry's activities were almost exclusively in the area of sponsored documentary, advertising, and educational film production. Before the formal incorporation of the Australian Film Institute in 1959, Australian Film Awards for 1958 were judged and presented as part of the Melbourne Film Festival (see Festivals).

The fledgling AFI was determined to make awards that encouraged excellence and recognised achievement in this small industry. The stated aim of the awards was to 'direct public attention to Australian films and to encourage high standards in their production'. The awards have continued since 1958 as one of the AFI's most important flagship activities. Although the size and nature of the Australian film industry and the methods of judging have changed over the past 36 years, the recognition of excellence and achievement is still the aim of the Awards.

In the late 1950s and early 1960s the AFI Awards and the Australian industry remained focused on the commercial areas of film production. Awards were created in categories such as travel, teaching, and advertising.

In 1963 Dusan Marek won the first Grand Prix for his animated experimental film **Adam and Eve**. Increasing numbers of experimental and short fiction works were entered for the awards in the mid 1960s, and by 1964 overseas festivals were asking to see AFI Award-winning films with a view to including them in their own festivals.

The Raymond Longford Award, which recognises individuals who have made significant contributions to Australian film-making, was established in 1968. The first recipient was documentary film-maker Ian •Dunlop.

The Grand Prix, however, was not awarded between 1964 and 1970. In 1970, it was won by an episode from the three-part feature film **Three to Go**. In the following year the fiction Grand Prix was awarded to Peter •Weir's **Homesdale**. 1970 marked the beginning of a new era in Australian film production and the emergence of a new generation of Australian film-makers, including Fred •Schepisi, Bruce •Beresford, Phillip •Noyce, Gillian •Armstrong, Russell •Boyd, Don •McAlpine, Bruce •Smeaton, and Peter •Best, all of whom were AFI winners in the 1970s.

Until 1970, with few exceptions, awards were presented in recognition of the films and not of individual film-makers. From 1971 onwards, an increasing number of awards recognised individual achievement, and from 1976 awards were given on this basis for all feature films. The same approach was subsequently adopted for short fiction, short animation, and documentary film awards.

The method of choosing recipients of AFI Awards has changed and evolved in response to changes in Australian film production since their inception. The early awards were judged by an invited panel drawn largely from critics, with some representation of film-makers.

The growth in Australian film production, aided by a measure of government funding inaugurated by John Gorton in 1969, meant that by 1974 the previously all-inclusive fiction section was split into Feature and Short Fiction categories. This was the last year that all awards were determind by the invited jury.

In 1976, Fred Schepisi's •**The Devil's Playground** won the newly instituted Best Film Award from the highly acclaimed •**Picnic at Hanging Rock**. Subsequent winners of this award included •**Storm Boy**, •**Newsfront**, •**My Brilliant Career**, •**'Breaker' Morant**, and •**Gallipoli**. The Jury Prize for a feature film was also instituted, and between 1978 and 1982, many significant low-budget films were recognised in this way. Recipients of the Jury Prize during this period included •**Mouth to Mouth**, •**Mad Max**, and **Hard Knocks**.

History of the Australian Film Institute Awards

1976 was also the year the AFI took the major step of redesigning the judging process for feature films, along the lines of the American Academy of Motion Picture Arts and Sciences Oscar-judging system. The various film-industry guilds, associations, and unions cooperated with the AFI to form panels to determine awards within their crafts. The wider general AFI membership voted only in the Best Film category. Other awards, including those for documentary, short fiction, and advertising, continued to be determined by a jury selected by the AFI.

The change to judging by a panel of peers for the majority of the feature film awards provoked some controversy. Craft versus art in film, and questions of subjectivity and objectivity, were thoroughly and often publicly canvassed. In 1977 further awards for craft achievements were added, for editing, art direction, and costume design.

The style of the awards presentation has at times been another subject of controversy. The awards were first telecast from a formal dinner at the Melbourne Hilton hotel in 1976 by Channel 9. The style of presentation and the sort of presenters appropriate to Australia's major film awards have been a regular subject of discussion in the following 18 years. In the early years of the telecast presentation ceremonies, presenters often included celebrities from the American and British film industries, and Hollywood production values were employed in the production. The Awards were telecast throughout most of the 1980s. However, following the restructuring of much of the television industry, the Awards were not able to secure a live telecast in 1991 or 1994, causing considerable comment and disappointment within the film and television industry.

In 1982 a form of preselection was introduced owing to the large number of entries. Panels narrowed the field and screenings were then held around Australia for the wider membership to determine award recipients. This arrangement was dropped when entry numbers fell in the following year. The first Byron Kennedy Award, to encourage unorthodox and visionary approaches to achieving excellence, was awarded to sound engineer Roger Savage. The award included a $10 000 cash prize.

In 1986 television categories were introduced in recognition of the important work done in the areas of miniseries, drama serials, serials, and children's drama. In 1990 a television documentary category was added in response to the shift from cinema to television as the major outlet for documentary production.

A different form of preselection was introduced in 1987. The new system gave appointed juries of practitioners control over the nominations in their specialist areas. Professionally accredited members were able to vote across the board for awards recipients in all craft categories, choosing from the four nominees in each category.

In 1997 the judging of all feature films reverted to the voting members of the AFI, eliminating the role of preselection juries. Voters with professional feature film accreditation vote only in their area of specialty and associated crafts. All voting members of the AFI may vote for Best Film, Best Short Fiction, Best Short Animation, Best Documentary, and Best Foreign Film.

SELECT BIBLIOGRAPHY

Anderson, Judith, *Australian Posters* 1906–1960, Currency Press, Sydney, 1978.

Baxter, John, *The Australian Cinema*, Angus & Robertson, Sydney, 1970.

Beilby, Peter, (ed.), *Australian Motion Picture Year Book 1980*, Cinema Papers and NSW Film Corporation, Melbourne, 1980.

—— (ed.), *Australian Motion Picture Year Book 1981/82*, Cinema Papers and NSW Film Corporation, Melbourne, 1981.

Beilby, Peter and Lansell, Ross (eds), *Australian Motion Picture Year Book 1983*, Four Seasons and Cinema Papers, Melbourne, 1982.

Benson, John, Berryman, Ken, and Levy, Wayne, *Screening the Past: The Sixth Australian History and Film Conference Papers*, La Trobe University Media Centre, Melbourne, 1994.

Bertrand, Ina, *Film Censorship in Australia*, University of Queensland Press, Brisbane, 1978.

—— (ed.), *Cinema in Australia: A Documentary History*, New South Wales University Press, Kensington, 1989.

Bertrand, Ina and Collins, Diane, *Government and Film in Australia*, Currency Press and Australian Film Institute, Sydney, 1981.

Blonski, Annette, Creed, Barbara, and Freiberg, Freida (eds), *Don't Shoot Darling!: Women's Independent Filmmaking in Australia*, Greenhouse Publications, Melbourne, 1987.

Brand, Simon, *Picture Palaces and Flea-Pits: Eighty Years of Australians at the Pictures*, Dreamweaver Books, Sydney, 1983.

——, *The Australian Film Book: 1930–Today*, Dreamweaver Books, Sydney, 1985.

Clark, Al (ed.) (Australian section edited by Tom Ryan), *The Film Yearbook*, vol. 1, Currey O'Neil Ross, Melbourne, 1984.

Coleman, Peter, *Bruce Beresford: Instincts of the Heart*, Angus & Robertson, Sydney, 1992.

Collins, Diane, *Hollywood Down Under: Australians at the* Movies, *1896 to the Present*, Angus & Robertson, Sydney, 1987.

Collins, Felicity, *The Films of Gillian Armstrong*, Australian Teachers of Media, 1999.

Cunningham, I.S. and Turner, G. (eds), *Media in Australia: Industries, Texts, Audiences*, Allen & Unwin, Sydney, 1993.

Dawson, Johnathon and Molloy, Bruce, *Queensland Images in Film and Television*, University of Queensland Press, Brisbane, 1990.

Select Bibliography

Dermody, Susan and Jacka, Elizabeth, *The Screening of Australia*, 2 vols, Currency Press, Sydney, 1987 and 1988.

—— (eds), *The Imaginary Industry: Australian Film in the Late 80s*, AFTRS Publications, Sydney, 1988.

Frow, John and Morris, Meaghan (eds), *Australian Cultural Studies: A Reader*, Allen & Unwin, Sydney, 1993.

Hall, Ken, G., *Directed by Ken G Hall: Autobiography of an Australian Film-maker*, Lansdowne Press, Sydney, 1977.

——, *Australian Film: The Inside Story*, Summit Books, Sydney, 1980.

Hall, Sandra, *Critical Business: The New Australian Cinema in Review*, Rigby Publishers, Adelaide, 1985.

——, *Australian Film Index: A Guide to Australian Feature Film Since 1900*, Thorpe, Melbourne, 1992.

Hamilton, Paul and Mathews, S., *American Dreams: Australian Movies*, Currency Press, Sydney, 1986.

Hutton, Anne (ed.), *The First Australian History and Film Conference Papers*, Australian Film and Television School, Sydney, 1982.

Jennings, Karen, *Sites of Difference: Cinematic Representations of Aboriginality and Gender*, Australian Film Institute, Melbourne, 1993.

Legg, F. *The Eyes of Damien Parer*, Rigby, Adelaide, 1963.

Levy, Wayne, *The Book of the Film and the Film of the Book: A Bibliography of Australian Cinema and TV, 1895–1995*, Academia Press, Melbourne, 1995.

Levy, Wayne, Graeme Cutts, and Sally Stockbridge (eds), *The Second Australian History and Film Conference Papers*, Australian Film and Television School, Sydney, 1984.

Long, Joan and Long, Martin, *The Pictures that Moved: A Picture History of the Australian Cinema 1896–1929*, Hutchison Group, Melbourne, 1982.

Marsh, Marion and Pip, Chris (eds), *Women in Australian Film, Video and Television Production*, the Australian Film Commission and the Australian Film and Television School, Sydney, 1987.

Mathews, Sue. *35mm Dreams: Conversations with Five Australian Directors*, Penguin, Melbourne, 1984.

McDonald, Neil, *War Cameraman: The Story of Damien Parer*, Lothian Books, Melbourne, 1994.

McFarlane, Brian, *Words and Images: Australian Novels into Film*, Heinemann, Melbourne, 1983.

——, *Australian Cinema 1970–1985*, Secker & Warburg, London, 1987.

—— (ed.), *The Australian Cinema, Literature/Film Quarterly*, vol. 21, no. 2, Salisbury State College, Maryland, USA, 1993.

McFarlane, Brian and Mayer, Geoff, *New Australian Cinema: Sources and Parallels in American and British Cinema*, Cambridge University Press, Melbourne, 1992.

Moran, Albert and O'Regan, Tom (eds), *An Australian Film Reader*, Currency Press, Sydney, 1989

——, *The Australian Screen*, Penguin, Ringwood, 1989.

Murray, Scott, *The New Australian Cinema*, Thomas Nelson Australia with *Cinema Papers*, Melbourne, 1980.

——, *Back of Beyond: Discovering Australian Film and Television*, the Australian Film Commission, Sydney, 1988.

—— (ed.), *Australian Film 1978–1994: A Survey of Theatrical Features*, Oxford University Press with *Cinema Papers* and the Australian Film Commission, Melbourne, 1995.

Myers, David, *Bleeding Battlers from Ironbark: Australian Myths in Fiction and Film, 1890s–1980s*, Capricornia Institute Publications, Rockhampton, 1987.

O'Regan, Tom, *Australian National Cinema*, Routledge, London and New York, 1996.

Pike, Andrew and Cooper, Ross, *Australian Film 1900–1977*, Oxford University Press with the Australian Film Institute, Melbourne, 1980.

Porter, Hal, *Stars of Australian Stage and Screen*, Rigby, Adelaide, 1965.

Rattigan, Neil, *Images of Australia: 100 Films of the New Australian Cinema*, Southern Methodist University Press, Dallas, USA, 1991.

Reade, Eric, *Australian Silent Films*, Lansdowne Press, Melbourne, 1970.

——, *The Talkies Era*, Lansdowne Press, Melbourne, 1972.

——, *The Australian Screen: A Pictorial History of Australian Film Making*, Lansdowne Press, Melbourne, 1976.

——, *History and Heartburn: The Saga of Australian Film, 1896–1978*, Harper & Row, Sydney, 1979.

Reis, Brian, *Australian Film: A Bibliography*, Mansell Publishing, London, 1997.

Sabine, James (ed.), *A Century of Australian Cinema*. William Heinemann Australia, Melbourne, 1995.

Shirley, G. and Adams, B., *Australian Cinema: The First 80 Years*, Angus & Robertson and Currency Press, Sydney, 1983.

Stewart, John, *An Encyclopedia of Australian Film*, Reed Books, Sydney, 1984.

Stratton, David, *The Last New Wave: The Australian Film Revival*, Angus & Robertson, Sydney, 1980.

——, *The Avocado Plantation*, Macmillan, Sydney, 1990.

Treole, Victoria (ed.), *Australian Independent Film*, the Australian Film Commission, Sydney, 1982.

Tulloch, John, *Legends on the Screen: The Australian Narrative Cinema 1919–1929*, Currency Press and the Australian Film Institute, Sydney, 1981.

——, *Australian Cinema; Industry, Narrative and Meaning*, George Allen & Unwin, Sydney, 1982.

Turner, Graeme, *National Fictions: Literature, Film and the Construction of Australian Narrative*, 2nd edn, Allen & Unwin, Sydney, 1993.

White, David (profiles of actors and directors by Debi Enker), *Australian Movies to the World: The International Success of Australian Films Since 1970*, Collins, Sydney, 1984.

SUBJECT INDEX